UK

CHRISTIAN HANDBOOK

2007/2008

Produced by a partnership between:

CHRISTIAN RESEARCH
Vision Building, 4 Footscray Road, Eltham, London SE9 2TZ UK
☎ 020 8294 1989 🖷 020 8294 0014
Web: www.christian-research.org.uk
E admin@christian-research.org.uk

CORNERSTONE VISION
28 Old Park Road, Peverell, Plymouth PL3 4PY
☎ 01752 225 623 🖷 01752 673 441
Web: www.cornerstonevision.com
E: info@cornerstonevision.com

EDEN INTERACTIVE Ltd
Chester Enterprise Centre, Hoole Bridge, Chester CH2 3NE
☎ 01244 350 994 🖷 01244 350 995
Web: www.edeninteractive.co.uk
E: info@edeninteractive.co.uk

VERITÉ CM Ltd
Moriah House, 124 Sea Place, Worthing BN12 4PY
☎ 01903 241 975 🖷 01903 521 959
Web: www.veritecm.com
E: enquiries@veritecm.com

www.ukchristianhandbook.org.uk

EDITOR
HEATHER WRAIGHT

ASSISTANT EDITOR
VICKY WHARTON

CONSULTING EDITOR
DR PETER BRIERLEY

CONSULTING EDITOR
DAVID LONGLEY

Supported by
EVANGELICAL ALLIANCE
186 Kennington Park Road, London SE11 4BT UK
☎ 020 7207 2100 🖷 020 7207 2150
Web: www.eauk.org
E enquiry@eauk.org

Sponsored by
ANSVAR INSURANCE COMPANY LTD
Ansvar House, 31 St Leonards Road, Eastbourne, BN21 3UR
☎ 01323 737 541 🖷 01323 430977
web: www.ansvar.co.uk
E ansvar.insurance@ansvar.co.uk

UK

CHRISTIAN HANDBOOK

2007/2008

Produced by a partnership between:

CHRISTIAN RESEARCH
Vision Building 4 Footscray Road, Eltham, London SE9 2TZ UK
☎ 020 8294 1989 🖷 020 8294 0014
Web: www.christian-research.org.uk
E admin@christian-research.org.uk

CORNERSTONE VISION
28 Old Park Road, Peverell, Plymouth PL3 4PY
☎ 01752 225 623 🖷 01752 673 441
Web: www.cornerstonevision.com
E: info@cornerstonevision.com

EDEN INTERACTIVE Ltd
Chester Enterprise Centre, Hoole Bridge, Chester CH2 3NE
☎ 01244 350 994 🖷 01244 350 995
Web: www.edeninteractive.co.uk
E: info@edeninteractive.co.uk

VERITÉ CM Ltd
Moriah House, 124 Sea Place, Worthing BN12 4PY
☎ 01903 241 975 🖷 01903 521 959
Web: www.veritecm.com
E: enquiries@veritecm.com

www.ukchristianhandbook.org.uk

EDITOR
HEATHER WRAIGHT

ASSISTANT EDITOR
VICKY WHARTON

CONSULTING EDITOR
DR PETER BRIERLEY

CONSULTING EDITOR
DAVID LONGLEY

Supported by
EVANGELICAL ALLIANCE
186 Kennington Park Road, London SE11 4BT UK
☎ 020 7207 2100 🖷 020 7207 2150
Web: www.eauk.org
E enquiry@eauk.org

Sponsored by
ANSVAR INSURANCE COMPANY LTD
Ansvar House, 31 St Leonards Road, Eastbourne, BN21 3UR
☎ 01323 737 541 🖷 01323 430977
web: www.ansvar.co.uk
E ansvar.insurance@ansvar.co.uk

Previous Volumes

Protestant Missions Handbook (compiled by Nancy Center)	First Edition	1964
Protestant Missions Handbook (compiled by Ernest Oliver)	Second Edition	1968
UK Protestant Missions Handbook (compiled by Peter Brierley)	Third Edition	September 1973
UK Protestant Missions Handbook Volume 1: Overseas	Fourth Edition	December 1976
UK Protestant Missions Handbook Volume 2: Home	First Edition	November 1977
	Reprinted	December 1978
UK Christian Handbook Volume 3: Agencies	First Edition	April 1980
UK Christian Handbook Volume 4: Indexes	First Edition	April 1980
UK Christian Handbook Volume 1: Overseas	Fifth Edition	November 1980
UK Christian Handbook (combined)	1983 Edition	November 1982
	Reprinted	May 1983
	1985/86 Edition	November 1984
	1987/88 Edition	October 1986
	Reprinted	January 1987
	1989/90 Edition	October 1988
	1992/93 Edition	October 1991
	1994/95 Edition	October 1993
	1996/97 Edition	October 1995
	1998/99 Edition	November 1997
	2000/01 Edition	November 1999
	2002/03 Edition	November 2001
	2004/05 Edition	February 2004
	2007/08 Edition	September 2005

British Library Cataloguing in Publication Data

UK Christian Handbook - 2007/08 ed.
1. Great Britain Christian church
I. Wraight, Heather, 1947 II. Brierley, Peter, 1938
274.1'0828

ISBN 978 1 85321 165 2

Credit: Advertising sales by Cornerstone Vision
Cover design by Verité CM Ltd
Web site by Eden Interactive Ltd

Christian Research aims to provide Christian leaders with factual information, surveys, and other resource material to help them, in the long-term in their strategic planning for evangelism and growth, and in the short-term with leadership consultancy and training for greater efficiency, effectiveness, and cost-effectiveness. Christian Research also publishes and distributes related books and papers. The Christian Research Association is a registered charity, number 2792246.

Typeset by WestKey Ltd, The Sycamores, Tremough Dale, Penryn, TR10 8JA
for Christian Research, Vision Building, 4 Footscray Road, Eltham, London SE9 2TZ
Printed by Goodman Baylis, The Trinity Press, London Road, Worcester WR5 2JH

FOREWORD

There are many reasons given for the apparent resurgence in interest in mainstream religion, but it seems to be a reality and the cynics' predictions regarding its demise seem premature. What the *UK Christian Handbook* helps to illustrate is just how vast, complex and varied the Christian life of these isles is. To the outsider, and even sometimes to the insider, Christian life can be seen simply as the local church and Sunday morning. What we see here is a vibrant, committed and enormous community of people who make such an important contribution to the life and well-being of our society. Often we are told that as Christians and believers we are irrelevant and - however well-meaning - of little significance. And we can easily be seduced into believing this. Yet here is evidence that everywhere you look the life of the Christian community is having its effect on the wider community.

I first got to know Peter Brierley and Heather Wraight over twelve years ago, and their enthusiasm and energy for Christian Research and the *UK Christian Handbook* has not diminished in that time. It is a pleasure to welcome another edition of the *Handbook*.

Once again congratulations are due to all those who have worked so hard to produce this panoramic view of the Christian churches and their mission. The mission will be all the more effective the more 'joined up' it is. The *UK Christian Handbook* will be of great assistance in joining the bits together.

I wish it continued success and growth.

+ Kieran

Kieran Conry
Bishop of Arundel & Brighton

ACKNOWLEDGMENTS

The *UK Christian Handbook* is approaching its 40th birthday! Over the years many people have come to rely on it for what we now call 'networking'. The *Handbook* is now online as well as in print and thus being used by many more churches, organisations and agencies - what would the Christian world do without the *UK Christian Handbook*! However, gathering the information and making sure it is as accurate as possible demands massive amounts of work, done within a very tight timescale by a highly committed team.

The *Handbook* is now co-produced, and so much 'blood, sweat, toil and tears' have gone into the project by:
Ian Pilkington and the staff of Cornerstone Vision
Gareth Mulholland and the staff of Eden Interactive
Chris Powell and the staff of Verité CM Ltd.

So here is a big thank you to all of them, and to the Christian Research staff whose life is at least in part ruled by the *Handbook* for several months:

Peter Brierley — Managing Editor who, although working mostly on *Religious Trends*, was available for discussion and advice as needed
Vicky Wharton — Assistant Editor, who meticulously handled much of the day-to-day work
Gwen Gowers — who dealt with all the invoicing for advertising and orders
Kim Miles — who helped as she was able between research projects.

The staff could not possibly complete the *Handbook* without short-term and part-time help:

Clara Bickford — who worked on the initial mailing
Joan Cheesman — who mailed forms, dealt with them as they came back and did the reminder phone calls
Jonathan Eades & James Lumgair — who did all the initial data entry
Josh Gowers — who helped in various ways during his school holidays
Peggy Hale — who helped in many ways.

The *Handbook* also draws on the expertise of several other people, and special thanks go to:

Derek Atkins — for the painstaking task of cross-checking proofs against original forms
David Longley — Consulting Editor, for his invaluable advice and detailed proofreading
John Marcus — for work on the database which holds the information
Lesley Reynolds — who researched potential new entries and mailed forms to them
Jim Henderson — at WestKey for the typesetting.

Thank you to these folk, without whom the *Handbook* would not happen! This is my last edition as Editor - I pray every success on whoever steps into my shoes.

Thank you also to everyone listed in this volume for completing forms on paper or online, sending faxes and emails, answering phone calls, and in one way or another helping to make sure the information contained here is as up-to-date, comprehensive and accurate as possible.

The reason we go on producing this *Handbook* is to serve the Kingdom of God by helping the Christian community in Britain - and wider afield. We pray this edition assists, even a little, in facilitating the networking which is now so much part of life for all of us.

Heather Wraight **Editor**

CRITERIA FOR INCLUSION

Organisations are normally only listed in this volume if they:

1. Are *Trinitarian*, that is, they accept the historic formulary of the Godhead as the three eternal persons, God the Father, God the Son and God the Holy Spirit, in one unchanging Essence. A fuller statement is available on request.
2. *Offer a definitive Christian product, service or function*, that is the nature of their output or work reflects their belief and could not be adequately performed without it.
3. *Do not operate or trade under their own individual name* (musical artistes, evangelists and similar occupations apart), so that their listing represents an identifiable organisation, however small, rather than the work or interest of one or two persons.
4. *Work in a wide geographical area*, that is they are serving the wider Body of Christ and not only one local church. Individual churches are usually only included if they are also the headquarters for their denomination in the UK.

Specific ministries within organisations are only included separately upon payment of a fee.

DISCLAIMER

1. No responsibility can be taken by the Editors for the omission of an organisation.
2. The inclusion of an organisation does not necessarily imply agreement by the Editors with its work.
3. The inclusion of an advert does not imply endorsement by the Editors of the content of the advert or the product or services advertised.
4. Entrants are required to sign a form signifying that they meet the above criteria; the Editors do not otherwise verify whether each entry fulfils all the criteria.

INFORMATION COLLECTION

Prior to the production of this edition each organisation listed in the previous edition was sent a form asking for up-to-date details of its work. A reminder letter was sent to each organisation which did not respond to the initial mailing. Reminders by telephone, fax or email were subsequently made to ensure that the data is as up-to-date as possible.

Organisations not previously listed, because either newly formed or unintentionally omitted from earlier volumes, were researched in a variety of ways and sent similar forms. These organisations were not reminded if they did not respond.

Information received up to June 2006 has been included.

Categories

The basic details of each organisation listed in this volume are shown once, under the most appropriate category. As many organisations have activities in more than one group, a number will be found in more than one category.

CONTENTS

CONTENTS BY SUBJECT

This list contains Section names and subjects which are part of a Category name in this or the previous edition. See also the Main Index on Page 524 which includes hundreds of additional subject entries.

UNDERSTANDING THIS BOOK

CONTENT

Contents are listed in the Table of Contents on Page 6

This edition of the *UK Christian Handbook* contains the same regular sections, each of which can be identified by a thumb tab:

Accommodation	(A)
Books	(B)
Churches	(C)
Evangelism	(E)
Media	(M)
Overseas	(O)
Services	(S)
Training	(T)
Extra Information	(X)

Within each section categories are listed in alphabetical order. There is one category change in this edition:

Bookshops now also includes **Other Retail Outlets.**

COLOUR ADVERTISEMENTS

These are all together and may be found between pages 544 and 545. Entries with a colour advert also have a black & white advert near their entry.

ORDER OF ENTRIES

Within each category entries are listed alphabetically. In finding an entry the following factors should be noted:

1. The order of entries is determined by the alphabetical sequence of the word in each entry rather than the letters, recognising spaces between them eg Alpha Book Shop comes before Alpha Bookroom, since Book precedes Bookroom word for word.

2. Where the name of an organisation consists of initials, the initials are treated as a word eg BMS World Mission follows Belgian Evangelical Mission, BMS being treated as Bms for order purposes.

3. The, A, Y for Welsh names, or Le for French ones etc, are ignored at the start of an organisation name for order purposes eg The Hayes Conference Centre will be found in the correct alphabetical order for Hayes and not for The.

4. Where the organisation name is that of an individual eg Independent Evangelists, the entry is indexed under the surname. This rule also applies to organisations eg Frank Wright Mundy will be found under Wright Mundy and not Frank.

5. St is indexed as Saint and Mc as Mac.

6. All Roman Catholic entries are indexed as Catholic whether or not the organisation name includes the word Roman.

ENTRIES

Layout

Entries are printed in a solid block of text, with the information always in the same order. Research has shown that people use the *Handbook* most often for four key items. These always appear in the same position in an entry:

Name of organisation starts the entry, in **bold**

Address immediately follows the organisation name

Phone and fax numbers follow the address, & then email and website addresses

The description of work *in italic* is on the next line/s

Chief Executive Officer starts a new line with the actual title in *italic*.

Lists

Seventeen categories have some information which does not fit into a standard entry, such as number of beds in the Accommodation section. Such information is given in a list at the start of the appropriate category. The following categories have such lists:

Where no relevant information is available, an organisation is listed in the category but not included in the list.

Abbreviations

M = men W = women
n/a = not answered, not available not applicable or unknown

Symbols

E = Email address
☎ = Telephone number
M = Mobile phone number
🖷 = Fax number
* = Member of Evangelical Alliance or Global Connections
† = Information not updated since last edition.

HOW TO FIND WHAT YOU WANT

If you know –	Use:
Organisation's current name	Main Index on Page 522
Organisation's previous name	Main Index on Page 522
Name of Chief Officer	Main Index on Page 522
Magazine's name	Main Index on Page 522
Postcode, county or town where located	Location Index on Page 471
Postcode, county or town and kind of work	List at start of appropriate category
Particular type of work undertaken	Contents in alphabetical order on Page 6
General type of work undertaken	Contents by Section on Page 6
Local name or address	Contents by Section or Location Index
Subject of data needed (eg schools)	Subject in Main Index on Page 522

In desperation, you are always welcome to telephone Christian Research on 020 8294 1989.
For latest updates see www.ukchristianhandbook.org.uk

QUICK GUIDE TO MEANING OF ENTRIES

2. Full legal title
1. Member of EA or GC
4. Telephone / Mobile phone, fax numbers
7. Description of work
8. Chief Officer
10. UK staff numbers
13. Denominational status
17. Other UK offices, if any

***Whatzits Church Services**, 56 Humpty Dumpty Street, Big Falls, XY9 2KM
☎ 01234 567 890 Ⓜ: 07890 123 456
🖷 01234 567 891
Ⓔ Email: joebloggs@whatzitseggs.com
Web: www.whatzitseggs.com
Providing eggs, posters and other products suitable for use in Easter Sunday church services.
Managing Director: Mr Joe Bloggs. *Rescue Manager:* Mr King. Executive staff 2. Other staff 9. ***CC*** No.1234567. Began 1972; non-denominational. (Previously Bloggs Eggs). Magazine: *Egg Collecting* (5,000 quarterly). Turnover £200,000 to year end Dec 02.
Also at:
Sales Manager: Josephine Bloggs, 97 Wall Street, Anywhere QP7 8HK
☎ 01987 654 321 🖷 01987 654 320

3. Address
5. Email address
6. Web site
9. Other senior staff
11. Registered Charity, Charity number
12. Date of foundation
14. Previous name
15. Magazine name, circulation, frequency
16. Income / turnover

LAYOUT OF ENTRIES

1. *A preceding asterisk indicates membership of the Evangelical Alliance or Global Connections, who have published or co-published the *UK Christian Handbook* since its inception. See Pages 16 to 20 for a full list of their group members.

† A preceding dagger indicates that no return was received or contact made and the information given may therefore be unreliable.

2. Organisation name is in **bold** and is usually the full legal title.

3. Correct postal address given is for the UK office. The address gives the Post Town and Postcode, a list of which can be found on Page 460 at the start of the Location Index.

4. Telephone, mobile phone and fax numbers always follow the address.

5. Email address follows phone and fax numbers. In most cases these are listed on one line, but where the address is too long for one line, it should be treated as one continuous number.

6. Website address is listed after the email address. In most cases the address is listed on one line, but in the occasional case where it is too long for one line, it should be treated as one continuous number. Web addresses are preceded by http:// but as this is automatically included by most Web Browsers it has not been printed for every web address.

7. Description of work is a maximum of 15 words and is the first item in the block of information printed in *italics*.

8. The Chief Executive Officer is given together with his/her actual designation (in *italics*). No academic degrees or other professional qualifications are shown except for Principals of Theological Colleges and Bible Schools. No title is shown for those belonging to the Society of Friends, and for others who requested the omission of a title. Normally only one name is shown.

9. Organisations with larger income/turnover were given the option of including a second or third name and designation. For mission agencies the international chief officer is included where known, but correspondence should normally be addressed to the first named person.

10. UK Staff numbers are as at 31st March 2003 and normally relate to full-time personnel only. Some organisations indicated part-time personnel and these have been combined to count as full-time equivalents. If there are no full-time staff, any part-time or voluntary staff are indicated as such. Executive or Admin (administrative) staff are usually those in management positions, while Other staff is not defined and may include a wide range of roles including clerical or manual.

11. ***CC*** indicates that the organisation is registered with the Charity Commission, and where known the Charity number follows immediately.

12. "Began xxxx" gives the year of foundation of the present or originating organisation.

13. Denominational status of organisation may be one of three: denominational (naming the denomination), interdenominational/ ecumenical/evangelical, or non-denominational. No definition is given on the questionnaire for these categories.

14. If the organisation has changed its name recently, the previous name will be found in the entry in brackets. If it has changed its name in the last 10 years, the old name is usually included in the Main Index.

15. Magazine name is given in *italics* followed by the circulation and frequency in brackets. Magazine name is indexed to help in identifying an Organisation (news letters are therefore not listed).

16. Income/Turnover. The term Turnover has been used throughout this volume, but for some organisations it refers to income. This figure relates to the latest (published) Income and Expenditure Account for the United Kingdom, and the month and year to which it refers is indicated. Where not known this is assumed to be December 2005.

17. Other UK Offices or additional information (eg Suffragan Bishops and Archdeacons for Church of England Dioceses) follow below the main entry.

Note:
Enhanced entries have a box round them.

TABLE 1: SUMMARY OF ORGANISATIONS BY FOUNDATION DATE, STAFF & FACILITIES

Category	Number[1]	Date of Foundation Percentage Founded: Before 1920	1920–1985	After 1985	Percentage with no Full Time Staff	Staff Percentage of: Admin Staff	Other Staff	Total Number of Full-time Staff	Average Number	Percentage with: Fax/ Phone	E-mail Address	Website
		%	%	%	%	%	%			%	%	%
Accommodation												
Camping, Caravan & Outdoor Centres	52	*0*	*63*	*37*	*6*	*20*	*80*	623	13	*81*	*92*	*90*
Conference Centres, Guest Houses & Hotels	181	*7*	*55*	*38*	*5*	*29*	*71*	1818	11	*80*	*92*	[illegible]
Hospices	6	*17*	*67*	*16*	*0*	*40*	*60*	1259	210	*100*	*100*	[illegible]
Hostels for Holiday Events	13	*8*	*77*	*15*	*46*	*76*	*24*	21	3	*38*	*85*	[illegible]
Hostels, Social Welfare	83	*8*	*24*	*68*	*4*	*29*	*71*	936	12	*86*	*41*	*35*
Hostels for Young People & Students	48	*35*	*50*	*15*	*0*	*19*	*81*	1856	39	*96*	*85*	*50*
Housing Associations	24	*9*	*48*	*43*	*9*	*2*	*98*	5463	261	*83*	*87*	*70*
Residential Homes for Disadvantaged People	13	*0*	*54*	*46*	*0*	*12*	*88*	237	18	*77*	*62*	*31*
Residential & Nursing Homes for Elderly People	142	*3*	*53*	*44*	*1*	*9*	*91*	2734	19	*73*	*56*	*45*
Retreat Houses	107	*27*	*51*	*22*	*13*	*65*	*35*	1105	12	*73*	*82*	*68*
Sheltered Housing	33	*3*	*33*	*64*	*0*	*92*	*8*	39	1	*85*	[illegible]	*88*
TOTAL ACCOMMODATION	**703**	***11***	***50***	***39***	***5***	***18***	***82***	**16,091**	**24**	***79***	***71***	***63***
Books												
Bible Distributors & Publishers	18	*53*	*40*	*7*	*20*	*40*	*60*	146	12	*80*	*8*	*80*
Bookshops & Other Retail Outlets	511	*4*	*59*	*37*	*10*	*36*	*64*	1722	4	*73*	*7*	*56*
Libraries	17	*43*	*14*	*43*	*14*	*42*	*58*	69	6	*57*	[illegible]	*36*
Publishers of Books	108	*15*	*50*	*35*	*9*	*38*	*62*	1598	16	*80*	*88*	*79*
Other Literature Producers & Distributors (UK)	94	*10*	*40*	*50*	*19*	*21*	*79*	894	12	*72*	*87*	*73*
TOTAL BOOKS	**748**	***8***	***54***	***38***	***12***	***34***	***66***	**4,429**	**7**	***74***	***75***	***63***
Churches												
Cathedrals	113	*6*	*8*	*86*	*n/a*	*n/a*	*n/a*	n/a	n/a	*88*	*84*	*79*
Chaplaincies	17	*35*	*41*	*24*	*6*	*95*	*5*	1,310	82	*82*	*82*	*53*
Councils of Churches & Churches Together	73	*4*	*41*	*55*	*59*	*53*	*47*	178	5	*49*	[illegible]	*47*
Denominational Headquarters, National & Local	359	*41*	*30*	*29*	*15*	*38*	*62*	7,839 [2]	11	*76*	[illegible]	*66*
Denominational Organisations	107	*26*	*50*	*24*	*52*	*36*	*64*	387	8	*64*	*32*	*66*
Evangelical Fellowships (Inter-Church)	37	*3*	*26*	*71*	*76*	*20*	*80*	71	9	*24*	*32*	*41*
Religious Orders (Anglican)	18	*71*	*24*	*5*	*0*	*92*	*8*	114 [3]	7	*59*	*76*	*41*
Religious Orders (Roman Catholic)	50	*63*	*27*	*10*	*2*	*6*	*94*	280 [3]	6	*83*	*56*	*31*
TOTAL CHURCHES	**774**	***31***	***31***	***38***	***39***	***61***	***3***	**10,179**	**9**	***71***	***78***	***62***
Evangelism												
Church Planting Organisations	10	*0*	*11*	*89*	*11*	*52*	*48*	60	7	*33*	*00*	*100*
City & Town Missions	36	*50*	*28*	*22*	*8*	*37*	*63*	759	23	*81*	*81*	*78*
Evangelistic Agencies (Primarily in the UK)	153	*16*	*40*	*44*	*12*	*28*	*72*	2,703	21	*70*	*93*	*87*
Evangelists (Independent)	30	*0*	*48*	*52*	*7*	*82*	*18*	51	2	*59*	*90*	*55*
Teaching & Preaching Agencies	29	*7*	*19*	*74*	*30*	*78*	*22*	65	3	*56*	*70*	*63*
TOTAL EVANGELISM	**258**	***18***	***36***	***46***	***13***	***32***	***68***	**3,638**	**17**	***67***	***88***	***80***
Media												
Art & Craft Producers & Suppliers	45	*0*	*36*	*64*	*7*	*29*	*71*	255	7	*76*	*90*	*71*
Computer and IT Services	36	*0*	*17*	*83*	*17*	*64*	*36*	146	5	*74*	*97*	*97*
Design, Layout & Editorial Services	48	*0*	*18*	*82*	*2*	*44*	*56*	177	4	*68*	*98*	*59*
Media Producers	68	*0*	*28*	*72*	*3*	*48*	*52*	729	11	*74*	*96*	*79*
Media Services (Incorporating Photographers)	90	*0*	*40*	*60*	*10*	*50*	*50*	422	5	*79*	*92*	*74*
Musical & Theatrical Performers	74	*1*	*40*	*59*	*43*	*64*	*36*	152	4	*47*	*86*	*67*
Musical & Theatrical Services	62	*3*	*35*	*62*	*19*	*42*	*58*	307	6	*69*	*94*	*76*
Newspapers & Periodicals	146	*27*	*35*	*38*	*55*	*31*	*69*	399	6	*80*	*85*	*77*
Video, Film & Cassette Libraries & Suppliers	11	*0*	*55*	*45*	*9*	*57*	*43*	30	3	*73*	*91*	*82*
TOTAL MEDIA	**580**	***7***	***34***	***59***	***25***	***45***	***55***	**2,617**	**6**	***72***	***91***	***75***
Overseas												
Evangelistic Agencies	44	*2*	*45*	*53*	*21*	*44*	*56*	304	9	*71*	*95*	*62*
Literature Producers & Distributors	23	*11*	*50*	*39*	*22*	*54*	*46*	130	9	*67*	*89*	[illegible]
Mission Sending Churches (Direct)	8	*25*	*63*	*12*	*0*	*99*	*1*	505	63	*88*	*88*	*88*
Mission Agencies	206	*54*	*30*	*16*	*4*	*86*	*14*	898 [4]	4	*85*	*81*	*62*
Mission Support Organisations	132	*16*	*42*	*42*	*23*	*59*	*41*	1,156	12	*74*	*93*	*78*
Relief & Development Agencies	103	*1*	*26*	*73*	*18*	*21*	*79*	1,673	20	*77*	*92*	*87*
TOTAL OVERSEAS	**515**	***28***	***35***	***37***	***14***	***75***	***25***	**4,666**	**11**	***79***	***88***	***72***

1. Excluding multiple entries
2. Excluding serving ministers
3. Excluding community members
4. Excluding serving members

TABLE 1: SUMMARY OF ORGANISATIONS BY RELIGIOUS AFFILIATION & INCOME

Category	Number[1]	Percentage registered with Charity Commission	Religious Affiliation Percentage who are				Income/Turnover	
			Anglican	Roman Catholic	Other Denominations	Inter[2]	Estimated Total £'000	Percentage[3]
		%	%	%	%	%		%
Accommodation								
Camping, Caravan & Outdoor Centres	52	67	10	0	19	71	£12,399	78
Conference Centres, Guest Houses & Hotels	181	58	11	2	24	63	£44,580	39
Hospices	7	100	0	0	17	83	£26,345	100
Hostels for Holiday Events	13	100	23	15	23	39	£996	38
Hostels, Social Welfare	83	96	4	1	66	29	£16,964	30
Hostels for Young People & Students	48	100	2	8	19	71	£35,977	85
Housing Associations	24	83	0	4	48	48	£194,208	75
Residential Homes for Disadvantaged People	13	85	0	0	46	54	£8,008	50
Residential & Nursing Homes for Elderly People	142	92	4	3	74	19	£53,915	10
Retreat Houses	107	91	35	35	17	13	£16,386	33
Sheltered Housing	33	100	3	0	94	3	£2,259	6
TOTAL ACCOMMODATION	**703**	**82**	**11**	**7**	**42**	**40**	**£412,037**	**38**
Books								
Bible Distributors & Publishers	18	93	0	0	0	100	£42,632	67
Bookshops & Other Retail Outlets	511	62	5	4	22	69	£75,197	45
Libraries	17	71	50	7	14	29	£2,465	12
Publishers of Books	108	38	6	7	29	58	£86,708	25
Other Literature Producers & Distributors (UK)	94	43	3	1	32	64	£47,198	26
TOTAL BOOKS	**748**	**57**	**6**	**4**	**24**	**66**	**£252,200**	**40**
Churches								
Cathedrals	113	19	46	22	32	0	£79,372	16
Chaplaincies	17	53	29	18	24	29	£1,172	24
Councils of Churches & Churches Together	73	32	0	0	27	73	£4,655	58
Denominational Headquarters, National & Local	359	57	20	11	68	1	n/a[4]	n/a
Denominational Organisations	107	64	41	18	36	5	£20,544	47
Evangelical Fellowships (Inter-Church)	37	35	0	0	38	62	£5,476	42
Religious Orders (Anglican)	18	94	76	6	6	12	£8,532	11
Religious Orders (Roman Catholic)	50	96	0	98	2	0	£2,500	4
TOTAL CHURCHES	**774**	**53**	**24**	**17**	**47**	**12**	**£122,251**	**32**
Evangelism								
Church Planting Organisations	10	100	0	0	78	22	£279	40
City & Town Missions	36	83	3	0	47	50	£20,386	83
Evangelistic Agencies (Primarily in the UK)	153	89	2	1	35	62	£51,240	61
Evangelists (Independent)	30	66	0	0	72	28	£859	33
Teaching & Preaching Agencies	29	48	0	0	70	30	£1,254	34
TOTAL EVANGELISM	**258**	**81**	**2**	**1**	**47**	**50**	**£74,018**	**57**
Media								
Art & Craft Producers & Suppliers	45	2	5	2	52	41	£20,881	33
Computer and IT Services	36	14	0	0	57	43	£9,481	67
Design, Layout & Editorial Services	48	5	0	0	52	48	£7,178	33
Media Producers	68	37	0	3	37	60	£25,448	54
Media Services	90	15	2	1	51	46	£20,719	45
Musical & Theatrical Performers	74	33	1	1	43	55	£2,774	34
Musical & Theatrical Services	62	31	2	0	45	53	£8,513	40
Newspapers & Periodicals	146	33	6	6	43	45	£26,618	13
Video, Film & Cassette Libraries & Suppliers	11	64	0	0	36	64	£341	18
TOTAL MEDIA	**580**	**25**	**3**	**2**	**46**	**49**	**£121,953**	**35**
Overseas								
Evangelistic Agencies	44	86	0	0	40	60	£13,232	61
Literature Producers & Distributors	23	89	0	0	33	67	£8,795	70
Mission Sending Churches (Direct)	8	100	0	0	50	50	£5,331	63
Mission Agencies	206	92	6	45	15	34	£206,348	50
Mission Support Organisations	132	83	7	6	32	55	£58,495	75
Relief & Development Agencies	102	93	0	3	55	42	£282,709	83
TOTAL OVERSEAS	**515**	**90**	**4**	**21**	**31**	**44**	**£574,910**	**65**

1. Excluding multiple entries
2. Interdenominational/non-denominational/ecumenical/evangelical
3. Percentage of organisations on which total figure is estimated
4. 46 denominations additionally supplied figures giving a total of £149,078,547, including one denomination with £60m and 8 Dioceses totalling £60.9m

TABLE 1: SUMMARY OF ORGANISATIONS BY FOUNDATION DATE, STAFF & FACILITIES (CONTINUED)

Category	Number[1]	Date of Foundation Percentage Founded: Before 1920	1920–1985	After 1985	Percentage with no Full Time Staff	Staff Percentage of: Admin Staff	Other Staff	Total Number of Full-time Staff	Average Number	Percentage with: Fax/ Phone	E-mail Address	Web site
		%	%	%	%	%	%			%	%	%
Services												
Addictions & Rehabilitation Services	36	*3*	*47*	*50*	*3*	*29*	*71*	704	20	*78*	*72*	[illegible]
Animal Welfare Agencies	4	*0*	*75*	*25*	*50*	*100*	*0*	2	1	*25*	*50*	[illegible]
Benevolent Organisations	38	*41*	*32*	*27*	*46*	*76*	*24*	394	20	*73*	*73*	[illegible]
Buildings & Church Design	30	*4*	*39*	*57*	*11*	*42*	*58*	227	9	*86*	*93*	[illegible]
Business Services	20	*12*	*29*	*59*	*0*	*31*	*69*	461	27	*88*	*88*	[illegible]
Children's Care & Adoption Societies	26	*50*	*23*	*27*	*0*	*2*	*98*	9,113	351	*92*	*81*	[illegible]
Counselling Organisations	87	*1*	*25*	*74*	*20*	*59*	*41*	516	8	*59*	*80*	[illegible]
Creation Movements	7	*0*	*43*	*57*	*57*	*18*	*82*	17	6	*57*	*100*	[illegible]
Organisations for People with Disabilities	27	*15*	*41*	*44*	*11*	*7*	*93*	1,665	69	*67*	*89*	[illegible]
Environment Movements	5	*0*	*40*	*60*	*40*	*77*	*23*	13	4	*60*	*100*	[illegible]
Ethnic Minority Associations	22	*14*	*32*	*54*	*18*	*76*	*24*	54	3	*82*	*73*	[illegible]
Family Care & Support Ministries	15	*21*	*29*	*50*	*21*	*7*	*93*	567	51	*71*	*79*	[illegible]
Financial Services	68	*12*	*37*	*51*	*8*	*24*	*76*	1,987	33	*82*	*94*	[illegible]
Furnishings, Fabric & Church Interiors	36	*22*	*47*	*31*	*0*	*14*	*86*	705	20	*94*	*94*	[illegible]
Health & Healing Organisations	40	*9*	*44*	*47*	*9*	*8*	*92*	1,161	38	*65*	*88*	[illegible]
Information & Telephone Organisations	23	*4*	*57*	*39*	*22*	*65*	*35*	51	3	*70*	*87*	[illegible]
Marketing & Fundraising Services	28	*0*	*19*	*81*	*12*	*40*	*60*	195	9	*81*	*96*	[illegible]
Marriage Ministries	19	*0*	*53*	*47*	*47*	*71*	*29*	42	4	*42*	*89*	[illegible]
Personnel Consultancy and Placement	24	*0*	*29*	*71*	*17*	*58*	*42*	77	4	*54*	*100*	[illegible]
Prayer Fellowships	39	*5*	*38*	*57*	*46*	*69*	*31*	81	4	*28*	*87*	[illegible]
Printers	18	*18*	*41*	*41*	*6*	*29*	*71*	243	15	*94*	*100*	[illegible]
Professional Christian Groups	78	*15*	*55*	*30*	*54*	*49*	*51*	101	3	*62*	*92*	[illegible]
Pro-Life Organisations	7	*0*	*43*	*57*	*43*	*23*	*77*	75	19	*71*	*100*	[illegible]
Reconciliation & Mediation Groups	33	*6*	*73*	*21*	*36*	*42*	*58*	224	11	*73*	*91*	[illegible]
Research & Development Organisations	23	*0*	*48*	*52*	*30*	*56*	*44*	77	5	*87*	*91*	[illegible]
Social Associations	49	*11*	*43*	*46*	*57*	*48*	*52*	230	11	*47*	*89*	[illegible]
Social Service & Welfare Organisations	62	*25*	*30*	*45*	*10*	*16*	*84*	9,849	182	*87*	*90*	[illegible]
Sports Organisations	10	*0*	*10*	*90*	*20*	*76*	*24*	54	7	*70*	*90*	[illegible]
Travel: Agents, Services, Tour Operators	38	*0*	*61*	*39*	*3*	*41*	*59*	413	12	*83*	*94*	[illegible]
Youth & Children's Organisations	91	*18*	*38*	*44*	*17*	*51*	*49*	1,173	16	*69*	*95*	[illegible]
TOTAL SERVICES	**1,003**	***12***	***40***	***48***	***22***	***17***	***83***	**30,471**	**41**	***71***	***89***	[illegible]
Training												
Bible Study Agencies	18	*6*	*61*	*33*	*39*	*24*	*76*	128	12	*61*	*78*	*72*
Conventions, Bible Weeks, Exhibitions and Festivals	30	*11*	*46*	*43*	*36*	*48*	*52*	131	7	*64*	*93*	*93*
Educational Agencies	65	*15*	*32*	*53*	*32*	*39*	*61*	309	7	*73*	*87*	*81*
Educational Resource Centres	33	*6*	*52*	*42*	*13*	*52*	*48*	100	4	*74*	*81*	*74*
Schools, Independent Christian	41	*62*	*21*	*17*	*0*	*49*	*51*	5,116	122	*100*	*90*	*95*
Teaching English as a Foreign Language Schools	7	*0*	*44*	*56*	*0*	*27*	*73*	85	9	*89*	*100*	*100*
Theological Colleges & Bible Schools (Full-time)	105	*45*	*36*	*19*	*4*	*53*	*47*	4,083	41	*89*	*90*	*87*
Theological Colleges and Bible Schools (Part-time)	42	*10*	*49*	*41*	*10*	*62*	*38*	291	8	*77*	*85*	*57*
Training Centres & Services	83	*0*	*32*	*68*	*11*	*46*	*54*	471	6	*68*	*91*	*81*
TOTAL TRAINING	**424**	***23***	***38***	***39***	***14***	***50***	***50***	**10,714**	**31**	***79***	***88***	***84***
GRAND TOTAL	**5,005**[2]	***16***	***41***	***43***	***19***	***55***	***45***	**82,805**	**20**	***74***	***83***	***70***
GRAND TOTAL 2003	5,055	15	41	44	19	53	47	82,129	19	77	[illegible]	59
GRAND TOTAL 2001	5,5014	15	40	45	21	50	50	77,471	18	75	[illegible]	46
GRAND TOTAL 1999	5,6002	15	41	44	28	41	59	72,378	19	69	[illegible]	23
GRAND TOTAL 1997	5,515	17	51	32	20	35	65	69,832	16	57	[illegible]	8
GRAND TOTAL 1995	5,593	22	57	21	19	34	66	64,333	14	48	[illegible]	n/a
GRAND TOTAL 1993	5,215	18[3]	41[4]	41[5]	20	36	64	57,133	14	40	n/a	n/a
GRAND TOTAL 1991	4,738	17[3]	43[4]	40[5]	22	36	64	62,012	17	26	n/a	n/a
GRAND TOTAL 1988	4,074	19[3]	24[4]	57[5]	24	38	62	48,781	16	3	n/a	n/a
GRAND TOTAL 1986	3,580	19[3]	26[4]	55[5]	27	38	62	45,944	14	n/a	n/a	n/a

1. Excluding multiple entries
2. Excluding 35 late Entries and addresses of 523 Other Organisations
3. Founded before 1900
4. Founded 1900–1975
5. Founded after 1975

TABLE 1: SUMMARY OF ORGANISATIONS BY RELIGIOUS AFFILIATION & INCOME (CONTINUED)

Category	Number[1]	Percentage registered with Charity Commission	Religious Affiliation: Percentage who are Anglican	Roman Catholic	Other Denominations	Inter[2]	Income/Turnover: Estimated Total £'000	Percentage[3]
		%	%	%	%	%		%
Services								
Addictions & Rehabilitation Services	36	*92*	*3*	*0*	*44*	*53*	£13,320	*58*
Animal Welfare Agencies	4	*50*	*25*	*0*	*0*	*75*	£54	*75*
Benevolent Organisations	38	*97*	*43*	*11*	*24*	*22*	£175,592	*76*
Buildings & Church Design	30	*21*	*11*	*0*	*36*	*53*	£8,207	*40*
Business Services	20	*18*	*6*	*0*	*35*	*59*	£38,892	*65*
Children's Care & Adoption Societies	26	*100*	*8*	*38*	*19*	*35*	£79,546	*83*
Counselling Organisations	87	*77*	*1*	*3*	*43*	*53*	£8,379	*68*
Creation Movements	7	*71*	*0*	*14*	*43*	*43*	£718	*86*
Organisations for People with Disabilities	27	*93*	*7*	*11*	*33*	*49*	£27,547	*67*
Environment Movements	5	*80*	*0*	*0*	*60*	*40*	£330	*60*
Ethnic Minority Associations	22	*77*	*0*	*18*	*27*	*55*	£1,968	*62*
Family Care & Support Ministries	15	*71*	*7*	*14*	*50*	*29*	£14,088	*64*
Financial Services	68	*28*	*6*	*0*	*51*	*43*	£434,236	*60*
Furnishings, Fabric & Church Interiors	36	*0*	*3*	*0*	*33*	*64*	£16,983	*42*
Health & Healing Organisations	40	*88*	*15*	*3*	*29*	*53*	£24,678	*70*
Information & Telephone Organisations	23	*48*	*9*	*17*	*35*	*39*	£1,528	*30*
Marketing & Fundraising Services	28	*8*	*0*	*0*	*38*	*62*	£4,478	*37*
Marriage Ministries	19	*68*	*16*	*16*	*37*	*31*	£2,032	*74*
Personnel Consultancy and Placement	24	*38*	*0*	*8*	*46*	*46*	£2,071	*50*
Prayer Fellowships	39	*67*	*3*	*0*	*46*	*51*	£1,288	*58*
Printers	18	*18*	*6*	*0*	*29*	*65*	£12,110	*56*
Professional Christian Groups	78	*70*	*5*	*4*	*20*	*71*	£5,003	*54*
Pro-Life Organisations	7	*14*	*0*	*0*	*29*	*71*	£2,350	*67*
Reconciliation & Mediation Groups	33	*58*	*3*	*21*	*21*	*55*	£9,410	*50*
Research & Development Organisations	23	*74*	*9*	*4*	*9*	*78*	£3,029	*42*
Social Associations	49	*53*	*0*	*11*	*30*	*59*	£5,437	*49*
Social Service & Welfare Organisations	62	*95*	*7*	*8*	*37*	*48*	£242,190	*77*
Sports Organisations	10	*90*	*0*	*0*	*80*	*20*	£3,187	*80*
Travel Agents Services, Tour Operators	38	*11*	*0*	*0*	*22*	*78*	£80,496	*54*
Youth & Children's Organisations	91	*79*	*7*	*2*	*44*	*47*	£63,409	*59*
TOTAL SERVICES	**1,003**	***62***	***6***	***6***	***35***	***53***	**£1,284,466**	***59***
Training								
Bible Study Agencies	18	*78*	*0*	*6*	*22*	*72*	£3,637	*41*
Conventions, Bible Weeks, Exhibitions and Festivals	30	*64*	*0*	*4*	*50*	*46*	£8,092	*48*
Educational Agencies	65	*71*	*8*	*6*	*40*	*46*	£7,550	*48*
Educational Resource Centres	33	*61*	*26*	*3*	*55*	*16*	£1,754	*38*
Schools, Independent Christian	41	*93*	*0*	*0*	*100*	*0*	£99,497	*61*
Teaching English as a Foreign Language Schools	7	*56*	*0*	*0*	*33*	*67*	£1,573	*75*
Theological Colleges & Bible Schools (Fulltime)	105	*85*	*14*	*11*	*43*	*32*	£90,635	*45*
Theological Colleges and Bible Schools (Part-time)	42	*77*	*21*	*0*	*41*	*38*	£4,952	*36*
Training Centres & Services	83	*70*	*3*	*1*	*50*	*46*	£9,149	*48*
TOTAL TRAINING	**424**	***76***	***9***	***5***	***50***	***36***	**£226,839**	***47***
GRAND TOTAL	**5,005**[5]	**57**	**8**	**8**	**45**	**39**	**£3,070,674**[4]	**46**
GRAND TOTAL 2003	5,055	61	9	9	36	46	£2,322,737	45
GRAND TOTAL 2001	5,501	60	10	9	31	50	£2,135,066	44
GRAND TOTAL 1999	5,600	55	9	8	33	50	£2,139,843	45
GRAND TOTAL 1997	5,515	59	12	9	18	61	£1,821,793	51
GRAND TOTAL 1995	5,593	54	14	9	19	58	£1,872,198	50
GRAND TOTAL 1993	5,215	58	14	9	18	59	£1,418,337	53
GRAND TOTAL 1991	4,738	55	11	10	18	61	£1,112,135	54
GRAND TOTAL 1988	4,074	48	10	10	16	64	£774,583	55
GRAND TOTAL 1986	3,580	48	11	11	14	64	£586,395	51

1. Excluding multiple entries
2. Interdenominational/non-denominational/ecumenical/evangelical
3. Percentage of organisations on which total figure is estimated
4. 46 denominations additionally supplied figures giving a total of £149,078,547, including one denomination with £60m and 8 Dioceses totalling £60.9m
5. Excluding 35 late Entries and addresses of 323 Other Organisations

TABLE 2: LARGEST ORGANISATION BY TURNOVER/INCOME

Organisations listed in the *UK Christian Handbook* and which reported their Turnover/Income as £2.2 million or more allowing for inflation on the 2003 level of £2.1 million and the 2001 level or £2.0 million). The organisations form 3.5% of the addresses in the *Handbook* but account for 73.2% of the total income, when allowance is made for denominational income. A further [illegible] organisations had income of £2.1 million and 27 organisations had income of £2.0 million. **Turnover/Income is given in millions**

Organisation	Turnover/Income
Ecclesiastical Insurance Group plc	£333.6
Church Commissioners	£145.0
English Churches Housing Group	£76.0
Help the Aged	£74.9
Christian Aid	£71.0
The Presbyterian Church in Ireland	£60.0
Tearfund	£53.0
Methodist Homes for the Aged	£52.7
World Vision UK	£49.2
Catholic Agency for Overseas Development (CAFOD)	£47.0
The Salvation Army Social Services Department	£42.0
CrossReach. Church of Scotland Social Care Council	£41.1
Finance Division of the Archbishops' Council	£40.0
The Children's Society	£40.0
World Emergency Relief	£34.8
The Shaftesbury Society	£34.4
YMCA, England	£33.0
Key Travel	£31.0
Stewardship	£30.6
Salvation Army Housing Association	£30.1
Send The Light Ltd	£30.0
Tours for Churches	£30.0
United Bible Societies, World Service Centre	£25.2
Chester College of Higher Education	£24.7
Samaritan's Purse International	£20.9
Eton College	£20.4
Autosave (UK) Ltd	£20.0
Congregational & General Insurance plc	£18.8
The College of St Mark and St John	£17.8
Shared Interest	£17.7
Traidcraft plc	£15.5
Creative Publishing	£15.0
Spurgeon's Child Care	£12.2
Roman Catholic Archdiocese of Glasgow	£12.0
Methodist Recorder	£11.5
Church of England Diocese of St Albans	£11.0
Mildmay Mission Hospital	£11.0
St Christopher's Hospice	£11.0
The Continuum International Publishing Group Ltd	£11.0
Methodist Insurance plc	£10.2
John Grooms	£10.0
Mission Care	£10.0
Adullam Homes Housing Association Ltd	£9.8
Bible Society (The British and Foreign Bible Society)	£9.5
Operation Mobilisation	£9.2
Lion Hudson plc	£8.8
Mission Aviation Fellowship	£8.6
Aldenham School	£8.0
Greencastle Pilgrimage Tours	£8.0
Mildmay International	£8.0
YMCA, London, West	£8.0
Church Mission Society	£7.9
PROSPECTS for People with Learning Disabilities	£7.8
Church Army	£7.7
Scripture Union	£7.6
Church of England Diocese of Liverpool	£7.6
Every Child	£7.4
Church of England Diocese of Gloucester	£7.0
Caterham School	£7.0
Church of England Diocese in Europe	£7.0
BMS World Mission	£6.9
Church of England Diocese of Bristol	£6.8
Religious Society of Friends (Quakers) in Britain	£6.7
The Langley House Trust	£6.6
United Christian Broadcasters Ltd	£6.5
London City Mission	£6.1
AFD Computers/AFD Software Ltd	£6.0
Auchlochan Trust	£6.0
CAHA Christian Alliance Housing Association Ltd	£6.0
Church of England Diocese of Peterborough	£6.0
Compassion	£6.0
MasterSun	£6.0
YWCA of England & Wales	£6.0
Wycliffe Bible Translators	£5.9
The Corporation of the Church House	£5.9
United Society for the Propagation of the Gospel	£5.5
Aldridge Print Group	£5.5
Royal Masonic School for Girls	£5.5
John Grooms Housing Association	£5.4
Blythswood Care	£5.3
Council for World Mission	£5.0
M Wood Insurance Services Ltd	£5.0
The Orange Grove Foster Care Agency	£5.0
Aid to the Church in Need	£4.9
L'Arche	£4.9
The Mission to Seafarers	£4.8
The Leprosy Mission, England and Wales Office	£4.7
Methodist Church World Church Office	£4.6
Father Hudson's Society (Archdiocese of Birmingham)	£4.5
Leicester Grammar School	£4.4
Catholic Institute for International Relations	£4.4
Catholic Children's Society (Arundel and Brighton, Portsmouth)	£4.3
OMF International (UK)	£4.3
Mercy Ships UK	£4.3
Pilgrim Homes	£4.2
Pontifical Missionary Societies	£4.2
Birmingham St Mary's Hospice	£4.1
Medair UK	£4.0
Home Words	£4.0
Scottish Catholic International Aid Fund (SCIAF)	£4.0
St Cuthbert's Care	£4.0
British & International Sailors' Society	£3.8
Premier Christian Radio	£3.8
Pecan Ltd	£3.7
St Joseph's College	£3.7
The Churches Conservation Trust	£3.7
Maxco Trust	£3.5
Catholic Caring Services (Diocese of Lancaster) Ltd	£3.5
Church of England Diocese of Hereford	£3.5
Echoes of Service	£3.5
HCPT The Pilgrimage Trust	£3.5
Haven's Christian Hospice	£3.5
Salvationist Publishing and Supplies Ltd	£3.5
YMCA, London, Waltham Forest	£3.5
Christian Blind Mission	£3.4
Free Church of Scotland	£3.4
Open Doors UK & Ireland	£3.4
International Fellowship of Evangelical Students	£3.2
SIM UK (Serving in Mission)	£3.2
Scope Productions Ltd	£3.2
BibleLands	£3.1
Adventist Development and Relief Agency (ADRA-UK)	£3.0
Belfast Central Mission	£3.0
Bolsius (UK) Ltd	£3.0
Care for the Family	£3.0
Co-operation Ireland	£3.0
Lifewords	£3.0
Westonbirt School	£3.0
Universities and Colleges Christian Fellowship (UCCF)	£2.9
CWR (Crusade for World Revival)	£2.9
Feba	£2.9
Rye St Antony School	£2.9
The Gideons International in the British Isles	£2.9
WEC International	£2.8
Newham Community Renewal Programme Ltd	£2.8
YMCA, National Centre	£2.8
A T Bell Insurance Brokers Ltd	£2.7
Catholic Children's Rescue Society (Diocese of Salford)	£2.7
Lifewords	£2.7
Newbold College	£2.7
Oasis Trust	£2.7
Church Pastoral Aid Society	£2.6
Baptist Insurance Company plc	£2.6
Keychange Charity	£2.5
Scripture Union Scotland	£2.5
Agapé	£2.5
CAHA Christian Alliance Housing Association Ltd	£2.5
Cathedral Church of the Holy and Undivided Trinity	£2.5
Catholic Children's Society (Diocese of Westminster)	£2.5
Central Hall Westminster	£2.5
Crusaders	£2.5
Ellenor Foundation	£2.5
Evangelical Alliance	£2.5
Habitat for Humanity Great Britain	£2.5
RG Jones Sound Engineering	£2.5
Royal National Mission to Deep Sea Fishermen	£2.5
Surecar Consultants	£2.5
Traidcraft plc	£2.5
WRS Limited Insurance Brokers	£2.5
West London Mission	£2.5
Youth With A Mission (YWAM)	£2.5
Mission Without Borders (UK) Ltd	£2.4
Christian Publishing & Outreach Ltd	£2.4
Interserve	£2.3
Church Urban Fund	£2.3
AIM International	£2.3
Crosslinks	£2.3
Hospitaller Order of St John of God	£2.3
Wigwam Acoustics Ltd	£2.3
Youth For Christ	£2.2
Church of the Nazarene	£2.2
Kenneth Copeland Ministries	£2.2
Castle Craig Hospital	£2.2
Total	**£2[illegible]49.1**

Total: 172 organisations in 2006
(180 of £2.1m + in 2003, [illegible]79 of £2.0m + in 1999, 149 in 1999,
144 in 1997 and 105 in 1995

MEMBERSHIP ORGANISATIONS

CHRISTIAN RESEARCH

CHRISTIAN RESEARCH

Christian Research undertakes a wide range of activities primarily designed for Christian leaders. It is well known for statistical data on church attendance but does a wide range of other quantitative and qualitative research, much of it commissioned by Christian organisations and denominations. Publication of resources such as the *UK Christian Handbook* and its companion volume *Religious Trends* is another aspect of the work. To help leaders understand and apply information to their particular context, Christian Research offers seminars and briefings based on research as well as consultancy. We are a membership organisation, and members of CRA get privileged access to the information and resources we have available.

Advocate Members
Ansvar Insurance Company Ltd
Archdeacon of Hampstead
CARE
Christ for the Nations UK
Church Army
CWR
Holy Ghost, Balham
Peniel Pentecostal Church
Salvation Army: Central North Division
St Nicholas', Durham
St Nicholas', Sevenoaks
Zondervan

Corporate Members
Action of Churches Together in Scotland (ACTS)
Adventist World Radio
Agapé
All Saints, Brixton
All Saints, Haywards Heath
Altrincham Baptist Church
Angel Foundation
Arab World Ministries
Archbishops' Council Research & Statistics
Archdeacon of Bradford
Ashburnham Christian Trust
Ashford Christian Fellowship
Aspley St Margaret

Barnabas Adventure Centres Ltd
Barnardo's
A J Bennewith & Co
Bible Reading Fellowship
BibleLands
Board of Mission in Ireland
Board for Social Responsibility, Liverpool Diocese
Boys' Brigade
Bracknell Family Church
Bridge Street Pentecostal Church
Bridge-Builders
British and Irish Association for Mission Studies
British & Foreign Bible Society
Bromley Christian Centre
Brook Lane Community Church

Cambridge Community Church
Capernwray Missionary Fellowship
Care For Mission
Care for the Family
CCM
Centre for Youth Ministry
Chapel House Publishing Oxford Limited
Chaplaincy Services, RAF
Charlotte Baptist Chapel, Edinburgh
Chinese Church in London
Christ Church, Bromley
Christ Church, Chineham
Christian Aid
Christian Art
Christian Communications Partnership Ltd
Christian Conference Trust
Christian Medical Fellowship
Christian Publicity Organisation
Christian Resources Exhibitions Ltd
Christian Youth Ministries
Christianity Today
Christians Aware
Christians in Sport
Church Administrator
Church Commissioners
Church of England Dioceses of:
Canterbury
Chelmsford
Chichester
Lichfield
Rochester
Salisbury
Church Pastoral Aid Society
Church Society
City Temple URC, London
Cliff College
The Coign Church, Woking
Congregational & General Insurance plc
Cornerstone Evangelical Church, Nottingham
CPL Chartered Architects (Church Projects Ltd)
Crawley Baptist Church
Crofton Lane Baptist Church, Orpington
Crown Nominations Commission
Crusaders / Urban Saints
Culham Institute

Deo Gloria Trust
Department for Research & Training in Mission, Baptist Union
DISCERN
Ealing Christian Fellowship
European Christian Mission
Evangelical Theological College of Wales
Evangelical Alliance

Feba Radio
Finchampstead Baptist Church
Fresh Expressions

Global Connections
Gold Hill Baptist Church
Gospel Light
Guildford Community Church

Haven Green Baptist Church
HEADWAY
Heart of England Baptist Association
Hillingdon Park Baptist Church
Holy Trinity, Aylesbury
Holy Trinity, Cheltenham
Hope UK
Hounslow Holy Trinity
Housing Justice
Huntingdonshire Community Church
Hymns Ancient & Modern Ltd

ICC
Immanuel Church, Romford
Independent Methodist Association
Irn Christian Ministries
International Christian College
International Nepal Fellowship
Interserve
Interserve Ireland

Jesmond Parish Church
Jesus Fellowship Central Office
Jubilee Community Church, Maidenhead

Kent Baptist Association
Kevin Mayhew Ltd
Key Travel
King's Church, Catford
Kingdom Bank Ltd

The Langham Partnership International
Latin Link UK
Leprosy Mission International
The Leprosy Mission Scotland
Librarians' Christian Fellowship
Life Changing Ministries International
Lifewords
Living Waters Church
London Baptist Association

London City Mission
London Institute for Contemporary Christianity
London School of Theology

Maybridge Christian Fellowship
Methodist Church Connexional Team
Mission Aviation Fellowship
Mission & Public Affairs Division
Moorlands College
Moorlands College Library
Moravian Church
The Mothers' Union
George Müller Foundation

National Mission Office, Church of Scotland
Nazarene Theological College
Network Church, St Albans
New Community Church, Sidcup
New Harvest Community Church, Brentwood
New Life Church, Cheltenham
New Tribes Mission
New Way of Being Church

OC International
OMF International (UK)
Open Doors UK & Ireland
Operation Mobilisation
Outlook Trust

Partnership
PCCA Christian Child Care
People's Christian Fellowship
Pip'n'Jay, Bristol
Potton Vineyard Church
Poynton Baptist Church

Premier Radio
Presbyterian Church in Ireland Board of Mission

Queens Park Baptist Church, Glasgow
Radipole & Melcombe Regis Benefice
Redcliffe College
Regents Park College
Regents Theological College
Rural Ministries

St Barnabas', Kensington
St James', Muswell Hill
St John's, West Ealing
St John's, Woodbridge
St Laurence's, Chorley
St Marks, Holloway
St Marks', Versailles
St Paul's, Salisbury
St Thomas', Blackpool
St Thomas', Sheffield
The Salvation Army: North Scotland Division
Samaritan's Purse International
SAO Cambodia
SASRA
Scripture Union
Scripture Union Scotland
Seventh-day Adventist Church
The Shepherd's Ministries, London
SIM International (UK)
Society for Promoting Christian Knowledge (SPCK)
Solihull Christian Fellowship
Southall Baptist Church
Spring Harvest
Spurgeon's College

Stewardship
Stewardship & Finance Department, Church of Scotland
Streatham Baptist Church
Surbiton Hill Christ Church

Tearfund
Traidcraft plc
True Freedom Trust

United Reformed Church in the United Kingdom
United Bible Societies
United Free Church of Scotland
United Reformed Church Windermere Centre
United Reformed Church Eastern Synod Office
University of Wolverhampton

Victoria Baptist Church, Eastbourne
Viva Network

WEC International
Wesley Institute Library
West of England Baptist Association
West Croydon Baptist Church
Wild Goose Resource Group
Woolwich Area Resource Exchange
World Vision UK
Wycliffe Bible Translators

Yeovil Community Church
YMCA, Bournemouth
Yorkshire Baptist Association
Youth With A Mission
Youth for Christ

In addition to the 250 members listed above Christian Research has nearly 650 Personal members.

CHURCHES TOGETHER IN BRITAIN & IRELAND

CHURCHES TOGETHER IN BRITAIN AND IRELAND

Churches Together in Britain and Ireland helps the Churches to think, work and pray together. It is the direct successor to the old British Council of Churches and is the official ecumenical body which brings together Catholic, Orthodox, Anglican, Protestant and Pentecostal traditions. Its work includes racial justice, inter faith relations, international affairs, global mission and spirituality. CTBI works closely with the Churches Together bodies which focus on Wales, Ireland, Scotland and England.

Full members (36)
Antiochian Orthodox Society of Britain
Baptist Union of Great Britain
Catholic Bishops' Conference of England and Wales
Catholic Bishops' Conference of Scotland
Cherubim and Seraphim Council of Churches
Church in Wales
Church of England
Church of God of Prophecy
Church of Ireland
Church of Scotland
Congregational Federation
Coptic Orthodox Church
Council of African and Caribbean Churches UK
Council of Oriental Orthodox Churches
Free Churches' Group
German-Speaking Congregation
Independent Methodist Churches
International Ministerial Council of Great Britain
Joint Council for Anglo and African-Caribbean Churches
Lutheran Council of Great Britain
Methodist Church
Methodist Church in Ireland
Moravian Church
New Testament Assembly
Oecumenical Patriarchate (Archdiocese of Thyateira and Great Britain)
Presbyterian Church of Wales
Religious Society of Friends
Russian Orthodox Church
Salvation Army
Scottish Episcopal Church
Serbian Orthodox Church
Trans-Atlantic & Pacific Alliance of Churches
Undeb Yr Annibynwyr / Union of Welsh Independents
United Free Church of Scotland
United Reformed Church
Wesleyan Holiness Church

Associated Members (2)
British Union Conference of Seventh-day Adventists
Roman Catholic Church of Ireland - Irish Episcopal Conference

Bodies in Association (33)
Action by Christians Against Torture
L'Arche
Association of Interchurch Families
Bible Society
Christian Council on Ageing
Christian Education
Christians Aware
Church Action on Disability
Church Action on Poverty
Churches Alert to Sex Trafficking across Europe
College of Preachers
Community of Aidan and Hilda
Corrymeela Community
Council on Christian Approaches to Defence and Disarmament
Ecumencial Council for Corporate Responsibility
Faith In Europe
Feed the Minds
Fellowship of Reconciliation
Fellowship of St Alban and St Sergius
Focolare Movement
The Industrial Mission Association
International Ecumenical Fellowship
Iona Community
Irish School of Ecumenics
Living Stones
Modem
NoATE (Network of Adult Theological Educators)
Retreat Association
Student Christian Movement
The Society of Ecumenical Studies
William Temple Foundation
Women's World Day of Prayer Movement
YMCA

THE EVANGELICAL ALLIANCE

Evangelical Alliance - Uniting to Change Society

The Evangelical Alliance UK, formed in 1846, is an umbrella group representing over one million evangelical Christians in the UK and is made up of member churches, organisations and individuals. As part of a movement 'uniting to change society' the Alliance promotes unity and truth, acts as an evangelical voice to the state, society and the wider Church, and provides resources to help members and other evangelicals live out their faith in their communities.

The Alliance's headquarters at Whitefield House in Kennington, London, houses a conference centre and hot desking facilities. For the latest evangelical news and access to resources and information about the work of the Alliance, log onto the Alliance's website at www.eauk.org or telephone 020 7207 2100.

Member Groups
= Organisation in membership of the Evangelical Alliance which is not listed in the UK Christian Handbook. All organisations which are listed have an asterisk (*) against their entry. If the entry is listed under another name this is given in brackets.

The 174 Trust
1904 Ltd
2K Plus International Sports Media
#2AMASE
The 40:3 Trust

AFD Software Ltd
Abernethy Trust Ltd
Acorn Christian Foundation
Across Havering
Activate
Adept Design
Adullam Homes Housing Association
#African Revival Ministries UK
#The Agapao Christian Trust
Agapé
Aglow International (Britain)
Aid to Romania
#All for Jesus Missions
All Nations Christian College
ALove
Alternatives Pregnancy Counselling Centres: Brighton, Inverness
#Amana Trust
AMAZE
Ambassadors for Christ in Britain
Ambassadors in Sport
Amersham Christian Housing Association Ltd
Amethyst Centre For Alcohol & Drug Education
Anchor Recordings Limited
Anglo-Japanese Christian Ministries
#Anglo Swiss Ministries
Anorexia and Bulimia Care
Anvil Trust
The Apostolic Church
#Aquasports
Aquila Way
Artisan Initiatives Charitable Trust
Ashburnham Christian Trust
Assemblies Of God
Assist Europe
Association of Christian Teachers: England, Scotland
At Home in the Community Ltd

Baptist Union - Department of Resources & Training in Mission
Baptist Union of Scotland
Barnabas Adventure Centres Ltd
Barnabas Fund
Barnabus Project
Bawtry Hall
#The Beacon Centre Trust
BeaconLight Trust
Bedwas Christian Resource Centre
AT Bell Insurance Brokers Ltd
Betel of Britain
Bethany Christian Trust
Bethany Ministries
John Bevere Ministries International
Bible Alive
The Bible Network
Bible Society
Bible Text Publicity Mission
Big Ideas Trust
Birmingham Christian College
Birmingham City Mission
Blue Skies Video Productions
The Boys' Brigade
Bridge Builders
Bridge Community Trust
Brighton & Hove City Mission
Bristol & District Evangelical Alliance
Bristol International Student Centre
#British National Temperance League
Bromley Evangelical Fellowship
Fiona Bruce & Co-Solicitors
Bruderhof Communities in the UK
Brunel Manor Christian Centre

Cambodian Communities out of Crisis
Campaigner Ministries
#Cantercare
Capernwray Missionary Fellowship
Cardiff Christian Healing Ministry
#Cardiff Institute for Contemporary Christianity
CARE (Christian Action Research & Education)
Care & Relief for the Young (CRY)
Care For the Family
Careforce
Centre for Christ Trust (Burstone Manor)
Centre For Contemporary Christianity In Ireland
Centre for Legal Aid Assistance
Charity Logistics
#Cheltenham Youth for Christ
Children Worldwide
Chinese Church Support Ministries
Christ for All Nations
Christ for the Nations
Christian Alliance Housing Association
#Christian Book Centre, Wirral
Christian Camping International UK
Christian Care Association
Christian Communications Network (Europe) Ltd
Christian Concern, Crewe

Christian Copyright Licensing
Christian Deaf Link UK
Christian Discipleship International
Christian Education Europe
Christian Endeavour Union: Great Britain & Ireland, Ireland
Christian English Language Centre
#Christian Family Centre
Christian Focus Publications
Christian Guidelines Ltd
Christian Healing Mission
Christian Housing Trust
Christian Insurance Service
Christian Literature Crusade
Christian Medical Fellowship
Christian Music Ministries
Christian Pages
Christian Police Association
Christian Prison Ministries-Scotland
Christian Publishing and Outreach Ltd
Christian Research Association
Christian Resources Exhibitions
Christian Resources Project
Christian Schools' Trust
Christian Solidarity Worldwide
Christian Surfers UK
Christian Television Association
Christian Viewpoint for Men
Christian Vision
Christian Vocations
Christian Women Communication International In UK
Christian Youth Enterprises
Christian Youth Ministries
Christians Against Poverty
Christians in Business
Christians in Caring Professions
Christians in Communications (POTCA)
Christians in Entertainment
Christians In Property
Christians In Road Transport
Christians in Science
Christians in Sport
Chrysalis Arts Trust
#Church Initiative UK
Church of England Evangelical Council
#Church of Ireland Evangelical Fellowship
Church Pastoral Aid Society
Church's Ministry Among Jewish People
Churches' Child Protection Advisory Service
Cities Network - Scotland
City Light Trust
#City of Joy
#Clerkenwell Medical Mission
#Clevedon Forbes Fund
Cliff College
Coastline Christian Resources
Anthony Collins Solicitors
Come Back to God Campaign
#Commission - Christian Radio
Community Bible Study, UK
Community of the Word of God
Compass Braille/Sightlink
Compassion UK
Compassionate Response
Connect Using Skills Changing Lives Limited
Connections
Containers of Hope (Christian Hope International)
Cornerstone

Counselling & Prayer Trust
Countess of Huntingdon's Connexion
Counties
Coventry City Mission
Creation Resources Trust
Creation Science Movement
Credit Action
CRIB (Christian Responses to Islam in Britain)
Crisis Centre Ministries
#Crisis Recovery UK
Crocus Ministries
Cross Rhythms
Crossline Central
CrossReach
Crossroads Christian Counselling Service
#Crown Jesus Ministries
Crusaders/Urban Saints
Crystal Clear Audio
Cutting Edge Ministries
CVG Television
CWR (Crusade for World Revival)

The Damaris Trust
Daventry Contact
Day One
Daybreak Drug Project
Daybreak Mission
#Dayspring Ministries
DCF Premier Workshops Trust
DCI Foundation
Deaf Christian Network - Hands Together
Deo Gloria Trust
Derbyshire Village Mission
#Dol Y Goleuni
#DPWE

Eagle Ministries
East European Literature Advisory Committee
The East to West Trust
Edinburgh City Mission
#Educational Insurance Services Ltd
Elam Ministries
Elim Pentecostal Churches England, Ireland, Scotland
Ellel Ministries
European Christian Mission
Eurovangelism
Evangelical Concern for People with Disabilities
Evangelical Fellowship in the Church in Wales
Evangelical Ministries
#Evangelical United Relief Organisation
Evangelism Explosion (GB) Ltd
Every Home for Christ
#Exodus Discipleship And Training Centre

The Faith Mission
Faith to Faith
Family Foundations Trust
#Family Relationship Workshop
#Family Space
The Family Trust
Farmers' Christian Postal Service
FCS Cassette Services
Fegans Child & Family Care
Fellowship for Evangelising British Villages

Fellowship of Christian Magicians
Fellowship of Churches of Christ
Ffald-y-Brenin Trust
Finnish Lutheran Mission
Fit Lives
Focus on Israel
Food for the Hungry UK
Fountain of Wisdom Ministries
Four Twelve Ministries
France Mission Trust
Free Church of England
Free Church of Scotland
Free Methodist Church in the UK
Freedom in Christ Ministries
#Freedom Road Ministries
Friends International
#Friends of Turkey (UK)
Frontiers Ireland
Fulani Ministries
Full Gospel Business Men's Fellowship International
Functional English
Fusion
#Fusion Youth Project

Gaines Christian Youth Centre
Peter Gammons Ministries International
#GHOBE Ministries
#Gifts for Romania
GiG - Hope for Wales
Gilead Foundations Training Centre
Girls' Brigade England & Wales
Glasgow City Mission
Global Care
#Global Focus
Go To The Nations Link
God TV
Going Public
#Good News Centre Ltd.
Good News Crusade
Good News Fellowship (As Africa Christian Press)
Good Shepherd Ministries UK
Gospel Cards
Grace Ministries Trust
Grandma's
Grassroots Trust
John Grooms Housing Association
Ground Level Network
Group for Evangelism and Renewal
Growing Through
Gypsies for Christ

Haggai Institute
Hand in Hand
Hants & Dorset Christian Youth Camp
Harvesters Trust
HCJB-UK
Headway: England, Ireland
Healthcare Christian Fellowship of Wales
Heart of England Outreach
Heartcry
Hebron Trust
The Heralds Trust (Ian Leitch)
Hi Kidz (part of Children's Ministry)
Home Evangelism
#Homeland Deliverance Centre
Hope (Counselling and Support)
Hope Now Ministries
Hope UK
Hothorpe Hall Conference Centre

ICC - International Christian Communications
Ichthus Christian Fellowship
Impact Giving UK Trust
In Yer Face Christian Theatre Co.
Independent Methodist Association
Inn Christian Ministries
Institute for Bible Translation
Integrity Music (Europe) Ltd
Intercessors for Britain
Interhealth
#International Aid Trust
International Bible Society (UK)
International Bible Training Institute
International Christian Chamber of Commerce
International Christian College
International Films
International Gospel Outreach
#International Outreach
International Teams UK
International Training Network
Interserve UK, Ireland, Scotland
Into The Light
Into The Light - London
Irish Mission
ISAAC
The Island Churches Guernsey Festival Chorus

#Jersey Evangelical Alliance
Jesus is Alive! Ministries
Jews For Jesus
Joshua Generation

#Kairos Youth Outreach
#Kent Baptist Association
#Kent For Christ Trust
Keswick Convention Centre
Keychange
Kilravock Castle Christian Trust (Ellel Ministries)
Kingdom Bank
The King's Foundation
Kings Communications
KingsCare
Kingsway Communications Ltd

Label of Love
Latin Link
Lay Witness Movement
#Leeds Faith in Schools
#Lenchwood Christian Centre
#Leyton Evangelical Fellowship
Librarians' Christian Fellowship
Life for the World Trust
#Life Transforming Ministries
Lifestyle International Ministries
Lifewords
The Light Project
Links International
#Liverpool Youth For Christ
#Living Hope Ministries
Living Waters Discipleship & Healing Trust
#Logos European College
London & Home Counties Festivals of Male Voice Praise
London Baptist Association
London Mennonite Centre Trust including Bridge Builders
London School Of Theology

#Look No Hands
Love Russia
Lydia Fellowship International
Mainstream
Mallon de Theological College
#Malvern Bible Ministry
Manchester City Mission
Manchester Network
Marriage Ministries International
MasterPlan Publishing Ltd (MasterSki)
Mattersey Hall Bible College
Matthew Project
MAXCO Trust
Media Support Services (Hebron Hall Christian Centre)
Medina Valley Centre
Mercy Ships UK
MESSAGE Christian Telephone Service
The Message Trust
Message on the Move (MEMO)
Messianic Testimony
Methodist Resource Centre (Salt Cellar Ltd)
Mid Cotswold Evangelical Alliance
Midwales Christian Holiday Centre (Cefn-Lea Park)
Mildmay Mission Hospital
Mill Grove
Mimeistry UK
Mission Aviation Fellowship UK
Mission Care Elmwood
#Mission Doncaster
Mission for Christ
Mission in Hounslow Trust
Mission India
Mission To Eastern Europe
Mission to Marriage
Missions To Prisons
Moorlands College
Morrison Daylight Projectors
Mulberry House
George Müller Foundation
Multiply Christian Network

National Marriage Week
Nations Trust
The Navigators
Nazarene Theological College
The Nehemiah Project
#The Net
New Hope Trust
#New Irish Arts
New Testament Assembly
Newfrontiers
Next Level International
Nexus Trust
NGM New Generation Music and Mission
Northamptonshire Association of Youth Clubs
#Norwich Youth for Christ
Novi Most International

OAC Ministries
Oak Hill College
Oasis Trust
Obsessive Behaviour Ltd (Christian Association for Youth)
Off The Fence
Old Baptist Union
The Olive Tree Centre
Olivet English Language School
OMS International

On the Move Trust
One Accord
Open Ears
Operation Mobilisation
Origin Scotland
OSCAR
Outlook Trust
#Overseas Fellowship of Nigerian Christians

Luis Palau Evangelistic Association
Palm Services
Paraclete Christian Network International
Parakaleo Ministry
Partnership
Partnership for Growth (Link Romania)
#Passion
#Peaceworks
Pecan
Pennefather Christian Medical Community Trust
Philo Trust
Pilgrim Hall Christian Trust
Pilgrim Hearts Trust
Pilgrims Hall Fellowship Ltd
Pioneer Trust
#Plain Truth
Plumbline Ministries
Plymouth City Mission (Crossline Plymouth)
#Power of Prayer Ministries International
Pray for Scotland
#Prayer Box Society
Prayer Expeditions
Prayer For The Nations
Prayer Trust
Premier Media Group
#Premier Network Ministries
Presbyterian Church in Ireland: Board of Social Witness, Youth Board

#Preston Evangelical Network
Prison Fellowship, England & Wales, Northern Ireland, Scotland
Probation Service Christian Fellowship
Proclaim Trust
Project Evangelism
Prospects
Purley & Andover Christian Trust
Purpose Driven Church Network UK

Quantock Christian Trust

Radstock Ministries
REACH Merseyside
Reaching the Unchurched Network
Redcliffe College
Regents Theological College
Relationships Foundation (Jubilee Centre)
Release Foundation
Release International
Reprotec (Office Solutions) Ltd
Resolve
Revival (The Hour of Revival Association)
Ridley Hall Theological College
Rivers of Life Trust

Michael Roberts Charitable Trust
A Rocha
#Rock House Trust (Doncaster)

#Romania Care
ROPE Charitable Trust
RSR - Royal Sailors' Rests
Rural Sunrise
Rushworth Literature Enterprise
The RZIM Zacharias Trust

St John's College - Durham
St John's College - Nottingham
#St Mary Magdalene School
Salmon Youth Centre
Salt & Light Ministries
Saltbox Christian Centre
Saltmine Trust
Sandes Soldiers' and Airmen's Centres
Scottish Christian Alliance Ltd
Scottish Crusaders
Scripture Union, England, Scotland
Seamen's Christian Friends Society
SEAN International
Send the Light Ltd
Servants Fellowship International
Servants to Asia's Urban Poor
Shaftesbury Society
Shankill Road Mission
Share Trust
#Silk Road Ministries International
SIM-UK
Smile International
Soapbox Communications Trust
#SOaR
Social Work Christian Fellowship
Soul Survivor
South Asian Concern
South Bristol Christian Centre
#South Bristol Outreach Trust
South Wessex Evangelical Alliance (SWEA)
#South West London Asian Outreach
Southampton Action For Employment
Southampton Christian Network
(Southampton Evangelical Alliance)
Southampton City Mission
#Southwark For Jesus
Sovereign World Trust
Speak Network
Spinnaker Trust Limited
Spring Harvest
#Springboard to Life
Springs Dance Company
SPUC Evangelicals

Spurgeons College
Stamps for Evangelism
Stapleford Centre
Stepping Stones Trust
Caladine Stevens
Stewardship
Storm Ministries
Sustain

Tandem TV & Film Limited
Teachers For China
Tearfund
Teen Challenge UK
Telephone Prayer Chain Ministry
TES
Thames Christian College
TBF Thompson Ministries
Through The Roof
TISCA (The Independent Schools
Christian Alliance)
Tiverton & District Evangelical Fellowship
Together
Together for the Harvest (Merseyside)
Torch Trust for the Blind
Toybox Charity
Trans World Radio
Treasures in Heaven Trust
Trinity College
True Freedom Trust
Tunbridge Wells Fellowship Of
Evangelicals
Twenty Thirty

UK Church Directory Ltd (Find a
Church)
United Christian Broadcasters
United Free Church of Scotland
Universal Prayer Group Ministries
Unlock
Upminster Christian Entertainment Ltd
(Fools Bookshop)
#Urban Action, North Manchester
Urban Presence
U-Turn Anglia Trust

Victory Tracts & Posters
Vinesong
#Vision Crusades Trust
Viva Network
Viz-a-Viz

Wales Awake
Wallington Missionary Mart & Auctions
Wanstead & Woodford Evangelical
Council
The War Cry
Watford New Hope Trust
Wellspring Christian Trust
Wesleyan Reform Union
West Sussex Bible Correspondence
College
West Yorkshire School of Christian
Studies
Willow Creek Association UK
#Wirral Youth for Christ
Word for Women, Swanwick
Word of Life
Word to the World Ministries
World Action Ministries
World Emergency Relief
World Horizons
World Outreach
World Prayer Centre
World Sport Ministries
World Vision UK
WorldShare
Worldwide Church of God - HQ
Worldwide Harvest Ministries
Frank Wright Mundy & Co. Ltd

Yeldall
Youth Connection
Youth For Christ, UK and Northern Ireland
YMCA:
- Bournemouth
- City of Belfast
- Hove
- Norwich
- Nottinghamshire

YWAM (Youth With A Mission), UK,
Northern Ireland, Scotland

#Zephaniah Trust

In addition to the 618 member organisations listed above, the Evangelical Alliance has nearly 7,000 church members, thousands of individual members and represents over one million evangelical churches in the UK.

GLOBAL CONNECTIONS

Global Connections is a growing network of over 250 evangelical agencies, colleges and churches that are involved in cross-cultural mission from, to and in the UK. As a network we seek to help God's people in the UK be active and effective in global mission. This is done in various ways including events, publications, codes and guidelines, and affinity schemes. Our hope is that in working together we will increasingly see mission at the heart of the church, the church at the heart of mission.

To discover more about what God is doing in the world, the breadth of Global Connections activities or how to engage with others who are passionate about mission, see our website - www.globalconnections.co.uk

#= Organisation in membership of Global Connections which is not listed in the *UK Christian Handbook*.
All organisations which are listed have an asterisk (*) against their entry.

Full members (169)
3P Ministries
A Rocha
ACET (AIDS Care, Education & Training)
Act4Africa
Action International Alliance
Action Partners Ministries
Acts on the Net
AE Evangelistic Enterprise

Africa Inland Mission International
African Pastors' Fellowship
Agapé
Ambassadors in Sport
Arab World Ministries
AsiaLink
Assemblies Of God World Ministries
The Association of Christian Resource Organisations Serving Sudan (UK)

#Barnabas (Outreach) Trust
Belgian Evangelical Mission
Bible Society (The British and Foreign Bible Society)
BMS World Mission
Book Aid
Breadline
Bridge-builders

Cambodian Communities out of Crisis
CEDARS (Charity Equipment for Development & Relief Services)
Central African Missions
Centre for Legal Assistance and Settlement
Chinese Overseas Christian Mission
Chosen People Ministries
Christian Hope International
Christian Literature Crusade
Christian Medical Fellowship
Christian Publicity Organisation
Christian Research
Christian Vocations (CV)
Christian Witness to Israel
Christians in Action
Church Mission Society
Church's Mission Among Jewish People
CORD (Christian Outreach – Relief & Development)
Crosslinks
Crusaders/Urban Saints

Dohnavur Fellowship

#East African Ministries Trust
East-West Fellowship
ECHO International Health Services
Echoes of Service
Edinburgh International Health Centre
Elam Ministries
Ellel Ministries International
Emmanuel Healthcare
Emmanuel International UK
Encourage International
EQUIP
European Christian Mission

#Familylink International
Feba
Fellowship of Faith for the Muslims (FFM)
Focus Radio
FOI Ministries
Fonic Trust
Food for the Hungry
France Mission Trust
Friends International
Frontiers UK, Ireland

Fulani Ministries

#GAP International
Global Outreach UK
Gorakhpur Nurseries Fellowship
Gospel Printing Mission

Haggai Institute for Advanced Leadership Training Ltd
HCJB-UK
Heart of the Father
Heartlink

Ichthus Christian Fellowship
IFES Trust
iNet
Intercontinental Church Society
InterHealth
International Fellowship of Evangelical Students
International Miners Mission
The Inter-National Needs Network
International Nepal Fellowship
International Teams UK
International Training Network
Interserve, England, Ireland, Scotland

Janz Team UK
Japan Christian Link
Jews For Jesus
Jian Hua Foundation

Langham Partnership Internaitonal
Latin Link
The Leprosy Mission, England and Wales Office, International Office, Northern Ireland, Scotland
Lifewords
Links International

Henry Martyn Trust
Media Associates International
Medical Service Ministries
The Messianic Testimony
Middle East Bible Outreach UK
Middle East Christian Outreach
Middle East Media
Mission Africa
Mission Aviation Fellowship UK + Europe
#Mission Encouragement Trust

The Navigators
Newfrontiers
North West Frontier Fellowship
Novi Most International

Oasis Trust
OC International UK
OMF International (UK)
OMS International
Open Doors UK
Operation Mobilisation
Orphaids UK
OSCAR

Penhurst Retreat Centre
People International
The Philippine Community Fund

Pioneer DNA Teams
Prayer Fellowship for South Asia
Preacher's Help
Presbyterian Church in Ireland

Radstock Ministries
#Ramabai Mukti Mission – English Council
Red Sea Mission Team
Release International
ReTRAK
Romanian Aid Fund

Samaritan's Purse International Limited
SAO Cambodia
SAT-7 Trust Ltd
Scripture Union
Servants to Asia's Urban Poor
Sierra Leone Mission
Sightlink / Compass Braille
SIM UK (Serving in Mission)
Soapbox Communications Trust
South American Mission Society (SAMS)
South Asian Concern
Sovereign World Trust
Stamps for Evangelism
Syzygy Mission Support Network

TASK (Training & Advice for Service in the Kingdom)
Teachers for China / Caring for China's Children / Health for China
Tearfund
Teso Development Trust
Torch Trust for the Blind
Trans World Radio Ltd

UFM Worldwide

Viva Network

WEC International
What4
WMA – UK
World Horizons (Britain)
World In Need
World Outreach
World Team UK
World Vision UK
WorldShare
#Worldwide Missions Outreach Ministries
Worldwide Missionary Convention
Wycliffe Associates (UK)
Wycliffe UK

Xenos

#YFCI/MENA
#Youth With A Mission (YWAM) England

Zambesi Mission

Member Colleges (17)
All Nations Christian College
Belfast Bible College
Bible College of Wales
Birmingham Christian College
The Evangelical Theological College of Wales

Member Bodies

Faith Mission Bible College
International Christian College, Glasgow
London School of Theology
The Missionary Training Service
Moorlands College
Nazarene Theological College
New Tribes Mission Bible & Missionary Training
Oak Hill Theological College
Redcliffe College
Southall School of Languages & Missionary Orientation
Trinity College, Bristol
#Veritas College

Affiliate Members (5)
Avant
Caleb Project Europe
Finnish Lutheran Mission
Friends of IEM (UK)
Pillar of Fire International

CHURCHES TOGETHER IN BRITAIN AND IRELAND

GLOBAL MISSION NETWORK

(Formerly The Churches' Commission on Mission)

CTBI's **Global Mission Network** is the ecumenical coordinating body for the mission departments and agencies of the churches in Britain and Ireland. It assists global witness and service through: world region networks, projects (China, missionary congregations), publications, and the Edinburgh Centenary Mission Fund. Read our Newsletter online at www.ccom.org.uk

Member Bodies (34)
Baptist Union of Great Britain
BMS World Mission
Catholic Church in England and Wales[1]
Catholic Agency for Overseas Development
Catholic Institute for International Relations
Cherubim and Seraphim Council of Churches
Christian Aid
Christian Education
Christians Abroad
Christians Aware
Church in Wales
Church of England
Church Mission Society and United Society for the Propagation of the Gospel
Church of Ireland/Council of the Church Overseas
Church of Scotland
CMS Ireland
Congregational Federation
Feed the Minds
Independent Methodist Churches
International Ministerial Council of Great Britain
Irish Missionary Union
Leprosy Mission
Methodist Church
Methodist Church in Ireland
Oecumenical Patriarchate (Archdiocese of Thyateira and Great Britain
Presbyterian Church of Wales
Religious Society of Friends/Quaker Peace and Social Witness
Salvation Army (UK Territory)
Scottish Episcopal Church
Union of Welsh Independents
United Reformed Church
YMCA

[1] Denominational organisations (eg mission societies) are included in this membership

PWM partnership for world mission

PARTNERSHIP FOR WORLD MISSION (PWM)

Partnership for World Mission (PWM) seeks to bring together and resource those involved in world mission and partnership links: the World Mission Agencies, the Diocesan Companion Links network and parts of the National Church Institutions of the Church of England.

Church Army
The Church's Ministry among Jewish People (CMJ)
Church Mission Society (CMS)
Church Pastoral Aid Society (CPAS)
Crosslinks
Intercontinental Church Society (ICS)
The Mission to Seafarers
The Mothers' Union
South American Mission Society (SAMS)
The Society for Promoting Christian Knowledge (SPCK)
The United Society for the Propagation of the Gospel (USPG)

A

ACCOMMODATION

CAMPING, CARAVAN & OUTDOOR CENTRES

By Country and Postcode – for location of Postcodes see map on Page 458
Venues which did not supply this information are not listed here
Only venues with 10 or more bed spaces are included

S = single rooms **D/T** = number of bed spaces in double/twin rooms **L** = number of bed spaces in rooms larger than double
TS = total bed spaces (not number of rooms) **DR** = Day Room, the capacity of the largest room suitable for group use
⇌ = nearest Railway station ⊖ = nearest London Underground station

Postcode	Location	Name	S	D/T	L	Other		TS	DR	Railway
ENGLAND										
CA16	**Appleby-in-Westmorland**	Chapel Farm Caravan Park	n/a	n/a	n/a			n/a	n/a	⇌ Kirkby Stephen or Appleby or Oxenholme
		Knock Christian Centre	-	4	56			60	-	⇌ Appleby or Penrith
CM 9	**Maldon**	The Cirdan Sailing Trust	-	-	-	boats (large vessels)		4	n/a	⇌ Witham
		Fellowship Afloat Charitable Trust	-	6	30	boats		36	60	⇌ Witham
CW10	**Middlewich**	Middlewich Narrowboats	-	-	-	2×12-berth narrowboats	24	24	-	⇌ Crewe
DL11	**Richmond**	Marrick Priory	n/a	n/a	n/a			38	n/a	⇌ Darlington
DL12	**Barnard Castle**	The Kingsway Adventure Centre	-	4	38	camping	20	62	50	⇌ Darlington
EX33	**Braunton**	St George's House	n/a	n/a	46			46	70	⇌ Barnstaple
GL15	**Lydney**	Viney Hill Christian Adventure Centre	-	-	37	camping	70	107	60	⇌ Lydney
HG 3	**Harrogate**	West End Outdoor Centre	-	8	52			60	-	⇌ Harrogate
LA12	**Newby Bridge**	YMCA National Centre	4	30	160	camping	150	344	150	⇌ Grange-over-Sands
LA23	**Ambleside**	Victor Training	n/a	n/a	n/a			n/a	n/a	⇌ Windermere
LA23	**Windermere**	Packway House	-	-	-	5 apartments		6	-	⇌ Windermere
ME 4	**Chatham**	Morning Star Trust	-	-	-	boats	14	14	-	⇌ Chatham
NN 9	**Wellingborough**	Frontier Centre	-	-	215	self or full catering		215	50	⇌ Wellingborough
NR12	**Norwich**	Horstead Centre	1	4	35			40	40	⇌ Norwich or Hoveton & Wroxham
OX 2	**Witney**	Adventure Plus	n/a	n/a	n/a	camping	n/a	n/a	100	⇌ Oxford
PL27	**Wadebridge**	The Laurels Holiday Park	-	-	-	self-catering units	14	25	-	⇌ Bodmin Parkway
PO18	**Chichester**	Christian Youth Enterprises Sailing Centre	-	6	30			36	40	⇌ Nutbourne or Bosham
PO21	**Bognor Regis**	Copthorne Caravans	-	-	-	holiday caravans		52	-	⇌ Bognor Regis
PO30	**Newport**	Medina Valley Centre for Outdoor Education	-	10	64			74	80	⇌ Ryde Esplanade
SO30	**Southampton**	YMCA Fairthorne	-	96	64	camping	180	340	60	⇌ Botley
SS3	**Southend-on-Sea**	Sky Lodge Christian Camp	-	-	24	Camping, self catering cabins	16	40	30	⇌ Shoeburyness
TN11	**Tonbridge**	Carroty Wood		-	200	self-catering units		200	-	⇌ Tonbridge
TN14	**Sevenoaks**	Halls Green		-	104	4 self-catering units		104	-	⇌ Sevenoaks
WR 6	**Worcester**	Gaines Christian Youth Centre	1	26	88			115	120	⇌ Worcester Shrub Hill
SCOTLAND										
DG 7	**Castle Douglas**	Abernethy Trust Barcaple	-	12	45			57	-	⇌ Dumfries
FK21	**Killin**	Abernethy Trust Ardeonaig	-	10	44			54	52	⇌ Crianlarich or Pitlochry
IV20	**Tain**	Tarbat Free Church (Continuing) Caravan Site	-	-	-	caravans	35	35	-	⇌ Fearn or Tain
KY13	**Kinross**	Lendrick Muir Centre	-	12	138		150	150	-	⇌ Stirling
ML12	**Biggar**	Tweedsmuir Scottish Crusaders Centre	-	-	30	self-catering		30	30	⇌ Carstairs
PA29	**Tarbert**	Port Ban Caravan Park	-	-	-	caravans	125	125	250	⇌ None near
PA67	**Isle of Mull**	Camas Adventure Camp	-	-	16			16	20	⇌ Oban
PH6	**Comrie**	Combruith Scottish Crusaders Centre	-	-	46			46	40	⇌ Dunblane
PH10	**Blairgowrie**	Compass Christian Centre	-	12	56	self-catering		68	-	⇌ Perth (30 miles)
PH14	**Perth**	Teen Ranch Scotland	-	-	66			66	n/a	⇌ Dundee
PH22	**Aviemore**	Alltnacriche Christian Centre	2	16	34			52	60	⇌ Aviemore
PH25	**Nethy Bridge**	Abernethy Trust Nethy Bridge	-	60	20			80	120	⇌ Aviemore
PH33	**Fort William**	Abernethy Trust Ardgour	n/a	4	28			32	n/a	⇌ Fort William
		Discovery Cruising				6-berth yachts	12	12	-	⇌ Fort William
PH49	**Ballachulish**	Glencoe Outdoor Centre	-	2	33			35	50	⇌ Fort William
TD 9	**Newcastleton**	Whithaugh Park	-	-	190	self-catering lodges	90	90	-	⇌ Carlisle
WALES										
LL23	**Bala**	Cornerstone Quest Achievement Centre	-	28	16	Self or full catering		40	40	⇌ Wrexham
LL39	**Arthog**	Min-Y-Don Christian Adventure Centre	3	14	30	self-catering flat	3	50	60	⇌ Fairbourne
LL45	**Llanbedr**	CMC Pensarn Harbour	-	10	40			50	120	⇌ Pensarn
		The Ranch Outdoor Discovery Centre	-	4	36			40	40	⇌ Pensarn or Barmouth
SA 3	**Swansea**	St Madoc Christian Youth Camp		-	80	self-catering		80	-	⇌ Swansea
SA33	**Carmarthen**	Cilcoed Christian Centre	-	-	-	bunkhouse	35	35	-	⇌ Carmarthen
SA44	**Llandysul**	The Long Barn	-	2	29	flat	3	34	30	⇌ Carmarthen

CAMPING, CARAVAN & OUTDOOR CENTRES

***Abernethy Trust Ardeonaig**, Killin FK21 8SY
☎01567 820 523 📠01567 820 955
E: at@ardeonaig.org
Web: www.abernethytrust.org.uk
Fully-staffed residential centre offering courses for groups to develop leadership and team skills.
Centre Director: Mr Philip A Simpson. *Deputy Centre Director:* Mrs Rosemary K Simpson. Executive staff 4, Other staff 20. ***CC*** No.SCO 06270. Began 1984; interdenominational. (Previously Ardeonaig Outdoor Centre). Turnover £400,000 to year end Oct 05.

***Abernethy Trust Ardgour**, School of Adventure Leadership, Ardgour, Fort William PH33 7AD
☎01967 411 222 📠01967 411 250
E: at@ardgour.org
Web: www.abernethytrust.org.uk
Providing a one-year instructor training course; schools and youth groups multi-activity programme.
Operations Director: Mr Barry Edmonson. *Deputy Operations Director:* Mrs Karen Edmondson. Admin staff 2, Other staff 6. ***CC*** No.SCO 06270. Began 1992; interdenominational. (Previously Ardgour Outdoor Centre). Turnover £156,000 to year end Nov 04.

***Abernethy Trust Barcaple**, Ringford, Castle Douglas DG7 2AP
☎01557 820 261 M:07736 830 909
📠01557 820 354
E: at@barcaple.org
Web: www.abernethytrust.org.uk
Fully-staffed outdoor adventure centre providing programmes for personal growth, team building and leadership development.
Operations Director: Mr David Pratt. *Deputy Operations Director:* Sylvia Pratt. Executive staff 2, Admin staff 2, Other staff 14. ***CC*** No.SCO 06270. Began 1983; interdenominational. (Previously Barcaple Christian Outdoor Centre). Turnover £300,000 to year end Mar 05.

***Abernethy Trust Nethy Bridge**, Nethy Bridge PH25 3ED
☎01479 821 279 📠01479 821 162
E: at@nethybridge.org
Web: www.abernethytrust.org.uk
Residential Christian outdoor centre using its people, properties and programmes to share Christ.
Executive Director: Mr J Lorimer Gray. *Operations Director:* Mr D Rutledge. Guest *Services Manager:* Mr Andrew Marrian. Admin staff 5, Other staff 35. ***CC*** No.SC 006270. Began 1971; interdenominational. (Previously Abernethy Outdoor Centre). Turnover £770,000 to year end Dec 04.

Adventure Plus, Hill Grove Farm, Crawley, Witney OX29 0NA
☎01993 703 308 📠01993 708 433
E: enquiries@adventureplus.org.uk
Web: www.adventureplus.org.uk
Providing adventure holidays, expeditions and training courses for young people, schools, adults; gap year training.
Director: Mr Jonathan Cox.
Secretary: Mrs Tessa Cox. Admin staff 2, Other staff 6. ***CC*** No.1081059. Began 1990; interdenominational. (Previously Fair Glade Trust). Turnover £300,000 to year end Dec 04.

Alltnacriche Christian Centre (Scripture Union Scotland), Lynwilg, Aviemore PH22 1PZ
☎01479 810 237 📠01479 811 383
E: alltnacriche@suscotland.org.uk
Web: www.suscotland.org.uk
Self-catering or catering; year-round activities, mid-week schools programmes, exploring Christianity. Centre Managers: Mr & Mrs Richard & Katherine Scarffe. Staff 8. ***CC*** Began 1988; interdenominational. Turnover £102 000 to year end Mar 02.

†Braemoor Christian Holiday Village, Torranyard, Kilwinning KA13 7RD
☎01294 850 286 📠01294 850 486
E: info@braemoorchv.com
Web: www.braemoorchv.com
Offering caravan ownership, holidays, conferences and retreats.
Sales and Marketing Coordinator: Name not supplied. Executive staff 1, Other staff 17. Began 1999; non-denominational. Turnover n/a.

Camas Adventure Camp (Iona Community), Ardfenaig, Bunessan, Isle of Mull PA67 6DX
☎01681 700 367/404
E: camas@iona.org.uk
Web: www.ionacommunity.org.uk
Outdoor adventure facilitating inner adventure, personal relationships and environmental awareness. ***Closed for renovation until Spring 2007.***
Coordinator: David Berger. Executive staff 1, Admin staff 1, Other staff 11. ***CC*** No.SCO 03794. Began 1938; ecumenical. Turnover n/a.

***Carroty Wood (Barnabas Adventure Centres)**, Carroty Wood, Higham Lane, Tonbridge TN11 9QX
☎01732 361 361 📠01732 360 429
E: carrotywood@barnabas.org.uk
Web: www.barnabas.org.uk
Outdoor adventure centre and conferences for youth groups, churches and schools.
Centre Manager: Mr Malcolm Maclean. Executive staff 1, Other staff 4. ***CC*** No.276346. Began 1978; interdenominational. Turnover £329,000 to year end Mar 05.

Chapel Farm Caravan Park, Little Asby, Appleby-in-Westmorland CA16 6QE
☎01539 623 665 M: 07789 418 377
Caravan park including 5 caravans to let.
Proprietor: Mr Williams. Admin staff 1. Began 1980; interdenominational. Turnover £20,000 to year end Dec 94.

The Christian Adventure Centre, The Old Vicarage, Viney Hill, Lydney GL15 4NA
☎01594 516 162 📠01594 510 091
E: info@vineyhilladventure.org
Web: www.vineyhilladventure.org
Open all year for camping and indoor accommodation.
Manager: Tony Williams. Executive staff 1, Other staff 8. Began 1983; Anglican. (Previously Viney Hill Adventure Centre). Turnover £170,000 to year end Dec 05.

For bed-spaces etc. see list on Page 24

***Christian Youth Enterprises Sailing Centre**, The Gerald Daniel, Chidham, Chichester PO18 8TE
☎01243 573 375 🖷01243 574 992
E: info@cye.org.uk
Web: www.cye.org.uk
Watersports activity centre catering for groups, schools and individuals on holiday, courses and field studies.
Director: Mr Norman Doney. *Centre Manager:* Mr Gavin Jones. Admin staff 1, Other staff 8. ***CC*** No.293781. Began 1986; non-denominational. Turnover £175,000 to year end Dec 02.

Cilcoed Christian Centre, Meidrim, Carmarthen SA33 5QA
☎01994 230 232 M: 07971 258 030
🖷01994 230 232
E: cilcoed2002@hotmail.com
Self-catering facilities for young people; sharing the Gospel in local schools and clubs.
Project Coordinator: Mrs Row Robinson. Executive staff 1, Other staff 3. ***CC*** No.1096649. Began 1996; non-denominational. Turnover £15,000 to year end Jan 03.

The Cirdan Sailing Trust, 3 Chandlers Quay, Fullbridge, Maldon CM9 4LS
☎01621 851 433 🖷01621 840 045
E: info@cirdansailing.com
Web: www.cirdansailing.com
Providing groups of young people with the challenge of sailing large historic vessels.
Chief Executive Officer: Mr Nicholas Back. *Head of Marketing and Fundraising:* Mrs Leonie Turner. Executive staff 1, Admin staff 4, Other staff 1. ***CC*** No.1091598. Began 1983; Anglican. Turnover £500,000 to year end Dec 02.

***CMC Pensarn Harbour**, Pensarn Harbour, Llanbedr LL45 2HS
☎01341 241 646 🖷01341 241 718
E: office@cmcpensarn.org.uk
Web: www.cmcpensarn.org.uk
Residential outdoor activity centre for all ages and abilities; accessible accommodation and activities.
Centre Director: Mr Mark Downey. Admin staff 2, Other staff 12. ***CC*** No.1062075. Began 1966; non-denominational. (Previously Christian Mountain Centre). Turnover £200,000 to year end Dec 00.

***Combruith Scottish Crusaders Centre**, Scottish Crusaders, Challenge House, 29 Canal Street, Glasgow G4 0AD
☎0141 331 2400
E: email@scottishcrusaders.org.uk
Web: www.crusaders.org.uk/scotland
Self-catering. Director: Mr Rob Rawson. No full-time staff. ***CC*** No.SCO 08518. Began 1980; interdenominational. Turnover n/a.

Compass Christian Centre, Glenshee Lodge, Blairgowrie PH10 7QD
☎01250 885 209 🖷01250 885 309
E: compass@compasschristian.co.uk
Web: www.compasschristian.co.uk
Winter skills, ski-touring, management & team training, conferences & retreats. Catered & self-catering.
Director: Ruth McBean. *Bookings Secretary:* Sally Gingell. Executive staff 3, Admin staff 1, Other staff 12. ***CC*** No.SCO 11797. Began 1967; interdenominational. Turnover £177,000 to year end May 00.

Copthorne Caravans, Rose Green Road, Bognor Regis PO21 3ER
☎01243 262 408 🖷01243 262 408
E: copthorne.caravans@dsl.pipex.com
Holiday caravan park; static caravans for hire, and privately owned caravans. No animals.
Proprietors: Mr & Mrs Tony & Lindsay Leney. Admin staff 2, Other staff 3. Began 1945; non-denominational. Turnover n/a.

Cornerstone Quest Achievement Centre, Gwern Genau, Arenig, Bala LL23 7PB
☎0121 643 1984
E: info@cornerstonequest.co.uk
Web: www.cornerstonequest.co.uk
Self or full-catering for achievement breaks on conservation estate.
Centre Manager: Mr Steve Weston. Executive staff 1, Other staff 2. ***CC*** No.501648. Began 1971; non-denominational. (Previously Quest Achievement Centre). Turnover £46,554 to year end Dec 04.

Discovery Cruising, Quiraing, Onich, Fort William PH33 6SB
☎01855 821 371 M: 07050 294 159
🖷01855 821 371
E: info@discoverycruising.co.uk
Web: www.discoverycruising.co.uk
Offering skippered cruises on the west coast of Scotland, particularly for young people and students.
Skipper: Mr Melville Paton. Admin staff 1. ***CC*** No.SCO 15412. Began 1986; interdenominational. Turnover £31,000 to year end Nov 04.

Fellowship Afloat Charitable Trust, The Sail Lofts, Woodrolfe Road, Tollesbury, Maldon CM9 8SE
☎01621 868 113 🖷01621 868 113
E: info@fact.org.uk
Web: www.fact.org.uk
Sharing the Christian faith through residential outdoor activities, dinghy sailing and education.
Director: David Hillyer. Admin staff 3, Other staff 10. ***CC*** No.1059143. Began 1966; non-denominational. Turnover £268,000 to year end Mar 05.

***Frontier Centre (Barnabas Adventure Centres)**, Addington Road, Irthlingborough, Wellingborough NN9 5UH
☎01933 651 718 🖷01933 651 893
E: frontier@barnabas.org.uk
Web: www.barnabas.org.uk
Outdoor adventure centre and conferences for youth groups, churches and schools. Self-catering or full board.
Centre Manager: Mr Mike Creese. Other staff 4. ***CC*** No.276346. Began 1997; interdenominational. Turnover £326,000 to year end Mar 05.

***Gaines Christian Youth Centre**, Whitbourne, Worcester WR6 5RD
☎01886 821 212 🖷01886 822 042
E: info@gaines-cyc.co.uk
Web: www.gaines-cyc.co.uk
Fully-catered residential youth centre.
Directors: Mr & Mrs Graham Woods. Admin staff 3, Other staff 7. ***CC*** No.1057267. Began 1963; non-denominational. Turnover £200,000 to year end Dec 02.

Glencoe Outdoor Centre Glencoe, Ballachulish PH49 4HS
☎01855 811 350 🖷01855 811 644
E: gocjezza@aol.com
Web: www.glencoeoutdoorcentre.org.uk
Residential centre offering multi-activity courses; wide range of outdoor activities.
Centre Director: Mr Chris Williams. Admin staff 4, Other staff 8. Began 1988; non-denominational. Turnover £89,000 to year end Sep 04.

***Halls Green (Barnabas Adventure Centres)**, Halls Green Centre, Hale Oak Road, Weald, Sevenoaks TN14 6NQ
☎01732 463 212 🖷01732 469 500
E: hallsgreen@barnabas.org.uk
Web: www.barnabas.org.uk
Outdoor adventure and conference centre for youth groups, churches and others.
Centre Manager: Mr Marcus Cameron. Executive staff 1, Other staff 3. ***CC*** No. 276346. Began 1980; interdenominational. Turnover £190,000 to year end Mar 05.

Horstead Centre, Rectory Road, Horstead, Norwich NR12 7EP
☎01603 737 215 🖷01603 737 494
E: mail@horsteadcentre.org.uk
Web: www.horsteadcentre.org.uk
Residential study/activity centre for young people to develop their physical, mental and spiritual capacities.
Warden: Mrs Val Khambatta. Executive staff 1, Other staff 13. ***CC*** No.303986. Began 1970; Anglican. Turnover £170,000 to year end Dec 04.

The Kingsway Adventure Centre, Alston Road, Middleton-in-Teesdale Barnard Castle DL12 0UU
☎01833 640 881
E: adam@kingswaycentre.co.uk
Web: www.kingswaycentre.co.uk
Family-run outdoor activity centre for groups of all ages.
Principal: Mr Adam Hearn. Admin staff 1, Other staff 2. Began 1990; non-denominational. Turnover £80,000 to year end Dec 05.

Knock Christian Centre, Dun Fell Christian Trust, Knock, Appleby-in-Westmorland CA16 6DL
☎01768 361 762 M: 07947 351 281
🖷01768 887 97
Web: www.dunfellchristiantrust.co.uk
Indoor and outdoor facilities.
Warden: Mr Trevor Wimbow. No full-time staff. ***CC*** No.510095. Began 1979; evangelical. Turnover n/a.
Bookings/Enquiries: Mr Philip Hem, Rigg End, Blencarn, Penrith CA10 1TX
E: riggend@enterprise.net
☎01768 887 97

For bed-spaces etc. see list on Page 24

The Laurels Holiday Park, Padstow Road, Whitecross, Wadebridge PL27 7JQ
☎01208 813 341 📠01208 816 590
E: anicholson@thelaurelsholidaypark.co.uk
Web: www.thelaurelsholidaypark.co.uk
Self-catering cottages, small touring caravan and camping site with individual pitches.
Proprietors. Mr & Mrs A Nicholson. Executive Staff 2. Began 1986; non-denominational. (Previously The Laurels, Holiday Cottages and Campsites). Turnover n/a.

***Lendrick Muir Centre (Scripture Union Scotland)**, Rumbling Bridge, Kinross KY13 0QA
☎01577 842 000 📠01577 840 164
E: lmoffice@suscotland.org.uk
Web: www.suscotland.org.uk
Self-catered, catered, 150 bed residential centre, year round activities, mid-week schools programmes, exploring Christian faith.
Centre Director: Christine Murison. Executive staff 2, Other staff 30. ***CC*** Began 1999; interdenominational. Turnover £315,000 to year end Mar 02.

The Long Barn, Penrhiw Farm, Capel Dewi, Llandysul SA44 4PG
☎01559 363 200 📠01559 363 200
E: cowcher@thelongbarn.co.uk
Web: www.thelongbarn.co.uk
Bunkhouse accommodation on working farm.
Proprietors: Mr & Mrs Tom & Eva Cowcher. Admin staff 2, Other staff 2. Began 1989; non-denominational. Turnover £4,800 to year end Mar 00.

Marrick Priory Outdoor Education and Residential Centre, Richmond DL11 7LD
☎01748 884 434 📠01748 884 434
E: office@marrickpriory.co.uk
Web: www.marrickpriory.co.uk
Providing educational, conference and outdoor pursuits facilities for church and secular groups.
Head of Centre: Jim Gleave. Admin staff 1, Other staff 11. Began 1970; Anglican but open to all. Turnover £200,000 to year end Mar 03.

***Medina Valley Centre for Outdoor Education**, Dodnor Lane, Newport PO30 5TE
☎01983 522 195 📠01983 825 962
E: info@medinavalleycentre.org.uk
Web: www.medinavalleycentre.org.uk
Field studies GCSE/'A' level, Geography/Biology; sailing courses for schools/individuals; church and youth holidays/retreats.
Executive Director: Mr Peter Savory. Admin staff 2, Other staff 9. ***CC*** No.235153. Began 1963; interdenominational. Turnover n/a.

Middlewich Narrowboats, Canal Terrace, Middlewich CW10 9BD
☎01606 832 460 📠01606 737 912
E: info@middlewichboats.co.uk
Web: www.middlewichboats.co.uk
Providing canal narrow boats for self-drive hire.
Proprietor: Mr Paul Foskett. Executive staff 1, Admin staff 1, Other staff 4. Began 1971; non-denominational. Turnover £270,000 to year end Dec 02.

Min-Y-Don Christian Adventure Centre, Arthog LL39 1BZ
☎01341 250 433 📠01341 250 686
E: holidays@minydon.com
Web: www.minydon.com
For schools, youth groups, church groups, families.
Administrators: Mr & Mrs Peter & Susan Cook. Admin staff 2, Other staff 15. Began 1961; interdenominational. AALA approved. Turnover £350,000 to year end Jan 05.

Morning Star Trust, Crews Quarters Offices, Historic Dockyard, Chatham ME4 4TZ
☎01634 403 890 📠01634 403 890
E: sailing@morningstar.org.uk
Web: www.morningstar.org.uk
Off-shore adventure sailing; Duke of Edinburgh awards; tall ships.
Manager: Miss Lynda Key. Admin staff 1, Other staff 2. ***CC*** No.328320. Began 1981; interdenominational. RYA registered. Turnover £101,000 to year end Dec 04.

Port Ban Caravan Park, Kilberry, Tarbert PA29 6YD
☎01880 770 224/388
E: portban@aol.com
Web: www.portban.com
Owners: The Sheldrick family. Director/Manager: Mr Ian T Jackson. Admin staff 1, Other staff 3. Began 1967; interdenominational. Turnover £300,000 to year end Dec 02.

Presbyterian Church of Wales Youth & Children's Centre, Coleg y Bala, Ffrydan Road, Bala LL23 7RY
☎01678 520 565 M: 07710 406 908
📠01678 520 849
E: colegybala@aol.com
Web: www.colegybala.org
Encouraging a personal faith in Jesus Christ through various outdoor activities.
Director of Youth & Children's Work: Rev W Bryn Williams. Executive staff 7, Other staff 5. ***CC*** Began 1967; Presbyterian Church of Wales. Turnover £100,000 to year end Dec 94.

***The Ranch Outdoor Discovery Centre**, Bryn-y-Moel, Llanbedr LL45 2HU
☎01341 241 358 📠01341 241 530
E: theranch@actioncentres.co.uk
Web: www.actioncentres.co.uk
Residential outdoor activity centre.
Head of Centre: Mr Andy Whittaker. Admin staff 2, Other staff 7. ***CC*** No.803431. Began 1973; interdenominational. Turnover n/a.

St George's House (Christian Outdoor Centre), Georgeham, Braunton EX33 1JN
☎01271 890 755 📠01271 890 060
E: enquiries@sghdevon.org
Web: www.sghdevon.org
Beach location offering range of activies; conference room.
Manager: Mr Martin Larrington. *Assistant Manager:* Mr Adam Austin. Admin staff 2, Other staff 6. ***CC*** No.279046. Began 1978; interdenominational. Turnover £105,000 to year end Dec 02.

†**St Madoc Christian Youth Camp**, Llanmadoc, Gower, Swansea SA3 1DE
☎01792 386 291
For self-contained youth groups.
Camp Managers: Mr & Mrs Steve & Julie Jenkins. Admin staff 2. ***CC*** No.260655. Began 1944; non-denominational. Turnover £20,000 to year end Dec 02.

Sky Lodge Christian Camp, Southend-on-Sea SS3
☎No telephone
Providing camping facilities.
The Manager: Name not supplied. Executive staff 2, Other staff 5. ***CC*** No.278996. Began 1972; interdenominational. Turnover n/a.
Bookings / Enquiries *The Manager:* Name not supplied, Europe for Christ, 80 Victoria Road, Romford RM1 2LA
☎01708 727 625 📠 01708 757 758

***Spring Harvest Holidays**, 14 Horsted Square, Uckfield TN22 1QG
☎0870 060 3322 📠0870 060 3330
E: info@springharvestholidays.com
Web: www.springharvestholidays.com
Holiday park in Vendée region of western France.
Managing Director: Mr Steven May-Miller. No UK staff. ***CC*** No.3509419. Began 2003; interdenominational. Part of Spring Harvest. Turnover included in Spring Harvest.

Standlake Holiday Ranch, Downs Road, Standlake, Witney OX29 7UH
☎01865 300 099 📠01865 300 099
E: wpillans@aol.com
Web: www.standlakeranch.co.uk
For young people.
Evangelist: Rev Suzanne Pillans. Executive staff 2, Other staff n/a. Began 2004; interdenominational. Turnover: first year of operation.

Tarbat Free Church (Continuing) Caravan Site, Portmahomack, Tain IV20 1YL
☎0845 129 7055 M: 07879 481 502
📠01862 871 467
E: caravansite@tarbat.org.uk
Web: www.highlander.zetnet.co.uk/caravan
35 holiday caravans (touring and static).
Manager: Rev John MacLeod. Admin staff 1, Other staff 2. ***CC*** Began 1955; Free Church of Scotland (Continuing). Turnover £14,000 to year end Dec 02.

For bed-spaces etc. see list on Page 24

Teen Ranch Scotland, Ballindean House, Inchture, Perth PH14 9SF
☎01828 686 227 🖷01828 686 227
E: trs@teenranch.org.uk
Web: www.teenranch.org.uk
Christian youth activity centre.
Directors: Mr & Mrs Robert Ockenden. *Trustee:* Mr Allan McCulloch. Executive staff 2, Admin staff 2, Other staff 14. Began 1984; interdenominational. Turnover £250,000 to year end Jan 01.

***Tweedsmuir Scottish Crusaders Centre**, Scottish Crusaders, Challenge House, 29 Canal Street, Glasgow G4 0AD
☎0141 331 2400
E: email@scottishcrusaders.org.uk
Web: www.crusaders.org.uk/scotland
Director: Mr Rob Rawson. Executive staff 1, Other staff n/a. Began 1997; interdenominational. Turnover n/a.

Victor Training, Dove Cragg, Birks Road, Windermere LA23 3PH
☎01539 530 417 ▯: 07900 943 603
E: info@victortraining.co.uk
Web: www.victortraining.co.uk
Outdoor activities and community development for church and youth organisations.
Managing Director: Name not supplied. Executive staff 1, Other staff 10. Began 1991; interdenominational. Turnover £40,000 to year end Apr 01.

West End Outdoor Centre, Wagtails, Thruscross, Harrogate HG3 4AH
☎01943 880 207 🖷01943 880 207
E: m.verity@virgin.net
Web: www.westendoutdoorcentre.co.uk
Self-catering. Proprietor: Mrs Margaret Verity. Admin staff 1, Other staff 1. Began n/a; non-denominational. Turnover £25,000 to year end May 98.

***Whithaugh Park (Barnabas Adventure Centres)**, Newcastleton TD9 0TY
☎01387 375 394 🖷01387 375 651
E: whithaugh@barnabas.org.uk
Web: www.barnabas.org.uk
Outdoor adventure and conference centre for youth groups, churches and others.
Centre Manager: Mr John Bailey. Executive staff 1, Other staff 5. **CC** No.276346. Began 1989; interdenominational. Turnover £306,000 to year end Mar 05.

YMCA, Fairthorne Group, Fairthorne Manor, Curdridge, Southampton SO30 2GH
☎01489 785 228 🖷01489 798 936
E: info@ymca-fg.org
Web: www.ymca-fg.org
Outdoor activities, play scheme and child care; for children and young people.
Centre Director: Mr Chris Hand. Executive staff 10, Other staff 60. ***CC*** 1090981. Began 1947; interdenominational. (Previously YMCA South East Hampshire National Centre). Incorporating YMCA, Portsmouth. Turnover n/a.

YMCA, National Centre, Lakeside, Newby Bridge, Ulverston LA12 8BD
☎08707 273 927 🖷01539 530 015
E: admin@lakesideymca.co.uk
Web: www.lakesideymca.co.uk
Outdoor education and training, holidays, conferences.
Chief Executive Officer: Mr Steve Taylor. *Operations Manager:* Mr Glen Duckes. Admin staff 10, Other staff 100. **CC** No.212810. Began 1951; non-denominational. (Previously Lakeside YMCA). Turnover £2,800,000 to year end Mar 05.

CONFERENCE CENTRES, GUEST HOUSES & HOTELS

By Country and Postcode – for location of Postcodes see map on Page 458
Venues which did not supply this information are not listed here
Only venues with 10 or more bed spaces are included

Does not include Bed & Breakfast or accommodation with less than 6 beds.

S = single rooms **D/T** = number of bed spaces in double/twin rooms **L** = number of bed spaces in rooms larger than double
TS = total bed spaces (not number of rooms) **DR** = Day Room, the capacity of the largest room suitable for group use
⇌ = nearest Railway station ⊖ = nearest London Underground station

Postcode	Location	Name	S	D/T	L	Other	TS	DR	Railway/Underground
ENGLAND									
B 15	**Birmingham**	The Queen's Foundation	54	4	-	one-bed flats 2	60	80	⇌ University
BA 2	**Bath**	Carfax Hotel	6	26	6		38	30	⇌ Bath Spa
BD 7	**Bradford**	St Columba's Horton Outreach	n/a	n/a	n/a	non-residential	n/a	50	⇌ Bradford
BD23	**Skipton**	Parcevall Hall	7	22	-		29	30	⇌ Skipton or Ilkley
		Scargill House Ltd	15	78	6		97	90	⇌ Skipton
BH4	**Bournemouth**	Daybreak Guest House	-	8	11		19	n/a	⇌ Branksome
		The Golden Sovereign Hotel	1	4	18		23	n/a	⇌ Branksome
BH 6	**Bournemouth**	Cliff House Holiday and Conference Centre	3	18	8		29	30	⇌ Pokesdown
BH13	**Poole**	Green Pastures Christian Centre	10	10	-		20	50	⇌ Branksome
BH19	**Swanage**	Bella Vista Hotel	-	6	12		18	n/a	⇌ Wareham
BN 6	**Hassocks**	North Acres Farm	1	4	15		20	30	⇌ Plumpton or Hassocks
BN21	**Eastbourne**	Arden Hotel	1	22	-		23	11	⇌ Eastbourne
		Beach Haven Private Hotel	2	10	-		12	12	⇌ Eastbourne
		Grays Hotel	-	10	4		14	n/a	⇌ Eastbourne
BN22	**Eastbourne**	Ranworth Christian Hotel	5	8	16		29	n/a	⇌ Eastbourne
BS 9	**Bristol**	Trinity College Conference Centre	55	8	-		63	150	⇌ Bristol Temple Mead
BS21	**Clevedon**	Cavell Christian Guest House	6	14	18		38	40	⇌ Yatton
BS23	**Weston-super-Mare**	Ashcroft Guest House	1	4	9		14	n/a	⇌ Weston-super-Mare

For bed-spaces etc. see list on Page 24

Postcode	Location	Name	S	D/T	L	Other		TS	DR	Railway/Underground
BS30	Bristol	Wick Court Centre	-	4	54			58	60	⇌ Bristol Temple Meads or Bath Spa
CA 6	Carlisle	Briar Lea House	-	4	10			14	n/a	⇌ Carlisle
CA 7	Wigton	Blaithwaite House	3	32	73			108	200	⇌ Wigton
CA12	Keswick	Bassenfell Manor Christian Centre	-	12	57	flat for disabled	2	71	70	⇌ Carlisle or Penrith
		Keswick Convention Centre	1	8	32			41	60	⇌ Penrith
CM 5	Ongar	Mulberry House	14	18	-			32	140	⇌ Harlow Town ⊖ Epping
CM15	Brentwood	Pilgrims Hall	1	6	-			7	60	⇌ Brentwood or Shenfield
CT 6	Herne Bay	Herne Bay Court Evangelical Centre	24	52	74			150	140	⇌ Herne Bay
CV 7	Coventry	Nettle Hill Training and Conference Centre	-	12	43			55	120	⇌ Coventry
CV36	Shipston-on-Stour	Green Hill Outreach	2	20	20			42	80	⇌ Moreton-in-Marsh
CW 5	Nantwich	Regents Park Conference Centre	9	26	15			50	100	⇌ Nantwich or Crewe
DE 4	Matlock	Alison House Training and Conference Centre	7	28	-			35	35	⇌ Cromford
		Willersley Castle	11	66	21			98	106	⇌ Cromford
DE6	Ashbourne	Dovedale House	-	10	50			60	60	⇌ Witham
DE7	Ilkeston	Morley Retreat and Conference House	25	12	-			37	40	⇌ Derby
DE55	Alfreton	The Hayes Conference Centre	192	154	76			416	400	⇌ Alfreton or Derby
DL 8	Leyburn	The Jonas Trust	-	60	24			84	80	⇌ Darlington
DN10	Doncaster	Bawtry Hall	10	50	10			70	200	⇌ Doncaster or Retford
DT2	Dorchester	Chantmarle Christian Resource Centre	17	190	-	self-catering Cottages	15	222	170	⇌ Maiden Newton
DY 1	Dudley	Saltmine Trust Conference Centre	-	-	-	non-residential		n/a	50	⇌ Sandwell and Dudley
DY14	Kidderminster	Pioneer Centre	7	32	206			245	250	⇌ Kidderminster
EN11	Hoddesdon	High Leigh Conference Centre	92	100	32			224	210	⇌ Broxbourne
EX 8	Exmouth	Haldon Court Christian Hotel and Conference Centre	6	36	56			98	120	⇌ Exmouth
EX10	Sidmouth	Sidholme	30	72	30			132	130	⇌ Exeter or Honiton
EX12	Seaton	Peacehaven Christian Centre	1	6	29			36	60	⇌ Axminster
		Upcott	1	-	39			40	40	⇌ Axminster
EX14	Honiton	Westcott Farm Christian Holiday Centre	31	18	-			49	80	⇌ Honiton
EX17	Crediton	Burstone Manor	1	20	30			51	70	⇌ Exeter or Crediton or Lapford
EX34	Ilfracombe	Lee Bay Hotel	4	46	6			56	100	⇌ Barnstaple
		Lower Campscott Farm	1	4	-	self-catering cottages	42	47	50	⇌ Barnstaple
		Sunnymeade Country Hotel	1	18	-			19	n/a	⇌ Barnstaple
EX35	Lynton	Lee Abbey	18	80	22			120	120	⇌ Barnstaple
EX39	Bideford	The Mount	2	6	2	wheelchair access		10	13	⇌ Barnstaple
GL15	Lydney	Lindors House	3	44	20			67	70	⇌ Lydney
GL54	Cheltenham	Glenfall House	8	36	-	self-catering cottage	1	45	45	⇌ Cheltenham
GU 9	Farnham	Waverley Abbey House	1	14	28			43	100	⇌ Farnham
GU29	Midhurst	YMCA, Dunford House	13	22	9			44	60	⇌ Haslemere or Chichester
GU35	Bordon	Acorn Christian Healing Foundation	n/a	n/a	n/a			30	60	⇌ Liphook
HA 1	Harrow	St Mary's Church House	0	8	4			12	15	⇌ Harrow-on-the-Hill ⊖ Harrow-on-the-Hill
HA3	Edgware	Convent of St Mary at the Cross	n/a	n/a	n/a			8	50	⇌ Mill Hill Broadway ⊖ Edgware
HD 7	Huddersfield	Westwood Christian Centre	-	-	30	self-contained flats	30	60	70	⇌ Slaithwaite
HP14	High Wycombe	Wycliffe Centre	9	38	43			90	200	⇌ High Wycombe
IP11	Felixstowe	Dorincourt Guest House	3	10	4			17	20	⇌ Felixstowe
IP16	Leiston	Sizewell Hall Ltd	5	26	49			80	150	⇌ Saxmundham
IP25	Thetford	Letton Hall	1	4	110	caravans, tents	n/a	115	70	⇌ Norwich
LA11	Grange-over-Sands	Abbot Hall	19	50	34			103	110	⇌ Kents Bank
		Boarbank Hall	20	10	-	nursing home	30	60	50	⇌ Grange-over-Sands
		Thornleigh Hotel	9	28	19			56	55	⇌ Grange-over-Sands
LA22	Ambleside	Rydal Hall	10	30	16	campsite	350	406	150	⇌ Windermere
LE 8	Leicester	Arnesby Christian Conference Centre	-	22	-	caravans, tent	n/a	n/a	30	⇌ Leicester
LE17	Lutterworth	Hothorpe Hall	2	64	70			136	200	⇌ Market Harborough
NE26	Whitley Bay	Livingstone Christian Centre	-	-	30			30	30	*Rail* Metro: Whitley Bay
NE43	Stocksfield	The Boys' Brigade Training Centre	n/a	n/a	n/a			62	n/a	⇌ Stocksfield
NE49	Haltwhistle	Featherstone Castle	-	-	-	self-catering		80	n/a	⇌ Haltwhistle
NN 3	Northampton	King's Park Conference and Sports Centre	-	100	-			100	200	⇌ Northampton
NR20	Dereham	Moor Farm Stable Cottages	6	12	-	self-catering		18	-	⇌ Norwich
NR22	Walsingham	Elmham House (Pilgrim Bureau)	52	66	9			127	100	⇌ Kings Lynn or Norwich
NR26	Sheringham	Greenhedges	-	-	30			30	30	⇌ Sheringham
NR27	Cromer	The Pleasaunce	5	22	53	self-catering bungalow	5	85	50	⇌ Cromer
NR33	Lowestoft	Fairhavens	1	2	9			12	n/a	⇌ Lowestoft
NR34	Beccles	Ringsfield Hall	2	4	35	self-catering cottage	9	50	50	⇌ Beccles
OX2	Oxford	Wycliffe Hall	35	28	-			63	65	⇌ Oxford
OX 7	Chipping Norton	Cotswold View Guest House	2	4	9			15	-	⇌ Kingham
OX11	Didcot	Baptist House	-	-	-	non-residential		n/a	100	⇌ Didcot Parkway
OX12	Wantage	Charney Manor	11	16	-			27	45	⇌ Didcot Parkway
OX18	Bampton	Windmill Farm Conference Centre	-	36	29			65	130	⇌ Oxford
PE37	Swaffham	Carey House	-	8	14			22	45	⇌ Downham Market
PL19	Tavistock	The Watering Hole Holiday Centre	-	20	-	3 cottages	5	25	25	⇌ Plymouth
PL27	Wadebridge	Lowenna Manor	6	32	62			100	100	⇌ Bodmin Parkway
		Trevanion House	4	22	-			26	20	⇌ Bodmin Parkway
PO19	Chichester	University of Chichester	218	40	-			258	350	⇌ Chichester
PO36	Sandown	Rowanhurst Christian Hotel	1	12	65			79	45	⇌ Lake
PO38	Ventnor	Hotel Picardie	2	14	8			24	n/a	⇌ Shanklin
		St Andrew's Hotel	-	14	12			26	n/a	⇌ Shanklin
		St Rhadagunds	5	12	87			104	n/a	⇌ Shanklin
PR 9	Southport	Beach House Private Hotel	4	12	10			26	n/a	⇌ Southport
RG23	Basingstoke	The Holy Trinity Malshanger Trust	1	12	18			31	30	⇌ Basingstoke
RH 5	Dorking	Felbury House	-	30	15			45	60	⇌ Gomshall
RH13	Horsham	Family Foundations Trust Ltd	-	2	62			64	100	⇌ Horsham
S 11	Sheffield	Whirlow Grange Conference and Training Centre	20	20	-			40	120	⇌ Sheffield or Dore
S 32	Hope Valley	Cliff College Conference Centre	n/a	n/a	n/a			286	n/a	⇌ Grindleford

Conference Centres, Guest Houses & Hotels

Postcode	Location	Name	S	D/T	L	Other		TS	DR	Railway/Underground
S 33	**Hope Valley**	Hollowford Centre	1	8	63	bungalow	10	82	80	⇌ Hope
SG 7	**Baldock**	Derek Prince Ministries – UK	-	20	4			24	100	⇌ Baldock or Letchworth
SL 4	**Windsor**	The Eton Dorney Centre	-	4	29			33	33	⇌ Windsor and Eton Riverside or Burnham
SL7	**Marlow**	Glade End Guest House	2	18	-			20	20	⇌ Marlow
SN 4	**Swindon**	Legge House	1	6	26			33	40	⇌ Swindon
SO24	**Alresford**	Old Alresford Place	6	34	9			49	0	⇌ Alton or Winchester
ST15	**Stone**	Shallowford House	15	22	3			40	40	⇌ Stafford or Norton Bridge
SY 8	**Ludlow**	Bishop Mascall Centre	16	8	24			48	100	⇌ Ludlow
SY10	**Oswestry**	Quinta Christian Centre	6	54	200	+ camping		260	400	⇌ Chirk or Gobowen
SY13	**Whitchurch**	Cloverley Hall Conference Centre	5	28	106			139	150	⇌ Whitchurch Salop
TA 4	**Taunton**	Harnham Farmhouse	-	2	12			14	n/a	⇌ Taunton
TA 5	**Bridgwater**	Hill House Christian Centre	2	28	69			99	150	⇌ Bridgwater
TA24	**Minehead**	Mayfair Hotel	2	14	12			28	20	⇌ Taunton
TD15	**Berwick-upon-Tweed**	Marygate House	6	6	19			31	40	⇌ Berwick-upon-Tweed
TN15	**Sevenoaks**	Oak Hall	3	20	50			73	100	⇌ Otford or Sevenoaks
TN22	**Uckfield**	Pilgrim Hall Christian Conference Centre	22	30	68			110	130	⇌ Uckfield
TN31	**Rye**	The Oast Houses	3	10	39			52	50	⇌ Etchingham
TN33	**Battle**	Ashburnham Christian Trust	20	186	40			246	220	⇌ Battle
TQ 1	**Torquay**	Brunel Manor	18	20	21	cottages	91	150	230	⇌ Newton Abbot
TQ 4	**Paignton**	Glencoe Holiday Flatlets	-	-	-	5 flats	25	25	-	⇌ Paignton
		Park Hotel	n/a	n/a	n/a			115	n/a	⇌ Paignton
TQ11	**Buckfastleigh**	Buckfast Abbey	4	30	3			33	150	⇌ Newton Abbot or Totnes
TQ12	**Newton Abbot**	Rora Christian Fellowship Trust	6	28	18			52	n/a	⇌ Newton Abbot
TQ14	**Teignmouth**	Thornley House	8	6	10			24	40	⇌ Teignmouth
TR 2	**Truro**	Trewince Manor	n/a	n/a	n/a	self-catering		n/a	35	⇌ St Austell or Truro
TR16	**Redruth**	Fountain Springs	1	6	10			17	50	⇌ Redruth
TR26	**St Ives**	Lamorna Lodge Hotel	4	20	9			33	33	⇌ Carbis Bay
		Treloyhan Manor	16	46	38			100	80	⇌ St Ives
TS12	**Saltburn-by-the-Sea**	Brockley Hall	15	30	15			60	60	⇌ Saltburn
TW 8	**Brentford**	St Paul's Parish Centre	-	-	-	non-residential		n/a	350	⇌ Brentford ⊖ Northfields
TW16	**Sunbury-on-Thames**	Sunbury Court and Recreation Centre	-	10	100			110	110	⇌ Hampton
WA 6	**Frodsham**	Foxhill	15	12	4			31	80	⇌ Frodsham or Runcorn
WR12	**Broadway**	House of the Open Door Community	-	-	32			32	70	⇌ Evesham
WR14	**Malvern**	The Christian Conference Centre	39	44	13			96	180	⇌ Malvern Link
YO11	**Scarborough**	Selbourne Licensed Hotel	1	14	19			34	34	⇌ Scarborough
YO12	**Scarborough**	Brincliffe Edge Hotel	2	10	10			22	12	⇌ Scarborough
YO13	**Scarborough**	Wydale	6	50	6			62	60	⇌ Scarborough
YO21	**Whitby**	Moorlands	13	30	8			51	60	⇌ Whitby
		Sneaton Castle Centre	58	24	38			120	140	⇌ Whitby or Scarborough
YO62	**York**	Redcar Farm	16	8	4			28	55	⇌ York or Malton or Thirsk
London										
E 14	**London**	The Royal Foundation of St Katharine	38	4	-			42	80	⇌ Limehouse (Docklands) ⊖ Shadwell
N 5	**London**	Foreign Missions Club	25	22	12	5 flats	-	59	30	⇌ Highbury and Islington ⊖ Highbury and Islington
N10	**London**	Guy Chester Centre	14	4	-	extra bunks	6	24	32	⊖ Bounds Green or Highgate
N 14	**London**	Oak Hill	30	20	0	flats	6	56	n/a	⊖ Cockfosters
SE11	**London**	The Evangelical Alliance Conference Centre	-	-	-	non-residential		n/a	60	⊖ Kennington
SW1	**London**	Emmanuel Centre	-	-	-	non-residential		n/a	n/a	⇌ Victoria ⊖ Westminster
SW16	**London**	Streatham Christian Conference Centre	-	-	-	non-residential		-	300	⇌ Streatham or Streatham Common
W 2	**London**	Ashley, Tregaron and Oasis Hotels	9	58	20			87	n/a	⇌ Paddington ⊖ Paddington
		Lancaster Hall Hotel Ltd	3	160	37			200	120	⇌ Paddington ⊖ Paddington or ⊖ Lancaster Gate
		Redland House Hotel	7	18	6			31	0	⊖ Marble Arch
W 10	**London**	Latymer Christian Centre	-	-	-	non-residential		-	200	⇌ Paddington ⊖ Latimer Road
WC1	**London**	Quaker International Centre	18	16	13			47	70	⇌ Euston ⊖ Euston Square or Goodge Street
CHANNEL ISLANDS										
GY 1	**Guernsey**	Les Cotils Ecumenical Centre	5	8	3			16	n/a	
JE 3	**Jersey**	Biarritz Christian Hotel	21	80	6			107	100	
		Highlands Hotel Ltd	19	50	33			102	100	
NORTHERN IRELAND										
BT31	**Castlewellan**	Castlewellan Castle Christian Conference Centre	1	8	141			150	130	⇌ Belfast Conference Centre
BT33	**Newcastle**	Glenada Holiday and Conference Centre	-	54	-			54	150	⇌ Belfast
BT34	**Newry**	Kilbroney Centre	1	2	75			78	n/a	⇌ Newry
BT47	**Londonderry**	YMCA, Londonderry	10	-	-			10	270	⇌ Londonderry
BT56	**Portrush**	Castle Erin	6	74	27			107	200	⇌ Portrush
BT66	**Craigavon**	YMCA, Lurgan	-	-	-	non-residential		n/a	25	⇌ Lurgan
BT71	**Dungannon**	Servite Priory	16	26	-			42	200	⇌ Portadown
SCOTLAND										
DD11	**Arbroath**	Windmill Christian Centre	2	8	36			46	100	⇌ Arbroath
EH 9	**Edinburgh**	Ben Doran Hotel	2	16	-			18	0	⇌ Edinburgh
EH21	**Musselburgh**	Carberry	14	36	42			92	100	⇌ Edinburgh or Musselburgh
FK 1	**Falkirk**	Falkirk Christian Centre	-	-	-	non-residential		-	100	⇌ Falkirk Grahamston
FK 8	**Stirling**	Gartmore House	1	48	140	+ caravans	-	189	300	⇌ Stirling
FK15	**Dunblane**	Scottish Churches' House	13	40	-			53	80	⇌ Dunblane

Postcode	Location	Name	S	D/T	L	Other		TS	DR	Railway/Underground
G 2	Glasgow	Adelaides	2	12	10			24	500	≈ Glasgow: Central or Queen Street
G 84	Helensburgh	The Way Christian Ministries	3	30	16	self-catering cottage, cabins	31	80	300	≈ Helensburgh or Gourock (via ferry)
IV 3	Inverness	Park Guest House	2	6	3			11	n/a	≈ Inverness
PA76	Isle of Iona	Bishops House	3	20	-			23	24	≈ Oban
PH 2	Perth	Perth Christian Centre	-	-	-	non-residential		n/a	130	≈ Perth
PH 8	Dunkeld	Waterbury Guest House	1	8	7			16	16	≈ Birnam or Dunkeld
PH16	Pitlochry	Atholl Centre	2	22	8			32	60	≈ Pitlochry
PH49	Ballachulish	Fern Villa Guest House and Cottages	-	10	-	self-catering cottages	12	22	0	≈ Fort William
TD 9	Hawick	Balcary House	4	10	34			48	80	≈ Carlisle or Edinburgh
		Whitchester Christian Guest House	1	14	9			24	n/a	≈ Carlisle or Edinburgh
WALES										
CF31	Bridgend	Bryntirion Christian Conference Centre	0	86	14			100	50	≈ Bridgend
CF64	Dinas Powis	Hebron Hall Ltd	n/a	n/a	n/a			139	n/a	≈ Dinas Powis
LD 3	Brecon	Coleg Trefeca	0	36	3			39	60	≈ Abergavenny
LL19	Prestatyn	Homefield	2	6	27			35	n/a	≈ Prestatyn
LL23	Bala	Bryn-y-Groes Christian Conference Centre	-	6	70			76	70	≈ Ruabon or Wrexham
LL28	Colwyn Bay	St Winifreds	6	36	20			62	62	≈ Colwyn Bay
LL29	Colwyn Bay	Llety lachad Hotel	-	10	-			10	n/a	≈ Colwyn Bay
LL30	Llandudno	Beth-Eden Christian Guest House	6	16	20			42	35	≈ Llandudno
		Fairhaven Christian Hotel	2	20	-			22	n/a	≈ Llandudno
LL32	Conwy	Beechwood Court	2	24	45			71	60	≈ Llandudno Junction
NP16	Chepstow	Woodcroft Christian Centre	0	2	48			50	50	≈ Chepstow
SA 3	Swansea	Nicholaston House	1	18	9			28	100	≈ Swansea
SA43	Cardigan	Croft Farm Celtic Cottages	1	26	11	self-catering cottages	40	78	15	≈ Haverfordwest
		Gorslwyd Farm	1	42	4			47	60	≈ Carmarthen or Aberystwyth
SA71	Pembroke	Haven Christian Holiday Centre	2	20	43			65	150	≈ Pembroke
SY15	Montgomery	Pentrenant Hall	0	2	50	tents	150	202	60	≈ Newtown (Powys)
SY16	Newtown	Cefn Lea Park	0	300	100			400	500	≈ Newtown (Powys)

CONFERENCE CENTRES, GUEST HOUSES & HOTELS

Does not include Bed & Breakfast or accommodation with less than 6 beds.

Abbot Hall (Christian Guild Holidays), Kents Bank, Grange-over-Sands LA11 7BG
☎01539 532 896 fax 01539 535 200
E: abbothall@cgholidays.co.uk
Web: www.cgholidays.co.uk
Holiday and conference centre open all year. For individuals, couples, families and groups.
Manager: Amanda Fogg. Executive staff [illegible], Other staff n/a. Began 1916; ecumenical. Turnover n/a.

***Acorn Christian Healing Foundation**, Whitehill Chase, High Street, Bordon GU35 0AP
☎01420 478 121 fax 01420 478 122
E: info@acornchristian.org
Web: www.acornchristian.org
For groups or individuals; retreats either led or self-run.
Director: Rev Dr Russ Parker. *Christian Listener Coordinator:* Rev Andrew Bradley. Executive staff 3, Other staff 16. **CC** No.1030011. Began 1983; interdenominational. Magazine: *Acorn News* (1,000 quarterly). Turnover £450,000 to year end Mar 05.

***Adelaides**, 209 Bath Street, Glasgow G2 4HZ
☎0141 248 4970 fax 0141 226 4247
E: info@adelaides.freeserve.co.uk
Web: www.adelaides.co.uk
Guesthouse, auditorium, nursery, church and small committee room.
Centre Director: Mr Sandy Meiklejohn. *Minister:* Rev Jack Quinn. Executive staff 2, Other staff 18. **CC** No.32260. Began 1995; Baptist. Turnover £410,000 to year end Dec 04.

Alison House Training and Conference Centre, Intake Lane, Cromford, Matlock DE4 3RH
☎01629 822 211
fax 01629 822 316
E: alisonhouse@toch.org.uk
Web: www.alison-house.co.uk
Providing residential conference facilities for church and other Christian groups.
Manager: Mr Richard Geldard. *Assistant to Manager:* Maggie Geldard. Executive staff 1, Admin staff 2, Other staff 2. **CC** No.1057232. Began 1968; interdenominational. (Operated by Toc H). Turnover £145,000 to year end Mar 02.

Arden Hotel, 17 Burlington Place, Eastbourne BN21 4AR
☎01323 639 639
M: 07791 700 939 fax 01323 417 840
E: mail@ardenhoteleastbourne.freeserve.co.uk Web: www.theardenhotel.co.uk
Proprietor: Mrs Patricia Lambert. Executive staff 1, Other staff 1. Began n/a; non-denominational. Turnover £40,000 to year end Dec 02.

***Arnesby Christian Conference Centre**, The Manse, St Peter's Road, Arnesby, Leicester LE8 5WJ
☎0116 247 8392
E: jhutton@fish.co.uk
Residential accommodation for children and young adults; day conferences; also self-catering.
Wardens: Mr & Mrs Johnny & Val Hutton. Executive staff 2. **CC** No.250068. Began 1974; non-denominational. Turnover £8,000 to year end Dec 00.

***Ashburnham Christian Trust**, Ashburnham Place, Battle TN33 9NF
☎01424 892 244 fax 01424 894 200
E: mail@ashburnham.org.uk
Web: www.ashburnham.org.uk
Offering facilities for churches and organisations to run conferences of up to 250.
Resident Director: Rev Andrew Wooding Jones. Admin staff 8, Other staff 21. **CC** No.212755. Began 1960; non-denominational. Turnover £1,500,000 to year end Mar 04.

Ashcroft Guest House, 13 Clevedon Road, Weston-super-Mare BS23 1DA
☎01934 621 737
Web: www.ashcroftguesth.co.uk
Proprietors: Mr & Mrs J R Hill. Admin staff 2. Began 1982; ecumenical. Turnover £37,000 to year end Apr 00.

Ashley, Tregaron and Oasis Hotels, 15 Norfolk Square, London W2 1RU
☎020 7723 3375/9966
fax 020 7723 0173
E: ashhot@btinternet.com
Web: www.ashleyhotels.com
Proprietors: Mr M George, Mr D George. Admin staff 4, Other staff 5. Began 1967; non-denominational. Turnover n/a.

Atholl Centre, Atholl Road, Pitlochry PH16 5BX
☎01796 473 044 fax 01796 473 844
E: admin@athollcentre.org.uk
Web: www.athollcentre.org.uk
Conference facilities and residential accommodation.
Manager: Adrienne Ruddock. Admin staff 1, Other staff 3. **CC** No.SCO 15113. Began 1970; interdenominational. Turnover £135,000 to year end Dec 02.

For bed-spaces etc. see list on Page 28

Balcary House Christian Conference and Ministry Support Centre, Buccleuch Road, Hawick TD9 0EH
☎01450 372 966 or 01738 639 792
🖷 01450 377 732
E: office@pwamm.com
Web: www.balcaryhouse.com
Conference, retreat and holiday facilities for groups, families and individuals. Bookshop, video library.
Manageress: Miss Val Garry. Executive staff 2, Other staff 2. ***CC*** No.SCO 14546. Began 1986; non-denominational. Part of People with a Mission Ministries. Turnover n/a.

Baptist Holiday Fellowship Ltd, 1 The Esplanade, Minehead TA24 5BE
☎01643 703 473
🖷 01643 703 473
E: christine@baptistholidayfellowship.co.uk
Web: www.baptistholidayfellowship.co.uk
Self-catering flats.
General Manager: Mrs Christine Lawrence. Executive staff 1, Other staff 2. ***CC*** No.270618. Began 1907; Baptist. Turnover n/a.

Baptist House, 129 Broadway, Didcot OX11 8XD
☎01235 517 700 🖷 01235 517 715
E: info@baptisthouse.org.uk
Web: www.baptisthouse.org.uk
Non-residential conference facilities.
Centre Manager: Mr Jonathan Spiller. Admin staff 5. Began 1989; Baptist. Turnover £220,000 to year end Oct 00.

Bassenfell Manor Christian Centre, Bassenthwaite, Keswick CA12 4RL
☎01768 776 366 🖷 01768 776 366
E: manager@bassenfell.org.uk
Web: www.bassenfell.org.uk
Group self-catering holidays, also childrens' adventure holidays, adult activity holidays and retreats.
Manager: Mr Chris Brook. Admin staff 4. ***CC*** No.283247. Began 1984; interdenominational. Turnover £83,000 to year end Mar 02.

***Bawtry Hall**, Bawtry, Doncaster DN10 6JH
☎01302 710 020 🖷 01302 710 027
E: info@bawtryhall.co.uk
Web: bawtryhall.co.uk
Centre for mission training; conference facilities; office accommodation for missionary organisations.
Director: Mr Nigel Spencer. *Conference Coordinator:* Andrea Fairchild. Admin staff 4, Other staff 10. ***CC*** No.225364. Began 1989; interdenominational. Turnover £440,000 to year end Dec 04.

Beach Haven Private Hotel, 61 Pevensey Road, Eastbourne BN21 3HS
☎01323 726 105
E: enquiries@beach-haven.co.uk
Web: www.beach-haven.co.uk
Also offering retreats and courses; own chapel; non-smoking.
Partner: Mr Ken Martin. Executive staff 1, No other full-time staff. Began n/a; non-denominational. Turnover n/a.

Beach House Private Hotel 4 Knowsley Road, Southport PR9 0HG
☎01704 500 100
E: james.beacho@tesco.net
Web: www.beach-house-hotel-southport.co.uk
Hotel also catering for church groups for study worship, Alpha weekends.
Owners: Mr & Mrs Edward & Janice James. Executive staff 2. Began n/a; non-denom- inational. Turnover n/a.

Beechwood Court (CE Holiday/Conference Centre Ltd), Mountain Road, Conwy LL32 8PY
☎01492 593 405 🖷 01492 593 4[illegible]4
E: beechwood@dialstart.net
Web: www.beechwoodcourt.com
or www.beechwoodcourt.net
Providing accommodation all year for holidays, conferences, retreats and outreach.
Manager: Mr John Bowgett. Executive staff 1, Other staff n/a. ***CC*** No.1039[illegible]70. Began n/a; interdenominational. Turnover n/a.

Bella Vista Hotel, Burlington Road, Swanage BH19 1LS
☎01929 422 873 🖷 01929 426 [illegible]0
E: mail@bellavista-hotel.co.uk
Web: www.bellavista-hotel.co.uk
Small private hotel catering for family holidays and short breaks.
Proprietor: Ms Deirdre McAlpine. Executive staff 2, Other staff 2. Began n/a; non-denominational. Turnover £52,000 to year end Oct 00.

For bed-spaces etc. see list on Page [illegible]3

Ben Doran Hotel, 11 Mayfield Gardens, Edinburgh EH9 2AX
☎0131 667 8488
📧 info@bendoran.com
Web: www.ben-doran.com
Family-run hotel.
Proprietor: Dr Joseph Labaki. Executive staff 1, Admin staff 2, Other staff 3. Began 1996; interdenominational. Turnover n/a.

Beth-Eden Christian Guest House, 4 West Parade, Llandudno LL30 2BB
☎01492 877 057 🖷 01492 873 595
📧: betheden@btinternet.com
Web: www.betheden.co.uk
Offering fellowship: groups welcome.
Proprietors: Lionel and Doreen Phillips. Executive staff 1, Other staff 4. Began 1972; interdenominational. Turnover n/a.

Biarritz Christian Hotel, Le Mont Sohier, St Brelade's Bay, Jersey JE3 8EA
☎01534 742 239
🖷 01534 747 433
📧: biarritzhotel@localdial.com
Web: www.biarritzhotel.co.uk
General Manager: Mr Duncan O'Neill. Full-time staff 2, Seasonal staff 25. Began 1959; Methodist. Turnover n/a.

Bishop Mascall Centre (Hereford Diocesan Centre), Lower Galdeford, Ludlow SY8 1RZ
☎01584 873 882 🖷 01584 877 945
📧: info@bmc.org.uk
Web: www.thebmc.org.uk
Residential and day conference centre.
Director: Mr George Reiss. *House Manager:* Miss Janet Haynes. Executive staff 2, Admin staff 3, Other staff 3. ***CC*** Began 1980; Anglican but open to all. Turnover n/a.

Bishops House, Isle of Iona PA76 6SJ
☎01681 700 800 🖷 01681 700 801
📧: bhiona@argyll.anglican.org
Web: www.scotland.anglican.org/retreats/bh.htm
Warden: Mrs Erica Meehan. Admin staff 1, Other staff 5. ***CC*** Began 1894; Episcopalian. Turnover £90,000 to year end Oct 98.

Blaithwaite House, Wigton CA7 0AZ
☎01697 342 319 🖷 01697 342 319
📧: manager@blaithwaite.co.uk
Web: www.blaithwaite.co.uk
Self-catering holiday and conference centre: outdoor activities provided by qualified staff.
Centre Manager: Mr Mal Tabb. Admin staff 2, Other staff 4. Began 1969; interdenominational. (Previously Blaithwaite Christian Centre). Turnover £135,270 to year end Apr 05.

Boarbank Hall, Grange-over-Sands LA11 7NH
☎01539 532 288 🖷 01539 535 386
📧: mail@boarbankhall.org.uk
Guest house, private retreats. Superior: Sister Imelda Gorman. Admin staff 5, Other staff 60. ***CC*** No.233499. Began 1921 Roman Catholic. Augustinian Sisters. Turnover n/a.

The Boys' Brigade Training Centre, Broomley Grange, Hindley Road, Stocksfield NE43 7RX
☎01661 842 299
🖷 01661 842 071
📧: boysbrigade@tiscali.co.uk
Web: www.broomleygrange.co.uk
Residential centre for youth, church and community-based organisations.
Manager: Alison Bolderson. Executive staff 1, Other staff 5. ***CC*** No.505386. Began 1976; interdenominational. (Previously North of England Training and Activity Centre). Turnover £125,000 to year end Feb 97.

Briar Lea House, Brampton Road, Longtown, Carlisle CA6 5TN
☎01228 791 538 Mobile: 07900 902 302 🖷 01228 791 538
📧: info@briarleahouse.co.uk
Web: www.briarleahouse.co.uk
Guest House.
Partner: Keith Mashiter. Executive staff 1. Began 2000; ecumenical. Turnover £20,000 to year end Dec 02.

Brincliffe Edge Hotel, 105 Queens Parade, Scarborough YO12 7HY
☎01723 364 834
📧: brincliffeedgehotel@yahoo.co.uk
Web: www.brincliffeedgehotel.co.uk
Family-run hotel.
Owner: Mrs B Sutcliffe. Executive staff 1, Other staff n/a. Began n/a; non-denominational. Turnover n/a.

Brockley Hall (CE Holiday/Conference Centre Ltd), Glenside, Saltburn-by-the-Sea TS12 1JS
☎01287 622 329 🖷 01287 622 329
📧: info@brockleyhall.co.uk
Web: www.christianholidays.co.uk
Centre Manager: Mr David Brooking. Executive staff 2, Admin staff 2, Other staff 2. ***CC*** No.1039170. Began 1934; interdenominational. Turnover n/a.

***Brunel Manor**, Teignmouth Road, Torquay TQ1 4SF
☎01803 329 333
🖷 01803 311 857
📧: info@brunelmanor.com
Web: www.brunelmanor.com
For spiritual and physical rest.
General Manager: Mr Rick Hillard. *Pastoral Leaders:* Mr & Mrs Peter & Jill du Feu. Admin staff 8, Other staff 26. ***CC*** No.209651. Began 1942; interdenominational. Turnover £800,000 to year end Sep 05.

Bryntirion Christian Conference Centre, Bryntirion, Bridgend CF31 4DX
☎01656 645 411
🖷 01656 641 987
📧: warden@etcw.ac.uk
Web: www.etcw.ac.uk
Conference centre at theological college.
Warden: Mr John Lang. Executive staff 1, Other staff 3. ***CC*** No.517324. Began 1970; non-denominational. Turnover £27,000 to year end Feb 05.

Bryn-y-Groes Christian Conference Centre, Bryn-y-Groes, Bala LL23 7YE
☎01678 520 752
M: 07721 758 831
E: conferencecentre@emw.org.uk
Web: www.emw.org.uk/conferencecentre
Manager: Mr David J Wilmot. Admin staff 1, Other staff 3. ***CC*** No.222407. Began 1960; non-denominational. Turnover £110,000 to year end Jan 05.

Buckfast Abbey, St Mary's Abbey, Buckfast, Buckfastleigh TQ11 0EE
☎01364 645 500 🖷 01364 643 891
E: enquiries@buckfast.org.uk
Web: www.buckfast.org.uk
Also shops and restaurant.
Liaison Officer: Mr Trevor Jarvis. Other staff 100. ***CC*** Began 1882; Roman Catholic. Turnover n/a.

***Burstone Manor, Centre for Christ Trust**, Burstone Manor, Bow, Crediton EX17 6LB
☎01363 822 61
E: centreforchrist@burstone.freeserve.co.uk
Web: www.burstone.freeserve.co.uk
Holiday, retreat and conference centre.
Trustees' Representatives: Rev & Mrs Howard Castle. Admin staff 3, Other staff 2. ***CC*** No.270327. Began 1977; interdenominational. Turnover £80,000 to year end Dec 02.

***Capernwray Hall**, Carnforth LA6 1AG
☎01524 733 908 🖷 01524 736 681
E: phil.burt@capernwray.org.uk
Web: www.capernwray.org.uk
Holidays for all ages, teens, families, 20s and 30s, men's and ladies conferences, Christmas and New Year.
Managing Director: Rev Mark Thomas. *Holiday Programme Director:* Mr Dougie Roy. *Business Director:* Mr Phil Burt. Admin staff 8, Other staff 25. ***CC*** No.1073139. Began 1947; interdenominational. (Previously Capernwray Missionary Fellowship of Torchbearers). Turnover included in Capernwray Bible School.

Carberry, Musselburgh EH21 8PY
☎0131 665 3135/3488
🖷 0131 653 2930
E: louise@carberrytower.com|
Web: www.carberrytower.com
Providing courses and conference facilities.
Chief Executive: Mr Peter Sunderland. *Office Activities Officer:* Ms Louise Morris. Executive staff 1, Other staff 19. ***CC*** No.SCO 24381. Began 1966; non-denominational. (Previously Carberry Tower). Gartmore House Trust. Magazine: *Carberry News* (1,500 half-yearly). Turnover n/a.

Carey House, Brecklands Green, North Pickenham, Swaffham PE37 8LG
☎01760 440 561 M: 07742 219 756
🖷 01760 440 561
E: peter@eastgate.org.uk
Web: www.eastgate.org.uk
Retreat and conference centre, prayer house, intercession meetings, teaching seminars, Alpha and away days.
Director: Mr Peter Gillett. Executive staff 1, Other staff n/a. ***CC*** No.1009279. Began 1974; interdenominational. Turnover n/a.

Carfax Hotel, 13 Great Pulteney Street, Bath BA2 4BS
☎01225 462 089 🖷 01225 443 257
E: reservations@carfaxhotel.co.uk
Web: www.carfaxhotel.co.uk
Temperance hotel; childcare provision.
General Manager: Mrs Sylvia Back. Admin staff 2, Other staff 16. ***CC*** No.214779. Began 1945; Salvation Army. Turnover £480,000 to year end Mar 02.

Castle Erin, Castle Erin Road, Portrush BT56 8DH
☎028 7082 2744 🖷 028 7082 2235
E: castleerin.guesthouse@btinternet.com
Web: www.findmeaccommodation.co.uk/castleerin/
Holiday and conference centre.
Manageress: Miss Avril Gracey. Admin staff 1, Other staff 14. Began 1926; interdenominational. Turnover n/a.

***Castlewellan Castle Christian Conference Centre**, Castlewellan BT31 9BU
☎028 4377 8733 🖷 028 4377 8733
Providing residential conference facilities for church, youth, school and activity groups.
Managers: Rev & Mrs Andrew Forson. Executive staff 1, Other staff 4. ***CC*** Began 1975; interdenominational. Operated by Cloverley Centres. Turnover n/a.

Cavell Christian Guest House, 1 Elton Road, Clevedon BS21 7RA
☎01275 874 477 🖷 01275 878 737
E: cavellguesthouse@onetel.net.uk
Web: www.cavellguesthouse.co.uk
Managers: Mr & Mrs George & Daphne Hamnett. Executive staff 2, Other staff 2. Began 1996; non-denominational. Turnover n/a.

***Cefn Lea Park Midwales Christian Holiday and Conference Complex**, Dolfor, Newtown SY16 4AJ
☎01686 625 275
🖷 01686 626 122
E: enquiries@cefnlea.co.uk
Web: www.cefnlea.co.uk
Conference venue; also summer family holidays, school groups.
Partner: Mr David Morgan. Admin staff 3, Other staff 7. Began 1978; interdenominational. Turnover n/a.

***Central Hall Westminster**, Storey's Gate, Westminster, London SW1H 9NH
☎020 7222 8010 🖷 020 7222 6[illegible]33
E: events@c-h-w.co.uk
Web: www.c-h-w.com
Historic venue and conference centre with various-sized meeting rooms.
General Manager: Mr Michael Sharp. Executive staff 6, Other staff 24. ***CC*** No.207463. Began 1912; Methodist. Turnover £2,500,000 to year end Aug 00.

Chantmarle Christian Resource Centre, Chantmarle Manor, Frome St Quintin, Dorchester DT2 0HD
☎01935 483 201 🖷 01935 838 [illegible]
E: resource.centre@chantmarle.co.uk
Web: www.chantmarle.co.uk
For seminars, meetings and retreats.
Managing Director: Mr John Glare. Executive staff 1, Other staff 15. Began 20[illegible]5; interdenominational. Turnover n/a.

Charney Manor, Charney Bassett, Wantage OX12 0EJ
☎01235 868 206 🖷 01235 868 832
Web: www.quaker.org.uk/charneymanor
Retreat house and conference centre.
Contact: Sheila Terry. Admin staff 3, Other staff 5. ***CC*** No.237267. Began 1947; Religious Society of Friends. Turnover £197,000 to year end Dec 02.

Compass Christian Centre, Glenshee Lodge, Blairgowrie PH10 7QD
☎01250 885 209 🖷01250 885 30[illegible]
E: compass@compasschristian.co.uk
Web: www.compasschristian.co.uk
Winter skills, ski-touring, management & team training, conferences & retreats. Catered & self-catering.
Director: Ruth McBean. *Bookings Secretary:* Sally Gingell. Executive staff 3, Admin staff 1, Other staff 12. ***CC*** No.SCO 11797. Began 1967; interdenominational. Turnover £177,000 to year end May 00.

Guy Chester Centre, Chesterhouse, Pages Lane, Muswell Hill, London N10 1PR
☎020 8883 8204
E: bookings@chestercentre.org.uk
Web: www.chestercentre.org.uk
Residential and day conference centre, organised retreats, quiet days, courses.
Bookings Officer: Ms Alison Campbell. Admin staff 10, Other staff 15. ***CC*** Began n/a; Methodist. Turnover n/a.

For bed-spaces etc. see list on Page 23

The Christian Conference Centre, Malvern, Ranelagh Road, Malvern WR14 1BQ
☎01684 568 241 🖷 01684 568 241
E: gordon.leveratt@talk21.com
Web: www.dofs.org.uk
Offering facilities for churches and organisations to run residential/day conferences and discipleship training courses.
Owners: Mr & Mrs Gordon & Maggie Leveratt. Executive staff 2, Other staff 3. Began 1998; non-denominational. Part of Day of Salvation Ministries. Turnover £70,000 to year end Nov 03.

*__The City Temple Conference Centre__, Holborn Viaduct, London EC1A 2DE
☎020 7583 5532 🖷 020 7353 1083
E: enquries@city-temple.com
Web: www.city-temple.com
Non-residential conference centre for up to 900 people.
Co-ordinator: Mr David DuRand. Admin staff 2, Other staff 5. ***CC*** No.235447. Began n/a; United Reformed. Turnover n/a.

Cliff College Conference Centre, Calver, Hope Valley S32 3XG
☎01246 584 206 🖷 01246 583 739
E: admin@cliffcollege.org
Web: www.cliffcollege.org
Bursar: Mr John Steer. *Conference Manager:* Mr Ian Phipps. Admin staff 1, Other staff 5. Began 1965; Methodist but open to all. Turnover £322,233 to year end Aug 04.

Cliff House Holiday & Conference Centre, 13 Belle Vue Road, Southbourne, Bournemouth BH6 3DA
☎01202 424 701
🖷 01202 426 995
E: info@cliffhouse-bournemouth.co.uk
Web: www.cliffhouse-bournemouth.co.uk
Manager: Mr Brian Wright. Executive staff 2, Other staff 6. ***CC*** No.214779. Began 1870; Salvation Army. Turnover n/a.

Cloverley Hall Christian Conference Centre, Whitchurch SY13 4PH
☎01948 890 688
🖷 01948 890 366
E: office@cloverleyhall.com
Web: www.cloverleyhall.com
Residential conference centre for churches, full-board.
Managers: Mr & Mrs Alan and Chris Scutt. *Group Administrator:* D E Burton. Admin staff 1, Other staff 10. ***CC*** No.528419. Began 1968; non-denominational. Operated by Cloverley Hall Group. Turnover £190,000 to year end Sep 98.

Coleg Trefeca, Trefeca, Brecon LD3 0PP
☎01874 711 423
🖷 01874 712 212
E: post@trefeca.org.uk
Web: www.trefeca.org.uk
Lay training centre; ecumenical conference and retreat centre.
Centre Manageress: Mair Jones. Executive staff 2, Admin staff 2, Other staff 4. ***CC*** No.258456. Began 1968; Presbyterian Church of Wales. Turnover n/a.

Convent of St Mary at the Cross, Priory Field Drive, Hale Lane, Edgware HA8 9PZ
☎020 8958 7868
🖷 020 8958 1920
E: nuns.osb.edgware@btclick.com
Providing guest house, day conference centre, care for the disabled and elderly.
Mother Abbess: Mother Mary Zelent. Other staff 3, Community 12. ***CC*** No.209261. Began 1866; Anglican, Benedictine. Turnover n/a.

Cotswold View Guest House, Nether Westcote, Kingham, Chipping Norton OX7 6SD
☎01993 830 699
E: info@cotswoldview-guesthouse.co.uk
Web: www.cotswoldview-guesthouse.co.uk
Directors: Mr & Mrs Anthony & Hazel Gibson. Executive staff 2. Began 1985; non-denominational. Turnover £50,000 to year end Dec 02.

Croft Farm Celtic Cottages, Croft, Cardigan SA43 3NT
☎01239 615 179
E: info@croft-holiday-cottages.co.uk
Web: www.croft-holiday-cottages.co.uk
Holiday cottages; various facilities.
Proprietors: Mr & Mrs Andrew & Sylvie Gow. Executive staff 2. Began 1988; non-denominational. Turnover n/a.

Daybreak Guest House, 6 Herbert Road, Alum Chine, Bournemouth BH4 8HD
☎01202 761 055
E: masondaybreak@aol.com
Web: www.daybreakguesthouse.co.uk
Proprietors: Mr & Mrs Alan and Agnes Mason. Executive staff 2. Began 1984; interdenominational. Turnover n/a.

Dorincourt Guest House, 41 Undercliff Road West, Felixstowe IP11 2AH
☎01394 270 447 🖷 01394 270 447
Family-run; ground floor rooms for disabled persons.
Proprietor: Mrs P Chambers. Executive staff 1. Began n/a; interdenominational. Turnover n/a.

Dovedale House, Ilam, Ashbourne DE6 2AZ
☎01335 350 365 🖷 01335 350 263
E: warden@dovedalehouse.org.uk
Web: www.dovedalehouse.org.uk
For schools, universities, churches and voluntary groups including disabled access.
Warden: Mr Arthur J H[illegible]ck. *Deputy Warden:* Mr Dave Lucas. Executive staff 2, Other staff 6. ***CC*** No.522677. Began 1966; Anglican but open to all. Turnover £120,000 to year end Dec 04.

Elmham House (Pilgrim Bureau), Friday Market Place, Walsingham NR22 6EB
☎01328 820 217 🖷 01328 821 087
E: rcnationalshrine@walsingham.org.uk
Web: www.walsingham.org.uk
For visitors to national shrine.
Director: Rev N Wynn. Admin staff 8, Other staff 21. ***CC*** No.265755. Began n/a; Roman Catholic. Turnover n/a.

*__Emmanuel Centre__, 9-23 Marsham Street, London SW1P 3DW
☎020 7222 9191 M: 07952 130 214
🖷 020 7233 1922
E: enquiry@emmanuelcentre.com
Web: www.emmanuelcentre.com
Providing non-residential facilities for day conferences, seminars and workshops for up to 1,000 people. Coffee shop.
Contact: Mr John Tan. Executive staff 1, Other staff 3. Began 1997; interdenominational. Turnover n/a.

The Eton Dorney Centre, Lake End Road, Dorney, Windsor SL4 6QS
☎01628 662 823
E: info@etondorney.org.uk
Web: www.etondorney.org.uk
Residential youth centre providing full-board accommodation for children's and young people's groups.
Warden: Mr Ged Pearce. Admin staff 1, Other staff 3. ***CC*** No.305994. Began 1971; Anglican but open to all. Turnover n/a.

For bed-spaces etc. see list on Page 28

***The Evangelical Alliance Conference Centre**, Whitefield House, 186 Kennington Park Road London SE11 4BT
☎020 7207 2100 📠 020 7207 2150
E: conference@eauk.org
Web: www.eauk.org
Non-residential, catering available.
Conference Centre Administrator: Margaret Jones. Executive staff 1. ***CC*** No.123448. Began 1995; interdenominational. Turnover included in Evangelical Alliance.

Fairhaven Christian Hotel, 3 Craig-y-don Parade, Promenade, Llandudno LL30 1BG
☎01492 878 447 📠 01492 870 185
E: andrew-paula@fairhaven-hotel.freeserve.co.uk
Proprietors: Mr & Mrs A Hammond. Admin staff 2. Began 1991; non-denominational. Turnover £63,000 to year end Dec 02.

Fairhavens, 8 Wellington Esplanade, Lowestoft NR33 0QQ
☎01502 574 927
E: fairhavens1@breathemail.net
Partners: Mr & Mrs Keith Clarke, Mr & Mrs Eric Mattless. Executive staff 4. Began 1972; interdenominational. (Previously Fairhavens Christian Guest House). Turnover n/a.

Falkirk Christian Centre, 1 Glebe Street, Falkirk FK1 1HX
☎01324 483 178 M: 07803 607 342
E: todd.john@talk21.com
Web: www.ye.co.uk/sites/falkirk-christianctr/
Providing halls, kitchen for conferences, seminars, exhibitions.
Secretary: Mr John Todd. No full-time staff. ***CC*** No.SCO 16770. Began 1987; non-denominational. Turnover £7,000 to year end Dec 00.

***Family Foundations Trust Ltd**, Dalesdown, Honeybridge Lane, Dial Post, Horsham RH13 8NX
☎01403 710 712 📠 01403 710 716
E: dalesdown@talk21.com
Web: www.dalesdown.org.uk
Conference centre.
Manager: Mr Cliff Powell. Executive staff 1. ***CC*** No.284006. Began 1987; non-denominational. Turnover £100,000 to year end Dec 04.

Featherstone Castle, Haltwhistle NE49 0JG
☎01434 320 202 📠 01434 320 785
E: john.clark@featherstonecastle.com
For young people and students; self-catering.
Owner: Mr John M Clark. Executive staff 1. Other staff 1. Began 1961; non-denominational. Turnover £50,000 to year end Dec 02.

Felbury House, Holmbury St Mary, Dorking RH5 6NL
☎01306 730 929 📠 01306 730 610
E: info@lifetrain.org.uk
Web: www.lifetrain.org.uk
Residential and training centre primarily for young people and disabled people.
Chief Executive: Mr Richard Bowden. *Centre Manager:* Mrs Liz Osborn. Executive staff 1, Admin staff 2, Other staff 1. ***CC*** No.803697. Began 1973; interdenominational. Turnover £500,000 to year end Mar 00.

Fern Villa Guest House and Cottages, Loanfern, Ballachulish PH49 4JE
☎01855 811 393 📠 01855 811 727
E: fernctg@aol.com
Web: www.fernvilla.com
Proprietor: Mr Kenneth Chandler. Executive staff 2. Began 1994; non-denominational. Turnover £49,000 to year end Dec 99.

Foreign Missions Club, The Highbury Centre, 26 Aberdeen Park, Highbury, London N5 2BJ
☎020 7226 2663 📠 020 7704 1853
E: fmc1893@aol.com
Web: www.theforeignmissionsclub.org
For visitors to London, public transport nearby.
Manager: Mrs Sue Scalora. Admin staff 4, Other staff 12. ***CC*** No.227866. Began 1893; interdenominational. Turnover £440,000 to year end Dec 04.

Fountain Springs, Glenfeadon House, Portreath, Redruth TR16 4JU
☎01209 842 650 📠 01209 842 650
Fellowship, counselling, hospitality and teaching from biblical roots. Family run.
Managers: Pastor & Mrs Anthony Keast. Began 1988; non-denominational. Turnover n/a.

Foxhill (Chester Diocesan Conference Centre), Tarvin Road, Frodsham WA6 6XB
☎01928 733 777 📠 01928 731 422
E: foxhillwarden@aol.com
Web: www.foxhillconferences.co.uk
Wardens: Mr & Mrs Ian & Sue Cameron. Admin staff 3, Other staff 5. ***CC*** Began 1969; Anglican. Turnover £100,000 to year end Dec 96.

Gartmore House Conference and Activity Centre, Gartmore, Stirling FK8 3RS
☎01877 382 991 📠 01877 382 725
E: mail@gartmorehouse.com
Web: www.gartmorehouse.com
Conference and activity centre, full-board; also restaurant.
Director: Peter Sunderland. Executive staff 1, Other staff n/a. ***CC*** No.SCO 29484. Began 1997; non-denominational. Turnover £500,000 to year end Dec 05.

Glade End Guest House, 2 Little Marlow Road, Marlow SL7 1DQ
☎01628 471 334 M: 07774 107 445
E: sue@gladeend.com
Web: www.gladeend.com
Proprietor: Mrs Susan Peperell. *Administration:* Mr Tony Peperell. Executive staff 2, Other staff 4. Began 1990; non-denominational. Turnover £150,000 to year end Mar 05.

Glenada Holiday and Conference Centre, 29 South Promenade, Newcastle BT33 0EX
☎028 4372 2402 M: 07720 049 555
📠 028 4372 6229
E: info@glenada.co.uk
Web: www.glenada.co.uk
Conferences, holiday and short breaks with guest speakers and coach trips.
Manager: Mrs Ellsye Rowell. Executive staff 1, Other staff n/a. ***CC*** No.XN 48517. Began 1900; interdenominational. Turnover n/a.

Glencoe Holiday Flatlets, 7 Esplanade Road, Paignton TQ4 6EB
☎01803 557 727 📠 01803 666 512
E: info@glencoeapartments.com
Web: www.glencoeapartments.com
Proprietor: Mrs P J Ayles. Executive staff 1. Began 1971; interdenominational. Turnover n/a.

For bed-spaces etc. see list on Page 28

A

Glenfall House, Mill Lane, Charlton Kings, Cheltenham GL54 4EP
☎01242 583 654 🖷 01242 251 314
E: enquiries@glenfallhouse.org
Web: www.glenfallhouse.org
Mainly for adults.
Resident Director: Mrs June Pratt. ***CC*** No.1029239. Began 1992; Anglican. Turnover n/a.

The Golden Sovereigns Hotel, 97 Alumhurst Road, Alum Chine, Westbourne, Bournemouth BH4 8HR
☎01202 762 088 🖷 01202 762 088
E: scott.p@talk21.com
Web: www.goldensovereignhotel.com
Family hotel.
Owner: Mr Stefano Pini. No full-time staff. Began 1989; non-denominational. Turnover n/a.

Gorslwyd Farm, Tanygroes, Cardigan SA43 2HZ
☎01239 810 593 M: 07801 978 492
E: info@gorslwyd.co.uk
Web: www.gorslwyd.co.uk
Self-catering cottages with accessible facilities for all visitors.
Proprietors: Mr & Mrs Rod & Rachel Hills. Executive staff 2, Other staff 1, Admin staff 2. Began 1982; Free Evangelical. Turnover n/a.

Grays Hotel, 18 Elms Avenue, Eastbourne BN21 3DN
☎01323 723 539
Family run.
Owners/Managers: Mr & Mrs R Waring. Admin staff 2. Began 1997; Methodist. Turnover n/a.

Green Hill Outreach, The Mill, Burmington, Shipston-on-Stour CV36 5AF
☎01608 663 952
E: GreenHillCentre@aol.com
Providing catered facilities for residential and non-residential Christian groups. Book/coffee shop
Manager: Miss Fran Wilson. Admin staff 1. ***CC*** No.1039041. Began 1990; non-denominational. Turnover n/a.

Green Pastures Christian Centre of Pastoral Care and Healing, 17 Burton Road, Branksome Park, Poole BH13 6DT
☎01202 764 776 🖷 01202 768 144
E: admin@green-pastures.org
Web: www.green-pastures.org
Short-term residential therapeutic environment for personal growth, healing, fellowship, counselling, spiritual direction, creativity, hands-on therapies.
Pastoral Director: Revd Colin Norris. *Centre Manager:* Audri Coleman. Executive staff 1, Other staff 10. ***CC*** No.1090568. Began 1955; interdenominational. Magazine: *Update* (3,000 quarterly). Turnover n/a.

Greenhedges, 15 Augusta Street, Sheringham NR26 8LB
☎01263 823 517
E: bobcumber@aol.com
Self-catering holiday house. Also base for SU beach mission, youth evangelism in north Norfolk.
Bookings Manager: Mrs D Burns. Admin staff 1, Other staff 1. ***CC*** No.250682. Began 1966; non-denominational. Turnover n/a.
Correspondence: Bob Cumber, Sheringham CSSM Trust, 16 St Nicholas Place, Sheringham NR26 8LF

Haldon Court Christian Hotel and Conference Centre, 34 Douglas Avenue, Exmouth EX8 2HB
☎01395 263 836 🖷 01395 263 836
E: paul@haldoncourt.freeserve.co.uk
Web: www.haldoncourt.co.uk
Managers: Mr & Mrs Paul & June Lambert. Admin staff 2, Other staff 2. Began 1957; interdenominational. Turnover £300,000 to year end Nov 98.

Harnham Farmhouse, Montys Court, Norton Fitzwarren, Taunton TA4 1BT
☎01823 432 255 🖷 01823 433 623
E: mitford-slade@montyscourt.freeserve.co.uk
Web: www.country-holidays2006. co.uk
Mainly self-catering, bed and breakfast available at Montys Court.
Proprietors: Major & Mrs Anthony C W Mitford-Slade. Admin staff 2, Other staff 1. Began n/a; non-denominational. Turnover n/a.

***Haven Christian Holiday Centre**, 1 Westgate Hill, Pembroke SA71 4LB
☎01646 685 469 🖷 01646 686 893
E: managers@havencentre.freeserve. co.uk
Web: www.havencentre.freeserve. co.uk
Group holidays, retreats and seminars; parent and toddler facilities.
Managers: Mr & Mrs Warren & Sheila Hodson. Admin staff 2, Other staff 4. ***CC*** Began 1979; interdenominational. Turnover £50,000 to year end Dec 00.

The Hayes Conference Centre, Swanwick, Alfreton DE55 1UY
☎01773 526 000 🖷 01773 540 841
E: peter.anderson@cct.org.uk
Web: www.cct.org.uk
Residential and day conference centre for up to 400 people; conference halls and delegate rooms.
Centre Manager: Mr Peter Anderson. Admin staff 9, Other staff 76. ***CC*** No.1056604. Began 1911; non-denominational. Part of The Christian Conference Trust - see also High Leigh Conference Centre. Turnover n/a.

Hebron Hall Ltd Christian Conference Centre, Cross Common Road, Dinas Powis CF64 4YB
☎029 2051 5665 🖷 029 2051 5776
E: admin@hebronhall.org
Web: www.hebronhall.org
Manager: Mr Jeff Lacey. Admin staff 4, Other staff 20. ***CC*** No.514184. Began 1983; interdenominational. Turnover n/a.

Herne Bay Court Evangelical Centre, Canterbury Road, Herne Bay CT6 5TD
☎01227 373 254 🖷 01227 741 581
E: enquiries@hernebaycourt.co.uk
Web: www.hernebaycourt.co.uk
Full board.
Manager: Mr D Paul Mitchell. Admin staff 2, Other staff 15. ***CC*** No.5[illegible]8419. Began 1948; interdenominational. Operated by Cloverley Hall Group. Turnover £5[illegible],000 to year end Sep 04.

High Leigh Conference Centre Lord Street, Hoddesdon EN11 8SG
☎01992 463 016 🖷 01992 44[illegible] 594
E: ian.andrews@cct.org.uk
Web: www.cct.org.uk
Residential and day conference centre for up to 200 people; conference halls and delegate rooms.
Manager: Mr Ian Andrews. Admin staff 5, Other staff 39. ***CC*** No.1056604. Began 1922; non-denominational. Part of The Christian Conference Trust - see also The Hayes Conference Centre. Turnover n/a.

Highlands Hotel Ltd, La Corbiere, Jersey JE3 8HN
☎01534 744 288 🖷 01534 747 273
E: enquiries@highlandshotel.com
Web: www.highlandshotel.com
Christian hotel with Bible Ministry speakers catering for individuals, families and groups. Temperance.
Hotel Manager: Mr A Irving. Admin staff 2, Other staff 24. Began 1966; interdenominational. Turnover £500,000 to year end Oct 05.

Hill House Christian Centre, Otterhampton, Bridgwater TA5 2PT
☎01278 652 289 M 077[illegible]0 359 083
🖷 01278 652 289
E: hillhouse@hillhouse.org.uk
Web: www.hillhouse.org.uk
Managers: Mr & Mrs Harry & Chris Jacobson. Admin staff 4, Other staff 5. ***CC*** No.1037604. Began 19[illegible]6; interdenominational. Part of Bristol Christian Youth Trust. Turnover n/a

***Hollowford Centre, Lindley Educational Trust Ltd**, Castleton, Hope Valley S33 8WB
☎01433 621 341 🖷 01433 621 717
E: enquiries@hollowford.org
Web: www.hollowford.org
For all age groups; outdoor activities with or without a trainer.
Centre Manager: Mr Mark Williams. *Bookings Administrator:* Vanessa Newton. Admin staff 2, Other staff 11. ***CC*** No.247662. Began 194[illegible]; interdenominational. (Previously Lindley Lodge). Turnover n/a.

†The Holy Trinity Malshanger Trust, Malshanger, Basingstoke RG23 7EU
☎01256 782 171 🖷 01256 5[illegible]4 853[illegible]
Warden: Mr Jeff Pink. Executive staff 1. ***CC*** Began 1982; Anglican. Turnover £20,000 to year end Dec 98.

For bed-spaces etc. see list on Page [illegible]8

A

†Homefield - Methodist Holiday and Conference Centre, 74 Gronant Road, Prestatyn LL19 9HW
☎01745 854 164 M: 07939 424 787
🖷 01745 854 164
Holidays, church away weekends and conferences.
Manager: Name not supplied. Staff n/a. ***CC*** No.248521. Began 1948; Methodist. Turnover n/a.

Hotel Picardie, Esplanade, Ventnor PO38 1JX
☎01983 852 647 M: 07974 778 082
🖷 01983 852 647
Web: www.picardie.f9.co.uk
Proprietor: Marcia Forsyth-Grant. Admin staff 2. Began 1986; non-denominational. Turnover n/a.

***Hothorpe Hall Christian Conference Centre**, Theddingworth, Lutterworth LE17 6QX
☎01858 881 500 🖷 01858 880 979
E: office@hothorpe.co.uk
Web: www.hothorpe.co.uk
Conference, holiday and wedding venue.
Chief Executive: Mr Brian Dunning. Admin staff 7, Other staff 33. Began 1984; non-denominational. Turnover n/a.

House of the Open Door Community, Childswickham House, Buckland Road, Childswickham, Broadway WR12 7HH
☎01386 852 084 🖷 01386 858 751
E: hod@houseoftheopendoor.org
Web: www.houseoftheopendoor.org
Discipleship training course, summer camps for teenagers, prison/schools ministry, retreat centre, music/drama team.
Founders: Mr & Mrs Roy Hendy. Community members 24. ***CC*** No.1064343. Began 1978; interdenominational. Turnover n/a.

The Jonas Trust, The Jonas Centre, Redmire, Leyburn DL8 4EW
☎01969 624 900 M: 07956 557 473
E: stay@jonascentre.org
Web: www.jonascentre.org
Conference, retreat and holiday centre.
Centre Managers: Mr Simon Eastwood, Mr Aiden Webster. Executive staff 2. ***CC*** No.1049167. Began 1995; interdenominational. Turnover £125,000 to year end Sep 05.

***Keswick Convention Centre**, Skiddaw Street, Keswick CA12 4BY
☎01768 780 075 🖷 01768 775 276
E: info@keswickministries.org
Web: www.keswickministries.org
Self-catering residential accommodation.
Operations Manager: Mr Simon Overend. Admin staff 4, Other staff 2. ***CC*** No.1083584. Began 1875; interdenominational. Turnover n/a.

Kilbroney Centre, 15 Kilbroney Road, Rostrevor, Newry BT34 3BH
☎028 4173 8293 🖷 028 4173 8293
E: jonesatkilbroney@hotmail.org.uk
For young people.
Warden: Rev Sam Jones. Admin staff 1, Other staff 3. ***CC*** Began 1975; Church of Ireland. Turnover £50,000 to year end Dec 00.

***King's Park Conference and Sports Centre**, Kings Park Road, Northampton NN3 6LL
☎01604 493 111 (conference centre only)
🖷 01604 493 559
E: kingspark@actioncentres.co.uk
Web: www.actioncentres.co.uk
Purpose-built centre, conference and seminar rooms, catering.
Head of Centre: Mrs Yvonne Whitaker. Admin staff 5, Other staff 20. ***CC*** No.803431. Began 1989; interdenominational. Turnover n/a.

Lamorna Lodge Hotel, Boskerris Road, Carbis Bay, St Ives TR26 2NG
☎01736 795 967
E: lamorna@tr26.wanadoo.co.uk
Web: www.lamorna.co.uk
Proprietors: Mr & Mrs Richard & Joanna Neil. Admin staff 2. Began 1960; interdenominational. (Previously Lamorna Christian Guest House). Turnover £60,000 to year end Aug 04.

Lancaster Hall Hotel Ltd, 35 Craven Terrace, Lancaster Gate, London W2 3EL
☎020 7723 9276 🖷 020 7706 2870
E: info@lancaster-hall-hotel.co.uk
Web: www.lancaster-hall-hotel.co.uk
Manager: Mr U Maynard. Admin staff 4, Other staff 34. Began 1973; interdenominational. (Subsidiary trading company of The German YMCA). Turnover n/a.

Lattendales Centre for Wellbeing, Berrier Road, Greystoke, Penrith CA11 0UE
☎01768 483 229 🖷 01768 483 058
E: info@lattendales.org
Web: www.lattendales.org
Manager: Ineke Gijsbers. Executive staff 1, Other staff 5. ***CC*** No.26-223. Began 1973; Religious Society of Friends but open to all. Turnover £44,000 to year end Mar 00. Offering place for healing, rest and relaxation to groups and individuals.

***Latymer Christian Centre**, 116 Bramley Road, Kensington, London W10 6SU
☎020 8969 2290 🖷 020 8960 5468
E: latymer@surefish.co.uk
Community centre providing activities that build relationships and bring wholeness; also conference facilities.
Centre Manager: Mary Johnson. Admin staff 1, Other staff 2. ***CC*** No.1041828. Began 1974; non-denominational. Turnover £85,000 to year end Mar 05.

Lee Abbey, Lynton EX35 6JJ
☎01598 752 621 🖷 01598 752 619
E: warden@leeabbey.org.uk
Web: www.leeabbey.org.uk
Holiday, retreat and conference centre; also outdoor centre. Catered and self-catering.
Warden: Rev Chris Edmondson. *Centre Manager:* Rev Andrew McCausland. *Finance Director:* Mr Stephen Scofield. Admin staff 19, Other staff 60. ***CC*** No.1094097. Began 1945; Anglican but open to all. Magazine: *Rapport* (4,500 quarterly). Turnover £1,500,000 to year end Dec 04.

For bed-spaces etc. see list on Page 28

A

Lee Bay Hotel, Lee, Ilfracombe EX34 8LP
☎01271 867 600 🖷 01271 863 956
E: accommodation@hotel7.freeserve.co.uk
Web: www.leebayhotel.com
Proprietor: Mr Douglas Turner. Admin staff 4, Other staff 30. Began 1991; non-denominational. Turnover n/a.

Legge House, Church Hill, Wroughton, Swindon SN4 9JS
☎01793 813 273 🖷 01793 814 582
E: legge.house@virgin.net
Web: www.leggehouse.com
For young people; also conferences.
Manager: Mr Chris Offord. Executive staff 1. **CC** No.305602. Began 1968; Anglican. Turnover £42,000 to year end Dec 04.

Les Cotils Ecumenical Centre, St Peter Port, Guernsey GY1 1UU
☎01481 727 793 🖷 01481 701 062
E: info@lescotils.com
Web: www.lescotils.com
Also coffee shop.
Manager: Mr Paul Chambers. *Assistant Managers:* Mr Peter Ahearn, Miss Ali Le Ray. Admin staff 3, Other staff n/a. Began n/a; ecumenical. Turnover £300,000 to year end Dec 00.

Letton Hall, Shipdham, Thetford IP25 7SA
☎01362 820 717 🖷 01362 820 877
E: info@lettonhall.org
Web: www.lettonhall.org
Conference, houseparty and activities centre offering catered or self-catering facilities.
Director of Trust: Mr John Currey. *Centre Managers:* Rev Gerald and Mrs June Rootham. Admin staff 1, Other staff 6. **CC** No.279817. Began 1980; interdenominational. Turnover £187,656 to year end Dec 04.

Lindors House (Christian Guild Holidays), St Briavels, Lydney GL15 6RB
☎01594 530 283 🖷 01594 530 559
E: cghlindors@aol.com
Web: www.lindors.cgholidays.co.uk
Holiday and conference centre open all year. For individuals, couples, families and groups.
General Manager: Joseph Donavon. *Hotel Manager:* James Sharp. Staff n/a. Began 1953; ecumenical. (Previously Lindors Country House). Turnover n/a.

Llety Iachad Hotel & Christian Centre, 12 Ellesmere Road, Colwyn Bay LL29 8RP
☎01492 530 528 🖷 01492 534 558
E: e wintringham@freeuk.com
Web: www.christianhotel.org.uk
Offering holidays, retreats, convalescence; non-smoking.
Joint Proprietors: Ms Esther Wintringham, Ms Jean Cotton. Executive staff 2, Admin staff 2. Began n/a; non-denominational. (Previously Fairways Hotel). Turnover n/a.

The Lodge on the Loch Hotel, Onich, Fort William PH33 6RY
☎08712 223 462 🖷 01855 821 190
E: reservation@lodgeontheloch.com
Web: www.lodgeontheloch.com
Person in charge: Daniel Goh. Admin staff 6, Other staff 4. Began 1977; non-denominational. Turnover n/a.

Lower Campscott Farm, Lee, Ilfracombe EX34 8LS
☎01271 863 479
🖷 01271 867 639
E: holidays@lowercampscott.co.uk
Web: www.lowercampscott.co.uk
Proprietor: Mrs Margaret Cowell. Staff n/a. Began 1981; Anglican. Turnover n/a.

Marygate House, Holy Island, Berwick-upon-Tweed TD15 2SD
☎01289 389 246 🖷 01289 389 246
E: ian@marygateho.freeserve.co.uk
Web: www.lindisfarne.org.uk/marygate/ or www.marygatehouse.org.uk
Providing group and individual programmes appropriate to Holy Island.
Warden: Mr Ian Mills. *Deputy Warden:* Maureen Bushnell. Executive staff 3. **CC** No.500051. Began 1970; interdenominational. Turnover £100,000 to year end Dec 02.

Mayfair Hotel, 25 The Avenue, Minehead TA24 5AP
☎01643 702 719
Web: www.hotelmayfair.com
Non-smoking.
Joint Proprietors: Mr & Mrs Jakob & Anne Segenhout. Other staff 2. Began 1977; non-denominational. Turnover £60,000 to year end Dec 00.

Moor Farm Stable Cottages, Moor Farm, Foxley, Dereham NR20 4QP
☎01362 688 523 🖷 01362 688 523
E: mail@moorfarmstablecottages.co.uk
Web: www.moorfarmstablecottages.co.uk
Manager: Mr Paul Davis. Admin staff 2, Other staff 2. Began 1992; interdenominational. Turnover n/a.

Moorlands (Christian Guild Holidays), 16 North Promenade, Whitby YO21 3JX
☎01947 603 584 🖷 01947 821 668
E: moorlands@cgholidays.co.uk
Web: www.moorlands.cgholidays.co.uk
Providing year-round holiday and conference facilities for individuals, couples and families; also coffee shop.
General Manager: John Key. Executive staff 2, Other staff n/a. Began 1955; ecumenical. Turnover n/a.

Morley Retreat and Conference House, Church Lane, Morley, Ilkeston DE7 6DE
☎01332 831 293 🖷 01332 834 944
E: morleyretreat@btconnect.com
Web: www.morleyretreat.co.uk
Providing welcome and hospitality for a wide range of day and residential events.
Warden: Mr Jeff Witts. *House Manager:* Mrs Catherine Witts. Admin staff 5, Other staff 12. **CC** No.1078494. Began 1959; Anglican. Turnover £179,000 to year end Dec 04.

The Mount, Northdown Road, Bideford EX39 3LP
☎01237 473 748 🖷 01271 373 813
E: andrew@themountbideford.fsnet.co.uk
Web: www.themount1.cjb.net
One room suitable for wheelchairs.
Owners: Mr & Mrs Andrew & Heather Laugharne. No full-time staff. Began 1953; non-denominational. Turnover £55,000 to year end Dec 00.

***Mulberry House**, Chelmsford Road, High Ongar, Ongar CM5 9NL
☎01277 365 398 🖷 01277 365 353
E: katie1@mulberry-house.com
Web: www.mulberry-house.com
Training facilities, church retreats, leisure breaks.
Centre Director: Mr Ray George. Admin staff 2, Other staff 5. **CC** No.282667. Began 1981; non-denominational. (Previously Woodford Wells Ministry Trust). Turnover £200,000 to year end Dec 96.

Nettle Hill Training and Conference Centre, Brinklow Road, Ansty, Coventry CV7 9JL
☎024 7662 1899 🖷 024 7660 2992
Manager: Mr Roger Stone. Executive staff 1, Other staff 6. **CC** No.328513. Began 1990; non-denominational. Turnover n/a.

Nicholaston House, Penmaen, Swansea SA3 2HL
☎01792 371 317 🖷 01792 371 217
E: managers@nicholastonhouse.org
Web: www.nicholastonhouse.org
Offering retreats, prayer ministry, time out, themed breaks and courses for overcoming eating disorders.
Ministry Manager: Mrs Anne Styants. *Training & Development Manager:* Helena Wilkinson. Admin staff 7. **CC** No.1096720. Began 1988; interdenominational. Turnover £165,000 to year end Dec 04.

***North Acres Farm**, North Acres, Streat, Hassocks BN6 8RX
☎01273 890 278 🖷 01273 890 278
E: eastwood_streat@yahoo.com
Web: www.northacres-streat.co.uk
Owners: Mr & Mrs John & Valerie Eastwood. **CC** No.268602. Began 1970; non-denominational. Operated by Streat Trust. Turnover n/a.

Oak Hall, Otford Manor, Otford, Sevenoaks TN15 6XF
☎01732 763 131 🖷 01732 763 136
E: office@oakhall.co.uk
Web: www.oakhall.co.uk
Home of Oak Hall Expeditions; conference accommodation for Christian groups, churches, mission organisations.
Director: Mrs Judy Mayo. Executive staff 1, Other staff n/a. Began 1986; non-denominational. Turnover n/a.

For bed-spaces etc. see list on Page 28

A

Oak Hill, Chase Side, Southgate, London N14 4PS
☎020 8449 0467 🖷 020 8441 5996
E: sodecho@oakhill.ac.uk
Web: www.oakhill.ac.uk
Residential and day conferences.
Conference Coordinator: Mrs Trixie Muirhead. ***CC*** No.1076618. Began 1932; Anglican. Turnover n/a.

The Oast Houses, Ewhurst Lane, Northiam, Rye TN31 6HL
☎01797 253 311 M: 07771 662 587
🖷 01797 253 586
E: info@theoasts.co.uk
Web: www.theoasts.co.uk
Providing residential and non-residential conferences, retreat facilities.
Manager: Sarah White. Executive staff 1, Other staff 12. ***CC*** No.801479. Began 1993; non-denominational. Turnover £150,000 to year end Dec 04.

Offa House (Coventry Diocesan Retreat House and Conference Centre), Offchurch, Leamington Spa CV33 9AS
☎01926 423 309 🖷 01926 330 350
E: offahouse@btconnect.com
Web: www.offahouseretreat.co.uk
Conferences for church organisations, parishes and groups; retreats for individuals and groups.
Warden: Rev Andrew De Smet. Admin staff 2, Other staff 7. ***CC*** Began 1962; Anglican. Turnover n/a.

Old Alresford Place (Winchester Diocesan Retreat and Conference Centre), Alresford SO24 9DH
☎01962 732 518 🖷 01962 732 593
E: enquiries@oldalresfordplace.co.uk
Web: www.oldalresfordplace.co.uk
Providing space for all seeking spiritual and personal growth and refreshment.
Administrator: Caroline Enderby. Admin staff 1, Other staff 4. ***CC*** No.1065509. Began 1964; Anglican. (Previously Winchester Diocesan House). Turnover n/a.

Packway House, Crook Road, Bowness-on-Windermere, Windermere LA23 3NE
☎01539 443 532
E: packwayhouse@nascr.net
Self-catering apartments.
Proprietors: Mr & Mrs W & M Robinson. Admin staff 2. Began 1971; non-denominational. Turnover n/a.

Parcevall Hall (Bradford Diocesan House), Skyreholme, Appletreewick, Skipton BD23 6DG
☎01756 720 213 🖷 01756 720 656
E: parcevall@bradford.anglican.org
Retreat and conference centre.
Warden: Mrs Beverley Seward. Admin staff 2, Other staff 6. ***CC*** No.247858. Began 1963; Anglican but open to all. Turnover £112,000 to year end Dec 98.

Park Guest House, 51 Glenurquhart Road, Inverness IV3 5PB
☎01463 231 858 M: 07929 766 102
E: hendry.robertson@connectfree.co.uk
Owner: Mrs Irene Robertson. Executive staff 1, Other staff 1. Began 1987; non-denominational. Turnover £40,000 to year end Apr 02.

Park Hotel, Esplanade Road, Paignton TQ4 6BQ
☎01803 557 856 🖷 01803 555 626
E: office@parkhotel.me.uk
Web: www.parkhotel.me.uk
Owners: Mr & Mrs D & S Schofield. Admin staff 3, Other staff 18. Began 1965; non-denominational. Turnover n/a.

Peacehaven Christian Centre, Harepath Hill, Seaton EX12 2TA
☎01297 216 81 🖷 07092 083 481
E: peacehaven@h4c.co.uk
Web: www.peacehaven.org.uk
Guest house and small conference centre for singles, families, groups, retreats; chapel.
Owner: Mr Graham P Board. Admin staff 1, Other staff 3. Began 1984; non-denominational. Turnover n/a.

***Pentrenant Hall**, Church Stoke, Montgomery SY15 6TG
☎01588 620 450 M: 07703 221 577
🖷 01588 620 150
E: info@christianholidaycentre.co.uk
Web: www.pentrenanthall.co.uk
Youth holiday conference and study centre; self-catering preferred; own programme encouraged.
Partner: Rev Peter A Rees. Executive staff 3, Other staff 3. Began 1984; interdenominational. Turnover n/a.

Perth Christian Centre, 28 Glasgow Road, Perth PH2 0NX
☎01738 639 792 🖷 01738 622 928
E: office@pwamm.com
Web: www.pwam.com
Non-residential conference facilities for hire; coffee shop; bookshop; video library; business offices to let.
Manager: Mr John Cameron. Executive staff 2, Other staff 28. ***CC*** No.SCO 14546. Began 1986; non-denominational. Turnover n/a.

***Pilgrim Hall Christian Conference Centre**, Easons Green, Uckfield TN22 5RE
☎01825 840 295 🖷 01825 840 017
E: pilghall@aol.com
Web: www.pilgrimhall.com
Wide range of conference facilities and events.
Executive Directors: Mr & Mrs Michael Lee. Admin staff 5, Other staff 25. ***CC*** No.262561. Began 1971; interdenominational. Turnover £500,000 to year end Dec 02.

***Pilgrims Hall**, Ongar Road, Brentwood CM15 9SA
☎01277 372 206
E: team@pilgrimshall.org.uk
Web: www.pilgrimshall.co.uk
Conferences, teaching, training, retreats, counselling.
Leader: Mr Doug Day. Admin staff 2, Other staff 8. ***CC*** No.257216. Began 1968; non-denominational. Turnover £70,000 to year end Dec 02.

***Pioneer Centre**, Cleobury Mortimer, Kidderminster DY14 8JG
☎01299 271 217 🖷 01299 270 948
E: enquiries@pioneercentre.org.uk
Web: www.actioncentres.co.uk
Canadian-themed residential activity, conference and training centre serving education, community, charity and church groups.
Head of Centre: Mr Ryland Robertshaw. *General Manager:* Mr Tim Stone. Admin staff 4, Other staff 25. ***CC*** No.803431. Began 1991; interdenominational. Turnover n/a.

The Pleasaunce (CE Holiday/Conference Centre Ltd) Harbord Road, Overstrand, Cromer NR27 0PN
☎01263 579 212 🖷 01263 578 606
E: thepleasaunce@cehc.fsnet.co.uk
Web: www.christianholidays.co.uk
Manager: Mrs A Powell. Executive staff 1, Other staff 11. ***CC*** No.1039170. Began 1936; interdenominational. Turnover £280,000 to year end Oct 04.

Quaker International Centre, 1 Byng Place, London WC1E 7JH
☎020 7387 5684 🖷 020 7383 3722
E: qicl@qic.org.uk
Web: www.quaker.org.uk
Manager: Fidelma Connolly. Admin staff 3, Other staff 4. ***CC*** Began n/a; Religious Society of Friends. Turnover n/a.

The Queen's Foundation for Ecumenical Theological Education Somerset Road, Edgbaston, Birmingham B15 2QH
☎ 0121 454 1527 🖷 0121 454 8171
E: enquire@queens.ac.uk
Web: www.queens.ac.uk
Conference Centre at Theological College.
Conference Secretary: Rona Earl. Conference staff 4. ***CC*** No.523989. Began 1828; ecumenical. Turnover n/a.

Quinta Christian Centre, Weston Rhyn, Oswestry SY10 7LR
☎01691 773 696 🖷 01691 774 687
E: admin@quinta.org
Web: www.quinta.org.uk
Providing self-catering conference facilities with catering and camping options. Outdoor activities, educational packages.
Centre Manager: Mr Peter Bevington. Admin staff 1, Other staff 5. ***CC*** No.528419. Began 1985; interdenominational. Cloverley Group. Turnover £295,000 to year end Sep 03.

For bed-spaces etc see list on Page 28

†Ranworth Christian Hotel, 86 Pevensey Road, Eastbourne BN22 8AE
☎01323 733 520 Ⓜ: 07961 899 992
Ⓔ: colmar159@aol.com
Web: www.ranworthhotel.co.uk
Proprietors: Mr & Mrs Colin & Daphne Marchant. Executive staff 2, Other staff 4. Began 1987; non-denominational. Turnover £45,000 to year end Apr 99.

†Redcar Farm, Hospitality Pastoral Office, Ampleforth, York YO62 4EN
☎01439 766 889 🖷 01439 766 755
Ⓔ: pastoral@ampleforth.org.uk
Web: www.ampleforth-hpo.com
Youth accommodation, field studies, church groups.
Administrator: Jan Fitzalan Howard. Admin staff 1, Other staff n/a. **CC** No.1026493. Began 1973; Roman Catholic. Turnover n/a.

Redland House Hotel, 52 Kendal Street, London W2 2BP
☎020 7723 7118 Ⓜ: 07754 842 323
🖷 020 7402 9049
Ⓔ: info@redlandhousehotel.co.uk
Web: www.redlandhousehotel.co.uk
Owners: Mr & Mrs H Newlands. Admin staff 2, Other staff 4. Began 1961; non-denominational. Turnover n/a.

***Regents Park Conference Centre**, London Road, Nantwich CW5 6LW
☎01270 615 409 🖷 01270 610 013
Ⓔ: info@rpcc.org.uk
Web: www.rpcc.org.uk
For church groups, missionary societies, specialist conferences.
Manager: Ms Ann Sylvester. Admin staff 2, Other staff 6. **CC** No.251549. Began 1987; Elim, but open to all. Turnover £250,000 to year end Jun 05.

***Ringsfield Hall**, Beccles NR34 8JR
☎01502 713 020 🖷 01502 710 615
Ⓔ: info@ringsfield-hall.co.uk
Web: www.ringsfield-hall.co.uk
Educational programmes for schools and Bible-based programmes for churches; also group retreats.
Centre Directors: Rev Ross Ashley, Rev Chris Walton. Executive staff 2, Other staff 5. **CC** No.1093404. Began 1972; interdenominational. Turnover n/a.

Rora Christian Fellowship Trust, Rora House, Halford, Liverton, Newton Abbot TQ12 6HZ
☎01626 821 746 🖷 01626 821 586
Ⓔ: roraaca@lineone.net
Web: www.rorahouse.org.uk
For groups; self-catering.
Manager: Mr M Ford. Executive staff 1, Other staff n/a. **CC** No.268281. Began 1968; interdenominational. Turnover £70,000 to year end Mar 00.

Rowanhurst Christian Hotel, 88 Sandown Road, Lake, Sandown PO36 9JX
☎01983 402 563
Proprietors: Mr & Mrs Peter & Eileen Atkinson. Admin staff 2, No other staff. Began 1984; non-denominational. Turnover n/a.

The Royal Foundation of St Katharine, 2 Butcher Row, London E14 8DS
☎020 7790 3540 🖷 020 7702 7603
Ⓔ: enquiries@stkatharine.org.uk
Web: www.stkatharine.org.uk
Master: Rev Preb Ron Swan. Admin staff 2, Other staff 1. **CC** Began 1147; Anglican. Turnover n/a.

Rydal Hall (Carlisle Diocesan Conference and Retreat House), Ambleside LA22 9LX
☎01539 432 050 🖷 01539 434 887
Ⓔ: bookings@rydalhall.org
Web: www.rydalhall.org
Community serving holiday, conference and retreat guests; coffee shop.
Booking Secretary: Alison Butland. Admin staff 4, Other staff 12. Began 1963; ecumenical. Turnover £350,000 to year end Dec 02.

St Andrew's Hotel, Belgrave Road, Ventnor PO38 1JH
☎01983 852 680
Ⓔ: novayoung@aol.com
Web: www.standrewsventor.com
Family run.
Proprietors: Mr and Mrs Mick Young. Admin staff 2. Began 1996; non-denominational. Turnover n/a.

St Columba's Horton Outreach, St Columba's Church, St Margaret's Place, Bradford BD7 3AW
☎01274 502 536
Ⓔ: hilarygreed@hortonoutreach.co.uk
Web: www.hortonoutreach.co.uk
Non-residential conference centre, restaurant; care of elderly, disabled, people with special needs.
Manager: Mrs Hilary Greed. Executive staff 1, Other staff 8. **CC** Began 1983; Anglican. Turnover n/a.

St Mark's College, Audley End, Saffron Walden CB11 4JD
☎01799 522 006 🖷 01799 520 326
Ⓔ: info@stmarkscollege.co.uk
Web: www.stmarkscollege.co.uk
Residential youth and conference centre.
Warden: Jonathan Wayper. Executive staff 3, Other staff 4. **CC** No.1031174. Began 1993; Anglican. Diocese of Chelmsford. Turnover n/a.

St Mary's Church House, Church Hill, Harrow HA1 3HL
☎020 8422 2652
Ⓔ: stmarys@harrowhill.org
Web: www.harrowhill.org
Administrator: Name not supplied. No full-time staff. Began n/a; Anglican. Turnover n/a.

St Paul's Parish Centre, St Paul's Road, Brentford TW8 0PN
☎020 8568 7442 🖷 020 8569 7864
Ⓔ: office@parishofbrentford.org.uk
Web: www.parishofbrentford.org.uk
Providing facilities for public, private and community meetings.
Administrator: Sue Hoad. Admin staff 1, Other staff 6. Began 1991; Anglican. Turnover n/a.

St Rhadagunds (CE Holiday/Conference Centre Ltd), St Lawrence, Ventnor PO38 1XQ
☎01983 852 160
Ⓔ: strhads@bigfoot.com
Web: www.strhads.co.uk
Providing holidays, retreats and conference facilitites for individuals, families and groups.
Manager: Andrew Gardner. Admin staff 2, Other staff 10. **CC** No.1039170. Began 1934; interdenominational. Turnover £250,000 to year end Nov 02.

St Winifreds (CE Holiday/Conference Centre Ltd), 35 Marine Drive, Rhos-on-Sea, Colwyn Bay LL28 4NL
☎01492 544 128 🖷 01492 544 460
Ⓔ: stwinifreds@bigfoot.com
Web: www.christianholidays.co.uk
Manager: Miss Linda Wadley. Admin staff 1, Other staff 12. **CC** No.1039170. Began 1912; interdenominational. Turnover n/a.

***Saltmine Trust Conference Centre**, St James House, Trinity Road, Dudley DY1 1JB
☎01384 454 800 🖷 01384 454 850
Ⓔ: mail@saltmine.org
Web: www.saltmine.org
Non-residential.
Admin. Director: Mr Laurie Fearon. Admin staff 1. **CC** No.1038007. Began 2001; interdenominational. Turnover included in Saltmine Trust.

Scargill House Ltd, Kettlewell, Skipton BD23 5HU
☎01756 760 234 🖷 01756 760 499
E: info@scargillhouse.co.uk and either
E: conference@scargillhouse.co.uk or
E: bookings@scargillhouse.co.uk
Web: www.scargillhouse.co.uk
Holidays, conferences, retreats, renewal, church weekends.
Warden: Dilly Baker. Admin staff 12, Other staff 26. ***CC*** No.228031. Began 1959; Anglican. Turnover £500,000 to year end Dec 02.

Scottish Churches' House, Kirk Street, Dunblane FK15 0AJ
☎01786 823 588 🖷 01786 825 844
E: warden@scottishchurcheshouse.org
Web: www.scottishchurcheshouse.org
Warden: Mr Alastair Hulbert. Admin staff 2, Other staff 7. ***CC*** No.SCO 00295. Began 1961; ecumenical. Turnover £127,000 to year end Dec 99.

Selbourne Licensed Hotel, 4 West Street, Scarborough YO11 2QL
☎01723 372 822 🖷 01723 372 822
E: selbournehotel@ukf.net
Family-run hotel; restaurant.
Owner: Mr Michael Broddle. Executive staff 2. Began 1986; Methodist. Turnover £50,000 to year end Apr 03.

Servite Priory, 10 Main Street, Benburb, Dungannon BT71 7JZ
☎028 3754 8241 🖷 028 3754 8524
E: servitepriory@btinternet.com
Web: www.servites-benburb.com
Retreat and conference centre.
Manager: Ms Noilin Mullin. Admin staff 2, Other staff 4. ***CC*** Began n/a; Roman Catholic but open to all. (Previously Benburb Conference Centre). Turnover n/a.

Shallowford House (Lichfield Diocesan Retreat and Conference House), Stone ST15 0NZ
☎01785 760 233
🖷 01785 760 390
E: warden@shallowfordhouse.freeserve.co.uk
Web: www.lichfield.anglican.org
Warden: Mr D C Shemilt. Admin staff 2, Other staff 9. ***CC*** Began 1939; Anglican. Turnover £166,000 to year end Dec 04.

Sidholme (Christian Guild Holidays), Elysian Fields, Sidmouth EX10 8UJ
☎01395 515 104 🖷 01395 579 321
E: sidholme@cgholidays.co.uk
Web: www.sidholme.cgholidays.co.uk
Holiday and conference centre open all year. For individuals, couples, families and groups.
Manager: Mrs Lesley Edghill. Executive staff 1, Other staff n/a. Began 1931; ecumenical. Turnover n/a.

Sizewell Hall Ltd, Leiston IP16 4TX
☎01728 830 715 🖷 01728 833 275
E: office@sizewellhall.com
Web: www.sizewellhall.com
Self-catering and camping.
Executive Adviser: Mr Victor Jack. Executive staff 1, Other staff 5. ***CC*** No.269157. Began 1975; interdenominational. Turnover n/a.

Sneaton Castle Centre (Order of the Holy Paraclete), Sneaton Castle, Whitby YO21 3QN
☎01947 600 051 🖷 01947 603 490 E: sneaton@globalnet.co.uk
Web: www.sneatoncastle.co.uk
Parish pilgrimages, conferences, seminars, bed and breakfast, workshops; also for schools and colleges.
Centre Manager: Mrs Linda Antill. Admin staff 4, Other staff 12. ***CC*** No.271117. Began 1998; Anglican. Turnover n/a.

***Streatham Christian Conference Centre**, 22 Lewin Road, Streatham, London SW16 6JR
☎020 8769 1515 🖷 020 8677 3486
E: mail@lewin.org.uk
Web: www.lewin.org.uk
Non-residential centre for private seminars up to major conferences.
Administrator: Mr Dave Kitchen. Executive staff 2, Other staff 8. Began 1996; Baptist. Turnover n/a.

†Sunbury Court, Lower Hampton Road, Sunbury-on-Thames TW16 5PL
☎01932 782 196 🖷 01932 770 910
E: andrew@sunburycourt.co.uk
Web: www.sunburycourt.co.uk
Manager: Mr A W Packham. Admin staff 2, Other staff 14. ***CC*** No.214779. Began 1920; Salvation Army. Turnover n/a.
Recreation Centre Harfield Road, Sunbury-on-Thames TW16 5PT
☎01932 786 198 🖷 01932 770 910
Self-catering only

Sunnymeade Country Hotel, Dean Cross, West Down, Ilfracombe EX34 8NT
☎01271 863 668 🖷 01271 863 668
E: info@sunnymeade.co.uk
Web: www.sunnymeade.co.uk
Suitable for wheelchair users.
Proprietor: Mrs Lynda Hunt. Executive staff 2, Other staff 2. Began 1994; interdenominational. Turnover n/a.

Thornleigh Hotel, The Esplanade, Grange-over-Sands LA11 7HH
☎01539 532 733 M: 07775 696 785
🖷 01539 536 088
E: thornleigh@christianholiday.co.uk
Web: www.thornleigh-hotel.co.uk
Manager: Mr David Mycock. Admin staff 4, Other staff 12. ***CC*** No.826993. Began 1973; interdenominational. Turnover £325,000 to year end Dec 02.

Thornley House, Thorney Drive, Teignmouth TQ14 9JH
☎01626 775 270 🖷 01626 775 270
Catering for fully active, partially disabled and elderly people; full disabled facilities; no overnight care.
Proprietor: Mr James H Chivers. Admin staff 1, Other staff 4. Began 1988 non-denominational. Turnover n/a.

Treloyhan Manor (Christian Guild Holidays), St Ives TR26 2AL
☎01736 796 240 🖷 01736 798 377
E: treloyhanmanor@cgholidays.co.uk
Web: www.treloyhanmanor.cgholidays.co.uk
Open all year; for individuals, couples, families and groups.
Manager: Keirnan Lynch. Admin staff 2, Other staff n/a. Began 1948 ecumenical. Turnover n/a.

Trevanion House, Trevanion Road, Wadebridge PL27 7PA
☎01208 814 903 🖷 0870 705 [illegible]582
E: enquiry@trevanion.co.uk
Web: www.trevanion.co.uk
CSCI-registered hotel specialising in holiday provision, adults with learning disabilities, care/escorted activities.
Care Manager: Tracy Barratt. Admin staff 5, Care staff 30. Began 1991 non-denominational. Turnover n/a.

Trewince Manor, Portscatho, Truro TR2 5ET
☎01872 580 289 M: 07966 625 550
🖷 01872 580 694
E: enquiries@trewince.co.uk
Web: www.trewince.co.uk
Self-catering holiday lodges. Timeshare.
Owner: Mr Peter Heywood. Admin staff 4, Other staff 12. Began 1985; non-denominational. Turnover n/a.

***Trinity College Conference Centre**, Trinity College, Stoke Hill, Stoke Bishop, Bristol BS9 1JP ☎0117 968 2[illegible]03 🖷 0117 968 7470 E: fran.breakey@trinity-bris.ac.uk
Web: www.trinity-bris.ac.uk
Day and residential conferences, retreats.
Executive Director: Mr Andrew Lucas. Conference staff 1. ***CC*** Began 1972; Anglican but open to all. Turnover £50,000 to year end Dec 04.

University of Chichester, Bishop Otter Campus, College Lane, Chichester PO19 6PE
☎01243 816 070 🖷 01243 81[illegible] 068
E: conference@chi.ac.uk
Web: www.chiuni.ac.uk
Conference and Accommodation Office Co-ordinator: Ms Julie Apps. Admin staff 2. ***CC*** Began n/a; Anglican. (Previously University College Chichester, Chichester Institute of Higher Education). Turnover n/a.

For bed-spaces etc. see list on Page 28

Upcott, Old Beer Road, Seaton EX12 2PZ
☎01297 217 49 🖷 01297 217 49
E: team@upcott.org.uk
Web: www.upcott.org.uk
For Alpha groups, young people's holidays, church groups.
Team Leader: Andrew Palmer. Admin staff 1, Other staff 1. **CC** No.285783. Began 1969; interdenominational. Turnover £100,000 to year end Dec 02.

Waterbury Guest House, Birnam, Dunkeld PH8 0BG
☎01350 727 324 🖷 01350 727 023
E: info@waterbury-guesthouse.co.uk
Web: www.waterbury-guesthouse.co.uk
Proprietors: Jane & David Murrell. Admin staff 2. Began 1987; non-denominational. Turnover £30,000 to year end Apr 98.

The Watering Hole Holiday Centre, Morwell, Tavistock PL19 8JH
☎01822 833 844 🖷 01822 833 688
E: colinbond@btinternet.com
Web: www.kingsnews.org.uk
Holidays, conferences, retreats. Also mission outreach to Africa.
Proprietors: Pastor & Mrs Colin & Joy Bond. Admin staff 2. **CC** No.801576. Began 1987; evangelical. Run by Tavistock Community Church. Turnover n/a.

***Waverley Abbey House (CWR)**, Waverley Lane, Farnham GU9 8EP
☎01252 784 733 🖷 01252 784 732
E: waverley@cwr.org.uk
Web: www.cwr.org.uk or www.waverleyabbeyhouse.org.uk
Day and residential conferences, in-house catering.
Chief Executive: Mr Mick Brooks. *House Manager:* Mrs Donna Brownlie. *Head of Sales & Marketing:* Mr Mike Ashford. Executive staff 6, Other staff 46. **CC** No.294387. Began 1987; interdenominational. Turnover £2,957,000 to year end Dec 04.

***The Way Christian Ministries**, Kilcreggan House, Argyll Road, Kilcreggan, Helensburgh G84 0JT
☎01436 842 318 M: 07775 966 880
E: thewaycm@aol.com
Web: www.thewaycm.com
Chief Executive: Rev Peter Stanway. Executive staff 1, Admin staff 1. **CC** No.SCO 27189. Began 1997; interdenominational. Turnover £80,534 to year end Mar 02.

Westcott Farm Christian Holiday Centre, Westcott Farm, Sheldon, Honiton EX14 4QS
☎01404 841 238
Self-catering, camping and caravans.
Proprietors: Mr & Mrs Luxmore. Admin staff 2. Began 1977; non-denominational. Turnover £30,000 to year end Apr 00.

Westwood Christian Centre, Westwood Edge, Golcar, Huddersfield HD7 4JY
☎01484 845 042
E: denvygale@lineone.net
Web: www.westwood-centre.org.uk
Self-catering; family, church, youth, student groups; also self-contained flats for retreats or holidays.
Secretary: Mr David Greenwood. Executive staff 2. **CC** No.1042699. Began 1994; interdenominational. Turnover n/a.

Whirlow Grange Conference & Training Centre (Diocese of Sheffield), 484 Ecclesall Road South, Whirlow, Sheffield S11 9PZ
☎0114 236 3173 🖷 0114 262 0717
E: manager@whirlowgrange.co.uk
Web: www.whirlowgrange.co.uk
General Manager: Mr Jonathon Green. Admin staff 4, Other staff 11. **CC** Began 1953; Anglican. Turnover £300,000 to year end Dec 02.

***Whitchester Christian Guest House and Retreat**, Borthaugh, Hawick TD9 7LN
☎01450 377 477 🖷 01450 371 080
E: enquiries@whitchester.org.uk
Web: www.whitchester.org.uk
Country house; daily worship, chapel.
Warden: Evelyn Jackson. Executive staff 1, Other staff 4. **CC** No.SCO 01436. Began 1984; interdenominational. ACC affiliated. Turnover n/a.

†**Wick Court Centre**, Court Lane, Wick, Bristol BS30 5RB
☎0117 937 3562 🖷 0117 303 9067
Director: Mrs Ann Garner. Admin staff 2, Other staff 2. **CC** No.279910. Began 1980; non-denominational. Turnover £63,000 to year end Apr 00.

For bed-spaces etc. see list on Page 28

Willersley Castle (Christian Guild Holidays), Cromford, Matlock DE4 5JH
☎01629 582 270
🖷 01629 582 329
E: willersley@cgholidays.co.uk
Web: www.cgholidays.co.uk
Holiday and conference centre, open all year.
General Manager: Mr Tim Rogers. Admin staff 6, Other staff 22. Began 1928; ecumenical. Turnover n/a.

Windmill Christian Centre, Millgate Loan, Arbroath DD11 1QG
☎01241 434 455
🖷 01241 434 466
E: dmp@windmillcentre.dabsol.co.uk
Web: www.windmillchristiancentre.org.uk
Providing self-catering accommodation for Christian groups who have Bible teaching as part of programme.
Centre Manager: Mrs Dorothy Parsons. Executive staff 1. ***CC*** No.SCO 22258. Began 1998; interdenominational. Turnover n/a.

Windmill Farm Conference Centre, Main Street, Clanfield, Bampton OX18 2SN
☎01367 810 258
🖷 01367 810 302
E: enquiries@windmillconferences.co.uk
Director: Mr Richard Pocock. Executive staff 2, Other staff 7. Began 2002; non-denominational. Turnover £125,000 to year end Jan 06.

***Wycliffe Centre**, Horsleys Green, High Wycombe HP14 3XL
☎01494 682 266 🖷 01494 682 300
E: centre_enquiries@wycliffe.org
Web: www.wycliffecentre.org
Conference Manager: Sarah Clark. Admin staff 3, Other staff 8. ***CC*** No.313854. Began 1973; interdenominational. Associated with Wycliffe Bible Translators. Turnover n/a.

Wycliffe Hall, 54 Banbury Road, Oxford OX2 6PW
☎01865 274 200 🖷 01865 274 215
E: enquiries@wycliffe.ox.ac.uk
Web: www.wycliffe.ox.ac.uk
Day or residential conferences for church groups and Christian organisations.
Principal: Rev Richard Turnbull. Conference staff n/a.
CC No.309703. Began 1877; Anglican. Turnover: included in Wycliffe Hall.

Wydale (York Diocesan Centre), Wydale, Brompton-by-Sawdon, Scarborough YO13 9DG
☎01723 859 270 🖷 01723 859 702
E: retreat@wydale.org
Retreat and conference centre, self-catering youth centre, multi-sports area.
Director: Rev Ann Coleman. Admin staff 2, Other staff 10. ***CC*** No.244976. Began 1963; Anglican. Turnover £280,000 to year end Dec 02.

YMCA, Dunford House, Midhurst GU29 0DG
☎01730 812 381 🖷 01730 817 042
E: info@dunfordhouse.org.uk
Web: www.dunfordhouse.org.uk
Conference and training venue, varied meeting rooms; historic house.
General Manager: Mrs Pauline Dey. Admin staff 2, Other staff 12. ***CC*** No.212810. Began 1951; non-denominational. Turnover £300,000 to year end Mar 00.

YMCA, Londonderry, 51 Glenshane Road, Drumahoe, Londonderry BT47 3SF
☎028 7130 1662 🖷 028 7130 1662
E: lderry@ymca-ireland.org
Executive Officer: Mr William Lamrock. Admin staff 1, Other staff 20. ***CC*** No.NI 15660. Began 1865; interdenominational. Turnover £150 000 to year end Mar 04.

YMCA, Lurgan, 42a High Street, Lurgan, Craigavon BT66 8AU
☎028 3832 1025 📱07742 464 300
E: info@ymcalurgan.com
Web: www.ymcalurgan.com
Providing personal and social development including cross-community work with at-risk youth. Non residential.
Director: Mr Hugo Dale. Executive staff 1, Other staff 5. ***CC*** No.X 052/88. Began 1986; interdenominational. Turnover £95,000 to year end Dec 05.

HOSPICES

Birmingham St Mary's Hospice, 176 Raddlebarn Road, Selly Park, Birmingham B29 7DA
☎0121 472 1191
🖷 0121 472 5075
E: info@st-marys-hospice.org.uk
Web: www.st-marys-hospice.org.uk
27 beds. Providing home care, day care, bereavement support, education centre.
Chief Executive: Mrs Tina Fisher. Staff 120, Volunteers 250. ***CC*** No.503456. Began 1979; non-denominational. No magazine. Turnover £4,100,000 to year end Mar 05.

Haven's Christian Hospice, 47 Second Avenue, Westcliff-on-Sea SS0 8HX
☎01702 220 350
🖷 01702 220 351
E: stewarthouse@havenshospices.org.uk
Web: www.havenshospices.org.uk
Adult and children's hospice.
Chief Executive: Mr Andy Smith. Executive staff 1, Other staff 189. ***CC*** No.102219. Began 1983; non-denominational. (Previously South East Essex Christian Hospice). No magazine. Turnover £3,500,000 to year end Apr 01.

Martin House Hospice for Children and Young People, Grove Road, Clifford, Wetherby LS23 6TX
☎01937 845 045 🖷 01937 541 363
E: admin@martinhouse.org.uk
Web: www.martinhouse.org.uk
Providing support to children and their families, including respite care, terminal care and bereavement support.
Head of Care: Sheila O'Leary. *Head of Finance & Administration:* Aase Somerscale. Executive staff 4, Other staff 50. ***CC*** Began 1987; non-denominational. Magazine: *Martin House News* (120,000 half-yearly). Turnover £2,000,000 to year end Apr 03.

***Mildmay Mission Hospital**, Hackney Road, Shoreditch, London E2 7NA
☎020 7613 6300 🖷 020 7613 5689
E: comms@mildmay.org
Web: www.mildmay.org
Providing specialist HIV/AIDs care for men, women and children; independent Christian charitable hospital.
Chief Executive and Medical Officer: Dr Veronica Moss. *UK Chaplain:* Rev Maria Schleger. Executive staff 4, Admin staff in UK 110, Other staff 140. ***CC*** No.292058. Began 1866, reopened 1985 as AIDS hospice; interdenominational. Magazine: *Highlights* (8,000 every four months). Turnover £11,000,000 [UK and international] to year end Mar 04.

St Christopher's Hospice, 51 Lawrie Park Road, Sydenham, London SE26 6DZ
☎020 8768 4500
🖷 020 8659 8680
E: info@stchristophers.org.uk
Web: www.stchristophers.org.uk
Control of pain and family support for patients with advanced cancer and other diseases.
Chief Executive: Barbara Monroe. *Medical Director:* Dr Nigel Sykes. *Director of Nursing:* Penny Hansford. Executive staff 7, Other staff 280. ***CC*** No.210667. Began 1967; interdenominational. Magazine: *Annual Report* (10,000 annually). Turnover £11,000,000 to year end Mar 05.

St Leonards Hospice, 185 Tadcaster Road, York YO24 1GL
☎01904 708 553
🖷 01904 704 337
E: enquiries@stleonardshospice.co.uk
Providing specialist palliative care for in-patients, day care and out-patients.
Chief Executive: Mr Martyn Callaghan. *Clinical Care Services Manager:* Mrs Sue Spence. *Medical Director:* Dr Sarah Anderson. Executive staff 4, Other staff 100. ***CC*** No.509294. Began 1984; interdenominational. Magazine: *St Leonards Hospice Newsletter* (3,000 quarterly). Turnover £1,800,000 to year end Mar 03.

HOSTELS FOR HOLIDAY EVENTS

By Postcode – for location of Postcodes see map on Page 458
Hostels which did not supply this information are not listed here
Only Hostels with 10 or more bed spaces are included

S = single rooms **D/T** = number of bed spaces in double/twin rooms **L** = number of bed spaces in rooms larger than double
TS = total bed spaces (not number of rooms) **DR** = Day Room, the capacity of the largest room suitable for group use
≠ = nearest Railway station ⊖ = nearest London Underground station

Postcode	Location	Name	S	D/T	L	Other	TS	DR	Railway/Underground
ENGLAND									
BS25	**Winscombe**	Barton Children's Centre and Conference Centre	5	6	59		70	n/a	≠ Bristol Temple Meads or Weston-super-Mare
CA12	**Keswick**	Braithwaite Methodist Youth Centre	-	-	26		26	n/a	≠ Penrith
		Carlisle Diocesan Youth Centre	-	4	35		39	39	≠ Penrith
		Castlerigg Manor	4	6	50		60	75	≠ Penrith (18 miles)
CM 0	**Chelmsford**	Asheldham Youth Church	-	-	36		36	n/a	≠ Southminster
CV37	**Stratford-upon-Avon**	Soli House	n/a	n/a	n/a		50	n/a	≠ Stratford-upon-Avon
LA21	**Coniston**	St Andrew's Youth Centre	-	8	40		48	100	≠ Ulverston or Windermere
NR26	**Sheringham**	Canaan Christian Centre	-	2	15	cottages, caravans	17	100	≠ Sheringham
TA22	**Dulverton**	Dulverton Residential Centre	-	6	29		35	n/a	≠ Taunton
WALES									
LL52	**Criccieth**	The Neptune	1	8	25		34	36	≠ Criccieth
LL53	**Pwllheli**	Olgra	-	4	24		28	28	≠ Pwllheli
		Pendorlan	2	2	16		20	n/a	≠ Pwllheli

HOSTELS FOR HOLIDAY EVENTS

Asheldham Youth Church, Hall Road, Asheldham, Southminster CM0 7JF
☎01621 743 536
E: brianjiggins@hotmail.com
Web: www.asheldhamcentre.com
Self-catering residential centre for young people.
Warden: Mr Brian Jiggins. Admin staff 1. **CC** Began 1976; Anglican. Turnover £15,200 to year end Mar 98.

Barton Children's Centre and Conference Centre, Barton, Winscombe BS25 1DY
☎01934 842 145
Fax 01179 621 757
E: bchsbarton@aol.com
Web: www.bartoncamp.co.uk
Holiday centre for deprived children, conference centre for church or other groups
Chairman: Mr M J Hardwick. Admin staff 1. **CC** No.1092921 Began 1884; non-denominational. Turnover n/a.
Bookings: 20 Southfield Road, Westbury-on-Trym, Bristol BS9 3BH
☎0117 962 1757 Fax 0117 962 1757

Braithwaite Methodist Youth Centre, The Methodist Church, The Green, Braithwaite, Keswick CA12 4QR
☎01768 774 314
E: byc@fish.co.uk
Web: www.dokeswick.com
Self-catering.
Warden: Mr Brian Watterson. No full-time staff. **CC** Began 1980; Methodist. Turnover n/a.
Bookings: Carlton House, 6 Southey Street, Keswick CA12 4EF
☎01768 774 314

***Canaan Christian Centre**, 21 Holt Road, Sheringham NR26 8NB
☎01263 824 300
E: menedek@talk21.com
Short breaks; groups welcome especially children and families; counselling service available.
Director: Miss Eve Smith. Admin staff 1. **CC** No.284117. Began 1978; interdenominational. Turnover £36,000 to year end Apr 05.

Carlisle Diocesan Youth Centre, St Johns-in-the-Vale, Keswick CA12 4UB
☎01768 779 714
E: chaplain@cdyc.org.uk
Web: www.cdyc.org.uk *Self-catering accommodation for youth organisations, churches and other organisations.*
Warden: Rev B Rothwell. No full-time staff. **CC** No.520363. Began 1950; Anglican. Turnover £45,000 to year end Dec 04.
Bookings: The Rectory, Threlkeld, Keswick CA12 4RT

Castlerigg Manor, Manor Brow, Keswick CA12 4AR
☎01768 772 711 Fax 01768 775 302
E: team@castleriggmanor.co.uk
Web: www.castleriggmanor.co.uk
For young people.
Bookings Officer: Mr Peter Dodd. Admin staff 8. **CC** No.234331. Began 1970; Roman Catholic. Turnover n/a.

Dulverton Residential Centre, 6 High Street, Dulverton TA22 9HB
☎01398 324 217 Fax 01398 324 217
Self-catering residential centre for church and other groups.
Director: Rev Robert Miller. No full-time staff. **CC** No.233977. Began n/a; Roman Catholic. Turnover n/a.

The Neptune, Criccieth, LL52
☎ No Telephone
E: bookings@theneptune.org.uk
On the Llynn Peninsular area of Wales.
Manager: Name not supplied. No full-time staff. **CC** No.1075391. Began 1999; non-denominational. Owned by CHCET. Turnover n/a.
Bookings Manager: Mrs Mary Blake 38 Manor Park, Histon, Cambridge CB4 9JT
☎01223 561 436 M: 07941 476 042
E: bookings@theneptune.org.uk

Olgra (Cambrian Coast Evangelical Trust), Llwyn, 5 Pistyll Terrace, Pistyll, Pwllheli LL53 6LS
☎01758 721 630
Self-catering.
Bookings Secretary: Anne Brookes. No full-time staff. **CC** Began 1969; interdenominational. Turnover n/a.

***Pendorlan (Cambrian Coast Evangelical Trust)**, Llwyn Rhug, Ffordd Dewi Saint, Nefyn, Pwllheli LL53 6EG
☎01758 720 834
E: mail@cgholidays.co.uk
Self-catering for up to 20 on the Lleyn peninsula.
Bookings Secretary: Name not supplied. No full-time staff. **CC** No.259100. Began 1969; interdenominational. Turnover n/a.

St Andrew's Youth Centre, The Vicarage, Yewdale Road, Coniston LA21 8DX
☎01539 441 262 Fax 01539 441 262
E: mark.east@standrewscdyc.org.uk
Web: www.standrewscdyc.org.uk
Residential centre for groups.
Warden: Rev Mark East. Admin staff 1, Other staff 2. **CC** Began 1981; Anglican. Turnover £47,000 to year end Dec 04

Soli House, Mill Lane, Stratford-upon-Avon CV37 6BJ
☎01789 267 011 🖷01789 267 011\
E: ann@solihouse.org.uk
Web: www.solihouse.org.uk
Youth retreat centre catering for secondary schools within Birmingham Diocese.
Secretary: Ann Morgan. Executive staff 3, Other staff 3. ***CC*** No.234218. Began 1950; Roman Catholic. Turnover £240,000 to year end Dec 02.

***Woodcroft Christian Centre**, Woodcroft, Chepstow NP16 7PZ
☎01291 624 114 📱07767 351 194
E: woodcroftchristiancentre@hotmail.com
Web: www.woodcroft-online.org.uk
Self-catering for young people and students; activity holidays, conferences, teaching, retreats. Also local youth outreach.
Manager: Mr Gareth Birt. Admin staff 1. ***CC*** No.237401. Began 1974; interdenominational. Turnover n/a.

HOSTELS, SOCIAL WELFARE

By Country and Postcode – for location of Postcodes see map on Page 458
Hostels which did not supply this information are not listed here
Only hostels with 10 or more bed spaces are included

S = single rooms **D/T** = number of bed spaces in double/twin rooms **L** = number of bed spaces in rooms larger than double
TS = total bed spaces (not number of rooms) **DR** = Day Room, the capacity of the largest room suitable for group use
⇌ = nearest Railway station ⊖ = nearest London Underground station

Postcode	Location	Name	S	D/T	L	Other		TS	DR	Railway/Underground
ENGLAND										
B 1	**Birmingham**	Washington Court	48	-	-	for homeless		48	n/a	⇌ Birmingham New Street
B 4	**Birmingham**	William Booth Lane Social Service Centre	n/a	n/a	n/a	for men		74	n/a	⇌ Birmingham Snow Hill
B 20	**Birmingham**	Lyncroft House	n/a	n/a	n/a	for mothers and children		36	n/a	⇌ Perry Bar
B 27	**Birmingham**	Pamela House Women's Hostel	n/a	n/a	n/a	for women		n/a	n/a	⇌ Acocks Green
BA20	**Yeovil**	The Christian Alliance Housing Association Hostel	13	-	-	for young low–medium level support people		13	-	⇌ Yeovil Junction or ⇌ Yeovil Pen Mill
BA21	**Yeovil**	The Christian Alliance Housing Association Hostel	n/a	n/a	n/a	+ flats	10	n/a	n/a	⇌ Yeovil Junction or ⇌ Yeovil Pen Mill
BB 2	**Blackburn**	Bramwell House Social Services Centre	n/a	n/a	n/a			54	n/a	⇌ Blackburn
BL 1	**Bolton**	Gilead House	n/a	n/a	n/a	for homeless men		67	n/a	⇌ Bolton
BS 2	**Bristol**	Little George Street Social Service Centre	n/a	n/a	n/a	for men		96	n/a	⇌ Bristol Temple Meads
BS23	**Weston-super-Mare**	The Christian Alliance Housing Association Hostel	13	-	-	for women		13	n/a	⇌ Weston-super-Mare
		The Christian Alliance Housing Association Hostel	n/a	n/a	n/a	8 flats for vulnerable young women and children		n/a	n/a	⇌ Weston-super-Mare
CT 9	**Margate**	The Christian Housing Trust	14	-	-	for mental health problems		14	n/a	⇌ Margate
CV11	**Nuneaton**	The Christian Alliance Housing Association Nuneaton Link-Up	8			for single, vulnerable men		8	n/a	⇌ Nuneaton
CV32	**Leamington Spa**	The Christian Alliance Housing Association Hostel	n/a	n/a	n/a	5 mother and baby units		n/a	28	⇌ Leamington Spa
		The Christian Alliance Housing Association Hostel	8	-	-	for young people		8	n/a	⇌ Leamington Spa
DL 1	**Darlington**	Tom Raine Court Social Service Centre	55	-	-	+ rehabilitation unit	n/a	n/a	n/a	⇌ Darlington
DN32	**Grimsby**	Brighowgate Social Service Centre	n/a	n/a	n/a			60	n/a	⇌ Grimsby Town
DY 7	**Stourbridge**	Living Springs Stourbridge	n/a	n/a	n/a	families child protection		n/a	n/a	⇌ Stourbridge
EX 4	**Exeter**	The Christian Alliance Housing Association Hostel	13	-	-			13	n/a	⇌ Exeter Central
		Esther Community	9					9	n/a	⇌ Exeter St David's or Exeter Central
EX 8	**Exmouth**	The Christian Alliance Housing Association Hostel	16	-	-	for mental health problems		16	n/a	⇌ Exmouth
		The Christian Alliance Housing Association Hostel	-	-	-	move on flats	8	8	n/a	⇌ Exmouth
GU 1	**Guildford**	The Christian Alliance Housing Association Hostel	15	-	-	for young women		15	n/a	⇌ Guildford
HU 1	**Hull**	William Booth House Social Service Centre	119		35			154	n/a	⇌ Hull
IP 4	**Ipswich**	Lyndon House	40			for homeless men		40	n/a	⇌ Ipswich
L 3	**Liverpool**	Ann Fowler House Social Service Centre	38	-	-	for women		38	n/a	⇌ Liverpool Lime Street
L 8	**Liverpool**	The Christian Alliance Housing Association Hostel	52	-	-	+ 6 s/c move-on flats	n/a	n/a	n/a	⇌ Liverpool Lime Street
L 13	**Liverpool**	Prescot Road Hostel	40					40	n/a	⇌ Liverpool Lime Street
LS 1	**Leeds**	St George's Crypt	22	2	-	for vulnerable people		24	50	⇌ Leeds
LS13	**Leeds**	Mount Cross Families Centre	-	-	-	family units	32	32	n/a	⇌ Leeds
M 3	**Salford**	James Street Centre Hostel	n/a	n/a	n/a	for homeless men		38	n/a	⇌ Salford or Salford Crescent
M 14	**Manchester**	The Christian Alliance Housing Association Hostel	18	8	-	for young men		26	n/a	⇌ Manchester Piccadilly
M 15	**Manchester**	Wilmott Street Social Service Centre	n/a	n/a	n/a	for homeless men		115	n/a	⇌ Manchester Oxford Road
NE 1	**Newcastle upon Tyne**	City Road Social Service Centre	n/a	n/a	n/a	for men		66	n/a	*Metro:* Byker
NG 1	**Nottingham**	Sneinton House Social Service Centre	n/a	n/a	n/a	for men		70	n/a	⇌ Nottingham
		YMCA	n/a	n/a	n/a	for young people		80	n/a	⇌ Nottingham
OL12	**Rochdale**	Providence House Social Service Centre	n/a	n/a	n/a	for men		73	n/a	⇌ Rochdale
PL 1	**Plymouth**	Devonport House Social Service Centre	n/a	n/a	n/a	for men		69	n/a	⇌ Devonport

Postcode	Location	Name	S	D/T	L	Other		TS	DR	Railway/Underground
PO 1	**Portsmouth**	Catherine Booth House Residential Centre	-	-	-	cluster flats	40	40	n/a	⇌ Portsmouth & Southsea
RH 2	**Reigate**	Wayside	10	4	-	disabled unit	3	17	-	⇌ Reigate
S 1	**Sheffield**	Charter Row Social Services Centre	n/a	n/a	n/a	for men		51	n/a	⇌ Sheffield
SK17	**Buxton**	Good News Family Care (Homes) Ltd	n/a	n/a	n/a	families in need		3	n/a	⇌ Buxton
SN 1	**Swindon**	Davis House Social Service Centre	-	-	-	flats, for men and women	121	121	100	⇌ Swindon
SO14	**Southampton**	The Christian Alliance Housing Association Hostel	-	-	-	mother & baby units / flats for young people	8 / 14	22	n/a	⇌ Southampton Central
SO40	**Southampton**	The Montfort Missionaries	17	2	-			19	60	⇌ Southampton Central
SP10	**Andover**	The Christian Alliance Housing Association Hostel	9	-	-	s/c for young people		9	-	⇌ Andover
SR 1	**Sunderland**	Swan Lodge	n/a	n/a	n/a	for men and women		65	n/a	⇌ Sunderland
ST 4	**Stoke-on-Trent**	Vale Street Hostel	56	-	8			64	n/a	⇌ Stoke-on-Trent
TN 1	**Tunbridge Wells**	The Christian Alliance Housing Association Hostel	17	-	-			17	n/a	⇌ Tunbridge Wells
TN38	**St Leonards-on-Sea**	The Christian Alliance Housing Association Hostel	10	-	-	s/c for young women		10	-	⇌ St Leonards Warrior Square
WA 1	**Warrington**	James Lee House Social Service Centre	n/a	n/a	n/a	for men		52	n/a	⇌ Warrington Bank Quay
WA 9	**St Helens**	Salisbury House Social Service Centre	n/a	n/a	n/a	for men		64	n/a	⇌ St Helens Central
London										
E 1	**London**	Booth House	n/a	n/a	n/a	for men		150	n/a	⊖ Whitechapel
E 13	**London**	House of the Divine Compassion	n/a	n/a	n/a	for homeless people		8	n/a	⊖ Plaistow or Canning Town
E 17	**London**	The Christian Alliance Housing Association Hostel	15	-	-			15	n/a	⇌ Walthamstow Central ⊖ Walthamstow
N 5	**London**	Newington Court	50	-	-			50	n/a	⇌ Canonbury ⊖ Manor House
NW 1	**London**	Marylebone Project	n/a	n/a	n/a	for homeless women		101	n/a	⇌ Marylebone ⊖ Marylebone
SE 5	**London**	Springfield Lodge	n/a	n/a	n/a	male ex-offenders		25	n/a	⇌ East Dulwich
SW1	**London**	Edward Alsop Court Social Services Centre	n/a	n/a	n/a	for homeless people		113	n/a	⊖ St James's Park
SW19	**London**	YMCA, Wimbledon	110	-	-			110	n/a	⇌ Wimbledon ⊖ Wimbledon or South Wimbledon
W 2	**London**	The Christian Alliance Housing Association Hostel	19	10	-	for women		29	n/a	⊖ Notting Hill Gate
W 14	**London**	Edith Road Social Services Centre	n/a	n/a	n/a	for rough sleepers		26	n/a	⊖ Barons Court or West Kensington
ISLE OF MAN										
IM 2	**Douglas**	David Gray House (Probation Hostel)	n/a	n/a	n/a			10	n/a	
NORTHERN IRELAND										
BT14	**Belfast**	Glen Alva Families Centre	-	-	-	family units		14	-	*Rail:* Belfast Central
		Thorndale Families Centre	4	-		for women family units	21	25	n/a	*Rail:* Belfast Central
SCOTLAND										
DD 1	**Dundee**	Strathmore Lodge Social Service Centre	-	-	-	resettlement flats		54	n/a	⇌ Dundee
DD 2	**Dundee**	Clement Park House Social Service Centre	-	-	-	family units		20	n/a	⇌ Dundee
EH 1	**Edinburgh**	Cunningham House	23	-	-			23	n/a	⇌ Edinburgh
EH 5	**Edinburgh**	Ashbrook Social Service Centre	n/a	n/a	n/a	for women		16	n/a	⇌ Edinburgh
EH 6	**Edinburgh**	Bethany Christian Trust	-	-	-	for homeless people		18	n/a	⇌ Edinburgh
EH 8	**Edinburgh**	The Pleasance Social Services Centre	n/a	n/a	n/a			38	n/a	⇌ Edinburgh
G 1	**Glasgow**	Hope House Social Service Centre	n/a	n/a	n/a	for men and women		121	n/a	*Underground:* St Enoch
	Glasgow	Wallace of Campsie House Social Service Centre	40	-	-	flats for disabled / cluster flats	2 / 10	52	n/a	⇌ Glasgow Central
G 5	**Glasgow**	William Hunter House Social Service Centre	5	12	20			37	37	*Underground:* Bridge Street
IV 3	**Inverness**	Huntly House Social Service Centre	-	-	-	units	22	22	n/a	⇌ Inverness
PH 1	**Perth**	Skinnergate Social Services Centre	n/a	n/a	n/a	re-settlement for homeless		36	n/a	⇌ Perth
PH21	**Kingussie**	Glen Feshie Hostel	-	2	8			10	n/a	⇌ Aviemore or Kingussie
WALES										
CF 5	**Cardiff**	Ty-Bronna Homeless Project	n/a	n/a	n/a	homeless young people		13	n/a	⇌ Cardiff Central
CF10	**Cardiff**	Ty Gobaith (Hope House)	n/a	n/a	n/a	for men		88	n/a	⇌ Cardiff Central
CF11	**Cardiff**	Danes Court House	n/a	n/a	n/a	for young people		n/a	n/a	⇌ Waun-gron Park

A

HOSTELS, SOCIAL WELFARE

Edward Alsop Court Social Services Centre, 19 Great Peter Street, Westminster, London SW1P 2BT
☎020 7233 0296 📠020 7233 0277
Web: www.saha.org.uk
For homeless people.
Officer-in-Charge: Centre Manager. Staff 25. ***CC*** Began 2000; Salvation Army. Turnover n/a.

Ashbrook Social Service Centre, 492 Ferry Road, Edinburgh EH5 2DL
☎0131 552 5705 📠0131 552 3891
For women.
Unit manager: Mr Frank O'Donald. Admin staff 1. ***CC*** Began n/a; Salvation Army. Turnover n/a.

***Bethany Christian Trust**, Bethany Hall, 18 Jane Street, Edinburgh EH6 5HD
☎0131 467 3030 📠0131 625 5300
E: info@bethanychristiantrust.com
Web: www.bethanychristiantrust.com
Holistic care for homeless people including streetwork, housing, addiction care, community education and charity shops.
Chief Executive: Mr Iain Gordon. *Housing and Development Manager:* Adrian Currie. Executive staff 2, Other staff 100. ***CC*** No.SCO 03783. Began 1983; interdenominational. Turnover £1,700,000 to year end Apr 00.
Also at: Bethany House, 12 Couper Street, Edinburgh EH6 6HH ☎0131 467 1010 📠 0131 467 1010
And: 6 Casselbank Street, Edinburgh EH6 5HA ☎0131 554 4071 📠 0131 554 4071
And: Bethany Supported Housing, 5 Casselbank Street, Edinburgh EH6 5HA ☎0131 553 1119 📠 0131 553 1119

Booth House, 153 Whitechapel Road, London E1 1DN
☎020 7392 9499 📠020 7247 7178
Web: www.saha.org.uk
For men.
Officer-in-Charge: Centre Manager. Admin staff 6. ***CC*** Began n/a; Salvation Army. Turnover n/a.

Catherine Booth House Residential Centre, 1 Aylward Street, Portsmouth PO1 3PH
☎023 9273 7226 📠023 9273 5238
Cluster flats for homeless families.
Officer-in-Charge: Centre Manager. Admin staff 4, Other staff 8. ***CC*** Began 1959; Salvation Army. Turnover n/a.

William Booth House Social Service Centre, 2 Hessle Road, Hull HU1 2QQ
☎01482 225 521 📠01482 322 483
Web: www.saha.org.uk *For men, women and children.*
Officer-in-Charge: Centre Manager. Executive staff 5. ***CC*** Began n/a; Salvation Army. Turnover n/a.

William Booth Lane Social Service Centre, William Booth Lane, Birmingham B4 6HA
☎0121 236 6554 📠0121 236 7135
For men.
Officer-in-Charge: Centre Manager. Executive staff 4. ***CC*** Began n/a; Salvation Army. Turnover n/a.

Bramwell House Social Services Centre, Heaton Street, Blackburn BB2 2EF
☎01254 677 338 📠01254 692 471
Web: www.saha.org.uk
Residential centre for men and women.
Officer-in-Charge: Centre Manager. Admin staff 5, Other staff 20. ***CC*** Began 1959; Salvation Army. Turnover £42,000 to year end Apr 98.

Brighowgate Social Service Centre, Brighowgate, Grimsby DN32 0QW
☎01472 242 648 📠01472 250 209
For men and women.
Officer-in-Charge: Centre Manager. Admin staff 3. ***CC*** Began n/a; Salvation Army. Turnover n/a.

Centenary House, 2 Victoria Street, Belfast BT1 3GE
☎028 9032 0320 / 9024 7304 📠028 9043 4944
For men; also charity shop.
Officer Chaplain: Centre Manager. Admin staff 3. ***CC*** Began n/a; Salvation Army. Turnover n/a.

Charter Row Social Services Centre, 126 Charter Row, Sheffield S1 4HR
☎0114 272 5158 📠0114 263 4475
Web: www.saha.org.uk
Residential centre and resettlement flats.
Officer-in-Charge: Centre Manager. Executive staff 4. ***CC*** Began n/a; Salvation Army. Turnover n/a.

***The Christian Alliance Housing Association Hostel, Andover**, 70 Junction Road, Andover SP10 3QX
☎01264 369 511 📠01264 369 512
E: manager.andover@caha.org.uk
Self-catering for young single people.
Manager: Ms Olly Simpson. Admin staff 1, Other staff 1. ***CC*** No.293232. Began 1992; interdenominational. Turnover £85,694 to year end Mar 03.

***The Christian Alliance Housing Association Hostel, Exeter**, The Grapevine Centre, 1 Culverland Road, Exeter EX4 6JH
☎01392 218 044 📠01392 217 068
E: manager.exeter@caha.org.uk
Self-catering for vulnerable young mothers and babies.
Manager: Miss Jenny Potter. Other staff 7. ***CC*** No.293232. Began 1991; interdenominational. Turnover £242,564 to year end Mar 03.

***The Christian Alliance Housing Association Hostel, Exmouth**, St Andrew's House, St Andrew's Road, Exmouth EX8 1AS
☎01395 223 737
📠01395 223 536
E: manager.exmouth@caha.org.uk
Self-catering for young single people with mental health difficulties.
Manager: Mrs Ruth Brinsden. Admin staff 1, Other staff 11. ***CC*** No.293232. Began 1995; interdenominational. Turnover £242,944 to year end Mar 03.

***The Christian Alliance Housing Association Hostel, Exmouth**, St Saviour's House, Church Street, Exmouth EX8 1PE
☎01395 223 737
E: manager.exmouth@caha.org.uk
For young single people with mental health difficulties, requiring minimal support and ready for independent living.
Manager: Mrs Ruth Brinsden. Admin staff 1, Other staff 1. ***CC*** No.293232. Began 1997; interdenominational. Turnover £41,204 to year end Mar 03.

***The Christian Alliance Housing Association Hostel, Guildford**, Mulberry House, 32 Epsom Road, Guildford GU1 3LE
☎01483 577 375
📠01483 577 474
E: manager.guildford@caha.org.uk
Self-catering for single women aged 16 to 35.
Manager: Mrs Goulden-Oliver. Admin staff 1, Other staff 4. ***CC*** No.293232. Began 1986; interdenominational. Turnover £198,450 to year end Mar 03.

***The Christian Alliance Housing Association Hostel, Leamington Spa**, Binswood Lodge, 44 Binswood Avenue, Leamington Spa CV32 5SG
☎01926 335 402
📠01926 335 402
E: manager.binswood@caha.org.uk
Self-catering facilities for single women and girls and vulnerable young mothers and babies.
Senior Manager: Ms Jane Chapman. Admin staff 1, Other staff 6. ***CC*** No.293232. Began 1920; interdenominational. Turnover £167,143 to year end Mar 03.

The Christian Alliance Housing Association Hostel, Leamington Spa, Warford Lodge, 79 Radford Road, Leamington Spa CV32 1NE
☎01926 336 435
📠01926 336 435
E: manager.warford@caha.org.uk
Mother and baby unit.
Manager: Mr Gez Baldwin. Admin staff 1, Other staff 2. Began n/a. Turnover £42,750 to year end Mar 03.

For bed-spaces etc. see list on Page 48

A

***The Christian Alliance Housing Association Hostel, Liverpool**, Mildmay House, 6 Blackburne Place, Liverpool L8 7PQ
☎0151 709 1417 🖷0151 707 8189
E: manager.liverpool@caha.org.uk
Self-catering for young single men and substance misusers; also move-on flats.
Manager: Mrs Pauline Gaye. Admin staff 2, Other staff 23. **CC** No.293232. Began n/a; interdenominational. Turnover £641,344 to year end Mar 03.

***The Christian Alliance Housing Association Hostel, London (Pembridge Square)**, Dashwood House, 6 Pembridge Square, Bayswater, London W2 4ED
☎020 7229 7848 🖷020 7229 3558
E: manager.pembridge@caha.org.uk
Medium-term, for women aged 16 to 30.
Acting Manager: Mrs De Perrins. Admin staff 1, Other staff 4. **CC** No.293232. Began 1920; interdenominational. Turnover £308,003 to year end Mar 03.

***The Christian Alliance Housing Association Hostel, London (Walthamstow)**, Stephen House, 1b Copeland Road, Walthamstow, London E17 9DB
☎020 8509 1090 🖷020 8223 0626
E: manager.walthamstow@caha.org.uk
Self-catering for 15 young single homeless people.
Manager: Ms S Cornhill. Admin staff 1, Other staff 4. **CC** No.293232. Began 1995; interdenominational. Turnover £160,548 to year end Mar 03.

***The Christian Alliance Housing Association Hostel, Manchester**, The Limes, 76 Daisy Bank Road, Victoria Park, Manchester M14 5GL
☎0161 224 5893 🖷0161 224 5893
E: manager.manchester@caha.org.uk
Self-catering for young single men.
Locality Manager: Ms Pauline Gaye. Admin staff 1, Other staff 15. **CC** No.293232. Began 1920; interdenominational. Turnover £299,234 to year end Mar 03.

Christian Alliance Housing Association, Newbold Lodge, 2 Newbold Street, Leamington Spa CV32 4HN
☎01926 885 491 🖷01926 885 491
E: manager.newbold@caha.org.uk
For young people leaving the care of the local authority.
Manager: Mr Stewart Gibson. Executive staff 1, Admin staff 6. **CC** No.293232. Began n/a; non-denominational. Turnover £170,134 to year end Mar 03.

The Christian Alliance Housing Association, Nuneaton Link-up, 3 Midland Road, Nuneaton CV11 5DU
☎024 7638 5501 🖷024 7638 5501
E: manager.nuneaton@caha.org.uk
Providing supported housing and accommodation for single, vulnerable men aged 16 and over.
Manager: Donna McCormick. Other staff 4. **CC** No.293232. Began 1976; interdenominational. Turnover £33,742 to year end Mar 03.

***The Christian Alliance Housing Association Hostel, St Leonards**, Turner House, 6 Pevensey Road, St Leonards-on-Sea TN38 0JZ
☎01424 427 613
🖷01424 427 613
E: manager.stleonards@caha.org.uk
Self-catering for vulnerable young mothers and babies and vulnerable single young women.
Manager: Mrs Anette Lovange. Admin staff 1, Other staff 5. **CC** No.293232. Began 1990; interdenominational. Turnover £157,770 to year end Mar 03.

***The Christian Alliance Housing Association Hostel, Southampton**, Kingsley House, 64 Alma Road, Southampton SO14 6UX
☎023 8023 2450
🖷023 8023 2450
E: manager.shampton@caha.org.uk
Self-catering for mothers and babies.
Manager: Ms Jo Cherriman. Admin staff 1, Other staff 5. **CC** No.293232. Began 1920; interdenominational. Turnover £242,408 to year end Mar 03.

***The Christian Alliance Housing Association Hostel, Tunbridge Wells**, Calverley Hill, 6 Clarence Road, Tunbridge Wells TN1 1HE
☎01892 530 676
E: manager.tunwells@caha.org.uk
For girls or single mothers and babies.
Manager: Mrs Fretha Biggs. Admin staff 1, Other staff 5. **CC** No.293232. Began 1920; interdenominational. Turnover £211,582 to year end Mar 03.

***The Christian Alliance Housing Association Hostel, Weston-super-Mare**, 20 Graham Road, Weston-super-Mare BS23 1YA
☎01934 416 804
🖷01934 413 976
E: manager.wsm@caha.org.uk
Self-catering for vulnerable young mothers and babies and single women.
Manager: Ms Helen Warwick. Admin staff 1, Other staff 12. **CC** No.293232. Began 1995; interdenominational. Turnover £205,348 to year end Mar 03.

Christian Alliance Housing Association, Margaret House, 76 Selworthy Road, Weston-Super-Mare BS23 3SB
☎01934 412 912
🖷01934 412 912
E: manager.wsm@caha.org.uk
Flats for vulnerable single young women and children, low level support.
Manager: Mrs Helen Warwick. *Senior Project Worker:* Miss Mel Bugler. Executive staff 1, Other staff 3. **CC** No.293232. Began 2002; interdenominational. Margaret House. Turnover £32,162 to year end Mar 03.

***The Christian Alliance Housing Association Hostel, Yeovil**, Christopher House, 93 Preston Road, Yeovil BA20 2DN
☎01935 423 456 🖷01935 471 897
E: anthonyj@caha.org.uk
For homeless people aged 16 to 25 with low-medium level of support.
Manager: Mr Anthony James. Admin staff 1, Other staff 5. **CC** No.293232. Began 1993; interdenominational. (Previously Hebron). Turnover £151,552 to year end Mar 03.

***The Christian Alliance Housing Association Hostel, Yeovil**, Elsinore, 57 The Avenue, Yeovil BA21 4BW
☎01935 423 456 🖷01935 471 897
E: anthonyj@caha.org.uk
Move-on flats housing young single people, aged 18 to 30.
Manager: Mr Anthony James. Admin staff 1, Other staff n/a. **CC** No.293232. Began 1997; interdenominational. Turnover £44,418 to year end Mar 03.

***The Christian Housing Trust**, 127 High Street, Margate CT9 1JT
☎01843 227 224
E: enquiries@chtrust.plus.com
Providing accommodation for homeless people with mental health problems; cafe, resource centre, counselling service.
Trust Manager: Miss Tina Wake. Admin staff 1, Other staff 12. **CC** No.1005330. Began 1988; interdenominational. Turnover £363,186 to year end Mar 02.

City Road Social Service Centre, 39 City Road, Newcastle upon Tyne NE1 2BR
☎0191 233 9150 🖷0191 232 5521
Web: www.saha.org.uk
Residential centre for men.
Officer-in-Charge: Centre Manager. Admin staff 4. **CC** Began n/a; Salvation Army. Turnover n/a.

Cunningham House, 205 Cowgate, Edinburgh EH1 1JH
☎0131 225 4795 🖷0131 220 1354
For vulnerable single adults.
Unit Manager: Andy Cashman. Admin staff 1, Other staff 15. **CC** Began 1994; Church of Scotland. Turnover n/a.

Danescourt House (Church Army), 62 Plasturton Avenue, Portcanna, Cardiff CF11 9HU
☎029 2023 6448
E: danescourt@churcharmy.org.uk
Web: www.churcharmy.org.uk
Providing a stepping stone to independent accommodation for young people aged 16 to 21.
Project Manager: Rev Jon Durley. Staff n/a. **CC** No.226226. Began 1882; Anglican. Turnover n/a.

For bed-spaces etc. see list on Page 48

Hostels, Social Welfare

Davis House Social Service Centre, Turl Street, Swindon SN1 1EF
☎01793 531 107 🖷01793 423 820
Web: www.saha.org.uk
Residential centre for men, women and families.
Officer-in-Charge: Centre Manager. Admin staff 5, Other staff 45. ***CC*** Began 1981; Salvation Army. Turnover n/a.

Devonport House Social Service Centre, Park Avenue, Devonport, Plymouth PL1 4BA
☎01752 562 170/564 545
🖷01752 605 901
For men.
Officer-in-Charge: Centre Manager. Admin staff 5. ***CC*** Began n/a; Salvation Army. Turnover n/a.

Edith Road Social Services Centre, 10 Edith Road, Hammersmith, London W14 8JG
☎020 7603 1692 🖷020 7602 4014
Web: www.saha.org.uk
Residential centre for men and women.
Officer-in-Charge: Centre Manager. Admin staff 1, Other staff 5. Began 2000; Salvation Army. Turnover n/a.

Esther Community (Keychange Charity), 12 Queen's Terrace, St David's, Exeter EX4 4HR
☎01392 203 336 🖷01392 203 337
Short-stay hostel for young single homeless women.
Manager: David Thomas. Admin staff 1, Other staff 8. ***CC*** Began 1998; interdenominational. Turnover n/a.

Ann Fowler House Social Service Centre, Fraser Street, Liverpool L3 8JX
☎0151 207 3815 🖷0151 207 3492
Web: www.saha.org.uk
Residential centre for women.
Officer-in-Charge: Centre Manager. Admin staff 3, Other staff 11. ***CC*** Began 1959; Salvation Army. Turnover n/a.

***Gilead House**, Gilead House, 17 Duke Street, Bolton BL1 2LU
☎01204 394 499 🖷01204 385 340
Web: www.saha.org.uk
For homeless men and women.
Officer-in-Charge: Centre Manager. Admin staff 3, Other staff 30. ***CC*** No.214779. Began 1959; Salvation Army. Turnover n/a.

Glen Alva Families Centre, 19 Cliftonville Road, Belfast BT14 6JN
☎028 9035 1185 🖷028 9035 2265
For families.
Officer-in-Charge: Centre Manager. Executive staff 1, Other staff 2. ***CC*** Began n/a; Salvation Army. Turnover n/a.

Glen Feshie Hostel, Kincraig, Kingussie PH21 1NH
☎01540 651 323
E: glenfeshie@totalise.co.uk
Owner: Jean Hamilton. No full-time staff. Began 1985; non-denominational. Turnover n/a.

Good News Family Care (Homes) Ltd, Charis House, Hardwick Square East, Buxton SK17 6PT
☎01298 247 61 🖷08701 319 152
E: mail@gnfc.org.uk
Web: www.gnfc.org.uk
Providing temporary accommodation, support and counselling for families in need; parenting resources, day nursery, work training.
Manager: Ms Hazel Guest. *Public Relations Officer:* Mr Keith Jones. Executive staff 5, Other staff 25. ***CC*** No.1042386. Began 1994; evangelical. Magazine: *Charis News* (500 quarterly). Turnover £250,000 to year end Dec 04.

David Gray House (Probation Hostel), 6 Drury Terrace, Douglas IM2 3HY
☎01624 662 814 Day care centre: 01624 675 702 🖷01624 613 787
For people on probation; also day care centre.
Officer-in-Charge: Centre Manager. Admin staff 2. ***CC*** Began n/a; Salvation Army. Turnover n/a.

Hope House Social Service Centre, 14 Clyde Street, Glasgow G1 5JH
☎0141 552 0537
For men and women.
Officer-in-Charge: Centre Manager. Executive staff 4. ***CC*** Began n/a; Salvation Army. Turnover n/a.

House of the Divine Compassion (Society of St Francis), 42 Balaam Street, Plaistow, London E13 8AQ
☎020 7476 5189
For people in need.
Contact: Brother Julian. No paid staff. ***CC*** Began 1894; Anglican. Turnover £15,000 to year end Jun 03.

William Hunter House Social Service Centre, 70 Oxford Street, Glasgow G5 9EP
☎0141 429 5201
Flats for families and individuals, 1 for disabled.
Officer-in-Charge: Centre Manager. Executive staff 3. ***CC*** Began n/a; Salvation Army. Turnover n/a.

Huntly House Social Service Centre, 1 Huntly Place, Inverness IV3 6HA
☎01463 234 123 🖷01463 717 469
For men and women; also resettlement project.
Officer-in-Charge: Centre Manager. Executive staff 1, Other staff n/a. ***CC*** Began n/a; Salvation Army. Turnover n/a.

International Care Network, 344a Holdenhurst Road, Bournemouth BH8 8BE
☎01202 301 173 🖷01202 301 177
E: info@int-care.net
Offering assistance and help to asylum seekers and refugees with accommodation, English, training, employment.
Executive Director: Mr Andrew Muir. *Director:* Mr Len Grates. Executive staff 3, Other staff 10. ***CC*** No.1099400. Began 1999; non-denominational. Turnover £630,000 to year end Dec 04.

James Street Centre Hostel, Oldfield Road, Salford M3 5HP
☎0161 831 7020 🖷0161 834 3699
For homeless men.
Team Leader: Centre Manager. Admin staff 6, Other staff 12. ***CC*** Began 1959; Salvation Army. Turnover n/a.

James Lee House Social Service Centre, Brick Street, Howley Warrington WA1 2PD
☎01925 636 496 🖷01925 570 502
For men.
Officer-in-Charge: Centre Manager. Admin staff 4. ***CC*** Began n/a; Salvation Army. Turnover n/a.

Little George Street Social Service Centre, Little George Street, Bristol BS2 9EL
☎0117 955 2821 🖷0117 954 1595
For men.
Officer-in-Charge: Centre Manager. Admin staff 3. ***CC*** Began n/a; Salvation Army. Turnover n/a.

***Living Springs**, Bridgnorth Road, Stourton, Stourbridge DY7 6QY
☎01384 872 817 M: 07855 309 777
🖷01384 872 817
E: info@livingsprings.co.uk
Web: www.livingsprings.co.uk
Residential and day support of mothers and children; social services referrals with child protection concerns.
Manager: Jane Chapman. Executive staff 1, Other staff n/a. ***CC*** No.108[illegible]726. Began n/a; interdenominational. Turnover n/a.

Lyncroft House, 99 Handsworth Wood Road, Handsworth, Birmingham B20 2PH
☎0121 357 9936 (Quarters)
🖷0121 523 4742
For mothers and children.
Officer-in-Charge: Centre Manager. Executive staff 3. ***CC*** Began n/a; Salvation Army. Turnover n/a.

Lyndon House, 107 Fore Street, Ipswich IP4 1LS
☎01473 251 070 🖷01473 225 613
Direct-access hostel for homeless men.
Officer-in-Charge: Centre Manager. Executive staff 1, Other staff n/a. ***CC*** Began 1959; Salvation Army. Turnover n/a.
Training flats: 12 St Clements Church Lane, Ipswich IP4 1JH

Marylebone Project, 1 Cosway Street, London NW1 5NR
☎020 7262 3818 🖷020 7402 8752
E: maryleboneproject@churcharmy.org.uk
Web: www.churcharmy.org.uk
For single homeless women; also day centre facilities.
Homeless Coordinator: Captain Edwin Bates. Admin staff 1, Other staff n/a. ***CC*** No.226226. Began 1882; Anglican. Church Army and Portman House Trust. Turnover n/a.

For bed-spaces etc. see list on Page 48

The Montfort Missionaries, St Joseph's, 8 Lyndhurst Road, Ashurst, Southampton SO40 7DL
☎023 8029 2337 🖷023 8029 2346
Superior of Community & Manager of Refuge: Father Danny Macavoy. Brother 1. ***CC*** No.1050485. Began 1942; Roman Catholic. (Previously Saint Joseph's House of Prayer) Turnover n/a.

***Mount Cross Families Centre**, 139 Broad Lane, Bramley, Leeds LS13 2JP
☎0113 257 0810 (Office) 0113 257 7552 (Annexe)
For families. Also Spring Grove Resettlement Unit.
Officer-in-Charge: Centre Manager. Executive staff 3. ***CC*** Began n/a; Salvation Army. Turnover n/a.

***Newington Court Ltd**, 1 Collins Road, London N5 2UF
☎020 7359 2495 🖷020 7288 1913
✉: info@newingtoncourt.org.uk
Web: www.newingtoncourt.org.uk
For women aged 18 to 40.
Manager: Name not supplied. Admin staff 3, Other staff 3. ***CC*** No.1074471. Began 1912; Baptist. Turnover £240,000 to year end Mar 04.

Pamela House Women's Hostel (Birmingham City Mission), 38 Flint Green Road, Birmingham B27 6QA
☎0121 706 5567 🖷0121 706 5572
✉: office@birminghamcitymission.co.uk
Web: www.birminghamcitymission.co.uk
For single, homeless women; support and resettlement services.
Project Manager: Mrs June Leonard. Admin staff 1, Other staff 7. ***CC*** No.1051023. Began 1991; interdenominational. Turnover n/a.

The Pleasance Social Service Centre, 1 The Pleasance, Edinburgh EH8 9UE
☎0131 556 9674
For homeless people.
Officer-in-Charge: Centre Manager. Executive staff 1, Other staff 12. ***CC*** Began 2000; Salvation Army. Turnover n/a.

Prescot Road Hostel, 380 Prescot Road, Liverpool L13 3DA
☎0151 228 0925 🖷0151 228 0927
Direct access hostel for homeless men.
Officer-in-Charge: Centre Manager. Executive staff 1, Other staff 22. ***CC*** Began 1989; Salvation Army. Turnover n/a.

Providence House Social Service Centre, High Street, Rochdale OL12 0NT
☎01706 645 151 🖷01706 759 466
✉: colin.mottershead@salvationarmy.org.uk
For men. Also charity shop.
Officer-in-Charge: Mr Colin Mottershead. Admin staff 4. ***CC*** Began n/a; Salvation Army. Turnover n/a.

Tom Raine Court Social Service Centre, Coburg Street, Darlington DL1 1SB
☎01325 489 242 🖷01325 465 603
Officer-in-Charge: Centre Manager. Other staff 3. ***CC*** Began 1987; Salvation Army. Turnover n/a.

St George's Crypt, Great George Street, Leeds LS1 3BR
☎0113 245 9061 🖷0113 244 3646
✉: admin@stgeorgescrypt.org.uk
Web: www.stgeorgescrypt.org.uk
Providing practical care and support for vulnerable and disadvantaged people.
Director: Mr John Flanders. *Executive Trustee:* Rev Jonathan Clarke. Executive staff 5, Other staff 30. ***CC*** No.250016. Began 1930; Anglican. Turnover £700,000 to year end Dec 02.

Salisbury House Social Service Centre, Parr Street, St Helens WA9 1JU
☎01744 744 800 🖷01744 744 808
For men.
Officer-in-Charge: Centre Manager. Admin staff 5. ***CC*** Began n/a Salvation Army. Turnover n/a.

Skinnergate Social Service Centre, 16 Skinnergate, Perth PH1 5JH
☎01738 624 360
Re-settlement for homeless people.
Officer-in-Charge: Centre Manager. Executive staff 1, Other staff 18. ***CC*** Began 2000; Salvation Army. Turnover n/a.

Sneinton House Social Service Centre, 2 Boston Street, Nottingham NG1 1ED
☎0115 950 4364 🖷0115 950 9605
For men.
Officer-in-Charge: Centre Manager. Admin staff 4. ***CC*** Began n/a; Salvation Army. Turnover n/a.

Springfield Lodge, 1 Grove Hill Road, Camberwell, London SE5 8DF
☎020 7274 7188 🖷020 7737 7707
Resettlement centre for men.
Officer-in-Charge: Centre Manager. Admin staff 3. ***CC*** Began n/a; Salvation Army. Turnover n/a.

Strathmore Lodge Social Service Centre, 31 Ward Road, Dundee DD1 1NG
☎01382 225 448 🖷01382 203 404
Also resettlement flats. Officer-in-Charge: Centre Manager. Admin staff 2. ***CC*** Began n/a; Salvation Army. Turnover n/a.

Swan Lodge, 5 High Street East, Sunderland SR1 2AU
☎0191 565 5411 🖷0191 514 7576
Web: www.saha.org.uk
Residential care for men and women.
Associate Officer-in-Charge: Centre Manager. Admin staff 6, Other staff 20. ***CC*** Began 1982; Salvation Army. (Previously High Street East Social Service Centre). Turnover n/a.

Thorndale Families Centre, Duncairn Avenue, Antrim Road, Belfast BT14 6BP
☎028 9035 1900 🖷028 9035 1310
Family units and women's hostel.
Officer-in-Charge: Centre Manager. Admin staff 4. ***CC*** Began n/a; Salvation Army. Turnover n/a.

Ty Gobaith (Hope House), 240 Bute Street, Cardiff CF10 5TY
☎029 2048 0187 🖷029 2048 0708
For men.
Officer-in-Charge: Centre Manager. Admin staff 3. ***CC*** Began n/a; Salvation Army. (Previously Bute Street Social Service Centre). Church Army and Cadwyn Housing Association. Turnover n/a.

Ty-Bronna Homeless Project, Clos Ty-Bronna, St Fagons Road, Freshwater, Cardiff CF5 3ER
☎029 2055 6929
✉: TyBronna@churcharmy.org.uk
Web: www.churcharmy.org.uk
Accommodation and support for homeless young people aged 16 to 21.
Project Manager: Rev Jon Durley. Executive staff 1, Other staff n/a. ***CC*** No.226226. Began 1882; Anglican. Church Army & Cadwyn Housing Association. Turnover n/a.

Vale Street Hostel, Vale Street, Stoke-on-Trent ST4 7RN
☎01782 744 374 🖷01782 749 512
Officer-in-Charge: Centre Manager. Admin staff 3, Other staff 25. ***CC*** Began 1987; Salvation Army. Turnover n/a.

Wallace of Campsie House Social Service Centre, 30 East Campbell Street, Glasgow G1 5DT
☎0141 552 4301 🖷0141 552 5910
Single and cluster flats for men and women, 2 for disabled.
Officer-in-Charge: Centre Manager. Executive staff 3. ***CC*** Began n/a; Salvation Army. Turnover n/a.

Washington Court (Birmingham City Mission), 38 Washington Street, Lee Bank, Birmingham B1 1LB
☎0121 643 6182 🖷0121 633 8258
✉: washington@birminghamcitymission. co.uk
Web: www.birminghamcitymission.co.uk
Direct access for single people. Support and resettlement services.
Senior Manager: Mr Derek Cotterill. Admin staff 5, Other staff 23. ***CC*** No.1051023. Began 1979; interdenominational. Turnover n/a.

***Wayside (Keychange Charity)**, Wayside, 42 Croydon Road, Reigate RH2 0PQ
☎01737 248 304 🖷01737 248 304
For single homeless women, stay up to two years.
Manager: Name not supplied. Executive staff 1, Other staff 5. ***CC*** Began 1996; interdenominational. Turnover n/a.

Willow House Social Service Centre, Willow Street, Fobney Street, Reading RG1 6BD
☎0118 959 0681 🖷0118 959 8663
For men and women.
Officer-in-Charge: Centre Manager. Admin staff 4. ***CC*** Began n/a; Salvation Army. Turnover n/a.

For bed-spaces etc. see list on Page 48

Wilmott Street Social Service Centre, 1 Wilmott Street, Chorlton-on-Medlock, Manchester M15 6BD
☎0161 236 7537 ℻0161 237 9782
Direct access hostel for homeless men.
Officer-in-Charge: Centre Manager. Admin staff 6, Other staff 25. ***CC*** Began 1977; Salvation Army. Turnover n/a.

YMCA, Doncaster, 31 Wood Street, Doncaster DN1 3LH
☎01302 342 148 ℻01302 342 148
Young single people needing support.
Hostel & Housing Manager: Olivia Britton. Admin staff 5, Other staff 12. ***CC*** Began 1989; interdenominational. Turnover £300,000 to year end Mar 02.

YMCA, Nottingham, 4 Shakespeare Street, Nottingham NG1 4FG
☎0115 956 7600 ℻0115 956 7601 E: admin@nottingham.ymca.org.uk
Web: www.nottinghamymca.org.uk
Supportive housing for young adults; conference centre; international community centre.
Chief Executive: Mr William Wakefield. Admin staff 5, Other staff 40. ***CC*** No.243044. Began 1871; interdenominational. Turnover £510,000 to year end Mar 98.

YMCA, Wimbledon, 200 The Broadway, Wimbledon, London SW19 1RY
☎020 8542 9055 ℻020 8542 1086
For homeless people and asylum seekers.
Chief Executive: M B Redfern. Full-time staff 40. ***CC*** No.250637. Began 1875; interdenominational. Turnover n/a.

HOSTELS FOR YOUNG PEOPLE & STUDENTS

By Country and Postcode – for location of Postcodes see map on Page 458
Hostels which did not supply this information are not listed here
Only hostels with 10 or more bed spaces are included

S = single rooms **D/T** = number of bed spaces in double/twin rooms **L** = number of bed spaces in rooms larger than double
TS = total bed spaces (not number of rooms) **DR** = Day Room, the capacity of the largest room suitable for group use
⇌ = nearest Railway station ⊖ = nearest London Underground station

Postcode	Location	Name	S	D/T	L	Other		TS	DR	Railway/Underground
ENGLAND										
AL 7	**Welwyn Garden City**	YMCA	115	-	34			149	n/a	⇌ Welwyn Garden City
B 29	**Birmingham**	Wesley International House	38	12	-			50	n/a	⇌ Selly Oak or Birmingham New Street
B 98	**Redditch**	YMCA	185	-	-			185	100	⇌ Redditch
BA 1	**Bath**	YMCA	32	58	120			210	30	⇌ Bath Spa
BH 1	**Bournemouth**	YMCA	63	-	-			63	n/a	⇌ Bournemouth
BS 8	**Bristol**	Methodist International House	32	8	-			40	n/a	⇌ Bristol Temple Meads
CB 1	**Cambridge**	YMCA	75	150	-	bedsits flatlets	18 22	265	150	⇌ Cambridge
CB 4	**Cambridge**	Link House Trust	15	20	-	for overseas students		35	n/a	⇌ Cambridge
CH41	**Birkenhead**	YMCA	53	-	-			53	n/a	⇌ Birkenhead Central
CR 0	**Croydon**	YWCA	n/a	n/a	n/a			115	n/a	⇌ East Croydon
CV 1	**Coventry**	YMCA	94	-	-			94	n/a	⇌ Coventry
CW 2	**Crewe**	YMCA	72	-	-			72	60	⇌ Crewe
DE24	**Derby**	YMCA	25	-	-	flatlets	57	82	50	⇌ Derby
DN32	**Grimsby**	YMCA	97	-	-			97	150	⇌ Grimsby Town
GL50	**Cheltenham**	YMCA	56	-	-			56	n/a	⇌ Cheltenham Spa
GU 1	**Guildford**	YMCA	114	12	-			126	n/a	⇌ Guildford
HG 4	**Ripon**	YMCA	16	-	-			16	90	⇌ Harrogate
HU 5	**Hull**	Hull International House	42	10	-			52	25	⇌ Hull
IP33	**Bury St Edmunds**	YMCA	23	-	-			23	n/a	⇌ Bury St Edmunds
LE 1	**Leicester**	YMCA	n/a	n/a	n/a			83	n/a	⇌ Leicester
LN 2	**Lincoln**	YMCA	81	-	-			81	120	⇌ Lincoln Central
M 14	**Manchester**	Methodist International House	62	-	-			62	n/a	⇌ Manchester Piccadilly
NR 2	**Norwich**	YMCA	90	-	-			90	n/a	⇌ Norwich
RG30	**Reading**	YMCA	42	8	-			50	100	⇌ Reading
RM 7	**Romford**	YMCA	173	-	-			173	100	⇌ Romford ⊖ Dagenham East
RM 9	**Dagenham**	YWCA	38	-	-			38	n/a	⊖ Dagenham Heathway
TR18	**Penzance**	YMCA	1	2	44			47	100	⇌ Penzance
WA10	**St Helens**	YMCA	120	-	-			120	100	⇌ St Helens Central
WD 3	**Rickmansworth**	Lay Community Centre	7	20	14	for lay people		41	n/a	⇌ Rickmansworth
WD 17	**Watford**	YMCA	n/a	n/a	n/a			177	n/a	⇌ Watford Junction
WR 2	**Worcester**	YMCA	71	-	-			71	n/a	⇌ Worcester Foregate Street or Worcester Shrub Hill
London										
E 17	**London**	YMCA, Waltham Forest	158	-	-			158	n/a	⇌ Walthamstow Central ⊖ Walthamstow
EC1	**London**	YMCA, City	108	8	-			116	n/a	⇌ Old Street ⊖ Barbican
N 8	**London**	YMCA, Hornsey	n/a	n/a	n/a	for people with special needs		158	n/a	⊖ Turnpike Lane or Finsbury Park or Archway
N 10	**London**	Chester House	116	8	-			124	n/a	⊖ Bounds Green or Highgate
NW 3	**London**	International Students Residence	17	2	16			35	n/a	⊖ Hampstead
NW 3	**London**	Netherhall House	93	-	-			93	n/a	⊖ Finchley Road
NW 6	**London**	Conway House	41	42	15			98	n/a	⊖ West Hampstead
NW 7	**London**	The Christian Alliance Housing Hostel	26	2	-			28	n/a	⇌ Mill Hill Broadway
SE 1	**London**	The Christian Alliance Housing Hostel	35	86	-			121	121	⇌ ⊖ Waterloo
SE18	**London**	The Christian Alliance Housing Hostel	81	-	-	flats	54	135	n/a	⇌ Woolwich Arsenal
SW 7	**London**	More House	20	22	-			64	n/a	⊖ South Kensington
SW 9	**London**	YMCA, South London	-	-	-	48 self contained units	125	125	n/a	⊖ Stockwell
W 1	**London**	St Vincent's Hostel	43	26	-			69	90	⊖ Baker Street or Bond Street
W 1	**London**	YMCA, Indian Student Hostel	98	10	6			114	200	⊖ Warren St or Great Portland St
W 5	**London**	Moullin House	2	10	-	other	38	50	n/a	⇌ ⊖ Ealing Broadway
W 8	**London**	Lee Abbey International Students' Club	67	82	31			180	60	⊖ Earl's Court
WC1	**London**	International Lutheran Student Centre	65	14	-			79	50	⇌ Kings Cross St Pancras ⊖ Russell Square

HOSTELS FOR YOUNG PEOPLE & STUDENTS

Chester House, Guy Chester Centre, Pages Lane, Muswel Hill, London N10 1PR
☎020 8883 8204
E: office@chesterhouse.org.uk
Web: www.chestercentre.org.uk
Halls of residence for students and workers aged 18 to 25.
Warden: Mr Andy Parkins. Admin staff 10, Other staff 15. ***CC*** Began 1960; Methodist. Turnover £540,371 to year end Sep 02.

***The Christian Alliance Housing Association Hostel, London (Waterloo)**, 2 Secker Street, Waterloo, London SE1 8UF
☎020 7450 4601 🖷020 7401 9945
E: manager.waterloo@caha.org.uk
Web: www.cahhousinguk.co.uk
Self-catering for single young people aged 18 to 36.
Manager: Name not supplied. Admin staff 5, Other staff 20. ***CC*** No.293232. Began 1978; interdenominational. Turnover £600,000 to year end Mar 05.

The Christian Alliance Housing Association, Mahon House, St Joseph's College, Lawrence Street, Mill Hill, London NW7 4JX
☎020 7450 4601 🖷020 8201 0344
E: cac.accom@boltblue.com
Web: cahhousinguk.co.uk
For international students.
Manager: Bruce Duncan. Admin staff 1, Other staff n/a. ***CC*** No.293232. Began 2003; interdenominational. (Previously Mahon House).

The Christian Alliance Housing Services Hostel, International House, 109 Brookhill Road, London SE18 6RZ
☎020 8854 1418 🖷020 8855 9257
E: manager.woolwich@caha.org.uk
For single and married students (families with up to 2 children), vacation visitors.
Manager: Mr Melvyn Gaunt. Executive staff 1, Other staff 12. ***CC*** No.15977. Began 1963; interdenominational. Being refurbished 2006. Turnover £361,464 to year end Mar 03.

†Conway House, 20 Quex Road, Kilburn, London NW6 4PG
☎020 7624 2918 🖷020 7624 2918
E: conway.house@irishcentrehousing.org
For young men new to London (mostly Irish).
Manager: Mr Aidan McLouglin. Admin staff 12, Other staff 16. ***CC*** Began 1974; Roman Catholic. Turnover n/a.

Hull International House, 96 Westbourne Avenue, Hull HU5 3HY
☎01482 342 104 🖷01482 447 729
Web: www.methodist.org.uk/hih
For overseas students.
Warden: Mrs Loretta Lynch. Admin staff 2, Other staff 4. ***CC*** Began 1961; Methodist. Turnover n/a.

For bed-spaces etc. see list on Page 54

International Lutheran Student Centre, 30 Thanet Street, London WC1H 9QH
☎020 7388 4044
🖷020 7383 5915
E: ilscaccomm@lutheran.org.uk
Web: www.lutheran.org.uk/student-centre.htm
For postgraduate students. Summer vacancies for others.
Warden: Ms Adelaide Nolan. Admin staff 5, Other staff 8. ***CC*** No.232042. Began 1963; Lutheran. Turnover £400,000 to year end Dec 05.

International Students Residence (Sisters of St Dorothy), 99 Frognal, Hampstead, London NW3 6XR
☎020 7794 6893
🖷020 7435 0724
E: st.dorothy@virgin.net
For full-time female students and young female tourists.
Sister-in-Charge: Sister Pauline Taylor. Admin staff 3, Other staff 5. ***CC*** No.266436. Began 1968; Roman Catholic but open to all. Turnover £50,000 to year end Dec 05.

Lee Abbey International Students' Club, 57 Lexham Gardens, London W8 6JJ
☎020 7373 7242
🖷020 7244 8702
E: accommodation@leeabbeylondon.com
Web: www.leeabbeylondon.com
Hostels for young people and students; holiday guests during summer.
Warden: Rev David Bainbridge. Admin staff 7, Other staff 34. ***CC*** No.232667. Began 1964; Anglican but open to all. Turnover £1,123,734 to year end Apr 05.

Link House Trust, 17 Chesterton Road, Cambridge CB4 3AL
☎01223 561 202
🖷01223 572 290
E: linkhouse@aol.com
Web: www.linkhousecambridge.info
For international graduate students.
Wardens: Paul & Hilary Drinkwater. Admin staff 2. ***CC*** No.296226. Began 1987; interdenominational. Turnover £170,000 to year end Dec 04.
Also at: 95 Gilbert Road, Cambridge CB4 3NZ
And: 7 East Hertford Street, Cambridge CB4 3AJ

Methodist International House, Bristol, Rodney House, Clifton Down Road, Clifton Village, Bristol BS8 4AL
☎0117 973 5179
🖷0117 973 1498
E: bristolm.i.h.4students@ukgateway.net
For students of all faiths, nationalities and ages.
Warden: Mr Mark Tubey. Admin staff 2, Other staff 5. ***CC*** No XN 8447. Began 1957; Methodist. Turnover n/a.

Methodist International House, Manchester, 68 Daisy Bank Road, Victoria Park, Manchester M14 5QP
☎0161 224 8041 🖷0161 225 0823
E: warden@mihmanchester.co.uk
Web: www.mihmanchester.co.uk
For postgraduate students mainly from overseas.
Warden: Mr Colin Morton. Admin staff 3. ***CC*** Began 1956; Methodist. Turnover n/a.

More House, 53 Cromwell Road, London SW7 2EH
☎020 7584 2040 🖷020 7581 5748
E: more-house@surf3.net
For university students; holiday guests in summer.
Warden: Sister Francoise Georgeault. *Bursar:* Victoria Franklin. Admin staff 2, Other staff 5. ***CC*** No.229051. Began 1950; Roman Catholic. (See also London University Catholic Chaplaincy). Turnover included in Canonesses of St Augustine Trust.

Moullin House, 24 Mount Park Road, Ealing, London W5 2RT
☎020 8997 4343 🖷020 8991 0254
E: moullinhouse1@hotmail.com
Web: www.moullinhouse.org.uk
House for International students and young workers.
Warden: Mr Stuart MacPherson. *Assistant Warden:* Mr Dasharet Palushi. Admin staff 2, Other staff 1. ***CC*** No.2074. Began 1951; Methodist. Turnover £225,000 to year end Jun 05.

Netherhall House, Nutley Terrace, Hampstead, London NW3 5SA
☎020 7435 8888
Director: Mr Peter Brown. Executive staff 4, Admin staff 2. ***CC*** Began n/a; Roman Catholic. Turnover £300,000 to year end Dec 05.

***Pillar of Fire Church**, 19 Brent Street, Hendon, London NW4 2EU
☎020 8202 3219/7618
M: 07767 356 307 🖷 020 8202 3277
E: bernarddawson36@aol.com
Web: www.pillaroffire.co.uk
For international students.
Administrator: Rev Bernard Dawson. *Assistant Administrator:* Jeffrey Olszyk. Admin staff 3. ***CC*** No.1015529. Began 1915; Pillar of Fire. Magazine: *British Isles Pillar of Fire* (600 monthly). Turnover £215,000 to year end Jun 00.

†St Vincent's Hostel, 14 Blandford Street, London W1V 4DR
☎020 7224 3616 🖷020 7935 8969
For women aged 18 to 25.
Manager: Sister Rosalie Hayes. Executive staff 1, Other staff 4. ***CC*** No.236803. Began 1938; Roman Catholic. Turnover £150,000 to year end Dec 02.

Wesley International House, Birmingham, 52 Oakfield Road, Selly Park, Birmingham B29 7EQ
☎0121 472 0109 🖷0121 472 1899
E: warden@wihbham.fsworld.co.uk
Web: www.bham-int-student-homes.org.uk
For full-time students and trainees.
Warden: Mr Peter Woodhill. *Lay Chairperson:* Dr Sue Balmer. Admin staff 1, Other staff 4. ***CC*** Began 1955; Methodist. Turnover £100,000 to year end Aug 00.

YMCA, Bath, International House, Broad Street Place, Bath BA1 5LH
☎01225 325 900 🖷01225 462 065
E: reservations@bathymca.co.uk
Web: www.bathymca.co.uk
Chief Executive: Mike Fairbeard. *Chairman:* Mr Mark Pitman. *Operations Manager:* Mrs Maggie King. Admin staff 12, Other staff 48. ***CC*** No.1106370. Began 1853; interdenominational. Turnover £900,000 to year end Dec 02.

YMCA, Birchwood, 46 Hamnett Court, Birchwood, Warrington WA3 7PL
☎01925 284 102 🖷01925 284 103
E: birchwoodymca@btconnect.com
Floating support services available on site.
Chief Executive: Mr Keith Fletcher. Executive staff 1, Managers 3, Other staff 3. ***CC*** Began 1981; interdenominational. (Previously YMCA, Warrington). No magazine. Turnover £230,000 to year end Mar 03.

YMCA, Birkenhead, 56 Whetstone Lane, Birkenhead CH41 2TJ
☎0151 647 8123 🖷0151 650 1944
E: ajoh100650@aol.com
For young adults.
Executive Director: Mrs Anne Johnson. Executive staff 1, Other staff 34. ***CC*** No.1000601. Began 1874; interdenominational. Turnover £350,000 to year end Dec 98.

***YMCA, Bournemouth**, Delta House, 56 Westover Road, Bournemouth BH1 2BS
☎01202 290 451 🖷01202 314 219
E: bmouthymca@aol.com
Special needs hostel; youth and community facilities.
Director: Mr B Crawford. *Chairman:* Mr David Williams. Admin staff 10, Other staff 31. ***CC*** No.1078728. Began n/a; interdenominational. Turnover £1,000,000 to year end Dec 02.

YMCA, Bury St Edmunds, Batt House, 56 Westgate Street, Bury St Edmunds IP33 1QG
☎01284 701 697 🖷01284 701 712
E: ymcaburysteds@btconnect.com
For young people aged 16 to 28, self-catering.
Chief Executive: Mr Ed Vaughan. Executive staff 1, Other staff 11. ***CC*** No.802285. Began 1989; interdenominational. Turnover £50,000 to year end Mar 97.

YMCA, Cambridgeshire, Queen Anne House, Gonville Place, Cambridge CB1 1ND
☎01223 356 998 🖷01223 312 749
E: admin@ymca.org.uk
Web: theymca.org.uk
Providing supportive and inclusive programmes in housing, youthwork, fitness, employment training, and other activities.
Chief Executive: Mr Jonathon Martin. *Director of Management Services:* Mr Robert Higginbottom. Admin staff 10, Other staff 24. ***CC*** No.1069810. Began 1852; interdenominational. Turnover £1,008,576 to year end Mar 02.

***YMCA, Cheltenham**, 6 Vittoria Walk, Cheltenham GL50 1TP
☎01242 524 024 🖷01242 232 635
E: admin@cheltenhamymca.com
Web: www.cheltenhamymca.com
For young people; also sports, health and fitness facilities; café.
Chief Executive: Mr David Wallace. *Assistant Chief Executive (Housing):* Mr Jerry Evans. *Assistant Chief Executive (Programme):* Mrs Angela Gilbert. Admin staff 5, Other staff 23. ***CC*** No.1079951. Began 1855; interdenominational. Turnover £530,593 to year end Apr 02.

YMCA, Coventry, 2nd Floor, Cash's Business Centre, Cash's Lane, Coventry CV1 4PB
☎024 7625 7312 🖷024 7663 2587
E: admin@coventry.ymca.org.uk
Manager: Tony Mawby. *Progress Manager:* Sean Colman. Admin staff 3, Other staff 5. ***CC*** Began 1889; interdenominational. Turnover £280,000 to year end Dec 90.
Accommodation at: Lucas House, 2a Craven Road, Rugby CV21 3HY
☎01788 537 700

YMCA Foyer, Crewe, Gresty Road, Crewe CW2 6EL
☎01270 257 673 🖷01270 586 200
E: admin@creweymca.com
Web: www.creweymca.com
Direct-access supported accommodation for single people aged 16 to 30; training.
Chief Executive: Mr Peter Speed. *Foyer Manager:* Mr Richard Holmes. Executive staff 5, Other staff 45. ***CC*** No.1030782. Began 1984; interdenominational. Turnover £1,000,000 to year end Mar 05.

YMCA, Derbyshire, London Road, Wilmorton, Derby DE24 8UT
☎01332 572 076 🖷01332 572 596
E: gilliansewell@ymcaderbyshire.org.uk
Short and medium stay for young men and women; youth and community facilities.
Chief Executive: Gillian Sewell. *Deputy Chief Executive:* Mr Justin Hill. Executive staff 2, Other staff 60. ***CC*** No.1049904. Began 1847; interdenominational. Turnover £1,000,000 to year end Mar 03.

YMCA, Grimsby and Cleethorpes, Peaks Lane, Grimsby DN32 9ET
☎01472 359 621 🖷01472 340 086
For young people.
Chief Executive: Mr Hywel Roberts. *Housing Officer:* Mr Steven Lea. *Programme Manager:* Mr Robyn Laurie. Admin staff 5, Other staff 60. ***CC*** No. 1058613. Began 19[illegible]6; interdenominational. Turnover £832,655 to year end Dec 02.

***YMCA, Guildford**, Bridge Street, Guildford GU1 4SB
☎01483 532 555 🖷01483 537 1[illegible]1
E: admin@guildfordymca.org.uk
Web: www.guildfordymca.org.uk
Providing housing, support counselling for young people; youth café, arts, information, advice, training, opportunities, development.
Chief Executive: Mr Pete Brayne. Admin staff 30, Other staff 70. ***CC*** No.29[illegible]314. Began 1894; interdenominational. Turnover £2,000,000 to year end Mar 05.

YMCA, Hornsey, 184 Tottenham Lane, London N8 8SG
☎020 8340 2345 🖷020 8342 51[illegible]8
E: ben@ymcahornsey.org.uk
Web: www.ymcahornsey.org.uk
For young homeless people with special needs.
General Secretary: Mr Louis A Lewis. *Hostel Manager:* Rev Ben O Badejo. *Programme Manager:* Mr Jim Shepley. Executive staff 3, Other staff 70. ***CC*** No.209492. Began 1929; interdenominational. Turnover £2,000,000 to year end Mar 97.

***YMCA, Leicester**, 7 East Street, Leicester LE1 6EY
☎0116 255 6507 🖷0116 255 65[illegible]9
E: humanresources@leicesterymca.co.uk
For homeless people aged 18 to 30.
Chief Executive: Mr Paul Brown. Executive staff 8, Other staff 50. ***CC*** No.21[illegible]13. Began 1844; interdenominational. Turnover n/a.

YMCA, Lincoln, St Rumbold's Street, Lincoln LN2 5AR
☎01522 888 200 🖷01522 888 2[illegible]
E: admin@lincolnymca.co.uk
Web: www.lincolnymca.co.uk
Providing housing and fitness services to young people in need.
Chief Executive: Mr Malcolm Barham. Admin staff 5, Other staff 25. ***CC*** No.243017. Began 1969; interdenominational. Turnover £900,000 to year end Dec 02.

YMCA, London, City, Luwum House, 8 Errol Street, London EC1Y 8SE
☎020 7614 5000 🖷020 7628 408[illegible]
E: reception@lcity.co.uk
Web: www.londoncityY.org
For young people in housing need; youth work projects.
Chief Executive: Mr Andy Wilson. *Deputy Chief Executive:* Mrs Sally Yousif. *Chairman:* Dr Simon Marcelli. Executive staff 3, Other staff 62. ***CC*** No.1053[illegible]64. Began 1988; interdenominational. Turnover £1,500,000 to year end Mar 03.

For bed-spaces etc. see list on Page 54

YMCA, London, Indian Student Hostel, 41 Fitzroy Square, London W1P 6AQ
☎020 7387 0411
📠020 7383 7651
E: indianymca@aol.com
Web: www.indianymca.org
For students and trainees.
General Secretary: Mr W I Judson. Admin staff 4, Other staff 13. **CC** Began 1920; interdenominational.
Turnover £1,000,000 to year end Dec 02.

YMCA, London Waltham Forest, 642 Forest Road, Walthamstow, London E17 3EF
☎020 8509 4600
📠020 8509 4590
E: clare.shinner@forestymca.org.uk
Web: www.forestymca.com
Housing, family, childcare and community services.
Chief Executive: Ms Clare Shinner. Executive staff 40, Other staff 180. **CC** No.803442. Began 1970; interdenominational. Turnover £3,500,000 to year end Dec 02.

***YMCA, Norfolk**, 48 St Giles Street, Norwich NR2 1LP
☎01603 620 269
📠01603 762 151
For single young men; pastoral care in Norfolk schools; floating support, supported lodgings.
General Secretary: Mr John Drake. Admin staff 40, Other staff 90. **CC** No.801606. Began 1856; interdenominational. Incorporating YMCAs King's Lynn and Norwich. Turnover £1,000,000 to year end Dec 00.

YMCA, Penzance, International House, Alverton, Penzance TR18 4TE
☎01736 365 016
📠01736 334 823
E: admin@cornwall.ymca.org.uk
Web: www.ymca.org.uk/gallery.cornwall
For homeless young people; working with the communities of Penwith
Chief Executive: Mr David Smith. *Chairman of Directors:* Mr Martyn Haley. Admin staff 1, Other staff 27. **CC** No.1073674. Began 1893; interdenominational. Turnover £320,000 to year end Jan 00.

YMCA, Redditch, Church Hill Centre, Loxley Close, Redditch B98 9JG
☎01527 616 43 📠01527 597 885
E: enquiries@redditchymca.org.uk
For singles and couples aged over 16.
Chief Executive: Mr Duncan Berry. *Chairman:* Rev Robin Baker. Admin staff 6, Other staff 20. **CC** No.516872. Began 1978; interdenominational. Turnover £922,000 to year end Mar 03.

YMCA, Ripon, Water Skelgate, Ripon HG4 1BQ
☎01765 607 609 📠01765 698 460
E: admin@ripon.ymca.org.uk
General Secretary: Mr David Gardener. Admin staff 1, Other staff 1. **CC** Began 1916; interdenominational. Turnover £90,238 to year end Mar 03.

YMCA, Romford, Rush Green Road, Romford RM7 0PH
☎01708 766 211 📠01708 754 211
E: info@romfordymca.org
Web: www.romfordymca.org
Community centre and sports, health and fitness provider.
Chief Executive: Mr Dave Ball. Executive staff 10, Other staff 140. **CC** No.299947. Began 1844; interdenominational. Turnover £2,000,000 to year end Dec 00.

YMCA, St Helens, North Road, St Helens WA10 2TJ
☎01744 225 29 📱07808 727 339
📠01744 291 12
E: admin@sthelensymca.org.uk
Web: www.sthelensymca.org.uk
Mainly for special needs.
Executive Director: Mr A Chick. *Deputy Executive Director:* Mr Brian Charlton. Admin staff 15. **CC** No.517144. Began 1876; interdenominational. Turnover £2,000,000 to year end Mar 98.

YMCA, South London, 40 Stockwell Road, London SW9 9ES
☎020 7501 9795 📠020 7501 8005
E: enquiries@eymca.org.uk
Chief Executive: Mrs Toni Letts. Executive staff 6, Other staff 96. **CC** No.294069. Began 1957; interdenominational. (Previously YMCA, London, Lambeth). Turnover £1,600,000 to year end Mar 98.

YMCA, Watford, Charter House, Charter Place, Watford WD17 2RT
☎01923 353 600 📠01923 353 606
E: admin@watfordymca.com
Chief Executive: Mr Phil Willerton. *Operations Director:* Ruth Ellis. *Chaplain:* Mr Wesley Van-Graan. Admin staff 30, Other staff 60. **CC** Began 1886; interdenominational. Turnover £1,230,000 to year end Mar 98.

YMCA, Welwyn/Hatfield, Maynard House, Peartree Lane, Welwyn Garden City AL7 3UL
☎01707 351 400 📠01707 351 401
E: admin@welwynymca.com
Web: www.welwynymca.com
General Secretary: Mr David Myles. *Housing Manager:* Mr Tim Fox. Admin staff 3, Other staff 77. **CC** No.1065875. Began 1967; interdenominational. Turnover £2,000,000 to year end Mar 05.

YMCA, Worcester, Henwick Road, St John's, Worcester WR2 5NS
☎01905 423 197 📠01905 422 969
E: admin@ymcaworcester.org.uk
Supporting and enabling independent living through vocational and work-related training.
Director: Mr B Kelly. Admin staff 3, Other staff 16. **CC** No.250213. Began 1869; interdenominational. Turnover £1,000,000 to year end Dec 02.

†**YWCA, Croydon**, The Cornerstone, 32 Dingwall Road, Croydon CR0 2NB
☎020 8688 0289 📠020 8667 9250
Self-catering hostel; offering benefit and resettlement support.
Manager: Ms Michelle Ferguson. Executive staff 2, Other staff 9. **CC** Began 1985; interdenominational. Turnover n/a.

YWCA, Dagenham, Bineries Young Women's Project, 321 Heathway, Dagenham RM9 5AF
☎020 8593 3931 📠020 8592 5423
E: edagenham@ywca.org.uk
For young women aged 11 to 30.
Director: Mrs Heather Pembroke. Executive staff 2, Other staff 3. **CC** No.217868. Began n/a; interdenominational. Turnover £100,000 to year end Mar 03.

For bed-spaces etc. see list on Page 54

HOUSING ASSOCIATIONS

A

Adullam Homes Housing Association Ltd, Peak House, Farm House Way, Birmingham B43 7SE
☎0121 358 3818 🖷0121 358 7218
E: info@adullam.org.uk
Web: www.adullam.uk.net
Housing and support for vunerable people.
Chief Executive: Mr Trevor Palfreyman. Executive staff 4, Other staff 200. ***CC*** No.326743. Began 1972; non-denominational. Magazine: *Lifebuilder* (5,000 annually). Turnover £9,830,201 to year end Dec 05.

***Amersham Christian Housing Association**, 28 Mottingham Road, Mottingham, London SE9 4QW
☎020 8857 4981 M: 07966 966 034
🖷020 8857 4981
E: admin@achal.fednet.org.uk
Web: www.achal.org.uk
Assisting key Christian workers to find affordable homes in under-resourced urban areas, primarily London.
Administrator: Mrs Judi Feasey. *Chairman:* Mr Graham Garner. No full-time staff. ***CC*** No.27367R. Began 1988; interdenominational. No magazine. Turnover £245,500 to year end Dec 04.

***Aquila Way**, Kings Court, Kingsway, Gateshead NE11 0SH
☎0191 491 5700 M: 07966 365 344
🖷0191 491 3334
E: info@aquilaway.org
Web: www.aquilaway.org
Providing housing with care and support for homeless young people.
Chief Executive: Mrs Jo Grant. *Project Director:* Phil Dobson. Executive staff 2, Other staff 44. ***CC*** No.24582R. Began 1984; non-denominational. (Previously Aquila Housing Association). Turnover £785,308 to year end Dec 04.

Baptist Housing Trust, 23 Hillway, Westcliff-on-Sea SS0 8QA
☎01702 473 373
Supporting the charitable work of English Churches Housing Group by funding housing and associated amenities.
Secretary: Mr J Barfield. Admin staff 1. ***CC*** No.1031620. Began 1994; Baptist. (Previously Baptist Housing Association Charitable Fund). No magazine. Turnover £62,000 to year end Mar 05.

***CAHA Christian Alliance Housing Association Ltd**, 2 Exton Street, London SE1 8UE
☎0870 458 4243
🖷0870 458 4245 / 020 7593 0478
E: mail@caha.org.uk
Sharing the Gospel of Christ with practical care through residential accommodation for those in special need.
Chief Executive: Mr Rob Taylor. Executive staff 6, Admin staff 6. ***CC*** No.293232. Began 1985; interdenominational. (Previously Christian Alliance). No magazine. Turnover £2,500,000 to year end Dec 98.

Christian Care Association, 4 Victoria Road, Bunny, Nottingham NG11 6QF
🖷0115 940 5648
E: sheilawalker@fish.co.uk
Association for providers of Christian residential care to share experience and expertise, promote quality care.
Coordinator: Sheila Walker. *Chairman:* Mr Brian James. Executive staff 1. Began 1999; interdenominational. No magazine. Turnover n/a.

†English Churches Housing Group, 3 Bede Island Road, Leicester LE2 7EA
☎0870 850 5577
E: contact@echg.org.uk
Web: www.echg.org.uk
Providing family housing, sheltered housing for elderly people, supported housing schemes for single homeless people.
Chief Executive: Mr Peter Walters. *Director of Operations:* Ms Karen Wilson. *Strategic Planning and Performance Director:* Ms Sue Witherspoon. Executive staff 7, Other staff 1400. ***CC*** Began n/a. (Baptist Housing Association (1966) and Church Housing Association (1924) merged 1991). No magazine. Turnover £76,000,000 to year end Mar 03.

Eothen Homes Ltd, 6 Lambton Road, Newcastle upon Tyne NE2 4RX
☎0191 281 9100 🖷0191 281 9264
E: enquiries@eothenhomes.org.uk
Web: www.eothenhomes.org.uk
Providing residential care homes for 108 elderley people in three locations.
General Manager: Mrs J M Hearl. Admin staff 4, Other staff 80. ***CC*** No.223262. Began 1950; interdenominational. No magazine. Turnover £2,149,237 to year end Mar 05.

The Fairfield Trust, Fairfield, Huxtable Hill, Torquay TQ2 6RN
☎01872 260 621 🖷01872 260 397
E: alex.w.h.dick@btinternet.com
Providing residential flats in Devon for 18 clergy and missionaries retired or on leave.
Chairman: Rev Alex W H Dick. No full-time staff. ***CC*** No.266699. Began 1974; non-denominational. No magazine. Turnover £90,000 to year end Oct 02.
Managed by Devon & Cornwall Housing Management Society Ltd, Kenwyn Street, Truro TR1 3BA

***John Grooms Housing Association**, 50 Scrutton Street, London EC2A 4XQ
☎020 7452 2000 🖷020 7452 2001
E: housing@johngrooms.org.uk
Web: www.johngrooms.org.uk
Specialist builder and manager of wheelchair-accessible housing for disabled people.
Chief Executive: Mr Tim Fallon. *Finance Director:* Mr Mutlow Marke. *Chairman:* Mr Ernest Picton. Executive staff 3, Other staff 60. ***CC*** Began 1970; interdenominational. Magazine: *Grooms News* (50,000 half-yearly). Turnover £5,414,000 to year end Mar 05.

Habitat for Humanity Northern Ireland, Unit 29, Farset Enterprise Park, 638 Springfield Road, Belfast BT12 7DY
☎028 9024 3686 🖷028 9[illegible]33 18[illegible]8
E: belfast@habitatni.co.uk
Web: www.habitatni.co.uk
Cross-community, Christian self-build housing organisation helping low-income families build and purchase their own homes.
Director: Mr Peter Farquharson. Executive staff 3, Other staff 15. ***CC*** No.XN 1[illegible]70. Began 1994; non-denominational. No magazine. Turnover £1 000,000 to year end Apr 04.

†Homes4Christians, PO Box 1[illegible]02, Hainault, Ilford IG6 2UQ
☎020 8500 7623
E: enquiries@homes4christians.co.uk
Web: www.homes4christians.co.uk
Providing Christians with details of rental accommodation including holiday and share accommodation.
Managing Director: Dr Eamicele Anjorin. Executive staff 2, Admin staff 2. Began 2003; non-denominational. No magazine. Turnover n/a.

Jericho Benedictines, Jericho House, 53 Lothian Street, Edinburgh EH1 1HB
☎0131 225 8230 🖷0131 225 2656
Providing housing across Scotland and northern England
Manager: Mrs June Balloch. Admin staff 6, Care staff 10. ***CC*** Began 19[illegible]0; Roman Catholic. No magazine. Turnover n/a.

***Keychange Charity**, 5 St George's Mews, 43 Westminster Bridge Road, London SE1 7JB
☎020 7633 0533 🖷020 792[illegible] 1872
E: info@keychange.org.uk
Web: www.keychange.org.uk
Providing residential care for frail elderly people and supported accommodation for vulnerable, homeless people.
Chief Executive: Mr David Shafik. *Operations Controller:* Barbara Barrett. *Financial Controller:* Mark Nixon. Executive staff [illegible], Other staff 3. ***CC*** No.10[illegible]134[illegible]. Began 1920; interdenominational. (Previously Christian Alliance). Magazine: *KeyChange News* (3,500 quarterly). Turnover £2,561,334 to year end Mar 0[illegible].

The Leaders of Worship and Preachers Homes, 89 High Street, Rickmansworth WD3 1EF
☎01923 775 856 🖷01923 71[illegible] 075
E: lwptoffice@lwpt.org.uk
Care homes primarily for elderly preachers and leaders of worship and their dependents.
Secretary: Mr Godfrey Talford. Executive staff 1, Other staff 90. Began 194[illegible]; Methodist but open to all(Previously Mutual Aid Homes and LPHA Homes). Turnover £1,638,713 to year end Aug 04.

†Manchester Methodist Housing Group, Hopeleigh, 1 Fairhope Avenue, Salford M6 8AR
☎0161 707 7147 🖷0161 707 7300
Web: www.mmhg.org.uk
Providing rented accommodation, low-cost homes for purchase, housing management services.
Chief Executive: Stephen Porter. Executive staff 1, Other staff n/a. **CC** No.19554. Began n/a; Methodist. No magazine. Turnover n/a.

Methodist Homes for the Aged, Epworth House, Stuart Street, Derby DE1 2EQ
☎01332 296 200 🖷01332 296 925
E: enquiries@mha.org.uk
Web: www.mha.org.uk
Providing care, accommodation and support services for 6,500 older people across the UK.
Chief Executive: Mr Roger Davies. *Senior Chaplain:* Rev Dr Keith Albans. Executive staff 6, Other staff 3000. **CC** No.1083995. Began 1943; Methodist. Part of MHA Care Group. Magazine: *Heart + Soul* (48,000 half-yearly). Turnover £52,700,000 to year end Mar 05.

MR Associates, 19 Wemyss Court, Leapmoor Drive, Wemyss Bay PA18 6BF
☎01475 522 962 M: 07967 963 806
E: info@mrassociates.org.uk
Web: www.mrassociates.org.uk
Advising the supported housing sector, specialising in housing benefit, supporting people and care commission issues.
Supported Housing Advisor: Mr Mark Rodgers. Executive staff 2, Admin staff 1. Began 2000; interdenominational. No magazine. Turnover n/a.

Nehemiah Housing, 5 Beacon Court, Birmingham Road, Great Barr, Birmingham B43 6NN
☎0121 358 0966 🖷0121 358 0934
E: contact@nehemiah.co.uk
Web: www.nehemiah.co.uk
Providing 500 housing units for elderly people, families, single people and young mothers
Chief Executive: Mr Llewellyn Graham. Executive staff 1, Admin staff 29. Began n/a; Church of God of Prophecy. No magazine. Turnover £2,000,000 to year end Dec 05.

***Pilgrim Homes**, Nasmith House, 175 Tower Bridge Road, London SE1 2AL
☎020 7407 5466 🖷020 7403 4533
E: info@pilgrimhomes.org.uk
Web: www.pilgrimhomes.org.uk
Residential and nursing care, and sheltered housing for elderly, Protestant Christians. Chief Executive: Mr P A Tervet. Executive staff 10, Other staff 202. **CC** No.242266. Began 1807; non-denominational. (Previously Aged Pilgrims' Friend Society). Magazine: *Quarterly* (5,000 quarterly), *Annual Report* (3,000 annually). Turnover £4,200,000 to year end Dec 02.

Retired Baptist Ministers Housing Society Ltd, Baptist House, PO Box 44, 129 Broadway, Didcot OX11 8RT
☎01202 548 890 M: 07760 261 357
🖷01202 548 890
E: stewart@rbmhs.fsworld.co.uk
Web: www.rbmhs.org.uk
Providing accommodation for retired Baptist ministers, missionaries and their spouses.
Manager: Mr Stewart Green. Executive staff 1. **CC** No.21462. Began 1975; Baptist. No magazine. Turnover £918,082 to year end Sept 04.

St Christopher's Fellowship, 1 Putney High Street, London SW15 1SZ
☎020 8720 7800 🖷020 8780 7801
E: generalenquiries@st-chris.org.uk
Providing hostels for men aged 16 to 21, women aged 16 to 65; 3 children's homes; 1 children's refuge.
Executive Manager: Louise Herring. *Personnel and Administration Manager:* L Morgan. Executive staff 3, Other staff 120. **CC** No.207782. Began 1870; non-denominational. No magazine. Turnover £1,000,000 to year end Mar 03.

Salvation Army Housing Association, Barber Surgeons Hall, 1a Monkwell Square, London EC2Y 5BL
☎020 7332 4800 🖷020 7332 4837
E: head.office@saha.org.uk
Web: www.saha.org.uk
Constructing and letting flats, houses and hostels for people in need.
Chief Executive: Mr Nigel Parrington. Executive staff 6, Other staff 104. **CC** Began 1959; Salvation Army. No magazine. Turnover £30,127,809 to year end Mar 03.
Also at: 33 Chorley New Road, Bolton BL1 4QR
☎01204 360 500 🖷 01204 360 509
And: Jarodale House, 7 Gregory Boulevard, Nottingham NG7 6LD
☎0115 985 6637 🖷 0115 956 5385
And: 39 Bath Road, Swindon SN1 $AS
☎01793 541 635 🖷 01793 420 159

***Scottish Christian Alliance**, 3 Nethercairn Place, Newton Mearns, Glasgow G77 5SZ
☎0141 571 3804 M: 07811 598 461
E: the.director@scottishchristianalliance.org
Web: www.scottishchristianalliance.org
Presenting the Gospel of Jesus Christ principally through offering supported accommodation.
Director: Mr Daniel McPhail-Smith. *Assistant Director:* Rev J E Cropley. Executive staff 2, Other staff 25. **CC** No.SCO 21765. Began 1993; interdenominational. (Previously KeyChange Scotland Ltd). No magazine. Turnover £638,000 to year end Mar 04.

RESIDENTIAL HOMES FOR DISADVANTAGED PEOPLE

Homes which did not supply this information are not listed here

⇌ = nearest Railway station

Name, Town	Type of resident	Number	Railway / Underground
Badgers, Leigh-on-Sea	learning disabilities	9	⇌ Leigh-on-Sea
Bethany Christian Trust, Edinburgh	homeless people	18	⇌ Edinburgh
Crossways Community, Tunbridge Wells	mental health	34	⇌ Tunbridge Wells
Gilven House, Scottish Christian Alliance Hostel, Glenrothes	homeless women	15	⇌ Markinch
Kilbirnie Centre, Kilbirnie	learning disabilities	25	⇌ Glengarnock
Leeds Autism Services	adults with autism	8	⇌ Leeds
The Lodge Trust, Oakham	learning disabilities	25	⇌ Oakham
Mayflower Centre, Plymouth	learning disabilities	15	⇌ Plymouth
Mercy Ministries UK, Bradford	women, life-controlling disorders	15	⇌ Bradford
Minstead Training Project, Lyndhurst	learning disabilities	23	⇌ Ashurst New Forest
Moorfield House, Liverpool	learning disabilities	31	⇌ Maghull
St Michael's Fellowship, London SW2	adolescent mothers and babies	8	⇌ Streatham Hill or Tulse Hill
Springfield Lodge, London SE5	male ex-offenders	25	⇌ East Dulwich
W J Thompson House, Belfast	male ex-offenders	16	*Rail:* Belfast Great Victoria Street
Westhaven, Glasgow	adults with epilepsy	18	⇌ Rutherglen

RESIDENTIAL HOMES FOR DISADVANTAGED PEOPLE

See also Addictions & Rehabilitation Centres on Page 318.

Badgers, 53 Rayleigh Avenue, Leigh-on-Sea SS9 5DN
☎01702 526 027 🖷01702 526 027
Supported by the Field Lane Foundation. For people with learning disabilities.
Manager: Ms Catherine Sutton. Other staff 30. ***CC*** No.207493. Began 1993; non-denominational. Turnover n/a.

Crossways Community, 8 Culverden Park Road, Tunbridge Wells TN4 9QX
☎01892 529 321 🖷01892 540 843
Supporting 34 people suffering from mental health difficulties in 2 residential settings.
Executive Manager: Mr Martin Granger. *Administrator:* Mr Stephen Howcroft. Executive staff 2, Other staff 8. ***CC*** No.1007156. Began 1967; interdenominational. Turnover £500,000 to year end Jan 02.

***Gilven House, Scottish Christian Alliance Hostel**, 22 Iona Park, Glenrothes KY7 6NU
☎01592 744 849 🖷01592 743 924
E: may.cropley@scottishchristianalliance.org
Web: www.scottishchristianalliance.org.
Project flats and community support for vulnerable people, teaching lifeskills principles leading to independent. living.
Project Manager: Mrs May Cropley. *Deputy Manager:* Mrs Trisha O'Brien. Executive staff 3, Other staff 17. ***CC*** No.SCO 21765. Began 1985; interdenominational. Turnover n/a.

Kilbirnie, 50 Holmhead, Kilbirnie KA25 6BS
☎01505 683 233
For adults with learning disabilities.
Officer-in-Charge: Centre Manager. Admin staff 1, Other staff n/a. ***CC*** No.215/174. Began n/a; Salvation Army. (Previously Redheugh Centre). Turnover n/a.

Leeds Autism Services, 76 Potternewton Lane, Leeds LS7 3LW
☎0113 226 2700 (home)/245 2736 (day services) 🖷0113 226 2700
E: admin@las.uk.net
Web: www.las.uk.net
Long-term care and development of adults with autism.
Manager: Name not supplied. Executive staff 3, Other staff 27. ***CC*** No.1047981. Began 1988; interdenominational. (Previously Ashlar House Autism Services). Turnover £639,000 to year end Dec 02.

The Lodge Trust, The Lodge, Market Overton, Oakham LE15 7PL
☎01572 767 234 🖷01572 767 503
E: admin@lodgetrust.org.uk
Web: www.lodgetrust.org.uk
Providing Christian homes and places of work for adults with learning disabilities.
Chief Executive: Mr Roy Palframan. *Care Manager:* Miss Elizabeth Irvine. Executive staff 2, Other staff 28. ***CC*** No.516835. Began 1984; evangelical. Turnover £602,000 to year end Mar 02.

Mayflower Centre, Courtfield Road, Plymouth PL3 5BB
☎01752 660 302
For adults with a learning disability; day centre and residential.
Centre Manager: Officer-in-Charge. Admin staff 1. ***CC*** Began n/a; Salvation Army. Turnover n/a.

Mercy Ministries UK, 4 James Street, Bradford BD1 3PZ
☎01274 745 427
E: admin@mercyministries.co.uk
Web: www.mercyministries.co.uk
For women aged 16 to 28 with life controlling disorders.
Chief Executive: Mrs Kerry Slater. Executive staff 2, Admin staff 2. ***CC*** No.1111377. Began 2004; non-denominational. Turnover: first year of operation.

Minstead Training Project, Minstead, Lyndhurst SO43 7FT
☎023 8081 2297 🖷023 8081 2297
E: mtp@milestonenet.co.uk
Training in work, life and social skills for people with learning disabilities.
Project Director: Mr Martin Lenaerts. *Administrator:* Ms Wendy Newton. Executive staff 2, Other staff 48. ***CC*** No.1053391. Began 1986; non-denominational. Turnover £1,[illegible]63,000 to year end Mar 05.

Moorfield House, Melling, Liverpool L31 1AQ
☎0151 549 2100 🖷0151 546 682[illegible]
E: moorfields.house@craigmore.co.uk
For young adults with learning difficulties.
Manageress: Mrs Clare Weston. Admin staff 1, Other staff 35. Began 1985; interdenominational. Turnover £1,000,000 to year end Dec 02.

St Michael's Fellowship, Streatham, 52 Palace Road, Streatham, London SW2 3NJ
☎020 8671 1252 🖷020 867[illegible] 501[illegible]
E: fifty.two@zetnet.com
Assessment of parenting skills; support and assistance to young mothers and children at risk. *Manager:* Mrs Liz Mitchell. Admin staff 1, Other staff 6. ***CC*** No.1035820. Began 1972; interdenominational. Turnover n/a.

W J Thompson House, 426 Antrim Road, Belfast BT15 5GA
☎028 9037 0923 🖷028 9077 5177
For male ex-offenders. Director: Mr David Farrow.
Deputy Director: Anne Calhearn. Resident social workers 6, Other staff [illegible]. Began 1984; Presbyterian Church in Ireland. Turnover £200,000 to year end Dec 0[illegible].

***Westhaven**, 2 Upper Bourtree Drive, High Burnside, Rutherglen, Glasgow G73 4EH
☎0141 634 4563 🖷0141 634 0599
E: westhaven.cos@uk.uumail.com
For adults with epilepsy.
Unit Manager: Mrs Elizabeth Gibb. Admin staff 1, Other staff 8. ***CC*** No.SCO 2436[illegible]. Began 1983; Church of Scotland. Turnover n/a.

A

RESIDENTIAL & NURSING HOMES FOR ELDERLY PEOPLE

By country and Postcode – for location of Postcodes see map on Page 458
Homes which did not supply this information are not listed here
Only homes with 10 or more places are included

S = single rooms **D/T** = number of bed spaces in double/twin rooms **Total** = total bed spaces (not number of rooms)
≉ = nearest Railway station ⊖ = nearest London Underground station

Postcode	Location	Name	S	D/T	Other		Total	Railway/Underground
ENGLAND								
B 9	**Birmingham**	Herondale	n/a	n/a	dementia care		36	≉Adderley Park
B 9	**Birmingham**	Kingfisher House	n/a	n/a			38	≉Adderley Park
BA 1	**Bath**	Stratton House	n/a	n/a	registered beds		33	≉Bath Spa
BA 2	**Bath**	Smallcombe House Eventide Home	n/a	n/a	care	26	30	≉Bath Spa
					flats	2		
					respite places	2		
BH15	**Poole**	Maidment Court	n/a	n/a	registered beds		46	≉Poole
BL 8	**Bury**	Epworth Grange	n/a	n/a	registered beds		39	*Metrolink:* Bury
BN 2	**Brighton**	Brighton and Lady Anne Treves Memorial Pilgrim Homes	n/a	n/a	care and nursing	23	38	≉brighton
					single sheltered flatlets	13		
					double sheltered flatlet	2		
BN 5	**Henfield**	Terry's Cross House	n/a	n/a			20	≉Horsham
BN11	**Worthing**	Koinomia (Sussex) Ltd	n/a	n/a	care		24	≉Worthing
BN14	**Worthing**	The Priory	41	2			43	≉West Worthing
BR 1	**Bromley**	Bromley and Sheppard's Colleges	n/a	n/a	flats	40	40	≉Bromley North or Bromley South
BR 4	**West Wickham**	Burrell Mead	20	2			22	≉West Wickham
BS 6	**Bristol**	The Müller Homes for the Elderly	22	2	residential		24	≉Bristol Temple Meads
BS 8	**Bristol**	St Angela's Residential Care Home	n/a	n/a			n/a	≉Bristol Temple Meads
BS13	**Bristol**	Hartcliffe	n/a	n/a			66	≉Bristol Temple Meads
BS23	**Weston-super-Mare**	Dewdown House	n/a	n/a			40	≉Weston-super-Mare
CB 2	**Cambridge**	Orchard House	n/a	n/a	also dementia care		35	≉Whittlesford
CB 5	**Cambridge**	Queens Court	n/a	n/a	dementia care		35	≉Cambridge
CH41	**Birkenhead**	Wirral Christian Centre Trust, Residential Home	n/a	n/a			39	≉Birkenhead Central
CH66	**South Wirral**	Mayfields	45	-	dementia care		45	≉Ellesmere Port
CO12	**Harwich**	Alexandra House	n/a	n/a			29	≉Dovercourt
CO14	**Walton on the Naze**	The Ernest Luff Homes Ltd	n/a	n/a	sheltered care		66	≉Frinton
CR 9	**Croydon**	Hall Grange	36	-	registered beds		36	≉East Croydon
CT 5	**Whitstable**	Cliff Dene	34	2	registered beds		36	≉whitstable
		Granary House	n/a	n/a			20	≉Whitstable
CV 1	**Coventry**	Newfield House Nursing Home	n/a	n/a			37	≉Coventry
CV 3	**Coventry**	Abbey Park Nursing Home	n/a	n/a			84	≉Coventry
		Youell Court Social Services Centre	n/a	n/a			40	≉Coventry
CV 5	**Coventry**	Allesley Hall	n/a	n/a			45	≉Coventry
CV 6	**Coventry**	Charnwood House	n/a	n/a	dementia care		57	≉Coventry
CV13	**Nuneaton**	Hornsey Rise Memorial Home Pilgrim Homes	n/a	n/a	care	32	42	≉Nuneaton
					sheltered	10		
CV32	**Leamington Spa**	Homewood	35	-	registered beds		35	≉Leamington Spa
CV37	**Stratford-upon-Avon**	Cedar Lawn	n/a	n/a			34	≉Stratford-upon-Avon
DE 5	**Ripley**	Maple Leaf House	n/a	n/a	nursing or dementia care		45	≉Ambergate or Alfreton
DH 8	**Consett**	St Mary's Convent Rest Home	20	-			20	≉Durham
DN 6	**Doncaster**	St Anne's Rest Home	30	-			30	≉Doncaster
DT 9	**Sherborne**	Bible Fellowship Eventide Trust	11	2			13	≉Sherborne
DY 9	**Stourbridge**	The Cedars Christian Residential Home	21	-	registered beds		21	≉Stourbridge
EX 8	**Exmouth**	Moreton	29	6	registered beds		35	≉Exmouth
EX10	**Sidmouth**	Rose Lawn Retirement Home	n/a	n/a			23	≉Honiton or Exeter
FY 8	**Lytham St Annes**	Starr Hills	n/a	n/a			36	≉Ansdell and Fairhaven
GL 3	**Gloucester**	Brockworth House	n/a	n/a			55	≉Gloucester
GU22	**Woking**	Woodbank	37	2	registered beds		39	≉Woking
GU27	**Haslemere**	Shottermill House Pilgrim Homes	n/a	n/a	care	27	32	≉Haslemere
					single flat	1		
					double flat	2		
					double very sheltered flats	2		
HG 2	**Harrogate**	Berwick Grange	n/a	n/a			32	≉Harrogate
		Emmaus House	18	16			34	≉Harrogate
HP11	**High Wycombe**	Keep Hill Rest Home	9	-	frail elderly		9	≉High Wycombe
HU10	**Hull**	Willersley House	29	6	registered beds		35	≉Hessle
IP1	**Ipswich**	Norwood	39		registered beds		39	≉ipswich
IP14	**Stowmarket**	Finborough Court Pilgrim Homes	n/a	n/a	residential care	20	49	≉Stowmarket
					bungalows	12		
					very sheltered double flats	16		
					house	1		
IP33	**Bury St Edmunds**	The Martins	n/a	n/a	dementia care		40	≉Bury St Edmunds
L 17	**Liverpool**	Fulwood Park	n/a	n/a			34	≉Aigburth
L 39	**Ormskirk**	Aughton Park Care Home	n/a	n/a	also people with dementia care		48	≉Aughton Park
LA11	**Grange over Sands**	Westerley	23	6			29	≉Grange over Sands
LE 2	**Leicester**	Aigburth	31	2			33	≉Leicester
LE 5	**Leicester**	Evington Home Pilgrim Homes	1	-	care	30	49	≉Leicester
					single bungalows	12		
					very sheltered flats	10		
		Foxton Grange Nursing Home	n/a	n/a	nursing or dementia care		36	≉Leicester
LN 6	**Lincoln**	Stones Place	40	2	registered beds		42	≉Lincoln Central
LN10	**Woodhall Spa**	Westerley	23	4			27	≉Lincoln

Residential & Nursing Homes for Elderly People

Postcode	Location	Name	S	D/T	Other		Total	Railway/Underground
LS29	**Ilkley**	Glen Rosa	n/a	n/a	dementia care		47	Ilkley
ME 4	**Chatham**	Agapé House	n/a	n/a			20	Chatham
MK16	**Newport Pagnell**	Westbury	30	-	dementia care		30	Milton Keynes Central
MK40	**Bedford**	The Dorothea Trust	16	-			16	Bedford
NE 3	**Newcastle upon Tyne**	Eothen Homes Ltd	35	2			37	Newcastle
NE23	**Cramlington**	Harwood Court	33	2			35	Cramlington
NE26	**Whitley Bay**	Eothen Homes Ltd	29	2	sheltered flats	2	33	*Metro:* Whitley Bay
NG 2	**Nottingham**	Notintone House Eventide Home	n/a	n/a			38	Nottingham
NG 9	**Nottingham**	Queenswood	41	-	registered beds		41	Nottingham or Beeston
NN10	**Rushden**	Rushden Park	n/a	n/a	nursing care		64	Wellingborough
NR 1	**Norwich**	Cromwell House	38	-	registered beds		38	Norwich
NR20	**Dereham**	Eckling Grange Ltd	n/a	n/a	residential	45	123	Dereham
					nursing care beds	20		
					sheltered bungalows	58		
NR27	**Cromer**	Upton Park	n/a	n/a			16	Cromer
NR28	**North Walsham**	The Mildred Duff Memorial Eventide Home	n/a	n/a			25	North Walsham
NR33	**Lowestoft**	The Dell Care Homel	17	10			27	Oulton Broad South
OX 4	**Oxford**	St John's Home	35	6			41	Oxford
OX12	**Wantage**	Framland Pilgrim Homes	2	2	care/sheltered housing	21	25	Didcot Parkway
		St Katharine's House	75	-	residential and nursing		75	Didcot Parkway
PE15	**March**	Kingswood Park	n/a	n/a	also dementia care		44	March
PL 4	**Plymouth**	Bethany Christian Home	22	4			26	Plymouth
PL 7	**Plymouth**	St Vincent's Nursing Home	20	4	respite	1	25	Plymouth
PO18	**Chichester**	Westhampnett Private Nursing Home	24	4			28	Chichester
PO20	**Chichester**	Nyton House	n/a	n/a			19	Barnham
PO21	**Bognor Regis**	Greenways	41	-	registered beds		41	Bognor Regis
PR 2	**Preston**	Bethany House	n/a	n/a			15	preston
PR 8	**Southport**	Connell Court	35	-	registered beds		35	Birkdale
PR 9	**Southport**	Orleans Residential Home for Elderly Christians	17	6			23	southport
RH 2	**Reigate**	Dovers	35	4			39	Reigate
S 7	**Sheffield**	Overdale Retirement Home	23	2			25	Sheffield
S 32	**Hope Valley**	Moorland House	33	-	registered beds		33	Hathersage
SG 5	**Hitchin**	Elmside	38	-	registered beds		38	Hitchin
SG 6	**Letchworth**	Trembaths	n/a	n/a	residential and nursing	40	40	Letchworth
SK17	**Buxton**	The Hawthorns Eventide Home	n/a	n/a			35	Buxton
SL 9	**Gerrards Cross**	Rock House	37	-	single flats	10	49	Gerrards Cross
					double flats	2		
SM 2	**Sutton**	Eothen Homes Ltd	36	2	sheltered bungalows	9	49	Sutton
SM 6	**Wallington**	Ryelands	46	2	registered beds		48	Wallington
SN 3	**Swindon**	Fitzwarren House	n/a	n/a	nursing or dementia care		60	Swindon
SN15	**Chippenham**	Leonora Home Pilgrim Homes	-	-	care	20	29	Chippenham
					single flats	7		
					double flats	2		
SO16	**Southampton**	Fair Havens	n/a	n/a	also nursing care		21	Southampton Central
SS0	**Westcliff on Sea**	Westerley	15	6			21	Westcliff on Sea
ST 6	**Stoke-on-Trent**	Claybourne	45	-			45	Stoke-on-Trent
ST16	**Stafford**	Weston/Queensway	n/a	n/a	nursing or dementia care		70	Stafford
TA24	**Minehead**	Westerley	23	4			27	Taunton
TN 2	**Tunbridge Wells**	Milward House Pilgrim Homes	n/a	n/a	care and nursing	28	46	Tunbridge Wells
					single flats	16		
					double flat	2		
		Rosset Holt Retirement Home	18	-			18	Tunbridge Wells
		Sunset Lodge	n/a	n/a			27	Tunbridge Wells
TN39	**Bexhill-on-Sea**	Richmond/Heatherbank	n/a	n/a	registered beds		52	Bexhill
TQ 1	**Torquay**	Walmer House Retirement Home	n/a	n/a			17	Torquay
TQ14	**Teignmouth**	Charterhouse Residential Home	n/a	n/a			20	Teignmouth
TR11	**Falmouth**	Langholme	n/a	n/a	registered beds		39	Falmouth Town
WA14	**Altrincham**	Handsworth	n/a	n/a	registered beds		41	Altrincham
WS 1	**Walsall**	Acorn Retirement Home	14	4	care of frail elderly		18	Walsall
WS15	**Rugeley**	Briar Hill House	n/a	n/a	nursing care		28	Rugeley Town
WV 3	**Wolverhampton**	Engelberg	32	-	registered beds		32	Wolverhampton
WV11	**Wolverhampton**	Waterside House	n/a	n/a	dementia care		60	Wolverhampton
YO12	**Scarborough**	Priceholme	31	2	registered beds		33	Scarborough
London								
N 10	**London**	The Meadow	40	-	dementia care		40	⊖Highgate
SE 1	**London**	South London Mission	n/a	n/a			38	⊖Borough
SE13	**London**	Glebe Court Eventide Home	n/a	n/a			41	Lewisham
SE26	**London**	Rookstone Eventide Home	n/a	n/a			32	Sydenham
SW 4	**London**	Alver Bank Eventide Home	25	2	sheltered housing	8	59	⊖Clapham Common
					independent housing	24		
SW19	**London**	Alexandra House	n/a	n/a			22	Wimbledon ⊖Wimbledon
SW20	**London**	St Theresa's Home	n/a	n/a			18	Wimbledon ⊖Wimbledon
NORTHERN IRELAND								
BT18	**Holywood**	Sir Samuel Kelly Memorial Eventide Home	n/a	n/a			32	*Rail:* Holywood
SCOTLAND								
AB 1	**Aberdeen**	Rubislaw Park	n/a	-		n/a	n/a	Aberdeen
AB 3	**Stonehaven**	Clashfarquhar House	-	-	flatlets	20	20	Stonehaven
AB10	**Aberdeen**	Ashley Lodge Home	40	-			40	Aberdeen
AB33	**Aberdeen**	Balmedie House	21	-			21	Aberdeen
AB31	**Banchory**	Bellfield Home	27	-			27	Aberdeen
EH 5	**Edinburgh**	Eagle Lodge Eventide Home	30	-			30	Edinburgh
EH 9	**Edinburgh**	The Elms Home	41	-			41	Edinburgh
EH10	**Edinburgh**	Morlich House	23	n/a			23	Edinburgh

Postcode	Location	Name	S	D/T	Other		Total	Railway/Underground
EH14	Edinburgh	Davidson House Eventide Home	n/a	n/a			30	⇌Edinburgh
EH15	Edinburgh	Queen's Bay Lodge	26	-			26	⇌Edinburgh
EH19	Bonnyrigg	Nazareth House	26	14			40	⇌Edinburgh
EH41	Haddington	Florabank Home Ltd	n/a	n/a			20	⇌Edinburgh
FK 2	Falkirk	St Margaret's	36	-	dementia care		36	⇌Polmont
G 32	Glasgow	Tollcross Mansionhouse	22	-	supported living		22	⇌Carntyne
G 44	Glasgow	Williamwood House	30	-	dementia care		30	⇌Muirend
G 46	Glasgow	Eastwoodhill Home	37	-			37	⇌Giffnock
G 72	Glasgow	Eva Burrows Social Services Centre	36	-			36	⇌Cambuslang
G 84	Helensburgh	Clyde View Home	28	-			28	⇌Helensburgh
IV 2	Inverness	Cameron House	28	-	dementia care		28	⇌Inverness
IV12	Nairn	Whinnieknowe Home	24	-			24	⇌Nairn
IV25	Dornoch	Oversteps Home	16	-			16	⇌Ardgay
IV51	Isle of Skye	Budhmor Home	30	-			30	⇌Kyle of Lochalsh
KA 7	Ayr	Ayr Baptist Homes	20	6	nursing	7	33	⇌Ayr
		Cumnor Hall Home	27	-	dementia care		27	⇌Ayr
KA22	Ardrossan	South Beach House Home	42	-			42	⇌Ardrossan South Beach
KW14	Thurso	Achvarasdal Home	16	6			22	⇌Thurso
ML11	Lanark	Auchlochan Trust	70	20	larger rooms	10	111	⇌Hamilton Central
					flats	11		
PA 5	Johnstone	Adams House	n/a	n/a	dementia care	28	30	⇌Johnstone
					respite care	2		
PA23	Dunoon	Invereck Home	23	-			23	⇌Gourock
PA28	Campbeltown	Auchinlee Home	20	-			20	⇌None near
PH12	Blairgowrie	Belmont Castle Home	20	-			20	⇌Perth
ZE 1	Shetland	Walter and Joan Gray Home	16	-			16	⇌None near
WALES								
CF64	Dinas Powis	Bethel House	n/a	n/a			39	⇌Dinas Powis
	Penarth	Morel Court	36	-			36	⇌Penarth
		Ty Gwyn	n/a	n/a	nursing care		45	⇌Dingle Road or Penarth
LL28	Colwyn Bay	Coed Craig	n/a	n/a	registered beds	41	45	⇌Colwyn Bay

RESIDENTIAL & NURSING HOMES FOR ELDERLY PEOPLE

See also Sheltered Housing on Page 80.

Abbey Park Nursing Home, Abbey Park, Humber Road, Coventry CV3 4FE
☎024 7650 6045 🖷024 7650 2260
E: home.abp@mha.org.uk
Web: www.mha.org.uk
Home Manager: Janet Pavlou. Admin staff 1, Other staff n/a. **CC** No.1083995. Began 1995; Methodist but open to all. Methodist Homes for the Aged. Turnover n/a.

***Achvarasdal Home**, Reay, Thurso KW14 7RR
☎01847 811 226 🖷01847 811 570
Unit Manager: Mrs Alison Cook. Admin staff 1, Other staff 25. **CC** No.SCO 24366. Began 1951; Church of Scotland. Turnover n/a.

Acorn Retirement Home, 102 Birmingham Road, Walsall WS1 2NJ
☎01922 524 314 M: 07767 426 700
🖷01922 534 549
E: bldavies@tiscali.co.uk
Proprietor: Mr Lloyd Davies. *Deputy Manager:* Miss Ruth Greenfield. Executive staff 4, Other staff 23. Began 1986; interdenominational. Turnover n/a.

***Adams House**, 136 Auchenlodment Road, Elderslie, Johnstone PA5 9NX
☎01505 337 322 🖷01505 337 872
For those with dementia.
Unit Manager: Brenda Torrance. Admin staff 1, Other staff 32. **CC** No.SCO 24366. Began 1992; Church of Scotland. Turnover n/a.

Agapé House, 45 Maidstone Road, Chatham ME4 6DP
☎01634 841 002 🖷01634 841 182
Proprietor: Mrs Siva. Admin staff 1, Other staff 20. Began 1989; non-denominational. Turnover £300,000 to year end Apr 03.

Aigburth, 21 Manor Road, Oadby, Leicester LE2 2LL
☎0116 271 5086 🖷0116 271 4288
E: home.lei@mha.org uk
Web: www.mha.org.uk
Home Manager: Mrs Sarah Haines. Admin staff 1, Other staff n/a. **CC** No.1083995. Began 1963; Methodist but open to all. Methodist Homes for the Aged. Turnover n/a.

Alexandra House, Marine Parade, Dovercourt, Harwich CO12 3JY
☎01255 503 340 🖷01255 554 693
E: home.dov@mha.org.uk
Web: www.mha.org.uk
Home Manager: Yvonne Hawkins. Admin staff 1, Other staff n/a. **CC** No.1083995. Began 1962; Methodist but open to all. Methodist Homes for the Aged. Turnover n/a.

***Alexandra House (Keychange Charity)**, 12 Clifton Road, Wimbledon, London SW19 4QT
☎020 8946 7147 🖷020 8879 1110
E: info@keychange.org.uk
Web: www.keychange.org.uk
Manager: Ms Elizabeth Dhlinayo. Executive staff 1, Other staff n/a. **CC** No.1061344. Began n/a; interdenominational. Turnover n/a.

Allesley Hall, Allesley Hall Drive, Allesley, Coventry CV5 9AD
☎024 7667 9977 🖷024 7671 7030
E: home.alh@mha.org.uk
Web: www.mha.org.uk
Home Manager: George Sampson. Admin staff 1, Other staff n/a. **CC** No.1083995. Began 2005; Methodist but open to all. Methodist Homes for the Aged. Turnover n/a.

Alver Bank Eventide Home, West Road, Clapham, London SW4 7DL
☎020 7627 8061 🖷020 7720 2150
For men and women.
Officer-in-Charge: Centre Manager. Admin staff 3, Other staff 14. **CC** Began 1959; Salvation Army. Turnover n/a.
Sheltered Housing: 1 Alver Bank, West Road, Clapham, London SW4 7DH
☎No telephone
Independent Housing: 2 Mayfield Close, West Road, Clapham, London SW4 7DH
☎No telephone
Liaison Officer: Brigadier Clifford Honeyball

***Ashley Lodge Home**, 253 Great Western Road, Aberdeen AB10 6PP
☎01224 585 558
Acting Unit Manager: Margaret Leadbetter. Executive staff 1, Other staff 35. **CC** No.SCO 24366. Began 1959; Church of Scotland. Turnover n/a.

***Auchinlee Home**, Campbeltown PA28 6EN
☎01586 552 568
Unit Manager: Miss Jill Slater. Admin staff 2, Other staff 17. **CC** No.SCO 24366. Began 1952; Church of Scotland. Turnover n/a.

Auchlochan Trust, Auchlochan House, New Trows Road, Lesmahagow, Lanark ML11 0GS
☎01555 893 592 🖷01555 894 919
🖃: mailbox@auchlochan.com
Web: www.auchlochantrust.com
Retirement village; range of care available.
Manager: Mr Andrew Brown. *Administrator:* Mr James Reid. *Admissions Manager:* Mrs Marie Dorricott. Admin staff 6, Other staff 200. ***CC*** No.SCO 11644. Began 1974; interdenominational. Turnover £6,000,000 to year end Dec 04.

Aughton Park Care Home, Aughton Park Road, Aughton, Ormskirk L39 5QE
☎01695 576 996 🖷01695 570 170
🖃: home.aug@mha.org.uk
Web: www.mha.org.uk
Also for people with dementia.
Home Manager: Michelle Morris. Admin staff 1, Other staff n/a. ***CC*** No.1083995. Began 2003; Methodist but open to all. Methodist Homes for the Aged. Turnover n/a.

Ayr Baptist Homes, Airlie House, 5 Victoria Park, Ayr KA7 2TR
☎01292 262 744 🖷01292 289 283
Also respite care.
Care Manager: Sharon Hendry. Executive staff 1, Other staff 50. ***CC*** No.SCO 111556. Began 1988; Baptist. Turnover n/a.

***Balmedie House**, Balmedie, Aberdeen AB33 8XU
☎01358 742 244
Unit Manager: Margaret McEwan. Other staff 22. ***CC*** No.SCO 24366. Began 1937; Church of Scotland. Turnover n/a.

***Bellfield Home**, 1 Dee Street, Banchory AB31 3XS
☎01330 822 692
Unit Manager: Kirsten Gill. Admin staff 1, Other staff 19. ***CC*** No.SCO 24366. Began 1971; Church of Scotland. Turnover n/a.

***Belmont Castle Home**, Meigle, Blairgowrie PH12 8TH
☎01828 640 244
Unit Manager: Dorothy Gautier. Admin staff 1, Other staff 28. ***CC*** No.SCO 24366. Began 1931; Church of Scotland. Turnover n/a.

Berwick Grange, 5 Otley Road, Harrogate HG2 0DJ
☎01423 566 196 🖷01423 536 790
🖃: home.har@mha.org.uk
Web: www.mha.org.uk
Home Manager: Mandy Scott. Admin staff 1, Other staff 28. ***CC*** No.1083995. Began 1946; Methodist but open to all. Methodist Homes for the Aged. Turnover n/a.

Bethany Christian Home, 2 Woodside, Lipson, Plymouth PL4 8QK
☎01752 220 692 🖷01752 220 692
🖃: bethanyhomepl4@btopenworld.com
Long and short-term care.
General Manager: Mr Graham Todd. Admin staff 2, Other staff 28. ***CC*** No.263727. Began 1972; non-denominational. Turnover £2[illegible]0,000 to year end Mar 05.

Bethany House, Gamull Lane, Ribbleton, Preston PR2 6TQ
☎01772 792 226 🖷01772 792 226
🖃: bethanyhouse2000@yahoo.co.uk
Manager: Gill Whitfield. *Chairman of Trustees:* Mr Andrew Wright. Admin staff 2, Other staff 30. ***CC*** No.511[illegible]5. Began 1987; non-denominational. Turnover £247,000 to year end Mar 05.

Bethel House, Cross Common Road, Dinas Powis CF64 4YB
☎029 2051 3162
Manager: Mrs Betty Iveson. Admin staff [illegible], Other staff 30. ***CC*** No.51418[illegible]. Began 1983; interdenominational. Hebron Hall Ltd. Turnover n/a.

Bible Fellowship Eventide Trust, Gainsborough House, 48 Gainsborough, Milborne Port, Sherborne DT9 5BB
☎01963 250 684
Housekeeper: Corrinne Vaughan. Admin staff 1, Other staff n/a. ***CC*** No.27373[illegible]. Began 1978; evangelical. Turnover n/a
Correspondence to: *Editor:* Mr Haines, 5 Simmonds Road, Hucclecote, Gloucester GL3 3WY
☎No telephone

For bed-spaces etc. see list on Page 6

A

Bradbury Eventide Home, 2 Roots Hall Drive, Southend-on-Sea SS2 6DA
☎01702 435 838
For men and women; disabled places.
Officer-in-Charge: Centre Manager. Admin staff 3. **CC** Began n/a; Salvation Army. Turnover n/a.

Briar Hill House, 51 Atlee Crescent, Rugeley WS15 1BP
☎01889 576 622 🖷01889 574 611
E: home.bhh@mha.org.uk
Web: www.mha.org.uk
Providing nursing care.
Home Manager: Pauline Kincaid. Admin staff 1, Other staff n/a. **CC** No.1083995. Began 2005; Methodist but open to all. Methodist Homes for the Aged. Turnover n/a.

Brighton and Lady Anne Treves Memorial Pilgrim Homes, 35 Egremont Place, Brighton BN2 2GB
☎01273 605 940 🖷01273 692 640
E: brighton@pilgrimhomes.org.uk
Web: www.pilgrimhomes.org.uk
Manager: Anne Gower. Admin staff 1, Other staff 24. **CC** No.242266. Began 1879; non-denominational. Turnover n/a.

Brockworth House, Mill Lane, Brockworh, Gloucester GL3 4QG
☎01452 864 066 🖷01452 863 366
E: home.brc@mha.org.uk
Web: www.mha.org.uk
Home Manager: Debbie Phillips. Admin staff 1, Other staff n/a. **CC** No.1083995. Began 2000; Methodist but open to all. Methodist Homes for the Aged. Turnover n/a.

†**Bromley and Sheppard's Colleges**, Chaplain's House, Bromley College, London Road, Bromley BR1 1PE
☎020 8464 3558 🖷020 8464 3558
E: admin@bromleycollege.org
Web: www.bromleycollege.org
Providing unfurnished flats for widow(er)s of Anglican clergy and retired Anglican clergy and their spouses.
Chaplain & Clerk to the Trustees: Rev George Baisley. Admin staff 2, Other staff 4. **CC** No.210337. Began 1666; Anglican. Turnover £166,060 to year end Dec 02.

***Budhmor Home**, Portree IV51 9DJ
☎01478 612 012
Unit Manager: Ms Ann Souter. Admin staff 1, Other staff 17. **CC** No.SCO 24366. Began 1954; Church of Scotland. Turnover n/a.

Burrell Mead, 47 Beckenham Road, West Wickham BR4 0QS
☎020 8776 0455 🖷020 8776 0858
Head of Home: Mrs June Parke. *Chairman:* Mr Alan Bowen. *Administrator:* Mr Paul Kendrick. Admin staff 2, Other staff 30. **CC** No.16397. Began 1964; Baptist. Turnover n/a.

Eva Burrows Social Services Centre, Clyde Place, Halfway, Cambuslang, Glasgow G72 7QT
☎0141 646 1461 🖷0141 646 1463
Officer-in-Charge: Centre Manager. Executive staff 1, Other staff 50. Began 2000; Salvation Army. Turnover n/a.

***Cameron House**, Culduthel, Inverness IV2 4YG
☎01463 243 241
For confused people and those with dementia.
Unit Manager: Kathleen McGeough. Admin staff 2, Other staff 26. **CC** No.SCO 24366. Began 1987; Church of Scotland. Turnover n/a.

Cedar Lawn, Cedar Close, Welcombe Road, Stratford-upon-Avon CV37 6UP
☎01789 205 882 🖷01789 292 752
E: home.str@mha.org.uk
Web: www.mha.org.uk
Home Manager: Pat Dean. Admin staff 1, Other staff n/a. **CC** No.1083995. Began 1975; Methodist but open to all. Methodist Homes for the Aged. Turnover n/a.

The Cedars Christian Residential Home, 22 Redlake Road, Pedmore, Stourbridge DY9 0SA
☎01562 882 299 🖷01562 882 299
Proprietor: Mrs Carole Jenkins. Admin staff 2, Other staff 24. Began 1983; interdenominational. Turnover n/a.

Charnwood House, 77a Beake Avenue, Radford, Coventry CV6 3AQ
☎024 7660 1404 🖷024 7659 6683
E: home.cov@mha.org.uk
Web: www.mha.org.uk
For people with dementia.
Home Manager: Dawn Hancox. Admin staff 1, Other staff n/a. **CC** No.1083995. Began 2004; Methodist but open to all. Methodist Homes for the Aged. Turnover n/a.

Charterhouse Residential Home, Second Drive, Dawlish Road, Teignmouth TQ14 8TL
☎01626 774 481 🖷01626 774 481
Also for mentally handicapped and infirm people. Proprietors: Mr & Mrs S Brett. Admin staff 1, Other staff 14. Began 1988; interdenominational. Turnover £250,000 to year end Jan 00.

***Clashfarquhar House**, Robert Street, Stonehaven AB3 2DJ
☎01569 762 438
Unit Manager: Ms Susan Hayward. Admin staff 5, Other staff 21. **CC** No.SCO 24366. Began 1970; Church of Scotland. Turnover n/a.

Claybourne, Turnhurst Road, Chell, Stoke-on-Trent ST6 6LA
☎01782 790 500 🖷01782 832 642
E: home.tun@mha.org.uk
Web: www.mha.org.uk
For people with dementia.
Home Manager: Zoe McCallum. Admin staff 1, Other staff 52. **CC** No.1083995. Began 1997; Methodist but open to all. Methodist Homes for the Aged. Turnover n/a.

Cliff Dene, 11 Marine Parade, Tankerton, Whitstable CT5 2BQ
☎01227 273 209 🖷01227 265 699
E: home.tan@mha.org.uk
Web: www.mha.org.uk
Home Manager: Richard Bass. Admin staff 1, Other staff n/a. **CC** No.1083995. Began 1946; Methodist but open to all. Methodist Homes for the Aged. Turnover n/a.

***Clyde View Home**, 12 East Montrose Street, Helensburgh G84 7HP
☎01436 674 529
Unit Manager: Claire Young. Admin staff 2, Other staff 21. **CC** No.SCO 24366. Began 1953; Church of Scotland. Turnover n/a.

Coed Craig, Tan y Bryn Road, Rhos-on-Sea, Colwyn Bay LL28 4AD
☎01492 544 075 🖷01492 543 353
E: home.col@mha.org.uk
Web: www.mha.org.uk
Also for people with dementia.
Home Manager: Mrs Nicola Caselton. Other staff n/a. **CC** No.1083995. Began 1994; Methodist but open to all. Methodist Homes for the Aged. Turnover n/a.

Connell Court, 22 Weld Road, Southport PR8 2DL
☎01704 560 651 🖷01704 551 983
E: home.sou@mha.org.uk
Web: www.mha.org.uk
Home Manager: Anne Glover. Admin staff 1, Other staff n/a. **CC** No.1083995. Began 1976; Methodist but open to all. Methodist Homes for the Aged. Turnover n/a.

Cromwell House, Cecil Road, Norwich NR1 2QJ
☎01603 625 961 🖷01603 660 581
E: home.nor@mha.org.uk
Web: www.mha.org.uk
Home Manager: Liz Pitcher. Admin staff 1, Other staff n/a. **CC** No.1083995. Began 1969; Methodist but open to all. Methodist Home for the Aged. Turnover n/a.

***Cumnor Hall Home**, 18 Racecourse View, Ayr KA7 2TY
☎01292 266 450
Unit Manager: Mr Wilson Meredith. Other staff 32. **CC** No.SCO 24366. Began 1957; Church of Scotland. Turnover n/a.

Davidson House Eventide Home, 266 Colinton Road, Edinburgh EH14 1DT
☎0131 441 2117
For men and women.
Officer-in-Charge: Centre Manager. Admin staff 4. **CC** Began n/a; Salvation Army. Turnover n/a.

The Dell Care Home, 45 Cotmer Road, Oulton Broad, Lowestoft NR33 9PL
☎01502 572 591 🖷01502 572 591
Manager: Mrs Jean Spoor. *Deputy Manager:* Mrs D Bestard. Admin staff 1, Other staff 32. Began 1955; Seventh-day Adventist. (Previously The Dell). Turnover n/a.

For bed-spaces etc. see list on Page 61

A

Dewdown House, 64 Beach Road, Weston-super-Mare BS23 4BE
☎01934 417 125
Officer-in-Charge: Centre Manager. Admin staff 1, Other staff n/a. ***CC*** Began 1959; Salvation Army. Turnover n/a.

†**The Dorothea Trust**, 32 Park Avenue, Bedford MK40 2LR
☎01234 359 103 🖷01234 342 116
Manager: To be appointed. Admin staff 1, Other staff 20. ***CC*** Began 1968; interdenominational. Turnover n/a.

Dovers, 9 Doversgreen Road, Reigate RH2 8BU
☎01737 225 737
Home Manager: Mrs Kerry Newton. Admin staff 2, Other staff 42. ***CC*** No.207493. Began 1948; non-denominational. Supported by the Field Lane Foundation. Turnover n/a.

The Mildred Duff Memorial Eventide Home, 73 Happisburgh Road, North Walsham NR28 9HD
☎01692 403 292 🖷01692 404 778
For men and women. Officer-in-Charge: Centre Manager. Executive staff 4. ***CC*** Began n/a; Salvation Army. Turnover n/a.

Eagle Lodge Eventide Home, 488 Ferry Road, Edinburgh EH5 2DL
☎0131 551 1611 🖷0131 552 5673
For men and women.
Officer-in-Charge: Centre Manager. Admin staff 4. ***CC*** Began n/a; Salvation Army. Turnover n/a.

***Eastwoodhill Home**, 238 Fenwick Road, Giffnock, Glasgow G46 6UU
☎0141 638 5127
Unit Manager: Anne Maclean. Admin staff 1, Other staff 21. ***CC*** No.SCO 24366. Began 1948; Church of Scotland. Turnover n/a.

Eckling Grange Ltd, Norwich Road, Dereham NR20 3BB
☎01362 692 520 🖷01362 690 278
E: eckling.grange5@btopenworld.com
Web: www.eclinggrange.org.uk
Also sheltered accommodation.
General Manager: Mr Peter Baldwin. *Care Manager:* Irene Launchbury. Admin staff 6, Other staff 80. ***CC*** No.251534. Began 1960; interdenominational. Turnover £1,000,000 to year end Mar 05.

***The Elms Home**, 148 Whitehouse Loan, Edinburgh EH9 2EZ
☎0131 447 4924
Unit Manager: Mrs Elizabeth Waddell. Admin staff 1, Other staff 24. ***CC*** No.SCO 24366. Began 1946; Church of Scotland. Turnover n/a.

Elmside, Elmside Walk, Hitchin SG5 1HB
☎01462 451 737 🖷01462 454 298
E: home.hit@mha.org.uk
Web: www.mha.org.uk
Home Manager: Mrs Lynn Carter. Admin staff 1, Other staff n/a. ***CC*** No.1083995. Began 1966; Methodist but open to all. Methodist Homes for the Aged. Turnover n/a.

Emmaus House, 115 Valley Drive, Harrogate HG2 0JS
☎01423 565 932 🖷01423 565 964
Matron/Manager: Mrs Christine Hornby. Admin staff 1, Other staff n/a. ***CC*** No.519535. Began 1987; evangelical. Turnover n/a.

Engelberg, Ash Hill, Compton, Wolverhampton WV3 9DR
☎01902 420 613 🖷01902 713 587
E: home.wol@mha.org.uk
Web: www.mha.org.uk
Home Manager: Mrs Angela Jevons. Admin staff 1, Other staff n/a. ***CC*** No.1083995. Began 1966; Methodist but open to all. Methodist Homes for the Aged. Turnover n/a.

Eothen Homes Ltd, Newcastle, 45 Elmfield Road, Gosforth, Newcastle upon Tyne NE3 4BB
☎0191 213 0707 🖷0191 213 0075
E: enquiries@eothenhomes.org.uk
Web: www.eothenhomes.org.uk
Manager: Name not supplied. Admin staff 1, Other staff 25. ***CC*** Began 1950; interdenominational. Turnover n/a.

Eothen Homes Ltd, Sutton, 31 Worcester Road, Sutton SM2 6PT
☎020 8642 2830 🖷020 8643 7961
E: eothenhomes@btopenworld.com
Web: www.eothenhomes.org.uk
Manager: Name not supplied. Admin staff 1, Other staff 25. ***CC*** No.223262. Began 1950; interdenominational. Turnover n/a.

Eothen Homes Ltd, Whitley Bay, Park Gardens, Whitley Bay NE26 2TX
☎0191 297 0707 🖷0191 251 0526
E: enquiries@eothenhomes.org.uk
Web: www.eothenhomes.org.uk
Manager: Name not supplied. Other staff 25. ***CC*** No.223262. Began 1950; interdenominational. Turnover n/a.

Epworth Grange, 1 Chirmside Street, Bury BL8 2BX
☎0161 763 7500 🖷0161 763 6630
E: home.bry@mha.org.uk
Web: www.mha.org.uk
Home Manager: Lesley Payne. Admin staff 1, Other staff n/a. ***CC*** No.1083995. Began 1990; Methodist but open to all. Methodist Homes for the Aged. Turnover n/a.

Evington Home Pilgrim Homes, Grocot Road, Evington, Leicester LE5 6AL
☎0116 273 8131
E: evington@pilgrimhomes.org.uk
Web: www.pilgrimhomes.org.uk
Manager: Jenny Leach. Admin staff 1, Other staff 21. ***CC*** No.242266. Began 1954; non-denominational. Turnover n/a.

***Fair Havens (Keychange Charity)**, 468 Winchester Road, Bassett, Southampton SO16 7DD
☎023 8079 0874 🖷023 8077 74[illegible]8
E: info@keychange.org.uk
Web: www.keychange.org.uk
Also nursing care.
Manager: Mrs Christine Newman. Executive staff 1, Other staff n/a. ***CC*** No.1061344. Began 1921; interdenominational. Turnover n/a.

Finborough Court Pilgrim Homes, Pilgrims' Way, Finborough, Stowmarket IP14 3AX
☎01449 676 336 🖷01449 672 4[illegible]8
E: finborough@pilgrimhomes.org.uk
Web: www.pilgrimhomes.org.uk
Manager: Lynne Durrant. Admin staff 1, Other staff 24. ***CC*** No.242266. Began 1982; non-denominational. Turnover n/a.

Fitzwarren House, Kingsdown Road, Swindon SN3 4TD
☎01793 836 920 🖷01793 836 921
E: home.swn@mha.org.uk
Web: www.mha.org.uk
Providing nursing care and care for people with dementia.
Home Manager: Wendy Champion. Admin staff 1, Other staff n/a. ***CC*** No.1083995. Began n/a; Methodist but open to all. Methodist Homes for the Aged.

Florabank Home Ltd, 18 Florabank Road, Haddington EH41 3LR
☎01620 823 259 🖷01620 823 066
Manager: Mr W Smith Flett. *Director:* Mr John Sinclair. Admin staff 3, Other staff 18. ***CC*** No.SCO 25515. Began 1984; interdenominational. Turnover £350,000 to year end Dec 02.

Foxton Grange Nursing Home, 571 Gipsy Lane, Leicester LE5 0TA
☎0116 246 0616 🖷0116 276 6598
E: home.fxg@mha.org.uk
Web: www.mha.org.uk
Providing nursing care and care for people with dementia.
Home Manager: Alison Plummer. Admin staff 1, Other staff n/a. ***CC*** No.1083995. Began 2005; Methodist but open to all. Methodist Homes for the Aged. Turnover n/a.

Framland Pilgrim Homes, Haldertown, Wantage OX12 9DL
☎01235 769 876 🖷01235 [illegible]62 09[illegible]
E: wantage@pilgrimhomes.org.uk
Web: www.pilgrimhomes.org.uk
Manager: Barbara Margetts. Admin staff 1, Other staff n/a. ***CC*** No.242266. Began 1986; non-denominational. Turnover n/a.

Fulwood Park, 19 Fulwood Park, Aigburth, Liverpool L17 5AD
☎0151 727 3840 🖷0151 72[illegible] 098[illegible]
E: home.liv@mha.org.uk
Web: www.mha.org.uk
Home Manager: Ester Markey. Admin staff 1, Other staff n/a. ***CC*** No.1083995. Began 1948; Methodist but open to all. Methodist Homes for the Aged. Turnover n/a.

For bed-spaces etc. see list on Page [illegible]1

A

Glebe Court Eventide Home, 2 Blackheath Rise, Lewisham, London SE13 7PN
☎020 8297 0637 🖷020 8852 7298
For men and women.
Officer-in-Charge: Centre Manager. Admin staff 3, Other staff n/a. ***CC*** Began n/a; Salvation Army. Turnover n/a.

Glen Rosa, 24 Grove Road, Ilkley LS29 9PH
☎01943 609 604 🖷01943 817 363
E: home.ilk@mha.org.uk
Web: www.mha.org.uk
Also for people with dementia
Home Manager: Sue Sullivan. Admin staff 1, Other staff n/a. ***CC*** No.1083995. Began 1947; Methodist but open to all. Methodist Homes for the Aged. Turnover n/a.

Granary House, 74 Canterbury Road, Whitstable CT5 4HE
☎01227 273 923
E: home.whi@mha.org.uk
Web: www.mha.org.uk
Home Manager: Terri Gill. Admin staff 1, Other staff n/a. ***CC*** No.1083995. Began 2005; Methodist but open to all. Methodist Homes for the Aged. Turnover n/a.

***Walter and Joan Gray Home**, Main Street, Scalloway, Shetland ZE1 0XJ
☎01595 880 691
Unit Manager: Ms Margaret Sandison. Other staff 13. ***CC*** No.SCO 24366. Began 1968; Church of Scotland. Turnover n/a.

Greenways, 227 Hawthorn Road, Bognor Regis PO21 2UW
☎01243 823 732 🖷01243 826 309
E: home.bog@mha.org.uk
Web: www.mha.org.uk
Home Manager: Mavis Stevens. Admin staff 1, Other staff 25. ***CC*** No.1083995. Began 1948; Methodist but open to all. Methodist Homes for the Aged. Turnover n/a.

Hall Grange, Shirley Church Road, Shirley, Croydon CR9 5AL
☎020 8654 1708 🖷020 8654 4982
E: home.shi@mha.org.uk
Web: www.mha.org.uk
Home Manager: Mrs Marion Evans. Admin staff 1, Other staff n/a. ***CC*** No.1083995. Began 1948; Methodist but open to all. Methodist Homes for the Aged. Turnover n/a.

Handsworth, West Road, Bowdon, Altrincham WA14 2LA
☎0161 928 5314 🖷0161 929 9048
E: home.bow@mha.org.uk
Web: www.mha.org.uk
Home Manager: Mark Greenhalgh. Admin staff 1, Other staff n/a. ***CC*** No.1083995. Began 1971; Methodist but open to all. Methodist Homes for the Aged. Turnover n/a.

Hartcliffe, 15 Murford Avenue, Hartcliffe, Bristol BS13 9JS
☎0117 964 1000 🖷0117 964 1100
E: home.hcl@mha.org.uk
Web: www.mha.org.uk
Home Manager: Ruth Andrews. Admin staff 1, Other staff n/a. ***CC*** No.1083995. Began 2000; Methodist but open to all. Methodist Homes for the Aged. Turnover n/a.

Harwood Court, Highburn, Cramlington NE23 6AZ
☎01670 712 492 🖷01670 735 626
E: home.cra@mha.org.uk
Web: www.mha.org.uk
Home Manager: Judith Moffat. Admin staff 1, Other staff n/a. ***CC*** No.1083995. Began 1969; Methodist but open to all. Methodist Homes for the Aged. Turnover n/a.

The Hawthorns Eventide Home, Burlington Road, Buxton SK17 9AR
☎01298 237 00 🖷01298 736 24
Officer-in-Charge: Centre Manager. Admin staff 3. ***CC*** Began n/a; Salvation Army. Turnover n/a.

Herondale, 175 Yardley Green Road, Birmingham B9 5PU
☎0121 753 1653 🖷0121 771 4188
E: home.her@mha.org.uk
Web: www.mha.org.uk
For people with dementia. Home Manager: Louise Jarvis. Admin staff 1, Other staff n/a. ***CC*** No.1083995. Began 2005; Methodist but open to all. Methodist Homes for the Aged. Turnover n/a.

Holt House Eventide Home, Headlands Drive, Hilton Lane, Prestwich, Manchester M25 9YF
☎0161 773 0220 🖷0161 798 6428
Men and women.
Officer-in-Charge: Centre Manager. Admin staff 3. ***CC*** Began n/a; Salvation Army. Turnover n/a.

Homewood, 19 Kenilworth Road, Leamington Spa CV32 5TR
☎01926 423 519 🖷01926 421 758
E: home.lea@mha.org.uk
Web: www.mha.org.uk
Home Manager: Wendy Cook. Other staff n/a. ***CC*** No.1083995. Began 1951; Methodist but open to all. Methodist Homes for the Aged. Turnover n/a.

Hornsey Rise Memorial Home Pilgrim Homes, Wellsborough, Nuneaton CV13 6PA
☎01455 290 219 🖷01455 292 867
E: wellsborough@pilgrimhomes.org.uk
Web: www.pilgrimhomes.org.uk
Managers: Philip & Sally Willis. Admin staff 1, Other staff 30. ***CC*** No.242266. Began 1974; non-denominational. Turnover n/a.

***Invereck Home**, Sandbank, Dunoon PA23 8QS
☎01369 706 231
Unit Manager: Sandra Marshall. Admin staff 1, Other staff 19. ***CC*** No.SCO 24366. Began 1947; Church of Scotland. Turnover n/a.

***Keep Hill Residential Home**, 17 Keep Hill Drive, High Wycombe HP1[illegible] 1DU
☎01494 528 627 M: 07[illegible]48 12[illegible] 002
E: keep-hill@fish.co.uk
For frail elderly people.
Manager: Mr Grahame Robinson. *Assistant Manager:* Mrs Robinson. Executive staff 2, Other staff 8. Began 198[illegible]; non-denominational. (Previously Keep Hill Rest Home). Turnover £15[illegible],00[illegible] to year end Dec 04.

Sir Samuel Kelly Memorial Eventide Home, 39 Bangor Road, Holywood BT18 0NE
☎028 9042 2293 🖷028 9042 7[illegible]61
For men and women.
Officer-in-Charge: Centre Manager. Admin staff 3. ***CC*** Began n/a; Salvation Army. Turnover n/a.

Kingfisher House, 171 Yardley Green Road, Birmingham B9 5PU
☎0121 753 0333 🖷0121 771 4[illegible]90
E: home.kgf@mha.org.uk
Web: www.mha.org.uk
Home Manager: Akin A[illegible]inpe[illegible]u. Admin staff 1, Other staff n/a. ***CC*** No.1083995. Began 2005; Methodist but open to all. Methodist Homes for the Aged. Turnover n/a.

Kingswood Park, Kingswood Road, March PE15 9RT
☎01354 652 381 🖷01354 660 [illegible]04
E: home.mar@mha.org.uk
Web: www.mha.org.uk
Also for people with dementia.
Home Manager: Sumiyo Berkeley. Admin staff 1, Other staff n/a. ***CC*** No.1083995. Began 2005; Methodist but open to all. Methodist homes for the Aged. Turnover n/a.

Koinonia (Sussex) Ltd, 4 Winchester Road, Worthing BN11 4DJ
☎01903 237 764
E: office@koinonia4.fsnet.co.uk
Web: www.koinonia4.fsnet.co.uk
Also do Residential Care.
Registered Manager: Mr John Ro[illegible]ston. Admin staff 2, Other staff 2[illegible]. ***CC*** Began 1977; FIEC. Turnover n/a.

Langholme, Arwenack Avenue, Falmouth TR11 3JP
☎01326 314 512 🖷01326 317 5[illegible]7
E: home.fal@mha.org.uk
Web: www.mha.org.uk
Home Manager: Mrs Susan [illegible]ings. Admin staff 1, Other staff n/a. ***CC*** No.1083995. Began 1969; Methodist but open to all. Methodist Homes for the Aged. Turnover n/a.

Leonora Home Pilgrim Homes, Wood Lane, Chippenham SN15 3D[illegible]
☎01249 651 613 🖷01249 460 0[illegible]7
E: chippenham@pilgrimhomes.org.uk
Web: www.pilgrimhomes.org.uk
Manager: Gaie Marshall. Admin staff 1, Other staff 14. ***CC*** No.242266. Began 1974; non-denominational. Turnover n/a.

For bed-spaces etc. see list on Page 61

The Ernest Luff Homes Ltd, 2 Luff Way, Garden Road, Walton on the Naze CO14 8SW
☎01255 679 212
🖷01255 674 414
Manager: Mr Derek Carpenter. Admin staff 1, Other staff 55. **CC** No.1045920. Began 1950; interdenominational. Turnover n/a.

Maidment Court, 47 Parkstone Road, Poole BH15 2NX
☎01202 674 423
🖷01202 676 410
E: home.poo@mha.org.uk
Web: www.mha.org.uk
Home Manager: Jackie Nelson. Admin staff 1, Other staff n/a. **CC** No.1083995. Began 1972; Methodist but open to all. Methodist Homes for the Aged. Turnover n/a.

Maple Leaf House, Kirk Close, Ripley DE5 3RY
☎01773 513 361
🖷01773 513 501
E: home.rpl@mha.org.uk
Web: www.mha.org.uk
Providing nursing care and care for people with dementia.
Home Manager: Michelle Whitmill. Admin staff 1, Other staff n/a. **CC** No.1083995. Began 2004; Methodist but open to all. Methodist Homes for the Aged. Turnover n/a.

The Martins, Vinefields, Bury St Edmunds IP33 1YA
☎01284 753 467
🖷01284 725 807
E: home.bur@mha.org.uk
Web: www.mha.org.uk
For people with dementia.
Home Manager: Mrs Wendy Tomlinson. Admin staff 1, Other staff n/a. **CC** No.1083995. Began 1962; Methodist but open to all. Methodist Homes for the Aged. Turnover n/a.

Mayfields, Naylor Crescent, Netherpool Road, Overpool, Ellesmere Port CH66 1TP
☎0151 356 4913
🖷0151 356 4915
E: home.ove@mha.org.uk
Web: www.mha.org.uk
For people with dementia.
Home Manager: Josephine Bell. Admin staff 1, Other staff n/a. **CC** No.1083995. Began 1997; Methodist but open to all. Methodist Homes for the Aged. Turnover n/a.

The Meadow, Meadow Drive, Muswell Hill, London N10 1PL
☎020 8883 2842
🖷020 8442 1394
E: home.mus@mha.org.uk
Web: www.mha.org.uk
Also for people with dementia.
Home Manager: Jeffrey Carnell. Admin staff 1, Other staff n/a. **CC** No.1083995. Began 1965; Methodist but open to all. Methodist Homes for the Aged. Turnover n/a.

Milward House Pilgrim Homes, 6 Madeira Park, Tunbridge Wells TN2 5SZ
☎01892 528 115 🖷01892 518 802
E: milward@pilgrimhomes.org.uk
Web: www.pilgrimhomes.org.uk
Manager: Ruth Meltz. Admin staff 1, Other staff 28. **CC** No.242265. Began 1972; non-denominational. Turnover n/a.

Moorland House, Station Road, Hathersage, Hope Valley S32 1DD
☎01433 650 582 🖷01433 650 795
E: home.hat@mha.org.uk
Web: www.mha.org.uk
Home Manager: Florence Doku. Admin staff 1, Other staff n/a. **CC** No.1083995. Began 1949; Methodist but open to all. Methodist Homes for the Aged. Turnover n/a.

Morel Court, Raisdale Road, Penarth CF64 5BN
☎029 2070 4811 🖷029 2070 0987
E: home.pen@mha.org.uk
Web: www.mha.org.uk
Home Manager: Mrs Sheila Bradbury. Admin staff 1, Other staff n/a. **CC** No.1083995. Began 1975; Methodist but open to all. Methodist Homes for the Aged. Turnover n/a.

Moreton, 13 Drakes Avenue, Exmouth EX8 4AA
☎01395 272 897 🖷01395 223 716
E: home.exm@mha.org.uk
Web: www.mha.org.uk
Home Manager: Tracey Nendic. Admin staff 1, Other staff n/a. **CC** No.1083995. Began 1953; Methodist but open to all. Methodist Homes for the Aged. Turnover n/a.

***Morlich House**, West Pavilion B, 11 Church Hill, Edinburgh EH10 4BG
☎0131 447 3239 🖷0131 447 2512
Unit Manager: Mr Glen Brady. Admin staff 1, Other staff 20. **CC** No.SCO 24366. Began 1970; Church of Scotland. Turnover n/a.

The Mount Eventide Home (Keychange Charity), 7 Lipson Terrace, Lipson, Plymouth PL4 7PR
☎01752 665 222 🖷01752 672 777
Manager: Mrs Margaret Barrett. Admin staff 1, Other staff 23. **CC** No.1061344. Began n/a; interdenominational. Turnover n/a.

***The Müller Homes for the Elderly**, 7 Cotham Park, Bristol BS6 6DA
☎0117 924 5001 🖷0117 924 4855
E: admin@mullers.org
Web: www.mullers.org
Chief Executive: Mr J P Marsh. Executive staff 1, Other staff 20. **CC** No.1066831. Began 1983; interdenominational. Part of the George Müller Foundation. Magazine: *Report on the work* (4,000 annually). Turnover £426,000 to year end Feb 05.

Nazareth House, Bonnyrigg, 13 Hillhead, Bonnyrigg EH19 2JF
☎0131 663 7191 🖷0131 663 0979
Manager: Mrs Pat McCann. Admin staff 1, Other staff 30. **CC** Began 1931; Roman Catholic. Turnover n/a.

Newfield House Nursing Home, Kingfield Road, Coventry CV1 4DW
☎024 7625 1800 🖷024 7625 1694
E: home.nfd@mha.org.uk
Web: www.mha.org.uk
Home Manager: Linda Carvell. Admin staff 1, Other staff n/a. **CC** No.1083995. Began 2005; Methodist but open to all. Methodist Homes for the Aged. Turnover n/a.

Norwood, 14 Park Road, Ipswich IP1 3ST
☎01473 257 502 🖷01473 216 697
E: home.ips@mha.org.uk
Web: www.mha.org.uk
Home Manager: Nikki Cantwell. Admin staff 1, Other staff n/a. **CC** No.1083995. Began 1979; Methodist but open to all. Methodist Homes for the Aged. Turnover n/a.

Notintone House Eventide Home, Sneinton Road, Nottingham NG2 4QG
☎0115 950 3788 🖷0115 959 8604
For men and women.
Officer-in-Charge: Centre Manager. Admin staff 3. **CC** Began n/a; Salvation Army. Turnover n/a.

Nyton House, Nyton Road, Westergate, Chichester PO20 3UL
☎01243 543 228 🖷01243 543 039
E: daviscarehomes.nyton@virgin.net
Proprietors: Mr & Mrs P & Mary Davis. Admin staff 3, Other staff 60. Began 1983; Christian Brethren. Turnover £950,000 to year end Apr 01.

Orchard House, 191 High Street, Sawston, Cambridge CB2 4HJ
☎01223 712 050 🖷01223 712 052
E: home.saw@mha.org.uk
Web: www.mha.org.uk
Also for people with dementia.
Home Manager: Alison Baggaley. Admin staff 1, Other staff n/a. **CC** No.1083995. Began 2001; Methodist but open to all. Methodist Homes for the Aged. Turnover n/a.

†Orleans Residential Home for Elderly Christians, 8 Lathom Road, Southport PR9 0JA
☎01704 530 440 🖷01704 549 995
E: petercleach@lineone.net
Owner-Manager: Mr P C Leach. Admin staff 1, Other staff 23. Began 1988; non-denominational. Turnover n/a.

Overdale Retirement Home, 29 Kenwood Park Road, Sheffield S7 1NE
☎0114 255 0257 🖷0114 255 0257
For frail elderly people.
Manager: Mrs Ruth Brown. Admin staff 2, Other staff 33. **CC** No.700301. Began n/a; interdenominational. Turnover n/a.

For bed-spaces etc. see list on Page 61

***Oversteps Home**, Earls Cross Road, Dornoch IV25 3PJ
☎01862 810 393
Acting Manager: Eileen Mackay. Admin staff 2, Other staff 13. ***CC*** No.SCO 24366. Began 1958; Church of Scotland. Turnover n/a.

Priceholme, Givendale Road, Scarborough YO12 6LE
☎01723 361 022 🖷01723 500 159
E: home.sca@mha.org.uk
Web: www.mha.org.uk
Home Manager: Mrs Elizabeth Dawson. Admin staff 1, Other staff n/a. ***CC*** No.1083995. Began 1963; Methodist but open to all. Methodist Homes for the Aged. Turnover n/a.

The Priory, South Street, Tarring, Worthing BN14 7NH
☎01903 237 027 🖷01903 204 253
E: priory@fieldlane.org.uk
Home Manager: Mrs Allena Edwards. Admin staff 1, Other staff 41. ***CC*** No.207493. Began 1951; non-denominational. Supported by the Field Lane Foundation. Turnover n/a.

***Queen's Bay Lodge**, 49 Milton Road East, Edinburgh EH15 2NN
☎0131 669 2828
Unit Manager: Morag Waring. Admin staff 1, Other staff 30. ***CC*** No.SCO 24366. Began 1962; Church of Scotland. Turnover n/a.

Queens Court, 2 Downing Close, Bottisham, Cambridge CB5 9DD
☎01223 811 905 🖷01223 812 517
E: home.bot@mha.org.uk
Web: www.mha.org.uk
For people with dementia.
Home Manager: Roz Wright. Admin staff 1, Other staff n/a. ***CC*** No.1083995. Began 2001; Methodist but open to all. Methodist Homes for the Aged. Turnover n/a.

Queenswood, Cliffgrove Avenue, Beeston, Nottingham NG9 4DP
☎0115 922 1037 🖷0115 943 6245
E: home.not@mha.org.uk
Web: www.mha.org.uk
Home Manager: Elizabeth Grognet. Admin staff 1, Other staff n/a. ***CC*** No.1083995. Began 1975; Methodist but open to all. Methodist Homes for the Aged. Turnover n/a.

Richmond / Heatherbank, Collington Lane East, Bexhill-on-Sea TN39 3RJ
☎01424 217 688 🖷01424 210 424
E: home.bex@mha.org.uk
Web: www.mha.org.uk
Also for people with dementia.
Home Manager: Debra Macklin. Admin staff 1, Other staff n/a. ***CC*** No.1083995. Began 1970; Methodist but open to all. (Previously Richmond). Methodist Homes for the Aged. Turnover n/a.

Rock House (Gold Hill Housing Association Ltd), Austenwood Lane, Chalfont St Peter, Gerrards Cross SL9 9DF
☎01753 882 194 🖷01753 893 395
Web: www.rockhouse.org.uk
Chief Executive: Dr Mike Nicholls. *Chairman:* Rev Keith King. *Care Manager:* Mrs Sue Shadloo. Admin staff 3, Other staff 100. ***CC*** No.XN 17205. Began 1966; Baptist. Associated with Gold Hill Baptist Church. Turnover £800,000 to year end Dec 02.

Rookstone Eventide Home, Lawrie Park Crescent, Sydenham, London SE26 6HH
☎020 8778 0317 🖷020 8778 5822
For men and women.
Officer-in-Charge: Centre Manager. Admin staff 3. ***CC*** Began n/a; Salvation Army. Turnover n/a.

Rose Lawn Retirement Home (Keychange Charity), All Saints Road, Sidmouth EX10 8EX
☎01395 513 876 🖷01395 579 519
E: info@keychange.org.uk
Web: www.keychange.org.uk
Manager: Mrs Margaret Haxton. Admin staff 1, Other staff 16. ***CC*** No.1061344. Began n/a; interdenominational. Turnover n/a.

***Rosset Holt Retirement Home (Keychange Charity)**, Pembury Road, Tunbridge Wells TN2 3RB
☎01892 526 077 🖷01892 526 077
E: info@keychange.org.uk
Web: www.keychange.org.uk
Manager: Mrs Marilyn Luck. Admin staff 2, Other staff 20. ***CC*** No.1061344. Began n/a; interdenominational. Turnover n/a.

***Rubislaw Park**, Rubislaw Park Road, Aberdeen AB1 8DA
☎01224 310 641
Closed 2004. Re-opening 2006. Unit Manager: To be appointed. Admin staff 1, Other staff n/a. ***CC*** No.SCO 24366. Began n/a; Church of Scotland. Turnover n/a.

Rushden Park, Melloway Road, Rushden NN10 6RP
☎01933 418 777 🖷01933 418 666
E: home.rus@mha.org.uk
Web: www.mha.org.uk
Providing nursing care.
Home Manager: Paul Draper. Admin staff 1, Other staff n/a. ***CC*** No.1083995. Began 2001; Methodist but open to all. Methodist Homes for the Aged. Turnover n/a.

Ryelands, 15 Beddington Gardens, Wallington SM6 0JF
☎020 8647 6837 🖷020 8647 8542
E: home.wal@mha.org.uk
Web: www.mha.org.uk
Also for people with dementia.
Home Manager: Sandra Roche. Admin staff 1, Other staff n/a. ***CC*** No.1083995. Began 1945; Methodist but open to all. Methodist Homes for the Aged. Turnover n/a.

St Angela's Residential Care Home, 5 Litfield Place, Clifton, Bristol BS8 [illegible]U
☎0117 973 5436 🖷0117 970 6[illegible]44
E: marielou39@btinternet.com
Matron: Sister Marie-Louise Levern. Admin staff 2, Other staff 2[illegible]. ***CC*** No.229049. Began 1920; Roman Catholic. Turnover n/a.

St Anne's Rest Home, Grange Lane, Burghwallis, Doncaster DN6 9JL
☎01302 700 319 🖷01302 708 [illegible]52
For ladies and gentlemen.
Manager: Gale Methorpe. *Assistant Manager:* Karen Oat. Admin staff [illegible], No other full-time staff. ***CC*** Began 1986; Roman Catholic. Turnover £220,000 to year end Dec 98.

St John's Home, St Mary's Road, Oxford OX4 1QE
☎01865 247 725 🖷01865 247 [illegible]20
E: admin@st-johns-home.org
Head of Home: Miss Mollie Burns. Admin staff 5, Other staff 39. ***CC*** Began 1874; Anglican. Turnover n/a.

St Katharine's House, Ormond Road, Wantage OX12 8EA
☎01235 762 739 🖷01235 772 [illegible]05
E: warden.stkatharines@talk21.com
Web: www.stkatharineshouse.co.uk
For ladies. Lay administration but under auspices of an Anglican religious Community.
Warden: Mr Tresham Gregg CBE. *Care Manager:* Mrs Doris Butler. *Community Sister:* Sr Jean Frances CSMV. Admin staff 9, Other staff 90. ***CC*** No.240513. Began 1848; Anglican. Turnover £1,800,000 to year end Mar 05.

***St Margaret's**, St Margaret's Crescent, Polmont, Falkirk FK2 0UP
☎01324 716 149 🖷0132[illegible] 711 [illegible]41
For people with senile dementia.
Unit Manager: Miss Elspeth McPheat. Admin staff 2, Other staff 2[illegible]. ***CC*** No. SCO 24366. Began 1987; Church of Scotland. Turnover n/a.

St Mary's Convent Residential Home, Ebchester, Consett DH8 0[illegible]
☎01207 560 288 🖷0120[illegible] 561 4[illegible]8
E: stmarysconvent@tiscali.co.uk
Manager: Sister Theresa Mary. *Assistant Manager:* Patricia Birkett. Admin staff 14, Other staff 9. ***CC*** No.23[illegible]440. Began 1934; Roman Catholic. Turnover n/a.

St Theresa's Home, 12 Lansdowne Road, London SW20 8AN
☎020 8879 7366 🖷020 8879 1[illegible]0
E: patriciakeller@btinternet.com
Matron: Mrs Goodsell. Admin staff 2, Other staff 35. ***CC*** Began [illegible]988; Roman Catholic, Congregation of the Sisters of St Anne. Turnover n/a.

For bed-spaces etc. see list on Page 61

St Vincent's Nursing Home, 79 Fore Street, Plympton St Maurice, Plymouth PL7 1NE
☎01752 336 205 🖷01752 336 206
E: stvincent@virgin.net
Respite and long term care.
Administrator: Sisters of Charity. Admin staff 2, Other staff 40. **CC** No.215027. Began 1944; Anglican. Turnover n/a.

Shottermill House Pilgrim Homes, Liphook Road, Haslemere GU27 1NX
☎01428 661 034 🖷01428 645 233
E: haslemere@pilgrimhomes.org.uk
Web: www.pilgrimhomes.org.uk
Manager: Diane Eldrett. Admin staff 1, Other staff 21. **CC** No.242266. Began 1990; non-denominational. Turnover n/a.

Smallcombe House Eventide Home, Oakwood Gardens, Bathwick Hill, Bath BA2 6EJ
☎01225 465 694 🖷01225 465 769
For men and women; also respite care.
Officer-in-Charge: Centre Manager. Admin staff 4. **CC** Began n/a; Salvation Army. Turnover n/a.

***South Beach House Home**, 7 South Crescent Road, Ardrossan KA22 8DU
☎01294 463 234
Acting Manager: Margaret Cassidy. Admin staff 1, Other staff 25. **CC** No.SCO 24366. Began 1959 Church of Scotland. Turnover n/a.

South London Mission, Cluny Place, London SE1 4QU
☎020 7407 2014 🖷020 7407 3885
Warden: Deacon Mark Attwood. Admin staff 1, Other staff 2. Began 1968; Methodist. Turnover n/a.

Starr Hills, 18 Ansdell Road South, Ansdell, Lytham St Annes FY8 5PQ
☎01253 735 037 🖷01253 732 466
E: home.lyt@mha.org.uk
Web: www.mha.org.uk
Home Manager: Annette Williams. Admin staff 1, Other staff n/a. **CC** No.1083995. Began 1948; Methodist but open to all. Methodist Homes for the Aged. Turnover n/a.

Stones Place Skellingthorpe Road, Lincoln LN6 0PA
☎01522 684 325 🖷01522 697 625
E: home.lin@mha.org.uk
Web: www.mha.org.uk
Home Manager: Carole Kus. Admin staff 1, Other staff n/a. **CC** No.1083995. Began 1972; Methodist but open to all. Methodist Homes for the Aged. Turnover n/a.

Stratton House, 16 Park Lane, Bath BA1 2XH
☎01225 421 196 🖷01225 443 432
E: home.bat@mha.org.uk
Web: www.mha.org.uk
Home Manager: Mrs Carol Britton. Admin staff 1, Other staff n/a. **CC** No.1083995. Began 1950; Methodist but open to all. Methodist Homes for the Aged. Turnover n/a.

Sunset Lodge, Pembury Road, Tunbridge Wells TN2 3QT
☎01892 530 861 🖷01892 533 769
For men and women.
Officer-in-Charge: Centre Manager. Admin staff 3. **CC** Began n/a; Salvation Army. Turnover n/a.

Terry's Cross House, Brighton Road, Woodmancote, Henfield BN5 9SX
☎01273 492 821
Retirement home for clergy, lay works, missionaries and their widows or dependants.
Warden: Miss Gillian Wheatley. Other staff 4. **CC** No.1011373. Began n/a; Anglican. Turnover £110,000 to year end Dec 04.

***Tollcross Mansionhouse**, 601 Tollcross Road, Glasgow G32 8TF
☎0141 778 5406
Unit Manager: Dorothy Millar. Admin staff 1, Other staff 19. **CC** No.SCO 24366. Began 1993; Church of Scotland. Turnover n/a.

Trembaths, Talbot Way, Norton, Letchworth SG6 1UA
☎01462 481 694 🖷01462 485 606
E: home.let@mha.org.uk
Web: www.mha.org.uk
Also nursing care and care for people with dementia
Home Manager: Mr Alan Dickinson. Admin staff 1, Other staff n/a. **CC** No.1083995. Began 1989; Methodist but open to all. Methodist Homes for the Aged. Turnover n/a.

Ty Gwyn, 221 Stanwell Road, Penarth CF64 2EZ
☎029 2070 3600 🖷029 2070 7250
E: home.tyg@mha.org.uk
Web: www.mha.org.uk
Providing nursing care.
Home Manager: Kath Burgoyne. Admin staff 1, Other staff n/a. **CC** No.1083995. Began 2003; Methodist but open to all. Methodist Homes for the Aged. Turnover n/a.

***Upton House (Keychange Charity)**, 2 St Margaret's Road, Cromer NR27 9DG
☎01263 512 172 🖷01263 512 693
E: uptonhouse2@aol.com
Web: www.keychange.org.uk
Manager: Miss Princess Williams. Executive staff 1, Other staff 16. **CC** No.1061344. Began n/a; interdenominational. Turnover n/a.

Villa Adastra Eventide Home, 79 Keymer Road, Hassocks BN6 8QH
☎01273 842 184 🖷01273 845 299
For men and women.
Officer-in-Charge: Centre Manager. Admin staff 3. **CC** Began n/a; Salvation Army. Turnover n/a.

Walmer House Retirement Home (Keychange Charity), 6 Ash Hill Road, Torquay TQ1 3HZ
☎01803 292 734 🖷01803 292 734
E: info@keychange.org.uk
Web: www.keychange.org.uk
Manager: Mrs Ena Bell. Admin staff 1, Other staff 15. **CC** No.1061344. Began n/a; interdenominational. Turnover n/a.

Waterside House, 41 Moathouse Lane West, Wolverhampton WV11 3HA
☎01902 727 766
E: home.wlv@mha.org.uk
Web: www.mha.org.uk
For people with dementia.
Home Manager: Susan Bishop. Admin staff 1, Other staff n/a. **CC** No.1083995. Began 2005; Methodist but open to all. Methodist Homes for the Aged. Turnover n/a.

Westbury, Westbury Lane, Newport Pagnell MK16 6QW
☎01908 210 885 🖷01908 218 428
E: home.pag@mha.org.uk
Web: www.mha.org.uk
Also for people with dementia.
Home Manager: To be appointed. Admin staff 1, Other staff n/a. **CC** No.1083995. Began 1989; Methodist but open to all. Methodist Homes for the Aged. Turnover n/a.

Westerley, Grange over Sands, The Esplanade, Grange-over-Sands LA11 7HH
☎01539 532 408
E: grange@lpma.co.uk
Manager: Mrs E Lynne Davey. Executive staff 1, Other staff 24. **CC** Began 1951; Methodist but open to all. The Leaders of Worship and Preachers Homes. Turnover n/a.

Westerley, Minehead, King Edward Road, Minehead TA24 5JB
☎01643 702 066
E: minehead@lpma.co.uk
Manager: Mr Vaughan C Ogden. Executive staff 1, Other staff 19. **CC** Began 1957; Methodist but open to all. The Leaders of Worship and Preachers Homes. Turnover n/a.

Westerley, Westcliff on Sea, 1 Winton Avenue, Westcliff-on-Sea SS0 7QU
☎01702 349 209
E: westcliff@lpma.co.uk
Manager: Mr Simon Lee. Executive staff 1, Other staff 20. **CC** Began 1949; Methodist but open to all. The Leaders of Worship and Preachers Homes. Turnover n/a.

Westerley, Woodhall Spa, The Broadway, Woodhall Spa LN10 6SQ
☎01526 352 231
E: woodhall@lpma.co.uk
Manager: Mr Ian Brown. Executive staff 1, Other staff 24. **CC** Began 1955; Methodist but now open to all. The Leaders of Worship and Preachers Homes. Turnover n/a.

For bed-spaces etc. see list on Page 61

A

Westhampnett Private Nursing Home, Westhampnett House, Westhampnett Road, Chichester PO18 0NT
☎01243 782 986
Proprietors: Mr & Mrs P & Mary Davis. Admin staff 3, Other staff 60. Began 1978; Christian Brethren. Turnover £600,000 to year end Apr 00.

Weston / Queensway, Weston Road, Stafford ST16 3TF
☎01785 228 324 🖷01785 220 815
E: home.weq@mha.org.uk
Web: www.mha.org.uk
Providing nursing care and care for people with dementia.
Home Manager: Jan Coulston. Admin staff 1, Other staff n/a. ***CC*** No.1083995. Began 2005; Methodist but open to all. Methodist Homes for the Aged. Turnover n/a.

***Whinnieknowe Home**, Mill Road, Nairn IV12 5EN
☎01667 452 387
Unit Manager: Pat Thackeray. Admin staff 2, Other staff 20. ***CC*** No.SCO 24366. Began 1946; Church of Scotland. Turnover n/a.

Willersley House, 85 Main Street, Willerby, Hull HU10 6BY
☎01482 653 353 🖷01482 659 668
E: home.hul@mha.org.uk
Web: www.mha.org.uk
Home Manager: Gill Bottomley. Admin staff 1, Other staff n/a. ***CC*** No.1083995. Began 1963; Methodist but open to all. Methodist Homes for the Aged. Turnover n/a.

***Williamwood House**, Strathtay Avenue, Netherlee, Glasgow G44 3YA
☎0141 637 1168
For people with senile dementia.
Unit Manager: Mr Neil Watson. Admin staff 1, Other staff 22. ***CC*** No.SCO 24366. Began 1983; Church of Scotland. Turnover n/a.

Wirral Christian Centre Trust, Residential Home, Woodchurch Road, Birkenhead CH41 2UE
☎0151 653 8307 🖷0151 653 4600
E: wcc@wccuk.org
Web: www.wccuk.org
Also day nursery. Manager: Mrs Evelyn Epton. Admin staff 1, Other staff 25. ***CC*** No.700269. Began 1983; Elim Pentecostal. Turnover n/a.

Woodbank, Holly Bank Road, Hook Heath, Woking GU22 0JP
☎01483 773 684 🖷01483 730 6[illegible]8
E: home.wok@mha.org.uk
Web: www.mha.org.uk
Home Manager: Melanie R[illegible]esch. Admin staff 1, Other staff n/a. ***CC*** No.1083995. Began 1952; Methodist but open to all. Methodist Homes for the Aged. Turnover n/a.

Youell Court Social Services Centre, Skipworth Road, Binley, Coventry CV3 2XA
☎024 7656 1300
Officer-in-Charge: Centre Manager. Admin staff 1, Other staff 42. Began 2000; Salvation Army. Turnover n/a.

RETREAT HOUSES

By Country and Postcode – for location of Postcodes see map on Page 458
Retreat houses which did not supply this information are not listed here
Only retreat houses with 10 or more bedspaces are included

S = single rooms **D/T** = number of bed spaces in double/twin rooms **L** = number of bed spaces in rooms larger than double
TS = total bed spaces (not number of rooms) **DR** = Day Room, the capacity of the largest room suitable for group use
⇌ = nearest Railway station ⊖ = nearest London Underground station

Postcode	Location	Name	S	D/T	L	Other		TS	DR	Railway/Underground
ENGLAND										
AL 2	**St Albans**	All Saints Pastoral Centre	72	48	-			120	120	⇌ Radlett
		SPEC Centre	-	40	20	for young people		60	70	⇌ Radlett or St Albans
B 61	**Bromsgrove**	Community for Reconciliation	4	16	18			38	60	⇌ Longbridge or Bromsgrove
BA 3	**Bath**	The Ammerdown Centre	16	22	38	self-catering flat	1	77	80	⇌ Bath Spa
		Bainesbury House	1	-	16			17	n/a	⇌ Bath Spa
BA 6	**Glastonbury**	The Abbey House	18	18	-			36	50	⇌ Castle Cary or Bristol Temple Meads
BA12	**Warminster**	Ivy House, St Denys Retreat Centre	16	12	-			28	25	⇌ Warminster
BB 7	**Clitheroe**	Whalley Abbey	10	18	6		34		100	⇌ Whalley
BH13	**Poole**	Green Pastures Christian Centre	10	10	-			20	50	⇌ Branksome
BH24	**Ringwood**	Crow Hill Day Retreat Centre	-	-	-	non-residential		-	30	⇌ Bournemouth
BN 6	**Hassocks**	Priory of Our Lady	18	14	4			36	40	⇌ Hassocks
BR 4	**West Wickham**	Emmaus Retreat and Conference Centre	9	64	-	3 flats	5	78	80	⇌ Hayes or Bromley South or East Croydon
CB 1	**Cambridge**	Mill Green House	-	4	-			4	30	⇌ Audley End or Cambridge
CB 7	**Ely**	Bishop Woodford House	32	4	-			36	60	⇌ Ely
CB 8	**Newmarket**	Sisters of St Louis	4	8	-			12	n/a	⇌ Newmarket
CH 1	**Chester**	Chester Retreat House	23	2	-			25	30	⇌ Chester
CH48	**Wirral**	Sisters of Jesus Way Retreat House	8	6	-			14	20	⇌ West Kirby
CM 3	**Chelmsford**	Diocesan House of Retreat	22	2	-	self-catering gatehouse	5	29	30	⇌ Chelmsford
CT 8	**Westgate-on-Sea**	St Christopher's Retreat & Respite Centre	1	4	-	2 or 3 bed flats	27	32	30	⇌ Westgate-on-Sea
CT12	**Ramsgate**	Minster Abbey Retreat/Guesthouse	8	4	4			16	40	⇌ Minster
CV33	**Leamington Spa**	Offa House	17	12	-	cottage	5	34	60	⇌ Leamington Spa
CW 2	**Crewe**	Wistaston Hall Oblate Retreat Centre	2	36	6			44	150	⇌ Crewe
DE 7	**Ilkeston**	Morley Retreat and Conference House	24	10	-			34	40	⇌ Derby
DH 8	**Consett**	Minsteracres Retreat Centre	18	58	2	other	21	99	n/a	⇌ Riding Mill
DN4	**Doncaster**	Doncaster Canaan Trust	4	8	-			12	20	⇌ Doncaster
DT 2	**Dorchester**	Chantmarle Christian Resource Centre	17	190	-	self-catering cottages	15	222	170	⇌ Maiden Newton
		Hilfield Friary	13	2	-			15	50	⇌ Sherborne
GL 4	**Gloucester**	Prinknash Abbey	5	-	-			5	n/a	⇌ Cheltenham or Stroud or Gloucester
GL10	**Stonehouse**	Marist Centre	10	18	-			28	n/a	⇌ Gloucester
GU22	**Woking**	St Columba's House	22	10	-	liturgical spaces	2	32	50	⇌ Woking
GU34	**Alton**	Alton Abbey	10	12	-			22	25	⇌ Alton
GU35	**Bordon**	Acorn Christian Healing Foundation	n/a	n/a	n/a			30	60	⇌ Liphook

Postcode	Location	Name	S	D/T	L	Other		TS	DR	Railway/Underground
L 15	**Liverpool**	Cenacle Retreat and Conference Centre	-	-	-	non-residential		-	30	⇌ Liverpool Lime Street
L 35	**Prescot**	Loyola Hall – Jesuit Spirituality Centre	43	2	-			45	100	⇌ Rainhill
LA 5	**Carnforth**	Monastery of Our Lady of Hyning	5	30	-			35	35	⇌ Carnforth
LE 7	**Leicester**	Launde Abbey	15	42	-			57	50	⇌ Oakham
LE67	**Coalville**	Mount St Bernard Abbey	20	-	-			20	n/a	⇌ Loughborough
LN 2	**Lincoln**	Edward King House	5	22	3			30	80	⇌ Lincoln Central
LS29	**Ilkley**	Myddelton Grange	29	20	-			49	70	⇌ Ilkley
ME20		The Friars Aylesford	20	68	12			100	100	⇌ Aylesford or Maidstone East
NE44	**Riding Mill**	Shepherds Dene	7	28	-			35	40	⇌ Riding Mill
NN 4	**Northampton**	Bouverie Court	-	-	-	non-residential		-	50	⇌ Northampton
NN 7	**Northampton**	Crossways Project	3	8	30			41	70	⇌ Northampton
NR35	**Bungay**	All Hallows House	3	6	-			9	n/a	⇌ Norwich or Beccles or Diss
		Holy Cross House	11	-	-			11	n/a	⇌ Norwich or Beccles or Diss
		Quiet Waters Christian Retreat House	1	34	-			35	30	⇌ Halesworth
		St Gabriel's Centre	46	48	16			110	110	⇌ Norwich or Beccles or Diss
		St Mary's Lodge	6	6	-			12	n/a	⇌ Norwich or Beccles or Diss
		St Michael's Centre	18	2	-			20	35	⇌ Norwich or Beccles or Diss
OX12	**Wantage**	St Mary's Convent	16	-	-			16	12	⇌ Didcot Parkway or Oxford
OX18	**Oxford**	Burford Priory	5	6	-			11	15	⇌ Charlbury or Oxford
OX33	**Oxford**	Stanton House	4	12	-			16	20	⇌ Oxford
PE28	**Huntingdon**	Houghton Chapel Centre	-	2	28	self-catering		30	50	⇌ Huntingdon
		St Francis' House	17	6	-			23	18	⇌ Huntingdon
PO33	**Ryde**	Quarr Abbey	9	-	-			9	n/a	⇌ Ryde Esplanade
RG 7	**Reading**	Douai Abbey	15	12	-	self-catering cottage	9	36	50	⇌ Reading
RG 9	**Henley-on-Thames**	Congregation of Marian Fathers	13	66	25			104	250	⇌ Henley-on-Thames
RG14	**Newbury**	Elmore Abbey	4	-	-			4	n/a	⇌ Newbury
RG17	**Hungerford**	St Cassian's Centre	5	58	-	cottage	1	64	50	⇌ Kintbury
RH 1	**Redhill**	Wychcroft	11	22	3			36	40	⇌ Redhill
RH10	**Crawley**	The Monastery of the Holy Trinity	6	-	-			6	n/a	⇌ Three Bridges
SK10	**Macclesfield**	Savio House	12	40	40			92	64	⇌ Macclesfield
SK23	**High Peak**	Whaley Hall	3	26	3			32	n/a	⇌ Whaley Bridge
SO31	**Southampton**	Cenacle Retreat House	6	-	-			6	n/a	⇌ Netley
SO51	**Romsey**	Hebron Christian Retreat	2	8	6			16	25	⇌ Romsey or Winchester
ST15	**Stone**	Shallowford House	15	22	3			40	40	⇌ Stafford or Norton Bridge
SY 4	**Shrewsbury**	Hawkstone Hall	60	6	-			66	90	⇌ Wem
SY14	**Malpas**	St Joseph's Retreat and Conference Centre	36	16	-			52	50	⇌ Chester or Whitchurch (Salop)
TA13	**South Petherton**	The Community of St Francis	14	4	-	self-catering cottage	5	23	40	⇌ Crewkerne
TN15	**Sevenoaks**	Society of Retreat Conductors	20	-	-			20	20	⇌ Swanley
TN33	**Penhurst**	Penhurst Retreat Centre	-	10	4			14	-	⇌ Battle
TQ11	**Buckfastleigh**	Buckfast Abbey	4	8	-			12	50	⇌ Newton Abbot or Totnes
TW10	**Richmond**	St Michael's Convent	13	4	-			17	30	⇌ Richmond ⊖ Richmond
WR 6	**Worcester**	Glasshampton	6	-	-			6	n/a	⇌ Worcester: Foregate Street or Shrub Hill
WR10	**Pershore**	Holland House	18	6	-			24	50	⇌ Evesham
YO21	**Whitby**	St Oswald's Pastoral Centre	10	6	-			16	16	⇌ Sleights
YO62	**York**	Ampleforth Abbey	n/a	n/a	n/a			120	55	⇌ York or Malton or Thirsk
London										
E 2	**London**	Society of St Margaret	6	2	-			8	25	⇌ Liverpool Street ⊖ Liverpool Street
N 14	**London**	Benedictine Centre for Spirituality	8	10	-			18	75	⊖ Oakwood
SE 4	**London**	The Fountain Gate Community	1	2	-	mainly non-residential		3	n/a	⇌ Greenwich
SW15	**London**	Kairos Centre	7	4	12			23	100	⊖ Putney Bridge
SW19	**London**	Marie Reparatrice Retreat Centre	30	2	-			32	n/a	⇌ Wimbledon ⊖ Wimbledon
NORTHERN IRELAND										
BT34	**Newry**	Our Lady of Apostles Retreat House	43	50	-			93	60	*Rail:* Newry *Bus:* Rostrevor
BT48	**Londonderry**	Iona Carmelite Retreat Centre	28	32	-			60	250	*Rail:* Londonderry
SCOTLAND										
AB56	**Buckie**	Letterfourie Retreats	-	-	-	3 self-contained flats	24	24	n/a	⇌ Keith
G 3	**Glasgow**	Ignatian Spirituality Centre	-	-	-	non-residential		-	40	⇌ Glasgow Central or Glasgow Queen Street
IV30	**Elgin**	Pluscarden Abbey	24	8	-			32	50	⇌ Elgin
PA33	**Dalmally**	Craig Lodge	n/a	n/a	n/a	for young people		30	n/a	⇌ Dalmally
PA76	**Isle of Iona**	Iona Community, Macleod Centre, Abbey	n/a	n/a	n/a			93	140	⇌ Oban (via 2 ferries)
PH 2	**Perth**	Institute of Spirituality	20	46	-			66	60	⇌ Perth
TD 9	**Hawick**	Whitchester Christian Guest House and Retreat	1	14	9			24	n/a	⇌ Carlisle or Edinburgh
WALES										
LD 3	**Brecon**	Llangasty Retreat House	6	16	-			22	25	⇌ Abergavenny
		Mill-Leat Ministries	1	2	-	mainly non-residential		3	20	⇌ Abergavenny
LL17	**St Asaph**	St Beuno's	48	2	n/a			50	80	⇌ Rhyl
LL21	**Corwen**	Coleg Y Groes	-	10	5			15	20	⇌ Wrexham
LL30	**Llandudno**	Loreto Centre	31	12	-	self-catering	12	55	160	⇌ Llandudno
LL34	**Penmaenmawr**	Noddfa Spirituality Centre	23	10	-	self-catering cottage	7	40	40	⇌ Penmaenmawr
NP25	**Monmouth**	Tymawr Convent	9	6	-			15	20	⇌ Newport (Gwent) or Chepstow
SA 3	**Swansea**	Nicholaston House	1	18	10			29	100	⇌ Swansea
SA65	**Fishguard**	Ffald-y-Brenin Retreat Centre	5	4	12	flat, cottage	10	31	50	⇌ Fishguard Harbour
SA70	**Tenby**	Caldey Abbey	18	2	-			20	n/a	⇌ Tenby
SY22	**Meifod**	Canolfan Cristionogol Anenwadol Cymru	-	-	-	non-residential		-	50	⇌ Welshpool

RETREAT HOUSES

For Religious Orders see also Religious Orders (Anglican) on Page 188,
Religious Orders (Roman Catholic) on Page 190,
Mission Agencies on Page 282.

The Abbey House (Bath and Wells Diocesan Retreat & Conference Centre), Chilkwell Street, Glastonbury BA6 8DH
☎01458 831 112 🖷01458 831 893
E: warden@abbeyhouse.org
Web: www.abbeyhouse.org
For all who are on a spiritual journey.
Warden: Mr David Hill. Admin staff 2, Other staff 6. ***CC*** No.224866. Began 1931; Anglican but open to all. Turnover n/a.

***Acorn Christian Healing Foundation**, Whitehill Chase, High Street, Bordon GU35 0AP
☎01420 478 121 🖷01420 478 122
E: info@acornchristian.org
Web: www.acornchristian.org
For groups or individuals; retreats either led or self-run.
Director: Rev Dr Russ Parker. *Christian Listener Coordinator:* Rev Andrew Bradley. Executive staff 3, Other staff 16. ***CC*** No.1080011. Began 1983; interdenominational. Magazine: *Acorn News* (1,000 quarterly). Turnover £450,000 to year end Mar 05.

All Hallows House (All Hallows Community Retreat Houses), Belsey Bridge Road, Ditchingham, Bungay NR35 2DT
☎01986 892 840 🖷01986 895 838
Offering a programme of retreats throughout the year; church groups, fellowships, individuals; full board.
Contact: Guest Sister. Staff n/a. ***CC*** No.230143. Began 1855; Anglican. Turnover n/a.

All Saints Pastoral Centre, Shenley Lane, London Colney, St Albans AL2 1AF
☎01727 822 010 🖷01727 822 880
E: conf.office@allsaintspc.org.uk
Director: Mgr Vladimir Felzmann. *Administrator:* Mr Alan Johnstone. Executive staff 1, Other staff 15. ***CC*** No.233699. Began 1973; Roman Catholic. Turnover £600,000 to year end Dec 00.

Alton Abbey, Beech, Alton GU34 4AP
☎01420 562 145 🖷01420 561 691
Web: www.starcourse.org/abbey
Contact: Bursar. Executive staff 1, Community n/a. ***CC*** No.229216. Began 1884; Anglican. Turnover n/a.

The Ammerdown Centre, Radstock, Bath BA3 5SW
☎01761 433 709 🖷01761 433 094
E: centre@ammerdown.org
Web: www.ammerdown.org
Retreat, conference centre and holiday facilities; private quiet days.
Director: Mrs Bénédicte Scholefield. Executive staff 3, Other staff 25. ***CC*** No.1010244. Began 1973; non-denominational but open to all. Turnover n/a.

†Ampleforth Abbey, Hospitality and Pastoral Office, Ampleforth Abbey, York YO62 4EN
☎01439 766 889 🖷01439 766 755
E: pastoral@ampleforth.org.uk
Web: www.ampleforth-hpo.org.uk
Accommodation in 6 centres.
Administrator: Jan Fitzalan Howard. Admin staff 1, Other staff n/a. ***CC*** No.1026493. Began n/a; Roman Catholic. Turnover n/a.

Bainesbury House, Downside Abbey, Stratton on the Fosse, Bath BA3 4RH
☎01761 235 114 🖷01761 235 124
Self-catering.
Warden: Rev Alexander George. Admin staff 1, Community n/a. ***CC*** No.232548. Began 1795; Roman Catholic, Benedictine. Turnover n/a.

Benedictine Centre for Spirituality, 29 Bramley Road, Oakwood, London N14 4HE
☎020 8449 2499
E: retreats@bcsuk.wanadoo.co.uk
Web: www.church-of-christ-the-king.com
Day, residential and personal retreats.
Administrator/Secretary: Name not supplied. Admin staff 2, Community 10. ***CC*** No.265126. Began 1995; Roman Catholic but open to all. Turnover n/a.

Bishop Woodford House (Ely Diocesan Retreat and Conference Centre), Barton Road, Ely CB7 4DX
☎01353 663 039 🖷01353 665 305
E: bpwoodford@e-l-y.freeserve.co.uk
Warden: Mrs Mary Streater. Admin staff 1, Other staff 3. ***CC*** No.311448. Began 1973; Anglican but open to all. Turnover £160,000 to year end Dec 02.

Bouverie Court (Peterborough Diocesan Conference Training & Resource Centre), The Lakes, Bedford Road, Northampton NN4 7YD
☎01604 887 000 🖷01604 887 077
E: bouverie@peterborough-diocese.org.uk
Web: www.peterborough-diocese.org.uk
Centre Manager: Mrs Elaine Syme. Executive staff 8, Admin staff 2. Began 2000; Anglican. Bouverie Court replaced Ecton House, 2000. Turnover n/a.

Burford Priory, 30 Priory Lane, Burford OX18 4SQ
☎01993 823 605
E: bookings@burfordosb.org.uk
Web: www.burfordosb.org.uk
Trying to maintain balance of work and prayer while exercising a ministry of hospitality.
Abbot: Rt Rev Stuart Burns. Community 10. ***CC*** No.221617. Began 1941; Anglican, Benedictine. Turnover n/a.

Caldey Abbey, Caldey Island, Tenby SA70 7UH
☎01834 844 453 🖷01834 845 9[illegible]2
E: info@caldey-island.co.uk
Web: www.caldey-island.co.uk
Guestmaster: Father Senan. Community 15. ***CC*** Began 1929; Roman Catholic. Turnover n/a.

Canolfan Cristionogol Anenwadol Cymru, Hen Gapel John Hughes, Pont Robert, Meifod SY22 6JA
☎01938 500 631
Ecumenical centre of Christian renewal and unity for Wales.
Guide: Nia Rhosier. No full-time staff. ***CC*** No.1001418. Began 1993; ecumenical. Turnover n/a.

Canonesses of the Holy Sepulchre, 48 Priory Street, Colchester CO1 2QB
E: priorynewhall1@aol.com
Web: www.newhall.org.uk
Retreat house closed. Temporary accommodation 2006
Prioress: Sister Teresa Len[illegible]an. Members 19, Other staff 2. ***CC*** No.229288. Began 1794. Founded in Belgium in 1642. Turnover n/a.
Also at: 23 Westdown Road, London E15 2BZ
☎020 8558 1464 🖷 020 8[illegible]57 12[illegible]2

†Cenacle Retreat and Conference Centre, Lance Lane, Wavertree, Liverpool L15 6TW
☎0151 722 2271
Day retreats for groups of 25 to 30 persons.
Warden: The Retreat Secretary. Community n/a. ***CC*** Began n/a; Roman Catholic but open to all. Turnover n/a.

Cenacle Retreat House, 48 Victoria Road, Netley Abbey, Southampton SO31 5DQ
☎023 8045 3718 🖷023 8045 371[illegible]
E: cenacle.netley@ntlworld.com
Web: www.cenaclesisters.co.uk
Retreat Secretary: Cenacle Sisters. Community 3. ***CC*** No 232[illegible]28. Began n/a; Roman Catholic. Turnover n/a.

Chantmarle Christian Resource Centre, Chantmarle Manor, Frome St Quintin, Dorchester DT2 0HD
☎01935 483 201 🖷01935 [illegible]38 95[illegible]
E: resource.centre@chantmarle.co.uk
Web: www.chantmarle.co.uk
Facilities for seminars meetings and retreats.
Managing Director: Mr John Clare. Executive staff 1, Other staff [illegible]6. Began 2005; interdenominational. Turnover n/a.

For bed-spaces etc. see list on Page 72

Chester Retreat House, 11 Abbey Square, Chester CH1 2HU
☎01244 321 801
E: chester.retreat@tiscali.co.uk
Web: www.chesterretreathouse.org
Devoted to prayer and reflection; counselling service available.
Warden: Mrs Valerie E Fisher. Executive staff 1, Other staff 3. ***CC*** No.248705. Began 1925 Anglican but open to all. Turnover £68,000 to year end Dec 04.

Coleg y Groes, Corwen LL21 0DR
☎01490 412 169 🖷01490 412 169
E: colegygroes@btopenworld.com
Web: www.colegygroes.co.uk
Retreats private, guided, Ignatian exercises, quiet space, individuals or small groups, quiet days.
Wardens: Rev Heather Fenton, Rev Margaret Harvey. Admin staff 2, No other staff. Began 1985 Anglican. Turnover n/a.

The College, Millport (Argyll Diocesan Conference Centre), Millport, Isle of Cumbrae KA28 0HE
☎01475 530 353 🖷01475 530 204
E: tccumbrae@argyll.anglican.org
Web: www.island-retreats.org
Retreat house and conference centre for groups and individuals.
Warden: Name not supplied, Other staff n/a. ***CC*** No.SCO 23281. Began 1851; Scottish Episcopalian. Turnover n/a

Community for Reconciliation, Barnes Close, Malthouse Lane, Chadwich, Bromsgrove B61 0RA
☎01562 710 231 🖷01562 710 278
E: cfrenquiry@aol.com
Web: www.cfrbarnesclose.co.uk
Conference, retreat and training centre, evangelistic missions, peace-building; East Africa, Croatia, Romania; reconciliation UK.
Company Secretary: Rev John Johansen-Berg. *Community Coordinator:* Rev Ian Ring. Executive staff 2, Other staff 4, Community n/a. ***CC*** No.295113. Began 1984; ecumenical. Turnover £105,000 to year end Mar 03.

The Community of St Francis, Manor House, Compton Durville, South Petherton TA13 5ES
☎01460 240 473 🖷01460 242 360
E: comptondurvillecsf@franciscans.org.uk
Web: www.franciscans.org.uk
Franciscan religious community; prayer, day visitors, retreats.
Warden: The Guardian. Community 8. ***CC*** No.286615. Began 1905; Anglican. Turnover £48,000 to year end June 02.

Community of Aidan & Hilda, The Open Gate, Holy Island, Berwick-upon-Tweed TD15 2SD
☎01289 389 222
E: aidan@theopengate.ndo.co.uk
Web: www.aidan.org.uk
Cradling a Christian spirituality for today, inspired by the Celtic saints.
Guardian: Rev Ray Simpson. Executive staff 3. ***CC*** No.1055305. Began 1994; Anglican but open to all. Magazine: *The Aidan Way* (Circulation n/a quarterly). Turnover £500 to year end Dec 00.

Congregation of Marian Fathers, Fawley Court, Henley-on-Thames RG9 3AE
☎01491 574 917 M: 07775 685 629
🖷01491 411 587
E: marian-f@dircon.co.uk
Web: www.marians-uk.org
Offering pastoral retreats, functions, weddings, christenings; museum, historical house and gardens; student exchange schemes.
Father Superior: Rev W Jasinski. Community 16. ***CC*** No.251717. Began 1950; Roman Catholic. Turnover n/a.

Craig Lodge, Dalmally PA33 1AR
☎01838 200 216 🖷01838 200 622
E: mail@craiglodge.org
Web: www.craiglodge.org
Family house of prayer and reflection; special ministries to young and disavantaged people.
Co-ordinator: Miss Sarah Morgan. Other staff 2, Volunters 9. ***CC*** No.SCO 23203. Began 1995; Roman Catholic, but open to all. Turnover £100,000 to year end Dec 98.

Crossways, Castle Ashby Road, Yardley Hastings, Northampton NN7 1EL
☎01604 696 307 🖷01604 696 030
E: nyrc@surfaid.org
Venue for conferences, retreats, training, seminars, team meetings, youth groups, school residentials and awaydays.
Acting Manager: Rev Rachel Pullman. Executive staff 2, Other staff 5. Began 1992; United Reformed. (Previously Yardley Hastings Centre). Turnover £200,000 to year end Dec 02.

Crowe Hill Day Retreat Centre, Bradbury Cottage, Crow Hill, Ringwood BH24 3DQ
☎01425 470 310
E: crowehill@hotmail.com
Web: www.crowehill.com
Wardens: Mr & Mrs Brian & Claire Skelley. Executive staff 3, No other staff. Began 1983; Methodist. Turnover £3,200 to year end Aug 00.

Diocesan House of Retreat, The Street, Pleshey, Chelmsford CM3 1HA
☎01245 237 251 🖷01245 237 594
E: retreathouse.pleshey@virgin.net
Web: www.retreathousepleshey.com
Warden: Rev Sheila Coughtrey. Admin staff 3, Other staff 10. ***CC*** No.249505. Began 1919; Anglican. Turnover £102,000 to year end Dec 98.

Doncaster Canaan Trust, The Manor House, Old Hexthorpe, Doncaster DN4 0HY
☎01302 818 184
🖷01302 818 184
E: office@hexthorpemanor.sagehost.co.uk
Pastoral care; day and residential retreats, conference facilities, respite and convalescent care.
Warden: To be appointed. Executive staff 1, Other staff 5. ***CC*** No.515927. Began 1984; interdenominational. Turnover £20,000 to year end Dec 02. Part of Centre for Health and Pastoral Care.

Douai Abbey, Upper Woolhampton, Reading RG7 5TQ
☎0118 971 5333
🖷0118 971 5303
E: pastoral@douaiabbey.org.uk
Web: www.douaiabbey.org.uk
Offering liturgical worship, retreats, conferences; also bookshop.
Abbot: Rev Dr Geoffrey Scott. Executive staff 1, Community 20. ***CC*** No.236962. Began 1903; Roman Catholic. Magazine: *Douai Magazine* (3,500 annually). Turnover £85,000 to year end Aug 03.

Elmore Abbey, Church Lane, Speen, Newbury RG14 1SA
☎01635 330 80
For men.
Prior: Fr Kenneth Newing. Community 8. ***CC*** Began 1914; Anglican, Benedictine. Turnover n/a.

Emmaus Retreat and Conference Centre, Layhams Road, West Wickham BR4 9QJ
☎020 8777 2000 📠020 8776 2022
E: dmj@emmaus.fsbusiness.co.uk
Web: www.rc.net/southwark/emmaus
Offering quiet days, counselling; also conference facilities.
Director: Sr Paula Spark. Admin staff 4, Other staff 9. ***CC*** Began 1979; Roman Catholic but open to all. Turnover n/a.

***Ffald-y-Brenin Retreat Centre**, Gwaun Valley, Fishguard SA65 9UA
☎01348 881 382
E: fy.b@virgin.net
Web: www.ffald-y-brenin.co.uk
Home of the Caleb prayer initiative; day retreats, prayer days; English/Welsh.
Wardens: Mr & Mrs Roy Godwin. Admin staff 2, Other staff n/a. ***CC*** No.516594. Began 1985; interdenominational. Turnover n/a.

***The Fountain Gate Community**, 58 Geoffrey Road, Brockley, London SE4 1NT
☎020 8694 2220
E: info@fountaingate.co.uk
Committed to community, hospitality, stillness, celebration, helping families, storytelling, leading retreats and pilgrimages.
Leader: Mr David Pott. Executive staff 2. ***CC*** No.264078. Began 1996; non-denominational. Part of YWAM. Turnover n/a.

The Friars Aylesford, Aylesford ME20 7BX
☎01622 717 272 📠01622 715 575
E: friarsreception@hotmail.com
Web: www.thefriars.org.uk
Also pilgrimage centre
Management Team Leader: Steve Hayden. Staff 30. ***CC*** No.1068518. Began 1242; Roman Catholic but open to all. Turnover n/a.

Glasshampton, Shrawley, Worcester WR6 6TQ
☎01299 896 345 📠01299 896 083
E: glasshamptonssf@franciscans.org.uk
Also spiritual direction, prayer.
The Guardian: Name not supplied. Community 4. ***CC*** No.236464. Began n/a; Anglican. Turnover n/a.

Green Pastures Christian Centre of Pastoral Care and Healing, 17 Burton Road, Branksome Park, Poole BH13 6DT
☎01202 764 776
📠01202 768 144
E: admin@green-pastures.org
Web: www.green-pastures.org
Short-term residential therapeutic environment for personal growth, healing, fellowship, counselling, spiritual direction, creativity, hands-on therapies.
Pastoral Director: Revd Colin Norris. Executive staff 1, Other staff 14. ***CC*** No.1090568. Began 1955; interdenominational. Magazine: *Update* (3,000 quarterly). Turnover n/a.

Hawkstone Hall International Pastoral Centre (Redemptorists), Marchamley, Shrewsbury SY4 5LG
☎01630 685 242
📠01630 685 565
E: hawkhall@aol.com
Web: www.hawkstone-hall.com
Renewal courses for people in ministry; retreats, short courses; groups and private retreats.
Rector: Very Rev M P O'Mahony CSSR. *Director of Courses:* Rev Fr D McBride CSSR. *Secretary:* Mrs J Kerr. Executive and academic staff 8, Community 70, Other staff 18. ***CC*** No.252041. Began 1973; Roman Catholic. Turnover £650,000 to year end Apr 03.

Hebron Christian Retreat, Broadgate House, Hook Road, Ampfield, Romsey SO51 9BY
☎023 8025 2673
Web: www.hebron-trust.org.uk
For groups; holiday weeks, quiet days, residential programme.
Manager: Mrs Julie Reeves. Executive staff 1, Other staff n/a. ***CC*** No.1086661. Began 1999; interdenominational. Turnover n/a.

Hilfield Friary, Dorchester DT2 7BE
☎01300 341 345
📠01300 341 293
E: hilfieldssf@franciscans.org.uk
Web: www.orders.anglican.org/ssf/
Contact: Guest Brother. Community 55. ***CC*** No.236464. Began 1921; Anglican. Turnover n/a.

Holland House, Cropthorne, Pershore WR10 3NB
☎01386 860 330
📠01386 861 208
E: laycentre@hollandhouse.org
Web: www.hollandhouse.org
Providing a venue for residential and non-residential courses; retreat, conference, and laity centre.
Warden: Mr Peter Middlemiss. *Deputy Warden:* Mrs Liz Palin. Admin staff 2, Other staff 2. ***CC*** No.504839. Began 1945; interdenominational. Turnover £155,000 to year end Dec 97.

Holy Cross House (All Hallows Community Retreat Houses), Belsey Bridge Road, Ditchingham, Bungay NR35 2DT
☎01986 894 092 📠01986 895 838
Offering a programme of retreats; for church groups, fellowships, individuals; full-board.
Contact: Guest Sister. Community n/a. ***CC*** No.230143. Began 1855; Anglican. Turnover n/a.

Houghton Chapel Centre, Chapel Lane, Houghton, Huntingdon PE28 2AY
☎01480 469 376
E: gerry.feakes@one-name.org
Web: www.houghtonchapelcentre.org.uk
Residential and day.
Wardens: Mr & Mrs Gerald & Sue Feakes. Executive staff 2, No other staff. ***CC*** Began 1986; United Reformed. Turnover n/a.

Ignatian Spirituality Centre, 7 Woodside Place, Glasgow G3 7QF
☎0141 354 0077 📠0141 354 0099
E: iscentre@btopenworld.com
Web: www.iscentre.btinternet.co.uk
Providing retreats and courses based on the spiritual exercises of Ignatius Loyola.
Director: Ruth Holgate. Executive staff 1, Other staff 7. ***CC*** No.230165. Began 1916; Roman Catholic. Turnover n/a.

Institute of Spirituality, St Mary's, Kinnoull, Perth PH2 7BP
☎01738 624 075 📠01738 442 071
E: copiosa@aol.com
Web: www.kinnoull.org
Also renewal courses.
Rector: Fr J McManus. Executive staff 1, Other staff 6. ***CC*** Began 1869; Roman Catholic. Turnover £300,000 to year end Apr 03.

Iona Carmelite Retreat Centre, Termonbacca, Londonderry BT48 9XE
☎028 7126 2512 📠028 7137 3589
E: fr.seanconlon@hotmail.com
For individuals and groups who wish to deepen their Christian lives.
Prior: Very Rev Sean Conlon. Other staff 3, Community 5. Began 1982; Roman Catholic. Turnover n/a.

Iona Community - Macleod Centre and Iona Abbey, Isle of Iona PA76 6SN
☎01681 700 404 📠01681 700 460
E: ionacomm@iona.org.uk
Web: www.iona.org.uk
Offering Christian experiment and renewal; prayer, politics, peace and healing in common life; creating community.
Warden: Rev Richard Sharples. *Deputy Warden:* Rowena Aberdeen De Voil. Admin staff 2, Other staff 20. ***CC*** No.SC0 03794. Began 1938; ecumenical but open to all. Magazine: *Coracle* (4,000 every two months). Turnover £1,400,000 to year end Dec 02.

For bed-spaces etc. see list on Page 72

Ivy House, St Denys Retreat Centre, 2 Church Street, Warminster BA12 8PG
☎01985 214 824
E: stdenys.ivyhouse@btopenworld.com
Web: www.ivyhouse.org
Christian hospitality to parishes, other groups and individuals; residential and days.
Warden: Name not supplied. Admin staff 2, Other staff 5. ***CC*** No.233026. Began 1879; Anglican but open to all. Turnover n/a.

Kairos Centre, Mount Angelus Road, Roehampton, London SW15 4JA
☎020 8788 4188 🖷020 8788 4198
E: director.kairos@psmgs.org
Web: www.thekairoscentre.co.uk
Offering resources for retreats, conferences, meetings, courses; for church groups, individuals; full board.
Director: Sister Mena O'Donnell. Community 160, Other staff 13. ***CC*** No.227931. Began 1369; Roman Catholic but open to all. (Previously Maryfield Convent). Turnover n/a.

Edward King House, The Old Palace, Minster Yard, Lincoln LN2 1PU
☎01522 528 778 🖷01522 527 308
E: enjoy@ekhs.org.uk
Web: www.ekhs.org.uk
Day and residential conference and retreat centre for church and the wider community.
Manager: Mr John Eames. *Deputy Manager:* Mrs Sue Brennan. Admin staff 2, Other staff 3. ***CC*** No.517930. Began 1960; Anglican. Turnover £176,000 to year end Mar 02.

Launde Abbey, East Norton, Launde, Leicester LE7 9XB
☎01572 717 254 🖷01572 717 454
E: laundeabbey@leicester.anglican.org
Web: www.launde.org.uk
Warden: Canon Tim Blewett. Admin staff 3, Other staff 19. ***CC*** Began 1958; Anglican. Leicester Diocesan Retreat House and Conference Centre. Turnover £350,000 to year end Dec 02.

Letterfourie Retreats, Letterfourie, Buckie AB56 2JP
☎01542 832 298
E: enquiries@letterfourie.com
Web: www.letterfourie.com
For self-organised groups and individuals; all self-catering.
Warden: Mr John Birch. Executive staff 1, Admin staff 1. Began 1996; non-denominational. Turnover n/a.

Llangasty Retreat House, Brecon LD3 7PJ
☎01874 658 250 🖷01874 658 250
E: llangasty.rh@btconnect.com
Web: www.llangasty.co.uk
Warden: Mr Andrew Perrin. Admin staff 1, Other staff 4. ***CC*** No.1060743. Began 1954; Anglican. Turnover n/a.

Loreto Centre (Institute of the Blessed Virgin Mary), Abbey Road, Llandudno LL30 2EL
☎01492 878 031
🖷01492 878 031
E: llandudno@loretocentre.wanadoo.co.uk
Web: www.loretollno.org.uk
Sister-in-Charge: Sister Brigid Kenny. Community 5. ***CC*** No.250607. Began 1919; Roman Catholic. Turnover £90,000 to year end Dec 04.

Loyola Hall - Jesuit Spirituality Centre, Warrington Road, Rainhill, Prescot L35 6NZ
☎0151 426 4137
🖷0151 431 0115
E: mail.loyolahall.co.uk
Web: www.loyolahall.co.uk
Retreats and courses in Ignatian spirituality.
Director: Rev Ian Tomlinson SJ. *Bursar:* Mrs Sheila Hanley. Admin staff 4, Other staff 20. ***CC*** No.230165. Began 1923; Roman Catholic but open to all. Turnover £450,000 to year end Dec 04.

Marie Reparatrice Retreat Centre, 115 Ridgway, London SW19 4RB
☎020 8946 1088
🖷020 8947 9820
E: retreathouse.wim@smcr.org
Sister Superior: Rev Sister. *Retreat Secretary:* Sister Maureen Peart. Admin staff 2, Other staff 3. ***CC*** No.233640. Began 1957; Roman Catholic. Turnover n/a.

Marist Centre, Nympsfield, Stonehouse GL10 3TY
☎01453 860 228
🖷01453 861 331
E: marissisters@tiscali.co.uk
Manager: Sister Helena Whelan. Community 8. ***CC*** Began 1858; Roman Catholic. Marist Sisters. Turnover n/a.

Mill Green House, Mill Green, Horseheath, Cambridge CB1 6QZ
☎01799 584 937
🖷01799 584 390
E: suewalker@nascr.net
For prayer and reflection.
Retreat Leaders & Administrators: Mr & Mrs Graeme & Sue Walker. Executive staff 2, No other staff. Began 1986; ecumenical. Turnover £5,000 to year end Dec 02.

Mill-Leat, Felindre Cottage, Abercynrig, Llanfrynach, Brecon LD3 7AQ
☎01874 665 208
E: info@mill-leat.org
Web: www.mill-leat.org
Offering personal retreats, sabbatical breaks, training, consultancy, spiritual guidance; for personal, ministerial and ecclesial regeneration.
Director: Jenny Joice. Executive staff 1, Other staff n/a. Began 2003; non-denominational. Turnover n/a.

Minster Abbey Retreat/Guesthouse, Minster, Ramsgate CT12 4HF
☎01843 821 254 🖷01843 821 254
Welcoming guests and retreatants into a monastic setting for rest and prayer.
The Guest Sister: Sister A Erwin. Community 13. ***CC*** No.232635. Began 1937; Roman Catholic. Turnover n/a.

Minsteracres Retreat Centre, Consett DH8 9RT
☎01434 673 248 🖷01434 673 540
E: info@minsteracres.co.uk
Web: www.minsteracres.com
Preached retreats (groups); individuals welcome, spiritual direction, conferences, youth centre.
Rector: Rev Jeroen Hoogland. Community 8, Other staff 11. ***CC*** No.234436. Began 1967; Roman Catholic but open to all. Turnover £200,000 to year end Dec 02.

Monastery of Our Lady of Hyning, Warton, Carnforth LA5 9SE
☎01524 732 684 🖷01524 720 287
E: hyningbookings@yahoo.co.uk
Web: www.bernadine.org
Monastic guest house welcoming individuals and groups to pray and reflect.
Prioress: Sister Elizabeth Mary. Community 12, Other staff 5. ***CC*** No.241743. Began 1974; Roman Catholic. Turnover n/a.

The Monastery of the Holy Trinity, Crawley Down, Crawley RH10 4LH
☎01342 712 074
Traditional monastic liturgy with instruction in the life of prayer, especially use of Jesus prayer.
Father Superior: Rev Fr Gregory. Community n/a. Began 1950; Anglican. Community of the Servants of the Will of God. Turnover n/a.

Morley Retreat and Conference House, Church Lane, Morley, Ilkeston DE7 6DE
☎01332 831 293 🖷01332 834 944
E: morleyretreat@btconnect.com
Web: www.morleyretreat.co.uk
Providing welcome and hospitality for a wide range of day and residential events.
Warden: Mr Jeff Witts. *House Manager:* Mrs Catherine Witts. Admin staff 5, Other staff 12. ***CC*** No.1078494. Began 1959; Anglican. Turnover £179,000 to year end Dec 04.

A

Mount St Bernard Abbey, Coalville LE67 5UL
☎01530 832 298 / 022
🖷01530 814 608
E: mountstbernardabbey@btinternet.com
Abbot: Rt Rev Joseph Delargy. *Guestmaster:* Fr Hilary Costello. Community 37. ***CC*** Began 1835; Roman Catholic. Order of Cistercians of the Strict Observance. Turnover n/a.

Myddelton Grange, Langbar Road, Ilkley LS29 0EB
☎01943 607 887 🖷01943 885 470
E: info@myddeltongrange.org.uk
Director: Rev Francis Smith. Admin staff 1, Other staff 10. ***CC*** Began 1922; Roman Catholic. Turnover n/a.

Nicholaston House, Penmaen, Swansea SA3 2HL
☎01792 371 317 🖷01792 371 217
E: managers@nicholastonhouse.org
Web: www.nicholastonhouse.org
Offering retreats, prayer ministry, time out, themed breaks, courses for overcoming eating disorders.
Resident Manager: Mr Derek Styants. *Ministry Manager:* Mrs Anne Styants. *Training & Development:* Helena Wilkinson. Admin staff 7. ***CC*** No.1096720. Began 1988; interdenominational. Turnover £165,000 to year end Dec 04.

Noddfa Spirituality Centre, Conwy Old Road, Penmaenmawr LL34 6YF
☎01492 623 473 🖷01492 622 517
E: noddfapen@aol.com
Web: www.noddfa.org.uk
Offering parish retreats, Ignatian retreats, short breaks for carers, conferences.
Retreat Programmer: Sister Patrice Power. Admin staff 3, Other staff 5. ***CC*** No.232190. Began 1970; Roman Catholic. (Previously Convent of the Sacred Heart of Mary). Turnover n/a.

Northumbria Community Trust Ltd, Nether Springs, Hetton Hall, Chatton, Alnwick NE66 5SD
☎01289 388 235 🖷01289 388 510
E: office@northumbriacommunity.org
Web: www.northumbriacommunity.org
Mother House of dispersed Christian community; open to visitors, retreatants, pilgrims, seekers.
Directors: Rev Roy Searle, Rev Trevor Miller. Executive staff 2, Admin staff 3, Other staff 17. ***CC*** No.1099503. Began 1988; interdenominational. Magazine: *CAIM* (1,500 quarterly). Turnover n/a.

Offa House (Coventry Diocesan Retreat House and Conference Centre), Offchurch, Leamington Spa CV33 9AS
☎01926 423 309 🖷01926 330 350
E: offahouse@btconnect.com
Web: www.offahouseretreat.co.uk
Conferences for church organisations, parishes and groups; retreats for individuals and groups.
Warden: Rev Andrew De Smet. Admin staff 2, Other staff 7. ***CC*** Began 1962; Anglican. Turnover n/a.

†Our Lady of Apostles Retreat House, 11 Greenpark Road, Rostrevor, Newry BT34 3EY
☎028 4173 8333
Sister-in-Charge: Sister Eugenius. Admin staff 2. ***CC*** Began 1976; Roman Catholic. Turnover n/a.

***Penhurst Retreat Centre**, The Manor House, Penhurst, Battle TN33 9QP
☎08454 580 602
🖷08454 580 602
E: info@penhurst.org.uk
Web: www.penhurst.org.uk
For individuals or small groups.
Wardens: Mr & Mrs Richard & Storm Hann. Executive staff 2. ***CC*** No.1060817. Began 1997; ecumenical. Turnover n/a.

Pluscarden Abbey, Elgin IV30 8UA
☎01343 890 257
🖷01343 890 258
E: monks@pluscardenabbey.org
Web: www.pluscardenabbey.org
Contemplative monastic community offering retreats, participation in worship and peace.
Guestmaster: Br Gabriel Potter. *Warden:* Dom Matthew Tylor. Community 25. ***CC*** No.SCO 13703. Began 1948; Roman Catholic, Benedictine. Turnover £80,000 to year end Dec 93.

Prinknash Abbey, Cranham, Gloucester GL4 8EX
☎01452 812 455
🖷01452 813 305
E: prinknash@waitrose.com
Web: www.prinknashabbey.org.uk
For men.
Guestmaster: Rev William Harwood. Community n/a. ***CC*** No.232863. Began 1928; Roman Catholic. Turnover n/a.

Priory of Our Lady, Sayers Common, Hassocks BN6 9HT
☎01273 832 901
E: prioryofourlady@btinternet.com
Secretary: The Sister Secretary. Community n/a. ***CC*** Began 1972; Roman Catholic. Turnover n/a.

Quarr Abbey, Ryde PO33 4ES
☎01983 882 420
🖷01983 884 402
E: guestmaster@quarrabbey.co.uk
Web: quarrabbey.co.uk
For men.
Guestmaster: Rev Francis Verry. Community 20. ***CC*** No.218731. Began 1908; Roman Catholic. Turnover n/a.

†Quiet Waters Christian Retreat House, Flixton Road, Bungay NR35 1PD
☎01986 893 201
E: mail@quietwaters.org.uk
Web: www.quietwaters.org.uk
Team Leader: Name not supplied. Admin staff 6, Other staff 2. ***CC*** No.269866. Began 1985; non-denominational. Turnover £48,000 to year end Sep 02.

St Beuno's, Spiritual Exercises Centre, St Asaph LL17 0AS
☎01745 583 444 🖷01745 584 1[illegible]1
E: info@beunos.com
Web: www.beunos.com
Silent individually guided retreats.
Director: Rev David Birchall. Admin staff 10. ***CC*** No.230165. Began 1848; Roman Catholic but open to all. Turnover n/a.

St Cassian's Centre, Wallington's Road, Kintbury, Hungerford RG17 [illegible]SR
☎01488 658 267 🖷01488 657 2[illegible]2
E: kintbury@aol.com
Web: www.kintbury.org
Mainly for people aged 15 to 18 in school groups.
Director: Mr Chanel Lally. Executive staff 1, Other staff 14. ***CC*** No.232632. Began 1946; Roman Catholic. De La Salle Brothers. Turnover n/a.

St Christopher's Retreat and Respite Centre, 15 Sea Road, Westgate-on-Sea CT8 8SA
☎01843 831 875 🖷01843 [illegible]31 82[illegible]
E: info@christophers-bythesea.co.uk
Web: www.christophers-bythesea.co.uk
Also coffee shop.
Manager: Mrs Marie Burr. Executive staff 1, Other staff 7. ***CC*** No.214[illegible]79. Began 1870; Salvation Army but open to all. Turnover n/a.

St Columba's House, Maybury Hill, Woking GU22 8AB
☎01483 766 498 M: 0797[illegible] 848 [illegible]41
🖷01483 740 441
E: retreats@st.columba.org.uk
Web: www.stcolumbashouse.org.uk
For religious and secular groups, individuals, businesses.
Director: Rev Canon Paul M Jenkins. Admin staff 1, Other staff 3. ***CC*** No.240675. Began 1958; Anglican. Owned by St. Peter's Convent Woking. Turnover n/a.

St Francis' House, Hemingford Grey, Huntingdon PE28 9BJ
☎01480 462 185
E: hemingford@mirfield.org.uk
Web: www.mirfield.org.uk
Providing peaceful atmosphere for all who seek spiritual refreshment.
Warden: Miss Mary Campbell. Admin staff 2, Other staff 8. ***CC*** No.2[illegible]2670. Began 1950; Anglican. Administered by the Community of the Resurrection, Mirfield. Turnover n/a.

St Gabriel's Centre (All Hallows Community Retreat Houses), Belsey Bridge Road, Ditchingham, Bungay NR35 2DT
☎01986 892 749 🖷01986 895 838
Offering a programme of retreats throughout the year; available to church groups, fellowships; full-board.
Contact: Convent Secretary. Admin staff 1, Other staff 8. ***CC*** No.230143. Began 1855; Anglican. Turnover n/a.

For bed-spaces etc. see list on Page 72

St Joseph's Retreat and Conference Centre, Tilston Road, Malpas SY14 7DD
☎01948 860 416 🖷01948 860 055
E: sgj@malpas2000.freeserve.co.uk
Web: www.malpas2000.freeserve.co.uk
Acting Director: Fr Michael Walshe. Other staff 6. ***CC*** No.215011. Began 1974; Roman Catholic but open to all. Turnover n/a.

St Mary's Convent, Wantage OX12 9DJ
☎01235 760 170
E: guestwing@csmv.co.uk
Religious community. Contact: The Guest Sister. Community n/a. ***CC*** No.240513. Began 1848; Anglican. Turnover n/a.

St Mary's Lodge (All Hallows Community Retreat Houses), Belsey Bridge Road, Ditchingham, Bungay NR35 2DT
☎01986 892 731 🖷01986 895 838
Offering a programme of retreats; for church groups, fellowships, individuals; self-catering, silent.
Contact: The Guest Sister. Community n/a. ***CC*** No.230143. Began 1855; Anglican. Turnover n/a.

St Michael's Centre (All Hallows Community Retreat Houses), Belsey Bridge Road, Ditchingham, Bungay NR35 2DT
☎01986 892 749 🖷01986 895 838
Offering a programme of retreats; for church groups, fellowships; full board.
Contact: Convent Secretary. Admin staff 1, Other staff 5. ***CC*** No.230143. Began 1855; Anglican. Turnover n/a.

St Michael's Convent, 56 Ham Common, Richmond TW10 7JH
☎020 8940 8711 🖷020 8332 2927
Welcoming groups and individuals (both men and women); day or residential.
Contact: Guest Sister. Admin staff 2, Other staff 3. ***CC*** No.271790. Began 1870; Anglican. Community of the Sisters of the Church. Turnover £700 to year end Dec 02.

St Oswald's Pastoral Centre, Woodlands Drive, Sleights, Whitby YO21 1RY
☎01947 810 496 🖷01947 810 750
E: ohpstos@globalnet.co.uk
Web: www.ohpwhitby.org/stoswalds
A place for prayer, quiet study and relaxation in the context of a religious community.
Sister-in-Charge: Sister Janet Elizabeth. Community n/a. ***CC*** No.231756. Began 1983; Anglican. Order of the Holy Paraclete. Turnover n/a.

Savio House, Ingersley Road, Bollington, Macclesfield SK10 5RW
☎01625 573 256 🖷01625 560 221
E: saviooffice@saviohouse.org.uk
Web: www.salesians.org.uk
Residential and day retreats, mainly for young people.
Rector: Fr Hugh Preston. *Administrator:* Mrs Margaret Rose. Admin staff 2, Other staff 12. ***CC*** No.233779. Began n/a; Roman Catholic but open to all. Turnover £230,000 to year end Dec 02.

Shallowford House (Lichfield Diocesan Retreat and Conference House), Stone ST15 0NZ
☎01785 760 233 🖷01785 760 390
E: warden@shallowfordhouse.freeserve.co.uk
Web: www.lichfield.anglican.org
Warden: Mr D C Shemilt. Admin staff 2, Other staff 9. ***CC*** Began 1939; Anglican. Turnover £166,000 to year end Dec 04.

Shepherds Dene (Retreat House and Conference Centre), Riding Mill NE44 6AF
☎01434 682 212 M: 07941 422 162
🖷01434 682 311
E: shepherdsdene@btconnect.com
Web: www.shepherdsdene.co.uk
For churches, other groups and individuals.
Warden: Mr P J Dodgson. Admin staff 1, Other staff 6. ***CC*** No.700258. Began 1946; Anglican. (Previously Shepherds Dene Newcastle and Durham Retreat House and Conference Centre). Turnover £140,000 to year end Dec 02.

Sisters of Jesus Way Retreat House, Red Acre, 24 Abbey Road, West Kirby, Wirral CH48 7EP
☎0151 625 8775
E: redacre@freeuk.com
For quiet, rest, fellowship; Sisters lead small day groups; small groups for prayer planning.
The Warden: Sister-in-Charge. Community n/a. ***CC*** No.509284. Began 1979; Anglican but open to all. Turnover n/a.

Sisters of St Louis, The Old Stable House, 3 Sussex Lodge, Fordham Road, Newmarket CB8 7AF
☎01638 667 190 🖷01638 667 190
Director: Sr Margaret Duggan. Admin staff 1, Other staff 2. ***CC*** No.255245. Began 1912; Roman Catholic Turnover n/a.

†**Society of Retreat Conductors**, Stacklands Retreat House, West Kingsdown, Sevenoaks TN15 6AN
☎01474 852 247
E: warden@stacklands.org.uk
Web: www.stacklands.org.uk
Providing Ignatian retreats for groups and individuals and conference use.
Warden: Rev Jim Bateman. Admin staff 1, Other staff 2. ***CC*** No.246045. Began 1927; Anglican but open to all. Turnover n/a.

Society of St Margaret, St Saviour's Priory, 18 Queensbridge Road, London E2 8NS
☎020 7739 9976
Leader of Community: Sr Helen Loder. Community 16. ***CC*** Began 1866; Anglican. Turnover n/a.

SPEC Centre, Shenley Lane, London Colney, St Albans AL2 1AF
☎01727 828 888 🖷01727 829 227
E: spec@rcdow.org.uk
For people aged 16 to 30.
Directors: Mr & Mrs David & Sandra Satchell. Executive staff 2, Other staff n/a. ***CC*** No.233699. Began n/a; Roman Catholic. Turnover n/a.

The Loft
☎01727 828 888 🖷 01727 822 927
For young people aged 9 to 15.
Directors: Mr & Mrs Jon & Roseanne Rogers

Stanton House, Stanton St John, Oxford OX33 1HQ
☎01865 358 807
E: office@stantonhouse.org.uk
Web: www.stantonhouse.org.uk
Offering space and quiet for spiritual rest, refreshment and renewal; also day groups.
Administrator: Elizabeth Spight. Admin staff 1, Other staff 5. ***CC*** No.275205. Began 1978; interdenominational. Turnover £56,000 to year end Dec 00.

The Tower House Christian Trust Ltd, 21 Collard Crescent, Barry CF62 9AQ
☎01446 420 025 🖷01446 420 025
E: enquiry@thetowerhouse.com
Web: www.thetowerhouse.com
Non-directed retreat centre on Greek Island of Kos; for individuals, couples and groups.
Retreat Managers: Mr & Mrs Roger & Felicity Carver. Admin staff 1, Centre staff 2. ***CC*** No.1091354. Began 2001; interdenominational. Turnover £19,000 to year end Apr 03.

Tymawr Convent, Lydart, Monmouth NP25 4RN
☎01600 860 244
Web: www.churchinwales.org.uk/tymawr
Anglican contemplative community living a life of prayer and offering hospitality.
The Warden: Guest Hostess. Community n/a. ***CC*** No.1047614. Began 1914; Church in Wales. Turnover n/a.

Whaley Hall Community of the King of Love, Whaley Hall, Reservoir Road, Whaley Bridge, High Peak SK23 7BL
☎01663 732 495 🖷01663 732 495
E: ckladmin@whaley23.freeserve.co.uk
Web: www.whaleyhallckl.org.uk
Offering programme of retreats and conferences; personal recreation, development and support available; day group facilities.
Guardian: Rev David B Hall. Executive staff 1, Other staff 2. ***CC*** No.271207. Began 1969; ecumenical. Turnover n/a.

Whalley Abbey (Blackburn Diocesan Conference & Retreat House), Whalley, Clitheroe BB7 9SS
☎01254 828 400 🖷01254 825 519
E: office@whalleyabbey.org
Retreats Manager: Mr John Wilson. *General Manager:* Claire Davies. Admin staff 4, Other staff 17. ***CC*** No.247647. Began 1926; Anglican but open to all. Turnover n/a.

For bed-spaces etc. see list on Page 72

Retreat Houses

***Whitchester Christian Guest House and Retreat**, Borthaugh, Hawick TD9 7LN
☎01450 377 477 🖷01450 371 080
E: enquiries@whitchester.org.uk
Web: www.whitchester.org.uk
Offering care, listening, prayer; daily worship, chapel.
Warden: Evelyn Jackson. Executive staff 1, Other staff 4. ***CC*** No.SCO 11436. Began 1984; interdenominational. ACC affiliated. No magazine. Turnover £75,000 to year end Jun 05.

Wistaston Hall Oblate Retreat Centre, 89 Broughton Lane, Crewe CW2 8JS
☎01270 568 653 🖷01270 650 776
E: director@oblateretreatcentre.org.uk
Web: www.oblateretreatcentre.org.uk
Providing facilities for and directing retreats, meetings and conferences.
Director: Oliver Barry OMI. Executive staff 1, Other staff 3. ***CC*** No.223318. Began 1943; Roman Catholic. Turnover n/a.

†Wychcroft (Southwark Diocesan Retreat House), Bletchingley, Redhill RH1 4NE
☎01883 743 041
Warden: Name not supplied Staff n/a. ***CC*** Began 1960; Anglican. Turnover n/a.

SHELTERED HOUSING

See also Residential & Nursing Homes for Elderly People on Page 61
Homes which did not supply this information are not listed here
Only homes with 10 or more spaces are included

🚆 = nearest Railway station ⊖ = nearest London Underground station

Name, Town	Number		Railway / Underground
Aldersgate, Nuneaton	Units	33	🚆 Nuneaton
Ash Court, Clapham	Units	12	🚆 Clapham Junction
			⊖ Clapham South
Bradley Court, Huddersfield	Units	46	🚆 Deighton
Bridge Court, Wolverhampton	Units	40	🚆 Wolverhampton
Callin Court, Chester	Units	42	🚆 Chester
Charles Court, Tunbridge Wells	single rooms	9	🚆 Tunbridge Wells
	double/twin rooms	8	
Church Court, Midsomer Norton, Bath	Units	20	🚆 Bath Spa
Coles Court, Tunbridge Wells	single rooms	13	🚆 Tunbridge Wells
	double/twin rooms	10	
Derham Court, Yatton, Bristol	Units	17	🚆 Yatton
Edina Court, Wisbech	Units	50	🚆 Peterborough or Kings Lynn
Epworth Court, Swindon	Units	25	🚆 Swindon
Field Court, York	Units	29	🚆 York
Gowan Park, Arbroath	Units	15	🚆 Arbroath
Grace Court, Folkestone	Units	27	🚆 Folkestone Central
The Hawthorns, Ellesmere Port	Units	41	🚆 Ellesmere Port
Hinton Court, Guisborough	Units	33	🚆 Middlesbrough
Jubilee Cottage Trust, Lytham St Annes	Places	17	🚆 St Annes-on-the-Sea
Naylor Court, Ellesmere Port	Units	21	🚆 Ellesmere Port
Norah Beliot Court, Barnstaple	Units	45	🚆 Barnstaple
The Paddock, Muswell Hill, London	Units	26	⊖ Highgate
Pilgrims Court, Newcastle upon Tyne	Units	41	🚆 Newcastle
Royd Court Pilgrim Homes, Mirfield	Flats	58	🚆 Mirfield
St Andrew's Court, East Kilbride	Units	32	🚆 East Kilbride
The Sheppard Trust, London W11	Sheltered flats	28	⊖ Holland Park
Southcroft, Sheffield	Units	37	🚆 Sheffield
Taransay Court, Glasgow	Units	36	🚆 Glasgow Central
Tranquility Court, Leeds	Units	22	🚆 Cross Gates
Walcot Court, Bath	Units	37	🚆 Bath Spa
Wesley Court, Edinburgh	Units	28	🚆 Edinburgh
West Court, Banbury	Units	22	🚆 Banbury
Willcox Close, Glastonbury	Units	21	🚆 Castle Cary or Bristol Temple Meads
Woodlands, Penrith	Units	28	🚆 Penrith
Yew Tree/Rosewood Court, Leeds	Units	70	🚆 Horsforth or Leeds

SHELTERED HOUSING

See also Residential & Nursing Homes for Elderly People on Page 61.

A

Aldersgate, Rose Lane, Nuneaton CV11 5TF
☎024 7664 2330 🖷024 7664 2330
Web: www.mha.org.uk
Specialist housing with support for older people.
Scheme Manager: Hilary Mountney. Admin staff 1, Other staff n/a. ***CC*** No.21860R. Began 1989; Methodist but open to all. Methodist Homes for the Aged. Turnover n/a.

Ash Court, 155 Broomwood Close, Clapham, London SW11 6JX
☎020 7223 0793
Web: www.mha.org.uk
Specialist housing with support for older people.
Scheme Manager: To be appointed. Admin staff 1, Other staff n/a. ***CC*** No.21680R. Began 1984; Methodist but open to all. Methodist homes for the Aged. Turnover n/a.

Norah Beliot Court, Vicarage Street, Barnstaple EX32 7ES
☎01271 379 787 🖷01271 374 139
Web: www.mha.org.uk
Specialist housing with support for older people.
Scheme Manager: Louise Thomas. Admin staff 1, Other staff n/a. ***CC*** No.21860R. Began 2000; Methodist but open to all. Methodist Homes for the Aged. Turnover n/a.

Bradley Court, Keldregate, Bradley, Huddersfield HD2 1WN
☎01484 519 748 🖷01484 519 758
Web: www.mha.org.uk
Specialist housing with support for older people.
Scheme Manager: Shibon Armstrong. Admin staff 1, Other staff n/a. ***CC*** No.21860R. Began 2004; Methodist but open to all. Methodist Homes for the Aged. Turnover n/a.

Bridge Court, 43 Moathouse Lane West, Wolverhampton WV11 3HE
☎01902 738 124 🖷01902 737 874
Web: www.mha.org.uk
Specialist housing with support for older people.
Scheme Manager: Margaret Lloyd. Admin staff 1, Other staff n/a. ***CC*** No.21860R. Began 2005; Methodist but open to all. Methodist Homes for the Aged. Turnover n/a.

Callin Court, Grey Friars, Chester CH1 2NW
☎01244 315 252 🖷01244 322 416
Web: www.mha.org.uk
Specialist housing with support for older people.
Scheme Manager: Mrs Carol Ward. Admin staff 1, Other staff n/a. ***CC*** No.1083995. Began 1983; Methodist but open to all. Methodist Homes for the Aged. Turnover n/a.

Charles Court, Pembury Road, Tunbridge Wells TN2 3QT
☎01892 547 439
Officer-in-Charge: Centre Manager. Executive staff 1, Other staff n/a. ***CC*** Began n/a; Salvation Army. Category 2. Turnover n/a.

Church Court, Church Lane, Midsomer Norton, Bath BA3 2JA
☎01761 414 927|
🖷01761 414 927
Web: www.mha.org.uk
Specialist housing with support for older people.
Scheme Manager: Lynn Lewis. Admin staff 1, Other staff n/a. ***CC*** No.1083995. Began 1978; Methodist but open to all. Methodist Homes for the Aged. Turnover n/a.

Coles Court, Kingswood Road, Tunbridge Wells TN2 4HW
☎01892 529 078
Officer-in-Charge: Centre Manager. Executive staff 1, Other staff n/a. ***CC*** Began n/a; Salvation Army. Category 1. Turnover n/a.

Derham Court, High Street, Yatton, Bristol BS49 4DW
☎01934 835 443
🖷01934 835 443
Web: www.mha.org.uk
Specialist housing with support for older people.
Scheme Manager: Karen Wood. Admin staff 1, Other staff n/a. ***CC*** No.21860R. Began 1982; Methodist but open to all. Methodist Homes for the Aged. Turnover n/a.

Edina Court, 57 Harecroft Road, Wisbech PE13 1RL
☎01945 463 419
🖷01945 465 358
Web: www.mha.org.uk
Specialist housing with support for older people.
Scheme Manager: Tony Pillow. Admin staff 1, Other staff n/a. ***CC*** No.1083995. Began 1986; Methodist but open to all. Methodist Homes for the Aged. Turnover n/a.

Epworth Court, Bath Road, Swindon SN1 4BA
☎01793 612 006
🖷01793 612 006
Web: www.mha.org.uk
Specialist housing with support for older people.
Scheme Manager: Hayley Atter. Admin staff 1, Other staff n/a. ***CC*** No.21860R. Began 1987; Methodist but open to all. Methodist Homes for the Aged. Turnover n/a.

Field Court, Hempland Lane, Heworth, York YO31 1DN
☎01904 430 147 🖷01904 430 147
Web: www.mha.org.uk
Specialist housing with support for older people.
Scheme Manager: Paul Nicholson. Admin staff 1, Other staff n/a. ***CC*** No.21860R. Began 1991; Methodist but open to all. Methodist Homes for the Aged. Turnover n/a.

Gowan Park, Gowan Street, Arbroath DD11 2BN
☎01241 879 432 🖷01241 879 432
Web: www.mha.org.uk
Specialist housing with support for older people.
Scheme Manager: Selena Milne. Admin staff 1, Other staff n/a. ***CC*** No.21860R. Began 1985; Methodist but open to all. Methodist Homes for the Aged. Turnover n/a.

Grace Court, Grace Hill, Folkestone CT20 1HG
☎01303 241 551 🖷01303 241 551
Web: www.mha.org.uk
Specialist housing with support for older people.
Scheme Manager: Barbara Wiffen. Admin staff 1, Other staff n/a. ***CC*** No.21860R. Began 1988; Methodist but open to all. Methodist Homes for the Aged. Turnover n/a.

The Hawthorns, Naylor Crescent, Netherpool Road, Overpool, Ellesmere Port CH66 1TW
☎0151 356 4630 🖷0151 356 1623
Web: www.mha.org.uk
Specialist housing support for older people.
Scheme Manager: Mr Paul Lilley. Admin staff 1, Other staff n/a. ***CC*** No.21860R. Began 1997; Methodist but open to all. Methodist Homes for the Aged. Turnover n/a.

Hinton Court, Lumley Terrace, Guisborough TS14 6HN
☎01287 636 719 🖷01287 636 719
Web: www.mha.org.uk
Specialist housing with support for older people.
Scheme Manager: Mrs Anita Wright. Admin staff 1, Other staff n/a. ***CC*** No.1083995. Began 1988; Methodist but open to all. Methodist Homes for the Aged. Turnover n/a.

***Jubilee Cottage Trust (Keychange Charity)**, 143 St Andrews Road South, Lytham St Annes FY8 1YB
☎01253 725 056
Sheltered flats.
Warden: Mrs Janet Hardie. Executive staff 1, Other staff n/a. ***CC*** No.1061344. Began 1978; interdenominational. Turnover £26,933 to year end Mar 02.

Naylor Court, Rossmore Road West, Ellesmere Port CH66 1SY
☎0151 355 8896 🖷0151 355 8896
Web: www.mha.org.uk
Specialist housing with support for older people.
Scheme Manager: Mrs Enid Gosden. Admin staff 1, Other staff n/a. ***CC*** No.21860R. Began 1984; Methodist but open to all. Methodist Homes for the Aged. Turnover n/a.

The Paddock, Meadow Drive, Muswell Hill, London N10 1PL
☎020 8444 1050 🖷020 8444 1050
Web: www.mha.org.uk
Specialist housing with support for older people.
Scheme Manager: Jackie Argent. Admin staff 1, Other staff n/a. ***CC*** No.21860R. Began 1987; Methodist but open to all. Methodist Homes for the Aged. Turnover n/a.

Pilgrims Court, Eslington Terrace, Jesmond, Newcastle upon Tyne NE2 4RL
☎0191 281 7800 🖷0191 281 7800
Web: www.mha.org.uk
Specialist housing with support for older people.
Scheme Manager: Chris Johnson. Admin staff 1, Other staff n/a. ***CC*** No.21860R. Began 1985; Methodist but open to all. Methodist Homes for the Aged. Turnover n/a.

***Royd Court Pilgrim Homes**, The Bungalow, 6 Royd Court, Huddersfield Road, Mirfield WF14 9DJ
☎01924 489 015
Web: www.pilgrimhomes.org.uk
To open in 2007.
Director of Housing and Care Services: Mrs Maureen Sim. Admin staff 1, Other staff n/a. ***CC*** No.242266. Began n/a; non-denominational. Turnover n/a.

St Andrew's Court, Sycamore Crescent, Greenhills, East Kilbride, Glasgow G75 9LN
☎01355 231 248 🖷01355 231 248
Web: www.mha.org.uk
Specialist housing with support for older people.
Scheme Manager: Karin Macdonald. Admin staff 1, Other staff n/a. ***CC*** No.21860R. Began 1981; Methodist but open to all. Methodist Homes for the Aged. Turnover n/a.

The Sheppard Trust, 12 Lansdowne Walk, London W11 3LN
☎020 7727 5500 🖷020 7727 7730
Providing unfurnished sheltered flats for gentlewomen aged over 65 of limited means.
Director: Mr David Cash. *Assistant to the Director:* Mrs Barbara V Ray. Admin staff 4, Other staff 3. ***CC*** No.205924. Began 1855; Anglican. Turnover £110,000 to year end Dec 04.

Southcroft, 33 Psalter Lane, Sheffield S11 8YL
☎0114 255 3978 🖷0114 255 3978
Web: www.mha.org.uk
Specialist housing with support for older people.
Scheme Manager: Margorie Merry. Admin staff 1, Other staff n/a. ***CC*** No.1083995. Began 1989; Methodist but open to all. Methodist Homes for the Aged. Turnover n/a.

Taransay Court, Liddesdale Square, Milton, Glasgow G22 7BT
☎0141 772 5384 🖷0141 772 5384
Web: www.mha.org.uk
Specialist housing with support for older people.
Scheme Manager: Bernadette McGovern. Executive staff 1, Other staff n/a. ***CC*** No.21860R. Began 1990; Methodist but open to all. Methodist Homes for the Aged. Turnover n/a.

Tranquility Court, 6 Tranquility Avenue, Crossgates, Leeds LS15 8QX
☎0113 260 6948 🖷0113 260 6948
Web: www.mha.org.uk
Specialist housing with support for older people.
Scheme Manager: Chris Maguire. Admin staff 1, Other staff n/a. ***CC*** No.21860R. Began 1989; Methodist but open to all. Methodist Homes for the Aged. Turnover n/a.

Walcot Court, Walcot Gate, Bath BA1 5UB
☎01225 428 476 🖷01225 428 476
Web: www.mha.org.uk
Specialist housing with support for older people.
Scheme Manager: Mrs Kerry Huggins. Admin staff 1, Other staff n/a. ***CC*** No.21860R. Began 1992; Methodist but open to all. Methodist Homes for the Aged. Turnover n/a.

Wesley Court, 13 Royston Mains Place, Granton, Edinburgh EH5 1LG
☎0131 552 4568 🖷0131 552 4568
Web: www.mha.org.uk
Specialist housing with support for older people.
Scheme Manager: Jim Gibson. Admin staff 1, Other staff n/a. ***CC*** No.21860R. Began 1982; Methodist but open to all. Methodist Homes for the Aged. Turnover n/a.

West Court, 45 West Street, Banbury OX16 3RA
☎01295 258 859 🖷01295 258 859
Web: www.mha.org.uk
Specialist housing with support for older people.
Scheme Manager: Mrs Yvonne Quinney. Admin staff 1, Other staff n/a. ***CC*** No.21860R. Began 1986; Methodist but open to all. Methodist Homes for the Aged. Turnover n/a.

Willcox Close, Glastonbury BA6 9AP
☎01458 831 123
🖷01458 831 123
Web: www.mha.org.uk
Specialist housing with support for older people.
Scheme Manager: Ann Partlow. Admin staff 1, Other staff n/a. ***CC*** No.21860R. Began 2005; Methodist but open to all. Methodist Homes for the Aged. Turnover n/a.

Woodlands, Bridge Lane, Penrith CA11 8GW
☎01768 867 490
🖷01768 868 997
Web: www.mha.org.uk *Specialist housing with support for older people. Scheme Manager:* Anne Timmins. Admin staff 1, Other staff n/a. ***CC*** No.1083995. Began 1983; Methodist but open to all. Methodist Homes for the Aged. Turnover n/a.

Yew Tree / Rosewood Court, 2 Cranmer Close, Leeds LS17 5PT
☎0113 288 8355
🖷0113 269 8319
Web: www.mha.org.uk
Specialist housing with support for older people.
Scheme Manager: Yasmin Coombes. Admin staff 1, Other staff n/a ***CC*** No.21860R. Began 2005; Methodist Homes for the Aged. Turnover n/a.

For number of units see list on Page 80

BOOKS

B

BIBLE DISTRIBUTORS & PUBLISHERS

R L Allan & Son Publishers, 53 Bothwell Street, Glasgow G2 6TS
☎0141 204 1285 🖷0141 204 1285
E: rlallan@btinternet.com
Web: www.bibles-direct.com
Specialist publisher and distributor of fine-bound Bibles and hymnbooks.
Manager: Mrs Margaret Milligan. *Managing Director:* Mr Nicholas Gray. Executive staff 1, Other staff 2. Began 1863; non-denominational. No magazine. Turnover £237,000 to year end Jan 05.

Bible Distributors, Fountain House, Conduit Mews, London SE18 7AP
☎020 8316 5389 🖷020 8854 5963
Publishing Scripture portions, tracts and Bible courses; distributing English and other language Bibles; archive (over 2,000 languages).
General Manager: Mr Edwin Cross. Executive staff 3, Other staff 4. **CC** No.1053047. Began 1976; interdenominational. Magazine: *Truth & Testimony* (2,500 every two months). Turnover £150,000 to year end Jul 99.

***Bible Society (The British and Foreign Bible Society)**, Stonehill Green, Westlea, Swindon SN5 7DG
☎01793 418 100 🖷01793 418 118
E: contactus@biblesociety.org.uk
Web: www.biblesociety.org.uk
Advocating the Bible in contemporary cultures; resourcing and influencing society.
Executive Director: James Catford. Executive staff 3, Other staff 77. **CC** No.232759. Began 1804; interdenominational. Magazine: *Word in Action* (100,000 every four months). Turnover £9,500,000 [Voluntary income £8m, Trade income £1.1m] to year end Mar 05.

The Bible Society in Northern Ireland, Bible House, 27 Howard Street, Belfast BT1 6NB
☎028 9032 6577
E: gsec@bsni.co.uk
Web: www.bsni.co.uk
Servicing churches; fundraising for Scripture translation and distribution worldwide; promoting Scripture use within Northern Ireland.
General Secretary: Mr John Doherty. *Office Manager:* Mr Campbell Moore. Executive staff 1, Other staff 2. **CC** No.XN 46187. Began 1807; interdenominational. Magazine: *Word at Work* (13,000 every four months). Turnover £314,050 to year end Dec 02.

Bible Spreading Union, 1 Donald Way, Chelmsford CM2 9JB
☎01245 268 815
E: satoms@sgat.fsnet.co.uk
Distributing Holy Scriptures.
Hon Secretary: Mr Stephen A Toms. No full-time staff. **CC** No.280847. Began 1894; interdenominational. No magazine. Turnover £50,306 to year end Aug 05.

Bibles for Children, 11 Southlands Drive, Timsbury, Bath BA2 0HB
☎01761 471 169 🖷01761 471 169
E: bibles4children2@aol.com
Web: www.biblesforchildren.org.uk
Providing Bibles and Bible-related materials to primary school children and their schools. Founder: Mr Ted Hudson. No paid staff. **CC** No.1063200. Began 1997; interdenominational. No magazine. Turnover £84,864 to year end Jun 05.

Cambridge University Press, Bible Department, Edinburgh Building, Shaftesbury Road, Cambridge CB2 2RU
☎01223 325 586 🖷01223 246 151
E: bibles@cambridge.org
Web: www.cambridge.org/bibles
Publishing Bibles in the KJV, REB, NIV, RSV, NRSV and TNIV translations; also BCP Prayer Books.
Bible Publishing Manager: Mr Christopher Wright. *Bible Marketing Controller:* Amanda Taylor. Executive staff 1, Other staff 1. **CC** Began 1591; non-denominational. No magazine. Turnover n/a.

The Gideons International in the British Isles, Western House, George Street, Lutterworth LE17 4EE
☎01455 554 241 🖷01455 206 978
E: hq@gideons.org.uk
Web: www.gideons.org.uk
Personal witnessing and free distribution of Scriptures in hotels, hospitals, schools in 176 countries.
Executive Director: Mr Iain Mair. *Finance Manager:* Mr Martin R Lowdon. Executive staff 5, Other staff 5. **CC** No.221605. Began 1949; interdenominational. Magazine: *Gideon News* (44,000 quarterly). Turnover £2,900,000 to year end Dec 02.

***International Bible Society (UK)**, 3 Howard Buildings, 69 Burpham Lane, Guildford GU4 7LX
☎01483 306 869 M: 07876 284 092
🖷01483 306 870
E: ibsuk@eur.ibs.org
Web: www.ibsdirect.co.uk
Providing low-cost NIV, TNIV and a wide range of foreign-language Bibles to churches.
UK Director: Mr Graham Sopp. *Ministry Resource Manager:* Ms Gill Hooper. Executive staff 1, Other staff 2. **CC** No.285319. Began 1982; non-denominational. (Incorporating Living Bibles International (UK)). No magazine. Turnover £213,000 to year end Dec 04.

***Lifewords**, Radstock House, 5 Eccleston Street, London SW1W 9LZ
☎020 7730 2155 🖷020 7730 0240
E: contact@lifewords.info
Web: www.lifewords.info
Resourcing God's people with culturally relevant multi-language, multi-media Bible tools for one-to-one use.
International Director: Mr Neil Crosbie. UK staff 32. **CC** No.219[illegible]55. Began [illegible]888; non-denominational. (Previously Scripture Gift Mission). Magazine: *Interact* (4[illegible],000 quarterly). Turnover £3,000,000 to year end Dec 04.

***Naval, Military & Air Force Bible Society**, Castaway House, 331 Twyford Avenue, Portsmouth PO2 8RN
☎023 9269 9873
E: rp@nmafbs.org
Web: www.nmafbs.org
Distributing Scriptures to armed forces and merchant navy personnel worldwide.
Director: Mr Richard Prendergast. *Chairman:* Sqn Ldr Paddy Gallaugher MBE RAFR. Executive staff 1, Other staff n/a. **CC** No.1102593. Began 1780; non-denominational. No magazine. Turnover £101,000 to year end Dec 99.

John Ritchie Ltd, 40 Beansburn, Kilmarnock KA3 1RH
☎01563 536 394 🖷01563 571 1[illegible]1
E: sales@johnritchie.co.uk
Web: www.johnritchie.co.uk
Wholesale distributors of books, Bibles, Scripture greetings cards and resource material.
General Manager: Mr John Watson. *Shop Manageress:* Mrs Elizabeth Wallace. Executive staff 3, Other staff 9. Began [illegible]880; non-denominational. No magazine. Turnover n/a.

Scottish Bible Society, Bible House, 7 Hampton Terrace, Edinburgh EH12 [illegible]XU
☎0131 337 9701 🖷0131 337 06[illegible]1
E: info@scottishbiblesociety.org
Web: www.scottishbiblesociety.org
Helping make the Word of God available to people everywhere at a price they can afford.
Chief Executive: Miss Elaine Duncan. *Director of Programmes:* Mr Colin Hay. *Director of Field Ministries:* Mrs Maisie Rendall. Executive staff 4, Office staff 24. **CC** No.SCO 10767. Began 1861 but Edinburgh Bible Society 1809; interdenominational. (Previously National Bible Society of Scotland). Magazine: *Word at Work* (70,000 every four months). Turnover n/a.

Society for Distributing Hebrew Scriptures, Joseph House, Bury Mead Road, Hitchin SG5 1RT
☎01462 457 486 🖷01462 451 5[illegible]8
E: sdhs1940@aol.com
Web: www.sdhs.co.uk
Publishing and distributing Hebrew bilingual Scriptures and CD-roms worldwide freely to Jewish people.
General Secretary: Mr Eric [illegible] Browning. Executive staff 1, Other staff 6. **CC** No.232692. Began 194[illegible]; interdenominational. Magazine: *Lamp & Light* (8[illegible]00 every two months). Turnover n/a.

Trinitarian Bible Society, Tyndale House, Dorset Road, London SW19 3NN
☎020 8543 7857 🖷020 8543 6370
E: tbs@trinitarianbiblesociety.org
Web: www.trinitarianbiblesociety.org
Sales / grants of the Bible (AV) and Scripture portions in many languages; worldwide. General Secretary: Mr D P Rowland. *Assistant General Secretary:* Mr David Larlham. *Editorial Manager:* Mr George Anderson. Executive staff 2, Other staff 24. ***CC*** No.233082. Began 1831; non-denominational. Magazine: *Quarterly Record* (13,000 quarterly). Turnover n/a.

United Bible Societies
Europe/Middle East Area Service Centre, Zurich House, East Park, Crawley RH10 6AS
☎01293 553 821 🖷01293 553 839
E: info@ubs-europe.org
Web: www.biblesociety.org
or www.opportunity21.org
Developing and coordinating Bible Society policy in the Middle East and Europe. Europe/Middle East Area Secretary: Mr P S Wigglesworth. Executive staff 9, Other staff 18. ***CC*** No.256255. Began 1946; interdenominational. No magazine. Turnover included in World Service Centre.
World Service Centre, 7th Floor, Reading Bridge House, Reading RG1 8PJ
☎0118 950 0200 🖷0118 950 0857
E: comms@ubs-wsc.org
Web: www.biblesociety.org
or www.opportunity21.org
Providing translation services, fundraising, communication development and financial support to national Bible societies worldwide. General Secretary: Rev Dr A Miller Milloy. *Director of Communications & Fundraising Development:* Dr Ashley Scott. *Deputy General Secretary:* Mr Somporn Sirikolkarn. Executive staff 6, Other staff 23. ***CC*** No.800058. Began 1946; interdenominational. Magazine: *World Report* (Circulation n/a monthly), *The Bible Translator* (Circulation n/a half-yearly). Turnover £25,200,000 [approx US$45,500,000] to year end Dec 04.

Lord Wharton's Charity, 30 Prentis Road, London SW16 1QD
☎020 8769 1924 🖷020 8769 1924
Distributing free Bibles and religious books to young people through Anglican and non-conformist churches. Clerk to the Trustees: Mrs W B N Edwards. No full-time staff. ***CC*** No.200298. Began 1696; non-denominational. No magazine. Turnover £11,124 to year end Dec 04.

BOOKSHOPS & OTHER RETAIL OUTLETS

By Country and Postcode – for location of Postcodes see map on Page 458
All shops are included, whether or not they supplied information, to enable users to locate those in a particular area
Internet distributors are not included. These can be found in Other Literature Producers & Distributors on page 129

Postcode	Location	Name	Titles Total	Titles Christian	Second-hand Total	Second-hand Christian	Space sq ft
ENGLAND							
AL 11	**St Albans**	St Andrews Bookshop Ltd	5,127	5,127	0	0	1,041
AL 2	**St Albans**	McCrimmons Bookshop	10,000	10,000	10,000	0	250
AL 3	**St Albans**	St Andrews Bookshop Ltd	5,127	5,127	0	0	1,041
AL 5	**Harpenden**	YWAM Books	1,000	1,000	0	0	500
B 2	**Birmingham**	CLC Bookshop	10,000	10,000	0	0	1,045
		SPCK Bookshop	14,000	14,000	0	0	1,150
B 4	**Birmingham**	St Pauls by St Chad's Cathedral Bookshop	6,000	6,000	0	0	60
		Wesley Owen Books and Music	10,000	10,000	0	0	3,000
B 8	**Birmingham**	Birmingham City Mission Bookshop/Video Library	3,000	3,000	1,600	1,600	400
B 29	**Birmingham**	Christian Education Book Sales	300	150	0	0	200
B 30	**Birmingham**	St Andrews Bookshop Ltd	3,000	3,000	0	0	300
B 97	**Redditch**	Christian Word Shop	798	798	0	0	500
BA 1	**Bath**	Wesley Owen Books and Music	5,000	5,000	0	0	800
BA 5	**Wells**	Wells Cathedral Publications Ltd	369	324	0	0	432
BA20	**Yeovil**	Oasis Christian Books	10,000	10,000	0	0	1,000
BB 2	**Blackburn**	Blackburn Bible Depot	200	200	100	100	1,000
BD 1	**Bradford**	Acorn Christian Bookshop	1,000	1,000	0	0	750
		SPCK Bookshop	8,000	8,000	0	0	2,000
BD23	**Skipton**	Cornerstone	4,000	4,000	200	200	750
BH 1	**Bournemouth**	Keith Jones Christian Bookshop	46,500	46,500	1,500	1,250	2,800
		The Living Stone Bookshop	6,000	6,000	0	0	500
BH 9	**Bournemouth**	Bible Truth Depot	1,000	1,000	400	400	n/a
BH15	**Poole**	St James' Bookshop	n/a	n/a	n/a	n/a	200
BH19	**Swanage**	Swanage Christian Centre	3,500	3,500	0	0	400
BL 1	**Bolton**	Wesley Owen Books and Music	2,000	2,000	0	0	856
BN 1	**Brighton**	Wesley Owen Books and Music	n/a	n/a	n/a	n/a	n/a
BN 3	**Hove**	Books Alive Christian Bookshop	4,500	4,500	0	0	500
BN11	**Worthing**	Wesley Owen Books and Music	3,000	3,000	0	0	750
BN21	**Eastbourne**	Eastbourne Christian Resource Centre	10,000	10,000	1,000	1,000	1,000
BN25	**Seaford**	Living Words	6,000	6,000	0	0	1,000
BR 1	**Bromley**	Wesley Owen Books and Music	10,000	10,000	0	0	2,000
BR 5	**Orpington**	Rainbow Christian Centre	2,500	2,500	0	0	300
BR 6	**Orpington**	The Christian Bookshop	11,000	11,000	0	0	860
BS 1	**Bristol**	SPCK Bookshop	10,000	10,000	3,000	0	1,450
	Bristol	Wesley Owen Books and Music	4,000	4,000	0	0	1,349
BS23	**Weston-super-Mare**	Wesley Owen Books and Music	n/a	n/a	n/a	n/a	735
BS31	**Bristol**	Family Books (Keynsham)	2,000	700	0	0	1,400
CA 3	**Carlisle**	SPCK Bookshop	10,000	10,000	0	0	610
		Wesley Owen Books and Music	3,500	3,500	0	0	750
CA15	**Maryport**	Time To	400	250	0	0	250
CA28	**Whitehaven**	Cornerstone Christian Bookshop	2,600	2,600	500	500	1,200
CB 1	**Cambridge**	SPCK Bookshop	17,500	17,500	0	0	n/a
CB 2	**Cambridge**	Wesley Owen Books and Music	3,500	3,500	0	0	680
CB 7	**Ely**	Ely Cathedral Shop Ltd	2,500	1,500	0	0	1,000
		Lighthouse Christian Books and Music	3,000	3,000	200	200	600
		Soham Books	2,500	2,000	0	0	900

Bookshops & Other Retail Outlets

Postcode	Location	Name	Titles Total	Titles Christian	Second-hand Total	Second-hand Christian	Space sq ft
CH 1	**Chester**	Chester Cathedral Shop	1,200	1,200	0	0	1,000
		SPCK Bookshop	650	550	0	0	200
		Wesley Owen Books and Music	12,000	12,000	0	0	902
CH5	**Deeside**	Bethany Books	2,250	2,250	n/a	n/a	260
CH41	**Birkenhead**	Christian Bookshop	10,000	10,000	0	0	750
CH44	**Wallasey**	Bethany Books	3,500	3,500	500	0	576
		Wallasey Christian Books	2,000	2,000	0	0	4,000
CH45	**Wallasey**	The Haven Christian Bookshop & Centre	500	500	0	0	540
CM 2	**Chelmsford**	Christian Bookshop	10,500	10,500	0	0	500
CM 9	**Maldon**	The Lighthouse	850	800	0	0	320
CM14	**Brentwood**	Christian Bookshop & The Edge Coffee Shop	10,500	10,500	0	0	800
		Michael Reid Ministries Bookshop	500	500	0	0	n/a
CM21	**Sawbridgeworth**	Chapter and Verse	5,000	5,000	0	0	700
CO 1	**Colchester**	Sign of the Fish Christian Bookshop	2,500	2,500	0	0	820
CO13	**Frinton-on-Sea**	Olive Luff Bible Bookshop Ltd	3,000	3,000	0	0	450
CR 0	**Croydon**	Wesley Owen Books and Music	4,500	4,500	0	0	883
CT 1	**Canterbury**	CLC Bookshop	10,000	10,000	0	0	1,625
		SPCK Bookshop	5,500	5,500	0	[illegible]	917
CT 9	**Margate**	Christian Book Centre	5,000	5,000	1,500	1,50[illegible]	850
CT14	**Deal**	Deal Christian Resource Centre	1,500	1,500	0	[illegible]	432
CT20	**Folkestone**	Vine Books	1,300	1,300	0	[illegible]	320
CV 1	**Coventry**	Coventry Cathedral Bookshop	1,100	1,000	0	[illegible]	n/a
		Wesley Owen Books and Music	4,000	4,000	0	[illegible]	200
CV 8	**Kenilworth**	Juteronomy	1,000	1,000	0	[illegible]	100
CV10	**Nuneaton**	YWAM Books	200	200	0	0	150
CV11	**Nuneaton**	The Sycamore Tree	2,000	2,000	0	0	450
CV21	**Rugby**	Christian Bookshop	2,000	2,000	0	0	60
CV31	**Leamington Spa**	Christian Resource Centre	3,500	3,500	0	0	500
CV37	**Stratford-upon-Avon**	Jubilate Christian Bookshop Ltd	4,500	4,500	0	0	620
CW 1	**Crewe**	Copnal Books	0	0	15,000	2,000	700
		The Way Bookshop	n/a	n/a	n/a	n/a	432
CW5	**Nantwich**	The Courtyard Shop	3,000	2,900	150	13[illegible]	[illegible]500
CW 9	**Northwich**	Ichthus Christian Books	2,000	2,000	0	0	390
DA 8	**Erith**	Ark Christian Bookshop & Cafe	1,000	1,000	0	0	500
DA12	**Gravesend**	Oasis Christian Bookshop	2,600	2,600	0	0	312
DA16	**Welling**	CLC Bookshop	7,000	7,000	0	0	500
DE 1	**Derby**	Derby Cathedral Shop Ltd	1,500	1,450	0	0	400
		Wesley Owen Books and Music	3,500	3,500	0	0	1[illegible]025
DE 4	**Matlock**	Cornerstone	2,085	2,085	100	100	[illegible]50
DE14	**Burton-on-Trent**	Linkup Christian Literature	1,800	1,800	0	0	[illegible]29
DH 1	**Durham**	SPCK Bookshop	10,000	10,000	0	0	[illegible]92
		Waterstones University Bookshop	72,000	8,000	10,000	4,000	6[illegible]000
DL 3	**Darlington**	Footprints	2,000	2,000	0	0	[illegible]00
DL12	**Barnard Castle**	Book Aid	0	0	5,000	5,000	[illegible]00
DN 1	**Doncaster**	Christian Outlook	3,500	3,500	0	0	[illegible]50
DN15	**Scunthorpe**	Kings Christian Bookshop	3,000	2,500	500	500	[illegible]00
DN22	**Retford**	Book Aid	0	0	20,000	15,000	1[illegible]00
DN32	**Grimsby**	Lifeline Christian Bookstore	4,500	4,500	0	0	3[illegible]00
DT 1	**Dorchester**	Frank Herring & Sons	2,000	2,000	0	0	[illegible]40
DT 4	**Weymouth**	Weymouth Christian Books	3,000	3,000	0	0	[illegible]00
DT 6	**Bridport**	Good Books	5,000	5,000	200	200	1,[illegible]00
DY 8	**Stourbridge**	Barogha Books Ltd	2,500	2,500	0	0	1,500
		The Well Trust	2,500	2,500	0	0	1,000
EN 3	**Enfield**	Watersprings	11,000	11,000	0	0	n/a
EX 1	**Exeter**	SPCK Bookshop	10,000	10,000	0	0	[illegible]21
		The Cathedral Shop	1,000	1,000	0	0	[illegible]70
		Wesley Owen Books and Music	3,500	3,500	0	0	1,[illegible]54
EX16	**Tiverton**	New Creation Trust Christian Book and Coffee Shop	1,300	1,300	40	40	[illegible]20
EX17	**Crediton**	Phillips Print & Stationery	1,600	600	0	0	n/a
EX23	**Bude**	The Ark Angel Christian Bookshop	2,000	2,000	50	50	[illegible]0
EX31	**Barnstaple**	Doves Christian Bookshop	4,000	4,000	0	0	1,000
EX34	**Ilfracombe**	Dovetails Christian Bookshop	700	700	30	30	300
EX39	**Bideford**	Goodliving Christian Bookshop	3,313	3,250	50	50	[illegible]0
FY 1	**Blackpool**	CLC Bookshop	6,000	6,000	0	0	[illegible]0
GL 5	**Stroud**	Centre Christian Bookshop	1,585	1,585	300	300	[illegible]0
GL 7	**Cirencester**	The Corner Stone	3,000	3,000	0	0	[illegible]0
GL18	**Newent**	Good News Centre (Bookshop and Coffeehouse)	3,000	3,000	5,000	5,000	1,[illegible]0
GL52	**Cheltenham**	Wesley Owen Books and Music	3,500	3,500	0	0	[illegible]
GU 1	**Guildford**	Wesley Owen Books and Music	3,000	3,000	0	0	[illegible]
GU 2	**Guildford**	Guildford Cathedral Bookshop	3,000	2,900	0	0	3[illegible]
GU 7	**Godalming**	Nathan's Christian Bookshop	3,000	3,000	0	0	6[illegible]5
GU12	**Aldershot**	The New Life Bookshop	3,500	3,500	0	0	430
GU14	**Farnborough**	The Triangle Christian Bookstore & Café	5,000	5,000	0	0	450
GU15	**Camberley**	High Cross Christian Bookshop	2,500	2,500	0	0	n/a
GU21	**Woking**	Wesley Owen Books and Music	3,000	3,000	300	300	5[illegible]
GU31	**Petersfield**	Unity Bookshop	3,000	3,000	0	0	4[illegible]
GU34	**Alton**	Just Looking Christian Bookshop	2,500	2,500	100	100	8[illegible]0
		Redemptorist Publications	3,000	3,000	0	0	6,0[illegible]
GU51	**Fleet**	Living Stones Christian Centre Ltd	3,000	3,000	0	0	1,5[illegible]
HA 3	**Harrow**	Wesley Owen Books and Music	3,500	3,500	0	0	1,156
HA 4	**Ruislip**	Priory Bookshop	1,000	1,000	2,000	500	n/a
HA 6	**Northwood**	London School of Theology Books and Resources	2,000	1,950	0	0	30[illegible]
HD 1	**Huddersfield**	Centre Books, Crafts and Coffee Shop	5,000	5,000	0	0	7,0[illegible]
		Christian Books	4,000	4,000	0	0	1,0[illegible]
HG 1	**Harrogate**	Wesley Owen Books and Music	7,000	7,000	0	0	1,6[illegible]
HG 4	**Ripon**	The Ark Christian Bookshop	800	800	200	200	2[illegible]

Postcode	Location	Name	Titles Total	Titles Christian	Second-hand Total	Second-hand Christian	Space sq ft
HP 1	Hemel Hempstead	The Mustard Seed	0	0	0	0	n/a
HP16	Great Missenden	St Andrews Bookshop Ltd	6,000	6,000	0	0	1,500
HR 1	Hereford	Hereford Cathedral Shop	20	10	0	0	400
HR 2	Hereford	English Benedictine Congregation Bookshop	600	600	0	0	200
HR 4	Hereford	SPCK Bookshop	4,000	4,000	0	0	389
HU 2	Hull	Wesley Owen Books and Music	5,000	5,000	5,000	5,000	1,100
HU13	Hessle	Our Lady's Bookshop	15,000	15,000	0	0	350
HU17	Beverley	Beverley Minster Shop Ltd	100	60	0	0	192
		Jacob's Well	5,000	5,000	3,000	400	600
HX 1	Halifax	Good Life Books (GLF)	2,000	2,000	0	0	1,000
IG 1	Ilford	The Bible Bookshop	4,000	4,000	400	400	1,200
IP 1	Ipswich	CLC Bookshop	6,000	6,000	0	0	550
		Revelations	4,000	4,000	0	0	425
IP14	Stowmarket	Nutshell Bookshop	3,000	2,800	0	0	500
IP33	Bury St Edmunds	The Cathedral Shop	2,000	1,500	0	0	144
		St Andrews Bookshop Ltd	2,000	2,000	500	500	480
KT 1	Kingston upon Thames	Wesley Owen Books and Music	6,000	6,000	0	0	900
KT18	Epsom	Dovecote Christian Bookshop	1,100	1,100	0	0	320
L 1	Liverpool	Gladstones Bookshop (Christian Media)	3,000	3,000	200	200	1,200
		Liverpool Cathedral Shop	8,500	8,200	0	0	2,000
		Pauline Books & Media	20,000	20,000	0	0	1,000
		Wesley Owen Books and Music	3,500	3,500	0	0	865
L 3	Liverpool	Metropolitan Cathedral Bookshop	n/a	n/a	n/a	n/a	400
L 17	Liverpool	Aigburth Christian Bookshop	5,000	5,000	0	0	n/a
L 31	Liverpool	Cornerstone	2,000	2,000	0	0	150
LA 1	Lancaster	Good News Christian Bookshop	2,000	2,000	0	0	310
LA 9	Kendal	Market Place Books	4,000	3,500	0	0	500
LA12	Ulverston	Lonsdale Bible Society	3,000	3,000	1,000	1,000	500
LE 1	Leicester	CLC Bookshop	10,000	10,000	0	0	1,195
		SPCK Bookshop	5,500	5,500	0	0	1,152
LE10	Hinkley	The Vine Christian Bookshop	1,000	1,000	50	50	250
LE11	Loughborough	Good News Centre	8,000	8,000	1,000	1,000	1,700
LE67	Coalville	Mount Saint Bernard Abbey Shop	6,000	4,000	0	0	280
LN 2	Lincoln	Advance Bookshop	6,500	4,500	0	0	700
		Lincoln Minster Shops Ltd	n/a	n/a	n/a	n/a	n/a
		SPCK Bookshop	9,000	9,000	0	0	1,173
LS 1	Leeds	Wesley Owen Books and Music	5,000	5,000	0	0	2,000
LS 2	Leeds	St Pauls by Leeds Cathedral	2,000	2,000	0	0	300
LS 6	Leeds	Acorn Books	3,000	3,000	500	500	400
LU 2	Luton	Luton Christian Book Centre	10,000	10,000	0	0	1,300
LU 6	Dunstable	Christian Books	4,000	4,000	0	0	400
M 1	Manchester	Wesley Owen Books and Music	3,500	3,500	0	0	4,500
M 2	Manchester	Catholic Truth Society Bookshop	8,500	8,500	100	0	1,400
M 3	Salford	Cathedral Books Ltd	2,200	2,200	0	0	1,750
M 4	Manchester	St Denys' Bookshop	5,000	5,000	0	0	1,200
M 41	Manchester	Taste & See Bookshop	800	800	0	0	50
ME 4	Chatham	CLC Bookshop	4,500	4,500	0	0	484
ME10	Sittingbourne	Sittingbourne Christian Bookshop	1,350	1,350	225	225	400
ME14	Maidstone	The Christian Bookshop	10,000	10,000	0	0	n/a
MK 6	Milton Keynes	Christian Centre Bookshop	1,500	1,500	0	0	440
MK12	Milton Keynes	St Andrews Bookshop Ltd	3,000	3,000	0	0	400
MK40	Bedford	Harmony Books	5,500	5,400	100	100	450
		Wesley Owen Books and Music	3,500	3,500	0	0	620
NE 1	Newcastle upon Tyne	Catholic Truth Society	n/a	n/a	n/a	n/a	n/a
		CLC Bookshop	10,000	10,000	0	0	1,980
		SPCK Bookshop	9,000	9,000	0	0	1,053
		SPCK Bookshop (The Bible House)	7,250	5,250	0	0	1,544
NE11	Gateshead	The Ocracy	10,000	10,000	0	0	n/a
NE26	Whitley Bay	Bethany Christian Bookshop and Coffeeshop	1,500	1,500	0	0	466
NE46	Hexham	Shalom The Good Book Shop	3,800	3,800	0	0	600
NE61	Morpeth	Lifestyle Christian Books and Music	7,000	7,000	0	0	700
NG 1	Nottingham	Castlegate Bookshop	4,800	4,800	0	0	144
		Wesley Owen Books and Music	6,000	6,000	0	0	950
NG 4	Nottingham	The Mustard Seed	10,000	10,000	0	0	600
NG 5	Nottingham	The Olive Tree Bookshop	3,000	3,000	0	0	500
NG 9	Nottingham	Christian Book Centre	6,000	6,000	0	0	2,500
		Trinity Books	n/a	n/a	n/a	n/a	n/a
NG17	Nottingham	The Ark Christian Bookshop	3,500	3,500	0	0	600
		Kyrios Books	15,000	13,000	15,000	13,000	396
NG18	Mansfield	Mansfield Christian Book Centre	n/a	n/a	n/a	n/a	900
NG24	Newark	Emmanuel Christian Bookshop	2,900	2,900	0	0	360
NN 1	Northampton	The Manna House Christian Bookshop	5,000	5,000	2,000	2,000	2,400
NR 1	Norwich	CLC Bookshop	8,500	8,500	0	0	720
		Norwich Cathedral Shop Ltd	1,000	1,000	0	0	n/a
NR 2	Norwich	SPCK Bookshop	14,000	14,000	0	0	883
NR11	Norwich	Sonshine Christian Bookshop	1,800	1,800	0	0	700
NR19	Dereham	Green Pastures Christian Bookshop	1,200	1,200	0	0	550
NR22	Walsingham	The Shrine Bookshop	1,500	1,500	0	0	300
NR32	Lowestoft	Oasis Christian Bookshop	2,000	2,000	0	0	600
OL 1	Oldham	King of Kings Christian Bookshop	3,000	3,000	0	0	400
OL 6	Ashton-under-Lyne	Spectrum Christian Books and Gifts	2,000	2,000	0	0	360
OL12	Rochdale	The Bible Bookshop	1,800	1,800	0	0	360
OL15	Littleborough	The Vine Christian Bookshop and Coffee House	800	800	0	0	90
OX 1	Oxford	B H Blackwell Ltd (Religion Dept)	6,939	6,005	1,420	1,420	169
OX 4	Oxford	St Andrews Bookshop Ltd	3,000	3,000	0	0	850
OX 8	Witney	St Andrews Bookshop Ltd	3,000	3,000	0	0	350
OX10	Wallingford	The Fountain (Wallingford) Ltd	2,000	2,000	0	0	360

B

Bookshops & Other Retail Outlets

Postcode	Location	Name	Titles Total	Titles Christian	Second-hand Total	Second-hand Christian	Space sq ft
PE 1	Peterborough	Peterborough Cathedral Enterprises Ltd	950	900	0	0	200
		Peterborough Christian Books Ltd	5,000	5,000	0	0	1,000
PE 9	Stamford	CLC Bookshop	3,000	3,000	0	0	525
PE13	Wisbech	GEM Books	1,000	1,000	0	0	200
		Oasis Christian Books	6,000	4,500	4,000	3,000	750
PE15	March	March Christian Bookshop	2,300	2,300	0	0	500
PE26	Ramsey	Christian Bookshop	1,000	1,000	0	0	225
PL 1	Plymouth	Christian Literature Centre	5,000	5,000	100	0	500
PL 4	Plymouth	Christian Resources Project	2,000	2,000	3,000	3,000	450
PL15	Launceston	Aquila Fellowship Trust (The Christian Bookshop)	5,500	5,500	1,000	980	1,122
PL25	St Austell	Good News Crusade Bookshop	5,000	5,000	800	800	450
PO 1	Portsmouth	Portsmouth Cathedral Bookshop	1,500	1,200	0	0	80
PO 5	Southsea	Acorn Book and Toy Shop	2,000	1,500	0	0	144
PO12	Gosport	Cornerstone Books (Gosport Cornerstone Trust)	2,500	2,500	0	0	900
PO16	Fareham	The Well	2,500	2,500	0	0	500
PO18	Chichester	Catholic Bible School Bookshop	1,000	1,000	0	0	25
PO19	Chichester	Living Word	3,500	3,500	150	150	500
		SPCK Bookshop	4,000	4,000	0	0	624
PO21	Bognor Regis	Living Word	4,000	4,000	100	100	600
PO30	Newport	Castlebooks	8,000	8,000	0	0	858
PO33	Ryde	Quarr Abbey Bookshop	400	400	100	100	600
PR 1	Preston	Christian Book Centre	8,000	8,000	0	0	900
PR 7	Chorley	Two Worlds Christian Bookshop	3,000	3,000	0	0	400
PR 8	Southport	Southport Christian Book Centre	8,000	8,000	0	0	200
RG 1	Reading	Greyfriars Christian Centre	1,200	1,200	0	0	[illegible]080
		St Andrews Bookshop Ltd	4,000	4,000	0	0	[illegible]300
RG12	Bracknell	Kerith Centre Bookshop	2,200	2,200	0	0	200
RG40	Wokingham	St Andrews Bookshop Ltd	3,000	3,000	0	0	350
RH 2	Reigate	Christian Bookshop	4,000	4,000	0	0	400
RH10	Crawley	Dabcec Bookshop	3,000	2,700	0	0	500
RH12	Horsham	Horsham Christian Centre	n/a	n/a	n/a	n/a	n/a
RH16	Haywards Heath	Haywards Heath Christian Book Centre	6,500	6,500	0	0	300
RM 1	Romford	Havering Christian Bookshop and Centre	7,000	7,000	0	0	[illegible]300
RM14	Upminster	Fools Bookshop	3,000	3,000	0	0	[illegible]275
S 1	Sheffield	CLC Bookshop	10,000	10,000	0	0	935
		Hallam Book Centre	1,000	1,000	0	0	500
		SPCK Bookshop	9,800	9,800	0	0	317
		Wesleyan Reform Union Bookshop	400	400	0	0	324
S 32	Hope Valley	Cliff College Bookshop	4,000	4,000	0	0	430
S 40	Chesterfield	Cornerstone Book and Coffee Shop	2,100	2,100	0	0	n/a
S 45	Chesterfield	Food for Thought	1,500	1,500	0	0	240
S 66	Rotherham	Full Life Christian Centre	400	400	0	0	600
SG 6	Letchworth	The Christian Bookshop	9,000	9,000	0	0	600
SG12	Ware	All Nations Christian Bookshop Ltd	2,000	2,000	0	0	[illegible]20
SK 1	Stockport	Wesley Owen Books and Music	3,500	3,500	0	0	1[illegible]85
SK11	Macclesfield	Wesley Owen Books and Music	3,000	3,000	0	0	689
SK17	Buxton	Buxton Christian Bookshop	1,750	1,750	500	500	[illegible]50
SL 1	Slough	St Andrews Bookshop	n/a	n/a	n/a	n/a	n/a
SL 6	Maidenhead	St Andrews Bookshop Ltd	3,000	3,000	0	0	[illegible]25
SL 9	Gerrards Cross	Gold Hill Church Books	1,000	1,000	0	0	n/a
		WEC Bookroom	1,000	1,000	0	0	[illegible]00
SM 1	Sutton	Wesley Owen Books and Music	6,200	6,200	0	0	1[illegible]00
SM 6	Wallington	The Oasis	6,000	6,000	0	0	1[illegible]00
SN 1	Swindon	Christian Bookshop	3,500	3,500	0	0	[illegible]50
		The Rainbow Bookshop	700	700	0	0	[illegible]20
SN 6	Swindon	Seekers Light Trust	3,000	3,000	0	0	[illegible]00
SN 8	Marlborough	Mustard Seed	2,000	2,000	0	0	[illegible]70
SN11	Calne	Calne Christian Bookshop	5,000	5,000	300	300	[illegible]00
SN15	Chippenham	Revelation Christian Resource Centre	5,000	5,000	0	0	[illegible]00
SN16	Malmesbury	Malmesbury Abbey Books Ltd	1,500	1,500	0	0	350
SO14	Southampton	Wesley Owen Books and Music	n/a	n/a	n/a	n/a	n/a
SO15	Southampton	CLC Bookshop	10,000	10,000	0	0	1,[illegible]00
SO16	Southampton	Southern Light Literature	800	800	100	0	[illegible]00
		The Fair Trade Shop	0	0	0	0	n/a
SO19	Southampton	Mayflower Christian Bookshop	1,990	1,990	135	135	[illegible]00
SO23	Winchester	SPCK Bookshop	12,500	12,500	0	0	[illegible]52
SO41	Lymington	The Ark	6,500	6,500	40	40	n/a
SO51	Romsey	The Oasis Christian Centre	10,000	10,000	0	0	[illegible]00
		Sozo Books	3,500	3,500	0	0	[illegible]00
SP 1	Salisbury	Sarum College Bookshop Ltd	7,000	7,000	1,000	1,000	[illegible]60
		SPCK Bookshop	12,500	12,500	0	0	[illegible]5
SP10	Andover	The Vine Trust Bookshop	2,000	2,000	0	0	4[illegible]0
SR 5	Sunderland	Bridge Books & Music	3,500	3,500	0	0	[illegible]2
SS 1	Southend-on-Sea	Southend Christian Bookshop Ltd	10,500	10,500	0	0	1,2[illegible]0
SS 9	Leigh-on-Sea	Church Shop	1,600	1,600	0	0	5[illegible]6
ST 1	Stoke-on-Trent	Bible Book Shop	4,000	4,000	0	0	4[illegible]0
		Methodist Book Centre	n/a	n/a	n/a	n/a	6,2[illegible]0
ST16	Stafford	Gateway Trust	4,500	4,500	0	0	[illegible]
SY 1	Shrewsbury	Illuminate	5,000	5,000	250	250	1,2[illegible]
SY11	Oswestry	Oswestry Christian Bookshop	4,000	4,000	500	500	6,9[illegible]
SY13	Whitchurch	Aletheia	8,000	8,000	0	0	5[illegible]
TA 1	Taunton	Good News – TCLC	5,000	5,000	0	0	6[illegible]
TA24	Minehead	Under The Rainbow	2,000	2,000	0	0	6[illegible]
TA 6	Bridgwater	Acorns Christian Resources	2,400	2,400	0	0	7[illegible]
TD15	Berwick-upon-Tweed	The Burning Light	n/a	n/a	n/a	n/a	n/a
		Faith Mission Christian Book Centre	6,000	6,000	0	0	2[illegible]

Postcode	Location	Name	Titles Total	Titles Christian	Second-hand Total	Second-hand Christian	Space sq ft
TF 3	Telford	Revelations	6,000	6,000	0	0	800
TN 1	Tunbridge Wells	The Christian Book Shop	11,000	11,000	0	0	500
		HoldFast Bible & Tract Depot	3,000	3,000	1,000	1,000	200
TN 9	Tonbridge	The Tonbridge Christian Book Centre Ltd	11,000	11,000	0	0	1,200
TN22	Uckfield	Pilgrim Hall Bookshop	1,500	1,500	0	0	300
TN33	Battle	Ashburnham Christian Trust Bookshop	1,500	1,500	0	0	300
TN34	Hastings	Pathway Books Ltd	4,000	4,000	0	0	440
TQ 4	Paignton	Choice Words Torbay	4,000	4,000	0	0	850
TQ 7	Kingsbridge	Wordwise	500	500	0	0	300
TQ12	Newton Abbot	Choice Words Christian Bookshop	4,000	4,000	0	0	650
		Rora Christian Fellowship Trust	600	600	150	150	n/a
TR 1	Truro	SPCK Bookshop	7,500	7,500	0	0	1,218
		Truro Cathedral Shop	2,000	1,500	0	0	500
TR13	Helston	Living Waters Christian Bookshop	8,000	8,000	0	0	1,050
TR15	Redruth	Christian Book Centre	8,500	8,500	0	0	400
TR18	Penzance	The Living Word	1,000	1,000	0	0	130
TR26	St Ives	Zion Christian Books	2,500	2,500	0	0	1,000
TS 1	Middlesbrough	CLC Bookshop	8,000	3,000	0	0	720
TS10	Redcar	Adeste Christian Trust	1,000	1,000	200	200	800
TS18	Stockton-on-Tees	Bridge Bookshop	5,000	5,000	0	0	1,028
TW 3	Hounslow	Bridge Christian Books	4,500	4,500	0	0	900
TW18	Staines	Canaan Christian Book Centre	5,000	5,000	0	0	600
UB 6	Greenford	Perivale Christian Bookshop	4,750	4,750	0	0	850
UB 8	Uxbridge	Maranatha Christian Bookshop	5,000	5,000	0	0	850
WA 1	Warrington	CLC Bookshop	4,000	4,000	0	0	700
WA10	St Helens	The Christian Bookshop	3,000	3,000	0	0	192
WD17	Watford	Wesley Owen Books and Music	3,500	3,500	0	0	683
WF 1	Wakefield	3's Company Bookshop	2,500	2,500	0	0	500
		Wakefield Cathedral Bookshop	350	350	0	0	130
WF 5	Ossett	Christian Bookshop	2,000	2,000	0	0	270
WF 8	Pontefract	Pontefract Christian Bookshop	2,000	2,000	0	0	700
WF13	Dewsbury	The Branch Christian Books	5,000	5,000	1,000	1,000	1,000
WN 1	Wigan	Words Bookshop	4,500	4,500	0	0	2,000
WR 1	Worcester	SPCK Bookshop	3,500	8,500	0	0	1,234
WR 9	Droitwich	Grace Cards and Books	4,000	4,000	0	0	500
WS 1	Walsall	Wesley Owen Books and Music	3,500	3,500	0	0	975
WS13	Lichfield	Lichfield Cathedral Bookshop	3,300	3,200	0	0	725
WV 2	Wolverhampton	CLC Bookshop	5,000	5,000	0	0	530
YO 1	York	Wesley Owen Books and Music	12,000	7,500	20,000	10,000	2,000
		SPCK Bookshop	9,000	9,000	0	0	1,507
		Spurriergate Centre	200	200	0	0	n/a
YO11	Scarborough	Immanuel Bookshop	3,000	3,000	100	100	400
YO15	Bridlington	Bethany Bookshop	2,000	2,000	500	500	600
London							
E 2	London	Books For Life	1,500	1,500	200	200	300
E 10	London	Good News Shop	10,000	10,000	0	0	1,500
E 18	London	Wesley Owen Books and Music	4,400	4,400	0	0	691
EC1	London	CLC Bookshop	16,000	16,000	0	0	5,000
EC4	London	Protestant Truth Society Bookshop	6,000	6,000	0	0	950
N 6	London	Metanoia Book Service	1,500	1,500	0	0	200
N 16	London	Pendlebury's	2,800	2,800	26,000	26,000	n/a
N 12	London	Bedford Books	2,000	2,000	0	0	500
		Cornerstone	5,000	5,000	0	0	1,500
N 14	London	Oak Hill Bookroom	1,000	1,000	0	0	250
NW 1	London	Methodist Bookshop	6,000	6,000	0	0	576
		Quaker Bookshop	5,000	2,000	500	0	900
SE 1	London	The Cathedral Shop	2,000	2,000	0	0	600
		New Covenant Bookshop	n/a	n/a	n/a	n/a	n/a
		Salvationist Publishing and Supplies Ltd	200	200	0	0	2,300
		Tabernacle Bookshop	2,000	2,000	0	0	2,000
SE 5	London	Urban Gospel UK	5,000	1,500	300	300	400
SE18	London	Chapter Two	8,000	8,000	200	190	400
SE25	London	Spurgeon's Book Room	4,000	4,000	0	0	500
SE26	London	Book Aid	30,000	20,000	30,000	20,000	1,000
SW1	London	Church House Bookshop	12,000	12,000	0	0	2,000
		St Pauls (Westminster Cathedral)	40,000	40,000	0	0	11,500
		Catholic Truth Society	2,000	2,000	0	0	750
		SPCK Bookshop	n/a	n/a	n/a	n/a	1,275
		SPCK Secondhand & Antiquarian Bookshop	0	0	10,000	10,000	600
SW 7	London	Holy Trinity Brompton Bookshop	3,662	3,662	0	0	1,000
		Russian Orthodox Cathedral Shop	n/a	n/a	n/a	n/a	n/a
SW 9	London	Beautiful Books LEF	5,000	5,000	0	0	650
		Christian Book Plus	40	40	0	0	n/a
SW16	London	Manna Christian Centre	10,000	5,000	0	0	700
W 3	London	Good News Christian Resource Centre Ltd	5,000	5,000	0	0	600
W 8	London	Pauline Books & Media	20,000	20,000	0	0	1,200
W 11	London	Christian Books & Music, Kensington Temple	5,000	5,000	0	0	450
W 1	London	The Regents Hall Café	1,000	1,000	0	0	250
		Waterstones Bookshop (incorporating Mowbrays)	45,000	10,000	0	0	3,000
		Wesley Owen Books and Music	5,000	5,000	0	0	2,721
WC1	London	United Reformed Church Bookshop	2,500	2,500	0	0	96
		Waterstones Bookshop	2,000	2,000	500	500	n/a

B

Bookshops & Other Retail Outlets

Postcode	Location	Name	Titles Total	Titles Christian	Second-hand Total	Second-hand Christian	Space sq ft
CHANNEL ISLANDS							
GY 1	**Guernsey**	Good News Christian Bookshop	1,500	1,500	0	[illegible]	300
JE 2	**Jersey**	Christian Bookshop Mission Ltd	2,000	2,000	0	[illegible]	210
ISLE OF MAN							
IM 1	**Douglas**	Churches Bookshop	4,000	4,000	70	70	200
IM 2	**Douglas**	The Well Bookshop & Coffee Shop	1,500	1,500	50	50	750
NORTHERN IRELAND							
BT 1	**Belfast**	Evangelical Book Shop	10,000	10,000	3,000	3,000	900
		Faith Mission Bookshop	10,000	10,000	2,000	2,000	[illegible]
		The Good Book shop	7,000	7,000	0	0	940
		Wesley Owen Books and Music	12,000	11,000	0	0	450
BT 4	**Belfast**	Belmont Christian Book Centre	7,000	7,000	200	[illegible]	n/a
BT 5	**Belfast**	Faith Mission Bookshop	n/a	n/a	n/a	n/a	n/a
		Scripture Union Resource Centre	1,500	1,500	0	0	[illegible]
BT 6	**Belfast**	Ebenezer Bible and Bookshop	1,500	1,500	0	0	300
BT 8	**Belfast**	Covenanter Bookshop	3,000	3,000	0	0	400
BT 9	**Belfast**	Number Nine Resource Centre	2,500	2,500	0	0	500
BT20	**Bangor**	Faith Mission Bookshop	10,000	10,000	0	0	750
BT23	**Newtownards**	Ards Evangelical Bookshop	20,000	20,000	0	0	[illegible]
BT28	**Lisburn**	Faith Mission Bookshop	10,000	10,000	0	0	750
BT32	**Banbridge**	Faith Mission Bookshop	5,000	5,000	0	0	750
BT33	**Newcastle**	Beulah Bookshop	4,000	4,000	300	300	300
BT34	**Newry**	Faith Mission Bookshop	10,000	10,000	0	0	500
BT39	**Ballyclare**	Book Aid	0	0	3,000	3,000	400
		Christian Book Centre	1,000	1,000	0	0	500
BT43	**Ballymena**	Faith Mission Bookshop	10,000	10,000	0	0	750
BT47	**Londonderry**	Faith Mission Bookshop	10,000	10,000	0	0	750
BT52	**Coleraine**	Wesley Owen Books and Music	6,000	6,000	0	0	500
BT61	**Armagh**	Faith Mission Bookshop	5,000	5,000	0	0	500
BT62	**Craigavon**	Faith Mission Bookshop	10,000	10,000	0	0	[illegible]
BT66	**Craigavon**	Faith Mission Bookshop	10,000	10,000	0	0	500
BT74	**Enniskillen**	Evangelical Bookshop	3,000	3,000	0	0	440
BT78	**Omagh**	Faith Mission Bookshop	10,000	10,000	0	0	500
BT80	**Cookstown**	Faith Mission Bookshop	10,000	10,000	0	0	500
BT92	**Eniskillen**	Oasis Bookshop	3,800	3,500	2,300	2,000	750
SCOTLAND							
AB 1	**Aberdeen**	CLC Bookshop	10,000	10,000	0	0	2,000
AB 24	**Aberdeen**	Blackwell's University Bookshop	500	500	0	0	2,000
AB25	**Aberdeen**	Wesley Owen Books and Music	15,000	12,500	0	0	1,350
AB42	**Peterhead**	Faith Mission Christian Book Centre	10,000	10,000	0	0	500
AB43	**Fraserburgh**	Faith Mission Christian Book Centre	5,000	5,000	0	0	360
AB56	**Buckie**	Cornerstone Bookshop	n/a	n/a	n/a	n/a	n/a
DD 1	**Dundee**	CLC Bookshop	5,000	5,000	0	0	500
		Wesley Owen Books and Music	2,500	2,500	0	0	570
DG 7	**Castle Douglas**	The Bible Shop	1,700	1,700	0	0	400
EH 1	**Edinburgh**	B McCall Barbour	10,000	10,000	300	300	300
		Free Church of Scotland Bookshop	10,880	10,880	0	0	300
EH 2	**Edinburgh**	Cornerstone Bookshop	n/a	n/a	n/a	n/a	n/a
		Wesley Owen Books and Music	21,000	17,500	0	0	[illegible]
FK 1	**Falkirk**	The Almond Tree Bookshop and Coffee House	1,000	1,000	0	0	2,500
		Wesley Owen Books and Music	3,000	3,000	0	0	500
FK 8	**Stirling**	Faith Mission Christian Book Centre	9,000	9,000	0	0	600
G 1	**Glasgow**	Pauline Books & Media	20,000	20,000	0	0	900
G 2	**Glasgow**	Wesley Owen Books and Music	22,000	20,000	0	0	5,500
G 3	**Glasgow**	Free Presbyterian Church of Scotland Bookroom	4,000	4,000	400	400	450
G 67	**Glasgow**	Cumbernauld Churches Bookshop Ltd	500	500	0	0	300
		New Dawn Bookshop and Connection Coffee House	800	800	0	0	1,200
HS 1	**Stornoway**	Blythswood Bookshop	1,100	1,100	0	0	550
		Stornoway Religious Bookshop	1,200	1,200	0	0	360
IV 1	**Inverness**	CLC Bookshop	4,500	4,500	0	0	430
IV 2	**Inverness**	Wesley Owen Books and Music	4,500	4,000	0	0	550
IV15	**Dingwall**	Blythswood Bookshop	850	850	50	50	216
IV16	**Dingwall**	Blythswood Bookshop	n/a	n/a	n/a	n/a	n/a
IV30	**Elgin**	Pluscarden Abbey Bookshop	1,000	1,000	200	200	430
IV51	**Portree**	Blythswood Bookshop	800	800	50	50	250
KA 7	**Ayr**	Wesley Owen Books and Music	4,000	3,250	0	0	1,157
KA21	**Saltcoats**	Bible Bookshop	322	322	0	0	400
KY12	**Dunfermline**	Faith Mission Christian Book Centre	20,000	20,000	0	0	[illegible]
KY15	**Cupar**	The Lighthouse	2,500	2,500	0	0	150
KY16	**St Andrews**	The Ladyhead Bookshop	3,000	2,800	0	0	300
ML 1	**Motherwell**	GLO Bookshop	20,000	20,000	0	0	[illegible]
PA15	**Greenock**	New Dawn Bookshop and Connection Coffee House	1,500	1,500	50	50	1,350
PA23	**Dunoon**	Dunoon Baptist Church Centre	1,300	1,300	0	0	500
PH 1	**Perth**	The Manna House	3,000	3,000	0	0	700
PH 2	**Perth**	Mustard Seed Bookshop	2,000	2,000	0	0	[illegible]
PH10	**Blairgowrie**	Emmaus Road Bookshop	1,000	1,000	0	0	700
PH16	**Pitlochry**	Atholl Centre Bookshop	300	300	50	50	247
TD 9	**Hawick**	Mustard Seed Bookshop	4,000	4,000	0	0	400
ZE 1	**Lerwick**	The Tanglewood Trust Christian Bookshop	2,500	2,500	0	0	295

B

Postcode	Location	Name	Titles Total	Titles Christian	Second-hand Total	Second-hand Christian	Space sq ft
WALES							
CF10	**Cardiff**	The Bible Depot	2,000	1,250	0	0	250
		Christian Bookshop	4,500	4,500	400	400	1,000
		SPCK Bookshop	4,000	4,000	0	0	700
CF14	**Cardiff**	Book Plus/Llyfrau Plus	4,900	3,900	0	0	1,000
		Heath Christian Bookshop Charitable Trust	2,500	2,500	500	500	750
		The Olive Branch Christian Book & Coffee Shop	3,000	3,000	0	0	400
CF31	**Bridgend**	Christian Bookshop	1,000	1,000	0	0	450
CF37	**Pontypridd**	Harvest Books and Crafts	450	400	0	40	400
CF44	**Aberdare**	Beulah Faith Mission & Christian Bookshop	2,000	2,000	0	0	500
CF83	**Caerphilly**	The Rock (Bedwas Christian Resource Centre)	2,500	2,500	500	500	500
CH 5	**Deeside**	Bethany Books	2,250	2,250	0	0	260
CH 7	**Mold**	Good News Centre	1,000	1,000	0	0	280
LD 1	**Llandrindod Wells**	Christian Bookshop (EMW)	1,200	1,200	0	0	275
LL11	**Wrexham**	The Christian Bookshop	1,000	1,000	0	0	275
LL18	**Rhyl**	Clwyd Christian Bookshop Ltd	4,000	4,000	20	20	700
LL34	**Penmaenmawr**	Oasis Christian Bookshop and Tearoom	950	950	0	0	760
LL57	**Bangor**	Bangor Christian Bookshop	3,174	3,174	0	0	270
		Siop Y Gair	2,000	2,000	n/a	n/a	200
NP 4	**Pontypool**	Christian Bookshop	1,000	1,000	300	300	n/a
NP20	**Newport**	Shepherd's Christian Bookshop	n/a	n/a	n/a	n/a	2,000
NP44	**Cwmbran**	Beacon Books and Crafts Ltd	3,250	3,250	700	700	800
SA 1	**Swansea**	Christian Bookshop	3,000	3,000	0	0	750
		CLC Bookshop	10,000	10,000	0	0	1,195
SA14	**Llanelli**	The Apostolic Church Training School Bookshop	1,200	1,200	0	0	850
SA31	**Carmarthen**	Christian Books	650	650	30	30	12
SA34	**Whitland**	Christian Connections	450	450	100	100	200
SA43	**Cardigan**	Teifi Christian Books	2,050	2,050	0	0	260
SA61	**Haverfordwest**	Emmanuel Christian Bookshop	2,500	2,500	0	0	450
SA62	**Haverfordwest**	St David's Cathedral Bookshop	850	850	0	0	250
SY16	**Newtown**	Emmanuel Books and Gifts	1,200	1,200	50	50	150
SY18	**Llanidloes**	Bethany Books	1,000	1,000	0	0	150
SY23	**Aberystwyth**	Christian Bookshop	2,000	2,000	0	0	200
		St Michael's Bookshop	1,238	1,238	0	0	250

B

BOOKSHOPS & OTHER RETAIL OUTLETS

Music, Fair Trade and other non-book shops are included. All shops are bookshops unless otherwise stated.
Most bookshops also stock cards, music, CDs, tapes and gifts.
Internet distributors can be found in Other Literature Producers & Distributors on Page 129.

†3's Company Bookshop, 3 Upper York Street, Wakefield WF1 3LQ
☎01924 201 022
Also coffee shop.
Manager: Mrs Bridie Watson. Executive staff 1, Other staff 3. ***CC*** No.1003233. Began 1991; interdenominational. Turnover n/a

Abbey Bookshop, Buckfast Abbey, Buckfastleigh TQ11 0EE
☎01364 645 506 🖷01364 645 524
E: bookshop@buckfast.org.uk
Manager: Mr David Ching. Executive staff 1, Admin staff 1. ***CC*** No.232497. Began n/a; ecumenical. Turnover n/a.

†Academy Books, 13 Marmion Road, Southsea PO5 2AT
☎023 9281 6632 🖷023 9281 6632
Web: www.book-academy.com
Proprietor: Mr William H Robinson. Executive staff 1, Other staff 2. Began 1972; non-denominational. Turnover n/a.

Acorn Book and Toy Shop, 109 Palmerston Road, Southsea PO5 3PS
☎023 9282 3925
Director: Miss Jean Pitts. Executive staff 1, Other staff 3. Began 1988; non-denominational. Turnover n/a.

Acorn Books, 1 Monkbridge Road, Headingley, Leeds LS6 4DX
☎0113 275 8233 🖷0113 275 8233
E: acornbooks@grobertson.freeserve.co.uk
Manager: Mrs Robertson. Executive staff 1, Other staff 2. Began 1998; interdenominational. Turnover £26,000 to year end Dec 04.

Acorn Christian Bookshop, 42 Sunbridge Road, Bradford BD1 2AB
☎01274 720 000
E: irenelam1@yahoo.co.uk
Web: www.christian-bookshop.com
Manager: Irene Charles. Executive staff 1, Other staff 1. Began 1997; interdenominational. (Previously Lambs Bookshop). Turnover £25,000 to year end Dec 04.

***Acorns Christian Resources**, 67 High Street, Bridgwater TA6 3BQ
☎01278 453 045
E: acornsresources@tiscali.co.uk
Also counselling service, coffee shop; Acorns Bible College.
Managers: Mrs Angela Cooper, Mrs Linda Heal. Executive staff 2. ***CC*** No.1071926. Began 1988; non-denominational. Part of Acorns Christian Trust. Turnover £70,000 to year end Dec 02.

Adeste Christian Trust, 8 Redcar Lane, Redcar TS10 3JF
☎01642 480 252
Manager: Miss P Rutherford. No full-time staff. ***CC*** Began 1982; interdenominational. Turnover n/a.

Advance Bookshop, 17 Monks Road, Lincoln LN2 5HL
☎01522 525 898
🖷01522 528 188
E: mail@advancebookshop.co.uk
Web: www.advancebookshop.co.uk
Also telephone, mail and online ordering facilities.
Proprietor: Mr Tim Leffler. No full-time staff. Began 1950; interdenominational. Turnover n/a.

Aigburth Christian Bookshop, 361 Aigburth Road, Liverpool L17 0BP
☎0151 727 0436
Selling of Reformed Christian books and other Christian products; also mail order.
Manager: Mrs P Barton. No full-time staff. ***CC*** No.278411. Began 1982; non-denominational. Turnover n/a.

Aletheia, 36 High Street, Whitchurch SY13 1BB
☎01948 663 770
M: 07718 684 113
🖷01948 662 772
E: office@apcommunications.freeserve.co.uk
Evangelical and Reformed books; also mail order, special events catered for.
Managing Director: Rev Kenneth T Lillie. *Office Manager:* Mrs Rosie Mee. Executive staff 1, Other staff 12. Began 1977; evangelical. Turnover £350,000 [50% Books 50% Other] to year end Dec 04.

For further details see list on page 85

***All Nations Christian Bookshop Ltd**, Easneye, Ware SG12 8LX
☎01920 469 126 🖷01920 462 997
E: bookshop@allnations.ac.uk
Manager: Mrs Lesley Moody. Executive staff 1, Other staff 1. Began 1972; interdenominational. Turnover £80,000 to year end Aug 02.

***The Almond Tree Bookshop and Coffee House**, Mission Lane, Falkirk FK1 1PN
☎01324 626 000 🖷01324 619 444
E: bookshop@struthers-church.org
Web: www.struthers-church.org
Also coffeeshop.
Manager: Miss Jennifer Jack. Executive staff 1, Other staff 5. ***CC*** No.SCO 06960. Began 2001; Struthers Memorial Churches. Turnover £200,000 to year end Dec 04.

The Anglican Catholic Bookshop, c/o Diocesan Office, 42 High Street, Lydd, Romney Marsh TN29 9AN
☎01797 321 704 🖷01797 321 704
E: acbooks@anglicancatholic.org.uk
Web: www.anglicancatholic.org.uk
Mail order only.
Manager: Very Rev Damien Mead. Executive staff 1, Other staff n/a. Began 1998; Anglican Catholic Church. Turnover n/a.

†The Apostolic Church Training School Bookshop, ACTS, Bryn Road, Penygroes, Llanelli SA14 7PH
☎01269 832 069
Manageress: Mrs Diane Horley. Executive staff 1. Began n/a; Apostolic. Turnover n/a.

Aquila Fellowship Trust (The Christian Bookshop), 9 Westgate Street, Launceston PL15 7AB
☎01566 772 047 🖷01566 772 047
Manager: Mr M Stearns. Executive staff 1, Other staff 2. ***CC*** No.253092. Began 1967; non-denominational. Turnover n/a.

Ards Evangelical Bookshop, Crimond House, 48 Frances Street, Newtownards BT23 7DN
☎028 9181 7530 🖷028 9181 5581
E: order@ardsbookshop.com
Web: www.ardsbookshop.com
Owner & Manager: Mr Richard M'Coubrey. Executive staff 4, Other staff 6. Began 1965; non-denominational. Turnover n/a.

The Ark, 11 St Thomas Street, Lymington SO41 9NA
☎01590 675 588 🖷01590 676 937
Web: theark@waitrose.com
Also coffee shop and restaurant.
Proprieter: Virginia Ayling. Executive staff 1, Other staff 10. Began 2004; non-denominational. (Previously The Archway). Turnover £118,000 to year end Apr 05.

The Ark Angel Christian Bookshop, 4 Lansdowne Mews, Lansdowne Road, Bude EX23 8BH
☎01288 356 886
E: sales@arkangeltrust.freeserve.co.uk
Web: www.arkangeltrust.org.uk
Also Traidcraft.
Manageress: Mrs B Raven. Executive staff 1. ***CC*** No.294313. Began 1986; interdenominational. Turnover £45,000 to year end Dec 04.

The Ark Christian Bookshop, 14 Ashfield Precinct, Kirby-in-Ashfield, Nottingham NG17 7BQ
☎01623 757 427
Church resource centre; all church requisites.
Manager: Mr John Cook. Executive Staff 1. Began 1979; non-denominational. (Previously The Jesus Centre). Turnover £47,000 to year end Dec 00.

Ark Christian Bookshop & Café, 19 Pier Road, Erith DA8 1TA
☎01322 332 515
Administrator: Mr Dennis Roberts. Admin staff 1, Other staff 2. ***CC*** No.1044047. Began 1988; interdenominational. Turnover n/a.

***Ashburnham Christian Trust Bookshop**, Ashburnham Place, Battle TN33 9NF
☎01424 892 244 🖷01424 894 200
E: mail@ashburnham.org.uk
Web: www.ashburnham.org.uk
Also coffee shop.
Manager: Mrs Susan Betts. No full-time staff. ***CC*** No.212755. Began 1960; non-denominational. Turnover included in Ashburnham Christian Trust.

Atholl Centre Bookshop, Atholl Road, Pitlochry PH16 5BX
☎01796 473 044 🖷01796 473 844
E: admin@athollcentre.org.uk
Web: www.athollcentre.org.uk
Also second-hand books.
Managers: Con & Adrienne Ruddock. Executive staff 2. ***CC*** No.SCO 15113. Began 1970; interdenominational. Turnover included in Atholl Centre.

Bangor Christian Bookshop, 31 Holyhead Road, Upper Bangor, Bangor LL57 2EU
☎01248 353 386 🖷01248 353 386
E: info@bangorchristianbookshop.co.uk
Web: www.bangorchristianbookshop.co.uk
Manager: Mr John P Gough. Executive staff 1, Other staff 1. ***CC*** No.222407. Began 1972; non-denominational. Turnover £44,851 to year end Jan 05.

Barogha Books Ltd, c/o Amblecote Christian Centre, 102 Brettell Lane, Amblecote, Stourbridge DY8 4BS
☎01384 370 365
Manager: Name not supplied. Executive staff 1, Other staff 2. ***CC*** Began 1984; interdenominational. (Previously Filling Station Christian Bookshop). Turnover n/a.

Beacon Books and Crafts Ltd, 2[illegible] The Parade, Cwmbran NP44 1PR
☎01633 484 587 🖷01633 484 [illegible]37
Manageress: Miss Tracey Downey. Executive staff 1, Other staff 2. ***CC*** No.51[illegible]778. Began 1983; non-denominational. Turnover £98,000 to year end Dec 04.

Beautiful Books LEF, 24 Brixton Station Road, London SW9 8PD
☎020 7738 3302 🖷020 7274 4[illegible]23
E: service@beautifulbooks.freeserve.co.uk
Web: www.lef-beautifulbooks.co.uk
Shop Manager: Johannes Weidenmüller. *Treasurer:* Mr Gunther Schmidt. Executive staff 1, Other staff 2. ***CC*** No.101[illegible]596. Began 1993; evangelical. Turnover £250,000 [65% books 35% other] to year end Dec 04.

Bedford Books, 45 Woodhouse Road, North Finchley, London N12 9ET
☎020 8446 3056
E: bedford@cornerstone.co.uk
Web: www.bedfordbooks.co.uk
Also wholesaling, college tours, special events.
Manager: Mr Andrew Franks. Executive staff 2. ***CC*** No.281838. Began 1958; non-denominational. Owned by Finchley Christian Bookshops Ltd. Turnover n/a.

†Belfast Family Books 64 Ann Street, Belfast BT1 4EG
☎028 9023 0064
Proprietor: Mr Michael J Penfold. Executive staff 1, Other staff 3. Began 1982; non-denominational. (Previously Belfast Book & Bible House). Turnover n/a.

Belmont Christian Book Centre, 49 Belmont Road, Belfast BT4 2[illegible]A
☎028 9065 3718 🖷028 9065 37[illegible]3
Manager: Mr Andrew Poots. Executive staff 1, Other staff 1. Began 1987; non-denominational. Turnover n/a.

Bethany Books, 5 Chester Road West, Shotton, Deeside CH5 1BX
☎01244 813 532 🖷01244 313 5[illegible]2
Also photocopying and faxing.
Manageress: Mrs Kath Kenyon. Executive staff 1. Began 1986; non-denominational. Turnover n/a.

Bethany Books, 1 High Street, Llanidloes SY18 6BY
☎01686 412 102
Managers: Mr & Mrs M Colpus. All voluntary staff. Began 1985; interdenominational. Turnover £6,000 to year end Dec 02.

Bethany Books, 7 Sherborne Road, Wallasey CH44 2EY
☎0151 638 3415 Mob: 0796[illegible] 119 0[illegible]7
E: brian@ghalgh.freeserve.co.uk
Also Traidcraft and counselling service.
Proprietor: Mr D Brian Greenhalgh. Executive staff 1. Began 1[illegible]82; non-denominational. Turnover n/a.

For further details see list on page 35

Bethany Bookshop, 48 Promenade, Bridlington YO15 2QQ
☎01262 604 758
E: chris@bethanybookshop.co.uk
Web: www.bethanybookshop.co.uk
Also mail order.
Manager: Mr Christopher J Heywood. Executive staff 2, Other staff 1. Began 1934; non-denominational. Turnover n/a.

Bethany Christian Bookshop and Coffeeshop, 26 Ilfracombe Gardens, Whitley Bay NE26 3SL
☎0191 297 0262 📠0191 297 0262
Also coffee, quiet room.
Shop Manager: Mrs Hilary Atkinson. Executive staff 1, Other staff 8. ***CC*** No.1009261. Began 1995; interdenominational. Churches Acting Together, Whitley Bay. Turnover n/a.

Beulah Bookshop, 67 Central Promenade, Newcastle BT33 0HH
☎028 4372 2629 📠07092 167 630
Manager: Mr G McConnell. Executive staff 1, Other staff 2. Began 1966; Free Presbyterian. Turnover n/a.

Beulah Faith Mission & Christian Bookshop, 30 Whitcombe Street, Aberdare CF44 7AU
☎01685 873 209
E: peter@beulahbooks.fsnet.co.uk
Web: www.beulahbooks.org.uk
Also coffee shop, mail order.
Manager: Mr Peter Mitchell. Executive staff 1. ***CC*** No.135597. Began 1927; interdenominational. Turnover n/a.

Beverley Minster Shop Ltd, Minster Yard North, Beverley HU17 0DP
☎01482 887 520 📠01482 887 520
Web: www.beverleyminster.co.uk
Also artefacts, site-specific and general souvenirs, guidebooks.
Manager: Mrs J Myers. Executive staff 1, Other staff 2. Began 1975; Anglican. Turnover £65,000 to year end Dec 02.

Bible Book Shop, 17 Huntbach Street, Hanley Stoke-on-Trent ST1 2BL
☎01782 214 709
E:
keith@biblebookshop.fsbusiness.co.uk
Manager: Mr Keith Galley. Executive staff 1, Other staff 1. Began 1963; interdenominational. Turnover n/a.

The Bible Bookshop, 20 Clements Lane, Ilford IG1 2QY
☎020 8478 3278 📠020 8478 3278
Partner: Miss Jill Black. Executive staff 1, Other staff 1. Began 1960; non-denominational. Turnover n/a.

***The Bible Bookshop**, 96 Whitworth Road, Rochdale OL12 0JJ
☎01706 631 253 📠01706 631 253
E: campaign@comebacktogod.org
Web: www.cbtg.org
Also counselling service.
Manager: Mr D Ferguson. Executive staff 2. ***CC*** No.240168. Began 1956; interdenominational. (Previously Campaign Christian Books). Linked to Come Back to God Campaign. Turnover £10,000 to year end Dec 00.

***Bible Bookshop**, Adelaide College, 3 Nineyard Street, Saltcoats KA21 5HS
☎01294 463 911 📠01294 463 366
E: campaign@cbtg.org
Web: www.cbtg.org
Manager: Miss Rachael Orme. Executive staff 2. ***CC*** No.240168. Began 1956; interdenominational. Linked to Come Back to God Campaign. Turnover £15,000 [60% books 40% other] to year end Dec 03.

The Bible Depot, Stall 228, Central Market, St Mary Street, Cardiff CF10 1AU
☎029 2022 4394 M: 07712 770 134
📠029 2022 4394
Web: www.bibledepot.co.uk
Partners: Mr B Anderson, Mr P Connolly. Executive staff 2. Began 1911; non-denominational. (Previously English, Welsh and Foreign Bible Depot). Turnover £62,000 to year end May 05.

The Bible Shop, 168 King Street, Castle Douglas DG7 1DA
☎01556 504 416 📠01556 504 416
Web:
www.castledouglas.net/thebibleshop
Also mail order, tracts, stationery.
Manager/Owner: Mr Jim Figgis. Executive staff 1. Began 1996; non-denominational. Turnover £18,500 to year end Aug 05.

Bible Truth Depot, 18 Namu Road, Bournemouth BH9 2QU
☎01202 516 739 📠01202 516 739
Also publishing 'Joyful News Gospel Calendar' and other evangelical literature.
Owner: Mr Philip Jenkins. Executive staff 1. Began 1980; non-denominational. Turnover n/a.

***Birmingham City Mission Bookshop/Video Library**, 832 Alum Rock Road, Ward End, Birmingham B8 2TX
☎0121 327 9305 📠0121 766 6727
E: bcm.bookshop@tiscali.co.uk
Web: www.birminghamcitymission.co.uk
Also second-hand books.
Manager: Mr Warwick Goulding. Executive staff 1. ***CC*** No.1051023. Began 1968; interdenominational. Turnover £20,000 to year end Mar 03.

Blackburn Bible Depot, 10 Stansfeld Street, Blackburn BB2 2NH
☎01254 663 874
Overseer: Mr Frank Thomas. No full-time staff. Began 1948; Christian Brethren. Turnover n/a.

†B H Blackwell Ltd (Religion Dept), 48 Broad Street, Oxford OX1 3BQ
☎01865 792 792 Ext 440
📠01865 794 143
E: extra@blackwellsbookshops.co.uk
Web: www.blackwell.co.uk
Also coffee shop.
Department Manager: Mr K R New. Executive staff 1, Other staff 2. Began n/a; non-denominational. Turnover n/a.

Blackwell's University Bookshop, 99 High Street, Old Aberdeen, Aberdeen AB24 3EN
☎01224 486 102 📠01224 276 162
E: aberdeen@blackwell.co.uk
Profit Centre Manager: Mr Colin Walker. Executive staff 1, Other staff 5. Began 1879; non-denominational. Turnover £800,000 to year end Dec 98.

Blythswood Bookshop, Station Square, Dingwall IV15 9JD
☎01349 864 608
Manager: Name not supplied. Executive staff 1. ***CC*** Began n/a; Reformed/evangelical. Turnover n/a.

Blythswood Bookshop, Deephaven Depot, Evanton, Dingwall IV16 9XJ
☎01349 830 777
E: peter.spittlehouse@blythswood.org
Co-ordinator: Mr Peter Spittlehouse. Executive staff 1. ***CC*** Began 1973; Reformed/evangelical. (Previously Christian Bookshop). Turnover n/a.

Blythswood Bookshop, Quay Street, Portree IV51 9DE
☎01478 612 198
Contact: Name not supplied. All voluntary staff. ***CC*** Began 1973; Reformed/evangelical. Turnover n/a.

Blythswood Bookshop, 16 Church Street, Stornoway HS1 2DH
☎01851 702 420
Contact: Mr Peter Spittlehouse. All voluntary staff. ***CC*** Began 2005; Reformed/evangelical. Turnover n/a.

***Book Aid**, Bromley House, Kangley Bridge Road, Sydenham, London SE26 5AQ
☎020 8778 2247 📠020 8778 2265
E: office@book-aid.org
Web: www.book-aid.org
Also coffee shop.
Shop Manager: Mrs Ada Hiley. Executive staff 2, Other staff 4. ***CC*** No.1039484. Began 1987; interdenominational. Turnover n/a.
Also at: *Shop Manager:* Mr Maurice Abrahams, 5 Galgate, Barnard Castle DL12 8EQ
☎01833 630 209
And: *Manager:* Mr Mark Freeman, North Road, Ranskill, Retford DN22 8NL
E: bookaid@tiscali.co.uk
☎01777 817 101 📠 01777 817 002
And: *Shop Manager:* Mr Frank Rea, The Haven Christian Centre, 44 Rickamore Road Upper, Templepatrick, Ballyclare BT39 0JE
E: bookaid@btinternet.com
☎028 9443 2061

For further details see list on page 85

Books Alive Christian Bookshop, 86 Elm Drive, Hove BN3 7JL
☎01273 738 818 🖷01273 738 818
E: info@booksalive.co.uk
Manager: Mr David Rees. Executive staff 1, Other staff 2. ***CC*** No.1077435. Began 1994; interdenominational. Turnover n/a.

***Books For Life**, Bethnal Green Mission Church, 305 Cambridge Heath Road, London E2 9LH
☎020 7729 4286 🖷020 7739 5079
E: books@bgmchurch.plus.com
Manager: Mr Richard G Farrell. Executive staff 1. ***CC*** No.222262. Began 1952; non-denominational. (Previously Bethnal Green Medical Mission Books). Turnover n/a.

Books Plus / Llyfrau Plus, Unit 6, The Concourse, University Hospital of Wales, Heath Park, Cardiff CF14 4XW
☎029 2074 6294 🖷029 2075 2800
E: info@books-plus.org.uk
Web: www.books-plus.org.uk
Manager: Mrs Sue Bevan. *Deputy Manager:* Mrs Mary Young. Executive staff 2. ***CC*** No.1074480. Began n/a; interdenominational. Turnover £180,000 to year end May 02.

The Branch Christian Books, 17 Halifax Road, Dewsbury WF13 2JH
☎01924 454 750 🖷01924 454 750
E: branchministries@lineone.net
Web: www.branchministries.org.uk
Also coffee shop.
Manager: Mrs Heather Ward. Executive staff 1, Other staff 2. Began 1984; non-denominational. Turnover n/a.

Bridge Books & Music, 14 North Bridge Street, Sunderland SR5 1AB
☎0191 567 3544 🖷0191 567 3544
E: bridgebooks@fsmail.net
Manager: Mrs Lynne Foreman. Executive staff 2, Other staff n/a. Began 1974; interdenominational. (Previously Scripture Union Bookshop). No magazine. Turnover n/a.

Bridge Bookshop, Stockton Baptist Tabernacle, The Square, Bishop's Gate, Stockton-on-Tees TS18 1TE
☎01642 675 297 🖷01642 604 840
E: sbt@stockton.netkonect.co.uk
Web: www.adlib.co.uk/sbt
Also coffee shop, restaurant and counselling.
Managers: Geoff & Joyce Burns. Executive staff 3. Began 1977; Baptist. (Previously Christian Literature Centre). Turnover n/a.

Bridge Christian Books, Holy Trinity Church, High Street, Hounslow TW3 1HG
☎020 8570 4586
E: bridgebooks@dialstart.net
Also coffee shop.
Manager: Cathy Allen. Executive staff 1, Other staff 2. ***CC*** Began 1983; Anglican. Turnover £160,000 to year end Dec 04.

The Burning Light, The Farne House, Marygate, Holy Island, Berwick-upon-Tweed TD15 2SJ
☎08707 451 172
E: mary@burninglight.co.uk
Web: www.burninglight.co.uk
Specialising in Celtic and Monastic spirituality.
Owner/Manager: Mrs Mary Fleeson. Executive staff 1, Admin staff 2. Began 1997; non-denominational. Turnover n/a.

Buxton Christian Bookshop, 2 Market Street, Buxton SK17 6JY
☎01298 268 43
E: enquiries@christianbux.org
Web: www.christianbux.org
Managers: Trustees. Staff 4. ***CC*** No.1046267. Began 1985; non-denominational. Turnover £37,000 to year end Dec 04.

Calne Christian Bookshop, 16 Phelps Parade, Calne SN11 0HA
☎No telephone
Manager: Mr H J Jarvis. All voluntary staff. ***CC*** No.298889. Began 1979; non-denominational. Turnover £33,500 to year end Feb 01.
Correspondence: 6 Poynder Place, Hilmarton, Calne SN11 8SQ
☎01249 760 398 M 07748 656 849

Canaan Christian Book Centre, 121 High Street, Staines TW18 4PD
☎01784 457 194 🖷01784 441 040
E: info@canaanbookshop.co.uk
Web: www.canaanbookshop.co.uk
Also coffee lounge, counselling, mail order.
Director/Manager: Mr A P Gilmour. Executive staff 2, Other staff 4. ***CC*** No.1015433. Began 1979; non-denominational. Turnover n/a.

Carmelite Book Service, Boars Hill, Oxford OX1 5HB
☎01865 730 183 🖷01865 326 478
E: priory@carmelite.org.uk
Web: www.carmelitebooks.com
Specialising in Carmelite material and prayer & spirituality; worldwide mail-order.
Secretary: Mrs Sandra Pooley. Executive staff 1, Other staff 1. ***CC*** No.207738. Began 1985; Roman Catholic. Turnover £50,000 to year end Dec 98.

Castlebooks, 82/83 High Street, Newport PO30 1BH
☎01983 525 885 🖷01983 521 950
E: castlebooks@btconnect.com
Also resource centre.
Manageress: Mrs Susan Young. Executive staff 1, Other staff 2. ***CC*** No.274901. Began 1976; interdenominational. Turnover £150,000 to year end Dec 02.

Castlegate Bookshop, 8 Castlegate, Nottingham NG1 7AS
☎0115 9111 1453
E: shop@congregational.org.uk
Web: www.congregational.org.uk
Manager: Name not supplied. Executive staff 1, Other staff 3. Began 1979; Congregational. Turnover n/a.

Cathedral Books Ltd, 250 Chapel Street, Salford M3 5LL
☎0161 833 0092 🖷0161 831 9[illegible]99
Also articles of devotion.
Manageress: Miss Catherine Astin. Executive staff 1, Other staff 2. ***CC*** No.2660084. Began 1988; Roman Catholic. Turnover £200,000 to year end Aug 05.

The Cathedral Shop, Angel Hill, Bury St Edmunds IP33 1LS
☎01284 754 933
Manageress: To be appointed. All voluntary staff. ***CC*** Began 199[illegible]; Anglican. Turnover n/a.

The Cathedral Shop, Exeter Cathedral, Exeter EX1 1HS
☎01392 271 354 🖷01392 285 9[illegible]5
E: shop@exeter-cathedral.org.uk
Web: www.exeter-cathedral.org.uk
Manager: Mr Paul Patch. Executive staff 2, Other staff 1. Began 1984; Anglican. Turnover n/a.

The Cathedral Shop, Southwark Cathedral, London Bridge, London SE1 9DA
☎020 7367 6710
🖷020 7367 6725/30
E: cathedral@southwark.anglican.org
Web: www.southwark.anglican.org
Manager: Janice Kimberly. Executive staff 1, Other staff n/a. Began 197[illegible]; Anglican. (Previously Southwark Cathedral Bookshop). Turnover £225,000 to year end Dec 02.

Catholic Bible School Bookshop, Nutbourne House, Farm Lane, Nutbourne, Chichester PO18 8SD
☎01243 371 766 🖷01243 371 45[illegible]
E: info@catholic-bible-school.org
Web: www.catholic-bible-school.org
Also counselling.
Directors: Geoff & Gina Poulter. Executive staff 2, Other staff 4. ***CC*** No.2626[illegible]9. Began 1988; Roman Catholic. Turnover n/a.

Catholic Truth Society, 25 Ashley Place, Westminster Cathedral Piazza, London SW1P 1LT
☎020 7834 1363 🖷020 782[illegible] 987[illegible]
E: bookshop@cts-online.org.uk
Web: www.cts-online.org.uk
Retailing Catholic publications and religious articles.
Manager: Ms G MacNiven-Johnston. Executive staff 1, Other staff 3. ***CC*** No.218951. Began 1926; Roman Catholic. Turnover n/a.

Catholic Truth Society, Brazennose House West, Brazennose Street, Manchester M2 5AS
☎0161 834 5115 🖷0161 834 5665
E: sales@cts-manchester.org.uk
Web: www.cts-manchester.org.uk
Manager: Mr Michael Silgram. Executive staff 1, Other staff n/a. ***CC*** No.105871[illegible]. Began 1891; Roman Catholic. Turnover n/a.

For further details see list on page [illegible]

Catholic Truth Society, Upper Level, Princess Square, Newcastle upon Tyne NE1 8ER
☎0191 232 1169 🖷0191 232 1169
Manageress: Mrs Kay Byrne. Executive staff 1. ***CC*** Began 1922; Roman Catholic. Turnover n/a.

Centre Books, Crafts and Coffee Shop, 5a Northumberland Street, Huddersfield HD1 1RL
☎01484 426 344 🖷01484 425 188
E: centrebooks@fs.com
Bookshop Manager: Mr Jeremy Lewis. Executive staff 1, Other staff 2. ***CC*** No.514595. Began 1991; non-denominational. Turnover n/a.

Centre Christian Bookshop, 5 London Road, Stroud GL5 2AG
☎01453 764 713 🖷01453 764 713
E: centrebooks@freeuk.com
Also second-hand books and counselling.
Manager: Mrs Yvonne Hobbs. Executive staff 2, Other staff 15. ***CC*** No.287501. Began 1981; non-denominational. Turnover £100,000 [55% books 45% other] to year end Feb 05.

Chapter and Verse, 49 Bell Street, Sawbridgeworth CM21 9AR
☎01279 724 929 M: 07734 128 430
E: enquiries@chapter-verse.co.uk
Web: www.chapter-verse.co.uk
Also resource centre.
Company Secretary: Gary Knott. Executive staff 1, Other staff 4. ***CC*** No.1080519. Began 1983; interdenominational. Turnover £108,762 to year end Dec 04.

Chapter Two, 199 Plumstead Common Road, Plumstead Common, London SE18 2UJ
☎020 8316 4972 🖷020 8854 5963
E: chapter2uk@aol.com
Web: www.chaptertwobooks.org.uk
Fundamental dispensational bookseller specialising in Plymouth Brethren publications, Bible sales and advice.
Principal: Mr Edwin Cross. Executive staff 3, Other staff 10. ***CC*** No.1053047. Began 1976; non-denominational. Turnover n/a.
Also at: Fountain House, Conduit Mews, Woolwich, London SE18 7AP
☎020 8316 5389 🖷 020 8854 5963

Chester Cathedral Shop, 12 Abbey Square, Chester CH1 2HU
☎01244 311 586 🖷01244 313 155
E: shop@chestercathedral.com
Web: www.chestercathedral.com
Manager: To be appointed. Executive staff 1, Other staff 4. Began 1977; Anglican. Turnover £613,000 to year end Dec 02.

Choice Words Christian Bookshop, 71 Queen Street, Newton Abbot TQ12 2AU
☎01626 334 027 M: 07798 694 318
🖷01626 334 027
E: newton@choicewords.co.uk
Also mail order, student discounts.
Proprietors: Roy and Pam Brittle. Executive staff 2. Began 1984; non-denominational. Turnover £118,000 to year end Dec 02.

Choice Words Torbay, 37 Hyde Road, Paignton TQ4 5BP
☎01803 551 316 M 07798 694 318
🖷01803 551 316
E: paignton@choicewords.co.uk
Also mail order, student discounts.
Proprietors: Roy and Pam Brittle. Executive staff 2. Began 1998; interdenominational. Linked with Choice Words Newton Abbot. Turnover £116,000 to year end Dec 02.

***Christian Book Centre**, 18 Rashee Road, Ballyclare BT39 9HJ
☎028 9335 2170
Proprietors: Mr & Mrs Harry Wilson. Executive staff 2. Began 1982; non-denominational. Turnover n/a.

Christian Book Centre, 5 Mary Street, Lancaster LA1 1UW
☎01524 841 655 🖷01524 841 655
E: cbcpreston@aol.com
Web: www.christian-book-centre.co.uk
Proprietors: Mr & Mrs R & C Hardman. Executive staff 2, Other staff 3. Began 1987; interdenominational. (Previously Good News Christian Bookshop). Turnover n/a.

Christian Book Centre, 45 Northdown Road, Margate CT9 2RN
☎01843 226 598
Manageress: Mrs D J Woodham. Executive staff 1, Other staff 1. Began 1975; interdenominational. Turnover n/a.

Christian Book Centre, 63 Chilwell Road, Beeston, Nottingham NG9 1EQ
☎0115 925 6961 🖷0115 925 6444
E: christianbookcentre@surefish.co.uk
Also software, church supplies.
Proprietor: Mrs Barbara Hayes. Executive staff 1, Other staff 1. Began 1966; non-denominational. Turnover n/a.

Christian Book Centre, 4 Fox Street, Preston PR1 2AB
☎01772 259 279 🖷01772 259 279
E: cbcpreston@aol.com
Web: www.christian-book-centre.co.uk
Owner/Manager: Mr Robert Hardman. Executive staff 1, Other staff 8. Began 1968; non-denominational. Turnover n/a.

Christian Book Centre, 13 Bond Street, Redruth TR15 2QA
☎01209 214 007 🖷01209 313 191
E: cbcred@globalnet.co.uk
Web: www.icbc.co.uk
Partner: Mr Chris Land. Executive staff 2. Began 1984; non-denominational. Turnover £85,000 to year end Dec 04.

The Christian Book Shop, 36 Grosvenor Road, Tunbridge Wells TN1 2AP
☎01892 527 557
Web: www.thechristianbookshop.co.uk
Proprietor: Mr Gordon Hoppé. Executive staff 2, Other staff 1. Began 1890; interdenominational. (Previously Hunts Christian Centre). Turnover n/a.
Sales and Correspondence:
Sevenoaks Road, Pratts Bottom, Orpington BR6 7SQ
E: mail@thechristianbookshop.co.uk
☎01689 854 117 🖷 01689 851 060

B

Christian Books, Unit 7, Provision Market, Carmarthen SA31 1QY
☎01267 234 953 M: 07813 360 764
Proprietor: Mr Albert Haynes. Executive staff 2. Began 1981; evangelical. Turnover n/a.

Christian Books, St Mary's Gate, Dunstable LU6 3SW
☎01582 601 945
E: books@christianbooks.uk.com
Web: www.christianbooks.uk.com
Manager: Mr John Snuggs. Executive staff 1, Other staff 1. ***CC*** No.801449. Began 1982; non-denominational. Turnover £97,000 to year end Dec 04.

Christian Books, 17 Byram Street, Huddersfield HD1 1DR
☎01484 534 377
Joint Managers: Mrs Kathryn Wilson, Mrs Catherine Reardon. No full-time paid staff. ***CC*** No.1029055. Began 1991; ecumenical. Turnover £956 to year end Jun 02.

Christian Books & Music, Kensington Temple, Kensington Park Road, London W11 3BY
☎020 8727 8684
E: abel.zea@kt.org
Web: www.dovewell.com
Bookshop Manager: Abel Zea. Executive staff 2, Other staff 6. ***CC*** No.251549. Began 1982; Elim Pentecostal. Turnover £540,000 to year end Dec 04.
Mail Order:
E: support@dovewell.com
☎0800 521 631 🖷 020 8799 6101

Christian Books Plus, 386 Brixton Road, London SW9 7AW
☎020 7737 1089 🖷020 7686 6008
E: info@christianbooks-plus.com
Web: www.uckg.org
Also 24-hour counselling.
Manager: Elaine Graham. Executive staff 1. Began 2000; Universal Church of the Kingdom of God. Turnover n/a.

Christian Bookshop, Alfred Place, Aberystwyth SY23 2BS
☎01970 625 005
Trustee: Mr Michael Keen. No full-time staff. ***CC*** Began 1975; non-denominational. Turnover n/a.

B

Christian Bookshop, 14 Grange Road West, Birkenhead CH41 4DA
☎0151 647 8743 🖷0151 647 8743
E: cbs_birkenhead@hotmail.com
Web: www.christian-bookshop.org
Manager: Mr Robert Purves. Executive staff 1, Other staff 3. ***CC*** No.1099726. Began 1946; interdenominational. Turnover £18,000 to year end Apr 04.

Christian Bookshop, Bryntirion, Bridgend CF31 4DX
☎01656 665 912 🖷01656 665 919
E: office@emw.org.uk
Web: www.emw.org.uk
Manageress: Miss M Elaine Harris. Executive staff 1, Other staff 1. ***CC*** No.222407. Began 1972; interdenominational. Evangelical Movement of Wales. Turnover £82,561 to year end Jan 05.

Christian Bookshop, 7 Wyndham Arcade, St Mary Street, Cardiff CF10 1FH
☎029 2022 0586 🖷029 2022 0586
Manager: Mr Stephen Potts. *Assistant Manager:* Mr Hywel George. Executive staff 1, Other staff 1. ***CC*** No.222407. Began 1961; interdenominational. Evangelical Movement of Wales. Turnover £180,000 to year end Dec 04.

Christian Bookshop, 8 Parkway, Chelmsford CM2 0NF
☎01245 257 054 🖷01245 257 054
Manager: Mr John Dawson. Executive staff 1, Other staff 3. Began 1977; interdenominational. Turnover n/a.

The Christian Bookshop, 63 Station Road, Letchworth SG6 3BJ
☎01462 481 285 🖷01462 481 285
Manager: Mrs Brendling. Executive staff 2, Other staff 3. ***CC*** No.253478. Began 1968; non-denominational. (Previously Letchworth Christian Bookshop). Turnover n/a.

The Christian Bookshop, 13 Brewer Street, Maidstone ME14 1RU
☎01622 761 440 🖷01622 761 440
Manager: Ed St Pier. Executive staff 1, Other staff 5. Began 1978; non-denominational. Linked to Tonbridge Christian Book Centre. Turnover n/a.

The Christian Bookshop, Sevenoaks Road, Pratts Bottom, Orpington BR6 7SQ
☎01689 854 117 🖷01689 851 060
E: mail@thechristianbookshop.co.uk
Web: www.thechristianbookshop.co.uk
Also coffee shop.
Owner: Mr Gordon Hoppé. Executive staff 1, Other staff n/a. Began 1990; non-denominational, Reformed. Turnover n/a.

Christian Bookshop, 21 Queen Street, Ossett WF5 8AS
☎01924 260 502 🖷01924 264 524
E: lorna@christianbookshopossett.co.uk
Web: www.christianbookshopossett.co.uk
Bookseller and publisher or Reformed literature under CBO publications imprint. Particular Baptist literature a speciality.
Partners: Mr N H Roe, Mr J Roe, Mrs L M Roe. Executive staff 3. Began 1983; Reformed evangelical. Turnover £30,000 to year end Dec 02.

***Christian Bookshop**, 23a Commercial Street, Pontypool NP4 6JQ
☎01495 750 680
Also centre for young people.
Shop Manager: Mr Alan Tucker. Executive staff 1, Other staff n/a. Began 1999; interdenominational. Turnover n/a.

Christian Bookshop, 90 High Street, Reigate RH2 9AP
☎01737 247 534
Organisers: Mr & Mrs Peter & Margare Robinson. No paid staff. ***CC*** No.800219. Began 1983; interdenominational. Turnover n/a.
Correspondence: 19 Hilltop Road, Reigate RH2 7HL

Christian Bookshop, 7 Castle Street, Rugby CV21 2TP
☎01788 542 852
Manager: Mr Richard Hannah. Executive staff 1, Other staff 3. Began 1972; interdenominational. Turnover n/a.

The Christian Bookshop, 121 Duke Street, St Helens WA10 2JG
☎01744 274 07
Owners: Mrs J Csutor, Mrs P Haselden. Executive staff 2. Began 1968; non-denominational. Turnover n/a.

†**Christian Bookshop**, 16e/f The Market, Swansea SA1 3PF
☎01792 650 773 🖷01792 650 773
Web: www.emw.org.uk
Manageress: Mrs Wynne Hess. Executive staff 1, Other staff 4. ***CC*** No.222407. Began 1962; interdenominational. Evangelical Movement of Wales. Turnover £155,000 to year end Jan 05.

Christian Bookshop, 45 Victoria Road, Swindon SN1 3AY
☎01793 520 528 🖷01793 520 528
E: johnblack@ntlworld.com
Proprietors: Mr & Mrs John Black. Executive staff 2. Began 1976; interdenominational. Turnover n/a.

The Christian Bookshop, 16 Central Arcade, Wrexham LL11 1AG
☎01978 364 405 🖷01978 366 754
Manageress: Miss Julie McIntosh. Executive staff 1, Other staff 4. ***CC*** Began 1950; non-denominational. Turnover n/a.

Christian Bookshop & The Edge Coffee Shop, 143 High Street, Brentwood CM14 4SA
☎01277 200 044 🖷01277 200 044
Also collecting point for Book Aid, coffee shop.
Manager: Mrs Valerie A Coulthard. Executive staff 1, Other staff 2. Began 1989; interdenominational. Turnover n/a.

Christian Bookshop (EMW), 1a Temple Street, Llandrindod Wells LD1 5DL
☎01597 823 171
🖷01597 823 171
E: christianbs@tiscali.co.uk
Manageress: Miss Gillian Davies. Executive staff 1. ***CC*** No.222407. Began 1974; non-denominational. (Previously Christian Books & Craft (EMW)). Evangelical Movement of Wales. Turnover £3[illegible],000 to year end Dec 04.

Christian Bookshop Mission Ltd, 78 Central Market, Halkett Place, St Helier, Jersey JE2 4WL
☎01534 733 380
🖷01534 780 868
E: items@christianbookshopmission.org.je
Web: www.christianbookshopmission.org.je
Also jewellery.
Manageress: Mrs M Bryans. *Assistant Manageress:* Mrs F Allaire. Executive staff 2, Other staff 4. ***CC*** Began 1972; non-denominational. Turnover £125,000 to year end Dec 00.

***Christian Centre Bookshop**, Strudwick Drive, Oldbrook, Milton Keynes MK6 2TG
☎01908 670 655
🖷01908 553 066
E: bookshop@mkcc.org.uk
Web: www.mkcc.org.uk
Also counselling.
Bookshop Assistant: Maryline Was[illegible]na. Executive staff 1, Other staff 1. ***CC*** No.1054324. Began 1986; Assemblies of God. Turnover n/a.

Christian Connections, Pengawsai Fach, Whitland SA34 0RB
☎01994 240 659
Also Bible garden.
Proprietor: Mrs Iris D Staniland. Executive staff 1. Began 1987; interdenominational. Member of Quiet Garden Trust. Turnover n/a.

Christian Education Book Sales, 1020 Bristol Road, Selly Oak, Birmingham B29 6LB
☎0121 472 4242
🖷0121 472 7575
E: enquiries@christianeducation.org.uk
Web: www.christianeducation.org.uk
Chief Executive: Peter Fishpool. *Office Manager:* Diane Horton. Executive staff 1, Other staff 13. ***CC*** No.1086990. Began 1803; non-denominational. Turnover n/a.

Christian Literature Centre, The Upper Room, 64 Cornwall Street, Plymouth PL1 1LR
☎01752 661 264
🖷01752 250 815
E: clcply@btconnect.com
Web: www.upperroombookshop.co.uk
Also mail order, out-of-print search, ordering service.
Partners: Mr & Mrs David & Anne Landricombe. Executive staff 2, Other staff 3. Began 1949; non-denominational. Turnover n/a.

For further details see list on page [illegible]5

†**Christian Outlook**, 44 Waterdale, Doncaster DN1 3EY
☎01302 363 033 🖷01302 363 033
✉: help@christianoutlookbooks.com
Also youth resources, mail order.
Manager: Ryan Price. Executive staff 1. ***CC*** No.10[illegible]1732. Began 1983; interdenominational. Turnover £75,000 to year end Mar 01.

Christian Resource Centre, 2 Radford Road, Leamington Spa CV31 1LX
☎01926 426 573 🖷01926 426 573
✉: info@leamington-crc.co.uk
Web: www.leamington-crc.co.uk
Proprietor: Mr Graham Allen. Executive staff 1, Other staff 1. Began 1954; interdenominational. Turnover n/a.

***Christian Resources Project**, 14 Lipson Road, Plymouth PL4 8PW
☎01752 224 012 🖷01752 222 814
✉: shop@christianresourcesproject.org.uk
Web: www.christianresourcesproject.org.uk
Specialising in children's and youth material.
Administrator: Mr Michael Law. *Centre Manager:* Mrs Audrey Burnham. Executive staff 1, Other staff 4. ***CC*** No.281735. Began 19[illegible]0; interdenominational. Magazine: *Mike's Musings* (500 five times a year). Turnover £132,000 to year end Dec 02.

Christian Word Shop, St Stephen's Church, Church Green West, Redditch B97 4DY
☎01527 520 773 / 585 386
✉: greg@diandgreg.com
Also Traidcraft. Profit donated to local youth and schools outreach work.
Manageress: Mrs Enid Drew. No full-time staff. ***CC*** No.518003. Began 1979; interdenominational. Turnover £30,000 to year end Mar 05.

Church House Bookshop, 31 Great Smith Street, London SW1P 3BN
☎020 7898 1300 🖷020 7898 1305
✉: bookshop@c-of-e.org.uk
Web: www.chbookshop.co.uk
The official bookshop of the Church of England; also mail order department, online shop.
Manager: Mr Melanie Tucker. Executive staff 2, Other staff 6. ***CC*** No.248711. Began n/a; Anglican but interdenominational. Turnover £850,000 to year end Dec 02.

Church Shop, 222 Leigh Road, Leigh-on-Sea SS9 1BF
☎01702 710 409 🖷01702 712 838
Manageress. Mrs E Burzynska. Executive staff 1. Began 1978; Roman Catholic. Turnover £60,000 to year end Jan 03.

Churches Bookshop, Howard Street, Douglas IM1 2EQ
☎01624 621 593
Also coffee lounge.
Manager Mr Colin Gurney. Executive staff 2. Began 1971; interdenominational. Turnover £36,000 to year end Dec 04.

***CLC Bookshop**, 22 Back Wynd, Aberdeen AB1 1JP
☎01224 641 620 🖷01224 626 332
✉: clc-aberdeen@btconnect.com
Web: www.clc.org.uk
Making evangelical literature available so that people may come to faith and maturity in Christ.
Manager: Mr Andrew Martin. Executive staff 1, Other staff 2. ***CC*** No.1015793. Began 1941; evangelical. Turnover n/a.

***CLC Bookshop**, 51 Stephenson Street, Birmingham B2 4DH
☎0121 643 6187 🖷0121 643 2471
✉: clcbirm@btconnect.com
Web: www.clc.org.uk
Making evangelical literature available so that people may come to faith and maturity in Christ.
Managers: Miss Naomi Thorp. Executive staff 1, Other staff 2. ***CC*** No.1015793. Began 1941; evangelical. Turnover n/a.

CLC Bookshop, 45 Abingdon Street, Blackpool FY1 1DH
☎01253 624 160 🖷01253 624 160
✉: clcblackpool@btconnect.com
Web: www.clc.org.uk
Making evangelical literature available so that people may come to faith and maturity in Christ.
Manager: Mrs Sheena Burwell. Executive staff 1. ***CC*** No.1015793. Began 1941; evangelical. (Previously Chapter & Verse Christian Bookshop). Turnover n/a.

***CLC Bookshop**, 22a Lower Bridge Street, Canterbury CT1 2LG
☎01227 463 535 🖷01227 768 098
✉: clc-canterbury@btconnect.com
Web: www.clc.org.uk
Making evangelical literature available so that people may come to faith and maturity in Christ.
Manager: Mr Paul Chandler. Executive staff 1, Other staff 2. ***CC*** No.1015793. Began 1941; evangelical. Turnover n/a.

***CLC Bookshop**, 118 High Street, Chatham ME4 4BY
☎01634 843 926 🖷01634 847 774
✉: clcchatham@btconnect.com
Web: www.clc.org.uk
Making evangelical literature available so that people may come to faith and maturity in Christ.
Manager: Miss Brenda Franklin. Executive staff 1, Other staff 1. ***CC*** No.1015793. Began 1941; evangelical. Turnover n/a.

***CLC Bookshop**, 26 Whitehall Crescent, Dundee DD1 4AY
☎01382 226 859 🖷01382 322 013
✉: clcdundee@btconnect.com
Web: www.clc.org.uk
Making evangelical literature available so that people may come to faith and maturity in Christ.
Manager: Mr Colin Waller. Executive staff 1, Other staff 1. ***CC*** No 1015793. Began 1941; evangelical. Turnover n/a.

***CLC Bookshop**, 98 Church Street, Inverness IV1 1EP
☎01463 238 876 🖷01463 242 486
✉: clc-inverness@btconnect.com
Web: www.clc.org.uk
Making evangelical literature available so that people may come to faith and maturity in Christ.
Manager: Mr Les Dowey. Executive staff 1, Other staff 1. ***CC*** No.1015793. Began 1941; evangelical. Turnover n/a.

***CLC Bookshop**, 16 St Matthews Street, Ipswich IP1 3EU
☎01473 255 346 🖷01473 255 649
✉: clcipswich@btconnect.com
Web: www.clc.org.uk
Making evangelical literature available so that people may come to faith and maturity in Christ.
Manager: To be appointed. Executive staff 1, Other staff n/a. ***CC*** No.1015793. Began 1941; evangelical. Turnover n/a.

***CLC Bookshop**, 43 Belvoir Street, Leicester LE1 6SL
☎0116 255 8481 🖷0116 285 5283
✉: clcleic@btconnect.com
Web: www.clc.org.uk
Making evangelical literature available so that people may come to faith and maturity in Christ.
Manager: Mrs Gina Inman. Executive staff 1, Other staff 1. ***CC*** No.1015793. Began 1941; evangelical. Turnover n/a.

***CLC Bookshop**, Morley House, 26 Holborn Viaduct, London EC1A 2AQ
☎020 7583 4835/4837 🖷020 7583 6059
✉: info.clclondon@btconnect.com
Web: www.clc.org.uk
Making evangelical literature available so that people may come to faith and maturity in Christ.
Manager: Miss Liz Patten. Executive staff 3, Other staff 8. ***CC*** No.1015793. Began 1941; evangelical. Turnover n/a.

***CLC Bookshop**, 22 Dundas Shopping Mall, Dundas Street, Middlesbrough TS1 1HT
☎01642 247 540 🖷01642 230 924
✉: clcmiddle@btconnect.com
Web: www.clc.org.uk
Making evangelical literature available so that people may come to faith and maturity in Christ.
Manager: Mrs Sue Brown. Executive staff 1, Other staff 1. ***CC*** No.1015793. Began 1986; evangelical. Turnover n/a.

***CLC Bookshop**, Higham Place, New Bridge Street, Newcastle upon Tyne NE1 8AF
☎0191 232 5301 🖷0191 233 0237
✉: clcnewcastleuk@btconnect.com
Web: www.clc.org.uk
Making evangelical literature available so that people may come to faith and maturity in Christ.
Manager: Mr Brian Taylor. Executive staff 1, Other staff 2. ***CC*** No.1015793. Began 1941; evangelical. Turnover n/a.

For further details see list on page 85

Bookshops & Other Retail Outlets

***CLC Bookshop**, 68 Prince of Wales Road, Norwich NR1 1LT
☎01603 623 875 🖷01603 616 286
E: clcnorwich@btconnect.com
Web: www.clc.org.uk
Making evangelical literature available so that people may come to faith and maturity in Christ.
Manager: Mr T M Bloomfield. Executive staff 1, Other staff 2. ***CC*** No.1015793. Began 1941; evangelical. Turnover n/a.

B

***CLC Bookshop**, 103 West Street, Sheffield S1 4EQ
☎0114 272 4663 🖷0114 276 5052
E: clcsheffield@btconnect.com
Web: www.clc.org.uk
Making evangelical literature available so that people may come to faith and maturity in Christ.
Manager: Mr Michael Shaw. Executive staff 1, Other staff 5. ***CC*** No.1015793. Began 1941; evangelical. Turnover n/a.

***CLC Bookshop**, Carlton House, Carlton Place, Southampton SO15 2DZ
☎023 8022 0844 🖷023 8033 1013
E: clcsouthampton@btconnect.com
Web: www.clc.org.uk
Making evangelical literature available so that people may come to faith and maturity in Christ.
Manager: Mr Chris Magee. Executive staff 1, Other staff 2. ***CC*** No.1015793. Began 1941; evangelical. Turnover n/a.

***CLC Bookshop**, 8 St George's Street, Stamford PE9 2BJ
☎01780 755 020 🖷01780 764 884
E: clcstamford@btconnect.com
Web: www.clc.org.uk
Making evangelical literature available so that people may come to faith and maturity in Christ.
Manager: To be appointed. Executive staff 1, Other staff 1. ***CC*** No.1015793. Began 1977; evangelical. (Previously The Ark, Stamford Christian Book Centre). Turnover n/a.

***CLC Bookshop**, 11 St Helens Road, Swansea SA1 4AL
☎01792 654 228 🖷01792 464 683
E: clcswanseauk@btconnect.com
Web: www.clc.org.uk
Making evangelical literature available so that people may come to faith and maturity in Christ.
Manager: Mr Peter Taylor. Executive staff 1. ***CC*** No.1015793. Began 1941; evangelical. Turnover n/a.

***CLC Bookshop**, 123 Bridge Street, Warrington WA1 2HS
☎01925 635 641 🖷01925 573 635
E: clcwarrington@btconnect.com
Web: www.clc.org.uk
Making evangelical literature available so that people may come to faith and maturity in Christ.
Manager: Mr Alan Middleton. Executive staff 1. ***CC*** No.1015793. Began 1963; evangelical. Turnover n/a.

***CLC Bookshop**, 13 Upper Wickham Lane, Welling DA16 3AA
☎020 8301 4641 🖷020 8301 6594
E: clcwelling@btconnect.com
Web: www.clc.org.uk
Making evangelical literature available so that people may come to faith and maturity in Christ.
Manager: Mrs Jose Seymour. Executive staff 1, Other staff 1. ***CC*** No.1015793. Began 1991; evangelical. Turnover n/a.

***CLC Bookshop**, 69 Worcester Street, Wolverhampton WV2 4LE
☎01902 424 020 🖷01902 421 416
Web: www.clc.org.uk
Making evangelical literature available so that people may come to faith and maturity in Christ.
Manager: Ms Jan Harris. Executive staff 1, Other staff 2. ***CC*** No.1015793. Began 1970; evangelical. (Previously Bible Book Shop). Turnover n/a.

Cliff College Bookshop, Calver, Hope Valley S32 3XG
☎01246 584 205 🖷01246 583 739
E: books@cliffcollege.org
Web: www.cliffcollege.org
Manager: Mr John Hogarth. Executive staff 1. ***CC*** No.529386. Began 1900; Methodist. Turnover £85,872 to year end Aug 04.

Clwyd Christian Bookshop Ltd, 4 Bedford Street, Rhyl LL18 1SY
☎01745 350 994
E: manager@ccbooks.com
Manager: Mr Stephen Dunning. Executive staff 1. Began 1969; non-denominational. Turnover £60,000 to year end Dec 04.

Copnal Books, 18 Meredith Street, Crewe CW1 2PW
☎01270 580 470
E: copnalbooks@yahoo.co.uk
Second-hand books only.
Partners: Mr & Mrs Peter & Rose Ollerhead. Executive staff 2, Other staff 1. Began 1984; Christian Brethren. Turnover n/a.

The Corner Stone, 1 Coxwell Street, Cirencester GL7 2BQ
☎01285 644 599 🖷01285 644 599
E: corner_stone@btinternet.com
Manager: Alison Brown. Executive staff 2, Other staff n/a. Began 1992; interdenominational. Ministry of Cirencester parish church. Turnover £115,000 to year end Dec 02.

Cornerstone, 102 Northway, Maghull, Liverpool L31 5NF
☎0151 531 9889 / 285 0111
🖷0151 531 9889
E: cornmag@aol.com
Web: www.merseyworld.com/cornerstone/
Also mobile bookstall.
Hon Resource Manager: Miss Isobel Turner. No paid staff. ***CC*** Began 1979; interdenominational. (Previously Miss Isobel Turner). Turnover £24,000 [50% books 50% other] to year end June 05.

Cornerstone, 45 Woodhouse Road, North Finchley, London N12 9ET
☎020 8446 3056
🖷020 8446 2227
E: books@cornerstone.co.uk
Web: www.cornerstone.co.uk
Business Manager: Mr Andrew Franks. *Bookshop Manager:* Mr John Duncan. Executive staff 2, Other staff [illegible]. ***CC*** No.281838. Began 1981; non-denominational. Head Office of Finchley Christian Bookshops Ltd. Turnover £250,000 to year end Dec 02.

Cornerstone, 2 Dale Road, Matlock DE4 3LT
☎01629 584 296
E: ebgbs90@hotmail.com
Chair: Mrs Bernice Smith. No full-time staff. ***CC*** No.16603. Began 198[illegible]; non-denominational. Turnover £50,000 to year end Dec 05.

Cornerstone, 17 Newmarket Street, Skipton BD23 2HX
☎01756 793 673
🖷01756 793 673
Also coffee shop.
Manager: Mr Jim Hope. Executive staff 1, Other staff 3. ***CC*** No.10[illegible]2329. Began 1993; ecumenical. Turnover £127,000 to year end Dec 04.

Cornerstone Book and Coffee Shop, Central Methodist Church, Saltergate, Chesterfield S40 1UH
☎01246 277 390
E: tony@catltd.co.uk
Web: www.saltergate.org
Also coffee shop.
Manager: Mr A J Fisher. No paid staff. Began n/a; Methodist. Turnover n/a.

Cornerstone Books (Gosport Cornerstone Trust), 9 Bemisters Lane, Gosport PO12 1HB
☎023 9258 3824
🖷023 9258 3824
Also crisis pregnancy counselling centre.
Manager: Mrs S Atkinson. No full-time staff. ***CC*** No.282517. Began 1979; non-denominational. Turnover £48,000 to year end Dec 04.

Cornerstone Bookshop, 11 West Church Street, Buckie AB56 1EN
☎01542 833 647
Manager: Mrs Catherine Addison. Executive staff 1, Other staff 1. Began n/a; interdenominational. Turnover n/a.

Cornerstone Bookshop, St John's Church Terrace, Princes Street, Edinburgh EH2 4BJ
☎0131 229 3776 🖷0131 229 03[illegible]2
E: edinburgh@cornerstonebooks.org.uk
Web: www.cornerstonebooks.org.uk
Also UK distributer of Seasons of the Spirit material.
Manager: David Smith. *Deputy Manager:* Mr William Blakemore. Executive staff 2, Other staff 5. ***CC*** No.SCO 21[illegible]95. Began 1991; ecumenical. Turnover £155,000 to year end Dec 00.

For further details see list on page 85

†**Cornerstone Bookshop**, Renfield St Stephen's Church Centre, 250 Bath Street, Glasgow G2 4JP
☎0141 353 2222
🖷0141 353 2222
Manager: Ms Margaret Saxon. Executive staff 1, Other staff n/a. Began n/a; Church of Scotland. Turnover n/a.

***Cornerstone Christian Bookshop**, 5 Church Street, Whitehaven CA28 7AY
☎01946 695 460 🖷01946 695 460
E: sheilacoupe@hotmail.com
Manager: Mrs Sheila Coupe. Executive staff 1, Other staff 1. **CC** No.507105. Began 1968; interdenominational. Turnover £25,000 to year end Dec 04.

***The Courtyard Shop**, Regents Park, London Road, Nantwich CW5 6LW
☎01270 615 444 🖷01270 615 445
E: bookshop@regents-tc.ac.uk
Web: www.regents-tc.ac.uk
Regents Theological College mail order service; second-hand book search.
Manager: Mr Tony Coles. Executive staff 1, Other staff. **CC** No.251549. Began 1987; interdenominational. Run by Regents Theological College. Turnover £70,000 to year end Jun 05.

Covenant Protestant Reformed Bookstore, 7 Leslunman Road, Kells, Ballymena BT42 3NR
☎028 2589 1851 🖷028 2589 1851
E: bookstore@cprf.co.uk
Web: www.cprf.co.uk/bookstore.htm
Distributing free pamphlets and Christian books.
Manager: Mrs Mary Stewart. Executive staff 1. Began 1989; non-denominational. Turnover n/a.

Covenanter Bookshop, 39 Knockbracken Road, Belfast BT8 4SF
☎028 9031 4110
Web: www.rpc.org/bookshop
Supervisor: Rev Prof Robert McCollum. Executive staff 1, Other staff 2. Began 1961; Reformed Presbyterian Church of Ireland. Turnover n/a.

†**Coventry Cathedral Bookshop**, 7 Priory Row, Coventry CV1 5ES
☎024 7622 7597 🖷024 7663 1448
E: information@coventrycathedral.org.uk
Web: www.coventrycathedral.org.uk
Manager: Mrs Penny Webb. No full-time staff. **CC** Began 1962; Anglican. Turnover n/a.

†**Cumbernauld Churches Bookshop Ltd**, 12 Ettrick Square, Town Centre, Cumbernauld, Glasgow G67 1ND
☎01236 723 851
Company Secretary: Mr John D Allan. Executive staff 1, Other staff 4. **CC** No.SCO 02361. Began 1981; interdenominational. Turnover n/a.

Dabcec Bookshop, Christian Education Centre, 4 Southgate Drive, Crawley RH10 6RP
☎01293 571 264 🖷01293 616 945
E: bookshop@dabcec.org.uk
Manager: Meg Rew. Executive staff 1, Other staff n/a. **CC** No.252878. Began 1980; ecumenical. Turnover £126,000 to year end Dec 00.

Deal Christian Resource Centre, 140 High Street, Deal CT14 6BE
☎01304 363 713 🖷01304 363 713
Manager: Mr S A Boyle. Executive staff 1. Began 1976; non-denominational. (Previously Good News Bookshop). Linked to Tonbridge Christian Book Centre. Turnover n/a.

Derby Cathedral Shop Ltd, Derby Cathedral Centre, 18 Iron Gate, Derby DE1 3GP
☎01332 381 685 🖷01332 203 991
E: shop@derbycathedral.org
Also coffee shop.
Manager: Mrs Linda Hampson. Executive staff 1, Other staff 4. Began 2003; Anglican. Turnover £253,000 to year end Dec 05.

Dovecote Christian Bookshop, 13 Ashley Road, Epsom KT18 7PF
☎01372 817 707
Manager: Mr Rudy Chan. Executive staff 1, Other staff n/a. **CC** No.296008. Began 1996; interdenominational. Turnover n/a.

Doves Christian Bookshop, 65 Boutport Street, Barnstaple EX31 1HG
☎01271 325 867 🖷01271 325 867
E: sales@doveschristianbookshop.com
Web: www.doveschristianbookshop.com
Manager: Mr Simon Gissing. Executive staff 1, Other staff 6. Began 1975; non-denominational. Turnover £140,000 to year end Dec 04.

***Dovetails Christian Bookshop**, 60 High Street, Ilfracombe EX34 9QB
☎01271 864 769 🖷01271 864 769
Manager: Mrs Christine Beckley. Executive staff 1. Began 1998; ecumenical. Linked to Doves Christian Bookshop, Barnstaple. Turnover £32,500 to year end Dec 02.

Dunoon Baptist Church Centre, 9 Alexandra Parade, Dunoon PA23 8AB
☎01369 706 665
Also coffee shop.
Manager: Mrs Helen Blair. Executive staff 1, Other staff 2. Began 1992; Baptist. Turnover n/a.

Eastbourne Christian Resource Centre, 91 Seaside Road, Eastbourne BN21 3PL
☎01323 732 070 🖷01323 647 832
E: christianresourcecentre@supanet.com
Manager: Mr Kevin Deeley. Executive staff 2, Other staff 2. **CC** No.259742. Began n/a; non-denominational. (Previously Eastbourne Bible Centre). Turnover n/a.

Ebenezer Bible and Bookshop, 353 Woodstock Road, Belfast BT6 8PT
☎028 9045 7048
Manager: Mr Jim Butler. Executive staff 1. **CC** No.516726. Began 1973; evangelical. Owned by Alethean Publications Trust. Turnover n/a.

Eden.co.uk. Christian Bookshop, Chester Enterprise Centre, Hoole Bridge, Chester CH2 3NE
☎01244 350 994 🖷01244 350 995
E: gareth@edeninteractive.co.uk
Web: www.eden.co.uk
Online Christian bookshop.
Managing Director: Mr Gareth Mulholland. Executive staff 2, Admin staff 10. Began 2004; non-denominational. Turnover included in Eden Interactive.

Ely Cathedral Shop Ltd, The Chapter House, The College, Ely CB7 4DL
☎01353 660 345 🖷01353 665 658
E: shop.office@catheral.ely.anglican.org
Web: www.cathedral.ely.anglican.org
Manager: Mrs Brenda Covell. *Book Buyer:* Mrs Sandra Firth. Executive staff 1, Other staff 4. Began 1971; Anglican. Turnover £435,483 to year end Dec 04.

Emmanuel Books and Gifts, Market Hall, Newtown SY16 2PQ
☎01686 624 835 M: 07929 751 464
🖷01686 626 665
Owners: Mr & Mrs A G & C M Roberts. Executive staff 2, Other staff n/a. Began 1984; non-denominational. Turnover n/a.

Emmanuel Christian Bookshop, 21 Market Courtyard, Haverfordwest SA61 2AL
☎01437 763 651
E: ecbookspembs@ukonline.co.uk
Manageress: Mrs Carol Smith. All voluntary staff. **CC** No.1087079. Began 1982; Emmanuel Holiness. (Previously Emmanuel Christian Centre). Turnover n/a.

Emmanuel Christian Bookshop, 6 Baptist Lane, Collingham, Newark NG23 7LT
☎01636 893 898 🖷01636 893 898
E: malcolm@pat&malcdavies.freeserve. co.uk
Manager: Malcolm Davies. Executive staff 2, Voluntary 5. **CC** No.1052628. Began 1987; Assemblies of God. (Previously Newark Christian Bookshop). Turnover £30,000 to year end Dec 02.

Emmaus Road Bookshop, 41 Leslie Street, Blairgowrie PH10 6AW
☎01250 876613
E: office@pwamm.com
Web: www.pwamm.org.uk
Also coffee shop.
Manager: Mr Peter Edwards. Staff 4. Began 2003; non-denominational. Part of People with a Mission Ministries. Turnover n/a.

For further details see list on page 85

English Benedictine Congregation, Belmont Abbey, Hereford HR2 9RZ
☎01432 374 718 📠01432 374 711
E: abbot@belmontabbey.org.uk
Web: www.belmontabbey.org.uk
Bookshop Manager: Name not supplied. All voluntary staff. ***CC*** No.226277. Began n/a; Roman Catholic. Turnover n/a.

Evangelical Book Shop, 15 College Square East, Belfast BT1 6DD
☎028 9032 0529 📠028 9043 8330
E: shop@evanbooks-belfast.fsnet.co. uk
Specialising in evangelical and Reformed books and associated products from USA and UK.
Manager: Mr John Grier. *Senior Assistant:* Miss Sheila Burns. Executive staff 3. ***CC*** Began 1926; interrelated trust with Evangelical Presbyterian Church. Turnover £261,800 to year end Jan 05.

Evangelical Bookshop, 8 Dublin Road, Enniskillen BT74 6HH
☎028 6632 2400 📠028 6632 2400
Manageress: Mrs L Moffitt. Executive staff 1, Other staff 2. ***CC*** Began 1936; interdenominational. Turnover n/a.

The Fair Trade Shop (Southampton) Ltd, 106 Shirley High Street, Southampton SO16 4FB
☎023 8051 3344
E: info@thefairtradeshop.org.uk
Specialising in fairly traded goods.
Directors: Mr Clem Mason, Mrs Anne Newton. No full-time paid staff. Began 2004; ecumenical. Turnover £150,000 to year end Aug 05.

Faith Mission Bookshop, 3b Dobbin Street, Armagh BT61 7QQ
☎028 3752 7927
General Manager: Mr Mark Conroy. Other staff 1. ***CC*** Began 1990; interdenominational. Turnover n/a.

Faith Mission Bookshop, 57 High Street, Ballymena BT43 6DT
☎028 2564 9443
General Manager: Mr Mark Conroy. Other staff 1. ***CC*** Began 1981; interdenominational. Turnover n/a.

Faith Mission Bookshop, 43 Bridge Street, Banbridge BT32 3JL
☎028 4062 6761
General Manager: Mr Mark Conroy. Other staff 1. ***CC*** Began 1990; interdenominational. Turnover n/a.

Faith Mission Bookshop, 73 High Street, Bangor BT20 5BD
☎028 9145 3222
General Manager: Mr Mark Conroy. Other staff 1. ***CC*** Began 1982; interdenominational. Turnover n/a.

Faith Mission Bookshop, 5 Queen Street, Belfast BT1 6EA
☎028 9023 3733 📠028 9023 3733
General Manager: Mr Mark Conroy. Executive staff 1, Other staff 7. ***CC*** Began 1889; interdenominational. Turnover n/a.

Faith Mission Bookshop, 15 Castlereagh Road, Belfast BT5 5FR
☎028 9073 1779
General Manager: Mr Mark Conroy. Other staff 1. ***CC*** Began 2003; interdenominational. Turnover n/a.

Faith Mission Bookshop, 20 Oldtown Street, Cookstown BT80 8EF
☎028 8676 6569
General Manager: Mr Mark Conroy. Other staff 1. ***CC*** Began 1974; interdenominational. Turnover n/a.

Faith Mission Bookshop, 20 Thomas Street, Portadown, Craigavon BT62 1HZ
☎028 3833 4123
General Manager: Mr Mark Conroy. Other staff 1. ***CC*** Began 1972; interdenominational. Turnover n/a.

Faith Mission Bookshop, 17 High Street, Lurgan, Craigavon BT66 8AA
☎028 3832 5304
General Manager: Mr Mark Conroy. Other staff 1. ***CC*** Began 1977; interdenominational. Turnover n/a.

Faith Mission Bookshop, 5 Chapel Hill, Lisburn BT28 1EP
☎028 9266 5888
General Manager: Mr Mark Conroy. Other staff 1. ***CC*** Began 1986; interdenominational. Turnover n/a.

Faith Mission Bookshop, 78 Spencer Road, Londonderry BT47 1AS
☎028 7134 5137
General Manager: Mr Mark Conroy. Other staff 1. ***CC*** Began 1986; interdenominational. Turnover n/a.

Faith Mission Bookshop, 33 Greencastle Street, Kilkeel, Newry BT34 4BH
☎028 4176 4934
General Manager: Mr Mark Conroy. Other staff 1. ***CC*** Began n/a; interdenominational. Turnover n/a.

Faith Mission Bookshop, 36 Market Street, Omagh BT78 1EH
☎028 8224 1334
General Manager: Mr Mark Conroy. Other staff 1. ***CC*** Began 1975; interdenominational. Turnover n/a.

Faith Mission Christian Book Centre, 31 Church Street, Berwick-upon-Tweed TD15 1EE
☎01289 304 505 📠01289 304 505
Manager: Mr Stan Forrest. Executive staff 1, Other staff 2. ***CC*** No.SCO 05119. Began 1985; interdenominational. Turnover n/a.

Faith Mission Christian Book Centre, 4 Canmore Street, Dunfermline KY12 7PX
☎01383 720 643 📠01383 720 643
E: fmbc@indunfermline.freeserve.co.uk
Manager: Mrs Marilyn Clunie. Executive staff 1, Other staff 3. ***CC*** No.SCO 05119. Began 1976; interdenominational. Turnover n/a.

Faith Mission Christian Book Centre, 40 Cross Street, Fraserburgh AB43 9EL
☎01346 517 088 📠01346 517 088
Manager: Ann Scott. Executive staff 1. ***CC*** No.SCO 05119. Began 1986; interdenominational. Turnover n/a.

Faith Mission Christian Book Centre, 2 Erroll Street, Peterhead AB42 1[illegible]X
☎01779 471 961 📠01779 471 961
Manager: Mrs Anne Urquhart. Executive staff 1, Other staff 3. ***CC*** No.SCO 05119. Began n/a; interdenominational. Turnover n/a.

Faith Mission Christian Book Centre, 36 Barnton Street, Stirling FK8 1NA
☎01786 451 152 📠01786 451 152
Manager: To be appointed. Executive staff 1, Other staff 3. ***CC*** No.SCO 05119. Began 1982; interdenominational. Turnover n/a.

Family Books (Keynsham), 3 Temple Court, Keynsham, Bristol BS31 1H[illegible]
☎0117 986 8747
E: david@familybooks.co.uk
Bookshop Manager: Mr David Brassington. Executive staff 1, Other staff 1. Began 1984; non-denominational. Turnover £76,000 to year end Dec 04.

***Family Christian Bookstore**, c/o 43 Kings Gate, Bishopric, Horsham RH12 1AE
☎01403 259 522 M: 07802 28[illegible] 112
E: word2theworld@waitrose.com
Web: www.word2theworld.co.uk
Also Spanish speaking ministry of translating, printing, literature distribution, personal ministry, London Spanish churches and overseas.
Director: Mrs Joanne Verkat. Executive staff 1, Other staff 4. ***CC*** No.110[illegible]062. Began 1986; non-denominational. Part of Word To The World Ministries Int.. Turnover n/a.

Food for Thought, 34 High Street Clay Cross, Chesterfield S45 9DY
☎01246 866 013
Also coffee shop, counselling.
Manager: Mr Mick Lowry-Fields. Executive staff 1. ***CC*** Began 1986; Fellowship of Independent Evangelical Churches. Turnover n/a.

***Fools Bookshop**, 14 Station Road, Upminster RM14 2UB
☎01708 640 391
Also coffee shop, High Street outreach.
Manageress: Mrs Alison Wilson. Admin staff 2, Other staff 1. ***CC*** No.290[illegible]60. Began 1991; interdenominational. Turnover £76,146 to year end Apr 04.

Footprints, 130a Newgate Street, Bishop Auckland DL14 7EH
☎01388 600 035
E: footprints@teesdaleonline.co.uk
Web: www.footprintscomputers.co.uk
Partners: Mr & Mrs John & Pam Ga[illegible]es. Executive staff 3. Began 1992. Turnover £30,000 to year end May 03.

For further details see list on page 85

B

B

Footprints, 6 Skinnergate, Darlington DL3 7NB
☎No Telephone
📠01325 487 366
E: footprints@teesdaleonline.co.uk
Web: www.footprintscomputers.co.uk
Also worldwide mail order.
Partner's: Mr & Mrs John & Pam Gaines. Executive staff 1, Other staff 4. Began 1995; interdenominational. (Previously Acorn Christian Bookshop). Turnover £200,000 to year end Dec 00.

***The Fountain (Wallingford) Ltd**, 21b St Mary's Street, Wallingford OX10 0EW
☎01491 839 511 📠01491 835 371
E: fountain@ridgeway-church.org.uk
Administrator: Kath Mobbs. Executive staff 1, Other staff 1. ***CC*** No.283919. Began 1980; Community Church. Turnover n/a.

Free Church of Scotland Bookshop, The Mound, Edinburgh EH1 2LS
☎0131 718 4144 📠0131 220 0597
E: bookshop@freechurchofscotland.org.uk
Extensive academic range.
Manager: C Douglas. Executive staff 1, Other staff 1. Began 1950; Free Church of Scotland. Turnover £93,000 to year end Dec 99.

Free Presbyterian Church of Scotland Bookroom, 133 Woodlands Road, Charing Cross, Glasgow G3 6LE
☎0141 332 1760 📠0141 332 4271
E: sales@fpbookroom.org
Web: www.fpbookroom.org
Also distributor.
Manager: Mr Kenneth Hutton. Executive staff 1. Began 1970; Free Presbyterian Church of Scotland. Turnover £54,000 to year end Dec 04.

Full Life Christian Centre, Rolleston House, High Street, Maltby, Rotherham S66 8LF
☎01709 818 213 📠01709 818 213
E: info@full-life.org.uk
Web: www.full-life.org.uk
Conference centre residential facilities for up to 30 people; also coffee shop.
Centre Administrator: Mr Paul Norris. Executive staff 1, Other staff 2. ***CC*** No.1052600. Began 1983; Assemblies of God. Turnover n/a.

†**Gateway Trust**, St Mary's Mews, St Mary's Place, Stafford ST16 2AR
☎01785 212 626 📠01785 229 457
E: info@gatewaytrust.co.uk
Also Third World food and crafts.
Manager: Mr Andrew Horsnall. Executive staff 1, Other staff 3. ***CC*** No.702181. Began 1990; interdenominational. Turnover n/a.

GEM Books, Christian Centre, 71 High Road, Gorefield, Wisbech PE13 4NZ
☎01945 870 149 📠01945 870 867
E: books@christian-centre.com
Web: www.christian-centre.com
Minister: Rev Leslie R Warren. Staff 4. Began 1981; Pentecostal. Part of Chapel Lodge Ministries. Turnover £30,000 to year end Dec 04.

Gladstones Bookshop (Christian Media), 18 Slater Street, Liverpool L1 4BS
☎0151 708 9550
E: gladstonestrust@tiscali.co.uk
Also mail order, coffee shop.
Manager: Mr William G Tonge. Executive staff 1, Admin staff 3, Other staff 8. ***CC*** No.232909. Began 1980; non-denominational. (Previously Contact Christian Books). Turnover n/a.

***GLO Bookshop**, 78 Muir Street, Motherwell ML1 1BN
☎01698 263 483 📠01698 275 418
E: books@glo-europe.org
Web: www.glo-europe.org
Resourcing local, national and international outreach. Also coffee shop.
Manager: Mr Andrew Lacey. *Assistant Manageress:* Miss Marion Mathers. Executive staff 2, Other staff 5. ***CC*** No.SCO 07355. Began 1973; non-denominational. Turnover £450,000 [60% Books 40% Other] to year end Dec 04.

Gold Hill Church Books, Gold Hill Baptist Church, Gold Hill Common East, Chalfont St Peter, Gerrards Cross SL9 9DG
☎01753 887 173 📠01753 892 572
E: office@goldhill.org
Web: www.goldhill.org
Manageress: Rita Harris. All voluntary staff. ***CC*** Began 1970; Baptist. Turnover n/a.

The Good Book Shop, Church of Ireland House, 61 Donegall Street, Belfast BT1 2QH
☎028 9024 4825 📠028 9023 7802
E: sales@goodbookshop.com
Web: www.goodbookshop.com
Manager: Mrs Evelyn Lewis. Executive staff 1, Other staff 6. Began 1978; Church of Ireland. (Previously APCK Book Centre). Turnover n/a.

Good Books, St Mary's Old School, Gundry Lane, Bridport DT6 3RL
☎01308 420 483 📠01308 420 483
E: goodbooksbridport@surefish.co.uk
Web: www.goodbooksbridport.co.uk
Also Traidcraft; Toybox, Book Aid collections point.
Manager: Ms Veronica Ziegler. No paid staff. ***CC*** No.1085241. Began 1985; interdenominational. (Previously Good Book Services Trust). Turnover n/a.

Good Life Books (GLF), 8 Cow Green, Halifax HX1 1JF
☎01422 351 361
E: shop@goodlifebooks.co.uk
Manager: Mr George Smith. Executive staff 1, Other staff 3. Began 1973; non-denominational. Turnover £78,000 to year end Dec 02.

Good News Centre, 47 Church Gate, Loughborough LE11 1UE
☎01509 236 057
E: mail@goodnews.uklinux.net
Also resource centre, coffee shop.
Manager: Mr John Pipet. Executive staff 1, Other staff 1. ***CC*** No.512100. Began 1980; interdenominational. Turnover £170,000 to year end Dec 05.

Good News Centre, 27 Wrexham Street, Mold CH7 1ET
☎01352 756 055
Proprietor: Mrs Geraldine R Seery. No full-time staff. Began 1989; non-denominational. Turnover £30,000 to year end Dec 05.

Good News Centre (Bookshop and Coffeehouse), High Street, Newent GL18 1AN
☎01531 821 456
E: sales@goodnewscentre.com
Web: www.goodnewscentre.com
Manager: Mr Peter A Wathen. Executive staff 1, Other staff 4. ***CC*** Began 1980; non-denominational. Turnover n/a.

Good News Christian Bookshop, 22 Fountain Street, St Peter Port, Guernsey GY1 1DA
☎01481 728 982
Proprietor: Mr Brian Leparme. Executive staff 1, No other staff. Began 1999; interdenominational. Turnover £55,5[illegible]0 to year end Dec 02.

***Good News Crusade Bookshop**, 1[illegible] High Cross Street, St Austell PL25 4AN
☎01726 722 82[illegible] 📠01726 722 8[illegible]
E: books@gnc.org.uk
Web: www.gnc.org.uk
Manager: Mr D Reynolds. Executive staff 1. ***CC*** No.225483. Began 1960; interdenominational. Turnover n/a.

Good News Shop, 654 High Road, Leyton, London E10 6RN
☎020 8539 2906 📠020 8988 0[illegible]75
E: elizabethburke1@btconnect.com
Web: www.goodnewsleyton.co.uk
Managers: Mr & Mrs Tom & Elizabeth Burke. Executive staff 2, Other staff 3. Began 1981; interdenominational. Turnover n/a.

Good News - TCLC, 25 East Reach, Taunton TA1 3EP
☎01823 282 429 📠01823 350 1[illegible]0
E: info@goodnewsbooks.co.uk
Also resource centre.
Partner: Mrs Lisa Westlake. Executive staff 4, Other staff n/a. Began 1965; non-denominational. Turnover n/a.

Goodliving Christian Bookshop, 20[illegible] Mill Street, Bideford EX39 2JR
☎01237 422 213 M: 07855 903 [illegible]63
📠01237 470 603
E: goodliving@btconnect.com
Also out-of-print books specialist.
Proprietor: Mrs Christina Harris. No full-time staff. Began 2000; non-denominational. Turnover £50,000 to year end Jan 05.

Goodnews Bookshop, 1 Thorpe Avenue, Tonbridge TN10 4PW
☎01732 369 303 📠020 8294 00[illegible]4
Manager: Mr W P Leyrie. Executive staff 1. Began 1969; interdenominational. Turnover n/a.

For further details see list on page 85

Goodnews Christian Resource Centre Ltd, 50 Churchfield Road, Acton, London W3 6DL
☎020 8992 7123 🖷020 8993 7616
E: info@getchristianbooks.com
Web: www.getchristianbooks.com
Also mail order, training resources.
Manager: Miss Nyuk Fong Lau. Executive staff 2, Other staff 2. Began 1954; non-denominational. Turnover n/a.

Gospel Light, 5 Deptford High Street, London SE8 4AF
☎020 8469 4152 🖷020 8469 4152
E: info@gospel-light.co.uk
Web: www.gospel-light.co.uk
Importing gospel music from around the world.
Owner: Mrs Angela Thomas. Admin staff 1. Began 1990; non-denominational. No magazine. Turnover n/a.

Grace Cards & Books, Unit 12, St Andrew's Square, Droitwich WR9 8HE
☎01905 774 856 M: 07712 163 646
🖷01905 798 137
E: gracecards@ukonline.co.uk
Proprietor: Mr Ernest Richardson. Executive staff 2, Other staff 3. Began 1991; Baptist. Turnover £300,000 to year end May 03.

Green Pastures Christian Bookshop, 20 High Street, Dereham NR19 1DR
☎01362 697 953 🖷01362 697 953
E: greenpastures@onetel.com
Manager: Mrs Jean Stroulger. Executive staff 1, Other staff 6. Began 1996; interdenominational. Turnover £75,000 to year end Dec 05.

***Greyfriars Christian Centre**, Friar Street, Reading RG1 1EH
☎0118 951 6703 🖷0118 951 6716
E: bookshop@greyfriars.org.uk
Web: www.greyfriars.org.uk
Also coffee shop.
Centre Administrator: Mr John R Brown. *Assistant Manager / Accounts:* Mr Dennis Parker. Executive staff 1, Other staff 5. Began 1983; interdenominational. Turnover £250,000 to year end Dec 04.

Guildford Cathedral Bookshop, Stag Hill, Guildford GU2 7UP
☎01483 547 873 🖷01483 303 350
E: bookshop@guildford-cathedral.org
Web: www.guildford-cathedral.org
Also wine, wafers and candles.
Manager: Mrs Janet Cruse. Executive staff 1, Other staff 2. **CC** Began 1984; Anglican. Turnover n/a.

Hallam Book Centre 22 Norfolk Row, Sheffield S1 2PA
☎0114 275 8225
Proprietor: Miss Casey. Executive staff 1. Began 1886; Roman Catholic. Turnover n/a.

†**Harmony Books**, 40 Harpur Street, Bedford MK40 2QT
☎01234 210 298
Also promoting religious and racial understanding.
Proprietor: Mrs Mary Shaw. No full-time staff. **CC** No.294509. Began 1984; interdenominational. Turnover £10,209 to year end Dec 00.

Harvest Books and Crafts, 2 Church Street, Market Square, Pontypridd CF37 2TH
☎01443 408 962
E: sheri@harvestbooks.co.uk
Also mail order, counselling.
Manager: Mrs Sheri Lollar. Executive staff 1, Other staff n/a. **CC** Began 1986; interdenominational. Turnover £33,000 to year end Dec 00.

The Haven Christian Bookshop & Centre, 142 Seabank Road, Wallasey CH45 1HG
☎0151 638 5910
Also coffee shop, counselling.
Secretary to the Trust: Mr D L Haynes. No full-time staff. **CC** No.510112. Began 1978; Baptist. Owned by New Brighton Baptist Church. Turnover £2,000 to year end Dec 02.

Havering Christian Bookshop and Centre, 80 Victoria Road, Romford RM1 2LA
☎01708 727 625 🖷01708 757 758
Also coffee shop, mail order.
Manager: Mrs D Reid. *Director:* Mr Colin Phillips. Executive staff 2, Other staff 6. **CC** No.277278. Began 1975; interdenominational. Turnover £160,000 to year end Dec 00.

***Haywards Heath Christian Book Centre**, 34 Sussex Road, Haywards Heath RH16 4EA
☎01444 412 300 🖷01444 412 300
Coordinator: Chris Gail. No full-time staff. Began 1983; interdenominational. (Previously Christian Book Centre). Linked to Tonbridge Christian Book Centre. Turnover £120,000 to year end Dec 98.

Heath Christian Bookshop Charitable Trust, 31 Whitchurch Road, Heath, Cardiff CF14 3JN
☎029 2062 1794
E: sales@christian-bookshop.co.uk
Web: www.christian-bookshop.co.uk
Also coffee shop.
Supervisor: Mr Geraint Jones. Executive staff 1, Other staff 2. **CC** No.504644. Began 1975; non-denominational. Turnover £100,000 to year end Dec 02.

Hereford Cathedral Shop, 5 College Cloisters, The Close, Hereford HR1 2NG
☎01432 374 208 🖷01432 374 220
E: shop@herefordcathedral.org
Web: www.herefordcathedral.org
Cathedral gift shop.
Shop Manager: Mrs Alison Chambers. Executive staff 2, Other staff 6. **CC** Began 1976; Anglican. Turnover n/a.

Frank Herring & Sons, 27 High West Street, Dorchester DT1 1UP
☎01305 264 449 🖷01305 250 675
E: info@frankherringandson.com
Also art and crafts.
Manager: Mr David Herring. Executive staff 3, Other staff 11. Began 1930; non-denominational. Turnover n/a.

High Cross Christian Bookshop, Knoll Road, Camberley GU15 3SY
☎01276 619 61 🖷01276 223 43
E: bookshop@highcross.org.uk
Web: www.highcross.org.uk
Manager: Mrs Linda Fry. Executive staff 1. Began 1990; United Reformed/Methodist. Turnover £60,000 to year end Dec 98.

HoldFast Bible & Tract Depot, 41 York Road, Tunbridge Wells TN1 1JX
☎01892 512 049 / 526 577
M: 07759 213 440
E: hbtd100@hotmail.com
Web: holdfast.seekbooks.co.uk
Publishing and distributing new and second-hand Christian literature; also multi-media.
Proprietor: Mr Nicholas R Fleet. No paid staff. Began 1991; non-denominational. Turnover £12,000 to year end Dec 00.

***Holy Trinity Brompton Bookshop**, Holy Trinity Brompton Church, Brompton Road, London SW7 1JA
☎0845 644 7533 🖷020 7589 3390
E: bookshop@htb.org.uk
Web: www.htb.org.uk
Also Alpha resources (including international resources), music, software, worldwide mail order.
Head of Bookshop and Technical: Rowan Miller. Executive staff 1, Other staff 2. **CC** Began 1991; Anglican. Turnover n/a.

Horsham Christian Centre, 4 South Street, Horsham RH12 1NR
☎01403 218 821 🖷01403 276 483
E: info@hcct.fsbusiness.co.uk
Also coffee shop, listening service.
Manager: Mr Doug Fletcher. Executive staff 1. **CC** No.1038233. Began 1994; ecumenical. Turnover £300,000 to year end Dec 04.

Ichthus Christian Books, 58 Station Road, Northwich CW9 5RB
☎01606 477 67
E: peter@ichthus.wanadoo.co.uk
Proprietors: Mr & Mrs Peter & Sue Southern. Executive staff 2. Began 1987; interdenominational. Turnover n/a.

Illuminate, 18 Wyle Cop, Shrewsbury SY1 1XB
☎01743 233 657 🖷01743 231 277
E: admin@illuminatebooks.co.uk
Web: www.illuminatebooks.co.uk
Christian media outlet and specialist art supplier.
Proprietor: Mr Phil Whittall. Executive staff 1, Other staff 3. Began 1957; non-denominational. (Previously Freemans Christian Bookshop). Turnover £200,000 to year end Jan 03.

B

***Immanuel Bookshop**, 24 Northway, Scarborough YO11 1JL
☎01723 500 261 🖷01723 500 261
E: immanuel@scarborough.co.uk
Proprietor: Mrs Kate Close. Executive staff 1, Other staff 1. Began 1987; non-denominational. Turnover n/a.

Jacob's Well, 2 Ladygate, Beverley HU17 8BH
☎01482 881 162
E: thejacobswell@aol.com
Web: www.thejacobswell.org
Also charity shop for Jacob's Well appeal.
Manager: Beryl Beynon. Executive staff 1. ***CC*** No.515235. Began 1981; non-denominational. Turnover n/a.

Jesus People Shop, Jesus Fellowship Central Offices, Nether Heyford, Northampton NN7 3LB
☎0845 166 8172 🖷0845 166 8178
E: info@jesuspeople.biz
Web: www.jesuspeople.biz
Also resources by mail order and at conferences.
Manager: Peter Taylor. Admin staff 3. Began n/a; Jesus Fellowship. (Previously Jesus Fellowship Resources). Turnover £35,000 to year end Dec 04.

Keith Jones Christian Bookshop, 2 Hinton Road, Bournemouth BH1 2EE
☎01202 292 272 🖷01202 316 947
E: kjinfo@btconnect.com
Web: www.keithjones.co.uk
Also online shopping, mail order.
Senior Partners: Mr Colin J Bailey, Mr Darren Peach. Executive staff 4, Other staff 4. Began 1955; evangelical. Turnover £840,000 [62% books 38% other] to year end Mar 04.

***Keith Jones Christian Bookshop**, 2 Park Road, Yeovil BA20 1DZ
☎01935 426 253
E: kjyeovil@btinternet.com
Web: www.keithjones.co.uk
Partners: Mr C J Bailey, Mr D P Peach. Executive staff 2, Other staff 10. Began 1976; non-denominational. Linked to Keith Jones Bookshop, Bournemouth. Turnover £155,000 to year end Sep 02.

Jubilate Christian Bookshop Ltd, 55 Ely Street, Stratford-upon-Avon CV37 6LN
☎01789 298 351 🖷01789 298 351
E: julie@jubilateshop.fsnet.co.uk
Web: www.jubilatebookshop.org.uk
Manager: Julie P Warren. Executive staff 1. ***CC*** No.1040890. Began 1986; interdenominational. Turnover £100,000 to year end Jul 02.

†*Just Looking Christian Bookshop, 8 Normandy Street, Alton GU34 1BX
☎01420 543 354 🖷01420 543 354
E: book@justlook.go-plus.net
Also coffee shop.
Manager: Mr Bruce Stevenson. Executive staff 2, Other staff 6. ***CC*** No.1096632. Began 1994; non-denominational. Turnover £60,000 to year end Dec 02.

†Juteronomy, 21 Talisman Square, Kenilworth CV8 1JB
☎01926 854 721 🖷01926 854 721
Also Third World crafts, Fairtrade foods.
Proprietor: Mrs K Shortley. Executive staff 2. Began 1980; non-denominational. Turnover £100,000 to year end Aug 02.

***Kerith Centre Bookshop**, Church Road, Bracknell RG12 1EH
☎01344 783 810 🖷01344 304 154
E: bookshop@kerith.co.uk
Manager: Mrs Heather West. Executive staff 1, Other staff 2. Began 1989; Newfrontiers. Turnover £84,676 to year end Mar 98.

King of Kings Christian Bookshop, 11a Church Lane, Oldham OL1 3AN
☎0161 626 3547
E: bob@kingofkings.freeserve.co.uk
Proprietor: Mr Steve Woolstencroft. Executive staff 1. Began 1982; non-denominational. Turnover £49,500 to year end July 02.

Kings Christian Bookshop, 74 Frodingham Road, Scunthorpe DN15 7JW
☎01724 865 410 🖷01724 865 410
E: kings@christianbooks.fsnet.co.uk
Also coffee shop, counselling service.
Manageress: Mrs A D Charlesworth. Executive staff 1, Other staff 2. ***CC*** No.505608. Began 1975; non-denominational. Turnover £100,000 to year end Dec 02.

Kyrios Books, 11 Kingsway, Kirkby-in-Ashfield, Nottingham NG17 7BB
☎01623 452 556
E: keith@kyriosbooks.co.uk
Web: www.kyriosbooks.co.uk
Mail-order second-hand Christian and religious theology, philosophy, church history.
Proprietor: Name not supplied. Executive staff 1. Began 1989; interdenominational. Turnover n/a.

The Ladyhead Bookshop, 35 North Street, St Andrews KY16 9AQ
☎01334 477 886
Also coffee shop.
Manager: Mr Jonathan Mason. All voluntary staff. ***CC*** No.32049. Began 1984; ecumenical. Turnover £10,000 to year end Dec 04.

Lichfield Cathedral Bookshop, 9 The Close, Lichfield WS13 7LD
☎01543 306 150 🖷01543 306 152
E: bookshop@lichfield-cathedral.org
Also mail order.
Manager: Mrs Pauline Cox. *Gift Buyer:* Mrs Wendy Paulson. Executive staff 1, Other staff 5. Began 1975; Anglican. Turnover £297,000 to year end Mar 05.

Lifeline Christian Bookstore, Ice House Christian Centre, Victor Street, Grimsby DN32 7QN
☎01472 349 917 🖷01472 349 [illegible]44
E: helen.lifeline@btinternet.com
Web: www.lifelinechristianresource.com
Also coffee shop, candles, wine, stationery.
Manageress: Mrs Helen M Carter. Executive staff 1, Other staff 3. ***CC*** No.50[illegible]169. Began 1982; non-denominational. Turnover n/a.

Lifestyle Christian Books and Music, 1 Chantry Place, Morpeth NE61 1FJ
☎01670 504 209 🖷01670 504 209
E: lifestylecbm@connectfree.co.uk
Proprietors: Mr & Mrs Douglas & Ruth Macfarlane. Executive staff 2. Began 1997; non-denominational. Turnover £120,000 to year end Mar 04.

The Lighthouse, 63 Bonnygate, Cupar KY15 4BY
☎01334 656 287
E: thelighthouse@ukgateway.net
Also coffee shop.
Manageress: Mrs Jane Crockett. Executive staff 1, Other staff 3. ***CC*** No.SCO 04123. Began 1987; interdenominational. Turnover £100,000 to year end Dec 04.

†The Lighthouse, 55a East Street, Tollesbury, Maldon CM9 8QE
☎01621 868 088
Chairman: Rev Keith Lovell. All voluntary staff. ***CC*** No.283085. Began 1980; interdenominational. Turnover n/a.

***Lighthouse Christian Books and Music**, 13 Lynn Road, Ely CB7 4EG
☎01353 667 004 🖷01353 662 17[illegible]
E: info@elychristianfellowship.org.uk
Web: www.elychristianfellowship.org.uk
Manager: Name not supplied. Executive staff 1, Other staff 1. ***CC*** No.1070[illegible]0. Began 1987; non-denominational. Turnover £35,000 to year end Mar 04.

Lincoln Minster Shops Ltd, Lincoln Cathedral, Lincoln LN2 1PX
☎01522 575 849 🖷01522 [illegible]68 41[illegible]
E: shop@lincolncathedral.com
Web: www.lincolncathedral.com
Shop Manager: Mrs J Osgodby. Executive staff 1, Other staff 5. ***CC*** Began 1972; non-denominational. Turnover n/a.

Linkup Christian Literature, The Kings Way Church, Queen Street, Burton-on-Trent DE14 3LW
☎01283 563 661 M: 07914 595 50[illegible]
🖷01283 563 661
E: linkup@fish.co.uk
Also Traidcraft, Tearcraft
Manageress: Mrs Linda Bateman. Executive staff 1, Other staff 1. ***CC*** No.5026[illegible]8. Began 1972; interdenominational. Turnover £72,438 to year end Jan [illegible]2.

For further details see list on page 35

Liverpool Cathedral Shop, Liverpool Cathedral, St James Mount, Liverpool L1 7AZ
☎0151 709 1897 🖷0151 708 6283
Manager: To be appointed. Executive staff 1, Other staff n/a. **CC** Began 1934; interdenominational. (Previously SPCK Bookshop, Liverpool Cathedral). Turnover n/a.

The Living Stone Bookshop, 44 Palmerston Road, Boscombe, Bournemouth BH1 4HS
☎01202 394 892 🖷01202 751 540
E: sales@livingstonebookshop.com
Web: www.livingstonebookshop.com
Proprietor: Mrs Susan Tibbs. Executive staff 2, Other staff 4. Began 1989; interdenominational. Turnover n/a.

Living Stones Christian Centre Ltd, 277 Fleet Road, Fleet GU51 3BT
☎01252 616 038 🖷01252 811 940
E: livingstonescc@btopenworld.com
Resource centre, multi media, rooms available for meetings.
Manager: Mrs Samantha Luscombe. *Assistant Manager:* Mrs Suzanne Lindsey Clark. Executive staff 2, Other staff 2. **CC** No.285509. Began 1982; interdenominational. Turnover £150,000 to year end Dec 99.

***Living Waters Christian Bookshop**, Harbourside, Porthleven, Helston TR13 9JA
☎01326 574 446 🖷01326 574 446
E: info@livingwaters.co.uk
Also outreach, mail order, coffee shop.
Proprietors: Mr & Mrs Trevor Darrell. Executive staff 2, Other staff 2. Began 1996; non-denominational. Turnover n/a.

Living Word, 30 Crescent Road, Bognor Regis PO21 1QG
☎01243 828 223 🖷01243 828 223
E: living.word@dsl.pipex.com
Owners: Mr & Mrs Tony & Lindsay Leney. Executive staff 2, Other staff 3. Began 1971; non-denominational. (Previously The Living Word Christian Bookshop). Turnover n/a.

The Living Word, 23 Wharfside Village, Wharf Road, Penzance TR18 2GA
☎01736 368 020
Manageress: Mrs L Carlin. Executive staff 1. Began 1982; non-denominational. Turnover £13,000 to year end Mar 04.

Living Words, 12 Place Lane, Seaford BN25 1LA
☎01323 893 699 🖷01323 490 940
E: enquiries@living-words.co.uk
Web: www.living-words.co.uk
Owner: Dr R E Atkinson. *Shop Manager:* Eliza Davies. Executive staff 2, Other staff 2. Began 1986; non-denominational. Turnover £120,000 to year end Dec 02.

†**Logos Christian Book Shop**, 97 Bathley Street, Meadows, Nottingham NG2 2EE
☎0115 952 0201 🖷0115 952 5240
Book Shop Manager: Rev Coke. Executive staff 1, Other staff 2. Began 2002; interdenominational. Turnover n/a.

***London School of Theology Books & Resources**, Green Lane, Northwood HA6 2UW
☎01923 456 130 🖷01923 456 131
E: bookshop@lst.ac.uk
Web: www.lst.ac.uk/bookshop
Specialist academic theological bookshop stocking titles on evangelism, music, worship, counselling, Islamic studies.
Manager: Phil Groom. Executive staff 1. **CC** No.312778. Began 1973; interdenominational. (Previously London Bible College Bookshop). Turnover included in London School of Theology.

Lonsdale Bible Society, The Bible Shop, Mill Street, Ulverston LA12 7EB
☎01229 583 563 📱07713 463 272
E: david@bibleshop.org.uk
Web: www.bibleshop.org.uk
Resource centre, primarily evangelical.
Manager: Mr David Parratt. Executive staff 1. **CC** No.230656. Began 1957; non-denominational. Turnover £54,000 to year end Mar 02.

†**Olive Luff Bible Bookshop Ltd**, 133 Connaught Avenue, Frinton-on-Sea CO13 9PS
☎01255 674 106 🖷01255 674 106
Manager: Mrs P McGowan. Executive staff 1, Other staff 2. **CC** No 289011. Began 1903; interdenominational. Turnover £75,000 to year end Mar 00.

Luton Christian Book Centre, Kestin House, 45 Crescent Road, Luton LU2 0AH
☎01582 723 210 🖷01582 721 702
E: shop@lutonchristianbookcentre.co.uk
Manager: Mr Alan Gilliam. Executive staff 1, Other staff 2. **CC** No.283511. Began 2004; interdenominational. (Previously Hightown Christian Books). Turnover £138,500 [57% books, 43% other] to year end Feb 05.

B McCall Barbour, 28 George IV Bridge, Edinburgh EH1 1ES
☎0131 225 4816 🖷0131 255 4816
Specialist in AV Bibles. Also counselling; publishing fundamental books; weekend ministry and evangelism.
Managing Partner: Rev Dr T C Danson-Smith. Executive staff 2, Other staff 3. Began 1900; non-denominational. Turnover n/a.

McCrimmons Bookshop, All Saints Pastoral Centre, Shenley Lane, London Colney, St Albans AL2 1AF
☎01727 827 612
Proprietor: McCrimmon Publishing Company Ltd. Staff 5. Began 1975; Roman Catholic. (Previously Anthony Clarke Books). Turnover n/a.

Malmesbury Abbey Books Ltd, c/o Abbey Office, Old Squash Court, Holloway, Malmesbury SN16 9BA
☎01666 824 339
E: abbeybooks@malmesburyabbey.com
Manager: Mr Robert Hitchings. Executive staff 1, Other staff 2. Began 1976; non-denominational. Turnover n/a.

Manna Christian Centre, 147/149 Streatham High Road, London SW16 6EG
☎020 8769 8588
🖷020 8677 0893
E: mannabookshop@btconnect.com
Web: www.mannachristiancentre.co.uk
Manager: Mr David Lock. Executive staff 1, Other staff 2. **CC** No.1092654. Began 1981; evangelical. Turnover £270,000 to year end Feb 05.

The Manna House, 240 Old High Street, Perth PH1 5QJ
☎01738 638 142
Also coffee shop, restaurant, music.
Manager: Mr Derek Everett. Executive staff 1. **CC** No.SCO 30213. Began 1990; non-denominational. Turnover £80,000 to year end Jan 00.

The Manna House Christian Bookshop, St Giles Street, Northampton NN1 1JW
☎01604 622 666
🖷01604 635 498
E: info@mannahouse.org.uk
Web: www.mannahouse.org.uk
Also wholesale.
Director & General Manager: Mr John Nightingale. *Commercial Manager:* Joe Story. Executive staff 2, Other staff 8. **CC** No.286358. Began 1983; interdenominational. Turnover £415,000 to year end Sep 04.

Mansfield Christian Book Centre, 2 Newgate Lane, Mansfield NG18 2LF
☎01623 636 582
🖷01623 636 582
Also resource centre, coffee bar.
Manager: Mr Andrew Shaw. Executive staff 1, Other staff 1. **CC** No.1068757. Began 1978; interdenominational. Turnover £50,000 to year end Dec 04.

Maranatha Christian Bookshop, 22 Windsor Street, Uxbridge UB8 1AB
☎01895 255 748
🖷01895 811 383
E: info@maranathabookshop.co.uk
Web: www.maranathabookshop.co.uk
Also resource centre, coffee shop.
Manager: Mr Geoffrey Wallace. *Music Manager:* Miss Jayne Holley. Executive staff 4. **CC** No.801808. Began 1976; evangelical. Turnover n/a.

For further details see list on page 85

March Christian Bookshop, 19a Station Road, March PE15 8LE
☎01354 650 336
Also coffee shop.
Manager: Mrs Rosemary Fuller. Executive staff 1, Admin staff 1, Other staff 5. Began 1992; non-denominational. Turnover n/a.

Market Place Books (Kendal & District Christian Literature Society), 35 Market Place, Kendal LA9 4TP
☎01539 724 532 🖷01539 724 532
E: manager@marketplacebooks.org.uk
Web: www.marketplacebooks.org.uk
Manager: Mr J William Allen. Executive staff 2. ***CC*** No.505981. Began 1977; interdenominational. Turnover £140,000 to year end Jan 02.

Mayflower Christian Bookshop, 114 Spring Road, Bitterne, Southampton SO19 2QB
☎023 8044 9398 🖷023 8044 9398
E: mcbs@springroad.org.uk
Web: mcbs.springroad.org.uk
Also publisher.
Manager: Mr Robin Lewis. Executive staff 1. ***CC*** No.282845. Began 1974; non-denominational. Turnover n/a.

***Metanoia Book Service**, London Mennonite Centre, 14 Shepherd's Hill, Highgate, London N6 5AQ
☎08454 500 214 M: 07736 256 265
🖷020 8341 6807
E: metanoia@menno.org.uk
Web: www.menno.org.uk
Primarily mail order.
Manager: Mr Will Newcomb. Executive staff 1, Other staff 1. ***CC*** No.227410. Began 1975; Mennonite. Turnover £38,000 to year end Dec 04.

Methodist Book Centre, Bemersley House, Gitana Street, Hanley, Stoke-on-Trent ST1 1DY
☎01782 212 146 🖷01782 212 146
E: methodistbookcen@btconnect.com
Web: www.methodistbookcentre.co.uk
Manager: Miss Julie Ann Ellis. Executive staff 1, Other staff 5. ***CC*** Began 1945; Methodist. Turnover £225,012 to year end Jan 99.

Methodist Bookshop, Methodist Church House, 25 Marylebone Road, London NW1 5JR
☎020 7486 5502 🖷020 7467 5229
Resources and Bookshop Manager: Mr David Rudiger. Executive staff 1, Other staff 3. ***CC*** Began n/a; Methodist. Turnover £150,000 to year end Dec 97.

†**Metropolitan Cathedral Bookshop**, Cathedral House, Mount Pleasant, Liverpool L3 5TQ
☎0151 707 2109 🖷0151 708 7242
Manager: Mrs Pat Stockley. Executive staff 1, Other staff 2. ***CC*** Began 1967; Roman Catholic. Turnover n/a.

Mount Saint Bernard Abbey Shop, Coalville LE67 5UL
☎01530 832 298/022
🖷01530 814 608
E: mountstbernardabbey@btinternet.com
Manager: Fr Mark Hartley. Executive staff 1. ***CC*** No.211004. Began 1835; Roman Catholic. Turnover n/a.

The Mustard Seed, 38 High Street, Hemel Hempstead HP1 3AE
☎01442 252 521 🖷01442 252 521
E: office@the-mustard-seed.org
Web: www.the-mustard-seed.org
Managers: Mrs Fiona Llewellyn, Margaret Elwick. Executive staff 2, No other paid staff. ***CC*** No.1077335. Began n/a; interdenominational. Turnover n/a.

Mustard Seed, The Old Boathouse, Hillier's Yard, Marlborough SN8 1BE
☎01672 511 611
E: mustardseed@waitrose.com
Web: www.mustardseedbooks.com
Also coffee shop.
General Manager: Mrs Deborah Reynolds.
Manager: Mrs Rachel Maurice. Executive staff 2, Other staff 5. ***CC*** No.1015804. Began 1990; non-denominational. Turnover n/a.

The Mustard Seed, 2 Main Road, Gedling, Nottingham NG4 3HP
☎0115 987 9819 🖷0115 987 9819
Also coffee shop.
Owner/Manager: Mrs C Stala. Executive staff 1, Other staff 3. Began 1986; non-denominational. Turnover £45,000 to year end Dec 00.

Mustard Seed Bookshop, Balcary House, Buccleugh Road, Hawick TD9 0EH
☎01450 372 966 🖷01450 377 732
E: office@pwamm.com
Web: www.balcaryhouse.com
Also coffee shop with garden; residential accommodation for groups.
Manager: Mr Peter Edwards. Executive staff 2. ***CC*** No.SCO 14546. Began 1986; non-denominational. Part of People with a Mission Ministries. Turnover n/a.

Mustard Seed Bookshop, Perth Christian Centre, 28 Glasgow Road, Perth PH2 0NX
☎01738 639 792 🖷01738 622 928
E: office@pwamm.com
Web: www.pwamm.com
Also mail order.
Manager: Mr Peter Edwards. Executive staff 2, Other staff 3. ***CC*** No.SCO 14546. Began 1986; non-denominational. Part of People with a Mission Ministries. Turnover n/a.

Nathan's Christian Bookshop, 15 Queen Street, Godalming GU7 1BA
☎01483 415 736 🖷01483 415 736
E: melkins@zoom.co.uk
Proprietor: Mr M Elkins. Executive staff 1. Began 1975; non-denominational. Turnover £75,000 to year end Dec 04.

***New Covenant Bookshop**, Unit 214, Elephant and Castle Shopping Centre, London SE1 6TE
☎020 7703 9363 🖷020 7277 0824
E: newcovenant.uk@aol.com
Web: www.newcovenant.org.uk
Also counselling.
Manager: Mr Ayo Daniel. Executive staff 1, Other staff n/a. ***CC*** No.1004343. Began 1991; New Covenant Church. Turnover £85,000 to year end Dec 05.

New Creation Trust Christian Book and Coffee Shop, 58 Bampton Street, Tiverton EX16 6AH
☎01884 255 769 🖷01884 255 [illegible]69
E: newcreation@tiscali.co.uk
Also coffee shop, resource centre, Tearcraft foods and gifts.
Manageress: Mrs Valerie Blo[illegible]ham. Executive staff 1, Other staff 1. ***CC*** No.1063294. Began 1988; non-denominational. Turnover £56,000 to year end Dec 04.

New Dawn Bookshop and Connection Coffee House, 36 Larch Road, Abronhill, Cumbernauld, Glasgow G67 3AZ
☎01236 781 102 🖷01236 781 1[illegible]2
E: bookshop@struthers-church.org
Web: www.struthers-church.org
Also coffee shop.
Manager: Miss Pauline Rough. Executive staff 1, Other staff 3. ***CC*** No.SCO 06960. Began 1997; Struthers Memorial Churches. Turnover n/a.

***New Dawn Bookshop and Connection Coffee House**, 10a Jamaica Street, Greenock PA15 1XX
☎01475 729 668 🖷01475 728 1[illegible]5
E: bookshop@struthers-church.org
Web: www.struthers-church.org
Also coffee shop.
Manager: Mr Chris Jewell. *Assistant:* Miss Ann Morris. Executive staff 2, Other staff 8. ***CC*** No.SCO 06960. Began 1[illegible]87; Struthers Memorial Churches. Turnover £250,000 to year end Dec 04.

The New Life Bookshop, 17a St Michael's Road, Aldershot GU12 4JW
☎01252 311 460 🖷01252 311 4[illegible]0
Owner: Mr Keith W Atkins. Executive staff 1, Other staff 1. Began 1975; non-denominational. Turnover n/a.

Norwich Cathedral Shop Ltd, The Close, Norwich NR1 4EH
☎01603 218 323 🖷01603 218 323
Web: www.cathedral.org.uk
Manager: Mr Michael Callow. Executive staff 1, Other staff 4. ***CC*** Began 1[illegible]73; Anglican. Turnover £23[illegible],000 to year end Mar 05.

Number Nine Resource Centre, Edgehill Christian Education Centre, 9 Lennoxvale, Belfast BT9 5BY
☎028 9068 6939 🖷028 9068 215[illegible]
E: No9@irishmethodist.org
Web: www.irishmethodist.org
Manager: Mr Sam Campbell Executive staff 1. ***CC*** No.XN46164. Began 20[illegible]2; Methodist. (Previously Methodist Bookroom). Turnover n/a.

For further details see list on page 35

Nutshell Bookshop, Milton Road South, Stowmarket IP14 1EZ
☎01449 616 464
🖷01449 616 464
E: nutshellbookshop@yahoo.com
Proprietor: Ray Meacham. Executive staff 2. Began 2000; interdenominational. Turnover n/a.

Oak Hill Bookroom, Chase Side, Southgate, London N14 4PS
☎020 8449 3162/8446 3056 (head office)
🖷020 8441 3996
Web: www.cornerstonebookshop.co.uk
Specialising in titles for theological students; also mail order.
Manager: Mrs Sarah Woodbridge. Executive staff 1, Other staff 1. **CC** No.281838. Began 1973; Anglican. Owned by Finchley Christian Bookshops Ltd. Turnover n/a.

The Oasis, 39 Woodcote Road, Wallington SM6 0LH
☎020 8773 1428
🖷020 8647 7536
E: paul@oasiswallington.freeserve.co.uk
Also Teacraft, Fair Trade food.
Manager: Paul Hawkins. *Sales Manager:* Brian Sherrell. Executive staff 2, Other staff 11. **CC** No.1055875. Began 1983; non-denominational. Turnover £195,000 to year end Aug 02.

Oasis Bookshop, 59 Lower Main Street, Lisnaskea, Enniskillen BT92 0JD
☎028 6772 2677
M: 07740 097 532
🖷028 6772 2677
E: oasisbookshop@hotmail.co.uk
Proprietress: Mrs Valerie Crozier. Executive staff 2, Admin staff 2. Began n/a; interdenominational. Turnover £26,000 to year end Nov 98.

***Oasis Christian Books**, 88 Norfolk Street, Wisbech PE13 2LF
☎01945 465 187
🖷01945 465 187
E: oasisbookswisbech@onetel.com
Web: www.oasisbookswisbech.co.uk
Also coffee shop, Traidcraft, second-hand books.
Partner: Mr Richard Welford. Executive staff 1. Began 1976; interdenominational. Turnover £42,000 to year end Dec 04.

***Oasis Christian Bookshop**, 55 Windmill Street, Gravesend DA12 1BA
☎01474 568 498
Manager: Mrs Margaret Hills. All voluntary staff. **CC** Began 1988; interdenominational. Turnover n/a.

Oasis Christian Bookshop, 124 Bevan Street East, Lowestoft NR32 2AQ
☎01502 512 302
🖷01502 512 302
E: oasisshop@aol.com
Manager: Mr David Willis. Executive staff 2. **CC** No.279718. Began 1970; non-denominational. (Previously Lowestoft Christian Bookshop Trust). Turnover £125,000 to year end Dec 00.

***Oasis Christian Bookshop and Tearoom**, Pant-yr-Afon, Penmaenmawr, Conwy LL34 6BY
☎01492 622 322 / 623 229
🖷01492 623 222
E: books@igoasis.co.uk
Web: www.undeb.org.uk
Also coffee shop.
Manager: Mr Bill Starr. Executive staff 1, Other staff 4. **CC** No.1048524. Began 1995; non-denominational. Turnover n/a.

The Oasis Christian Centre, 25 Church Street, Romsey SO51 8BT
☎01794 512 194 🖷01794 512 194
Web: www.oasisromsey.co.uk
Manageress: Mrs Angie Nelson. Executive staff 4. **CC** No.295266. Began 1984; interdenominational. Turnover £135,000 to year end Sep 03.

The Olive Branch Christian Book & Coffee Shop, 17 Heol-y-Deri, Rhiwbina, Cardiff CF14 6HA
☎029 2061 4659
E: olivebranchrhiwbina@btconnect.com
Web: theolivebranchbookshop.org.uk
Also coffee shop.
Bookshop Manager: Mrs Sharon Price. Executive staff 1. **CC** No.516782. Began 1984; non-denominational. Turnover £150,000 to year end Dec 02.

The Olive Tree Bookshop, 513 Mansfield Road, Sherwood, Nottingham NG5 2JL
☎0115 985 7803 🖷0115 962 3715
E: olivetree@congyah.co.uk
Manager: Mr David Hayes. Executive staff 1, Other staff 2. **CC** No.245132. Began 1978; interdenominational. (Previously Beech Avenue Bible Shop). Turnover n/a.

Olive Tree Christian Resource Centre, High Mill, Kirkby Hill, Old Bolingbroke, Spilsby PE23 4HP
☎01790 763 627 M 07870 646 015 / 07866 092 318
Also resource centre.
Partner: Mr Peter Strickland. Executive staff 2, Other staff n/a. Began 1991; non-denominational. Turnover n/a.

Oswestry Christian Bookshop, Lower Brook Street, Oswestry SY11 2HG
☎01691 661 936 🖷01691 662 299
E: info@ocbooks.co.uk
Web: www.ocbooks.co.uk
Also coffee shop.
Manager: Mrs Maria Palmer. Executive staff 1, No other full-time staff. **CC** No.1102538. Began 1979; evangelical. Turnover £70,000 to year end Feb 03.

Our Lady's Bookshop, 23 Northgate, Hessle HU13 0LW
☎01482 641 835 🖷01482 640 740
E: hesslebookshop@yahoo.co.uk
Owners: Mrs Sheila Chambers, Miss Lucy Chambers. Executive staff 2, Other staff 1. Began 1980; Roman Catholic. Turnover £280,000 to year end Mar 04.

Pathway Books Ltd, 34 Robertson Street, Hastings TN34 1HT
☎01424 431 387 🖷01424 442 847
Manager: Name not supplied. No paid staff. **CC** Began 1970; non-denominational. (Previously Christian Book Mission). Turnover n/a.

Pauline Books & Media, 5-7a Royal Exchange Square, Glasgow G1 3AH
☎0141 226 3391 🖷0141 226 4719
E: glasgow@pauline-uk.org
Web: www.pauline-uk.org
Sister-in-Charge: Sr Betty Twamley. Executive staff 1, Other staff 9. **CC** No.296042. Began 1969; Roman Catholic. (Previously St Paul MultiMedia). Turnover £406,000 to year end Dec 98.

Pauline Books & Media, 82 Bold Street, Liverpool L1 4HR
☎0151 494 1328 🖷0151 707 1371
E: liverpool@pauline-uk.org
Web: ww.pauline-uk.org
Sister in Charge: Sr Noreen O'Rourke. Executive staff 1, Other staff 7. **CC** No.296042. Began 1969; Roman Catholic. (Previously St Paul MultiMedia). Turnover £409,000 to year end Dec 98.

Pauline Books & Media, 199 Kensington High Street, London W8 6BA
☎020 7937 9591 🖷020 7937 9910
E: london@pauline-uk.org
Web: www.pauline-uk.org
Sister in Charge: Sr Virginia Marras. Executive staff 1, Other staff 9. **CC** No.296042. Began 1955; Roman Catholic. (Previously St Paul MultiMedia). Turnover £772,000 to year end Dec 98.

Pauline Books & Media, Clayton Street West, Newcastle upon Tyne NE1 5HH
☎0191 239 5702 🖷0191 239 5707
E: newcastle@pauline-uk.org
Web: www.pauline-uk.org
Sister-in-Charge: Sr Angela Grant. Executive staff 1, Other staff 2. **CC** No.296042. Began 2003; Roman Catholic. Turnover n/a.

Pendlebury's, Church House, Portland Avenue, Stamford Hill, London N16 6HJ
☎020 8809 4922
E: books@pendleburys.com
Web: www.pendleburys.com
Specialising in second-hand theological books.
Proprietor: Mr John Pendlebury. Executive staff 2, Admin staff 2. Began 1984; non-denominational. Turnover £160,000 to year end Apr 02.

Perivale Christian Bookshop, 90 Bilton Road, Perivale, Greenford UB6 7BN
☎020 8998 2933 🖷020 8998 2940
E: peribooks@christnetbooks.co.uk
Web: www.christnetbooks.co.uk
Also mail order, counselling.
Manager: Mr Martin Deadman. Executive staff 1, Other staff 3. **CC** No.293404. Began 1984; non-denominational. (Previously Perivale Christian Centre). Turnover £60,000 to year end Dec 02.

B

For further details see list on page 85

Bookshops & Other Retail Outlets

Peterborough Cathedral Enterprises Ltd, 2 Minster Precincts, Peterborough PE1 1XS
☎01733 555 098
Web:www.peterborough-cathedral.org.uk
Cathedral souvenir and gift shop; also liturgical and church supplies.
Manager: Mrs Sylvia Gower. Executive staff 1. Began 1988; Anglican. Turnover £175,000 to year end Dec 05.

Peterborough Christian Books Ltd, 68 Westgate, Peterborough PE1 1RG
☎01733 551 915 📠01733 558 520
E: frankpcb@fs.com
Web: www.p-christianbooks.co.uk
Directors: Mrs Annette Smith, Mrs Ruth Grenfell. Executive staff 2, Other staff 1. Began 1978; non-denominational. Turnover £225,000 to year end Mar 01.

Phillips Print + Stationery, 115 High Street, Crediton EX17 3LG
☎01363 772 060 📠01363 774 030
Web: www.phillipsprint.co.uk
Christian resource centre.
Manageress: Mrs C Turner. Executive staff 2, Other staff 8. Began n/a; non-denominational. (Previously Phillips & Company). Turnover £250,000 to year end Dec 02.

The Phoenix Bookshop, 19 North Street, Winchcombe, Cheltenham GL54 5LH
☎01242 602 795 📠01242 604 095
Owners/Partners: Mr & Mrs Adlington. Executive staff 1, Admin staff 1. Began 2000; interdenominational. Turnover £130,000 to year end Mar 03.

***Pilgrim Hall Bookshop**, Easons Green, Uckfield TN22 5RE
☎01825 841 342 M: 07768 511 297
📠01825 841 342
E: nnibloe@compuserve.com
Web: www.tcbconline.co.uk
Bookshop Manager: Mrs B Trickey. Executive staff 1. ***CC*** Began n/a; interdenominational. Linked to Tonbridge Christian Book Centre. Turnover n/a.

Pluscarden Abbey Bookshop, Pluscarden Abbey, Elgin IV30 8UA
☎01343 890 257 📠01343 890 258
E: monks@pluscardenabbey.org
Web: www.pluscardenabbey.org
Cellarer: Name not supplied. Executive staff 1. ***CC*** No.SCO 13703. Began 1948; Roman Catholic, Benedictine. Turnover n/a.

Pontefract Christian Bookshop, Unit A, Mauds Yard, Pontefract WF8 1AQ
☎01977 701 405 📠01977 701 405
Manageress: Mrs Beryl Suggitt. No full-time staff. Began 1980; evangelical. Turnover n/a.

Portsmouth Cathedral Bookshop, St Thomas' Street, Old Portsmouth, Portsmouth PO1 2HH
☎023 9236 7747
Managers: Mr & Mrs Derek & Myrna Hall. No full-time staff. Began 1983; Anglican. Turnover n/a.

Priory Bookshop, 1 High Street, Ruislip HA4 7AU
☎01895 624 498 📠01895 624 498
E: ampriory@aol.com
Web: www.smartins-ruislip.co.uk /Priory_Bookshx.html
Also counselling.
Managers: Mr & Mrs A Seymour. Project Leaders 2, Other staff n/a. Began 1995; interdenominational. Turnover n/a.

Protestant Truth Society Bookshop, 184 Fleet Street, London EC4A 2HJ
☎020 7405 4960
E: ptslondon@btinternet.com
Web: www.protestant-truth.org
Promoting the Protestant Reformed religion and faith.
Bookshop Manager: Mr George Rae. Executive staff 1, Other staff n/a. ***CC*** No.248505. Began 1889; non-denominational. Turnover n/a.

Quaker Bookshop, Friends House, Euston Road, London NW1 2BJ
☎020 7663 1030/1031
📠020 7663 1008
E: bookshop@quaker.org.uk
Web: www.quaker.org.uk
Manager: Phillip Arnold. Executive staff 1, Other staff 2. ***CC*** Began 1926; Religious Society of Friends. (Previously Friends Book Centre). Turnover £250,000 to year end Dec 00.

Quarr Abbey Bookshop, Quarr Abbey, Ryde PO33 4ES
☎01983 882 420
Manager: Br Charles Gilman. No full-time staff. ***CC*** No.218731. Began n/a; Roman Catholic. Turnover n/a.

The Rainbow Bookshop, St Aldhelm's Centre, Edgeware Road, Swindon SN1 1QS
☎01793 694 583 📠01793 694 583
E: rainbowbookshop@btinternet.com
Manageress: Mrs Helen Watt. Executive staff 1, Other staff 1. ***CC*** Began 1979; ecumenical. Turnover n/a.

Rainbow Christian Centre, 87 Queensway, Petts Wood, Orpington BR5 1DQ
☎01689 821 789 📠01689 890 136
E: rainbowcentre@aol.com
Web: www.rainbowchristiancentre.org.uk
Also coffee shop, office services.
Partner: Miss Diana Pattison. Other staff 3. Began 1984; non-denominational. Turnover £200,000 to year end Dec 02.

Redemptorist Publications, Alphonsus House, Chawton, Alton GU34 3HQ
☎01420 88 222 📠01420 88 805
E: sales@shineonline.net
Web: www.redempt.org
Executive Director: Fr Timothy Buckland. Executive staff 3, Other staff 19. ***CC*** No.3261721. Began 1957; Roman Catholic/Anglican. (Previously Redemptorist Book Room). Turnover n/a.

The Regent Hall Café, Regent Hall, 275 Oxford Street, London W1C 2DJ
☎020 7629 5424
📠020 7629 4917
E: hallhire@regenthall.co.uk
Also day conference facilities, coffee shop, training, meeting rooms.
Centre Director: Mr Richard Heathman. Staff n/a. ***CC*** No.214779. Began 1994; Salvation Army. Turnover n/a.

Michael Reid Ministries Bookshop, 49 Coxtie Green Road, Brentwood CM14 5PS
☎01277 373 436
📠01277 375 578
E: info@michaelreidministries.org
Web: www.aliveuk.com
Manager: Mrs Diane Wilkinson. Executive staff 1, Other staff n/a. Began 1988; Pentecostal. (Previously Peniel Bookshop). Part of Peniel Pentecostal Church. Turnover n/a.

Revelation Christian Resource Centre, 1 River Street, Chippenham SN15 3ED
☎01249 659 432
📠01249 463 227
E: andrea@revelationcrc.com
Manager: Mrs Andrea Alner. *Assistant Manager:* Mrs Anne Showering. No full-time staff. ***CC*** No.1015148. Began 1985; non-denominational. Turnover £110,000 to year end Jul 04.

Revelations, St Nicolas Centre, 4 Cutler Street, Ipswich IP1 1UQ
☎01473 298 507
📠01473 298 501
E: revelations@stedmundsbury.anglican.org
Manager: Shirley Nichols. All voluntary staff. Began 1998; non-denominational. (Previously Church Centre Ltd). Turnover £100,000 to year end Dec 02.

Revelations, Meeting Point House, Southwater Square, Telford TF3 4HS
☎01952 291 634
📠01952 213 555
E: revelations@telfordchristiancouncil.co.uk
Manager: Mr Steve Aston. Executive staff 1. ***CC*** No.1084035. Began 1974; ecumenical. (Previously Telford Christian Council Bookshop). Turnover n/a.

***The Rock (Bedwas Christian Resource Centre)**, 1 Church Street, Bedwas, Caerphilly CF83 8EA
☎029 2088 1101
📠029 2088 5004
E: therocksec@aol.com
Web: bedwasrock.org.uk
Also tea room, respite flat for full-time or retired Christian workers, conference centre.
Manageress: Mrs Ford. Executive staff 1. ***CC*** No.1042285. Began 1994; interdenominational. Turnover £50,000 to year end Dec 04.

For further details see list on page 35

Rora Christian Fellowship Trust, Rora House, Halford, Liverton, Newton Abbot TQ12 6HZ
☎01626 821 746 📠01626 821 586
E: roraaca@lineone.net
Web: www.rorahouse.org.uk
Also conference facilities for group bookings including self-catering.
Manager: Mr J Ford. All voluntary staff. ***CC*** No.268681. Began 1968; non-denominational. (Previously Brexwise Ltd). Turnover n/a.

Russian Orthodox Cathedral Shop, 67 Ennismore Gardens, London SW7 1NH
☎020 7584 0096 📠020 7584 9864
E: info@ikon-records.com
Web: www.cathedral.sourozh.org or www.ikon-records.com
Also icons, mail order.
Manager: Miss Honor Stephenson. No full-time staff. ***CC*** No.254025. Began n/a; Orthodox. Turnover n/a.

St Andrews Bookshop Ltd, 126 Mary Vale Road, Bournville, Birmingham B30 1PJ
☎0121 459 7000 📠0121 459 7000
E: birmingham@standrewsbookshop.co.uk
Web: www.standrewsbookshop.co.uk
Manager: Lizzy Hunting. Executive staff 1, Other staff 3. Began 1998; non-denominational. (Previously Mother Goose). Linked to St Andrews Bookshop Ltd, Great Missenden. Turnover £50,000 to year end Dec 98.

St Andrews Bookshop Ltd, 70 St Johns Street, Bury St Edmunds IP33 1SJ
☎01284 769 517 📠01284 769 517
E: bury@standrewsbookshop.co.uk
Web: www.standrewsbookshop.co.uk
Manager: Mr Darren Bullen. Executive staff 1, Other staff 2. Began 1962; non-denominational. (Previously P A Cook Christian Books). Linked to St Andrews Bookshop Ltd, Great Missenden. Turnover n/a.

St Andrews Bookshop Ltd, 61 High Street, Great Missenden HP16 0AA
☎01494 862 168 Mail order 01494 865 510 📠01494 862 068
E: gm@standrewsbookshop.co.uk
Web: www.standrewsbookshop.co.uk
Manager: Greg Hassell. Executive staff 4, Other staff 9. Began 1957; non-denominational. Head Office of St Andrews Bookshops Ltd. Turnover £900,000 to year end Dec 02.

St Andrews Bookshop Ltd, 19 Queen Street, Maidenhead SL6 1NB
☎01628 621 985 📠01628 621 985
E: maidenhead@standrewsbookshop.co.uk
Web: www.standrewsbookshop.co.uk
Manager: Name not supplied. Executive staff 1, Other staff 3. Began 1981; non-denominational. Linked to St Andrews Bookshop Ltd, Great Missenden. Turnover £200,000 to year end Dec 02.

St Andrews Bookshop Ltd, 50 Church Street, Wolverton, Milton Keynes MK12 5JW
☎01908 221 331 📠01908 221 331
E: wolverton@standrewsbookshop.co.uk
Web: www.standrewsbookshop.co.uk
Manager: Name not supplied. Executive staff 1, Other staff 4. Began 1980; non-denominational. Linked to St Andrews Bookshop Ltd, Great Missenden. Turnover £200,000 to year end Dec 02.

St Andrews Bookshop Ltd, 57c St Clements, Oxford OX4 1AG
☎01865 247 567 📠01865 247 567
E: oxford@standrewsbookshop.co.uk
Web: www.standrewsbookshop.co.uk
Manager: Name not supplied. Executive staff 1, Other staff 3. Began 1948; non-denominational. Linked to St Andrews Bookshop Ltd, Great Missenden. Turnover £200,000 to year end Dec 02.

St Andrews Bookshop Ltd, 60 London Street, Reading RG1 4SQ
☎0118 957 6078 📠0118 957 6078
E: reading@standrewsbookshop.co.uk
Web: www.standrewsbookshop.co.uk
Manager: Name not supplied. Executive staff 1, Other staff 6. Began 1967; non-denominational. (Previously Gateway Outreach). Linked to St Andrews Bookshop Ltd, Great Missenden. Turnover £200,000-300,000 to year end Dec 02.

St Andrews Bookshop Ltd, 97 London Road, St Albans AL1 1LN
☎01727 834 236 📠01727 834 236
E: stalbans@standrewsbookshop.co.uk
Web: www.standrewsbookshop.co.uk
Manager: Mr Guy Marshall. Executive staff 1, Other staff 2. Began 2003; non-denominational. (Previously Crusaders Bookshop). Linked to St Andrews Bookshop Ltd, Great Missenden. Turnover n/a.

St Andrews Bookshop Ltd, Kingsway Church, Church Street, Slough SL1 1SZ
☎01753 538 999 📠01753 538 999
E: slough@standrewsbookshop.co.uk
Web: www.standrewsbookshop.co.uk
Manager: Name not supplied. Executive staff 1, Other staff 1. Began 2002; non-denominational. Linked to St Andrews Bookshop Ltd, Great Missenden. Turnover n/a.

***St Andrews Bookshop Ltd**, 384 Stratford Road, Shirley, Solihull B90 4AQ
☎0121 744 1722 📠0121 733 3400
E: shirley@standrewsbookshop.co.uk
Web: www.standrewsbookshop.co.uk
CDs, Cassettes, videos, gifts, cards. Also mail order.
Manager: Hillary Beaumont. Executive staff 1, Other staff 5. Began 1977; non-denominational. (Previously Revelation Books). Solihull Christian Fellowship. Linked to St Andrews Bookshop Ltd, Great Missenden.Turnover n/a.

St Andrews Bookshop Ltd, 31 High Street, Witney OX8 6LP
☎01993 709 429
E: witney@standrewsbookshop.co.uk
Web: www.standrewsbookshop.co.uk
Manager: Name not supplied. Executive staff 1, Other staff 3. Began 1994; non-denominational. Linked to St Andrews Bookshop Ltd, Great Missenden. Turnover £80,000 to year end Dec 02.

St Andrews Bookshop Ltd, Holme Grange Craft Village, Heathlands Road, Wokingham RG40 3AW
☎0118 977 6715 📠0118 977 6715
E: wokingham@standrewsbookshop.co.uk
Web: www.standrewsbookshop.co.uk
Manager: Name not supplied. Executive staff 1, Other staff 3. Began 1996; non-denominational. Linked to St Andrews Bookshop Ltd, Great Missenden. Turnover £80,000 to year end Dec 02.

St David's Cathedral Bookshop, The Cathedral Close, St Davids, Haverfordwest SA62 6RH
☎01437 720 199
Web: info@stdavidscathedral.org.uk
Also a restaurant.
Administrator: Miss Moyra Skenfield. Executive staff 1, Other staff 6. ***CC*** Began n/a; Church in Wales. Turnover n/a.

***St Denys' Bookshop**, 11 Oak Street, Manchester M4 5JD
☎0161 835 1069 📠0161 839 7661
E: stdenysbookshop@btconnect.com
Web: www.stdenysbookshop.com
Partner: Mrs Susan Usher. Executive staff 2, Other staff 3. Began 1982; non-denominational. Turnover n/a.

St Michael's Bookshop, St Michael's Church, Laura Place, Aberystwyth SY23 2AU
☎01970 617 184 📠01970 610 133
E: ruth@stmikes.net
Web: www.stmikes.net
Manager: Ruth Wood. Executive staff 1, Other staff 1. Began 1983; Church in Wales. Turnover £11,500 [75% Books 25% Other] to year end Dec 04.

St Pauls at Hinsley Hall, 62 Headingley Lane, Leeds LS6 2BX
☎0113 275 4043 📠0113 275 3207
Web: www.stpauls.org.uk
Also multi-media centre.
Manager: Mr Tom Kala. Executive staff 1, Other staff n/a. ***CC*** No.230948. Began 2001; Roman Catholic but ecumenical stock. Turnover n/a.

St Pauls by Leeds Cathedral, 25 Cookridge Street, Leeds LS2 3AG
☎0113 245 0850 📠0113 245 2987
Also gifts, church artifacts.
Manager: Mr Tom Kala. Other staff 3. ***CC*** No.230948. Began 1953; Roman Catholic but ecumenical stock. Turnover n/a.

For further details see list on page 85

St Pauls by St Chad's Cathedral, St Chad's Queensway, Birmingham B4 6ET
☎0121 236 6336 🖷0121 236 2332
Web: www.stpauls.org.uk
Also candles, posters, rosaries, church furnishings.
Manager: Mr Lorenzo Torri. , Other staff 3. Began 2001; Roman Catholic but ecumenical stock. (Previously St Chad's Cathedral Bookshop). Turnover n/a.

St Pauls by Westminster Cathedral, Morpeth Terrace, Victoria, London SW1P 1EP
☎020 7828 5582 🖷020 7828 3329
E: bookshop@stpauls.org.uk
Web: www.stpauls.org.uk/bookshop
Managing Director: Sebastian Karamvelil. *Systems Coordinator:* Steven Mosling. Executive staff 2, Other staff 11. ***CC*** No.230948. Began 1990; Roman Catholic but ecumenical stock. Turnover £1,200,000 to year end Dec 98.

Salvationist Publishing and Supplies Ltd, 1 Tiverton Street, London SE1 6NT
☎020 7366 6571 🖷020 7367 6576
E: mail_order@sp-s.co.uk
Web: www.sps-shop.com
Managing Director: Mr Trevor P Caffull. Executive staff 5, Other staff 23. Began 1911; interdenominational. Turnover £3,500,000 to year end Mar 02.

†Sancta Maria Abbey Bookshop, Garvald, Haddington EH41 4LW
☎01620 830 223 / 335
🖷01620 830 304
Manager: Rev Philip Bell. Admin staff 1, No other paid staff. Began 1946; Roman Catholic. Turnover £35,000 to year end Oct 02.

Sarum College Bookshop, 19 The Close, Salisbury SP1 2EE
☎01722 326 899 🖷01722 338 508
E: bookshop@sarum.ac.uk
Web: www.sarumcollegebookshop.co.uk or www.sarum.ac.uk/bookshop
Specialising in new and second-hand theological books; mail order. Also coffee shop and restaurant.
Manager: Mr Mark Clifford. Executive staff 1, Admin staff 3. ***CC*** Began 1985; ecumenical. (Previously Swells Bookshop Ltd). Turnover £330,000 to year end Jul 05.

Scripture Union Resource Centre, 157 Albertbridge Road, Belfast BT5 4PS
☎028 9073 4360 🖷028 9073 9758
E: resources@suni.co.uk
Web: www.suni.co.uk
Resouces for young people and to promote reading the Bible.
Manager: Mr Michael Gibson. *General Director:* Ms Helen Warnock. Executive staff 5, Other staff 3. ***CC*** No.XN 47412. Began 1954; interdenominational. Turnover £200,000 to year end Mar 05.

Second Chance, 379 Aspley Lane, Aspley, Nottingham NG8 5RR
☎0115 929 2500
Selling greetings cards and good quality second-hand clothing and furniture.
Chairman: Mrs Doris A Lilley. Executive staff 1. ***CC*** No.506775. Began 1978; interdenominational. (Previously The Lord's Shop Trust). No magazine. Turnover n/a.

Seekers Light Trust, The Lighthouse, 40 High Street, Highworth, Swindon SN6 7AQ
☎01793 763 337 🖷01793 763 337
E: malcolm.swift@care4free.net
Web: www.lighthousebooks.net
Manager: Mr Malcolm Swift. Executive staff 1. ***CC*** No.289860. Began 1984; non-denominational. Turnover n/a.

Shalom The Good Book Shop, Central Chambers, Beaumont Street, Hexham NE46 3LS
☎01434 604 004
Manager: Mrs Stephanie Young. Executive staff 1, No other paid staff. Began 1996; interdenominational. Turnover £54,000 to year end Dec 04.

Shepherd's Christian Bookshop, 131-132 Lower Dock Street, Newport NP20 1EG
☎01633 259 222 M: 07974 120 048
Web: www.shepherdschristian bookshop.co.uk
Also coffee shop.
Manager: Miss Emma Brownhill. Executive staff 1, Other staff 2. ***CC*** No.1051834. Began 2001. Turnover n/a.

The Shrine Bookshop, 2 Common Place, Walsingham NR22 6EE
☎01328 824 201
E: shop@olw-shrine.org.uk
Web: www.walsingham.org.uk
Manager: Heather Deive. Executive staff 1, Other staff 2. ***CC*** No.215863. Began 1935; Anglican. (Previously The Shrine Shop). Turnover n/a.

†Sign of the Fish Christian Bookshop, 30 Eld Lane, Colchester CO1 1LS
☎01206 579 665
Proprietor: Mr Dexter Slatter. Executive staff 1. Began 1967; interdenominational. Turnover n/a.

Siop Y Gair, Rhos Building, School of Education, University of Wales Bangor, Normal Site, Bangor LL57 2PX
☎01248 382 947 🖷01248 382 155
E: aled.davies@bangor.ac.uk
Web: www.ysgolsul.com
Focusing on children's and youth work, also resource centre.
Director: Rev Aled Davies. *Manager:* Mr E. Hughes. Executive staff 2, Other staff 6. Began 2000; non-denominational. (Previously RE Bookshop / Llyfrfa). Turnover n/a.

Sittingbourne Christian Bookshop, Baptist Church, High Street, Sittingbourne ME10 4AQ
☎01795 422 315
E: scbookshop@tiscali.co.uk
Manager: Mrs Joan Hammond. Executive staff 2, No other paid staff. ***CC*** No.1070071. Began 1976; non-denominational. Turnover £36,000 to year end Dec 00.

Soham Books, 38 High Street, Soham, Ely CB7 5HE
☎01353 722 259 🖷01353 722 259
E: sohbooks@fish.co.uk
Proprietor: Mrs Joy Dean. Executive staff 1, Other staff 3. Began 1986; non-denominational. Turnover £74,000 to year end Mar 02.

†Sonshine Christian Bookshop, Burgh Road, Aylsham, Norwich NR11 6AJ
☎01263 734 420
E: sonshine-bookshop@lineone.net
Manager: Mr Dave Pelham. Executive staff 1. Began 1984; non-denominational. Turnover £60,000 to year end May 00.

Southend Christian Bookshop Ltd, 57 London Road, Southend-on-Sea SS1 [illegible]PF
☎01702 344 008 🖷01702 390 5[illegible]0
E: scbookshop@aol.com
Director: Mr P J Slennett. Executive staff 2, Other staff 6. Began 1971; interdenominational. Turnover n/a.

†Southerden Books, Sheriff Place, Market Square, Hailsham BN27 1AD
☎01323 441 079 🖷01323 441 0[illegible]9
E: southerdenbooks@aol.com
Proprietor: Mrs Kay Timms. Executive staff 1, Other staff 3. Began 1994; non-denominational. Turnover £38,000 to year end Sep 02.

Southern Light Literature, 51a Wimpson Lane, Millbrook, Southampton SO16 4[illegible]F
☎023 8039 9894
E: info@millbookchristiancentre.com
Web: www.millbrookchristiancentre.com
Senior Minister: Pastor Mark [illegible] Starbuck. Executive staff 1. ***CC*** No.1036[illegible]09. Began 1990; Assemblies of God. (Previously Southern Light Ministries). Turnover n/a.

Southport Christian Book Centre 3 Wesley Street, Southport PR8 1BN
☎01704 542 226 🖷01704 542 22[illegible]
E: christianbooks@btconnect.com
Web: www.southportchristianbooks.co.uk
Proprietors: Mr C C Arch, Mrs L J Arch. Executive staff 2, Other staff 3. Began 1955; non-denominational. Turnover n/a.

Sozo Books, Sozo House, Alma Road, Romsey SO51 8ED
☎01794 522 511 🖷01794 522 57[illegible]
E: Email@sozo.org
Web: www.sozo.org
Specialising in conference and public meeting bookstalls; also online ordering.
Partner: Mr A S Daniel. Executive staff 1, Other staff 4. ***CC*** No.104242[illegible]. Began 1989; non-denominational. Turnover n/a.

For further details see list on page [illegible]5

SPCK Bookshop, 12 Ethel Street, Birmingham B2 4BG
☎0121 643 2617 🖷0121 633 3459
E: birmingham@spck.org.uk
Web: www.spck.org.uk
Manager: Mr David C Stokes. Executive staff 1, Other staff 4. **CC** No.231144. Began 1858; interdenominational. (Previously Mowbrays Bookshop). Society for Promoting Christian Knowledge. Turnover n/a.

SPCK Bookshop, 14 North Parade, Bradford BD1 3HY
☎01274 728 669 🖷01274 759 982
E: bradford@spck.org.uk
Web: www.spck.org.uk
Manager: Mr Nicholas Johnson. Executive staff 1, Other staff 2. **CC** No.231144. Began 1936; interdenominational. Society for Promoting Christian Knowledge. Turnover n/a.

SPCK Bookshop, 79 Park Street, Bristol BS1 5PF
☎0117 927 3461 🖷0117 929 3525
E: bristol@spck.org.uk
Web: www.spck.org.uk
Manager: Rev Richard Greatrex. Executive staff 1, Other staff 3. **CC** No.231144. Began 1948; interdenominational. Society for Promoting Christian Knowledge. Turnover n/a.

SPCK Bookshop, 15 Sussex Street, Cambridge CB1 1PA
☎01223 358 452 🖷01223 366 316
E: cambridge@spck.org.uk
Web: www.spck.org.uk
Manager: Mrs Christina Lang. Executive staff 1, Other staff n/a. **CC** No.231144. Began n/a; interdenominational. Society for Promoting Christian Knowledge. Turnover n/a.

SPCK Bookshop, 7 St Peter's Street, Canterbury CT1 2EF
☎01227 462 881 🖷01227 456 297
E: canterbury@spck.org.uk
Web: www.spck.org.uk
Manager: Mr David Rose. Executive staff 1, Other staff 3. **CC** No.231144. Began 1932; interdenominational. Society for Promoting Christian Knowledge. Turnover n/a.

SPCK Bookshop, City Church, Windsor Place, Cardiff CF10 3BZ
☎029 2022 7736 🖷029 2022 7515
E: cardiff@spck.org.uk
Web: www.spck.org.uk
Manager: Mr Roger Spencer. Executive staff 1, Other staff 3. **CC** No.231144. Began 1937; interdenominational. Society for Promoting Christian Knowledge. Turnover n/a.

SPCK Bookshop, The Lodge, Carlisle Cathedral, Carlisle CA3 8TZ
☎01228 543 498 🖷01228 402 857
E: carlisle@spck.org.uk
Web: www.spck.org.uk
Manager: Mr Raymond Witty. Executive staff 1, Other staff 2. **CC** No.231144. Began 1979; interdenominational. Society for Promoting Christian Knowledge. Turnover n/a.

SPCK Bookshop, 7/11 St Werburgh Street, Chester CH1 2EJ
☎01244 404 010 🖷01244 404 019
E: chester@spck.org.uk
Web: www.spck.org.uk
Manager: Mr Ian Vollands. Executive staff 1, Other staff 3. **CC** No.231144. Began 1946; interdenominational. Society for Promoting Christian Knowledge. Turnover n/a.

SPCK Bookshop, St Olave's Church, North Street, Chichester PO19 1LQ
☎01243 782 790 🖷01243 784 604
E: chichester@spck.org.uk
Web: www.spck.org.uk
Manager: Miss Barbara Scott. Executive staff 1, Other staff 2. **CC** No.231144. Began 1957; interdenominational. Society for Promoting Christian Knowledge. Turnover n/a.

SPCK Bookshop, The Great Kitchen, Durham Cathedral, Durham DH1 3EQ
☎0191 386 2972 🖷0191 384 2834
E: durham@spck.org.uk
Web: www.spck.org.uk
Manager: Mrs C Burrows. Executive staff 1, Other staff 3. **CC** No.231144. Began 1954; interdenominational. Society for Promoting Christian Knowledge. Turnover n/a.

SPCK Bookshop, 1/2 Catherine Street, Cathedral Yard, Exeter EX1 1EX
☎01392 260 270 🖷01392 260 279
E: exeter@spck.org.uk
Web: www.spck.org.uk
Manager: Mr Crispin Heath. Executive staff 1, Other staff 4. **CC** No.231144. Began 1932; interdenominational. Society for Promoting Christian Knowledge. Turnover n/a.

SPCK Bookshop, Palace Yard, Hereford HR4 9BJ
☎01432 266 785 🖷01432 279 040
E: hereford@spck.org.uk
Web: www.spck.org.uk
Manager: Ms Hannah Jameson. Executive staff 1, Other staff 1. **CC** No.231144. Began 1982; interdenominational. Society for Promoting Christian Knowledge. Turnover n/a.

SPCK The Pilgrim Shop, First Floor, 20 Newmarket Street, Leeds LS1 6DG
☎0113 237 6480 🖷0113 237 6486
E: leeds@spck.org.uk
Manager: Miss Rachael Franklin. Executive staff 1, Other staff 2. Began 2001; interdenominational. Society for Promoting Christian Knowledge. Turnover n/a.

SPCK Bookshop, Pilgrim House, 10 Bishop Street, Leicester LE1 6AF
☎0116 285 4499 🖷0116 275 5948
E: leicester@spck.org.uk
Web: www.spck.org.uk
Manager: Rev Peter Hebden. Executive staff 1, Other staff 3. **CC** No.231144. Began 1974; interdenominational. Society for Promoting Christian Knowledge. Turnover n/a.

SPCK Bookshop, 30a Sincil Street, Lincoln LN5 7ET
☎01522 527 486 🖷01522 587 849
E: lincoln@spck.org.uk
Web: www.spck.org.uk
Manager: Miss Melanie Caroll. Executive staff 1, Other staff 7. **CC** No.231144. Began 1946; interdenominational. Society for Promoting Christian Knowledge. Turnover n/a.

SPCK Bookshop, Faith House, 7 Tufton Street, London SW1P 3QN
☎020 7799 5083 🖷020 7233 4297
E: london@spck.org.uk
Web: www.spck.org.uk
Manager: Miss Aude Pasquier. Executive staff 1, Other staff 4. **CC** No.231144. Began 1836; interdenominational. Society for Promoting Christian Knowledge. Turnover n/a.

SPCK Secondhand & Antiquarian Bookshop, Faith House, 7 Tufton Street, London SW1P 3QN
☎020 7799 5083 🖷020 7233 4297
E: secondhand@spck.org.uk
Web: www.spck.org.uk
Specialising in antiquarian, out-of-print and second-hand theology and Christian literature, maps and prints.
Manager: Rev Basil Youdell. Executive staff 1, Other staff 2. **CC** No.231144. Began 1976; interdenominational. (Previously Charles Higham Bookshop). Society for Promoting Christian Knowledge. Turnover n/a.

SPCK The Bible House, 14 Pilgrim Street, Newcastle upon Tyne NE1 6QD
☎0191 232 0335 🖷0191 233 0869
E: newcastle@spck.org.uk
Web: www.spck.org.uk
Manageress: Mrs H Place. Executive staff 1, Other staff 8. **CC** No.231144. Began 1864; non-denominational. (Previously The Bible House). Turnover £400,000 to year end Jan 03.

SPCK Bookshop, 8 Ridley Place, Newcastle upon Tyne NE1 8JW
☎0191 232 3466 🖷0191 230 2265
E: newcastle@spck.org.uk
Web: www.spck.org.uk
Manager: Mrs Heather Place. Executive staff 1, Other staff 3. **CC** No.231144. Began 1943; interdenominational. Society for Promoting Christian Knowledge. Turnover n/a.

SPCK Bookshop, St Michael at Plea Church, Redwell Street, Norwich NR2 4SN
☎01603 627 332 🖷01603 627 332
E: norwich@spck.org.uk
Web: www.spck.org.uk
Manager: Mr Steven Foyster. Executive staff 1, Other staff 2. **CC** No.231144. Began 1978; interdenominational. Society for Promoting Christian Knowledge. Turnover n/a.

For further details see list on page 85

SPCK Bookshop, 51 High Street, Salisbury SP1 2PE
☎01722 334 535 🖷01722 414 904
E: salisbury@spck.org.uk
Web: www.spck.org.uk
Manager: Miss Sarah Hargreaves. Executive staff 1, Other staff 3. ***CC*** No.231144. Began 1941; interdenominational. Society for Promoting Christian Knowledge. Turnover n/a.

SPCK Bookshop, 8 East Parade, Sheffield S1 2ET
☎0114 272 3454 🖷0114 279 7751
E: sheffield@spck.org.uk
Web: www.spck.org.uk
Manager: Mrs Janette Cloke. Executive staff 1, Other staff 2. ***CC*** No.231144. Began 1936; interdenominational. Society for Promoting Christian Knowledge. Turnover n/a.

SPCK Bookshop, 8 St Mary's Street, Truro TR1 2AF
☎01872 272 771 🖷01872 260 491
E: truro@spck.org.uk
Web: www.spck.org.uk
Manager: Mr David Ivall. Executive staff 1, Other staff 2. ***CC*** No.231144. Began 1950; interdenominational. Society for Promoting Christian Knowledge. Turnover n/a.

SPCK Bookshop, 24 The Square, Winchester SO23 9EX
☎01962 866 617 🖷01962 890 312
E: winchester@spck.org.uk
Web: www.spck.org.uk
Manager: Mr William Cole. Executive staff 1, Other staff 2. ***CC*** No.231144. Began 1977; interdenominational. Society for Promoting Christian Knowledge. Turnover n/a.

SPCK Bookshop, 105 High Street, Worcester WR1 2HS
☎01905 243 96 🖷01905 243 96
E: worcester@spck.org.uk
Web: www.spck.org.uk
Manager: Mr Stephen Jeynes. Executive staff 1, Other staff 2. ***CC*** No.231144. Began 1937; interdenominational. Society for Promoting Christian Knowledge. Turnover n/a.

SPCK Bookshop, 28 Goodramgate, York YO1 7LG
☎01904 654 176 🖷01904 670 931
E: york@spck.org.uk
Web: www.spck.org.uk
Manager: Mr Paul Walker. Executive staff 1, Other staff 2. ***CC*** No.231144. Began 1947; interdenominational. Society for Promoting Christian Knowledge. Turnover n/a.

Spectrum Christian Books and Gifts, 167 Stamford Street, Ashton-Under-Lyne OL6 6XW
☎0161 344 5991
Senior Trustee: Mr Allan Taylor. No paid staff. ***CC*** No.509290. Began 1975; non-denominational. (Previously Jesus Family Bookshop). Turnover £30,000 to year end Dec 04.

Spurgeon's Book Room, 189 South Norwood Hill, London SE25 6DJ
☎020 8653 3640 🖷020 8653 0850
Web: www.tcbconline.co.uk
Managing Director: Mr Norman E Nibloe. Executive staff 1, Other staff 1. Began 1981; Baptist. (Linked to Tonbridge Christian Book Centre). Turnover £48,000 to year end Jun 98.

Spurriergate Centre, St Michael's Church, Spurriergate, York YO1 9QR
☎01904 629 393 🖷01904 629 383
E: general@thespurriergatecentre.com
Web: www.thespurriergatecentre.com
Also restaurant, coffee shop, counselling service, evangelism, listening, prayer.
Centre Manager: Simon Watterson. Executive staff 3, Other staff 33. ***CC*** No.519912. Began 1989; Anglican. Turnover £380,000 to year end Mar 03.

***St James' Bookshop**, 7 Sterte Avenue, Poole BH15 2AJ
☎01202 667 267
Manager: Mrs J M MacGregor. Admin staff 1. Began 2002; interdenominational. Turnover £2,000 [50% books, 50% other products] to year end Dec 05.

Stornoway Religious Bookshop, 30 Kenneth Street, Stornoway HS1 2DR
☎01851 703 334
Manager: William Forsyth. Executive staff 1. ***CC*** No.SCO 30274. Began 1956; non-denominational. Turnover n/a.

Swanage Christian Centre, The Old Stable, 37 Commercial Road, Swanage BH19 1DF
☎01929 424 544 🖷01929 424 544
Web: www.swanagechristiancentre.org.uk
Also coffee shop.
Manager: Mrs Pauline Wisker. Executive staff 2. ***CC*** No.276495. Began 1977; non-denominational. Turnover n/a.

The Sycamore Tree, 2 Chapel Street, Nuneaton CV11 5QH
☎024 7638 5448 Counselling 024 7674 4544 🖷024 7638 5448
E: books@sycamoretree.ctlconnect.co.uk
Also coffee shop, counselling.
Manager: Mrs Pat Bull. *Counselling:* Mrs Carol French. Executive staff 3, Other staff 1. ***CC*** No.519317. Began 1990; non-denominational. Turnover £100,000 to year end Oct 00.

Tabernacle Bookshop, Metropolitan Tabernacle, Elephant and Castle, London SE1 6SD
☎020 7735 7076 🖷020 7735 7989
E:bookshop@metropolitantabernacle.org
Web: www.tabernaclebookshop.org
Conservative Christian books and media recommended by Dr Peter Masters, Pastor Metropolitan Tabernacle. Bookshop Manager: Name not supplied. Executive staff 1, Other staff 1. ***CC*** Began 1976; non-denominational. Turnover n/a.

Talents Music Shop, 9 Brockley Rise, Forest Hill, London SE23 1JG
☎020 8699 4216 🖷020 8291 9799
E: martin@talents.co.uk
Web: www.talents.co.uk
Retailing musical instruments, computers, musical instrument tuition, computer tuition; financial services.
Senior Partner: Pastor Martin Powell. Executive staff 3, Other staff 10. Began 1989; non-denominational. No magazine. Turnover £250,000 to year end Oct 04.

Taste & See Bookshop, 102 Irlam Road, Flixton, Manchester M41 6JT
☎0161 747 5672 🖷0161 747 7379
E: shop@tasteandsee.freeserve.co.uk
Web: www.maranathacommunity.org.uk
Manager: Ms Sylvia Middlemist. Executive staff 1, No other paid staff. ***CC*** Began 1994; interdenominational. (Affiliated to Maranatha Community). Turnover n/a.

***Teifi Christian Books**, Unit 2, Priory Court, Priory Street, Cardigan SA43 1BZ
☎01239 615 516 🖷01239 615 516
Manager: Mr Chris Bacon. Executive staff 1. Began n/a; non-denominational. Turnover n/a.

The Tanglewood Trust Christian Bookshop, 30 Market Street, Lerwick, Shetland ZE1 0JP
☎01595 694 816
E: sales@ttcb.org.uk
Web: www.ttcb.org.uk
Manager: Mrs Mary Smith. Executive staff 1, No other full-time staff. ***CC*** No.SCO 26549. Began n/a; interdenominational. Turnover n/a.

***This Way Up**, Croft Cottage, The Square, Magor, Caldicot NP26 3HY
☎01633 882 525 📱07788 830 84[illegible]
E: drews@fish.co.uk
Co-Director: Mrs Jayne Drew. Executive staff 2, Admin staff 1. Began 2000; interdenominational. Turnover n/a.

Time To, 89 Crosby Street, Maryport CA15 6BP
☎01900 812 363 🖷01900 812 363
E: snowtiger@talktalk.net
Web: www.timetocumbria.co.uk
Also counselling.
Manager/Owner: Pastor William Roberts. Executive staff 1, Other staff 1. Began 1966; interdenominational. (Previously The Bookshop, Maryport). Turnover n/a.

The Tonbridge Christian Book Centre Ltd, 9 Quarry Hill Parade, Tonbridge TN9 2HR
☎01732 364 897 📱07758 511 297
🖷01732 365 437
E: nnibloe@compuserve.com
Web: www.tcbconline.co.uk
Managing Director: Mr Norman E Nibloe. Executive staff 3, Other staff 5. Began 1976; interdenominational. Turnover £200,000 to year end Dec 02.

For further details see list on page 35

The Triangle Christian Bookstore & Café, 64 Kingsmead, Farnborough GU14 7SL
☎01252 519 172 🖷01252 549 220
Web: www.thetriangle.org.uk
Also fair trade with over 30,000 products.
Manager: Mr Paul Taylor. All voluntary staff except café. ***CC*** Began 1986; interdenominational. Turnover £136,000 to year end Dec 04.

Trinity Books, St John's College, Chilwell Lane, Bramcote, Beeston, Nottingham NG9 3DS
☎0115 925 1839 🖷0115 925 1839
Proprietor: Rev Mary Essex. Executive staff 2. ***CC*** No 231144. Began n/a; interdenominational. (Previously SPCK Bookshop, Nottingham). Turnover n/a.

Truro Cathedral Shop, Wilkes Walk, Truro TR1 2UF
☎01872 275 125 🖷01872 245 012
Manager: Mr James Barker. Executive staff 1, No other full-time staff. Began 1987; Anglican. Turnover n/a.

Two Worlds Christian Bookshop, 2 Avondale Road, Chorley PR7 2ED
☎01257 263 880 🖷01257 263 880
Web: www.twoworldschorley.org.uk
Also outreach, a "listening ear".
Manager: Mrs M Ogden, All voluntary workers. ***CC*** No.518002. Began 1978; non-denominational. Turnover £56,000 [75% books, 25% other] to year end Dec 04.

UK Christian Bookshops Directory, 93 High Street, Yiewsley, West Drayton UB7 7QH
E: ukcbd.enquiries@christianbookshops.org.uk
Web: www.christianbookshops.org.uk
Free online guide to UK Christian bookshops and cafés with book reviews and shop.
Webmaster: Mr Phil Groom. No full-time staff. Began 2001; non-denominational. Turnover £1,000 to year end Apr 05.

Under The Rainbow, 7 Friday Street, Minehead TA24 5UB
☎01643 709 410
E: jrloescher@undertherainbow.freeserve.co.uk
Also coffee shop.
Proprietor: Mrs Rachael Loescher. Executive staff 2. Began 1998; non-denominational. Turnover £52,000 to year end Jan 05.

United Reformed Church Bookshop, 86 Tavistock Place, London WC1H 9RT
☎020 7916 8629 🖷020 7916 2021
E: bookshop@urc.org.uk
Web: books.urc2.org.uk
Communications Officer: Mrs Carol Rogers. Executive staff 2, Other staff 1. ***CC*** Began n/a; United Reformed. Turnover n/a.

Unity Bookshop, 15 Folly Lane, Petersfield GU31 4AU
☎01730 262 572
Part-time Manager: Ms Sharon Lack. Executive staff 1. ***CC*** No.296533. Began 1987; interdenominational. Turnover n/a.

***Urban Gospel UK**, 76 Bolton Crescent, Camberwell New Road, Kennington, London SE5 0SE
☎020 7582 1299 🖷020 7820 1508
E: dunamisbrixton@aol.com
Web: urbangospel.co.uk
Also ministry centre.
Team Leader: Mr John Bedingfield. Admin staff 2. ***CC*** No.264078. Began 1993; interdenominational. (Previously Christian City Books). Turnover n/a.

Vine Books, 23 Cheriton Place, Folkestone CT20 2AY
☎01303 210 900
E: shop@vinebooks.co.uk
Also local crafts, coffee shop.
Contact: Ms Mary Tapper. Staff n/a. Began 1999; interdenominational. Turnover £100,000 [50% books 50% other] to year end Dec 04.

The Vine Christian Bookshop, Hinckley United Reformed Church, The Borough, Hinckley LE10 1NL
☎01455 612 345 🖷01455 612 345
E: thevinehinckley@btconnect.com
Manageress: Mrs Sharon Deeming. Executive staff 1, Other staff 5. ***CC*** No.1094075. Began 2001; non-denominational. Turnover £53,000 to year end Dec 04.

The Vine Christian Bookshop and Coffee House, 6 Albert Street, Littleborough OL15 8BS
☎01706 374 534 🖷01706 377 322
E: info@thevinefellowship.co.uk
Web: www.thevinefellowship.co.uk
Also coffee shop, counselling.
Manager: Mr Geoff Hopcroft. Executive staff 1. ***CC*** No.515709. Began 1981; non-denominational. Turnover £45,000 to year end Mar 00.

The Vine Trust Bookshop, 31 Bridge Street, Andover SP10 1BE
☎01264 355 706 M: 07770 421 535
E: andoverbaptist@bigfoot.com
Manager: Mr Brian Percey. Executive staff 1. ***CC*** No.288706. Began 1984; non-denominational. Partnership with the Bridge Coffee Shop. Turnover £42,000 to year end Dec 98.

Wakefield Cathedral Bookshop, The Cathedral, Northgate, Wakefield WF1 1HG
☎01924 373 923 🖷01924 315 054
Managers: Mrs Sue Robinson, Mrs Christine Haigh. All voluntary staff. Began 1982; Anglican. Turnover £39,000 to year end Jan 04.

Wallasey Christian Books, 100 Liscard Road, Wallasey CH44 0AA
☎0151 630 5114 🖷0151 630 5114
Managers: Mrs Lynne Clark, Rev Andrew Funnell. No full-time staff. ***CC*** No.517003. Began 1985; interdenominational. Turnover £28,000 to year end Sep 02.

Watersprings, 170 High Street, Ponders End, Enfield EN3 4EU
☎020 8805 1320
M: 07788 581 193
🖷020 8805 1383
E: dafadipe@aol.com
Also coffee shop, counselling; wholesaling.
Directors: Mr & Mrs D A & H A Fadipe. Executive staff 2, Administrative staff 1, Other staff 1. Began 2001; Pentecostal. Turnover £69,550 to year end Mar 03.

Waterstones Bookshop (incorporating Mowbrays), 28 Margaret Street, London W1N 7LB
☎020 7436 0294
🖷020 7637 1790
E: enquiries@margaretstreet.waterstones.co.uk
Web: www.waterstones.co.uk
Manager Theology: Mr Frank Nugent. Staff n/a. Began 1903; non-denominational. (Previously Dillons the Bookshop). Turnover n/a.

Waterstones Bookshop (Theology Department), 82 Gower Street, London WC1E 6EQ
☎020 7636 1577
🖷020 7580 7680
E: enquiries@gowerst.waterstones.co.uk
Web: www.waterstones.co.uk
Manager Theology: Mike Long. Staff n/a. Began n/a; non-denominational. (Previously Dillons Bookstore). Turnover n/a.

Waterstones University Bookshop, 55 Sadler Street, Durham DH1 3EJ
☎0191 384 2095
🖷0191 383 1551
E: enquiries@durham-academic.waterstones.co.uk
Manager: Sue Hume. Executive staff 2, Other staff 6. ***CC*** Began 1954; interdenominational. (Previously Dillons University Bookshop and SPCK). Turnover n/a.

The Way Bookshop, West Street, Crewe CW1 3HE
☎01270 257 623
Also coffee shop.
Managers: Mrs Jill Buchan, Mrs Clarissa Shackleton. Executive staff 2. Began 1984; non-denominational. Turnover n/a.

For further details see list on page 85

†WDY Bookshop, Aberdeen Street, Winson Green, Birmingham B18 7DL
☎0121 551 3919
🖷0121 551 3934
E: wdybookshop@aol.com
Senior Pastor: Rev Wilma Folayan. Executive staff 1, Other staff 4. Began n/a; Church of God of Prophecy. Turnover n/a.

***WEC Bookroom**, Bulstrode, Oxford Road, Gerrards Cross SL9 8SZ
☎01753 884 631
🖷01753 278 166
E: bulstrode.bookroom@btopenworld.com
Web: www.wec-int.org.uk
Also mail order.
Manager: Judy Parker. No full-time staff. ***CC*** No.237005. Began 1978; interdenominational. Turnover n/a.

The Well, 116-118 West Street, Fareham PO16 0EP
☎01329 318 731 🖷01329 318 732
E: manager@thefarehamwell.co.uk
Web: www.thefarehamwell.co.uk
Also coffee shop.
General Manager: Mrs June Haye. Executive staff 1, Admin staff 7. ***CC*** No.1074048. Began 2000; ecumenical. Turnover £100,000 to year end Dec 04.

The Well Bookshop & Coffee Shop, Alpha Centre, Broadway, Douglas IM2 4EN
☎01624 622 284 🖷01624 622 284
E: thewell@ukgateway.net
Web: www.manx.net/thewell
Also listening ministry, coffee shop, counselling.
Manageress: Mrs Sheila Sutton. No full-time staff. ***CC*** Began 1984; non-denominational. Turnover £45,000 to year end Dec 00.

***The Well Trust**, 105 High Street, Stourbridge DY8 1EE
☎01384 444 649 🖷01384 443 636
E: books@thewelltrust.org.uk
Also coffee shop, counselling, pregnancy crisis centre.
Director: Mr Roger Eames. Executive staff 4, Other staff 7. ***CC*** No.1100362. Began 1989; interdenominational. Turnover n/a.

Wells Cathedral Publications Ltd, The West Cloister, Wells BA5 2PA
☎01749 672 773 🖷01749 676 543
Web: www.wellscathedral.org.uk
Manager: Mrs Elizabeth Stafford. Executive staff 2, Other staff 6. Began 1971; Anglican. Turnover n/a.

***Wesley Owen Books and Music**, 205 George Street, Aberdeen AB25 1HY
☎01224 644 464 🖷01224 644 989
E: aberdeen@wesley-owen.com
Web: www.wesleyowen.com
Manager: Meta Chalmers. Executive staff 1, Other staff 6. ***CC*** No.270162. Began n/a; interdenominational. Turnover £214,000 to year end Jan 03.

***Wesley Owen Books and Music**, 57-59 Kyle Street, Ayr KA7 1RS
☎01292 264 548 🖷01292 880 691
E: ayr@wesley-owen.com
Web: www.wesleyowen.com
Manager: Jennifer Wilson. Executive staff 1, Other staff 6. ***CC*** No.270162. Began n/a; interdenominational. Turnover £120,000 to year end Jan 03.

Wesley Owen Books and Music, 3 Forum Buildings, St James Parade, Bath BA1 1UG
☎01225 315 179 🖷01225 315 059
E: bath@wesley-owen.com
Web: www.wesleyowen.com
Manager: Mr Peter Slee. Executive staff 1, Other staff n/a. ***CC*** No.270162. Began 1983; interdenominational. Turnover n/a.

***Wesley Owen Books and Music**, 30 St Loyes Street, Bedford MK40 1EP
☎01234 262 517 🖷01234 349 587
E: bedford@wesley-owen.com
Web: www.wesleyowen.com
Manager: Mr Alun Jones. Executive staff 1, Other staff 3. ***CC*** No.270162. Began 1978; interdenominational. Turnover £259,000 to year end Jan 03.

Wesley Owen Books and Music, The Spires, Church House, Fisherwick Place, Belfast BT1 6DW
☎028 9032 1323 🖷028 9023 3533
E: belfast@wesley-owen.com
Web: www.wesleyowen.com
Manager: Alan Hamilton. Executive staff 1, Other staff 3. ***CC*** No.270162. Began n/a; interdenominational. Turnover n/a.

***Wesley Owen Books and Music**, 7 Carrs Lane, Birmingham B4 7TG
☎0121 643 9235 🖷0121 633 4311
E: birmingham@wesley-owen.com
Web: www.wesleyowen.com
Manager: Mr David J Chant. Executive staff 1, Other staff 12. ***CC*** No.270162. Began 1893; interdenominational. Turnover £607,000 to year end Jan 03.

***Wesley Owen Books and Music**, 129 Deansgate, Bolton BL1 1HA
☎01204 532 384 🖷01204 525 424
E: bolton@wesley-owen.com
Web: www.wesleyowen.com
Manager: Julian Gittings. Executive staff 1, Other staff 2. ***CC*** No.270162. Began 1963; interdenominational. Turnover £175,000 to year end Jan 03.

***Wesley Owen Books and Music**, 123-124 Queens Road, Brighton BN1 3WB
☎01273 626 944 / 234 567 🖷01273 620 636
E: brighton@wesley-owen.com
Web: www.wesleyowen.com
Also music, videos, mail order.
Manager: Vicky MacFarlane. Executive staff 1, Other staff n/a. ***CC*** No.270162. Began 1996; interdenominational. (Previously Jubilee Books and Music). Turnover n/a.

***Wesley Owen Books and Music**, [illegible]0 Park Street, Bristol BS1 5JN
☎0117 926 4426 🖷0117 929 [illegible]068
E: bristol@wesley-owen.com
Web: www.wesleyowen.com
Manager: Olivia Murray. Executive staff 1, Other staff 8. ***CC*** No.270162. Began 1834; interdenominational. Turnover £525,000 to year end Jan 03.

***Wesley Owen Books and Music**, [illegible]a The Mall, Bromley BR1 1TR
☎020 8464 1191 🖷020 8466 [illegible]66
E: bromley@wesley-owen.com
Web: www.wesleyowen.com
Manager: Mr Dave Brown. Executive staff 1, Other staff 9. ***CC*** No.270162. Began 1966; interdenominational. Turnover £603,000 to year end Jan 03.

***Wesley Owen Books and Music**, 88a Regent Street, Cambridge CB2 1D[illegible]
☎01223 352 727 🖷01223 302 [illegible]53
E: cambridge@wesley-owen.com
Web: www.wesleyowen.com
Manager: Sarah MacKenzie. Executive staff 1, Other staff 4. ***CC*** No.270162. Began 1984; interdenominational. Turnover £278,000 to year end Jan 03.

***Wesley Owen Books and Music**, 22 Fisher Street, Carlisle CA3 8FH
☎01228 534 919 🖷01228 631 [illegible]91
E: carlisle@wesley-owen.com
Web: www.wesleyowen.com
Manager: Jenny Beattie. Executive staff 1, Other staff 4. ***CC*** No.270162. Began 1974; interdenominational. Turnover £170,000 to year end Jan 03.

***Wesley Owen Books and Music**, 51 Winchcombe Street, Cheltenham GL52 2NE
☎01242 513 686 🖷01242 228 6[illegible]6
E: cheltenham@wesley-owen.com
Web: www.wesleyowen.com
Manager: Simon Monk. Executive staff 1, Other staff 3. ***CC*** No.270162. Began 1971; interdenominational. Turnover £218,000 to year end Jan 03.

Wesley Owen Books and Music, 53 Watergate Street, Chester CH1 2L[illegible]
☎01244 317 664 🖷01244 342 6[illegible]9
E: chester@wesley-owen.com
Web: www.wesleyowen.com
Manager: Chantal Proctor. Executive staff 1, Other staff 1. Began 2002; interdenominational. (Previously Acorn Christian Bookshop). Turnover n/a.

Wesley Owen Books and Music, 22a Railway Road, Coleraine BT52 1[illegible]
☎028 7034 3857 🖷028 7035 940[illegible]
E: coleraine@wesley-owen.com
Web: www.wesleyowen.com
Manager: Ann Harrison. Executive staff 2, Other staff 2. ***CC*** No.270162. Began 1965; interdenominational. (Previously Mizpah Bible and Bookshop). Turnover n/a.

For further details see list on page 35

B

***Wesley Owen Books and Music**, 21 City Arcade, Coventry CV1 3HX
☎024 7622 2064
🖷024 7655 3744
E: coventry@wesley-owen.com
Web: www.wesleyowen.com
Manager: Mr Richard Morris. Executive staff 1, Other staff 7. ***CC*** No.270162. Began 1978; interdenominational. Turnover £295,000 to year end Jan 03.

***Wesley Owen Books and Music**, 16 Park Street, Croydon CR0 1YE
☎020 8686 2772
🖷020 8681 3463
E: croydon@wesley-owen.com
Web: www.wesleyowen.com
Manager: James Batterbee. Executive staff 1, Other staff 6. ***CC*** No.270162. Began 1965; interdenominational. Turnover £410,000 to year end Jan 03.

***Wesley Owen Books and Music**, 48 Queen Street, Derby DE1 3GN
☎01332 345 936
🖷01332 296 674
E: derby@wesley-owen.com
Web: www.wesleyowen.com
Manager: Mr Ian McLaren. Executive staff 1, Other staff 3. ***CC*** No.270162. Began 1810; interdenominational. Turnover £330,000 to year end Jan 03.

***Wesley Owen Books and Music**, 112 Nethergate, Dundee DD1 4EH
☎01382 200 075
🖷01382 200 091
E: dundee@wesley-owen.com
Web: www.wesleyowen.com
Manager: Miss Fiona Elder. Executive staff 1, Other staff 6. ***CC*** No.270162. Began n/a; interdenominational. Turnover £156,000 to year end Jan 03.

***Wesley Owen Books and Music**, 117-119 George Street, Edinburgh EH2 4JN
☎0131 225 2229
🖷0131 225 8167
E: edinburgh@wesley-owen.com
Web: www.wesleyowen.com
Manager: Julie Downie. Executive staff 1, Other staff 14. ***CC*** No.270162. Began n/a; interdenominational. Turnover £818,000 to year end Jan 03.

***Wesley Owen Books and Music**, 15 Paris Street, Exeter EX1 2JB
☎01392 254 024
🖷01392 425 558
E: exeter@wesley-owen.com
Web: www.wesleyowen.com
Manager: Mr Stuart Skinner. Executive staff 1, Other staff 5. ***CC*** No.270162. Began 1985; interdenominational. Turnover £232,000 to year end Jan 03.

***Wesley Owen Books and Music**, 1 Glebe Street, Falkirk FK1 1HX
☎01324 612 955
🖷01324 634 961
E: falkirk@wesley-owen.com
Web: www.wesleyowen.com
Manager: Mr John Marshall. Executive staff 1, Other staff 2. ***CC*** No.270162. Began 1970; interdenominational. Turnover £139,000 to year end Jan 03.

***Wesley Owen Books and Music**, 24-28 Bothwell Street, Glasgow G2 6PA
☎0141 221 8913
🖷0141 227 2707
E: glasgow@wesley-owen.com
Web: www.wesleyowen.com
Also restaurant.
Manager: Mary MacLeod. Executive staff 3, Other staff 30. ***CC*** No.270162. Began 1893; interdenominational. Turnover £1,122,000 to year end Jan 03.

***Wesley Owen Books and Music**, 60 Quarry Street, Guildford GU1 3UA
☎01483 573 707
🖷01483 455 214
E: guildford@wesley-owen.com
Web: www.wesleyowen.com
Manager: Nan MacFarlene. Executive staff 1, Other staff 3. ***CC*** No.270162. Began 1930; interdenominational. Turnover £224,000 to year end Jan 03.

For further details see list on page 85

***Wesley Owen Books and Music**, 11 Commercial Street, Harrogate HG1 1UB
☎01423 521 662 🖷01423 528 961
E: harrogate@wesley-owen.com
Web: www.wesleyowen.com
Manager: Mrs Julie Jowett. Executive staff 1, Other staff 4. ***CC*** No.270162. Began 1990; non-denominational. (Previously Branchlines Christian Resource Centre). Turnover n/a.

***Wesley Owen Books and Music**, 11 Masons Avenue, Wealdstone, Harrow HA3 5AH
☎020 8861 3259 🖷020 8863 8015
E: harrow@wesley-owen.com
Web: www.wesleyowen.com
Manager: Caroline Jenkins. Executive staff 1, Other staff 5. ***CC*** No.270162. Began 1978; interdenominational. Turnover £201,000 to year end Jan 03.

***Wesley Owen Books and Music**, 66 Wright Street, Hull HU2 8JD
☎01482 328 135 🖷01482 324 040
E: hull@wesley-owen.com
Web: www.wesleyowen.com
Manager: Alistair Crompton. Executive staff 1, Other staff 3. ***CC*** No.270162. Began 1972; interdenominational. Turnover £191,000 to year end Jan 03.

***Wesley Owen Books and Music**, 23 Castle Street, Inverness IV2 3EP
☎01463 226 152 🖷01463 237 432
E: inverness@wesley-owen.com
Web: www.wesleyowen.com
Manager: Fiona Thompson. Executive staff 1, Other staff 6. ***CC*** No.270162. Began n/a; interdenominational. Turnover £181,000 to year end Jan 03.

***Wesley Owen Books and Music**, 32 Fife Road, Kingston upon Thames KT1 1SU
☎020 8547 2617 🖷020 8546 3331
E: kingston@wesley-owen.com
Web: www.wesleyowen.com
Manager: Edward Neyt. Executive staff 1, Other staff 1. ***CC*** No.270162. Began n/a; interdenominational. (Previously Chapter & Verse). Turnover n/a.

***Wesley Owen Books and Music**, 113 Vicar Lane, Leeds LS1 6PJ
☎0113 245 8264 🖷0113 244 2600
E: leeds@wesley-owen.com
Web: www.wesleyowen.com
Manager: Carl Rayner. Executive staff 1, Other staff 6. ***CC*** No.270162. Began 1968; interdenominational. Turnover £346,000 to year end Jan 03.

***Wesley Owen Books and Music**, 6 Roe Street, St John's Centre, Liverpool L1 1EP
☎0151 709 1029 🖷0151 709 1194
E: liverpool@wesley-owen.com
Web: www.wesleyowen.com
Manager: Mr Andrew Stott. Executive staff 1, Other staff 4. ***CC*** No.270162. Began 1973; interdenominational. Turnover £295,000 to year end Jan 03.

***Wesley Owen Books and Music**, 82 High Road, South Woodford, London E18 2NA
☎020 8530 4244 🖷020 8518 8924
E: southwoodford@wesley-owen.com
Web: www.wesleyowen.com
Manager: Dominic Stinchcombe. Executive staff 1, Other staff 4. ***CC*** No.270162. Began n/a; interdenominational. Turnover £188,000 to year end Jan 03.

***Wesley Owen Books and Music**, 16-18 Park Green, Macclesfield SK11 7NA
☎01625 431 684 🖷01625 869 206
E: macclesfield@wesley-owen.com
Web: www.wesleyowen.com
Manager: Ian Carrington. Executive staff 1, Other staff 3. ***CC*** No.270162. Began 1978; interdenominational. (Previously The Christian Bookshop). Turnover £159,000 to year end Jan 03.

***Wesley Owen Books and Music**, 123 Deansgate, Manchester M3 2BY
☎0161 834 4655 🖷0161 839 3472
E: manchester@wesley-owen.com
Web: www.wesleyowen.com
Also coffee shop.
Manager: Janet Crooks-Jones. Executive staff 1, Other staff 5. ***CC*** No.270162. Began n/a; interdenominational. Turnover £616,000 to year end Jan 03.

***Wesley Owen Books and Music**, 24 Heathcote Street, Nottingham NG1 3AA
☎0115 950 1919 🖷0115 941 4624
E: nottingham@wesley-owen.com
Web: www.wesleyowen.com
Manager: Julia Copilet. Executive staff 1, Other staff 5. ***CC*** No.270162. Began 1966; interdenominational. Turnover £182,000 to year end Jan 03

***Wesley Owen Books and Music**, Unit 31, The Bargate Centre, Southampton SO14 1HF
☎023 8082 9676
E: southampton@wesley-owen.com
Web: www.wesleyowen.com
Manager: Paul Smith. Executive staff 1, Other staff n/a. ***CC*** No.270162. Began 2005; interdenominational. Turnover: first year in operation.

***Wesley Owen Books and Music**, 11 Lower Hillgate, Stockport SK1 1JQ
☎0161 480 1467 🖷0161 477 7275
E: stockport@wesley-owen.com
Web: www.wesleyowen.com
Manager: Mr John Watkins. Executive staff 1, Other staff 4. ***CC*** No.270162. Began 1976; interdenominational. Turnover £291,000 to year end Jan 03.

***Wesley Owen Books and Music**, 5 Grove Road, Sutton SM1 1BB
☎020 8642 6511 🖷020 8642 4080
E: sutton@wesley-owen.com
Web: www.wesleyowen.com
Manager: Mr Kevin Ahronson. Executive staff 1, Other staff 4. ***CC*** No.270162. Began 1974; interdenominational. Turnover £199,000 to year end Jan 03.

***Wesley Owen Books and Music**, Unit 6, The Crossing at St Paul's, Darwall Street, Walsall WS1 1DA
☎01922 631 230 🖷01922 632 [illegible]99
E: walsall@wesley-owen.com
Web: www.wesleyowen.com
Manager: Mr Matt Humpage. Executive staff 1, Other staff 6. ***CC*** No.270162. Began 1969; interdenominational. Turnover £179,000 to year end Jan 03.

***Wesley Owen Books and Music**, The Broadway, 66 Queen's Road, Watford WD17 2LA
☎01923 248 727 🖷01923 221 [illegible]54
E: watford@wesley-owen.com
Web: www.wesleyowen.com
Manager: Jill Willimott Executive staff 1, Other staff 3. ***CC*** No.270162. Began 1982; interdenominational. Turnover £206,000 to year end Jan 03.

***Wesley Owen Books and Music**, 1[illegible] The Centre, Walliscote Road, Weston-super-Mare BS23 1UW
☎01934 418 109 🖷0193[illegible] 644 [illegible]54
E: weston@wesley-owen.com
Web: www.wesleyowen.com
Manager: Caroline Jones. Executive staff 1, Other staff 4. ***CC*** No.270162. Began 1984; interdenominational. Turnover £133,000 to year end Jan 03.

***Wesley Owen Books and Music**, Christ Church, Town Square, Woking GU21 [illegible]YG
☎01483 770 806
E: woking@wesley-owen.com
Web: www.wesleyowen.com
Manager: Mr Tim Brown Executive staff 1, Other staff 3. ***CC*** No.270162. Began 1956; interdenominational. (Previously Berean Bookshop). Turnover n/a.

***Wesley Owen Books and Music**, [illegible]-11 Chatsworth Road, Worthing BN11 1[illegible]
☎01903 234 566 🖷01903 236 8[illegible]7
E: worthing@wesley-owen.com
Web: www.wesleyowen.com
Manager: Janet Ashton. Executive staff 1, Other staff 7. ***CC*** No 270162. Began 1968; interdenominational. Turnover £260,000 to year end Jan 03.

***Wesley Owen Books and Music**, 24 Fossgate, York YO1 9TA
☎01904 653 643 🖷01904 653 64[illegible]
E: mail@barbicanbookshop.co.uk
Web: www.barbicanbookshop.co.uk
Also mail order.
Directors: Mr & Mrs Les & Jean Bingham. Executive staff 1, Other staff 6. Began 1962; non-denominational. Turnover n/a.

***Wesleyan Reform Union Bookshop**, [illegible]23 Queen Street, Sheffield S1 2DU
☎0114 272 1938 🖷0114 2[illegible]2 193[illegible]
E: gen.sec@wesleyan-reform.freeserve.co.uk
Web: www.thewru.com
General Secretary: Rev Colin Braithwaite. Executive staff 1, Other staff 1. ***CC*** No.250315. Began 1849; Wesleyan Reform. Turnover n/a.

For further details see list on page 35

Weymouth Christian Books, 25a Trinity Road, Weymouth DT4 8TJ
☎01305 788 555
Reformed and evangelical titles.
Co-owner: Dr John H Mann. No full-time staff. Began 1982; non-denominational. Turnover n/a.

Words Bookshop, 68 Wallgate, Wigan WN1 1BA
☎01942 495 402 M: 07916 150 579
🖷01942 820 566
E: words@btinternet.com
Web: www.words-bookshop.com
Also gifts, cards and multimedia.
Owner: Mr & Mrs Paul Williamson. Executive staff 2, Other staff 5. Began 1982; non-denominational. Turnover £100,000 to year end Mar 05.

Wordwise, 41 Fore Street, Kingsbridge TQ7 1PG
☎01548 856 571
🖷01458 856 573
E: wordwise@fish.co.uk
Also coffee shop, second-hand books.
Manager: Mrs Sally Veise Executive staff 1. ***CC*** No.1098305. Began 2003; interdenominational. Turnover n/a.

YWAM Books, Highfield Oval, Ambrose Lane, Harpenden AL5 4BX
☎01582 463 242
🖷01582 463 305
E: bookshop@oval.com
Web: www.ywamharpenden.org
Manager: Ms Charlotte Sattler. Executive staff 2. ***CC*** No.264078. Began 1983; interdenominational. Turnover n/a.

***YWAM Books**, The King's Lodge, Watling Street, Nuneaton CV10 0TZ
☎024 7634 8128
🖷024 7634 4464
E: admin@thekingslodge.com
Web: www.thekingslodge.com
Manager: Mr Darren Lyons. Executive staff 1. ***CC*** No.264078. Began 1983; interdenominational. Turnover n/a.

Zion Christian Books, Fore Street, St Ives TR26 1HW
☎01736 798 291
E: jan.oshea@tesco.net
Manager: Mr Ralph O'Shea. All voluntary staff. ***CC*** Began n/a; Evangelical Fellowship of Congregational Churches and Countess of Huntingdon's Connexion. Turnover n/a.

LIBRARIES

Web: www.christian-research.org.uk and www.ukchristianhandbook.org.uk
Statistical and other reference sources relating to the Church around the world.
Information Officer: Kim Miles. Library staff 1. ***CC*** No.1017701. Began 1983; interdenominational. Magazine: *Quadrant* (2,600 every two months). Turnover £260,000 to year end Dec 05.

The Ark Resource Library, 12 Ellesmere Road, Colwyn Bay LL29 8RP
☎01492 530 528 🖷01492 534 558
E: christianresourcesint@yahoo.com
Web: www.christianresourcesinternational.com
Cross section of theological books; residential facilities available.
Librarian: Rev Esther Wintringham. No full-time staff. Began 2003; non-denominational. No magazine. Turnover n/a.

Canterbury Cathedral Library, The Precincts, Canterbury CT1 2EH
☎01227 865 287 🖷01227 865 222
E: library@canterbury-cathedral.org
Web: www.canterbury-cathedral.org
Historical library of 35,000 pre-1900 books and 20,000 20th century books.
Cathedral Librarian: Mr Keith M C O'Sullivan. Executive staff 1, Other staff 5. ***CC*** Began n/a; Anglican. No magazine. Turnover n/a.

The Cathedral Library, The College, Durham DH1 3EH
☎0191 386 2489
E: library@durhamcathedral.co.uk
Historical books and Archdeacon Sharp Library of current theological books.
Chapter Librarian: Rev Canon Prof David Brown. Executive staff 1, Other staff 1. Began 995; Anglican. (Previously The Chapter Library). No magazine. Turnover n/a.

Catholic Central Library, St Michael's Abbey, Farnborough Road, Farnborough GU14 7NQ
☎01252 543 818
E: librarian@catholic-library.org.uk
Web: www.catholic-library.org.uk
Religious subscription library open to people of all denominations.
Librarian: Mrs Joan Bond. Executive staff 1. ***CC*** No.1064460. Began n/a; Roman Catholic. No magazine. Turnover n/a.

Christian World Library, Christian Research, Vision Building, 4 Footscray Road, Eltham, London SE9 2TZ
☎020 8294 1989 🖷020 8294 0014
E: research@christian-research.org.uk

The Evangelical Library, 78a Chiltern Street, London W1U 5HE
☎020 7935 6997 🖷020 7935 6997
E: stlibrary@btinternet.com
Web: www.elib.org.uk
Lending, reference, research and subscription library for ministers, students, authors; postal service.
Librarian: Mr S J Taylor. Executive staff 1, Other staff 3. ***CC*** No.1091654. Began 1928; non-denominational. Magazine: *In WRITING* (1,500 half-yearly). Turnover £30,000 to year end Dec 00.

Evangelical Library West, PO Box 170, Fishponds, Bristol BS16 5XN
☎0117 910 9308
E: ELWinBath@aol.com
Subscription lending, reference, research library, located at Bethel Chapel, St Johns Road, Bath; annual lecture.
Hon Secretary: Chris J Mansfield. No full-time staff. Began 1992; non-denominational. Magazine: *Bulletin* (Circulation n/a half-yearly). Turnover n/a.

Lambeth Palace Library, Lambeth Palace, London SE1 7JU
☎020 7898 1400 🖷020 7928 7932
Web: www.lambethpalacelibrary.org
Principal library and archive for the history of the Church of England.
Librarian & Archivist: Dr Richard J Palmer. Executive staff 7, Other staff 4. ***CC*** Began 1610; Anglican. No magazine. Turnover n/a.

***Methodist Studies Unit, Wesley Centre Oxford**, Westminster Institute of Education, Oxford Brookes University, Harcourt Hill Campus, Oxford OX2 9AT
☎01865 488 319 🖷01865 488 317
E: pforsaith@brookes.ac.uk
Web: www.brookes.ac.uk/schools/wco
Resources for the study of Wesley and Methodism including archives, papers and art collections.
Keeper: Peter Forsaith. Staff 1. ***CC*** Began n/a; Methodist. (Previously Wesley Centre, Oxford (Library, Archive & Art)). No magazine. Turnover n/a.

Partnership House Mission Studies Library, 157 Waterloo Road, London SE1 8XA
☎020 7803 3215 🖷020 7928 3627
E: library.phmslib@cms-uk.org
Web: phmsl.soutron.com
History and theology of mission, including former CMS and USPG collections.
Librarian: Miss Elizabeth Williams. Executive staff 1. ***CC*** No.297154. Began 1987; Anglican. Magazine: *Bulletin* (Circulation n/a every two months). Turnover n/a.

Pusey House Library, Pusey House, St Giles, Oxford OX1 3LZ
☎01865 278 415
E: pusey.house@irc24.net
Web: www.puseyhouse.org.uk
Church history and philosophy, theology, patristics; access by appointment.
Custodian: Rev W E P Davage. Executive staff 3. ***CC*** Began 1884; Anglican. No magazine. Turnover n/a.

St Deiniol's Residential Library, Church Lane, Hawarden, Deeside CH5 3DF
☎01244 532 350 🖷01244 520 643
E: deiniol.visitors@btconnect.com
Web: www.st-deiniols.org
Library open to all genuine students - laity or clergy; accommodation for 36.
Warden & Chief Librarian: Rev P B Francis. Executive staff 5, Other staff 20. ***CC*** No.701399. Began 1902; ecumenical. No magazine. Turnover n/a.

St Paul's Cathedral Library, St Paul's Cathedral, London EC4M 8AE
☎020 7246 8345/8342
E: library@stpaulscathedral.org.uk
Web: www.stpauls.co.uk
Collection of rare books; by appointment.
Librarian: Mr J J Wisdom. Executive staff 1. Began n/a; Anglican. No magazine. Turnover n/a.

Tyndale House Library, 36 Selwyn Gardens, Cambridge CB3 9BA
☎01223 566 604 🖷01223 566 608
🖂: librarian@tyndale.cam.ac.uk
Web: www.tyndalehouse.com
Biblical and theological research centre and library; 42 rented desks and 12 places for occasional visitors.
Warden: Rev Dr B W Winter. Executive staff 5, Other staff 3. ***CC*** No.273458. Began 1944; non-denominational. Magazine: *Academic Journal* (Circulation & frequency n/a). Turnover n/a.

Westminster Abbey Library, Westminster Abbey, London SW1P 3PA
☎020 7654 4830 🖷020 7654 4827
🖂: library@westminster-abbey.org
Web: www.westminster-abbey.org
Archives of books and manuscripts relating to the history of Westminster Abbey; access by appointment.
Librarian: Dr Tony Trowles. Executive staff 2, Other staff 1. ***CC*** Began 1065; Anglican. No magazine. Turnover n/a.

Dr Williams's Library, 14 Gordon Square, London WC1H 0AR
☎020 7387 3727
🖂: enquiries@dwlib.co.uk
Web: www.dwlib.co.uk
Part of work of Dr Williams's Trust which was established to benefit English Protestant Dissenters.
Director: Dr David Wykes. Executive staff 1, Other staff 3. ***CC*** Began 172[illegible] non-denominational. No magazine. Turnover n/a.

PUBLISHERS OF BOOKS

Titles Published Year by Year

Listed by number of Christian titles published in 2005 (last column)

Publishers which have not supplied any of this information are not listed here

	1999		2000		2001		2002		2003		2004		2005	
	All	Chr	All	Chr	All	Chr	All	Chr	All	Chr	All	Chr	All	Chr
Kevin Mayhew	250	120	280	150	302	140	310	160	227	227	216	216	300	300
Christian Focus Publications	74	74	82	82	95	95	98	98	187	187	152	152	180	180
Hodder & Stoughton Religious Books	120	120	136	136	94	94	87	87	84	50	71	43	98	73
IVP	n/a	n/a	n/a	n/a	40	40	47	47	65	65	66	66	67	67
Feather Books	92	92	117	117	62	60	49	44	65	65	66	66	67	67
Paternoster	n/a	n/a	n/a	n/a	n/a	n/a	n/a	n/a	55	55	55	55	55	55
The Banner of Truth Trust	16	16	13	13	17	17	12	12	48	48	66	66	48	48
Evangelical Press	23	23	25	25	25	25	30	30	37	37	39	39	39	39
Go Teach Publications Ltd	n/a	n/a	n/a	n/a	34	34	34	34	36	36	36	36	36	36
Day One Publications	10	8	10	8	16	16	19	19	12	12	25	25	35	35
SCM-Canterbury Press	30	30	30	30	n/a	n/a	n/a	n/a	30	30	35	35	35	35
Ambassador Productions	n/a	n/a	n/a	n/a	n/a	n/a	n/a	n/a	37	33	31	29	34	31
Grove Books Ltd	29	29	29	29	33	33	33	33	32	32	29	29	31	31
Creative Publishing	n/a	n/a	1,000	30	1,000	30	1,000	40	1,000	30	1,000	30	1,000	30
New Dawn Books	21	21	21	21	21	21	22	22	n/a	n/a	n/a	n/a	25	25
Chapter Two (Publishing Division)	42	42	48	48	45	45	40	40	33	33	27	27	24	24
Sovereign World	16	16	22	22	30	30	40	40	20	20	20	20	20	20
St Pauls	n/a	n/a	n/a	n/a	n/a	n/a	n/a	n/a	20	20	20	20	20	20
Roy Hession Book Trust	5	5	4	4	7	7	8	8	8	8	10	10	13	13
Two-Edged Sword Publications	n/a	n/a	n/a	n/a	n/a	n/a	n/a	n/a	n/a	n/a	4	4	13	13
Piquant	n/a	n/a	6	6	4	4	4	4	6	6	1	1	11	11
John Hunt Publishing	n/a	n/a	n/a	n/a	n/a	n/a	n/a	n/a	40	10	50	10	60	10
Christian Education Publications	28	28	19	19	17	11	14	5	6	6	7	7	7	7
Gospel Standard Trust	3	3	4	4	5	5	7	7	5	5	6	6	7	7
The Open Bible Trust	7	7	8	8	7	7	8	8	7	7	7	7	7	7
Terra Nova Publications Ltd	3	3	4	4	4	4	5	5	n/a	n/a	n/a	n/a	6	6
Christian Research	2	2	4	4	5	5	3	3	5	5	4	4	5	5
Regnum International	n/a	n/a	n/a	n/a	3	3	3	3	2	2	0	0	5	5
Highland Books	4	4	9	9	7	7	7	7	8	8	6	6	4	4
Scripture Truth Publications	1	1	n/a	n/a	n/a	n/a	n/a	n/a	4	4	4	4	4	4
Handsel Press	n/a	n/a	n/a	n/a	n/a	n/a	n/a	n/a	0	0	1	1	3	3
New City	3	3	4	4	4	4	5	5	3	3	4	4	3	3
St Matthew Publishing Ltd	3	3	2	2	n/a	n/a	n/a	n/a	n/a	n/a	n/a	n/a	3	3
Chapter House Ltd	2	2	3	3	4	4	2	2	n/a	n/a	n/a	n/a	2	2
Christian Year Publications	2	2	2	2	1	1	2	2	2	2	2	2	2	2
Hayes Press	6	6	4	4	4	4	2	2	6	6	4	4	2	2
New Living Publishers	1	1	1	1	n/a	n/a	n/a	n/a	1	1	1	1	2	2
The Rushworth Enterprise Ltd	n/a	n/a	n/a	n/a	2	2	2	2	n/a	n/a	n/a	n/a	2	2
Teresian Press	n/a	n/a	n/a	n/a	n/a	n/a	n/a	n/a	0	0	0	0	2	2
The James Begg Society	2	2	1	1	n/a	n/a	n/a	n/a	4	4	2	2	1	1
Modern Welsh Publications Ltd	n/a	n/a	n/a	n/a	n/a	n/a	n/a	n/a	4	4	3	3	1	1
Precious Seed Publications	1	1	n/a	n/a	0	0	1	1	1	1	1	1	1	1
Bunyan Press	1	1	1	1	1	1	1	1	0	0	0	0	0	0
Coastline Christian Resources	n/a	n/a	n/a	n/a	n/a	n/a	n/a	n/a	0	0	0	0	0	0
John Metcalfe Publishing Trust	1	1	2	2	5	5	2	2	1	1	1	1	0	0
Jubilate Hymns Ltd	n/a	n/a	n/a	n/a	n/a	n/a	n/a	n/a	1	1	0	0	0	0
K & M Books	1	1	1	1	n/a	n/a	n/a	n/a	0	0	0	0	0	0
Loxwood Press	n/a	n/a	2	2	1	1	1	1	3	3	3	3	0	0
ALIVE UK	n/a	n/a	n/a	n/a	1	1	1	1	n/a	n/a	n/a	n/a	n/a	n/a
Baptist Union Publications	6	6	5	5	n/a	n/a	n/a	n/a	n/a	n/a	n/a	n/a	n/a	n/a

Publishers of Books

	1999		2000		2001		2002		2003		2004		2005	
	All	Chr	All	Chr	All	Chr	All	Chr	All	Chr	All	Chr	All	Chr
Belmont House Publishing	1	1	1	1	1	1	n/a	n/a	n/a	n/a	n/a	n/a	n/a	n/a
Bethel Publications	n/a	n/a	n/a	n/a	n/a	n/a	n/a	n/a	n/a	n/a	n/a	n/a	n/a	n/a
Bible Reading Fellowship	n/a	n/a	n/a	n/a	n/a	n/a	n/a	n/a	n/a	n/a	n/a	n/a	n/a	n/a
Bryntirion Press/Gwasg Bryntirion	4	4	6	6	n/a	n/a	40	40	n/a	n/a	n/a	n/a	n/a	n/a
Christina Press Ltd	12	12	12	12	12	12	12	12	n/a	n/a	6	6	n/a	n/a
Church House Publishing	n/a	n/a	n/a	n/a	n/a	n/a	60	n/a	n/a	n/a	n/a	n/a	n/a	n/a
Chyvourder Consolidated Publishing	n/a	n/a	n/a	n/a	n/a	n/a	n/a	n/a	n/a	n/a	n/a	n/a	n/a	n/a
James Clarke and Co Ltd	2	1	2	1	n/a	n/a	n/a	n/a	n/a	n/a	n/a	n/a	n/a	n/a
Continuum	75	75	75	75	n/a	n/a	n/a	n/a	n/a	n/a	n/a	n/a	n/a	n/a
Covenant Publications Ltd	n/a	n/a	n/a	n/a	2	2	3	3	n/a	n/a	n/a	n/a	n/a	n/a
Crossbridge Books	2	2	2	2	3	3	3	3	n/a	n/a	n/a	n/a	n/a	n/a
CTBI Publications	n/a	n/a	n/a	n/a	n/a	n/a	n/a	n/a	n/a	n/a	n/a	n/a	n/a	n/a
CWR (Crusade for World Revival)	25	25	45	45	n/a	n/a	n/a	n/a	n/a	n/a	n/a	n/a	n/a	n/a
Cyhoeddiadau'r Gair	34	34	41	41	40	40	75	75	n/a	n/a	n/a	n/a	n/a	n/a
Darton, Longman and Todd Ltd	40	40	40	40	40	40	75	75	n/a	n/a	n/a	n/a	n/a	n/a
Eagle	36	36	30	30	36	36	26	26	24	24	n/a	n/a	n/a	n/a
Family Publications	n/a	n/a	n/a	n/a	n/a	n/a	n/a	n/a	n/a	n/a	5	5	n/a	n/a
The Good Book Company	22	22	30	30	54	54	58	58	n/a	n/a	n/a	n/a	n/a	n/a
Grace Publications Trust	2	2	3	3	n/a	n/a	n/a	n/a	n/a	n/a	n/a	n/a	n/a	n/a
Gracewing Publishing	20	20	31	29	33	33	31	30	n/a	n/a	n/a	n/a	n/a	n/a
The Grail	n/a	n/a	n/a	n/a	n/a	n/a	n/a	n/a	1	1	0	0	0	0
John Ritchie Ltd	4	4	7	7	5	5	9	9	n/a	n/a	n/a	n/a	n/a	n/a
Janus Publishing Company	n/a	n/a	n/a	n/a	n/a	n/a	n/a	n/a	n/a	n/a	n/a	n/a	n/a	n/a
Kings Highway Books	n/a	n/a	n/a	n/a	n/a	n/a	3	3	n/a	n/a	n/a	n/a	n/a	n/a
Kingsway Publications	39	39	39	39	n/a	n/a	n/a	n/a	n/a	n/a	n/a	n/a	n/a	n/a
Lion Hudson plc[1]	190	190	195	195	205	205	215	215	n/a	n/a	n/a	n/a	n/a	n/a
Mirfield Publications	n/a	n/a	n/a	n/a	5	5	7	7	n/a	n/a	n/a	n/a	n/a	n/a
Moorley's Print and Publishing Ltd	19	19	9	9	9	9	8	8	n/a	n/a	n/a	n/a	n/a	n/a
MPH	30	30	40	40	25	25	26	26	n/a	n/a	n/a	n/a	n/a	n/a
Nelson Thornes (Publishers) Ltd	n/a	n/a	n/a	n/a	n/a	n/a	n/a	n/a	n/a	n/a	n/a	n/a	n/a	n/a
New Wine Ministries	n/a	n/a	n/a	n/a	n/a	n/a	n/a	n/a	n/a	n/a	n/a	n/a	n/a	n/a
Plough Publishing House	6	6	8	8	n/a	n/a	n/a	n/a	n/a	n/a	2	2	n/a	n/a
Printforce Ltd	n/a	n/a	n/a	n/a	49	2	49	2	n/a	n/a	n/a	n/a	n/a	n/a
Quinta Press	1	1	2	1	3	3	4	4	n/a	n/a	2	2	n/a	n/a
Saint Andrew Press	n/a	n/a	15	15	20	20	n/a	n/a	n/a	n/a	n/a	n/a	n/a	n/a
Salvationist Publishing and Supplies Ltd	n/a	n/a	n/a	n/a	n/a	n/a	n/a	n/a	n/a	n/a	n/a	n/a	n/a	n/a
Save The Church of England Foundation	n/a	n/a	1	1	n/a	n/a	n/a	n/a	n/a	n/a	n/a	n/a	n/a	n/a
Scripture Union Publishing	n/a	n/a	n/a	n/a	n/a	n/a	n/a	n/a	n/a	n/a	n/a	n/a	n/a	n/a
Sessions of York, The Ebor Press	n/a	n/a	n/a	n/a	n/a	n/a	n/a	n/a	n/a	n/a	n/a	n/a	n/a	n/a
Silvertree Publishing	n/a	n/a	2	2	3	3	1	1	n/a	n/a	3	3	n/a	n/a
Sovereign Press	n/a	1	n/a	n/a	n/a	n/a	2	1	n/a	n/a	n/a	n/a	n/a	n/a
SPCK	n/a	n/a	n/a	n/a	n/a	n/a	n/a	n/a	n/a	n/a	n/a	n/a	n/a	n/a
St Stephen's Press	n/a	n/a	n/a	n/a	n/a	n/a	n/a	n/a	n/a	n/a	n/a	n/a	n/a	n/a
Stainer & Bell Ltd	21	8	34	6	29	6	25	7	34	7	20	4	n/a	n/a
Stanborough Press	n/a	n/a	n/a	n/a	n/a	n/a	n/a	n/a	n/a	n/a	n/a	n/a	n/a	n/a
Tufton Books (Church Union Publications)	n/a	n/a	n/a	n/a	n/a	n/a	n/a	n/a	n/a	n/a	n/a	n/a	n/a	n/a
Westminster John Knox Press (UK Office)	n/a	n/a	80	80	n/a	n/a	n/a	n/a	n/a	n/a	n/a	n/a	n/a	n/a
Wild Goose Publications	80	80	85	85	n/a	n/a	n/a	n/a	n/a	n/a	n/a	n/a	n/a	n/a
Zondervan	n/a	n/a	n/a	n/a	n/a	n/a	n/a	n/a	n/a	n/a	n/a	n/a	n/a	n/a
TOTAL[2]	1,631	1,399	2,919	1,681	2,477	1,220	2,537	1,293	2,106	1,068	2,113	1,057	2,280	1,232

[1] These numbers combine previous listings for Lion Publishing plc with those for Candle Books and Monarch Books (Angus Hudson)

[2] No estimate is made for publishers not showing data in a particular category or year.

B

PUBLISHERS OF BOOKS

See also Other Literature Producers & Distributors (Primarily in the UK) on Page 129,
Newspapers & Periodicals on Page 246, Literature Producers & Distributors (Primarily Overseas) on Page 261.
For publishers of Music see Musical & Theatrical Services on Page 241.

B

ALIVE UK, 49 Coxtie Green Road, Brentwood CM14 5PS
☎01277 373 436 🖷01277 375 578
Web: www.aliveuk.com
Manager: Mrs Diane Wilkinson. Executive staff 6, Other staff 6. Began 1988; Pentecostal. Turnover n/a.

Ambassador Productions, Providence House, Ardenlee Street, Belfast BT6 8QJ
☎028 9045 0010 🖷028 9073 9659
E: sales@ambassador-productions.com
Web: www.ambassador-productions.com
Contact: Mr Samuel Lowry. Staff 7. Began 1980; interdenominational. Turnover n/a.

Apologia Publications, PO Box 3005, Eastbourne BN21 9BS
☎No telephone
Web: www.apologia.free-online.co.uk
Publishing Christian apologetic, revival and science-related books.
Director: Dr Herbert H Osborn. Executive staff 1. Began 1995; interdenominational. Turnover n/a.

Ashgate Publishing Ltd, Gower House, Croft Road, Aldershot GU11 3HR
☎01252 331 551
E: slloyd@ashgatepublishing.com
Web: www.ashgate.com
Publishers of academic and wider interest theology and religious studies books worldwide.
Publisher: Ms Sarah Lloyd. Executive staff 1, Other staff n/a. Began 1967; ecumenical. Turnover n/a.

The Banner of Truth Trust, The Grey House, 3 Murrayfield Road, Edinburgh EH12 6EL
☎0131 337 7310
🖷0131 346 7484
E: info@banneroftruth.co.uk
Web: www.banneroftruth.co.uk
Publishing Christian literature in the historic Reformed tradition.
General Manager: Mr John Rawlinson. Executive staff 4, Other staff 7. ***CC*** No.235652. Began 1957; non-denominational. Turnover n/a.

Baptist Union Publications, Baptist House, PO Box 44, 129 Broadway, Didcot OX11 8RT
☎01235 517 700
🖷01235 517 715
E: info@baptist.org.uk *Manager:* Mr Chris Mepham. Executive staff 1, Other staff 2. Began 1992; Baptist. Turnover n/a.

The James Begg Society, Yr Hen Ysgol, Abergwyngregyn, Llanfairfechan LL33 0LR
☎01224 895 979
E: jbeggsoc@mwfree.net
Web: www.jbeggsoc.org.uk
Promoting the Reformed understanding of the Scriptures in doctrine, worship and practice.
President: Rev James Gracie. No full time staff. ***CC*** No.SCO 25349. Began 1994; Presbyterian. Magazine: *Presbyterian Standard* (250 quarterly). Turnover £7,071 to year end Dec 04.

Belmont House Publishing, 36 The Crescent, Belmont, Sutton SM2 6BJ
☎020 8642 9330
🖷020 8286 3655
E: belmonthouse1@aol.com
Web: www.belmonthouse.co.uk
Promoting biblical morality.
Director: Dr E S Williams. Executive staff 1, Other staff n/a. Began 1997; non-denominational. Turnover n/a.

Bethel Publications, Bethel, 30 Beacon Street, Lichfield WS13 7AJ
☎01543 253 505
Director: Mr Philip M Horton. Executive staff 1. Began 1992; interdenominational. Turnover n/a.

Bible Reading Fellowship, First Floor, Elsfield Hall, 15-17 Elsfield Way, Oxford OX2 8FG
☎01865 319 700
🖷01865 319 701
E: enquiries@brf.org.uk
Web: www.brf.org.uk
Helping people of all ages to encounter the living God through Bible reading and prayer.
Chief Executive Officer: Mr Richard Fisher. *General Manager:* Mrs Karen Laister. Executive staff 2, Other staff 1[illegible]. ***CC*** No.233280. Began 1922; interdenominational. Imprints: Barnabas, Bible Reading Fellowship. Turnover n/a.

Bishopsgate Press Ltd, Bartholomew House, 15 Tonbridge Road, Hildenborough, Tonbridge TN11 9BH
☎01732 833 778
🖷01732 833 090
Supplying greetings cards and notecards.
Managing Director: Mr Ian Straker. *Sales Director:* Mr Robert Wilson. Executive staff 4, Other staff 6. Began 1800; non-denominational. Turnover n/a.

Bryntirion Press/Gwasg Bryntirion, Bryntirion, Bridgend CF31 4DX
☎01656 655 886
🖷01656 665 919
E: huw@emw.org.uk
Web: www.emw.org.uk
Press Manager: Mr Huw Kinsey. Executive staff 1, Other staff 2. ***CC*** No.222[illegible]07. Began 1955; non-denominational. (Previously Evangelical Press of Wales/Gwasg Efengylaidd Cymru). Turnover n/a.

Bunyan Press, 23 Haslingden Close, Harpenden AL5 3EW
☎01582 760 545
E: caleb@themutual.net
Web: www.bunyanpress.co.uk
Publishing Reformed books.
Manager: Mr Caleb Pearce. Executive staff 1, Other staff 1. Began 1980; non-denominational. Turnover £9,000 to year end Dec 05.

Cambridge University Press, Edinburgh Building, Shaftesbury Road, Cambridge CB2 2RU
☎01223 325 586
🖷01223 246 151
E: bibles@cambridge.org
Web: www.cambridge.org
Publishing in various educational subjects including Bibles and prayer books, theology and religious studies.
Bible Publishing Manager: Mr Christopher Wright. Executive staff 1, Other staff 2. ***CC*** Began 1591; non-denominational. Turnover n/a.

For number of books published see list on Page 1[illegible]3

Catholic Truth Society, 40 Harleyford Road, Vauxhall, London SE11 5AY
☎020 7640 0042 🖷020 7640 0046
E: info@cts-online.org.uk
Web: www.cts-online.org.uk
Publishing distributing and retailing accessible materials for Christians and the wider community.
General Secretary: Mr Fergal Martin. Executive staff 10. ***CC*** No.218951. Began 1869; Roman Catholic. Imprints: CTS Publications, Catholic Truth Society. Turnover n/a.

Chapter House Ltd, 53 Bothwell Street, Glasgow G2 6TS
☎0141 204 1285 🖷0141 204 1285
E: rlallan@btinternet.com
Web: www.bibles-direct.com
Publishing Bibles and reference works; mail order and online.
Publisher: Mr Nicholas Gray. *Administrator:* Mrs Margaret Milligan. Executive staff 1, Other staff 2. Began 1985; non-denominational. Incorporating R L Allan & Son. Turnover £237,000 to year end Jan 05.

Chapter Two (Publishing Division), Fountain House, Conduit Mews, Woolwich, London SE18 7AP
☎020 8316 5389 🖷020 8854 5963
E: chapter2uk@aol.com
Web: www.chaptertwo.org.uk
Propagating Christianity by literature, outreach, Bible distribution, conferences. Worldwide distribution in many languages.
Principal: Mr Edwin Cross. *Office Manager:* Miss A Meister. Executive staff 3, Other staff 10. ***CC*** No.1053047. Began 1976; Christian Brethren. Turnover £200,000 to year end Dec 00.

***Children's Ministry**, 26 Lottbridge Drove, Eastbourne BN23 6NT
☎01323 437 748
🖷01323 411 970
E: childrensministry@kingsway.co.uk
Web: www.childrensministry.co.uk
Teaching programme, conferences, training days, books, music, puppets and other resources for children/children's workers.
Brand Manager: Mr Phil Parekh. Executive staff 1, Other staff 8. Began n/a; non-denominational. Turnover included in Kingsway.

Christian Education Publications, 1020 Bristol Road, Selly Oak, Birmingham B29 6LB
☎0121 472 4242
🖷0121 472 7575
E: enquiries@christianeducation.org.uk
Web: www.christianeducation.org.uk
Working to improve education in church, home and school.
Chief Executive: Peter Fishpool. Executive staff 1, Other staff 13. ***CC*** No.1086990. Began 1803; non-denominational. Turnover £300,000 to year end Feb 00.

***Christian Focus Publications**, Geanies House, Fearn, Tain IV20 1TW
☎01862 871 011
🖷01862 871 699
E: info@christianfocus.com
Web: www.christianfocus.com
Publishing classic, study and children's/adult books.
Director: Mr William MacKenzie. *General Manager:* Mr Ian Thompson. *Editorial Manager:* Mr Willie Mackenzie. Executive staff 4, Other staff 16. Began 1979; non-denominational. Imprints: Christian Focus, Christian Heritage, Mentor. Turnover n/a.

* **Christian Research**, Vision Building, 4 Footscray Road, Eltham, London SE9 2TZ
☎020 8294 1989
🖷020 8294 0014
E: admin@christian-research.org.uk
Web: www.christian-research.org.uk and www.ukchristianhandbook.org.uk
Publishing reference works and research-based books, such as Religious Trends.
Executive Director: Dr Peter Brierley. *Deputy Director:* Heather Wraight. Executive staff 3, Other staff 3. ***CC*** No.1017701. Began 1993; interdenominational. (Previously MARC Europe). Magazine: *Quadrant* (2,600 every two months). Turnover £260,000 to year end Dec 05.

Christian Year Publications, The Glebe House, Stanton Drew, Bristol BS39 4EH
☎01275 332 475
M: 07986 059 335
🖷01275 333 596
E: roy@royhill.com
Partners: Mr & Mrs Roy and Margaret Hill. Executive staff 1, Other staff 1. Began 1988; non-denominational. Turnover n/a.

Christina Press Ltd, 17 Church Road, Tunbridge Wells TN1 1LG
☎01892 774 774
🖷01892 774 775
E: philip.edwards@footdavson.co.uk
Publishing books by women for women and discerning men; daily readings for women with Bible Reading Fellowship.
Publisher: Mr David J Hanes. Executive staff 2, Other staff n/a. Began 1996; interdenominational. Turnover n/a.

Church House Publishing, Church House, Great Smith Street, London SW1P 3NZ
☎020 7898 1451
🖷020 7898 1449
E: publishing@c-of-e.org.uk
Web: www.chpublishing.co.uk
Official publisher of the Divisions of the Archbishop's Council, Church of England; also book publisher.
Publishing Manager: Mr Thomas Allain-Chapman. Executive staff 9. ***CC*** No.248711. Began 1923; Anglican. Turnover n/a.

Church in Wales Publications, 39a Cathedral Road, Cardiff CF11 9XF
☎029 2034 8259 🖷029 2038 7835
E: publications@churchinwales.org.uk
Web: www.churchinwales.org.uk
Business Manager: Mr Hendrik Haye. Executive staff 1, Other staff 2. ***CC*** Began 1960; Church in Wales. Turnover n/a.

Chyvounder Consolidated Publishing, Coombe Lane, Bissoe, Truro TR4 8RE
☎01872 865 844 🖷01872 865 844
E: ccp@chyvounder.ndirect.co.uk
Web: www.ndirect.co.uk/~chyvounder
Proprietor: Mr A S Darlington. Executive staff 1. Began 1994; Methodist. Turnover n/a.

James Clarke and Co Ltd, PO Box 60, Cambridge CB1 2NT
☎01223 350 865 🖷01223 366 951
E: publishing@jamesclarke.co.uk
Web: www.jamesclarke.co.uk
Theology and church history.
Managing Director: Mr Adrian Brink. *Acting Sales & Publicity Manager:* Max Espley. Executive staff 2, Other staff 4. Began 1859; non-denominational. Imprints: James Clarke, The Lutterworth Press. Turnover n/a.

***Coastline Christian Resources**, 263 Arbury Road, Cambridge CB4 2JL
☎01223 355 931 M: 07980 966 867
E: info@coastline.org.uk
Web: www.coastline.org.uk
Writing, publishing Bible study material.
Director: Dr John Robertshaw. Executive staff 1. Began 1992; non-denominational. Turnover n/a.

†**The Continuum International Publishing Group Ltd**, The Tower Building, 11 York Road, London SE1 7NX
☎020 7922 0880 🖷020 7922 0881
E: info@continuumbooks.com
Web: www.continuumbooks.com
Managing Director: Mr Phillip Sturrock. *Publishing Director:* Mr Robin Baird-Smith. *UK Sales Manager:* Ms Georgina Brindley. Executive staff 3, Other staff 80. Began 2001; non-denominational. (Previously Cassell & Co). Imprints: Burns & Oates, Geoffrey Chapman, Mowbray, T & T Clark. Turnover £11,000,000 to year end Dec 00.

Covenant Publishing Co Ltd, 121 Low Etherley, Bishop Auckland DL14 0HA
☎01388 835 753 🖷01388 835 957
E: admin@covpub.co.uk
Web: www.britishisrael.co.uk
Manager: Name not supplied. Executive staff 5, Admin staff 2. Began 1922; non-denominational. Turnover £20,000 to year end Apr 05.

Creative Publishing, Downwood, Claverton Down Road, Bath BA2 6DT
☎01225 445 595 🖷01225 445 121
Sponsoring Bibles and Gospels worldwide; producing TV / video Bible teaching programme.
Founder: Mr Robert Hicks. Executive staff 10, Admin staff 10, Other staff 80. Began 1982; interdenominational. Turnover £15,000,000 to year end Apr 01.

Cressrelles Publishing Company Ltd, 10 Station Road, Colwall, Malvern WR13 6RN
☎01684 540 154 🖷01684 540 154
E: simonsmith@cressrelles4drama fsbusiness.co.uk
Publishing plays including religious drama.
Director: Mr Simon Smith. Executive staff 1. Began 1973; non-denominational. Turnover n/a.

Crossbridge Books, 345 Old Birmingham Road, Bromsgrove B60 1NX
☎0121 447 7897 🖷0121 445 1053
E: crossbridgebooks@btinternet.com
Web: www.crossbridgebooks.com
Publishing Christian books for adults and children, with an emphasis on divine miracles.
Publisher: Mrs Eileen Mohr. Executive staff 1. Began 1995; interdenominational. Turnover £13,000 to year end Dec 04.

CTBI Publications, Bastille Court, 2 Paris Garden, London SE1 8ND
☎020 7654 7254 🖷020 7654 7222
E: info@ctbi.org.uk
Web: www.ctbi.org.uk
Producing ecumenical resources and publications arising from the work of Churches Together.
Sales Manager: Name not supplied. Staff n/a. ***CC*** No.259688 Began 1940; ecumenical. (Previously BCC Publications). Turnover n/a.

***CWR (Crusade for World Revival)**, Waverley Abbey House, Waverley Lane, Farnham GU9 8EP
☎01252 784 700 🖷01252 784 73[illegible]
E: mail@cwr.org.uk
Web: www.cwr.org.uk
Publishing books, videos and daily devotionals including Every Day with Jesus.
Chief Executive: Mr Mick Brooks. *Head of Sales & Marketing:* Mr Mike Ashford. *Business Manager:* Mr Eddie Olliffe. Executive staff 6, Other staff 46. ***CC*** No.294387. Began 1965; interdenominational. Turnover £2,957,000 to year end Dec 04

***Cyhoeddiadau'r Gair**, School of Education, University College of North Wales, Normal Site, Bangor LL57 2PX
☎01248 382 947 🖷01248 382 15[illegible]
E: aled.davies@bangor.ac.uk
Web: www.bangor.ac.uk
Publishers of Welsh language Christian books and resources for churches, schools and home.
Director: Rev Aled Davies. Executive staff 1, Other staff 5. ***CC*** No.525766. Began 1991; interdenominational. Imprints: Gydan Gilydd, Cyfres y Gair. Turnover £150,000 to year end Dec 02.

Darton, Longman and Todd Ltd, 1 Spencer Court, 140 Wandsworth High Street, London SW18 4JJ
☎020 8875 0155 🖷020 8875 0133
E: tradesales@darton-longman-todd.co.uk
Web: www.darton-longman-todd.co.uk
Manager: Common ownership company. Staff 12. Began 1959; interdenominational. Turnover n/a.

For number of books published see list on Page 1[illegible]

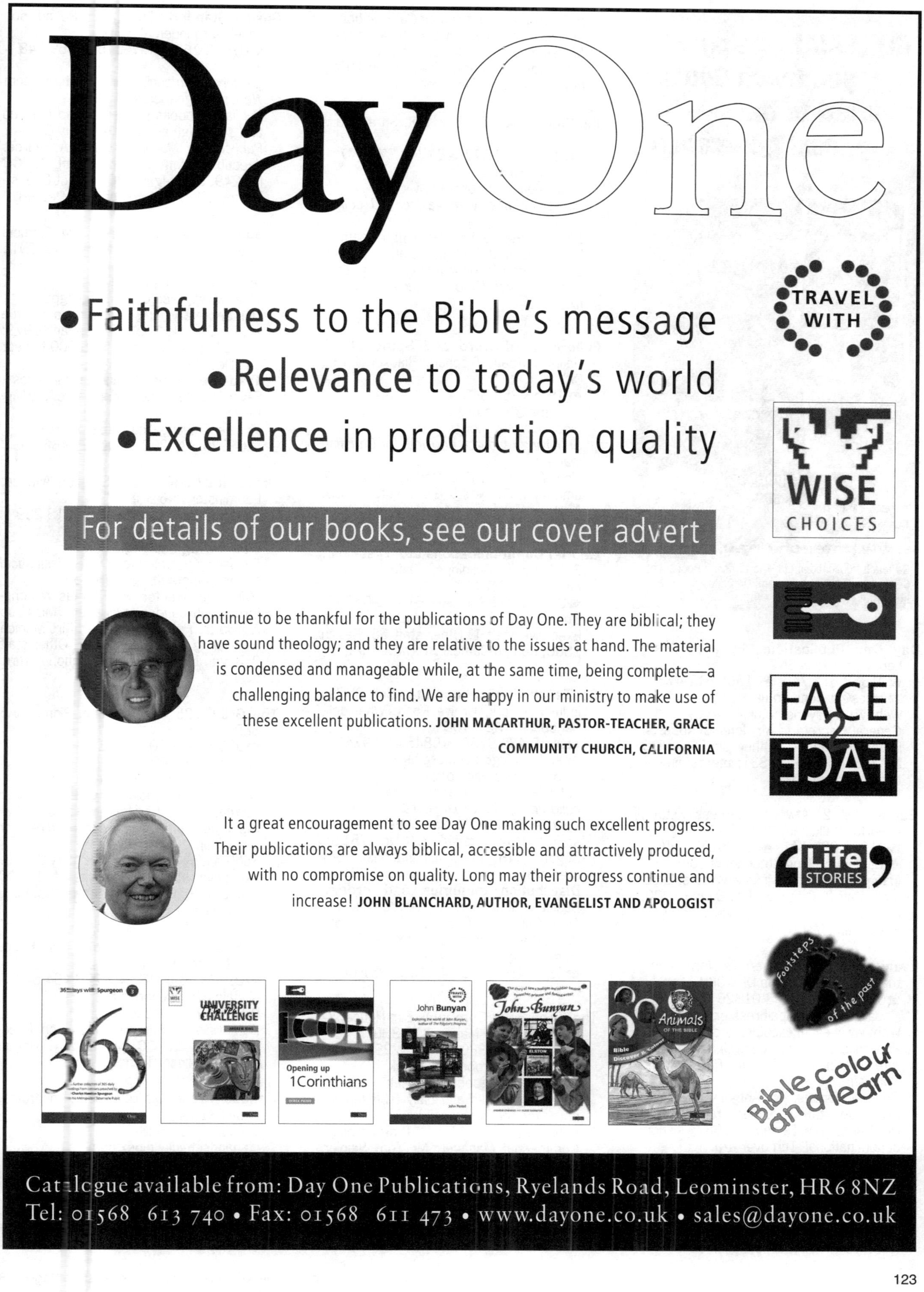
Day One
• Faithfulness to the Bible's message
• Relevance to today's world
• Excellence in production quality
For details of our books, see our cover advert
I continue to be thankful for the publications of Day One. They are biblical; they have sound theology; and they are relative to the issues at hand. The material is condensed and manageable while, at the same time, being complete—a challenging balance to find. We are happy in our ministry to make use of these excellent publications. JOHN MACARTHUR, PASTOR-TEACHER, GRACE COMMUNITY CHURCH, CALIFORNIA
It a great encouragement to see Day One making such excellent progress. Their publications are always biblical, accessible and attractively produced, with no compromise on quality. Long may their progress continue and increase! JOHN BLANCHARD, AUTHOR, EVANGELIST AND APOLOGIST
TRAVEL WITH
WISE CHOICES
FACE 2 FACE
Life STORIES
Footsteps of the past
Bible colour and learn
365
UNIVERSITY CHALLENGE
Opening up 1Corinthians
John Bunyan
Animals OF THE BIBLE
Catalogue available from: Day One Publications, Ryelands Road, Leominster, HR6 8NZ
Tel: 01568 613 740 • Fax: 01568 611 473 • www.dayone.co.uk • sales@dayone.co.uk

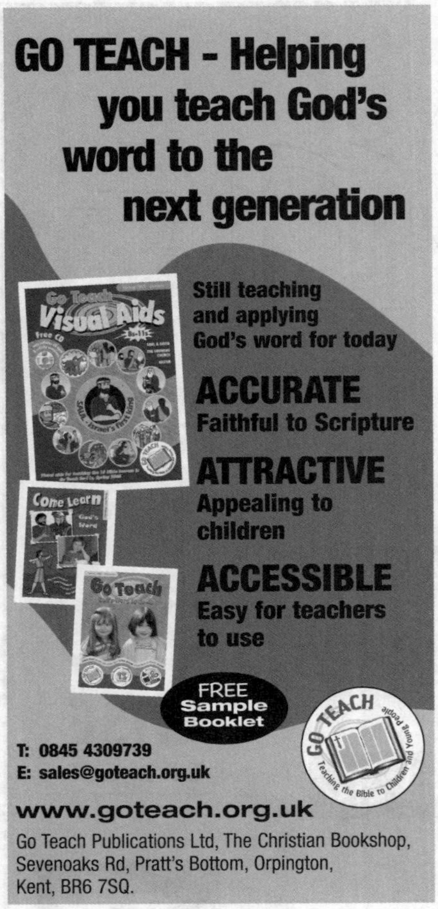

Day One Publications, Ryelands Road, Leominster HR6 8NZ
☎01568 613 740 🖷01568 611 473
🄴: sales@dayone.co.uk
Web: www.dayone.co.uk
General Secretary: Mr John G Roberts. Executive staff 2, Other staff 10. ***CC*** No.233465. Began 1831; interdenominational. Turnover n/a.

***Eagle**, Unit 2, Atworth Business Estate, Atworth, Melksham SN12 8SB
☎01225 899 141 🖷01225 790 746
🄴: Eaglepublishing@btconnect.com
Managing Director: Mr David Wavre. Executive staff 2, Other staff 1. Began 2000; non-denominational. Turnover £250,000 to year end Mar 05.

Evangelical Press, Faverdale North Industrial Estate, Darlington DL3 0PH
☎01325 380 232 🖷01325 466 153
🄴: sales@evangelicalpress.org
Web: www.evangelicalpress.org
Publishing and distributing Christian literature in English, French, Russian and Spanish.
General Manager: Mr Anthony L Gosling. Executive staff 3, Other staff 12. ***CC*** No.254335. Began 1967; non-denominational. Turnover n/a.

Family Publications, 6a King Street, Jericho, Oxford OX2 6DF
☎01865 558 336 🖷01865 316 951
🄴: sales@familypublications.co.uk
Web: www.familypublications.co.uk
Publishing and distributing Catholic books and books about family and social issues.
Managing Director: Mr Colin Mason. Executive staff 4, Other staff 4. Began 1988; Roman Catholic. Turnover n/a.

***Feather Books**, PO Box 438, Shrewsbury SY3 0WN
☎01743 872 177 🖷01743 872 177
🄴: john@waddys
Web.freeuk.com or www.waddys
Publishing poetry magazine and collections.
Director: Rev John Waddington-Feather. Executive staff 3, Other staff 5. Began 1980; interdenominational. Magazine: *Poetry Church* (500 quarterly). Turnover n/a.

Fellowship of Word and Spirit, 86 All Hallows Road, Bisphan, Blackpool FY2 0AY
☎01253 353 648
🄴: admin@fows.org
Web: www.fows.org
Supplying resource booklets for Christian leaders.
Hon. Secretary: Paul Darlington. No full-time staff. ***CC*** No.293159. Began 1983; Anglican. Turnover n/a.

Gabriel Communications Ltd, First Floor, St James's Buildings, Oxford Street, Manchester M1 6FP
☎0161 236 8856 🖷0161 236 8530
Commercial Director: Mr David Bould. Executive staff 1, Other staff 56. Began 1860; Roman Catholic. Turnover n/a.

Go Teach Publications Ltd, Unit 3t Zan Industrial Park, Crewe Road, Wheelock, Sandbach CW11 4QD
☎0845 430 9739 🖷0845 430 9741
🄴: editorial@goteach.org.uk
Web: www.goteach.org.uk
Publishing Bible teaching materials for children aged 3 to 14 years.
Editorial Director: Mr Ray Tibbs. Executive staff 1, Other staff 4. ***CC*** No.275116. Began 1946; interdenominational. Turnover n/a.
Distribution enquiries and orders: *Business Manager:* Mr Gordon Hoppé, The Christian Bookshop, Sevenoaks Road, Pratts Bottom, Orpington BR6 7SQ
🄴: sales@goteach.org.uk
☎0845 430 9739 🖷 01689 851 060

The Good Book Company, Elm House, 37 Elm Road, New Malden KT3 3HB
☎0845 225 0880 🖷0845 225 0990
🄴: admin@thegoodbook.co.uk
Web: www.thegoodbook.co.uk
Publishing books and daily Bible-reading notes for adults and children.
Publisher: Mr Tim Thornborough. *Commercial Manager:* Mr Tom Seidler. *Administrator:* Mr Anton Joubert. Executive staff 4, Other staff 8. Began 1990; interdenominational. Imprints: St Matthias Press, Narrowgate Press, Matthias Media. Turnover £800,000 to year end Dec 04.

Gospel Standard Trust, 125 Roundwood Lane, Harpenden AL5 3DD
☎01582 765 448 🖷01582 469 148
🄴: gospelstandardpublications@btinternet.com
Web: www.gospelstandard.org
Publishing books that commend the free and sovereign grace of Almighty God.
Publications Manager: Caleb A Pearce. Executive staff 1, Other staff 1. ***CC*** No.249781. Began 1966; Strict Baptist. Turnover £27,000 to year end Dec 98.

Grace Publications Trust, 104 Fairfield Road, Borough Green, Sevenoaks TN15 8DS
☎01732 780 077
Web: www.grace.org.uk/orgs/gpt/
Hon Secretary: Mr E C Porter. No full-time staff. ***CC*** No.285237. Began 1979; Grace Baptist. Turnover £45,000 to year end Dec 00.
Trade enquiries: Evangelical Press, Faverdale North Industrial Estate, Darlington DL3 0PH
🄴: sales@evangelical-press.org
☎01325 380 232 🖷 01325 466 153

Gracewing Publishing, 2 Southern Avenue, Leominster HR6 0QF
☎01568 616 835 🖷01568 613 289
🄴: gracewingx@aol.com
Web: www.gracewing.co.uk
Publishing theology, ecclesiastical history, biographies, prayer books.
Managing Director: Mr Thomas W Longford. *Publications Manager:* Miss Jo Ashworth. *Publicity Manager.* Mrs Monica Manwaring. Executive staff 3, Other staff 2. Began 1951; non-denominational. Turnover n/a.

The Grail, 125 Waxwell Lane, Pinner HA5 3ER
☎020 8866 0505/2195
🖷020 8866 1408
🄴: grailcentre@compuserve.com
Web: www.grailsociety.org.uk
Formation of Christian leaders; small resource centre which can be hired for day groups.
Publications Secretary: Miss Mary Grasar. Executive staff 2, Other staff 1. ***CC*** No.221076. Began n/a; Roman Catholic. Turnover n/a.

Grove Books Ltd, Ridley Hall Road, Cambridge CB3 9HU
☎01223 464 748 🖷01223 464 849
🄴: sales@grovebooks.co.uk
Web: www.grovebooks.co.uk
Administrator: Susanne Thompson. Executive staff 1. ***CC*** No.327014. Began 1970; Anglican. Turnover n/a.

Handsel Press, 62 Toll Road, Kincardine, Alloa FK10 4QZ
☎01259 730 538
🄴: handsel@dial.pipex.com
Web: www.handselpress.co.uk
Publishing Christian theology.
Editor: Rev Jock Stein. No full-time staff. ***CC*** No.SCO 14135. Began 1973; non-denominational. Turnover £9,000 to year end Aug 05.

For number of books published see list on Page 1[illegible]8

Hayes Press, Essex Road, Leicester LE4 9EE
☎0116 294 9949 M: 07801 683 183
E: sales@hayespress.org
Web: www.hayespress.org
Supplying Christian literature, gospel tracts, calenders, hymn books, gifts and Christian children's comic.
General Manager: Mr Kevin S Hickling. Executive staff 1, Other staff 5. ***CC*** No 242257. Began 1904; non-denominational. Magazine: *Plus/Eagles Wings* (10 000 monthly). Turnover n/a.

Roy Hession Book Trust, 3 Florence Road, Bromley BR1 3NU
☎020 8454 3460 📠020 8313 1373
E: gerry@daveygm.freeserve.co.uk
Promoting the translation, publication and distribution worldwide of books by the late Roy Hession.
General Secretary: Mr Gerry Davey. Executive staff 1. ***CC*** No.1031304. Began 1994; non-denominational. Turnover n/a.

Highland Books, 2 High Pines, Knoll Road, Godalming GU7 2EP
☎01483 424 560 📠01483 424 388
E: info@highlandbks.com
Web: www.highlandbks.com
Publisher Mr Philip Ralli. Executive staff 2, Other staff 1. Began 1983; non-denominational. Turnover £40,000 to year end Mar 04.

Hodder & Stoughton Religious Books, 338 Euston Road, London NW1 3BH
☎020 7873 6000 📠020 7873 6059
E: religious_sales@hodder.co.uk
Web: www.hodderreligious.co.uk
Bibles and other Christian books.
Managing Director: Mr Martin Mullin. *Publishing Director:* Ms Judith Longman. Executive staff 2, Other staff 10. Began 1868; non-denominational. Imprints: Hodder Christian Books, Hodder & Stoughton. Turnover n/a.

John Hunt Publishing, The Bothy, Deershot Lodge, Park Lane, Ropley, Alresford SO24 0BE
☎No telephone 📠01962 773 769
E: john@johnhunt-publishing.com
Web: www.johnhunt-publishing.com
Publishing Christian books plus those on spirituality and other world religions.
Proprietor: Mr John Hunt. *Sales Manager:* Mrs Kate Rowlandson. *Promotions Manager:* Mrs Marie-Claire Watson. Executive staff 3. Began 1989; non-denominational. Imprints: Hunt & Thorpe, Arthur James Ltd, O Books. Turnover £1,000,000 to year end Dec. 04.

Hymns Ancient & Modern Ltd, St Mary's Works, St Mary's Plain, Norwich NR3 3BH
☎01603 612 914 📠01603 624 483
E: admin@scm-canterburypress.co.uk
Web: www.scm-canterburypress.co.uk
The parent company of SCM-Canterbury Press and G J Palmer.
Group Chief Executive: Mr Andrew Moore. *Financial Controller:* Mrs Brenda Medhurst. *Customer Services Manager:* Loise Hopcroft. Executive staff 3, Other staff 55. ***CC*** No.270060. Began 1975; Anglican. Turnover n/a.

IVP, Norton Street, Nottingham NG7 3HR
☎0115 978 1054 📠0115 942 2694
E: ivp@ivpbooks.com
Web: www.ivpbooks.com
Chief Executive: Mr Brian Wilson. Executive staff 11, Other staff 19. ***CC*** Began 1935; non-denominational. Imprints: Apollos, Crossway, IVP. Turnover n/a.

†Janus Publishing Company Ltd, 105-107 Gloucester Place, London W1U 6BY
☎020 7580 7664 📠020 7636 5756
E: publisher@januspublishing.co.uk
Web: www.januspublishing.co.uk
Managing Director: Mr Sandy Leung. Executive staff 5. Began 1991; non-denominational. Turnover £200,000 to year end Dec 00.

Jubilate Hymns Ltd, Southwick House, 4 Thorne Park Road, Chelston, Torquay TQ2 6RX
☎01803 607 754 📠01803 605 682
E: copyrightmanager@jubilate.co.uk
Web: www.jubilate.co.uk
Publishing hymnbooks; copyright agency.
Copyright & Financial Managers: Mrs Merrilyn Williams, Mr Paul Williams. Executive staff 1, Other staff 1. Began 1960; interdenominational. Turnover n/a.

K & M Books, Plas Gwyn, High Street, Trelawnyd, Rhyl LL18 6DT
☎01745 571 707 📠01745 571 707
E: kandmbooks@aol.com
Web: www.kandmbooks.co.uk
Publisher: Mr Michael Kimmitt. Executive staff 1. Began 1994; non-denominational. Turnover n/a.

King's Highway Books, PO Box 789, Sutton Coldfield B73 5FX
☎0121 355 8333 📠0121 355 3833
E: worldaction@aol.com
Web: worldactionministries.org.uk
Producing Christian devotional books and booklets.
Managing Director: Mr Philip B. South. Admin staff 3. Began 2001; interdenominational. Part of World Action Ministries. Turnover £10,000 to year end Dec 04.

***Kingsway Publications**, Lottbridge Drove, Eastbourne BN23 6NT
☎01323 437 700 📠01323 411 970
E: books@kingsway.co.uk
Web: www.kingsway.co.uk
Publishing Director: Mr Richard Herkes. *Managing Director:* Mr John Paculabo. Executive Staff 2, Other staff 63. Began 1977; interdenominational. Part of Kingsway Communications Ltd. Turnover n/a.

***Lion Hudson plc**, Mayfield House, 256 Banbury Road, Oxford OX2 7DH
☎01865 302 750 📠01865 302 757
E: enquiries@lionhudson.co.uk
Web: www.lionhudson.co.uk
Designing and publishing books for general and international markets; colour coeditions in over 160 languages.
Managing Director: Mr Paul Clifford. *International Rights Director:* Mr Tony Wales. *Sales Director:* Mr John O'Nions. Executive staff 6, Other staff 55. Began 1971 as Lion Publishing plc, merged with Angus Hudson 2003; non-denominational. Imprints: Candle, Lion, Lion Children's, Monarch. Turnover £8,800,000 to year end Mar 05.

Loxwood Press, 50 Loxwood Avenue, Worthing BN14 7RA
☎01903 232 208
Publishing music and academic monographs by Asian and African Christians.
Directors: Mr & Mrs Donald & Ruth Banks. Executive staff 2. Began 1992; interdenominational. Turnover n/a.

Lutterworth Press, PO Box 60, Cambridge CB1 2NT
☎01223 350 865 📠01223 366 951
E: publishing@lutterworth.com
Web: www.lutterworth.com
Managing Director: Mr Adrian Brink. Executive staff 2, Other staff 2. Began 1799; non-denominational. Imprints: Hardy Patrick, Acorn Additions. Turnover n/a.

McCrimmon Publishing Co Ltd, 10 High Street, Great Wakering, Southend-on-Sea SS3 0EQ
☎01702 218 956 📠01702 216 082
E: mccrimmons@dial.pipex.com
Web: www.mccrimmons.com
Publishing liturgical and religious education resources; also CDs, posters, banners, cards and music.
Managing Director: Mrs Joan McCrimmon. *Sales Director:* Mr Don McCrimmon. Executive staff 2, Other staff 1. Began 1969; ecumenical. Turnover £800,000 to year end Dec 02.

Marcham Manor Press, Appleford, Abingdon OX14 4PB
☎01235 848 319
Evangelical specialist academic publishing house; mainly church history and historical theology at PhD level.
Director: Mr Gervase E Duffield. Executive staff 1, Other staff 2. Began 1963; non-denominational. Turnover n/a.

Kevin Mayhew, Buxhall, Stowmarket IP14 3BW
☎01449 737 978 📠01449 737 834
E: sales@kevinmayhewltd.com
Web: www.kevinmayhew.com
Managing Director: Mr Kevin Whomes. Executive staff 3, Other staff 50. Began 1976; non-denominational. Imprints: Kevin Mayhew, Palm Tree Press, World Wide Worship. Turnover n/a.

John Metcalfe Publishing Trust, Church Road, Tylers Green, Penn, High Wycombe HP10 8LN
☎01494 813 174
Managing Director: Mr John Metcalfe. Executive staff 3, Other staff 10. ***CC*** No.263381. Began 1971; non-denominational. Turnover n/a.

B

Mirfield Publications, House of the Resurrection, Stocks Bank Road, Mirfield WF14 0BN
☎01924 483 307 🖷01924 490 489
E: publications@mirfield.org.uk
Web: www.mirfield.org.uk
Publications Secretary: Br Alan Brown. Executive staff 1. ***CC*** No.232670. Began 1958; Anglican. Turnover £25,000 to year end Dec 02.

Modern Welsh Publications Ltd, 32 Garth Drive, Liverpool L18 6HW
☎0151 724 1989 🖷0151 724 5691
E: ben@garthdrive.fsnet.co.uk
Web: www.liverpool-welsh.co.uk
General Secretary: Rev Dr D Ben Rees. No full-time staff. Began 1963; non-denominational. Turnover n/a.

Moorley's Print and Publishing Ltd, 23 Park Road, Ilkeston DE7 5DA
☎0115 932 0643 🖷0115 932 0643
E: info@moorleys.co.uk
Web: www.moorleys.co.uk
Publishers and printers specialising in Christian drama, school assembly material; church and charity work.
Founding Directors: Mr & Mrs John & Jean Moorley. Executive staff 2, Other staff 5. Began 1969; interdenominational. Turnover n/a.

MPH, 4 John Wesley Road, Werrington, Peterborough PE4 6ZP
☎01733 325 002 🖷01733 384 180
E: chief.exec@mph.org.uk
Web: www.mph.org.uk *Publishing house of the Methodist Church. Chief Executive:* Mr Martin Stone. Executive staff 1, Other staff 28. ***CC*** Began 1750; Methodist. (Previously Methodist Publishing House). Imprints: Epworth, Methodist Publishing House, Inspire. Turnover n/a.

Nelson Thornes (Publishers) Ltd, Delta Place, 27 Bath Road, Cheltenham GL53 7TH
☎01242 267 100 🖷01242 221 914
E: cservices@nelsonthornes.com
Web: www.nelsonthornes.com
Commissioning Editor: Mr Robert Bircher. Executive staff 5, Other staff 200. Began 1986; non-denominational. (Previously Stanley Thornes (Publishers) Ltd). Incorporating Simon and Schuster Education and Thomas Nelson. Turnover n/a.

New City, Unit 17, Sovereign Park, Coronation Road, London NW10 7QP
☎020 8453 1558 🖷020 8453 1621
E: newcity@care4free.net
Business Manager: Mr Tomeu Mayans. Executive staff 1, Other staff 4. ***CC*** No.257912. Began 1968; interdenominational. Turnover n/a.

***New Dawn Books**, 10a Jamaica Street, Greenock PA15 1XX
☎01475 729 668 🖷01475 728 145
E: bookshop@struthers-church.org
Web: www.struthers-church.org
Publishing Pentecostal books dealing with salvation, baptism in the Spirit, healing, deliverance and related topics.
Manager: Mr Chris Jewell. No full-time staff. ***CC*** No.SCO 06960. Began 1987; Pentecostal. Turnover n/a.

†***The New Hope Trust**, Faith Acres, Peterhead AB42 3DQ
☎01779 838 251 M: 07977 137 920
🖷01779 838 549
E: info@newhopetrust.org
Web: www.newhopetrust.org
Director: Mr Phillip Cameron. Executive staff 1, Other staff 22. ***CC*** No.276520. Began 1974; interdenominational. (Previously New Hope Publications). Turnover n/a.

***New Living Publishers**, 164 Radcliffe New Road, Whitefield, Manchester M45 7TU
☎0161 766 1166
E: theway@newlivingpublishers.co.uk
Web: www.newlivingpublishers.co.uk
Publishing Pentecostal books.
Manager: Steve Martin. Executive staff 1. Began 1995; Pentecostal. Turnover n/a.

New Wine Ministries, New Wine Ministries, Unit 22, Arun Business Park, Bognor Regis PO22 9SX
☎01243 867 227 🖷01243 867 292
E: newwine@xalt.co.uk
Web: www.newwineministries.co.uk
Publishing charismatic Word and Spirit books; distributing and importing 2000 titles from USA.
Partners: Mr Ed Harding, Dr Elizabeth Harding. *Publishing Director:* Mr Tim Pettingale. Executive staff 2, Other staff 5. Began 1984; non-denominational. Turnover £800,000 to year end Dec 04.

The Open Bible Trust, Fordland Mount, Upper Basildon, Reading RG8 8LU
☎01491 671 357
E: admin@obt.org.uk
Web: www.obt.org.uk
Aiding understanding of Scripture by publishing Bible study resources, commentaries, tapes and CDs.
Administrator: Mr Michael Denny.
Executive staff 2. ***CC*** No.326717. Began 1984; non-denominational. Magazine: *Search* (500 every two months). Turnover £21,000 to year end Aug 00.

Oxford University Press, Great Clarendon Street, Oxford OX2 6DP
☎01865 353 808 (Bibles/books) 353 349 (Music) 🖷01865 353 741
E: bibles.uk@oup.com
Web: www.oup.co.uk
Publishing hymn books, Bibles, music, religious and theological books.
Marketing Manager, Bibles: Mr Phil Henderson. *Sales and Marketing Manager, Music:* Ms Suzy Gooch. Executive staff 4, Other staff 1. ***CC*** Began 1478; non-denominational. No magazine. Turnover n/a.
Also at: Distribution Services, Saxon Way West, Corby NN18 9ES
☎01536 741 727 🖷 01536 454 577

Paternoster, 9 Holdom Avenue, Milton Keynes MK1 1QR
☎01905 357 780 / 01908 364 2[illegible]9
🖷01908 277 169
E: paternoster@authenticmedia.co.uk
Web: www.authenticmedia.co.uk/paternoster
Acquisitions Editor: Dr Robin Parry. Executive staff 1. ***CC*** Began 1935; interdenominational. Imprint of Authentic Media. Turnover n/a.

Piquant Editions Ltd, 4 Thornton Road, PO Box 83, Carlisle CA3 9GR
☎01228 525 075
🖷01228 380 441
E: info@piquant.net
Web: www.piquanteditions.com
Specialing in books on arts and mission.
Publisher: Mr Pieter Kwant. *Editorial Director:* Mrs Elria Kwant. Executive staff 2, Other staff 1. Began 1999; interdenominational. Turnover £100,000 to year end Dec 00.

***Plough Publishing House of the Bruderhof Communities in the UK**, Darvell Bruderhof, Robertsbridge TN32 5DR
☎01580 883 344/0800 01[illegible] 0799
🖷01580 883 319/0800 018 3347
E: contact@plough.com
Web: www.bruderhof.co.uk
Distributing literature, mainly from the Plough Publishing House.
Secretary: Name not supplied. Community 350. ***CC*** No.2292[illegible]6. Began 1[illegible]36; non-denominational. Magazine: *The Plough-Reader* (2,800 quarterly). Turnover n/a.

Precious Seed Publications, 5 Turnham Green, Penylan, Cardiff CF23 9DL
☎029 2049 2346
E: info@preciousseed.org
Web: www.preciousseed.org
Publishing Bible study books.
Treasurer: Mr Michael Jones. No full-time staff. ***CC*** No.326157. Began 1945; interdenominational. Turnover n/a.

Printforce Ltd, Drovers Way, Ugford, Wilton, Salisbury SP2 0EB
☎01722 743 295
🖷01722 743 295
Publishing books for youth leaders.
Director: Mr Paul Wade. Executive staff 1. Began 1983; non-denominational. Turnover n/a.

Quinta Press, Meadow View, Weston Rhyn, Oswestry SY10 7RN
☎01691 778 659
M: 07970 678 144
🖷01691 777 638
E: info@quintapress.com
Web: www.quintapress.com
Proprietor: Dr Digby L James. Executive staff 1. Began 1992; evangelical. Turnover n/a.

For number of books published see list on Page 1[illegible]3

Redemptorist Publications, Alphonsus House, Chawton, Alton GU34 3HQ
☎01420 882 22
🖷01420 888 05
E: sales@shineonline.net
Web: www.redempt.org
Executive Director: Fr Timothy Buckland. Executive staff 3, Other staff 19. ***CC*** Began 1954; Roman Catholic. Turnover n/a.

Regnum International, PO Box 70, Oxford OX2 6HB
☎01865 556 071
🖷01865 510 823
E: regnum@ocms.ac.uk
Publisher: Rev Canon Dr Chris Sugden. Other staff 1. ***CC*** No.290112. Began 1986; non-denominational. Turnover n/a.

John Ritchie Ltd, 40 Beansburn, Kilmarnock KA3 1RH
☎01563 536 394
🖷01563 571 191
E: sales@johnritchie.co.uk
Web: www.johnritchie.co.uk
Wholesale distribution of Bibles, Scripture greetings cards and resource material.
General Manager: Mr John Watson. *Shop Manageress:* Mrs Elizabeth Wallace. Executive staff 3, Other staff 9. Began 1880; non-denominational. Turnover n/a.

***The Rushworth Enterprise Ltd**, 2 Dimple Lane, Crich, Matlock DE4 5BQ
☎01773 857 313 🖷01773 856 062
E: rushworth.lit@virgin.net
Web: www.rushworth.org.uk
Publishing and donating Christian study books to pastors in overseas countries.
General Secretary: Miss Catherine S Cheetham. Executive staff 3. ***CC*** No.241364. Began 1953; non-denominational. Turnover £34,000 [excluding second-hand books] to year end Mar 05.

†Saint Andrew Press, 121 George Street, Edinburgh EH2 4YN
☎0131 240 2253 🖷0131 220 3113
E: standrewpress@cofscotland.org.uk
Web: www.standrewpress.com
Publishing an ecumenical range of titles.
Head of Publishing: Ms Ann Crawford. *Editorial Manager:* Mr Richard Allen. Executive staff 3, Admin staff 3. Began 1954; Church of Scotland. Turnover £215,000 to year end Feb 03.

St Matthew Publishing Ltd, 24 Geldart Street, Cambridge CB1 2LX
☎01223 504 871 🖷01223 512 304
E: pf.smp@dial.pipex.com
Web: www.stmatthewpublishing.co.uk
Providing materials warning the churches of the rapidly growing apostasy within them.
Director: Rev Philip Foster. No full-time staff. Began 1995; interdenominational. Turnover £25,000 to year end Dec 04.

St Pauls Publishing, 187 Battersea Bridge Road, London SW11 3AS
☎020 7978 4300
M: 07799 818 705
🖷020 7978 4370
E: editions@stpauls.org.uk
Web: www.stpauls.ie
Publishing books which promote the Gospel and Christian vision.
Editorial Director: Rev Andrew Pudussery. Members of religious order 2, Other staff 2. ***CC*** No.230948. Began 1947; Roman Catholic. Turnover n/a.

†St Stephen's Press, 31 Warnborough Road, Oxford OX2 6JA
E: ssp@sourozh.org
Web: www.sourozh.org
Publishing on behalf of the Russian Orthodox Patriarchal Church in Great Britain. Theological and liturgical texts.
Managing Director: Mrs Jessica Rose. Executive staff 1, Other staff 1. ***CC*** Began 1992; Orthodox. Turnover n/a.

Salvationist Publishing and Supplies Ltd, 1 Tiverton Street, London SE1 6NT
☎020 7366 6571
🖷020 7367 6576
E: mail_order@sp-s.co.uk
Web: www.worldofbrass.com
Managing Director: Mr Trevor P Caffull. Executive staff 6, Other staff 32. Began 1867; Salvation Army. Turnover £3,500,000 to year end Mar 00.

For number of books published see list on Page 118

Save The Church of England Foundation, West Ella House, 15 Tunnelwood Road, Watford WD17 4SN
☎01923 229 045
Campaigning for the Doctrine of the Church of England as expressed in the 39 Articles.
Chief Executive: Mr Malcolm J W Barker Esq. Executive staff 1. Began 1979; Anglican. Turnover n/a.

B

SCM-Canterbury Press Ltd, Editorial, Production & Marketing Departments, 9 St Albans Place, London N1 0NX
☎020 7359 8033/01502 711 171
🖷020 7359 0049
E: office@scm-canterburypress.co.uk or admin@scm-cant
Web: www.scm-canterburypress.co.uk
The book publishing subsidiary of Hymns Ancient & Modern, Norwich.
Publishing Director: Mrs Christine Smith. *Senior Marketing Manager:* Michael Addison. *Production Manager:* Stephen Rogers. Executive staff 3, Other staff 7. Began 1929; non-denominational. Imprints: Canterbury Press, Hymns Ancient & Modern, SCM Press, RMEP, Church Times. Turnover £1,900,000 to year end Dec 02.

Scripture Truth Publications, Coopies Way, Coopies Lane, Morpeth NE61 6JN
☎01670 511 615
M: 07957 776 046
🖷01670 516 620
E: scripturetruth@compuserve.com
Web: www.scripture-truth.org.uk
Manager: Mr John Keable. Executive staff 3. ***CC*** No.223327. Began 1909; interdenominational. Turnover £55,000 to year end Dec 02.

***Scripture Union**, 207 Queensway, Bletchley, Milton Keynes MK2 2EB
☎01908 856 000
Mail order 0845 070 6006
🖷01908 856 111
Mail order 01908 856 020
E: info@scriptureunion.org.uk
Web: www.scriptureunion.org.uk
Publishing Bible reading and study materials, children's and youth curriculum, adult / children's books, church resources.
Head of Resources Development: Mr Terry Clutterham. Executive staff 6, Commissioning staff 29. ***CC*** No.213422. Began 1867; interdenominational. Turnover included in Scripture Union.

Sessions of York, The Ebor Press, Huntington Road, York YO31 9HS
☎01904 659 224
🖷01904 637 068
E: ebor.info@sessionsofyork.co.uk
Web: www.sessionsofyork.co.uk
Publishing Manager: Mr Robert Jarrett. Executive staff 1, Other staff n/a. Began 1811; non-denominational. Turnover n/a.

Silvertree Publishing, PO Box 2768, Yeovil BA22 8XZ
☎01935 862 127 🖷01935 862 127
E: editor@minney74.freeserve.co.uk
Applying biblical and psychological insights to personal problem areas; poetry; biography.
Editor: Mr Brian Minney. Executive staff 1. Began 2000; interdenominational. Turnover n/a.

Society for Promoting Christian Knowledge (SPCK), 36 Causton Street, London SW1P 4ST
☎020 7592 3900 🖷020 7592 3939
E: publishing@spck.org.uk
General Secretary: Mr Simon Kingston. Executive staff 4, Other staff 14. ***CC*** No.231144. Began 1698; Anglican. Turnover n/a.

Sovereign Publications, PO Box 88, Bromley BR2 9PF
☎020 8460 7503 🖷020 8460 7503
E: mb@mbowden.info
Web: www.mbowden.info
Publishing books mainly on creation and biblical counselling.
Principal: Mr M Bowden. No full-time staff. Began 1977; Free evangelical. Turnover n/a.

Sovereign World, PO Box 777, Tonbridge TN11 0ZS
☎01732 850 598 🖷01732 851 077
E: chrismungeam@btconnect.com
Web: www.sovereign-world.com
Publishing Christian teaching books especially related to Word and Spirit.
Managing Director & President: Mr Chris Mungeam. Executive staff 2, Other staff 2. Began 1986; non-denominational. Turnover n/a.
Distribution: New Wine Ministries, Unit 22, Arun Business Park, Bognor Regis PO22 9SX
E: newwine@xalt.co.uk
☎01243 867 227 🖷 01243 867 292

Stainer & Bell Ltd, PO Box 110, Victoria House, 23 Gruneisen Road, London N3 1DZ
☎020 8343 3303 🖷020 8343 3024
E: post@stainer.co.uk
Web: www.stainer.co.uk
Managing Directors: Mr & Mrs Keith & Carol Wakefield. *Publishing Director:* Mr Nicholas Williams. Executive staff 4, Other staff 6. Began 1907; non-denominational. Turnover £832,000 to year end Dec 04.

Stanborough Press, Alma Park, Grantham NG31 9SL
☎01476 591 700 🖷01476 577 144
E: stanborg@aol.com
Manager: Mr Paul Hammond. Executive staff 1, Other staff 19. ***CC*** Began 1890; Seventh-day Adventist. Turnover n/a.

Talking Points, 34 Whinchat Tail, Galley Hill, Guisborough TS14 8PW
☎01287 630 835
Publications Director: Mr Philip M Bancroft. Executive staff 1. Began 1992; non-denominational. Turnover n/a.

Tentmaker Publications, 121 Hartshill Road, Stoke-on-Trent ST4 7LU
☎01782 746 879
M: 07723 349 389
🖷01782 414 805
E: sales@tentmaker.org.uk
Web: www.tentmaker.org.uk
Printing and publishing short print run books; republishing classic Christian titles.
Manager: Mr Phil Roberts. Executive staff 1, Other staff 2. Began 1996; non-denominational. Turnover £68,000 to year end Apr 03.

Teresian Press, Carmelite Priory, Boars Hill, Oxford OX1 5HB
☎01865 730 183
🖷01865 326 478
E: priory@carmelite.org.uk
Web: www.carmelitebooks.com
Specialising in Carmelite titles.
Secretary: Mrs Sandra Pooley. Executive staff 2. ***CC*** No.2077[illegible]8. Began 1985; Roman Catholic. Turnover n/a.

Terra Nova Publications International Ltd, PO Box 2400, Bradford-on-Avon BA15 2YN
☎01225 868 723
E: terranovabooks@aol.com
www.terranovapress.com
Publishing charismatic evangelical books.
Publisher Administrator: Name not supplied. Staff 2. Began n/a; interdenominational. Turnover n/a.

Triumph House, Remus House, Coltsfoot Drive, Woodston, Peterborough PE2 9JX
☎01733 898 102
🖷01733 313 524
E: triumphhouse@forwardpress.co.uk
Web: www.forwardpress.co.uk
Publishing poetry of Christian and other faiths.
Managing Editor: Mr Simon Harwin. Executive staff 1, Other staff 1. Began 1993; interdenominational. Turnover n/a.

Tufton Books (Church Union Publications), 7 Tufton Street, London SW1P 3QN
☎020 7222 6952
🖷020 7976 7180
E: churchunion@care4free.net
Coordinator: Rev John Fitchford. Executive staff 1, Other staff 1. ***CC*** Began 1995; Anglican. Turnover n/a

Twoedged Sword Publications, PO Box 266, Waterlooville PO7 5ZT
☎023 9220 0569
E: paul@twoedgedswordpublications.co.uk
Web: www.twoedgedswordpublications.co.uk
Publishing "biblically correct" books.
Publications Manager: Mr Paul Rose. Admin staff 1, Other staff 1. Began 200[illegible]; non-denominational. Turnover n/a.

For number of books published see list on Page 113

B

Verité CM Ltd, 8 St John's Parade, Alinora Crescent, Goring-by-Sea, Worthing BN12 4HJ
☎01903 241 975 M: 07818 091 723
🖷01903 521 959
E: info@veritecm.com
Web: www.veritecm.com
Specialising in evangelistic books and booklets; short run, on demand, personalised publications.
Director: Mr Chris Powell. Executive staff 2, Admin staff 2. Began 2003; non-denominational. Turnover n/a.

Wild Goose Publications (The Iona Community), Savoy House, 140 Sauchiehall Street, Glasgow G2 3DH
☎0141 332 6292 🖷0141 332 1090
E: admin@ionabooks.com
Web: www.ionabooks.com
Publishing house of the Iona Community established in the Celtic Christian tradition of St Columba.
Managing Editor: Sandra Kramer. *Assistant Publishing Manager Marketing:* Alex O'Neill. Executive staff 2, Other staff 2. ***CC*** No.SCO 03794. Began 1938; ecumenical. Turnover £250,000 to year end Dec 04.

Zondervan, PO Box 630, Shrewsbury SY3 9WZ
☎0870 199 3419 or 020 7384 2481
🖷020 8930 0073
E: ian.matthews@zondervan.com
Web: www.zondervan.com
Publishing resources that glorify Christ and promote biblical principles.
UK Sales and Marketing Manager: Mr Ian Matthews. Staff n/a. Began 1931; non-denominational. Turnover n/a.

OTHER LITERATURE PRODUCERS & DISTRIBUTORS

Alban Books Ltd, 14 Belford Road, Edinburgh EH4 3BL
☎0131 226 2217 🖷0131 225 5999
E: sales@albanbooks.com
Web: www.albanbooks.com
Managing sales, promotion, marketing and distribution in Europe of books on religious studies, and social issues.
Managing Director: Ms Jane Grounsell. Executive staff 1, Other staff 5. Began 1995; non-denominational. Distributors for: Abingdon Press, Augsburg Fortress Publishers, The Crossroad Publishing, WmB Hendrickson Publishers, Orbis Books, WmB Eerdmans Publishing Co and Ave Maria Press. No magazine. Turnover n/a.

AP Communications Ltd, 36 High Street, Whitchurch SY13 1EB
☎01948 663 770 🖷01948 662 772
E: office@ap-communications.freeserve.co.uk
Distributing of Christian literature, cards and stationery from us and UK suppliers.
Managing Director: Rev Kenneth T Lillie. *Office Manager:* Mrs Rosie Mee. Executive staff 1, Other staff 12. Began 1983; interdenominational. No magazine. Turnover £350,000 to year end Apr 05.

Appleford Publishing Group, Appleford House, Appleford, Abingdon OX14 4PB
☎01235 848 319
Holding company for evangelical and other academic books, magazines and pastoralia; sale of antiquarian books.
Editorial Director: Mr Gervase E Duffield. Executive staff 1, Other staff 2. Began 1963; Anglican, Reformed and Evangelical. No magazine. Turnover n/a.

Articles of Faith Ltd, Resource House, Kay Street, Bury BL9 6BU
☎0161 763 6232
🖷0161 763 5366
E: hello@articlesoffaith.co.uk
Web: www.articlesoffaith.co.uk
Supplying artefacts, books and resources for religious education to schools and colleges by mail order.
Managing Director: Ms Christine Howard. *Director:* Mr Leslie Howard. Total work force 22. Began 1991; non-denominational. No magazine. Turnover £800,000 to year end Jul 05.

Asian Books (South Asian Concern), PO Box 43, Sutton SM2 5WL
☎020 8770 9717
🖷020 8770 9747
E: southasianconcern@tiscali.co.uk and info@southasianconcern.org.uk
Web: www.southasianconcern.org.uk
Supplying Asian Christian resources in many languages.
Coordinator: Ms Helen Adams. All voluntary staff. ***CC*** No.1002270. Began 1994; interdenominational. No magazine. Turnover £5,000 to year end Mar 02.

AT Publications, PO Box 41, Derby DE1 9ZR
☎0870 027 3656
🖷0870 027 3656
E: manjit@advent-truth.co.uk
Web: www.advent-truth.co.uk
Distributing books and tracts for evangelism; organising religious and health tours and seminars.
Director: Mr Manjit Biant. Executive staff 1, Other staff 1. Began 1990; non-denominational. (Previously The Advent Truth). No magazine. Turnover £25,000 to year end Apr 98.

@tracts Ltd, PO Box 6212, Kirkwall KW15 1YB
☎0870 777 2329
E: info@attracts.co.uk
Web: www.attracts.co.uk
Providing evangelistic literature; designing and hosting Web sites.
General Manager: Mr Mark Nixon. Executive staff 2. Began 2001; non-denominational. No magazine. Turnover £15,000 to year end Jul 04.

***Authentic Media**, 9 Holdom Avenue, Bletchley, Milton Keynes MK1 1QR
☎01908 364 200
🖷01908 648 592
E: info@authenticmedia.co.uk
Web: www.authenticmedia.co.uk
Publishing Bibles, books, music, video and software.
General Manager: Mr David Withers. Executive staff 7, Other staff 10. Began 2001; non-denominational. (Previously Word Music & Publishing, Nelson Word, Paternoster Publishing, Alliance Music). A Division of Send the Light. Product Divisions: Authentic Publishing (Authentic Books, Paternoster), Authentic Music, Authentic Software, Authentic DVD: Magazine *Premier* (30,000 monthly). Turnover n/a.

Other Literature Producers & Distributors

AVEC Resources, 125 Waxwell Lane, Pinner HA5 3ER
☎020 8866 2195
🖷020 8866 1408
E: grailpublications@compuserve.org
Web: www.avecresources.org
Books and catalogued archives on work with groups, communities, religious, church and community development; consultancy.
Secretary: Ms Catherine Widdicombe. **CC** No.226023. Began 1994; ecumenical. (Previously AVEC (A Service Agency for Church and Community Work)). No magazine. Turnover £11,000 to year end Aug 05.

Basyl Books, Tapes and Videos, PO Box 9077, London E1 6QU
☎020 7729 4985
E: sales@basyl.org.uk
Web: www.basyl.org.uk
Producing and distributing Christian resources for the Bangladeshi community in Britain.
Director: Mr David Mear. Executive staff 1. Began 1998; interdenominational. No magazine. Turnover n/a.

Berean Publishing Trust, The Chapel of the Opened Book, 52a Wilson Street, London EC2A 2ER
☎020 7247 1467
E: bptonline@btinternet.com
Web: www.bereanonline.org
Publishing and distributing Bible study books and booklets.
Distribution Secretary: Mr Jim Clift. Executive staff 2, Other staff 1. **CC** No.232856. Began 1909; non-denominational. Associated with Berean Forward Movement Trust. Magazine: *The Berean Expositor* (550 every two months). Turnover £14,159 to year end Dec 00.

The Bible & Tract Depot, 219 Mary Street, Birmingham B12 9RN
☎0121 440 1422
Mail order distribution of Bible deliverance literature.
Manager: Miss O G M Everitt. Executive staff 1. Began 1946; interdenominational. No magazine. Turnover n/a.

The Bible League Trust, 46 Bulbridge Road, Wilton, Salisbury SP2 0LE
☎No telephone
E: ruth.ward@ukonline.co.uk
Web: www.bibleleaguetrust.org
Proclaiming the inspiration, infallibility and sole sufficiency of Scripture; promoting its reverent study.
Hon Secretary: Mrs Ruth Ward. All voluntary staff. **CC** No.281867. Began 1892; non-denominational. Magazine: *Bible League Quarterly* (1,450 quarterly). Turnover £14,700 to year end Dec 04.

***The Bible Text Publicity Mission**, PO Box 2677, Romford RM7 8XF
☎01708 733 293 📱07952 045 717
E: billturner@tiscali.co.uk
Web: www.btpm.org.uk
Displaying Bible texts on UK railways, Underground, prisons and internet; also telephone counselling service.
Administrator: Rev Bill Turner. No paid staff. **CC** No.235773. Began 1923; interdenominational. Magazine: *Annual Report* (400 annually). Turnover £18,271 to year end Dec 04.

BibleLands Trading Ltd (BibleLands), PO Box 1117, Wilstead, Bedford MK45 3ZQ
☎01234 740 000 🖷01234 743 113
E: salesenq@biblelands.co.uk
Web: www.biblelands.co.uk
Mail order Easter and Christmas season Christian cards, gifts, church folders and Bethlehem Carol Sheet.
Director: Nigel Edward-Few. *Head of Finance:* Rev Nick Plant. Executive staff 2, Other staff 2. Began 1967; non-denominational. No magazine. Turnover £480,000 to year end Apr 05.

Birmingham Gospel Outreach, PO Box 5681, Birmingham B1 1SD
☎0121 458 6582 🖷0121 458 6582
Web: www.birminghamgospeloutreach.co.uk
Producing English and Romanian Gospel tracts, Scripture memory verse cards, bookmarks, posters, Gospel booklets, cards.
Director: Mr Michael Simpson. Executive staff 1, Other staff 1. Began 1995; non-denominational. No magazine. Turnover n/a.

Don Bosco Publications, Thornleigh House, Sharples Park, Bolton BL1 6PQ
☎01204 308 811 🖷012[illegible]4 386 [illegible]68
E: joan@don-bosco-publications.co.uk
Web: www.don-bosco-publications
Supplying books mainly for children, teenagers, youth workers, schools and parishes.
Manager: Joan Rankin. Executive staff 2, No other paid staff **CC** No.2[illegible]3779. Began 1892; Roman Catholic. (Previously Salesian Publications (UK)). Linked with European Salesian Publications. Magazine: *Don Bosco Today* (18,000 quarterly), *Salesian Calendar* (2[illegible],000 quarterly). Turnover n/a.

P Brengle Crowhurst Pastoral Trust, 88 Railton Jones Close, Stoke Gifford, Bristol BS34 8BF
☎0117 979 3619
E: peter@pastor-peter.org.uk
Web: www.pastor-peter.org.uk
Encouraging isolated believers by correspondence and literature.
Secretary: Rev Peter B Crowhurst. No full-time staff. **CC** No.289[illegible]20. Began [illegible]984; interdenominational. Magazine: *Peter's Pastoral Letter* (1,000 half-yearly). Turnover n/a.

Bridge Books & Music 14 North Bridge Street, Sunderland SR5 1AB
☎0191 567 3544 🖷0191 567 35[illegible]4
E: bridgebooks@fsmail.net
Also music, cards, CDs, gifts, Bibles Sunday school materials.
Manager: Mrs Lynne Foreman. Executive staff 2, Other staff n/a. Began 1974; interdenominational. (Previously Scripture Union Bookshop). No magazine. Turnover n/a.

By All Means Gospel Trust, 353 Station Road, Dorridge, Solihull B93 8EY
☎01564 771 185 🖷01564 771 1[illegible]5
E: info@bam-gospeltrust.org
Web: bam-gospeltrust.org
Daily readings in English, Romanian, Hungarian. Studies, Books, Greek Christian newspaper.
General Secretary: Maurice J W Paine. Executive staff 1. **CC** No.231070. Began 1962; interdenominational. Break And Meditate. Magazine: *BAM News* (3,000 every two months). Turnover n/a.

***Challenge Newsline**, 8 St John's Parade, Alinora Crescent, Goring-by-Sea, Worthing BN12 4HJ
☎0845 166 8463 🖷0845 166 8459
E: challenge@veritecm.com
Web: www.challengenewsline.com
Publishing evangelistic newspaper.
Editor: Mrs Debbie Bunn. *Publisher:* Mr Chris Powell. Executive staff 1. **CC** No.270162. Began 1958; interdenominational. (Previously Challenge Literature Fellowship) Magazine: *Challenge* (70,000 monthly). Turnover n/a.

***Oswald Chambers Publications Association Ltd**, St Paul's Centre, Christian Concern, Hightown, Crewe CW1 3BY
☎01270 586 186 🖷01270 250 683
E: ocpal@christianconcern.co.uk
Web: www.oswaldchambers.co.uk
Publishing and distributing material by Oswald Chambers.
Treasurer: Mr Rob Wykes. No full time staff. **CC** No.244995. Began 1934; non-denominational. No magazine. Turnover £80,000 to year end Sept 05.

Christian Bits, 5 Underwood Road, Haslemere GU27 1JQ
☎01428 653 853 M: 07785 734 600
🖷08717 333 884
E: enquiries@christianbits.co.uk
Web: www.christianbits.co.uk
Distributing Christian books, Bibles, CDs, videos, software, gifts; mail order and online.
Managing Director: Mr Andy Rigby. Executive staff 1, Admin staff 1. Began 2003; non-denominational. (Previously Soft Approach Ltd). Turnover n/a.

Christian Book Club, 18 Slater Street, Liverpool L1 4BS
☎0151 708 9550
E: gladstonetrust@tiscali.co.uk
Providing book service to customers' home.
Manager: Mr William G Tonge. Executive staff 1. **CC** Began 1976; non-denominational. No magazine Turnover n/a.

The Christian Book Club, Unit 2, Atworth Business Estate, Atworth, Melksham SN12 8SB
☎0870 990 8277 🖷01225 790 746
E: christianbookclub@btconnect.com
Web: www.christianbookclub.co.uk
Offering wide range of adult and children's Christian books by mail.
Business Manager: Mr David Wavre. Executive staff 2, Other staff 8. Began 1997; non-denominational. Magazine: *The Christian Book Club* (Circulation n/a every two months). Turnover £900,000 to year end Dec 04.

Christian Books Direct, 54 Roseford Road, Cambridge CB4 2HD
☎01223 300 065 🖷01223 322 277
E: sales@christianbooksdirect.co.uk
Supplying books, CDs in the UK.
Proprietor: Mr Trevor Hames. Other staff 1. Began 1994; interdenominational. No magazine. Turnover £38,000 to year end Apr 05.

Christian Centre Services, Christian Centre, 71 High Road, Gorefield, Wisbech PE13 4NZ
☎01945 870 149
🖷01945 870 867
E: centre@christian-centre.com
Web: www.christian-centre.com
Distributing Christian books to bookshops; representing mainly USA and Canadian publishers; also Christian genealogy, crafts.
Trustee: Rev Leslie Warren. Executive Staff 1, Other staff 3. Began 1993; interdenominational. No magazine. Turnover £70,000 to year end Aug 04.

***Christian Communications Partnership Ltd**, PO Box 17911, London SW1P 4YX
☎020 7316 1300
🖷020 7316 1453
E: ccp@premier.org.uk
Web: www.youthwork.co.uk
Christian periodicals Publishing.
Chairman: David Heron. *Editoral Director:* John Buckeridge. *Advertising Manager:* Candy O'Donovon. Executive staff 2, Other staff 12. Began 1998; interdenominational. owned by Premier Radio and Spring Harvest. Turnover £1,100,000 to year end Sep 05.
Also at: Broadway House, The Broadway, Crowborough TN6 1HQ
☎01892 652 364

***Christian Literature Crusade**, 51 The Dean, Alresford SO24 9BJ
☎01962 733 142
🖷01962 733 141
E: clcwsale@aol.com
Web: www.clc.org.uk
Making evangelical literature available so that people may come to faith and maturity in Christ.
Head of Wholesale: Mr Roger Page. Executive staff 1, Other staff 9. **CC** No.1015793. Began 1941; evangelical. Magazine: *CLC World* (6,000 every two months). Turnover n/a.

Christian Music Ministries, 325 Bromford Road, Hodge Hill, Birmingham B36 8ET
☎0121 783 3291
🖷0121 785 0500
E: office@cmm.org.uk
Web: www.cmm.org.uk
Providing resources through mail-order catalogue, conferences training courses; publishing and recording Roger Jones' music.
Directors: Mr & Mrs Roger & Mary Jones. Executive staff 3, Other staff 4. **CC** No.516643. Began 1983; non-denominational. No magazine. Turnover £45,000 to year end Mar 96.

***Christian Pages**, PO Box 266, Staines TW18 4GP
☎0870 286 3190
🖷0870 286 3136
E: info@christianpages.org.uk
Web: www.christianpages.org.uk
Publishing local directories around the UK advertising Christian businesses and resourcing Christians in their locality.

Managing Directors: Katie Dodsworth, Barry Mockford. Executive staff 2, Other staff 1. Began 1997; interdenominational. (Previously Christian Business Directories & Christian Business Pages). Incorporating London Christian Business Directory. No magazine. Turnover £50,000 to year end Dec 04.

Christian Publishers' Representatives, 36 Causton Street, London SW1P 4ST
☎020 7592 3900
🖷020 7592 3939
E: sales@spck.org.uk
Representing a wide range of Christian publishers to the UK book trade.
Manager: Mr Alan Mordue. Executive staff 1, Other staff 5. Began 1972; non-denominational. No magazine. Turnover n/a.

***Christian Publishing & Outreach**, Garcia Estate, Canterbury Road, Worthing BN13 1BW
☎01903 264 556
ISDN 01903 830 005
🖷01903 830 066
E: enquiries@cpo.org.uk
Web: www.cpo.org.uk
Distributing Christian literature for evangelistic, pastoral and educational use.
Chief Executive: Mr Paul Slide. *Director of Production:* Mike Axell. Executive staff 4, Other staff 41. **CC** No.221462. Began 1957; non-denominational. Turnover n/a. Previously Christian Publicity Organisation.

B

Other Literature Producers & Distributors

B

Christian Weekly Newspapers Ltd, Fourth Floor, Central House, 142 Central Street, London EC1V 8AR
☎020 7417 5800 M: 07941 041 959
🖷020 7216 6410
E: cen@parlicom.com
Web: www.churchnewspaper.com
Trustees of The Church of England Newspaper.
Chairman: Mr Robert Leach. Executive staff 1, Other staff n/a. ***CC*** No.270655. Began 1976; Anglican. No magazine. Turnover n/a.

***Christmas Letters to Prisoners**, 52a Whitehorse Lane, London SE25 6RE
☎020 8653 3563
E: info@christmasletters.org.uk
Sending hand-written Christmas letters to prisoners.
Administrator: Mr Graham Tullett. Executive staff 1. ***CC*** No.210053. Began 1880; non-denominational. No magazine. Turnover n/a.

Churchwarden Publications Ltd, 36 High Street, Sutton Veny, Warminster BA12 7AW
☎01985 840 189 🖷01985 840 243
E: churchwardens@btinternet.com
Publishing and distributing books for churchwardens and PCC members.
Managing Director: Mr John Stidolph. Executive staff 2, Admin staff 1. Began 1998; Anglican. Magazine: *The Churchwarden's Yearbook* (5,000 annually). Turnover £60,000 to year end Sep 02.

***Cloisters**, Northumbria Community Trading Ltd, Hetton Hall, Chatton, Alnwick NE66 5SD
☎01289 388 235 🖷01289 388 510
E: cloisters@northumbriacommunity.org
Web: www.northumbriacommunity.org
Mail order sales of items from the Northumbria Community: books, music, cards, stained glass ornaments.
Administrator: Brenda Grace. Staff 1. Began 1994; non-denominational. No magazine. Turnover n/a.

Courtenay Bindery, Acacia Court, Appleford, Abingdon OX14 4PA
☎01235 848 319
Specialising in restoration and sale of high quality and leather books, antiquarian and modern.
Director: Ms Elizabeth Collie. Executive staff 1, Other staff n/a. Began 1963; non-denominational. Part of Appleford Publishing Group. No magazine. Turnover n/a.

†**Cross Publications**, The Old Bakehouse, 1242a Evesham Road, Astwood Bank, Redditch B96 6AA
☎01527 892 945 🖷01527 892 152
E: cross.publications@virgin.net
Publishing and producing diocesan newspapers.
Advertising Manager: Mrs S Williams. Executive staff 1, Admin staff 6. Began 2002; non-denominational. No magazine. Turnover n/a.

Crux Press, Gwelfryn, Llanidloes Road, Newtown SY16 4HX
☎01686 623 484
Web: booksmid-wales.net
Stocking titles previously published by Crux Press.
Proprietor: Mr Alick Hartley. Executive staff 1. Began 1988; non-denominational. Part of Impart Books. No magazine. Turnover n/a.

Decani Music Ltd, Oak House, 70 High Street, Brandon IP27 0AU
☎0845 456 8392 🖷01842 819 832
E: sue@decanimusic.co.uk
Web: www.decanimusic.co.uk
Publishing and distributing liturgy and music resources.
Editor/Director: Mr Stephen Dean. Executive staff 3, Other staff 2. Began 1991; non-denominational. Magazine: *The Liturgy Planner* (1,700 every four months), *Pastoral Patterns* (Circulation n/a every four months). Turnover n/a.

***Deo Gloria Trust**, Selsdon House, 212-220 Addington Road, South Croydon CR2 8LD
☎020 8651 6428 🖷020 8651 6429
E: lit@deo-gloria.co.uk
Web: www.deo-gloria.co.uk
Producing and distributing outreach materials; providing small grants for evangelistic purposes.
Director: Mr Eric Thompson. Executive staff 2, Other staff 4. ***CC*** No.243305. Began 1965; non-denominational. Magazine: *Newsletter* (7,500 annually). Turnover n/a.

†**James A Dickson Books**, Unit 25, Eldin Industrial Estate, Edgefield Road, Loanhead EH20 9QX
☎0131 448 0701
Mail order of new, antiquarian and second-hand theological books.
Manager: Mr J Dickson. Executive staff 1, Other staff 2. Began 1970; interdenominational. No magazine. Turnover n/a.

Dorchester House Publications, PO Box 67, Rickmansworth WD3 5SJ
☎01923 286 080 🖷01923 286 080
E: spiritof88@hotmail.com
Web: www.dorchesterhouse.net
Publishing books about Roman Catholicism and Islam in the light of the Christian Gospel.
Director: Mr Michael de Semlyen. Executive staff 1. ***CC*** No.327574. Began 1993; non-denominational. No magazine. Turnover n/a.

Dovewell Communications, Monarch House, PO Box 9161, London W3 6GS
☎020 7727 8684 🖷020 8799 6101
Web: www.dovewell.com
Producing and publishing Christian books, audio and video products; bookshop, mail order and online.
Head of Publications, Sales & Marketing: Mr Marko Joensuu. Executive staff 2, Other staff 14. ***CC*** No.251549. Began 1982; Pentecostal. Magazine: *Revival Times* (10,000 monthly). Turnover £400,000 to year end Dec 00.

Drummond Trust (Incorporating Stirling Tract Enterprise), 3 Pitt Terrace, Stirling FK8 2EY
☎01786 450 985 🖷01786 451 360
E: douglaswhyte@hillandrobb.co.uk
Giving financial assistance for publications of Christian doctrine and outreach.
Secretaries: Hill & Robb, Solicitors. No full-time staff. ***CC*** No.SCO 11077. Began 1848; non-denominational. No magazine. Turnover £18,000 to year end Dec 04.

Eden.co.uk. Christian Bookshop, Chester Enterprise Centre, Hoole Bridge, Chester CH2 3NE
☎01244 350 994 🖷01244 350 995
E: gareth@edeninteractive.co.uk
Web: www.eden.co.uk
Online Christian bookshop.
Managing Director: Mr Gareth Mulholland. Executive staff 2, Admin staff 10. Began 2004; non-denominational. Turnover included in Eden Interactive.

Educational Resources, 23 Woodcote Road, Wallington SM6 0LH
☎020 8669 5961 M: 07869 127 191
E: edresources@fsmail.net
Retailing educational learning aids, books, Bible games, health guides, school and church, tuition centre, resource centre.
Proprietor: Mrs Joyce Morrison. Executive staff 1, Other staff n/a. Began 2000; interdenominational. No magazine. Turnover n/a.

Alan & Margaret Edwards, 10 Meteor Avenue, Whitstable CT5 4DH
☎01227 262 276 🖷01227 261 1[illegible]8
E: a.m.books@lineone.net
Selling second-hand and new books (church history, theology, liturgy) by post, finding out-of-print titles.
Partners: Mr & Mrs Alan & Margaret Edwards. Executive staff 2. Began 1988; non-denominational. No magazine. Turnover n/a.

†**Egon Publishers Ltd**, Royston Road, Baldock SG7 6NW
☎01462 894 498 🖷01462 894 6[illegible]0
E: information@egon.co.uk
Web: www.egon.co.uk
Marketing Christian books and educational books, primary schools numeracy and literature.
Managing Director: Mr John Street. Executive staff 5, Other staff 6. Began 1974; non-denominational. No magazine. Turnover n/a.

Evangelical Sisterhood of Mary, 17 Gills Hill Lane, Radlett WD7 8DE
☎01923 856 316 🖷01923 853 25[illegible]
E: sisters@marysisters.freeserve.co.uk
Web: www.kanaan.org
Distributing literature, cassettes, videos by M Basilea Schlink.
Sister-in-Charge: Sr Thekla [illegible]ildner. All voluntary staff. ***CC*** No.259421. Began 1969; interdenominational. No magazine. Turnover n/a.

Everlasting Books & Music Ltd, PO Box 2793, Walsall WS2 7YE
☎0870 745 5793 M: 07968 836 664
Fax 0870 745 5794
E: info@everlastingbooks.com
Web: www.everlastingbooks.com
Importing, distributing and publishing books, Bibles, video; UK and worldwide.
Managing Director: Mr David J Graham. Executive staff 2, Admin staff 2. Began 1996; interdenominational. No magazine. Turnover n/a.

Fairway Marketing Ltd, Rebecca Springs, Nadderwater, Exeter EX4 2JH
☎01392 424 610 M 07779 789 470
Fax 01392 274 396
E: sales@fairwaymarketing.ltd.uk
Marketing and distributing remainder and promotional Christian books and resources to the book trade.
Director: Mr John Robertson. Executive staff 2, Other staff 5. Began 1995; non-denominational. No magazine. Turnover n/a.

Faith Builders, PO Box 40, Knutsford WA16 9EW
☎01565 654 414 Fax 01565 652 706
E: enquiries@faithbuilders.co.uk
Web: www.faithbuilders.co.uk
Importing Christian faith building teaching books, audio and video tapes, calendars.
Partner: Miss Susan Spilman. Executive staff 5, Other staff 8. Began 1980; non-denominational. No magazine. Turnover n/a.

***Faith Mission Bookshop (Scotland)**, 548 Gilmerton Road, Edinburgh EH17 7JD
☎0131 672 2152 Fax 0131 672 2149
E: bookshops.scot@faithmission.org
Web: www.faithmission.org
Headquarters for Faith Mission bookshops in Scotland; Coffee shop.
General Manager, Bookshops: Norman Liddle. Executive staff 1, Other Staff 2. ***CC*** Began 1886; non-denominational. No magazine. Turnover n/a.

Family Worship Resources, 60 Kendale Road, Bromley BR1 4NH
☎020 8698 7201 Fax 020 8698 7201
E: mikeburn@familyworship.org.uk
Web: www.familyworship.org.uk
Providing resources to help the whole church to worship together.
Director: Mr Mike Burn. Executive staff 1. Began 1998; interdenominational. No magazine. Turnover £20,000 to year end Dec 05.

Free Presbyterian Publications, 133 Woodlands Road, Glasgow G3 6LE
☎0141 332 9283 Fax 0141 332 4271
E: fpchurch@btconnect.com
Web: www.fpchurch.org.uk
Publishing Christian literature.
General Treasurer: Mr Roderick A Campbell. Executive staff 1. ***CC*** No.SCO 03545. Began 1893; Presbyterian. Magazine: *Free Presbyterian Magazine* (2,000 monthly), *Young Peoples' Magazine* (1,800 monthly). Turnover £58,034 to year end Dec 04.

Gage Postal Books, PO Box 105, Westcliff-on-Sea SS0 8EQ
☎01702 715 133 Fax 01702 715 133
E: gagebooks@clara.net
Web: www.gagebooks.com
Buying and selling second-hand church history and theological books.
Proprietor: Mr Simon A Routh. Executive staff 1, Other staff 2. Began 1971; non-denominational. No magazine. Turnover £110,000 to year end Dec 04.

***Gates of Praise**, Vine Christian Centre, Australian Terrace, Bridgend CF31 1LY
☎01656 664 245 Fax 01656 662 252
E: sales@gatesofpraise.co.uk
Importing and distributing Christian literature and tapes to bookshops and churches.
Sales Manager: Mrs Wendy Perkins. Executive staff 1, Other staff 5. ***CC*** Began 1993; non-denominational. No magazine. Turnover n/a.

The Good Bookstall, 60 Godiva Road, Leominster HR6 8UQ
☎01568 615 989 Fax 01568 615 989
E: editor@thegoodbookstall.org.uk
Web: www.thegoodbookstall.org.uk
Online independent reviews for book agents and others to help in choice from Christian bookshops.
Editor: Mrs Mary Bartholomew. No paid staff. Began 1964; non-denominational. (Previously A Bookstalls Newsletter). No magazine. Turnover n/a.

Gospel Literature Outreach, 78 Muir Street, Motherwell ML1 1BN
☎01698 263 483 Fax 01698 275 418
E: admin@glo-europe.org
Web: www.glo-europe.org
Distributing Christian literature through teams operating worldwide; church planting; training for Christian service.
Co-ordinator, Europe: Mr John Speirs. All voluntary staff. ***CC*** No.SCO 41802. Began 1974; Christian Brethren. Magazine: *Spearhead* (4,500 every four months). Turnover n/a.

Guardian Gifts, Saxon's Farm, Birch, Heywood OL10 2QB
☎01706 625 258 Fax 01706 622 628
E: sales@guardiangifts.com
Web: www.guardiangifts.com
Supplying Christian books, music and gifts online or mail order.
Director: Mr D Court. Executive staff 1, Other staff n/a. Began 2000; interdenominational. No magazine. Turnover n/a.

Harvest Field Distributors, Harvest Fields, Unit 17, Churchill Business Park, Churchill Road, Doncaster DN1 2TF
☎01302 367 868 Fax 01302 361 006
E: harvestfields@theway.co.uk
Web: www.harvestfieldsuk.co.uk
Distributing Bibles, books, cards, CDs, cassettes, games, pictures and gift ideas to Christian bookshops.
Manager: Mr Andrew Golba. Executive staff 1, Other staff 9. Began 1990; non-denominational. No magazine. Turnover n/a.

Heartworks Ltd, B21 Valley Business Centre, 67 Church Road, Newtownabbey BT36 7LS
☎028 9055 2789
M: 7802 466 302
Fax 028 9055 2789
E: mail@heartworks.co.uk
Web: www.heartworks.co.uk
Wholesale distributor of greeting cards, gifts, stationery to Christian book trade.
Director: Rev Robert McEvoy. Executive staff 2, Other staff 2. Began 1990; non-denominational. (Previously OBS Print). No magazine. Turnover n/a.

B

Humber Books, Rozel House, 4 St Marys Lane, Barton-upon-Humber DN18 5EX
☎01652 634 958
Fax 01652 634 965
E: pmc@humberbooks.co.uk
Web: www.humberbooks.co.uk
Retailing antiquarian theological books and Bibles; specialising in the Protestant Reformation and English Puritanism. Nonconforming.
Proprietors: Mr & Mrs P M Cresswell. Executive staff 2. Began 1972; non-denominational. Magazine: *Antiquarian Theology* (Circulation n/a every two months), *Antiquarian Bibles* (Circulation n/a twice yearly). Turnover n/a.

Jarom Books, 18 Rigby Close, Croydon CR0 4JU
☎020 8680 3635
Fax 07971 117 510
E: mail@jarom.net
Web: www.jarom.net
Publishing new Christian monographs, booklets and books.
Manager: Mr Jacques R More. No full-time staff. Began 1993; non-denominational. No magazine. Turnover n/a.

***Kitab**, PO Box 315, Oldham OL1 3YW
☎0161 678 6838
Fax 0161 678 6838
E: kitab.uk@domini.org
Web: www.kitab.org.uk
Supplying Christian and secular books, videos, on the Muslim world, including foreign and minority languages.
Manager: Mr Alan Howell. Executive staff 1, Other staff 4. ***CC*** No.1020758. Began 1989; non-denominational. Owned by Interserve. Magazine: *Ahl-i-Kitab* (1,400 every four months). Turnover £15,000 to year end Dec 04.

A M Laverty & Co Ltd, Marian House, Otley LS21 3JG
☎01943 462 032
Fax 01943 462 032
Web: www.amlaverty.co.uk
Wholesaling devotional and religious articles.
Director: Mr E C Laverty. Executive staff 2, Other staff 4. Began 1955; Roman Catholic. No magazine. Turnover n/a.

Other Literature Producers & Distributors

***Leadership Bookclub**, 6 Norton Street, Nottingham NG7 3HR
☎0115 978 1054 🖷0115 942 2694
E: ivp@ivpbooks.com
Web: www.ivpbooks.com
Bookclub exclusively for church leaders.
Bookclub Editor: Mr Daryl Wearring. Executive staff 1, Admin staff 2. ***CC*** No.273458. Began 1936; non-denominational. Part of IVP. Magazine: Name not supplied (Circulation n/a quarterly). Turnover included in IVP.

Liberty Books, 31 Hambledon Gardens, Blandford Forum DT11 7SE
☎01258 450 097 🖷01258 450 097
E: sales@libertybooks.co.uk
Web: www.libertybooks.co.uk
Selling second-hand Christian books by catalogue and internet to finance mission.
Manager: Mr Steve Green. Executive staff 1. Began 2002; non-denominational. No magazine. Turnover n/a.

†Maranatha Christian Ministries Resource Centre International, PO Box 506, Portslade, Brighton BN41 2ZG
☎01273 414 990 🖷01273 700 116
Supplying Bibles, cassettes, electronic Bibles, books, greeting cards, gifts.
Director: Mr Eric Long. No full-time staff. Began 1987; interdenominational. No magazine. Turnover n/a.

New Life Publishing, PO Box 777, Nottingham NG11 6ZZ
☎0115 921 7280 🖷0115 984 5251
E: info@newlifepublishing.co.uk
Web: www.newlifepublishing.co.uk
Publishers of New Life Newspaper, *Christian magazines and books.*
Editor: Mr Peter Wreford. Executive staff 2, Other staff 5. Began 1982; interdenominational. No magazine. Turnover n/a.

Onesimus Books and Music, PO Box 170, Fishponds, Bristol BS16 5XN
☎01179 109 308
E: OnesimusBooksUK@aol.com
Mail order book service with 2,000 new and 6,000 second-hand titles.
Proprietor: Mr Chris J Mansfield. Executive staff 2, Other staff 1. Began 1986; non-denominational. No magazine. Turnover n/a.

Orthodox Christian Books Ltd, Unit 1, High Carr Network Centre, Millennium Way, High Carr Business Park, Newcastle ST5 7XE
☎01782 576 933 🖷01782 576 930
E: orthbook@aol.com
Web: www.orthodoxbooks .co.uk
European distributors, book wholesalers, mail order, retail (over 5,000 titles); CDs, greeting cards, mounted icon-prints.
Managing Director: Nicholas Chapman. Executive staff 7, Other staff 3. Began 1993; Orthodox. No magazine. Turnover n/a.

Overseas Tract Mission, 109 Avondale Crescent, Grange, Cardiff CF11 7DF
☎029 2034 5342
Publishing and distributing foreign Gospel literature in Britain.
Director: Mr Fred K Dodds. Executive staff 1, Other staff 1. Began 1940; interdenominational. No magazine. Turnover n/a.

Parish & People, The Old Mill, Spetisbury, Blandford Forum DT11 9DF
☎01258 453 939
E: pandpeople@tiscali.co.uk
Web: www.parishandpeople.org.uk
Producing the Deanery Exchange *to help deaneries work more effectively.*
Secretary/Partner: Rev Jimmy Hamilton-Brown. No full-time staff. Began 1980; Anglican. Imprints: Parish & People. Turnover n/a.

Penfold Book and Bible House Ltd, Unit M3, Telford Road, Industrial Estate, Bicester OX26 4LD
☎01869 249 574 🖷01869 244 033
E: penfoldbooks@characterlink.net
Web: www.penfoldbooks.com or www.webtruth.org
Distributing evangelical books, videos, dvds.
Managing Director: Mr Michael J Penfold. *Warehouse Manager:* Mr Nicholas Harvey. *Secretary:* Mrs Lucy West. Executive staff 1, Other staff 2. Began 1986; non-denominational. No magazine. Turnover £513,000 to year end Nov 04.

Perivale Christian Distributors, 184 Horsenden Lane South, Perivale, Greenford UB6 7NT
☎020 8998 2940 🖷020 8998 2940
E: peribooks@christnetbooks.co.uk
Web: www.christnetbooks.co.uk/peribooks
Distributing Christian products to Christian bookshops throughout the UK.
Director: Rev Colin Taylor. Executive staff 1, Other staff 2. ***CC*** No.293404. Began 1986; non-denominational. No magazine. Turnover n/a.

Pewsey Christian Bookshop, The Old Rectory, River Street, Pewsey SN9 5DB
☎01672 564 938 🖷01672 565 030
E: info@barnabasfund.org
Specialising in books on Islam and Christianity; mail order only.
Manager: Mrs R Sookhdeo. Executive staff 1. Began 1979; interdenominational. (Previously St Andrews Bookshop (SFI) Ltd). No magazine. Turnover £54,000 to year end Aug 98.

Praise Him Ltd, 46a Constitution Street, Edinburgh EH6 6RS
☎0131 467 2827 🖷0131 467 2829
E: support@praise-him.org
Web: www.praise-him.org
Online bookshop.
Manager: Miss Carol Dawson. Executive staff 1, Admin staff 1. Began 2000; non-denominational. Turnover n/a.

Praise Trust, PO Box 359, Darlington DL3 8YD
☎01325 380 232 (sales only)
Web: www.praise.org.uk
Publisher of Praise! Hymnbook, Praise!.
Secretary: Mr Bob Campen. No full-time staff. ***CC*** No.1056529. Began 1996; interdenominational. No magazine. Turnover £20,000 to year end Dec 04.

Derek Prince Ministries - UK, Kingsfield, Hadrian Way, Baldock SG7 6AN
☎01462 492 100
🖷 01462 492 102
E: enquiries@dpmuk.org
Web: www.dpmuk.org
Conference facilities, accommodation, seminar rooms; prayer and training events; church, Alpha, youth weekends.
Director: Neil Cornick. Executive staff 3, Other staff 6. ***CC*** No.32[illegible]763. Began 1983; interdenominational. (Previously (Derek Prince Ministries - UK) DPM-UK). Magazine: *Proclamation* (Circulation n/a quarterly). Turnover n/a.

Protestant Truth Society Inc and the Wickliffe Preachers, 184 Fleet Street, London EC4A 2HJ
☎020 7405 4960
E: ptslondon@btconnect.com
Web: www.protestant-truth.org
Furthering of Christ's gospel and promoting the Protestant Reformed religion and faith.
Secretary: Mr George Rae. Trustees 12. ***CC*** No.248505. Began 1[illegible]89; interdenominational. No magazine. Turnover £78,000 to year end Mar 0[illegible].

Rosemary Pugh Second Hand Books, 59b Old Sarum Airfield, Salisbury SP4 6DZ
☎01722 330 132
🖷01722 330 132
E: rosemarypugh@btopenworld.com
Web: www.rosemarypughbooks.com
Mail order distribution of secondhand books with 15,000 titles in stock.
Owner: Mrs Rosemary M Pugh. Staff 1. Began 1991; non-denominational. (Previously Pugh & Greatrex Second Hand Books). No magazine. Turnover n/a.

Renewal Servicing, PO Box [illegible]53, Staines TW18 3WL
☎No telephone
E:richards@renewal-servicing.freeserve.co.uk
Web: www.helpforchristians.co.uk
Providing articles, hymns on renewal, healing and Christian living copyright waived.
Hon Director: Rev John Richards. All voluntary staff. ***CC*** No.2830[illegible]4. Began 1[illegible]81; interdenominational. No magazine. Turnover £2,700 to year end Jan 96.

Roots for Churches Ltd, Bastille Court, 2 Paris Garden, London SE1 8ND
☎020 7654 7254
🖷020 7654 7222
E: roots@ctbi.org.uk
Web: www.rootsontheweb.com
Publishing magazines of lectionary-based resources for worship leaders and children's/youth leaders in all churches.
Project Director: Ms Elizabeth Marsh. Executive staff 3. ***CC*** No.1097[illegible]66. Began 2002; ecumenical. Magazine: *Roots* (16,000 every two months). Turnover n/a.

***The RZIM Zacharias Trust**, 97a St Aldates, Oxford OX1 1BT
☎01865 203 951 🖷01865 203 950
E: office@zactrust.org
Web: www.zactrust.org
Involved in evangelism, apologetics, training; aiming to reach the sceptic with the Gospel.
European Director: Mr Michael Ramsden. Executive staff 2, Other staff 5. ***CC*** No.1067314. Began 1998; non-denominational. (Previously Zacharias Trust). Magazine: *Just Thinking* (65,000 every four months). Turnover £334,000 to year end Dec 04.

***Send The Light Ltd**, PO Box 300, Kingstown Broadway, Carlisle CA3 0QS
☎01228 512 512 🖷01228 514 949
E: info@stl.org
Web: www.stl.org
Distributing, wholesaling, publishing and retailing of Christian books, music and software.
Chief Executive: Mr Keith Danby. *Deputy Chief Executive:* Mr Eddie Olliffe. *Director of Finance:* Ms Janet Rusk. Executive staff 24, Other staff 515. ***CC*** No.270162. Began 1963; non-denominational. Magazine: *The Bulletin* (25,000 monthly). Turnover £30,000,000 to year end Dec 00.

Shiloh House Distribution, PO Box 10147, Birmingham B14 6WD
M: 07866 747 387 🖷07866 747 387
E:tim@shilohhousedistribution.wanadoo.co.uk
Distributing new and second-hand christian literature by mail order.
Manager: Mr Tim MacLeod. Executive staff 1. Began 2004; non-denominational. No magazine. Turnover n/a.

***South Park Community Trust**, Church Farm House, Wokingham Road, Hurst, Reading RG10 0RX
☎0118 934 0944
E: PgaviganSPCT@aol.com
Administrator: Ms Patricia Beall Gavigan. Admin staff 1, Other staff n/a. ***CC*** No.292234. Began 1985; ecumenical. No magazine. Turnover n/a.

Sovereign Grace Advent Testimony, 1 Donald Way, Chelmsford CM2 9JB
☎01245 268 815
E: satoms@sgat.fsnet.co.uk
Web: www.sgat.org
Providing exposition of Bible doctrine and prophecy by literature and meetings.
Hon Secretary: Mr Stephen A Toms. No full-time staff. ***CC*** No.261489. Began 1918; interdenominational. Magazine: *Watching and Waiting* (3,000 quarterly). Turnover n/a.

SPCK Bookshops Head Office, 36 Causton Street, London SW1P 4ST
☎020 7592 3900 🖷020 7643 0389
E: spck@spck.org.uk
Web: www.spck.org.uk
Supplying Christian books, gifts and resources through SPCK's bookshops, mail order , and SPCK online.
Bookshop & Finance Manager: Mr Malcolm Munro-Faure. *General Secretary:* Mr Simon Kingston. Executive staff 1. ***CC*** No.231144. Began 1698; interdenominational. Society for Promoting Christian Knowledge. No magazine. Turnover included in SPCK.
SPCK Bookshops Mail Order
E: mailorder@spck.org.uk
Web: www.spckonline.com

Speaking Volumes (CBPT), 54 Roseford Road, Cambridge CB4 2HD
☎01223 300 065 🖷01223 322 277
E: info@speakingvolumes.org.uk
Web: www.speakingvolumes.org.uk
Helping Churches donate Christian books to libraries by offering 50% off ; bi-annual UK Christian Book Awards.
Proprietor: Mr Trevor Hames. Executive staff 1, Other staff 1. ***CC*** No.255001. Began 1972; interdenominational. (Previously Christian Book Promotion Trust). No magazine. Turnover n/a.

†***Startwrite**, New Life Bible Church, 1 Graham Road, Wealdstone, Harrow HA3 5RP
☎020 8427 0985 🖷020 8427 6297
E: jeyu@talk21.com
Specialising in leadership, counselling and teaching books; distributor for City Bible Publishing; audio tapes ministry.
IT Manager: Mr John Udoh. Other staff 4. ***CC*** No.295876. Began 1982; non-denominational. No magazine. Turnover n/a.

Stone Publishing Trust, The Eagles, Headcorn Road, Staplehurst, Tonbridge TN12 0BU
☎01580 892 843
Publishing two Christian magazines and free distribution of Christian literature.
Secretary: Mr Mark Lemon. No full-time staff. ***CC*** No.1034689. Began 1993; non-denominational. Magazine: *Living Water* (1,000 every two months). Turnover £15,000 to year end Dec 04.

Symphony Sales & Distribution Ltd, 5b Arrow Trading Estate, Corporation Road, Audenshaw, Manchester M34 5LR
☎0161 320 7684 🖷0161 320 4162
E: info@symphonysalesanddistribution.co.uk
Web: www.symphonysalesand distribution.co.uk
Distributing Bibles, books, music, software, baptismal and dedication certificates, cards, crafts, gifts and novelties.
Director: Mr Keith Todhunter. Executive staff 1, Other staff 4. Began 1993. (Previously Horizons Distributors). No magazine. Turnover n/a.

Teal Press Ltd, Unit 12, Bunns Bank, Old Buckenham, Attleborough NR17 1QD
☎01953 455 718 🖷01953 455 190
E: info@tealpress.co.uk
Web: www.tealpress.co.uk
Greetings card and gift publishers and wholesalers.
Director: Mr A Sayers. Executive staff 3, Other staff 10. Began 1985; non-denominational. Incorporating Spearhead Publishers. No magazine. Turnover n/a.

***TELit,** 144a Ferry Road, Edinburgh EH6 4NX ☎0131 554 0339
🖷0131 554 2330
E: info@telitquick.org
Web: telitquick.org
Publishing thematic evangelistic literature in a contemporary format for specific places, events and everyday activities.
Managing Director: Mr Barry Sprott. Executive staff 1, Other staff 1. ***CC*** No.SCO 08979. Began 1990; non-denominational. Magazine: *Newsletter* (Circulation n/a quarterly). Turnover n/a.

Ten Of Those, 7 Silverstream Close, Bangor BT20 3GZ
☎028 9127 7117
Web: www.tenofthose.com
Website selling Christian books at discounts for quantities over 10.
Proprietor: Mr Jonathan Carswell. No full-time staff. Began 2006; non-denominational. Turnover n/a.

Tim Tiley Products, 33 Zetland Road, Bristol BS6 7AH
☎0117 942 3397
🖷0117 942 0433
E: sales@timtiley.com
Web: www.timtiley.com
Producing and importing verse cards, bookmarks, small posters, frames, Christian gifts and novelties.
Managing Director: Mr Timothy F T Tiley. *Administration Manager:* Mrs Margaret Tiley. Executive staff 3, Other staff 8. Began 1974; non-denominational. No magazine. Turnover £578,000 to year end Dec 04.

Victory European Ministries, PO Box 204, Southfleet, Gravesend DA13 9LG
☎01474 833 107
🖷01474 833 107
E: faith@victoryeuropeanmins.freeserve.co.uk
European distribution of materials by Dr Hobart E Freeman, Faith Ministries & Publications, Dr Russell K Tardo, Faithful Word Ministries & Publications.
Directors: Mr & Mrs Roger & Wendy Harris. Executive staff 1. Began 1988; non-denominational. No magazine. Turnover n/a.

***Victory Tracts and Posters**, Victory House, Portland Road, London SE25 4PN
☎0845 330 6745
M: 07984 467 151
🖷0845 330 6746
E: info@victorytracts.co.uk
Web: www.victorytracts.co.uk
Publishing salvation Gospel tracts, Bible text posters and a range of Answer Series booklets.
Director: Mr Mark Walford. Executive staff 1, Other staff 2. *CC* No.229741. Began 1945; interdenominational. No magazine. Turnover £15,000 to year end Jan 01.

B

Wesley Owen Direct, PO Box 19, Kingstown Broadway, Carlisle CA3 0BR
☎0800 834 315 🖷01228 514 949
E: wesleyowen@stl.org
Web: www.wesleyowen.com
Mail order department for Wesley Owen Books and Music.
Manager: Mr Mick Goodman. Executive staff 1, Other staff 8. ***CC*** Began n/a; interdenominational. No magazine. Turnover n/a.

***Word to the World Ministries International**, 20 Bishopric, Horsham RH12 1QN
☎0845 241 0991 M: 07802 287 112
E: word2theworld@waitrose.com
Web: www.word2theworld.co.uk
Director: Mrs Joanne Venkat. Executive staff 1, Other staff 4. ***CC*** No.1105062. Began 1986; non-denominational. (Previously Family Christian Bookstore) Turnover n/a. Supplying books online; Spanish speaking ministry: translating, printing, literature distribution, personal ministry; churches UK, overseas.

B

ROMAN CATHOLIC CATHEDRALS

(OMITTED IN ERROR FROM PAGE 138)

Aberdeen, Cathedral of St Mary of the Assumption, Cathedral Clergy House, 20 Huntly Street, Aberdeen AB1 1SH
☎01224-640160
Administrator: Very Rev Stuart Chalmers.

Argyll and the Isles, St Columba Cathedral, Cathedral House, Esplanade, Oban PA34 5AB
☎01631 562 123
Administrator: Very Rev Donald J MacKay.

Armagh, St Patrick's Cathedral, Parochial House, Abbey Street, Armagh BT61 7DZ
☎028 3752 2802
Administrator: Very Rev Pádraig Murphy.

Clogher, St Macartan's Cathedral, The Presbytery, Park Street, Monaghan, Republic of Ireland
☎00 353 478 1220
E: presbytery@eircom.net
Web: www.clogherdiocese.ie
Administrator: Very Rev Joseph McEaneny.

Down and Connor, St Peter's Cathedral, The Cathedral Presbytery, St Peter's Square, Belfast BT12 4BU
☎028 9032 7573 🖷 028 9032 5570
E: stpeterscathedralbelfast@hotmail.co.uk
Administrator: Rt Rev Mgr Thomas Toner.

Dromore, Cathedral of St Patrick and St Colman, The Presbytery, Hill Street, Newry BT34 1AT
☎028 3026 2586
Administrator: Rev Terence Rafferty.

Dunkeld, St Andrew's Cathedral, 150 Nethergate, Dundee DD1 4EA
☎01382 225 228
Administrator: Very Rev Steven P Mulholland.

Galloway, Good Shepherd Cathedral, Cathedral House, 37 Dalmilling Crescent, Ayr KA8 0QL
☎01292 265 716
Administrator: Very Rev John McGee.

Glasgow, St Andrew's Metropolitan Cathedral, 90 Dunlop Street, Glasgow G1 4ER
☎0141 221 3096
E: administrator@cathedral12.freeserve.co.uk
Administer: Very Rev Christopher J McElroy.

Motherwell, Our Lady of Good Aid Cathedral, Cathedral House, 31 Coursington Road, Motherwell ML1 1PW
☎01698 263 045
E: motherwellcathedral@supanet.com
Administrator: Very Rev Noel Carey

Paisley, St Mirin's Cathedral, Cathedral House, 8 East Buchanan Street, Paisley PA1 1HS
☎0141 889 2404
Administrator: Very Rev Mgr Gerard Brennan.

CHURCHES

C

CATHEDRALS

ROMAN CATHOLIC DIOCESES

For Roman Catholic Cathedrals not listed here see page 136

Arundel and Brighton, Cathedral Church of Our Lady and St Philip Howard, Cathedral House, Parsons Hill, Arundel BN18 9AY
☎01903 882 297 🖷01903 885 335
E: aruncath1@aol.com
Web: www.arundelcathedral.org
Dean: Rev Timothy Madeley. ***CC*** No.252878. Began 1873.

Birmingham, Metropolitan Cathedral Church of St Chad, Cathedral House, St Chads Queensway, Birmingham B4 6EU
☎0121 236 2251 🖷0121 230 6279
E: cathedral.dean@rc-birmingham.org
Web: www.birminghamdiocese.org.uk
Mother Church of Roman Catholic Archdiocese of Birmingham and Minor Basilica. Dean: Rev Father Brian Doolan. *Cathedral Secretary:* Mrs Alwen Griffiths. ***CC*** No.234216.

Brentwood, Cathedral Church of St Mary and St Helen, Clergy House, 28 Ingrave Road, Brentwood CM15 8AT
☎01277 265 235
Web: www.brentwood-cathedral.co.uk
Dean: Mgr William Nix. ***CC*** No.234092.

Cardiff, Metropolitan Cathedral Church of St David, Cathedral Clergy House, St David's Cathedral, Charles Street, Cardiff CF10 2SF
☎029 2023 1407 🖷029 2023 1407
Dean: Rev Canon Peter Collins.

Clifton, Cathedral Church of St Peter and St Paul, Clifton Cathedral House, Clifton Park, Bristol BS8 3BX
☎0117 973 8411 🖷0117 974 4897
E: cathedral@cliftondiocese.com
Web: www.cliftoncathedral.org.uk
Parish Priest: Rev Canon Robert Corrigan. ***CC*** No.233977.

Derry, Cathedral Church of St Eugene, Parochial House, Francis Street, Londonderry BT48 9AP
☎028 7126 2894/7136 5712
🖷028 7137 7494
E: steugenesderry@btconnect.com
Administrator: Very Rev Michael Canny.

East Anglia, Cathedral Church of St John the Baptist, Cathedral House, Unthank Road, Norwich NR2 2PA
☎01603 624 615 🖷01603 623 684
E: enq@stjohncathedral.co.uk
Web: www.stjohncathedral.co.uk
Dean: Rev James Walsh.

Hallam, Cathedral Church of Saint Marie, Cathedral House, Norfolk Street, Sheffield S1 2JB
☎0114 272 2522 🖷0114 276 3861
E: office@stmariecathedral.org
Web: www.stmariecathedral.org
Administrator: Rev Father Desmond Sexton.

Hexham and Newcastle, Cathedral Church of St Mary, Clayton Street West, Newcastle upon Tyne NE1 5HH
☎0191 232 6953 🖷0191 239 5708
E: office@stmaryscathedral.org.uk
Web: www.stmaryscathedral.org.uk
Also bookshop.
Dean: Rev Michael Campion. ***CC*** No.235686. Began 1844.

Lancaster, Cathedral Church of St Peter, Cathedral House Presbytery, Balmoral Road, Lancaster LA1 3BT
☎01524 384 820 🖷01524 384 831
E: clergy@lancastercathedral.org.uk
Web: www.lancastercathedral.org.uk
Administrator: Very Rev Canon Stephen Shield. ***CC*** No.234331.

Leeds, Cathedral Church of St Anne, Cathedral House, Great George Street, Leeds LS2 8BE
☎0113 245 4545 🖷0113 245 3626
E: info@leedscathedral.com
Web: www.dioceseofleeds.org.uk/cathedral
Dean: Rev Martin Kelly.

Liverpool, Metropolitan Cathedral of Christ the King, Cathedral House, Mount Pleasant, Liverpool L3 5TQ
☎0151 709 9222 🖷0151 708 7274
E: enquiries@metcathedral.org.uk
Web: www.liverpoolmetcathedral.org.uk
Administrator: Mgr Canon Peter Cookson. ***CC*** No.232709.

Menevia, Cathedral Church of St Joseph, Convent Street, Greenhill, Swansea SA1 2BX
☎01792 652 683
E: stjosephscathedral@btinternet.com
Dean: Rev Canon Michael Flook. Menevia.

Middlesbrough, Cathedral Church of St Mary, Cathedral House, Dalby Way, Coulby Newham, Middlesbrough TS8 0TW
☎01642 597 750 🖷01642 576 971
Dean: Mgr Canon Ricardo Morgan.

Northampton, Cathedral of Our Lady and St Thomas, Cathedral House, Kingsthorpe Road, Northampton NN2 6AG
☎01604 714 556
E: office@northamptoncathedral.org
Web: www.northamptoncathedral.org
Dean: Canon Fr John Udris.

Nottingham, Cathedral Church of St Barnabas, North Circus Street, Nottingham NG1 5AE
☎0115 953 9839/9840 🖷0115 959 8112
E: stbarnabas@tiscali.co.uk
Web: www.stbarnabasnottingham.org.uk
Dean: Mgr Tom McGovern VG.

Plymouth, Cathedral Church of St Mary and St Boniface, Cathedral House, 45 Cecil Street, Plymouth PL1 5HW
☎01752 662 537 🖷01752 223 [illegible]50
E: parish@plycathedral.f9.co.uk
Web: www.plymouthcathedral.co.uk
Dean: Rev Canon Bartholomew Nannery.

Portsmouth, Cathedral Church of St John the Evangelist, Edinburgh Road, Portsmouth PO1 3HG
☎023 9282 6170 🖷023 9283 9[illegible]43
E: stjcath@btconnect.com
Web: www.portsmouthcatholiccathedral.org
Dean: Rev Canon David Hopgood. *Cathedral Priest:* Fr Steven Restori ***CC*** No.246871.

St Andrews and Edinburgh, Metropolitan Cathedral of St Mary, Cathedral House, 61 York Place, Edinburgh EH1 3JD
☎0131 556 1798 / 0027
🖷0131 556 4281
E: cathedralhouse@stmaryscathedral.co.uk
Web: www.stmaryscathedral.co.uk
Also restaurant and coffee shop.
Administrator: Very Rev David Gemmell.

Salford, Cathedral Church of St John the Evangelist
Information withheld

Shrewsbury, Cathedral Church of our Lady Help of Christians and St Peter of Alcantara, Cathedral House, 11 Belmont, Shrewsbury SY1 1TE
☎01743 362 366
E: shrewsbury.cathedral@btinternet.com
Web: www.shrewsburycathedral.org
Dean: Rev Stephen Coonan.

Southwark, Metropolitan Cathedral of St George, Clergy House, Westminster Bridge Road, Southwark, London SE1 7HY
☎020 7928 5256 🖷020 7202 21[illegible]
E: info@southwark-rc-cathedral.org.uk
Web: www.southwark-rc-cathedral.org.uk
Dean: Rev Canon James Cronin. ***CC*** No.235468. Began 1848.

Westminster, Metropolitan Cathedral of the Most Precious Blood, Cathedral Clergy House, 42 Francis Street, London SW1P 1QW
☎020 7798 9055 🖷020 7798 90[illegible]0
E: mlangham@rcdow.org.uk
Web: www.westminstercathedral.org.uk
Administrator: Rev Mark Langham. ***CC*** No.233699.

Wrexham, Cathedral Church of Our Lady of Sorrows, Regent Street Wrexham LL11 1RB
☎01978 263 943 🖷01978 352 27[illegible]
E: office@wrexhamcathedral.org.uk
Web: www.wrexhamcathedral.org.uk
Dean: Rev Peter M Brignall. ***CC*** No.700426.

CHURCH IN WALES DIOCESES

Bangor, Cathedral Church of St Deiniol, Diocesan Centre, Cathedral Close, Bangor LL57 1RL
☎01248 353 983 ℻01248 353 983
E: martinbrown@churchinwales.org.uk
Web: www.esgobaethbangordiocese.org
Also bookshop.
Dean: Very Rev Alun Hawkins. *Cathedral Administrator:* Mr Martin Brown.

Llandaff, Cathedral Church of St Peter and St Paul, Administrative Office, Perbenbal House, Llandaff, Cardiff CF5 2LA
☎029 2056 4554 ℻029 2056 3897
E: office@llandaffcathedral.org.uk
Web: www.llandaffcathedral.org.uk
Dean: Very Rev John T Lewis.

Monmouth, Cathedral Church of St Woolos, Stow Hill, Newport NP20 4EA
☎01633 212 077 ℻01633 254 896
Dean: Very Rev Richard Fenwick. *Administrator:* Mr Brian Cox. ***CC*** No.X28607.

St Asaph, Cathedral Church of St Asaph, Cathedral Office, High Street, St Asaph LL17 0RD
☎01745 583 429 ℻01745 583 566
E: adminstasaph@churchinwales.org.uk
Web: www.dioceseofstasaph.org.uk
Dean: Very Rev Christopher Potter. *Administrator:* Karen Williams.

St Davids, Cathedral Church of St David and St Andrew, The Deanery, St Davids, Haverfordwest SA62 6RU
☎01437 720 199 ℻01437 721 194
E: info@stdavidscathedral.org.uk
Web: www.stdavidscathedral.org.uk
Dean: Very Rev J Wyn Evans. *Administrator:* Moyra Skenfield.

Swansea and Brecon, Cathedral Church of St John the Evangelist, Cathedral Office, Cathedral Close, Brecon LD3 9DP
☎01874 623 857 ℻01874 623 716
E: admin@breconcathedral.org.uk
Web: www.breconcathedral.org.uk
Dean: Very Rev John D E Davies.

CHURCH OF ENGLAND DIOCESES

Bath and Wells, Cathedral Church of St Andrew in Wells, Cathedral Office, Chain Gate, Cathedral Green, Wells BA5 2UE
☎01749 674 483 ℻01749 832 210
E: office@wellscathedral.uk.net
Web: www.wellscathedral.org.uk
Dean: To be appointed. Turnover n/a.

***Birmingham**, Cathedral Church of St Philip, Birmingham Cathedral, Colmore Row, Birmingham B3 2QB
☎0121 262 1840 ℻0121 262 1860
E: enquiries@birminghamcathedral.com
Web: www.birminghamcathedral.com
Dean: Very Rev Robert Wilkes. Turnover n/a.

Blackburn, Cathedral Church of St Mary the Virgin, Cathedral Close, Blackburn BB1 5AA
☎01254 503 090 ℻01254 689 666
E: cathedral@blackburn.anglican.org
Web: www.blackburn.anglican.org
Dean: Very Rev Christopher Armstrong. *Chapter Clerk:* Rev Canon Michael Wedgeworth. Turnover n/a.

Bradford, Cathedral Church of St Peter, Cathedral Office, 1 Stott Hill, Bradford BD1 4EH
☎01274 777 720 ℻01274 777 730
E: secretary@cathedral.bradford.anglican.org
Web: www.bradfordcathedral.co.uk
Dean: Very Rev David Ison. Turnover n/a.

Bristol, Cathedral Church of the Holy and Undivided Trinity, Cathedral Office, College Green, Bristol BS1 5TJ
☎0117 926 4879 ℻0117 925 3678
E: reception@bristol-cathedral.co.uk
Web: www.bristol-cathedral.co.uk
Also coffee shop.
Dean: Very Rev Robert Grimley. Began 1542. Turnover n/a.

†**Canterbury**, Cathedral and Metropolitical Church of Christ, Cathedral Office, Cathedral House, 11 The Precincts, Canterbury CT1 2EH
☎01227 762 862 ℻01227 865 222
Dean: Very Rev Robert Willis. *Receiver General:* Brigadier John Meardon. Turnover n/a.

Carlisle, Cathedral Church of the Holy and Undivided Trinity, Cathedral Office, 7 The Abbey, Carlisle CA3 8TZ
☎01228 548 151 ℻01228 547 049
E: office@carlislecathedral.org.uk
Web: www.carlislecathedral.org.uk
Treasury exhibition, shop, restaurant, education centre, disabled access.
Dean: Very Rev Mark Boyling. Turnover n/a.

Chelmsford, Cathedral Church of St Mary The Virgin, St Peter and St Cedd, Cathedral Office, New Street, Chelmsford CM1 1TY
☎01245 294 489 ℻01245 294 499
E: dean@chelmsfordcathedral.org.uk
Web: www.chelmsfordcathedral.org.uk
Dean: Very Rev Peter Judd. Turnover n/a.

Chester, Cathedral Church of Christ and the Blessed Virgin Mary, Cathedral Office, 12 Abbey Square, Chester CH1 2HU
☎01244 324 756 ℻01244 341 110
E: office@chestercathedral.com
Web: www.chestercathedral.com
Also coffee shop.
Dean: Very Rev Prof Gordon McPhate. Turnover £1,740,000 to year end Dec 02.

Chichester, Cathedral Church of the Holy Trinity, The Royal Chantry, Cathedral Cloisters, Chichester PO19 1PX
☎01243 812 482 ℻01243 812 499
E: visitors@chichestercathedral.org.uk
Web: www.chichestercathedral.org.uk
Dean: Very Rev Nicholas Frayling. Turnover n/a.

Coventry, Cathedral Church of St Michael, 1 Hill Top, Coventry CV1 5AB
☎024 7652 1200 ℻024 7652 1200
E: information@coventrycathedral.org
Web: www.coventrycathedral.org
Rebuilt after its destruction to the glory of God and testimony to reconciliation.
Dean: Very Rev John Irvine. *Marketing/Promotions Manager:* Mrs V Meredith. Turnover £500,000 to year end Dec 98.

Derby, Cathedral Church of All Saints, Cathedral Office, 18 Iron Gate, Derby DE1 3GP
☎01332 341 201 ℻01332 203 991
E: dean@derbycathedral.org.uk
Web: www.derbycathedral.org
Linked with Church of North India.
Administrator: Mr David Lane. ***CC*** No.X41380. Turnover n/a.
Dean: Very Rev Dr Martin Kitchen, The Dean's House, 9 Highfield Road, Derby DE22 1GX

Durham, Cathedral Church of Christ and Blessed Mary the Virgin of Durham, The Chapter Office, The College, Durham DH1 3EH
☎0191 386 4266 ℻0191 386 4267
E: enquiries@durhamcathedral.org.uk
Web: www.durhamcathedral.org.uk
Dean: Very Rev Michael Sadgrove. Turnover n/a.

Ely, Cathedral Church of The Holy and Undivided Trinity, The Chapter House, The College, Ely CB7 4DL
☎01353 667 735 ℻01353 665 658
Web: www.cathedral.ely.org
Dean: Very Rev Dr Michael J Chandler. Turnover n/a.

Exeter, Cathedral Church of St Peter, Cathedral Office, 1 The Cloisters, Exeter EX1 1HS
☎01392 255 573 ℻01392 285 986
E: admin@exeter-cathedral.org.uk
Web: www.exeter-cathedral.org.uk
Dean: Very Rev Jonathan Meyrick. Turnover n/a.

Gloucester, Cathedral Church of St Peter and the Holy Indivisible Trinity, Cathedral Office, 2 College Green, Gloucester GL1 2LR
☎01452 528 095 ℻01452 300 469
E: office@gloucestercathedral.org.uk
Web: www.gloucestercathedral.org.uk
Strong musical tradition; also coffee shop.
Dean: Very Rev Nicholas Bury. Turnover n/a.

Cathedrals

Guildford, Cathedral Church of the Holy Spirit, Cathedral Office, Stag Hill, Guildford GU2 7UP
☎01483 547860 📠01483 303 350
E: info@guildford-cathedral.org
Web: www.guildford-cathedral.org
Dean: Very Rev Victor Stock. Turnover n/a.

Hereford, Cathedral Church of the Blessed Virgin Mary and St Ethelbert, Cathedral Office, 5 College Cloisters, Hereford HR1 2NG
☎01432 374 200 📠01432 374 220
E: office@herefordcathedral.org
Web: www.herefordcathedral.org
Dean: Very Rev Michael Tavinor. Turnover n/a.

Leicester, Cathedral Church of St Martin, Cathedral Centre, 21 St Martins, Leicester LE1 5DE
☎0116 262 5294 📠0116 262 5295
E: leicestercathedral@leccofe.org
Web: www.cathedral.leicester.anglican.org
Also coffee shop; counselling for those living with cancer and for asylum seekers.
Dean: Very Rev Vivienne Faull. Turnover £450,000 to year end Dec 02.

Lichfield, Cathedral Church of the Blessed Virgin Mary & St Chad, Chapter Office, 19a The Close, Lichfield WS13 7LD
☎01543 306 100 📠01543 306 109
E: enquiries@lichfield-cathedral.org
Web: www.lichfield-cathedral.org
Dean: Very Rev Adrian Dorber.

Lincoln, Cathedral Church of the Blessed Virgin Mary, Chapter Office, 4 Priorygate, Lincoln LN2 1PL
☎01522 544 544 📠01522 511 307
E: chiefexecutive@lincolncathedral.com
Web: www.lincolncathedral.com
Dean: To be appointed. ***CC*** No.X7802. Turnover n/a.

Liverpool, Cathedral Church of Christ, St James' Mount, Liverpool L1 7AZ
☎0151 709 6271 📠0151 702 7292
E: info@liverpoolcathedral.org.uk
Web: www.liverpoolcathedral.org.uk
Dean: Rt Rev Dr Rupert Hoare. *Treasurer:* Rev Canon Anthony Hawley. *Administrator:* Mr Andy Chittenden. Turnover £1,000,000 to year end Dec 02.

London, Cathedral Church of St Paul, Chapter House, St Paul's Churchyard, London EC4M 8AD
☎020 7236 4128 📠020 7248 3104
E: chapter@stpaulscathedral.org.uk
Web: www.stpauls.co.uk
Dean: To be appointed. Turnover n/a.

Manchester, Cathedral and Collegiate Church of St Mary St Denys and St George, Cathedral Yard, Manchester M3 1SX
☎0161 833 2220 📠0161 839 6218
E: office@manchestercathedral.com
Web: www.manchestercathedral.com
Dean: Very Rev Rogers Morgan Govender. Turnover n/a.

Newcastle, Cathedral Church of St Nicholas, The Cathedral Office, St Nicholas Churchyard, Newcastle upon Tyne NE1 1PF
☎0191 232 1939 📠0191 230 0735
E: office@stnicnewsastle.co.uk
Web: www.newcastle-ang-cathedral-stnicholas.org.uk
Focus on the spirituality of childhood; also coffee shop.
Dean: Very Rev Christopher Dalliston. Turnover n/a.

Norwich, Cathedral Church of the Holy and Undivided Trinity, Cathedral Office, 12 The Close, Norwich NR1 4DH
☎01603 218 300 📠01603 766 032
Web: www.cathedral.org.uk
Also restaurant.
Dean: Very Rev Graham Smith. *Vice-Dean:* Rev Canon Jeremy Haselock. *Chapter Clerk:* Tim Cawkwell. Turnover £2,500,000 to year end Mar 05.

Oxford, Cathedral Church of Christ, The Deanery, Christ Church, Oxford OX1 1DP
☎01865 276 161 📠01865 276 238
E: jan.bolongaro@chch.ox.ac.uk
Web: www.chchox.ac.uk
Dean: Very Rev Christopher Lewis. Turnover n/a.

***Peterborough**, Cathedral Church of St Peter, St Paul and St Andrew, Chapter Office, Minster Precincts, Peterborough PE1 1XS
☎01733 343 342 📠01733 355 316
E: info@peterborough-cathedral.org.uk
Web: www.peterborough-cathedral.org.uk
Dean: To be appointed. Turnover n/a.

Portsmouth, Cathedral Church of St Thomas of Canterbury, Cathedral Office, St Thomas's Street, Portsmouth PO1 2HH
☎023 9282 3300 📠023 9229 5480
E: administrator@portsmouthcathedral.org.uk
Web: www.portsmouthcathedral.org.uk
Dean: Very Rev David Brindley. Began 1927. Turnover n/a.

Ripon and Leeds, Cathedral Church of St Peter and St Wilfrid, The Chapter House, Ripon Cathedral, Ripon HG4 1QT
☎01765 602 072 📠01765 690 530
E: postmaster@riponcathedral.org.uk
Web: www.riponcathedral.org.uk
Acting Dean: Rev Canon Michael Glanville-Smith. Turnover n/a.

Rochester, Cathedral Church of Christ and the Blessed Virgin Mary, The Cathedral Office, Garth House, The Precincts, Rochester ME1 1SX
☎01634 843 366 📠01634 401 410
E: dean@rochestercathedraluk.org
Web: www.rochestercathedral.org
Dean: Very Rev Adrian Newman. Turnover n/a.

St Albans, Cathedral and Abbey Church of St Alban, Cathedral Office, The Chapter House, Sumpter Yard, St Albans AL1 1BY
☎01727 860 780 📠01727 850 944
E: mail@stalbanscathedral.org.uk
Web: www.stalbanscathedral.org.uk
Pilgrimage focus; also café, shop.
Dean: Very Rev Dr Jeffery John. *Sub-Dean:* Rev Canon Stephen Lake. *Cathedral Administrator:* Mr Nicholas Bates. Turnover £1,700,000 to year end Dec 04.

St Edmundsbury and Ipswich, Cathedral Church of St James, Cathedral Office, Angel Hill, Bury St Edmunds IP33 1LS
☎01284 754 933 📠01284 768 655
E: provost@btconnect.com
Dean: Very Rev Neil Collings. Turnover n/a.

Salisbury, Cathedral Church of the Blessed Virgin Mary, Cathedral Office, 5 The Close, Salisbury SP1 2EF
☎01722 555 110 📠01722 555 1[illegible]5
E: chapter@salcath.co.uk
Web: www.salisburycathedral.org.uk
Dean: Very Rev June Osborne. Turnover n/a.

Sheffield, Cathedral Church of St Peter and St Paul, Cathedral Office, Church Street, Sheffield S1 1HA
☎0114 275 3434 📠0114 278 02[illegible]
E: enquiries@sheffield-cathedral.org.uk
Web: www.sheffield-cathedral.org.uk
Dean: Very Rev Peter Bradley. Turnover n/a.

Sodor and Man, Cathedral Church of St German, Cathedral Vicarage, Albany Road, Peel IM5 1JS
☎01624 626 994 📠01624 626 99[illegible]
Web: www.sodorman.anglican.org
Dean: Rev B H Kelly. Turnover n/a.

Southwark, The Collegiate Church of St Saviour and St Mary Overie, Cathedral Office, London Bridge, Southwark, London SE1 9DA
☎020 7367 6700
📠020 7367 6725/6730
E: cathedral@southwark.anglican.org
Web: www.southwark.anglican.org/cathedral
Also coffee shop, restaurant, bookshop.
Dean: Very Rev Colin Slee. *Sub Dean:* Rev Canon Andrew Nunn. *Administrator:* Mr Matthew Knight. ***CC*** No X61565. Turnover £1,190,000 to year end Dec 04.

†Southwell and Nottingham, Cathedral and Parish Church of the Blessed Virgin Mary, The Minster Centre, Church Street, Southwell NG25 0HD
☎01636 812 649 📠01636 815 904
E: mail@southwellminster.org.uk
Web: www.southwellminster.org.uk
Dean of Southwell: Very Rev David Leaning. Turnover n/a.

Truro, Cathedral Church of St Mary, Cathedral Office, 14 St Mary's Street, Truro TR1 2AF
☎01872 276 782 📠01872 277 788
E: admin@trurocathedral.org.uk
Web: www.trurocathedral.org.uk
Dean: Very Rev Dr Christopher Hardwick. *Chief Executive Office:* Mr Richard Glover. Turnover n/a.

Wakefield, Cathedral Church of All Saints, Cathedral Office, Northgate, Wakefield WF1 1HG
☎01924 373 923 🖷01924 215 054
E: admin@wakefield-cathedral.org.uk
Web: www.wakefield-cathedral.org.uk
Dean: Very Rev George Nairn-Briggs. Turnover n/a.

Winchester, Cathedral Church of the Holy Trinity and of St Peter, Cathedral Office, 1 The Close, Winchester SO23 9LS
☎01962 857 200 🖷01962 857 201
E: cathedral.office@winchester-cathedral.org.uk
Web: www.winchester-cathedral.org.uk
Dean: Very Rev James Atwell. Turnover n/a.

Worcester, Cathedral Church of Christ and the Blessed Virgin Mary, Cathedral Office, 10a College Green, Worcester WR1 2LH
☎01905 28854 🖷01905 611 139
E: info@worcestercathedral.org.uk
Web: www.worcestercathedral.org.uk
Dean: To be appointed. Turnover n/a.

York, Cathedral Church of St Peter, Church House, Ogleforth, York YO1 7JN
☎01904 557 200 🖷01904 557 201
E: info@yorkminster.org
Web: www.yorkminster.org
Dean: Very Rev Keith Brynmor Jones. Turnover n/a.

CHURCH OF IRELAND DIOCESES

Armagh, Cathedral Church of St Patrick, The Library, Abbey Street, Armagh BT61 7DY
☎028 3752 3142 🖷028 3752 4177
E: armroblib@aol.com
Dean: Very Rev Patrick Rooke.

***Clogher**, The Cathedral Churches of St Macartan, The Cathedral Rectory, 10 Augher Road, Clogher BT76 0AD
☎028 8554 9797
E: dean@clogher.anglican.org
Dean: Very Rev Raymond C Thompson.

Connor, Cathedral Church of St Saviour, The Rectory, 49 Rectory Gardens, Broughshane, Ballymena BT42 4LF
☎028 2586 1215 🖷028 2586 1215
E: dean@connor.anglican.org
Dean: Very Rev John F A Bond.

Derry and Raphoe, Cathedral Church of St Columb, The Deanery, 30 Bishop Street, Londonderry BT48 6PP
☎028 7126 2746
E: dean@derry.anglican.org
Web: www.stcolumbcathedral.org
Dean: Very Rev Dr William Wright Morton.

Down and Dromore, Connor, Cathedral Church of St Anne, Donegal Street, Belfast BT1 2HB
☎028 9032 8332 🖷028 9023 8855
E: assist@belfastcathedral.org
Web: www.belfastcathedral.org
Belfast Cathedral.
Dean: Very Rev Houston McKelvey. *Dean's Vicar:* Rev Timothy Close. *Director of Music:* Mr Philip Stopford. Began 1904.

Down and Dromore, Cathedral Church of Christ the Redeemer, 30 Church Street, Dromore BT25 1AA
☎028 9269 3968 🖷028 9269 2275
E: dean@dromore.anglican.org
Web: www.dromorecathedral.co.uk
Dean: Rev Stephen H Lowry.

CHURCH OF SCOTLAND

Edinburgh, St Giles Cathedral, Royal Mile, Edinburgh EH1 1RE
☎0131 225 9442 🖷0131 225 9576
E: info@stgilescathedral.org.uk
Web: www.stgilescathedral.org.uk
Also restaurant.
Minister: Very Rev Gilleasbuig Macmillan.

ORTHODOX

Antiochian Orthodox

Antiochian Orthodox Cathedral of St George, 1a Redhill Street, London NW1 4BE
☎020 7383 0403
E: frsgholam@msn.com
Web: www.antiochian-orthodox.co.uk
Priest: Father Samir Gholam. ***CC*** No.801540. Began 1939.

Greek Orthodox

Greek Orthodox Cathedral, Bayswater, Cathedral of the Divine Wisdom, Moscow Road, Bayswater, London W2 4LQ
☎020 7229 7260 🖷020 7243 6144
Web: www.stsophia.org.uk
Bishop of Nazianzos: Rt Rev Dr Theodoritos. Began 1878.

Greek Orthodox Cathedral, Birmingham, Cathedral of the Dormition of the Mother of God and St Andrew, 8 Arthur Place, Summer Hill, Birmingham B1 3DA
☎0121 236 3274 🖷0121 236 3274
Dean: Name not supplied. ***CC*** No.506188. Began 1939.

Greek Orthodox Cathedral, Camberwell, Cathedral of the Nativity of the Mother of God, 305 Camberwell New Road, Camberwell, London SE5 0TF
☎020 7703 0137
Bishop of Telmissos: To be appointed. Began 1962.

Greek Orthodox Cathedral, Camden Town, Cathedral of All Saints, Camden Street, Camden Town, London NW1 0JA
☎020 7485 2149 🖷020 7485 2149
Dean: To be appointed. Began 1948.

Greek Orthodox Cathedral, Glasgow, Cathedral of St Luke the Evangelist, 27 Dundonald Road, Dowanhill, Glasgow G12 9LL
☎0141 339 7386
E: nondas.pitticas@ntlworld.com
Priest: Rev Constantinos Papageorgiou. Began 1944.

Greek Orthodox Cathedral, Golders Green and Hendon, Cathedral of the Holy Cross and St Michael, Golders Green Road, London NW11 8DA
☎020 8455 7510 🖷020 8458 4752
Bishop of Zenoupolis: To be appointed. Began 1965.

Greek Orthodox Cathedral, Kentish Town, Cathedral of St Andrew, Kentish Town Road, London NW1 9QA
☎020 7485 6385/0198 🖷020 7485 9972
Bishop of Kyanea: Rt Rev Chrysostomos. Began 1957.

Greek Orthodox Cathedral, Shepherd's Bush, Cathedral of St Nicholas, 60 Godolphin Road, London W12 8JW
☎020 8743 3968 🖷020 8743 3968
E: saintnicholas@greekorthodox.fsnet.co.uk
Dean: Very Rev Archmandrite Isaias Simonopetritis. ***CC*** No.1024869. Began 1965.

Greek Orthodox Cathedral, Wood Green, Cathedral of St Mary, Trinity Road, London N22 8LB
☎020 8888 2295 / 8889 1122 🖷020 8881 4455
Bishop of Tropaeou: Rt Rev Athanasios. Began 1970.

Russian Orthodox

Russian Orthodox Cathedral, London, Russian Orthodox Cathedral, 67 Ennismore Gardens, London SW7 1NH
☎020 7584 0096 🖷020 7584 9864
Web: www.sourozh.org
Dean: Very Rev John Lee. Turnover n/a.

SCOTTISH EPISCOPAL CHURCH DIOCESES

Aberdeen and Orkney, St Andrew's Cathedral, Saint Andrew's Cathedral Office, 28 King Street, Aberdeen AB24 5AX
☎01224 640 119
E: cathedral@aberdeen.anglican.org
Web: www.cathedral.aberdeen.anglican.org
Provost: Very Rev Richard Eifl Kilgour.

Argyll and the Isles, St John the Divine Cathedral, The Rectory, Ardconnel Terrace, Oban PA34 5DJ
☎01631 562 323
E: provostoban@argyll.anglican.org
Provost: Very Rev Norman D MacCallum.

†**Argyll and the Isles**, Collegiate Church of the Holy Spirit (The Cathedral of the Isles), St Andrew's Rectory, Parade Road, Fort William PH33 6BA
☎01397 702 979
Dean: Very Rev G Alexander Guinness.

Brechin, St Paul's Cathedral, Cathedral Office, 1 High Street, Dundee DD1 1TD
☎01382 224 486 🖷01382 202 200
E: admin@stpaulscathedraldundee.org
Web: www.stpaulscathedraldundee.org
Provost: Very Rev Miriam Byrne.

Edinburgh, St Mary's Cathedral, Palmerston Place, Edinburgh EH12 5AW
☎0131 225 2978 🖷0131 225 3181
Provost: Very Rev Graham Forbes.

Glasgow and Galloway, St Mary's Episcopal Cathedral, 300 Great Western Road, Glasgow G4 9JB
☎0141 339 6691 🖷0141 334 5669
E: office@thecathedral.org.uk
Web: www.cathedral.glasgow.anglican.org
Provost: Very Rev Kelvin Holdsworth.

Moray, Ross and Caithness, St Andrew's Cathedral, 15 Ardross Street, Inverness IV3 5NS
☎01463 225 553 (enquiries) 🖷01463 225 553
E: office@invernesscathedral.net
Web: www.invernesscathedral.net
Also coffee shop.
Provost: Very Rev Alexander Gordon. *Administrator:* Mr Edward Barbieri. Turnover £100,000 to year end Dec 02.

St Andrews, Dunkeld and Dunblane, St Ninian's Cathedral, St Ninian's House, North Methuen Street, Perth PH1 5PP
☎01738 623 053 🖷01738 639 311
E: stninians.cathedral@btinternet.com
Web: www.perthcathedral.co.uk
Provost: Very Rev Hunter Farquharson. St Andrews.

CHAPLAINCIES

Anglican Chaplaincy to the Universities, London, 30b Farrington Square, London WC1E 7JL
☎020 7580 9812 🖷020 7631 3219
E: chaplaincy@lon.ac.uk
Providing a ministry to students and staff within London's universities.
Senior Chaplain: Rev Stephen Williams. Executive staff 1, Other staff 36. Began 1962; Anglican. No magazine. Turnover n/a.

Chaplaincy Services in the Royal Navy, MP 1.2 Leach Building, Whale Island, Portsmouth PO2 8BY
☎023 9262 5049
E: peter.keat271@mod.uk
Providing ministry of the Gospel by word and sacrament to Royal Navy personnel.
Chaplain of the Fleet: Ven John Green QHC. Full-time chaplains 75. Began 1177; Anglican, Church of Scotland, Free Churches, Roman Catholic. Magazine: *Church Pennant* (2,500 quarterly). Turnover n/a.

Church of England Chaplaincies in Further and Higher Education, Church House, Great Smith Street, London SW1P 3NZ
☎020 7898 1513 🖷020 7898 1520
E: alan.murray@c-of-e.org.uk
Web: www.cofe.anglican.org/info/education/hefe
Developing the Church's engagement with HE/FE sectors and its presence in university/college chaplaincies.
Churches' National Adviser for Further Education: Mr Alan Murray. Executive staff 1, HE Chaplains 227, FE (Ecumenical and Multifaith) Chaplains 450. ***CC*** Began 1550; Anglican. No magazine. Turnover n/a.
Also at: *National Adviser in Higher Education:* Mr Hugh Shilson-Thomas.
E: hugh.shilson-thomas@c-of-e.org.uk
☎020 7898 1517 🖷 020 7898 1520

The Guild of St Helena, Wellington Barracks, Birdcage Walk, London SW1E 6HQ
☎020 7414 3461
Web: www.army.mod.uk/army/press
Offering Christian fellowship and charitable giving to members of the Armed Services and their families.
Chief Secretary: Mrs Janice Carson. Executive staff 2. ***CC*** No.267656. Began 1875; ecumenical. Magazine: *Guild of St Helena* (Circulation n/a annually). Turnover £30,000 to year end Mar 05.

Health Care Chaplaincy Steering Committee, Free Churches Group, 27 Tavistock Square, London WC1H 9HH
☎020 7529 8130/8136
🖷020 7529 8134
E: chaplaincy@cte.org.uk
Official body for all matters relating to Free Church health care chaplaincy work.
Secretary: Rev Debbie Hodge. Staff n/a. Began 1950; interdenominational. Part of Churches Together in England. No magazine. Turnover n/a.

Hospital Chaplaincies Council (General Synod), Church House, Great Smith Street, London SW1P 3NZ
☎020 7898 1892 🖷020 7898 1891
E: edward.lewis@c-of-e.org.uk
Web: www.nhs-chaplaincy-spiritualcare.org.uk
Advisory body for chaplaincy work in health care.
Secretary/Chief Executive: Rev Edward Lewis. Executive staff 2, Other staff 1. Began 1952; Anglican. No magazine. Turnover n/a.

Hungarian Roman Catholic Chaplaincy, Dunstan House, 141 Gunnersbury Avenue, London W3 8LE
☎020 8992 2054 🖷020 8992 2054
E: hungarian.chaplaincy@btinternet.com
Chaplain: Rev Mgr George Tüttö. *Assistant Chaplain:* Fr Joseph Viragh. No full-time staff. ***CC*** No.WRCDT.233699. Began 1948; Roman Catholic. No magazine. Turnover n/a.

Lincolnshire Chaplaincy Services, Church House, The Old Palace, Lincoln LN2 1PU
☎01522 504 070
E: john.tomlinson@lincoln.anglican.org
Web: www.ctal.org.uk
Promoting the expansion of chaplaincy in a variety of workplaces and educational establishments.
Director: Rev John Tomlinson. Executive staff 12. Began n/a; ecumenical. No magazine. Turnover £500,000 to year end Dec 05.

Lutheran Student Chaplaincy, 30 Thanet Street, London WC1H 9QH
☎020 7554 2901 🖷020 7383 3081
E: chaplaincy@lutheran.org.uk
Web: www.lutheran.org.uk
Providing pastoral care to international students in the UK.
Chaplain: Rev Jennifer Welsh. Executive staff 1. ***CC*** No.232042. Began 1961; Lutheran. No magazine. Turnover n/a.

Methodist Church Forces Work, 13 Park Road, St Dominic, Saltash PL12 6TL
☎01579 351 286
E: andjing@aol.com
Coordinating Methodist service chaplains and Wesley Houses.
Secretary: Rev J K Watson. Executive staff 1, Other staff 1. ***CC*** Began n/a; Methodist. Magazine: *Over To You* (2,000 half-yearly). Turnover £40,000 to year end Dec 02.

Ministry of Defence Chaplains (Army), MOD Chaplains (A), Building 183, Trenchard Lines, Upavon, Pewsey SN9 6BE
☎01980 615 804 🖷01980 615 800
E: modchaplainsarmy@tiscali.co.uk
Web: www.army.mod.uk/chaps
Exercising the Church's ministry within the Army.
The Chaplain General to the Forces: Rev David Wilkes. Executive staff 4, Other staff 7. Began n/a; interdenominational. No magazine. Turnover n/a.

The Nigerian Chaplaincy, 82 Keslake Road, London NW6 6DG
☎020 7935 9478 🖷020 7485 5493
E: nigerianchaplaincy@yahoo.co.uk
Counselling Nigerian students and residents; preaching, teaching and enabling churches and mission agencies.
Chaplain: Rev Ben Enwuchola. Executive staff 1, Other staff 1. ***CC*** No.1031806. Began 1981; interdenominational. Mission partner with Church Mission Society. Magazine: *Announcer* (250 quarterly). Turnover n/a.

Prison Chaplaincy, Horseferry House, Dean Ryle Street, London SW1P 2AW
☎020 7217 8201 🖷020 7217 3980
E: william.noblett@hmps.gsi.gov.uk
Web: www.hmprisonservice.gov.uk
Ensuring the provision of religious facilities within penal establishments.
Chaplain General of Prisons: Ven William Noblett. Executive staff 13, Chaplains 300. Began n/a; interdenominational. No magazine. Turnover n/a.

Pusey House, Pusey House, Oxford OX1 3LZ
☎01865 278 415 🖷01865 278 416
Providing pastoral care for undergraduates, chapel services, theology and philosophy library, writing and research.
Principal: Rev J M R Baker. Executive staff 7, Other staff 2. ***CC*** Began 1884; Anglican. No magazine. Turnover n/a.

RAF Chaplains Branch, HQ, Personnel and Training Command, RAF Innsworth, Gloucester GL3 1EZ
☎01452 712 612 ext 5164
🖷01452 510 828
E: ray.pentland929@mod.uk
Providing spiritual, moral and welfare support to the personnel of the Royal Air Force.
Director of Chaplaincy: Ven Raymond Pentland. Chaplains 79. Began 1918; interdenominational. No magazine. Turnover n/a.

St Wenceslaus House - Velehrad, 22 Ladbroke Square, London W11 3NA
☎020 7727 7849 🖷020 7229 2739
E: info@velehrad.org
Web: www.velehrad.org
Offering pastoral work, social care, help to au-pairs, students, visitors from Czech and Slovak Republics.
Chaplains: Rev John Lang, Rev Joseph Vojtek. Executive staff 2, Other staff 1. **CC** No.241281. Began 1964; Roman Catholic but ecumenical. Magazine: *CM Vestnik* (Circulation n/a monthly). Turnover £56,000 to year end Dec 02.

Universities of London Catholic Chaplaincy, Newman House, 111 Gower Street, London WC1E 6AR
☎020 7387 6370 🖷020 7388 6431
E: enquiries@universitycatholic.net
Web: www.universitycatholic.net
Providing pastoral services to students and staff in tertiary education in London; also accommodation.
Senior Chaplain: Fr Peter Wilson. Chaplains 5, Other staff 5. **CC** No.233699. Began 1908; Roman Catholic. (Previously London Universities Catholic Chaplaincy). No magazine. Turnover n/a.

COUNCILS OF CHURCHES & CHURCHES TOGETHER

Action of Churches Together in Scotland (ACTS), 7 Forrester Lodge, Inglewood, Alloa FK10 2HU
☎01259 216 980 🖷01259 215 964
E: ecumenical@acts-scotland.org
Web: www.acts-scotland.org
Encouraging and expressing the unity of the Christian churches in Scotland.
General Secretary: Very Rev Dr Kevin Franz. *Convener of ACTS:* Alison Elliot OBE. Executive staff 2, Other staff 2. **CC** No.SC000295. Began 1990; interdenominational. No magazine. Turnover £200,000 to year end Dec 04.

Affinity, PO Box 2119, Reading RG1 7WS
☎0118 956 9103 🖷0118 959 0058
E: admin@affinity.org.uk
Web: www.affinity.org.uk
Church-centred partnership for Bible-centred Christianity; promoting evangelical church unity and testimony, locally and nationally.
Director: Mr Jonathan Stephen. Executive staff 1, Other staff 1. **CC** No.258924. Began 1952, re-launched 2004; non-denominational. (Previously British Evangelical Council). Turnover £66,000 to year end Aug 04.
Also at: *Administrator:* Mr Ian Herring, 37 Clifton Gardens, West End, Southampton SO18 3DA ☎023 8046 6235

†Afro-West Indian United Council of Churches, NTCGod, Arcadian Gardens, High Road, London N22 5AA
☎020 8888 9427 🖷020 8888 2877
Promoting, co-ordinating and fostering Christian ideals and action between member churches and the community.
General Secretary: Bishop Eric A Brown. No full-time staff. **CC** Began 1976; evangelical. No magazine. Turnover n/a.

Birmingham Churches Together, The Place of Welcome, 172 Herbert Road, Small Heath, Birmingham B10 0PR
☎0121 766 5522
E: office@birminghamchurches.org.uk
Web: www.birminghamchurches.org.uk
Coordinating body for all Roman Catholic, Anglican and Free Church denominations.
Development Officer: Rev Dr Colin Marsh. Executive staff 1, Other staff 3. **CC** No.243931. Began 1951; interdenominational. Magazine: *BEN* (1,500 quarterly). Turnover £63,000 to year end Dec 04.

Black Country Churches Engaged, 18 Selman's Hill, Bloxwich, Walsall WS3 3RJ
☎01922 475 932
E: jmtopliss@fish.co.uk
Facilitating engagement in shared mission, social concern, worship, theological reflection; forum; church leaders' meeting.
Ecumenical Officer: Mr Michael Topliss. No full-time staff. Began 2000; interdenominational. Magazine: *Ecumentions* (Circulation n/a occasional). Turnover n/a.

Cambridgeshire Ecumenical Council, Silverlands, Church Street, Litlington, Royston SG8 0QB
☎01763 852 841
E: priscilla.barlow@easynet.co.uk
Intermediate body of Churches Together in England; strengthening cooperation, supporting and initiating local ecumenical partnerships.
County Ecumenical Officer: Mrs Priscilla Barlow. No full-time staff. Began 1988; ecumenical. No magazine. Turnover n/a.

Cherubim & Seraphim Church Council
See page 442

Christians Together in Jersey, Ocean View, La Route de L'Etacq, St Ouen, Jersey JE3 2FB
☎01534 482 366
E: jpir@oceanviewjersey.freeserve.co.uk
Web: www.ctj.org.je
Furthering ecumenical cooperation in Jersey.
Secretary: Mr Michael J Ruskin. No full-time staff. Began n/a; ecumenical. Magazine: *The Jersey Link* (5,000 half-yearly). Turnover n/a.

Churches Together in Bedfordshire, 36 Cainloe Road, Clophill, Bedford MK45 4AQ
☎01525 860 0986 🖷01525 860 0986
E: ian.gordon@ukgateway.net
Promoting Christian unity and joint action of the churches in Bedfordshire.
County Ecumenical Officer: Ian Gordon. *Secretary:* Adrienne Gordon. Executive staff 1, Admin staff 1. Began n/a; ecumenical. No magazine. Turnover n/a.

Churches Together in Berkshire, 2 Ash Grove, Guildford GU2 8UT
☎0118 926 1062 🖷0118 926 1063
E: reading@corrymeela.org
Initiating, enabling and supporting efforts towards full unity in the Christian church.
County Ecumenical Officer: Mrs Honor Alleyne. No full-time staff. Began 1986; interdenominational. Magazine: *Together* (Circulation n/a half-yearly). Turnover n/a.

Churches Together in Greater Bristol, 6 Bampton Drive, Bristol BS16 6BJ
☎0117 956 5447
E: cac@fish.co.uk
Fostering and oversight of regional and local ecumenical activity and action.
Ecumenical Officer: Mr David Carter. Executive staff 1. Began 1987; interdenominational. (Previously Greater Bristol Ecumenical Council). Magazine: *Bristol Christian Quarterly* (510 quarterly). Turnover £20,000 to year end Dec 04.

Churches Together in Britain and Ireland, Bastille Court, 2 Paris Garden, London SE1 8ND
☎020 7654 7254 🖷020 7654 7222
E: info@ctbi.org.uk
Web: www.ctbi.org.uk
Coordinating the work of the churches and national ecumenical instruments and bodies.
General Secretary: Rev Canon Bob Fyffe. Executive staff 10, Admin staff 16. **CC** No.259688. Began 1990; interdenominational. (Previously Council of Churches for Britain and Ireland). No magazine. Turnover n/a.
Note: For member organisations see Page 16
See also:
CTBI Publications on Page 122
Churches' Commission for Inter Faith Relations on Page 181
Churches' Commission for International Students on Page 181
Churches' Commission for Racial Justice on Page 379
Global Mission Network on Page 300

See also in this category
Action of Churches Together in Scotland (ACTS) on Page 143
Churches Together in England on Page 144
CYTUN: Churches Together in Wales on Page 146
Irish Council of Churches on Page 146

C

Churches Together in Buckinghamshire
3 Criss Grove, Chalfont St Peter, Gerrards Cross SL9 9HG
Furthering ecumenical cooperation within the county.
Ecumenical Development Officer: Major David Scott. No full-time staff. Began n/a; ecumenical. (Previously Buckinghamshire Ecumenical Council). No magazine. Turnover n/a.

Churches Together in Cheshire, District Centre, Bishop's Wood, Nantwich CW5 7QD
☎01270 627 774
E: do.chestoke@fish.co.uk
Encouraging cooperation, mutual support and evangelism by the churches in the county and related areas.
County Ecumenical Officer: Mr Mark Thompson. No full-time staff. Began 1975; interdenominational. Magazine: *Cheshire United* (1,000 half-yearly). Turnover £7,500 to year end Dec 02.

Churches Together in Cornwall, St Hilary, Higher West Polgus, Redruth TR15 3TP
☎01209 213 698
E: dyer4kernow@btinternet.com
Furthering ecumenical cooperation within the county.
County Ecumenical Officer: Rev Adrian Dyer. No full-time staff. ***CC*** No.1053899. Began 1990; interdenominational. No magazine. Turnover £8,000 to year end Dec 00.

Churches Together in Coventry & Warwickshire, 6 Sycamore Close, Stratford-upon-Avon CV37 0DZ
☎01789 298 299 Fax 08715 227 280
E: ctcw@fish.co.uk
Web: www.ctcw.org.uk
Furthering ecumenical cooperation in Coventry and Warwickshire.
County Ecumenical Officer: Rev Bryan Alderson. No full-time staff. ***CC*** No.1060171. Began n/a; ecumenical. No magazine. Turnover n/a.

Churches Together in Cumbria, Chapel Cottage, Hawkshead Hill, Ambleside LA22 0PW
☎01539 436 451
M: 07971 636 319 Fax 01539 360 32
E: andrew.dodd1@btinternet.com
Web: www.churchestogethercumbria.co.uk
Promoting and enabling ecumencial work and witness county-wide; social responsibility forum.
County Ecumenical Officer: Rev Andrew Dodd. Executive staff 2. Began 1984; interdenominational. No magazine. Turnover £2,500 to year end Dec 02.
Also at: *Social Responsibility Coordinator:* Helen Boothroyd, Chapel View, Milton, Brampton CA8 1JD
E: helen.boothroyd@ntlworld.com
☎01697 465 671

Churches Together in Derbyshire, 52 South Avenue, Chellaston, Derby DE73 6RS
☎01332 705 078
E: dovedale.revs@virgin.net
Web: www.churchestogetherderbyshire.org.uk
Furthering ecumenical cooperation within the county.
Ecumenical Development Officer: Rev Philip Webb. Staff 1. Began 1985; interdenominational. No magazine. Turnover £1,000 to year end Dec 04.

Churches Together in Devon, 1 Albert Terrace, Two Bridges Road, Princetown, Yelverton PL20 6QP
☎01822 890 412
E: staylor921@aol.com
Furthering ecumenical cooperation within the county.
County Ecumenical Officer: Rev Simon Taylor. No full-time staff. Began 1991; ecumenical. (Previously Christians Together in Devon). Magazine: *Devon Christians Together* (720 quarterly). Turnover £20,000 to year end Dec 06.

Churches Together in Dorset, 22 D'Urberville Close, Dorchester DT1 2JT
☎01305 264 416
E: ctdorset@clara.net
Web: www.ctdorset.org.uk
Encouraging joint worship, study and social action among the churches of Dorset.
County Ecumenical Officer: Mrs Val Potter. No full-time staff. ***CC*** No.1103400. Began 1990; interdenominational. Magazine: *Pilgrim Post in Dorset* (900 every four months). Turnover £14,000 to year end Dec 02.

Churches Together in England, 27 Tavistock Square, London WC1H 9HH
☎020 7529 8141 Fax 020 7529 8134
E: office@cte.org.uk
Web: www.churches-together.org.uk
Official body enabling its 23 member churches to work together for Christian unity.
General Secretary: Rev Bill Snelson. *Associate General Secretary (Free Churches):* Rev Geoffrey Roper. *Field Officer for the South:* Rev John Bradley. Executive staff 8, Other staff 5. ***CC*** No.1005368. Began 1990; interdenominational. Magazine: *Pilgrim Post* (2,300 every two months). Turnover £809,263 to year end Dec 99.
Field Officer for the North and Midlands Ms Jenny Bond, Luther King House, Brighton Grove, Manchester M14 5JP
☎0161 249 2515 Fax 0870 121 5613

Churches Together in Essex & East London, 5 Lesney Gardens, Rochford SS4 1TY
☎01702 543 794 M: 07811 433 518
E: edo@cteel.org.uk
Sponsoring and overseeing local ecumenical partnerships, specialist ecumenical ministries and work of Churches Together.
Ecumenical Development Officer: Rev Geoff Wright. No full-time staff. Began 1978; interdenominational. No magazine. Turnover n/a.

Churches Together in Guernsey, Woodlands, Houmet Lane, Vale, Guernsey GY6 8JG
☎01481 247 492
Fax 01481 247 492
E: iharvey@supanet.com
Furthering ecumenical cooperation in Guernsey.
Chairman: Mrs Irene Harvey. No full-time staff. Began n/a; ecumenical. (Previously Guernsey Council of Churches). No magazine. Turnover n/a.

Churches Together in Hampshire and the Isle of Wight, 71 Andover Road, Winchester SO22 6AU
☎01962 849 623
Fax 01962 849 623
E: cthi@rolph.freeuk.com
Web: www.hants.gov.uk/cthi
Forum for ecumenical matters in Hampshire and the Isle of Wight.
Counties Ecumenical Officer: Dr Paul Rolph. No full-time staff. Began 1987; interdenominational. No magazine. Turnover n/a.

Churches Together in Herefordshire, 1 Holme Lacy Road, Hereford HR2 6DD
☎01432 353 275
E: lynnjohnson@orange.net
Promoting ecumenism within the county.
County Ecumenical Officer: Lynn Johnson. No full-time staff. Began 1999; interdenominational. (Previously Hereford- shire Ecumenical Sponsoring Body). No magazine. Turnover £3,800 to year end Dec 02.

Churches Together in Hertfordshire, 6 The Round, Mawsley, Kettering NN14 1GR
☎01536 791 496
M: 07788 404 695
Fax 01536 791 496
E: geraldpeacock39@btinternet.com
Promoting Christian unity and joint action of the churches in the county.
County Ecumenical Officer: Major Gerald Peacock. No full-time staff. Began 1967; interdenominational. Magazine: *Together* (800 quarterly). Turnover £7,735 to year end Dec 04.

Churches Together in Kent, St Lawrence Vicarage, Stone Street, Seal, Sevenoaks TN15 0LQ
☎01732 761 766
Fax 01732 761 766
E: info@ctkent.org.uk
Web: www.ctkent.org.uk
Encouraging and promoting ecumenism throughout the county and providing forum for church leaders.
County Ecumenical Officer: Rev Dr Michael Cooke. No full-time staff. Began 1984; interdenominational. Magazine: *Together* (150 quarterly). Turnover £13,600 to year end Dec 02.

Churches Together in Lancashire, Wesley Hall, Feilden Street, Blackburn BB2 1LQ
☎01254 699 833 🖷01254 699 833
E: ctloffice@btinternet.com
Furthering ecumenical cooperation in the county.
County Ecumenical Development Officer: Mrs Terry Garley. Executive staff 1, Other staff 1. Began 1994; ecumenical. No magazine. Turnover £81,507 to year end Dec 05.

Churches Together in Leicestershire, 18 Stanley Road, Leicester LE2 1RE
☎0116 270 8764 🖷0116 253 2889
E: cedo@dial.org.uk
Furthering ecumenical cooperation in the county.
County Ecumenical Officer: John Downing. No full-time staff. Began 1980; interdenominational. No magazine. Turnover £12,629 to year end Dec 98.

Churches Together in All Lincolnshire, Church House, The Old Palace, Lincoln LN2 1PU
☎01522 529241
E: john.tomlinson@lincoln.anglican.org
Web: www.ctal.org.uk
Promoting the growth of mission and unity among churches through local and county ecumenical projects.
Ecumenical Coordinator for Mission: Rev John Tomlinson. Executive staff 2. Began n/a; interdenominational. Magazine: *Notepad* (Circulation & frequency n/a). Turnover £40 000 to year end Dec 05.

Churches Together in Man, Tarnalforn, 12 Ballagarey Road, Glen Vine, Douglas IM4 4EA
☎01624 851 693
Local ecumenical body.
Secretary: Mrs Mavis Matthewman. Staff n/a. Began n/a; interdenominational. No magazine. Turnover n/a.

Churches Together in the Merseyside Region, Quaker Meeting House, 22 School Lane, Liverpool L1 3BT
☎0151 709 0125 🖷0871 916 7098
E: ctmr@fish.co.uk
Web: www.ctmr.ik.com
Enabling the churches to work together both regionally and locally.
Ecumenical Officer: Rev Martyn Newman. Executive staff 1. **CC** No.519061. Began 1974; ecumenical. (Previously The Merseyside and Region Churches Ecumenical Assembly). Magazine: *Merseyside Ecumenical News* (1,200 quarterly). Turnover £40,000 to year end Dec 04

Churches Together in North Thames
Contact Churches Together in England
Sponsoring ecumenical resources for churches in the boroughs of Brent, Ealing, Harrow and Hillingdon.
Convenor: To be appointed. No paid staff. Began 1990; interdenominational. No magazine. Turnover £1,500 to year end Dec 00.

Churches Together in the North York Moors, 18 North End, Osmotherley, Northallerton DL6 3BB
☎01609 883 308
Furthering ecumenical cooperation in north-east Yorkshire.
Hon Secretary: Rev Terence Richardson. No full-time staff. Began n/a; ecumenical. No magazine. Turnover n/a.

Churches Together in Northamptonshire and Peterborough (Shire & Soke)
21 Main Street, Thurning, Oundle Peterborough PE8 5RB
Furthering ecumenical cooperation within the county.
Ecumenical Development Officer: Teresa Brown. No full-time staff. Began n/a; ecumenical. No magazine. Turnover n/a

Churches Together in Nottinghamshire, 52 South Avenue, Challaston, Derby DE73 6RS
☎01332 705 078
E: dovedale.revs@virgin.net
Web: www.churchestogethernottinghamshire.org.uk
Furthering ecumenical cooperation within the county.
Ecumenical Development Officer: Rev Philip Webb. Staff 1. Began 1984; interdenominational. No magazine. Turnover £1,000 to year end Dec 05.

***Churches Together in Orpington**, 26 Charterhouse Road, Orpington BR6 9EL
☎01689 875 867
E: yvonne.pressdee@htmlworld.com
Forum for churches in Orpington to discuss mutual concerns and interests and organise united events.
President: Rev Paul Cockburn. No full-time staff. Began n/a; interdenominational. No magazine. Turnover £5 000 to year end Dec 04.

Churches Together in Oxfordshire, St Columba's URC, Alfred Street, Oxford OX1 4EH
☎01865 723 801 / 864 805
E: bede.gerrard@care4free.net
Web: www.communigate.co.uk/oxford/churchinoxon
Pastoral oversight of local ecumenical projects in Oxfordshire and advancement of ecumenical matters generally.
County Ecumenical Officer: M R Bede Gerrard. No full-time staff. Began 1993; interdenominational. (Previously Oxfordshire Ecumenical Council). Magazine: *Between the Lines* (Circulation n/a every two months). Turnover £17,500 to year end Dec 02.

Churches Together in Shropshire, Fern Villa, Four Crosses, Llanymynech SY22 6PR
☎01691 831 374
E: gedcliffe@worldonline.co.uk
Web: www.chtogshropshire.co.uk
Uniting in mission the Christian churches in the county of Shropshire.
Ecumenical Secretary: Mr Gerard Cliffe. No full-time staff. Began 1993; ecumenical. Magazine: *The Shropshire Christian* (Circulation n/a every two months). Turnover n/a.

Churches Together in South Yorkshire, Victoria Hall Methodist Church, Norfolk Street, Sheffield S1 2JB
☎0114 278 8308
E: louise@ctsy.freeserve.co.uk
Web: www.ctsy.freeserve.co.uk
Encouraging and promoting local unity; sponsoring and overseeing local ecumenical partnerships in the county.
Ecumenical Development Officer: Rev Louise Dawson. Executive staff 1. Began 1991; interdenominational. No magazine. Turnover n/a.

Churches Together in Suffolk, 34 Rectory Lane, Kirton, Ipswich IP10 0PY
☎01394 448 576
Web: www.ctsuffolk.org.uk
Encouraging a deeper commitment between member churches.
Ecumenical Officer: Mrs Margaret Condick. No full-time staff. Began 1970; interdenominational. Magazine: *Together* (Circulation & frequency n/a). Turnover £7,000 figures end of Dec 04.

Churches Together in Surrey, 10 Abbey Gardens, Chertsey KT16 8RQ
☎01932 566 920
E: sue.loveday.ctsurrey@lineone.net
Coordinating and enabling ecumenical activities throughout the county.
Ecumenical Coordinator: Rev Sue Loveday. No full-time staff. Began 1976; interdenominational. No magazine. Turnover n/a.

Churches Together in Sussex, 85 Hollingbury Rise, Brighton BN1 7HH
M: 07976 811 654
E: ianpchisnall@aol.com
Web: www.ctsussex.org.uk
Coordinating ecumenical activity throughout Sussex.
Ecumenical Officer: Mr Ian Chisnall. No full-time staff. Began 1955; interdenominational. (Previously Sussex Council of Churches). Magazine: *Together* (3,000 every four months). Turnover £22,000 to year end Dec 02.

Churches Together in Swindon, 14 The Mall, Swindon SN1 4JG
☎01793 320 238
E: rpower@surefish.co.uk
Web: www.swindonchurchestogether.org.uk
Furthering ecumenical cooperation in Swindon and surrounding areas.
Ecumenical Development Officer: Dr Rosemary Power. No full-time staff. Began 2003; ecumenical. No magazine. Turnover n/a.

Churches Together in Worcestershire, 4 Dalycroft, Home Meadow, Worcester WR4 0JB
☎01905 616 109 🖷01905 612 302
E: dpryangb@aol.com
Coordinating the churches' work and witness in the county, organising ecumenical events.
County Ecumenical Office: Rev David Ryan. No full-time staff. Began 2000; interdenominational. No magazine. Turnover £500 to year end Dec 00.

C

Councils of Churches & Churches Together

Churches' Regional Commission in the North East, Ushaw College, Durham DH7 9RH
☎0191 373 5453 🖷0191 373 7804
E: crcnortheast@btconnect.com
Web: www.northeastchurches.org.uk
Encouraging and supporting social action by church and faith communities together in North East England.
Chief Officer: Mr Paul Southgate. Executive staff 1, Admin staff 2. ***CC*** No.1047745. Began 1995; ecumenical. No magazine. Turnover £165,000 to year end Dec 04.

Churchlink West London, Flat 6, 147 Cromwell Road, London SW7 4DW
☎020 7370 4327
Furthering ecumenical cooperation in boroughs of Chelsea, Fulham, Hammersmith, Hampton, Hounslow, Kensington, Richmond (north), Spelthorne.
Convenor: Ms Annemarie DeVisser. No full-time staff. Began n/a; ecumenical. No magazine. Turnover n/a.

CLASP - Churches Linked Across Staffordshire & The Potteries, 18 Selman's Hill, Bloxwich, Walsall WS3 3RJ
☎01922 475 932
E: jmtopliss@fish.co.uk
Facilitating engagement in shared mission, social concern, worship, theological reflection; forum; church leaders' meeting.
Ecumenical Officer: Mr Michael Topliss. No full-time staff. Began 1993; interdenominational. (Previously Staffordshire Plus Ecumenical Council). Magazine: *Ecumentions* (Circulation n/a occasional). Turnover n/a.

Council of African and Afro-Caribbean Churches UK, 31 Norton House, Sidney Road, London SW9 0UJ
☎020 7274 5589 🖷020 7274 4726
Fostering mutual understanding and cooperation between member churches to make possible common witness and evangelism.
Chairman: His Grace the Most Rev Father Olu A Abiola OBE. No full-time staff. Began 1979; Pentecostal. No magazine. Turnover under £10,000 to year end Dec 00.

The Council of Oriental Orthodox Churches, 34 Chertsey Road, Church Square, Shepperton TW17 9LF
☎020 8368 8447 🖷020 8368 8447
E: nour@antaccia.u-net.com
Secretary: Deacon Aziz M Nour. No full-time staff. Began n/a. No magazine. Turnover n/a.

Covenanted Churches in Wales, 39 Cathedral Road, Cardiff CF11 9XF
☎029 2034 8200 🖷029 2038 7835
E: sion@cytun.org.uk
Web: www.cytun.org.uk
Being brought by the Spirit into one visible church to serve together in mission.
Secretary: Mr Sion Rhys Evans. Executive staff 1. ***CC*** No.506315. Began 1975; interdenominational. (Previously ENFYS). No magazine. Turnover n/a.

CYTUN: Churches Together in Wales, 58 Richmond Road, Cardiff CF24 3UR
☎029 2046 4204 🖷029 2045 5427
E: post@cytun.org.uk or churches@nationalassembly.freeserve.co.uk
Web: www.cytun.org.uk or www.nationalassembly.freeserve.co.uk
Churches together in Wales at national, regional and local level.
General Secretary: To be appointed. Executive staff 1, Other staff 4. ***CC*** No.246209. Began 1956; interdenominational. Magazine: *CYTÛN News/Newyddion CYTUN* (4,500 every four months). Turnover £80,000 to year end Dec 00.

†East Midlands Churches Forum, YMCA, St Rumbold Street, Lincoln LN2 5AR
☎01522 870 017 🖷01522 870 017
E: emcf@tesco.net
Web: www.emcf.org.uk
Coordinating advice and comment to the regional assembly and other appropriate regional agencies.
Administrative Officer: Mrs Pauline Nichols. Admin staff 1. Began 1998; ecumenical. No magazine. Turnover n/a.

ENVOY (Ecumenical Network in the Vale of York), The Manor, Moss End Farm, Hawkhills, Easingwold, York YO61 3EW
☎01347 838 593 🖷01347 838 710
E: jeanabbey@hotmail.co.uk
Futhering ecumenical projects in York and surrounding area.
Secretary: Mrs Jean Abbey. No full-time staff. Began n/a; ecumenical. No magazine. Turnover n/a.

Free Church Women's Forum, 27 Tavistock Square, London WC1H 9HH
☎020 7529 8132 🖷020 7529 8134
E: pauline@cte.org.uk
Bringing together Free Church women from national churches and local groups.
Secretary: Mrs Pauline Main. No full time staff. ***CC*** Began 1907; interdenominational. (Previously National Free Church Women's Council). No magazine. Turnover n/a.

Free Churches Group, Churches Together in England, 27 Tavistock Square, London WC1H 9HH
☎020 7529 8130 🖷020 7529 8134
E: mark.fisher@cte.org.uk
Representating and coordinating activities of the Free Church denominations in chaplaincy, education and ecumenical affairs.
Secretary: Rev Mark Fisher. *Moderator:* Rev David Coffey. Executive staff 3. ***CC*** No.236878. Began 1896; interdenominational. Linked with Churches Together in England. No magazine. Turnover £368,000 to year end Dec 02.

Gloucestershire Churches Together, Britannia Cottage, High Street, King's Stanley, Stonehouse GL10 3JD
☎01453 824 034
E: malcolm.alison@btinternet.com
Web: www.gloucestershirechurches together.co.uk
Fostering ecumenical relationships in the county, and links with national ecumenism.
County Ecumenical Officer: Rev Dr Alison R Evans. Executive staff 1. Began 1985; interdenominational. (Previously Churches Together in Gloucestershire). No magazine. Turnover £24,000 to year end Dec 02.

Greater Manchester Churches Together, St Peter's House, Oxford Road, Manchester M13 9GH
☎0161 273 5508
Coordinating the churches' service and witness within Greater Manchester and promoting Christian unity.
County Ecumenical Oficer: Rev Graham R Kent. Executive staff 3. ***CC*** Began 1924; ecumenical (interdenominational). Magazine: *Together* (Circulation & frequency n/a). Turnover £34,000 to year end Apr [illegible]5.

International Ministerial Council of Great Britain, 217 Langhedge Lane, Edmonton, London N18 2TG
☎020 8345 5376 🖷020 8887 6[illegible]59
E: imcgb@aol.com
Web: www.imcgb.com
Membership body for black and minority ethnic churches; fostering unity, respect and understanding.
General Secretary: Rt Rev Onye [illegible]bika. Executive staff 2, Admin staff 1. ***CC*** No.269440. Began 1968; ecumenical. No magazine. Turnover n/a

Irish Council of Churches, Inter-Church Centre, 48 Elmwood Avenue, Belfast BT9 6AZ
☎028 9066 3145 🖷028 9066 41[illegible]0
E: irish.churches@btconnect.com
Web: www.irishchurches.org
Partnership of Protestant and Orthodox Churches, working in cooperation with the Roman Catholic Church.
General Secretary: Mr Michael Earle. Executive staff 2, Other staff 1. ***CC*** Began 1922; interdenominational. Magazine: *Irish Ecumenical News* (Circulation & frequency n/a). Turnover £100,000 to year end Dec 99.

Joint Council for Anglo-Caribbean Churches, 141 Railton Road, London SE24 0LT
☎020 7737 6542 🖷020 7737 654[illegible]
Offering advice and consultancy services to member churches on administrative and social issues.
General Secretary: Rev Esme Beswick MBE. No full-time staff. ***CC*** Began 1985; interdenominational. No magazine. Turnover £21,000 to year end Aug 98.

KEY Churches Together, Methodist Central Hall, King Edward Street, Hull HU1 3SQ
☎01482 328 196 🖷01482 328 19[illegible]
E: cathy@keyct.karoo.co.uk
Web: www.keyct.org.uk
Covering all churches in Hull, East Yorkshire, Scarborough and Filey area; encouraging ecumenical development.
Administrative Secretary: Mrs Cathy Crumpton. No full-time staff. Began 19[illegible]1; interdenominational. (Previously Humberside Churches Council). Magazine: *Newsletter* (1,300 quarterly). Turnover £13,400 to year end Dec 02.

C

Lutheran Council of Great Britain, 30 Thanet Street, London WC1H 9QH
☎020 7554 2900 🖷020 7383 3081
E: enquiries@lutheran.org.uk
Web: www.lutheran.org.uk
Representing and coordinating common work of 10 national Lutheran churches with congregations in Britain.
Chairman: Very Rev Lennart Sjöström. *General Secretary:* Rev Thomas Bruch. *Treasurer:* Rev Juhaa Rintamäki. Executive staff 2, Other staff 15, Serving ministers n/a. **CC** No.232042. Began 1948. Turnover £[illegible]66,000 to year end Dec 04.

Mission Partnership of the Milton Keynes Churches Council, Christian Foundation, The Square, Aylesbury Street, Milton Keynes MK2 2HX
☎01908 331 310 🖷01908 311 310
E: admin@mkcc.fsnet.co.uk
Facilitating the working together of Milton Keynes' 100 churches.
Ecumenical Moderator: Rev Dr Mary Cotes. Executive staff 5, Other staff 2. **CC** No.29372[illegible]. Began 1967; interdenominational. (Previously Milton Keynes Christian Council). No magazine. Turnover £100,000 to year end Dec 02.

NECCT (North East Christian Churches Together), Ushaw College, Durham DH7 9RJ
☎01429 428 558
E: necct@northeastchurches.org.uk
Web: www.northeastchurches.org.uk
Oversight body for local ecumenical projects; encouraging coordination between denominations.
Secretary: Mrs Susan Atkinson. No full-time staff. Began 2001; interdenominational. (Previously Newcastle Church Relations Group). No magazine. Turnover £9,500 to year end Dec 02.

Norfolk & Waveney Churches Together, 21 Homefield Paddock, Beccles NR34 9NE
☎01502 717 744
E: aplatt@waitrose.com
Sponsoring body for local ecumenical partnerships to encourage churches to work together.
Executive Officer: Rev Andrew Platt. No full-time staff. Began 1990; interdenominational. (Previously Norfolk Churches Together). No magazine. Turnover n/a.

Somerset Churches Together, 25 Claverton Road West, Saltford, Bristol BS31 3AL
☎01225 872 903 🖷01225 872 903
E: sctog@blueyonder.co.uk
Web: www.sctog.org.uk
Encouraging and initiating ecumenical work.
Ecumenical Officer: Mr Robin Dixon. No full-time staff. Began 1983; interdenominational. (Previously Somerset and South Avon Ecumenical Council). Magazine: *Churches Together in Somerset* (1,200 quarterly). Turnover £14,000 to year end Jan 02.

South Devon District of the Congregational Federation, 85 Bowden Park Road, Crownhill, Plymouth PL6 5NQ
☎01752 708 903
Mutual support group for five Congregational churches; organising rallies, meetings.
Secretary: Mrs Greta M White. No full-time staff. **CC** No.268559. Began 1974; Congregational Federation. Magazine: *Newsletter* (30 occasionally). Turnover n/a.

Telford Christian Council, Meeting Point House, Southwater Square, Town Centre, Telford TF3 4HS
☎01952 291 904 🖷01952 213 555
E: davidlavender@telfordchristiancouncil.co.uk
Ecumenical council for Telford, sponsoring sector ministries, local ecumenical partnerships, bookshop, community and housing projects.
Ecumenical Dean: Rev David Lavender. *Director of Community and Housing Projects:* Mr Neil Finch. Executive staff 13, Other staff 37. **CC** No.510321. Began 1972; interdenominational. No magazine. Turnover £800,000 to year end Dec 02.

Trans-Atlantic & Pacific Alliance of Churches, 281 Rye Lane, Peckham, London SE15 4UA
☎020 7639 4058 M: 07949 945 540
E: tapacglobal@aol.com
Fostering visible unity and cooperation among churches as an umbrella organisation.
President: Archbishop Paul Hackman. Executive staff 3, Admin staff 2. **CC** No.04256140. Began n/a; Pentecostal. (Previously Christians Together in Visible Action for Global Missions). Magazine: *Tapac News* (100 quarterly). Turnover n/a.

United Protestant Council, Flat 3, Canford, 6 Dittons Road, Eastbourne BN21 1DN
☎01323 722 727
E: davidndyer@yahoo.co.uk
Web: www.unitedprotestantcouncil.com
Federal body supporting and coordinating approx 15 Protestant societies through corporate meetings and council.
Hon Secretary: David N Dyer. No full-time staff. Began 1898; interdenominational. No magazine. Turnover £3,000 to year end Dec 05.

West Midlands Region Churches Forum, The Place of Welcome, 172 Herbert Road, Small Heath, Birmingham B10 0PR
☎0121 766 5522
E: office@wmchurches.org.uk
Web: www.birminghamchurches.org.uk
Coordinating body for Birmingham, Herefordshire, Shropshire, Staffordshire, Warwickshire and Worcestershire.
General Secretary: To be appointed. Staff n/a. Began 1973; interdenominational. No magazine. Turnover n/a.

West Yorkshire Ecumenical Council, Hinsley Hall, 62 Headingley Lane, Leeds LS6 2BX
☎0113 261 8053 🖷0113 261 8054
E: office@wyec.co.uk
Proclaiming the Gospel by committed relationships, common witness and service in the world.
Acting County Ecumenical Officer: Rev David Rowland. Executive staff 1. Began 1986; interdenominational. Newspaper: *Unity Post* (30,000 annually). Turnover £50,000 to year end Dec 05.

Wiltshire Churches Together, 104 St Marks Avenue, Salisbury SP1 3DW
☎01722 328 686
E: morrismunns@aol.com
Oversight, care and support of local ecumenical partnership and other ecumenical activities.
County Ecumenical Officer: Rev Morris Munns. No full-time staff. Began 1987; interdenominational. No magazine. Turnover £14,000 to year end Aug 98.

Women's Co-ordinating Group for Churches Together in England, 27 Tavistock Square, London WC1H 9HH
☎020 7529 8132 🖷020 7529 8134
E: pauline@cte.org.uk
Secretary: Mrs Pauline Main. *Moderators:* Mrs Sheila Brain, Rev Celia Midgley. Executive staff 1, Other staff n/a. Began n/a; ecumenical. (Previously Women's Inter-Church Consultative Committee). No magazine. Turnover n/a.

C

DENOMINATIONAL HEADQUARTERS, NATIONAL & LOCAL

Other Churches & Religious Headquarters, Multi-faith Organisations in Section X on page 444, 445

Abundant Life Ministries, Abundant Life Centre, Wapping Road, Bradford BD3 0EQ
☎01274 307 233 🖷01274 303 008
E: network@alm.org.uk
Web: www.alm.org.uk
Network of churches linked to Abundant Life Church, England.
Senior Pastor: Mr Paul Scanlon. Executive staff 3, Admin staff 20, Serving ministers n/a. **CC** No.701289. Began 1989. Magazine: *Voice to the Nations* (15,000 quarterly). Turnover n/a.

C

American Church in London, Whitefield Memorial Church, 79a Tottenham Court Road, London W1T 4TD
☎020 7580 2791 🖷020 7580 5013
E: americanchurch@amchurch.fsnet.co.uk
Web: www.americanchurchinlondon.org
Sharing Christ with the international community.
Senior Minister: Rev Dr Ron F Allison. *Associate Minister:* Rev Logan Dunn. Executive staff 3, Admin staff 2, Serving ministers 2. Began 1969. Part of United Reformed Church English-speaking churches, Europe and the Middle East. Magazine: *Open Door* (450 monthly). Turnover £300,000 to year end Dec 06.

Ancient Orthodox Church (Canonical), Church House, 26 Hillside Terrace, Milton of Campsie, Glasgow G66 8BP
☎01360 311 903
Contact: Mr Ronald T P Harwood. Executive staff 2, Serving ministers n/a. Began 1970. No magazine. Turnover n/a.

Anglian Apostolic Episcopal Free Church, 50 Bells Place, Coleford GL16 8BX
☎Number not supplied
Administrator: Rt Rev Dr Terence Bovill. *Archbishop and Principal:* Most Rev Dr Bruno Von Ehrenberg. Executive staff 3, Serving ministers 23. Began 1840. No magazine. Turnover n/a.

The Anglican Catholic Church (Original Province) Diocese of the United Kingdom, Diocesan Office, 42 High Street, Lydd, Romney Marsh TN29 9AN
☎01797 321 704 🖷01797 321 704
E: enquiries@anglicancatholic.org.uk
Web: www.anglicancatholic.org.uk
Vicar General: Very Rev Damien Mead. *Episcopal Visitor:* Rt Rev Rommie M Starks. Executive staff 3, Serving ministers 9. **CC** No.1068168. Began 1992. Magazine: *ACC-UK* (20,000 quarterly). Turnover n/a.

Anglican Churches
See
Church in Wales Page 153
Church of England Page 154
Church of Ireland Page 163
Scottish Episcopal Church Page 175

†The Anglican Independent Communion in the British Isles & Europe, 11 Malpas Drive, Timperley, Altrincham WA14 5BH
☎0161 926 2642
M: 07762 240 193 🖷0161 926 2642
Presiding Bishop: Rt Rev Norman Dutton. Executive staff 1, Serving ministers 37. Began 1997. (Previously The Traditional Episcopal Church in the United Kingdom). No magazine. Turnover n/a.

Antiochian Orthodox Church, Church of Saint George, 1a Redhill Street, London NW1 4BG
☎020 783 0403 🖷020 783 0403
E: frsgholam@msn.com
Priest: Father Samir Gholam. *Chairman:* Dr Samir Hraiki. Executive staff 1, Serving ministers n/a. **CC** No.801540. Began 1989. No magazine. Turnover n/a.

Antiochian Orthodox Deanery of the United Kingdom and Ireland, 16 Pightle Close, Harston, Cambridge CB2 5NN
☎01223 872 433
E: aslanharper@clara.co.uk
Web: www.antiochian-orthodox.co.uk
Developing a British Orthodox presence and outreach rooted in the church of the apostles.
Dean: Fr Michael Harper. Executive staff 1, Serving ministers 16. **CC** No.1057533. Began n/a. (Previously British Antiochian Orthodox Deanery). No magazine. Turnover £22,000 to year end Apr 05.

***The Apostolic Church**, 17 Tawe Business Village, Phoenix Way, Enterprise Park, Swansea SA7 9LA
☎01792 790 300 🖷01792 790 363
E: admin@apostolic-church.org
Web: www.apostolic-church.org
National Leader: Rev Warren Jones. *Administrator:* Rev Andrew Saunders. Executive staff 7, Admin staff 3, Serving ministers 85. **CC** No.284789. Began 1916. No magazine. Turnover n/a.

Apostolic Faith Church, 66 Muscliffe Road, Winton, Bournemouth BH9 1NW
☎01202 528 270 🖷01202 528 270
E: afc-bmth@supanet.com
Pastor: Rev Duncan Lee. Serving ministers 3, Other staff 3. **CC** No.238009. Began 1908. Magazine: *Showers of Blessing* (10,000 weekly). Turnover n/a.

Apostolic Faith Mission UK, 95 Fenham Road, Peckham, London SE15 1AE
☎020 7639 8897 M: 07956 822 363 🖷020 7625 8685
E: worship@apostolic.org.uk
Web: www.apostolicfaith.org.uk
Pastor: Rev Isaac O Adigun. Admin staff 4, Serving ministers 9. **CC** No.1087489. Began 1906. Magazines: *Light of Hope* (3,000 every two months), *Higher Way* (3,000 every two months), *London News Report* (1,000 quarterly). Turnover n/a.

The Armenian Orthodox Church (Patriarchate of Etchmiadzin), Armenian Vicarage, Iverna Gardens, London W8 6TP
☎020 7937 0152
🖷020 7937 9049
E: arajnortaram@aol.com
Web: www.accc.org.uk
Also Pontifical Legate and a President of Churches Together in England.
Bishop: Rt Rev Nathan Hovhanissian. Executive staff n/a, Serving ministers n/a. Began n/a. No magazine. Turnover n/a.

***Assemblies of God Inc.**, PO Box 7634, Nottingham NG11 6ZY
☎0115 921 7272
🖷0115 921 7273
E: info@aog.org.uk
Web: www.aog.org.uk
General Administrator: Mr David [illegible] Gill. Admin staff 7, Serving ministers 1200. **CC** No.1032245. Began 1924. Magazine: *Joy* (5,000 monthly). Turnover n/a.
Central Region *Superintendent:* Pastor Calvin Young, Aston Christian Centre, Thomas Street, Birmingham B6 4T[illegible]
E: admin@astoncc.org.uk
☎0121 554 9638
www.astoncc.org.uk
East Midlands Region *Superintendent:* Pastor Philip Pye, Jacksdale Christian Centre, Franklin Road, Jacksdale, Nottingham NG16 5LG
☎01773 781 558
East Pennine Region *Superintendent:* Pastor John Morgan, Bethel Community Church, Royston Lane, Royston, Barnsley S71 4NJ
E: andrew@byteroyston.freeserve.co.uk
☎01226 723 298 🖷01226 723 298
Eastern Region *Superintendent:* Mr Dave Puddle, Grays Pentecostal Church, PO Box 164, Tilbury RM18 7WA
E: office@gpconline.org.uk
☎01375 843 261
www.gpconline.org.uk
Greater London Region *Superintendent:* Pastor Doug Williams, Emmanuel Christian Centre, 102 Erskine Road, Walthamstow, London E17 6SA
E: admin@eccaog.org
☎020 8509 3128 🖷020 8509 99[illegible]8
www.eccaog.org
North Wales and Midlands Region *Superintendent:* Pastor Jim Bowler, Carmel Christian Centre, Seymour Street, Denton, Manchester M34 3RW
E: carmelcc@talk21.com
☎0161 320 7308 🖷0161 366 96[illegible]8
www.carmelchristiancentre.org.uk
North West Region *Superintendent:* Pastor Bruce Millar, Bethesda, 11 Parkhills Road, Bury BL9 9AU
E: bethesda.pc@virgin.net
☎0161 761 6942
Northumbria Region *Superintendent:* Pastor Ken Gott, Metro Church International, Park Road, Sunderland SR2 8HR
E: kengott12@hotmail.com
☎0191 564 2000

Scottish Region *Superintendent:* Pastor Andrew Smith, Whitburn Pentecostal Church, Reveston Lane, Croftmalloch Road, Whitburn EH47 8HJ
E: wburnacg@aol.com
☎01501 741 447 📠 01501 745 064
www.whpc[illegible].com
South East Region *Superintendent:* Pastor Dario Bucceri, New Life Christian Fellowship, 8 Church Street, Margate CT9 1ST
E: admin@nlcfthanet.org
☎01843 221 259
www.nlcfthanet.org
South Wales Region *Superintendent:* Pastor Rae Galloway, Cardiff Christian Life Centre, PO Box 408, Cardiff CF10 2YN
E: admin@cardiff-clc.org
☎029 2047 0037
www.cardiff-clc.org
West Country Region *Superintendent:* Pastor Ian Williams, Living Waters Christian Centre, 527 Babbacombe Road, Torquay TQ1 1HG
E: williams@cherith6.freeserve.co.uk
☎01803 291 156 📠 01803 296 454

Assemblies of God Ireland, Carrig Eden, 1 Marine Road, Greystones, Co Wicklow, Republic of Ireland
☎00 353 1 201 6961
E: aogi@eircom.net
Web: www.agireland.org
National Director: Mr Gary Davidson. Executive staff 1, Admin staff n/a, Serving ministers n/a. Began n/a. No magazine. Turnover n/a.

Assemblies of the First Born, St Stephen's Church, Battersea Bridge Road, London SW11 3AE
☎020 7223 3099 📠020 7978 4135
Overseer: Rev Charles Wright. No full-time staff, Serving ministers n/a. **CC** No.258457. Began 1960. No magazine. Turnover n/a.

Associated Presbyterian Churches, APC Manse, 36 Newvalley, Stornoway, Isle of Lewis HS2 0DN
☎01851 703 217 📠01851 703 775
E: gimacaskill@mailblocks.com
Web: www.apchurches.org
Assistant Clerk of Presbytery: Rev George I Macaskill. Executive staff 1, Serving ministers 8. **CC** No.SCO 2313. Began 1989. Magazine: *APC News* (1,500 nine times per year). Turnover £110,000 to year end Dec 02.

Association of Baptist Churches in Ireland, The Baptist Centre, 19 Hillsborough Road, Moira, Craigavon BT67 0HG
☎028 9261 9267 📠028 9261 0150
E: abc@thebaptistcentre.org
Web: www.baptistinireland.org
Secretary: Rev W Colville. *Missions Secretary:* Rev Gordon Darragh. *Youth Secretary:* Mr Dave Ramsey. Executive staff 4, Other staff 7, Serving ministers n/a. **CC** No.XN 45793. Began 1895. (Previously Baptist Union of Ireland). Magazine: *Irish Baptist Life* (2,600 monthly). Turnover n/a.

†Assyrian Church of the East, Westminster Road, Hanwell, London W7 3TU
☎020 8567 1814 📠020 8567 1814
Archdeacon: Rev Stephen Yalda Turkhan. Serving ministers 2. Began 1977. No magazine. Turnover n/a.

Baptist Union of Great Britain, Baptist House, PO Box 44, 129 Broadway, Didcot OX11 8RT
☎01235 517 700 📠01235 517 715
E: info@baptist.org.uk
Web: www.baptist.org.uk
General Secretary: Rev Jonathan Edwards. Executive staff 1, Other staff 40. **CC** Began 1812. Magazine: *Baptist Times* (10,000 weekly), *Transform* (8,000 every four months). Turnover n/a.

See also:
Baptist House on Page 32
(BMS) World Mission on Page 284
Baptist Missions on Page 283
Baptist Times on Page 247
Baptist Union Corporation Ltd on Page 344
Baptist Union Publications Ltd on Page 120
Retired Baptist Ministers Housing Society Ltd on Page 59

Also see under
Baptist in Main Index on Page 522

***Baptist Union of Great Britain*: Central Association**, 17 Emmett Close, Emerson Valley, Milton Keynes MK4 2DY
☎01908 503 501 M: 07929 001 283
E: geoff@colmer77.fsnet.co.uk
Serving the churches of Bedfordshire, Buckinghamshire, Hertfordshire and Northamptonshire.
Team Leader: Rev Geoffrey Colmer. Executive staff 4, Serving ministers 160. **CC** No.1090606. Began 1915. No magazine. Turnover £135,000 to year end Dec 02.
General Secretary: Rev Stephen Copson, 60 Strathmore Avenue, Hitchin SG5 1ST
E: stephen.copson@dsl.pipex.com
☎01462 442 548

***Baptist Union of Great Britain*: East Midland Association**, 25 Coningsby Road, Woodthorpe, Nottingham NG5 4LH
☎0115 967 9679
Team Leader: Rev Peter Grange. *Administrator:* Mrs Rachel Tole. Executive staff 1, Other staff 2, Serving ministers n/a. Began n/a. No magazine. Turnover n/a.

***Baptist Union of Great Britain*: Eastern Association**, 7 The Furrells, Linton, Cambridge CB1 6JJ
☎01223 890 141 📠01223 890 141
E: paul.hills@easternbaptist.org.uk
Web: www.easternbaptist.org.uk
Comprising former Cambridgeshire, Norfolk, Suffolk and Essex Associations.
Team Leader: Rev Paul Hills. Executive staff 3, Admin staff 3, Serving ministers 157. **CC** No.1089795. Began n/a. No magazine. Turnover n/a.

***Baptist Union of Great Britain*: Heart of England Association**, Unit 8, 137 Newhall Street, Birmingham B3 1SF
☎0121 212 4842 📠0121 212 4512
E: mailbox@baptist-heartofengland.org
Web: www.baptist-heartofengland.org
Team Leader: To be appointed. *Administrator:* Karen Martindale. Executive staff 7, Admin staff 3, Serving ministers 160. **CC** No.1080529. Began 2001. No magazine. Turnover n/a.

******Baptist Union of Great Britain*: London Association**, 28 Chadwick Road, Leytonstone, London E11 1NF
☎020 8530 8179
E: pmtook@aol.com
Web: ourworld.compuserve.com/homepages/cphicks/lbahome.htm
Team Leader: Rev Dr Patricia Took. Executive staff 5, Admin staff 4, Serving ministers 320. **CC** No.1091160. Began n/a. No magazine. Turnover £255,000 to year end Dec 05.
Association Secretary: Rev Paul Martin, 235 Shaftesbury Avenue, London WC2H 8EP
E: lbaoffice@londonbaptist.org.uk
☎020 7692 5592 📠 020 7692 5593

***Baptist Union of Great Britain*: North Western Association**, The Resource Centre, Fleet Street, Wigan WN5 0DS
☎01942 221 595 📠01942 227 768
E: baptnw1@aol.com
Regional Ministers: Rev Phil Jump, Rev Andrew Funnell (Church Life), Rev Sandra Crawford (Youth). Executive staff 2, Other staff 1, Serving ministers 125. **CC** No.247113. Began n/a. No magazine. Turnover n/a.

***Baptist Union of Great Britain*: Northern Association**, 23 Church Wynd, Sherburn, Durham DH6 1QU
☎0191 372 3727
E: johnclaydon@thenba.org.uk
Web: www.thenba.org.uk
Team Leader: Rev John Claydon. *Association Secretary:* Mr David Lennox. Executive staff 3, Serving ministers 43. **CC** No.1092595. Began 1690. No magazine. Turnover n/a.

***Baptist Union of Great Britain*: South Eastern Association**, 40 Ashden Walk, Tonbridge TN10 3RL
☎01732 361 005 M: 07984 951 530
E: normantharby@btopenworld.com
Comprising Kent, North Downs Association and Sussex Association.
Team Leader: Rev Norman Tharby. Executive staff 1, Serving ministers 115. **CC** No.1093252. Began n/a. No magazine. Turnover n/a.

******Baptist Union of Great Britain*: South Wales English Association**, 54 Richmond Road, Cardiff CF24 3UR
☎029 2021 9691
E: nickbradshaw@btconnect.com
Regional Minister & Team Leader: Rev Nick Bradshaw. Executive staff 3, Serving ministers 150. Began 1915. No magazine. Turnover n/a.
Note: For other Baptists in Wales see Baptist Union of Wales

C

***Baptist Union of Great Britain*: South West Association**, Regional Office, Wonford Baptist Chapel, 36 Wonford Street, Exeter EX2 5DL
☎01392 433 533
E: office@swbaptists.org.uk
Web: www.swbaptists.org.uk
Comprising the former Devon and Cornwall and Western Associations.
Team Leader: Rev Jez Brown. Executive staff 1, Serving ministers 80. Began 2002. No magazine. Turnover n/a.

***Baptist Union of Great Britain*: Southern Counties Association**, 138 Barkham Ride, Finchampstead, Wokingham RG40 4EL
☎0118 973 3049
E: r.standing@scba.org.uk
Web: www.scba.org.uk
Berkshire, Buckinghamshire, Dorset, Gloucestershire, Guernsey, Hampshire, Isle of Wight, Middlesex, Northamptonshire, Oxfordshire, Surrey, Sussex, Warwickshire.
Regional Ministers: Rev Dr Roger Standing, Rev Kathryn Morgan, Mrs Gill Crippen. Executive staff 4, Serving ministers 173. ***CC*** No.1091066. Began n/a. No magazine. Turnover n/a.

***Baptist Union of Great Britain*: West of England Association**, The Old Forge, Broom Hill, Stapleton, Bristol BS16 1DN
☎0117 965 8828 🖷0117 965 8838
E: office@webassoc.org.uk
Web: www.webassoc.org.uk
Comprising Bristol, Gloucestershire, Wiltshire and East Somerset Associations.
Team Leader: Rev Nigel Coles. Executive staff 3, Serving ministers 90. ***CC*** No.1092443. Began n/a. No magazine. Turnover n/a.

***Baptist Union of Great Britain*: Yorkshire Association**, 1 South Parade, Headingley, Leeds LS6 3LF
☎0113 278 4954 🖷0113 230 7950
E: debbie.gamble@yba.org.uk
Web: www.yba.org.uk
Regional Minister: Rev Ernie Whalley. *Regional Minister (Mission):* Rev Graham Brownlee. Executive staff 2, Other staff 7, Serving ministers 110. ***CC*** No.247173. Began n/a. No magazine. Turnover £190,000 to year end Dec 05.

***Baptist Union of Scotland**, 14 Aytoun Road, Glasgow G41 5RT
☎0141 423 6169 🖷0141 424 1422
E: admin@scottishbaptist.org.uk
Web: www.scottishbaptist.org.uk
For details of local churches contact the Union or see listings on website.
Director: Rev Bill Slack. Executive staff 5, Admin staff 7, Serving ministers 150. ***CC*** No.SCO 04960. Began 1869. Magazine: *BUS News* (Circulation n/a monthly (on website)). Turnover n/a.

Baptist Union of Wales, Ty Ilston, 94 Mansel Street, Swansea SA1 5TZ
☎01792 655 468 🖷01792 469 489
E: peter@bedyddwyrcymru.co.uk
General Secretary: Rev Peter Thomas. Executive staff 3, Serving ministers 100. Began 1866. Magazine: *Seren Cymru* (1,000 weekly), *Cristion* (350 every two months), *Ilston Newsfile* (800 quarterly). Turnover n/a.
Anglesey Association *Association Secretary:* Rev Ienan E Jones, Pen Parc, 12 New Park Road, Holyhead LL65 1PH
☎01407 761 231
Arfon Association *Association Secretary:* Mrs Katie Pritchard, Rhosydd, 66 Ffordd Iorwerth, Nefyn, Pwllheli LL53 6NE
☎01758 720 424
Brecon Association *Association Secretary:* Mrs Betty Williams, Wern Willm Cottage, Erwood, Builth Wells LD2 3AY
☎01982 560 421
Carmarthenshire and Cardigan Association *Association Secretary:* Rev Wynn Vittle, 2 Bryn Tywi, Llangynnwr, Carmarthen SA31 2NZ
☎01267 236 572
Denbigh, Flint and Merioneth Association *Association Secretary:* Miss Einwen Jones, Rhyd Lafar, Glyn Ceiriog, Llangollen LL20 7EY
☎01691 718 383
East Glamorgan Association *Association Secretary:* Rev Eifion Wynne, Golygfa, 17 Ivor Terrace, Dowlais, Merthyr Tydfil CF48 3SW
☎01685 377 896
Gwent Welsh Association *Association Secretary:* Rev Dr Peter Baines, Greenfield, School Lane, Govilion, Abergavenny NP7 9NT
☎01873 831 619
Pembrokeshire English Association *Secretary:* Rev Roger Hart, Bethany Manse, 3 Treowen, Pembroke SA72 6NY
☎01646 686 044
Pembrokeshire Welsh Association *Association Secretary:* Rev D Carl Williams, 78 Stryd Fawr, Abergwaun, Fishguard SA65 9AU
☎01348 872 190
Radnor and Montgomery Association *Association Secretary:* Rev Meredith Powell, Arosta, Hillfield, Llanidloes SY18 6ET
E: wo@meredithpowel.freeserve.co.uk
☎01686 412 452 🖷 01686 412 452
West Glamorgan Association *Association Secretary:* Rev Alan Jones, 10 Park Howard Avenue, Llanelli SA15 3JY
☎01554 774 537

Beneficial Veracious Christ Church, 281 Rye Lane, Peckham, London SE15 4UA
☎020 7639 4058 🖷020 7639 4058
E: bvcchurch@aol.com
Archbishop: Bishop Paul Hackman. Executive staff 9, Other staff 5, Serving ministers 14. ***CC*** No.1028128. Began 1988. Magazine: *Beneficial Trumpet* (3,000 quarterly). Turnover n/a.

B'nai Maccabim Messianic Synagogue (Yeshua Ministries), 36 Clydesdale Close, Borehamwood WD6 2SD
☎020 8236 0995
🖷020 8236 0995
E: DrRF1997@aol.com
Supporting spiritual revival among Messianic Jews; annual conferences; book publication and distribution; teaching; temporal support.
Messianic Rabbi: Dr Ruth Fleischer. Executive staff 1, Serving ministers n/a. Began 1981. (Previously London Messianic Congregation). Magazine: *Yeshua Journal* (500 quarterly). Turnover £40,000 to year end Mar 05.

†Born Again Christ Healing Church International, 77 Beechwood Road, Hornsey, London N8 7NE
☎020 8340 9962
🖷020 8341 5323
E: bachci@aol.com
Chief Prophet: Most Rev Prophetess Fidilia N Onyuku-Opukiri. Executive staff 4, Admin staff 2, Serving ministers 5. Began 1979. Magazine: *BAJ* (150 quarterly). Turnover n/a.

British Conference of Mennonites, 14 Shepherds Hill, Highgate, London N6 5AQ
☎0845 450 0214
🖷020 8341 6807
E: director@menno.org.uk
Web: www.menno.org.uk
Contact: Vic Thiessen. Executive staff 1, No serving ministers. Began 198[illegible]. No magazine. Turnover n/a.

***Bruderhof Communities in the UK**, Darvell Bruderhof, Robertsbridge TN32 5DR
☎01580 883 300
🖷01580 883 317
Web: www.bruderhof.co.uk
Minister: Name not supplied. Executive staff 1, Serving ministers 3. ***CC*** No.229226. Began 1936; Anabaptist. Magazine: *The Plough* 1,500 quarterly). Turnover n/a.

Byelorussian Autocephalic Orthodox Church, Address not supplied
☎01394 273 820
Administrator: Very Rev Fr John Abab[illegible]ko. Executive staff 2, Admin staff 2, Serving ministers n/a. Began 1948. No magazine. Turnover n/a.

Catholic Bishops' Conference Secretariat, 39 Eccleston Square, London SW1V 1BX
☎020 7901 4810
🖷020 7901 4819
E: secretariat@cbcew.org.uk
Web: www.catholicchurch.org.uk
Supporting the Catholic Bishops' conference of England and Wales.
General Secretary: Mgr Andrew Summersgill. Executive Staff 6, Other staff 12. **CC** No.1097482. Began 19[illegible]4. No magazine. Turnover n/a.

See also:
Roman Catholic Bishops' Conference
Departments for:
Catholic Education and Formation on Page 410
International Affairs on Page 180
Mission and Unity on Page 298
Responsibility and Citizenship on Page 130
Consultative Bodies:
Catholic Youth Services on Page 398
National Justice and Peace Network on Page 380

***Roman Catholic* Diocese of Aberdeen**, Bishop's House, 3 Queen's Cross, Aberdeen AB15 4XU
☎01224 319 154 🖷01224 325 570
🖃: administrator.rcdioceseofaberdeen@dial.pipex.com
Bishop of Aberdeen: Rt Rev Peter Moran. Executive staff n/a, Serving ministers n/a. Began 1131. Province of St Andrews and Edinburgh. No magazine. Turnover n/a.

***Roman Catholic* Diocese of Argyll and the Isles**, Bishop's House, Esplanade, Oban PA34 5AB
☎01631 567 436 🖷01631 564 986
🖃: rcdargyllandisles@supanet.com
Web: www.dioceseofargyllandtheisles.org
Bishop of Argyll & the Isles: Rt Rev Ian Murray. Executive staff n/a, Serving ministers 33. Began 1878. No magazine. Turnover n/a.

***Roman Catholic* Archdiocese of Armagh**, Ara Coeli, Armagh BT61 7QY
☎028 3752 2045 🖷028 3752 6182
🖃: admin@aracoeli.com
Web: www.armagharchdiocese.org
Archbishop of Armagh & Primate of All Ireland: Most Rev Seán Brady. Executive staff 2, Serving ministers 172. Began 444. No magazine. Turnover n/a.
Auxiliary Bishop of Armagh: Most Rev Gerard Clifford, Annaskeagh, Ravensdale, Dundalk, Co Louth, Republic of Ireland
☎00 353 42 71012

***Roman Catholic* Diocese of Arundel & Brighton**, Highoaks, Old Brighton Road North, Pease Pottage, Crawley RH11 9AJ
☎01293 526 428 🖷01293 614 714
🖃: bishop@dabnet.org
Bishop of Arundel & Brighton: Rt Rev Kieran Conry. Executive staff 14, Pastoral and Admin staff 28, Serving ministers 143. ***CC*** No.252878. Began 1965. Province of Southwark. Magazine: *A & B News* (5,000 monthly). Turnover n/a.
Vicar General: Rt Rev Mgr Canon John Hull, Bishop's House, Upper Drive, Hove BN3 6NE
☎01273 506 387 🖷 01273 501 527

***Roman Catholic* Archdiocese of Birmingham**, Archbishop's House, 8 Shadwell Street, Birmingham B4 6EY
☎0121 236 9090 🖷0121 212 0171
🖃: archbishop@rc-birmingham.org
Web: www.birminghamdiocese.org.uk
Archbishop of Birmingham: Most Rev Vincent Nichols. Executive staff n/a, Serving ministers 444. ***CC*** No.234216. Began 1850. No magazine. Turnover n/a.
Auxiliary Bishop: Rt Rev Philip Pargeter, Grove House, 90 College Road, Sutton Coldfield B73 5AH
☎0121 354 4363
Auxiliary Bishop: Rt Rev David McGough, The Rocks, 106 Draycott Road, Tean, Stoke-on-Trent ST10 4JF
☎01538 722 433

***Roman Catholic* Diocese of Brentwood**, Bishop's House, Stock, Ingatestone CM4 9BU
☎01277 840 268
Web: www.dioceseofbrentwood.net
Bishop of Brentwood: Rt Rev Thomas McMahon. Executive staff n/a, Serving ministers 181. Began 1917. Province of Westminster. No magazine. Turnover n/a.
Chancellor: Rev G Read, Cathedral House, Ingrave Road, Brentwood CM15 8AT
☎01227 265 213

***Roman Catholic* Archdiocese of Cardiff**, Archbishop's House, 43 Cathedral Road, Cardiff CF11 9HD
☎029 2022 0411 🖷029 2039 9036
🖃: arch@rcadc.org or secretary@rcadc.org
Archbishop of Cardiff: Most Rev Peter Smith. Executive staff 5, Other staff 7, Serving ministers 139. ***CC*** No.242380. Began 1895. Magazine: *Cardiff People* (Circulation n/a monthly). Turnover n/a.

***Roman Catholic* Diocese of Clifton**, St Ambrose, North Road, Leigh Woods, Bristol BS8 3PW
☎0117 973 3072
Web: www.cliftondiocese.com
Bishop: Rt Rev Declan Langham. *Vicars General:* Rev Mgr Canon Gabrial Leydon, Rev Mgr Canon Jeremy Rigden. Executive staff 3, Admin staff 11, Serving ministers 142. ***CC*** No.233977. Began 1850. Province of Birmingham. No magazine. Turnover n/a.

***Roman Catholic* Diocese of Clogher**, Bishop's House, Monaghan, Republic of Ireland
☎00 353 478 1019
🖷00 353 478 4773
🖃: cloghdiocoffmon@eircom.net
Web: www.clogherdiocese.ie
Bishop of Clogher: Most Rev Joseph Duffy. Executive staff n/a, Serving ministers 94. Began n/a. Province of Armagh. No magazine. Turnover n/a.

***Roman Catholic* Diocese of Derry**, PO Box 227, Londonderry BT48 9YG
☎028 7126 2302 🖷028 7137 1960
🖃: office@derrydiocese.org
Bishop of Derry: Most Rev Seamus Hegarty. Executive staff n/a, Serving ministers 134. Began n/a. Province of Armagh. No magazine. Turnover n/a.
Auxiliary Bishop of Derry: Most Rev Francis Lagan, 9 Glen Road, Strabane BT82 8BX
☎028 7188 4553 🖷 028 7188 4551

***Roman Catholic* Diocese of Down and Connor**, Lisbreen, 73 Somerton Road, Belfast BT15 4DE
☎028 9077 6185 🖷028 9077 9377
🖃: dccuria@downandconnor.org
Web: www.downandconnor.org
Bishop of Down and Connor: Most Rev Patrick Walsh. Executive staff n/a, Serving ministers 236. Began n/a. Province of Armagh. No magazine. Turnover n/a.
Auxiliary Bishop: Most Rev Anthony Farquhar, 24 Fruithill Park, Andersonstown, Belfast BT11 8GE
☎028 9077 6185 🖷 028 9077 9377
Auxiliary Bishop: Most Rev Donal McKeown, 96 Downview Park West, Belfast BT15 5HZ
☎028 9078 1642 🖷 028 9077 9377

***Roman Catholic* Diocese of Dromore**, Bishop's House, Violet Hill, Newry BT35 6PN
☎028 3026 2444 🖷028 3060 3026
🖃: bishopofdromore@btinternet.com
Bishop of Dromore: Most Rev John McAreavey. Executive staff n/a, Serving ministers 45. Began n/a. Province of Armagh. No magazine. Turnover n/a.

***Roman Catholic* Diocese of Dunkeld**, 24 Lawside Road, Dundee DD3 6XY
☎01382 225 453 🖷01382 204 585
🖃: bishop.logan@dunkelddio.org
Web: www.dunkelddiocese.org.uk
Bishop of Dunkeld: Rt Rev Vincent Logan. Admin staff 10, Serving ministers 44, Deacons 11. ***CC*** No.CR 33859. Began 1878. Province of St Andrews and Edinburgh. Magazine: *Dunkeld News* (3,000 quarterly). Turnover n/a.

***Roman Catholic* Diocese of East Anglia**, The White House, 21 Upgate, Poringland, Norwich NR14 7SH
☎01508 492 202/493 956
🖷01508 495 358
🖃: office@east-angliadiocese.org.uk
Web: www.catholiceastanglia.org
Bishop of East Anglia: Rt Rev Michael Evans. Admin staff 7, Serving ministers 129. ***CC*** No.278742. Began 1976. Province of Westminster. Magazine: *Our Diocesan Family* (3,000 frequency n/a). Turnover n/a.

***Roman Catholic* Diocese of Galloway**, 8 Corsehill Road, Ayr KA7 2ST
☎01292 266 750/289 888
🖷01292 289 888
E: administration@gallowaydiocese.org.uk
Web: www.gallowaydiocese.org.uk
Bishop of Galloway: Rt Rev John Cunningham. *Vicar General:* Rt Rev Joseph Boyd. *Diocesan Secretary:* Mrs Ann Tierney. Executive staff 2, Serving ministers 36. ***CC*** No.CR 35354. Began 398. Province of St Andrews and Edinburgh. Magazine: *The Galloway Newsletter* (10,000 half-yearly). Turnover £750,000 to year end Dec 02.

***Roman Catholic* Archdiocese of Glasgow**, Curial Offices, 196 Clyde Street, Glasgow G1 4JY
☎0141 226 5898
🖷0141 225 2600
E: curia@rcag.org.uk
Web: www.rcag.org.uk
Archbishop of Glasgow: Most Rev Mario J Conti. *Vicar General:* Mgr John Gilmartin. *Chancellor:* Mgr Peter Smith. Executive staff 8, Admin staff 40, Serving ministers 589. ***CC*** No.CR 35422. Began 1492. Magazine: *Flourish* (15,000 monthly). Turnover £12,000,000 to year end Dec 02.

***Roman Catholic* Diocese of Hallam**, Bishop's House, 75 Norfolk Road, Sheffield S2 2SZ
☎0114 278 7988
🖷0114 278 7988
E: bishopofhallam@btinternet.com
Web: www.hallam-diocese.com
Bishop of Hallam: Rt Rev John Rawsthorne. Admin staff 10, Serving ministers 69. Began 1980. Province of Liverpool. Magazine: *Hallam News* (10,000 monthly). Turnover n/a.

***Roman Catholic* Diocese of Hexham and Newcastle**, Bishop's House, East Denton Hall, 800 West Road, Newcastle upon Tyne NE5 2BJ
☎0191 228 0003
🖷0191 274 0432
E: office@rcdhn.org.uk
Web: www.rcdhn.org.uk
Bishop of Hexham and Newcastle: Rt Rev Kevin Dunn. Executive staff n/a, Serving ministers 221. ***CC*** No.235686. Began 1850. Province of Liverpool. Magazine: *Northern Cross* (7,200 monthly). Turnover n/a.

***Roman Catholic* Diocese of Lancaster**, Bishop's Apartment, Cathedral House, Balmoral Road, Lancaster LA1 3BT
☎01524 596 050
🖷01524 596 053
E: bishop@lancasterrcdiocese.org.uk
Web: www.churchnet.ucsm.ac.uk/lancs_rc
Bishop of Lancaster: Rt Rev Patrick O'Donoghue. Executive staff n/a, Serving ministers 250. ***CC*** No.234331. Began 1924. Province of Liverpool. Magazine: *The Voice* (Circulation n/a monthly). Turnover n/a.

***Roman Catholic* Diocese of Leeds**, Bishop's House, 13 North Grange Road, Headingley, Leeds LS6 2BR
☎0113 230 4533 🖷0113 278 9890
E: leedscathport@aol.com
Web: www.dioceseofleeds.org.uk
Bishop of Leeds: Rt Rev Arthur Roche. Executive staff 7, Admin staff 10, Serving ministers 170. Began 1878. Province of Liverpool. Magazine: *Catholic Post* (20,000 monthly). Turnover n/a.
Pastoral Centre *General Manager:* Mr Austin Smith, Hinsley Hall, 62 Headingley Lane, Leeds LS6 2BX
E: info@hinsley-hall.co.uk
☎0113 261 8000 🖷 0113 224 2406

***Roman Catholic* Archdiocese of Liverpool**, Archbishop's House, Carnatic Road, Liverpool L18 8BY
☎0151 724 6398 🖷0151 724 6405
E: archbishop.liverpool@rcaolp.co.uk
Archbishop of Liverpool: Most Rev Patrick Kelly. Executive staff n/a, Serving ministers 412. Began 1850. Magazine: *Pictorial* (15,000 weekly). Turnover n/a.
Auxiliary Bishop: Rt Rev Vincent Malone, 17 Westoak, Oakhill Park, Liverpool L13 1BN
E: vmalone@onetel.com
☎0151 228 7637
Auxiliary Bishop: Rt Rev Thomas A Williams, 14 Hope Place, Liverpool L1 9BG
E: bpwilliams@rcaolp.co.uk
☎0151 703 0109 🖷 0151 703 0267

***Roman Catholic* Diocese of Menevia**, Curial Office, 27 Convent Street, Swansea SA1 2BX
☎01792 644 017 🖷01792 458 641
Bishop of Menevia: Rt Rev Mark Jabale. *Coadjutore Bishop:* To be appointed. Executive staff 3, Admin staff 3, Serving ministers 62. ***CC*** No.234168. Began 1987. Province of Cardiff. Magazine: *Menevia News-Dolen Mynyw* (Circulation & frequency n/a). Turnover n/a.
Vicar General: Rt Rev Mgr Provost David Bottrill, Maes-Gwyn, 63 Margam Road, Margam, Port Talbot SA13 2HR
☎01639 883 323

***Roman Catholic* Diocese of Middlesbrough**, Bishop's House, 16 Cambridge Road, Middlesbrough TS5 5NN
☎01642 818 253 🖷01642 850 548
E: bishopsecretary@dioceseofmiddlesborough.co.uk
Bishop of Middlesbrough: Rt Rev John Crowley. Admin staff 20, Serving ministers 80. Began 1875. Province of Liverpool. Magazine: *Catholic Voice* (20,000 monthly). Turnover n/a.
Financial Secretary: Dr James Whiston, Curial Office, 50a The Avenue, Linthorpe, Middlesbrough TS5 6QT
E: bishopsecretary@dioceseofmiddlesborough.co.uk
☎01642 850 505 🖷 01642 851 404

***Roman Catholic* Diocese of Motherwell**, Diocesan Centre, Coursington Road, Motherwell ML1 1PP
☎01698 269 114 🖷01698 275 [illegible]30
E: chancellor@rcdom.org.uk
Web: www.rcdom.org.uk
Bishop of Motherwell: Rt Rev Joseph Devine. *Vicars General:* Rt Rev John J Burns, Rev Thomas O'Hare. Executive staff 3, Admin staff 15, Serving ministers 134. ***CC*** No.CR37435. Began 1948. Province of Glasgow. No magazine. Turnover n/a.

***Roman Catholic* Diocese of Northampton**, Bishop's House, Marriott Street, Northampton NN2 6AW
☎01604 715 635 🖷01604 792 [illegible]86
E: admin@northamptondiocese.com
Web: www.northamptondiocese.org
Bishop of Northampton: Rt Rev Peter Doyle. Executive staff 2, Serving ministers 131. ***CC*** No.234091. Began 1850. Province of Westminster. Magazine: *The Vine* (Circulation n/a monthly). Turnover n/a.

***Roman Catholic* Diocese of Nottingham**, 27 Cavendish Road East, The Park, Nottingham NG7 1BB
☎0115 947 4786 🖷0115 947 52[illegible]5
E: bishopsecretary@nrcdt.org.uk
Web: www.nottinghamdiocese.org.uk
Bishop of Nottingham: Rt Rev Malcolm McMahon OP. Admin staff 2, Serving ministers 100. ***CC*** No.234064. Began 1850. Province of Westminster. No magazine. Turnover n/a.

***Roman Catholic* Diocese of Paisley**, Diocesan Centre, Cathedral Precinct, Incle Street, Paisley PA1 1HR
☎0141 847 6130 🖷0141 847 614[illegible]
E: diocesanoffice@paisleydiocese.org.uk
Web: www.paisleydiocese.org.uk
Bishop of Paisley: Rt Rev Philip Tartaglia. *Vicar General:* Mgr Gerald Gallagher. Admin staff 3, Serving ministers 67. ***CC*** No.SCO 13514. Began 1947. Province of Glasgow. No magazine. Turnover n/a.

***Roman Catholic* Diocese of Plymouth**, Bishop's House, 31 Wyndham Street West, Plymouth PL1 5RZ
☎01752 224 414 🖷01752 223 75[illegible]
E: bishop@plymouth-diocese.org.uk
Web: www.plymouth-diocese.org.uk
Bishop of Plymouth: Rt Rev Christopher Budd. Admin staff 23, Serving ministers 100. ***CC*** No.213227. Began 1850. Province of Southwark. No magazine. Turnover n/a.

***Roman Catholic* Diocese of Portsmouth**, Bishop's House, Edinburgh Road, Portsmouth PO1 3HG
☎023 9282 0894 🖷023 9286 3086
E: bishop@rcdp.org.uk
Web: www.portsmouth-dio.org.uk
Bishop of Portsmouth: Rt Rev Crispian Hollis. Admin staff n/a, Serving ministers 150. Began 1882. Province of Southwark. No magazine. Turnover n/a.

C

***Roman Catholic* Archdiocese of St Andrews & Edinburgh**, Archbishop's House, 42 Greenhill Gardens, Edinburgh EH10 4BJ
☎0131 447 3337
Archbishop of St Andrews & Edinburgh: His Eminence Most Rev Cardinal Keith P O'Brien. Executive staff 5, Admin staff 10, Serving ministers 130. Began 1878. No magazine. Turnover n/a.
Diocesan Secretary: To be appointed, Chancery Offices, 100 Strathearne Road, Edinburgh EH9 1BB
E: chancery@staned.org.uk
☎0131 623 8900
🖷0131 623 8399

***Roman Catholic* Diocese of Salford**, Wardley Hall, Worsley, Manchester M28 2ND
☎0161 794 2325
🖷0161 727 8592
E: revsec@wardleyhall.org.uk
Web: www.wardleyhall.org.uk
Bishop of Salford: Rt Rev Terence J Brain. Executive staff n/a, Serving ministers 281. ***CC*** No.250037. Began 1850. Province of Liverpool No magazine. Turnover n/a.

***Roman Catholic* Diocese of Shrewsbury**, Laburnum Cottage, 97 Barnston Road, Barnston, Heswall, Wirral CH61 1BW
☎0151 648 0623
🖷0151 648 0624
E: curia@dioceseofshrewsbury.org
Web: www.dioceseofshrewsbury.org
Bishop of Shrewsbury: Rt Rev Brian M Noble. Executive staff n/a, Serving ministers 132. ***CC*** No.234025. Began 1850. Province of Birmingham. Magazine: *Catholic Voice* (Circulation n/a monthly). Turnover n/a.
Bishop's Secretary: Miss M Lightbound, Curial Offices, 2 Park Road South, Prenton CH43 4UX
☎0151 652 9855
🖷 0151 653 5172

***Roman Catholic* Archdiocese of Southwark**, Archbishop's House, St George's Road, Southwark, London SE1 6HX
☎020 7928 2495/5592
🖷020 7928 7833
E: aps@rcsouthwark.co.uk
Web: www.rcsouthwark.co.uk
Archbishop: Most Rev Kevin McDonald. Admin staff 4, Other staff 8, Serving ministers 509. ***CC*** No.235468. Began 1850. No magazine. Turnover n/a.
Auxiliary Bishop of Southwark: Rt Rev John Hine, Bishop's Flat, The Hermitage, More Park, West Malling ME19 6HN
☎01732 845 486
Auxiliary Bishop of Southwark: Rt Rev Paul Hendricks VG, The Friary, Friary Road, Peckham, London SE15 1RH

***Roman Catholic* Archdiocese of Westminster**, Archbishop's House, Ambrosden Avenue, London SW1P 1QJ
☎020 7798 9033 🖷020 7798 9077
E: enquiries@rcdow.org.uk
Web: www.rcdow.org.uk
Cardinal Archbishop of Westminster: His Eminence Cormac Murphy-O'Connor. *Private Secretary:* Rev Mark O'Toole. *Auxiliary Bishops:* Rt Rev John Arnold, Rt Rev George Stack, Rt Rev Alan Hopes, Rt Rev Barnard Longley also at above address. Admin staff 152, Serving ministers 800. ***CC*** No.233699. Began 1850. Magazine: *Westminster Record* (Circulation & frequency n/a). Turnover n/a.

***Roman Catholic* Diocese of Wrexham**, Bishop's House, Sontley Road, Wrexham LL13 7EW
☎01978 262 726 🖷01978 354 257
E: diowxm@globalnet.co.uk
Web: www.wrexham.diocese.btinternet.co.uk
Bishop of Wrexham: Rt Rev Edwin Regan. *Vicar General:* Rev Peter Brignall. Admin staff 2, Serving ministers 40. ***CC*** No.700426. Began n/a. Province of Cardiff. Magazine: *North Wales Catholic* (Circulation & frequency n/a). Turnover n/a.

Celtic Orthodox Church: British Eparchy, Saint Anne's Monastic House, 33 Brownlow Street, York YO31 8LW
☎01904 626 599 M: 07867 561 386
Web: www.celticorthodox.org
British Eparch: His Grace, Bishop Stephen. Executive staff n/a, Serving ministers 14. ***CC*** No.1064510. Began 1866. Magazine: *Parish News and Newsletters* (Circulation n/a monthly). Turnover n/a.

***Chinese Church in London**, 69 Brook Green, Hammersmith, London W6 7BE
☎020 7602 9092 🖷020 7602 0092
E: admin@ccil.org.uk
Web: www.ccil.org.uk
Administrator: Mr Yip. *Senior Pastor:* Rev S H Ong. *Associate Senior Pastor:* Rev Robert Tang. Admin staff 4, Serving ministers 10. ***CC*** No.1107558. Began 1951. No magazine. Turnover £500,000 to year end Dec 02.

†Christ Apostolic Church of Great Britain, 64 Gifford Street, London N1 0DF
☎020 8365 1842 🖷020 8365 1842
E: admin@cac-7sister.org.uk
Web: www.cac-7sister.org.uk
Minister-in-Charge: Pastor M Akkinola. Executive staff 16, Serving ministers 2. Began 1979. No magazine. Turnover n/a.

Christ Apostolic Church Mount Bethel, 215 Kingsland Road, London E2 8AN
☎020 7729 4375
M: 07770 304 604 🖷020 7613 4204
E: info@cacbethel.org
Web: www.cacbethel.org
Apostle: Apostle Ayo Omideyi. Executive staff 3, Admin staff 8, Serving ministers 2. ***CC*** No.274154. Began 1974. Magazine: *Sower Outreach* (1,000 quarterly). Turnover n/a.

Christian Brethren, Abbey Court, Cove, Tiverton EX16 7RT
☎01398 331 105 or 01590 676 407
E: neil.summerton@ruralinternet.co.uk
A contact point for the Christian Brethren, who have no central or regional denominational bodies.
Chairman & Executive Director, Partnership: Dr Neil Summerton. No full-time staff, Full-time pastoral leaders 190. Began 1830. Magazine: *Partnership Perspectives* (520 every four months), *International Partnership Perspectives* (800 annually). Turnover n/a.

C

The Christian Community (London West), Temple Lodge, 51 Queen Caroline Street, Hammersmith, London W6 9QL
☎020 8748 8388
🖷020 8748 8327
E: templelodgeclub@btconnect.com
Priest: Rev Peter van Breda. Executive staff n/a, Serving ministers 17. ***CC*** No.210905. Began 1961. Magazine: *Perspectives* (Circulation n/a every two months). Turnover n/a.

Christian Outreach Centre (European Office), North Street, Portslade, Brighton BN41 1DG
☎01273 433 422
🖷01273 433 423
E: coceurope@coc.org.uk
Administrative headquarters for Christian Outreach Centres across Europe and UK. Also Global Compassion (caring arm).
European Administrator: Mr Ashley Gullo. *European Chairman:* Pastor Ashley Schmierer. Admin staff 2, Serving ministers 26. ***CC*** No.1107128. Began 1994. No magazine. Turnover n/a.

Church in Wales, 39 Cathedral Road, Cardiff CF11 9XF
☎029 2034 8200
🖷029 2038 7835
E: information@churchinwales.org.uk
Web: www.churchinwales.org.uk
Archbishop of Wales: Most Rev Dr Barry Morgan. *Provincial Secretary:* Mr J M Shirley. *Principal Officer for Mission and Ministry:* Rev Robert Paterson. Executive staff 2, Serving ministers - see dioceses. Began n/a. (Disestablished 1920). Magazines: *Highlights* (6,000 half-yearly), *Llan* (800 monthly). Turnover n/a.
Provincial Assistant Bishop: Rt Rev David Thomas, Bodfair, 3 White's Close, Abergavenny NP7 5HZ
E: pab@churchinwales.org.uk
☎01873 858 780
🖷 01873 858 269

***Church in Wales* Diocese of Bangor**, Diocesan Centre, Cathedral Close, Bangor LL57 1RL
☎01248 354 999 🖷01248 353 882
Web: www.esgobaethbangordiocese.org
Diocesan Secretary: Ms Stella Schultz. *Chapter Clerk and Cathedral Administrator:* Mr Martin J Brown. Executive staff 3, Admin staff 5, Serving ministers 80. ***CC*** No.1075931. Began 550. Magazine: *Y Ddolen/The Link* (3,000 every four months). Turnover £1,405,536 to year end Dec 04.
Bishop of Bangor: Rt Rev Anthony Crockett, Church in Wales, Ty'r Esgob, Bangor LL57 2SS
E: dbf.bangor@churchinwales.org.uk
☎01248 354 999 🖷 01248 372 454
Archdeacon of Bangor: Ven Meurig Llwyd Williams, The Archdeaconry, 1 Belmont Road, Bangor LL57 2LL
☎01248 354 369
Archdeacon of Merioneth: Ven Emyr W Rowlands, The Rectory, Newtown Road, Machynlleth SY20 8HE
☎01654 702 261

C

***Church in Wales* Diocese of Llandaff**, The Diocesan Office, The Court, Coychurch, Bridgend CF35 5EH
☎01656 868 868 🖷01656 868 869
E: peteratkins@churchinwales.org
Web: www.churchinwales.org.uk/Llandaff
Diocesan Secretary: Mr Peter Atkins. Executive staff 4, Admin staff 3, Serving ministers 189. Began 460. Magazine: *Diocesan Leaflet* (26,000 quarterly). Turnover n/a.
Bishop of Llandaff & Archbishop of Wales: The Most Rev Dr Barry Morgan, Llys Esgob, The Cathedral Green, Llandaff, Cardiff CF5 2YE
E: archbishop@churchinwales.org.uk
☎029 2056 2400 🖷 029 2056 8410
Assistant Bishop of Llandaff & Archdeacon of Morgannwg: Ven Dr David Yeoman, 3 Dennison Way, Michaelston-super-Ely, Cardiff CF5 4SF
E: asstbishop@churchinwales.org.uk
☎029 2059 8110
Archdeacon of Llandaff: Ven Bill Thomas, 6 Rachel Close, Danescourt, Llandaff, Cardiff CF5 2SH
☎029 2056 2991 🖷 029 2056 2991
Archdeacon of Margam: Ven Philip G Morris, The Vicarage, Southerndown Road, St Brides Major, Bridgend CF32 0SD
E: archdeacon.margam@llandaff.org.uk
☎01656 880 108

***Church in Wales* Diocese of Monmouth**, 64 Caerau Road, Newport NP20 4HJ
☎01633 267 490 🖷01633 265 586
Web: www.churchinwales.org.uk
Diocesan Secretary: Mr R J Tarran. Executive staff 4, Serving ministers 104. Began 1921. Magazine: *Diocesan Newsletter* (12,000 every two months). Turnover £2,000,000 to year end Dec 02.
Bishop of Monmouth: Rt Rev Dominic Walker, Bishopstow, Stow Hill, Newport NP20 4EA
E: bishop.monmouth@churchinwales.org.uk
☎01633 263 510 🖷 01633 259 946
Archdeacon of Monmouth: Ven Glyndwr Hackett, The Rectory, 1 Millbrook Court, Little Hill, Pontypool NP4 0HT
E: glyndwrhackett@tiscali.co.uk
☎01495 785 528 🖷 01495 785 528
Archdeacon of Newport: Ven Kenneth W Sharpe, The Archdeaconry, 93 Stow Hill, Newport NP20 4EA
☎01633 215 012

***Church in Wales* Diocese of St Asaph**, Diocesan Office, High Street, St Asaph LL17 0RD
☎01745 584 321
Web: www.churchinwales.org.uk
Diocesan Secretary: Rev Brian Harvey. Executive staff 1, Serving ministers 112. Began 1921. Magazine: *Diocesan News* (15,500 quarterly). Turnover n/a.
Bishop of St Asaph: Rt Rev John S Davies, Esgobty, Upper Denbigh Road, St Asaph LL17 0TW
☎01745 583 503 🖷 01745 584 301
Archdeacon of Montgomery: Ven John Thelwell, The Vicarage, Berriew, Welshpool SY21 8PL
☎01686 640 223
Archdeacon of St Asaph: Ven E. Bernard Thomas, The Rectory, Ffordd Las, Llandyrnog, Denbigh LL16 4LT
☎01824 790 777
Archdeacon of Wrexham: Ven Malcolm Squires, The Rectory, Llandeyla, Wrexham LL11 3AW
☎01978 790 362

***Church in Wales* Diocese of St Davids**, Diocesan Office, Abergwili, Carmarthen SA31 2JG
☎01267 236 145 🖷01267 223 046
E: mandywp@churchinwales.org.uk
Web: www.churchinwales.org.uk
Diocesan Secretary: Mrs Valerie Hockey. Executive staff 2, Admin staff 6, Serving ministers 139. ***CC*** No.231239. Began 590. Magazine: *Pobl Dewi* (Circulation & frequency n/a). Turnover n/a.
Bishop of St Davids: Rt Rev Carl Cooper, Llys Esgob, Abergwili, Carmarthen SA31 2JG
E: bishop.stdavid@churchinwales.org.uk
☎01267 236 597 🖷 01267 237 482
Archdeacon of Cardigan: Ven Andrew John, The Vicarage, Cwmann, Lampeter SA48 8DV
☎01267 236 145
Archdeacon of Carmarthen: Ven Alun W Evans, The Vicarage, Cynwyl Elfed, Carmarthen SA33 6TH
E: archdeacon.alun@tiscali.co.uk
☎01267 281 605
Archdeacon of St Davids: Ven Dr John Holdsworth, The Vicarage, Steynton, Milford Haven SA73 1AW
☎01646 692 867

***Church in Wales* Diocese of Swansea & Brecon**, The Diocesan Centre, The Cathedral Close, Brecon LD3 9DP
☎01874 623 716 🖷01874 623 716
E: dbf@sandb.org.uk
Web: www.churchinwales.org.uk
Diocesan Secretary: Mrs Heather Price. Executive staff n/a, Serving ministers 90. Began 1923. Magazine: *Yr Eryr* (Circulation n/a every two months). Turnover n/a.
Bishop of Swansea and Brecon: Rt Rev Anthony E Pierce, Diocesan Centre, The Cathedral Close, Brecon LD3 9DP
E: dbf@sandb.org.uk
☎01874 623 716 🖷 01874 623 716
Archdeacon of Brecon: Ven Randolph Thomas, The Vicarage, Bronllys, Brecon LD3 0HS
E: RevThomasStPeter@aol.com
☎01874 711 200
Archdeacon of Gower: Ven Robert Williams, 56 Pinewood Road, Uplands, Swansea SA2 0LT
E: archdeaconofgower@swansea andbrecon.org.uk
☎01792 297 817

Church of Christ, 64 Grenville Road, Southcourt, Aylesbury HP21 8EZ
☎01296 421 064
E: gafisher888@aol.com
Web: www.christian-worker.org.uk
Magazine Editor: Mr Graham Fisher. No full-time staff. Began 1969. The address and person given are solely as information points. Magazine: *The Christian Worker* (1,100 monthly). Turnover n/a.

Church of England Archbishops' Council and General Synod Church House, Great Smith Street, London SW1P 3NZ
☎020 7898 1000 🖷020 7898 13[illegible]9
E: <firstname.surname>@c-of-e.org.uk
Web: www.cofe.anglican.org
Secretary General: Mr William Fittall. Full-time staff 279. Began n/a. Archbishops' Council, 1999. No Relevant Journals. Turnover n/a.

See also:
Anglican Religious Communities on Page 179
Archbishop's Council - Committee for Ministry among Deaf People on Page 337
Archbishop's Council and Research and Statistics on Page 381
Association of Ordinands and Candidates for Ministry on Page [illegible]79
The Cathedrals Fabric Commission for England on Page 3[illegible]4
Central Readers' Council on Page [illegible]80
Church House Publishing on Page 121
Church of England Chaplaincies in Further and Higher Education on Page 142
Church of England National Youth Office on Page 398
Communications Department on Page 358
The Corporation of the Church House on Page 181
Council for Christian Unity on Page 182
Council for the Care of Churches on Page 182
Dioceses Commission on Page 1[illegible]2
Enquiry Centre on Page [illegible]58
Finance Division of the Archbishops' Council on Page 347
Hospital Chaplaincies Council on Page 142
Legal Advisory Commission on Page 183

See also entry under
Church of England in Main Index on Page 522

***Church of England* Diocese in Europe**, 14 Tufton Street, London SW1P 3QZ
☎020 7898 1155 🖷020 7898 1166
E: diocesan.office@europe.c-of-e.org.uk
Web: www.europe.anglican.org
Serving 280 congregations in 43 countries.
Diocesan Secretary: Mr Adrian Mumford.
Assistant Diocesan Secretary: Mrs Jeanne French. Executive staff n/a, Serving ministers 140. ***CC*** No.250186. Began 1980. Province of Canterbury. Magazine: *The European Anglican* (7,000 quarterly). Turnover £7,000,000 to year end Dec 05.
Bishop of Gibraltar in Europe: Rt Rev Dr Geoffrey Rowell, Bishop's Lodge, Church Road, Worth, Crawley RH10 7RT
E: diocesan.office@europe.c-of-e.org.uk
☎01293 883 051 🖷 020 7898 1166
Suffragan Bishop in Europe: Rt Rev David Hamid
Archdeacon in the Gulf: Ven Alan Hayday
Archdeacon of Cyprus: Very Rev Steve Collis
Archdeacon of the Eastern Archdeaconry: Ven Patrick Curran
Archdeacon of Germany & North Europe: Ven Mark Oakley
Archdeacon of Gibraltar: Ven Alan Woods
Archdeacon of Italy & Malta: Ven Arthur Siddall
Archdeacon of North West Europe: Ven Dirk Van Leeuwen
Archdeacon of France: To be appointed
Archdeacon of Switzerland: To be appointed

***Church of England* Diocese of Bath and Wells**, The Old Deanery, Wells BA5 2UG
☎01749 670 777 🖷01749 674 240
E: nick.denison@bathwells.anglican.org
Web: www.bathwells.anglican.org
Diocesan Secretary: Mr Nicholas Denison. Executive staff 20, Serving ministers 319. ***CC*** No.249398. Began 909. Province of Canterbury. Magazine: *The Grapevine* (62,000 monthly). Turnover n/a.
Bishop of Bath and Wells: Rt Rev Peter Price, Bishop's Palace, Wells BA5 2PD
E: bishop@bathwells.anglican.org
☎01749 672 341 🖷 01749 679 355
Suffragan Bishop of Taunton: To be appointed, Bishop's Lodge, Monkton Heights, West Monkton, Taunton TA2 8LU
E: bishoptaunton@talk21.com
☎01823 413 526 🖷 01823 412 805
Archdeacon of Bath: Ven Andrew Piggott, 56 Grange Road, Saltford, Bristol BS31 3AG
E: adbath@bathwells.anglican.org
☎01225 873 609 🖷 01225 874 110
Archdeacon of Taunton: Ven John Reed, 4 Westerkirk Gate, Staplegrove, Taunton TA2 6BQ
E: adtaunton@bathwells.anglican.org
☎01823 323 838 🖷 01823 325 420
Archdeacon of Wells: Ven Peter Maurice, 6 The Liberty, Wells BA5 2SU
E: adwells@bathwells.anglican.org
☎01749 685 147

***Church of England* Diocese of Birmingham**, 175 Harborne Park Road, Birmingham B17 0BH
☎0121 426 0400 🖷0121 428 1114
Diocesan Secretary: Mr Jim Drennan. Admin staff 34, Serving ministers 270. ***CC*** Began 1905. Province of Canterbury. Magazine: *Bulletin* (830 monthly). Turnover n/a.
Bishop of Birmingham: Rt Rev David Urquhart, Bishop's Croft, Old Church Road, Harborne, Birmingham B17 0BG
E: bishop@birmingham.anglican.org
☎0121 427 1163 🖷 0121 426 1322
Suffragan Bishop of Aston: To be appointed, Diocesan Office, 175 Harborne Park Road, Birmingham B17 0BH
E: bishopofaston@birmingham.anglican.org
☎0121 426 0400 🖷 0121 428 1114
Archdeacon of Aston: Ven Dr Brian Russell, Diocesan Office, 175 Harborne Park Road, Birmingham B17 0BH
E: archdeaconofaston@birmingham.anglican.org
☎0121 426 0400 🖷 0121 428 1114
Archdeacon of Birmingham: Ven Hayward Osborne, Diocesan Office, 175 Harborne Park Road, Birmingham B17 0BH
E: archdeaconofbham@birmingham.anglican.org
☎0121 426 0400 🖷 0121 428 1114

***Church of England* Diocese of Blackburn**, Diocesan Offices, Cathedral Close, Blackburn BB1 5AA
☎01254 503 070 🖷01254 667 309
Web: www.blackburn.anglican.org
Diocesan Secretary: Mr Graeme Pollard. Executive staff 10, Other staff 10, Serving ministers 246. Began 1926. Province of York. Magazine: *The See* (49,000 monthly). Turnover n/a.
Bishop of Blackburn: Rt Rev Nicholas Reade, Bishop's House, Ribchester Road, Blackburn BB1 9EF
E: secretary@bishopofblackburn.org.uk
☎01254 248 234 🖷 01254 246 668
Suffragan Bishop of Burnley: Rt Rev John Goddard, Dean House, 449 Padiham Road, Burnley BB12 6TE
☎01282 470 360 🖷 01282 470 361
Suffragan Bishop of Lancaster: To Be Appointed, The Vicarage, Shireshead, Forton, Preston PR3 0AE
☎01524 799 900 🖷 01524 799 901
Archdeacon of Blackburn: Ven John Hawley, 19 Clarence Park, Blackburn BB2 7FA
E: archdeacon.blackburn@milestonenet.co.uk
☎01254 262 571 🖷 01254 263 394
Archdeacon of Lancaster: Ven Peter Ballard, Wheatfield, 7 Dallas Road, Lancaster LA1 1TN
E: peter.ballard@blackburn.anglican.org
☎01524 328 97

***Church of England* Diocese of Bradford**, Diocesan Offices, Kadugli House, Elmsley Street, Steeton, Keighley BD20 6SE
☎01535 650 555 🖷01535 650 550
E: office@kadugli.org.uk
Web: www.bradford.anglican.org
Diocesan Secretary: Mr Malcolm K Halliday. Executive staff 1, Serving ministers 140, Other staff 10. ***CC*** No.247858. Began 1919. Province of York. Magazine: *Newsround* (25,000 quarterly). Turnover n/a.
Bishop of Bradford: Rt Rev David James, Bishopcroft, Ashwell Road, Bradford BD9 4AO
E: office@kadugli.org.uk
☎01274 545 414
Archdeacon of Bradford: Ven Dr David Lee, 14 Park Cliffe Road, Undercliffe, Bradford BD2 4NS
E: davidjlee@blueyonder.co.uk
☎01274 641 337 🖷 01274 641 337
Archdeacon of Craven: Ven Paul Slater, Woodlands, Netherghyll Lane, Cononley, Keighley BD20 8PB
E: paul.slater@bradford.anglican.org
☎01535 635 133

***Church of England* Diocese of Bristol**, Church House, 23 Great George Street, Bristol BS1 5QZ
☎0117 906 0100 🖷0117 925 0460
E: lesley.farrall@bristoldiocese.org or web-verger@bristoldiocese.org
Web: www.bristol.anglican.org
Diocesan Secretary: Mrs Lesley Farrall.
Finance Manager: Mr D Hargrave. Admin staff 15, Serving ministers 157. ***CC*** No.248502. Began 1524. Province of Canterbury. Magazine: *Newspaper* (20,000 monthly). Turnover £6,800,000 to year end Dec 04.
Bishop of Bristol: Rt Rev Mike Hill, Church House, 23 Great George Street, Bristol BS1 5QZ
E: bishop@bristoldiocese.org
☎0117 906 0100 🖷 0117 925 0460
Suffragan Bishop of Swindon: Rt Rev Lee Rayfield, Mark House, Field Rise, Swindon SN1 4HP
☎01793 538 654
Archdeacon of Bristol: Ven Timothy McClure, Church House, 23 Great George Street, Bristol BS1 5QZ
E: tim.mcclure@bristoldiocese.org
☎0117 906 0102 🖷 0117 925 0460
Archdeacon of Malmesbury: Ven Alan F Hawker, Church Paddock, Church Lane, Kington Langley, Chippenham SN15 5NR
E: alan@venjen.fsnet.co.uk
☎01249 750 085

***Church of England* Diocese of Canterbury**, Lady Woottons Green, Canterbury CT1 1NQ
☎01227 459 401 🖷01227 450 964
E: reception@diocant.org
Web: www.canterbury.anglican.org
Diocesan Secretary: Mr David S Kemp. Executive staff 6, Admin staff 20, Serving ministers 170. ***CC*** No.249972. Began 597. Province of Canterbury. Magazine: *Outlook* (25,000 monthly). Turnover n/a.
Archbishop of Canterbury: Most Rev & Rt Hon Dr Rowan Williams, Lady Woottons Green, Canterbury CT1 1NQ
E: reception@diocant.org
☎01227 459 401 🖷 01227 450 964
Also at: *Primate of All England & Metropolitan:* Most Rev & Rt Hon Dr Rowan Williams, Lambeth Palace, London SE1 7JU
☎020 7928 1200 🖷 020 7898 1281
Suffragan Bishop of Dover: Rt Rev Stephen Venner, Bishop's Office, Old Palace, Canterbury CT1 2EE
E: bishop@bishcant.org
☎01227 459 382
Suffragan Bishop of Maidstone: Rt Rev Graham Cray, Bishop's House, Pett Lane, Charing, Ashford TN27 0DL
E: bishop@bishmaid.org
☎01233 712 950
Archdeacon of Canterbury: Ven Patrick Evans, 29 The Precincts, Canterbury CT1 2EP
E: patrick@canterbury-cathedral.org
☎01227 865 238 🖷 01227 785 209
Archdeacon of Maidstone: Ven Philip Down, The Old Rectory, The Street, Pluckley, Ashford TN27 9AT
E: pdown@archdeacmaid.org
☎01233 840 291 🖷 01233 840 759

***Church of England* Diocese of Carlisle**, Church House, West Walls, Carlisle CA3 8UE
☎01228 522 573 🖷01228 815 400
E: enquiries@carlislediocese.org.uk
Web: www.carlislediocese.org.uk
Diocesan Secretary: Mr Derek Hurton. Executive staff 4, Other staff 10, Serving ministers 183. ***CC*** No.251977. Began 1133. Province of York. Magazine: *Carlisle Diocesan News* (35,000 monthly). Turnover n/a.
Bishop of Carlisle: Rt Rev Graham Dow, Rose Castle, Dalston, Carlisle CA5 7BZ
E: resources@carlislediocese.org.uk
☎01228 522 573 🖷 01228 594 899
Suffragan Bishop of Penrith: Rt Rev James Newcome, Holm Croft, 13 Castle Road, Penrith LA9 7AU
E: bishop.penrith@carlislediocese.org.uk
☎01539 727 836 🖷 01539 734 380
Archdeacon of Carlisle: Ven Dr David Thomson, 2 The Abbey, Carlisle CA3 8TZ
E: archdeacon.north@carlislediocese.org.uk
☎01228 523 026 🖷 01228 594 899
Archdeacon of West Cumberland: Ven Colin Hill, 50 Stainburn Road, Workington CA14 1SN
E: adcnwest@primex.org.uk
☎01900 661 90 🖷 01900 603 534
Archdeacon of Westmoreland and Furness: Ven George Howe, The Vicarage, Windermere Road, Lindale, Grange-over-Sands LA11 6LB
E: archdeacon.south@carlislediocese. org.uk
☎01539 534 717 🖷 01539 535 090

***Church of England* Diocese of Chelmsford**, Diocesan Office, 53 New Street, Chelmsford CM1 1AT
☎01245 294 400 🖷01245 294 477
Web: www.chelmsford.anglican.org
Chief Executive: Mr Steven Webb. Executive staff 28, Admin staff 28, Serving ministers 411. ***CC*** No.249505. Began 1914. Province of Canterbury. Magazine: *East Window* (47,500 monthly). Turnover n/a.
Bishop of Chelmsford: Rt Rev John Gladwin, Bishopscourt, Main Road, Margaretting, Ingatestone CM4 0HD
E: bishopscourt@chelmsford.anglican.org
☎01277 352 001 🖷 01277 355 374
Area Bishop of Barking: Rt Rev David Hawkins, Verulam Avenue, Walthamstow, London E17 8ES
E: b.barking@chelmsford.anglican.org
☎020 8509 7377 🖷 020 8521 4097
Area Bishop of Bradwell: Rt Rev Dr Laurie Green, Bishop's House, Orsett Road, Horndon-on-the-Hill, Stanford-le-Hope SS17 8NS
E: b.bradwell@chelmsford.anglican.org
☎01375 673 806 🖷 01375 674 222
Area Bishop of Colchester: Rt Rev Christopher Morgan, 1 Fitzwalter Road, Lexden, Colchester CO3 3SS
☎01206 576 648 🖷 01206 576 648
E: b.colchester@chelmsford.anglican.org
Archdeacon of Colchester: Ven Annette Cooper, 63 Powers Hall End, Witham CM8 1NH
E: a.colchester@chelmsford.anglican.org
☎01376 513 130 🖷 01376 500 789
Archdeacon of Harlow: Ven Peter Taylor, Glebe House, Church Lane, Sheering, Bishop's Stortford CM22 7NR
E: a.harlow@chelmsford.anglican.org
☎01279 734 524 🖷 01279 734 426
Archdeacon of Southend: Ven David Lowman, Archdeacon's Lodge, 136 Broomfield Road, Chelmsford CM1 1RN
E: a.southend@chelmsford.anglican.org
☎01245 258 257 🖷 01245 250 845
Archdeacon of West Ham: Ven Michael Fox, 86 Aldersbrook Road, Manor Park, London E12 5DH
E: a.westham@chelmsford.anglican.org
☎020 8989 8557 🖷 020 8530 1311

***Church of England* Diocese of Chester**, Church House, Lower Lane, Aldford, Chester CH3 6HP
☎01244 620 444 🖷01244 620 456
E: stephen.marriott@chester.anglican.org
Web: www.chester.anglican.org
Diocesan Secretary: Rev Canon Stephen Marriott. Executive staff n/a, Serving ministers 267. ***CC*** No.248968. Began 1541. Province of York. Magazine: *Chester Diocesan News* (70,000 monthly). Turnover n/a.
Bishop of Chester: Rt Rev Dr Peter Forster, Bishop's House, Abbey Square, Chester CH1 2JD
E: bpchester@chester.anglican.org
☎01244 350 864 🖷 01244 314 187
Suffragan Bishop of Birkenhead: To be appointed, Bishop's Lodge, 67 Biston Road, Oxton, Prenton CH43 6TR
E: bpbirkenhead@chester.anglican.org
☎0151 652 2741 🖷 0151 651 2330
Suffragan Bishop of Stockport: Rt Rev Nigel Stock, Bishop's Lodge, Back Lane, Dunham Town, Altrincham WA14 4SG
E: bpstockport@chester.anglican.org
☎0161 928 5611 🖷 0161 929 0692
Archdeacon of Chester: Ven Donald Allister, Church House, Lower Lane, Aldford, Chester CH3 6HP
E: donald.allister@chester.anglican.org
☎01244 620 444 🖷 01244 620 456
Archdeacon of Macclesfield: Ven Richard J Gillings, 5 Robins Lane, Bramhall, Stockport SK7 2PE
E: richard.gillings@chester.anglican.org
☎0161 439 2254 🖷 0161 439 0378

***Church of England* Diocese of Chichester**, Church House, 211 New Church Road, Hove BN3 4ED
☎01273 421 021 🖷01273 421 041
E: diosec@diochi.org.uk
Web: www.diochi.org.uk
Diocesan Secretary: Mr J M R Prichard. Executive staff 10, Other staff 29, Serving ministers 521. ***CC*** No.243134. Began 681. Province of Canterbury. Magazine: *The Chichester Leaflet* (28,000 monthly), *The Chichester Magazine* (7,000 quarterly). Turnover n/a.
Bishop of Chichester: Rt Rev John Hind, The Palace, Chichester PO19 1PY
E: bishchichester@diochi.org.uk
☎01243 782 161 🖷 01243 531 332
Area Bishop of Horsham: Rt Rev Lindsay G Urwin, Bishop's House, 21 Guildford Road, Horsham RH12 1LU
E: bishhorsham@diochi.org.uk
☎01403 211 139 🖷 01403 217 349
Area Bishop of Lewes: Rt Rev Wallace Benn, Bishop's Lodge, 16a Prideaux Road, Eastbourne BN21 2NB
E: bishlewes@diochi.org.uk
☎01323 648 462 🖷 01323 641 514
Archdeacon of Chichester: Ven Douglas McKittrick, 2 Yorklands, Dyke Road Avenue, Hove BN3 6RW
E: archchichester@diochi.org.uk
☎01273 421 021 🖷 01273 421 041
Archdeacon of Horsham: Ven Roger Combes, 3 Danehurst Crescent, Horsham RH13 5HS
E: archhorsham@diochi.org.uk
☎01403 262 710 🖷 01403 210 778
Archdeacon of Lewes & Hastings: Ven Philip Jones, 27 The Avenue, Lewes BN7 1DT
E: archlandh@diochi.org.uk
☎01273 479 530 🖷 01273 476 529

***Church of England* Diocese of Coventry**, Cathedral and Diocesan Offices, 1 Hill Top, Coventry CV1 5AB
☎024 7652 1200 🖷024 7652 1300
Web: www.coventry.anglican.org
Diocesan Secretary: Mrs Simon Lloyd. Executive staff 8, Serving ministers 200. ***CC*** No.247828. Began 1918. Province of Canterbury. Turnover n/a.
Bishop of Coventry: Rt Rev Colin Bennetts, Bishop's House, 23 Davenport Road, Coventry CV5 6PW
☎024 7667 2244 🖷 024 7671 3271
Suffragan Bishop of Warwick: Rt Rev John Stroyan, Warwick House, 139 Kenilworth Road, Coventry CV4 7AF
☎024 7641 2627 🖷 024 7641 5254

Archdeacon of Coventry: Ven Mark W Bryant, Cathedral and Diocesan Offices, 1 Hill Top, Coventry CV1 5AB
E: mark.bryant@covcofe.org
☎024 7652 1200 🖷 024 7652 1300
Archdeacon of Warwick: Ven Michael J J Paget-Wilkes, 10 Northumberland Road, Leamington Spa CV32 6HA
E: michael.pagetwilkes@covcofe.org
☎024 7652 1200 🖷 024 7652 1300

***Church of England* Diocese of Derby**, Derby Church House, Full Street, Derby DE1 3DR
☎01332 388 650 🖷01332 292 969
E: finance@derby.anglican.org
Web: www.derby.anglican.org
Diocesan Secretary: Mr Bob Carey. Executive staff n/a, Serving ministers n/a. **CC** No.249767. Began 1927. Province of Canterbury. Magazine: *Our Diocese* (Circulation & frequency n/a). Turnover n/a.
Bishop of Derby: Rt Rev Alastair Redfern, The Bishop's House, 6 King Street, Duffield, Belper DE56 4EU
E: pa@bishopofderby.org
☎01332 840 132 🖷 01332 842 743
Suffragan Bishop of Repton: To be appointed. Derby Church House, Full Street, Derby DE1 3DR
☎01332 388 650 🖷01332 292 969
Archdeacon of Chesterfield: Ven David Garnett, The Old Vicarage, Church Street, Baslow, Bakewell DE45 1RY
E: davidcgarnett@yahoo.co.uk
☎01246 583 928
Archdeacon of Derby: Ven Dr Christopher Cunliffe, 1 Thatch Close, Derby DE22 1EA
E: archderby@talk21.com
☎01332 383 676 🖷 01332 292 969

***Church of England* Diocese of Durham**, Diocesan Office, Auckland Castle, Bishop Auckland DL14 7QJ
☎01388 604 515 🖷01388 603 695
E: diocesan.secretary@durham.anglican.org
Web: www.durham.anglican.org
Diocesan Secretary: Mr Ian Boothroyd. Executive staff 7, Admin staff 8, Serving ministers 235. **CC** No.248287. Began 635. Province of York. Magazine: *Durham Newslink* (27,000 monthly). Turnover n/a.
Bishop of Durham: Rt Rev Tom Wright, Auckland Castle, Bishop Auckland DL14 7NR
E: bishop@bishopdunelm.co.uk
☎01388 602 576 🖷 01388 605 264
Suffragan Bishop of Jarrow: Rt Rev John Pritchard, Bishop House, Ivy Lane, Low Fell, Gateshead NE9 6QD
E: bishop.of.jarrow@durham.anglican.org
☎0191 491 0917 🖷 0191 491 5116
Archdeacon of Auckland: To be appointed, Diocesan Office, Auckland Castle, Bishop Auckland DL14 7QJ
E: archdeacon.of.auckland@durham.anglican.org
☎01388 604 515 🖷01388 603 695
Archdeacon of Durham: Ven Ian Jagger, 15 The College, Durham DH1 3EQ
E: archdeacon.of.durham@durham.anglican.org
☎0191 384 7534 🖷 0191 386 6915

Archdeacon of Sunderland: Ven Stuart Bain, St Nicholas' Vicarage, Hedworth Lane, Boldon Colliery NE35 9JA
E: archdeacon.of.sunderland@durham.anglican.org
☎0191 536 2300 🖷 0191 519 3369

***Church of England* Diocese of Ely**, Diocesan Office, Bishop Woodford House, Barton Road, Ely CB7 4DX
☎01353 652 702 🖷01353 652 745
E: matthew.lavis@office.ely.anglican.org
Web: www.ely.anglican.org
Diocesan Secretary: Dr Matthew Lavis. Admin staff 6, Other staff 6, Serving ministers 127. **CC** Began 1109. Province of Canterbury. Magazine: *Ely Ensign* (11,000 monthly). Turnover n/a.
Bishop of Ely: Rt Rev Dr Anthony Russell, Bishop's House, Ely CB7 4DW
E: bishop@ely.anglican.org
☎01353 662 749 🖷 01353 669 477
Suffragan Bishop of Huntingdon: Rt Rev Dr John Inge, 14 Lynn Road, Ely CB6 1DA
E: suffragan@ely.anglican.org
☎01353 662 137 🖷 01353 669 357
Archdeacon of Ely: Ven John Beer, St Botolph's Rectory, 1a Summerfield, Cambridge CB3 9HE
E: archdeacon.ely@ely.anglican.org
☎01223 515 725 🖷 01223 571 322
Archdeacon of Huntingdon and Wisbech: Ven Hugh McCurdy, 12 Boadicea Court, Chatteris PE16 6BN
E: archdeacon.handw@ely.anglican.org
☎01354 692 142 🖷 01354 692 142

***Church of England* Diocese of Exeter**, Diocesan House, Palace Gate, Exeter EX1 1HX
☎01392 272 686 🖷01392 499 594
E: dsec@exeter.anglican.org
Web: www.exeter.anglican.org
Diocesan Secretary: Mr Mark Beedell. Executive staff 6, Other staff 7, Serving ministers 302. **CC** Began 909. Province of Canterbury. Magazine: *Exeter Diocesan News* (34,000 monthly). Turnover n/a.
Bishop of Exeter: Rt Rev Michael Langrish, The Palace, Exeter EX1 1HY
☎01392 272 686 🖷 01392 499 594
Suffragan Bishop of Crediton: Rt Rev Robert Evens, 32 The Avenue, Tiverton EX16 4HW
E: bishop.of.crediton@exeter.anglican.org
☎01884 250 038 🖷 01884 257 454
Suffragan Bishop of Plymouth: Rt Rev John Ford, 31 Riverside Walk, Tamerton Foliot, Plymouth PL5 4AQ
E: bishop.of.plymouth@exeter.anglican.org
☎01392 273 509 🖷 01392 431 266
Archdeacon of Barnstaple: Ven David Gunn-Johnson, Stage Cross, Sanders Lane, Whitmoor Hill, Bishops Tawton, Barnstaple EX32 0BE
E: archdeacon.of.barnstaple@exeter.anglican.org
☎01271 375 475 🖷 01271 377 934
Archdeacon of Exeter: Ven Penelope Driver, St Matthew's House, 45 Spicer Road, Exeter EX1 1TA
E: archdeaon.of.exeter@exeter.anglican.org
☎01392 425 432 🖷 01392 425 783

Archdeacon of Plymouth: Ven Tony Wilds, 33 Leat Walk, Roborough, Plymouth PL6 7AT
E: archdeacon.of.plymouth@exeter.anglican.org
☎01752 793 397 🖷 01752 774 618
Archdeacon of Totnes: Ven John Rawlings, Blue Hills, Bradley Road, Bovey Tracey, Newton Abbot TQ13 9EU
E: archdeacon.of.totnes@exeter.anglican.org
☎01626 832 064 🖷 01626 834 947

***Church of England* Diocese of Gloucester**, Church House, College Green, Gloucester GL1 2LY
☎01452 410 022 🖷01452 308 324
E: church.house@glosdioc.org.uk
Web: www.glosdioc.org.uk
Diocesan Secretary: Dr Kevin Brown. *Financial Secretary:* Mr B Preece-Smith. Executive staff 4, Other staff 12, Serving ministers 145. **CC** No.251234. Began 1541. Province of Canterbury. No magazine. Turnover £7,015,000 to year end Dec 04.
Bishop of Gloucester: Rt Rev Michael Perham, Church House, College Green, Gloucester GL1 2LY
E: church.house@glosdioc.org.uk
☎01452 410 022 🖷 01452 308 324
Suffragan Bishop of Tewkesbury: Rt Rev John Went, Bishops House, Church Road, Staverton, Cheltenham GL51 0TW
E: bshptewk@star.co.uk
☎01242 680 188 🖷 01242 680 233
Archdeacon of Cheltenham: Ven Hedley Ringrose, The Sanderlings, Thorncliffe Drive, Cheltenham GL51 6PY
E: archdchelt@star.co.uk
☎01242 522 923 🖷 01242 235 925
Archdeacon of Gloucester: Ven Geoffrey Sidaway, Glebe House, Church Road, Maisemore, Gloucester GL2 8EY
E: archdglos@star.co.uk
☎01452 528 500 🖷 01452 381 528

***Church of England* Diocese of Guildford**, Diocesan House, Quarry Street, Guildford GU1 3XG
☎01483 571 826 🖷01483 790 333
Web: www.cofeguildford.org.uk
Diocesan Secretary: Mr Stephen Marriott. Admin staff 3, Serving ministers 328. **CC** No.590500. Began 1927. Province of Canterbury. Magazine: *The Wey* (30,000 ten times a year). Turnover n/a.
Bishop of Guildford: Rt Rev Christopher Hill, Willow Grange, Woking Road, Guildford GU4 7QS
E: marymorris@cofeguildford.org.uk
☎01483 590 500 🖷 01483 590 501
Suffragan Bishop of Dorking: Rt Rev Ian Brackley, Dayspring, 13 Pilgrims Way, Guildford GU4 8AD
E: bishop.ian@cofeguildford.org.uk
☎01483 570 829 🖷 01483 567 268
Archdeacon of Dorking: Ven Julian Henderson, Diocesan House, Quarry Street, Guildford GU1 3XG
☎01483 571 826 🖷 01483 790 333
Archdeacon of Surrey: Ven Stuart Beake, Diocesan House, Quarry Street, Guildford GU1 3XG
☎01483 571 826 🖷 01483 790 333

***Church of England* Diocese of Hereford**, Diocesan Office, The Palace, Hereford HR4 9BL
☎01432 353 863 🖷01432 352 952
Diocesan Secretary: Rev Sylvia Green. *Financial Secretary:* Mr Gordon Powell. Executive staff 8, Admin staff 5, Serving ministers 160. ***CC*** No.249685. Began 676. Province of Canterbury. Magazine: *The NEWS paper* (18,000 quarterly). Turnover £3,500,000 to year end Dec 00.
Bishop of Hereford: Rt Rev Anthony Priddis, Diocesan Office, The Palace, Hereford HR4 9BL
E: hereford@diooffice.freeserve.co.uk
☎01432 353 863 🖷01432 352 952
Suffragan Bishop & Archdeacon of Ludlow: Rt Rev Michael Hooper, Bishop's House, Corvedale Road, Craven Arms SY7 9BT
E: bishopofludlow@ukf.net
☎01588 673 571 🖷 01588 673 585
Archdeacon of Hereford: Ven Malcolm Colmer, Diocesan Office, The Palace, Hereford HR4 9BL
E: archdeacon@hereford.anglican.org
☎01432 373 324 🖷 01432 352 952

***Church of England* Diocese of Leicester**, Church House, St Martins East, Leicester LE1 5FX
☎0116 248 7400 🖷0116 253 2889
Web: www.leicester.anglican.org
Diocesan Secretary: Mrs Jane Easton. Executive staff 15, Serving ministers 200. ***CC*** No.249100. Began 1926. Province of Canterbury. Magazine: *News and Views* (Circulation n/a monthly). Turnover n/a.
Bishop of Leicester: Rt Rev Timothy Stevens, Bishop's Lodge, 10 Springfield Road, Leicester LE2 3BD
E: bpsec@leicester.anglican.org
☎0116 270 8985 🖷 0116 270 3288
Archdeacon of Leicester: Ven Richard Atkinson, Church House, St Martin's East, Leicester LE1 5FT
E: richard.atkinson@leccofe.org
☎0116 248 7400 🖷 0116 253 2889
Archdeacon of Loughborough: Ven Paul Hackwood, Church House, St Martins East LE1 5FX
E: paul.hackwood@leccofe.org
☎0116 248 7400 🖷 0116 253 2889

***Church of England* Diocese of Lichfield**, St Mary's House, The Close, Lichfield WS13 7LD
☎01543 306 030 🖷01543 306 039
E: info@lichfield.anglican.org
Web: www.lichfield.anglican.org
Diocesan Secretary: Mr D R Taylor. Executive staff 33, Admin staff 50, Serving ministers 528. ***CC*** No.1107827. Began 656. Province of Canterbury. Magazine: *Gazette* (60,000 monthly), *Spotlight* (30,000 every two months). Turnover n/a.
Bishop of Lichfield: Rt Rev Jonathan Gledhill, Bishop's House, 22 The Close, Lichfield WS13 7LG
E: bishop.lichfield@lichfield.anglican.org
☎01543 306 000 🖷 01543 306 009
Area Bishop of Shrewsbury: Rt Rev Dr Alan G C Smith, Athlone House, 68 London Road, Shrewsbury SY2 6PG
E: bishop.shrewsbury@lichfield.anglican.org
☎01743 235 867 🖷 01743 243 296
Area Bishop of Stafford: Rt Rev Gordon Mursell, Ash Garth, 6 Broughton Crescent, Barlaston, Stoke-on-Trent ST12 9DD
E: bishop.stafford@lichfield.anglican.org
☎01782 373 308 🖷 01782 373 705
Area Bishop of Wolverhampton: Rt Rev Michael G Bourke, 61 Richmond Road, Merridale, Wolverhampton WV3 9JH
E: bishop.wolverhampton@lichfield.anglican.org
☎01902 824 503 🖷 01902 824 504
Archdeacon of Lichfield: Ven Christopher Liley, 24 The Close, Lichfield WS13 7LD
E: archdeacon.lichfield@lichfield.anglican.org
☎01543 306 145 🖷 01543 306 147
Archdeacon of Salop: Ven John Hall, The Vicarage, Tong, Shifnal TF11 8PW
E: archdeacon.salop@lichfield.anglican.org
☎01902 372 622 🖷 01902 374 021
Archdeacon of Stoke: Ven Godfrey Stone, 39 The Brackens, Clayton, Newcastle ST5 4JL
E: archdeacon.stoke@lichfield.anglican.org
☎01782 663 066 🖷 01782 711 165
Archdeacon of Walsall: Ven Robert Jackson, 55b Highgate Road, Walsall WS1 3JE
E: archdeacon.walsall@lichfield.anglican.org
☎01922 620 153 🖷 01922 445 354

***Church of England* Diocese of Lincoln**, The Old Palace, Lincoln LN2 1PU
☎01522 504 050 🖷01525 512 717
E: administration@lincoln.anglican.org
Web: www.lincoln.anglican.org
Chief Executive: Mr Maximilian Mann. Executive staff 20, Other staff 6, Serving ministers 234. ***CC*** Began 886. Province of Canterbury. Magazine: *Crosslincs* (Circulation & frequency n/a). Turnover n/a.
Bishop of Lincoln: Rt Rev John Saxbee, Bishop's House, Eastgate, Lincoln LN2 1QQ
E: bishop-lincoln@lincoln.anglican.org
☎01522 534 701 🖷 01522 511 095
Suffragan Bishop of Grantham: Rt Rev Dr Timothy Ellis, Fairacre, 243 Barrowby Road, Grantham NG31 8NP
E: bishop.grantham@lincoln.anglican.org
☎01476 647 22 🖷 01476 592 468
Suffragan Bishop of Grimsby: Rt Rev David Rossdale, Bishop's House, Church Lane, Irby-upon-Humber, Grimsby DN37 7JR
E: bishop.grimsby@lincoln.anglican.org
☎01472 371 715 🖷 01472 371 716
Archdeacon of Lincoln: Ven Arthur J Hawes, Archdeacon's House, Northfield Road, Quarrington, Sleaford NG34 8RT
E: archdeacon.lincoln@lincoln.anglican.org
☎01529 304 348 🖷 01529 304 354
Archdeacon of Stow and Lindsey: To be appointed, The Old Palace, Lincoln LN2 1PU
☎01522 529 241 🖷01525 512 717
E: arch.stowlind@lincoln.anglican.org
☎01522 529 241 🖷 01525 512 717

***Church of England* Diocese of Liverpool**, Church House, 1 Hanover Street, Liverpool L1 3DW
☎0151 709 9722 🖷0151 709 2885
Diocesan Secretary: Mr Mike Eastwood. Executive staff 12, Admin staff 18, Serving ministers 245. ***CC*** No.249740. Began 1880. Province of York. Magazine: *Crosscurrents*(Circulation & frequency n/a). Turnover £7,600,000 to year end Dec 01.
Bishop of Liverpool: Rt Rev James S Jones, Church House, 1 Hanover Street, Liverpool L1 3DW
☎0151 709 9722 🖷 0151 709 2335
Suffragan Bishop of Warrington: Rt Rev David Jennings, 34 Central Avenue, Eccleston Park, Prescot L34 2QP
☎0151 724 3956 🖷 0151 705 2140
Archdeacon of Liverpool: Ven Richard J G Panter, Church House, 1 Hanover Street, Liverpool L1 3DW
E: archdeaconricky@blueyonder.co.uk
☎0151 709 9722 🖷 0151 709 2385
Archdeacon of Warrington: Ven Peter Bradley, Church House 1 Hanover Street, Liverpool L1 3DW
E: archdeacon@peterbradley.fsnet.co.uk
☎0151 705 2144 🖷 0151 709 2385

***Church of England* Diocese of London**, London Diocesan House, 30 Causton Street, London SW1P 4AU
☎020 7932 1100 🖷020 7932 1112
E: info@london.anglican.org
Web: www.london.anglican.org
Diocesan Secretary: Mr Keith Robinson. Executive staff 25, Serving ministers n/a. ***CC*** Began 314. Province of Canterbury. Magazine: *London Link* (60,000 quarterly). Turnover n/a.
Bishop of London: Rt Rev & Rt Hon Richard Chartres, The Old Deanery, Dean's Court, London EC4V 5AA
E: bishop@london.clara.co.uk
☎020 7248 6233
Suffragan Bishop of Fulham: Rt Rev John C Broadhurst, 26 Canonbury Park South, London N1 2FN
E: bpfulham@compuserve.com
☎020 7354 2334 🖷 020 7354 2335
Area Bishop of Edmonton: Rt Rev Peter W Wheatley, 27 Thurlow Road, London NW3 5PP
E: bishop.edmonton@london.anglican.org
☎020 7435 5890 🖷 020 7435 6049
Area Bishop of Kensington: Rt Rev Michael J Colclough, Dial House, Riverside, Twickenham TW1 3DT
E: bishop.kensington@london.anglican.org
☎020 8892 7781
Area Bishop of Stepney: Rt Rev Stephen Oliver, 63 Coborn Road, Bow, London E3 2DB
E: bishop.stepney@london.anglican.org
☎020 8981 2323 🖷 020 8981 8015
Area Bishop of Willesden: Rt Rev Peter Broadbent, 173 Willesden Lane, Brondesbury, London NW6 7YN
E: bishop.willesden@btinternet.com
☎020 8451 0189 🖷 020 8451 4606
Archdeacon of Charing Cross: Ven William M Jacob, St Giles in the Fields Church, St Giles High Street, London WC2H 8LG
E: archdeacon.charingcross@london.anglican.org
☎020 7379 5649 🖷 020 7379 5649
Archdeacon of Hackney: Ven Dr Lyle Dennen, St Andrew's Vicarage, 5 St Andrew Street, London EC4A 3AB
E: archdeacon.hackney@london.anglican.org
☎020 7353 3544 🖷 020 7583 2750
Archdeacon of Hampstead: Ven Michael Lawson, London Diocesan House, 36 Causton Street, London SW1P 4AU
E: archdeacon.hampstead@london.anglican.org
☎020 7932 1190 🖷 020 7932 1192

Archdeacon of London: Ven Peter Delaney, The Old Deanery, Dean's Court, London EC4V 5AA
E: archdeacon.london@london.anglican.org
☎020 7236 7891 🖷 020 7248 7455
Archdeacon of Middlesex: Ven Stephan Welch, Archdeacon's Office, Dial House, Riverside, Twickenham TW1 3DT
E: archdeacon.middlesex@london.anglican.org
☎020 8607 9483 🖷 020 8607 9483
Archdeacon of Northolt: Ven Rachel Treweek, 16 Baldwyn Gardens, Acton, London W3 6HL
E: archdeacon.northolt@london.anglican.org
☎020 8993 5415

***Church of England* Diocese of Manchester**, Bishopscourt, Bury New Road, Manchester M7 4LE
☎0161 792 2096 🖷0161 792 6826
E: manchesterdbf@manchester.anglican.org
Web: www.manchester.anglican.org
Diocesan Secretary: Mr Nigel Spraggins. Executive staff 5, Admin staff 13, Serving ministers 319. ***CC*** Began 1847. Province of York. Magazine: *Crux Magazine* (20,000 monthly). Turnover n/a.
Bishop of Manchester: Rt Rev Nigel McCulloch, Bishopscourt, Bury New Road, Manchester M7 4LE
E: pa@bishopscourt.manchester.anglican.org
☎0161 792 2096 🖷 0161 792 6826
Suffragan Bishop of Bolton: Rt Rev David Gillett, Bishop's Lodge, Bolton Road, Hawkshaw, Bury BL8 4JN
E: david.gillett@ukgateway.net
☎01204 882 955 🖷 01204 882 988
Suffragan Bishop of Hulme: Rt Rev Stephen Lowe, 14 Moorgate Avenue, Withington, Manchester M20 1HE
E: lowehulme@btinternet.com
☎0161 445 5922 🖷 0161 448 9687
Suffragan Bishop of Middleton: Rt Rev Michael Lewis, The Hollies, Manchester Road, Rochdale OL11 3QY
E: maolewis_2000@yahoo.com
☎0161 792 6117
Archdeacon of Bolton: Ven Dr John Applegate, 45 Rudgwick Drive, Brandlesholme, Bury BL8 1YA
E: archdeacon.bolton@rudgwickdr.fsnet.co.uk
☎0161 761 6117 🖷 0161 763 7973
Archdeacon of Manchester: Ven Andrew Ballard, 2 The Walled Garden, Ewhurst Avenue, Swinton, Manchester M27 0FR
E: andrew.ballard@virgin.net
☎0161 794 2401 🖷 0161 794 2411
Archdeacon of Rochdale: Ven Mark Davies, 57 Melling Road, Oldham OL4 1PN
☎0161 678 1455 🖷 0161 678 1455

***Church of England* Diocese of Newcastle**, Church House, St John's Terrace, North Shields NE29 6HS
☎0191 270 4100 🖷0191 270 4101
E: church_house@newcastle.anglican.org
Web: www.newcastle.anglican.org
Diocesan Secretary: Mr Philip Davies. *Communications Officer:* Mrs Sue Scott. Executive staff 11, Admin staff 7, Serving ministers 180. ***CC*** No.247233. Began 1882. Province of York. Magazine: *Link* (13,000 monthly). Turnover n/a.
Assistant Bishop of Newcastle: Rt Rev Martin Wharton, Church House, St John's Terrace, North Shields NE29 6HS
E: bishop@newcastle.anglican.org
☎0191 270 4100 🖷 0191 270 4101
Suffragan Bishop of Newcastle: Rt Rev Paul Richardson, Close House, St George's Close, Jesmond, Newcastle upon Tyne NE2 2TF
E: p.richardson@newcastle.anglican.org
☎0191 281 2556
Archdeacon of Lindisfarne: Ven Robert Langley, 4 Acomb Close, Stobhill Manor, Morpeth NE61 2YH
E: kca85@dial.pipex.com
☎01670 503 810 🖷 01670 503 469
Archdeacon of Northumberland: Ven Geoffrey Miller, 80 Moorside North, Fenham, Newcastle upon Tyne NE4 9DU
E: g.miller@newcastle.anglican.org
☎0191 273 8245 🖷 0191 226 0286

***Church of England* Diocese of Norwich**, Diocesan House, 109 Dereham Road, Easton, Norwich NR9 5ES
☎01603 880 853 🖷01603 881 083
E: diocesanhouse@norwich.anglican.org
Web: www.norwich.anglican.org
Diocesan Secretary: Rev Canon Richard Bowett. Executive staff 8, Admin staff 24, Serving ministers 320. ***CC*** No.249318. Began 630. Province of Canterbury. Magazine: *Across the See* (75,000 monthly). Turnover n/a.
Bishop of Norwich: Rt Rev Graham James, Diocesan House, 109 Dereham Road, Easton, Norwich NR9 5ES
E: diocesanhouse@norwich.anglican.org
☎01603 880 853 🖷 01603 881 083
Suffragan Bishop of Lynn: Rt Rev James Langstaff, The Old Vicarage, Castle Acre, King's Lynn PE32 2AA
E: bishoplynn@norwich.anglican.org
☎01760 755 553 🖷 01760 755 085
Suffragan Bishop of Thetford: Rt Rev David Atkinson, Rectory Meadow, Bramerton, Norwich NR14 7DW
E: bishop@bishopofthetford.fslife.co.uk
☎01508 538 251 🖷 01508 538 371
Archdeacon of Lynn: Ven Martin Gray, Holly Tree House, Whitwell Road, Sparham, Norwich NR9 5PN
E: martin.gray@lynnarch.freeserve.co.uk
☎01362 688 032 🖷 01362 688 032
Archdeacon of Norfolk: Ven David F Hayden, 8 Boulton Road, Thorpe St Andrew, Norwich NR7 0DF
E: david_hayden@lineone.net
☎01603 702 477 🖷 01603 702 477
Archdeacon of Norwich: Ven Clifford Offer, 26 The Close, Norwich NR1 4DZ
E: archdeaconclifford@norwichcathedral.fsnet.co.uk
☎01603 620 007 🖷 01603 661 104

***Church of England* Diocese of Oxford**, Diocesan Church House, North Hinksey, Oxford OX2 0NB
☎01865 208 200 🖷01865 790 470
E: diosec@oxford.anglican.org and Diocesan Secretary:
E: diosec@oxford.anglican.org
Web: www.oxford.anglican.org
Diocesan Secretary: Mrs Rosemary Pearce. Executive staff 10, Serving ministers 408, Other staff 47. ***CC*** No.247954. Began 1542. Province of Canterbury. Magazine: *The Door* (40,000 ten times a year). Turnover n/a.
Bishop of Oxford: To be appointed, Diocesan Church House, North Hinksey, Oxford OX2 0NB
E: bishopoxon@oxford.anglican.org
☎01865 208 200 🖷 01865 790 470
Area Bishop of Buckingham: Rt Rev Dr Alan Wilson, Sheridan, Grimms Hill, Great Missenden HP16 9BD
E: bishopbucks@oxford.anglican.org
☎01494 862 173 🖷 01494 890 508
Area Bishop of Dorchester: Rt Rev Colin Fletcher, Arran House, Sandy Lane, Yarnton, Kidlington OX5 1PB
E: bishop.dorchester@oxford.anglican.org
☎01865 375 541 🖷 01865 379 980
Area Bishop of Reading: Rt Rev Stephen Cottrell, Bishop's House, Tidmarsh Lane, Tidmarsh, Reading RG8 8HA
E: bishop.reading@oxford.anglican.org
☎0118 984 1216 🖷 0118 984 1218
Archdeacon of Berkshire: Ven Norman Russell, Foxglove House, Love Lane, Donnington, Newbury RG14 2JG
E: archdber@oxford.anglican.org
☎01635 552 820 🖷 01635 522 165
Archdeacon of Buckingham: Ven Sheila Watson, Bede House, Paul's Hill, Penn, High Wycombe HP10 8NZ
E: archdbuc@oxford.anglican org
☎01494 814 571 🖷 01494 817 057
Archdeacon of Oxford: Ven Julian Hubbard, Archdeacon's Lodgings, Christ Church, Oxford OX1 1DP
E: archdoxf@oxford.anglican.org
☎01865 276 185 🖷 01865 204 465

***Church of England* Diocese of Peterborough**, The Palace, Peterborough PE1 1YA
☎01733 887 000 🖷01733 555 271
E: communications@peterborough-diocese.org.uk
Web: www.peterborough-diocese.org.uk
Diocesan Secretary: Mr Richard Pestle. Executive staff 3, Serving ministers 160. ***CC*** Began 1541. Province of Canterbury. No magazine. Turnover £6,000,000 to year end Dec 04.
Bishop of Peterborough: Rt Rev Ian Cundy, The Palace, Peterborough PE1 1YA
E: communications@peterborough-diocese.org.uk
☎01733 887 000 🖷 01733 555 271
Bishop of Brixworth: Rt Rev Frank White, 4 The Avenue, Dallington, Northampton NN5 7AN
E: fw@bpofbrixworth.free-online.co.uk
☎01604 759 423 🖷 01604 750 925
Archdeacon of Northampton: Ven Christine Allsopp, Westbrook, 11 The Drive, Northampton NN1 4RZ
E: archdeacon@aofn.wanadoo.co.uk
☎01604 714 015 🖷 01604 792 016
Archdeacon of Oakham: Ven David Painter, 7 Minster Precincts, Peterborough PE1 1XS
E: david.painter@peterborough-cathedral.org.uk
☎01733 891 360 🖷 01733 554 524

***Church of England* Diocese of Portsmouth**, Cathedral House, St Thomas Street, Portsmouth PO1 2HA
☎023 9282 5731 🖷023 9229 3423
E: admin@portsmouth.anglican.org
Web: www.portsmouth.anglican.org
Diocesan Secretary: Mr Michael Jordan. Executive staff 3, Admin staff 4, Serving ministers 135. ***CC*** Began 1927. Province of Canterbury. Magazine: *The Pompey Chimes* (9,000 monthly). Turnover n/a.
Bishop of Portsmouth: Rt Rev Kenneth Stevenson, Bishopsgrove, 26 Osborn Road, Fareham PO16 7DQ
E: bishports@portsmouth.anglican.org
☎01329 280 247 🖷 01329 231 538
Archdeacon of the Isle of Wight: Ven Caroline Baston, 5 The Boltons, Wootton Bridge, Ryde PO33 4PB
☎01983 884 432 🖷 01983 884 432
E: adiow@portsmouth.anglican.org
☎023 9282 5731 🖷023 9229 3423
Archdeacon of the Meon: Ven Peter Hancock, Victoria Lodge, 36 Osborn Road, Fareham PO16 7DS
E: admeon@portsmouth.anglican.org
☎01329 280 101 🖷 01329 281 603
Archdeacon of Portsdown: Ven Dr Trevor Reader, Diocesan Office, Cathedral House, St Thomas' Street, Portsmouth PO1 2HA
E: adportsdown@portsmouth.anglican.org
☎023 9828 5731 🖷 023 9229 3423

***Church of England* Diocese of Ripon and Leeds**, Diocesan Office, St Mary's Street, Leeds LS9 7DP
☎0113 200 0540 🖷0113 249 1129
E: philipa@riponleeds-diocese.org.uk
Web: www.riponleeds.anglican.org
Diocesan Secretary: Mr Philip M Arundel. Executive staff 4, Other staff 10, Serving ministers n/a. ***CC*** No.249860. Began 1836. Province of York. Magazine: *Together* (21,000 monthly). Turnover n/a.
Bishop of Ripon and Leeds: Rt Rev John Packer, Diocesan Office, St Mary's Street, Leeds LS9 7DP
E: philipa@riponleeds-diocese.org.uk
☎0113 200 0540 🖷 0113 249 1129
Suffragan Bishop of Knaresborough: Rt Rev James Bell, Thistletown, Exelby, Bedale DL8 2HD
E: bishop.knaresb@btinternet.com
☎01677 423 525
Archdeacon of Leeds: Ven Peter Burrows, Archdeacon's Lodge, 3 West Park Grove, Roundhay, Leeds LS8 2HQ
E: archdeacon.leeds@riponleeds.anglican.org
☎0113 269 0594
Archdeacon of Richmond: To be appointed, Diocesan Office, St Mary's Street, Leeds LS9 7DP
☎0113 200 0540 🖷0113 249 1129

***Church of England* Diocese of Rochester**, St Nicholas Church, Boley Hill, Rochester ME1 1SL
☎01634 830 333 🖷01634 829 463
E: louise.gilbert@rochester.anglican.org
Web: www.rochester.anglican.org
Diocesan Secretary: Mrs Louise Gilbert. Executive staff 5, Admin staff 15, Serving ministers 295. ***CC*** No.249339. Began 604. Province of Canterbury. Magazine: *Rochester Link* (25,000 ten times a year). Turnover n/a.
Bishop of Rochester: Rt Rev Dr Michael Nazir-Ali, Bishopscourt, 24 St Margaret's Street, Rochester ME1 1TS
E: bishops.secretary@rochester.anglican.org
☎01634 842 721 🖷 01634 831 136
Suffragan Bishop of Tonbridge: Rt Rev Dr Brian Castle, Bishop's Lodge, 48 St Botolph's Road, Sevenoaks TN13 3AG
E: bishop.tonbridge@rochester.anglican.org
☎01732 456 070 🖷 01732 741 449
Archdeacon of Bromley and Bexley: Ven Paul Wright, The Archdeaconry, The Glebe, Chislehurst BR7 5PQ
E: archdeacon.bromley@rochester.anglican.org
☎020 8467 8743 🖷 020 8467 8743
Archdeacon of Rochester: Ven Peter Lock, The Archdeaconry, Kings Orchard, The Precinct, Rochester ME1 1TG
E: archdeacon.rochester@rochester.anglican.org
☎01634 843 366 ext 111 🖷 01634 401 410
Archdeacon of Tonbridge: Ven Clive Mansell, 3 The Ridings, Blackhurst Lane, Tunbridge Wells TN2 4RU
E: archdeacon.tonbridge@rochester.anglican.org
☎01892 520 660 🖷 01892 520 660

***Church of England* Diocese of St Albans**, Holywell Lodge, 41 Holywell Hill, St Albans AL1 1HE
☎01727 854 532 🖷01727 844 [illegible]59
E: mail@stalbans.anglican.org
Web: www.stalbans.anglican.org
Diocesan Secretary: Miss Susan Pope. Executive staff 7, Admin staff 5, Serving ministers 270. ***CC*** No.24[illegible]887. Began 1877. Province of Canterbury. Magazine: *See Round* (19,000 monthly). Turnover £11,000,000 to year end Dec 04.
Bishop of St Albans: Rt Rev Christopher Herbert, Holywell Lodge, 41 Holywell Hill, St Albans AL1 1HE
E: mail@stalbans.anglican.org
☎01727 854 532 🖷 01727 844 [illegible]69
Suffragan Bishop of Bedford: Rt Rev Richard Inwood, Bishop's Lodge, Bedford Road, Cardington, Bedford MK44 3[illegible]S
E: bishopbedford@stalbans.anglican.org
☎01234 831 432 🖷 01234 831 [illegible]4
Suffragan Bishop of Hertford: Rt Rev Christopher Foster, Hertford House, Abbey Mill Lane, St Albans AL3 4HE
E: bishophertford@stalbans.anglican.org
☎01727 866 420
Archdeacon of Bedford: Ven Paul Hughes, 17 Lansdowne Road, Luton LU3 1E[illegible]
E: archbedf@stalbans.anglican.org
☎01582 730 722 🖷 0158[illegible] 877 [illegible]54
Archdeacon of Hertford: Ven Trevor P Jones, St Mary's House, Stapleford, Hertford SG14 3NB
E: archdhert@stalbans.anglican.org
☎01992 581 629 🖷 0199[illegible] 558 [illegible]45
Archdeacon of St Albans: Ven Helen Cunliffe, 6 Sopwell Lane, St Albans AL1 1RR
E: archdstalbans@stalbans.anglican.org
☎01727 847 212 🖷 01727 848 [illegible]1

***Church of England* Diocese of St Edmundsbury & Ipswich**, Diocesan Office, Churchgates House, Cutler Street, Ipswich IP1 1UQ
☎01473 298 500 🖷01473 298 5[illegible]
E: nicholas@stedmundsbury.anglican.org
Web: www.stedmundsbury.anglican.org
Diocesan Secretary: Mr Nicholas Edgell. Executive staff 9, Serving ministers [illegible]45. ***CC*** Began 1914. Province of Canterbury. Magazine: *East Anglican* (14,000 monthly). Turnover n/a.
Bishop of St Edmundsbury and Ipswich: Rt Rev Richard Lewis, Bishop's House, 4 Park Road, Ipswich IP1 3ST
E: bishop.richard@stedmundsbury.anglican. org
☎01473 252 829 🖷 01473 232 5[illegible]2
Suffragan Bishop of Dunwich: Rt Rev Clive Young, 28 Westerfield Road, Ipswich IP4 2UJ
E: bishop.clive@stedmundsbury.anglican.org
☎01473 222 276 🖷 01473 210 3[illegible]3
Archdeacon of Ipswich: To be appointed, Diocesan Office, Churchgates House, Cutler Street, Ipswich IP1 1UQ
☎01473 298 500 🖷 01473 298 5[illegible]
Archdeacon of Sudbury: Ven David Brierley, Diocesan Office, Churchgates House, Cutler Street, Ipswich IP1 1UQ
E: archdeacon.david@stedmundsbury.anglican.org
☎01473 298 500 🖷 01473 298 5[illegible]

Archdeacon of Suffolk: Ven Geoffrey Arrand, Glebe House, The Street, Ashfield, Stowmarket IP14 6LX
E: archdeacon.geoffrey@stedmundsbury.anglican.org
☎01728 685 497 🖷 01728 685 969

***Church of England* Diocese of Salisbury**, Church House, Crane Street, Salisbury SP1 2QB
☎01722 411 922 🖷01722 411 990
E: lucinda.herklots@salisbury.anglican.org
Web: www.salisbury.anglican.org
Diocesan Secretary: Mrs Lucinda Herklots. Executive staff 6, Other staff 8, Serving ministers 301. ***CC*** No.240833. Began 1075. Province of Canterbury. Magazine: *The Sarum Link* (50,000 monthly). Turnover n/a.
Bishop of Salisbury: Rt Rev David Stancliffe, South Canonry, 71 The Close, Salisbury SP1 2ER
E: dsarum@salisbury.anglican.org
☎01722 334 031 🖷 01722 413 112
Suffragan Bishop of Ramsbury: Rt Rev Stephen Conway, Southbroom House, London Road, Devizes SN10 1LT
E: ramsbury.office@salisbury.anglican.org
☎01380 729 808
Suffragan Bishop of Sherborne: Rt Rev Tim Thornton, Little Bailie, Duller Lane, Sturminster Marshall, Wimborne BH21 4AD
E: sherborne.office@salisbury.anglican.org
☎01258 859 110 🖷 01258 859 118
Archdeacon of Dorset: Ven Alistair J Magowen, Little Bailie, Duller Lane, Sturminster Marshall, Wimborne BH21 4AD
E: alistair@magowan55.fsnet.co.uk
☎01258 859 110
Archdeacon of Sarum: Ven Alan Jeans, Southbroom House, London Road, Devizes SN10 1LT
E: adsarum@salisbury.anglican.org
☎01380 729 808
Archdeacon of Sherborne: Ven Paul Taylor, The Rectory, West Stafford, Dorchester DT2 8AE
E: adsherborne@salisbury.anglican.org
☎01305 264 637 🖷 01305 260 640
Archdeacon of Wiltshire: Ven John Wraw, Southbroom House, London Road, Devizes SN10 1LT
E: adwilts@salisbury.anglican.org
☎01380 729 808 🖷 01380 848 247

***Church of England* Diocese of Sheffield**, Diocesan Church House, 95 Effingham Street, Rotherham S65 1BL
☎01709 309 100 🖷01709 512 550
E: tony.beck@sheffield-diocese.org.uk
Web: www.sheffield.anglican.org
Diocesan Secretary: Mr Tony Beck. Admin staff 12, Serving ministers 206. ***CC*** No.245361. Began 1914. Province of York. Magazine: *Sheffield Diocesan News* (9,000 monthly). Turnover n/a.
Bishop of Sheffield. Rt Rev John Nicholls, Bishopscroft, Snaithing Lane, Sheffield S10 3LG
E: reception@sheffield.anglican.org
☎01709 309 100 🖷 01709 512 550
Suffragan Bishop of Doncaster: Rt Rev Cyril Ashton, Bishop's House, 3 Farrington Court, Wickersley, Rotherham S66 1JQ
E: m.powell1@virgin.net
☎01709 730 130 🖷 01709 730 230
Archdeacon of Doncaster: Ven Robert Fitzharris, Diocesan Church House, 95 Effingham Street, Rotherham S65 1BL
E: archdeacon.of.doncaster@sheffield-diocese.org.uk
☎01709 309 110 🖷 01709 309 107
Archdeacon of Sheffield: Ven Richard Blackburn, Diocesan Church House, 95 Effingham Street, Rotherham S65 1BL
E: archdeacons.office@sheffield.anglican. org
☎01709 309 110 🖷 01709 309 107

***Church of England* Diocese of Sodor & Man**, Holly Cottage, Ballaughton Meadows, Douglas IM2 1JG
☎01624 626 994 🖷01624 626 994
Diocesan Secretary: Mrs Christine Roberts. Executive staff 1, Serving ministers 19. ***CC*** Began 447. Province of York. Magazine: *The Church Leader* (20,000 monthly). Turnover n/a.
Bishop of Sodor and Man: Rt Rev Graeme Knowles, Bishop's House, The Falls, Tromode Road, Cronkbourne, Douglas IM4 4PZ
E: bishop-sodor@mcb.net
☎01624 622 108 🖷 01624 672 890
Archdeacon of the Isle of Man: Ven Brian Smith, St George's Vicarage, 16 Devonshire Road, Douglas IM2 3RB
E: archd-sodor@mcb.net
☎01624 675 430

***Church of England* Diocese of Southwark**, Trinity House, 4 Chapel Court, Borough High Street, London SE1 1HW
☎020 7939 9400 🖷020 7939 9468
E: simon.parton@southwark.anglican.org
Web: www.southwark.anglican.org
Diocesan Secretary: Mr Simon Parton. Executive staff 28, Serving ministers 450. ***CC*** No.249678. Began 1905. Province of Canterbury. Magazine: *The Bridge* (25,000 monthly). Turnover n/a.
Bishop of Southwark: Rt Rev Thomas F Butler, Bishop's House, 38 Tooting Bec Gardens, Streatham, London SW16 1QZ
E: bishop.tom@southwark.anglican.org
☎020 8769 3256 🖷 020 8769 4126
Area Bishop of Croydon: Rt Rev Nicholas Baines, St Matthew's House, 100 George Street, Croydon CR0 1PE
E: bishop.nick@southwark.anglican.org
☎020 8256 9630 🖷 020 8256 9631
Area Bishop of Kingston: Rt Rev Richard Cheetham, Kingston Episcopal Area Office, Saint Cecilia's C of E School, Sutherland Grove, London SW18 5JR
E: bishop.richard@southwark.anglican.org
☎020 8785 1980 🖷 020 8785 1981
Area Bishop of Woolwich: Rt Rev Christopher Chessun, Trinity House, 4 Chapel Court, Borough High Street, London SE1 1HW
E: bishop.christopher@southwark.anglican.org
☎020 7939 9400 🖷 020 7939 9467
Archdeacon of Croydon: Ven V Anthony Davies, St Matthew's House, 100 George Street, Croydon CR0 1PE
E: tony.davies@southwark.anglican.org
☎020 8256 9630 🖷 020 8256 9631
Archdeacon of Lambeth: Ven Christopher Skilton, Kingston Episcopal Area Office, Saint Cecilia's C of E School, Sutherland Grove, London SW18 5JR
E: christopher.skilton@southwark.anglican.org
☎020 8785 1980 🖷 020 8785 1981
Archdeacon of Lewisham: Ven Christine Hardman, Trinity House, 4 Chapel Court, Borough High Street, London SE1 1HW
E: christine.hardman@southwark.anglican. org
☎020 7939 9400 🖷 020 7939 9467
Archdeacon of Reigate: Ven Daniel Kajumba, St Matthew's House, 100 George Street, Croydon CR0 1PE
E: daniel.kajumba@southwark.anglican.org
☎020 8256 9630 🖷 020 8256 9631
Archdeacon of Southwark: Ven Dr Michael Ipgrave, Trinity House, 4 Chapel Court, Borough High Street, London SE1 1HW
E: michael.ipgrave@southwark.anglican.org
☎020 7939 9400 🖷 020 7939 9467
Archdeacon of Wandsworth: Ven Stephen S Roberts, Kingston Episcopal Area Office, Saint Cecilia's C of E School, Sutherland Grove, London SW18 5JR
E: stephen.roberts@southwark.anglican.org
☎020 8785 1980 🖷 020 8785 1981

C

***Church of England* Diocese of Southwell and Nottingham**, Dunham House, 8 Westgate, Southwell NG25 0JL
☎01636 814 331 🖷01636 815 084
Web: www.southwell.anglican.org
Chief Executive: Rev Canon Peter Hill. Executive staff 13, Other staff 30, Serving ministers 200. ***CC*** No.249359. Began 1884. (Previously Church of England Diocese of Southwell). Province of York. Magazine: *C* (30,000 quarterly). Turnover n/a.
Bishop of Southwell: Rt Rev George Cassidy, Dunham House, 8 Westgate, Southwell NG25 0JL
E: bishop@southwell.anglican.org
☎01636 814 331 🖷 01636 815 084
Suffragan Bishop of Sherwood: Ven Anthony Porter, Sherwood House, 34 Glebe Park, London Road, Balderton, Newark NG24 3GN
E: bishopsherwood@southwell.anglican.org
☎01636 700 791
Archdeacon of Newark: Ven Nigel Peyton, 4 The Woodwards, London Road, New Balderton, Newark NG24 0JL
E: archdeacon-newark@southwell.anglican.org
☎01636 612 249 🖷 01636 611 952
Archdeacon of Nottingham: Ven Gordon Ogilvie, 2b Spencer Avenue, Mapperley, Nottingham NG3 5SP
E: gogilvie@southwell.anglican.org
☎0115 967 0875 🖷 0115 967 1014

***Church of England* Diocese of Truro**, Diocesan House, Kenwyn, Truro TR1 1JQ
☎01872 274 351 🖷01872 222 510
Web: www.truro.anglican.org
Diocesan Secretary: Mrs S J Sturgess. Executive staff 6, Other staff 32, Serving ministers 177. ***CC*** Began 1877. Province of Canterbury. Magazine: *The Coracle* (10,000 monthly). Turnover n/a.
Bishop of Truro: Rt Rev William Ind, Lis Escop, Feock, Truro TR3 6QQ
E: bishop@truro.anglican.org
☎01872 862 657 🖷 01872 862 037
Suffragan Bishop of St Germans: Rt Rev Roydon Screech, 32 Falmouth Road, Truro TR1 2HX
E: bishop@stgermans.truro.anglican.org
☎01872 273 190
Archdeacon of Bodmin: Ven Clive Cohen, Archdeacon's House, Cardinham, Bodmin PL30 4BL
E: adbodmin.trurodio@virgin.net
☎01208 821 614
Archdeacon of Cornwall: Ven Roger Bush, Westwood House, Tremorvah Crescent, Truro TR1 1NL
E: roger@truro.anglican.org
☎01872 225 630

***Church of England* Diocese of Wakefield**, Church House, 1 South Parade, Wakefield WF1 1LP
☎01924 371 802 🖷01924 364 834
E: diocesan.secretary@wakefield.anglican.org
Web: www.wakefield.anglican.org
Diocesan Secretary: Mr Ashley Ellis. Executive staff 10, Other staff 12, Serving ministers 200. ***CC*** Began 1888. Province of York. Magazine: *Awake* (Circulation & frequency n/a). Turnover n/a. *Bishop of Wakefield:* Rt Rev Stephen Platten, Bishop's Lodge, Woodthorpe Lane, Wakefield WF2 6JL
E: bishop@bishopofwakefield.org.uk
☎01924 255 349 🖷 01924 250 202
Suffragan Bishop of Pontefract: Rt Rev Tony Robinson, Pontefract House, 181a Manygates Lane, Sandal, Wakefield WF2 7DR
E: bishop.pontefract@wakefield.anglican.org
☎01924 250 781 🖷 01924 250 781
Archdeacon of Halifax: Ven Robert Freeman, 2 Vicarage Gardens, Rastrick, Brighouse HD6 3HD
E: archdeacon.halifax@wakefield.anglican.org
☎01484 714 553 🖷 01484 711 897
Archdeacon of Pontefract: Ven Jonathan Greener, 24 Pledwick Lane, Sandal, Wakefield WF2 6DN
E: archdeacon.pontefract@wakefield.anglican.org
☎01924 240 547 🖷 01924 364 834

***Church of England* Diocese of Winchester**, Church House, 9 The Close, Winchester SO23 9LS
☎01962 844 644 🖷01962 841 815
E: andrew.howard@winchester.anglican.org
Web: www.winchester.anglican.org
Diocesan Secretary: Mr Andrew Howard. Executive staff 6, Serving ministers 253. ***CC*** Began 676. Province of Canterbury. No magazine. Turnover n/a.
Bishop of Winchester: Rt Rev M C Scott-Joynt, Wolvesey, Winchester SO23 9ND
E: joyce.cockell@dial.pipex.com
☎01962 854 050 🖷 01962 842 376
Suffragan Bishop of Basingstoke: Rt Rev Trevor Willmott, Bishopswood End, 40 Kingswood Rise, Four Marks, Alton GU34 5BD
E: trevor.willmott@dial.pipex.com
☎01420 562 925 🖷 01420 561 251
Suffragan Bishop of Southampton: Rt Rev Paul Butler, Ham House, The Crescent, Romsey SO51 7NG
E: paul.butler@bpsotonoffice.clara.co.uk
☎01794 516 005 🖷 01794 830 242
Archdeacon of Bournemouth: Ven Adrian Harbidge, Glebe House, 22 Bellflower Way, Chandlers Ford, Eastleigh SO53 4HN
E: adrian.harbidge@dial.pipex.com
☎023 8026 0955
Archdeacon of Winchester: Ven John Guille, 6 The Close, Winchester SO23 9LS
E: john.guille@winchester-cathedral.org.uk
☎01962 857 263 🖷 01962 857 242
Dean of Guernsey: Very Reverend Paul Mellor, The Deanery, Cornet Street, St Peter Port, Guernsey GY1 1BZ
E: paul@townchurch.org.gg
☎01481 720 036 🖷 01481 722 948
Dean of Jersey: Very Rev Bob Key, The Deanery, David Place, St Helier, Jersey JE2 4TB
E: deanofjersey@jerseymail.co.uk
☎01534 720 001 🖷 01534 617 488

***Church of England* Diocese of Worcester**, The Old Palace, Deansway, Worcester WR1 2JE
☎01905 205 37 🖷01905 612 302
E: generalinfo@cofe-worcester.org.uk
Web: www.cofe-worcester.org.uk
Diocesan Secretary: Mr R Higham. Executive staff 10, Other staff 20, Serving ministers 220. ***CC*** No.247778. Began 679. Province of Canterbury. Magazine: *Worcester Diocesan News* (22,000 ten times a year). Turnover n/a.
Bishop of Worcester: Rt Rev Dr Peter Selby, Bishop's House, Hartlebury Castle, Kidderminster DY11 7XX
☎01299 250 214 🖷 01299 250 027
Suffragan Bishop of Dudley: Rt Rev David Walker, Bishop's House, Bishop's Walk, Cradley Heath B64 7RH
E: bishop.david@cofe-worcester.org.uk
☎0121 550 3407 🖷 0121 550 7340
Archdeacon of Dudley: Ven Frederick Trethewey, Archdeacon's House, 15 Worcester Road, Droitwich WR9 8AA
E: fred.trethewey@ntlworld.com
☎01905 773 301 🖷 01905 773 301
Archdeacon of Worcester: Ven Dr Joy Tetley, The Old Palace, Deansway, Worcester WR1 2JE
E: jtetley@cofe-worcester.org.uk
☎01905 20537 🖷 01905 612 302

***Church of England* Diocese of York**, Diocesan House, Aviator Court, Clifton Moor, York YO30 4WJ
☎01904 699 500 🖷01904 699 501
E: yorkdbf@yorkdiocese.org
Diocesan Secretary: Mr Peter Warry. Senior staff 9, Admin staff 8, Serving ministers 257. Began 627. Province of York. Magazine: *York Diocesan News* (Circulation n/a monthly). Turnover n/a.
Archbishop of York: Most Rev & Rt Hon Dr John Sentamu, Bishopthorpe Palace, Bishopthorpe, York YO23 2QE
E: office@bishopthorpepalace.co.uk
☎01904 707 021 🖷 01904 709 204
Suffragan Bishop of Hull: Rt Rev Richard Frith, Hullen House, Woodfield Lane, Hessle HU13 0ES
E: richard@bishop.karoo.co.uk
☎01482 649 019 🖷 01482 647 [illegible]49
Suffragan Bishop of Selby: Rt Rev Martin Wallace, Bishop's House, Barton le Street, Malton YO17 6PL
E: bishselby@clara.net
Suffragan Bishop of Whitby: Rt Rev Robert Ladds, 60 West Green, Stokesley, Middlesbrough TS9 5ED
E: bishopofwhitby@episcopus.co.uk
☎01642 714 475 🖷 01642 714 [illegible]72
Archdeacon of Cleveland: Ven Paul Ferguson, 2 Langbaurgh Road, Hutton Rudby, Yarm TS15 0HZ
☎01642 706 005 🖷 01642 706 [illegible]97
Archdeacon of the East Riding: To be appointed, Diocesan House, Aviator Court, Clifton Moor, York YO30 4WJ
☎01904 699 500 🖷 01904 699 501
Archdeacon of York: Ven Richard Seed, Holy Trinity Rectory, 81 Micklegate, York YO1 6LE
E: richard-seed@archdeaconyork.fsnet.co.uk
☎01904 623 798 🖷 01904 628 [illegible]55

***Church of England* Bishop to the Forces**, The Deanery, Windsor Castle, Windsor SL4 1NJ
☎01753 865 561 🖷01753 819 0[illegible]2
Bishop to the Forces and Dean of Windsor: Rt Rev David Conner. No full-time staff.

***Church of England* Provincial Episcopal Visitors**
Pastoral care of those opposed to ordination of women priests.
No full-time staff. Began 2000. No magazine. Turnover n/a.
Bishop of Beverley: Rt Rev Martyn W Jarrett, 3 North Lane, Roundhay, Leeds LS8 2QJ
E: bishop-of-beverley@3-north-lane.fsnet.co.uk
☎0113 265 4280 🖷 0113 265 428[illegible]
Bishop of Ebbsfleet: Rt Rev Andrew Burnham, Bishop's House, Dry Sandford, Abingdon OX13 6JP
E: bishop.andrew@ebbsfleet.org.uk
☎01865 390 746 🖷 01865 390 61[illegible]
Bishop of Richborough Rt Rev Keith Newton, 6 Mellish Gardens, Woodford Green IG8 0BH
E: pev@btinternet.com
☎020 8505 7259 M: 07976 585 8[illegible]1
🖷 020 8504 3349

***Church of England* (Continuing)**, 15 Bridge Street, Knighton LD7 1BT
☎01547 528 815 M: 07976 358 611
E: edward@revmalcolm.freeserve.co.uk
Web: www.continuingcofe.org
Presiding Bishop: Rt Rev Edward Malcolm. Executive staff n/a, Serving ministers 6. ***CC*** No.1055010. Began 1995. Magazine: *Journal of the Continuing Church* (400 periodically). Turnover n/a.

†Church of God (European Office), 14 Clark's Mead, Bushey Heath, Bushey, Watford WD23 4JZ
☎020 8950 6539 🖷020 8950 6539
Maintaining links with Church of God in Europe.
Superintendent: Rev Ron Brown. *Field Director:* Grant McClung. Executive staff 2, Other staff n/a. Began 1954; New Testament Church of God. No magazine. Turnover n/a.

Church of God Ground of Truth, 91 Cairnfield Avenue, Neasden, London NW2 7PH
☎020 8452 8863
Bishop: Rt Rev Lionel Bailey. No full-time staff. Began 1975. No magazine. Turnover n/a.

†Church of God in Christ Congregational (Independent), 217 Maryon Road, Prospect Vale, Woolwich, London SE7 8DB
☎No telephone
Bishop: Bishop Campbell. No full-time staff. Serving ministers 8. Began 1972. No magazine. Turnover n/a.

†Church of God of Prophecy, 6 Beacon Court, Birmingham Road, Great Barr, Birmingham B43 6NN
☎0121 358 2231 🖷0121 358 1065
E: admin@cogop.org.uk
Web www.cogop.org.uk
National Overseer: Bishop Wilton R Powell OBE Executive staff 8, Admin staff 4, Serving ministers 81. ***CC*** No.287868. Began 1953. Magazine: *Messenger of Truth* (1,600 quarterly). Turnover n/a.

†Church of God Reformation Movement, Community Church of God, St Ann's Road, Tottenham, London N15 6NG
☎020 8800 9119 🖷020 8514 1280
E: cogtottenham@aol.com
Chairman of Assembly: Rev John Pemberton. No full-time staff, Serving ministers 4. ***CC*** No.280378. Began 1894. No magazine. Turnover n/a.

Church of Ireland, Church of Ireland House, Church Avenue, Rathmines, Dublin 6, Republic of Ireland
☎00 353 1 497 8422 🖷00 353 1 497 8821
Web: www.ireland.anglican.org
Chief Officer & Secretary: Mr D C Reardon. Executive staff 5, Admin staff 27, Serving ministers - see dioceses. Began n/a. (Disestablished 1870). Magazine: *Church of Ireland Gazette* (6,000 weekly). Turnover n/a.

***Church of Ireland* Archdiocese of Armagh**, Diocesan Office, Church House, 46 Abbey Street, Armagh BT61 7DZ
☎028 3752 7144 🖷028 3752 7823
E: archbishop@armagh.anglican.org
Archbishop of Armagh, Primate of All Ireland & Metropolitan: Most Rev Dr Robert H A Eames. Executive staff n/a, Serving ministers 50. Began n/a. Magazine: *Armagh Diocesan Magazine* (Circulation n/a monthly). Turnover n/a.
Archdeacon of Armagh: Ven Raymond G Hoey, The Rectory, 2 Maytown Road, Bessbrook, Newry BT35 7LY
E: archdeacon@armagh.anglican.org
☎028 3083 0302 🖷 028 3083 0302

***Church of Ireland* Diocese of Clogher**, St Macartan's Cathedral Offices, Hall's Lane, Enniskillen BT74 4DR
☎028 6634 7879 🖷028 6634 7879
E: secretary@clogher.anglican.org
Diocesan Secretary: Mr Glenn Moore. Executive staff 1, Serving ministers 36. Began 453. Magazine: *Diocesan Magazine* (Circulation n/a ten times a year). Turnover n/a.
Bishop of Clogher: Rt Rev Michael Jackson, The See House, 152a Ballagh Road, Fivemiletown BT75 0QP
E: bishop@clogher.anglican.org
☎028 8952 2475 🖷 028 8952 2475
Archdeacon of Clogher: Ven Cecil T Pringle, The Rectory, Derrygonnelly Road, Rossory, Enniskillen BT74 7JE
☎028 6632 2874 🖷 028 6632 2874

***Church of Ireland* Diocese of Connor**, Diocesan Office, Church of Ireland House, 61 Donegall Street, Belfast BT1 2QH
☎028 9032 2268/3188 🖷028 9032 1635
Bishop: Rt Rev Alan E Harper. Executive staff 2, Admin staff 6, Serving ministers 105. Began n/a. Magazine: *Connor Contact* (Circulation n/a quarterly). Turnover n/a.
Archdeacon of Connor: Ven Stephen McBride, The Vicarage, 10 Vicarage Gardens, Station Road, Antrim BT41 4JP
☎028 9446 2186
Archdeacon of Dalriada: Ven P W Rooke, The Rectory, 59 Strand Road, Portstewart BT55 7LU
☎028 7083 2538

†*Church of Ireland* Diocese of Derry and Raphoe, The See House, Culmore Road, Londonderry BT48 8JF
☎028 7135 1206 🖷028 7135 2554
E: bishop@derry.anglican.org
Web: www.derry.anglican.org
Bishop: Rt Rev Kenneth Good. Executive staff n/a, Serving ministers 55. Began n/a. Magazine: *Vision* (10,000 quarterly). Turnover n/a.
Diocesan Secretary: Mr Geoffrey Kelly, Diocesan Office, London Street, Londonderry BT48 6RQ
☎028 7126 2440
Archdeacon of Derry: Ven Donald S McLean, Christ Church Rectory, 80 Northland Road, Londonderry BT48 0AL
E: archdeacon@derry.anglican.org
☎028 7126 3279 🖷 028 7127 1621
Archdeacon of Raphoe: Ven Matthew S Harte, The Rectory, Horn Head Road, Dunfanaghy, Letterkenny,Republic of Ireland
☎00 353 74 36 187 🖷 00 353 74 36 061

***Church of Ireland* Diocese of Down and Dromore**, Diocesan Office, Church of Ireland House, 61 Donegall Street, Belfast BT1 2QH
☎028 9032 2268 / 3188 🖷028 9032 1635
E: bishop@down.anglican.org
Bishop: Rt Rev H C Miller. Executive staff 2, Admin staff 8, Serving ministers 111, Began n/a. No magazine. Turnover n/a.
Archdeacon of Down: Ven Gregory McCamley, The Rectory, 29 King's Road, Belfast BT5 6JG
☎028 9047 1514
Archdeacon of Dromore: Ven William J Scott, The Rectory, 63 Lurgan Road, Banbridge BT32 4LY
☎028 4062 2612

C

Church of Scotland Council of Assembly, 121 George Street, Edinburgh EH2 4YN
☎0131 225 5722 🖷0131 220 3113
Principal Clerk of the General Asse: Very Rev Dr Finlay A J Macdonald. Executive staff n/a, Serving ministers 1,081. Began 1560. Magazine: *Life and Work* (46,000 monthly). Turnover n/a.

See also:
Church of Scotland Council of Assembly on Page 180
Church of Scotland Mission and Discipleship Council Page 200
Church of Scotland Board of Principal Clerks Department on Page 181
Church of Scotland Stewardship & Finance Committee on Page 346
Church of Scotland Department of Education Page 411
Church of Scotland Guild on Page 181
Church of Scotland Ecumenical Relations on Page 180
Life & Work on Page 251

Presbytery of Aberdeen *Clerk:* Rev Ian McLean, Mastrick Parish Church, Greenfern Road, Aberdeen AB16 6TR
E: akph34@uk.uumail.com
☎01224 690 494 🖷 01224 690 494
Presbytery of Abernethy *Clerk:* Rev James A I MacEwan, The Manse, Nethy Bridge PH25 3DG
E: akph35@uk.uumail.com
☎01479 821 280
Presbytery of Angus *Clerk:* Rev Malcolm Rooney, St Margaret's Church, West High Street, Forfar DD8 1BJ
E: akph36@uk.uumail.com
☎01307 464 224 🖷 01307 465 589
Presbytery of Annandale and Eskdale *Clerk:* Rev C Bryan Haston, The Manse, Gretna Green, Gretna DG16 5DU
E: akph37@uk.uumail.com
☎01461 338 313 🖷 08701 640 119

Presbytery of Ardrossan *Clerk:* Rev Johnstone McKay, Upper Burnfoot, 27 Stanlane Place, Largs KA30 8DD
E: akph38@uk.uumail.com
☎01475 672 960 🖷 01475 674 380

Presbytery of Argyll *Clerk:* Mr Hugh W Paterson, Carmonadh, Eastlands Road, Rothesay, Isle of Bute PA20 9JZ
E: akph73@uk.uumail.com
☎Number not supplied

Presbytery of Ayr *Clerk:* Rev James Crichton, 30 Garden Street, Dalrymple, Ayr KA6 6DG
E: akph40@uk.uumail.com
☎01292 560 263 🖷 01292 560 574

Presbytery of Buchan *Clerk:* Mr George Berstan, Faithlie, Victoria Terrace, Turriff AB53 4EE
E: akph41@uk.uumail.com
☎01888 862 392

Presbytery of Caithness *Clerk:* Mrs Myrtle Gillies, Ardchadh, Halladale, Forsinard KW13 6YT
E: akph42@uk.uumail.com
☎01641 571 241 🖷 01641 571 288

Presbytery of Dumbarton *Clerk:* Rev Colin Caskie, The Manse, 11 Ardenconnel Way, Rhu, Helensburgh G84 8LX
E: akph43@uk.uumail.com
☎01436 820 213

Presbytery of Dumfries and Galloway *Clerk:* Rev Gordon M A Savage, Maxwelltown West Manse, 11 Laurieknowe, Dumfries DG2 7AH
E: akph44@uk.uumail.com
☎01387 252 929

Presbytery of Dundee *Clerk:* Rev James L Wilson, 53 Old Craigie Road, Dundee DD4 7JD
E: akph45@uk.uumail.com
☎01382 459 249

Presbytery of Dunfermline *Clerk:* Rev William E Farquhar, Townhill Manse, 161 Main Street, Dunfermline KY12 0EZ
E: akph46@uk.uumail.com
☎01383 723 835 🖷 01383 723 835

Presbytery of Dunkeld and Meigle *Clerk:* Rev John Russell, Kilblaan, Gladstone Terrace, Birnam, Dunkeld PH8 0DP
E: akph47@uk.uumail.com
☎01350 728 896

Presbytery of Duns *Clerk:* Mr Peter Johnson, Todlaw, Duns TD11 3EJ
E: akph49@uk.uumail.com
☎01361 883 724

Presbytery of Edinburgh *Clerk:* Rev W Peter Graham, 10 Palmerston Place, Edinburgh EH12 5AA
E: akph50@uk.uumail.com
☎0131 225 9137 🖷 0131 225 3312

Presbytery of England *Clerk:* Rev Andrew J Jolly, Chaplaincy Services (RAF), RAF Uxbridge, Uxbridge UB10 0RZ
E: akph14@uk.uumail.com
☎01895 815 387

Presbytery of Falkirk *Clerk:* Rev Ian W Black, Zetland Manse, Ronaldshay Crescent, Grangemouth FK3 9JH
E: akph51@uk.uumail.com
☎01324 472 868

Presbytery of Glasgow *Clerk:* Rev David W Lunan, 260 Bath Street, Glasgow G2 4JP
E: akph84@uk.uumail.com
☎0141 332 6606 🖷 0141 332 6606

Presbytery of Gordon *Clerk:* Rev Euan Glen, The Manse, 26 St Ninian's, Monymusk, Inverurie AB51 7HF
E: akph52@uk.uumail.com
☎01467 651 941

Presbytery of Greenock and Paisley *Clerk:* Rev David Kay, 6 Southfield Avenue, Paisley PA2 8BY
E: akph69@uk.uumail.com
☎0141 884 3600 🖷 0141 884 3600

Presbytery of Hamilton *Clerk:* Rev Shaw J Paterson, 15 Lethame Road, Strathaven ML10 6AD
E: akph54@uk.uumail.com
☎01357 520 019

Presbytery of Inverness *Clerk:* Rev Alastair Younger, St Columba High Manse, 3 Elm Park, Inverness IV2 4WN
E: akph55@uk.uumail.com
☎01463 232 462 🖷 01463 232 462

Presbytery of Irvine and Kilmarnock *Clerk:* Rev Colin G F Brockie, Grange Manse, 51 Portland Road, Kilmarnock KA1 2EQ
E: akph57@uk.uumail.com
☎01563 525 311

Presbytery of Jedburgh *Clerk:* Rev Frank Campbell, 22 The Glebe, Ancrum, Jedburgh TD8 6UX
E: akph56@uk.uumail.com
☎01835 830 318

Presbytery of Kincardine and Deeside *Clerk:* Rev Jack Holt, The Manse, Finzean, Banchory AB31 6PB
E: akph58@uk.uumail.com
☎01330 850 339

Presbytery of Kirkcaldy *Clerk:* Mr Andrew Moore, Anandale, Linksfield Street, Leven KY8 4HX
E: akph59@uk.uumail.com
☎01333 422 644

Presbytery of Lanark *Clerk:* Rev James S H Cutler, 17 Mercat Loan, Biggar ML12 6DG
E: akph60@uk.uumail.com
☎01899 220 625

Presbytery of Lewis *Clerk:* Rev Thomas S Sinclair, An Caladh, East Tarbert, Tarbert, Isle of Harris HS3 3DB
E: akph61@uk.uumail.com
☎01859 502 849 M: 07766 700 100

Presbytery of Lochaber *Clerk:* Rev David M Anderson, Mirlos, 1 Dumfries Place, Fort William PH33 6UQ
☎01397 703 203

Presbytery of Lochcarron-Skye *Clerk:* Rev Allan J Macarthur, High Barn, Croft Road, Lochcarron, Strathcarron IV54 8YA
E: akph63@uk.uumail.com
☎01520 722 278 🖷 01520 722 674

Presbytery of Lothian *Clerk:* Mr John D McCulloch, Auchindinny House, Penicuik EH26 8PE
E: akph65@uk.uumail.com
☎01968 676 300 🖷 01968 676 300

Presbytery of Melrose and Peebles *Clerk:* Mr Jack Stewart, 3 St Cuthbert's Drive, St Boswells, Melrose TD6 0DF
E: akph66@uk.uumail.com
☎01835 822 600

Presbytery of Moray *Clerk:* Rev Hugh M C Smith, Mort Lach, Dufftown, Keith AB55 4AR
E: akph67@uk.uumail.com
☎01340 820 538

Presbytery of Orkney *Clerk:* Rev Trevor G Hunt, The Manse, Finstown, Orkney KW17 2EG
E: akph68@uk.uumail.com
☎01856 761 328 🖷 01856 761 328

Presbytery of Perth *Clerk:* Rev Derek G Lawson, 209 High Street, Perth PH1 5PB
E: akph70@uk.uumail.com
☎01738 451 177 🖷 01738 638 226

Presbytery of Ross *Clerk:* Rev Thomas M McWilliam, Guidhadden, 7 Woodholme Crescent, Culbokie, Dingwall IV7 8JH
E: akph71@uk.uumail.com
☎01349 877 014

Presbytery of St Andrews *Clerk:* Dr Mackie, c/o Church and Society, Church of Scotland, 121 George Street, Edinburgh EH2 4YN
E: akph74@uk.uumail.com
☎Number not supplied

Presbytery of Shetland *Clerk:* Rev Charles H M Greig, The Manse, Sandwick, Shetland ZE2 9HW
E: akph72@uk.uumail.com
☎01950 431 244

Presbytery of Stirling *Clerk:* Rev Moira MacCormick, St Columba's Church, Park Terrace, Stirling FK8 2NA
E: akph75@uk.uumail.com
☎01786 449 522 🖷 01786 473 930

Presbytery of Sutherland *Clerk:* Rev J Leslie Goskirk, The Manse, Lairg IV27 4EH
E: akph76@uk.uumail.com
☎01549 402 373

Presbytery of Uist *Clerk:* Rev Murdo Smith, The Manse, Scarista, Isle of Harris HS3 3HX
E: akph77@uk.uumail.com
☎01859 550 200 🖷 01859 550 200

Presbytery of West Lothian *Clerk:* Rev Duncan Shaw, St John's Manse, Mid Street, Bathgate EH48 1QD
E: akph78@uk.uumail.com
☎01506 653 146

Presbytery of Wigtown and Stranraer *Clerk:* Rev David W Dutton, High Kirk Manse, Leswalt High Road, Stranraer DG9 0AA
E: akph79@uumail.com
☎01776 703 268

Presbytery Clerk of Jerusalem: Rev Clarence W Musgrace

Presbytery Clerk of Europe: Rev John A Cowie

†***Church of the Nazarene** 29 Parkway, Westhoughton, Bolton BL5 2RY
☎01942 815 036 🖷01942 810 613
E: burrclive1@aol.com
South District Superintendent: Rev Clive Burrows. *District Business Manager:* Mr David Barnes. Executive staff 2, Other staff 1, Serving ministers 6[illegible]. **CC** No.SCO 06321. Began 1908 as Pentecostal Church of Scotland, name changed 1915, united with International Holiness Mission 1952 and Calvary Holiness Church 1955. Member of the World Methodist Council. Magazine: *Holiness Today* (Circulation n/a monthly), *Nazarene News* (2,000 quarterly). Turnover £2,272,730 to year end Dec 02.
North District Superintendent: Rev Colin H Wood, 8 Blackcroft Road, Glasgow G32 0RB
E: revcwood@compuserve.com
☎0141 778 3262 🖷0141 778 3262

Congregational Federation, Congregational Centre, 8 Castle Gate, Nottingham NG1 7AS
☎0115 911 1460 🖷0115 911 1462
E: admin@congregational.org.uk
Web: www.congregational.org.uk
General Secretary: Rev Michael Heaney. Executive staff 1, Admin staff 4, Serving ministers 77. ***CC*** No.264839. Began 1972. Magazine: *Congregationalist* (2,500 every two months). Turnover n/a.

Congregational Union of Ireland, 1 Bradford Heights, Carrickfergus BT38 9EB
☎028 9336 8292
Secretary: Mr Sydney Johnston. No full-time staff, Serving ministers 31. Began 1829. Magazine: *The Congregationalist* (2,000 quarterly). Turnover n/a.

†**Continuing Church of England (Diocese of Lambeth)**, 113 Fortess Road, London NW5 2HR
☎020 7267 4015
General Secretary: Rev Michael J Plant. Executive staff 1, Serving ministers n/a. Began 1994 No magazine. Turnover £2,000 to year end Dec 00.

Coptic Orthodox Church, Hill Park House, Lapworth Street, Lapworth, Solihull B94 5QS
☎01564 783 926 🖷01564 784 236
Coptic Orthodox Patriarchate, Bishop of Birmingham: His Grace Bishop Missaiel. Executive staff n/a, Serving ministers 2. ***CC*** No.267387. Began 1866. No magazine. Turnover n/a.
Diocese of Ireland, Scotland, North East England & affiliated Territories *Bishop*: His Grace Bishop Antony, 40 Kingston Drive, Whitley Bay NE26 1JJ
E: banton@blueyonder.co.uk
☎0191 297 2155 / 253 5558
🖷 0191 253 5558
The British Orthodox Church *Metropolitan of Glastonbury:* His Grace Abba Seraphim, Church Secretariat, 10 Heathwood Gardens, Charlton, London SE7 8EP
E: boc@mildram.co.uk
www.britishorthodox.org
☎020 8854 3090 M: 07770 304 925
🖷 020 8244 7888
Executive staff 1, Admin staff 2, Serving ministers 18. Magazine: *The Glastonbury Review* (1,000 every four months) Website
Churches directly under Pope Shenouda II His Grace Angaelos, Archangel Michael & St Anthony Coptic Orthodox Church Centre, Shephalbury Manor, Broadhall Way, Stevenage SG2 8RH
E: angaelos@copticcentre.com
☎01438 748 473 / 534 🖷 01438 313 879

***Countess of Huntingdon's Connexion**, 27 St Marys Road, Mortimer, Reading RG7 3UE
☎0118 933 2569
E: generalsecretary@cofhconnexion.org.uk
Web: www.cofhconnexion.org.uk
Secretary: Dr Brian Baldwin. No full-time staff, Serving ministers 14. ***CC*** No.232674 Began 1781. Magazine: *Voice* (750 quarterly). Turnover £60,000 to year end Jun 04.

Croatian Roman Catholic Church, 17 Boutflower Road, London SW11 1RE
☎020 7223 3530
🖷020 7223 3530
E: hrvkatmisja@yahoo.com
Croatian Catholic Mission: Rev Fr Drago Berisic. No full-time staff. Serving ministers n/a. Began 1969. Magazine: *Prisutnost* (Circulation & frequency n/a). Turnover n/a.

Danish Church of St Katharine, 4 St Katharine's Precinct, Regents Park, London NW1 4HH
☎020 7935 1723
🖷020 7486 9737
Web: www.danskekirke.org
Chaplain to Seamen's Mission and Embassy: To be appointed. Executive staff 2, Admin staff 2, Serving ministers 2. Began 1692. Magazine: *Kirkehilsen* (2,500 quarterly). Turnover n/a.

***Deeper Christian Life Ministry**, 82 Borough Road, London SE1 1DN
☎020 7357 7558 🖷020 7378 8550
E: admin@dclm.freeserve.co.uk
Web: www.deeperlife.org.uk
National Overseer: Rev Pre Ovia. Executive staff 1, Other staff 5, Serving ministers (part-time) 50. ***CC*** No.297359. Began 1985. No magazine. Turnover n/a.

Dutch Church, 7 Austin Friars, London EC2N 2HA
☎020 7588 1684
🖷020 7374 0790
E: info@dutchchurch.org.uk
Web: www.dutchchurch.org.uk
Minister: Rev Henk ten Napel. Admin staff 6, Serving minister 1. ***CC*** No.214686. Began 1550. Magazine: *Kerknieuws* (550 monthly). Turnover n/a.

***Elim Pentecostal Churches**, PO Box 38, Cheltenham GL50 3HN
☎01242 519 904 🖷01242 222 279
E: info@elimhq.net
Web: www.elim.org.uk
General Superintendent: Rev John Glass. *Administrator:* Rev Bruce Hunter. Executive staff 3, Admin staff 16, Serving ministers 650. ***CC*** No.251549. Began 1915. Magazine: *Direction* (9,000 monthly). Turnover n/a.
Ireland Region *Irish Superintendent:* Rev E McComb, Conference & Corporate Centre, 13 Balloo Crescent, Bangor BT19 7WP
☎028 9147 8003
M: 07866 500 813 🖷 028 9147 0070
Kensington Temple *Regional Superintendent:* Rev Colin Dye, London City Church, PO Box 54108 London W5 9AE
E: info@kt.org
www.kt.org
☎020 8799 6100
🖷 020 8799 6101
Metropolitan East Region *Regional Superintendent:* Rev Mervyn Tilley, 29 Clarendon Road, Leytonstone, London E11 1BZ
E: mervyntilley@compuserve.com
☎020 8556 3229
M: 07721 360 492
🖷 020 8556 3582

Metropolitan West Region *Regional Superintendent:* Rev David Campbell, 60 Linden Crescent, St Albans AL1 5DD
E: davecampbell@ntlworld.com
☎01727 764 558
M: 07887 991 138
🖷 01727 844 812
Midland Region *Regional Superintendent:* Rev Gordon H Neale, 220 Warwick Avenue, Derby DE23 6HP
E: ghneale@aol.com
☎01332 273 212
M: 07973 163 169
🖷 01332 273 214
North Midlands and North West Region *Regional Superintendent:* Rev David G Woodfield, Regional Office, Regents Park, London Road, Nantwich CW5 6LW
E: david-woodfield@charis.co.uk
☎01270 611 550
M: 07770 692 110
North East Region *Regional Superintendent:* Rev Geoff J Feasey, Muirfield, Sheep Cote Road, Shrogs Wood, Brecks, Rotherham S60 4BZ
E: gjfeasey@aol.com
www.elim.org.uk/northeast
☎01709 700 819
M: 07767 211 533
🖷 01709 703 174
Scotland Region *Regional Superintendent:* Rev Kevin M Peat, 10 Ochil Court, East Kilbride, Glasgow G75 9GJ
E: kmpeat@aol.com
☎01355 241 578
M: 07720 439 792
Southern Region *Regional Superintendent:* Rev Michael C Epton, 7 Carsworth Way, Canford Heath, Poole BH17 8SP
E: Eptoncme1942@aol.com
www.elimsouthernregion.org.uk
☎01202 381 933
M: 07860 700 825
🖷 01202 248 786
Wales and South West Midlands Region *Regional Superintendent:* Rev Denis Phillips, Maranatha, 135 Vivian Road, Sketty, Swansea SA2 0UP
E: elim@denis-phillips.co.uk
☎01792 204 826
M: 07831 245 269
🖷 01792 203 117

English Catholic Church (The Archdiocese of Our Lady of England), 68 Bowhill, Kettering NN16 8TU
☎01536 520 324
E: robertmcbride@btinternet.com
Web: www.english-catholic-church.org
Metropolitan Archbishop: Most Rev Robert McBride. Admin staff 3, Serving ministers n/a. ***CC*** Began 2000. No magazine. Turnover £15,000 to year end Mar 03.

Eritrean Orthodox Church, 78 Edmund Street, Camberwell, London SE5 7NR
☎020 7703 5147 🖷020 7703 5147
Priest: Father Yohannes Sibhatu. No full-time staff, Serving ministers n/a. ***CC*** No.1044068. Began 1989. No magazine. Turnover n/a.

†Ethiopian Evangelical Church Mekane Yesus in Great Britain, 5 Gilpin Close, Porteus Road, London W2 1AD
☎020 7724 9675 🖷020 7600 8984
Services at St Anne's Lutheran Church, Gresham Street, London EC2.
Pastor: Rev Barnabas Daniel. No full-time staff, Serving ministers 1. Began n/a; Lutheran. No magazine. Turnover n/a.

Ethiopian Orthodox Tewahido Church, St Mary of Debre Tision, PO Box 4112, London W1A 6GX
☎020 7243 0659
Acting Head of Church: Rev Berhanu Besarat. No full-time staff, Serving ministers 4. ***CC*** No.1060394. Began 1974. No magazine. Turnover n/a.

Evangelical Fellowship of Congregational Churches, PO Box 34, Beverley HU17 0YY
☎01482 860 324 🖷01482 860 324
E: efcc@cix.co.uk
Web: www.efcc.org.uk
General Secretary: Rev Mike Plant. *Administrative Secretary:* Mr Peter Moss. Executive staff 4, Serving ministers n/a. ***CC*** No.262802. Began 1967. Magazine: *Concern* (2,200 quarterly). Turnover n/a.

Evangelical Lutheran Church of England, 28 Huntingdon Road, Cambridge CB3 0HH
☎01223 355 265 🖷01223 355 265
E: elce.central@ntlworld.com
Web: www.lutheran.co.uk
Chairman: Rev R C Quirk. Executive staff 2, Serving ministers 14. ***CC*** No.220466. Began 1896. Magazine: *The British Lutheran* (600 every two months). Turnover n/a.

Evangelical Presbyterian Church in England and Wales, 15 Key Avenue, Worcester WR4 0LT
☎01905 612 830
E: clerk@epcew.org.uk
Web: www.epcew.org.uk
Clerk of the Presbytery: Rev David L Cross. Executive staff n/a, Serving ministers 13. ***CC*** No.801935. Began 1987. (Previously Presbyterian Association in England). Magazine: *Presbyterian Network* (600 half-yearly). Turnover £400,000 to year end Dec 05.

†Evangelical Presbyterian Church in Ireland, 16 Huntingdale, Ballyclare BT39 9XB
☎028 9332 2926/9032 0529
🖷028 9071 4820
E: epc@ukonline.co.uk
Web: web.ukonline.co.uk/epc
Clerk of Presbytery: Rev Stephen Roger. Executive staff 1, Serving ministers 10. Began 1927. Magazine: *Evangelical Presbyterian* (1,000 every two months). Turnover n/a.

***Fellowship of Churches of Christ in Great Britain & Ireland**, 101 Redstone Close, Church Hill North, Redditch B98 9AF
☎01527 455 446 🖷07092 138 798
E: dan.yarnell@blueyonder.co.uk
National Co-ordinator: Rev Dan Yarnell. Executive staff 1, Serving ministers 20. ***CC*** No.SCO 10258. Began 1842. Magazine: *The Christian* (250 quarterly). Turnover n/a.

Fellowship of Independent Evangelical Churches, 39 The Point, Market Harborough LE16 7QU
☎01858 434 540 M: 07952 880 222
🖷01858 411 550
E: admin@fiec.org.uk
Web: www.fiec.org.uk
Supporting independent evangelical churches in the UK.
General Secretary: Richard Underwood. *Administrator:* Rod Badams. *Conference Manager:* Andrew Nicholson. Admin staff 7, Other staff 6, Serving ministers 335. ***CC*** No.263354. Began 1922. Magazine: *Together* (12,000 half-yearly). Turnover £648,000 to year end Oct 04.

†*The Finnish Church in London, 33 Albion Street, London SE16 7JG
☎020 7237 1261 🖷020 7237 1245
E: lomtoo@merimieskirkko.fi or webmaster@scj.org.uk
Senior Chaplain: Rev Tapani Rantala. *Chaplain:* Rev Ulla Kosonen. Admin staff 1, Serving ministers 2. ***CC*** No.283594. Began 1882. Magazine: *Horisontti* (12,000 quarterly). Turnover n/a.

Foursquare Church Great Britain, PO Box 264, Hastings TN34 9BL
☎01424 712 097 M: 07899 962 089
E: gb4square@aol.com
Web: www.foursquaregb.org
National Leader: Rev Kenneth Baird. Executive staff 3, Admin staff 2, Serving ministers 23. ***CC*** No.1069564. Began 1981. (Previously Foursquare Gospel Church of Great Britain). No magazine. Turnover £27,000 to year end Mar 05.

***Free Church of England**, 329 Wolverhampton Road West, Willenhall WV13 2RL
☎01902 607 335 M: 07830 279 744
🖷01902 607 335
E: church@revpaulhunt.wanadoo.co.uk
Web: www.fcofe.org.uk
Diocesan Bishops: Rt Rev K J W Powell, Rt Rev J D M McLean. *General Secretary:* Rev P Hunt. Executive staff 3, Serving ministers 3[illegible]. ***CC*** No.366710. Began 1844, Reformed Episcopal Evangelical Church united with Reformed Episcopal Church in 19[illegible]7. No magazine. Turnover n/a.

***Free Church of Scotland**, Free Church Offices, 15 Bank Street, The Mound, Edinburgh EH1 2LS
☎0131 226 5286 🖷0131 220 [illegible]97
E: offices@freechurchofscotland.org.uk
Web: www.freechurch.org
Principal Clerk of Assembly: Rev James Maciver. *Chief Administrative Officer:* Mr Rod Morrison. *Media Officer:* Rev Alex J Macdonald. Executive staff 1, Other staff 10, Serving ministers 79. ***CC*** No.SCO 12925. Began 1843. Magazines: *Monthly Record* (4,300 monthly), *The Instructor* (1,800 monthly), *From the Frontiers* (2,500 annually), *Free* (1,800 every two months). Turnover £3,400,000 to year end Dec 04.

Edinburgh & Perth Presbytery *Clerk:* Rev David A Robertson, 14 Shamrock Street, Dundee DD4 7AQ
E: darobertson@blueyonder.co.uk
☎01382 861401

Glasgow & Argyll Presbytery *Clerk:* Mr Norman Smith, 48 Crofthead Road, Ayr KA7 3ND
☎01242 267 740

Inverness, Lochaber & Ross Presbytery *Clerk:* Rev Angus MacRae, Free Church Manse, Firth View, Dingwall IV15 9PF
☎01349 862 183

Northern Presbytery *Clerk:* Rev Kenneth A Macleod, Free Church Manse, Millbank Road, Thurso KW14 8PS
E: kenny@kirktons.freeserve.co.uk
☎01847 890 322

Skye & Wester Ross Presbytery *Clerk:* Mr Angus I Campbell, Sonas, 24 Culloden Road, Balloch, Inverness IV2 7HQ
☎01463 790 220

Western Isles Presbytery *Clerk:* Rev Malcolm MacLeod, Free Church Manse, North Shawbost, Isle of Lewis HS2 [illegible]BD
☎01851 710 216

Free Church of Scotland (Continuing), Assembly Clerks' Office, Portmahomack, Tain IV20 1YL
☎0845 129 7055
M: 07879 481 502
🖷01862 871 467
E: enquiries@fccontinuing.org
Web: www.fccontinuing.org
Principal Clerk of Assembly: Rev John MacLeod. Executive staff 1, Serving ministers 36. Began 1843. Separated from Free Church of Scotland, 2000. Magazine: *Free Church Witness* (1[illegible]000 monthly). Turnover n/a.

Northern Synod

Presbytery of Caithness & Sutherland
Clerk: Mr John MacKenzie, 307 Culkein, Drumbeg, Lairg IV27 4NL
E: john@cabarfeidh.freeuk.com
☎01571 833 258

Presbytery of Inverness *Clerk:* Rev John Macleod, Free Church Manse, Tomatin IV13 7XY
E: johnmacleodtomatin@fccontinuing.org
☎01808 511 294
Presbytery of Ross *Clerk:* Rev Harry Woods, Free Church Manse, Beauly IV4 7EX
E: harrywoods@fccontinuing.org
☎01463 782 303
Southern Synod
Presbytery of Argyll & Lochaber *Clerk:* Rev Graeme Craig, Free Church Manse, Ardelve, Kyle IV40 8DY
E: greamecraig@fccontinuing.org
☎01599 555 372
Presbytery of Edinburgh & Perth *Clerk:* Mr Maurice A Grant, 8 Nantwich Drive, Edinburgh EH7 6QS
E: mgrant@ecn96.freeserve.co.uk
☎0131 669 7347
Presbytery of Glasgow *Clerk:* Rev Murdo A N MacLeod, Free Church Manse, 64 Woodend Drive, Glasgow G13 1TG
E: murdomacleod@fccontinuing.org
☎0141 959 5648
Western Synod
Presbytery of Lewis *Clerk:* Capt Callum MacLean, 19 Barony Square, Stornoway, Isle of Lewis HS1 2TQ
E: callum.maclean@btinternet.com
☎01851 702 958
Presbytery of Lochcarron *Clerk:* Rev Graeme Craig, Free Church Manse, Ardelve, Kyle IV40 8DY
E: greamecraig@fccontinuing.org
☎01599 555 372
Presbytery of Skye & Uist *Clerk:* Rev Allan I M Maciver, Free Church Manse, Broadford, Isle of Skye IV49 9AE
☎01471 822 341

***Free Methodist Church in the United Kingdom**, 36 Fairways, Fulwood, Preston PR2 8FY
☎01772 719 422 / 713 607 🖷01772 719 422 / 713 607
E: office@freemethodist.org.uk
Web: www.freemethodist.org.uk
Conference Superintendent: Rev J Allan Ellershaw. Executive staff 1, Other staff 2, Serving ministers 22. ***CC*** No.518173. Began 1960. Magazine: *Light and Life* (Circulation n/a monthly, published in USA). Turnover £70,000 to year end Dec 00.

Free Presbyterian Church of Scotland, 133 Woodlands Road, Glasgow G3 6LE
☎0141 332 9283 🖷0141 332 4271
E: fpchurch@btconnect.com
Web: www.fpchurch.org.uk
Clerk of Synod: Rev John Macleod. *General Treasurer:* Mr R A Campbell. Admin Staff 2, Serving ministers 20. ***CC*** No.SCO 03545. Began 1893. Magazine: *Free Presbyterian* (1,900 monthly), *Young People* (1,700 monthly). Turnover £2,137,239 to year end Dec 04.

Free Presbyterian Church of Ulster, Church House, 356 Ravenhill Road, Belfast BT6 8GL
☎028 9045 7106
Web: www.ianpaisley.org or www.freeprayers.org
Clerk of Presbytery: Dr John Douglas. Executive staff 4, Admin staff 9, Serving ministers n/a. Began 1951. Magazine: *The Revivalist* (6,000 monthly), *Truth for Youth* (3,500 every two months). Turnover n/a.
Correspondence: 117 Banbridge Road, Gilford, Craigavon BT28 2UP
☎028 4066 2232

French Protestant Church of Brighton, Queensbury Mews, Brighton BN1 2FE
☎01273 725 098
Pastor: To be appointed. No full-time staff, Serving minister 1. ***CC*** No.1063644. Began n/a. Magazine: *The Bulletin* (120 every four months). Turnover n/a.

French Protestant Church of Canterbury, 4 The Precinct, Canterbury CT1 2EE
☎01227 762 372 M: 07906 235 392
Pastor: Rev Lusa Nseng-Ngoy. *Secretary of the Consistory:* Mr Michael H Peters. Executive staff 1, Other staff 2, Serving ministers n/a. ***CC*** No.252693. Began 1550. No magazine. Turnover n/a.

†French Protestant Church of London, 8 Soho Square, London W1D 3QD
☎020 7437 5311 🖷020 7434 4579
E: eglisoho@globalnet.co.uk
Pastor: Ms Leila Hamrat. Admin staff 2, Serving minister 1. Began 1550. Magazine: *Le Lien* (450 quarterly). Turnover n/a.

German Christ Church, 19 Montpelier Place, London SW7 1HL
☎020 8876 6366 🖷020 8876 6366
E: evkirchelondonw.e.@aol.com
Pastors: Wolfgand & Anne Kruse. No full-time staff, Serving ministers 2. ***CC*** No.251120. Began 1904. Magazine: *Gemeindebriefe* (450 every two months). Turnover n/a.

†German Roman Catholic Church (St Boniface's), 47 Adler Street, London E1 1EE
☎020 7247 9529 🖷020 7247 3879
Rector of Church & Mission: Rev Heinz Medoch. No full-time staff, Serving minister 1. Began 1809. Magazine: *OASE* (500 quarterly). Turnover n/a.

German Speaking Evangelical Lutheran Synod in Great Britain, German YMCA, 35 Craven Terrace, London W2 3EL
☎020 7706 8589 🖷020 7706 2870
Administrator: Mr Uwe-Kai Maynard. Admin staff 1, Serving ministers 7. ***CC*** No.266600. Began 1955. No magazine. Turnover n/a.

†The Gospel Faith Mission International, 583 Commercial Road, Stepney, London E1 0HJ
☎020 7729 1939 M: 07956 875 488
E: admin@gospelfaithmission.org
Web: www.gospelfaithmission.org
Minister-in-Charge: Rev Jospeh Adeyemo. Admin staff 2, Serving minister 1. ***CC*** No.293765. Began 1984. No magazine. Turnover £20,000 to year end Dec 98.

†Gospel Standard Strict Baptists, 8 Fairleigh Rise, Kington Langley, Chippenham SN15 5QF
☎01249 758 877
🖷01249 758 877
Secretary: Mr H Mercer. No full-time staff, Serving ministers n/a. Began 1872. Magazine: *Gospel Standard* (1,800 monthly), *Friendly Companion* (1,300 monthly). Turnover n/a.

Gospel Tabernacle Assembly, 41 Upper Tulse Hill, London SW2 2SG
☎020 7622 8803
E: agagospeltab@aol.com
Pastor: Pastor Warren Reid. No full-time staff, Serving minister 1. Began 1960. No magazine. Turnover n/a.

Grace Baptist Assembly, 4 Beechwood Road, Caterham CR3 6NA
☎01883 342 711
M: 07950 036 637
🖷01883 342 711
E: keithjohns@onetel.com
Secretary: Mr Keith A Johns. No full-time staff, Serving ministers n/a. Began 1977; but as Particular or Strict Baptists 1620. Magazine: *Grace Magazine* (2,000 eleven times a year). Turnover n/a.

Greek Orthodox Archdiocese of Thyateira & Great Britain, Thyateira House, 5 Craven Hill, London W2 3EN
☎020 7723 4787 🖷020 7224 9301
E: thyateiragb@yahoo.com
Archbishop: Archbishop Gregorios. *Chancellor:* Bishop Athanasios of Tropaeou. Admin staff 7, Serving ministers 117. ***CC*** No.243715. Began 1922. Magazine: *Orthodox Herald* (2,000 bi-monthly), *Bulletin of Spiritual Edification* (10,000 weekly). Turnover n/a.
Assistant Bishop of Diokleia: Rt Rev Kallistos, 19b Northmoor Road, Oxford OX2 6UW
☎01865 554 023 🖷 01865 554 023
Assistant Bishop of Kyanea: Rt Rev Chrysostomos, Cathedral of St Andrew, Kentish Town Road, London NW1 9QA
☎020 7485 6385 / 0198 🖷 020 7485 9972
Assistant Bishop of Nazianzos: Rt Rev Theodoritos, Cathedral of the Divine Wisdom, Moscow Road, London W2 4LQ
☎020 7243 4893 🖷 020 7243 6144
Assistant Bishop of Tropaeou: Rt Rev Athanasios, Cathedral of St Mary, Trinity Road, London N22 8LB
☎020 8888 2295 / 8889 1122 🖷 020 8881 4455

***Ground Level Network**, 1a Beaumontree, Lincoln LN1 1UH
☎01522 533 535 🖷01522 533 636
E: admin@groundlevel.org.uk
Web: www.groundlevel.org.uk
Team Leader: Mr Stuart Bell. *Operations Manager:* Mr Paul Benger. Executive staff 14, Admin staff 3, Serving ministers 68. ***CC*** No.1001599. Began 1985. No magazine. Turnover £250,000 to year end Dec 99.

†**Hackney Pentecostal Apostolic Faith Church**, 27 Middleton Road, Hackney, London E8 4PL
☎020 7275 0074 🖷020 7254 9648
Leader: Pastor E M Douglas. No full-time staff, Serving minister 1. ***CC*** No.76175. Began 1970. No magazine. Turnover n/a.

Harvest Community Network, The Gospel Centre, Wightman Road, London N8 0LZ
☎020 8374 7708 🖷020 8374 7709
E: thegospelcentre@blueyonder.co.uk
Web: www.harvestcc.net
Pastor: Graeme Hotter. No full-time staff, Serving ministers n/a. ***CC*** Began 1935. (Previously The United Apostolic Faith Church). No magazine. Turnover n/a.

The Holy Catholic Church (Western Rite), Archbishop's Office, St Mary's House, Byatts Grove, Longton, Stoke-on-Trent ST3 2RH
☎01782 330 743 🖷01782 255 221
Web: www.holycatholicchurch-wr.org
Metropolitan Archbishop: Most Rev Leslie Hamlett. Executive staff 1, Serving ministers n/a. Began 1992. (Previously Anglican Catholic Church: Missionary Diocese of UK). Magazine: *Unreformed* (500 every two months). Turnover n/a.

Hungarian Reformed Church in the UK (Presbyterian), 17 St Dunstan's Road, London W6 8RD
☎020 8748 8858 🖷020 8445 0879
Also counselling services.
Minister: Rev Istvan Salanki. No full-time staff, Serving minister 1. Began 1948. Magazine: *Circular Letters* (210 quarterly). Turnover n/a.

Icelandic Church in London, 2a Hans Street, London SW1X 0JE
☎020 7259 3999 🖷020 7245 9649
E: chaplain@mfa.is
Web: www.kirkjan.is/london
Embassy Chaplain: Rev Sigudur Arnarson. Executive staff 1, Serving minister 1. Began 1995; Evangelical Lutheran. Magazine: *Molda - Newsletter of the Icelandic Society* (Circulation n/a quarterly). Turnover n/a.

***Ichthus Christian Fellowship**, 7 Greenwich Quay, Clarence Road, Greenwich, London SE8 3EY
☎020 8694 7171 🖷020 8694 7172
E: admin@ichthus.org.uk
Web: www.ichthus.org.uk
Team Leader: Mr Roger T Forster. Executive staff 22, Serving ministers 30. ***CC*** No.1099412. Began 1974. No magazine. Turnover n/a.

***Iglesia Evangelica**, St Pauls Church, Robert Adam Street, London W1M 5AH
☎020 8968 5152 M: 07939 621 456
E: cevangelic@aol.com
Senior Minister: Pastor Jose Dominguez. Executive staff 3, Serving ministers 3. ***CC*** No.280694. Began 1960. (Previously Spanish Evangelical Church). Magazine: *Church Bulletin* (500 monthly). Turnover n/a.

***Independent Methodist Connexion of Churches**, Office and Resource Centre, Fleet Street, Pemberton, Wigan WN5 0DS
☎01942 223 526 🖷01942 227 768
E: resourcecentre@imcgb.org.uk
Web: imcgb.org.uk
Also resource centre.
General Secretary: Mr William Gabb. Admin staff 2, Serving ministers 89. ***CC*** No.254007. Began 1805. Magazine: *Connexion* (1,500 monthly). Turnover n/a.

***International Gospel Outreach**, The Oasis, Dwygyfylchi, Penmaenmawr LL34 6PS
☎0845 226 7027/01492 622 473 (prayerline) 🖷0845 226 7037
E: admin@igo.org.uk
Web: www.igo.org.uk
General Secretary: Rev Bob Searle. Executive staff 9, Other staff 4, Serving ministers 270. ***CC*** No.252872. Began 1967. Magazine: *Vision* (600 monthly). Turnover n/a.

***International Presbyterian Church**, 53 Drayton Green, Ealing London W1[illegible] 0JE
☎020 8997 4706
E: paullevy@onetel.com
Web: www.ipc-ealing.co.uk
Pastor: Mr Paul Levy No full-time staff, Serving minister 1. Began 196[illegible] No magazine. Turnover n/a.

†**International Presbyterian Church, Korean Congregation**, 3[illegible] Grove Crescent, Kingston upon Thames KT1 [illegible]DG
☎020 8397 1202
E: bhyoo44@hotmail.com
Minister: Rev B H Yoo. Executive staff n/a, Serving ministers 5. Began 197[illegible] No magazine. Turnover n/a.

***Iranian Christian Fellowship** 158 Sutton Court Road, Chiswick, London W4 [illegible]HR
☎020 8995 4966
Pastor: Rev Edward Hovsep[illegible]an-Me[illegible]r. No full-time staff, Serving ministers 2. Began 1985. No magazine. Turnover n/a.

Italian Pentecostal Church, Marlborough Road, Woking GU21 5[illegible]G
☎01932 341 653
Pastor: Rev Joseph D[illegible]Aloia No full-time staff, Serving ministers n/a. ***CC*** No.285192. Began 196[illegible]. Magazine: *Notiziario Pentecostale* (1,4[illegible]0 quarterly, Swiss publication). Turnover £12,[illegible]0 to year end Dec 00.

***Jesus Fellowship**, Jesus Fellowship Central Offices, Nether Heyford, Northampton NN7 3LB
☎08451 235 550 🖷08451 668 [illegible]9
E: info@jesus.org.uk
Web: www.jesus.org.uk
A charismatic and evangelical church of radical 24-7 Christians from around the UK.
Senior Pastor: Noel Stanton. Executive staff 1, Admin staff 4, Serving ministers n/a. ***CC*** Began 1969. Affiliated to Multiply Christian Network. Magazine: *Jesus Life* (18,000 every four months), *Modern Jesus Army Streetpaper* (8[illegible],000 every four months). Turnover n/a.

***KC21**, The King's Centre, High Street, Aldershot GU11 1DJ
☎01252 333 767 🖷01252 310 8[illegible]4
E: administration@kc21.net
Web: www.kc21.net
Leader: Mr Derek Brown. Executive staff n/a, Serving ministers 10. ***CC*** No.1107682. Began 1984. (Previously The King's Church). No magazine. Turnover n/a.

***Kensington Temple, London City Church**, Kensington Park Road, London W11 3BY
☎020 8799 6100 🖷020 8[illegible]99 61[illegible]
E: info@kt.org
Web: www.kt.org
Also responsible for several congregations of overseas nationals.
Senior Minister: Pastor Colin W Dye. Executive staff 16, Other staff [illegible]5, Serving ministers 10. ***CC*** No.25[illegible]549. Began n/a. Magazine: *Revival Times* (10,[illegible]00 monthly). Turnover n/a.

Kingdom Faith Church, National Revival Centre, Foundry Lane, Horsham RH13 5PX
☎01293 851 543 🖷01293 854 610
E: info@kingdomfaith.com
Web: www.kingdomfaith.com
Pastor: Clive Urquhart. Executive staff n/a, Serving ministers 10. ***CC*** No.278746. Began 1992. Magazine: *Impact* (20,000 quarterly). Turnover n/a.

†The Latter-Rain Outpouring Revival Ministry 242 Hoxton Street, London N1 5LX
☎020 7739 5389
Overseer/Bishop: Rev C L Green. Executive staff 2, Other staff 5, Serving ministers 3. Began 1964. No magazine. Turnover n/a.

Latvian Lutheran Church, 65 Northcote Road, Leicester LE2 3FJ
☎0113 217 6879
Spiritual Head & Dean: Very Rev Dean Juris Jurgis. *Dean:* Dean Gita Putce. Executive staff 5, Other staff 5, Serving ministers 4. Began 1947. Magazine: *Cela Biedrs* (500 monthly), *Pie Svetavota* (475 quarterly). Turnover n/a.

†The Liberal Catholic Church, 2 Dairy Farm, Goring Street, Goring-by-Sea, Worthing BN12 5AE
☎01903 501 281 M: 07960 964 032
E: gw.lcc@btinternet.com
Vicar General: Very Rev Graham Wale. *Presiding Bishop:* Most Rev Yohannes van Alphen. All voluntary staff, Serving ministers 23 Began 1916. Magazine: *Albanus* (500 half-yearly). Turnover n/a.

Liberal Catholic Church Grail Community, Bishop's House and Oratory of Our Lady, Chalice House, Torridge Hill, Bideford EX39 2AZ
☎01237 424 737 🖷01237 424 737
E: grailcommunity@care4free.net
Web: www.lccgrail.co.uk
Bishop-in-Charge: Rt Rev Roy Bannister. No full-time staff, Serving ministers 4. Began 1991. Magazine: *The Grail* (Circulation n/a half-yearly). Turnover n/a.

***Life Changing Ministries**, Bemersley House, Gitana Street, Hanley, Stoke-on-Trent ST1 1DY
☎01782 287 940 M: 07931 735 132
Apostle & Senior Pastor: Rev Trevor Newport. Admin staff 1, Serving ministers 10. ***CC*** No.1049129. Began 1992. Magazine: *Life Changing News* (250 quarterly). Turnover £70,000 to year end Dec 04.

Lithuanian Roman Catholic Church of St Casimir, 21 The Oval Hackney Road, London E2 9DT
☎020 7739 8735 M: 07939 126 505
E: ptverijonas@btinternet.com
Web: www.londonas.co.uk
Chaplain: Rev Petras Tverijonas. No full-time staff, Serving ministers 1. ***CC*** No.233699. Began 1901. No magazine. Turnover n/a.

†Lutheran Church in Great Britain, Lutheran Church House, 9 Alma Road, Headingley, Leeds LS6 2AH
☎0113 275 9042 🖷0113 275 9042
E: info@lutheransinleeds.freeserve.co.uk
Web: www.lutheran.org.uk
Bishop: Rt Rev Walter Jagucki. Executive staff 1, Serving ministers 18. Began 1961. Magazine: *Lutherans in Britain* (Circulation n/a half-yearly). Turnover n/a.

†Mar Thoma Syrian Church UK Congregation, Office Mar Thoma Centre, 22 Altmore Avenue, London E6 2BY
☎020 8471 2446 🖷020 8471 2446
E: achen@marthomachurch.org.uk
Web: www.marthomachurch.org.uk
Vicar: Rev Prasab Mathew. Executive staff 1, Other staff 1, Serving minister 1. Began 1957. Magazine: *Mar Thoma Messenger* (200 quarterly). Turnover n/a.

Methodist Church, Methodist Church House, 25 Marylebone Road, London NW1 5JR
☎020 7486 5502 🖷020 7467 5226
E: enquiries@methodistchurch.org.uk
Web: www.methodist.org.uk
General Secretary of Conference: Rev David G Deeks. Executive staff n/a, Admin staff n/a. The Wesleyan, Primitive and United Methodist Churches united in 1932. Magazine: *Momentum* (Circulation n/a half-yearly). Turnover n/a.

See also:
Children's Work on Page 401
Church House on Page 183
Experience Exchange on Page 308
MAYC - Methodist Association of Youth Clubs on Page 401
Methodist Bookshop on Page 106
Relief and Development Fund on Page 312
World Church Office on Page 290

See also listings under **Methodist** in Main Index on Page 522

***Methodist Church*: Bedfordshire, Essex, Hertfordshire District**, 37 Long Buflers, Harpenden AL5 1JF
☎01582 760 567/460 732
🖷01582 460 128
E: anne.brown@districtnet.org.uk
Web: www.districtnet.org.uk
Likely to move late 2006/early 2007
District Chair: Rev Anne E Brown. Executive staff 2, Serving ministers 80. Began n/a No magazine. Turnover n/a.
Secretary: Miss Kathleen Burrell, 17 Oakfield Road, Benfleet SS7 5NS
☎01268 794 741
E: burrellkm@aol.com

***Methodist Church*: Birmingham District**, 36 Amesbury Road, Moseley, Birmingham B13 8LE
☎0121 449 0131 🖷0121 449 0131
E: bhammeth@fish.co.uk
Web: www.bhammeth.org.uk
Chair: Rev William H Anderson. Executive staff 1, Admin staff 1, Serving ministers 45. Began n/a. No magazine. Turnover n/a.
Secretary: Mr John Nodding, 6 Midgley Drive, Sutton Coldfield B74 2TW
☎0121 323 3508

***Methodist Church*: Bolton and Rochdale District**, 5 Hill Side, Heaton, Bolton BL1 5DT
☎01204 843 302 🖷01204 843 302
Web: www.barmd.org
Chairman: Rev David King. No full-time staff, Serving ministers 59. Began n/a. No magazine. Turnover n/a.
Secretary: Miss Margaret Higson, 10 Heatherfield, Edgeworth, Bolton BL7 0DJ
☎01204 852 538

***Methodist Church*: Bristol District**, District Office, c/o Wesley Church, Wesley Slope, Frome BA11 1HP
☎01373 452 383
Web: www.bristolmethodist.org.uk
Covering Bristol, Gloucestershire, northern parts of Wiltshire and Somerset.
Chairman: Rev A Ward Jones. Executive staff 10, Serving ministers 78. Began 1739. No magazine. Turnover n/a.
Secretary: Rev Carrie Seaton, 7 Towbury Court, Kilmore Lane, Twyning, Tewkesbury GL20 6EN
☎01684 293 227

***Methodist Church*: Channel Islands District**, Les Pipots, Les Petites Rues, St Lawrence, Jersey JE3 1FD
☎01534 743 933 🖷01534 743 933
E: david@cooteonline.com
Web: www.ci-methodist.org.uk
Chairman: Rev David Coote. Executive staff 1, Serving ministers 10. Began n/a. Magazine: *Jersey Methodist* (250 quarterly). Turnover n/a.
Secretary: Rev Stephen J Robinson, Aldersgate, Rue de la Ronde Chemineé, Castel, Guernsey GY5 7GB
E: rkabisa@aol.com
☎01481 257 178

***Methodist Church*: Chester and Stoke-on-Trent District**, Methodist District Centre, Bishops Wood, Nantwich CW5 7QD
☎01270 627 774
E: do.chestoke@fish.co.uk
Also book centre (Hanley), Primitive Methodist Museum (Englesea Brook).
Chairman: Rev Canon John D Walker. *Synod Secretary:* David Scott. Executive staff 5, Serving ministers 60. Began n/a. No magazine. Turnover n/a.
Secretary: Mr David Scott, 5 White Hart Lane, Wistaston, Crewe CW2 8EX
E: do.chestoke@fish.co.uk
☎01270 568 550

***Methodist Church*: Cornwall District**, 4 Upland Crescent, Truro TR1 1LU
☎01872 272 514 🖷01872 262 554
E: chrisblake@clara.net
Web: www.cornish-methodists.org
Chairman: Rev Dr Chris Blake. Executive staff n/a, Serving ministers 50. Began n/a. Magazine: *District Chronicle* (7,000 every four months). Turnover n/a.
Secretary: Rev Celia Phillips, The Manse, 56 Hilgrove Road, Newquay TR7 2QT
☎01637 873 087

***Methodist Church*: Cumbria District**, 14 Monnington Way, Penrith CA11 8QJ
☎01768 866 342 M: 07977 900 215 🖷01768 866 342
E: david@cumbriadistrict.u-net.com
Web: www.cumbriamethodists.org.uk
Chair: Rev David Emison. Executive staff n/a, Serving ministers 35. Began n/a. No magazine. Turnover n/a.
Secretary: Rev Keith Burrow, 25 Beechwood Avenue, Carlisle CA3 9BW
E: burrow@fish.co.uk
☎01228 522 645 🖷 01228 526 318

***Methodist Church*: Cymru District**, Heulfryn, Ffordd Tyn-y-Coed, Dolgellau LL40 2YT
☎01341 422 524
E: ps@penllwyn3.fsnet.co.uk
Web: www.westwales.co.uk/methodism
Chairman: Rev Patrick Slattery. Admin staff 2, Serving ministers 12. Began n/a. Magazine: *Y Gwyliedydd* (2,500 every two months). Turnover n/a.
Secretary: Rev Dennis Griffiths, 65 Ruabon Road, Wrexham LL13 7PL
☎01978 263 955

***Methodist Church*: Darlington District**, 2 Edinburgh Drive, Darlington DL3 8AW
☎01325 468 119 🖷01325 468 119
Web: www.darlingtonmethodist.web space.surefish.co.uk
Chairman: Rev Graham Carter. Executive staff 1, Serving ministers 66. Began n/a. No magazine. Turnover n/a.
Secretary: Rev D Paul Wood, 52 The Avenue, Durham DH1 4EB
☎0191 384 7950

***Methodist Church*: East Anglia District**, 26 Wentworth Green, Sunningdale, Norwich NR4 6AE
☎01603 452 257
Chairman: Rev Graham Thompson. Admin staff 3, Serving ministers 79. Began n/a. No magazine. Turnover n/a.
Secretary: Mr Graham Lindsay, 38 Bowthorpe Road, Wisbech PE13 2DX
☎01945 475 366

***Methodist Church*: Isle of Man District**, Yn Conney, Shore Road, Castletown IM9 1BF
☎01624 822 541 🖷01624 822 541
Chairman: Rev Stephen Caddy. *Secretary:* Rev M Peacock. Executive staff 1, Serving ministers 7. Began n/a. No magazine. Turnover n/a.

***Methodist Church*: Leeds District**, 281 Otley Road, Leeds LS16 5LN
☎0113 278 5546 🖷0113 274 5611
E: leedschair@ntlworld.com
Web: www.leedsmethodist.org.uk
Chairman: Rev Michael J Townsend. Executive staff 1, Serving ministers 75. Began n/a. No magazine. Turnover n/a.
Secretary: Rev Richard Oldroyd, 142 Balne Lane, Wakefield WF2 0DN
E: richardoldroyd@tiscali.co.uk
☎01924 373 287

***Methodist Church*: Lincoln and Grimsby District**, 27 Woodland View, The Bridles, Barnetby DN38 6FE
☎01652 680 858
E: revdwperry@btinternet.com
Web: www.lgmethodistdistrict.org.uk
Chairman: Rev Dr David W Perry. Executive staff 3, Admin staff 2, Serving ministers 43. Began n/a. Magazine: *Link-It*(Circulation & frequency n/a). Turnover n/a.
Secretary: Mr Mike Childs, 5 Rowan Close, Keelby, Grimsby DN41 8SA
☎01469 560 115

†***Methodist Church*: Liverpool District**, 49 Queen's Drive, Mossley Hill, Liverpool L18 2DT
☎0151 722 1219 🖷0151 722 1[illegible]19
E: liv.meth.dist@rapid.co.uk
Chairman: Rev James A Booth. *Secretary:* Rev Neil A Stubbens. Executive staff 2, Serving ministers 64. Began n/a. No magazine. Turnover n/a.

***Methodist Church*: London District**, London District Resource Centre, 1 Central Buildings, London SW1H 9NH
☎020 7654 3850 🖷020 7799 14[illegible]2
E: admin@methodistlondon.org.uk
Chairman: Rev Ermal Kirby. Executive staff 5, Serving ministers 156. Began n/a No magazine. Turnover n/a.
Secretary: Mr Bala Gnanapragasam, 25 Inchmery Road, London SE6 2NA
☎020 8698 6710
E: bala@balasylvia.com

***Methodist Church*: Manchester and Stockport District**, 15 Woodlands Road, Handforth, Wilmslow SK9 3AW
☎01625 523 480 🖷01625 523 4[illegible]0
E: kjs.davies63@btopenworld.com
Chairman: Rev Keith Davies. Executive staff 1, Serving ministers 90. Began n/a. No magazine. Turnover n/a.
Secretary: Mr T Fred Bell, 198 Turf Lane, Royton, Oldham OL2 6EU
E: bellfred@btinternet.com
☎0161 626 5703

***Methodist Church*: Newcastle upon Tyne District**, 246 Wingrove Road North, Fenham, Newcastle upon Tyne NE4 [illegible]EJ
☎0191 273 9790 🖷0191 273 97[illegible]
E: leo.osborn@talk21.com
Chair: Rev L E Osborn. Executive staff 1, Serving ministers 88. Began n/a. No magazine. Turnover n/a.
Secretary: Mrs E Edwards, 18 Weston Avenue, Fellside Park, Whickham, Newcastle upon Tyne NE16 5[illegible]S
☎0191 488 1969 🖷 0191 273 97[illegible]9

†***Methodist Church*: North Lancashire District**, 47 Greenacres, Fulwood, Preston PR2 7DB
☎01772 861 110 / 862 482
E: sjpoxon@aol.com
Chairman: Rev Stephen Poxon. Executive staff 1, Serving ministers 65. Began n/a. No magazine. Turnover n/a.
Secretary: Rev Andrew Horsfall, 12 Hall Drive, Torrisholme, Morecambe LA4 [illegible]X
E: revhors@aol.com
☎01524 410 072 🖷 01524 410 07[illegible]

†***Methodist Church*: Nottingham and Derby District**, 37 Sutton Passey's Crescent, Nottingham NG8 1BX
☎0115 978 7598 🖷0115 978 759[illegible]
E: wes@jwwblakey.fsnet.co.uk
Web: www.nddistrict.oc-tech.co.uk
Chairman: Rev J W Wesley Blakey. *Secretary:* Ms A George. Executive staff [illegible], Serving ministers 86. Began n/a. No magazine. Turnover n/a.

***Methodist Church*: Oxford and Leicester District**, 291 Billing Road East, Northampton NN3 3LG
☎01604 530 128
E: altomlin@fish.co.uk
Web: www.methodistdistrict23.org.uk
Chair: Rev Alison Tomlin. Executive staff 1, Serving ministers 86. Began n/a. No magazine. Turnover n/a.
Secretary: Rev Dr Martin Wellings, 53 Oxford Road, Kidlington OX5 2BP
☎01865 373 958 🖷 01865 373 958

***Methodist Church*: Plymouth and Exeter District**, 18 Velwell Road, Exeter EX4 4LE
☎01392 272 541
E: carne@manse99.freeserve.co.uk
Chairman: Rev Frederick J Carne. Executive staff 1, Serving ministers 75. Began n/a. Magazine: *Newsletter* (Circulation n/a every four months). Turnover n/a.
Secretary: Rev Linda Barriball, 13 King Edward Road, Minehead TA24 5EA
E: lbarriball.freespace@virgin.net
☎01643 705 175

***Methodist Church*: Scotland District**, Methodist Centre, Scottish Churches House, Kirk Street, Dunblane FK15 0AJ
☎01786 823 295 🖷01786 820 295
E: meth@scottishchurches.org
Proclaiming the conviction of God's love and action in Christ for all the world.
Chairman: Rev James W Jones. *Secretary:* Mrs Margaret Brown. Executive staff 5, Serving ministers 40. Began n/a. No magazine. Turnover n/a.

***Methodist Church*: Sheffield District**, Victoria Hall Methodist Church, Norfolk Street, Sheffield S1 2JB
☎0114 281 2733 🖷0114 281 2734
E: admin@sheffieldmethodist.org
Web: www.sheffieldmethodist.org
Covering South Yorkshire, north Nottinghamshire, north-east Derbyshire.
Chairman: Rev Vernon Marsh. *Secretary:* Rev Gill Newton. Executive staff 1, Serving ministers 97. Began n/a. No magazine. Turnover n/a.

***Methodist Church*: Shetland District**, Wesley Manse, 9 Hillhead, Lerwick, Shetland ZE1 0EJ
☎01595 692 874
E: JeremyDare@aol.com
Chairman: Rev Jeremy Dare. Executive staff 1, Serving ministers 4. ***CC*** Began n/a. No magazine. Turnover n/a.
Secretary: Mrs Sylvia White, Croft House, Railsbrough, Skellister, Shetland ZE2 9PS
☎01595 890 349

***Methodist Church*: South East District**, 39 Limes Avenue, Horley RH6 9DG
☎01293 774 119
E: chair.sedist@ntlworld.com
District Chair: Rev John Hellyer. Executive staff 5, Serving ministers 88. Began n/a Magazine: *District News-sheet* (500 half-yearly). Turnover n/a.
Secretary: Mr David Ridley, 11 Tamarisk Rise, Wokingham RG40 1WG
☎0118 377 8088
E: synodsec.sedist@ntlworld.com

***Methodist Church*: South Wales District**, 12 Llwyn-y-Grant Road, Penylan, Cardiff CF23 9ET
☎029 2048 6751 🖷029 2048 6751
E: districtchairsouth@methodistwales.org.uk
Web: www.methodistwales.org.uk/south
Chairman: Rev Will Morrey. Executive staff 1, Serving ministers 60. Began n/a. (Previously Cardiff and Swansea District). Magazine: *South Wales District Issues* (400 half-yearly). Turnover n/a.
Secretary: Mr Graham Illingworth, 38 Britway Road, Dinas Powys CF64 4AF
E: synodsecretarysouth@methodistwales.org.uk
☎029 2051 3878

†*Methodist Church*: Southampton District, 4 The Glade, Thornbury Wood, Chandler's Ford, Eastleigh SO53 5AZ
☎023 8027 0519
Chairman: Rev Thomas J Stuckey. Executive staff 1, Serving ministers 88. Began n/a. Magazine: *District Newsletter* (Circulation n/a quarterly). Turnover n/a.

***Methodist Church*: West Yorkshire District**, 19 Wentworth Court, Rastrick, Brighouse HD6 3XD
☎01484 719 993
E: pwwyks@aol.com
Web: www.westyorkshiremethodist.inuk.com
Chairman: Rev Peter Whittaker. Staff 1, Serving ministers 65. Began n/a. Magazine: *District Newsletter* (6,000 quarterly). Turnover n/a.
Secretary: Rev Ruth M Gee, 9 The Crescent, Hipperholme, Halifax HX3 8NQ
E: ruth@rmgee.freeserve.co.uk
☎01422 202 564

***Methodist Church*: Wolverhampton and Shrewsbury District**, Beckminster Methodist Church, Birches Barn Road, Wolverhampton WV3 7BQ
☎01902 332 508/424 430 (home)
Chair: Rev John D Howard. No full-time staff, Serving ministers 30. Began n/a. No magazine. Turnover n/a.
Secretary: Mrs Brenda Shuttleworth, 19 Tudor Crescent, Wolverhampton WV2 4PX
E: bs@wsmeth.org.uk
☎01902 330 002

***Methodist Church*: York and Hull District**, 13 Lawn Way, Stockton Lane, York YO31 1JD
☎01904 424 739 🖷01904 426 268
Chairman: Rev Stephen Burgess. Admin staff 1, Serving ministers 72. Began n/a. No magazine. Turnover n/a.
Secretary: Mrs Rosemary Harrison, 21 Mile End Park, Pocklington, York YO42 2TH
E: roseh@fish.co.uk
☎01759 303 888

Methodist Church in Ireland, 1 Fountainville Avenue, Belfast BT9 6AN
☎028 9032 4554 🖷028 9023 9467
E: secretary@irishmethodist.org
Web: www.irishmethodist.org
Secretary: Rev Winston Graham. Executive staff 4, Serving ministers 125. Began 1738. Magazine: *Methodist Newsletter* (4,750 monthly). Turnover n/a.

***Methodist Church in Ireland*: Belfast District**, Belfast Central Mission, Grosvenor House, 5 Glengall Street, Belfast BT12 5AD
☎028 9024 1917
District Superintendent: Rev Donald Ker. Executive staff 1, Serving ministers 46. Began 1750. No magazine. Turnover n/a.
Secretary: Rev Derek Johnston, 54 Grangewood Road, Dundonald, Belfast BT16 1GW
☎028 9029 5237

C

***Methodist Church in Ireland*: Down District**, 9 Maxwell Park, Bangor BT20 3SH
☎028 9145 5185
District Superintendent: Rev Ken Todd. Executive staff 1, Serving ministers 16. Began 1973. No magazine. Turnover n/a.
Secretary: Rev Thomas R McKnight, 9a Chippendale Avenue, Bangor BT20 4PT
☎028 9146 0098

***Methodist Church in Ireland*: Lakelands District**, Aldersgate, 47 Chanterhill Road, Enniskillen BT74 6DE
☎028 6632 2244
District Superintendent: Rev Ken Robinson. Executive staff 1, Serving ministers 10. ***CC*** Began n/a. (Previously Mid-Western District). No magazine. Turnover n/a.
Secretary: Rev Philip Agnew, 67 Main Street, Ballinamallard, Enniskillen BT94 2FZ
☎028 6638 8200

***Methodist Church in Ireland*: North East District**, 32 Harwood Gardens, Carrickfergus BT38 7US
☎028 9336 2202
E: methcomm@talk21.com
Chairman: Rev Aian Ferguson. Executive staff 1, Serving ministers 25. Began 1747. No magazine. Turnover n/a.
Secretary: Rev Trevor Jamieson, 1 Glenagherty Drive, Old Galgorm Road, Ballymena BT42 1AG
☎028 2565 6693

***Methodist Church in Ireland*: North West District**, 9 Dergmoney Place, Omagh BT78 1HS
☎028 8224 2372
E: haroldagnew@freeinternet.co.uk
District Superintendent: Rev Harold M Agnew. Executive staff 1, Serving ministers 13. Began n/a. (Previously Londonderry District). No magazine. Turnover n/a.
Secretary: Rev Alan Macaulay, 33 Grange Road, Coleraine BT52 1NG
☎028 7034 3158

***Methodist Church in Ireland*: Portadown District**, 5 The Hollows, Gilford Road, Lurgan, Craigavon BT66 7FF
☎028 3832 3367
District Superintendent: Rev J A Maurice Laverty. Executive staff 1, Serving ministers 22. Began 1747. No magazine. Turnover n/a.
Secretary: Rev Brian Sweeney, 28 Loy Street, Cookstown BT80 8PE
☎028 8676 2639

Metropolitan Community Churches, Office 3, Green Park Offices, Johnson's Building, James Street West, Bath BA1 2BU
☎01225 320 833 ℻01225 320 880
E: ceciliaeggleston@MCCchurch.org
Web: www.MCCchurch.org
Affirming ministry to lesbians, gays, bisexual and transgendered community.
Regional Elder: Rev Cecilia Eggleston. Executive staff 1, Serving ministers n/a. Began 1972. No magazine. Turnover n/a.

C

Miracle Church of God in Christ, 36 Alexandra Road, Bedford MK40 1JB
☎01234 215 081
E: miraclechurch1@aol.com
Web: www.miraclelogic.org
Overseer: Mr Francis Vaughan. *Administrator:* Mrs Lynn Ashman. Executive staff 9, Admin staff 4, Serving ministers 4. ***CC*** No.291224. Began 1960. No magazine. Turnover n/a.

Moravian Church in Great Britain and Ireland, 5 Muswell Hill, London N10 3TJ
☎020 8883 3409 ℻020 8365 3371
E: office@moravian.org.uk
Web: www.moravian.org.uk
Chairman, Provincial Board: Mrs J K Morten. Executive staff 2, Admin staff 5, Serving ministers 25. ***CC*** No.251211. Began 1737. Magazine: *The Moravian Messenger* (2,000 monthly). Turnover n/a.

***Multiply Christian Network**, Jesus Fellowship Central Offices, Nether Heyford, Northampton NN7 3LB
☎08451 668 175 ℻08451 668 178
E: info@multiply.org.uk
Web: www.multiply.org.uk
Multiply Director: Huw Lewis. Admin staff 2, Serving ministers 150. Began 1992. No magazine. Turnover n/a.

New Apostolic Church UK, Administration Office, 19 Southwell Park Road, Camberley GU15 3PU
☎01276 614 16 ℻01276 677 971
E: nacadmin@nacukie.net
Web: www.nacukie.net
District Elder: Rev David Middleton. *Administrator:* Rev Jack Muggeridge. Executive staff 1, Serving ministers 175. ***CC*** No.239664. Began 1948. No magazine. Turnover n/a.

***New Covenant Church**, 214 Elephant and Castle Shopping Centre, London SE1 6TE
☎020 7277 0272
℻020 7277 0824
E: newcovuk@aol.com
Web: www.newcovenant.org.uk
National Overseers: Rev Timothy Kolade, Rev Niyi Kolade. *National Administrator:* Rev Obafemi Omisade. Admin staff 6, Serving ministers 31. ***CC*** No.1004343. Began 1988. Magazine: *U-turn* (2,000 quarterly). Turnover n/a.

***New Testament Assembly (Pentecostal)**, 5 Woodstock Avenue, Ealing, London W13 9UQ
☎020 8579 3841
E: njsterlnta@aol.com
General Secretary: Rev Nezlin Sterling. *Presiding Bishops:* Bishop Melvin Powell, Bishop David Greeves. Executive staff 4, Serving ministers n/a. Began 1961. No magazine. Turnover n/a.

***New Testament Church of God**, Main House, Overstone Park, Overstone, Northampton NN6 0AD
☎01604 643 311 / 645 944
℻01604 790 254
Web: www.ntcg.org.uk
National Overseer: Rev Eric Arthur Brown. Executive staff 12, Admin staff 15, Serving ministers 282. ***CC*** No.250306. Began 1953. No magazine. Turnover n/a.

***Newfrontiers**, 17 Clarendon Villas, Hove BN3 3RE
☎01273 234 555
℻01273 234 556
E: office@newfrontiers.xtn.org
Web: www.newfrontiers.xtn.org
International Team Leader: Mr Terry Virgo. *National Team Leader:* Mr David Holden. Executive staff 8, Serving ministers 400. ***CC*** No.1060001. Began 1980. (Previously New Frontiers). Magazine: *New Frontiers Magazine* (15,000 every two months). Turnover n/a.
Administration and Training *Administrator:* Mr Steve Blaber, New Community Church Sidcup, 24 Station Road, Sidcup DA15 7DU
E: office@newfrontiers.xtn.org
☎020 8300 0333

†Non-subscribing Presbyterian Church of Ireland, 1 Sherwood Avenue, Newtownabbey BT36 8GF
☎028 9084 3592
Clerk to the General Synod: Rev T N Playfair. *Editor:* Rev A D G Steers. No full-time staff, Serving ministers 15. ***CC*** Began 1910. Magazine: *The Non-subscribing Presbyterian* (1,100 monthly). Turnover n/a.

Norwegian Church and Seamen's Mission, St Olav's Church, 1 St Olav's Square, Albion Street, Rotherhithe, London SE16 7JB
☎020 7740 3900
M: 07711 223 059
℻020 7237 7280
E: london@sjomannskirken.no
Web: www.sjomannskirken.no/london
Rector: Rev Torbjørn Holt. Executive staff 7, Serving ministers [illegible]. ***CC*** No.22[illegible]235. Began 1692; Lutheran. Magazine: *Månedsbladet* (2,200 every two months). Turnover n/a.

***Old Baptist Union**, 64 Kennedy Avenue, Macclesfield SK10 3DE
☎01625 422 404
M: 07780 692 808
℻01625 422 404
E: cnwhiteley@xalt.co.uk
Web: www.members.aol.com/obulinc
Secretary: Rev C Whiteley. No full-time staff, Serving ministers 12. ***CC*** No.233642. Began 1830. No magazine. Turnover n/a.

The Open Episcopal Church, Bishop's Haven, 105 Danson Crescent, Welling DA16 2AS
☎020 8304 7605
M: 07767 687 711
E: bishopjonathanblake@ntlworld.com
Web: www.openepiscopalchurch.com
Bishop of Greater London: Rt Rev Jonathan Blake. Executive staff 2, Admin staff 3, Serving ministers 40. Began 2001. Magazine: *The Open Episcopalian* ([illegible]300 every four months). Turnover £65[illegible] to year end Mar 02.
Bishop of Romsey: Rt Rev Prof Elizabeth Stuart, 143 North East Road, Sholing, Southampton SO19 8AW
E: DrEBStuart@aol.com
☎023 8032 9743
M: 07711 607 234

Orthodox Church in Wales, Orthodox Church of the Holy Protection, 11 Manod Road, Blaenau Ffestiniog LL41 4DE
☎01766 831 272
℻01766 831 272
E: deiniol@copticmail.com
Administrator: Very Rev Archimandrite Fr Deiniol. No full-time staff, Serving ministers 3. Began n/a. No magazine. Turnover n/a.

***Peniel Church**, 49 Coxtie Green Road, Pilgrim's Hatch, Brentwood CM14 5P[illegible]
☎01277 372 996
℻01277 375 046
E: Sunday10am@peniel.org
Web: www.michaelreidministries.org
Bishop: Dr Michael S B Reid. Staff [illegible]4, Serving ministers 9. ***CC*** No.1112[illegible]5. Began 1976. (Previously Peniel Pentecostal Church). Operated by Michael Reid Ministries. Magazine: *Miracles, Healing, Faith* (100,000 quarterly). Turnover n/a.

Pentecostal Revival Church of Christ, 220 Ellison Road, Streatham, London SW16 5DJ
☎020 8764 2643
President: Rt Rev Akinola O Ajibode. Admin staff 18, Serving ministers 6. Began 1973. No magazine. Turnover n/a.

***The People's Christian Fellowship**, Springfield Hall, 89 Broad Lane, London N15 4DW
☎020 8801 1873
📠020 8808 9007
E: pastordave@tpcf.org.uk
Web: www.tpcf.org.uk
Pastor: Rev Joseph A Daniel. *Co-Pastor:* Rev David Daniel. No full-time staff, Serving ministers 2. *CC* No.1031255. Began 1956. No magazine. Turnover n/a.

***Pillar of Fire Church**, 19 Brent Street, Hendon, London NW4 2EU
☎020 8202 3219/7618
M: 07767 356 307
📠020 8202 3277
E: bernarddawson36@aol.com
Web: www.pillaroffice.co.uk
Senior Pastor: Rev Bernard Dawson. *Assistant Pastor:* Jeffrey Olszyk. Admin staff 4, Other staff 5, Serving ministers 4. *CC* No.1015529. Began 1915. Magazine: *British Isles Pillar of Fire* (800 every two months). Turnover £205,000 to year end Jun 03.

Pioneer Trust, Rayleigh House, 32 High Street, Bookham, Leatherhead KT23 4AG
☎01372 459 413
📠01372 459 413
E: admin@pioneer.org.uk
Web: www.pioneer.org.uk
Team Leader: Mr Gerald Coates. Executive staff 3, Other staff 6, Serving ministers 100. *CC* No.327160. Began 1982. (Previously Pioneer). Magazine: *Library of Lives* (5,000 every two months). Turnover £250,000 to year end Dec 04.

***Plumbline Ministries**, 83a High Street, Huntingdon PE29 3DP
☎01480 411 665
📠01480 414 442
E: hcc@plumbline.org.uk
Web: www.plumbline.org.uk
Team Leader: Mr Simon Matthews. Executive staff 5, Admin staff 6, Serving ministers 30. *CC* No.327271. Began 1986. Magazine: *Newsletter* (700 every four months). Turnover n/a.

Plymouth Brethren No 4, Chelwood House, Cox Lane, Chessington KT9 1DN
☎020 8391 8822
Contact: Name not supplied. No full-time staff. Began 1828. No magazine. Turnover n/a

The Presbyterian Church in Ireland, Church House, Fisherwick Place, Belfast BT1 6DW
☎028 9032 2284 M: 07703 467 706 📠028 9041 7301
E: clerk@presbyterianireland.org
Web: www.presbyterianireland.org
Clerk of Assembly & General Secretary: Rev Dr Donald Watts. *Financial Secretary:* Mr Clive Knox. *Board of Mission Overseas Secretary:* Rev Uel Marrs. Executive staff 12, Admin staff 50, Serving ministers 430. Bega 1662. Synods united 1840. Magazine: *The Presbyterian Herald* (17,000 monthly). Turnover £60,000,000 to year end Dec 02.

See also:
Belfast City Mission on Page 195
Irish Mission on Page 203
Presbyterian Church in Ireland Overseas Board on Page 292
Presbyterian Herald on Page 253
Presbyterian Board of Youth & Children's Ministry on Page 402

Ards Presbytery *Clerk:* Rev Dr R Alan Russell, 46 Dunover Road, Ballywalter, Newtownards BT22 2LE
☎028 4275 8788
Armagh Presbytery *Clerk:* Rev Colin G Harris, 155 Ahorey Road, Portadown, Craigavon BT62 3SX
☎028 3887 0458
Ballymena Presbytery *Clerk:* Rev Joseph J Andrews, 1 Forthill Park, Ballymena BT42 2HL
☎028 2564 5544
Belfast East Presbytery *Clerk:* Mr Douglas C Cowan, 16 Ferndene Gardens, Dundonald, Belfast BT16 2EP
☎028 9048 1292
Belfast North Presbytery *Clerk:* Rev Colin T Morrison, 39 Old Cavehill Road, Belfast BT15 5FH
☎028 9077 0301
Belfast South Presbytery *Clerk:* Rev Robert T Anderson, 71d Movilla Road, Newtownards BT23 8EZ
☎028 9182 3545
Carrickfergus Presbytery *Clerk:* Rev William J Johnstone, 22 Brustin Braes, Larne BT40 2HS
☎028 2827 2083
Coleraine Presbytery *Clerk:* Rev Ivan Hunter, The Manse, 8 Ballywatt Road, Cloyfin, Coleraine BT52 2LT
☎028 2073 1310
Derry and Strabane Presbytery *Clerk:* Rev Dr Joseph Fell, 19 Clearwater, Caw, Londonderry BT47 6BE
☎028 7131 1425
Down Presbytery *Clerk:* Rev Norman A L Cameron, 10 Seaside Road, Killyleagh, Downpatrick BT30 9QY
☎028 4482 8167
Dromore Presbytery *Clerk:* Rev John Davey, 2 Lisburn Road, Hillsborough BT26 6AA
☎028 9268 3696
Foyle Presbytery *Clerk:* Rev Dr Steward R Jones, 249 Duncastle Road, Donemana, Strabane BT82 0LR
☎028 7139 8663
Newry Presbytery *Clerk:* Rev Stuart A Finlay, 156 Glassdrumman Road, Annalong, Newry BT34 4QL
☎028 4376 8232
Omagh Presbytery *Clerk:* Rev Robert Herron, 16 Beltany Road, Omagh BT78 5NA
☎028 8224 3776

Route Presbytery *Clerk:* Rev Hugh B Wallace, 134 Fivey Road, Ballymoney BT53 8HY
☎028 2074 1694
Templepatrick Presbytery *Clerk:* Rev W Derek Weir, 37 Village Green, Doagh, Ballyclare BT39 0UD
☎028 9332 3588
Tyrone Presbytery *Clerk:* Rev Thomas J Conway, 74 Ballymacilcurr Road, Upperlands, Maghera BT46 5TT
☎028 7964 2278

Presbyterian Church of Wales, 81 Merthyr Road, Whitchurch, Cardiff CF14 1DD
☎029 2062 7465 📠029 2061 6188
E: swyddfa.office@ebcpcw.org.uk
Web: www.ebcpcw.org.uk
General Secretary: Rev Ifan Roberts. Executive staff 5, Other staff 6, Serving Ministers 94. Began n/a. First ordination 1811; incorporated 1826. Magazine: *Y Goleuad* (1,950 weekly, in Welsh), *The Treasury* (1,400 monthly). Turnover n/a.
Association in the East *Clerk:* Rev Iain Hidgins, Tabernacle Church, Pen-Clawdd, Swansea SA4 3YX
☎01792 850 314
Association in the North *Clerk:* Mr Meurig Royles, Cartref, Trelawnyd, Rhyl LL18 6DL
☎01792 850 314
Association in the South *Clerk:* Dr D Huw Owen, Gelligylyd, Fford Llanbadarn, Aberystwyth SY23 1EY
☎01970 611 644

C

Protestant Evangelical Church of England, PO Box 3066, Goring-by-Sea, Worthing BN12 4NQ
☎01903 505 919
Joint Co-ordinator: Rev Kenneth Whittaker. Executive staff 2, Serving ministers 5. Began 1922. (Previously Protestant Episcopal Reformed Church (The Protestant Evangelical Church of England)). Magazine: *The Cranmer Record* (100 annually). Turnover n/a.

†***Rainbow Churches**, PO Box 1908, London N17 6ZN
☎020 8885 5488 🖷020 8885 5007
E: rainbow.admin@virgin.net
Web: www.rainbowinternational.org
Executive Leader: Mr Charles Traty. *Administrator:* Mr Gareth Hawkes. Executive staff 4, Admin staff 14, Serving ministers n/a. ***CC*** No.1023328. Began 1991; affiliated to Pioneer Trust. No magazine. Turnover £65,000 to year end Dec 98.

***Ransom Church of God Universal Fellowship**, 78 Albacore Crescent, Lewisham, London SE13 7HP
☎020 8690 7563 / 1890
General Overseer: Bishop Owen O Douce. Executive staff 7, Other staff 8, Serving ministers 5. Began 1965. Magazine: *Ransom Bulletin* (200 frequency n/a), *The Dove* (Circulation n/a quarterly). Turnover n/a.

Redemption Church of God, 1 Lealand Road, Tottenham, London N15 6JS
☎020 8802 1206 M: 07930 423 916 🖷020 8802 1206
Pastor: Pastor B W Scott. No full-time staff, Serving minister 1. Began 1961. No magazine. Turnover n/a.

The Reformed Liberal Catholic Church (Old Catholic), Diocese of England & The Channel Islands, 9 Lyon Street, Southampton SO14 0LD
☎023 8021 1838 🖷023 8022 4251
E: bishoprichard uk@yahoo.co.uk
Diocesan Bishop: Rt Rev Richard Palmer. No full-time staff, Serving ministers n/a. Began 1999. No magazine. Turnover n/a.

Reformed Presbyterian Church of Ireland, 37 Knockbracken Road, Belfast BT8 6SE
☎Number not supplied
Web: www.rpc.org
Clerk of Synod: Rev E M McCollum. *Inter-Church Correspondent:* Prof David McKay. Executive staff n/a, Serving ministers 25. Began 1763. Magazine: *Covenanter Witness* (500 monthly), *The Messenger* (500 every two months (youth)). Turnover n/a.

†**Reformed Presbyterian Church of Scotland**, Church Manse, 15 Mavisbank Street, Airdrie ML6 0JA
☎01236 620 107
E: airdrierpes@aol.com
Clerk of Synod: Rev A Sinclair Horne. Admin staff 1, Serving ministers 3. Began 1743. Magazines: *Tidings* (Circulation & frequency n/a), *Covenanter Witness* (3,000 monthly). Turnover n/a.

Religious Society of Friends (Quakers) in Britain, Friends House, Euston Road, London NW1 2BJ
☎020 7633 1000
🖷020 7633 1001
E: enquiries@quaker.org.uk
Web: www.quaker.org.uk
Recording Clerk: Elsa Dicks. *Meeting for Sufferings:* Caroline Nursey. *Britain Yearly Meeting:* Peter Eccles. Staff 96. Began 1652. Magazine: *Quaker News* (15,000 quarterly). Turnover £6,700,000 to year end Dec 00.

Restored Covenant Churches of God, 3 Benson Lane, Hawkinge, Folkestone CT18 7AQ
☎01303 894 069
🖷01303 894 069
E: bishop@homecall.co.uk
Web: www.gilson-ministries.5v.com
Presiding Prelate: Bishop J-M Gilson-Levi. Executive staff 9, Admin staff 2, Serving ministers 63. Began 2000. (Previously Kingdom of God in Christ). Magazine: *The Altar Call* (500 monthly). Turnover n/a.

Romanian Orthodox Church in London, Parish House, 250 Clapham Road, London SW9 0PZ
☎020 7735 3515
M: 07941 134 748
🖷020 7735 9535
E: ppufulete@romanianchurch.freeserve.co.uk
Priest-in-Charge: Rev S P Pufulete. Executive staff 1, Serving ministers 3. ***CC*** No.269405. Began 1965. No magazine. Turnover n/a.

Russian Orthodox Diocese of Sourozh, 6 Maiden Place, London NW5 1HZ
☎020 7272 9898
E: diocesan.secretary@sourozh.org.
Web: www.sourozh.org
Diocesan Secretary: Mrs Gillian Crow. Executive staff n/a, Serving ministers 26. ***CC*** No.277508. Began 1945. Magazine: *Sourozh* (Circulation n/a quarterly). Turnover n/a.
Bishop of Sergievo: Bishop Basil, 94a Banbury Road, Oxford OX2 6JT
E: basil.sergievo@sourozh.org
☎01865 512 701
Assistant Bishop of Kerch: Archbishop Anatoly, 14a Bloom Park Road, Fulham, London SW6 7BG
☎020 7386 7837

St Gregorios Indian Orthodox Church, Cranfield Road, Brockley, London SE4 1UE
☎020 8691 9456 M: 07957 440 736
E: vicar@indian-orthodoxchurch.uk or abrahamthomas1969@gmail.com
Web: www.indian-orthodox.co.uk
Also worship at St Andrew by the Wardrobe, Queen Victoria Street, London EC4. Metropolitan's Representative: Rev Abraham Thomas. No full-time staff, Serving minister 1. ***CC*** No.1000[illegible]23. Began 1975. (Previously Malankara Orthodox Syrian Church). Magazine: *Parish Circular* (150 half-yearly). Turnover £45,000 to year end Dec 02.

***Salt and Light Ministries**, The King's Centre, Osney Mead, Oxford OX2 0ES
☎01865 297 440 🖷01865 297 401
E: european@saltlight.org
Web: www.saltlight.org
UK Team Leader: Rev Stephen Thomas. Executive staff 14, Other staff 4, Serving ministers 90. ***CC*** No.107[illegible]500. Began 1985. No magazine. Turnover £256,000 to year end Jul 04.

***The Salvation Army**, UK Territorial Headquarters, 101 Newington Causeway, London SE1 6BN
☎020 7367 4500 🖷020 7367 4728
E: thq@salvationarmy.org.uk
Web: www.salvationarmy.org.uk
UK Territorial Commander: Commissioner John Matear. *Chief Secretary, UK:* Lt Col Victor Poke. Serving Officers 2,794, Employees (UK & Ireland) 4,097 ***CC*** No.214779. Began 1865. Magazine: *The War Cry* (66,000 weekly), *Kids Alive!* (25,000 weekly), *Salvationist* (22,000 weekly). Turnover n/a.

See also:
Kids Alive on Page 251
Salvation Army Social Services on Page 391
Salvationist on Page 254
The War Cry on Page 25[illegible]

See also entries under
Salvation Army in Main Index on Page 524

***The Salvation Army: Anglia Division**, 2 Barton Way, Norwich NR1 1DL
☎01603 724 400 🖷01603 724 4[illegible]1
E: anglia@salvationarmy.org.uk
Web: www.salvationarmy.org.uk
Divisional Commander: Major Alan Burns. Admin staff n/a, Serving officers n/a. ***CC*** No.214779. Began 1865. No magazine. Turnover n/a.

***The Salvation Army: Central North Division**, 80 Eccles New Road, Salford M5 4DU
☎0161 743 3900 🖷0161 743 3911
E: centralnorth@salvationarmy.org.uk
Web: www.salvationarmy.org.uk
Divisional Commander: Major Chick Yuill. Admin staff n/a, Serving officers n/a. ***CC*** No.214779. Began 1865. No magazine. Turnover n/a.

***The Salvation Army*: Central South Division**, 16c Cowley Road, Uxbridge UB8 2LT
☎01895 208 800 🖷01895 208 811
E: centralsouth@salvationarmy.org.uk
Web: www.salvationarmy.org.uk
Divisional Commander: Major Christine Bailey. Admin staff n/a, Serving officers n/a. ***CC*** No.214779 Began 1865. No magazine. Turnover n/a.

***The Salvation Army*: East Midlands Division**, Paisley Grove, Chilwell, Meadows Business Park, Nottingham NG9 6DJ
☎0115 983 5000 🖷0115 983 5011
E: eastmidlands@salvationarmy.org.uk
Web: www.salvationarmy.org.uk
Divisional Commander: Lt Col Trevor Davis. Admin staff n/a, Serving officers n/a. ***CC*** No.214779. Began 1865. No magazine. Turnover n/a.

***The Salvation Army*: East Scotland Division**, 12a Dryden Road, Loanhead EH20 9LZ
☎0131 440 9100 🖷0131 440 9111
E: eastscotland@salvationarmy.org.uk
Web: www.salvationarmy.org.uk
Divisional Commander: Major Robert McIntyre. Admin staff n/a, Serving officers n/a. ***CC*** No.214779. Began 1865. No magazine. Turnover n/a.

***The Salvation Army*: Ireland Division**, 12 Station Mews, Sydenham, Belfast BT4 1TL
☎028 9067 5000 🖷028 9067 5011
E: ireland@salvationarmy.org.uk
Web: www.salvationarmy.org.uk
Divisional Commander: Major David Jackson. Admin staff n/a, Serving officers 49. ***CC*** No.214779. Began 1865. No magazine. Turnover n/a.
Also at: PO Box 2098, 114 Marlborough Street, Dublin, Republic of Ireland
☎00 353 1874 0987
🖷00 353 1874 7478

***The Salvation Army*: London Central Division**, 2nd Floor, 33/35 Kings Exchange, Tileyard Road, London N7 9AH
☎020 7619 6100 🖷020 7619 6111
E: londoncentral@salvationarmy.org.uk
Web: www.salvationarmy.org.uk
Divisional Commander: Major George Pilkington. Admin staff n/a, Serving officers n/a. ***CC*** No.214779. Began 1865. No magazine. Turnover n/a.

***The Salvation Army*: London North East Division**, Maldon Road, Hatfield Peverel, Chelmsford CM3 2HL
☎01245 383 000 🖷01245 383 011
E: londonnortheast@salvationarmy.org.uk
Web: www.salvationarmy.org.uk
Divisional Commander: Major Michael Highton. Admin staff n/a, Serving officers n/a. ***CC*** No.214779. Began 1865. No magazine. Turnover n/a.

***The Salvation Army*: London South East Division**, 1 East Court, Enterprise Road, Maidstone ME15 6JF
☎01622 775 000 🖷01622 775 011
E: londonsoutheast@salvationarmy.org.uk
Web: www.salvationarmy.org.uk
Divisional Commander: Major Anthony Cotterill. Admin staff n/a, Serving officers n/a. ***CC*** No.214779. Began 1865. No magazine. Turnover n/a.

***The Salvation Army*: North Scotland Division**, Deer Road, Woodside, Aberdeen AB24 2BL
☎01224 496 000 🖷01224 496 011
E: northscotland@salvationarmy.org.uk
Web: www.salvationarmy.org.uk
Divisional Commander: Major Martin Hill. Admin staff n/a, Serving officers n/a. ***CC*** No.214779. Began 1865. No magazine. Turnover n/a.

***The Salvation Army*: North Western Division**, 16 Faraday Road, Wavertree Technology Park, Liverpool L13 1EH
☎0151 252 6100 🖷0151 252 6111
E: northwestern@salvationarmy.org.uk
Web: www.salvationarmy.org.uk
Divisional Commander: Major Marion Drew. Admin staff n/a, Serving officers n/a. ***CC*** No.214779. Began 1865. No magazine. Turnover n/a

***The Salvation Army*: Northern Division**, Balliol Business Park West, Newcastle upon Tyne NE12 8EW
☎0191 238 1800 🖷0191 238 1811
E: northern@salvationarmy.org.uk
Web: www.salvationarmy.org.uk
Divisional Commander: Major Melvin Fincham. Admin staff n/a, Serving officers n/a. ***CC*** No.214779. Began 1865. No magazine. Turnover n/a.

***The Salvation Army*: South & Mid Wales Division**, East Moors Road, Ocean Park, Cardiff CF24 5SA
☎029 2044 0600 🖷029 2044 0611
E: southmidwales@salvationarmy.org.uk
Web: www.salvationarmy.org.uk
Divisional Commander: Major Peter Moran. Admin staff n/a, Serving officers n/a. ***CC*** No.214779. Began 1865. No magazine. Turnover n/a.

***The Salvation Army*: South Western Division**, 6 Marlborough Court, Manaton Close, Matford Business Park, Exeter EX2 8PF
☎01392 822 100 🖷01392 822 111
E: southwestern@salvationarmy.org.uk
Web: www.salvationarmy.org.uk
Divisional Commander: Major Cliff Bradbury. Admin staff n/a, Serving officers n/a. ***CC*** No.214779. Began 1865. No magazine. Turnover n/a.

***The Salvation Army*: Southern Division**, 6 Little Park Farm Road, Segensworth, Fareham PO15 5TD
☎01489 566 800 🖷01489 566 811
E: southern@salvationarmy.org.uk
Web: www.salvationarmy.org.uk
Divisional Commander: Major Ian Barr. Admin staff n/a, Serving officers n/a. ***CC*** No.214779. Began 1865. No magazine. Turnover n/a.

***The Salvation Army*: West Midlands Division**, 102 Unett Street, Hockley, Birmingham B19 3BZ
☎0121 507 8500 🖷0121 507 8511
E: westmidlands@salvationarmy.org.uk
Web: www.salvationarmy.org.uk
Divisional Commander: Major William Heeley. Admin staff n/a, Serving officers n/a. ***CC*** No.214779. Began 1865. No magazine. Turnover n/a.

***The Salvation Army*: West Scotland Division**, 4 Buchanan Court, Cumbernauld Road, Stepps, Glasgow G33 6HZ
☎0141 779 5000 🖷0141 779 5011
E: westscotland@salvationarmy.org.uk
Web: www.salvationarmy.org.uk
Divisional Commander: Major Ivor Telfer. Admin staff n/a, Serving officers n/a. ***CC*** No.214779. Began 1865. No magazine. Turnover n/a.

***The Salvation Army*: Yorkshire Division**, 1 Cadman Court, Hanley Road, Morley, Leeds LS27 0RX
☎0113 281 0100 🖷0113 281 0111
E: yorkshire@salvationarmy.org.uk
Web: www.salvationarmy.org.uk
Divisional Commander: Lt Col John Hassard. Admin staff n/a, Serving officers n/a. ***CC*** No.214779. Began 1865. No magazine. Turnover n/a.

†Scottish Asian Christian Fellowship, 5c Kilwinning Street, Musselburgh EH21 7EB
☎0131 665 9708 M: 07719 611 109 🖷0131 665 9708
E: chilerat@aol.com
Asian ethnic congregation with English, Urdu, Punjabi speaking fellowship.
Pastor: Rev Shamaun Tufail. No full-time staff, Serving ministers 2. Began 1998. No magazine. Turnover n/a.

Scottish Episcopal Church, The Office of the General Synod, 21 Grosvenor Crescent, Edinburgh EH12 5EE
☎0131 225 6357 🖷0131 346 7247
E: office@scotland.anglican.org
Web: www.scottishepiscopal.com
Primus: Most Rev Dr Idris Jones. *Secretary General:* Mr John Stuart. Executive staff 4, Admin staff 9. ***CC*** No.SCO 13463. Began n/a. Magazine: *Inspires* (5,000 ten times a year). Turnover n/a.

***Scottish Episcopal Church*: Diocese of Aberdeen and Orkney**, Diocesan Office, 39 King's Crescent, Aberdeen AB24 3HP
☎01224 636 653 🖷01224 636 186
E: office@aberdeen.anglican.org
Web: www.scotland.anglican.org
Bishop: To be appointed. *Hon Secretary:* Mr Andrew Armstrong. *Hon Treasurer:* Rev Canon Alex MacGillivray. Admin staff 2, Serving ministers 44. ***CC*** No.SCO 22180. Aberdeen 1100; Orkney 1087. Magazine: *Northern Light* (2,000 quarterly). Turnover n/a.

***Scottish Episcopal Church*: Diocese of Argyll and the Isles**, St Moluag's Diocesan Centre, Croft Avenue, Oban PA34 5JJ
☎01631 570 870 🖷01631 570 411
E: office@argyll.anglican.org or bishop@argyll.anglican.org
Web: www.argyll.anglican.org
Bishop: Rt Rev Martin Shaw. *Diocesan Administrator:* Mr Chris Todhunter. Executive staff 2, Serving ministers 10. ***CC*** No.SCO 05375. Began 1848. Magazine: *Argyll and the Isles* (2,000 quarterly). Turnover n/a.

***Scottish Episcopal Church*: Diocese of Brechin**, c/o St Salvador's Church, Church Street, Dundee DD3 7HL
☎01382 228 781 🖷01382 228 782
E: office@brechin.anglican.org
Web: www.thedioceseofbrechin.org
Bishop: Rt Rev Dr John A C Mantle. *Diocesan Secretary:* Miss Hilary Gibson. Executive staff n/a, Serving ministers 28. ***CC*** No.SCO 016813. Began 1150. Magazine: *Grapevine* (Circulation n/a quarterly). Turnover n/a.

***Scottish Episcopal Church*: Diocese of Edinburgh**, Diocesan Centre, 21a Grosvenor Crescent, Edinburgh EH12 5EL
☎0131 538 7033 🖷0131 538 7088
E: office@edinburgh.anglican.org
Bishop: Rt Rev Brian Smith. *Diocesan Secretary:* Dr Christine Shepherd. Executive staff 2, Admin staff 2, Serving ministers 125. ***CC*** Began 1633. Magazine: *The Edge* (1,750 five times a year). Turnover n/a.

***Scottish Episcopal Church*: United Diocese of Glasgow and Galloway**, Diocesan Office, 5 St Vincent Place, Glasgow G1 2DH
☎0141 221 5720 🖷0141 221 7014
E: office@glasgow.anglican.org
Web: www.scotland.anglican.org
Bishop: Rt Rev Idris Jones. *Diocesan Secretary:* Mr G FitzGibbon. Executive staff 2, Admin staff 3, Serving ministers 90. ***CC*** Began 1837. Magazines: *Travelling Together in Glasgow and Galloway* (4,750 half-yearly), *Diocesan News Service* (4,750 ten times a year). Turnover n/a.

***Scottish Episcopal Church*: Diocese of Moray, Ross and Caithness**, 11 Kenneth Street, Inverness IV3 5NR
☎01463 226 255 🖷01463 221 056
E: office@moray.anglican.org
Web: www.moray.anglican.org
Bishop: Rt Rev John M Crook. *Diocesan Secretary:* Mrs Norma Higgott. No full-time staff, Serving ministers 42. Began 1110. No magazine. Turnover n/a.

***Scottish Episcopal Church*: Diocese of St Andrews, Dunkeld and Dunblane**, 28 Balhousie Street, Perth PH1 5HJ
☎01738 632 053 🖷01738 632 053
E: office@standrews.anglican.org
Web: www.standrews.anglican.org
Bishop: Rt Rev David Chillingworth. *Diocesan Secretary:* Mrs Alicia Rootes. Executive staff 2, Serving ministers 87. Began n/a. Magazine: *St Andrews Diocesan News* (Circulation n/a quarterly). Turnover n/a.

Serbian Orthodox Church Diocese of Great Britain and Scandinavia, 131 Cob Lane, Bourneville, Birmingham B30 1QE
☎0121 458 5273 🖷0121 458 4986
E: lazarica.church@virgin.net
Episcopal Vicar: Very Rev Milenko Zebic. *Serving Vicar:* Rev Aleksander Zebic. No full-time staff, Serving ministers 2. Began 1952. Magazine: *Lazarisa* (1,500 every four months). Turnover n/a.

Seventh-day Adventist Church, British Union Conference, Stanborough Park, Watford WD25 9JZ
☎01923 672 251 🖷01923 893 212
E: buc@adventist.org.uk
Web: www.adventist.org.uk
President: Pastor Cecil R Perry. Executive staff 24, Admin staff 54, Serving ministers 123. ***CC*** No.1044071. Began 1878. Magazine: *Messenger* (10,000 fortnightly). Turnover n/a.
Irish Mission Office *President:* Pastor Curtis G Murphy, 9 Newry Road, Banbridge BT32 3HF
E: sdaireland@aol.com
☎028 4062 6361 🖷 028 4062 6361
North England Conference *President:* Pastor E R Francis, 22 Zulla Road, Mapperley Park, Nottingham NG3 5DB
E: admin@necadventist.org.uk
www.necadventist.org.uk
☎0115 960 6312 🖷 0115 969 1476
Scottish Mission Office *President:* Pastor L R Edwards, Gwydyr Road, Crieff PH7 4BS
E: sdascotland@onetel.com
☎01764 653 257
South England Conference *President:* Pastor H Walters, 25 St John's Road, Watford WD17 1PZ
E: reception@ted-adventist.org
☎01923 232 728 🖷 01923 250 582
www.secadventist.org.uk
Trans European Division *President:* Dr Bertil Wiklander, 119 St Peter's Street, St Albans AL1 3EY
E: info@ted-adventist.org
☎01727 860 331 🖷 01727 866 312
www.ted-adventist.org
Welsh Mission Office *President:* Dr B P Philips, Ty Capel, Twyn Road, Ystrad Mynach, Caerphilly CF82 7EU
E: bpphdd@sdanw.fsnet.co.uk
☎01443 814 582 🖷 01443 814 582

Slovenian Roman Catholic Mission, 62 Offley Road, London SW9 0LS
☎020 7735 6655 🖷020 7735 6[illegible]55
E: cikanek@msn.com
Chaplain to Slovenian Community in UK: Rev Stanislav Cikanek. Admin staff 1, Serving minister 1. Began 1948. Magazine: *Nasa Luc* (150 monthly). Turnover n/a.

***Struthers Memorial Churches**, 3[illegible] West Stewart Street, Greenock PA15 1S[illegible]
☎01475 729 668 🖷01475 728 [illegible]45
E: smc@struthers-church.org
Web: www.struthers-church.org
Also bookshops, coffee shops, private Christian school.
Minister: Mrs Grace Gault. *Secretary:* Mr Robert M Cleary. *Central Treasurer:* Mr Chris Jewell. Executive staff 6, Serving ministers 16. ***CC*** No.SCO 06960. Began 1955. No magazine. Turnover £1,160,000 to year end Dec 04.

†Swahili-Speaking Christian Congregation, St Anne's Lutheran Church, Church of St Anne & St Agnes, Gresham Street, London EC2V 7BX
☎020 7606 4986 🖷020 7600 8[illegible]4
E: stanneluthch@lutheran.fsnet.co.uk
Web: www.stanneslutheranchurch.org
Pastor: Rev Jana Jeruma-Grinberga. No full-time staff, Serving ministers 2. Began 1973. No magazine. Turnover n/a.

Swedish Church (Lutheran), 6 Harcourt Street, London W1H 4AG
☎020 7723 5681 M: 07785 308 [illegible]57
🖷020 7724 2178
E: rector@swedish-church.org.uk
Web: www.swedish-church.org.uk
Rector: Very Rev Lennart Sjöström. Executive staff 2, Serving ministers 2. ***CC*** No.19989. Began 1710. Magazine: *Kyrkobladet* (11,000 every four months). Turnover n/a.

Swiss Church in London, 79 Endell Street, London WC2H 9DY
☎020 7836 1418 🖷020 7379 10[illegible]
E: info@swisschurchlondon.org.uk
Web: www.swisschurchlondon.org.uk
Minister: Rev David Leuenberger. Executive staff 2, Serving minister 1. ***CC*** No.1094992. Began 1762. Magazine: *Swiss Church News* (1,000 quarterly). Turnover n/a.

Swiss Evangelical Brotherhood Church, 25 Calabria Road, London N5 1HZ
☎020 7226 7341
E: ebclondon@onetel.com
Also foreign students ministry.
Minister: Mr Matthias Roggli. Executive staff 2, Serving minister 1. ***CC*** No.1097799. Began 1960. Magazine: *The Message of Peace* (5,000 every two months). Turnover n/a.

Syrian Orthodox Church, Antiochian, 5 Canning Road, Croydon CR0 6QA
☎020 8654 7531 🖷020 8654 7531
E: fatherdomadawod@yahoo.co.uk
Web: www.syrianorthodoxchurch.net
Worship at St Andrew's Church, Star Road, West Kensington, London W14. Patriarchal Vicar's Representative: Fr Doma Dawod. No full-time staff, Serving ministers n/a. **CC** No.1107634. Began n/a. No magazine. Turnover n/a.

Tamil Language Congregations, 35 Woodhouse Grove, London E12 6SR
☎020 8552 9911 / 8470 4990
Web: www.tamilchurchlondon.org
Contact: Pastor G I Ebenezer. No full-time staff, Serving ministers 16. Began 1970. No magazine. Turnover n/a.

Together, Nettle Hill, Brinklow Road, Ansty, Coventry CV7 9JL
☎024 7660 2777 🖷024 7660 3276
E: info@togetherweb.net
Web: www.togetherweb.net
Director: Mr Jonathan Carvell. Executive staff 1, Other staff 6, Serving ministers 50. **CC** No.328513. Began 1977. (Previously Covenant Ministries International). No magazine. Turnover n/a.

The Traditional Anglican Church, 7 Hereford Street, Presteigne LD8 2AW
☎01544 267 063
Web: www.thetraditionalanglicanchurch.org.uk
Vicar General: Rev Brian Gill. Executive staff 5, Serving ministers 20. Began 1995. Magazine: *The Messenger* (Circulation & frequency n/a). Turnover £100,000 to year end Apr 00.

***Traditional Roman Catholic Church**, 52 Parliament Hill, Hampstead, London NW3 2TL
☎020 7435 4288
E: anthony-earl-williams@hotmail.com
Bishop & Chancellor of Archdiocese: Rt Rev Anthony Earl-Williams. No full-time staff, Serving ministers 3. Began 2003. (Previously English Catholic Church). No magazine. Turnover £18,000 to year end Dec 03.

Ukrainian Catholic Church, Bishop's House, 22 Binney Street, London W1K 5BQ
☎020 7629 1534
E: paulospm@catholic.org
Bishop/Apostolic Exarch: Rt Rev Paul Chomnycky. No full-time staff, Serving ministers 2. **CC** No.240088. Began 1947; Apostolic Exarchate in Great Britain 1957. No magazine. Turnover n/a.

Union of Evangelical Churches (UEC), 36 Eastwood Road, Rayleigh SS6 7JQ
☎01268 742 293
E: john@unicnec.freeserve.co.uk
Chairman: Rev R E Werrett. *Administrator:* Rev J A Pease. Executive staff n/a, Serving ministers 25. **CC** No.227498. Began 1956; but as the Peculiar People 1838. Associated with FIEC. Magazine: *UEC Fellowship Link* (Circulation n/a quarterly). Turnover n/a.

Union of Welsh Independents/ Annibynwyr (Welsh Congregational Union), Ty John Penri, 5 Axis Court, Riverside Business Park, Swansea Vale, Swansea SA7 0AJ
☎01792 795 888 🖷01792 795 376
E: undeb@annibynwyr.org
Web: www.annibynwyr.org
General Secretary: Rev Dewi M Hughes. Admin staff 3, Serving ministers 105. **CC** No.248076. Began 1872. Magazine: *Y Tyst* (1,000 weekly). Turnover n/a.

The United Episcopal Church in the Province of Great Britain & Ireland, 9 Lyon Street, Southampton SO14 0LD
☎023 8022 9560 🖷023 8022 4251
E: bishoprichárduk@yahoo.co.uk
Web: www.unitedepiscopalchurch.org
Archbishop, Metropolitan, Diocesan Bishop for Central Southern England & The Channel Islands: Most Rev Richard A Palmer. Executive staff 3 Admin staff 1, Serving ministers n/a. Began 2006. No magazine. Turnover n/a.
Provincial Administrator: Rev Canon Pam Lees, 37 Lomas Drive, Northfield, Birmingham B31 5LR
E: revpamlees@hotmail.com
☎0121 604 9188 🖷 0121 604 9188
Bishop for the North of Britain: Rt Rev Charles Michael Wilson, 41 Ingleborough Way, Leyland, Preston PR25 4ZS
E: revmichael@lineone.net
☎01722 436 817 🖷 01722 452 578
Bishop for the West of Britain: Rt Rev Dr Roger Whatley, 496a Semington Road, Melksham SN12 6DX
E: Tyfurog@aol.com
☎01225 702 436

***United Free Church of Scotland**, 11 Newton Place, Glasgow G3 7PR
☎0141 332 3435 🖷0141 333 1973
E: office@ufcos.org.uk
Web: www.ufcos.org.uk
General Secretary: Rev John O Fulton. *Principal Clerk:* Rev M C Keane. Executive staff 3, Serving ministers 41. **CC** No.SCO 08167. Began 1900. Magazine: *Steadfast* (1,400 every two months). Turnover £793,392 to year end Dec 04.

United Reformed Church in the United Kingdom, 86 Tavistock Place, London WC1H 9RT
☎020 7916 2020 🖷020 7916 2021
E: urc@urc.org.uk
Web: www.urc.org.uk
General Secretary: Rev Dr David Cornick. Executive staff 17, Admin staff 26, Serving missionaries 4. Began 1972. Magazine: *Reform* (13,000 monthly). Turnover n/a.

See also:
Fellowship of United Reformed Youth (FURY) on Page 399
Pilots on Page 402
Reform on Page 254
URC Bookshop on Page 113

See also entries under
United Reformed in Main Index on Page 522

***United Reformed Church*: East Midlands Synod**, Sherwood United Reformed Church, 1 Edwards Lane, Sherwood, Nottingham NG5 3AA
☎0115 960 9241 🖷0115 960 9202
E: emd@urc.org.uk
Web: www.lineone.net/~office.urceastmid
Synod Moderator: Rev Terry Oakley. *Synod Clerk:* Mrs Irene Wren. Executive staff 4, Admin staff 4, Serving ministers 72. Began 1972. Turnover n/a.

***United Reformed Church*: Eastern Synod**, Synod Office, United Reformed Church, Whittlesford, Cambridge CB2 4ND
☎01223 830 770 🖷01223 830 771
E: eastern.admin@urc.org.uk
Web: www.urc-eastern.org.uk
Synod Moderator: Rev Elizabeth Caswell. *Synod Clerk:* Mr Mick J Barnes. *Training and Development Officer:* Rev Richard Church. Executive staff 4, Admin staff 3, Serving ministers 65. Began 1972. Magazine: *Eastwords* (3,500 half-yearly). Turnover £2,000,000 to year end Dec 02.

***United Reformed Church*: Mersey Synod**, 1 Fingall Road, Wavertree, Liverpool L15 9JE
☎0151 722 6590 🖷0151 722 1883
E: admin@mersey.urc2.org.uk
Synod Moderator: Rev Howard Sharp. *Synod Clerk:* Mr D C Swift. Executive staff 1, Admin staff 3, Serving ministers 61. Began 1972. Magazine: *Lookout* (6,500 every two months). Turnover n/a.

***United Reformed Church*: North Western Synod**, Franklin Street, Patricroft, Eccles, Manchester M30 0QZ
☎0161 789 5583 🖷0161 707 9117
E: admin.nwsynod@urc.org.uk
Web: www.nwsynod.org.uk
Synod Moderator: Rev P J Brain. *Synod Clerk:* Mr George Morton. Executive staff 3, Admin staff 2, Serving ministers 70. Began 1972. No magazine. Turnover n/a.

***United Reformed Church*: Northern Synod**, 4 College Lane, Newcastle upon Tyne NE1 8JJ
☎0191 232 1168 🖷0191 232 1811
E: office@urc-northernsynod.org.uk
Web: www.urc-northernsynod.org.uk
Synod Moderator until Dec 06: Rev Peter Poulter. *Synod Clerk:* Rev John Durell. *Synod Moderator from Jan 07:* Rev Rowena Francis. Executive staff 1, Admin staff 4, Serving ministers 54. Began 1972. Magazine: *Synod Hotline* (100 half-yearly). Turnover n/a.

***United Reformed Church*: Scotland Synod**, 340 Cathedral Street, Glasgow G1 2BQ
☎0141 332 7667 🖷0141 332 8463
E: scotland@urc.org.uk
Synod Moderator: Rev John L I Humphreys. *Synod Clerk:* Mr James Merrilees. Executive staff 2, Admin staff 2, Serving ministers 34. **CC** Began 2000. Magazine: *Syn News* (5,000 quarterly). Turnover n/a.

***United Reformed Church*: South Western Synod**, Synod Office, The Manse, Norton Fitzwarren, Taunton TA2 6RU
☎01823 275 470
🖷01823 334 522
E: synodoffice@urcsouthwest.co.uk
Web: www.urcsouthwest.org.uk
Synod Moderator: Rev David Grosch-Miller. Executive staff 3, Admin staff 3, Serving ministers 69. Began 1972. Magazine: *Southwesterly*(Circulation & frequency n/a). Turnover n/a.
Synod Clerk: Rev Roz Harrison, 21 Barton Close, Exton, Exeter EX3 0PE
E: synodclerk@urcsouthwest.org.uk
☎01392 876 744

C

***United Reformed Church*: Southern Synod**, Synod Office, East Croydon United Reformed Church, Addiscombe Grove, Croydon CR0 5LP
☎020 8688 3730
🖷020 8688 2698
E: office@urcsouthern.org.uk
Web: www.urcsouthern.org.uk
Synod Moderator: Rev Nigel Uden. *Synod Clerk:* Dr Graham Campling. Executive staff 2, Admin staff 4, Serving ministers 100. Began 1972. No magazine. Turnover n/a.

***United Reformed Church*: Thames North Synod**, Ipalo House, 32 Great Peter Street, London SW1P 2DB
☎020 7799 5000
🖷020 7799 5555
E: office@urc10.org
Web: www.urc10.org
Synod Moderator: Rev Roberta Rominger. *Synod Clerk:* Rev Martin Hazell. Executive staff 3, Admin staff 3, Serving ministers 99. Began 1972. No magazine. Turnover n/a.

***United Reformed Church*: Wales Synod / Roath Yr Eg Lwys Ddiwgiedig Unedig Synod Cenedlaethol Cymru**, Synod Office, United Reformed Church, Minster Road, Cardiff CF23 5AS
☎029 2019 5728/5729
E: admin@urcwales.org.uk
Web: www.urcwales.org.uk
Synod Moderator: Rev Peter Noble. *Synod Clerk:* Rev David Fox. Executive staff 19, Admin staff 4, Serving ministers 38. ***CC*** No.1063214. Began 1972. No magazine. Turnover n/a.

***United Reformed Church*: Wessex Synod**, 120 Alma Road, Southampton SO14 6UW
☎023 8067 8570 🖷023 8067 7820
E: office@urcwessex.org.uk
Web: www.urcwessex.org.uk
Synod Moderator: Rev Adrian Bulley. *Synod Clerk:* Mr Peter Pay. Executive staff 1, Admin staff 2, Serving ministers 87. Began 1972. No magazine. Turnover n/a.

***United Reformed Church*: West Midlands Synod**, Digbeth-in-the-Field United Reformed Church, Moat Lane, Yardley, Birmingham B26 1TW
☎0121 783 1177 🖷0121 789 8500
E: admin@urcwestmidlands.org.uk
Web: www.urcwestmidlands.org.uk
Synod Moderator: Rev Elizabeth Welch. *Synod Clerk:* Mr Bill Robson. Executive staff 2, Admin staff 4, Serving ministers 75. Began 1972. Magazine: *Connect* (5,000 frequency n/a). Turnover n/a.

***United Reformed Church*: Yorkshire Synod**, Somerset House, St Paul's Street, Morley, Leeds LS27 9EP
☎0113 289 8490 🖷0113 289 8491
E: office@urcyorkshire.org.uk
Web: www.urcyorkshire.org.uk
Synod Moderator: Rev Arnold Harrison. *Synod Clerk:* Mrs V Morrison. Executive staff 2, Admin staff 2, Serving ministers 53. ***CC*** No.1068103. Began 1972. Magazine: *Four Yorkshire* (Circulation n/a every four months). Turnover n/a.

Universal Church of the Kingdom of God (UCKG Help Centre), Rainbow Theatre, 232 Seven Sisters Road, Finsbury Park, London N4 3NX
☎020 7686 6000 🖷020 7686 6008
E: info@christianbooks-plus.com
Web: www.uckg.org
Bishop: Bishop Renato Cardoso. Executive staff 20, Serving ministers n/a. ***CC*** No.1043985. Began 1995. Magazine: *Faith in Action* (5,000 weekly), *City News* (200,000 every two months). Turnover n/a.

***Universal Prayer Group Ministries**, Dominion Centre, 9 The Broadway, Wood Green, London N22 6DS
☎020 8829 0080 🖷020 8829 0081
E: info@dominioncentre.org
Web: www.dominioncentre.org
Worshipping at Edmonton Temple, Grove Street, London N18.
Senior Minister: Rev Samuel Ohene-Apraku. Executive staff 5, Admin staff 5, Serving ministers n/a. ***CC*** No.298368. Began 1986. No magazine. Turnover n/a.

***Vineyard Churches UK & Ireland**, 23 Blagdon Road, New Malden KT3 4AH
☎020 8336 1734 🖷020 8336 [illegible]319
E: office@vineyardchurchesuk.com
Web: www.vineyardchurchesuk.com
National Director: John Mumford. Admin staff 3, Serving ministers 7[illegible]. ***CC*** No.1099748. Began 19[illegible]7. Magazine: *Cutting Edge* (Circulation n/a half-yearly). Turnover n/a.

Wesleyan Holiness Church, The New Life Wesleyan Church, Holyhead Road, Handsworth, Birmingham B21 0LA
☎0121 551 2802
E: JoycePGray@aol.com
District Superintendent: Rev Joyce Gray. Executive staff 1, Serving ministers n/a. Began 1958. No magazine. Turnover n/a.

***Wesleyan Reform Union**, 123 Queen Street, Sheffield S1 2DU
☎0114 272 1938
🖷0114 272 1938
E: gen.sec@wesleyan-reform.freeserve.co.uk
Web: www.thewru.com
General Secretary: Rev Colin Braithwaite. Executive staff 1, Other staff 1, Serving ministers 20. ***CC*** No.25[illegible]315. Began 1849. Magazine: *Contact* (1,250 monthly). Turnover n/a.

***Winners Christian Centre**, 16 Clive Road, West Dulwich, London SE21 8BY
☎020 8761 5445
M: 07956 019 161
🖷020 8761 5445
E: winnerscc@aol.com
Pastor: Rev Anthony C I U[illegible]oka. No full-time staff, Serving minister 1. ***CC*** No. 1002281. Began 1987. No magazine. Turnover n/a.

The Worldwide Church of God (UK), [illegible] The Point, Rockingham Road, Market Harborough LE16 7QU
☎01858 438 282
🖷01858 438 289
Web: www.wcg.org.uk
National Director: Mr James Henderson. *Company Secretary & Business Manager:* Mr David Stirk. Executive staff 2, Admin staff 5, Serving ministers 70. ***CC*** No.311098. Began 1957. Magazine: *The Plain Truth* (20,000 every two months). Turnover £1,729,000 to year end Dec 01.

DENOMINATIONAL ORGANISATIONS

Alcuin Club, Ty Nant, 6 Parc Bach, Trefnant, Denbigh LL16 4YE
☎01745 730 585
E: alcuinclub@waitrose.com
Web: www.alcuin.mcmail.com
Promoting study of liturgy of the Christian church, especially by publishing works of scholarship.
Secretary: Mr J Ryding. No full-time staff. **CC** No.274203. Began 1897; Anglican. Magazine: *Joint Liturgical Studies* (450 half-yearly). Turnover £15,000 to year end Dec 04.

The Anabaptist Network, 14 Shepherd's Hill, Highgate, London N6 5AQ
☎0845 450 0214 or 01865 250 914
Fax: 0208 341 6807
E: admin@anabaptistnetwork.com
Web: www.anabaptistnetwork.com
Encouraging a Christ-centred approach to discipleship and a radical missionary engagement with contemporary society.
Chair: Dr Stuart Murray Williams. No full-time staff. **CC** No.1021760. Began 1991; interdenominational. No magazine. Turnover £5,000 to year end Dec 04.

Anglican Catechumenate Network, Upper House Grosmont, Abergavenny NP7 8EP
☎01981 241 383 Fax: 01981 241 387
E: andrewk@harter.co.uk
Enabling adult initiation by experiential learning or accompanied journey.
Chairman: Rev Dr John Railton. No full-time staff. Began 1980; Anglican. (Previously Catechumenate Network). No magazine. Turnover n/a.

Anglican Communion Office, St Andrew's House, 16 Tavistock Crescent, London W11 1AP
☎020 7313 3900 Fax: 020 7313 3999
E: aco@anglicancommunion.org
Web: www.anglicancommunion.org
Coordinating body for the Anglican Communion worldwide.
Secretary General: Rev Canon Kenneth Kearon. Executive staff 7, Other staff 12. **CC** No.276591. Began 1969; Anglican. Magazine: *Anglican World* (20,000 quarterly). Turnover n/a.

Anglican Evangelical Assembly, c/o Oak Hill College, Chase Side, Southgate, London N14 4PS
☎020 8449 0467 ext 254
E: ChrisG@oakhill.ac.uk
Promoting effective consultation and fostering leadership amongst Anglican evangelical leaders.
Organiser: Rev Chris Green. Executive staff 1, Other staff 1. **CC** No.212315. Began 1982; Anglican. Magazine: *CEEC Newsletter* (Circulation & frequency n/a). Turnover included under Church of England Evangelical Council.

Anglican-Lutheran Society, 15 Hampden, Kimpton, Hitchin SG4 8QH
☎01438 832 649
Developing better understanding and closer links between Anglicans and Lutherans.
Secretary: Mrs Valerie Phillips. No full-time staff. **CC** No.1015153. Began 1984; Anglican and Lutheran. Magazine: *The Window* (600 quarterly). Turnover £7,000 to year end Dec 99.

Anglican Mainstream, 21 High Street, Eynsham, Witney OX29 4HE
☎01865 883 388 M: 07808 297 043
Fax: 01865 570 823
E: p.j.giddings@reading.ac.uk or csugden@ocms.ac.uk
Web: www.anglican-mainstream.net
A network of networks within the Anglican communion teaching and preserving Scripture truths.
UK Convenor: Dr Philip Giddings. *International Secretary:* Rev Dr Canon Chris Sugden. No full-time staff. Began 2003; Anglican. No magazine. Turnover n/a.

Anglican Religious Communities, c/o Miss Jane Melrose CSF, Church House, Great Smith Street, London SW1P 3NZ
☎No telephone
E: arc@fish.co.uk
Web: www.orders.anglican.org/arcyb
Supporting and encouraging members of religious orders in the Church of England, promoting religious life.
Secretary: Sr Christine James. No full-time staff. **CC** No.1097586. Began 1975; Anglican. (Previously Communities Consultative Council). Magazine: *ARC Year Book* (Circulation n/a every 2 years). Turnover n/a.

Anglican Renewal Ministries (Wales), Adnewyddiad Eglwyswyr Cymru, 5 Gwelfryn, Llanymynech SY22 6LJ
☎01691 830 590
E: secretary@anglicanrenewalministries-wales.org.uk
Web: www.anglicanrenewalministries-wales.org.uk
Advancing the Christian religion through the promotion and encouragement of spiritual renewal.
Secretary: Mr Brian Newsom. Admin staff n/a. **CC** No.1053180. Began 1984; Anglican. Magazine: *Anglican Renewal Ministries (Wales) Magazine* (500 quarterly). Turnover £61,845 to year end Jun 04.

†The Archbishop of Canterbury's Department for Ecumenical Affairs, Lambeth Palace, London SE1 7JU
☎020 7898 1200 Fax: 020 7401 9886
E: jonathon.gough@lampal.c-of-e.org.uk
Assisting the Archbishop on ecumenical affairs and acting ecumenically on his behalf.
Archbishop of Canterbury's Secretary: Rev Canon Jonathan Gough. Executive staff 2, Other staff 3. Began 1933; Anglican. No magazine. Turnover n/a.

Association of Church Fellowships, Bickenhill House, 154 Lode Lane, Solihull B91 2HP
☎0121 704 9281
Encouraging Christian evangelistic charitable fellowship by fostering and forming church groups for men and women.
Head of Secretariat: Rev Canon Stanley Owen. Executive staff 2. **CC** Began 1960; Anglican. Magazine: *ACF National Newsletter* (1,000 quarterly). Turnover £10,000 to year end Dec 00.

Association of Denominational Historical Societies & Cognate Libraries, c/o Library of the Society of Friends, Friends House, Euston Road, London NW1 2BJ
☎020 7663 1129
E: heatherr@quaker.org.uk
Exchanging information and encouraging research into denominational histories and related traditions.
Secretary: Ms Heather Rowland. *Convenor:* Rev Dr Martin Wellings. No full-time staff. Began 1993; interdenominational. No magazine. Turnover n/a.

Association of Ordinands & Candidates for Ministry (AOCM), c/o Ministry Division, Church House, Great Smith Street, Westminster, London SW1P 3NZ
☎020 7898 1404 Fax: 020 7898 1421
E: chair@aocm.org.uk
Web: www.aocm.org.uk
Representing the interests of Anglican ordinands and candidates for accredited lay ministry.
Chair: Changes annually. No full-time staff. Began n/a; Anglican. Magazine: *Training for Ministry* (1,500 annually). Turnover n/a.

Baptist Historical Society, 60 Strathmore Avenue, Hitchin SG5 1ST
☎01462 442 548
E: stephen.copson@dsl.pipex.com
Web: www.baptisthistory.org.uk
Encouraging the study and recording of Baptist history.
Secretary: Rev Stephen Copson. No full-time staff. **CC** No.271367. Began 1908; Baptist. Magazine: *The Baptist Quarterly* (650 quarterly). Turnover £25,000 to year end Dec 98.

Baptist Men's Movement, 5 Elizabeth Drive, Wantage OX12 9YA
☎01235 768 660
E: secretary@baptistmen.org.uk
Web: www.baptistmen.org.uk
Promoting faith, commitment, service and giving among Baptist men; fellowship and reconciliation worldwide.
National Secretary: Mr Bryan Orchard. Admin staff 1. **CC** No.250334. Began 1917; Baptist. Magazine: *World Outlook* (1,200 quarterly). Turnover n/a.

Denominational Organisations

Canon Law Society of Great Britain and Ireland, Westminster Metropolitan Tribunal, Vaughan House, 46 Francis Street, London SW1P 1QN
☎020 7798 9003
Web: www.clsgbi.org
Disseminating information concerning the Canon Law to members of the society and interested groups.
Secretary: Rev J Conneely. Admin staff 1. ***CC*** No.266263. Began 1957; Roman Catholic. Magazine: *Canon Law Society Newsletter* (Circulation n/a members only), *Canon Law Abstracts* (1,000 half-yearly). Turnover n/a.

Caritas-social action, 39 Eccleston Square, London SW1V 1BX
☎020 7901 4875
E: caritas@cbcew.org.uk
Web: www.caritas-socialaction.org.uk
The voice of the catholic church on social justice and care in England and Wales.
Director: Sarah Lindsell. Executive staff 1, Other staff 1. ***CC*** No.4505111. Began 1929; Roman Catholic. (Previously Catholic Child Welfare Council). No magazine. Turnover n/a.

Catholic Bishops' Conference Department for Christian Life & Worship, 39 Eccleston Square, London SW1V 1PL
☎020 7901 4850 Fax 020 7901 4821
E: lifeworsh@cbcew.org.uk
Web: www.liturgyoffice.org.uk
Supporting the work of the Bishops of England and Wales.
Secretary, Liturgy Office: Fr Allen Morris. *Assistant Secretary:* Mr Martin Foster. Executive staff 2. ***CC*** No.257239. Began 1984; Roman Catholic. No magazine. Turnover n/a.
Each diocese has an Officer for this area of ministry. Contact them via the appropriate Curial Office.

Catholic Bishops' Conference Department for Christian Responsibility and Citizenship, 39 Eccleston Square, London SW1V 1BX
☎020 7901 4828 Fax 020 7901 4821
Supporting marriage and family life, marginalised and vulnerable peoples, life issues.
Chairman: Rt Rev Peter Smith. Executive staff 3. ***CC*** No.257239. Began 1984; Roman Catholic. No magazine. Turnover n/a.
Each diocese has an Officer for this area of ministry. Contact them via the appropriate Curial Office.

Catholic Bishops' Conference Department of International Affairs, 39 Eccleston Square, London SW1V 1BX
☎020 7901 4865 Fax 020 7901 4821
E: international@cbcew.org.uk
Web: www.catholicchurch.org.uk
Concerned with international justice, peace, development, European affairs, migrants and nuclear issues.
Chairman: Rt Rev Crispian Hollis. Executive staff 3. Began 1984; Roman Catholic. No magazine. Turnover n/a.

†Catholic Record Society, 12 Melbourne Place, Wolsingham, Bishop Auckland DL13 3EH
☎01388 527 747
Web: www.catholic-history.org.uk/crs
Researching post-reformation history of Roman Catholicism in England and Wales.
Hon Secretary: Dr L Gooch. No full-time staff. ***CC*** Began 1904; ecumenical. Journal: *Recusant History* (800 half-yearly). Turnover n/a.

†Catholic Union of Great Britain, St Maximilian Kolbe House, 63 Jeddo Road, London W12 9EE
☎020 8749 1321 Fax 020 8735 0816
E: phiggs@cathunion.fsnet.co.uk
Web: www.catholicunion.org
Secretary: Mr Peter Higgs. Executive staff 1. Began 1870; Roman Catholic. No magazine. Turnover n/a.

†Catholic Women's League, PO Box 49, Orpington BR5 1WT
☎01689 897 107 Fax 01689 896 534
E: cwl@cwlhq.fsnet.co.uk
Non-political organisation for charitable religious intellectual work, ensuring representation of Catholic interests on public bodies.
General Secretary: Mrs Breda Ford. Executive staff 1. ***CC*** No.250120. Began 1906; Roman Catholic. Magazine: *CWL News* (8,000 quarterly). Turnover n/a.

Catholics for a Changing Church, 14 West Halkin Street, London SW1X 8JS
☎020 7235 2841
E: brydenbrook@talk21.com
Web: www.c-c-c.freeserve.co.uk
Promoting church reform and renewal in the spirit of Vatican II.
Chair: Mr Frank Pycroft. No full-time staff. Began 1969; Roman Catholic. (Previously Catholic Renewal Movement). Magazine: *Renew* (400 quarterly). Turnover £3,400 to year end Apr 05.

Central Readers' Council, Church House, Great Smith Street, Westminster, London SW1P 3NZ
☎020 7898 1415/1416
Fax 020 7898 1421
E: alan.wakely@c-of-e.org.uk or thereader@c-of-e.org.uk
Web: www.readers.cofe.anglican.uk
Advising dioceses and enhancing Readers' overall contribution to the Church's ministry.
Hon Secretary: Dr Alan Wakely. No full-time staff. ***CC*** No.271916. Began 1922; Anglican. Magazine: *The Reader* (10,000 quarterly). Turnover n/a.

Christian Life Community, St Joseph's, Watford Way, London NW4 4TY
☎020 7511 6331 Fax 020 7901 4874
E: clcew@iname.com
Web: www.clcew.org.uk
Promoting integration of faith and everyday life through companionship, seeking God together and loving service.
Development Worker: Ms Teresa House. *Director:* Sarah Lindsell. Executive staff 2, Other staff n/a. ***CC*** No.1056891. Began 1563; Roman Catholic (Ignatian), but open to all. Magazine: *Focus* ([illegible]00 monthly). Turnover £300,000 to year end Mar 02.

Church in Danger, PO Box 132, East Rudham, King's Lynn PE31 8QT
☎01485 528 664 Mobile: 07[illegible]50 03[illegible] 620
Fax 01485 528 155
E: r.b-e@virgin.net
Promoting the Christian faith in accordance with traditions, ancient and received orders, teachings of Church of England.
Director: Mr Rodney Bennett-England. No full-time staff. ***CC*** No.327963. Began 1988; Anglican. No magazine. Turnover under £10,000 to year end Dec 98.

†*Church of England Evangelical Council, PO Box 93, Heaton, Newcastle upon Tyne NE6 5WL
☎0191 240 2084 Fax 0191 240 2[illegible]84
E: ceec@blueyonder.co.uk
Web: www.ceec.info
Promoting effective consultation between evangelical Anglican leaders; organising Anglican Evangelical Assembly and National Evangelical Anglican Congress.
Executive Officer: Mr Frank Knaggs. Executive staff 1. ***CC*** No.21[illegible]315. Began 1960; Anglican. No magazine. Turnover £13,000 to year end Mar 98.

Church of Scotland Church and Society Council, 121 George Street, Edinburgh EH2 4YN
☎0131 225 5722 Fax 0131 220 3[illegible]13
E: dsinclair@cofscotland.org.uk
Facilitating the Church of Scotland's engagement with and comment upon national, political and social issues.
Secretary: Rev Dr David Sinclair. Executive staff 5. Began n/a; Church of Scotland. (Previously Church of Scotland Church and Nation Committee). No magazine. Turnover: included in Church of Scotland.

Church of Scotland Council of Assembly, 121 George Street, Edinburgh EH2 4YN
☎0131 225 5722 Fax 0131 220 31[illegible]3
Assessing changing needs and priorities of the Church of Scotland.
The Secretary: Very Rev Dr Finlay A J Macdonald. Executive staff [illegible]. Began n/a; Church of Scotland. (Previously Church of Scotland Assembly Council). No magazine. Turnover n/a.

Church of Scotland Ecumenical Relations, 121 George Street, Edinburgh EH2 4YN
☎0131 225 5722 Fax 0131 220 31[illegible]3
E: skesting@cofscotland.org.uk
Promoting cooperation between churches of different traditions in a spirit of reconciliation and joint worship.
Secretary for Ecumenical Relations: Rev Sheilagh M Kesting. Executive staff 1, Admin staff 1. ***CC*** No.SCO 1[illegible]353. Began n/a; Church of Scotland. Magazine: *Ecumenical Relations Newletter* (Circulation n/a quarterly). Turnover: included in Church of Scotland.

Church of Scotland Guild, 121 George Street, Edinburgh EH2 4YN
☎0131 225 5722 🖷0131 220 3113
🖃: guild@cofscotland.org.uk
Developing faith and Christian responses to current issues through worship, prayer and action
General Secretary: Mrs Alison Twaddle. Executive staff 2, Other staff 4. **CC** No.SCO 11353. Began 1887; Church of Scotland. (Previously Church of Scotland Woman's Guild). Magazine: *Newsletter* (45,000 every four months). Turnover: included in Church of Scotland.

Church of Scotland Ministries Council, 121 George Street, Edinburgh EH2 4YN
☎0131 225 5722 🖷0131 240 2201
🖃: ministries@cofscotland.org.uk
Web: www.churchofscotland.org.uk
Recruiting, locating, training and supporting ordained and commissioned ministries in the Church of Scotland.
Council Secretary: Rev Dr Martin Scott. Executive staff 13, Admin staff 13. Began n/a; Church of Scotland. (Previously Church of Scotland Board of Ministry). No magazine. Turnover: included in Church of Scotland.

Church of Scotland Principal Clerk's Department, 121 George Street, Edinburgh EH2 4YN
☎0131 240 2240 🖷0131 240 2239
🖃: pracproc@cofscotland.org.uk
Servicing General Assembly, related church-law responsibilities, church-state relations, providing support for Moderator.
Principal Clerk: Very Rev Dr Finlay Macdonald. Executive staff 2, Other staff 3. Began n/a; Church of Scotland. (Previously Church of Scotland Board of Practice and Procedure). No magazine. Turnover: included in Church of Scotland.

Church Patronage Trust, Truckers Ghyll, Horsham Road, Handcross, Haywards Heath RH17 6DT
☎01444 400 274
Nominating incumbents to 120 Anglican churches.
Secretary: Rev K W Habershon. No full-time staff. Began 1870; Anglican. No magazine. Turnover n/a.

Church Society, Dean Wace House, 16 Rosslyn Road, Watford WD18 0NY
☎01923 235 111 🖷01923 800 362
🖃: admin@churchsociety.org
Web: www.churchsociety.org
Campaigning to keep the Church of England established, Protestant and Reformed. Parish patronage and support.
Director: Rev David Phillips. Executive staff 1, Other staff 2. **CC** No.249574. Began 1835; Anglican. Magazine: *Churchman* (1,000 quarterly), *Cross+Way* (1,000 quarterly). Turnover n/a.

†The Church Union, 7 Tufton Street, London SW1P 3QN
☎020 7222 6952 🖷020 7976 7180
🖃: churchunion@care4free.net
Web: www.churchunion.care4free.net
Promoting Catholic faith, publishing literature.
Administrator: Mrs Jenny Miller. Executive staff 1. **CC** No.243535. Began 1859; Anglican. Magazine: *Church Observer* (3,000 quarterly). Turnover n/a.

†The Churches Conservation Trust, 89 Fleet Street, London EC4Y 1DH
☎020 7213 0660 🖷020 7936 2284
🖃: central@tcct.org.uk
Web: www.visitchurches.org.uk
Preserving historic Church of England churches of architectural and historical importance, surplus to pastoral requirements.
Director: Miss C Cullis. *Chief Financial Officer:* Mr Charles Williams. *Chief Caseworker:* Ms Sarah Robinson. Executive staff 3, Other staff 15. **CC** No.258612. Began 1969; Anglican. (Previously Redundant Churches Fund). Magazine: *Annual Report* (3,500 annually). Turnover £3,700,000 to year end Mar 00.

Churches Main Committee, 1 Millbank, London SW1P 3JZ
☎020 7898 1878 🖷020 7898 1798
🖃: cmc@c-of-e.org.uk
Web: www.cmain.org.uk
Representing churches in their dealings with Government on matters affecting churches.
Secretary: Mr Derek Taylor Thompson. Executive staff 1, Other staff 1. **CC** No.256303. Began 1941; ecumenical. No magazine. Turnover £45,000 to year end Dec 05.

Churches' Commission for Inter Faith Relations, CTBI, 2 Paris Garden, Bastille Court, London SE1 8ND
☎020 7654 7211
🖃: joan.poole@ctbi.org.uk
Web: www.ctbi.org.uk
Working to enable churches to engage effectively in relations and dialogue with other faith communities
Commission Secretary: To be appointed. Executive staff 1, Admin staff 1. Began n/a; ecumenical. A Commission of Churches Together in Britain and Ireland. No magazine. Turnover n/a.

Churches' Commission on International Students, CTBI, Bastille Court, 2 Paris Garden, London SE1 8ND
☎020 7654 7254 🖷020 7654 7222
🖃: ccis@ctbi.org.uk
Web: www.ctbi.org.uk
Representing the churches and other Christian bodies on international students' concerns in Britain and Ireland.
Commission Secretary: Ms Gillian Court. **CC** No.259688. Began 1975; ecumenical. (Previously Churches' Commission on Overseas Students). A commission of Churches Together in Britain and Ireland. No magazine. Turnover £40,000 to year end Mar 98.

Churches' Council for Industry and Social Responsibility (ISR), St Nicholas House, Lawfords Gate, Bristol BS5 0RE
☎0117 955 7430 🖷0117 941 3252
🖃: Administration@ccisr.org.uk
Advising, representing and supporting churches in relating faith to life, work, society, and providing chaplains.
Director: Rev Harold Clarke. Executive staff 1, Other staff 13. Began 1994; ecumenical. Magazine: *ISR News* (1,500 quarterly). Turnover £260,000 to year end Dec 00.
Also at: The Pilgrim Centre, Regent Circus, Swindon SN1 1PX
🖃: isrswindon@btconnect.com
☎01793 491 454 🖷 01793 491 454

C

The Congregational History Circle, Trinity Congregational Church, St Matthew's Road, Brixton, London SW2 1NF
☎020 7274 5541 / 8640 8192
Stimulating study and research into the history of Congregational churches, ministers and members.
Editor: Dr Alan Argent. All voluntary staff. Began 1978; Congregational. Magazine: *Congregational History Circle Magazine* (400 annually). Turnover £1,000 to year end Apr 98.

Connexion, The Manse, 11 Barns Close, Kirby Muxloe, Leicester LE9 2BA
☎0116 239 2731 🖷0116 239 5222
🖃: ang@revbob.org
Web: www.visitweb.com/connexion
Offering fellowship and support for those married to Baptists in ministry and mission.
Secretary: Mrs Angela Almond. No full-time staff. Began 1890; Baptist. (Previously Baptist Ministers and Missionaries Wives Fellowship). Magazine: *Connexion* (1,000 half-yearly). Turnover n/a.

The Corporation of the Church House, Great Smith Street, London SW1P 3AZ
☎020 7898 1310 🖷020 7898 1321
🖃: colin.menzies@c-of-e.org.uk
Operating the administrative headquarters and conference centre of the Church of England.
Company Secretary: Mr Colin Menzies. Executive staff 4, Other staff 21. **CC** No.213252. Began 1888; Anglican. No magazine. Turnover £5,903,000 to year end Dec 04.

Cost of Conscience, 79 Maze Hill, London SE10 8XQ
☎020 8858 7052
🖃: francisgardom@aol.com
Web: www.trushare.com
Seeking welfare of Anglican clergy unable to accept ordination of women as priests or bishops.
Administrator: Rev Francis Gardom. No full-time staff. Began 1986; Anglican. Magazine: *Costings* (300 half-yearly). Turnover £12,000 to year end Dec 98.

Council for Christian Unity, Church House, Great Smith Street, London SW1P 3NZ
☎020 7898 1471 🖷020 7898 1483
E: ccu@c-of-e.org.uk
Web: www.cofe.anglican.uk
Promoting Christian unity between Anglican and other Churches in the UK and elsewhere.
General Secretary: Rev Preb Dr Paul Avis. Executive staff 4, Other staff 2. Began 1991; Anglican. No magazine. Turnover n/a.

Crown Nominations Commission, Cowley House, 9 Little College Street, London SW1P 3SH
☎020 7898 1877 🖷020 7898 1867
E: caroline.boddington@c-of-e.org.uk
Nominating priests for diocesan bishoprics to the Prime Minister.
Secretary: Ms Caroline Boddington. Executive staff 1, Other staff 1. Began 1977; Anglican. (Previously Crown Appointments Commission). No magazine. Turnover n/a.

Diaconal Association of the Church of England, 55 Vicarage Lane, Marton, Blackpool FY4 4EF
☎0870 321 3260
E: secretary@dace.societies.anglican.org
Web: www.societies.anglican.org/dace
Supporting diaconal ministry in the Church of England, promoting diaconate as full and equal order.
Secretary: Rev Deacon Ann Wren. No full-time staff. ***CC*** No.1042999. Began 1988; Anglican. No magazine. Turnover £2,300 to year end Aug 00.

Dioceses Commission, Church House, Great Smith Street, London SW1P 3NZ
☎020 7898 1385 🖷020 7898 1369
E: colin.podmore@c-of-e.org.uk
Web: www.cofe.anglican.org
Considering proposals under the Dioceses Measure and advising on matters affecting the diocesan structures.
Secretary: Dr Colin Podmore. No full-time staff. Began 1978; Anglican. No magazine. Turnover n/a.

***Evangelical Fellowship in the Church in Wales**, The Rectory, Broadway, Llandrindod Wells LD1 5HT
☎01597 822 043 M: 07859 013 452
🖷01597 823 171
E: postmaster@efcw.org.uk
Web: www.efcw.org.uk
Witnessing to evangelical principles; day conferences and twice-yearly meetings.
Secretary: Rev Canon Andrew Loat. No full-time staff. ***CC*** No.1047004. Began 1967; Anglican. Magazine: *Bulletin* (260 quarterly). Turnover n/a.

Fellowship of Word and Spirit, 86 All Hallows Road, Bispham, Blackpool FY2 0AY
☎01253 351 886 🖷01253 351 886
E: admin@fows.org
Web: www.fows.org
Reforming Church of England for 21st Century by systematic Reformed theology and practice.
Hon Secretary: Paul Darlington. No full-time staff. ***CC*** No.293159. Began 1983; Anglican. Magazine: *Orthos* (400 quarterly). Turnover n/a.

Forward in Faith, 2a The Cloisters, Gordon Square, London WC1H 0AG
☎020 7388 3588 🖷020 7387 3539
E: fif.uk@forwardinfaith.com
Web: www.forwardinfaith.com
Organisation for Church of England groups opposed to the ordination of women.
National Director: Mr Stephen Parkinson. *Chairman:* Rt Rev John Broadhurst. Executive staff 1, Other staff 1. ***CC*** No.1057246. Began 1992; Anglican. Magazines: *New Directions* (8,000 monthly), *Forward Plus!* (18,000 quarterly). Turnover £300,000 to year end Dec 04.

Forward Together, The Manse, 2 Lanark Road, Kirkmuirhill, Lanark ML11 9RB
☎01555 892 409
E: ian.watson21@btopenworld.com
Web: www.forwardtogether.org
Giving a voice for evangelicals in the Church of Scotland.
Chairman: Rev Gordon Kennedy. No full-time staff. Began 2005; Church of Scotland. No magazine. Turnover n/a.

The Friends of Cardinal Newman, The Oratory, Hagley Road, Edgbaston, Birmingham B16 8UE
☎0121 454 0496 🖷0121 455 8160
E: jhn@oratory.globalnet.co.uk
Web: www.birmingham-oratory.org.uk
Disseminating knowledge of Cardinal Newman's life, teaching and philosophy; furthering the cause of his canonisation.
Director: Rev Gregory Winterton. Executive staff 1. ***CC*** No.274474. Began 1976; Roman Catholic but ecumenical. No magazine. Turnover £10,000 to year end Dec 04.

†Fulcrum, 23 Cowper Road, Wimbledon, London SW19 1AA
☎020 7704 1895 🖷020 7226 3400
E: admin@fulcrum-anglican.org.uk
Web: www.fulcrum-anglican.org.uk
Representing and stimulating evangelical Anglican orthodoxy in the church and media.
Chair: Rev Dr Francis Bridger. No full-time staff. ***CC*** Began 2003; Anglican. No magazine. Turnover n/a.

Grace Baptist Trust Corporation, 19 Croydon Road, Caterham CR3 6PA
☎01883 345 488 🖷01883 345 129
E: admin@gbtc.org.uk
Advancing the Christian religion especially Particular Baptist churches practising strict communion.
General Secretary: Mr E Cousins. Executive staff 1, Other staff 1. ***CC*** No.251675. Began 1909; Particular Baptist (Strict Communion). (Previously Strict and Particular Baptist Trust Corporation). No magazine. Turnover n/a.

***Group for Evangelism and Renewal**, Barnes Close, Malthouse Lane, Chadwich, Bromsgrove B61 0RA
☎01562 710 231
E: info@gear.org.uk
Web: www.gear.org.uk
Promoting renewal and evangelism in the URC, emphasising again the reality and Lordship of Christ.
Secretary & Treasurer: Rev Ian Ring. Executive staff 1, Other staff 1. ***CC*** Began 1974; United Reformed. Magazine: *In Gear* (3,300 every four months). Turnover £13,000 to year end Dec 02.

***Headway**, 33 Old Hexthorpe, Doncaster DN4 0JD
☎01302 855 389
E: headway@beeb.net
Web: www.headway.org
Evangelical Methodists in prayer and action.
General Secretary: Mr Richard Ibal[illegible]. No full-time staff. ***CC*** No.29[illegible]087. Began 1987; Methodist. Magazine: *Headline* (2,700 quarterly). Turnover £40,000 to year end Aug 02.

Historic Churches Preservation Trust, 31 Newbury Street, London EC1A [illegible]HU
☎020 7600 6090
🖷020 7796 2442
E: info@historicchurches.org.uk
Web: www.historicchurches.org.uk
Assisting with grants and loans towards building and repairs to Anglican churches in England and Wales.
Assistant Director: Judith Leigh. Executive staff 5. ***CC*** No.2127[illegible]2. Began 1818; Anglican. (Previously Incorporated Church Building Society). Magazine: *Annual Report* (4,500 annually). Turnover n/a.

The Hope Trust, 31 Moray Place, Edinburgh EH3 6BY
☎0131 226 5151
🖷0131 225 2608
Upholding the Reformed tradition in Scotland and worldwide. Gap year projects not funded.
Secretary: Robert Miller. No full-time staff. ***CC*** Began 1890; Church of Scotland. No magazine. Turnover n/a.

Kingdom Faith Church Offices, Roffey Place, Old Crawley Road, Horsham RH12 4RU
☎01293 851 543
🖷01293 854 610
E: info@kingdomfaith.com
Web: www.kingdomfaith.com
Also Bible College, publications, conferences.
Director: Rev Colin Urquhart. Executive staff 5, Other staff 40. ***CC*** No.278[illegible]46. Began 1980. Magazine: *Impact* (Circulation & frequency n/a). Turnover n/a.

Latin Mass Society, 11 Macklin Street, London WC2B 5NH
☎020 7404 7284 🖷020 7831 5585
E: thelatinmasssociety@snmail.co.uk
Web: www.latin-mass-society.org
Working for the preservation of the traditional Roman rite.
Secretary: Mr Paul Beardsmore. *General Manager:* Mr John Medlin. Admin staff 2. ***CC*** No.248388. Began 1965; Roman Catholic. No magazine. Turnover £130,000 to year end Mar 04.

Legal Advisory Commission (General Synod), Church House, Great Smith Street, London SW1P 3NZ
☎020 7898 1368
🖷020 7898 1718/1721
E: ingrid.slaughter@c-of-e.org.uk
Advising central church bodies and diocesan authorities of the Church of England on legal matters.
Secretary to the Commission: Miss Ingrid E Slaughter. No full-time staff. Began 1925; Anglican. Magazine: *Supplements to Legal Opinions Concerning the Church of England* (Circulation & frequency n/a). Turnover n/a

Liturgical Commission (General Synod), Church House, Great Smith Street, London SW1P 3NZ
☎020 7898 1385 🖷020 7898 1369
E: colin.podmore@c-of-e.org.uk
Web: www.cofe.anglican.org
Advising on and preparing forms of worship in the Church of England.
Secretary: Dr Colin Podmore. No full-time staff. Began 1954; Anglican. No magazine. Turnover n/a.

London Days of Renewal, 4 Beechwood Road, Sanderstead, South Croydon CR2 0AA
☎020 8657 1285
Promoting renewal in the Holy Spirit with prayer and praise and ministry of healing.
Secretary: Mrs Rosemary Radley. No full-time staff. Began 1967; Anglican. (Previously Anglo-Catholic Charismatic Renewal Committee) No magazine. Turnover £700 to year end Dec 05.

***Mainstream - A Word and Spirit Network**, 16 Ambleside Avenue, Rawtenstall, Rossendale BB4 6RY
☎01706 831 195
Web: www.mainstream-uk.com
Committed to getting passionate about God, getting real in relationships, getting stuck into God's mission.
Secretary: Rev Adrian Argile. No full-time staff. ***CC*** No.280032. Began 1979; Baptist (Previously Mainstream - Baptists for Life and Growth). No magazine. Turnover £44,148 to year end Apr 04.

Methodist Church, Methodist Church House, 25 Marylebone Road, London NW1 5JR
☎020 7486 5502 🖷020 7467 5226
E: enquiries@methodistchurch.org.uk
Web: www.methodist.org.uk
Servicing the Methodist Conference and ensuring its legislation as the Church's governing body is implemented.
General Secretary of Conference: Rev David G Deeks. Executive staff 1. Began 1932. No magazine. Turnover n/a.
Coordinating Secretaries: *Conference & Communication:* Rev K Howcroft
Human & Financial Resources: Ms Ruby Beech
Legal & Constitutional Practice: Rev David Gamble
Public Life for Social Justice: Mrs Anthea Cox
Unity in Mission: Rev Peter Sulston,
Worship & Learning: Rev Jonathan W Kerry

Methodist Church Music Society, 23a The Quadrant, Totley, Sheffield S17 4DB
☎0114 236 7196 🖷0114 236 7196
E: john.baileymcms@btopenworld.com
Web: www.methodistmusic.org
Developing, enabling and encouraging vocal and instrumental worship music in all its formats throughout the Church.
Secretary: Mr John Bailey. All voluntary staff. ***CC*** No.1098545. Began 1935; Methodist. Magazine: *Notes* (1,100 half-yearly). Turnover n/a.

Methodist Church Property Office, Central Buildings, Oldham Street, Manchester M1 1JQ
☎0161 236 5194 🖷0161 236 8908
E: secretaries@property.methodist.org.uk
Web: www.methodist.org.uk
Providing administration, advice and financial assistance for Methodist church property.
Secretary: Mr G Alan Pimlott. Executive staff 6, Other staff 17. Began 1854; Methodist. Magazine: *Property Points* (15,000 half-yearly). Turnover £1,500,000 to year end Dec 98.

Methodist Sacramental Fellowship, 107 Wellholme Avenue, Grimsby DN32 0BP
☎01472 877 644
E: chris@humblec.freeserve.co.uk
Fostering the study and practice of theology, liturgy and ecumenism in Methodism.
Secretary: Rev Chris Humble. No full-time staff. Began 1935; Methodist. Magazine: *The Bulletin* (325 annually). Turnover £3,000 to year end Mar 96.

Ministry Division (Archbishops' Council), Church House, Great Smith Street, Westminster, London SW1P 3NZ
☎020 7898 1390 🖷020 7898 1421
E: christopher.lowson@mindiv.c-of-e.org.uk
Web: www.cofe.anglican.org
Advising Church of England regarding selection, training, deployment, remuneration, for ordained ministers and lay readers.
Director: Ven Christopher Lowson. Executive staff 20, Other staff 14. ***CC*** Began 1912; Anglican. (Previously Advisory Board of Ministry (General Synod)). No magazine. Turnover n/a.

The Modern Churchpeople's Union, 9 Westward View, Liverpool L17 7EE
☎0151 726 9730 / 0845 345 1909
E: office@modchurchunion.org
Web: www.modchurchunion.org
Encouraging freedom and informed enquiry in the Church of England and Anglican Communion.
General Secretary: Rev Jonathan Clatworthy. No full-time staff. ***CC*** No.281573. Began 1898; Anglican. Magazine: *Modern Believing* (800 quarterly). Turnover £25,000 to year end Dec 02.

†The Mothers' Union, Mary Sumner House, 24 Tufton Street, London SW1P 3RB
☎020 7222 5533 🖷020 7222 1591
E: mu@themothersunion.org
Web: www.themothersunion.org
Strengthening marriage and family life; facilities for day conferences; gift shop.
Chief Executive: Mr Reg Bailey. Executive staff 6, Other staff 36. ***CC*** No.240531. Began 1876; Anglican but open to all. Magazine: *Home and Family* (95,000 quarterly). Turnover £1,400,000 to year end Dec 95.

†Movement for the Reform of Infant Baptism, 18 Taylors Lane, Lindford, Bordon GU35 0SW
☎01420 477 508
Web: www.baptism.org.uk
Fostering better understanding and practice of baptism administration within the Church of England.
Secretary: Ms Carol Snipe. No full-time staff. ***CC*** No.1067112. Began 1986; Anglican. Magazine: *Baptismal Integrity*(Circulation & frequency n/a). Turnover n/a.

†National Board of Catholic Women, 12 Worsall Road, Yarm TS15 9DF
☎01642 791 840 🖷01642 791 840
E: enquiries@nbcw.org
Web: www.nbcw.org
Forum for Catholic women; consultative body to Bishops' Conference of England and Wales & UN (ECSOC).
Development Officer: Angela Perkins. Executive staff 1, Other staff n/a. Began 1938; Roman Catholic. Incorporating National Catholic Women's Network. Magazine: *Catholic Omnibus* (15,000 quarterly). Turnover n/a.

National Council for Lay Associations, 21 Bassett Crescent West, Bassett, Southampton SO16 7EB
☎023 8079 0942 M: 07774 400 115
E: malcolm-rita@talk21.com
Web: www.ncla.org.uk
Network of Apostolic lay Catholic organisations and consultative body to Bishops' Conference.
President: Mr Malcolm Forster. No full-time staff. Began 1951; Roman Catholic. No magazine. Turnover £7,000 to year end Dec 05.

C

National Office for Vocation of England and Wales, The Chase Centre, 114 West Heath Road, London NW3 7TX
☎020 8458 6017 🖷020 8458 6017
E: enquiries@ukvocation.org
Web: www.ukvocation.org
Building a stronger culture of vocation throughout the church, promoting ordained ministry and consecrated life.
Director: Rev Paul Embery. Executive staff 1, Other staff 2. ***CC*** No.1097482. Began 2002; Roman Catholic. (Previously Diocesan Vocations Service of England and Wales). No magazine. Turnover £45,000 to year end Dec 02.

National Religious Vocation Centre, PO Box 37602, The Ridgeway, Mill Hill, London NW7 4XG
☎020 8201 1871 🖷020 8201 1988
E: formation@corew.org
Web: www.corew.org
Promoting and informing about religious life in England and Wales for men and women.
Director: Sr Karen Marguerit d'Artois. Executive staff 1. ***CC*** No.277024. Began 1979; Roman Catholic. No magazine. Turnover n/a.

***New Creation Christian Community**, Jesus Fellowship Central Offices, Nether Heyford, Northampton NN7 3LB
☎08451 668 172 🖷08451 668 178
E: info@newcreation.org.uk
Web: www.newcreation.org.uk
Charismatic Christian community throughout the UK.
Senior Pastor: Noel Stanton. Admin staff 2. Began 1974; Jesus Fellowship. No magazine. Turnover n/a.

Nikaean Club, Lambeth Palace, London SE1 7JU
☎020 7898 1221 🖷020 7401 9886
Extending world ecumenical hospitality on behalf of the Archbishop of Canterbury to church leaders from abroad.
The Secretary: Name not supplied. Admin staff 1. Began 1925; Anglican. No magazine. Turnover £17,000 to year end Dec 02.

†Open Synod Group, Plowman's Corner, The Square, Westbury sub Mendip, Wells BA5 1HJ
☎01749 870 356
E: tim.hind@lineone.net
Enhancing and assisting the proclamation of the Gospel through the synodical process.
Secretary: Mr Tim Hind. No full-time staff. ***CC*** No.297315. Began 1970; Anglican. Magazine: *OSG Magazine* (400 half-yearly). Turnover £1,200 to year end Dec 02.

Orthodox Fellowship of St John the Baptist, c/o 26 Denton Close, Oxford OX2 9BW
☎01865 864 805
E: bjgerrard@compuserve.com
Web: www.ofsjb.org
Providing conferences and publications for Orthodox clergy and parishes in Britain and Ireland.
Chair: Bishop Kallistos of Diokleia. No full-time staff. ***CC*** No.106713. Began n/a; Orthodox. No magazine. Turnover £9,000 to year end Mar 03.

***Oxfordshire Community Churches**, The King's Centre, Osney Mead, Oxford OX2 0ES
☎01865 297 400 🖷01865 297 401
E: office@occ.org.uk
Web: www.occ.org.uk
Group of Churches and Christian schools in Oxfordshire.
Senior Pastor: Rev Stephen Thomas. *Area Administrator:* Mr Andy O'Connell. Executive staff 15, Admin staff 4. ***CC*** No.1056921. Began 1982; Salt & Light. Magazine: *Area News* (500 every two months). Turnover £1,800,000 to year end Aug 01.

***Partnership**, Abbey Court, Cove, Tiverton EX16 7RT
☎01398 331 105
E: neil.summerton@ruralinternet.co.uk
Web: www.partnershipuk.org
Providing networking, support, encouragement, training to churches of Christian Brethren background and other independent churches.
Chairman & Executive Director: Dr Neil Summerton. Paid staff member 1. ***CC*** No.802564. Began 1987; Christian Brethren. Including Partnership Link-Up Service (Plus), Brethren Archivists and Historians Network (BAHN) and Christian Brethren Research Fellowship. Magazine: *Partnership Perspectives* (520 every four months), *International Partnership Perspectives* (800 annually). Turnover £46,050 to year end Mar 03.

Peache Trust, Truckers Ghyll, Horsham Road, Handcross, Haywards Heath RH17 6DT
☎01444 400 274
Appointing incumbents to 45 Anglican churches.
Secretary: Rev K W Habershon. No full-time staff. Began 1878; Anglican. No magazine. Turnover n/a.

People of God Trust, 14 West Halkin Street, London SW1X 8JS
☎020 7235 2841 🖷020 7823 2110
E: brydenbrook@talk21.com
Promoting the Second Vatican Council's idea of renewal in the Catholic Church.
Hon Secretary: Mr Simon Bryden-Brook. No full-time staff. ***CC*** No.1013830. Began 1992; Roman Catholic. No magazine. Turnover £4,900 to year end Apr 05.

Praxis, Cleveland Lodge, Westhumble, Dorking RH5 6BW
☎01306 872 829 🖷01306 887 [illegible]60
E: praxis@praxisworship.org.uk
Web: www.praxisworship.org.uk
Liturgical formation; study days and conferences on liturgy and worship.
Chairman: Rev Paul Roberts. *Administrator:* Penny Neary. No full-time staff. Began 1990; Anglican. Magazine: *Praxis News* (Circulation n/a every two months). Turnover n/a.

The Prayer Book Society, The Studio, Copyhole Farm, Goring Heath, Reading RG8 7RT
☎0118 984 2582 🖷0118 984 5[illegible]20
E: pbsadmin@prayerbook.org.uk
Web: www.prayerbook.org.uk
Promoting the Book of Common Prayer as the principal form of worship in the Church of England.
Chairman: Mr Roger Evans. No full-time staff. ***CC*** No.10992[illegible]5. Began 1975; Anglican. Magazine: *PBS Journal* ([illegible],000 quarterly), *Faith and Worship* (10,000 annually). Turnover £194,000 to year end Dec 02.

Protestant Dissenting Deputies of Three Denominations, 27 Tavistock Square, London WC1H 9HH
☎020 7529 8141 🖷020 7529 81[illegible]4
E: freechurch@cte.org.uk
Defending the civil rights of nonconformists and maintaining the right of access to the throne. Annual lecture.
Secretary: Rev Geoffrey H Roper. No full-time staff. Began 1732; represents Baptists, Congregationalists and United Reformed. No magazine. Turnover £[illegible]00 to year end Dec 97.

Quaker Life, Friends House, Euston Road, London NW1 2BJ
☎020 7633 1000 🖷020 7[illegible]3 100[illegible]
E: michaelh@quaker.org.uk
Web: www.quaker.org.uk
Nurturing Quakers and outreach to others through conferences, correspondence, literature and advertising
General Secretary: Michael Hutchinson. Executive staff 1, Other staff 27. ***CC*** Began 1978; Religious Society of Friends. (Previously Quaker Home Service). Magazine: *Quaker Monthly* (2,000 monthly). Turnover £610,000 to year end Dec 04.

Reform, PO Box 1183, Sheffield S10 3Y[illegible]
☎0114 230 9256 🖷0114 230 9256
E: administrator@reform.org.uk
Web: www.reform.org.uk
Promoting biblically-based ideas and action for reforming the Church of England.
Chairman: Rev David Banting. Executive staff 1, Admin staff 1. ***CC*** No.103619[illegible]. Began 1993; Anglican. No magazine. Turnover £85,000 to year end Dec 02.

Reformation Today Trust, 75 Woodhill Road, Leeds LS16 7BZ
☎0113 251 2513
Web: www.reformation-today.org
Distributing Reformed Baptist literature worldwide; organising conferences.
Editor: Rev Erroll Hulse. All voluntary staff. **CC** No.10[illegible]7000. Began 1970; Reformed Baptist. Magazine: *Reformation Today* (2,200 every two months). Turnover £[illegible]6,000 to year end Dec 02.

ReSource, 4 Old Station Yard, Abingdon OX14 3LD
☎01235 553 722 🖷01235 553 922
E: office@resource-arm.net
Web: www.resource-arm.net
Helping leaders, dioceses and churches to be more effective in their mission.
Director: Mr Martin Cavender. Executive staff 2, No other full-time staff. **CC** No.327035. Began 2004; Anglican. (Previously Anglican Renewal Ministries). Magazine *ReSource* (Circulation n/a every four months). Turnover £150,000 to year end Dec 05.

Retired Clergy Association, Kiggon Cottage, Pencalenick, St Clement, Truro TR1 1TE
☎01872 520 471
E: johnandpauline@kiggoncottage.fsnet.co.uk
Encouraging retired clergy and assisting them to form groups for discussion and further study.
Hon Secretary: Mr John Sansom. No full-time staff. Began 1934; Anglican. No magazine. Turnover £9,800 to year end Dec 04.

Royal Martyr Church Union, 7 Nunnery Stables, St Albans, St Albans AL1 2AS
☎01727 856 626
Revering the memory of Charles I and bringing together descendants of Cavaliers and those interested in Caroline history.
Hon Secretary: David Roberts. No full-time staff. Began 1906; Anglican. Magazine: *Royal Martyr Annual* (Circulation n/a annually). Turnover n/a.

Russian Orthodox Monastery of St Seraphim of Sarov, 158 Elmbridge Road, Perry Barr, Birmingham B44 8AE
☎0121 356 5176 🖷0121 356 5176
Web: russian-orthodox-church.org.uk
Missionary spiritual centre: monastic life, prayers, advice, lectures, social services. Translation: French, German, Latvian, Russian.
Abbot: Very Rev Archimandrite Seraphim. *Reader:* Alexander Suscento. Community n/a. Began 1986. (Previously Latvian Autonomous Orthodox Church). Russian Orthodox Church Outside Russia - Metropolitan Vitaly. No magazine. Turnover n/a.

Saint Edward Brotherhood, Saint Cyprian's Avenue, Brookwood, Woking GU24 0BL
☎01483 487 763 🖷01483 487 763
E: theshepherd@mac.com
Web: www.saintedwardbrotherhood.org
Monastic community, missionary work, care of Orthodox Christian cemetery and shrine of Saint Edward the martyr.
Superior: Very Rev Archimandrite Alexis. Order members 5. **CC** No.284929/0. Began 1981; Orthodox. Magazine: *The Shepherd* (750 monthly). Turnover £6,000 to year end Apr 00.

Scottish Baptist Men's Movement, 5 Murchland Way, Irvine KA12 0XN
☎01294 278 700
E: andrew.harvey@tiscali.co.uk
Web: www.scottish-baptist-mens-movement.co.uk
Annual men's conference; annual dinner; promoting men's work in Baptist churches; books for pastors abroad.
Secretary: Mr Andrew Harvey. No full-time staff. **CC** No.SCO 28288. Began 1947; Baptist. No magazine. Turnover £5,020 to year end Dec 99.

Scottish National Tribunal, 22 Woodrow Road, Glasgow G41 5PN
☎0141 427 3036 🖷0141 427 7715
E: nationaltribunal@btopenworld.com
Dealing with issues of canon law, principally concerning the bond of marriage.
Officialis: Rev James O'Kane. Executive staff 2, Other staff 23. **CC** Began 1970; Roman Catholic. No magazine. Turnover n/a.

Simeon's Trustees and Hyndman's Trustees, c/o Mrs A Brown, 6 Angerford Avenue, Sheffield S8 9BG
☎0114 255 8522 🖷0114 255 8522
E: ann.brown@simeons.org.uk
Patronage trust nominating incumbents for vacant benefices in the Trust's gift.
Chairman: Rev Canon Dr Peter Williams. No full-time staff. **CC** No.06293. Began 1836; Anglican. No magazine. Turnover n/a.

Society of King Charles the Martyr, 22 Tyning Road, Winsley, Bradford-on-Avon BA15 2JJ
☎01225 862 965
Web: www.skcm.org
Promoting idea of King Charles as a saint and martyr.
Chairman: Mr Robin Davies. No full-time staff. Began 1894; Anglican. Magazine: *Church and King* (500 half-yearly). Turnover £1,000 to year end Dec 02.

†**Society of St Willibrord**, 57 Maltese Road, Chelmsford CM1 2PB
☎01245 353 914 🖷01245 353 914
E: il.morris@virgin.net
Fostering good relationships between the Anglican Church and the Old Catholic Churches in Europe.
Secretary: Rev Ivor Morris. No full-time staff. **CC** Began 1908; Anglican. No magazine. Turnover n/a.

Society Pontifical of St John Chrysostom, 1 St James' Close, Bishop's Street, London N1 8PH
☎020 7359 0250
Making known to Western Christians the history, worship and spirituality of Eastern Christendom.
Chairman: Rev A T J Salter. No full-time staff. Began 1926; Roman Catholic but ecumenical. (Previously Society of St John Chrysostom). Magazine: *Chrysostom* (800 half-yearly). Turnover n/a.

The Strict Baptist Historical Society, 33 Addison Road, Caterham CR3 5LU
☎01883 341 909
E: thesecretary@sbhs.org.uk
Web: www.strictbaptisthistory.org.uk
Studying Baptist history; preserving books, documents and other historical material.
Hon Secretary: Mrs Pauline J Johns. No full-time staff. **CC** No.1061908. Began 1960; Strict Baptist. Magazine: *Bulletin* (150 annually). Turnover £1,804 to year end Oct 04.

Ukrainian Religious Society of St Sophia, 79 Holland Park, London W11 3SW
☎020 7221 1890 🖷020 7221 1890
E: sophia_soc@yahoo.co.uk
Promoting religious knowledge, Christian practice and education with reference to Ukrainian Catholic Church teachings.
Director: Rev I Muzychka. All voluntary staff. **CC** No.275483. Began 1977; Ukrainian Catholic. No magazine. Turnover n/a.

***United Reformed Church History Society**, c/o Westminster College, Madingley Road, Cambridge CB3 0AA
☎01223 741 300 🖷01223 300 765
E: mt212@cam.ac.uk
Promoting study of Congregational and Presbyterian history, especially in England.
Hon Secretary: Rev Elizabeth Brown. No full-time staff. Began 1972; United Reformed Church. Magazine: *Journal of the United Reformed Church History Society* (200 half-yearly). Turnover n/a.

Wesley Historical Society, 34 Spiceland Road, Birmingham B31 1NJ
☎0121 475 4914
Web: www.wesleyhistoricalsociety.org.uk
Encouraging interest and research into the history and literature of all branches of Methodism.
General Secretary: Dr E Dorothy Graham. No full-time staff. **CC** No.283012. Began 1893; Methodist. Magazine: *Proceedings of the Wesley Historical Society* (700 every four months). Turnover £10,000 to year end Dec 04.

C

†The Wesley Historical Society (Ireland), 5 Aberdelghy Gardens, Lisburn BT27 4QQ
☎No telephone
E: archives@irishmethodist.org
Library and archives.
Secretary: Mrs Maureen Weir. No full-time staff. Began n/a; Methodist. No magazine. Turnover n/a.
Library at: Edgehill College, 9 Lennoxvale, Malone Road, Belfast BT9 5BY
☎028 9066 5870
Archivist: Rev Robin P Roddie, Epworth, 16 Brooklands Road, Newtownards BT23 4TL
E: robin@roddie.plus.com
☎028 9181 5959

Wesley's Chapel, The Museum of Methodism and John Wesley's House, 49 City Road, London EC1Y 1AU
☎020 7253 2262 🖷020 7608 3825
E: administration@welseyschapel.org.uk
Web: www.wesleyschapel.org.uk
Providing information about the Wesleys and Methodism to visitors worldwide of all denominations. Non-residential conference centre.
Office Manager: Mrs Joy Cruickshank. Admin staff 1, Other staff 5. ***CC*** Began 1778; Methodist. Magazine: *Wesley's Chapel Magazine* (2,500 annually). Turnover n/a.

Westminster Interfaith, 23 Kensington Square, London W8 5HN
☎020 7361 4740 🖷020 7361 4741
E: alfredagius@rcdow.org.uk
Fostering relations between Roman Catholics and other world faiths.
Director: Mr Alfred Agius. Executive staff 1, Other staff 4. ***CC*** No.233699. Began 1981; Roman Catholic. No magazine. Turnover n/a.

The Worshipful Company of Parish Clerks, Acreholt, 33 Medstead Road, Beech, Alton GU34 4AD
☎01420 543 913 🖷01420 590 [illegible]41
Assisting the work of the Anglican Church in the City of London (Westminster and Southwark).
Clerk of the Company: Mr B [illegible] N Coombes. Executive staff 1. Began 12[illegible]4; Anglican. No magazine. Turnover £27,500 to year end Mar 00.

EVANGELICAL FELLOWSHIPS (INTER-CHURCH)

***Across Havering**, 24 Lower Bedfords Road, Rise Park, Romford RM1 5DF
☎01708 721 310
Building relationships between church leaders/member churches to encourage evangelism in London Borough of Havering.
Chairman: Rev Roger Garnet. Executive staff 1. ***CC*** No.1051811. Began 1989; interdenominational. (Previously Havering Mission 2000). No magazine. Turnover £1,080 to year end Mar 98.

***Alliance of Asian Christians**, PO Box 1375, Headington, Oxford OX3 0WJ
☎01865 741 400 🖷01865 741 400
E: raj@patelz.net
Supporting and representing Asian individuals and churches.
Executive Secretary: Mr Pradip Sudra. Executive staff 1, Other staff 3. ***CC*** No.1020767. Began 1989; non-denominational. In partnership with Evangelical Alliance. Magazine: *Aaeki Haae* (2,000 half-yearly). Turnover £10,000 to year end Jun 05.

Associating Evangelical Churches of Wales, 11 Brook Street, Maerdy, Ferndale CF43 4AF
☎01443 757 655
E: secretary@aecw.org.uk
Web: www.aecw.org.uk
Linking 62 like-minded churches in Wales for interchurch church planting and mutual encouragement.
Secretary: Rev Graham John. No full-time staff. Began 1988; interdenominational. Magazine: *Contact* (2,000 half-yearly). Turnover n/a.

***Bath Evangelical Fellowship**, The Church Office, Avenue Place, Combe Down, Bath BA2 5EE
☎01225 835 835
E: admin@htcd.org
Coordinating evangelical fellowship and work in the Bath area.
Hon Secretary: Rev Paul Langham. No full-time staff. Began n/a; interdenominational. No magazine. Turnover n/a.

***Breakthrough**, PO Box 25, Scarborough YO11 1JF
☎01723 378 045 M: 07977 229 039
E: david@dnellist.freeserve.co.uk
Inter-church initiative encouraging leaders and churches to pray and work together for revival.
Leader: Rev David Nellist. No full-time staff. ***CC*** No.1052790. Began 1996; interdenominational. No magazine. Turnover n/a.

***Brentwood and District Evangelical Fellowship (BADEF)**, 2 Magnolia Way, Pilgrims Hatch, Brentwood CM15 9QS
☎01277 233 769
E: admin@sawyerschurch.org
Promoting fellowship between Evangelical Alliance churches in the area and coordinating joint projects.
Chair: Mr David Matthews. No full-time staff. Began 1990; interdenominational. No magazine. Turnover n/a.

***Brighton and District Evangelical Alliance**, City Gate Church, 84 London Road, Brighton BN1 4JF
☎01273 693 807 🖷01273 682 248
E: karen@citygatechurch.org.uk
Coordinating evangelical fellowship and work in the Brighton and East Sussex area.
Secretary: Karen Peck. No full-time staff. Began n/a; interdenominational. No magazine. Turnover n/a.

***Bristol Evangelical Alliance**, South Bristol Centre, Churchlands Road, Bristol BS3 3PW
☎0117 964 2506
Web: www.beaming.org.uk
Expressing the unity God has given in Christ to Christians of all denominations.
Secretary: Mr Les Potter. No full-time staff. Began 1965; interdenominational. No magazine. Turnover n/a.

British Reformed Fellowship, 50 Brookfield Heights, Burnside, Ballyclare BT39 0TS
☎028 9334 1198
E: briancrossett@hotmail.com
Web: www.britishreformedfellowship.org.uk
Promoting the Reformed faith in the British Isles through biennial conferences, journal, website.
Secretary: Mr Brian Crossett. Executive staff 2. Began 1990; interdenominational. Magazine: *British Reformed Journal* ([illegible]125 quarterly). Turnover £30,000 to year end Apr 05.

***Bromley Evangelical Fellowship**, c/o Bromley Town Church, 2 Ethelbert Road, Bromley BR1 1JA
☎020 8466 0191
E: bromch@aol.com
Acting as a channel for united Christian prayer fellowship and outreach in Bromley.
Chairman: Mr Jonathan McGill. No full-time staff. ***CC*** Began 1970; interdenominational. No magazine. Turnover n/a.

***Cities Network Scotland**, Ardcraig, Bankhead Grove, Dalmeny, South Queensferry EH30 9JZ
☎0131 331 3310 🖷0131 331 33[illegible]
E: dgj.flett@uk.iccc.net
Bringing together networkers from Scottish cities; providing events and information on the city challenge.
Trustees: Mr Douglas Flett. No full-time staff. Began n/a; interdenominational. Magazine: *Cities Network* (Circulation & frequency n/a). Turnover n/a.

Essex Protestant Council, 3[illegible]3 Baddow Road, Chelmsford CM2 7QF
☎No telephone
Web: www.essexprotestantcouncil.co.uk
Raising a testimony on Protestant issues through correspondence, publicity, open-air and other public meetings.
Hon Secretary: Mr Stephen Evans. No full-time staff. Began 1982; non-denominational. No magazine. Turnover n/a.

***European Evangelical Alliance**, Whitefield House, 186 Kennington Park Road, London SE11 4BT
☎020 7582 7276 🖷020 7582 2043
E: eeaoffice@aol.com
Web: www.europeanea.org
Uniting national Evangelical Alliances and other agencies to serve Christ around Europe.
General Secretary: Mr Gordon Showell-Rogers. Executive staff 1, Other staff 3. **CC** No.33351 Guernsey. Began 1952; interdenominational. No magazine. Turnover n/a.

***Evangelical Alliance**, Whitefield House, 186 Kennington Park Road, London SE11 4BT
☎020 7207 2100 🖷020 7207 2150
E: london@eauk.org
Web: www.eauk.org
Uniting evangelicals, presenting Christ credibly and evangelism as good news; bringing spiritual and social transformation.
General Director: Rev Joel Edwards. *Executive Director:* Mr Mike Morris. *Public Policy Director:* Rev R David Muir. Executive staff 3, Other staff 47. **CC** No.212325. Began 1846; interdenominational. Incorporating ACUTE. Magazine: *idea* (38,000 every two months). Turnover £2,500,000 to year end Mar 05.
Ireland *General Secretary:* Rev Stephen Cave, Downview House, 440 Shore Road, Newtownabbey BT37 9RU
E: nireland@eauk.org
☎028 9029 2266 🖷 028 9029 2277
Scotland *General Secretary:* Rev Fred Drummond, Challenge House, 29 Canal Street, Glasgow G4 0AD
E: scotland@eauk.org
☎0141 332 8700 🖷 0141 332 8704
Wales *General Secretary:* Rev Elfed Godding 20 High Street, Cardiff CF10 1PT
E: wales@eauk.org
☎029 2022 9822 🖷 029 2022 9741

See also:
African and Caribbean Evangelical Alliance on Page 340
European Evangelical Alliance on Page 187
Evangelical Alliance Conference Centre on Page 37
idea on Page 250

Note: For member groups see Page 17

The Evangelical Movement of Wales, Bryntirion, Bridgend CF31 4DX
☎01656 655 886 🖷01656 665 919
E: office@emw.org.uk
Web: www.emw.org.uk
Pursuing fellowship, evangelical unity, services of mutual benefit at church level and evangelism.
Office Manager: Mrs Joan Pells Cocks. *Pastoral Director* Rev Stuart Olyott. *Chairman of the Management Committee:* Rev Gwynn Williams. Executive staff 2, Other staff 7. **CC** No.222407. Began 1948; non-denominational. Magazine: *Y Cylchgrawn Efengylaidd* (800 quarterly), *The Evangelical Magazine of Wales* (1,600 every two months). Turnover £1,097,834 to year end Jan 05.

See Also:
Bryntirion Christian Conference Centre on Page 33
Bryntirion Press/Gwasg Bryntirion on Page 120
Christian Bookshop on Page 96
Y Cylchgrawn Efengylaidd on Page 248
The Evangelical Magazine of Wales on Page 249
The Evangelical Theological College of Wales on Page 425
Theological Training Course on Page 434

***Global Connections**, Whitefield House, 186 Kennington Park Road, London SE11 4BT
☎0870 774 3806 🖷0870 774 3809
E: info@globalconnections.co.uk
Web: www.globalconnections.co.uk
Global Options offering a consultancy service for churches in an age of bewildering choice.
Executive Director: Mr Martin Lee. *Church Relations Director:* Mr Bryan Knell. Executive staff 2, Other staff 4. **CC** No.274521. Began 1958; interdenominational. Registered as Evangelical Missionary Alliance. Magazine: *Global Connections* (2,000 quarterly), *World Prayer News* (1,600 every two months). Turnover £292,660 to year end Dec 05.

Note: For members groups see Page 20

***Grampian Evangelical Fellowship**, 76 Kirk Brae, Cults, Aberdeen AB15 9QQ
☎01224 868 532
E: wmain45343@aol.com
Encouraging communication and cooperation between evangelical churches and organisations in Aberdeen and North East Scotland.
Administrator: Mrs Main. No full-time staff. Began 1998; interdenominational. Magazine: *Aberdeen Christian Diary* (Circulation & frequency n/a). Turnover £1,000 to year end Dec 00.

***Guernsey Evangelical Alliance**, The King's Centre, New Road, St Sampson, Guernsey GY2 4QE
☎01481 242 282 🖷01481 242 292
E: jon@kcg.org.uk
Bringing churches, leaders, agencies together; extending the influence of the Gospel in the Channel Islands.
Chairman: Mr Jonathan Le Tocq. No full-time staff. Began 1965; interdenominational. No magazine. Turnover n/a.

Ipswich Partnership of Evangelical Churches, 12 Houghton Place, Rushmere St Andrew, Ipswich IP4 5UX
☎01473 274 622
E: burton@fish.co.uk
Coordinating evangelical churches fellowship and work in the area.
Chairman: Mr Tony Burton. No full-time staff. Began 1995; interdenominational. (Previously Ipswich Evangelical Fellowship). No magazine. Turnover n/a.

†***Manchester Network**, Nazarene Theological College, Dene Road, Didsbury, Manchester M20 2GU
☎07762 627 568
E: info@network-ea.org.uk
Web: www.network-ea.org.uk
Churches in Manchester working together in social action, prayer, media, sport ministries, evangelism.
Chairman: Mr Michael Harvey. Admin staff 1. **CC** No.504453. Began n/a; interdenominational. No magazine. Turnover n/a.

***Mid-Cotswolds Evangelical Alliance (MCEA)**, 16 Sydenham Road South, Cheltenham GL52 6EF
☎01242 245 597
E: j-esmuts@tiscali.co.uk
Coordinating evangelical fellowship and work in the area.
Hon Secretary: Mr John Smuts. *Hon Chairman:* Mr Simon Measures. No full-time staff. Began n/a; interdenominational. No magazine. Turnover n/a.

North West Partnership Trust, St Andrew's Parish Office, Worden Lane, Leyland PR25 3EL
☎01772 422 266
E: info@northwestpartnership.com
Web: www.northwestpartnership.com
Training, supporting and equipping people for Gospel ministry in the North West.
Ministry Training Course Director: Rev Justin Mote. Executive staff 1, Admin staff 1. **CC** No.1104423. Began 2003; interdenominational. No magazine. Turnover £61,378 to year end May 05.

***Paisley & District Evangelical Alliance**, 20 Gordon Street, Paisley PA1 1XD
☎0141 561 0118
E: pdea@pdea.freeserve.co.uk
Web: www.pdea.org.uk
Linking evangelical Christians in Renfrewshire to pray, proclaim and praise.
Chairman: Mr Phil Arbon. No full-time staff 1. Began 1992; interdenominational. Magazine: *Grapevine* (110 every two months). Turnover £3,500 to year end Feb 00.

***The Penge and Beckenham Evangelical Fellowship**, The Vicarage, St John's Road, London SE20 7EQ
☎020 8778 6176
Coordinating evangelical fellowship and work in the area.
Hon Chairman: Rev P Venables. No full-time staff. Began n/a; interdenominational. (Previously Beckenham and Penge Evangelical Fellowship). No magazine. Turnover n/a.

Seedtime and Harvest, 11 Woodburn Crescent, Aberdeen AB15 8JX
☎01224 319 158 Ⓜ:07791 605 134
E: seedtime@totalise.co.uk
Facilitating city-reaching events; working toward transformation in church and community.
Director: Mr Gordon Shewan. No full-time staff. **CC** Began 1996; non-denominational. No magazine. Turnover £2,640 to year end Dec 02.

***South East Essex Evangelical Fellowship**, 20 Lascelles Gardens, Ashingdon, Rochford SS4 3BP
☎01702 548 438 🖷01702 548 438
E: redbond@btopenworld.com
Coordinating evangelical fellowship and work in the area.
Hon Chairman: Rev David M Redbond. No full-time staff. **CC** No.1014671. Began n/a; interdenominational. No magazine. Turnover n/a.

***South Wessex Evangelical Alliance**, c/o 55 Curzon Road, Springbourne, Bournemouth BH1 4PN
☎01202 303 036
E: office@swea.net
Web: www.swea.net
Equipping evangelical Christians to be a prophetic voice through teaching, fellowship, networking, outreach, prayer, communication.
Chairman: Rev M Stear. No full-time staff. Began 1988; interdenominational. No magazine. Turnover £3,000 to year end Dec 04.

***Southampton Evangelical Alliance**, The Vicarage, 37 Brockdale Road, Southampton SO17 1QR
☎023 8055 4277
E: vicarbiker@aol.com
Alliance of evangelical church leaders in the area.
Chair: Rev Graham Archer. No full-time staff. Began 1987; interdenominational. No magazine. Turnover n/a.

***Sustain**, 61 Chandos Road, Newbury RG14 7EG
☎01635 42 239
E: chair@sustain-worship.org.uk
Web: www.sustain-worship.org.uk
Organising non-denominational celebrations, training and outreach events; providing worship resources for Christians in Newbury.
Chair: Mrs J Green. No full-time staff. **CC** No.1076859. Began 1999; non-denominational. No magazine. Turnover £1,000 to year end Dec 02.

***Taunton Evangelical Alliance**, 68 Smithy, Bishops Hull, Taunton TA1 5BP
☎01823 325 553
E: chris@b-hull.fsnet.co.uk
Coordinating evangelical fellowship and work in the Taunton Deane area.
Chairman: Mr Chris Stone. No full-time staff. Began 1987; interdenominational. No magazine. Turnover n/a.

†***Tell Torbay**, Thatcher Brake, 37 Whidborne Avenue, Torquay TQ1 2PG
☎01803 380 399
E: info@telltorbay.co.uk
Web: www.telltorbay.co.uk
Partnership of 20 churches of all denominations, working together to impact the community of Torbay.
Chairman: Adrian Huxham. No full-time staff. Began 2001; interdenominational. Incorporating Torbay Evangelical Fellowship. No magazine. Turnover n/a.

***Tiverton & District Evangelical Fellowship**, Sellake Farm, Uplowman, Tiverton EX16 7DJ
☎01884 820 210 Ⓜ: 07720 034 667
🖷01884 820 210
Fellowship of local churches; building up Christians; evangelistic outreach; united services.
Hon Chairman: Mr Mike Britton. No full-time staff. Began 1967; interdenominational. No magazine. Turnover £2,000 to year end Mar 93.

***Together for the Harvest**, PO Box 155, Liverpool L15 0JH
☎0151 525 6316 Ⓜ: 07711 556 369
E: jcc@tfth.org.uk
Web: www.tfth.merseyside.org
Promoting unity, leadership and church relationships for the purpose of communicating the gospel.

Chairman: Mr John Cavanagh. Staff 2. Began 1990; interdenominational. (Previously Merseyside Evangelical Alliance Trust). Magazine: *Leaders' Bulletin* (350 monthly). Turnover £2[illegible],000 to year end Dec 01.

Toxteth Evangelical Association, St Cleopas' Vicarage, Beresford Road, Liverpool L8 4SG
☎0151 727 0633
Coordinating and sharing in the work and witness of member churches by united action and prayer.
Chairman: Rev David G Gavin. No full-time staff. Began 1973; interdenominational. No magazine. Turnover n/a.

***Tunbridge Wells Fellowship of Evangelicals**, 36 Beulah Road Tunbridge Wells TN1 2NR
☎01892 514 050
E: cllyallen@aol.com
Drawing evangelicals together for prayer, outreach and evangelism; a voice in the community.
Secretary: Name not supplied. No full-time staff. **CC** No.1090774. Began 1997; interdenominational. No magazine. Turnover £3,000 to year end Dec 02.

***Wanstead & Woodford Evangelical Council**, 9 Gascoigne Gardens, Woodford Green IG8 9NT
☎020 8504 5725
E: richard@richvera.freeserve.co.uk
Promoting united events for local fellowship and evangelism.
Chairman: Mr Richard Thomas. No full-time staff. Began 1958; interdenominational. No magazine. Turnover n/a.

Yorkshire Gospel Partnership St John's Vicarage, Clough Road, Hull HU6 7PA
☎01482 343 658 🖷01482 345 027
E: melvin@stjohnnewland.org.uk
Partnership of evangelical churches seeking to establish biblical, outward-looking churches.
Chairman of the Steering Committee: Rev Melvin Tinker. No full-time staff. Began 2005; interdenominational. No magazine. Turnover: first year of operation.

RELIGIOUS ORDERS (ANGLICAN)

See also Retreat Houses on Page 72.

†Alnmouth Friary, Society of St Francis, Alnwick NE66 3NJ
☎01665 830 213 🖷01665 830 213
E: alnmouthssf@franciscans.org.uk
Web: www.orders.anglican.org/ssf
Ministry of hospitality, spiritual direction, other sacramental ministries, retreats by arrangement.
Guardian: Brother Paschal SF. Members 7. **CC** No.236464. Began n/a. No magazine. Turnover n/a.

Community of St Andrew, 8 Verona Court, Chiswick Lane, Chiswick, London W4 2JD
☎020 8987 2799
Prayer and evangelism, carried out in parish and specialised ministry.
Contact: Mother Superior. Members 8. **CC** No.244321. Began 1861. Magazine: *Annual Review* (350 frequency n/a). Turnover n/a.

Community of St Clare, St Mary's Convent, 178 Wroslyn Road, Freeland, Witney OX29 8AJ
☎01993 881 225 🖷01993 886 912
E: community@oscfreeland.co.uk
Prayer, printing, producing Communion wafers, guest house (calls about guest house, 6-7pm Mon-Sat).
Contact: Abbess. Members 13. Began 1950. No magazine. Turnover n/a.

The Community of St Francis, Manor House, Compton Durville, South Petherton TA13 5ES
☎01460 240 473 🖷01460 242 360
E: comptondurvillecsf@franciscans.org.uk
Web: www.franciscans.org.uk
Pastoral work, hospitality, retreats, evangelism, chaplaincy, community life, prayer, worship. Four UK houses.
Minister Provincial: Helen Julian CSF. Members 25. ***CC*** No.286615. Began 1905. Magazine: *Franciscan* (3,000 every four months). Turnover £48,000 to year end June 02.

Community of St Mary the Virgin, St Mary's Convent, Wantage OX12 9DJ
☎01235 763 141
E: convent.sisters@csmv.co.uk
Reverend Mother: Mother Barbara Claire. Community 62. ***CC*** No.240513. Began 1848. No magazine. Turnover n/a.

Community of St Peter, St Peter's Convent, Maybury Hill, Woking GU22 8AB
☎01483 750 739 🖷01483 776 208
E: rosamond.davidson@btinternet.com
Retreats and conferences, counselling, caring in the community.
Mother Superior: Rev Mother Rosamond Davidson. *Director of St Columba's Retreat House:* Rev Paul Jenkins. Members 7, Other staff 5. ***CC*** No.240675. Began 1861. No magazine. Turnover £900,000 to year end Dec 02.

Community of the Glorious Ascension, The Priory, Lamacraft Farm, Start Point, Kingsbridge TQ7 2NG
☎01548 511 474 🖷01548 511 474
The brothers unite a working life with monastic community life.
Prior: Brother Simon. Members 9. ***CC*** Began 1960. No magazine. Turnover n/a.

Community of the Holy Cross, Holy Cross Convent, Rempstone Hall, Rempstone, Loughborough LE12 6RG
☎01509 880 336
Benedictine community; producing prayer and greeting cards and meditation leaflets.
Mother Superior: Rev Mother Mary Luke Wise. Members 9. ***CC*** Began 1857. No magazine. Turnover n/a.

Community of the Holy Name, Morley Road, Oakwood, Derby DE21 4QZ
☎01332 671 716 🖷01332 669 712
E: bursarsoffice@tiscali.co.uk
Web: www.chnderby.org
Pastoral and evangelistic work, hospitality and prayer.
Provincial Superior: Sr Monica Jane. Members 42. ***CC*** No.250256. Began 1865. No magazine. Turnover n/a.

†The Community of the Sacred Passion, The Convent, Lower Road, Effingham, Leatherhead KT24 5JP
☎01372 457 091
Prayer and service in the community.
Contact: Mother Superior. Members 21. ***CC*** No.800080. Began 1911. No magazine. Turnover n/a.

Community of the Sisters of the Church, 56 Ham Common, Richmond TW10 7JH
☎020 8940 8711 🖷020 8332 2927
E: sisters.csm.ham@fish.co.uk
Web: www.tap.net/csc
Promoting growth and fulness of life of God's people by work, worship, hospitality, education and reconciliation.
Mother Superior: Sister Anita. Members 26. ***CC*** No.271790. Began 1870. No magazine. Turnover n/a.
Also at: 82 Ashley Road, St Paul's, Bristol BS6 5NT
And: Well Cottage, Upper Street, Kingsdown, Deal CT14 8BH
And: 10 Furness Road, Harrow HA2 0RL

†*Community of the Word of God, 90 Kenworthy Road, London E9 5RA
☎020 8986 8511
E: cwg@fish.co.uk
Prayer, hospitality, service and evangelism; retreats and quiet days; involvement in work of local church.
Servant: Miss Jenny Brailsford. Members 5, Prayer companions 50. ***CC*** No.269209. Began 1972. Magazine: *Community of the Word of God Magazine* (200 annually). Turnover n/a.

Order of the Holy Paraclete, St Hilda's Priory, Sneaton Castle, Whitby YO21 3QN
☎01947 602 079 🖷01947 820 854
E: ohppriorywhitby@btinternet.com
Web: www.ohpwhitby.org
Benedictine community involved in education, hospital chaplaincy, retreats, conferences, missions, urban priority work.
Prioress: Sr Dorothy Stella. Members 55. ***CC*** No.271117. Began 1915. No magazine. Turnover n/a.

St Margaret's Convent, Hooke Hall, 250 High Street, Uckfield TN22 1EN
☎01825 766 808
E: egmotherssm@hotmail.com
Prayer and service in hospitality, care of the elderly, guest and retreat facilities and quiet days.
Mother Superior: Rev Mother Cynthia Clare. Members 16. ***CC*** No.231926. Began 1855. Magazine: *St Margaret's Chronicle* (320 every four months). Turnover n/a.

Society of All Saints Sisters of the Poor, All Saints Convent, St Mary's Road, Oxford OX4 1RU
☎01865 249 127
🖷01865 726 547
E: admin@socallss.co.uk
Working with elderly, homeless, sick people, children, students; church embroidery; small guest house.
Mother Superior: Sister Helen J F Chappell. Members 12. ***CC*** No.228383. Began 1851. Magazine: *New Venture* (Circulation n/a annually). Turnover n/a.
Also at: 19 Mulready Walk, Hemel Hempstead HP3 9FS
☎01443 243 447
🖷 01443 243 447

C

Society of St Francis, The Friary, Hilfield, Dorchester DT2 7BE
☎01300 341 345
🖷01300 341 293
E: hifieldssf@franciscans.org.uk
Web: www.franciscans.org.uk
Following the traditions of the Franciscan orders: prayer, hospitality, mission, concern for the poor.
Minister Provincial: Br Samuel. Staff 55. ***CC*** No.236464. Began 1921. Magazine: *Franciscan* (Circulation n/a every four months). Turnover n/a.

Society of the Precious Blood, Burnham Abbey, Lake End Road, Taplow, Maidenhead SL6 0PW
☎01628 604 080
🖷01628 604 080
E: burnhamabbey@tiscali.co.uk
Web: www.parishes.oxford.anglican.org/burnhamabbey
Prayer and intercession.
Mother Superior: Sr Mary Bernard. Members 16. ***CC*** No.900512. Began 1905. No magazine. Turnover n/a.

Society of the Sisters of Bethany, House of Bethany, 7 Nelson Road, Southsea PO5 2AR
☎023 9283 3498
E: ssb@sistersofbethany.org.uk
Web: www.sistersofbethany.org.uk
Retreat work, hospitality, prayer and work for unity.
Mother Superior: Sr Gwenyth. Members 11, Other staff 4. ***CC*** No.226582. Began 1866. No magazine. Turnover n/a.

RELIGIOUS ORDERS (ROMAN CATHOLIC)

See also Retreat Houses on Page 72, Mission Agencies on Page 282.

Augustinian Nursing Sisters, Ince Blundell Hall, Ince Blundell, Liverpool L38 6JL
☎0151 929 2596 🖷0151 929 2188
Nursing the elderly infirm and terminally ill, sick and retired priests and lay people.
Prioress: Sr Marie Laura Hughes. Sisters 8, Other staff 36. ***CC*** No.251782. Began 1961. No magazine. Turnover n/a.

†The Canons Regular of Premontre (The White Canons), Our Lady of England Priory, School Lane, Storrington, Pulborough RH20 4LN
☎01903 742 150 🖷01903 740 821
E: norbertines@pavilion.co.uk
Caring for Roman Catholics in the area; schools work; pastoral work; guest house.
Contact: Prior. Members 6. ***CC*** Began 1147. No magazine. Turnover n/a.

Carthusians, St Hugh's Charterhouse, Henfield Road, Partridge Green, Horsham RH13 8EB
☎No telephone 🖷01403 864 231
E: simon.brennan@chartreus.info
Web: www.parkminister.org.uk
Leading a life of prayer and worship.
Prior: Rev John Beabeau. Members 26. Began 1084. No magazine. Turnover n/a.

Congregation of the Blessed Sacrament, 4 Dawson Street, Liverpool L1 1LE
☎0151 709 5528 🖷0151 709 5977
E: peterezmard@aol.com
Adoration shrine of the Blessed Sacrament.
Provincial Superior: Fr Gary Walsh. Members 6. ***CC*** Began 1936. No magazine. Turnover n/a.

†Congregation of the Mission (Vincentians), Vincentian Community, Sacred Heart Presbyterion, 2 Flower Lane, Mill Hill, London NW7 2JB
☎020 8959 1021
Retreats, missions, parish work, chaplaincies, formation; working with homeless people.
Regional Superior: Fr C M Aiden Galvin. Members 25. ***CC*** No.233777. Began 1853. No magazine. Turnover n/a.

Congregation of the Sisters of St Anne, 14a The Downs, London SW20 8HS
☎020 8946 1094/4794 🖷020 8947 7602
Parish assistance and home for elderly people.
Superior General: Sr Barbara O'Mahony. Members 14. ***CC*** No.233808. Began 1927. No magazine. Turnover n/a.

†Corpus Christi Carmelites, 15 Sevenhay Close, Leicester LE2 3TW
☎0116 2270 4564
E: teresategas@ssmail.net
A contemplative lifestyle and active apostolates.
Regional Superior: Sr Teresa Joseph. Members 3. ***CC*** Began 1908. No magazine. Turnover n/a.

Daughters of Our Lady of Providence, Convent of Our Lady of Providence, Anstey Lane, Alton GU34 2NG
☎01420 541 545 🖷01420 541 711
A teaching/nursing order, undertaking any apostolate which is needed.
Sister Superior: Sr Helen. Members 9. ***CC*** Began 1938. No magazine. Turnover n/a.

†Daughters of the Cross (of Torquay), Stoodley Knowle Convent, Anstey's Cove Road, Torquay TQ1 2JB
☎01803 215 865/290 880 M: 07970 888 837 🖷01803 290 880
E: benignus@stoodley.fsbusiness.co.uk
Web: www.stoodleyknowle.devon.sch.uk
Education and other religious and pastoral activities.
Superior General: Sr Benignus O'Brien. Members 37, Other staff 50. ***CC*** No.232014. Began 1640. No magazine. Turnover n/a.

Dominican Sisters of St Catherine of King Williams Town, St Martin's Convent, Stoke Golding, Nuneaton CV13 6HT
☎01455 212 207 🖷01455 213 476
E: stmartinop@aol.com
Working in education, clinics, prisons; pastoral work, retreat work, guests.
Sister-in-Charge: Sr Louise Curran. Members 400. ***CC*** No.231235. Began 1933. No magazine. Turnover n/a.

Dominican Sisters of the English Congregation of St Catherine of Siena, 21 Station Road, Stone ST15 8EN
☎01785 813 552 🖷01785 813 852
E: opsisters.stone@lineone.net
Web: www.stone-dominican.org.uk
Trying, like St Dominic, 'to praise, to bless, to preach' by prayer and service.
Prioress General: Sr Angela Mary Leydon. Members 60. ***CC*** Began 1854. No magazine. Turnover n/a.

Dominican Sisters of the Presentation, Presentation Convent, Easthampstead Road, Wokingham RG40 2ED
☎0118 978 2553 🖷0118 989 3822
E: Poussepin@aol.com
Parish work, foreign student care.
Superior: Sr Veronica Mary Jackson. Members 3. ***CC*** Began 1904. No magazine. Turnover £80,000 to year end Dec 00.

Downside Abbey, Stratton on the Fosse, Bath BA3 4RH
☎01761 235 161 🖷01761 235 124
E: monks@downside.co.uk
Web: www.downside.co.uk
Benedictine; teaching in school, parish work, giving retreats, academic research, publication.
Abbot: Dom Richard Yeo. Members 30, Other staff 150. ***CC*** No.232548. Began 1795. No magazine. Turnover n/a.

Ealing Abbey, Charlbury Grove, Ealing, London W5 2DY
☎020 8862 2100 🖷020 8862 22[illegible]6
E: ealingmonk@aol.com
Web: members.aol.com/ealingmonk
Benedictines; teaching in school, parish work, adult teaching in art, liturgy.
Abbot: Rt Rev M Shipperlee. Community 23, Other staff n/a. ***CC*** No.242[illegible]15. Began 1897. No magazine. Turnover n/a.

Franciscan Friars of the Atonement, 47 Francis Street, London SW1P 1QR
☎020 7828 4163 🖷020 7821 22[illegible]9
Mission and ecumenism
Brother-in-Charge: Fr Michael Seed. Members 2. ***CC*** No.231951. Began 1957. No magazine. Turnover n/a.

Franciscan Missionary Sisters, 2 Broad Road, Braintree CM7 9RS
☎01376 326 654 🖷01376 340 40[illegible]
E: maryfinuala@aol.com
Providing residential care for elderly people.
Sister Superior: Sr Helen Connolly. Members 6. ***CC*** Began n/a. No magazine. Turnover n/a.

†Franciscan Missionary Sisters of Littlehampton, The Generalate, St Joseph's Franciscan Convent, East Street, Littlehampton BN17 6AU
☎01903 714 039 🖷01903 731 09[illegible]
Nursing, visiting and pastoral work, parish and prison work, retreats, hostels for students.
Superior General: Sr Anne Mclaughlin. Members 54. ***CC*** No.232931. Began 1890. No magazine. Turnover n/a.

†Franciscan Sisters of the Immaculate Conception, St Anthony's Convent, [illegible]3 Belle Vue Road, Cinderford GL14 2AA
☎01594 822 310 🖷01594 824 79[illegible]
Teaching, parish work, caring for mothers and babies and those who are mentally handicapped.
Sister-in-charge: Sr Mary Celestine McKenna. Members 1. ***CC*** No.3590[illegible]. Began n/a. (Previously Missionary Franciscan Sisters of the Immaculate Conception). No magazine. Turnover n/a.

Little Brothers of the Good Shepherd, Montini House, 2 Richmond Road, Wolverhampton WV3 9HY
☎01902 422 218
Distribute lunch pack six days week from Wolverhampton Centre in middle of town; no accommodation.
Local Superior: Br William Cahill. Community 2. ***CC*** No.703163. Began 1971; Roman Catholic. (Previously Good Shepherd Centre). No magazine. Turnover n/a.

Little Company of Mary, 28 Trinity Crescent, Tooting Bec, London SW17 7AE
☎020 8682 0928 🖷020 8682 0552
E: adminsecretary@lcmgenerlate.org
Web: www.lcmglobal.org
Praying for the sick and dying, chaplaincy work and nursing where it is needed.
Congregational Leader: Sr Jeanette Connell. Members 410. ***CC*** No.327867. Began 1877. No magazine. Turnover n/a.

Little Sisters of the Poor, St Peter's Residence, 2a Meadow Road, London SW8 1QH
☎020 7735 0788 🖷020 7820 9647
Care until death of elderly poor people of all denominations; eight residential homes in England.
Mother Provincial: Sr Stephen. Members 150. ***CC*** No.234434. Began 1851. No magazine. Turnover n/a.

Olivetan Benedictines, Priory of Our Lady of Peace, Turvey Abbey, Turvey, Bedford MK43 8DE
☎01234 881 432 🖷01234 881 432
Web: www.turveyabbey.org.uk
Prayer, hospitality, ecumenism, liturgy, retreats, making liturgical vestments and wall hangings.
Prioress: Sr Zoë Davis. Members 14. ***CC*** No.246754. Began 1936. No magazine. Turnover n/a.

Our Lady of Providence, Convent of Our Lady of Providence, Anstey Lane, Alton GU34 2NG
☎01420 541 545 🖷01420 541 711
Teaching, chaplaincy, pastoral supervision, pastoral work, nursing, counselling, caring for homeless people.
Regional Superior: Sr Helen. Members 7. ***CC*** No.232908. Began 1938. No magazine. Turnover n/a.

Poor Handmaids of Jesus Christ, The Convent, 46 Draycott Road, Bournemouth BH10 5AR
☎01202 513 555
Parish pastoral work and spiritual direction.
Sister-in-Charge: Sr Paul Snell. Members 7. ***CC*** No.234423. Began 1876. No magazine. Turnover n/a.

Poor Servants of the Mother of God, Maryfield Convent, Mount Angelus Road, Roehampton, London SW15 4JA
☎020 8788 4351 🖷020 8789 9281
E: maryfield@psmgs.org
Web: www.poorservants.com
Working in education and healthcare; social and pastoral work.
Superior General: Sr Elizabeth Crehane. Members in UK 158. ***CC*** No.227931. Began 1869. No magazine. Turnover n/a.

Presentation Brothers, 63 Bath Road, Reading RG30 2BB
☎0118 956 0232
Involved in education for less well-off people, social work.
Provincial Delegate: Br Richard English. *Secretary General Republic of Ireland:* Fr Bede Minehane. Members 10. ***CC*** Began 1872. No magazine. Turnover n/a.

Presentation Sisters, Provincial House, 4 King's End, Bicester OX26 6DT
☎01869 323 660 🖷01869 323 659
E: pbvmepro@clara.co.uk
Web: www.presentationsisters.co.uk
Christian education of youth, social work, parish work and counselling.
Provincial Superior: Sr Susan Richert. Members 106. ***CC*** Began 1836. No magazine. Turnover n/a

Prinknash Benedictines, Prinknash Abbey, Cranham, Gloucester GL4 8EX
☎01452 812 455 🖷01452 813 305
E: prinknash@waitrose.com
Web: www.prinknashabbey.org.uk
Prayer, study and manual work; retreats and hospitality.
Abbot: Rt Rev Francis Baird. Members 18, Other staff n/a. ***CC*** No.232863. Began 1928. Magazine: *Pax* (Circulation n/a quarterly). Turnover n/a.

Religious of the Sacred Heart of Mary, 64 Little Ealing Lane, London W5 4XF
☎020 8567 3148 🖷020 8579 8072
Pastoral and social outreach, community development, homelessness, education. Communities in over 20 locations.
Provincial Superior: Sr Barbara Bailey. Members 144. ***CC*** No.232190. Began 1849. No magazine. Turnover n/a.

Salesian Sisters of St John Bosco, 13 Streatham Common North, London SW16 3HG
☎020 8677 4515 🖷020 8677 4523
E: provincialoffice.fma@ukonline.co.uk
Web: www.salesiansistersuk.com
Youth work, schools, education and development projects, volunteering, scholastic/social recuperation, parish ministry, overseas missions.
Provincial Superior: Sr Elizabeth Purcell. Community 65, Serving missionaries 5. ***CC*** No.250888. Began 1872. Magazine: *Don Bosco Today* (Circulation n/a quarterly). Turnover n/a.

Sisters of Marie Auxiliatrice, 20 Elgin Road, London N22 7UE
☎020 8881 8547
🖷020 8883 6299
E: marieaux@eircom.net
Web: www.marieuk.org
Serving the needs of young people, especially those underprivileged.
Regional Co-ordinator: Sr Mary O'Dea. Members 23. Began 1920. No magazine. Turnover n/a.

Sisters of Mercy, Convent of Mercy, Newcastle ST5 1LH
☎01782 614 459
🖷01782 711 446
Prison work, social work, parish work, care of the poor, sacristy work, hospital ministry.
Mother Superior: To be appointed. Members 9, Other staff 2. ***CC*** No.233969. Began 1839. No magazine. Turnover n/a.

C

†Sisters of Our Lady, Convent of Our Lady, Hall Lane, Kettering NN15 7LR
☎01536 513 711
🖷01536 392 599
Administration, catechetical and pastoral ministry, nursing and chaplaincy work.
District Superior: Sr Marion Connaughty. Members 7. ***CC*** No.221865. Began 1933. No magazine. Turnover n/a.

†Sisters of Providence (Ruillé sur Loire), The Mount, Wragby Road, Lincoln LN2 5SL
☎01522 540 894
🖷01522 568 321
E: sisterstephanie@prov15.ssnet.co.uk
Dedicating their lives to God through varied ministries in the Catholic Church.
Regional Superior: Sr Stephanie Dalton. Members n/a. ***CC*** Began 1896. No magazine. Turnover n/a.

Sisters of Providence of Rouen, Convent of Providence, 10 Sutton Avenue, Seaford BN25 4LA
☎01323 892 178
Parish work, visiting sick people.
Sister Superior: Sr Odile Deswarte. Members 4. ***CC*** Began n/a. No magazine. Turnover n/a.

Sisters of St Marcellina, Hampstead Towers, 6 Ellerdale Road, London NW3 6BD
☎020 7435 0181
🖷020 7433 3459
E: stmarcellina@btconnect.com
School of English for foreign students; accommodation for girls only.
Sister Superior: Sr Giuliana Carrara. Members 5. ***CC*** No.211414. Began 1955. No magazine. Turnover n/a.

Sisters of the Christian Retreat, House of Prayer, 35 Seymour Road, East Molesey KT8 0PB
☎020 8941 2313 Ⓜ: 07752 369 902 🖷020 8941 2313
E: houseofprayerem@aol.com
Web: www.christian-retreat.org
House of prayer, residential retreats, individual quiet days; counselling and spiritual direction available.
Regional Superior: Sr Melanie. Members 10. ***CC*** No.232567. Began 1789. No magazine. Turnover £20,000 to year end Dec 02.

†Sisters of the Divine Saviour, 9c Boreham Road, Warminster BA12 9JP
☎01985 217 647 🖷01985 218 007
Nursing, parish work and social work.
Regional Superior: Sr Paula Langton. Members 8. ***CC*** No.228082. Began 1888. (Previously Salvatorian Sisters). No magazine. Turnover n/a.

Sisters of the Gospel of Life, Our Lady & St Joseph's, 106 Dixon Avenue, Crosshill, Glasgow G42 8EL
☎0141 422 2634
E: gospeloflife@btinternet.com
Community defending respect for the right to life for all.
Sister in Charge: Sr Roseann Reddy. Community 2. ***CC*** No.SCO 30667. Began 2000; Roman Catholic. No magazine. Turnover n/a.

Sisters of the Holy Family of Nazareth, Holy Family Convent, 52 London Road, Enfield EN2 6EN
☎020 8363 4483 🖷020 8363 2583
Teaching, hospital chaplaincies, parish and pastoral work.
Sister-in-Charge: Sr Mercedés. Enfield members 10, Northampton members 7. ***CC*** No.234201. Began 1895. No magazine. Turnover n/a.

†Sisters of the Presentation of Mary, Mount St Mary Convent, Wonford Road, Exeter EX2 4PF
☎01392 433 301 🖷01392 490 859
Teaching, marriage tribunals, chaplaincies, hospital and pastoral work, working with dying people.
Regional Superior: Sr Guy-Marie. Members 10. ***CC*** Began 1896. No magazine. Turnover n/a.

Sisters of the Sacred Heart of Jesus, 6 Oakleigh Park South, Whetstone, London N20 9JU
☎020 8445 9299 🖷020 8445 9299
E: conv@sscj.freeserve.co.uk
Apostolic Religious, working in teaching, nursing, parish work, chaplaincy, social work, pastoral work.
District Superior: Sr Mary Paul Ewen. Members in UK 15. ***CC*** No.230335. Began 1816, 1903 England. No magazine. Turnover n/a.

Sisters of the Temple, St Angela's Convent, 5 Litfield Place, Clifton, Bristol BS8 3LU
☎0117 973 5436 🖷0117 970 6844
E: marielou39@btinternet.com
Caring for elderly people.
Sister Provincial: Sr Marie-Louise Levern. Members 4, Sisters 6, Other staff 20. ***CC*** No.229049. Began 1862. No magazine. Turnover n/a.

Society of Christ, 196 Lloyd Street North, Manchester M14 4QB
☎0161 226 1588 🖷0161 232 0450
Spiritual, social and cultural welfare of Poles living away from their homeland.
Father Provincial: Rev Czeslaw Osika. Members 22. ***CC*** No.298723. Began 1988. No magazine. Turnover n/a.

The Sons of Divine Providence, 13 Lower Teddington Road, Kingston upon Thames KT1 4EU
☎020 8977 5130 🖷020 8977 0105
E: pkehoe@sonsofdivine.org
Web: www.sonsofdivineprovidence.org
Running day-care facilities and 7 residential homes for the elderly and people with learning disabilities.
Regional Superior: Rev Philip Kehoe. Members 8, Other staff 120. ***CC*** No.1088675. Began 1952. Magazine: *The Bridge* (6,000 quarterly). Turnover n/a.

Subiaco Congregation, St Augustine's Abbey, Ramsgate CT11 9P[illegible]
☎01843 593 045 🖷01843 582 [illegible]32
E: staugabbey@aol.com
Web: www.ramsgatebenedictines.com
Parochial and retreat work; monastic hospitality; spiritual guidance; courses on Sacred Scripture.
Abbot: Rt Rev Laurence O'Keeffe. Members 12. ***CC*** No.24[illegible]415. Began 1856. Benedictine. No magazine. Turnover n/a.

Trinitarian Sisters, Holy Trinity Convent, 81 Plaistow Lane, Bromley BR1 3LL
☎020 8402 2785 🖷020 8466 0[illegible]51
E: sisterjmt@tiscali.co.uk
Working in the UK in parishes, prison chaplaincies and fostering Christian education.
Superior: Sr J Madeleine Timmins. Members 13. ***CC*** Began 18[illegible]6. No magazine. Turnover n/a.

Ursulines of Brentwood, Ursuline Generalate, 93 Queen's Road, Brentwood CM14 4EY
☎01277 260 156 🖷0127[illegible] 263 [illegible]18
E: admin@ursulinesistersbrentwood.org
Companioning women, young people through local church, prison chaplaincy, hospital visiting, school support.
Congregation Leader: Sr Margaret Soper. Members 26, Associate Members 30. ***CC*** No.223378. Began 1900. No magazine. Turnover n/a.

Worth Abbey, Turners Hill, Crawley RH10 4SB
☎01342 710 310 🖷01342 710 311
E: enquiries@worthabbey.net
Web: www.worthabbey.net
Benedictine monastic community offering prayer and sanctuary.
Abbot: Rt Rev Christopher Jamison. Members 25. ***CC*** No.[illegible]093[illegible]13. Began 1933. No magazine. Turnover n/a.

†Xaverian Brothers, 20 Be[illegible]field Road, Didsbury, Manchester M20 6[illegible]H
☎0161 445 5273
Local education and prison work.
Area Coordinator: Br Donald Bi[illegible]les. Members 6, Other staff 4. ***CC*** No.239240. Began 1848. No magazine. Turnover n/a.

EVANGELISM

E

CHURCH PLANTING ORGANISATIONS

Anglican Church Planting Initiatives, Philadelphia Campus, 6 Gilpin Street, Sheffield S6 3BL
☎0114 278 9378 🖷0114 278 9600
E: admin@acpi.org.uk
Web: www.acpi.org.uk
Serving tomorrow's churches today by encouraging and assisting the planting of healthy missionary-minded churches.
Co-Leader: Rev Bob Hopkins. Admin staff 2, Training and consulting staff 4. ***CC*** No.1060703. Began 1993; Anglican. Magazine: *News from Anglican Church Planting Initiatives* (1,000 half-yearly). Turnover £25,000 to year end Dec 04.

***The Bible Network**, 6 Clarendon House, 117 George Lane, South Woodford, London E18 1AN
☎No telephone
E: johntbn@aol.com
Web: www.thebiblenetwork.org.uk
Bible distribution and church planting.
Director: John Savage. Executive staff 1, Other staff n/a. ***CC*** No.299943. Began 1985; interdenominational. (Previously Christian Mission Fellowship). Magazine: *Report* (10,000 every four months). Turnover n/a.

***Days of Wonder Trust**, New Life Christian Centre, Bridlington Avenue, Hull HU2 0DU
☎01482 610 705 🖷01482 221 090
E: office@daysofwonder.org.uk
Web: www.daysofwonder.org.uk
Promoting revival through missions, signs and wonders, leadership training, music and media ministries.
Director: Rev Jarrod Cooper. Executive staff 2, Other staff 8. ***CC*** No.1076045. Began 1997; interdenominational. Magazine: *Days of Wonder* (1,500 occasionally). Turnover £17,000 to year end Apr 00.

Destiny Ministries, 1120 Pollockshaws Road, Glasgow G41 3QP
☎0141 616 6777 🖷0141 616 6300
E: info@destiny-church.com
Web: www.destiny-church.com or www.destiny-college.com
Church planting, Bible college, publishing, social action ministries, teaching resources.
Chairman of Trustees: Mr Andrew Owen. *Business Manager:* Mr Liam Smith. Executive staff 5, Admin staff 3, Other staff 7. ***CC*** No.SCO 20228. Began 1992; non-denominational. (Previously Reapers Trust). Magazine: *Days of Destiny* (Circulation n/a quarterly). Turnover £121,557 to year end May 04.

Fresh Expressions, 15 Fyfield Rd, Oxford OX2 6QE
☎01865 311838
E: contact@freshexpressions.org.uk
Web: www.freshexpressions.org.uk
Encouraging fresh expressions of church across the UK.
Archbishops' Missioner: Rev Dr Steven Croft. Executive staff 6, Admin staff 2. ***CC*** No.1080103. Began 2004; Anglican/Methodist. An Archbishop's initiative. Turnover n/a.

***Grace Ministries Trust**, 141 Cleveland Street, London W1T 6QG
☎020 7388 7475 M: 07734 101 776
E: info@gracelondon.co.uk
Web: www.gracelondon.co.uk
Planting the seed of the Gospel into relational networks of unchurched urban people.
Regional Coordinator: Rev Paul Klawitter. Executive staff 1, Other staff 9. ***CC*** No.700373. Began 1986; Grace Brethren. No magazine. Turnover nil.

MR Associates, 19 Wemyss Court, Leapmoor Drive, Wemyss Bay PA18 6BF
☎01475 522 962M: 07967 963 806
E: info@mrassociates.org.uk
Web: www.mrassociates.org.uk
Helping newly-planted churches where they set up accommodation-based services for vulnerable adults.
Supported Housing Advisor: Mr Mark Rodgers. Executive staff 2, Admin staff 1. Began 2000; interdenominational. No magazine. Turnover n/a.

Peace Foundation Ministries - Christ Fellowship (UKHQ), 65 Fullbrook Road, Walsall WS5 4PB
☎01922 620 776
M: 07960 118 265
E: pfm4mails@aol.com
Web: pfm-missions.org
Undertaking church planting, evangelism, discipleship, urban missions, community projects, reaching children and young people.
Missions Director: Pastor Isi Agboaye. Executive staff 2, Admin staff 2. ***CC*** No.1069974. Began 1995; interdenominational. No magazine. Turnover n/a.

Together in Mission, Rowheath Pavilion, Heath Road, Birmingham B30 1HH
☎0121 433 3912
E: martin.robinson@togetherinmission.org
Web: www.togetherinmission.org
Promoting a DAWN strategy in England involving church Mobilisation and multiplication.
Coordinator: Mr Martin Robinson. Other Staff 5. ***CC*** No.1049296. Began 1991; non-denominational. (Previously Challenge 2000). No magazine. Turnover n/a.

Urban Expression, PO Box 35238, London E1 0YA
☎01865 250 914
M: 07780 690 536
E: enquiries@urbanexpression.org.uk
Web: www.urbanexpression.org.uk
Recruiting, equipping, deploying and networking self-financing teams to plant churches in under-churched urban communities.
Director: Dr Stuart Murray Williams. No full-time staff. ***CC*** No.1090734. Began 1997; non-denominational. No magazine. Turnover £10,000 to year end Dec 04

CITY & TOWN MISSIONS

Bath Christian Trust, 1a Forum Buildings, St James's Parade, Bath BA1 1UG
☎01225 463 556 🖷01225 460 651
E: enquiries@bathcitychurch.org.uk
Web: www.bathcitychurch.org.uk
Coordinating the work of Bath City Church and serving related churches in the region.
Leaders: Mr Simon Neal, Mr Stephen Wood, Mr Stewart Keiller. Total Staff 17. ***CC*** No.4122782. Began 1976; non-denominational. No magazine. Turnover £1,000,000 to year end Mar 03.

Battersea Central Methodist Mission, PO BOX 17, 20 York Road, London SW11 3QE
☎020 7207 6663 🖷020 7924 1491
E: contactus@batterseamission.info
Web: www.batterseamission.info
Cancer resource centre, citizens advice bureaux, chiropody clinic, imani project, Learning Ladder pre-school.
Superintendant: Rev David Gillman. Executive staff 1, Other staff 8. ***CC*** Began 1940; Methodist. Magazine: *Reflections* (150 monthly). Turnover £280,000 to year end Aug 02.

Belfast Central Mission, Grosvenor House, 5 Glengall Street, Belfast BT12 5AD
☎028 9024 1917 🖷028 9024 05[illegible]7
E: dker@belfastcentralmission.org
Web: www.belfastcentralmission.org
Chaplaincy, social work, counselling, pastoral care, accommodation for children and elderly people, conference facilities.
Superintendent: Rev Donald Ker. Executive 7, Other staff 140. ***CC*** No.XN 46[illegible]01. Began 1889; Methodist. Magazine: *BCM in Focus* (3,000 frequency n/a). Turnover £3,000,000 to year end Dec 04.

Belfast City Mission, Church House, Fisherwick Place, Belfast BT1 6DW
☎028 9032 0557 🖷028 9043 9950
E: info@belfastcitymission.com
Web: www.belfastcitymission.com
Evangelism through home visitation, door-to-door, hospitals, prisons, open air witness, Gospel, youth, children's meetings.
Executive Secretary: Mr George Ferguson. *Assistant Secretary:* Mr Robin Fairbairn. Executive staff 2, Other staff 25. **CC** No.XN 45106. Began 1827; Presbyterian. Magazine: *Annual Report* (7,500 annually). Turnover £500,000 to year end Dec 02.

***Birmingham City Mission**, 75 Watery Lane, Middleway, Bordesley, Birmingham B9 4HN
☎0121 766 6603 🖷0121 766 6727
E: office@birminghamcitymission.co.uk
Web: www.birminghamcitymission.co.uk
Reaching all with the Gospel through evangelistic and social work.
Executive Director: Mr Wesley Erpen. *Company Secretary:* Mr Alan Cutler. *Finance Director:* Mr Rob Warner. Executive staff 6, Other staff 77. **CC** No.1051023. Began 1966; interdenominational. No magazine. Turnover £1,524,800 to year end Mar 05.

***Bridge Community Trust**, 135 Ravenhill Road, Belfast BT6 8DR
☎028 9045 2321
Providing support and spiritual focus in partnership with local churches to lower Ravenhill area of Belfast.
Chairperson: Dr Connor Mulholland. No paid staff. **CC** No.XN 69937. Began 1997; non-denominational. (Previously Bridge Christian Community). No magazine. Turnover £30,000 to year end Dec 02.

Brighton & Hove City Mission, 88 London Road, Brighton BN1 4JF
☎01273 609 484
E: office@bhcm.org.uk
Web: www.brightonandhovecitymission.org.uk
Evangelistic ministry to schools (assemblies, clubs); communities (visiting, literature); disadvantaged people (food, children's clothes).
City Mission Co-ordinator: Mr Tony Smith. Executive staff 2, Evangelists 4. **CC** No.251768. Began 1849; non-denominational. Magazine: *BHCM Newsletter* (800 quarterly) Turnover £86,000 to year end Dec 04.

British Association of City Missions, 47 Copse Hill, Brighton BN1 5GA
☎01273 503 344
Web: www.bacm.org.uk
Network of city missions giving mutual support, training and sharing of resources.
Hon Secretary: Mr Harold W Oakley. No paid staff. Began 1991; interdenominational. No magazine. Turnover n/a.

Coventry City Mission, PO Box 40, Coventry CV6 2PR
☎024 7661 5931 🖷024 7661 1000
E: office@covcitymission.org.uk
Web: www.covcitymission.org.uk
Evangelistic ministry to the whole city with additional concern for those with practical needs.
Director: Mr Neville Carpmail. Executive staff 1, Other staff 11. **CC** No.1090102. Began 1983; interdenominational. No magazine. Turnover £242,813 to year end Dec 04.

Darlington Town Mission, 18 Hartford Road, Darlington DL3 8HE
☎01325 356 454
Web: www.communigate.co.uk/ne/dtm
Giving Christian fellowship and practical aid to needy local people.
Hon Secretary: Mrs Margaret Senior. Missioners 2. **CC** No.235572. Began 1838; interdenominational. No magazine. Turnover £21,000 to year end Jun 00.

Derby City Mission, 32 Quarn Drive, Allestree, Derby DE22 2NQ
☎01332 606 488/489 🖷01332 606 489
E: derbycitymission@gmail.com
Web: www.derbycitymission.org.uk
Advancing the Gospel through evangelism; practical concern for people of Derby.
Director: Mr Geoffrey Holland. Executive staff 2, Other staff 5. **CC** No.702027. Began 1989; interdenominational. Magazine: *Newsletter* (1,000 every two months). Turnover £89,455 to year end Jun 05.

***East Belfast Mission**, 239 Newtownards Road, Belfast BT4 1AF
☎028 9045 8560 🖷028 9045 2561
E: info@ebm.org.uk
Web: www.ebm.org.uk
Caring for the needy, day centre, housing for homeless people, youth ministy.
Superintendent: Rev Dr Gary Mason. *Director of Care and Training Services:* Peter Quigley. Executive staff 3, Other staff n/a. **CC** No.XN 68566. Began 1988; Methodist. No magazine. Turnover £1,200,000 to year end Dec 04.

†***Edinburgh City Mission**, 9 Pilrig Street, Edinburgh EH6 5AH
☎0131 554 6140 🖷0131 467 0010
E: billstaig@ecm.org.uk
Web: www.ecm.org.uk
Evangelistic outreach, telephone helpline, counselling service, caring for poor, needy and homeless people, mission support.
Director in Residence: Mr Alan Barlow. *Administrator:* Mr Bill Staig. Executive staff 2, Other staff 17. **CC** No.SCO 12385. Began 1832; non-denominational. Magazine: *Sharing Life* (1,000 frequency n/a). Turnover £229,168 to year end Dec 02.

Evangelical Coalition for Urban Mission, 305 Cambridge Heath Road, London E2 9LH
☎020 7729 6262 🖷020 7739 5079
Partnership of networks and agencies to further the evangelical thrust in urban mission.
Secretary: Mr Michael Eastman OBE. Executive staff 1. **CC** No.326300. Began 1980; interdenominational. Magazine: *Urban Bulletin Incorporating City Cries* (500 half-yearly). Turnover £5,520 to year end Dec 01.

Friends International Oxford, Lamorna, 13 The Paddocks, Yarnton, Kidlington OX5 1TF
☎01865 559 370 Home: 01865 841 702 🖷01865 559 370
E: oxford@f-i.org.uk
Web: www.friendsinternational.org.uk
Evangelism and care of international students, equipping local churches to do likewise.
Team Leader: Mr Christopher Band. Executive staff 5, Admin staff 1. Began 1983; non-denominational. (Previously Oxford Ministry among Overseas Students). No magazine. Turnover £36,000 to year end Dec 04.

†***Glasgow City Mission**, 19 Elderpark Workspace, 100 Elderpark Street, Glasgow G51 3TR
☎0141 419 9090 🖷0141 419 9222
E: info@glasgowcitymission.com
Web: www.glasgowcitymission.com
Caring for hungry and homeless people, drug addicts, street girls, children and families.
Chief Executive Director: Mr Stuart Valentine. *Administrator:* Miss Susan Creighton. *Finance Manager:* Mr Iain MacDonald. Executive staff 3, Other staff 17. **CC** No.SCO 01499. Began 1826; interdenominational. Magazine: *Carer Magazine* (3,000 quarterly). Turnover £515,000 to year end Dec 02.

Lambeth Mission & St Mary's (LEP), 3 Lambeth Road, London SE1 7DQ
☎020 7735 2166 M: 07900 606 534 🖷020 7735 5814
E: emsm@fish.co.uk
Web: www.crossoverlambeth.com
Pastoral and community work in Lambeth and Vauxhall.
Superintendent Minister: Rev Michael Faulkner. Executive staff 1, Other staff 3. **CC** Began 1778; Methodist/Anglican since 1972. No magazine. Turnover £115,000 to year end Dec 04.

Leeds City Mission, Hunslet Hall Road, Leeds LS11 6TT
☎0113 271 8180
E: admin@leedscitymission.org.uk
Web: www.leedscitymission.org.uk
Proclaiming the Gospel to the inhabitants of the district. Chaplains to prison and police.
Superintendent: To be appointed. Executive staff 1, Other staff 2. **CC** No.234431. Began 1837; interdenominational. Magazine: *Prayer News* (500 monthly). Turnover £60,000 to year end Mar 04.

E

***The Light Project**, 1 The Mount, Boughton, Chester CH3 5UD
☎01244 400 221 Ⓜ: 07775 901 855
🖷0870 762 6371
E: info@lightproject.org.uk
Web: www.lightproject.org.uk
Working with 15 Chester churches in 30 community and youth projects; demonstrating good news relevantly.
Project Coordinator: Mr Chris Duffett. Executive staff 1, No other paid staff. ***CC*** No.1084941. Began 2000; interdenominational. No magazine. Turnover £15,000 to year end Dec 04.

Liverpool City Mission, 20 Mount Pleasant, Liverpool L3 5RY
☎0151 702 5399 (24-hour)
🖷0151 709 8886
E: admin@livercm.org.uk
Web: www.livercm.org.uk
Social and evangelistic work through mission centres, telephone ministry and chaplaincies, bookshop and coffee shop.
Director: Stan Chedgzoy. Executive staff 3, Other staff 13. ***CC*** No.234521. Began 1829; interdenominational. Magazine: *Voice in the City* (3,000 half-yearly). Turnover n/a.

London City Mission, 175 Tower Bridge Road, London SE1 2AH
☎020 7407 7585 🖷020 7403 6711
E: enquiries@lcm.org.uk
Web: www.lcm.org.uk
Extending the knowledge of the Gospel among the inhabitants of London and its vicinity.
Chief Executive: Rev Dr John Nicholls. Executive staff 8, Mission staff 20, Evangelists 127. ***CC*** No.247186. Began 1835; non-denominational. Magazine: *Changing London* (35,000 quarterly). Turnover £6,100,000 to year end Dec 04.

London Methodist Mission (North West Circuit), 32 Kingswood Avenue, London NW6 6LR
☎020 8969 4004 🖷020 8969 4004
Web: www.frmethodistchurch.moonfruit.com
Inner-city ministry and community projects based on 4 church centres. Rooms for hire.
Superintendent Minister: Rev Martin Tullett. Executive staff 3, Admin staff 1. ***CC*** Began n/a; Methodist. No magazine. Turnover n/a.

***Macclesfield Christian Mission**, 20 Arlington Drive, Macclesfield SK11 8QL
☎01625 266 300 Ⓜ: 07708 571 750
E: darren.hodkinson@ntlworld.com
Evangelistic outreach, hospital radio, schools/youth work, resource to churches, elderly people's homes.
Director: Mr Darren Hodkinson. Executive staff 6, Other staff 2. ***CC*** No.514550. Began 1889; non-denominational. No magazine. Turnover £20,000 to year end Apr 00.

***Manchester City Mission**, Windsor Christian Centre, Churchill Way, Salford M6 5BU
☎0161 736 7959 🖷0161 736 7959
E: mancitmis@aol.com
Web: www.manchestercitymission.com
City centre and district evangelism, social concern, district visitation, literature distribution, work with asylum seekers.
Evangelism Leader: Duncan Hunter. *Office Manager:* Mr M Beere. Executive staff 1, Other Staff 11. ***CC*** No.224626. Began 1837; interdenominational. Magazine: *Newsline* (3,000 every two months). Turnover £230,000 to year end Dec 04.

***Mission in Hounslow Trust**, 201 Nelson Road, Twickenham TW2 7BB
☎020 8744 5333 🖷020 8894 1917
E: hounslow.mission@btinternet.com
Web: www.hounslowmission.org.uk
Relief of sickness and poverty to share the Christian message.
Trustees: Mr & Mrs Colin & Madeleine Windsor. Executive staff 2. ***CC*** No.1031597. Began 1993; non-denominational. No magazine. Turnover £100,000.

Newtownabbey Methodist Mission, 35a Rathcoole Drive, Newtownabbey BT37 9AQ
☎028 9085 2546 🖷028 9085 9956
E: office@newtownabbeymethodist.org.uk
Web: www.newtownabbeymethodist.org.uk
Evangelistic outreach, worship and training, social caring, retirement flats for elderly people.
Superintendent: Rev Andrew Boucher. Executive staff 3, Other staff 7. ***CC*** No.XN 47068. Began 1898; Methodist. Incorporating North Belfast Mission. No magazine. Turnover £95,000 to year end Dec 02.

***Plymouth Methodist Central Hall**, Eastlake Street, Plymouth PL1 1BA
☎01752 660 997 🖷01752 229 911
E: pmch@surefish.co.uk
Web: www.plymouthcentralhall.co.uk
City centre evangelism among young and old people; including day centres and chaplaincies.
Superintendent Minister: Rev D Paul C Smith. Ministerial staff 3, Other staff 15. Began 1940; Methodist. No magazine. Turnover £500,000 to year end Dec 02.

St Giles Christian Mission, 62 Bride Street, London N7 8AZ
☎020 7607 4370 🖷020 7607 2522
E: admin@sgcm.co.uk
Web: www.sgcm.co.uk
Church ministry with social work in north of London.
Superintendent: Rev David M Page. Executive staff 3, Other staff 4. ***CC*** No.208434. Began 1860; evangelical. Magazine: *Annual Report* (500 annually). Turnover n/a.

***Shankill Road Mission**, 116 Shankill Road, Belfast BT13 2BD
☎028 9032 4345 🖷028 9023 6843
E: shankillroadmission@btopenworld.com
Promoting the welfare of local people through evangelism and social witness.
Superintendent: Rev W M Campbell. Executive staff 4, Other staff [illegible]4. ***CC*** No.XN 45423. Began 1898; Presbyterian Church in Ireland. No magazine. Turnover n/a.

Sheffield Inner-City Ecumenical Mission, 178 Abbeyfield Road, Sheffield S4 7AY
☎0114 243 6688 🖷0114 243 [illegible]56
E: office@utusheffield.fsnet.co.uk
Alliance of ten denominational and ecumenical churches; mission units and educational and community facilities.
Co-ordinator: Rev Dr John Vincent. Staff n/a. Began 1971; ecumenical. Magazine: *Where and When* (250 quarterly). Turnover n/a.

South London Mission, The Central Hall, 256 Bermondsey Street, London SE1 3UJ
☎020 7407 2014 🖷020 7407 3[illegible]85
E: secretary@slm-bermondsey.org.uk
Evangelism, worship, social welfare, accommodation for students and elderly women, supplementary school for children aged 5 to 8.
Director: Rev Sheryl Anderson. Executive staff 4. ***CC*** Began 1889; Methodist. No magazine. Turnover £300,000 to year end Aug 00.

South West London Evangelistic Mobile Unit, 56 Chestnut Copse, Hurst Green, Oxted RH8 0JJ
☎01883 722 037
Open air Gospel witness.
Hon Secretary: Mr R Reed. No paid staff. ***CC*** No.1074735. Began 1947; non-denominational. No magazine. Turnover £1,300 to year end Dec 05.

Southampton City Mission, Brooklands Courtyard, First Avenue, Millbrook, Southampton SO15 0LJ
☎023 8077 3132 🖷023 8077 7040
E: scm2scratch@tiscali.co.uk
City-wide evangelism through social action, schools, holiday clubs, training and teaching for churches. Coffee shop.
Projects Director: Name not supplied. Executive staff 2, Other staff 3. ***CC*** No.251142. Began 1963; interdenominational. No magazine. Turnover £70,000 to year end Mar 02.

Touchstone Centre, 32 Merton Road, Bradford BD7 1RE
☎01274 721 626 🖷01274 395 [illegible]4
E: resources@touchstone-bradford.org.uk
Web: www.touchstone-bradford.org.uk
City-wide community and interfaith work; student chaplaincy, resource centre.
Team Leader: Rev Geoff Reid. *Chaplain:* Deacon Marian Sharp. Executive staff 1, Other staff 4. Began 198[illegible]; Methodist. Magazine: *Touchlines* (450 every four months). Turnover £120,000 to year end Aug 04.

West London Mission, 19 Thayer Street, London W1U 2QJ
☎020 7935 6179 🖷020 7487 3965
Web: www.wlm.org.uk
University chaplaincy, day centres; projects for alcohol misusers, offenders, young homeless people; Chinese ministry.
Superintendent Minister: Rev Geoff Cornell. Executive staff 16, Other staff 80. Began 1887; Methodist. Magazine: *Cross Currents* (500 every two months). Turnover £2,500,000 to year end Mar 05.

Whitechapel Mission, 212 Whitechapel Road, London E1 1BJ
☎020 7247 8280 🖷020 7392 2726
E: mission@whitechapel.org.uk
Web: www.whitechapel.org.uk
Caring for homeless people, church activities.
Director: Mr Tony Miller. Executive staff 3, Office staff 2. **CC** No.227905. Began 1896; Methodist. Magazine: *Annual Report* (4,500 annually). Turnover £380,000 to year end Aug 02.

EVANGELISTIC AGENCIES (PRIMARILY IN THE UK)

***The 40:3 Trust**, PO Box 403, Coventry CV5 8WW
☎024 7650 4792
E: office@fortythreetrust.com
Web: www.fortythreetrust.com
Church-based and area wide evangelism within the UK and elsewhere.
Trust Director: Rev Canon Ian Knox. *Trust Manager:* Mr Darren Burgess. Executive staff 3, Other staff 1. **CC** No.327205. Began 1986; interdenominational. No magazine. Turnover £110,000 to year end Sep 02.

***Action Bookshare**, PO Box 144, Wallasey CH44 5WE
☎0151 630 2451
E: actionuk@btinternet.com
Web: www.actionintl.org
Training in personal evangelism and follow-up to produce mature believers through Bible study; also publishing.
UK Director: Mr Ingo Abraham. Executive staff 1, Other staff 4. **CC** No.1058661. Began 1959; interdenominational. Magazine: *Actionpoint* (1,500 quarterly). Turnover n/a.

***Activate**, 9 Criss Grove, Chalfont St Peter, Gerrards Cross SL9 9HG
☎01753 399 388 M: 07946 612 480 🖷01753 899 388
E: info@activatecv.org.uk
Web: www.activatecv.org.uk
Resourcing and inspiring Christian women to take God's love into the community.
National Co-ordinator: Mrs Ruth Adams. Executive staff 3. **CC** No.295075. Began 1966; interdenominational. (Previously Christian Viewpoint). Magazine: *Viewpoint* (2,500 quarterly). Turnover £75,000 to year end Aug 05.

***Aglow International**, PO Box 122, South Shields NE33 4WU
☎08702 407 934 🖷08702 407 934
Woman-to-woman full Gospel evangelistic ministry; Bible studies, literature; also in Ukraine, Belarus, Moldova, Romania.
National President: Evanne McVeigh. Executive staff 2, Other staff 2. **CC** No.327825. Began 1980; interdenominational. (Previously Women's Aglow Fellowship). Magazine: *Aglow* (6,500 twice yearly). Turnover £250,000 to year end Dec 98.

***Ambassadors for Christ**, The Elms, 61 Green Lane, Redruth TR15 1LS
☎01209 217 927 🖷01209 217 927
E: office.afcbritain@freeserve.co.uk
Web: www.afciworld.org
Evangelistic team working mainly in Cornwall.
National Director: Mr John Hills. Executive staff 3, Admin staff 2. **CC** No.249782. Began 1963; interdenominational. Magazine: *AFC Britain News* (1,800 every four months). Turnover £144,000 to year end Jun 01.

†Associated Bus Ministries Trust, 128b Westwood Road, Tilehurst, Reading RG31 5PZ
☎0118 941 9044
E: enquiries@busministries.org
Web: www.busministries.org
Mobile facility for evangelism with coffee lounge, video, displays explaining the Christian message.
National Administrator: Mrs Orla McBride. Administrative staff 3, Other staff 2. **CC** No.1002455. Began 1991; interdenominational. Magazine: *Bus Route* (2,000 every six months). Turnover £56,000 to year end Dec 02.

Biblical Ministries Worldwide, 17 Stuart Close, Brandon IP27 0HE
☎01842 815 479 M: 07763 378 759
E: evolsemaj52@yahoo.co.uk
Web: www.biblicalministries.org
Church-planting mission society from the USA.
England Field Leader: Rev James Love. Serving missionaries 18. Began n/a; evangelical. (Previously Worldwide European Fellowship). No magazine. Turnover n/a.
Scotland Field Leader: Rev Howard Davidson, 14 St Martin's Place, Haddington EH41 4NF
☎01620 826 699
Also at: Rev Fred Stonehouse, 20 Bankpark Grove, Tranent EH33 1AU
☎01875 615 507

***Big Ideas**, PO Box 39, Dinas Powys CF64 4ZX
☎029 2051 2247 🖷029 2051 1183
E: info@igniteme.org
Web: www.igniteme.org
Providing creative evangelism and training for churches, youth organisations; performing arts; youth discipleship initiative Ignite.
Directors: Mr Nigel James, Mr Gary Smith. Executive staff 4, Other staff 10. **CC** No.1047757. Began 1994; interdenominational. Magazine: *Yes* (2,500 quarterly). Turnover n/a.

***Blowing your Cover**, Christchurch Business Centre, Grange Road, Christchurch BH23 4JD
☎01425 280 425
E: admin@blowingyourcover.com
Web: www.blowingyourcover.com
Training Christians to confidently and effectively share their faith in their everyday lives.
Director: Mr Kevin Higham. Executive staff 1, Admin staff 1. Began 2005; interdenominational. No magazine. Turnover: first year of operation.

Alex Bowler Evangelistic Association (ABEA), The Exchange, Hamilton Road, Taunton TA1 2EQ
☎01823 338 440 🖷01823 338 440
E: alex@abea.org.uk
Web: www.abea.org.uk
Undertaking city-wide evangelistic missions and festivals.
Evangelist: Mr Alex Bowler. Executive staff 2, Other staff 2. **CC** No.1110930. Began 2005; interdenominational. No magazine. Turnover: first year in operation.

***Bridge-Builders**, Vision Building, 4 Footscray Road, Eltham, London SE9 2TZ
☎020 8850 0111 🖷020 8850 0777
E: admin@bridge-builders.net
Web: www.bridge-builders.net
Providing free gospels and training to encourage personal evangelism.
General Director: Rev Graham R Woolgar. Executive staff 1, Other staff 4. **CC** No.281910. Began 1908; interdenominational. (Previously Pocket Testament League). Magazine: *Bridge-Builders* (3,500 every two months). Turnover n/a.

***Bristol International Student Centre**, 45 Woodland Road, Clifton, Bristol BS8 1UT
☎0117 915 9826
E: bisc@bisc.org.uk
Web: www.bisc.org.uk
Offering friendship and events to international students of all faiths or no faith.
Coordinator: Miss Hannah Birtill. Executive staff 1, Other staff 2. **CC** No.298035. Began 1976; non-denominational. No magazine. Turnover £30,000 to year end Aug 99.

E

†**The Brotherhood and Sisterhood Movement**, Penge Congregational Church, 172 High Street, London SE20 7QS
☎020 8659 7899 🖷020 8659 1260
E: jtsocres@pengecc.freeserve.co.uk
Seeking to win men and women for Christ through informal worship, fellowship and community work.
General Secretary: Rev John Taylor. Executive staff 1. ***CC*** No.207686. Began 1875; interdenominational. Magazine: *Outlook* (800 every two months). Turnover n/a.

***Careforce**, 35 Elm Road, New Malden KT3 3HB
☎020 8942 3331 🖷020 8942 3331
E: enquiry@careforce.co.uk
Web: www.careforce.co.uk
Placing volunteers aged 17 to 30 with UK evangelical churches and caring projects for a year.
Director: Rev Ian R L Prior. Executive staff 4. ***CC*** No.279443. Began 1980; interdenominational. Magazine: *Annual Magazine* (5,000 annually). Turnover £134,000 to year end Mar 05.

Catholic Agency to Support Evangelisation (CASE), The Chase Centre, 114 West Heath Road, London NW3 7TX
☎020 8458 3316 🖷020 8905 5780
E: info@life4seekers.co.uk
Web: www.caseresources.org.uk
Promoting and fostering evangelisation in England and Wales.
Director: Mgr Keith Barltrop. Executive staff 4, Admin staff 3. ***CC*** No.233699. Began 1902; Roman Catholic. Incorporating Catholic Missionary Society and Office for Evangelisation. No magazine. Turnover n/a.

***Causeway PROSPECTS**, PO Box 351, Reading RG30 4XQ
☎0118 951 6978 🖷0118 939 1683
E: causeway@prospects.org.uk
Web: www.prospects.org.uk
Raising awareness, training and resource materials for effective spiritual ministry among people with learning disabilities.
Director: Mr Tony Phelps-Jones. Executive staff 1, Other staff 6. ***CC*** No.1060571. Began 1989; interdenominational. (Previously Causeway). Part of PROSPECTS for People with Learning Disabilities. No magazine. Turnover £150,000 to year end Mar 04.

***Chapel Lodge Ministries (Go Evangelise Mission)**, 71 High Road, Gorefield, Wisbech PE13 4NZ
☎01945 870 149 🖷01945 870 867
E: clm@christian-centre.com
Web: www.christian-centre.com
International revival and healing ministry; Christian book publishing. In fellowship with International Gospel Outreach.
Minister: Rev Les Warren. Executive staff 2, Other staff 2. Began 1976; Full Gospel. Incorporating Gem Books. Magazine: *Living Water* (1,000 quarterly). Turnover £20,000 to year end Dec 04.

***Chosen People Ministries**, PO Box 47871, Golders Green, London NW11 1AL
☎07886 324 869 M: 07886 324 869
E: info@chosenpeople.co.uk
Web: www.chosenpeople.co.uk
Evangelism and discipleship among Jewish people; UK and worldwide.
Chief Officer: Mr Daniel Nessim. Executive staff 1, Part time 1. ***CC*** No.1095644. Began UK 1999; non-denominational. (Previously American Board of Mission to the Jews). Magazine: *The Chosen People* (300 monthly). Turnover £30,000 to year end Jun 05.

***Christian Association for Youth**, 52 Lonnen Road, Colehill, Wimborne BH21 7AX
☎01202 881 334 🖷01202 881 334
E: info@obsessivebehaviour.com
Communicating the Gospel to postmodern culture through relational evangelism.
Chairman: Mr Bryan Mills. Full-time staff 1. ***CC*** No.295519. Began 1986; interdenominational. (Previously The Barn Christian Association for Youth). No Magazine. Turnover £60,000 to year end Apr 03.

Christian Business Men's Committee (CBMC), 29 Greyhound Road, London W6 8NH
☎020 7610 2191
Sharing Christ with business and professional people.
Chairman: Mr Steven Moussavi. No full-time staff. ***CC*** Began 1967; interdenominational. Magazine: *Businessmen & Christianity* (Circulation & frequency n/a). Turnover n/a.

Christian Enquiry Agency, 27 Tavistock Square, London WC1H 9HH
☎020 7387 3659 🖷020 7529 8134
E: cea@christianity.org.uk
Web: www.christianity.org.uk
Providing opportunities for people to enquire about the Christian faith; offering information and advice.
Director: Mr Jeff Bonser. Executive staff 1. ***CC*** No.297393. Began 1985; interdenominational. Magazine: *Newsletter* (20,000 half-yearly). Turnover £59,000 to year end Dec 04.

Christian Family Ministries, 32 Norfolk Road, Erdington, Birmingham B23 6NA
☎0121 350 6151 M: 07910 190 755
E: petecfm@aol.com
Web: www.askalfred.org.uk
Conducting evangelistic programmes to reach the whole family; training in evangelism; conducting non-threatening marriage seminars.
Director: Rev Peter Green. Executive staff 1, Other staff 1. ***CC*** No.516947. Began 1985; interdenominational. No magazine. Turnover £18,801 to year end Dec 00.

Christian Heritage, Round Church Vestry, Bridge Street, Cambridge CB2 1UB
☎01223 311 602 🖷01223 306 693
E: admin@christianheritageuk.org.uk
Web: www.christianheritageuk.org.uk
Explaining Cambridge's contribution to Christianity through video, walking tours, exhibition; apologetic and theological training.
Coordinator: Rev Ranald Macaulay. *Administrator:* Mr Martin Lo[illegible]n. Executive staff 1, Admin staff 1. ***CC*** No.10[illegible]6750. Began 1999; interdenominational. (Previously Cambridge Christian Heritage). No magazine. Turnover £100,000 to year end Dec 05.

The Christian Jew Foundation, PO Box 28775, London E18 2WT
☎01959 565 955
E: uk@cjfministries.org
Evangelism among Jews, preaching and teaching God's purposes for Israel and the Jews.
Representative & Evangelist: Rev Robert Weissman. Executive staff 1. ***CC*** No.1056947. Began 1989 (UK); interdenominational. Magazine: *Message of the Christian Jew* (300 frequency n/a). Turnover n/a.

***Christian Viewpoint for Men**, Isabella House, The Avenue, Combe Down, Bath BA2 5EH
☎01225 833 748
E: admin@cvmen.org.uk
Web: www.cvmen.org.uk or www.gg2w.org.uk
Providing training, encouragement and resources to men seeking to bring others to faith in Jesus.
Executive Director: Mr Richard Maryon. Executive staff 3, Other staff [illegible]. ***CC*** No.1071663. Began 1989; interdenominational. Magazine: *MOTA* (2,500 frequency n/a), *REACH* (2,500 frequency n/a). Turnover £145,000 to year end Oct 04.

Christian Witness Ministries, PO Box 179, Chatham ME4 6YA
☎01634 847 477
🖷01634 407 657
Reaching unchurched people through roadshows, using music, drama and contemporary preaching.
Director: Pastor Matthew Guest. Executive staff 1, Other staff 1. ***CC*** No.1062660. Began 1998; interdenominational. No magazine. Turnover n/a.

Church Army, Marlowe House, 109 Station Road, Sidcup DA15 7AD
☎020 8309 3519
M: 07958 997 455
🖷020 8309 3500
E: info@churcharmy.org.uk
Web: www.churcharmy.org.uk
Sharing faith through words and action, and encouraging Christians in their everyday witness.
Chief Executive: Mr Mark Russell. *International Secretary:* (from Feb 07). *Director of Evangelism:* Neil Biles. Executive staff 5, Other staff 500. ***CC*** No.226[illegible]26. Began 1882; Anglican. Magazine: *Share It!* (20,000 quarterly). Turnover £7,700,000 to year end Mar 00.

***Church Pastoral Aid Society**, Athena Drive, Tachbrook Park, Warwick CV34 6NG
☎01926 458 458 🖷01926 458 459
E: mail@cpas.org.uk
Web: www.cpas.org.uk
Inspiring and enabling churches to reach everyone in their communities through training, consultancy and publications.
General Director: Rev John Dunnett. Executive staff 7, Other staff 55. ***CC*** No.1007820. Began 1836; Anglican. Magazine: *Together* (10,000 half-yearly). Turnover £2,650,000 to year end Apr 05.

Church of Scotland Mission and Discipleship Council, 121 George Street, Edinburgh EH2 4YN
☎0131 225 5722 🖷0131 226 6121
E: mandd@cofscotland.org.uk
Web: www.churchofscotland.org.uk
Resourcing congregations for mission and discipleship.
Council Secretary: Rev Douglas A O Nicol. Executive staff 4, Other staff 40. ***CC*** Began 2005; Church of Scotland. (Previously Church of Scotland Board of National Mission). No magazine. Turnover n/a.

E

***Come Back to God Campaign**, Adelaide College, 3 Nineyards Street, Saltcoats KA21 5HS
☎01294 463 911 🖷01294 463 366
E: feedback@comebacktogod.org
Web: www.comebacktogod.org
Bible training college, postal enquiry, pastoral aid, conferences and literature.
Director: To be appointed. *Administrator:* Mrs Marilyn E Paterson. Executive staff 12. ***CC*** No.240168. Began 1956; interdenominational. Magazine: *Teamwork* (2,000 every two months). Turnover £145,500 to year end Dec 04.

Community of Celebration Christian Trust, 35 Cavendish Road, Redhill RH1 4AL
☎01737 778 760
E: celebration@ccct.co.uk
Web: www.ccct.co.uk
Promoting the Christian faith through support for ministry of members of Community of Celebration.
Secretary: Rev P Bradshaw. No full-time staff. ***CC*** No.266564. Began 1973; non-denominational. No magazine. Turnover £25,000 to year end Mar 05.

***Contact for Christ**, Selsdon House, 212 Addington Road, South Croydon CR2 8LD
☎020 8651 6246 🖷020 8651 6429
E: cfc@deo-gloria.co.uk
Web: www.deo-gloria.co.uk
Providing personal contact and follow-up service throughout UK.
Administrator: Mr Rob Bradshaw. Executive staff 1, Other staff 2. ***CC*** No.243305. Began 1975; non-denominational. A ministry of Deo Gloria Trust. No magazine. Turnover n/a.

Co-ordinating Group for Evangelism, 232 Browns Lane, Allesley, Coventry CV5 9ED
☎No telephone
E: secretary@gfe.org.uk
Web: www.gfe.org.uk
Coordinating evangelisation strategies, policies and programmes between denominations, para-church groups and Christian agencies.
Executive Secretary: Captain Jim Currin. Executive staff 1, Other staff n/a. ***CC*** No.1052321. Began 1990; ecumenical. No magazine. Turnover £25,000 to year end Dec 04.

Kenneth Copeland Ministries, PO Box 15, Bath BA1 3XN
☎01225 448 374 🖷01225 335 983
Web: www.kcm-org.uk
Teaching victorious Bible Christian living using events, broadcasting, teaching on digital media and prison ministry.
UK Director: Mr Martin Hawkins. Executive staff 1, Other staff 20. ***CC*** No.326392. Began 1983; non-denominational. Magazine: *Believers' Voice of Victory* (22,000 monthly). Turnover £2,221,000 to year end Dec 04.

***Cornerstone**, Cornerstone House, 5 Ethel Street, Birmingham B2 4BG
☎0121 643 1984 🖷0121 632 5136
E: admin@cornerstone.uk.com
Web: www.cornerstone.uk.com
Evangelism and social action through community centres, coffee shops, hostels, children's/youth work, family care.
Services Director: Mr Robert Lawley. *Community Director:* Mrs Susan Allchin. Executive staff 2, Other staff 42. ***CC*** No.510971. Began 1980; non-denominational. No magazine. Turnover £759,593 to year end May 05.

***Counties**, 30 Haynes Road, Westbury BA13 3HD
☎01373 823 013
E: office@countiesuk.org
Web: www.countiesuk.org
Helping county-based evangelists and churches with their evangelism programmes.
Chief Executive Officer: Mr John Wilkes. *Office Manager:* Jonathan Brooks-Martin. Executive staff 2, Other staff 45. ***CC*** No.264278. Began 1899; non-denominational. (Previously Counties Evangelistic Work). No magazine. Turnover n/a.

***CRIB (Christian Response to Islam in Britain)**, Global Connections, 186 Kennington Park Road, London SE11 4BT
☎0870 774 3806 🖷0870 774 3809
E: crib@globalconnections.co.uk
A fellowship of Christians involved in evangelising, dialoguing, debating and building relationships with UK Muslims.
Chair: Mr Bryan Knell. No full-time staff. Began 1998; interdenominational. No magazine. Turnover n/a.

***Cutting Edge Ministries**, 32 Farrant Avenue, Churchdown, Gloucester GL3 2BP
☎01452 536 328
E: RLeighUK@aol.com
Web: www.cuttingedgeministries.org.uk
Providing extended support to local churches for evangelism.
Evangelists: Rev Roger Leigh, Paul Arblaster. Staff 2. ***CC*** No.105[illegible]563. Began 1995; interdenominational. No magazine. Turnover £36,500 to year end Apr 05.

Damaris Trust, PO Box 200, Southampton SO17 2DL
☎023 8031 5319 🖷023 8031 53[illegible]9
E: office@damaris.org
Web: www.damaris.org
Developing resources which relate Christian faith and contemporary culture.
Director: Mr Nick Pollard. Executive staff 2, Other staff 6. ***CC*** No 1082499. Began 2000; interdenominational. Linked to Damaris Publishing. Turnover n/a.

Miss Daniell's Soldiers' Homes, Havelock House, Barrack Road, Aldershot GU11 3NP
☎01252 310 033 M: 0788[illegible] 554 [illegible]4
🖷01252 350 722
E: admin@sasra.org.uk
Providing a home-from-home environment where the Gospel can be proclaimed to soldiers.
Hon Secretary: Sqn Ldr Colin Woodland. *Missioner:* Mr Bill Woolfall. *Administrator:* Mr John Tucker. Executive staff 1, Other staff 2. ***CC*** No.23368[illegible]. Began 1[illegible]51; interdenominational. No magazine. Turnover £150,000 to year end Dec 02.

Daylight Christian Prison Trust, PO Box 82, Leominster HR6 6AD
☎01252 312 144 M 07909 966 7[illegible]
E: prison@daylightcpt.org
Web: www.daylightcpt.org
Preaching the Gospel in prisons, producing evangelistic materials for prisons, linking evangelical churches with prisons.
General Director: Mr Gerard A Chrispin. Executive staff 1, No other paid staff. ***CC*** No.1104726. Began 2004; interdenominational. No magazine. Turnover n/a.

***Department for Research & Training in Mission**, Baptist Union of Great Britain, Baptist House, PO Box 44, Didcot OX11 8RT
☎01235 517 700 🖷01235 517 715
E: mission@baptist.org.uk
Web: www.baptist.org.uk
Providing research and training in holistic mission.
Head of Department: To be appointed. Executive staff 4, Other staff 3. ***CC*** Began 1996; Baptist. Magazine: *Transform* (5,000 every four months). Turnover n/a.

*__Derbyshire Village Mission__, Epworth House, New Street, Matlock DE4 3FE
☎01629 760 735
E: info@derbyshirevillagemission.org
Web: www.derbyshirevillagemission.org
Rural evangelism uniting Christian schools work; prayer, praise celebration, children's mission social action.
Director: Rev Alf Waite. Executive staff 1, Other staff 4. **CC** No.504965. Began 1916; non-denominational. Magazine: *DVM Newsletter* (1,300 quarterly). Turnover £10,000 to year end Apr 02.

Door To Door Mission, 3 Church Hill View, Sydling St Nicholas, Dorchester DT2 9SY
☎01300 341 670
E: mail@doortodoormission.org
Web: www.doortodoormission.org
Enabling and supporting church-based door-to-door evangelism; supporting full-time evangelists.
General Secretary: Rev Frederick Serjeant. Executive staff 1, Other staff n/a. **CC** No.274796. Began 2005; non-denominational. No magazine. Turnover : first year of operation.

*__The Earls Court Community Project__, 24 Collingham Road, London SW5 0LX
☎020 7370 4424 🖷020 7370 4424
E: earlscourt@ywamlondon.com
Web: eccp-ywam.org.uk or www.ywam-england.com
Outreach to homeless drug or alcohol addicts, prostitutes and Arabic people. Also counselling centre.
Project Leader: Mr Samy Mansour. Executive staff 4, Other staff 8. **CC** No.264078. Began 1985; interdenominational. Part of YWAM. Magazine: *Earls Court Newsletter* (400 quarterly). Turnover £40,000 to year end Dec 04.

East + West Trust, Cornerstone House, 5 Ethel Street, Birmingham B2 4BG
☎0121 632 4462 M 07813 038 756 🖷0121 243 3339
E: eastandwesttrust@aol.com
Web: www.eastandwest.co.uk
Reaching, discipling British Asians for Christ; safe house for Asian women; training churches fusion music.
Team Leader: Mr Pall Singh. Executive staff 1, Other staff 1. **CC** No.1076444. Began 1999 interdenominational. Magazine: *East – West News* (5,000 half-yearly). Turnover £42,000 to year end Mar 03.

Ekklesia Foundation, PO Box 5244, Leicester LE5 3ZP
☎0845 004 9277 🖷0871 504 7007
E: miracles@EkklesiaFoundation.org.uk
Web: www.ekklesiafoundation.org.uk or www.ekklesiaonline.net
International multi-cultural prophetic & deliverance healing ministry; multiple internet sites.
Director: Rev Marshall W Durrance. Executive staff 1, Other staff 5. **CC** No.290127. Began 1981; interdenominational. (Previously Ekklesia Gold). Magazine: *Newsletter* (200 quarterly). Turnover n/a.

*__Evangelical Ministries__, 114a Holywood Road, Belfast BT4 1NU
☎028 9047 1100 🖷028 9047 1190
E: info@emins.com
Web: www.emins.com
Church faith planning, evangelism, discipleship advice, resources and training; Focusfest, The Mandate conferences, women's ministry.
Director: Mr David Millen. Executive staff 8, Other staff 5. **CC** No.XN 48447. Began 1965; interdenominational. (Previously Evangelical (Youth Movement) Ministries). Magazine: *In Contact* (2,000 quarterly). Turnover n/a.

*__Evangelism Explosion__, PO Box 363, Epsom KT19 9XR
☎020 8391 5200 🖷020 8391 5200
E: info@ee-gb.org.uk
Web: www.ee-gb.org.uk
Equipping churches to train their members in effective personal witnessing and discipleship.
National Director: Mr Peter Crook. Admin staff 1. **CC** No.269722. Began 1975; non-denominational. Magazine: *Update* (1,400 half-yearly). Turnover n/a.

†**Exploits**, PO Box 109, Hereford HR4 9XR
☎01432 265 432 🖷01432 263 408
E: exploits@compuserve.com
Web: www.olivetree.org
Using TV, radio, internet, conference halls, tents, open air meetings to fulfil Acts 1:8.
Evangelist: Rev Dr Christine Darg. Executive staff 1, Other staff 4. Began 1989; non-denominational. Magazine: *Exploits* (2,000 every two months). Turnover n/a.

*__The Faith Mission__, Govan House, 548 Gilmerton Road, Edinburgh EH7 7JD
☎0131 664 5814 🖷0131 664 2260
E: hq@faithmission.org
Web: www.faithmission.org
Evangelistic movement geared to reach all ages in rural areas; UK and Republic of Ireland.
General Director: Mr John Townend. Executive staff 5, Other staff 100. **CC** No.SCO 05119. Began 1886; non-denominational. No magazine. Turnover n/a.
Also at: *England Director:* Mr David Bennett, 10 Millgates, York YO26 6AT
☎01904 330 120
And: *Ireland Director:* Mr Trevor Matthews, 62 Glenavy Road, Lisburn BT28 3UT
E: hq.belfast@faithmission.org
☎028 9262 8286

*__Farmer's Christian Postal Service__, 53 High Street, Kimpton, Hitchin SG4 8PU
☎01442 240 511
E: secretary@fcps.freeserve.co.uk
Web: www.farmingchristianlink.co.uk
Promoting and encouraging Christian faith among farming community via internet; pastoring in rural Britain.
Hon General Secretary: David Shillitoe. No full-time staff. **CC** No.251982. Began 1934; interdenominational. Magazine: *Farmers Post* (3,000 annually), *Women's Circle Magazine* (400 quarterly). Turnover £3,367 to year end Dec 04.

*__Fellowship for Evangelising Britain's Villages__, 38 Griffin Road, Braybrooke, Market Harborough LE16 8LH
☎01823 321 016
🖷01823 321 016
E: hq@febv.org.uk
Web: www.febv.org.uk
Assisting village churches; rural evangelism to establish groups of living witnesses for Jesus Christ.
Director: Rev Graham Wise. Executive staff 7, Other staff 21. **CC** No.232793. Began 1919; interdenominational. Magazine: *Village News* (2,300 every two months). Turnover n/a.

Fellowship of Evangelistic Ministries, PO Box 187, Knottingley WF11 9XT
☎01977 674 244
E: morningwatch2@aol.com
Web: femonline.co.uk
Proclaiming and teaching the Bible-based message through its members, associates and our Academy students.
General Secretary: Rev David Moody. Executive staff 3. Began 1896; non-denominational. Magazine: *Sounding the Trumpet* (Circulation & frequency n/a). Turnover n/a.

E

The Festivals of Male Voice Praise, 90 Crookston Avenue, Glasgow G52 3PR
☎0141 882 2009
E: bill.rodger@ukonline.co.uk
Web: www.fmvp.org
Gospel witness through the medium of male voice song and related music publications.
Secretary: Mr William Rodger. No full-time staff. Began 1934; non-denominational. Magazine: *Interlink* (3,000 half-yearly). Turnover n/a.

*__Finnish Lutheran Mission__, PO Box 40, Lyndsey Road, Dagenham RM8 2RJ
☎020 8924 4136
Bringing the Gospel to people of other faiths in the UK. Funded from Finland.
Field Director: Name not supplied. Field staff 1. Began 1973; Lutheran. Magazine: *DelightNoor* (340,000 (worldwide) frequency n/a). Turnover n/a.

Firm Foundation Trust, 14 Hurst Way, Sevenoaks TN13 1QN
☎01732 741 581
🖷01732 459 918
E: rogerhm@attglobal.net
Web: www.firmfoundation.org.uk
Producing evangelistic and Bible teaching media for Muslims in English, Turkish and other languages.
Director: Mr Roger Malstead. Executive staff 1, Other staff 1. **CC** No.277298. Began 1992; interdenominational. (Previously Spear Trust). No magazine. Turnover n/a.

***Friends International**, 3 Crescent Stables, 139 Upper Richmond Road, London SW15 2TN
☎020 8780 3511 🖷020 8785 1174
E: info@friendsinternational.org.uk
Web: www.friendsinternational.org.uk
Mobilising and equipping churches to reach international students in the UK for Christ.
Director of Ministries: Mr Bob Dawson. *National Field Director:* Mr Peter Hayden. *Director of Operations:* Mr Stephen Knowles. Executive staff 3, Other staff 60. ***CC*** No.1094095. Began 1985; non-denominational. (Previously International Student Christian Services). Magazine: *Opportunity* (2,000 quarterly). Turnover £986,000 to year end Mar 05.

***Full Gospel Business Men's Fellowship International**, PO Box 11, Knutsford WA16 6QP
☎01565 632 667
E: fgbmfi.uk@NTLBusiness.com
Web: www.fgbmfi.org.uk
Reaching men for Christ through dinners, breakfasts and outreach events. Chapters (branches) throughout UK.
Chairman of National Council: John Walker. *National Executive Officer:* Mr Terry Waters. Executive staff 2. ***CC*** No.275987. Began 1976; non-denominational. Magazine: *Voice* (40,000 quarterly). Turnover £90,000 to year end Dec 04.

†**Genesis Arts Trust**, PO Box 8, Sandown PO37 6DY
☎01983 868 542 🖷01983 868 542
E: nigel@genesisartstrust.org.uk
Web: www.genesisartstrust.org.uk
Supporting the ministry of Nigel Goodwin in the professional world of arts, media and entertainment.
International Director: Mr Nigel Goodwin. Executive staff 1, Other staff 1. ***CC*** No.326035. Began 1982; non-denominational. No magazine. Turnover n/a.

***GiG - Hope for Wales**, 15 Violet Place, Whitchurch, Cardiff CF14 1HT
☎029 2062 3513
E: gig.cymru@virgin.net
Web: www.gobaith.org or www.beibl.net
Promoting evangelism, supporting local churches, encouraging growth, mentoring young people in Welsh-speaking communities.
Field Officer: Mr Arfon Jones. Executive staff 1. ***CC*** No.1078107. Began 1999; interdenominational. No magazine. Turnover £30,000 to year end Dec 04.

God's Squad Christian Motorcycle Club (UK Chapter), PO Box 437, Reading RG30 3DF
☎01792 480 391
Web: www.godssquad.org
Evangelism and chaplaincy among 'outlaw' motorcycle fraternity and associated fringe groups.
President: Sean Stillman. No staff. Began 1994; non-denominational. Associated with Care and Communication Concern, Australia. Magazine: *Squad Supporter* (Circulation & frequency n/a). Turnover n/a.

***Going Public**, Glenwood Centre, Circle Way West, Cardiff CF23 6UW
☎029 2033 7890 🖷029 2033 7881
E: info@goingpublic.org.uk
Web: www.goingpublic.org.uk
Evangelism in South Wales and Valleys; sex/drugs education for youth and adults; professional media services.
Directors: Paul Francis, Mark Stavers. Admin staff 2, Other staff 9. ***CC*** No.1019789. Began 1990; non-denominational. No magazine. Turnover £248,000 to year end Aug 04.

***Good News Crusade**, 15 High Cross Street, St Austell PL25 4AN
☎01726 639 45 🖷01726 722 82
E: info@gnc.org.uk
Web: www.gnc.org.uk
Evangelism through missions; equipping the Church worldwide; conferences, training courses, publications.
Director: Rev Don Double. Executive staff 2, Other staff 3. ***CC*** No.225483. Began 1960; interdenominational. Magazine: *Frontline Connections* (10,000 quarterly), *Frontline News* (2,500 quarterly). Turnover £285,000 to year end Mar 04.

Gospel Outreach International, South View House, Station Terrace, Fence Houses, Houghton le Spring DH4 6HR
☎0191 385 6655 M: 07951 713 295
🖷0191 385 8521
E: gordon@stoves-goi.freeserve.co.uk
Work and training in evangelism, Bible teaching.
Evangelist: Mr Gordon K Stoves. Executive staff 1. ***CC*** No.517006. Began 1985; interdenominational. No magazine. Turnover £10,000 to year end Mar 04.

Billy Graham Evangelistic Association Ltd, PO Box 2032, Woodford Green IG9 5AP
☎020 8559 0342 🖷020 8502 9062
E: ukoffice@bgea.org
Web: www.billygraham.org
London contact with Billy Graham and his team.
Director & Company Secretary: Miss Jean Wilson. Executive staff 1, Other staff 1. ***CC*** No.233381. Began 1956; interdenominational. Incorporating World Wide Films. Magazine: *Decision* (15,000 eleven times a year). Turnover n/a.

***Grassroots**, 8 Meadow Way, Rowledge, Farnham GU10 4DY
☎01252 792 387 M: 07899 894 199
E: info@grassroots.org.uk
Web: www.grassroots.org.uk
Evangelism, church leadership/planting, humanitarian aid agency; Grassroots Tanzania, The Living Room (Tenerife).
Directors: Hugo & Sharon Anson. Executive staff 2, Other staff 6. ***CC*** No.1060034. Began 1997; interdenominational. Magazine: *Grassroots* (2,000 quarterly). Turnover £60,000 to year end Dec 05.

***Gypsies for Christ Travelling With the Romani Gospel Waggon**, 36 C[illegible]nville Road, London E18 1L[illegible]
☎020 8491 0176
Web: www.gypsiesforchrist.org
Coordinating humanitarian aid and evangelism amongst gypsies in Eastern Europe and UK.
Chairman: Mr David Morgan. Admin staff 2. ***CC*** No.273789. Began [illegible]975; interdenominational. No magazine. Turnover £4,000 to year end Nov 05.

***Heart of England Outreach**, PO Box 470, Meriden, Coventry CV7 7YT
☎01676 523 050
🖷01676 523 050
E: heartofenglandoutreach@fsnet.co.uk
Pioneer evangelism; training and assisting existing churches; Christian centre and charity shop.
Director: Rev John Yates. Executive staff 4, Other staff 3. ***CC*** No.32[illegible]046. Began 1979; non-denominational. Magazine: *Central Vision* (500 quarterly). Turnover £11,451 to year end Dec 0[illegible].

Holy Fools, 93 Horns Road, Barkingside, Ilford IG6 1DQ
☎020 8554 7986
E: rokeytheclown@hotmail.com
Web: www.holyfools.co.uk
Proclaiming the Good News through clowning and circus skills; performances and workshops.
Director: Mr Richard James. No full-time staff. Began 1983; interdenominational. Magazine: *Foolish Times* (100 quarterly). Turnover £2,000 to year end Oct 05.

***Home Evangelism**, Tyndale House, 3 Grange Road, Egham TW20 [illegible]QW
☎01784 432 558
🖷01784 432 064
E: hq@home-evangelism.fsnet.co.uk
Web: www.home-evangelism.com
One-to-one evangelism; training and mobilising church teams; associate evangelists - HEAT.
Field Director: Rev Robin A Wood. *Administrative Director:* Mr Gerald Matthewman. Executive staff 2, Other staff 2, Field staff 22. ***CC*** No.223[illegible]73. Began 1874; interdenominational. Magazine: *BLAZE* (7,000 twice a year). Turnover £382,501 to year end Mar 05.

ICC, 4-5 Regency Mews, Silverdale Road, Eastbourne BN20 7AB
☎01323 643 341
🖷01323 649 240
E: info@icc.org.uk
Web: www.icc.org.uk
Spreading the Gospel through modern media.
Chief Executive: Mr Peter Martin. Executive staff 2, Other staff 40. ***CC*** No.1079801. Began 1976; interdenominational. No magazine. Turnover n/a.

***International Gospel Outreach**, The Oasis, Dwygyfylchi, Penmaenmawr LL34 6FS
☎0845 226 7027/01492 622 473 (Prayerline) Fax 0845 226 7037
E: admin@igo.org.uk
Web: www.igo.org.uk
Fellowship of ministers, Christian workers, intercessors; network of churches and Christian organisations; worldwide missionary link-up.
General Secretary: Rev Bob Searle. Executive staff 9, Office staff 4, Field staff 270. **CC** No.1048524. Began 1967; interdenominational. Incorporating North Wales Gospel Outreach (NOWGO). Magazine: *Vision* (600 monthly). Turnover n/a.
Also at: *President:* Rev Kingsley Armstrong, Joshua House, 27 Crestbrooke, Northallerton DL7 8YP
☎01609 771 027
M: 07712 323 027 7305
E: kingsley@thejoshuaproject.co.uk

The Internet Mission, Green Garth, Lowick Green, Ulverston LA12 8DT
☎01229 885 249
E: office@theinternetmission.com
Web: www.theinternetmission.com
Using the internet to tell people about Jesus; encouraging others to do the same.
Administrator: Mr Matthew Rich. Executive staff 1. **CC** No.1092215. Began 2000; non-denominational. (Previously E-vangelism). No magazine. Turnover n/a.

***Interserve - Urban Vision**, Cornerstone House, 5 Ethel Street, Birmingham B2 4BG
☎0121 643 7771
E: urbanvision@mabham.globalnet.co.uk
Providing specialist help to churches and Christian projects in multi-cultural urban areas of Britain.
Team Leader: To be appointed. Executive staff 1, Admin staff 1, Mission partners 24. **CC** No.1020758. Began 1984; interdenominational. (Previously Interserve - Ministry Among Asians in Britain). Magazine: *Streetwise* (1,500 half-yearly). Turnover included with Interserve.

***Into The Light**, PO Box 107, Glossop SK13 3WU
☎0161 620 8991 Fax 0161 620 8991
E: info@itl.org.uk
Web: www.itl.org.uk
Outreach to Muslims using the internet; distributing free literature; providing teaching and training for Christians.
Hon Secretary: Mr Philip Ronson. Executive staff 1. **CC** No.1082032. Began 1999; non-denominational. No magazine. Turnover £3,210 to year end Mar 03.

***Irish Mission**, Church House, Fisherwick Place, Belfast BT1 6DW
☎028 9032 2284
M: 07710 074 712 Fax 028 9041 7305
E: irishmission@presbyterianireland.org
Web: www.presbyterianireland.org/bmi
Evangelism, Bible teaching, children's work, youth clubs, video library, summer missions, church planting.
Superintendent: Rev David J Temple. *Office and Finance Manager:* Mr Nehru Dass. Executive staff 3, Other staff 4, Field Workers 12. **CC** No.XN 45376. Began 1710; Presbyterian. No magazine. Turnover £620,000 to year end Dec 04.

***Jesus Army (Modern Jesus Army)**, Jesus Fellowship Central Offices, Nether Heyford, Northampton NN7 3LB
☎0845 123 5550
Fax 0845 166 8179
E: info@jesus.org.uk
Web: www.jesus.org.uk
Campaigning evangelism on streets of towns and cities around the UK.
Senior Pastor: Noel Stanton. No full-time staff. Began 1987; Jesus Fellowship. Magazine: *Modern Jesus Army Streetpaper* (100,000 every four months). Turnover n/a.

***Jesus is Alive! Ministries**, 57 London Road, Southend-on-Sea SS1 1PF
☎01702 343 749
Fax 01702 394 077
E: jiaminsuk@aol.com
Web: www.jesusisalive.org.uk
Evangelistic campaigns nationally, internationally; ministering to Jewish people, inmates of prisons, borstals; relief.
Executive Director: Mr Paul Slennett. Executive staff 1, Other staff 3. **CC** No.1036183. Began 1994; interdenominational. No magazine. Turnover n/a.

***Jews for Jesus**, 106 Kentish Town Road, Camden Town, London NW1 9PX
☎020 7267 5597
Fax 020 7284 0302
E: uk@jews-for-jesus.org.uk
Web: www.jewsforjesus.org.uk
Making the Messiahship of Jesus an unavoidable issue for Jewish people worldwide.
UK Director: Mr Stephen Pacht. Executive staff 1, Other staff 4. **CC** No.1110425. Began 1992; non-denominational. Magazine: *Newsletter* (15,000 quarterly). Turnover £439,519 to year end Dec 04.

Kairos Trust, 30 St Matthews Street, Cambridge CB1 2LT
☎01223 311 130
E: bartow.wylie@friendsinternational.org.uk
Web: www.friendsinternational.org.uk
Evangelising and discipling overseas students in Cambridge and training those involved.
Coordinator: Mr Bartow Wylie. Executive staff 1, Other staff 3. **CC** No.279068. Began 1981; interdenominational. In partnership with Friends International. No magazine. Turnover £39,000 to year end Apr 03.

***Label of Love**, The Good News Centre, 67 Wright Street, Hull HU2 8JD
☎01482 211 379
Fax 01482 322 692
E: john@labeloflove.co.uk
Web: www.labeloflove.org
Undertaking evangelistic events and work in secondary schools; videos, music.
Project Manager: John Flavell. Executive staff 1, Other staff 5. **CC** No.1061328. Began 1996; non-denominational. Turnover n/a.

***Lay Witness Movement**, 7 Sandown Road, Toton, Beeston, Nottingham NG9 6GL
☎0115 877 3827
E: lwm@laywitness.org.uk
Web: www.laywitness.org.uk
Spiritual stocktaking weekends for churches and individuals based on small group discussion and testimony.
Acting General Secretaries: Alan & Jennifer Goulden. Executive staff 2. **CC** No.328365. Began 1976; interdenominational. No magazine. Turnover n/a.

Light for the Last Days, Box BM-4226, London WC1N 3XX
☎020 8445 1451 Fax 020 8445 1451
E: enquiries@lightforthelastdays.co.uk
Web: www.lightforthelastdays.co.uk
Producing evangelistic material, Bible studies and tapes about current affairs and prophecy.
Editor: Mr Antony Pearce. Executive staff 1, Other staff 3. Began 1989; interdenominational. Magazine: *Light for the Last Days* (6,000 quarterly). Turnover £60,000 to year end Dec 04.

LMI – Logos Ministries International, PO Box 1131, Belfast BT5 4UD
☎028 9045 8362 M: 07802 844 610
Fax 028 9045 8362
E: info@logosministries.org.uk
Web: www.logosministries.org.uk
Church missions programme; youth and schools outreach; Bible teaching worldwide; training leaders for tomorrow's church.
Director: Rev Thomas McClean. Executive staff 4, Other staff 8. **CC** No.XN 46135. Began 1977; interdenominational. (Previously Logos Ministries). Magazine: *Edge* (3,000 quarterly). Turnover £163,000 to year end Dec 02.

Lord's Day Observance Society (Day One Publications), Ryelands Road, Leominster HR6 8NZ
☎01568 613 740 Fax 01568 611 473
E: info@lordsday.co.uk
Web: www.dayone.co.uk
Evangelism; exhibitions, children's missions; Sunday observance; book publishing, selling; religious, social, political meetings; prison ministry.
General Secretary: Mr John G Roberts. Executive staff 2, Other staff 10. **CC** No.233465. Began 1831; interdenominational. Magazine: *Day One* (12,000 frequency n/a). Turnover n/a.

***Love & Joy Ministries**, Bethel House, 77a Durning Road, Liverpool L7 5ND
☎0151 475 6878 Fax 0151 475 0005
E: info@loveandjoy.freeserve.co.uk
Web: www.loveandjoy.org.uk
Reaching communities with the Gospel through the medium of the arts and caring projects.
Director: Rev Dr Tani Omideyi. *Trustee:* Dr Modupe Omideyi. Executive staff 6, Admin staff 8. **CC** No.1050222. Began 1991; non-denominational. No magazine. Turnover £399,156 to year end Mar 02.

E

Evangelistic Agencies (Primarily in the UK)

Maritime Christian Ministries, 11 Worcester Road, Bootle L20 9AA
☎0151 922 5543 🖷0151 922 1415
E: stanmcm@aol.com
Web: www.mcmuk.org
Ministering to seafarers of all nations and their families, distributing the scriptures in 120 languages.
Director/Port Missionary: Mr Stan Sherrington. Executive staff 2, Other staff 1. ***CC*** No.1071480. Began 1998; non-denominational. Magazine: *Mersey Tidings* (2,500 quarterly). Turnover n/a.

***MEMO (Message On The Move)**, PO Box 199, Bognor Regis PO21 4PB
☎01243 263 717 🖷01243 266 389
E: info@me-mo.org
Web: www.me-mo.org
Displaying Scripture posters to the travelling public throughout the UK.
Administrator: Mr Peter Martin. No full-time staff. ***CC*** No.233136. Began 1883; Protestant. No magazine. Turnover n/a.

†***Men's Ministry (UK)**, 15 Highfield, Tebay, Penrith CA10 3TJ
☎01539 624 434 🖷01539 624 223
E: rod.readhead@btopenworld.com
Web: www.promisekeepers.org
Evangelism and discipling men by resourcing the local church.
Board Member: Mr Rod Readhead. Executive staff 1, Other staff 1. Began 1997; interdenominational. (Previously Promise Keepers (UK)). No magazine. Turnover n/a.

***Mission for Christ (Rural Evangelism)**, PO Box 69, Pond Cottage, Peasmarsh, Rye TN31 9AR
☎01797 230 888/230 886
M: 07801 334 281
E: admin@ruralevangelism.org
Web: www.ruralevangelism.org
Enabling the rural church in their mission to their local community.
Administrator: Mr Philip Stainer. Executive staff 2. ***CC*** No.242198. Began 1959; interdenominational. Magazine: *Action* (3,500 quarterly). Turnover £64,000 to year end Dec 04.

***Missions to Prisons**, PO Box 37, Kendal LA9 6GF
☎01539 724 075
M: 07754 160 138 🖷01539 720 475
E: m2p@greenstones.fsnet.co.uk
Holistic and evangelistic Christian ministry amongst people affected by imprisonment; mostly in the UK.
Founder Trustee/Hon Director: Rev Bob Spratt. No full-time staff. ***CC*** No.513862. Began 1974; non-denominational. Also Friends of Prison Fellowship Ethiopia. Magazine: *Prayer and Newsletter* (750 ten times a year). Turnover £31,000 to year end Dec 02.

NISCU (Northern Inter Schools Christian Union), 57 Lancaster Road, Carnforth LA5 9LE
☎01524 732 764
E: info@niscu.org.uk
Web: www.niscu.org.uk
Evangelism through area-based schools.
Secretary: Mrs Rosie Leavers. Executive staff 1, Other staff 14. ***CC*** No.246661. Began 1962; non-denominational. North West Evangelistic Trust Charity. No magazine. Turnover £341,000 to year end Dec 04.

***NGM (New Generation Music and Mission)**, Caedmon Complex, Bristol Road, Thornbury, Bristol BS35 3JA
☎01454 414 880 🖷01454 414 812
E: ngm@ngm.org.uk
Web: www.ngm.org.uk
Engaging young people in their own culture through mission, training and the media.
Directors: Ray & Nancy Goudie. Executive staff 3, Other staff 110. ***CC*** No.292923. Began 1981; non-denominational. (Previously New Generation Ministries). Magazine: *The Gen* (7,000 half-yearly). Turnover n/a.

***OAC Ministries**, 30 Garth Twenty, Killingworth, Newcastle upon Tyne NE12 6LN
☎0191 268 2829 🖷0191 268 2829
E: dave.glover@oaci.org
Web: www.oacgb.org.uk
Presenting Christ by all means everywhere.
National Director: Mr Dave Glover. *General Secretary:* Mr Norman Moderate. Admin staff 2, Other staff 22. ***CC*** No.295432. Began 1968; interdenominational. (Previously Open Air Campaigners). No magazine. Turnover £500,000 to year end Dec 04.

***Oasis Trust**, 115 Southwark Bridge Road, London SE1 0AX
☎020 7450 9000 🖷020 7450 9001
E: enquiries@oasistrust.org
Web: www.oasistrust.org
Demonstrating that Christian faith works by delivering practical solutions to people's needs.
International Director: Rev Steve Chalke. Executive staff 7, Other staff 60. ***CC*** No.1026487. Began 1985; interdenominational. Magazine: *Oasis News* (23,000 quarterly). Turnover £2,700,000 to year end Aug 02.

***Off The Fence**, PO Box 2206, Hove BN3 8LY
☎01273 733 732 M: 07843 356 016 🖷01273 719 249
E: paul.young@offthefence.org.uk
Web: www.offthefence.org.uk
Social action and enterprise; children in care, women at risk, homeless people; schools education.
Director: Rev Paul Young. *Director of Social Projects:* Mr Mervyn Weeks. Executive staff 2, Other staff 13. ***CC*** No.1108777. Began 1997; evangelical. No magazine. Turnover £350,000 to year end Mar 05.

***OM LUKE**, LUKE Training Centre, Little Cornbow, Halesowen B63 3AJ
☎0121 585 5662 🖷0121 585 0271
E: info@luke.om.org
Web: www.luke.om.org
Country-wide team-based evangelism, city outreaches, ethnic outreach, evangelistic training for local churches and foreign nationals.
Director: Mr Steve Critchlow. Executive staff 8, Other staff 37. ***CC*** No.100[illegible]196. Began 1989; interdenominational. (Previously LUKE (Love UK Evangelism)). A ministry of Operation Mobilisation. No magazine. Turnover £648,[illegible]00 to year end Dec 04.

***On the Move**, PO Box 7761, Birmingham B17 0BW
☎0121 427 3300 🖷0121 427 34[illegible]4
E: onthemove@btinternet.com
Web: onthemove.org.uk
Bringing churches together in evangelistic outreach to their community through free barbecues; international.
Director: Mr Martin Graham. *Missioners:* Mr & Mrs Nick & Cristina Hoult. Executive staff 4, Admin staff 1. ***CC*** No.1087[illegible]98. Began 1998; interdenominational. No magazine. Turnover £[illegible]91,000 to year end Apr 05.

Open Air Mission, 4 Harrier Court, Woodside Road, Slip End, Luton LU1 4DQ
☎01582 841 141 🖷01582 841 14[illegible]
E: oamission@btinternet.com
Web: www.oamission.com
Organising and encouraging open-air evangelism in the crowded places of the UK.
General Secretary: Mr Andy N Barton. Executive staff 1, Other staff 15. ***CC*** No.215409. Began 1853; interdenominational. Magazine: *The Master and the Multitude* (4,800 quarterly). Turnover £400,000 to year end Dec 02.

Our Inheritance Bible Ministries, The Old Post Office, 12 High Street, Polegate BN26 3AA
☎01323 484 052 🖷01323 484 07[illegible]
Web: www.oibm.co.uk
Undertaking evangelism, seminars, Christian Heritage exhibition, literature, outreach to all ages.
Field Director: David Driver. Executive staff 2. ***CC*** No.252040. Began 18[illegible]1; non-denominational. Magazine: *Our Inheritance* (1,400 quarterly), *Today Contender* (300 quarterly). Turnover n/a.

***Outlook Trust**, The Wycliffe Centre, Horsleys Green, High Wycombe HP14 3XL
☎01494 485 222
E: mail@outlook-trust.org.uk
Web: www.outlook-trust.org.uk
Bringing the Gospel to older people, working through volunteers and local churches throughout the UK.
Director: Mr David Heydon. Executive Staff 1, Other Staff 1. ***CC*** No.10231[illegible]. Began 1992; interdenominational. No magazine. Turnover £62,[illegible]00 to year end Dec 04.

E

Luis Palau Evangelistic Association, 120 Broad Street, Chesham HP5 3ED
☎01494 782 020 M 07958 907 598 🖷01494 786 507
E: info@lpea.org.uk
Web: www.palau.org.uk
Evangelism with church-based preparation and follow-up.
European Director: Mr Nigel Gordon. *NGA Mission Director:* Mr John Grant. Executive staff 2, Other staff 1. **CC** No.285474. Began 1979; non-denominational. Magazine: *Proclaim* (Circulation & frequency n/a). Turnover £220,000 to year end Dec 02.

†**Partnership Missions**, PO Box 783, Maidenhead SL6 CBL
☎01628 633 433 🖷01628 633 433
E: pmukusa@aol.com
Sending key teams to churches in the UK and abroad.
Liaison Officer: Mrs M L Clements. No full-time staff. **CC** No.281345. Began 1981; primarily Baptist. Magazine: *PM News* (3,000 occasionally). Turnover £40,000 to year end Dec 02.

People with a Mission Ministries, Perth Christian Centre, 28 Glasgow Road, Perth PH2 0NX
☎01738 639 792 🖷01738 622 928
E: office@pwamm.com
Web: www.pwamm.com
Evangelism in Scotland; teaching and training Christians; Spring Bible School; video ministries; ministry support centres.
Directors: Mr & Mrs Mervyn & Jane Milne. Executive staff 2, Other staff 30. **CC** No.SCO 14546. Began 1986; non-denominational. No magazine. Turnover n/a.
Also at: Mustard Seed Bookshop, Balcary House, Buccleugh Road, Hawick TD9 0EH
E: office@pwamm.com
☎01450 372 966 🖷 01450 377 732
And: Emmaus Road Bookshop, 41 Leslie Street, Blairgowrie PH10 6AW
☎01250 876 613

***The Philo Trust**, 141 High Street, Rickmansworth WD3 1AR
☎01923 772 288 🖷01923 770 088
E: admin@philotrust.com
Web: www.philotrust.com
Inter-church area-wide missions teaching the Church to communicate; mentoring young evangelists.
Director: Mr J John. Executive staff 1, Other staff 6. **CC** No.285762. Began 1981; interdenominational. No magazine. Turnover n/a.

***Pilgrim Hearts Trust**, 24 Yorkshire Place, Warfield, Bracknell RG42 3XE
☎01344 3[illegible]7 030 🖷01344 426 286
E: pilgrimhearts@ntlworld.com
Web: www.pilgrimhearts.org
Liberating, encouraging, promoting creative gifts in evangelism; art exhibitions, retreats, creative days; events, prison work.
UK Director: Elaine Chalmers-Brown. No full-time staff. **CC** No.1085766. Began 2000; non-denominational. No magazine. Turnover £3,000 to year end Dec 04.

Pilgrims Community, St Joseph's Convent, Brockhurst Lane, Monks Kirby, Rugby CV23 0RA
☎01788 834 633 🖷01788 834 635
E: info@pilgrimscommunity.com
Web: www.pilgrimscommunity.com
Evangelising, training and equipping youth and adults to evangelise in effective and creative ways.
Director: Fr Jonathan Cotton. Community members 6. **CC** No.1086358. Began 1989; Roman Catholic. No magazine. Turnover n/a.

***Proclaimers Church**, 38 Morgan Way, Bowthorpe, Norwich NR5 9JJ
☎01603 740 064 🖷01603 740 363
E: office@proclaimerschurch.com
Web: www.proclaimerschurch.com
Value-based business consultancy, audio and multimedia solutions, motivational speaking and generational communicational techniques.
Pastor: Mr Tom Rawls. Executive staff 1, No other paid staff. **CC** No.1108722. Began 1991; non-denominational. (Previously Kerygma International Christian Ministries). No magazine. Turnover £150,000 [Proclaimers International] to year end Dec 05.

***Project Evangelism**, Murlough House, Keel Point, Dundrum, Newcastle BT33 0NQ
☎028 4375 1480 🖷028 4375 1232
E: murlough@projectmh.org
Web: www.projectmh.org
Discipleship and outreach training in evangelism; Bible School; conference centre.
Director: Mr John Moxen. Executive staff 2, Other staff 3. **CC** No.XN 48651. Began 1969; interdenominational. Magazine: *Newsletter* (1,500 quarterly). Turnover £114,000 to year end Mar 03.

†**The Protestant Alliance**, 77 Ampthill Road, Flitwick, Bedford MK45 1BD
☎01525 712 348 🖷01525 712 348
Protestant evangelistic educational body engaged in answering the teaching of Roman Catholicism.
General Secretary: Dr Stephen J Scott-Pearson. Executive staff 3, Other staff 3. **CC** Began 1845; non-denominational. Magazine: *Reformer* (5,000 every two months), *Young Reformer* (Circulation n/a every two months). Turnover n/a.

The Railway Mission, PO Box 495, Bedford MK41 9WQ
☎01234 214 790 M 07718 971 919 🖷01234 214 790
E: DickLCrane@aol.com
Web: www.railwaymission.org
Offering Christian ministry to staff working in the railway industry throughout Great Britain.
Mission Manager: Dick Crane. *Chairman:* Mr Ian Markey. Executive staff 1, Full-time chaplains 8, Associate chaplains 6. **CC** No.248988. Began 1881; non-denominational. No magazine. Turnover £150,000 to year end Dec 04.

***Reaching The Unchurched Network**, PO Box 387, Aylesbury HP21 8WH
☎08707 873 635
🖷01296 434 143
E: info@run.org.uk
Web: www.run.org.uk
Envisioning, networking and resourcing; to prioritise unchurched in the mission strategies of the church.
Development Director: Rev Chris Stoddard. Admin staff 3. **CC** No.1080435. Began 1994; interdenominational. Magazine: *Runway* (750 every four months). Turnover n/a.

Reachout Trust, 24 Ormond Road, Richmond TW10 6TH
☎0870 770 3258
M: 07790 434 791
🖷0870 770 3259
E: rt@reachouttrust.org
Web: www.reachouttrust.org
Equipping and resourcing Christians; helping those in the cults and occult come to know Christ.
Director: Mr Douglas Harris. Executive staff 1, Other staff 2. **CC** No.1087085. Began 1985; non-denominational. Magazine: *Newsletter* (2,500 quarterly). Turnover £60,000 to year end May 04.

Reconciliation Ministries International, Zion Christian Centre, Little Cornbow, Halesowen B63 3AJ
☎ 0121 585 5294 🖷0121 585 5374
E: admin@rmiuk.org
Web: www.rmiuk.org
Advancing the Christian faith and relief of distressed people in the UK, Caribbean, Africa.
Evangelist: Rev George Miller. Executive staff 2, Other staff 1. **CC** No.800894. Began 1987; interdenominational. No magazine. Turnover £47,000 to year end Dec 99.

Reformation Ireland, 15 Lakeview Avenue, Mossley, Newtownabbey BT36 5ZG
☎028 9083 9117
M: 07801 756 112
E: raymond1517@utvinternet.com
Web: www.reformationireland.com
Calling churches and individuals back to the simplicity of Puritan theology and practice.
Secretary: Mr Raymond Stewart. Admin staff 1, No other full-time staff. Began 1992; Reformed and Calvinistic. (Previously Reformation Ireland: South East Antrim Reformation Movement). No magazine. Turnover £500 to year end Dec 04.

Rejesus.co.uk, 27 Tavistock Square, London WC1H 9HH
☎020 7387 3659
🖷020 7529 8134
E: info@rejesus.co.uk
Web: www.rejesus.co.uk
Website for people not involved with church to explore Jesus Christ and Christian faith today.
Director: Jeff Bonser. No full-time staff. **CC** No.1093647. Began 2002; ecumenical. No magazine. Turnover £33,000 to year end Dec 04.

E

Evangelistic Agencies (Primarily in the UK)

***River Christian Centre**, Vincent Street, Canning Town, London E16 1LZ
☎020 7476 1171
M: 07970 811 410
🖷020 7511 1019
E: info@riverchristiancentre.org.uk
Web: www.riverchristiancentre.org.uk
Outreach to young people, elderly people, 2 keyworker hostels, sports and community facilities.
Managing Director: Rev Roger Grassham. *Associate Minister:* Rev David Gill. Executive staff 3, Other staff 8. ***CC*** No.231370. Began 2003; Pentecostal but open to all. (Previously Mayflower Family Centre). Magazine: *River News* (500 quarterly). Turnover £215,000 to year end Apr 04.

Rural Evangelism Network, 4 Clarence Street, Market Harborough LE16 7NE
☎01858 414 930
M: 07720 322 213
E: ren@ruralmissions.org.uk
Web: www.ruralmissions.org.uk
Networking those involved from denominations and mission agencies in or concerned for effective rural evangelism.
Secretary: Rev Barry Osborne. No full-time staff. Began 1982; non-denominational. (Previously Federation For Rural Evangelism). Magazine: *Country Way* (4,000 every four months). Turnover n/a.

Rural Ministries, Wellingborough Innovation Centre, Church Street, Wellingborough NN8 4PD
☎01933 303 050
🖷01933 303 049
E: office@ruralministries.org.uk
Web: www.ruralministries.org.uk
Partnership of rural churches working together to establish an evangelical witness in Britain's villages.
Chief Executive: Rev Declan Flanagan. *Operations Manager:* Mr Robert Webb. Executive staff 2. ***CC*** No.200027. Began 1962; non-denominational. (Previously Datchet Evangelical Fellowship). Magazine: *Rural Challenge* (3,000 half-yearly). Turnover £130,000 to year end Mar 04.

***Rural Sunrise**, 4 Clarence Street, Market Harborough LE16 7NE
☎01858 414 930
M: 07720 322 213
E: sunrise@ruralmission.org.uk
Web: www.ruralmissions.org.uk
Enabling and assisting rural churches in total mission and evangelism; researching and publishing related material.
Director: Rev Barry Osborne. Executive staff 2. ***CC*** No.802305. Began 1988; non-denominational. (A division of Sunrise Ministries). Magazine: *Sunrise* (700 quarterly). Turnover £30,000 to year end Dec 00.

***The RZIM Zacharias Trust**, 97a St Aldates, Oxford OX1 1BT
☎01865 203 951 🖷01865 203 950
E: office@zactrust.org
Web: www.zactrust.org
Understanding evangelism, apologetics, training; aiming to reach the sceptic with the Gospel.
European Director: Mr Michael Ramsden. Executive staff 2, Other staff 5. ***CC*** No.1067314. Began 1998; non-denominational. (Previously The Zacharias Trust). Magazine: *Just Thinking* (65,000 every four months). Turnover £334,000 to year end Dec 04.

***Saltbox Christian Centre**, Bemersley House, Gitana Street, Hanley, Stoke-on-Trent ST1 1DY
☎01782 207 200 🖷01782 207 300
E: email@saltbox.org.uk
Web: www.saltbox.org.uk
Organising united prayer, renewal and evangelistic initiatives, and encouraging societal transformation.
Director: Mr Lloyd Cooke. Executive staff 2, Other staff 2. ***CC*** No.517299. Began 1982; interdenominational. Magazine: *Information Service* (1,000 monthly). Turnover £64,000 to year end Dec 01.

***Saltmine Trust**, St James House, Trinity Road, Dudley DY1 1JB
☎01384 454 800 🖷01384 454 850
E: mail@saltmine.org
Web: www.saltmine.org
Church-based missions, schools work, theatre company, family holidays, Trailblazers challenges; conference/meetings/dance studio facilities.
Chairman: Mr Dave Pope. *Ministry Coordinator:* Miss Jessica Poupart. Executive staff 4, Other staff 34. ***CC*** No.1038007. Began 1980; interdenominational. Magazine: *Saltshaker* (12,000 half-yearly). Turnover £1,000,000 to year end Mar 05.

***Sandes Soldiers' and Airmen's Centres**, 30a Belmont Road, Belfast BT4 2AN
☎028 9050 0250 🖷028 9065 2592
E: info@sandes.org.uk
Web: www.sandes.org.uk
Offering Christian mission to the Armed Forces, especially the Army and the RAF.
Mission Director: Mr T R Mearns. *Finance Manager:* Mrs G Jordan. Executive staff 2, Other staff 50. ***CC*** No.250718. Began 1869; non-denominational. Magazine: *Focus* (3,000 every two months). Turnover £600,000 to year end Dec 04.

Scottish Counties Evangelistic Movement, Challenge House, 29 Canal Street, Glasgow G4 0AD
☎0141 333 9900
E: office@scem.org.uk
Web: www.scem.org.uk
Evangelising in Scotland.
Committee Chairman: Mr John Allan. No full-time staff. ***CC*** No.SCO 15845. Began 1965; Christian Brethren. Magazine: *SCEM Gen* (2,000 quarterly). Turnover £20,000 to year end Dec 02.

***Scripture Union**, 207 Queensway, Bletchley, Milton Keynes MK2 2EB
☎01908 856 000 🖷01908 856 1[illegible]1
E: info@scriptureunion.org.uk
Web: www.scriptureunion.org.uk
Working with young people, families; schools work, missions, holidays, Bible ministries, training, resources.
Chief Executive/Team Leader: Mr Keith Civval. *Director of Field Ministries:* Ms Lesley Blight. *Director of Theology/Hermeneutics:* Mr John Grayston. Executive staff 4, Other staff 110. ***CC*** No.21[illegible]22. Began 1867; interdenominational. Magazine: *The Life* (25,000 quarterly). Turnover £7,611,000 to year end Mar [illegible].

†Scripture Union Northern Ireland, 157 Albertbridge Road, Belfast BT5 4PS
☎028 9045 4806 🖷028 9[illegible]73 97[illegible]
E: info@suni.co.uk
Web: www.suni.co.uk
Reaching children and young people, publishing and distributing resources and teaching materials; holiday missions and camps.
General Director: To be appointed. Executive staff 5, Other staff 5. ***CC*** Began 1954; interdenominational. No magazine. Turnover £320,000 to year end Mar 02.

***Scripture Union Scotland**, 70 Milton Street, Glasgow G4 0HR
☎0141 332 1162 🖷0141 332 760[illegible]
E: info@suscotland.org.uk
Web: www.suscotland.org.uk
Schools, churches and holidays based ministry reaching Scotland's young people with Christ's Gospel.
Chief Executive: Mr Andy Bathgate. Executive staff 4, Other staff 19. ***CC*** No.SCO 11222. Began 1867; interdenominational. Magazine: *@SU* (10,000 quarterly). Turnover £2,532,632 to year end Mar 04.

***Share Jesus International**, Tolverne Road, Raynes Park, London SW20 8RA
☎020 8944 5678 🖷020 89[illegible]7 51[illegible]
E: robfrost@sharejesusinternational.com
Web: www.sharejesusinternational.com
Evangelism and church renewal through Easter People; youth missions, leadership training and vision teams.
Director: Rev Dr Rob Frost. Executive staff 4, Other staff 6. ***CC*** No.1089[illegible]84. Began 1983; Methodist. (Previously Rob Frost Team). No magazine. Turnover n/a.
Easter People
☎020 8288 1966

Sion Catholic Community for Evangelism, Sawyers Hall Lane, Brentwood CM15 9BX
☎01277 215 011 🖷01277 234 40[illegible]
E: admin@sioncommunity.org.uk
Web: www.sioncommunity.org.uk
Providing prophetic, effective and innovative approach to evangelisation within the Catholic Church.
Ministry Director: Mrs Michelle Moran. *President:* Rev Gerard Kelly. Executive staff 37, Other staff 5. ***CC*** No.3279[illegible]7. Began 1984; Roman Catholic. No magazine. Turnover £250,000 to year end Mar 02.

***Soapbox Communications Trust**, PO Box 169, Cranleigh GU6 7WX
☎01483 268 467 M: 07739 966 805
E: admin@soapboxtrust.com
Web: www.soapboxtrust.com
Third world short-term projects, child care, prison ministry, worship ministry support.
Executive Director: Mr John Russell. *Project Officers:* Kathy and Shaun Murphy. Executive staff 2, Other staff 4. **CC** No.1088937. Began 1989; interdenominational. (Previously Soapbox Communications). Magazine: *SoapBox News Update* (Circulation & frequency n/a). Turnover £323,000 to year end Dec 04.

The Soldiers' and Airmens' Scripture Readers Association (SASRA), Havelock House, Barrack Road, Aldershot GU11 3NF
☎01252 310 033 ℻01252 350 722
E: admin@sasra.org.uk
Web: www.sasra.org.uk
Evangelism among Army and RAF personne and their families.
General Secretary: Sqn Ldr Colin Woodlard. *Administrator:* Mr John Tucker. *Members Secretary:* Miss Helen Black. Executive staff 9, Other staff 17. **CC** No.235708. Began 1838; interdenominational. Magazine: *Ready* (13,000 half-yearly). Turnover £650,000 to year end Dec 99.

***Sound of the Underground**, 37 Springfield Drive, Cinderford GL14 2TE
☎01594 824 011
M: 07774 273 420 ℻01594 827 372
E: pfl020865@aol.com
Evangelistic roadshow involving and encouraging local churches in outreach to youth using contemporary media.
Project Co-ordinator: Mr John Webster. Executive staff 1, Other staff 1. **CC** No.1057385. Began 1995; non-denominational. No magazine. Turnover n/a.

Sozo Ministries International, Sozo House, Alma Road, Romsey SO51 8ED
☎01794 522 511 ℻01794 522 577
E: email@sozo.org
Web: www.sozo.org
Preaching salvation, healing and deliverance to the church and to the world.
Director: Mrs Marion Daniel. Executive staff 6, Other staff 2. **CC** No.1042420. Began 1983; non-denominational. Magazine: *Newsletter* (300 every three weeks). Turnover n/a.

***Speak Network**, The Crypt, St Peter's Church, Northchurch Terrace, London N1 4DA
☎020 7249 4309 ℻020 7241 3248
E: speak@speak.org.uk
Web: www.speak.org.uk
Sharing faith through creative prayer and campaigning on issues of global injustice.
Director: Ms Louise Donkin. Executive staff 3, Other staff 6. Began 1998; interdenominational. Magazine: *Volumize* (3,500 quarterly). Turnover n/a.

Strangers' Rest Mission, 131 The Highway, London E1W 2BP
☎020 7488 4427
Evangelistic ministry and charitable work.
Pastor: Rev Gerald Daley. Executive staff 1, Other staff 2. **CC** No.209117. Began 1877; non-denominational. Magazine: *Occasional Notes* (800 every four months). Turnover n/a.

***TES (The Evangelization Society)**, PO Box 63, Cullompton EX15 2YQ
☎01884 356 58 ℻01884 356 58
E: office@tes.org.uk
Web: www.tes.org.uk
Supporting evangelists and evangelism in the UK.
Trust Manager: Mr Peter Day. Executive staff 1. **CC** No.245273. Began 1864; interdenominational. Magazine: *News Updates* (6,000 half-yearly). Turnover £36,000 to year end Mar 05.

Through Faith Missions, 73 High Street, Coton, Cambridge CB3 7PL
☎01954 210 239 ℻08707 062 062
E: admin@through-faith-missions.org
Web: www.through-faith-missions.org
Conducting interdenominational missions in towns and villages; large and small scale; training in evangelism.
Evangelists: Rev Daniel H Cozens, Rev Peter Adams. Executive staff 2, Other staff 5. **CC** No.801113. Began 1992; interdenominational. (Previously Walk of 1000 men). Magazine: *Through Faith Prayerletter* (6,500 frequency n/a). Turnover £258,000 to year end Dec 04.

***Treasures in Heaven Trust**, PO Box 26, Sevenoaks TN15 0ZP
☎01732 834 297 ℻01732 834 298
E: treasuresheaven1@btconnect.com
Offering cringe-free evangelism, training, Bible teaching, church weekends; presentations to enrich marriage and family life.
Director: Mr Max Sinclair. Executive staff 2, Admin staff 1. **CC** No.1073068. Began 1998; interdenominational. No magazine. Turnover £45,000 to year end Dec 04.

United Beach Missions, Spring Cottage, Spring Road, Leeds LS6 1AD
☎0113 230 4362 ℻0113 230 4363
E: office@ubm.org.uk
Web: ubm.org.uk
Reaching families for Christ on the beaches of UK, Ireland, France and Belgium.
Executive Officer: Mr Graham Kneale. *Office Manager:* Adele Anderton. Executive staff 1, Other staff 1. **CC** No.273912. Began 1952; non-denominational. Associated with Young Life. No magazine. Turnover £230,000 to year end Sep 04.
Also at: *Office Manager:* Mr Bertie Coffey, 218 York Street, Belfast BT15 1GY
E: irishoffice@ubm.org.uk
☎028 9074 7677

***Universities and Colleges Christian Fellowship (UCCF)**, 38 De Montfort Street, Leicester LE1 7GP
☎0116 255 1700 ℻0116 255 5672
E: email@uccf.org.uk
Web: www.uccf.org.uk
Supporting CUs in universities and colleges; evangelism; training student leaders; overseas student work; publishing (IVP).
Director: Mr Richard Cunningham. Executive staff 2, Other staff 83. **CC** No.273458. Began 1928; non-denominational. Linked to IVP. Magazine: *NB* (15,000 quarterly). Turnover £2,961,000 to year end Apr 05.

***Viz-A-Viz, Phoenix Court**, Christopher Martin Road, Basildon SS14 3EZ
☎01268 530 531 ℻01268 530 999
E: info@vizaviz.org
Web: www.vizaviz.org
Evangelising unchurched people and helping the church to do the same.
General Director: Rev Dennis Pethers. *Executive Director:* Mr Simon Parish. *Finance Director:* Mr Ian Rudd. Executive staff 4, Admin staff 4, Other staff 30. **CC** No.1031486. Began 1993; non-denominational. No magazine. Turnover £500,000 to year end May 05.

***Wales Lausanne Cymru**, 23 Cherry Tree Road, The Bryn, Pontllanfraith, Blackwood NP12 2PY
☎01495 223 255
M: 07960 165 548 ℻01495 226 054
E: ronspillards@btopenworld.com
Web: www.lausanne.org
Furthering in Wales the purposes of the International Lausanne movement.
Executive Chair: Mr Ron Spillards. No full-time staff. Began 1994; interdenominational. No magazine. Turnover n/a.

†***Walk Like Jesus Walked**, The Gateway, Addlewell Lane, Yeovil BA20 1AQ
☎0870 749 4147
M: 07974 975 064
E: admin@wljw.org
Web: www.wljw.org
Mobilising and equipping Christians to walk like Jesus walked; through media, community, conferences, speaking, worship.
Director: Mr Mark Bowness. Executive staff 1, Other staff 11. **CC** Began 1998; interdenominational. Magazine: *The Walk Magazine* (10,000 quarterly). Turnover n/a.

***Willow Creek Association (UK)**, PO Box 966, Southampton SO15 2WT
☎0845 130 0909 ℻023 8082 9765
E: info@willowcreek.org.uk
Web: www.willowcreek.org.uk
Helping churches build biblically-functioning communities through resources, training, seminars, conferences and membership.
Chairman: Mr Wallace Pepper. Admin staff 5. **CC** No.1069726. Began 1994; interdenominational. (Previously WCA (UK)). Magazine: *Willow* (1,000 quarterly). Turnover n/a.

E

Women in Mission, 7 Barleyfield Way, Witney OX28 1AA
☎01993 772 544
E: info@women-in-mission.co.uk
Web: www.women-in-mission.co.uk
Equipping and encouraging women in evangelism and mission through national and regional conferences and events.
Chair: Rev Penny Joyce. Executive staff 3. **CC** No.1067727. Began 1995; interdenominational. No magazine. Turnover £18,000 to year end Dec 02.

The Word for Life Trust, The House of Bread, Ross Road, Christchurch, Coleford GL16 7NS
☎01594 837 744 🖷01594 837 742
E: wflt@wflt.org
Web: www.wflt.org
Providing counselling, prayer ministry, healing, retreats, quiet days, training programmes; home and away.
Director: Rev Elizabeth Brazell. *Chairman:* Mr Harvey Bromley. Executive staff 4, Other staff 4. **CC** No.1071313. Began 1998; non-denominational. ACC affiliated. No magazine. Turnover £240,000 to year end Dec 04.

WorkNet, 56 Baldry Gardens, London SW16 3DJ
☎020 8764 8080 🖷020 8764 8080
E: info@worknetuk.org
Web: www.worknetuk.org
Providing spiritual resources for the work place including the Work Talk course.
National Director: Geoff Shattock. Executive staff 1. **CC** No.1069411. Began 1997; non-denominational. No magazine. Turnover n/a.

***World Team UK**, 10 Pringle Gardens, London SW16 1SH
☎020 8769 6343
E: adrianfricker@worldteam.org
Web: www.worldteam.org
Evangelism, discipleship and church planting among ethnic minorities in relationship with local churches.
Field Director: Mr Adrian Fricker. Executive staff 1, Other staff 9. **CC** No.327703. Began 1986; interdenominational. Magazine: *World Team Advance* (1,000 quarterly). Turnover £6,000 to year end Dec 96.

World Vision for Christ, 70 Sixth Avenue, Manor Park, London E12 5PR
☎020 8478 1073 / 8514 1820
🖷020 8553 9855
E: info@wvfc.co.uk
Web: www.wvfc.co.uk
International full gospel ministry; presenting Christ to all.
Director: Dr Albert Chambers. Executive staff 5. **CC** No.288179. Began 1969; interdenominational. Magazine: *Unlimited Horizons* (4,000 every two months). Turnover n/a.

***Worldwide Harvest Ministries**, 41 Marlow Road, Maidenhead SL6 7AQ
☎01628 621 727
🖷01628 777 084
E: wwhuk@compuserve.com
Web: www.worldwideharvest.org
Evangelism and church planting through Gospel crusades.
President: Rev Eric Cowley. Admin staff 1. **CC** No.1005119. Began 1990; interdenominational. No magazine. Turnover £16,203 to year end Dec 93.

Youth For Christ, PO Box 5254, Halesowen B63 3DG
☎0121 550 8055
🖷0121 550 9979
E: yfc@yfc.co.uk
Web: www.yfc.co.uk
Evangelistic youth outreach through creative arts, church-based missions, schools work, community involvement and training.
National Director: Mr Roy Crowne. *Director of Local Ministries:* Mr Richard Bromley. *Director of Evangelism:* Mr Dave Newton. Executive staff 5. Other staff 145. **CC** No.263446. Began 1947; interdenominational. (Previously British Youth For Christ. Merged with Covenanters April 2000). Magazine: *Into View* (4,500 termly). Turnover £2,276,000 to year end Dec 04.

EVANGELISTS (INDEPENDENT)

†Ian and Rosemary Andrews (Citadel Ministries), PO Box 28, Chard TA20 1LT
☎01460 625 42
E: citmin@ntlworld.com
Signs, wonders, teaching and equipping; worldwide.
Leader: Mr Ian Andrews. Executive staff 1, Other staff 1. **CC** No.802969. Began 1969; Independent. No magazine. Turnover n/a.

Association of Evangelists, 15 Stirling Crescent, Horsforth, Leeds LS18 5SJ
☎0113 258 1183 🖷0113 258 1183
E: assocevang@aol.com
Web: www.theevangelist.org.uk
Association of independent evangelists. Linked to the Metropolitan Mission in Andra Pradesh, India.
Director: Name not supplied. Executive staff 4, Other staff 2. **CC** No.266005. Began 1983; interdenominational. No magazine. Turnover n/a.

***Ann Baker**, 60 Earlham Grove, Weston-super-Mare BS23 3JJ
☎01934 627 789
Missions, camps, Bible teaching for children, youth, adults; leadership training; Great Britain and Europe.
Evangelist: Miss Ann Baker. Executive staff 1. Began 1971; Baptist. No magazine. Turnover n/a.

***Blessed Hope of Christ Evangelistic Ministry**, 14 Nine Acres Close, Manor Park, London E12 6AU
☎020 8478 1769 🖷020 8478 1769
E: williamptey@lineone.net
Holding city crusades and revivals; teaching seminars on evangelism, cults, Islam, spiritual warfare prayer, intercession.
Evangelist: Rev William Lamptey. Executive staff 1. **CC** No.1082061. Began 1993; non-denominational. No magazine. Turnover £8,000 to year end Dec 04.

Christopher Brown, 11 Brownings Road, Cannington, Bridgwater TA5 2RH
☎01278 653 586 🖷01278 653 706
E: chris@my-church.co.uk
Web: www.webchristian.org.uk
Bible-based teaching and evangelism; nationwide.
Evangelist: Rev Christopher Brown. Executive staff 1. Began 1999; interdenominational. No magazine. Turnover n/a.

Roger Carswell, 15 Stirling Crescent, Horsforth, Leeds LS18 5SJ
☎0113 258 1183 🖷0113 258 1183
E: carswell77@aol.com
Web: www.tell-me-more.org
Preaching the Gospel, writing and publishing evangelistic literature, evangelism training.
Evangelist: Mr Roger Carswell. Executive staff 1. Began 1983; Independent. Magazine: *Newsletter* (2,000 quarterly). Turnover n/a.

Crossfire Trust, 95 Darkley Road, Keady, Armagh BT60 3AY
☎028 3753 1636 🖷028 3753 88[illegible]
E: admin@crossfiretrust.net
Web: www.crossfiretrust.net
Making God's love real to the people of south Armagh.
Director: Mr Ian Bothwell. Executive staff 2, Other staff 2. **CC** No.XO 84[illegible]85. Began 1980; Independent. (Previously Ian Bothwell (Crossfire Trust)). Magazine: *Crossfire Trust News* (700 quarterly). Turnover n/a.

Exousia Trust (Sean Stillman), PO Box 437, Reading RG30 3DF
☎01792 480 391 🖷01792 480 39[illegible]
E: office@exousia.demon.co.uk
Web: www.exousia.demon.co.uk or www.zacsplace.org
Supporting Sean Stillman and associated projects including 'Bibles for Bikers' and 'Zac's Place'.
Evangelist: Rev Sean Stillman. Executive staff 1. **CC** No.100258[illegible]. Began 19[illegible]1; interdenominational. Magazine: *Newsletter* (600 half-yearly). Turnover £27,000 to year end Apr 02.

Gus Eyre (Cedarwood Ministries - Association of Evangelists), 23 Warwick Road, Lytham St Annes FY8 1TX
☎01253 728 465 M: 07951 831 893 Fax 01253 728 465
E: guseyre@carcon.co.uk
Contemporary singer/songwriter and preacher; themed audio-visual presentations for all ages; churches, prisons, students, overseas.
Evangelist: Mr Gus Eyre. Executive staff 2. Began 1976; interdenominational. Magazine: *Newsletter* (300 every four months). Turnover n/a.

Paul Gunstone, 48 St Peter's Crescent, Bexhill-on-Sea TN40 2EJ
☎01424 222 224
Evangelist to elderly people, going into homes with the Gospel, in Bexhill, Hastings and St Leonards.
Evangelist: Paul Gunstone. Executive staff 1. Began 1981; interdenominational. No magazine. Turnover n/a.

***Alyn Haskey (Freedom Ministries)**, PO Box 24, Nottingham NG3 4LD
☎0115 960 5489
E: alynhaskey@freedomministries.freeserve.co.uk
Web: www.freedomministries.co.uk
Local and itinerant evangelism and missions in schools, colleges, churches, clubs, conferences.
Director: Rev Alyn Haskey. Executive staff 1. **CC** No.327526. Began 1986; interdenominational. No magazine. Turnover £15,000 to year end Dec 04.

Tony Jasper, 29 Harvard Court, Honeybourne Road, London NW6 1HL
☎020 7435 4246 M: 07941 616 177
E: tony.jasper@blueyonder.co.uk
Speaking, preaching, conference organising, magazine compiling; visiting churches, schools, secular organisations.
Evangelist: Tony Jasper. No full-time staff. Began n/a; non-denominational. No magazine. Turnover n/a.

***Steve Legg (Breakout Trust)**, PO Box 3070, Littlehampton BN17 6WX
☎01903 732 190 M: 07966 484 754 Fax 01903 733 492
E: steve@breakout.org.uk
Web: www.breakout.org.uk
Creative evangelism in schools, colleges, universities, prisons and events in UK and abroad.
Director: Mr Steve Legg. Executive staff 1, Other staff 1. **CC** No.1070960. Began 1989; interdenominational. Magazine: *Breakout Update* (1,000 quarterly). Turnover n/a.

***Ian Leitch (The Heralds Trust)**, PO Box 813, Edinburgh EH14 7LR
☎01506 882 892 Fax 0131 449 6910
E: IL011F6147@blueyonder.co.uk
Web: www.theheraldstrust.org
Evangelism and Bible teaching, New Life seminars; UK, Europe, India, North America.
Evangelist/Bible teacher: Mr Ian B Leitch. Executive staff 2. **CC** No.SCO 06798. Began 1969; interdenominational. Magazine: *The Heralds Trust News Report* (3,000 quarterly). Turnover £90,000 to year end Mar 05.

***Life Discovery**, Cherry Tree Cottage, 55 Lee Street, Horley RH6 6HD
☎01293 823 823/774 260 M: 07850 445 398
Fax 01293 774 261
E: info@lifediscovery.co.uk
Web: www.lifediscovery.co.uk
Using activity programmes for adults to provide a platform for evangelism.
Director: Mr Jonathan Crouch. Executive staff 1. **CC** No.1064911. Began 1995; non-denominational. (Previously Discovery Ministries). No magazine. Turnover £30,000 to year end Dec 00.

†***Manna Ministries International**, 40 Stratheden Heights, Newtownards BT23 8TD
Fax 028 9181 2275
E: alanmanna1@aol.com
Web: www.heartbeat-music.com/manna
Ministering healing, wholeness, deliverance through music, preaching God's Word, prayer, counselling.
Founder: Mr Alan Cunningham. Executive staff 1, Admin staff 2. **CC** No.XR 15980. Began 1995; non-denominational. Magazine: *Manna Mail* (1,500 quarterly). Turnover n/a.

Mission Link International, PO Box 2214, Bristol BS99 7HL
☎0870 860 4973 M: 07779 606 279
Fax 0117 937 4545
E: info@missionlinkinternational.com
Web: www.missionlinkinternational.com
Ministry to churches through mission, evangelism, linking projects; emergency disaster team; child sponsorship; author.
Director Executive: Rev John Delaney. Executive staff 1, Admin staff 2. **CC** No.10099168. Began 2003; interdenominational. No magazine. Turnover £15,766 to year end Feb 05.

***Derek Moon**, 34 Fletcher Close, Torquay TQ2 6DD
☎01803 405 333
E: derekmoon@blueyonder.co.uk
Evangelism through organ/keyboard concerts with personal testimony.
Evangelist: Rev Derek J Moon. No full-time staff. Began n/a; interdenominational. No magazine. Turnover n/a.

†**Paul Morley**, 91 Green Street, Middleton, Manchester M24 2TB
☎0161 653 6626 M: 07860 470 812
E: Paul@morley54.freeserve.co.uk
Evangelism in schools, open air, missions, church planting, Gospel magic; UK, Europe, Africa and India.
Evangelist: Mr Paul Morley. Executive staff 1. Began 1980; Assemblies of God. Magazine: *Newsletter* (350 quarterly). Turnover n/a.

†**New Life in Jesus Gospel Crusade**, 50 Gilbard Road, Norwich NR5 8TL
☎01603 452 962
E: newlife@gospelcrusade.freeserve.co.uk
Undertaking evangelistic crusades, missions, Gospel singing, tent missions, men's outreach; throughout UK.
Evangelist: Gary Moore. Evangelist 1. Began 2000; interdenominational. No magazine. Turnover n/a.

Evangelists (Independent)

†***Proclaim Trust**, Champness Hall, Drake Street, Rochdale OL16 1PB
☎01706 638 803 Ⓜ: 07867 533 247
Ⓔ: admin@proclaim.trust.org
Web: www.proclaim.trust.org
Assisting local churches in UK and overseas in evangelism and equipping through teaching and training.
Evangelist/Director: Mr Barry Woodward. Executive staff 1. ***CC*** No.1076342. Began 1999; interdenominational. Turnover £3,767 to year end Feb 00.

***RSVP**, PO Box 55, Stowmarket IP14 1UG
☎01449 677 058
Ⓔ: office@rsvptrust.co.uk
Web: www.rsvptrust.co.uk
Evangelism and ministry to prostitutes, prisoners and poor; evangelism resources, healing ministry; UK, Africa.
Director: Rev Don Egan. Executive staff 1, Other staff 2. ***CC*** No.1093860. Began 1994; non-denominational. (Previously The Evangelism Fellowship). Magazine: *RSVP News* (4,000 annually). Turnover £87,000 to year end Dec 04.

Soteria Trust, 2 New Town, Chichester PO19 1UG
☎01243 771 494 ℻01243 771 240
Ⓔ: admin@soteriatrust.org.uk
Web: www.soteriatrust.org.uk
Effective missions for local churches in UK and abroad, helping poor in Nigeria.
Director: Mr Andy Economides. Executive staff 1, Admin staff 2. ***CC*** No.1040766. Began 1994; interdenominational. Magazine: *Soteria News* (600 every four months). Turnover n/a.

***Ron Spillards Ministries**, 23 Cherry Tree Road, The Bryn, Pontllanfraith, Blackwood NP12 2PY
☎01495 223 255 Ⓜ: 07960 165 548 ℻01495 226 054
Ⓔ: ronspillards@btopenworld.com
Itinerant ministry of evangelism and Bible teaching nationwide and overseas.
Evangelist: Ron Spillards. Executive staff 1, No other full-time staff. Began 1970; interdenominational. Linked to The Evangelization Society. No magazine. Turnover n/a.

David Stillman Evangelistic Association, PO Box 102, Reading RG30 3NP
☎0118 983 2221
Ⓔ: davidstillman@waitrose.com
Web: www.davidstillman.org.uk
International ministry of evangelism and Bible teaching; prison ministry in UK.
Evangelist: Rev David Stillman. Executive staff 1, Volunteer staff 1. ***CC*** No.269396. Began 1968; interdenominational. No magazine. Turnover n/a.

Time For Truth!, PO Box 1146, Kidderminster DY10 1WG
☎01562 824 337
Ⓜ: 07958 489 994
℻01562 824 337
Encouraging Christians to evangelise; christian literature.
Partner: Mr John E Davis. Executive staff 2. Began 1998; interdenominational. No magazine. Turnover n/a.

***The Twenty Five Trust**, PO Box 250, Sutton SM2 5AZ
☎020 8395 4951
Ⓔ: The25Trust@aol.com
Prison evangelism in UK and overseas.
Director: Rev Brian Greenaway. Executive staff 1, Other staff 1. ***CC*** No.327483. Began 1987; interdenominational. No magazine. Turnover £35,000 to year end Aug 98.

Keith and Maureen Venables (Living Word (Evangelistic) Ministries), 35 Croftson Avenue, Ormskirk L39 1NL
☎01695 574 462 ℻01695 574 452
Ⓔ: ven-ork@hotmail.co.uk
Preaching, teaching, evangelism, healing; nationwide and international.
Director: Mr Keith Venables. Executive staff 2. ***CC*** No.326359. Began 1976; interdenominational. No magazine. Turnover n/a.

†***Phillip Willer (In-Sight Communication Trust)**, 76 Fore Street, Chudleigh, Newton Abbot TQ13 0HT
☎01626 853 693
Ⓜ: 07762 738 018 ℻01626 853 693
Ⓔ: willer@in-sight.freeserve.co.uk
Web: www.in-sight.freeserve.co.uk
Evangelism, sport, holiday clubs, training, camps, open air, encouragement, preaching, schools, inter-denominational Bible teaching.
Evangelist: Rev Phillip Willer. Executive staff 1. ***CC*** No.801351. Began 1979. Magazine: *Newsletter* (200 quarterly). Turnover £15,000 to year end Mar 03.

***Keith Wills Evangelism Trust (Spearhead)**, Victoria Hall, Knowsley Street, Bolton BL1 2AS
☎01204 399 363 ℻01204 399 363
Ⓔ: keith.wills@virgin.net
Web: homepage.virgin.net/keith.wills/index.htm
Helping churches to reach a whole community for Christ.
Evangelist: Mr Keith Wills. Executive staff 1. ***CC*** No.327150. Began 1974; interdenominational. Magazine: *Spearhead Communication* (600 every four months). Turnover n/a.

TEACHING & PREACHING AGENCIES

All-Age Christian Ministries, PO Box 55, Newport NP19 8XT
☎01633 277 167 ℻01633 277 167
Evangelising and Bible teaching through missions, holidays, publications, audio tapes.
Evangelist: Mr Glyn Morgan. Executive staff 3, Other staff 4. Began 1966; interdenominational. Magazine: *Alive News* (20,000 quarterly). Turnover n/a.

Barratt Ministries, 114 Daisybank Road, Manchester M14 5QH
☎0161 224 2620 ℻0161 224 0265
Ⓔ: info@barrattministries.org.uk
Web: www.barrattministries.org.uk
Teaching discipleship, music ministry, prison work, publishing books/videos/CDs.
Director: Mr William M Barratt. Executive staff 2, Other staff 3. Began 1983; Independent. Magazine: *Challenge* (500 every two months). Turnover £75,000 to year end Feb 00.

C L Ministries, 24 The Street, Capel St Mary, Ipswich IP9 2EE
☎01473 311 128 ℻01473 311 128
Ⓔ: admin@clministries.org.uk
Web: www.clministries.org.uk
Bible teaching through preaching and other means; Bible Tours of Israel.
Director: Mr Christopher Hill. Executive staff 1, Admin staff 3. Began 1990; non-denominational. Magazine: *C L Update* (800 quarterly). Turnover n/a.

CHIEF (Christian Hope Indian Eskimo Fellowship), PO Box 789, Sutton Coldfield B73 5FX
☎0121 355 8333 ℻0121 355 3833
Ⓔ: worldactmin@aol.com
Providing Bible teaching, evangelism and leadership training (Schools Without Walls) among Native American Indians.
Executive Director: Mr Philip B South. No full-time staff. Began n/a; interdenominational. Administered in the UK by World Action Ministries. No magazine. Turnover n/a.

Damascus Trust, 51 Clockhouse Way, Braintree CM7 3RD
☎01376 342 529 ℻01376 342 529
Ⓔ: info@damascustrust.org
Web: www.damascustrust.org
Enthusing, enabling, establishing local churches in evangelism and discipleship through Bible teaching and outreach programmes.
Director: Mr Andy Paine. Executive staff 1, Other staff 2. ***CC*** No 1013236. Began 1990; interdenominational. Magazine: *News-Line* (1,000 quarterly). Turnover n/a.

***Eagle Ministries**, 69 East Park Road, Blackburn BB1 8DW
☎01254 521 44 Ⓜ 07891 483 4[illegible]3
Working with existing churches in evangelism, teaching and discipling.
Director: Mr Vincent J Purcell. Executive staff 2. ***CC*** No.1017740. Began 1988; non-denominational. No magazine. Turnover n/a.

Encounter Ministries, PO Box 789, Sutton Coldfield B73 5FX
☎0121 355 8333 🖷0121 355 3833
E: worldactmin@aol.com
Bible teaching ministry of the late Dr Stephen Olford; also occasional seminars for preachers, pastors.
Executive Director: Mr Philip B South. No full-time staff. Began n/a; interdenominational. Administered in the UK and Europe by World Action Ministries. Magazine: *Angelos* (Circulation n/a quarterly). Turnover n/a.

European Institute of Protestant Studies, The Paisley Jubilee Complex, 356 Ravenhill Road, Belfast BT6 8GL
☎028 9045 7106/8761 🖷028 9045 7783
Web: www.ianpaisley.org
Exposing the papacy, promoting, defending and maintaining the Bible and Protestantism worldwide.
President: Rev Dr Ian R K Paisley MP, MEP. Executive staff 1, Other staff 2. Began 1998; Free Presbyterian. No magazine. Turnover n/a.

Evangelical Protestant Society, PO Box 306, Belfast BT5 7WA
☎028 9048 1920
Propagating the Protestant Reformed faith and heritage, evangelism.
Chair of Council: Mr Vincent Shortt. Executive staff 1. **CC** No.XN 48166. Began 1948; non-denominational. Magazine: *Ulster Bulwark* (2,800 every three months). Turnover n/a.

Evidence Ministries, 25 Priory Road, Keynsham, Bristol BS31 2BX
☎0117 986 2394
E: jim@valian.fsnet.co.uk
Presenting lectures on archaeological biblical discoveries, with supporting follow-up books and videos.
Director: Rev Jim Elmer. No full-time staff. Began 2001; Elim Pentecostal. No magazine. Turnover n/a.

Forthtell, 1 Grove Gardens, Boston Spa, Wetherby LS23 6BG
☎01937 845 027
Presenting Christian perspectives on current issues through public meetings, rallies, the media.
Convener: Mrs Sally Coulby. Executive staff 1, Admin staff 1. Began 1997; non-denominational. No magazine. Turnover n/a.

The Framework Trust, The Old Rectory, Carr Lane, Great Moulton, Norwich NR15 2LA
☎01379 674 473 🖷01379 674 340
E: TAatFT@aol.com
Web: www.frameworktrust.org
Providing training to help Christians apply their faith; books, resources and opportunities to minister worldwide.
Director: Terry-Anne Preston. Executive staff 3. **CC** No.1063405. Began 1997; non-denominational. Magazine: *Framework* (Circulation n/a quarterly). Turnover n/a.

In Touch Ministries, PO Box 1643, Croydon CR9 1UX
☎0845 070 1643
Web: www.intouch.org
Bible teaching ministry of Dr Charles Stanley; TV, radio, books, tapes, daily Bible reading notes.
Executive Director: Mr Stephen Maxted. No full-time staff. Began n/a; interdenominational. Magazine: *In Touch* (10,000 monthly). Turnover n/a.

***Lifestyle International Ministries**, 10 Clairmont Road, Colchester CO3 5BE
☎01206 523 923
Web: www.lifestyleint.co.uk
Evangelism and teaching, UK and overseas.
International Director: Rev Eric Graham. Executive staff 1, Other staff 3. **CC** No.1071735. Began 1998; non-denominational. Magazine: *Lifestyle News* (700 quarterly). Turnover n/a.

Lifestyle Ministries, PO Box 789, Sutton Coldfield B73 5FX
☎0121 355 8333 🖷0121 355 3833
E: worldactmin@aol.com
Bible teaching ministry of the late Dr Ron Dunn; books and tapes.
Executive Director: Mr Philip B South. No full-time staff. Began n/a; interdenominational. Administered in the UK by World Action Ministries. No magazine. Turnover n/a.

Messenger International, PO Box 622, Newport NP19 8ZJ
☎08707 455 790
🖷08707 455 791
E: dhowells@messengerintl.org
Web: www.messengerinternational.org
Revival ministries to the church, Bible teaching, Christian leaders meetings, books, videos, resources.
European Manager: Mrs Donna Howells. Executive staff 2, Admin staff 2. ***CC*** No.1077247. Began 1999; interdenominational. (Previously John Bevere Ministries International). Magazine: *The Messenger* (6,000 every two months). Turnover n/a.

E

***Paraclete Christian Network International**, 1 Roman Crescent, Southwick, Brighton BN42 4TY
☎01903 522 279
M: 07703 770 138
E: lynda@paraclete.org.uk
Web: www.paraclete.org.uk
Supporting evangelical and evangelistic work in UK, Zimbabwe and Spain; providing oversight, Bible teaching, training.
Executive Director: Rev Lynda Hulcoop. No full-time staff. ***CC*** No.1019767. Began 1991; interdenominational. No magazine. Turnover £10,000 to year end Mar 05.

***Prophetic Witness Movement International**, PO Box 109, Leyland, Preston PR25 1XE
☎01772 452 846
🖷01772 452 846
E: info@pwmi.org
Web: www.pwmi.org
Proclaiming the return of Christ through teaching, evangelism and Christian literature.
General Secretary: Rev Colin Le Noury. Executive staff 1, Other staff n/a. ***CC*** No.228941. Began 1917; non-denominational. Magazine: *Prophetic Witness* (1,800 monthly). Turnover £56,000 to year end May 98.

***Purpose Driven UK**, 12 Pace Centre, Stephenson Road, Clacton-on-Sea CO15 4XA
☎01255 435 577 🖷01235 435 863
E: info@purposedrivenuk.com
Web: www.purposedrivenuk.com
Providing teaching and support materials to help churches develop.
Regional Coordinator: Rev David Beer. *Commercial Director:* Mr Peter Simpson. Admin staff 7. Began 2004; interdenominational. No magazine. Turnover £250,000 to year end Jan 05.

†***Rivers of Life Trust**, 36 Pond Avenue, Lisburn BT28 3JL
☎028 9267 5206 M 07977 928 719
E: mapinkerton@compuserve.com
Web: www.domini.org/riveroflife
Bible teaching, space for God days, counselling, training seminars, workshop.
Director: Miss Meriel Pinkerton. Executive staff 1, Admin staff 1. ***CC*** No.XR 59022. Began 1995; interdenominational. No magazine. Turnover £25,000 to year end Dec 98.

***The RZIM Zacharias Trust**, 97a St Aldates, Oxford OX1 1BT
☎01865 203 951 🖷01865 203 950
E: office@zactrust.org
Web: www.zactrust.org
Involved in evangelism, apologetics, training; aiming to reach the sceptic with the Gospel.
European Director: Mr Michael Ramsden. Executive staff 2, Other staff 5. ***CC*** No.1067314. Began 1998; non-denominational. (Previously Zacharias Trust). Magazine: *Just Thinking* (65,000 every four months). Turnover £334,000 to year end Dec 04.

Sovereign Grace Union, 43 Warwick Road, Rayleigh SS6 8PQ
☎01268 775 041
Web: www.sgu.org.uk
Promoting the doctrines of grace and testifying against the evils of priestcraft, arminianism and liberalism.
General Secretary: Mr C N Banks. No full-time staff. ***CC*** No.247867. Began 1914; interdenominational. Magazine: *Peace and Truth* (650 quarterly). Turnover £10,000 to year end Dec 02.

†**Storehouse Ministries**, PO Box 777, Bromley BR1 3XZ
☎020 8289 1684 🖷020 8289 1685
E: c.pick1@ntlworld.com
Web: www.storehouseministries.org.uk
Teaching ministry on biblical economics, releasing individuals, ministries and the churches into financial blessing.
Founder: Mr Clive Pick. Executive staff 2. ***CC*** No.1017926. Began 1992; Pentecostal. No magazine. Turnover n/a.

The Tehillah Trust, 49 St Mary's Park, Nailsea, Bristol BS48 4RP
☎01275 543 000 M 07740 797 933 🖷01275 543 000
E: jap@living-waters.org.uk
Teaching and leading praise and worship meetings, seminars and courses including Psalmody International; music publishing.
Administrator: Mr Julian Perkins. Executive staff 2, Admin staff 1. Began [illegible]989; non-denominational. No magazine. Turnover £1,000 to year end Aug 04.

Telling The Truth, PO Box [illegible]950, Sutton Coldfield B73 5FZ
☎0121 354 6914 🖷0121 355 3[illegible]33
E: worldactmin@aol.com
Bible teaching ministry of Stuart and Jill Briscoe; TV, radio, books, tapes, worldwide ministry.
Executive Director: Mr Philip B Sou[illegible]. No full-time staff. Began n/a; interdenominational. Administered in the UK by World Action Ministries. No magazine. Turnover n/a.

The Wesley Fellowship, Stonebridge Cottage, Back Lane, Sheersby, Lutterworth LE17 6PN
☎0116 247 8679
E: pt@westfel.freeserve.co.uk
Web: www.wesley-fellowship.org.uk
Providing a contemporary expression and interpretation of Wesleyan teaching and experience.
Secretary: Mr Paul S Taylor. Executive staff 1. Began 1985; interdenominational. Magazine: *The Wesley Quarterly* ([illegible]250 quarterly). Turnover £3,500 to year end Mar 05.

Andrew Wommack Ministries (Europe), PO Box 4392, Walsall WS1 [illegible]AR
☎01922 473300
E: inquiries@awme.net
Web: www.awme.net
Providing audio teaching tapes, Bible study programmes, Bible correspondence courses, annual ministers' conference.
Director: Mr Will Graham. Executive staff 9. ***CC*** No.1032438. Began 1991; interdenominational. No magazine. Turnover n/a.

Words of Life Ministries, PO Box [illegible]34, Eastleigh SO53 2UB
☎023 8026 9681
E: dt@wordsoflife.co.uk
Web: www.wordsoflife.co.uk
Distributing Bible study materials by Francis Dixon in various languages, promoting David Tucker's teaching ministry.
Chief Officer: Rev David A Tucker. Executive staff 2. ***CC*** No.269[illegible]81. Began 1[illegible]75; interdenominational. No magazine. Turnover n/a.

MEDIA

M

ART & CRAFT PRODUCERS

Heather Bartlett Calligraphy, The Orchard, Great Corby, Carlisle CA4 8LS
☎01228 561 844 🖷01228 561 844
E: heatherb@orchard6.force9.co.uk
Creative calligraphy, commissions: greetings cards, posters, texts illuminated in various styles and languages.
Scribe: Heather Bartlett. No full-time staff. Began 1999; interdenominational. No magazine. Turnover n/a.

Biblicus Publications Ltd, 215 Hatch Road, Brentwood CM15 9QN
☎01277 260 729 M: 07950 039 167
🖷01277 260 729
E: enquiries@biblicus.co.uk
Web: www.biblicus.co.uk
Designing and supplying Bible study charts, clocks, games.
Director: Mr Roy Hossack. Executive staff 2. Began 2003; non-denominational. No magazine. Turnover £5,000 to year end Mar 05.

Jacquie Binns, 1 Cargill Road, Earlsfield, London SW18 3EF
☎020 8874 0895
E: jb@jacquiebinns.com
Web: www.jacquiebinns.com
Making vestments and hangings richly embroidered in original designs, creating individual works of art.
Artist/Embroiderer: Ms Jacquie Binns. No full-time staff. Began 1987; non-denominational. No magazine. Turnover n/a.

Boo Cards, The Woodlands, Fauld Lane, Fauld, Burton-on-Trent DE13 9GU
☎01283 520 502 🖷01283 520 502
E: boodesigns@btopenworld.com
Writing, illustrating, designing, printing range of cards with spiritual verses. Also song writing.
Designer Director: Mrs Sandra Robinson. Executive staff 3. Began 1995; Anglican. No magazine. Turnover n/a.

Brotherhood of St Seraphim, Station Road, Walsingham NR22 6DG
☎01328 820 610
E: obwal@tiscali.co.uk
Web: www.stseraphim.inspiron.co.uk
Making traditional icons in egg tempera and gold leaf; commissions accepted.
Iconographer: Mr Leon Liddament. Executive staff 1. Began 1966; Russian Orthodox. No magazine. Turnover n/a.

Cards of Encouragement, Beth Ruach, Heathlands Road, Wokingham RG40 3AP
☎0845 1082 054 🖷0700 5800 681
E: info@cards-of-encouragement.co.uk
Web: www.cards-of-encouragement.co.uk
Designing, publishing and marketing cards for spiritual encouragement and for use in pastoral ministry.
Proprietors: Mr & Mrs John & Jan Hall. Executive staff 2. Began 1990; non-denominational. No magazine. Turnover n/a.

†**Cathcard**, 49 Russell Hill Road, Purley CR8 2XB
☎020 8668 2181 🖷020 8763 2274
Publishing and selling Christian Christmas cards for a group of UK Catholic social work agencies.
Company Secretary: Mr T Connor. Executive staff 1, Administrative staff 2. Began 1992; Roman Catholic. No magazine. Turnover £170,000 to year end Mar 98.

CBC Distributors, Greenbank Industrial Estate, Newry BT34 2JP
☎028 3026 5216 🖷028 3026 3927
E: info@cbcdistributors.co.uk
Manufacturing, publishing and distributing religious and inspirational gifts, books and cards.
Managing Director: Mr Des Woods. Executive staff 1, Other staff n/a. Began 1957; non-denominational. No magazine. Turnover n/a.

Cedar Trading International Ltd, PO Box 247, Farnham GU9 8XY
☎01252 790 636 🖷01252 790 639
E: sales@cedartrading.com
Web: www.cedartrading.com
Manufacturing and distributing Christian gifts and communion items.
Operations Manager: Mrs A E Nelson. Executive staff 2, Other Staff 3. Began 1996; non-denominational. No magazine. Turnover n/a.

Chapel House Publishing Oxford Limited, The Studio, Boundary Cottage, Letcombe Regis, Wantage OX12 9LJ
☎01235 772 922 M 07836 238 026 🖷01235 772 923
E: info@chapel-house.org
Web: www.chapel-house.org
Distributing inspirational greetings cards, stationery, gifts and posters.
Managing Director: Ms Wendy Robinson. Executive staff 1, Other staff n/a. Began n/a; non-denominational. No magazine. Turnover n/a.

Creative Solutions, 2 Uplyme Road Business Park, Lyme Regis DT7 3LS
☎01297 444 665/890 🖷01297 444 690
E: sales@c-s.uk.com
Web: www.c-s.uk.com
Designing and manufacturing banners, signage, notice boards, pavement signs, exhibition equipment and display panels.
Proprietor: Mr Mark Shurey. Executive staff 2, Other staff 8. Began 1998; non-denominational. (Previously The Banner Company). No magazine. Turnover £876,000 to year end Aug 05.

Custom Ideas, PO Box 58, Watford WD24 6BA
☎01923 248 154
E: info@customideas.co.uk
Web: www.customideas.co.uk
Customising T-shirts and other leisure wear; promotional products.
Managing Director: Mr Martyn Francis. Executive staff 2. Began 1990; interdenominational. (Previously Top Flight, Kingscourt Enterprises). No magazine. Turnover n/a.

Elenis Hand-Painted Icons, Pilgrims Rest, 34 Guildhall Street, Bury St Edmunds IP33 1QF
☎01284 723 722
E: elenisicons@btopenworld.com
Traditional and contemporary icon commissions; icon painting and religious art history tuition.
Artist: Mrs Helen Mcllcowie-Jenkins. Executive staff 1. Began 1994; Roman Catholic. (Previously Helen Mcllcowie-Jenkins). No magazine. Turnover n/a.

Faith & Hope, 12 Rutland Grove, Farnworth, Bolton BL4 9QL
M: 07776 282 980
Supplying verse cards, fridge magnets, keyrings and bookmarks.
Partner: Mr John Butterworth. Admin staff 1, Other staff n/a. Began 1950; interdenominational. (Previously Bees & Co Ltd). No magazine. Turnover n/a.

Genesis UK.Com Ltd, 18 Pendre Industrial Estate, Tywyn LL36 9LW
☎01654 710 137
🖷01654 712 461
E: info@genesis-uk.com
Web: www.genesis-uk.com or
Online shop: www.inyerfaith.co.uk
T-shirts, sweatshirts, clothing, hats, bags, mugs, balloons, pens, stickers, printed to any design.
Managing Director: Mr G Michael Stevens. Executive staff 2, Other staff 13. Began 1973; non-denominational. Incorporating Texstyle Graphics Ltd. No magazine. Turnover n/a.

***Gospel Cards**, PO Box 56, Bridgend CF31 1WG
☎01656 647 551
🖷01656 647 551
E: office@gospelcardsetc.com
Web: www.gospelcardsetc.com
Producing evangelistic and devotional greetings cards and calendars; percentage of sales given to missionary organisations.
Director: Mr Michael Hart. Executive staff 1, Other staff 2. Began 1982; evangelical. No magazine. Turnover n/a.

Holy Socks, Faith on your Feet, 68 Queen Street, Newton Stewart, Castle Douglas DG8 6JL
☎01671 404 043
M: 07918 184 539
🖷01671 404 043
E: info@holysocks.co.uk
Web: www.holysocks.co.uk
Socks with biblical designs and an original story; golf balls, brollies; for sale through churches.
Manager: Mrs Margaret Wylie. Executive staff 1, Other staff 1. Began 2000; non-denominational. No magazine. Turnover n/a.

Hughes & Coleman Ltd, Delta Close, Norwich NR6 6BG
☎01603 426 159 🖷01603 486 853
E: sales@hughesandcoleman.co.uk
Web: www.hughesandcoleman.co.uk
Producing and distributing Christian gifts and greetings cards.
Managing Director: Mr John Hughes. *Buying Director:* Mrs J Wastell. *General Manager:* Mr Roger Everett. Executive staff 3, Other staff 15. Began 1957; evangelical. Incorporating Christian Crafts. No magazine Turnover £1,000,000 to year end Mar 98.

†IGWIT Cards of Encouragement, The Old Parish Clerk's Office, Grappenhall Youth & Community Centre, Bellhouse Lane, Grappenhall, Warrington WA4 2SG
☎01925 453 941 🖷01925 453 941
E: claire@igwit.co.uk
Web: www.igwit.com
Designing and supplying Christian greetings cards.
Managing Director and Designer: Ms Claire Hawksworth. Executive staff 1, Other staff 2. Began 2003; non-denominational. No magazine. Turnover n/a.

Impressions, 18 Rosebery Road, Stanwix, Carlisle CA3 9HU
☎01228 525 310 M 07887 933 474
🖷01228 526 310
Manufacturing framed texts; wholesale distribution of Christian literature.
Managing Director: Mr John Smith. Executive staff 2, Other staff 4. Began 1980; non-denominational. No magazine. Turnover n/a.

†JCP Community Business Project Ltd, Edward Road Baptist Church, 196 Edward Road, Balsall Heath, Birmingham B12 9LY
☎0121 440 7919 🖷0121 446 5228
E: admin@jcp.org.uk
Web: www.jcp.org.uk
Charity business for socially disadvantaged people, supplying printed and embroidered T-shirts, sweatshirts and similar items.
Project Manager: Mr Ben Parkinson. Executive staff 6, Other staff 6, Beneficiary Placements 35. **CC** No.1037084. Began 1998; interdenominational. No magazine. Turnover £493,000 to year end Dec 01.

Kenex Bible Citation Markers, 18 Main Street, Kirkby Lonsdale, Carnforth LA6 2AG
☎01524 271 603 🖷01524 271 841
E: woodsjack@btopenworld.com
Web: www.theartstore.org.uk
Manufacturing and distributing Bible citation clip-on markers.
Managing Director: Mr Bruce E Woods-Jack. Executive staff 4, Other staff 2. Began 1969; non-denominational. No magazine. Turnover £100,000 to year end Dec 05.

The Lindisfarne Scriptorium, The Farne House, Marygate, Holy Island, Berwick-upon-Tweed TD15 2SJ
☎0870 745 1172 🖷0870 460 1523
E: mary@lindisfarne-scriptorium.co.uk
Web: www.lindisfarne-scriptorium.co.uk
Producing modern illuminated calligraphy and Celtic-inspired artwork.
Proprietors: Mr & Mrs Mark & Mary Fleeson. Executive staff 2. Began 1997; non-denominational. No magazine. Turnover n/a.

LJ Designs Ltd, 2 Priddy Close, Frome BA11 2XZ
☎01373 462 069 M: 07962 301 950
🖷01373 451 205
E: info@ljdesigns.ndo.co.uk
Web: www.ljdjewellery.co.uk
Manufacturing and supplying witness jewellery including Austrian crystal, 9ct gold and sterling silver.
Director: Mrs Karen Brown. Executive staff 2, Admin staff 1. Began 2000; non-denominational. No magazine. Turnover n/a.

Matabeleland Church Linens, 7 The Daedings, Deddington, Banbury OX15 0RT
☎01869 337 761
E: hughm@fish.co.uk
Web: www.deddington.org.uk/community/matabelelandlinens.html
Selling church linens made by Zimbabwe Mother's Union; all proceeds to Matabeleland MU.
Manager: Rev Canon Hugh Marshall. No full-time staff. Began 1997; Anglican. No magazine. Turnover £8,000 to year end Dec 04.

Newday Calendars, The Old Post Office, Evertown, Canonbie DG14 0TJ
☎01387 371 693
E: info@novellos.net
Web: www.newdaycalendars.com
Publishing and promoting calendars to help find still points in life.
Proprietor: Dr Daan Van Belzen. Executive staff 1, Other staff 6. Began 2005; non-denominational. (Previously Novellos). No magazine. Turnover n/a.

Origins, Artro House, Gwynfryn, Llanbedr LL45 2PA
☎01341 241 538 🖷01341 241 538
E: origins@davenewbould.co.uk
Web: www.davenewbould.co.uk
Producing greetings cards, postcards, posters and calendars from Dave Newbould's photography.
Partners: Mr & Mrs Dave & Ali Newbould. Executive staff 1, Other staff 2. Began 1993; non-denominational. No magazine. Turnover £200,000 to year end Apr 05.

†Painted Fishes.com, 60 Winchester Road, Romsey SO51 8JA
☎01794 512 914 🖷01794 521 077
E: allison@paintedfishes.com
Web: www.paintedfishes.com
Providing Fair Trade crafts with a fishy flavour through website.
Managing Director: Mrs Allison Hartley. Executive staff 1, Other staff 1. Began 2000; non-denominational. No magazine. Turnover £3,000 to year end Apr 03.

Pinnacle Creative, 143 The Gardens, Southwick, Brighton BN42 4AR
☎01273 870 221
🖷 01273 870 229
E: design@pinnaclecreative.co.uk
Web: www.pinnaclecreative.co.uk
Administrator: Mr Roland Brown. Executive staff 4, Other staff 4. **CC** Began 1980; non-denominational. (Previously Jubilee Traiding) No magazine. Turnover n/a. Undertaking graphic design and magazine production; producing design-led greeting cards and gifts.

Herbert Ramsden, 4 Saxony Road, Worthing BN14 7AT
☎01903 206 039
M: 07976 644 393
🖷01903 206 039
E: herbert.ramsden@btopenworld.com
Distributing books, gift items and pictures to Christian bookshops.
Proprietor: Mr Herbert Ramsden. Executive staff 1, Other staff 2. Began 1984; interdenominational. No magazine. Turnover n/a.

Religious T-Shirts, Unit B1, Hazleton Interchange, Horndean, Waterlooville PO8 9JU
☎0870 770 2677
🖷023 9259 2528
E: enquiries@religioustshirts.co.uk
Web: www.religioustshirts.co.uk
Designing and printing garments with Christian designs.
Operations & Sales Administrator: Mr Oliver Lea. Executive staff 1, Other staff 3. Began 2001; non-denominational. Turnover £55,000 to year end Dec 05.

Rock Cottage Crafts, Cockshades Farm, Stock Lane, Wybunbury, Nantwich CW5 7HA
☎01270 842 030/302
M: 07932 150 053
🖷01270 841 678
E: info@rockcottagecrafts.com
Producing coasters, magnets, Scriptural texts and verse cards, pictures, tea towels, bookmarks, posters.
Partner: Miss Helen Piddock. Executive staff 3. Began 1980; Anglican. No magazine. Turnover n/a.

Shades of Time, Scotch Corner House, Huntsmead, Alton GU34 2SF
☎01420 827 25
M: 07740 099 374
🖷01420 827 25
E: carl@shadesoftime.net
Web: www.shadesoftime.net
Distributing Christian art and giftware from a wide variety of sources.
Managing Director: Mr Jim McKell. *General Manager:* Mr Carl Saunders. Executive staff 2, Admin staff 1. Began 2003; non-denominational. No magazine. Turnover n/a.

†Silverfish Jewellery, Studio 12, Middleton Hall Craft Centre, Middleton, Tamworth B78 2AE
☎0121 354 3257
E: norma.dmurrain@globalnet.co.uk
Web: www.silverfishjewellery.com
Communicating the Gospel of our Lord Jesus Christ with designer-made jewellery.
Jewellery Designer & Maker: Mrs Norma Jean Murrain. Executive staff 1, Other staff 2. Began 2002; non-denominational. No magazine. Turnover n/a.

Leonard Smith, The Courtyard, Marks Hall Road, Coggeshall, Colchester CO6 1TE
☎01376 562 727 🖷01376 563 737
E: sales@leonardsmith.co.uk
Web: www.leonardsmith.co.uk
Designing and producing photographic greetings cards; commissioned photography; picture library.
Owner: Mr Leonard Smith. Executive staff 5, Other staff 2. Began 1985; non-denominational. (Previously The Lens Ideas Studio). No magazine. Turnover £400,000 to year end Dec 96.

Stamps Unlimited, 148 Kings Road, Newbury RG14 5RG
☎01635 447 17 🖷01635 327 07
E: enquiries@stampsunlimited.com
Web: www.stampsunlimited.com
Manufacturing and supplying rubber stamps and marking devices for commercial and recreational use.
Managing Director: Mr Michael Payne. Executive staff 1, Other staff 1. Began 1986; United Reformed. No magazine. Turnover £80,000 to year end Dec 04.

Stanelli Designs, 95 Ullswater Road, Urmston, Manchester M41 8SQ
☎0161 748 9364 🖷0161 748 9364
E: info@stanelli.co.uk
Web: www.stanelli.co.uk
Manufacturing greetings cards and supplying to trade and churches.
Proprietor: Mr Mike Bayley-Sanderson. Executive staff 2, Other staff 3. Began 1997; non-denominational. No magazine. Turnover n/a.

†Steave's Shirts, The Gaines, Whitbourne, Worcester WR6 5RD
☎01886 821 624 M: 07971 474 310
🖷01886 821 624
E: steave@steaveshirt.freeserve.co.uk
Screen printing T-shirts, sweatshirts, polo shirts, baseball caps, jog pants, scarves, badges; design available.
Sole Proprietor: Mr Steve Marshall. Executive staff 2, Other staff 2. Began 1982; non-denominational. No magazine. Turnover £12,000 to year end Dec 02.

Traidcraft plc, Kingsway, Team Valley Trading Estate, Gateshead NE11 0NE
☎0191 491 0591 🖷0191 497 6562
E: comms@traidcraft.co.uk
Web: www.traidcraft.co.uk
Direct sales and mail order business giving market opportunities to producers in 30 developing countries.
Chief Executive: Mr Paul Chandler. *Board Chairman:* Mr David Nussbaum. *Public Relations Manager:* Mr Peter Collins. Executive staff 4, Other staff 89. Began 1979; non-denominational. Magazine: *Traid Bulletin* (5,000 monthly). Turnover £15,500,000 to year end Mar 05.

Veritasse (Oxford) Ltd, PO Box 325, Witney OX28 1ZP
☎0845 123 5884 🖷01993 708 844
E: info@veritasse.co.uk
Web: www.veritasse.co.uk
Publishing and distributing work in the Christian arts; also Veritasse Arts Society.
Business Manager: Aidan Meller. Executive staff 2, Other staff 5. Began 1998; non-denominational. Magazine: *Veritasse Magazine* (18,000 annually). Turnover n/a.

Vision International Products, Ide Lane, Ide, Exeter EX2 9RY
☎01392 423 839 🖷01392 424 262
Producing gift and stationery items including plaques, keyrings, sticker books.
Partners: Mr & Mrs Paul & Michelle Ablett. Executive staff 2, Other staff 8. Began 1995; non-denominational. No magazine. Turnover n/a.

†The Visionary Art of Carleton, The Studio, 1 Shaw Street, Gowerton, Swansea SA4 3ER
M: 07791 947 677 🖷01792 522 [illegible]19
E: hand-of-creation@orange.net
Web: www.thevisionaryartofcarleton.com
Original acrylic and oil paintings with powerful visionary elements suitable for promotions, marketing and retail.
Proprietor: Mr Carleton D Watts. Executive staff 1, Other staff 1. Began [illegible]989; non-denominational. (Previously Lifestyle Designs). No magazine. Turnover n/a.

Mike Williams Publicity and Promotion, Perrowford, Trefusis Road, Redruth TR1[illegible] 2JN
☎01209 213 912
E: mike@mikewilliamspromotions.co.uk
Web: www.mikewilliamspromotions.co.uk
Publicity, promotion, fundraising items including colour laser, foil, transfer printing; badgemaking, pens, keyfobs and more.
Sole Trader: Mr Michael Williams. Executive staff 1. Began [illegible]990; non-denominational. No magazine. Turnover £20,000 to year end Mar 00.

Wirral Textile Motifs Ltd, 113 Roden Road, Overchurch, Upton, Wirral CH4[illegible] 4LX
☎0151 678 6076 🖷0151 678 60[illegible]6
Manufacturing general motifs, embroidered badges and logos for Christian organisations, churches, companies, clubs, schools.
Director: Mr Bernard Gallivan. Executive staff 2. Began 1982; non-denominational. No magazine. Turnover n/a.

†Alexandra Zvi Textile Design, 21d Buckland Hill, Maidstone ME[illegible]6 0SG
☎01622 681 543 M: 0780[illegible] 099 [illegible]94
E: advi@lineone.net
Designing and producing art textiles with a Christian theme for domestic and public spaces.
Designer: Miss Alexandra Zvi. Artist 1. Began 2004; non-denominational. No magazine. Turnover n/a

COMPUTER, IT SERVICES & WEB LISTINGS

***Acts on the Net**, 4 Bracken Close, Copthorne, Crawley RH10 3QE
☎01342 713 117
M: 07876 047 016
E: sharonmartin@john-3-16.wanadoo.co.uk
Web: www.acts-on-the-net.org
Internet mission society equipping, training and resourcing the church in online mission and evangelism.
Founder Trustee: Mrs Sharon Martin. No full-time staff. ***CC*** No.1085649. Began 2001; interdenominational. Turnover £8,000 to year end Mar 03.

***AFD Computers/AFD Software Ltd**, Lough House, Approach Road, Ramsey IM8 1RG
☎01624 811 711 🖷01624 817 695
E: postcode@afd.co.uk
Web: www.afd.co.uk
Supplying address list management and postcoding software.
Managing Director: Mr David Dorricott. *Secretary:* Dru Hamm. Executive staff 30, Other staff 5. Began 1983; non-denominational. Magazine: *Postcode News* (10,000 quarterly). Turnover £6,000,000 to year end Mar 05.

†Britannia Systems Ltd, Britannia House, Albion Street, Clifford, Wetherby LS23 6HY
☎01937 840 440
🖷01937 840 441
E: sales@britsys.co.uk
Web: www.britanniasystems.co.uk
Supplying computer systems and software to support churches, charities, other Christian organisations.
Managing Director: Dr David Barlow. Executive staff 4, Other staff 1. Began 1991; non-denominational. Turnover £150,000 to year end May 02.

Browncow Media, 11 Brownings Road, Cannington, Bridgwater TA5 2RH
☎01278 653 586
E: info@browncow.co.uk
Web: www.browncow.co.uk
Website design, e-commerce, SEO.
Proprietor: Rev Christopher Brown. Executive staff 1, Other staff 1. Began 1998; non-denominational. (Previously Covenant Technology). Turnover n/a.

Capstone Systems Ltd, Oak Mead, Malting Row, Honington, Bury St Edmunds IP31 1RE
☎01359 268 711 🖷01359 268 870
E: deg@capstonesystems.co.uk
Web: www.capstonesystems.co.uk
ReadyRiter software for charities and hospices; business consultancy offering software development.
Director: Mr D C Godfrey. Admin staff 2. Began 1986; non-denominational. Turnover n/a.

CCI Venue Finding Service, 2 Leon House, Queensway, Bletchley, Milton Keynes MK2 2SS
☎01908 641 641 🖷01908 641 641
E: office@cci.org.uk
Web: www.cci.org.uk/venues
Web-based venue finding service for group leaders looking for a group residential venue.
Chief Executive: Jim Hammett. Admin staff 2. ***CC*** No.326637. Began 1986; non-denominational. Magazine: *Getaway* (700 every four months). Turnover £82,000 to year end Dec 04.

ChristianChurches.co.uk, PO Box 266, Staines TW18 4GP
☎0870 286 3190 🖷0870 286 3136
E: info@ChristianChurches.co.uk
Web: www.ChristianChurches.co.uk
Providing an internet listing of churches and activities across the UK.
Managing Directors: Barry Mockford. No full-time staff. Began 2002. Turnover £2,500 to year end Dec 04.

Christian Computer Art, 33 Bramley Way, Hardwick, Cambridge CB3 7XD
☎01954 210 009
E: gallery@cc-art.com
Web: www.biblepicturegallery.com
Providing clip art and Bible background pictures as an internet download service for church publicity and teaching.
Owner: Mrs Enid Instone-Brewer. Executive staff 1. Began 1992; non-denominational. Turnover £12,000 to year end Apr 05.

Christian Technology, The Royal Stores, 152 Offmore Road, Kidderminster DY10 1SB
☎0870 742 0530 🖷0870 742 0535
E: sales@christiantechnology.co.uk
Web: www.christiantechnology.co.uk
Providing internet services, web and server hosting and network security solutions to Christian organisations nationwide.
Director: Mr Paul Sillars. Executive staff 3, Other staff 7. Began 2000; non-denominational. Turnover n/a.

Church 123.com Church Websites, Blueberry House, 113 Dukes Avenue, New Malden KT3 4HR
☎020 8949 6005 🖷0870 138 6000
E: ukch@church123.com
Web: www.church123.com
Providing easily updatable church websites.
Director: Mr Gordon Thorn. Executive staff 2. Began 2001; interdenominational. Turnover £70,000 to year end Dec 02.

Computers for Charities, Cemetery Lodge, Ersham Road, Hailsham BN27 3LJ
☎01323 840 641
E: info@computersforcharities.org
Web: www.computersforcharities.org
Non-profit making retail for mission and churches; computer recycling scheme; consultancy IT projects; also overseas.
Principal: Mr Simon Rooksby. No paid staff. ***CC*** No.1107802. Began 1994; interdenominational. Turnover £34,000 to year end Dec 02.

Data Developments (UK) Ltd, Wolverhampton Science Park, Stafford Road, Wolverhampton WV10 9RU
☎01902 824 044 🖷01902 824 046
E: sales@datadevelopments.co.uk
Web: www.datadevelopments.co.uk
Supplying software to churches and charities including for Gift Aid, accounting, membership, clipart.
Directors: Mr Alan Redmond, Mr Stephen Ibbs. Other staff 3. Began 1985; non-denominational. Turnover n/a.

†***Daystar Computing Solutions**, Daystar House, Burnage Lane, Manchester M19 2NG
☎0161 248 8088 🖷0161 224 2522
Web: www.daystar.co.uk
Advice, installation and support of Microsoft and Novell servers, printers and internet connectivity.
Partners: Mr & Mrs Stephen & Heather Noller. Executive staff 2, Other staff 1. Began 1991; non-denominational. Turnover £180,000 to year end Dec 02.

Downs Associates, 2 South View Place, Midsomer Norton, Bath BA3 2AX
☎07050 320 822 M: 07958 578 417
E: michael@downs-associates.co.uk
Web: www.downs-associates.co.uk
Consultancy, training and supplying computer systems; project management for a wide variety of purposes.
Partner: Mr E Michael Jakins. Executive staff 1, Other staff 1. Began 1984; non-denominational. Turnover n/a.

Eden Interactive Ltd, Chester Enterprise Centre, Hoole Bridge, Chester CH2 3NE
☎01244 350 994 🖷01244 350 995
E: info@edeninteractive.co.uk
Web: www.edeninteractive.co.uk
Interactive design and communications agency.
Director: Mr Gareth Mulholland. Executive staff 1, Other staff 8. Began 1999; inter-denominational. (Previously ChurchUK.net). Turnover n/a.

†**EIS Ltd**, PO Box 1125, Croydon CR0 6XJ
☎0845 456 1228 M: 07721 074 073
E: info@euvisol.co.uk
Web: www.euvisol.co.uk
Providing IT support to charitable organisations.
Director: Mr Tim Eveleigh. Executive staff 1, Admin staff 3. Began 1998; non-denominational. Turnover £75,000 to year end Mar 02.

Explan Computers Ltd, PO Box 32, Tavistock PL19 8YU
☎01822 613 868 🖷01822 610 868
E: info@explan.co.uk
Web: www.explan.co.uk
Bible software publishers; multi-lingual software and project managers for Solo, solar-powered computer equipment.
Director: Mr Paul Richardson. Executive staff 2, Other staff 2. Began 1994; non-denominational. Turnover £80,000 to year end Nov 00.

GCD Technologies, Trinity House, Lisburn BT28 2YY
☎0845 200 5129 M: 07767 392 989
🖷028 9260 6953
E: omega@gcdtech.com
Web: www.omega-system.co.uk
Developing administration software for churches and charities to help maintain supporter/donor records.
Partners: Mr Andrew Cuthbert, Mr Andrew Gough. Executive staff 2, Admin staff 9. Began 1995; non-denominational. No magazine. Turnover £220,000 to year end Apr 00.

†***IT Helper**, 15 Holland Road, South Norwood, London SE25 5RF
☎0870 350 4357 M: 07970 923 536
🖷0871 277 1912
E: mail@ithelper.net
Trouble-shooting, repairing and building computers and networks for Christians and others.
Director: Mr Geoffrey Roberts. Executive staff 1, Other staff 1. Began n/a; non-denominational. No magazine. Turnover £8,000 to year end Apr 03.

Jentech Computers Ltd, Smithfield Christian Centre, Whitburn Street, Bridgnorth WV16 4QT
☎01746 761 458 M: 07831 230 182
🖷01746 768 710
E: alan@jentech.co.uk
Web: www.jentech.co.uk
Specialists in computer systems, supply, maintenance, support, accounts, internet, intranet, rural wireless broadband in Shropshire.
Managing Director: Mr A S Vincent. Executive staff 2, Other staff 3. Began n/a; non-denominational. Turnover £500,000 to year end Jan 03.

†Jireh.co.uk, 18 Park Lane, Cottingham HU16 5RD
☎01482 875 532 📠0845 345 6561
E: ajb@jireh.co.uk
Web: www.jireh.co.uk
Providing a cost effective internet service. Specialists in name registration and web hosting.
Owner: Mr Andrew John Bruce. Executive staff 1, Other staff n/a. Began 1997; interdenominational. Turnover n/a.

Marcus Systems Ltd, 16 Orchard Grove, Chalfont St Peter, Gerrards Cross SL9 9EY
☎01753 886 882
E: john.marcus@maracc.com
Web: www.maracc.com
Supplying accounting and mailing software to charities and churches.
Consultant: Mr John Marcus. No full-time staff. Began 1982; non-denominational. Turnover £80,000 to year end Nov 02.

Mickwood.com, 82 St Andrews Road South, St Annes, Lytham St Annes FY8 1PS
☎ M: 07932 894 260
E: mick@mickwood.com
Web: www.mickwood.com
Domain name registration, web design and hosting for organisations, churches, businesses, individuals.
Owner: Mr Michael Wood. Executive staff 1, Other staff n/a. Began 2002; non-denominational. Turnover n/a.

Mission Computers, Manor Farm, 14 Alms Hill, Bourn, Cambridge CB3 7SH
☎01954 718 076 📠01954 719 703
E: services@miscom.co.uk
Web: www.miscom.co.uk
Office support services including desktop publishing, database management, mailing services and administration.
Partner: Mr Paul Gildersleve. Executive staff 2, Other staff 1. Began 1987; non-denominational. Turnover £30,000 to year end May 03.

Online Bible Foundation, 12 Birkfield Place, Carluke ML8 4PZ
☎01555 752 943 📠01555 752 943
E: Biblefound@aol.com
Web: onlinebible.co.uk
Christian computer software and Sunday School supplies.
Director: Mr James G Black. Executive staff 1, Admin staff 1. ***CC*** No.SCO 23693. Began 1990; non-denominational. Turnover £15,000 to year end Dec 04.

†P & W Enterprises, 21 Gallows Hill, Kings Langley WD4 8PG
☎01923 266 964 M: 07802 486 100
📠01923 443 607
E: info@pandwi.com
Web: www.pandwi.com
Producing Alpha & Omega church computer system.
Owner: Mr Paul Vernon. Executive staff 2, Other staff 5. Began n/a; non-denominational. Turnover £100,000 to year end Apr 98.

Saltshakers, PO Box 16817, London E13 8TR
☎020 8550 7519 M 07885 941 848
📠020 8551 1719
E: steve@saltshakers.com
Web: www.kesherweb.com
Design and marketing of websites.
Manager: Mr Steve Maltz. Executive staff 1, Other staff 3. Began 1990; non-denominational. (Previously Shards Software). Turnover n/a.

Tim Sibley Web Design, Peacehaven, Harepath Hill, Seaton EX12 2TA
☎01297 625 773 M: 07796 976 170
📠07092 083 481
E: info@timsibley.co.uk or info@webdesign4christians.co.uk
Web: www.timsibley.co.uk or www.webdesign4christians.co.uk
Website design, hosting, maintenance for business, churches, Christian organisations; internet directory of Christian holiday accommodation.
Proprietor: Mr Tim Sibley. Executive staff 1. Began 2000; non-denominational. (Previously Webdesign4Christians). Incorporating Holidays4Christians. Turnover n/a.

Think Interactive Ltd, Priory Lodge, Ruperra Close, Old St Mellons, Cardiff CF3 9HX
☎029 2036 3311 📠029 2036 3315
E: phil@thinkinteractive.co.uk
Web: www.thinkinteractive.co.uk
Website design and hosting; multimedia and DVD authoring and replication; video, CD, cassette duplication.
Technical Director: Mr Philip Silver. Executive staff 2. Began 1999; interdenominational. Incorporating Media Transcript Services. Turnover £300,000 to year end Dec 02.

†*Timperley Evangelical Trust, 183 Wythenshawe Road, Northern Moor, Wythenshawe, Manchester M23 0AD
☎0161 374 1089 📠0161 374 1089
E: info@tetrust.org
Web: www.tetrust.org
Encouraging Holy Spirit empowered study of the word of God, especially by computer software.
Hon Secretary: Mr A M Bolton. No paid staff. ***CC*** No.273710. Began 1977; non-denominational. Turnover n/a.

Truedata Computer Services, 23 Park Road, Ilkeston DE7 5DA
☎0115 932 0643 📠0115 932 0643
E: enquiries@truedata.org.uk
Web: www.truedata.org.uk
Mailing list services, subscription handling, typesetting, data storage and retrieval for Christian organisations.
Chairman/Administrator: Mr John R Moorley. Executive staff 3. Began 1983; interdenominational. Turnover n/a.

UK-Church.net (1st-Web), 37 Thisselt Road, Canvey Island SS8 9EP
☎01268 692 982 M: 07850 692 982
📠01268 510 100
E: ian@first-group.com
Web: www.1st-web.co.uk
Internet services to UK Christians, including uk-church.net database listing UK churches of all denominations.
Director: Mr Ian C Walmsley. Executive staff 1, Other staff 4. Began 1997; ecumenical. Turnover £30,000 to year end Dec 98.

Vermont Systems Ltd, Unit 12, BPC House, Romsey Industrial Estate, Romsey SO51 0HR
☎01794 521 201 📠01794 514 [illegible]21
E: info@vermont.co.uk
Web: www.vermont.co.uk
Specialising in accounting, database and network systems.
Managing Director: Mr Richard Mills. *Director:* Mr David Gill. Other staff 9. Began 1997; non-denominational. Turnover £470,000 to year end Dec 04

Windrush, 7 Pyle Close, Cowplain, Waterlooville PO8 8JN
☎0845 644 0717 M: 0778[illegible] 987 [illegible]38
📠0870 766 2713
E: enquiries@windrush-holidays.com or www.christianholiday.co.uk
Web: www.windrush-holidays.com
Advertising and bookings for Christian holiday accommodation
Company Secretary & Director: Mr & Mrs Andy & Margaret Stevens. Executive staff 2, Admin staff 3. Began 2000; non-denominational. Turnover £17,000 to year end Sep 04.

Worldwide Webdesign, 22 Manvers Road, Old Town, Eastbourne BN20 [illegible]HJ
☎01323 732 788 M: 0794[illegible] 020 6[illegible]6
E: office@worldwidewebdesign.co.uk
Web: www.worldwidewebdesign.co.uk
Web design and online shops for charities, business and individuals.
Principal: Mr K J Duursma. Executive staff 1, No other full-time staff. Began 20[illegible]2; non-denominational. Turnover £25,000 to year end Jun 05.

Wyattgraphics, 5 Wren Close, St Mellons, Cardiff CF3 0PD
☎029 2033 7603 M: 07767 883 2[illegible]4
📠029 2079 8447
E: robert.wyatt3@ntlworld.com
Web: www.wyattgraphics.co.uk
Large format digital printing, mounting and encapsulating, pop-up display systems, roller banners.
Designer: Mr Robert Wyatt. Executive staff 1. Began 1992; non-denominational. Turnover £80,000 to year end Apr 01

DESIGN, LAYOUT & EDITORIAL SERVICES

See also Marketing & Fundraising Services on Page 360.

Aaron Editorial, 19 Albemarle Road, Gorleston-on-Sea, Great Yarmouth NR31 7AE
☎01493 444 556 🖷01493 444 556
E: eldo@words4profit.com
Web: www.1stcalleditorial.com
Copywriting for fundraising, on screen editing.
Editor: Mr Eldo Barkhuizen. Executive staff 1. Began 1997; non-denominational. Turnover n/a.

***Adept Design (Norfolk) Limited**, 15 White Hart Street, Aylsham, Norwich NR11 6HG
☎01263 734 198 🖷01263 734 822
E: admin@adeptdesign.co.uk
Web: www.adeptdesign.co.uk
Offering design and creative consultancy in literature, advertising, display exhibition, corporate identity, marketing and website.
Director: Mr Derek Blois. Executive staff 2, Other staff 8. Began 1976; non-denominational. Turnover n/a.

†Amadi Design Co, Tottenham Green Enterprise Centre, Town Hall Approach Road, London N15 4RX
☎020 8375 3465 M: 07899 990372
🖷020 8375 3466
E: info@amadidesign.co.uk
Web: www.amadidesign.co.uk
Providing graphic design, marketing, advertising, corporate identity, web design, multimedia and print.
Managing Director: Mr Kelechi Amadi. Executive staff 2. Began 1999; non-denominational. Turnover £100,000 to year end Sep 02.

†Arcus Design and Publishing, The Oast House, 5 Mead Lane, Farnham GU9 7DY
☎01252 727 929
🖷01252 727 929
E: arcus@nildram.co.uk
Offering creative design and publishing for print and other media.
Proprietor: Mr Nick Mills. Executive staff 1, Other staff 1. Began 1993; ecumenical. Turnover n/a.

Artlines, 465 West Wycombe Road, High Wycombe HP12 4AQ
☎01494 442 988
🖷01494 452 949
E: tom@artlines.co.uk
Web: www.artlines.co.uk
Providing graphic design, website design and maintenance, email marketing.
Designer: Mr Tom Van Aurich. Executive staff 3, Other staff 1. Began 1985; non-denominational. Turnover n/a.

***AWM Media**, PO Box 4006, Worthing BN13 1AP
☎01903 215 345
🖷01903 215 456
E: info@media.awm.org
Web: www.media.awm.org
Proclaiming the Gospel through television, radio, and internet. Providing evangelistic courses & discipleship for seekers.
UK Media Manager: Mr Richard Lackey. Executive staff 1, Other staff 9. ***CC*** No.1095167. Began 1986; interdenominational. (Previously AWM Graphics). Part of AWM International. Turnover £80,000 to year end Dec 00.

***Catherine Butcher**, 6 Milton Crescent, Eastbourne BN21 1SP
☎01323 647 195
M:07974 798 529
🖷01323 721 549
E: cathbutcher@aol.com
Writing, editing and producing magazines and literature particularly for use in evanglism and community work.
Writer/Editor: Mrs Catherine Butcher. Executive staff 1. Began 1986; interdenominational. Turnover n/a.

M

Design, Layout & Editorial Services

Christian Publishing & Outreach Ltd, Garcia Estate, Canterbury Road, Worthing BN13 1BW
☎01903 264 556 ISDN: 01903 537 308
🖷01903 830 066
E: enquiries@cpo.org.uk
Web: www.cpo.org.uk or www.cpo-online.org.uk
Magazine editorial, production, distribution, advertising; subscription service using same systems as Woman Alive.
Managing Director: Mr Paul Slide. *Production Director:* Mr Mike Axell. Executive staff 5, Other staff 30. ***CC*** No.221462. Began 1990; interdenominational. (Previously Christian Media Centre). Turnover n/a.

Creative Media Ltd, 35 Woodland Park, Paignton TQ3 2JT
☎01803 390 055 M: 07792 241 356
🖷01803 390 055
E: martin@mhcreativemedia.co.uk
Web: www.mhcreativemedia.co.uk
Design and advertising agency supplying production and promotion services to the Christian and publishing sectors.
Director: Mr Martin Harris. Executive staff 2, Other staff 3. Began 1998; non-denominational. Turnover n/a.

Creative Pages, 20 Napier Street, Bletchley, Milton Keynes MK2 2NF
☎01908 371 372 M: 07917 573 548
E: john@creativepages.co.uk
Web: www.creativepages.co.uk
Providing publishing consultancy, skills development training, project management, book typesetting and production.
Director: Mr John Ball. Executive staff 1, Admin staff 1. Began 2005; non-denominational. Turnover n/a.

Creative Stream Ltd, Aizlewood's Mill, Sheffield S3 8GG
☎0114 282 3413
E: info@creativestream.co.uk
Web: www.creativestream.co.uk
Graphic Designer: Mr Cliff Hewson. Executive staff 1. Began 1998; interdenominational. (Previously Cliff Hewson Graphic Design Ltd) Turnover n/a. Providing graphic design and print services, mainly to churches, charities and Christian organisations.

D'Art Design, Broadoak House, Horsham Road, Cranleigh GU6 8DJ
☎01483 275 054 🖷01483 268 173
E: inform@dartdesign.co.uk
Web: www.dartdesign.co.uk
Corporate design, logos, advertising campaigns, packaging and print, website design.
Designer: Mr Paul Higgins. Executive staff 1, Other staff 1. Began 1989; non-denominational. Turnover £54,000 to year end Oct 04.

Design Jazz, Smithfield Christian Centre, Whitburn Street, Bridgnorth WV16 4QT
☎01746 767 319 🖷01746 768 710
E: alan@design-jazz.com
Web: www.design-jazz.com
Graphic, website design; exhibition graphics; photography; specialising in school prospectus design and e-commerce websites.
Senior Designer: Mr Alan Muscat. Executive staff 1, Other staff n/a. Began 1995; interdenominational. (Previously Grapevine Digital Arts). Turnover n/a.

Steve English, Cartoonist, 1 White Cottage, Frankfort, Sloley, Norwich NR12 8HG
☎01692 535 826
E: steve_english@macunlimited.net
Writing and illustrating cartoons, gags, and Sunday School resources for publishers, churches and individuals.
Cartoonist: Mr Steve English. Staff 1. Began 2000; non-denominational. Turnover £1,600 to year end Apr 05.

Sylvia Evans and Associates, York House, 44 Hawthorn Road, Redcar TS10 3PA
☎01642 473 207 🖷01642 492 254
E: syl@sylviaevans.fsbusiness.co.uk
Undertaking public relations consultancy; television, press, seminars, conferences, brochures, publishing, advertising, strategic marketing.
Owner: Mrs Sylvia Evans. Executive staff 1, Other staff 1. Began 1972; non-denominational. Turnover n/a.

Getting It Across!, 1 Garden House Court, 142 Sandgate Road, Folkestone CT20 2FF
☎01303 253 195 🖷01303 253 195
E: david.3longley@btinternet.com
Editing, copywriting, proof-reading and indexing service for Christian organisations of all sizes.
Principal: Mr David Longley. Executive staff 1. Began 1985; interdenominational. Turnover n/a.

Go Publishing, The Flat, Park Lane, Wembley HA9 7SG
☎020 8903 3024 🖷020 8903 3024
Providing editing and publishing services.
Hon Secretary: Mr Chris Road. No full-time staff. Began 2002; interdenominational. Turnover n/a.

Stephen Goddard Associates, 1 Ellison's Cottages, Crank Road, St Helens WA11 7RQ
☎01744 733 898 M: 07930 198 209
🖷01744 733 898
E: steve@shipoffools.com
Public relations consultants; product and service launches to Christian and mainstream media; promotional newspaper production.
Principal: Mr Stephen Goddard. Executive staff 1, Other staff 3. Began 1987; interdenominational. Turnover n/a.

H&B Enterprises, 276 South Lambeth Road, London SW8 1UJ
☎020 7627 4862 🖷020 7978 20[illegible]0
E: haydn_and_beulah@onetel.com
Foreign language desktop publishing, booksales, record label, producing tracts for outreach.
Directors: Rev & Mrs Haydn & Beulah Wood. Executive staff 2, Other staff 2. Began 1990; non-denominational. (Previously Beulah Graphics) Turnover n/a.

Iden Design Associates, 1[illegible]3 Crescent Drive, Petts Wood, Orpington BR5 1[illegible]Z
☎01689 876 191 🖷01689 810 [illegible]1
E: iden@i-d2.fsnet.co.uk
Graphic design, copy and print solutions for leaflets, brochures, advertising, packaging and corporate identity.
Director: Mr Ron Iden. Executive staff 1, Other staff 1. Began n/a; non-denominational. (Previously Crescent Graphics). Turnover n/a.

Image-on Artworks, Suite 14a, Hull Road, Hessle HU13 0AH
☎01482 629 933 🖷01482 629 7[illegible]7
E: admin@imageonartworks.co.uk
Web: www.imageonartworks.co.uk
Creating graphic design, print and multimedia for Christian organisation and charities.
Proprietor: Mr Jonathan Richards. Executive staff 1, Other staff 2. Began 1[illegible]94; non-denominational. Turnover £100,000 to year end Dec 04.

†**Simon Jenkins Associates**, 14 Hillcrest Road, Acton, London W3 9RZ
☎020 8993 3936 🖷020 8752 09[illegible]9
E: simonj@shipoffools.com
Web: www.shipoffools.com
Creating concepts, copywriting, design for all forms of print media and the internet.
Partner: Mr Simon Jenkins. Admin staff 1. Began 1988; non-denominational. Turnover n/a.

keithjones.net, Charis House, Hardwick Square East, Buxton SK17 6PT
☎0129 825 849 M: 07813 449 52[illegible]
🖷08701 319 152
E: mail@keithjones.net
Web: www.keithjones.net
Providing web design, various internet services, photography, digital image manipulation, electronic publications, graphic design, colour printing.
Partner: Keith Jones. Executive staff 2, Other staff 2. Began 1992; interdenominational. Turnover n/a.

***Paul Jones Associates**, 98 Eden Way, Beckenham BR3 3DH
☎020 8663 3963 M 07956 383 1[illegible]
🖷020 8663 3964
E: pj@pja.u-net.com
Design and fundraising consultancy for Christian charities and organisations, including newsletters, magazines and direct mail.
Managing Director: Mr Paul Jones. Executive staff 1. Began 1979 interdenominational. Turnover n/a.

Just Words, 39 Thanet Lee Close, Cliviger, Burnley BB10 4TX
☎01282 459 498
E: davidbhall@compuserve.com
Freelance writing of press releases, company features; publicity advice and editorial for fundraising.
Director: Mr David B Hall. No other staff. Began 1986; interdenominational. Turnover n/a.

Lazy Daisy, 28 Abbas Walk, Great Cornard, Sudbury CO10 0YW
☎01787 315 742 M: 07808 760 379
E: info@lazydaisy.biz
Web: www.lazydaisy.biz
Providing graphic print and design services; publishing photography and illustration work.
Designer: Mrs Rachael Banham. Executive staff 2. Began 1999; interdenominational. Turnover £12,000 to year end Nov 01.

Stephen Lown, Graphic Designer, 23 Gwydir Street, Cambridge CB1 2LG
☎01223 576 706 M: 07702 346 114
🖷01223 576 706
E: slowngd@aol.com
Graphic design, artwork and print production for corporate identity, advertising, promotional literature, magazines and books.
Graphic Designer: Mr Stephen Lown. Executive staff 1. Began 1991; interdenominational. Turnover n/a.

MHM Grax, 19 Garrick Street, London WC2E 9AX
☎020 7240 7767 🖷020 7379 7119
E: info@mhmgrax.com
Web: www.mhmgrax.com
Designing and producing websites, printed literature, logos, exhibitions; design for publishing and advertising.
Design Director: Mrs Heather Knight. Executive staff 2, Other Staff 3. Began 1992; non-denominational. Turnover £250,000 to year end Apr 03.

Jeremy Mudditt Publishing Services, 3 Longlands Road, Carlisle CA3 9AD
☎01228 547 937
E: jmudditt@aol.com
Book and magazine project, editorial and production management services for authors and publishers.
Partner: Mr Jeremy H L Mudditt. Executive staff 1, Other staff 1. Began 1997; non-denominational. Turnover £30,000 to year end Mar 05.

†***Elizabeth Nicoll**, 7 Allan Way, Acton, London W3 0PW
☎020 8993 8455 M: 07958 763 448
🖷020 8993 7071
E: elizabeth.r.nicoll@btinternet.com
Graphic design and print for all sales, marketing and administration purposes.
Designer: Mrs Elizabeth Nicoll. *Partner:* Mr Colin Nicoll. Executive staff 2. Began 1996; interdenominational. Turnover £100,000 to year end Dec 02.

Outer Space Commercial Illustration, Moonfleet Cottage, Polgreen, St Newlyn East, Newquay TR8 5HR
☎ M: 07763 321 777
E: outer-space@lycos.co.uk
Illustrating in colour and monochrome for books, packaging, education; cartoon styles; greeting card illustration, publishing.
Artist and Illustrator: Mr David Stansfield. Artist 1, No other staff. Began 2005; non-denominational. Turnover n/a.

***Page '90 Publishing Services**, 48 The Crescent, Kettering NN15 7HW
☎01536 483 800
E: david.page@zetnet.co.uk
Providing freelance editorial services, consultancy for publishers of books, journals, training material.
Proprietor: Mr David Page. Executive staff 1. Began 1990; non-denominational. Turnover n/a.

Pencil-Sharp Editors, Unit F8, Rake Industries, Rake, Petersfield GU31 5DU
☎01730 895 222 🖷01730 895 222
E: info@pencil-sharp.com
Web: www.pencil-sharp.com
Publishing and project management.
Editorial Manager: Mr James Croft. Executive staff 1, No other full-time staff. Began 2004; non-denominational. Turnover n/a.

Phase, Willow Court, Cordy Lane, Underwood, Nottingham NG16 5FD
☎01773 764 288 🖷01773 764 282
E: sales@phaseprint.com
Web: www.phaseprint.com
Marketing, designing and producing material for Christian organisations across the UK; print, websites, exhibitions.
Managing Director: Mr Kevin Marks. *Sales Executive:* Mr Philip Dobson. Executive staff 2, Admin staff 5, Other staff 20. Began 2000; interdenominational. (Previously Phase Print Ltd). Turnover £700,000 to year end May 00.

The Piquant Agency, 4 Thornton Road, Carlisle CA3 9HZ
☎01228 525 075 🖷01228 380 441
E: info@piquant.net
Web: www.piquant.net
Literary agents for Christian authors and artists.
Partners: Mr & Mrs Pieter & Elria Kwant. Executive staff 2, Admin staff 1. Began 2004; interdenominational. Turnover n/a.

Portfolio Associates, 517a Hagley Road, Bearwood, Smetwick B66 4AX
☎0121 429 4400 🖷0121 429 4400
E: steve@portfolioassociates.co.uk
Web: www.portfolioassociates.co.uk
Providing graphic design and marketing consultancy for charitable organisations, Christian and non-Christian businesses, government bodies.
Managing Director: Mr Steve Bamford. Executive staff 2, Admin staff 1. Began 1985; interdenominational. Turnover £150,000 to year end Dec 05.

Design, Layout & Editorial Services

Profile Design, 4 East Pallant, Chichester PO19 1TS
☎01243 537 444 🖷01243 537 440
E: sales@profiledesign.net
Web: www.profiledesign.net
Designing and printing brochures, magazines, stationery, leaflets and reports for the Christian and secular community.
Proprietor: Mr Peter Hamilton. Executive staff 1, Other staff 2. Began 1989; House Church. Turnover £260,000 to year end Oct 02.

Red & Green Marketing Ltd, 12 Montacute Road, Tunbridge Wells TN2 5QR
☎01892 512 900 🖷01892 517 067
E: info@redandgreenmarketing.com
Web: www.redandgreenmarketing.com
Providing marketing, project management and creative services to the charitable and commercial sectors.
Managing Director: Mr Nigel Saunders. *Director:* Roger Hulbert. Executive staff 2, Other staff 7. Began 2001; interdenominational. (Previously Greenleaf Communications Ltd). Turnover £900,000 to year end Jun 03.

Sovereign Creative Marketing Ltd, Stanley House, 15 Ladybridge Road, Cheadle Hulme, Cheadle SK8 5BL
☎0161 485 4488 🖷0161 486 1886
E: n.tedford@sovereign.uk.com
Web: www.sovereign.uk.com
Marketing campaigns, advertisement design and media buying, web design/hosting, web marketing campaigns, donor recruitment.
Managing Director: Mr Nigel Tedford. *Financial Director:* Mrs Dianne Tedford. Executive staff 2, Other staff 4. Began 1984; interdenominational. (Previously Sovereign Advertising & Marketing (CH) Ltd). Turnover £1,000,000 to year end Dec 04.

Sticky New Media & Design, The Clocktower, Great Southsea Street, Southsea PO5 3BY
☎023 9273 4201 🖷023 9273 4020
E: info@stickynewmedia.co.uk
Web: www.stickydesign.co.uk or www.stickynewmedia.co.uk
Graphic design, advertising and web design.
Partner: Mr Phillip Owen. Partners 2, Other staff 4. Began 1993; Elim Pentecostal. Turnover n/a.

Teamwork, 44 Rectory Walk, Sompting, Lancing BN15 0DU
☎01903 750 946
E: thelawthers@ntlworld.com
Web: www.gails-quilts-plus.co.uk
Design, editorial and production services for books, booklets, periodicals, publicity; also specialist church banner design.
Joint Partners: Mr & Mrs Christopher & Gail Lawther. Executive staff 2. Began 1985; non-denominational. Turnover n/a.

Vantage Graphics & Design Ltd, 9 Vicarage Lane, Harbury, Leamington Spa CV33 9HA
☎01926 614 211
E: studio@vgd.co.uk
Web: www.vgd.co.uk
Creative service in design, computer graphics and digital illustration for print, multimedia, internet and TV.
Director: Mr Michael D Abbott. Executive staff 1, Other staff 2. Began 1986; non-denominational. (Previously Vantage Advertising and Design Ltd). Turnover £50,000 to year end Dec 00.

Verité CM Ltd, 8 St John's Parade, Alinora Crescent, Goring-by-Sea, Worthing BN12 4HJ
☎01903 241 975
M: 07818 091 723
🖷01903 521 959
E: info@veritecm.com
Web: www.veritecm.com
Providing graphic design, layout and editorial services including personalisation, book production, print management.
Director: Mr Chris Powell. Executive staff 2, Admin staff 2. Began 2003; non-denominational. Turnover n/a.

Watermark, Norfolk House, 1 Hamilton Road, Cromer NR27 9HJ
☎01263 515 575
E: watermark@britishlibrary.net
Writing, editing, indexing, typesetting and design.
Managing Director: Rev Robert Backhouse. Executive staff 4. Began 1984; non-denominational. Turnover n/a.

Wellspring Design, 26 Rydale, Kirkheaton, Huddersfield HD5 0HT
☎01484 316 678 M: 07890 371 836
E: info@wellspringdesign.co.uk
Web: www.wellspringdesign.co.uk
Providing graphic and web design; specialising in exhibition projects.
Designer: Mr Adam Knowles. Executive staff 2. Began 2002; non-denominational. Turnover n/a.

Wingfinger Graphics, 1st Floor, 13 Queen Square, Leeds LS2 8AJ
☎0113 245 0469 🖷0113 244 46[illegible]8
E: pteri@wingfinger.co.uk
Web: www.wingfinger.co.uk
Designing and printing magazines, leaflets, publicity, stationery; reports, workbooks; branding, copywriting, editing, multi-language work.
Partners: Mr Bill Phelps, Mr Richard Lether. Executive staff 4. Began 1973; non-denominational. Turnover £250,000 to year end Mar 05.

Word Alive Telos Translations, PO Box 21261, Maida Hill, London W9 2YR
☎020 7286 7682
E: J.Chevellier@wordalive.co.uk or telostranslations@wordalive.fsbusiness.co.uk
Undertaking English/French translation and interpretation of printed, audio, video Bible-related material.
Director: Mr Jean Chevellier. Executive staff 1, Other staff 3. Began 1999; interdenominational. Turnover n/a.

Write Now, BM Box 3684, London WC1N 3XX
☎020 8883 9600
E: info@writenow.me.uk
Writing, editing articles, educational resources; radio, DVD scripts; press releases; church / media relations; communications strategy.
Communications Co-ordinator: Miss Deborah Steiner. Executive staff 1. Began 2004; non-denominational. Turnover n/a.

MEDIA PRODUCERS

***2K Plus International Sports Media**, PO Box 4436, Worthing BN14 7WH
☎01903 217 727 🖷01903 217 727
E: office@2Kplus.org.uk
Web: www.2Kplus.org.uk
Providing news, comment and interviews with a Christian perspective from major sporting events.
Chief Executive Officer: Mr Adrian Barnard. Executive staff 1. ***CC*** No.1091911. Began 2001; non-denominational. Magazine: *2K Plus News* (2,000 half-yearly). Turnover £30,000 to year end 2003.

†A and C Audio Visual, 98 Goremire Road, Carluke ML8 4PF
☎01555 772 648 🖷01555 752 060
E: enquiries@aandcaudio.co.uk
Web: www.aandcaudio.co.uk
Supplying audio and visual equipment, projectors, screens, cassette copiers, recorders, loop systems; UK and worldwide.
Partner: Mr Alex Borthwick. Executive staff 3. Began 1990; non-denominational. No magazine. Turnover n/a.

Abstract Images, 117 Willoughby House, Barbican, London EC2Y 8BL
☎020 7638 5123 🖷020 7638 5123
E: productions@abstract-images.co.uk
Producing television acts of worship, single documentaries, factual drama series; radio discussion, current/religious affairs.
Managing Director: Mr Howard Ross. Executive staff 1. Began 1990; non-denominational. No magazine. Turnover £300,000 to year end Dec 99.

Active Media, 42a High Street North, Dunstable LU6 1LA
☎01582 503 413 M: 07791 635 682
🖷01582 502 233
E: info@ampublishing.net
Web: www.ampublishing.net
Designing and producing video, DVD, CD, web, and print resources; training services.
Directors: Mr Richard Armiger, Mr Brian Holmes. Executive staff 2, Other staff 4. Began 2003; non-denominational. No magazine. Turnover £150,000 to year end Mar 05.

†*Alitapes, 73 Apton Road, Bishop's Stortford CM23 3ST
☎01279 651 195 🖷01279 651 195
E: burnett@ntlworld.com
Helping Christian organisations use media to become a presence locally.
Proprietor: Ms Alison Burnett. Executive staff 1. Began 1994; non-denominational. No magazine. Turnover n/a.

Anglo-Nordic Productions Trust, 2 Thornton Close, Girton, Cambridge CB3 0NQ
☎01223 276 504 🖷01223 563 821
E: patrick.colquhoun@ntlworld.com
Web: anptrust.org.uk
Producing and distributing Christian film and video; emphasis on education, churches and Eastern Europe.
Secretary: Mr Patrick Colquhoun. Executive staff 1. ***CC*** No.280052. Began 1980; non-denominational. No magazine. Turnover £9,717 to year end Apr 02.

BBC School Radio, Room 340, Henry Wood House, 3 & 6 Langham Place, London W1A 1AA
☎020 7765 0632
E: andrew.barnes@bbc.co.uk
Web: www.bbc.co.uk/schoolradio
Producing TV/radio programmes, print and on-line resources for schools. Christian and non-Christian faiths.
Editor: Mr Andrew Barnes. Executive staff 10. Began n/a; non-denominational. No magazine. Turnover n/a.

Bethel Communications, 2 Johnston Park, Inverkeithing KY11 1BT
☎01383 411 066 🖷01383 420 397
E: deb@bethelcommunications.com
Web: www.bethelcommunications.com
Producing video, radio, TV programmes, multi media on CD ROM, web including photography, design.
Director: Deborah Menelaws. Executive staff 2, Other staff 3. Began 1986; non-denominational. No magazine. Turnover £250,000 to year end Dec 02.

†BYKmedia, 19a Endlesham Road, London SW12 8JX
☎020 8673 7567 M: 07931 736 653
E: camilla@bykmedia.com
Web: www.bykmedia.com
Filming, editing, producing video and multimedia projects for charities and educational establishments.
Producer/Director: Mrs Camilla Byk. Executive staff 1. Began 2000; non-denominational. No magazine. Turnover £15,000 to year end Apr 02.

Callister Communications Ltd, 88 Causeway End Road, Lisburn BT28 2ED
☎028 9267 3717 🖷028 9267 3652
E: john@callister.tv
Web: www.callister.tv
Producing film and videos to broadcasting standard for Christian organisations and charities.
Director: Mr John Callister. Executive staff 1, Other staff 2. Began 1990; interdenominational. No magazine. Turnover n/a.

†Cambridge Film and Television Productions, Middlewhite Barn, St George's Way, Impington, Cambridge CB4 9AF
☎01223 236 007 🖷01223 237 555
E: lester@cftp.co.uk
Web: www.cftp.co.uk
Producing video for church organisations, charities and broadcasters; CD ROMs; free-loan video library.
Director/Producer: Mr Lester Milbank. *Assistant Producer:* Mrs Jenny Urwin. Admin staff 2, Technical staff 2. Began 1989; interdenominational. (Previously Lester Milbank Productions). No magazine. Turnover £550,000 to year end Mar 02.

Catholic Evangelisation Services, PO Box 333, St Albans AL2 1EL
☎01727 822 837 🖷01727 822 837
E: info@faithcafe.org
Web: www.faithcafe.org
Producing and distributing Catholic teaching videos for parish renewal and evangelisation.
Director: Mr David Payne. Executive staff 1, Other staff 4. ***CC*** No.277425. Began 1996; Roman Catholic. No magazine. Turnover £115,600 to year end Apr 03.

Media Producers

***Centre for Christian Broadcasting**, 27 Leveson Road, Stoke-on-Trent ST4 4QP
M: 07901 670 019
Christian radio production and broadcasting.
Directors: Mr Gareth Littler, Ms Patricia Hargreaves. Executive staff 2. Began 2005; interdenominational. (Previously Centre for Justice and Liberty). No magazine. Turnover n/a.

***Christian Communications Network (Europe) Ltd**, 646 Shore Road, Whiteabbey, Newtownabbey BT37 0PR
☎028 9085 3997
🖷028 9036 5536
E: info@ccneurope.org.uk
Web: www.ccneurope.org.uk
Broadcast-quality Christian production centre, producing videos for television and radio stations.
President: Dr C Stewart OBE. Executive staff 2, Other staff 8. ***CC*** No.XR 14124. Began 1996; interdenominational. No magazine. Turnover n/a.

***Christian Television Association**, Wraxall, Bristol BS48 1PG
☎01275 851 222/555
🖷01275 851 550
E: info@cta.uk.com
Web: www.cta.uk.com
Producing video programmes for sale, on commission and for broadcasting; also video library.
Executive Director: Mr Malcolm Turner. Executive staff 2, Other staff 1. ***CC*** No.280329. Began 1978; interdenominational. Magazine: *CTA News* (4,000 half-yearly). Turnover £200,000 to year end Dec 02.

Clearwater Communications, 163 Marshall Lake Road, Shirley, Solihull B90 4RB
☎0121 744 3122
M: 07901 773 279
🖷0121 624 3866
E: don.sanders@bigfoot.com
Producing evangelistic programmes for television, and video materials for churches and schools.
Director: Mr Don Sanders. Executive staff 1, Other staff 1. Began 1984; interdenominational. No magazine. Turnover £15,000 to year end Aug 04.

Cloak Productions, PO Box 101, East Boldon NE36 0WY
☎0191 519 4466
M: 07811 197 452
🖷0191 519 4466
E: enquiries@cloakproductions.com
Web: www.cloakproductions.com
Television and video production and other media services.
Producer / Director: Mr Graeme Spencer. Executive staff 2. Began 2002; non-denominational. No magazine. Turnover n/a.

Contrapositive New Media, 1 Theatre Place, 489a New Cross Road, London SE14 6TQ
☎020 8692 8882
🖷020 8692 9828
E: studio@contrapositive.tv
Web: www.contrapositive.tv
Web design, video production and graphic design for charities, Christian Organisations and public and private sectors.
Business Development Manager: Mr Adam Kensington. Executive staff 3, Other staff 3. Began 2000; non-denominational. No magazine. Turnover £75,000 to year end Mar 02.

***Cross Rhythms**, PO Box 1110, Stoke-on-Trent ST1 1XR
☎08700 118 008
🖷08700 117 002
E: admin@crossrhythms.co.uk
Web: www.crossrhythms.co.uk
24-hour FM and digital radio station, magazine, festivals, outside events, TV and website ministries.
Chief Executive Officer: Mr Jonathan Bellamy. Executive staff 1, Other staff 12. ***CC*** No.1069357. Began 1990; interdenominational. Magazine: *Cross Rhythms* (6,000 every two months). Turnover £480,000 to year end Dec 04.

***CrossView Audio Visual**, PO Box 22, Felixstowe IP11 9EU
☎01394 270 110
E: mail@crossview.co.uk
Web: www.crossview.co.uk
Producing evangelistic, promotional and teaching videos and multi-media; training, consultancy.
Director: Dr Terry Smith. Executive staff 2, Other staff 1. Began 1993; interdenominational. No magazine. Turnover n/a.

CTVC, 9 Copper Row, Tower Bridge, London SE1 2LH
☎020 7940 8480
🖷020 7940 8490
E: info@ctvc.co.uk
Web: www.ctvc.co.uk
Television production.
Chief Executive Officer: Mr Nick Stuart. Executive staff 6, Other staff 15. ***CC*** No.1375941. Began 1959; non-denominational. No magazine. Turnover n/a.

***Cutting Edge Productions**, Unit 19 Lymington Barn, 27 Lymington Bottom Road, Medstead, Alton GU34 5EW
☎01420 563 737
🖷01420 568 292
E: info@cuttingedgeuk.com
Web: www.cuttingedgeuk.com
Specialising in live multi-camera events, single-camera productions, OB truck and post-production, DVD/CD-ROM authoring.
Proprietor: Mr Alan Matthews. Admin staff 5. Began 1994; interdenominational. No magazine. Turnover n/a.

†Dales Broadcast Ltd, Nettle Hill, B[illegible]nklow Road, Ansty, Coventry CV7 9JL
☎024 7662 1763 M: 07[illegible]03 58[illegible] 925
🖷024 7660 2732
E: sales@dales-ltd.com
Web: www.dales-ltd.com
Producing religious and moral videos and television broadcast programmes.
Managing Director: Mr Julian [illegible]oden. *Marketing Director:* Mrs Kate [illegible]oden. Executive staff 3, Other staff 2. Began 1984; non-denominational. (Previously Dales Television). No magazine. Turnover £250,000 to year end Mar 00.

***Delta Lights Multimedia Communications**, 23 Cherington Close, Northern Moor, Manchester M23 0FE
☎0161 613 0373
E: info@deltalights.co.uk
Web: deltalights.co.uk
Providing Worship Session song projection software; video production, CD-ROM, internet streaming, training.
Principal: Mr Tim Ingham. Executive staff 1, Admin staff 1. Began 1984; non-denominational. No magazine. Turnover £19,000 to year end Mar 0[illegible].

Dovetail Productions, Dovecote House, Walcot, Sleaford NG34 0SU
☎01529 497 081
M: 07770 893 455 🖷01529 497 [illegible]81
E: emival@dovetail.nildram.co.uk
Producing films, television programmes and videos, special interest in education, training in basic video skills.
Director: Mr Eric Mival. Executive staff 1, Other staff 1. Began [illegible]988; non-denominational. No magazine. Turnover n/a.

Encounter Video, PO Box 28, Marple, Stockport SK6 6JE
☎0161 427 0661 M: 07754 393 [illegible]14
E: encounter@vidtech.fsnet.co.uk
Web: www.encountervideo.co.uk
Free lance cameraman, multi-camera shoots, conferences, events, video production and editing facilites,.
Director: Mr Dennis Cooper. Executive staff 1. Began 2002; Pentecostal. (Previously Encounter Video & Technical. No magazine. Turnover £10,000 to year end Mar 05.

†FLT Films / MRA Productions, 24 Greencoat Place, London SW[illegible]P 1RD
☎020 7828 6591
E: info@fltfilms.org.uk
Producing films and videos offering broad perspective on and practical approach to social and moral issues.
Director: Mr David Channer. Executive staff 1, Other staff 3. ***CC*** No.226[illegible]11. Began 1952; interdenominational. FLT: For the Love of Tomorrow. Magazine: *For a Change* (5,000 every two months). Turnover £113,000 to year end Mar 02.

M

FRIENDS
AND
HEROES

***Focus Radio**, 54 The Avenue, Southampton SO17 1XQ
☎023 8067 6911
E: office@focus.org.uk
Web: www.focus.org.uk
Making radio programmes for international evangelism and leadership training.
Director: Mr David A Couchman. Executive staff 1, Other staff 2. ***CC*** No.298007. Began 1976; interdenominational. No magazine. Turnover £66,000 to year end Mar 02.

Forward Vision Communications Ltd, 215 Greenhouse, Custard Factory, Gibb Street, Birmingham B9 4AA
☎0121 224 7575 🖷0121 224 7585
E: action@forwardvision.co.uk
Web: www.forwardvision.co.uk
Multi-media content creation and delivery company including video, CD ROM, DVD, web design, print design and e-learning.
Operations Coordinator: Sarah Lowther. Executive staff 1, Other staff n/a. Began 1991; non-denominational. No magazine. Turnover n/a.

***Friends and Heroes**, Lough House, Approach Road, Ramsey IM8 1RG
☎01624 811 747 🖷01624 811 733
E: mail@friendsandheroes.com
Web: www.friendsandheroes.com
Producing television animation series for broadcast and DVD distribution in UK and worldwide.
Chairman: Mrs Alison Dorricott. *Managing Director:* Mr David Dorricott. *General Manager:* Mrs Judy Mills. Admin staff 5, Production staff 195. Began 2004; non-denominational. No magazine. Turnover £2,000,000 to year end Jun 05.

God TV, Angel House, Borough Road, Sunderland SR1 1HW
☎0191 568 0800 🖷0191 568 0808
E: info@god.tv
Web: www.god.tv
Producing and distributing Christian television programmes.
Chief Executive Office: Mr & Mrs Rory & Wendy Alec. Executive staff 5, Other staff 100. Began 1995; non-denominational. (Previously Christian Channel (Europe) Ltd). Magazine: *Partner News*(Circulation & frequency n/a). Turnover n/a.

***Good News Broadcasting Association (Great Britain) Ltd**, Back Lane, Ranskill, Retford DN22 8NN
☎01777 817 138 Radio response line 08000 927 892 M: 07711 522 872
E: info@gnba.net
Web: www.gbna.net
International, national, local radio programme production; resource centre: books, tapes, videos, CDs, internet audio ministry.
Business Manager: Chalmers Dobson. *National Director:* Rev Dr Derek Stringer. Executive staff 2, Admin staff 8. ***CC*** No.275115. Began 1954; non-denominational. Affiliated to Back to the Bible. Magazine: *Sounding Out* (3,700 monthly). Turnover £181,203 to year end June 04.

Gospel Broadcasting System Ltd (GBS Radio), 14 Grange Road West, Birkenhead CH41 4DA
☎0151 639 2450 🖷0151 639 2450
E: enquiries@gbsradio.org.uk
Web: www.gbsradio.org.uk
Producing Bible teaching and evangelical radio programmes for Africa, India and elsewhere.
Director/Secretary: Mr J K Stuffins. All voluntary staff. ***CC*** No.218947. Began 1956; interdenominational. No magazine. Turnover £25,000 to year end June 05.

GRF Christian Radio, GRF Studios, 342 Argyle Street, Glasgow G2 8LY
☎0141 221 9447 🖷0141 221 8298
E: the.team@grf.org.uk
Web: www.grf.org.uk
Producing programmes for worldwide radio networks, BBC radio, ILR and hospital radio.
Programme Controller: Mr Brian W Muir. No full-time staff. ***CC*** No.SCO 40269. Began 1948; non-denominational. No magazine. Turnover £34,000 to year end Mar 05.

Hatikvah Film Trust, PO Box 2025, Steyning BN44 3QW
☎0845 230 8788 🖷0845 230 8788
E: mail@hatikvah.co.uk
Web: ww.hatikvah.co.uk
Producing educational and documentary programmes.
Producer: Mr Hugh Kitson. Admin staff 1, No other paid staff. ***CC*** No.1104887. Began 2004; non-denominational. (Previously Hatikvah Film Foundation). No magazine. Turnover £5,000 to year end Jun 05.

†Hope FM, Delta House, 56 Westover Road, Bournemouth BH1 2BS
☎01202 315 200 🖷01202 317 751
Web: www.hopefm.com
Community Christian radio serving Bournemouth, Christchurch and Poole.
Director: Mr B Crawford. Executive staff 1. ***CC*** No.250619. Began n/a; interdenominational. Part of Bournemouth YMCA. No magazine. Turnover £30,000 to year end Dec 02.

Housetop, 111a High Street, Rickmansworth WD3 1AN
☎01923 779 446 🖷01923 779 447
E: jos@womenpriests.org
Web: www.womenpriests.org
Christian communications centre; raising the question of women's ordination in the church.
Director: Dr John Wijngaards. Executive staff 2, Other staff 6. ***CC*** No.1053251. Began 1982; Roman Catholic. No magazine. Turnover £50,259 to year end Dec 02.

Ignite Creative, The Way of the Goose Building, 32 East Street, Coventry CV1 5LS
☎024 7622 5226
E: info@ignitecreative.co.uk
Web: www.ignitecreative.co.uk
Producing film and video for a wide range of clients.
Director: Mr Stephen Holdsworth. Executive staff 2, Admin staff 1. Began 2003; interdenominational. Turnover n/a.

***International Films**, 36 High Street, Princes Risborough HP27 0AX
☎01844 346 471 M: 07[illegible]74 45[illegible] 191
🖷01844 274 207
E: info@internationalfilms.org
Web: www.internationalfilms.org
Producing and distributing Christian videos and broadcast programmes.
Chief Executive Officer: Mr Mike Pritchard. Executive staff 3. ***CC*** No.26[illegible]968. Began 1970; interdenominational. No magazine. Turnover n/a.

Irish Christian Broadcasters, 18 Ba[illegible]lehill Road, Portadown, Craigavon BT62 [illegible]ER
☎028 3835 4503 M: 077[illegible]3 693 [illegible]53
🖷028 3835 4503
E: icbireland@btinternet.com
Re-broadcasting Christian radio programmes throughout Ireland on 549 medium wave and FM frequencies.
Director: Mr David Robinson. Executive staff 1, Other staff 3. Began 2000; interdenominational. No magazine. Turnover n/a.

†Lamplight Productions, 30 Horton View, Banbury OX16 9HP
☎01295 275 708
E: mark@lamplight-uk.com
Broadcast-quality video production and consultation; camera crew hire.
Contact: Mr Mark Howe. Executive staff 2. Began 1987; non-denominational. No magazine. Turnover £100,000 to year end Apr 98.

LangMedia, East Waterside Studios, Upton Marina, Upton-upon-Severn, Worcester WR8 0PB
☎01684 591 077 🖷01684 591 07[illegible]
E: langm90@aol.com
Producing radio and TV programmes, audio visuals (Christian and commercial); media training; scriptwriting; music productions.
Executive Producer: Mr Clive Langmead. Executive staff 2. Began 1988; non-denominational. No magazine. Turnover n/a.

†Magnetic Pictures, First House, 1 Sutton Street, Birmingham B1 1PE
☎0121 622 1582 🖷0121 622 308[illegible]
E: aprice@magpix.co.uk
Web: www.magpix.co.uk
Producing video, broadcast and multi-media material for the charity sector, education and TV.
Producer: Sally Murcott. *Marketing Manager:* Andy Price. Executive staff 2, Other staff 5. Began 1989; non-denominational. No magazine. Turnover n/a.

New Life Radio, 29 Sydney Road, Exeter EX2 9AH
☎01392 219 499 🖷01392 275 296
E: radio@newliferadio.co.uk
Web: www.newliferadio.co.uk
Broadcasting the Christian message with good news and music in Devon and on the internet.
Director of Operations: Mr Mike Coles. Executive staff 2, Other staff 1. Began 1998; interdenominational. No magazine. Turnover n/a.

M

M

***Oasis Media**, 115 Southwark Bridge Road, London SE1 0AX
☎020 7450 9057 🖷020 7450 9060
E: debbie.hyde@oasismedia.co.uk
Web: www.oasismedia.co.uk
PR communications for companies & organisations.
Director: Ms Debbie Hyde. Executive staff 4. Began 1996; non-denominational. No magazine. Turnover n/a.

OCM Films Ltd, 3 Lawn Road, Exmouth EX8 1QJ
☎0870 760 2076 M: 07703 172 994
E: info@ocmfilms.co.uk
Web: www.ocmfilms.co.uk
TV, DVD and internet video production company. Specialists in internet video delivery.
Director: Mr Tim Finch. Executive staff 2, Other staff 4. Began 1994; interdenominational. (Previously FosterFinch Ltd). No magazine. Turnover n/a.

One Mediator Ltd, 6 Bawn Meadows, Hamiltonsbawn, Armagh BT60 1LU
☎028 3887 1727 M: 07970 777 475
E: info@onemediator.com
Web: www.onemediator.com
Producing films and documentaries, telling interesting and meaningful stories to a universal audience.
Director: Mr Jeff Marshall. Executive staff 1, Other staff n/a. Began 1997; non-denominational. (Previously One Mediator Communications). No magazine. Turnover n/a.

Pauline Books & Media, Middle Green, Langley, Slough SL3 6BS
☎01753 577 629 🖷01753 511 809
E: slough@pauline-uk.org
Web: www.pauline-uk.org
Producing and marketing DVDs, CDs, visual products, videos, posters.
Sister-in-Charge: Sister Rina Risitano. Executive staff 1, Other staff 5. ***CC*** No.296042. Began 1987; Roman Catholic. (Previously St Paul MultiMedia Productions). No magazine. Turnover £350,000 to year end Dec 98.

Plankton Records, PO Box 13533, Forest Gate, London E7 0SG
☎020 8534 8500
E: plankton.records@virgin.net
Record label and music publisher for Christian-orientated bands and songwriters.
Senior Partner: Mr Keith Dixon. Executive staff 2. Began 1977; non-denominational. No magazine. Turnover n/a.

***Premier Christian Radio**, 22 Chapter Street, London SW1P 4NP
☎020 7316 1300 🖷020 7233 6706
E: premier@premier.org.uk
Web: www.premier.org.uk
Broadcasting publishing and internet resources for London and the UK.
Chairman: Mr David Heron. *Chief Executive:* Mr Peter Kerridge. Executive staff 4, Other staff 50. ***CC*** No.287610. Began 1991; interdenominational. Magazine: *On Air* (40,000 quarterly). Turnover £3,800,000 to year end Sep 05.

R M Freelance, 43 Chevin Avenue, Leicester LE3 6PX
☎0116 287 0489 M: 07774 735 538
🖷0116 299 6304
E: r_marsh@btinternet.com
Video and audio production for events; training; news releases; audio production for puppetry, radio adverts.
Producer/Director: Mr Rob Marsh. Executive staff 1, Admin staff 1. Began 1993; interdenominational. (Previously Burning Bush Productions). No magazine. Turnover £38,000 to year end Aug 00.

***Radio Worldwide**, Springhead Park House, Park Lane, Rothwell, Leeds LS26 0ET
☎0113 282 2291 🖷0113 282 3908
E: enquiries@radioworldwide.org
Web: www.radioworldwide.org
Producing radio programmes; media training UK and overseas; internet radio.
Directors: Mr & Mrs Christopher & Bela Singh. Executive staff 2, Other staff 14. ***CC*** No.237005. Began 1961; interdenominational. A WEC international ministry. No magazine. Turnover £76,382 to year end Mar 02.

Revelation Christian Resources, 6 Cedar Close, Worthing BN13 2HZ
☎01903 694 433
E: johnray@onetel.onetel.com
Promoting, marketing and producing Christian videos.
Director: Mr John Ray. Executive staff 1. ***CC*** Began 1988; interdenominational. Also known as Sunrise Video Productions. No magazine. Turnover n/a.

***Revival (The Hour of Revival Association)**, 13 Lismore Road, Eastbourne BN21 3AY
☎01323 725 231 🖷013[illegible]3 412 [illegible]50
E: info@revivalmedia.org
Web: www.revivalmedia.org
Producing worldwide Gospel radio, correspondence courses, cassettes, radio production facilities, Christian advertising campaigns on secular radio.
General Secretary: Mr Ian M[illegible]lmine. *Director of Programmes:* Mr Patrick Woodward. Executive staff [illegible], Other staff [illegible]. ***CC*** No.232509. Began 19[illegible]3; interdenominational. (Previously Hour of Revival Association). Magazine: *International Daily Prayer Bulletin* (8,000 every two months). Turnover £198,000 to year end Mar 0[illegible].

†**Scope Productions Ltd**, 12[illegible] Blythswood Street, Glasgow G2 4[illegible]N
☎0141 275 3320 🖷0141 [illegible]75 3[illegible]21
E: annahannigan@scopeproductions.co.uk
Web: www.scopeproductions.co.uk
Producing television resources worldwide.
Producer/Director: Mrs Anna Hannigan. Executive staff 4, Other staff 8. Began 1984; interdenominational. No magazine. Turnover £3,200,000 to year end Dec 02.

Spark Productions Ltd, Brook Place, Bagshot Road, Chobham, Woking GU2[illegible] [illegible]SJ
☎01276 855 571 🖷01276 855 5[illegible]5
E: spark@sparkproductions.co.uk
Freelance commissioned work in audio, television, film; publishing house; editing suite; media seminars.
Directors: Mr Bart Gavigan, Mrs Patricia Beall. Executive staff 2. Other staff n/a. Began 1990; non-denominational. No magazine. Turnover n/a.

Studio 18 Productions Ltd, [illegible]6 Battlehill Road, Portadown, Craigavon BT62 4[illegible]R
☎028 3835 4503 M: 077[illegible]3 683 [illegible]3
🖷028 3835 4503
E: david.studio18@btinternet.com
Web: godspot.ie
Producing Christian programmes for secular radio stations throughout Ireland; also CDs with music / message.
Managing Director: Mr David Robinson. Executive staff 1, Other staff [illegible]. ***CC*** No.XR 35470. Began 2000; interdenominational. No magazine. Turnover n/a.

***STV Videos**, PO Box 299, Bromley BR2 [illegible]XB
☎020 8464 4287 M 07770 918 8[illegible]
🖷020 8464 4287
Web: www.stvvideos.co.uk
Video and audio productions; duplication, mastering, editing; large screen OB vehicle; bulk CDs, VCDs, DVDs.
Director: Mr Dave Armstrong. Executive staff 2, Other staff 3. Began [illegible]989; interdenominational. No magazine. Turnover n/a.

***Such and Such Productions**, 18 Queens Road, Steepleview, Laindon, Basildon SS15 4AN
☎01268 490 241 🖷01268 459 054
E: davidaldous@blueyonder.co.uk
Web: www.suchandsuchproductions.org.uk
Voice-overs, radio and television presenter makers of documentaries and short films, drama specialists.
Director: David Aldous. Executive staff 2, Other Staff 2. Began 1994; non-denominational. (Previously Voice in the Dark Production Co Ltd). No magazine. Turnover n/a

***Tandem TV and Film Ltd**, Charleston House, 13 High Street, Hemel Hempstead HP1 3AA
☎01442 261 576 🖷01442 219 250
E: terry@tandemtv.com
Web: www.tandemtv.com
Producing video, television and DVD for a wide range of Christian and secular clients.
Directors: Mr & Mrs Terry & Barbara Page. Executive staff 2, Other staff 3. Began 1979; non-denominational. No magazine. Turnover £300,000 to year end Dec 04.

†Telling Pictures, 6 Waitemeads, Purton, Swindon SN5 4ET
☎01793 770 171 M: 07890 002 175
🖷01793 770 171
E: info@tellingpictures.org.uk
Web: www.tellingpictures.org.uk
Producing promotional and Christian educational programmes for video distribution and broadcast.
Creative Director: Mr David Martin. Executive staff 2, Other staff 2. Began 1995; non-denominational. No magazine. Turnover n/a

†TVA Productions, 47 Moorfield Road, Irlams O Th Height, Salford M6 7EY
☎0161 736 1168 🖷0161 736 1168
E: info@tva-productions.com
Web: www.tva-productions.com
Producing videos on tape, DVD, CD ROM, web; for churches, charities and missions.
Producer: Mr Frank Walsh. Executive staff 1. Began 1994; non-denominational. No magazine. Turnover n/a.

UK Christian News, PO Box 758, Taunton TA4 3WZ
☎0870 760 7614
E: info@ukchristiannews.tv
Web: www.ukchristiannews.tv
Team-based television news reporting agency making current affairs programmes for the UK.
Editor: Mr Tim Finch. Executive staff 1. Began 2003; non-denominational. No magazine. Turnover n/a.

***United Christian Broadcasters Ltd**, Broadcast Centre, Hanchurch Lane, Stoke-on-Trent ST4 8RY
☎01782 642 000 🖷01782 641 121
E: ucb@ucb.co.uk
Web: www.ucb.co.uk
Radio and TV broadcasting by satellite, cable, internet. Printing/distribution of The Word For Today.
Chief Executive: Mr Ian Mackie. *Company Secretary:* Richard Willoughby. *Communications Director:* Brian Bennett. Executive staff 4, Other staff 100. ***CC*** No.299128. Began 1986; interdenominational. (Previously UCB Europe). Magazine: *The Word for Today* (850,000 quarterly). Turnover £6,500,000 to year end Dec 04.

†Vision Broadcasting, The Vision Studios, Shaftesbury Centre, Percy Street, Swindon SN2 2AZ
☎01793 511 244 🖷01793 511 211
E: info@visionchannel.co.uk
Web: www.visionchannel.co.uk
Christian TV channel on Sky digital.
Director: Mrs Fran Wildish. Executive staff 1, Other staff 3. ***CC*** No.802553. Began 1986; non-denominational. Magazine: *Vision for Today* (500 every two months). Turnover £20,000 to year end Dec 02.

†Vision Productions, 111 Ecclesall Road South, Sheffield S11 9PH
☎0114 262 0700 🖷0114 236 3031
E: visionproductions@easynet.co.uk
Producing films, videos drama, documentary; training; working exclusively for government training.
Studio Director: Mr Gordon Ramsay. Executive staff 1, Other staff 2. Began 1979; interdenominational. No magazine. Turnover £200,000 to year end Dec 02.

Vivid Broadcast Ltd, The NRC, Foundry Lane, Horsham RH13 5PX
☎01403 213 020 🖷07958 071 438
E: info@vividbroadcast.co.uk
Web: www.vividbroadcast.co.uk
Producing TV and film programmes, promotional films; live events, emerging technologies, DVD production, stage design.
Director: Mr Rory Springthorpe. Executive staff 2, Admin staff 2. Began 2005; interdenominational. No magazine. Turnover £60,000 to year end May 05.

***Wirral Christian Media Ltd**, PO Box 53, Upton, Wirral CH49 3WB
☎0151 643 1696
E: office@flamefmwirral.org.uk
Web: www.flamefmwirral.org.uk
Local Christian and community radio station, Flame FM; media training, radio programme production.
Station Manager Managing Director: Mr Norman Polden. Executive staff 3, Admin staff 2, Other staff 10. ***CC*** No.1088763. Began 2001; non-denominational. No magazine. Turnover £25,000 to year end Apr 05.

XSolve Media Ltd, Holy Trinity, Boar lane, Leeds LS1 6HW
☎0113 245 4099 M: 07989 234 031
E: info@xsolve.co.uk
Web: www.xsolve.co.uk
Providing media solutions including web and graphic design to missions and churches.
Director: Mr Anthony Trivino. Executive staff 2, Admin staff 2. Began 2002; non-denominational. (Previously iMedia). No magazine. Turnover £35,000 to year end Jun 03.

MEDIA SERVICES

21st Century Video, Hollybush Christian Fellowship, Hollybush Farm, Newsham, Thirsk YO7 4DH
☎01845 587 386 🖷01845 587 103
E: hollybushcf@aol.com
Web: www.hollybushchristianfellowship.co.uk
Recording live meetings, producing and distributing tapes in UK and beyond.
Director: Mr Arthur Bennison. No full-time staff. Began 1981; non-denominational. No magazine. Turnover £12,000 to year end Oct 00.

Acts Sound & Lighting, Riversdene, Howley Lane, Warrington WA1 2DJ
☎01925 656 469 M: 07711 841 641
🖷01925 656 469
E: acts@fsbdial.co.uk
Web: www.actssoundandlighting.co.uk
Hireing, selling, installing, repairing of sound and lighting equipment; complete productions services for events.
Owner: Mr Martin Naylor. Executive staff 1, Other staff 2. Began 1986; non-denominational. No magazine. Turnover £200,000 to year end Aug 05.

†AG Photography (Adam Greene), 36a Shadwell Road, Portsmouth PO2 9EJ
☎023 9265 5657 M: 07775 624 445
E: adamgreene@tiscali.co.uk
Press, publicity and promotional photographic services; weddings, portraits, digital imaging, picture repairs; training in photoshop.
Freelance Photographer: Mr Adam Greene. Executive staff 1. Began 1983; Anglican. No magazine. Turnover n/a.

Alive Church Systems Ltd, Brookhampton, North Cadbury, Yeovil BA22 7DA
☎01925 656 469 M: 07711 841 641
E: info@actssoundandlighting.co.uk
Web: www.actssoundandlighting.co.uk
Design and installation of remote control sound enhancement systems; NXT flat sound panel specialist.
Director: Mr Christopher Fone. Executive staff 1, Personnel 5. Began 1995; ecumenical. No magazine. Turnover £135,000 to year end Jul 04.

***Ambassador Enterprises**, Victory House, Portland Road, London SE25 4PN
☎0845 330 6745 M: 07984 467 151
🖷0845 330 6746
E: info@ambassadorenterprises.co.uk
Web: www.ambassadorenterprises.co.uk
Supplying public address systems, overhead and video projectors, musical instruments, church requirements including perspex lecterns.
Manager: Mr Mark Walford. Executive staff 2. ***CC*** No.229741. Began 1972; interdenominational. No magazine. Turnover £98,729 to year end Jan 98.

***Anchor Recordings Ltd**, 72 The Street, Kennington, Ashford TN24 9HS
☎01233 620 958 🖷01233 620 958
E: info@anchor-recordings.com
Web: www.anchor-recordings.com
Recording and distributing Christian messages; worship and video cassettes.
General Manager: Mr James Harris. Executive staff 3, Other staff 3. ***CC*** No.224579. Began 1973; interdenominational. No magazine. Turnover n/a.

Angel Talk Limited, 9a Shaftesbury Close, Harmans Water, Bracknell RG12 9PX
☎01344 425 200 🖷01344 869 589
E: sales@angeltalk.co.uk
Web: www.angeltalk.co.uk
Low-volume CD/R and DVD+R duplication, audio digital editing, CD mastering, various associated supplies.
Managing Director: Mr Malcolm D Powell. Executive staff 2. Began 1981; interdenominational. No magazine. Turnover £40,000 to year end Sept 02.

Ark-T Centre, Crowell Road, Oxford OX4 3LN
☎01865 773 499 / 396 778
🖷01865 773 499
E: mail@ark-t.org
Web: www.ark-t.org
Creating space for the arts through music, dance, the visual arts and food.
Director: Mr James Grote. Executive staff 2, Other staff 5. ***CC*** No.1079495. Began 1994; non-denominational. No magazine. Turnover £120,000 to year end Dec 04.

ARM Services, 79 Haycroft Drive, St Leonards Park, Gloucester GL4 6XX
☎01452 418 418 M: 07985 583 373
🖷01452 418 418
E: info@armaudio.co.uk
Web: www.armaudio.co.uk
Live recording for conferences and special services, PA hire, equipment supply, loop amplification, church installations.
Principal: Mr Kelly Gibson. Executive staff 1. Began 1986; Newfrontiers. (Previously Audio and Recording Ministries (ARM)). No magazine. Turnover £100,000 to year end Dec 05.

Art and Christianity Enquiry (ACE), 107 Crundale Avenue, London NW9 9PS
☎020 8206 2253 🖷020 8206 2253
E: enquiries@acetrust.org
Web: www.acetrust.org
Reaching all for whom visual arts are vital in understanding, teaching and practice of faith.
Director: Rev Tom Devonshire Jones. Executive staff 1. ***CC*** No.1035221. Began 1991; ecumenical. Magazine: *Art and Christianity* (1,400 quarterly). Turnover n/a.

B & H Sound Services Ltd, The Old School Studio, Crowland Road, Eye, Peterborough PE6 7TN
☎01733 223 535 🖷01733 223 545
E: sound@bhsound.co.uk
Web: www.bhsound.co.uk or www.audioplan.co.uk
Designing and installing sound systems; studio and on-location recording facilities; duplication; sound equipment hire.
Managing Director: Mr Brian Hillson. *Financial Director:* Mr I B Dunkley. *Recording Services Manager:* Mrs Nicki Sager. Executive staff 5, Other staff 7. Began 1978; interdenominational. Incorporating Audioplan. No magazine. Turnover £1,200,000 to year end Dec 02.

***Blue Skies Video Productions**, Blue Skies Studios, 31 Shire Lane, Chorleywood, Rickmansworth WD3 5NP
☎01923 282 686 🖷01923 282 386
E: info@blueskiesvideo.co.uk
Web: www.blueskiesvideo.co.uk
Exploring Bible Sites *DVD series; producing promotional and teaching programmes for Christian organisations.*
Director: Mr David Nunn. Executive staff 1, Admin staff 1. Began 1993; non-denominational. No magazine. Turnover n/a.

Roman Catholic Diocesan Communication Officers, *England and Wales.*
Arundel and Brighton *Diocesan Communications Officer:* Rev Stuart Geary, Tulp Cottage, Old Lane, Tatsfield, Westerham TN16 2LJ
E: dabcec@dabnet.org
☎01293 515 666 M 079[illegible]4 18[illegible] 169
Birmingham *Diocesan Communications Officer:* Mr Peter Jennings, 47 Regent Road, Harborne, Birmingham B17 9[illegible]U
E: imc@peterjennings.co.uk
☎0121 427 2780 M: 07[illegible]57 639 556
Brentwood *Diocesan Communications Officer:* Fr John Harvey, 9 Trap's Hill, Loughton IG10 1SZ
E: jjh152@aol.com
☎020 8508 3492 🖷 020 8532 0[illegible]38
Cardiff *Diocesan Communications Officer:* Rev Canon Robert Reardon, 910 Newport Road, Rumney, Cardiff CF3 4LL
E: r-c-chaplaincy@cardiff.ac.uk
☎029 2036 0044 M: 07774 410 [illegible]57
🖷 029 2079 3172
Clifton *Diocesan Communications Officer:* Rev Robert D Corrigan, Clifton Cathedral House, Clifton Park, Bristol BS8 3BX
E: PressandMedia@CliftonDiocese.com
☎0117 973 8411 🖷 0117 974 4[illegible]97
East Anglia *Diocesan Communications Officer:* Rev John Warrington, The White House, 21 Upgate, Poringland, Norwich NR14 7SH
E: office@east-angliadiocese.org.uk
☎01508 492 202 Home 01508 493 919 🖷 01508 495 358
Hallam *Diocesan Communications Officer:* To be appointed, Hallam CYS, St Charles Street, Attercliffe, Sheffield S9 3WU
E: youthservice@hallam-diocese.com
☎0114 256 6460 🖷 0114 256 26[illegible]3
Hexham and Newcastle *Diocesan Communications Officer:* Mrs Pat Campbell, Bishop's House, 800 West Road, Newcastle upon Tyne NE5 2BJ
E: office@rcdhn.org.uk
☎0191 228 0003/4 🖷0191 274 0[illegible]32

Lancaster *Diocesan Communications Officer:* Rev Denis Blackledge SJ, Church House, 17 Talbot Road, Blackpool FY1 1LB
E: denisblackledge@compuserve.com
☎01253 297 666 🖷 01253 297 888
Leeds *Diocesan Communications Officer:* Mr John Grady, Hinsley Hall, 62 Headingley Lane, Leeds LS6 2BU
E: dolposs@aol.com
☎0113 261 8022 M: 07703 341 527
🖷 0113 261 8035
Liverpool *Diocesan Communications Officer:* Mr Peter Heneghan, Centre of Evangelisation, Croxteth Drive, Sefton Park, Liverpool L17 1AA
☎0151 522 1042 🖷 0151 522 1060
Menevia *Diocesan Communications Officer:* Fr Michael Burke, Sacred Heart Church, School Road, Moriston, Swansea SA6 6HZ
E: michael@w-burke.freeserve.co.uk
☎01792 771 053
Middlesbrough *Diocesan Communications Officer:* Rev Jim Whiston, Diocesan Curia, 50a The Avenue, Middlesbrough TS5 6QT
E: Jim.Whiston@btinternet.com
☎01642 850 505 🖷 01642 851 404
Northampton *Diocesan Communications Officer:* Rev David Barrett, Bishop's House, Marriott Street, Northampton NN2 6AW
E: david.barrett15@btopenworld.com
☎01604 715 635 🖷 01604 792 186
Nottingham *Diocesan Communications Officer:* Rev Philip McBrien, Bishop's House, 27 Cavendish Road East, The Park, Nottingham NG7 1BB
E: bishop.secretary@nottinghamdiocese.org.uk
☎0115 947 4786 🖷 0115 947 5235
Plymouth *Diocesan Communications Officer:* Rev Michael Fay, 106 Steed Close, Paignton TQ4 7SP
E: michael.fay@btinternet.com
☎01803 845 023
Portsmouth *Diocesan Communications Officer:* Mr Barry Hudd, Night Owls, 100 Enborne Road, Newbury RG14 6AN
E: bhudd@portsmouth-dio.org.uk
☎01635 443 26 M: 07770 538 693
🖷 01635 443 26
Salford *Diocesan Communications Officer:* Rev Michael Walsh, 285 Stockport Road, Guide Bridge, Ashton-Under-Lyne OL7 0NT
E: MWalsh1402@aol.com
☎0161 330 2777 🖷 0161 343 5595
Shrewsbury *Diocesan Communications Officer:* Rev John Joyce, St Vincent's, Tatton Street, Knutsford WA16 6HB
E: Jjoycepat@aol.com
☎01565 633 040
Southwark *Diocesan Communications Officer:* Rev William Saunders, Archbishop's House, St George's Road, Southwark, London SE1 6HX
E: aps@rcsouthwark.co.uk
☎020 7928 2495 🖷 020 7928 7833
Westminster None
Wrexham *Diocesan Communications Officer:* Mrs Vicky Barlow, 1 Newmarket Rise, Llwyn Onn Park, Wrexham LL13 0QL
E: vibarlow@supanet.com
☎01978 311 420 M: 07802 894 817

The Forces *Communications Officer:* Fr David Conroy, HMS Collingwood, Fareham PO14 1AS
E: da.conroy@virgin.net
☎01329 332 239

CEVMA, Wraxall, Bristol BS48 1PG
☎01275 851 222
E: cevma@erf.de
Web: www.cevma.com
Association of Christians in film, television and new media, from across Europe.
Chairman: Mr Wolf-Dieter Kretschmer. No full-time staff. Began 1980; interdenominational. Magazine: *CEVMA News* (800 every six months). Turnover n/a.
Head Office PO Box 1444, D-35614, Wetzlar, Germany
E: info@cevma.com
☎+49 6441 957 261 🖷 –49 6441 957 130

CHAD Media Trust, PO Box 3456, Henley-in-Arden B95 6DZ
☎01926 426 922
E: chad@chadmedia.org
Web: www.chadmedia.org
Supporting Christian media practitioners in the Midlands; offering media education to the churches.
Secretary: Rev Mervyn Roberts. No full-time staff. ***CC*** No.519033. Began 1971; ecumenical. (Previously Coventry & Warwickshire Churches Broadcasting Committee). No magazine. Turnover £5,000 to year end Dec 05.

†**Chapel Lane Ministries/Chapel Lane Studios**, Hampton Bishop, Hereford HR1 4JR
☎01432 870 437 🖷01432 870 430
E: chapellane@aol.com
Web: www.chapellane.co.uk
Christian recording studio services; complete productions undertaken.
Managing Director: Mr Rob Andrews. Executive staff 2, Other staff 1. Began 1976; Pentecostal. No magazine. Turnover n/a.

***Cheltenham Stage Services**, Unit 5, Churchill Industrial Estate, Cheltenham GL53 7EG
☎01242 244 978 🖷01242 250 618
E: css@ullenwood.co.uk
Web: www.cheltenhamstageservices.co.uk
Hiring PA systems to 25kw and stage lighting to 150kw; pull rigging, production facilities, transport.
Proprietor: Mr Peter J Allison. *General Manager:* Mr Steve Roskilly. Executive staff 2, Other staff 4. Began 1981; Anglican. No magazine. Turnover n/a.

Christian Broadcasting Council of UK, PO Box 1110, Stoke-on-Trent ST1 1XR
E: enquiries@cbc.org uk
Web: www.cbc.org.uk
Promoting the Christian faith by supporting and sponsoring Christians in broadcasting, electronic and other media.
General Secretary: To be appointed. No full-time staff. ***CC*** No.327340. Began 1983; non-denominational. No magazine. Turnover n/a.

Christian Fabrications Ltd, 5 Chase Side Crescent, Enfield EN2 0JQ
☎020 8364 6411 M: 07973 734 811
🖷020 8364 6488
E: gwyates@blueyonder.co.uk
Web: www.christianfabrications.co.uk
Designing and installing amplification and induction-loop systems for churches and schools. Audio tape suppliers.
Managing Director: Mr Geoffrey W Yates. *Administrator:* Mrs Sue Taylor. Executive staff 1, Other staff 3. Began 1974; non-denominational. (Previously Christian Communication Services Ltd). No magazine. Turnover £300,000 to year end May 99.

***Christian TV**, Virtual Business Centre, Buxhall, Stowmarket IP14 3DX
☎01449 737 377 M: 07808 888 733
🖷01449 737 677
E: ctv@buxhall.co.uk
Web: christianTV.org.uk
Providing statellite equipment to receive Christian television and radio channels plus other wholesome family viewing.
Managing Director: Rev David Green. Executive staff 1, Other staff 3. Began 2002; interdenominational. No magazine. Turnover £46,000 to year end Dec 02.

***Christian-Sat Satellite Services**, 25 Albert Road, Hounslow TW3 3RW
☎0800 075 8113 M: 07932 620 966
🖷020 8569 5939
E: info@christian-sat.co.uk
Web: christian-sat.co.uk
Supplying and installing satellite TV systems for receiving Christian and family TV and radio programmes.
Managing Director: Mr Silas Mante. Executive staff 5, Admin staff 2. Began 2004; non-denominational. Turnover £47,000 to year end Jun 04.

Church of England Diocesan Communications Officers
Each diocese has a Communications Officer, who can be contacted via the Diocesan Office. See pages 155-162 in Church Headquarters.

Circle Sound Services, Circle House, 14 Waveney Close, Bicester OX26 2GP
☎01869 240 051 M: 07973 633 634
🖷08707 059 679
E: sound@circlesound.net
Web: www.circlesound.net
Location digital recording, digital editing and mastering, sound equipment supply, consultancy.
Contact: John Willett. Executive staff 1. Began 1978; non-denominational. No magazine. Turnover n/a.

Cloak Productions, PO Box 101, East Boldon NE36 0WY
☎0191 519 4466 M: 07811 197 452
🖷0191 519 4466
E: enquiries@cloakproductions.com
Web: www.cloakproductions.com
Television and video production and other media services.
Producer / Director: Mr Graeme Spencer. Executive staff 2. Began 2002; non-denominational. No magazine. Turnover n/a.

M

Media Services

†CN Productions Ltd, 5 Little Way, Moortown, Leeds LS17 6JN
☎0113 269 3930 M: 07802 785 450
℻0113 266 2075
E: c.norton@btclick.com
Web: www.cnproductions.com
Producing and licensing master tapes internationally; background music for television/film; publishing and music engraving.
Managing Director: Mr Christopher Norton. Executive staff 1, No other staff. Began 1982; non-denominational. No magazine. Turnover £400,000 to year end Dec 02.

Communications Training, Church House, Great Smith Street, London SW1P 3NZ
☎020 7898 1465 / 1458
E: comms.training@c-of-e.org.uk
Web: www.commstraining.cofe.anglican.org
Providing ecumenical communications training for individuals and organisations associated with the Churches.
Senior Information Officer: Mr Martin Short. Executive staff 1, Other staff 1. Began n/a; Anglican. No magazine. Turnover n/a.

***Crystal Clear Audio**, 62 Princes Park Lane, Hayes UB3 1JX
☎0845 330 1578 M: 07974 439 664
℻0845 330 1868
E: info@crystalclearaudio.co.uk
Web: www.crystalclearaudio.co.uk
Providing audio/visual design and installation services for churches and conference venues in south east England.
Partner: Mr Nick Fatkin. Executive staff 3, Other staff 2. Began 1989; interdenominational. No magazine. Turnover n/a.

CTJTS Ltd, Oakwood House, 4 St John's Street, Chichester PO19 1UR
☎01243 788 220 M: 07733 145 620
E: cleland.thom@tesco.net
Web: www.ctfts.com
Providing online accredited journalism courses for Christians, with personal tuition.
Director: Mr Cleland Thom. Executive staff 1, Admin staff 1. Began 2002; interdenominational. No magazine. Turnover £20,000 to year end Apr 05.

Cunnings Recording Associates, Brodrick Hall, Brodrick Road, London SW17 7DY
☎020 8767 3533 ℻020 8767 8525
E: info@cunnings.co.uk
Web: www.cunnings.co.uk
Selling, installing, servicing and hiring professional audio and video equipment for churches.
Proprietor: Mr Malcolm J Cunnings. Executive staff 3, Other staff 6. Began n/a; non-denominational. No magazine. Turnover n/a.

†Jean Dawkins, 39 Pavilion Drive, Leigh-on-Sea SS9 3JR
☎01702 714 655
E: jeandawkins@onetel.com
Supplying photographic images for posters, cards, magazines and weddings.
Photographer: Mrs Jean Dawkins. Executive staff 1. Began 2000; evangelical. No magazine. Turnover n/a.

***Day One Radio**, PO Box 4289, Wolverhampton WV10 8WX
☎01902 404 289 M: 07941 035 903
E: info@dayoneradio.co.uk
Web: www.dayoneradio.co.uk
Contemporary Christian & gospel music radio; local DAB digital radio broadcaster licenced by Ofcom.
Director: Mr J Peter Wilson. Executive staff 1. Began 1998; non-denominational. (Previously Day One Projects). No magazine. Turnover n/a.

†DCM Studios, Dovetales Christian Centre, Gospel Mission, Maygate, Westwood, Oldham OL9 6TR
☎0161 628 3838 ℻0161 628 3838
E: admin@dovetails.org
Recording studio available for Christian artistes.
Directors: Mr & Mrs WE, JA & Marcus Heap. Executive staff 3. Began n/a; interdenominational. No magazine. Turnover n/a.

†Roger Dey Sound & Communications Engineers, PO Box 492, Canterbury CT2 7GS
☎01227 768 778 ℻01227 768 778
E: sales@rogerdey.co.uk
Web: www.rogerdey.co.uk
Designing, installing and maintaining church sound and loop systems; specialists in medieval buildings.
Proprietor: Mr Roger Dey. Executive staff 2, Admin staff 2. Began 1982; non-denominational. No magazine. Turnover £250,000 to year end Sep 00.

Ecumenical Olympus Network (EON), The Vicarage, Epping Green, Epping CM16 6PN
☎01992 572 949 ℻01992 578 892
E: chrisbard@hotmail.com
Advancing ecumenical education through the use of communications satellites and advanced communications technology.
Company Secretary: Rev Canon Chris Bard. All voluntary staff. ***CC*** No.803448. Began 1989; ecumenical. No magazine. Turnover n/a.

Edenfield Communications Ltd, 2 South View Place, Midsomer Norton, Bath BA3 2AX
☎01761 414 992 M: 07958 578 417
E: info@edenfield-communications.co.uk
Web: www.edenfield-communications.co.uk
Hiring and installing audio-visual and public address equipment.
Director: Mr E Michael Jakins. Executive staff 2. Began 1985; non-denominational. No magazine. Turnover n/a.

Edvicron Electronic Services, 70 Charlesfield Road, Horley RH6 8BL
☎01293 821 824 ℻0129[illegible] 786 [illegible]5
Designing, supplying and installing sound reinforcement PA, loop systems for churches. Remote control specialists.
Director: Mr Ron Hall. Executive staff 4, Other staff 5. Began 1981; interdenominational. No magazine. Turnover n/a.

†Fastforward Music Ltd 1 Sorrel Horse Mews, Ipswich IP4 1LN
☎01473 210 555 M: 077[illegible] 608 [illegible]40
℻01473 210 500
E: sales@fastforwardmusic.co.uk
Marketing and selling family audio cassettes and CD releases to religious retailers.
Sales Director: Mr Neil Read. Executive staff 2, Admin staff 7. Began 1990; non-denominational. No magazine. Turnover £1,125,000 to year end Jul [illegible]0.

f f g, Bredon Fields, Eckington Road, Bredon, Tewkesbury GL20 7HE
☎01684 772 664 ℻01684 772 9[illegible]2
E: david@ffg.org.uk
Web: www.ffg.org.uk
Producing Christian records; residential recording studio; music for video and broadcasting.
Partner: Mr David Pick. Executive staff 3. Began 1977; non-denominational. Free For Good. No magazine. Turnover n/a.

The Focus Trust, 25 Spencer Gardens, Shillingstone, Blandford Forum DT11 [illegible]L
☎01258 860 301
Supporting the production and distribution of quality visual and print media reflecting and promoting Christianity.
Administrator: Mr Tony [illegible]ew. No full-time staff. ***CC*** No.282542. Began [illegible]979; non-denominational. No magazine. Turnover n/a.

Roy Francis Productions Ltd, [illegible]27 Cherry Orchard Road, Croydon CR0 6BE
☎020 8681 0345 ℻020 86[illegible]1 044[illegible]
E: info@RFProductions.co.uk
Web: www.RFProductions.co.uk
Events, media, marketing, promotions serving the needs of the Christian and business community.
Director: Mr Roy Francis. Admin staff 2, Other staff 3. Began 19[illegible]9; interdenominational. No magazine. Turnover £80,[illegible]0 to year end Aug 02.

Freelance Journalism Correspondence Exchange, 9 The Lodge, 3 Blackwater Road, Eastbourne BN21 4JF
☎01323 638 234
E: wendy@whiteheadw.freeserve.co.uk
Providing free Correspondence Exchange on preparing and submitting church information to local and national press.
Trainer: Mrs Wendy Whitehead. Executive staff 1. Began n/a; interdenominational. (Previously Freelance Journalism Workshops). No magazine. Turnover n/a.

M

Future Media, Unit 2, Grange Road Industrial Estate, Christchurch BH23 4JD
☎01425 270 511 M: 07714 761 023
📠01425 278 615
E: enquiries@futuremediasystems.com
Web: www.futuremediasystems.com
Sound, video and lighting services for churches, live events and recording; sales, hire training.
Director: Mr Luke Siemaszko. *Sales Manager:* Mr Simon Dodridge. Executive staff 1, Admin staff 2, Other staff 2. Began 1994; non-denominational. (Previously Lookpine Ltd). No magazine. Turnover £158,000 to year end Mar 03.

†Ghetto Blasters, 73 Apton Road, Bishop's Stortford CM23 3ST
☎01279 651 195 📠01279 651 195
E: burnett@ntlworld.com
Workshop to help churches use media and become a presence in local radio/newspapers.
Producer: Ms Alison Burnett. Executive staff 1. Began 1989; non-denominational. No magazine. Turnover n/a.

Grenville Educational Media Ltd, 25 Spencer Gardens, Shillingstone, Blandford Forum DT11 0TL
☎01258 860 088 📠01258 860 099
E: grenvillemedia@aol.com
Web: www.grenville-media.com
Distributing religious educational videos and books for use in school, church and home.
Director: Mr Tony Tew. Executive staff 1, Other staff 2. Began 2003; non-denominational. No magazine. Turnover n/a.

†Hartmusic Studios, Newhaven, Easton, Wells BA5 1EH
☎01749 870 424 📠01749 870 424
E: info@hartmusic-studios.co.uk
Web: www.hartmusic-studios.co.uk
Providing professional recording and production for Christian bands and artists.
Production Engineer: Mr Steve Hart. Executive staff 1, Admin staff 1. Began 2000; ecumenical. No magazine. Turnover £10,000 to year end Apr 03.

†HCVF Television & Video Productions, 67 Kenneth Street, Inverness IV3 5QF
☎01463 224 788 M: 07860 285 872
📠01463 711 460
E: hcvf@aol.com
Web: www.hcvf.co.uk
Television and video production, multimedia, conference support.
Partner Mr Jim Eglinton. Executive staff 2, Other staff 4. Began 1981; non-denominational. No magazine. Turnover £250,000 to year end Dec 98.

Hope Press Agency, PO Box 777, Nottingham NG11 6ZZ
☎0115 921 7280 📠0115 984 5251
E: hope@newlifepublishing.co.uk
Web: www.hopepressagency.co.uk
Providing Good News stories and Christian features to secular and religious media.
Editor: Mr Peter Wreford. Executive staff 2, Other staff 3. Began 1983; non-denominational. No magazine. Turnover n/a.

†HW Audio Ltd, 180 St Georges Road, Bolton BL1 2PH
☎01204 385 199 📠01204 364 057
E: sales@hwaudio.co.uk
Web: www.hwaudio.co.uk
Installing PA and audio induction-loop equipment.
Director: Mr Stephen D Harfield. Executive staff 2, Other staff 8. Began 1976; interdenominational. No magazine. Turnover £800,000 to year end Dec 00.

ICC Multimedia, 4-5 Regency Mews, Silverdale Road, Eastbourne BN20 7AB
☎01323 647 880 📠01323 645 095
E: sales@iccduplication.co.uk
Web: www.iccmultimedia.co.uk
Recording, audio media manufacturing centre, blank/duplicated cassettes and videos, CD, CD-ROM, Minidisc, DVD replication.
Duplication Manager: Mr Andy Thorpe. Executive staff 2, Other staff 40. ***CC*** No.1079801. Began 1976; interdenominational. Part of ICC. No magazine. Turnover [included in ICC]. CD, DVD, cassette, video duplication and replication, authoring, CD ROM, graphic design, print, multimedia, studios, editing.

ICC Studios, 4-5 Regency Mews, Silverdale Road, Eastbourne BN20 7AB
☎01323 643 341 📠01323 649 240
E: info@icc.org.uk
Web: www.iccstudios.co.uk
Recording, audio media manufacturing centre; blank/duplicated cassettes and videos; replication and multimedia services.
Studio Manager: Mr Neil Costello. Executive staff 2, Other staff 40. ***CC*** No.1079801. Began 1976; interdenominational. No magazine. Turnover n/a.

Images, 146 Two Butt Lane, Rainhill, Prescot L35 8PT
☎0151 426 1693 📠0151 493 0229
E: info@fotographicimages.co.uk
Web: www.fotographicimages.co.uk
Photographers specialising in events, conferences and the natural world.
Photographers: Mr & Mrs John & Carol Fairclough. Staff 2. Began 2003; non-denominational. No magazine. Turnover £150,000 to year end Jun 04.

International Christian Media Commission (ICMC), PO Box 154, Keighley BD20 6UU
☎08703 218 446 📠07092 316 711
E: ukadmin@icmc.org
Web: www.icmc.org
Providing consultancy, training and co-ordination. Association of media professionals and trainers from around the world.
Senior UK Associate: Mr Andrew Steele. Executive staff 2. ***CC*** No.1014870. Began 1990; non-denominational. No magazine. Turnover n/a.

ISIS Duplicating Co Ltd, Unit M2, Albany Road, Prescot L34 2UP
☎0151 430 9001 M: 0779 903 0500
📠0151 430 7441
E: john@isis-uk.com
Web: www.isis-uk.com
Divisonal Director: Mr John Fairclough. *Sales & Production Coordinator:* Mrs Sue Carr. Management staff 5, Admin staff 6, Studio staff 29. Began 1979; non-denominational. (Previously RTS One Stop) No magazine. Turnover n/a. Manufacturing CDs and audio cassettes, mastering, DVD, authoring, printing, distributing; mail order.

ITC Productions, Cefn Lea Park, Dolfor, Newtown SY16 4AJ
☎01686 625 040 📠01686 626 122
E: office@itcproductions.com
Web: www.itcproductions.co.uk or www.soundforchurches.co.uk
Consulting, selling and installing sound, lighting and visual for churches.
Director: Name not supplied. Executive staff 2, Other staff 2. Began 1998; interdenominational. No magazine. Turnover n/a.

ITV Teletext Religious Pages, 14 Oakleigh Park South, London N20 9JU
☎020 8445 4654 / 8388
📠020 8445 6831
E: allsaints.net@boltblue.com
Providing five pages of Godlines on ITV Teletext (Channel 4 page 149 and 1 London page).
Editor: Rev Adrian V Benjamin. Executive staff 1. Began 1979; interdenominational. (Previously British Churches Teletext Project). No magazine. Turnover n/a.

†RG Jones Sound Engineering, 16 Endeavour Way, Wimbledon, London SW19 8UH
☎020 8971 3100 📠020 8971 3101
E: sales@rgjones.co.uk
Web: www.rgjones.co.uk
Selling, installing and hiring audio equipment to churches; acoustic consultancy.
Managing Director: Mr Stephen Hall. *Sales/Installations:* Mr Scott Fraser, Mr Adam Villiers. Executive staff 1, Admin staff 3, Other staff 12. Began 1930; non-denominational. No magazine. Turnover £2,500,000 to year end Jun 03.

KBS Sound, Unit 6 and 7, Sandwich Industrial Estate, Sandwich CT13 9LY
☎01304 611 158 🖷01304 611 178
E: sales@kbs-sound.com
Web: www.kbs-sound.com
Supplying UK churches with sound, multimedia and musical instrument equipment.
Sales & Marketing Director: Mr Bob Forder. Executive staff 2, Other staff 3. Began 1987; non-denominational. No magazine. Turnover n/a.

†**Kings Audio**, 15 Oxford Road, Pen Mill Trading Estate, Yeovil BA21 5HR
☎01935 411 322 M 07714 767 966
🖷01935 706 008
E: mac@kingsaudio.co.uk
Web: www.kingsaudio.co.uk
Distributing and servicing CD-R, DVD-R, cassette copiers, blank media; on-site and in-house duplication.
Proprietor: Rev Mac Kingsbury. *Partner:* Mrs Angela Kingsbury. Executive staff 2, Other staff 4. Began 1989; interdenominational. No magazine. Turnover n/a.

Roy Kirkpatrick Sound Engineering, 1 Clover Drive, Pickmere, Knutsford WA16 0WF
☎01565 733 200 M: 07831 504 404
🖷01565 733 200
E: roy@kirkpatrick4sound.fsbusiness.co.uk
Web: www.kirkpatrick4sound.co.uk
Designing, supplying and installing specialised sound systems and magnetic induction loop systems.
Proprietor: Mr Roy D Kirkpatrick. Executive staff 1. Began 1976; non-denominational. No magazine. Turnover n/a.

LBC Productions, London School of Theology, Green Lane, Northwood HA6 2UW
☎01923 456 456 🖷01923 456 455
E: lbcproductions@lbc.uk.com
Providing video production to Christian organisations and local churches.
Director: Rob Purbrick. Executive staff 2. Began 1996; interdenominational. No magazine. Turnover n/a.

Let the Bible Speak, 11 Westland Avenue, Ballymoney BT53 6PE
☎028 2766 2896 🖷028 2766 2896
E: ltbs@dsl.pipex.com
Web: www.ltbs.org
Broadcasting the Gospel in USA, Canada, India, Africa, China, Asia, Republic of Ireland and London.
Programme Director: Rev Leslie Curran. Executive staff 1, Other staff 1. ***CC*** No.XN 48598. Began 1973; Free Presbyterian Church of Ulster. Magazine: *Let the Bible Speak* (5,000 quarterly). Turnover £100,000 to year end Mar 05.

†***Lighting and Sound Services**, Unit 3, Stanney, 10 Industrial Estate, Mill Lane, Little Stanney, Chester CH2 4JZ
☎0151 357 3502 🖷0151 357 3501
Designing, supplying, hiring and installing PA, lighting, effects, staging and generators.
Partner: Mr Phil Johnson. Executive staff 2, Other staff 6. Began 1978; non-denominational. No magazine. Turnover n/a.

***Logos Services**, 30 Barrack Lane, Nottingham NG7 1AN
☎0115 985 9795 🖷0115 985 9795
E: logos.services@dsl.pipex.com
Supplying overhead and slide projectors, screens, accessories, other visual aids; repair of OHPs.
Director: Mr John Churchill. Executive staff 1, Other staff 1. Began 1980; non-denominational. (Previously Logos Graphics and Logos Services Ltd). No magazine. Turnover n/a.

Look & Listen Multimedia, 20 Manor Road, Ruislip HA4 7LB
☎01895 624 774 M: 07941 942 579
🖷01895 473 649
E: info@llmedia.com
Web: www.llmedia.com
Supplying laptops and video/data projectors with song management software; installation.
Director: Mr Bill Upchurch. Executive staff 1. Began 1999; non-denominational. No magazine. Turnover £102,223 to year end Mar 00.

†**The Media Suite**, St Leonards Road, Amersham HP6 6DR
☎01494 431 232 🖷01494 431 233
E: info@themediasuite.co.uk
Web: www.themediasuite.co.uk
Media training specialists.
Managing Director: Mr Chris Doggett. Executive staff 6. Began 1986; interdenominational. No magazine. Turnover n/a.

MFJ Productions, 2 Johnston Park, Inverkeithing KY11 1BT
☎01383 420 397
E: mfjradio@aol.com
Christian radio programming; parent company of MFJ-FM radio broadcasting on RSL in Scotland.
Director: Deborah Menelaws. Executive staff 2, Other staff 2. ***CC*** No.24170. Began 1994; non-denominational. No magazine. Turnover n/a.

Keith Monks Sound Systems, Brodrick Hall, Brodrick Road, London SW17 7DY
☎020 8682 3456 🖷020 8767 8525
E: info@keithmonks.co.uk
Web: www.keithmonks.co.uk
Installing of Seamless Sound systems and loop systems for churches.
Proprietor: Mr Malcolm J Cunnings. Executive staff 3, Other staff 5. Began 1968; non-denominational. No magazine. Turnover n/a.

***Morrison Daylight Projectors**, The Gatehouse, Holme Industrial Estate, Holme-on-Spalding-Moor, York YO43 4BB
☎01430 861 561 M 07957 356 086
🖷01430 861 841
E: info@morrisonprojectors.co.uk
Web: www.morrisonprojectors.co.uk
Supplying churches with ex-conference data projectors and screens.
Director: Mr Malcolm Morrison. Executive staff 2, Other staff 4. Began 1986; non-denominational. No magazine. Turnover £1,800,000 to year end Dec 01.

†**Moving Art**, 131 Chilton Street, Bridgwater TA6 3HZ
☎01278 450 496
M: 07971 356 303
🖷01278 450 496
E: geoff@movingart.demon.co.uk
Total production services for events, documentaries; media-100 editing, multi-camera outside broadcasts, worldwide.
Director: Mr Geoff Sherring. Executive staff 2, Other staff 3. Began 1968; non-denominational. No magazine. Turnover n/a.

MVS Video Productions, Rehoboth, Alkham Valley Road, Folkestone CT18 7EH
☎01303 891 468
M: 07831 183 256
🖷07092 094 431
E: info@mvsvideo.co.uk
Web: www.mvsvideo.com
Video production, filming, editing, duplication services, equipment sales and service, outside broadcast vehicle.
Partner: Mr Paul Marshall. Executive staff 2, Other staff 1. Began 1989; interdenominational. No magazine. Turnover n/a.

New Day, 152 Courtfield Road, Quedgeley, Gloucester GL2 4UF
☎01452 618 619
M: 07976 076 356
🖷0870 402 9941
E: sales@newday.co.uk
Web: www.newdayvisual.co.uk or www.newdayaudio.co.uk
Audio-visual supplier, installations and hire, including conference support. Church specialists in video projection systems.
Partners: Mr & Mrs D J & P K Clare. Executive staff 2. Began 1999; interdenominational. No magazine. Turnover n/a.

PMH Productions, 69 Holyrood Close, Spondon, Derby DE21 7QB
☎01332 738 341
M: 07711 259 450
🖷01332 749 546
E: pmhprods@aol.com
Web: www.pmhproductions.com
Producing video and broadcast programmes in DVD format using digital broadcast technology.
Producer/Director: Mr Philip Holmes. Executive staff 1, Other staff 1. Began 1997; interdenominational. No magazine. Turnover n/a.

†**Psalm 96 Productions**, Video & Production, 7 Wortley Road, Croydon CR0 3E[illegible]
☎020 8684 5231
M: 07710 020 227
Video and audio production for TV programmes, events, weddings, adverts, music; multi-camera shoots undertaken.
Proprietors: Simon & Marie Yousaf. Executive staff 2. Began 1996; interdenominational. (Previously Sound 96). No magazine. Turnover n/a.

M

re:creation sound, Unit B2, 83 Copers Cope Road, Beckenham BR3 1NR
☎020 8658 2260 🖷020 8658 2261
E: enquiries@recreationsound.co.uk
Web: www.recreationsound.co.uk
Hiring, installing and selling public address equipment; event management services.
Director: Mr Mark Trigg. Admin staff 1, Other staff 2. Began 1994; non-denominational. (Previously Ichthus Sound Services) No magazine. Turnover £287,000 to year end Dec 04.

†Reelife Recordings, Laverick Hall, Halton, Lancaster LA2 6PH
☎01524 811 282 🖷01524 811 959
E: sales@reelife.org.uk
Web: www.reelife.org.uk
Conference recording, PA, audio and video, duplication. High-speed copier specialists, reelife recording and sound systems.
Director: Mr William I Towers. Executive staff 1, Other staff 5. ***CC*** No.265626. Began 1972; non-denominational. No magazine. Turnover £350,000 to year end Dec 02.

***Replicate**, Unit 38, Commerce Court, Challenge Way, Bradford BD4 8NW
☎01274 661 744 🖷01274 782 006
E: replicate@legend.co.uk
Web: replicate-media.co.uk
Software duplication of CD, DVD, floppy disks; digital print, packaging & distribution.
Proprietor: Mr John Wilson. Executive staff 2. Began 1993; Anglican. No magazine. Turnover n/a.

Revival Radio Ltd, PO Box 106, Cumbernauld, Glasgow G67 1JX
☎01236 721 110 🖷01236 725 849
E: info@revivalradio.org.uk
Web: www.revivalradio.org.uk
Broadcasting full-time in west central Scotland as Revival FM.
Chairman: Ian Dunlop. Other Staff 2. ***CC*** No.SCO 24130. Began 1995; interdenominational. No magazine. Turnover £23,500 to year end Oct 98.

rMaudio, The Model Bakery, 183 Barnbygate, Newark NG24 1RJ
☎01636 613 094 🖷01636 613 094
E: richard@rmaudio.co.uk
Web: www.rmaudio.co.uk
Designing, supplying and installing professional sound-reinforcement and induction-loop systems (BS 7594) for churches.
General Manager: Mr Richard Miller. Executive staff 1, Other staff 2. Began 1992; non-denominational. No magazine. Turnover £55,000 to year end May 05.

†Room 3, 4 Hamilton Drive West, Edinburgh EH15 1NR
☎0131 620 1235
E: info@room3.co.uk
Resourcing Christian events through hire of professional quality technical equipment: sound, video lighting, staging.
Director: Mr Fraser McClaren. Executive staff 1, Other staff n/a. Began 1996; interdenominational. No magazine. Turnover n/a.

Sain Fflur, Is Y Bryn, Borth Road, Porthmadog LL49 9UP
☎01766 810 092 🖷01766 810 092
E: aled.davies@bangor.ac.uk
Hiring PA sound systems.
Director: Rev Aled Davies. No full-time staff. Began 1987; non-denominational. No magazine. Turnover n/a.

Selecta Sound, 52 Rockingham Avenue, Hornchurch RM11 1HH
☎01708 453 424 M: 07779 140 311
🖷01708 455 565
E: info@selecta-sound.co.uk
Web: www.selecta-sound.co.uk
Manufacturing and duplicating audio cassettes, videos, DVDs and compact discs for studios, churches, businesses and schools.
Proprietor: Mr John Smailes. *Director:* Mrs Carol Smailes. Executive staff 2. Began 1979; non-denominational. No magazine. Turnover £140,000 to year end Dec 04.

†Shaw Sounds, 5 Douglas Avenue, Harold Wood, Romford RM3 0UT
☎01708 342 553 M: 07941 556 912
E: john@jshaw40.freeserve.co.uk
Web: www.mysite.freeserve.com/shawsounds
Video, television, audio, public address sales and service; transfering of records and tapes to CD.
Audio Engineer: Mr John L G Shaw. Executive staff 1. Began 1982; interdenominational. No magazine. Turnover £75,000 to year end Dec 96.

Sixth Sense Solutions, Unit 23, Headley Park Ten, Woodley, Reading RG5 4SW
☎08707 424 393 🖷08707 441 551
E: info@6thsensesolutions.co.uk
Web: www.6thsensesolutions.co.uk
Video production for corporate festivals, events and touring productions.
Senior AV Manager: Mr Craig Lawrence. Executive staff 4. Began 1997; non-denominational. No magazine. Turnover £1,200,000 to year end Oct 04.

†Sound by Design, Unit 1d, Lansbury Estate, Lower Guildford Road, Knaphill, Woking GU21 2EP
☎01483 797 242 🖷01483 797 256
E: office@soundbydesign.net
Web: www.soundbydesign.net
Sound installation hire and design, induction loop specialist.
Managing Director: Mr Andy Callin. Executive staff 2, Other staff 9. Began 1991; interdenominational. (Previously B & H Production Services). No magazine. Turnover n/a.

†Sound Foundation, Unit A4, Acre Business Park, Acre Road, Reading RG2 0SA
☎0118 986 6566 🖷0118 986 6221
E: sales@soundfoundation.com
Providing engineered sound, lighting, video systems for events, conferences, concerts; also dry-hire
Logistics Director: Mr Graham Preston. Executive staff 3, Other staff 5. Began n/a; non-denominational. No magazine. Turnover £800,000 to year end Dec 02.

†Sounds Professional, 4 Goss Barton, Kingsgrove, Nailsea, Bristol BS48 2XD
☎01275 858 156
E: mikebird@soundspro.com
Web: www.soundspro.com
Audio architect; designing, supplying and installing audio, hi-fi, audio visual and PA equipment.
Director: Mr Mike Bird. Executive staff 1, Other staff 1. Began 1993; non-denominational. No magazine. Turnover £70,000 to year end Dec 02.

Spirit of Caleb Ministries, 2 Great Quarry, Guildford GU1 3XN
☎01483 504 539 M 07748 944 027
E: info@spiritofcaleb.co.uk
Web: www.spiritofcaleb.co.uk or www.impatica.com
Envisioning older Christians to have Spirit of Caleb; *television interviews, DVDs, books.*
Sole Executive: Mr David Falkus. Executive staff 1, Other staff n/a. Began 2004; non-denominational. (Previously Inspired Media.biz, Spacebridge Communications). No magazine. Turnover £2,000 to year end Dec 04.

†TMH Media, 10 St Peters Court, Colchester CO1 1WD
☎01206 506 123 🖷01206 500 106
E: emma@tmhtelemedia.co.uk
Representing Christian media; selling TV air-time and advertising space.
Manager: Emma Freeman. Executive staff 3, Other staff 6. Began 1989; non-denominational. Magazine: *TV 4 Life* (15,000 every two months). Turnover n/a.

Ultrasound, 60 Reynolds Avenue, Chadwell Heath, Romford RM6 4NS
☎020 8599 6690 M: 07957 880 916
🖷07092 221 523
E: vince@ultrasoundpro.com
Web: www.ultrasoundpro.com
Professional sound installation; sound systems for concerts, corporate events; audio sales, consultancy, freelance engineering.
Director: Mr Vince Gray. Executive staff 1. Began 1988; interdenominational. No magazine. Turnover £80,000 to year end Dec 02.

†Vision Screen Services, Clayton Villa, 9 St Jude's Road, Newbridge, Wolverhampton WV6 0EB
☎01902 747 007 M: 07836 674 582
🖷01902 658 184
Web: www.visionav.com
Specialist suppliers of audio-visual equipment to churches, education and charities supporting Christian ministry and outreach.
Director: Martin Thomas. Executive staff 2. Began 1959; interdenominational. No magazine. Turnover £150,000 to year end Jun 02.

Vivid Communications, 349 North Circular Road, London N13 5JJ
☎020 8360 4008 Ⓜ: 07970 914 896
🖷020 8350 0901
Ⓔ: david@vividav.co.uk
Web: www.vividav.co.uk
Audio visual production, presentation, installation; creative solutions for churches, conferences or events.
Partner: Mr David Wisker. Executive staff 2, Admin staff 1. Began 1997; non-denominational. No magazine. Turnover £350,000 to year end Apr 05.

Wigwam Acoustics Ltd, Unit 6, Junction 19, Industrial Estate, Heywood OL10 1NB
☎ 01706 363 400 (sales)/800 (hire)
🖷 01706 363 410 (sales)/810 (hire)
Ⓔ: sales@wigwam.co.uk or rental@wigwamhire.co.uk
Web: www.wigwam.co.uk
Supplying professional sound equipment for hire, sale and installations, consultancy service.
Managing Director: Mr Mike Spratt. Executive staff 4, Other staff 30. Began 1978; non-denominational. No magazine. Turnover £2,300,000 to year end Feb 96.

†World of Music Church Services, 28 Denmark Street, London WC2H 8NJ
☎020 7240 7696 🖷020 7379 3398
Ⓔ: info@wom.co.uk
Installing and advising on sound / public address systems, musical instruments, pianos, organs; for churches and Christian school.
Chief Executive Officer: Cliff Cooper. *Sales Executive:* Fabrice Vonkaenel. Executive staff 2, Other staff n/a. Began 1968; Anglican. No magazine. Turnover n/a.

MUSICAL & THEATRICAL PERFORMERS

4 Real, Unit 5, Churchill Industrial Estate, Churchill Road, Cheltenham GL53 7EG
☎01242 245 444 🖷01242 250 618
Ⓔ: ems@ullenwood.co.uk
Web: www.eventandmanagement services.com
Folk group specialising in Celtic music.
Director: Mr Peter Allison. Executive staff 1. Began 1997; non-denominational. No magazine. Turnover n/a.

Acacia, BCC, 2 Masons Hill, Bromley BR2 9HA
☎020 8313 0367
Ⓔ: annahopelittler@yahoo.co.uk
Original songs and monologues for Christians and non-Christians; worship leader; multi-linguist: overseas missions.
Singer/Songwriter/Actor: Miss Anna Littler. Musician 1. Began 1995; interdenominational. No magazine. Turnover n/a.

M

***Adosia Records**, PO Box 403, Nottingham NG7 5QS
☎0115 841 2092 🖷0115 841 2092
Ⓔ: info@adosia.co.uk
Web: www.adosia.co.uk
Gospel music label; writing songs, performing, producing CDs and DVDs.
Director: Miss Esther Stapleton. Executive staff 1, Other staff 7. Began 2000; ecumenical. No magazine. Turnover n/a.

AG and Kate, Meredale, The Dell, Reach Lane, Leighton Buzzard LU7 0AL
☎01525 237 700 🖷01525 237 700
Singer/songwriter; concerts in clubs, churches and prisons.
Administrator: Rev Dr Paul Davis. No full-time staff. Began n/a; interdenominational. No magazine. Turnover n/a.

†Alpha Recordings Ltd, 12 Tilgarsley Road, Eynsham, Witney OX8 1PP
☎01865 880 240 🖷01865 880 240
Producing and distributing records, church, organ and choral music.
Managing Director: Mr H F Mudd. Executive staff 1, Other staff n/a. Began 1964; non-denominational. No magazine. Turnover n/a.

***Jerry Arhelger**, Meredale, The Dell, Reach Lane, Leighton Buzzard LU7 0AL
☎01525 237 700 🖷01525 237 700
Singer/songwriter.
Administrator: Rev Dr Paul Davis. No full-time staff. Began 1975; interdenominational. No magazine. Turnover n/a.

Arts Ecclesia, Morning Star, 9 Grange Court, Stratton, Cirencester GL7 2JS
☎01285 659 450
Ⓔ: shirley.collins@virgin.net
Web: artsecclesia.org.uk
Offering peripatetic training in artistic skills; dance, drama, fine arts, music, video, writing.
Director: Miss Shirley Collins. Executive staff 1, Other staff 9. Began 1998; interdenominational. (Previously Christian Choreographics). No magazine. Turnover n/a.

†As If, Glebe Farm, Ludgershall, Aylesbury HP18 9PL
☎01844 237 916
Ⓔ: as-if@as-if.co.uk
Web: www.as-if.co.uk
Christian rock/dance band playing youth-based music; also Appletree Studios.
Band Leader: Philip Goss. Band members 3. Began 1994; non-denominational. No magazine. Turnover n/a.

Marilyn Baker Ministries, PO Box 393, Tonbridge TN9 9AY
☎08707 501 720 🖷08707 501 721
Ⓔ: rachel@marilynbakerministries.org
Web: www.marilynbakerministries.org
Christian singer/songwriter with particular emphasis in encouraging Christians through live performance and recorded material.
Administrator: Rachel Barr. *Musician:* Marilyn Baker. Executive staff 1, Other staff 3. ***CC*** No.326553. Began 1984; evangelical. No magazine. Turnover n/a.

†*Cliff and Char Bergdahl, 105 Victoria Avenue, Hillingdon, Uxbridge UB10 9AJ
☎01895 238 499
Ⓔ: cbergdahl@compuserve.com
Christian music ministry, particularly to schools and prisons; Bible teaching.
Musicians: Rev & Mrs C Clifford & Charlotte Bergdahl. No full-time staff. Began 1973; Presbyterian Church, USA. In association with London Youth for Christ. No magazine. Turnover n/a.

Cambrensis Ministries, 21 Windsor Road, Porthcawl CF36 3LR
☎01656 784 376
🖷01656 784 376
Ⓔ: admin@cambrensis.org.uk
Web: www.cambrensis.org.uk
Choir, children's choir, concert band and orchestra, productions company, praise events; CDs, music books.
Administrator: Mrs Anne Brown. Admin staff 1, Other staff 1. ***CC*** No.1026060. Began 1982; interdenominational. No magazine. Turnover n/a.

†Cedar Dance, 42 Gunton Road, London E5 9JS
☎020 8806 4609
Ⓔ: janet_randell@lineone.net
Web: www.danceanimations.com
Professional freelance choreographer, qualified dance teacher; workshops in worship, dance therapy, dance for disabled people.
Artistic Director: Ms Janet Randell. No full-time staff. Began 1974; interdenominational. No magazine. Turnover n/a.

†CJM Music Ltd, Don Bosco House, Coventry Road, Coleshill, Birmingham B46 3EA
☎01675 466 254
Ⓜ: 07801 375 138
🖷01675 466 448
Ⓔ: admin@cjmmusic.com
Web: www.cjmmusic.com
Contemporary Christian musicians; youth ministry, concerts, workshops, publishing, recording.
Directors: Mr Michael Stanley, Ms Joanne Boyce. Executive staff 3, Other staff 3. Began 1996; Roman Catholic. No magazine. Turnover n/a.

†Frances Clarke, 274 Harborne Park Road, Harborne, Birmingham B17 0BL
☎0121 427 1681 M: 07711 140 104
Professional dancer, choreographer, dance teacher; sharing the Christian faith through dance in worship, evangelism; workshops.
Professional Dancer: Frances Clarke. Executive staff 1. Began n/a; interdenominational. No magazine. Turnover n/a.

***Rodney Cordner with Jean-Pierre Rudolph**, 21 Tandragee Road, Portadown, Craigavon BT62 3BQ
M: 07748 187 776
E: rodneycordner@hotmail.com
Web: www.cordner.net/rodney
Evangelist and singer using Irish music as vehicle for Gospel; UK, Europe and USA.
Singer/Evangelist: Mr Rodney Cordner. No full-time staff. Began 1976; Church of Ireland. No magazine. Turnover n/a.

Covenant Players, The Manse, Clarence Place, Pontypool NP4 8AP
☎01495 740 481 M: 07904 868 822
℻01495 757 422
E: cp.bio@covenantplayers.org
Web: www.covenantplayers.org
Communications resource for churches, schools, community; 5 full-time touring drama teams; 1,000 plays; music.
National Directors: Mr & Mrs D & G Allen. Executive staff 2, Other staff 13. ***CC*** No.1059359. Began 1972; interdenominational. Magazine: *Covenant World* (2,500 quarterly). Turnover £69,000 to year end Dec 04.

Crying Out Loud, 2 Princes Crescent North, Dollar FK14 7BX
☎01259 742 425 M: 07962 648 953
E: eddie@eddiewilliamson.co.uk
Web: www.eddiewilliamson.co.uk
Performances of dramas, mysteries for adults and children's outreach; books, resources.
Director: Mr Eddie Williamson. Executive staff 1. ***CC*** No.SCO 25267. Began 1996; interdenominational. No magazine. Turnover n/a.

David Daltrey, 3 Hughesdon House, 122 Northgate Street, Bury St Edmunds IP33 1HG
☎01284 762 076 M: 07714 763 260
E: yazzpeachey@aol.com
Web: www.byor.com
Musician composer; performing guitar, lute, keyboard music; traditional, contemporary, liturgical styles; tuition, audio consultant.
Musician: David Daltrey. Musician 1, No other staff. Began 1967; interdenominational. No magazine. Turnover n/a.

†Dance for Christ, The Farne House, Marygate, Holy Island, Berwick-upon-Tweed TD15 2SJ
☎01289 389 247
E: mary@burninglight.co.uk
Web: www.danceforchrist.org
Collating and providing resources in dance, mime, movement and puppetry; advice; local workshops (north east).
Coordinator: Mr Mark Fleeson. No full-time staff. Began 1988; non-denominational. No magazine. Turnover n/a.

†Clive Davenport, 57 Altrincham Road, Gatley, Cheadle SK8 4EG
☎0161 718 8596
℻0161 718 8596
E: clive.davenport@bigfoot.com
Web: www.bigfoot.com/~clive.davenport
Worship leading, multimedia events; recording, technical support, soundtracks, PA, lighting and training.
Musician/Technician/Engineer: Mr Clive Davenport. Executive staff 1, No other staff. Began 1984; interdenominational. No magazine. Turnover n/a.

***Wes Davis**, 4 Willowbank Walk, Leighton Buzzard LU7 3UR
☎01525 237 700
℻01525 237 700
Web: www.wesdavis.co.uk
Singer/songwriter.
Administrator: Rev Dr Paul Davis. No full-time staff. Began 1975; interdenominational. No magazine. Turnover n/a.

†*Daybreak, Glenmuir, 17 Glen Road, Parkstone, Poole BH14 0HF
☎01202 743 813
℻01202 743 813
E: aline.larkin@ntlworld.com
Worship evangelism in prisons, churches and other locations, UK and France.
Secretary: A Larkin. No full-time staff. Began 1984; interdenominational. No magazine. Turnover n/a.

***Excel School of Performing Arts**, KT Summit House, 100 Hanger Lane, Ealing, London W5 1EZ
☎020 8799 6117
E: excel@kt.org
Web: www.kt.org or www.ktioe-excel.org
Providing professional full-time courses in drama, singing, music and technical production.
Administrator: Jodi Desouza. Executive staff 1. ***CC*** No.251549. Began 1982; Elim Pentecostal. (Previously School of Creative Ministries (Kensington Temple)). No magazine. Turnover n/a.

***Fellowship of Christian Magicians (UK)**, 58 Langley Park Road, Iver SL0 9QS
☎No telephone
E: info@fcmuk.org
Web: www.fcmuk.org
Proclaiming the Gospel and illustrating Christian truth using sleight of hand, illusion and other visual aids.
Secretary: Major Ron Smith. No full-time staff. Began 1987; interdenominational. Magazine: *"Voila!"* (140 quarterly). Turnover n/a.

David Fitzgerald, Columcille, Dereham Road, Norwich NR2 3UT
☎01603 632 444 M: 07768 573 284
℻01603 632 444
E: davidftz@aol.com
Web: www.davidfitzgerald.co.uk
Musician, teacher of saxophones & woodwind, co-founder of Celtic band IONA; recordings, tours, seminars, adjudication.
Tutor/Performer: Mr David Fitzgerald. Musician 1. Began 1994; interdenominational. No magazine. Turnover n/a.

Footprints Trust, St Nicholas Centre, 79 Maid Marian Way, Nottingham NG1 6AE
☎0115 958 6554 ℻0115 952 4624
E: admin@footprintstheatre.co.uk
Web: www.footprintstheatre.co.uk
Educational and community Arts provision and consultancy promoting the values of God's kingdom.
Executives: Robin Crawford, Steve & Janet Stickley, Sarah Woodall. Executive staff 4. ***CC*** No.277884. Began 1978; non-denominational. (Previously Footprints Theatre Company). No magazine. Turnover n/a.

†The Free Church Choir Union, 94 Goddington Lane, Orpington BR6 9DY
☎01689 602 397
E: jean.shacklady@virgin.net
Organising choral religious services at 3-yearly intervals, usually in cathedrals.
Secretary: Mrs J M Shacklady. No full-time staff. Began 1888; non-conformist. No magazine. Turnover n/a.

M

Freedom Music Ministries, 17 The Quadrant, Romiley, Stockport SK6 3AY
☎0161 430 8401 M: 07803 012 678
E: scottfellows@onetel.com
Duo playing free of charge a wide range of music with a strong Gospel message.
Musicians: Dorike Adensunloye, Scott Fellows. Musicians 2. Began 1984; interdenominational. No magazine. Turnover n/a.

Fresh Claim, 185 Lodge Avenue, Dagenham RM8 2HQ
☎020 8592 5900 ℻020 8592 5900
E: law@fish.co.uk
Christian rock band; evangelism through words and music in schools, youth clubs and missions.
Leader: Rev Simon Law. No full-time staff. Began 1986; interdenominational. No magazine. Turnover £4,712 to year end Dec 04.

***Garden Music Duet**, 10 Mayfield, Welwyn Garden City AL8 7EL
☎01707 887 393
E: burden.garden@ntlworld.com
Professional musicians communicating the message of Christ through the language of music; Christian, classical, contemporary.
Musicians: David & Rachel Burden. Musicians 2. Began n/a; non-denominational. No magazine. Turnover n/a.

†Gem Records, 20a Richmond Park Road, Kingston Upon Thames KT2 6AH
☎020 8974 5755
E: gem@gemrecords.co.uk
Web: www.gemrecords.co.uk
Record label, music school; artist teaching, songwriting and performing.
Musician: Miss Gemma Ingram. Musician 1. Began 2000; non-denominational. No magazine. Turnover n/a.

***George Hamilton IV**, Meredale, The Dell, Reach Lane, Leighton Buzzard LU7 0AL
☎01525 237 700 📠01525 237 700
E: enq@newmusicenterprises.com
Web: www.newmusicenterprises.com
Singer/songwriter.
Administrator: Rev Dr Paul Davis. No full-time staff. Began 1975; interdenominational. No magazine. Turnover n/a.

Hands Up! Puppet Team, 24 Old Street, Clevedon BS21 6BY
☎01275 797 999 📠01275 797 999
E: info@living-waters.org.uk
Web: www.living-waters.org.uk
Presenting the Gospel with puppets, songs, sketches to schools, festivals, within BS postcode area.
Coordinator: Valerie Bennett. Executive staff 1. ***CC*** No.1042944. Began 1993; non-denominational. No magazine. Turnover n/a.

M

Judy Herring Leigh, Meredale, The Dell, Reach Lane, Leighton Buzzard LU7 0AL
☎01525 237 700 📠01525 237 700
Singer/songwriter.
Administrator: Rev Dr Paul Davis. No full-time staff. Began n/a; interdenominational. No magazine. Turnover n/a.

Garth Hewitt, Amos Trust, All Hallows on the Wall, 83 London Wall, London EC2M 5ND
☎020 7588 2638 📠020 7588 2663
E: garth@amostrust.org
Web: www.amostrust.org
Freelance music ministry promoting justice and peace through music and storytelling.
Administrator: Rachel Wilkinson. No full-time staff. ***CC*** No.292592. Began n/a; interdenominational. No magazine. Turnover n/a.

***Paul Heyman**, 26 Mavis Court, Raven Close, Colindale, London NW9 5BJ
☎020 8203 3130
E: heyman@icc.org.uk
Web: www.iccrecords.com
Electric violinist; performing ministry featuring Messianic Jewish/Christian worship music, Jewish roots teaching, testimony, dance.
Manager: Jan Heyman. No full-time staff. Began 1989; non-denominational. No magazine. Turnover n/a.

†Phil Holburt, 35 Patterdale Avenue, Richmond, Whitehaven CA28 8RX
M: 07929 179 628
E: philholburt@fish.co.uk
Worship leader, singer/songwriter.
Singer/songwriter: Phil Holburt. Musician 1. Began 1994; interdenominational. No magazine. Turnover n/a.

†*In Yer Face Theatre Company, Mill House, Mill Lane, Cheadle SK8 2NT
☎0161 491 3090 M: 07958 605 575
E: inyerface@domini.org
Web: www.inyerface.org.uk
Evangelistic theatre presentations; drama and life skills workshops, secondary school assemblies, RE and drama lessons.
Administrative Director: Karen Arnold. Executive staff 1, Other staff 5. ***CC*** Began 1996; non-denominational. No magazine. Turnover £80,000 to year end Jul 02.

Iona, PO Box 232, Leeds LS17 6YH
☎01652 678 065 📠01652 678 065
Web: www.iona.uk.com
Contemporary folk / rock / progressive / ambient band; music inspired by Celtic Christian saints.
Coordinator: Dave Bainbridge. Band 4. Began 1989; interdenominational. Magazine: *Friends of Iona* (Circulation n/a quarterly). Turnover n/a.

***The Island Churches Guernsey Festival Chorus**, Le Campere, Les Villets, Forest, Guernsey GY8 0HP
☎01481 263 930 M: 07781 421 400
📠01481 265 004
Web: www.festivalchorus.org.gg
Specialising in Christian music reflecting biblical festivals; local festival, guest programmes in concert hall.
Musical Directors: Mr & Mrs Roy & Maddie Sarre. No full-time staff. Began 1985; interdenominational. Magazine: *Christian Arts Newsnotes* (50 quarterly). Turnover £11,000 to year end Mar 02.

Jasperian Theatre Company, 29 Harvard Court, Honeybourne Road, London NW6 1HL
☎020 7435 4246 / 7813 4362
M: 07941 616 177
E: tony.jasper@blueyonder.co.uk
Performing traditional and modern drama placing people within God's dealings; also evangelist.
Administrator: Mr Tony Jasper. Executive staff 1. Began 1992; interdenominational. No magazine. Turnover £25,000 to year end Mar 04.

***Kettle of Fish Theatre**, Holmfield, Bank Villas, High Street, Mold CH7 1BN
☎01352 756 547 📠01352 756 547
E: marc.cavallini@talk21.com
Scriptwriters, advisers, workshop leaders, pioneering theatre forms, community theatre, education and awareness, available for commissions.
Artistic Directors: Mr & Mrs Marc & Karen Cavallini. Executive staff 2. ***CC*** No.1000655. Began 1991; non-denominational. Magazine: *No Magazine*(Circulation & frequency n/a). Turnover £30,000 to year end Aug 00.

Keynote Trust, Townhaven, Pound Square, Cullompton EX15 1DN
☎01884 343 89
📠01884 343 89
E: maries@keynotetrust.org.uk
Web: www.keynotetrust.org.uk
Offering music and worship workshops, presentations, teaching, training, consultancy, covering breadth of style and approach.
Executive Officer: Mr Andrew Maries. Executive staff 1. ***CC*** No.1015152. Began 1992; ecumenical Magazine: *Keynote newsletter* (300 quarterly). Turnover n/a.

***Kingsway Music**, Lottbridge Drove, Eastbourne BN23 6NT
☎01323 437 700
📠01323 411 970
E: music@kingsway.co.uk
Web: www.kingsway.co.uk
Producing worship recordings, songbooks and seminars.
Label Manager: Mr Stephen Doherty. ***CC*** No.265612. Began 19[illegible]7; interdenominational. Magazine: *Worship Together* (6,000 every two months). Turnover n/a.

Langham Arts, St Paul's Church, Robert Adam Street, London W1U 3HW
☎020 7935 7246
📠020 7935 7486
E: office@langhamarts.org
Web: www.allsoulsorchestra.org
Musical and theatrical performances connected with the music ministry of All Souls Church Langham Place.
General Manager: Janet O'Brien. Admin staff 2, Other staff 2. ***CC*** No.1059[illegible]11. Began 1987; non-denominational. Magazine: *Langham Arts News* (7,000 quarterly). Turnover £240,000 to year end June 98.

***Lantern Arts Centre**, Tolverne Road, Raynes Park, London SW20 [illegible]RA
☎020 8944 5794
📠020 8947 5152
E: lac@lanternarts.org
Web: www.lanternarts.org
Productions, theatre in education, children's theatre clubs, café studio, café church, rehearsal space available.
Artistic Director: Angela Smith. Executive staff 2, Other staff 2. ***CC*** No.1098[illegible]80. Began 1995; ecumenical. No magazine. Turnover £30,000 to year end Apr 0[illegible].

Peter Lewis (Family Folk), 22 Marlborough Rise, Aston, Sheffield S26 2ET
☎0114 287 3087
E: antifession@aol.com
Sing Life - school assemblies, Sing Love - family folk concerts; Sing Jesus - family services, other events.
Singer/Musician: Peter Lewis. No full-time staff. Began n/a; non-denominational. No magazine. Turnover n/a.

***Living Stones Drama Group**, 49 Bell Street, Sawbridgeworth CM21 9AR
☎01279 724 515 M: 07734 128 430
E: enquiries@mrct.org.uk
Web: www.mrct.org.uk
Able-bodied/disabled Christian drama group performing drama to mime, music and narration.
Director of Community Services: Mr Gary Knott. No full-time staff. **CC** No.1065006. Began 1991; non-denominational. Magazine: *Capstone* (500 three times a year). Turnover £59,299 to year end Mar 04.

***The London & Home Counties Festivals of Male Voice Praise**, 7 Common Lane, Benfleet SS7 3TB
M: 07778 488 369
E: john@jpease.wanadoo.co.uk
Gospel witness and outreach through singing male voice Gospel songs and other Christian musical arrangements.
Area Organiser/Secretary: Mr John A Pease. No full-time staff. **CC** No.263429. Began 1951; interdenominational. Part of The Festivals of Male Voice Praise. No magazine. Turnover n/a.

***London Community Gospel Choir (LCGC)**, Brockdale House, 75 Brookdale Road, London E17 6QH
☎020 8509 7288 M: 07973 327 955
🖷020 8509 7299
E: choirconnexion@btconnect.com
Web: www.lcgc.org.uk
Promotion of the Christian faith through Gospel music.
President: Rev Bazil Meade. *Office Manager* Yvonne White. Executive staff 1, Admin staff 1. Began 1982; non-denominational. No magazine. Turnover £100,000 to year end Dec 05.

***London Crusader Chorale**, 48 Beresford Road, Cheam, Sutton SM2 6ER
☎020 8770 3896 🖷020 8643 8267
E: janishomewood@blueyonder.co.uk
Musical evangelism to prisons, churches, homes for elderly and disabled in London and south east.
Leader: Mrs Janis Homewood. No full-time staff. **CC** No.287915. Began 1979; non-denominational. No magazine. Turnover n/a.

Mid-Scotland Evangelical Choir, 48 Brown Street, Camelon, Falkirk FK1 4QF
☎01324 623 933
Gospel outreach; ministering mainly to residential care homes for elderly people.
Conductor: Mr Alan M McIntyre. No full-time staff. Began 1972; non-denominational with Christian Brethren links. No magazine. Turnover n/a.

Mid-Sussex Christian Outreach, The Pippins, 29 Beckworth Lane, Lindfield, Haywards Heath RH16 2EH
☎01444 483 294 M: 07746 176 936
🖷01444 483 294
E: ford@peterandkath.wanadoo.co.uk
Promoting Christian arts in concerts, festivals.
Administrator: Mr Peter D Ford. No full-time staff. **CC** Began 1986; interdenominational. No magazine. Turnover £3,000 to year end Mar 03.

New English Orchestra, 4 Link Road, Edgbaston, Birmingham B16 0EP
☎0121 455 8197
🖷0121 455 8197
Web: www.newenglishorchestra.org
Professional orchestra with singers and dancers performing in major venues in the UK and abroad.
Artistic/Musical Director: Mr Nigel Swinford. Executive staff 1, Musicians 35. **CC** No.1078424. Began 1976; interdenominational. Magazine: *NEO Friends* (1,000 half-yearly). Turnover £55,000 to year end Dec 00.

†**New Horizons Choir**, 16 Braemar Gardens, West Wickham BR4 0JW
☎020 8777 8523
E: andrewking@btopenworld.com
Web: www.members.tripodco.uk/newhorizons
Encouraging and helping the local church through the ministry of music.
Leader: Mr Andrew King. No full-time staff. Began 1983; interdenominational. No magazine. Turnover n/a.

Anamcaras, 9 Miles Meadow Close, Willenhall WV12 5YE
☎01922 403 033
E: MillStjm@aol.com
Web: www.anamcaras.co.uk
Performing roots/worship/contemplation to help churches and institutions raise funds for worthy causes.
Singer/Songwriters: Mr & Mrs Terry & Jackie Mills, Terry Braithwaite. No full-time staff. Began 2004; interdenominational. (Previously NUFFSED) No magazine. Turnover n/a.

†**Oddments Theatre Co**, 39 Orchard Street, Yeovil BA20 1BB
☎01935 433 481
M: 07961 8789 800
E: boytons@oddments-theatre.co.uk
Web: www.oddments-theatre.co.uk
Performing Christian theatre at churches, outreach events and prisons, around southern England.
Director: Mr Barry Boyton. No full-time staff. Began 1981; interdenominational. No magazine. Turnover £6,500 to year end Mar 03.

***Origin Scotland**, 65 High Street, Edinburgh EH1 1SR
☎Mobile 07745 915 311
🖷07092 187 716
E: info@originscotland.org
Web: www.originscotland.org
Undertaking contemporary evangelism using the arts; promoting Christian unity through praise and worship events.
Managing Director: Mr Colin Peckham. Executive staff 4, No other full-time staff 3. **CC** No.SCO 32754. Began 1997; non-denominational. No magazine. Turnover £125,000 to year end May 05.

Simon Peter, 48 Woodfield Drive, Harrogate HG1 5LS
M: 07816 140 133
E: simonpeterpro@yahoo.co.uk
Web: www.simonpeterpro.co.uk
Providing music books of praise and worship. Songwriter, composer, worship leader.
Solo Artist: Mr Darren Warner. No full-time staff. Began 2000; non-denominational. No magazine. Turnover n/a.

Lance Pierson, 48 Peterborough Road, London SW6 3EB
☎020 7731 6544 🖷020 7731 1858
E: lance@lancepierson.org
Web: www.lancepierson.org
Bringing the Bible, poetry and other words to life; performing for churches and secular groups.
Performer: Mr Lance Pierson. Executive staff 2. Began 1978; interdenominational. (Previously Freelance Wordwright). No magazine. Turnover £25,000 to year end April 02.

Rascal Productions, 52 Colmer Road, Streatham, London SW16 5JZ
☎020 8764 5571 M: 07970 771 591
🖷01737 248 645
E: john.n.talbot@talk21.com
Web: rascalproductions.com
Low-key evangelistic resource theatre company.
Director/Producer: Mr John Talbot. No full-time staff. Began 1997; interdenominational. No magazine. Turnover £2,000 to year end Apr 00.

Reconcilers Evangelical Ministries (REM), Scotney Hall, 17 Sharratt Street, Ilderton Road, London SE15 1NR
☎020 7639 3337 M: 07956 651 365
🖷020 7639 3337
E: reconcilers@yahoo.co.uk
Web: www.reconcilers.org
Teaching, preaching, broadcasting the Gospel; songwriting academy, Saturday school, after school club, Sunday scripture forum.
Evangelist: Rev Vincent Onwukanjo. Musician 1. **CC** No.1003914. Began 1985; non-denominational. Magazine: *REM News* (150 every two months). Turnover £36,000 to year end Dec 02.

***Riverside School of Performing Arts**, 21 Alcester Road, Moseley, Birmingham B13 8AR
☎0121 442 2586/4484 🖷0121 442 4481
E: info@rspa.org.uk
Web: www.rspa.org.uk
Christian theatre training with performing arts, and discipleship elements, performing locally and nationally.
Course Director: Mrs Sarah Auger. *Administrator:* Mr Audy Westcott. Executive staff 1, Other staff 3. **CC** No.1099487. Began 1996; interdenominational. No magazine. Turnover £60,000 to year end Jul 05.

M

†*Rodd & Marco - The Acts Drama Trust, 28 Moray Park, Dalgety Bay, Dunfermline KY11 9UN
☎01383 824 533 M: 07753 764 393
E: marco@uberdudc.fsnet.co.uk
Web: www.rodd&marco.com
Using comedy, drama and music in ministry in UK and worldwide.
Directors: Rodd Christensen, Marco Palmer. Executive staff 2. ***CC*** No.SCO 23654. Began 1995; interdenominational. No magazine. Turnover £28,000 to year end Dec 98.

Solo Plus Theatre Company, 222 Cooks Lane, Kingshurst, Birmingham B37 6NH
☎0121 770 8893
M: 07799 683 148
E: linda@soloplus.fsnet.co.uk
Web: www.geocities.com/soloplusuk
Writing and performing biblical and other drama.
Administrator: Miss Linda Mae. Admin staff 1. Began 1988; interdenominational. No magazine. Turnover £5,000 to year end Apr 05.

Songs of Worship by Howard Dobson, The Forge, Station Road, Newton le Willows, Bedale DL8 1SP
☎01677 450 518 🖷01677 450 525
E: worship@howarddobson.co.uk
Web: www.howarddobson.co.uk/worship
Worship music resource featuring praise and worship songs written by Howard Dobson.
Songwriter: Mr Howard Dobson. No full-time staff. Began 2003; non-denominational. No magazine. Turnover n/a.

Springs Dance Company, 10 College Road, The Historic Dockyard, Chatham ME4 4QX
☎01634 817 523 M: 07775 628 442
E: springsdc@aol.com
Web: www.springsdancecompany.org.uk
Professional Christian dance company, performing and teaching in schools and churches across the world.
Artistic Director: Ruth Hughes. Executive staff 1, Admin staff 2, Other staff 3. ***CC*** No.326521. Began 1979; interdenominational. No magazine. Turnover £67,000 to year end Dec 02.

Stage-Fright: Faith in Theatre, The Cornerstone, Norreys Avenue, Wokingham RG40 1UE
☎0118 979 0098 M: 07737 477 193
E: info@stage-fright.org.uk
Web: www.stage-fright.org.uk
Exploring and expressing Christian spirituality through theatre, improvisation; team-building workshops for churches, schools; residentials.
Director: Michael Johnson. No full-time staff. Began 1999; non-denominational. No magazine. Turnover n/a.

The Still Time Band, Still Time Music, PO Box 27, Feltham TW14 0YN
☎07776 482 452 M: 07776 482 452
E: info@stilltime.com
Web: www.stilltime.com
Professional jazz Gospel band specialising in evangelism; also worship and entertainment.
Artistic Director: Mr Mike Roberts. Executive staff 1, Other staff 3. Began 1999; interdenominational. No magazine. Turnover £20,000 to year end Jul 05.

†Strictly Personal, 30 The Willows, Daventry NN11 5PY
☎01327 706 244 M: 07802 419 815
E: jsritter@aol.com
Web: members.aol.com/jsritter
Youth evangelism and training with a specialised ministry for musicians.
Partners: Mr & Mrs John & Sue Ritter. Executive staff 2. Began 1985; interdenominational. No magazine. Turnover £20,000 to year end Dec 96.

Theatre Roundabout Ltd, 859 Finchley Road, London NW11 8LX
☎020 8455 4752 M: 07774 638 800
E: info@theatreroundabout.co.uk
Web: www.theatreroundabout.co.uk
Two person touring theatre visiting churches, cathedrals, colleges, arts centres.
Director: Mr William Fry. Executive staff 2. ***CC*** No.234999. Began 1964; Anglican. No magazine. Turnover £21,000 to year end July 05.

†The Urban Gospel Music Ministry, DJK, 47 Trulock Court, Trulock Road, London N17 0PE
M: 07899 990 372
E: kelechi@dj-k.com
Web: www.dj-k.com
Urban Gospel DJ playing R'n'B, Hip-Hop, Garage, Ragga, Soca music.
Gospel DJ: Mr Kelechi Amadi. Musician 1. Began 2002; non-denominational. No magazine. Turnover £2,000 to year end Jun 03.

Valentine International Clown Ministry, Carineve, Ythanbank, Ellon AB41 7TU
☎01358 761 459
E: clownbarni@aol.com
Clown, storyteller, mime artist bridging the gap between church and unchurched; working with emerging church.
Artistic Director: Mrs Olive M Fleming-Drane. No full-time staff. Began 1985; ecumenical. Turnover n/a.

†Whiteraven, 48 Silkmore Crescent, Stafford ST17 4JL
☎01785 212 115
E: ianjen@supanet.com
Four-piece melodic rock band, challenging and encouraging; particular interest in China; audience aged 20 to 50.
Manager: Mr Ian Whyte. No full-time staff. Began n/a; interdenominational. No magazine. Turnover n/a.

MUSICAL & THEATRICAL SERVICES

Abinger Organs, Little Hoe, Hoe Lane, Abinger Hammer, Dorking RH5 6RH
☎01306 730 277 M: 07831 858 999
📠01306 731 483
E: peter@abinger.globalnet.co.uk
Web: www.abinger-organs.co.uk
Selling and hiring church organs, keyboards, electric pianos, digital hymn recording and playback units.
Partners: Mr Peter Flatau, Mrs Susan Flatau. Executive staff 1, Other staff 2. Began 1983; interdenominational. No magazine. Turnover n/a.

†Acoustic Arrangements, 14 Hammond Business Centre, Hammond Close, Nuneaton CV11 6RY
☎0845 125 9406 📠0871 717 7324
E: mail@a-a.uk.com
Selling, installing and hiring audio, video and stage lighting to churches and Christian organisations.
Managing Director: Mr Glyn Chapman. *System Consultant:* Mr Nick Wilmot. Executive staff 2, Admin staff 2. Began 1994; non-denominational. No magazine. Turnover £300,000 to year end Mar 04.

***ACTS (Audio Consultancy & Technical Services)**, 1 Beddington Grove, Wallington SM6 9LB
☎07984 467 151 📠020 8408 0547
E: acts@blueyonder.co.uk
Providing audio and video consultancy, supply and installation.
Director: Mr Mark Walford. Executive staff 1, Admin staff 1. Began 1986; interdenominational. (Previously Mewtech). No magazine. Turnover n/a.

Allen Organs, TRADA Business Campus, Stocking Lane, Hughenden Valley, High Wycombe HP14 4ND
☎01494 563 833 📠01494 563 546
E: sales@allenorgans.co.uk
Web: allenorgans.co.uk
Supplying, servicing and hiring Allen digital computer organs.
Managing Director: Mr Emyr Davies. *Sales Consultants:* Giles Williams, Richard Goodall. Executive staff 4, Other staff 3. Began 1968; non-denominational. No magazine. Turnover £900,000 to year end Dec 02.

***Artisan Initiatives Charitable Trust**, 245 Old Marylebone Road, London NW1 5QT
☎020 8398 0138 M: 07989 300 134
E: backstage@dial.pipex.com
Web: www.artisaninitiatives.org
Supporting Christians in media, arts and entertainment through personal relationships, publications and events.
Director: Mr Stephen Cole. Executive staff 1. ***CC*** No.1056949. Began 1995; interdenominational. Magazine: *Backstage* (1,200 quarterly). Turnover £18,000 to year end Apr 03.

Arts in Mission, The House of Bread, Ross Road, Christchurch, Coleford GL16 7NS
☎01594 837 744 📠01594 837 742
E: artsim@wflt.org
Web: www.artsinmission.org
Encouraging, enabling and equipping Christian artists, assisting churches in mission through the creative arts.
Contact: Rev Elizabeth Brazell. *Administrator:* Keith Hawkins. Executive staff 1, Other staff 2. ***CC*** No.1071313. Began 1996; non-denominational. Part of The Word For Life Trust. No magazine. Turnover n/a.

***Authentic Media**, 9 Holdom Avenue, Bletchley, Milton Keynes MK1 1QR
☎01908 364 200 📠01908 648 592
E: info@authenticmedia.co.uk
Web: www.authenticmedia.co.uk
Publishing Bibles, books, music, video and software.
General Director: Mr David Withers. *A&R Director:* Mr David Bruce. *Publishing Director:* Mr Mark Finnie. Executive staff 12, Other staff 38. Began 1967; non-denominational. (Previously Word Music & Publishing, Nelson Word). A Division of Send the Light. Magazine: *Premier* (30,000 monthly). Turnover n/a.

British Association of Christian Brass Bands, Rosslyn House, 370 Bloomfield Road, Odd Down, Bath BA2 2PD
☎01225 832 041
E: mikepriscottbath@aol.com
Offering Christian fellowship to musicians; meetings half-yearly at High Wycombe; branches: Andover, Faversham, Northampton, Teesside.
Secretary: Mr Mike Priscott. No full-time staff. Began 1988; interdenominational. No magazine. Turnover n/a.

Calamus, Oak House, 70 High Street, Brandon IP27 0AU
☎0845 456 8392 📠01842 819 832
E: sue@decanimusic.com
Web: www.decanimusic.co.uk
Church music copyright licensing agency.
Administrators: Mrs Susan Dean, Mr Nicholas Blackford. Executive staff 2, Other staff 2. Began 1991; non-denominational. No magazine. Turnover n/a.

CHIME - The Churches' Initiative in Music Education, 52 Victoria Road, Wilton, Salisbury SP2 0DY
☎01722 741 154 M: 07879 443 060
E: fieldings4@btopenworld.com
Web: www.chime.org.uk
Providing ecumenical training forum for UK church musicians.
Secretary: Mr Robert Fielding. No full-time staff. ***CC*** No.1058585. Began 1991; ecumenical. No magazine. Turnover n/a.

***Christian Copyright Licensing (Europe) Ltd**, Chantry House, 22 Upperton Road, Eastbourne BN21 1BF
☎01323 417 711 📠01323 417 722
E: info@ccli.co.uk
Web: www.ccli.com
Copyright licensing resource to churches, schools, oranisations and individuals; serving the church in worship.
Managing Director: Mr Andy Bodkin. Executive staff 1, Other staff 35. Began 1991; non-denominational. No magazine. Turnover n/a.

***Chrysalis**, 78 The Broadway, Chesham HP5 1EG
☎01494 581 115 📠01494 581 114
E: office@chrysalis.org.uk
Web: www.chrysalis.org.uk
Resourcing churches to present the Gospel relevantly through cabaret-style outreach events using the performing arts.
Chairman: Mrs Nicki Pulen. Admin staff 2, Other staff 1. ***CC*** No.1049294. Began 1995; non-denominational. No magazine. Turnover n/a.

†City of Gold Outreach, 9 Woodleighton Grove, Uttoxeter ST14 8BY
☎01869 563 930 M: 07881 781 547
📠01869 563 930
E: cityofgold@lineone.net
Encouraging and supporting local churches to use City of Gold productions in their outreach.
Evangelists: Mr & Mrs Graham & Judy White. Executive staff 2. Began 2000; interdenominational. No magazine. Turnover n/a.

Cleaford Services Ltd, 46 Hazell Road, Farnham GU9 7BP
☎01252 717 166 M: 07713 322 290
📠01252 717 137
E: cleaver@cleaford.co.uk
Web: www.cleaford.co.uk/puppet.htm
Supplying puppets, scripts and training workshops for evangelism, school assemblies and all-age worship.
Director: Mr Angus Cleaver. Executive staff 2. Began 1994; non-denominational. No magazine. Turnover £40,000 to year end Jul 04.

Copeman Hart and Company Ltd, Organ Builders, Finedon Road, Irthlingborough, Wellingborough NN9 5TZ
☎01933 652 600 📠01933 652 288
E: info@copemanhart.co.uk
Web: www.copemanhart.co.uk
Custom-built pipeless organs for cathedrals, churches and schools.
Managing Director: Mr Ernest C Hart. *Production Manager:* Mr R Alan Foster. Executive staff 2, Other staff 10. ***CC*** No.696548. Began 1960; non-denominational. No magazine. Turnover £500,000 to year end Mar 03.

Crosswaysmusic.com, 43 Fillebrook Avenue, Leigh-on-Sea SS9 3NS
☎01702 711 020 M: 07771 646 327
Fax 01702 472 163
E: diana@crosswaysmusic.com
Web: www.crosswaysmusic.com
Selling music by mail order, internet at concerts and events; web searches for deletions, current, hard-to-find.
Senior Partner: Ms Diana Causton. Executive staff 1, Admin staff 1. Began 1989; interdenominational. (Previously Crossways Records and Crossways Music). No magazine. Turnover n/a.

Cymdeithas Emynau Cymru (Welsh Hymn Society), 11 Heol Alun, Waunfawr, Aberystwyth SY23 3BB
☎01970 617 897
E: morgans@blaenfallen.fsnet.co.uk
Furthering study of Welsh hymnody in its spiritual, cultural and historical context.
Secretary: Mrs Delyth Morgans. No full-time staff. ***CC*** No.700609. Began 1967; non-denominational. Magazine: *Bulletin Cymdeithas Emynau* (Circulation & frequency n/a). Turnover £8,000 to year end Apr 98.

†Stephen Deal, 24 Devonshire Road, Carshalton SM5 2TJ
☎020 8773 9604 Fax 020 8773 9604
Web: www.stevendeal.org
Humorous quick sketch drama, tried and tested by professional actors.
Writer: Mr Stephen Deal. Executive staff 1. Began 1984; non-denominational. No magazine. Turnover £25,000 to year end Dec 02.

***DM Music for Churches**, Unit 4, Riverside Estate, Coldharbour Lane, Harpenden AL5 4UN
☎01582 761 122 Freephone 0500 026 930 Fax 01582 768 811
E: info@dmmusic.com
Web: www.dmmusic.com
Supplying and installing PA, audio visual and musical equipment to churches and schools. Arranging training seminars.
Managing Director: Mr David Moore. Executive staff 2, Other staff 12. Began 1991; non-denominational. No magazine. Turnover £1,500,000 to year end Dec 02.

Eternal Sound & Light, 7 Corinthian Way, Victoria Dock, Hull HU9 1UF
☎01482 212 216 M: 07812 833 390
E: esl@ganney.net
Web: www.ganney.net/esl.htm
Providing sound, lighting and discos to churches and other groups.
Director: Mr Paul Ganney. Executive staff 1. Began 1989; Anglican. (Previously Small & Hairy). No magazine. Turnover £3,000 to year end Oct 02.

Event & Management Services, Unit 5, Churchill Industrial Estate, Churchill Road, Cheltenham GL53 7EG
☎01242 245 444 Fax 01242 250 618
E: ems@ullenwood.co.uk
Organising conferences, music and corporate events; Christian music artists.
Partner: Mr Peter Allison. Executive staff 4. Began 1997; non-denominational. No magazine. Turnover £80,000 to year end Mar 99.

†Festivals of Christian Music, 57 Ashwell Street, Ashwell, Baldock SG7 5QT
☎01462 742 185
E: gonjurney@aol.com
Promoting the Gospel through Christian music in four-part harmony; encouraging preservation of church choirs.
Chairman: Norman J Gurney. Executive staff 1. Began 1989; non-denominational. No magazine. Turnover £2,000 to year end Dec 02.

FHG Music That Matters, Searrach, Grange Road, Fort William PH33 6JF
☎01397 700 724 M: 0788 580 723
Fax 01491 639 371
E: chris@fhgmusic.co.uk
Web: www.chris-adams.biz
Music production, promotion, sales. Film, TV, composition. Christian music online sales outlet.
Directors: Mr C Adams. Executive staff 2, Other staff 1. Began 1998; interdenominational. No magazine. Turnover n/a.

†Gold Records, 9 Woodleighton Grove, Uttoxeter ST14 8BY
☎01889 563 930 M: 07881 781 547
Fax 01889 563 930
E: sales@goldrecords.co.uk
Independent Christian record label producting concept albums created by Phil Baggaley and friends.
Partner, Sales and Information: Mr Graham White. Executive staff 6. Began n/a; interdenominational. No magazine. Turnover n/a.

The Gregorian Association, 26 The Grove, Ealing, London W5 5LH
☎020 8840 5832 Fax 08700 553 684
E: pjsw@beaufort.demon.co.uk
Web: www.beaufort.demon.co.uk/chant.html
Promoting study and use of plainsong and its suitability to the English language.
Chairman: Mr A G Ellison-Macartney. All voluntary staff. ***CC*** No.1003775. Began 1870; interdenominational. Magazine: *The Gregorian* (200 occasionally). Turnover n/a.

Guild of Church Musicians, St Katharine Cree, 86 Leadenhall Street, London EC3A 3DH
☎01883 743 168 Fax 01883 740 570
E: JohnMusicsure@orbix.co.uk
Web: www.churchmusicians.org
Examining body for Church Music especially for Archbishops of Canterbury and Westminster.
General Secretary: Mr John Ewington OBE. Executive staff 4, Other staff 2. ***CC*** Began 1888; ecumenical. Magazine: *Laudate* (800 every four months). Turnover n/a.

Hymn Society of Great Britain and Ireland, 99 Barton Road, Lancaster LA1 4EN
☎01524 667 40 Fax 01524 667 4[illegible]
E: robcanham@haystacks.fsnet.co.uk
Web: www.hymnsocietygbi.org.uk
Encouraging study and research into hymns and promoting their good and discerning use in worship.
Secretary: Rev Robert A Canham. No full-time staff. ***CC*** No.248225. Began 1936; interdenominational. See also Welsh Hymn Society). Magazine: *The Bulletin* (450 quarterly). Turnover n/a.

Hymn Technology Ltd, 9 South End, Croydon CR0 1BE
☎0800 043 0503 Fax 020 8680 9[illegible]71
E: info@hymntechnology.com
Web: www.hymntechnology.com
Providing pre-recorded accompaniments for the singing of hymns and other worship music.
Director: Mr Martin Phelps. Executive staff 2, Other staff 4. Began 1995; interdenominational. (Previously Digital Hymnals UK Ltd). No magazine. Turnover n/a.

ICC Records, 4-5 Regency Mews, Silverdale Road, Eastbourne BN20 7AB
☎01323 643 341 Fax 01323 649 2[illegible]0
E: info@icc.org.uk
Web: www.iccrecords.com
Supporting new and existing Christian artists of all styles of music.
Record Label Manager: Mr Phil Loose. Executive staff 2, Other staff 40. ***CC*** No.1079801. Began 1976; interdenominational. Part of ICC. No magazine. Turnover included in ICC.

***Integrity Music (Europe) Ltd**, Berkeley House, 26 Gildredge Road, Eastbourne BN21 4SA
☎01323 430 033 Fax 01323 411 9[illegible]1
E: jonathanb@integrityeurope.com
Web: www.integrityeurope.com or www.gospel-direct.com
Christian media company creating and distributing books, CDs, DVDs, videos, software and music books.
Managing Director: Jonathan Bugden. Executive staff 5, Other staff 14. Began 1986; interdenominational. Magazine: *gospel-direct.com* (Circulation n/a online). Turnover n/a.

†Joshua Music, St Luke's House, 1[illegible] St Luke's Road, Maidstone ME14 5AW
☎01622 661 200 Fax 01622 663 1[illegible]9
E: admin@joshuamusic.com
Web: www.joshuamusic.com
Publishing and administering the musical ministry of Russ Hughes and other worship leaders.
Director: Mr Russ Hughes. Executive staff 1. Began 1994; non-denominational. No magazine. Turnover n/a.

John Keys, 61 Sherwood Rise, Nottingham NG7 6JE
☎0115 962 0367 Ⓜ: 07779 039 356
🖷0115 962 0367
Ⓔ: JohnKeysMusic@aol.com
Web: www.johnkeys.co.uk
Providing church music organ accompaniments on CD.
Organist: Mr John Keys. No full-time staff. Began 2005; interdenominational. No magazine. Turnover n/a.

Kingship, PO Box 7981, Birmingham B23 5PL
☎0121 386 1831
Ⓔ: gospel.music@kingship.co.uk
Web: www.kingship.co.uk
Recording and producing Christian music; training courses.
Director: Mr Ruben King. Admin staff 1. Began 1997; non-denominational. No magazine. Turnover n/a.

†**The Leaveners**, Ground Floor, 1 The Lodge, 1046 Bristol Road, Birmingham B29 6LJ
☎0121 414 0099 🖷0121 414 0090
Ⓔ: enquiry@leaveners.org
Web: www.leaveners.org
Training and live arts projects exploring social issues, conflict, non-violence, spirituality, especially with young people.
Co-ordinator: Alison Jones. Admin staff 2, Other staff 2. **CC** No.292499. Began 1978; Religious Society of Friends. Incorporating Quaker Youth Theatre, Quaker Music Makers, Words, signs, vibes.. Magazine: *Leavenings* (2,000 half-yearly). Turnover n/a.

***The Lighthouse Agency**, PO Box 1941, Barnston, Dunmow CM6 1YP
☎01371 874 544
🖷01371 874 544
Ⓔ: dave@bemmentlh.fsnet.co.uk
Web: www.lighthouseagency.co.uk
Agency for many leading performers and sportsmen for testimony evenings.
Director: Mr David Bemment. Executive staff 1. Began 1998; interdenominational. No magazine. Turnover n/a.

***Make Way Music Ltd**, PO Box 263, Croydon CR9 5AP
Ⓔ: info@makewaymusic.com
Web: www.makewaymusic.com
Publishing and administering the musical ministry of Graham Kendrick.
Managing Director: Mr Graham Kendrick. Executive staff 2, Other staff 1. Began 1988; non-denominational. No magazine. Turnover n/a.

Makin Organs Ltd, Sovereign House, 30 Manchester Road, Shaw, Oldham OL2 7DE
☎01706 888 100
🖷01706 888 109
Ⓔ: sales@makinorgans.co.uk
Web: www.makinorgans.co.uk
Manufacturing and distributing English and European pipeless classical organs.
Managing Director: Dr Keith Harrington. Executive staff 3, Other staff 5. Began 1970; non-denominational. Magazine: *Makin News* (5,000 half-yearly). Turnover £1,200,000 to year end Dec 05.

Mercia Theatre Services, PO Box 2222, Coalville LE67 2YW
☎01530 263 454 🖷01530 260 206
Ⓔ: merciatheatre@aol.com
Supplying theatre equipment; suppling and installing church sound systems.
Managing Partner: Mr Simon Nickerson. Executive staff 2, Admin staff 1. Began 1989; non-denominational. (Previously Theatrehouse). Turnover n/a.

***Mimeistry UK**, The Coach House, Woodhill, Congresbury, Bristol BS49 5AF
☎01934 833 652 Ⓜ: 07967 974 137
🖷01934 833 652
Ⓔ: europe@mimeistry.com
Web: www.mimeistry.com
International performances combining mime, drama, dance; training programme, workshops. European contact for Todd Farley.
European Director: Jacque Hyde. Executive staff 1. Began 1982; interdenominational. No Magazine. Turnover n/a.

†**M.i.T.Ch Puppet Ministries**, 18 New Street, Dudley DY1 1LP
☎01384 234 408
Ⓔ: puppetmansl@blueyonder.co.uk
Teaching skills in puppetry; workshops, presentations, resources, scripts, videos; supplying hand-made puppets.
Training Manager: Rev Simon Grove. No full-time staff. Began n/a; interdenominational. No magazine. Turnover n/a.

M

†MLM Records Ltd, PO Box 653, Bolton BL1 4WR
☎0151 430 9002 🖷0151 430 7441
E: nadine@rtsonestop.co.uk
Web: www.marilla.com
Sales and distribution department of the music of Marilla Ness.
Marketing Director: Mrs Barbara Ainscough. Executive staff 2, Other staff 6. Began 1990; interdenominational. (Previously Merciful Love Music). No magazine. Turnover n/a.

Music and Worship Foundation, 8 Silverdale, Fleet GU52 7TT
☎01252 614 604 🖷01252 614 604
E: info@mwf.org.uk
Web: www.mwf.org.uk
Training, resourcing churches in music/worship, training to degree level with London School of Theology.
Administrator: Mr Granville Lovat. No full-time staff. ***CC*** No.290417. Began 1984; ecumenical. Magazine: *Baseline* (Circulation n/a quarterly). Turnover £26,000 to year end Mar 05.

The Netherbow Scottish Storytelling Centre, 43 High Street, Edinburgh EH1 1SR
☎0131 556 9579 / 2647
🖷0131 557 5224
E: netherbow-storytelling@dial.pipex.com
Web: www.scottishstorytellingcentre.co.uk
Arts centre programme, M workshops in drama, storytelling, worship, church arts; John Knox House Museum.
Director: Dr Donald Smith. *General Manager:* Moira Hay. Executive staff 2, Other staff 7. ***CC*** No.SCO 11353. Began 1972; Church of Scotland. No magazine. Turnover £480,000 to year end Dec 02.

***New Christian Music**, Meredale, The Dell, Reach Lane, Heath and Reach, Leighton Buzzard LU7 0AL
☎01525 237 700 🖷01525 237 700
E: enq@newchristianmusic.co.uk or enq@newmusicenterprises.comand
Web: www.newchristianmusic.co.uk or www.newmusicenterprises.com
Promoting Christian recording to media worldwide; publishing songs, arranging Gospel concerts, producing Christian recordings.
Manager: Rev Dr Paul Davis. No full-time staff. Began 1975; interdenominational. Incorporating New Music Enterprises. No magazine. Turnover n/a.

Newby Entertainments, 100 Fotheringham Road, Enfield EN1 1QE
☎020 8366 6051
Entertainment for Sunday Schools, adults, private parties; Gospel and close-up magic, clowns, puppets.
Managing Director: Mr Dave Newby. Executive staff 1, No other full-time staff. Began 1981; non-denominational. No magazine. Turnover £15,000 to year end Apr 95.

†Norwich Organs, Unit 10, Bure Valley Business Centre, The Street, Lamas, Norwich NR10 5AF
☎01603 278 078
🖷01603 278 078
E: sales@norwich-organs.co.uk
Web: www.norwich-organs.co.uk
Manufacturing classical electronic organs.
Partners: Mr Muttock, Mr Plummer. Executive staff 2, Other staff 5. Began 1974; non-denominational. No magazine. Turnover n/a.

Orange Room Music, 4 Kendal Court, Railway Road, Newhaven BN9 0AY
☎01273 612 825
🖷01273 612 811
E: office@orangeroommusic.co.uk
Web: www.orangeroommusic.co.uk
Music production company; recording studio.
Directors: Mr Colin Walker, Mr Mark Edwards. Executive staff 2, Admin staff 2. Began 1998; non-denominational. (Previously Modern Gospel Ltd). No magazine. Turnover £200,000 to year end Mar 03.

Peak Music Ltd, 3 Tapton House Road, Sheffield S10 5BY
☎0845 890 4452
E: enquiries@peakmusic.co.uk
Web: www.peakmusic.co.uk
Arranging Christian songs for choirs and instruments; typesetting specialising in music; music arranging.
Production Manager: Ruth Milsom. Executive staff 1, No other staff. Began 1981; interdenominational. (Previously Jaw Music Ltd). No magazine. Turnover n/a.

Pratt Green Trust, 12 Heol Tyn Cae, Cardiff CF14 6DJ
☎029 2061 6023
🖷029 2061 6023
E: alanluff@fish.co.uk
Web: www.hymnquest.com
Furthering the cause of hymnody.
Chairman of Trustees: Rev Canon Alan Luff. Admin staff 2. ***CC*** No.290556. Began n/a; ecumenical. No magazine. Turnover £35,000 to year end Mar 00.

Psalmody International, PO Box 5222, Burton-on-Trent DE14 3WT
☎01283 534 375
M: 07764 606 572
E: info@psalmody.org, or info@ci-ministries.org.uk
Web: www.psalmody.org
Teaching and developing praise and worship as a lifestyle; supplying resources, books, tapes, CDs.
UK Directors: Mr & Mrs Stephen & Jenny Watson. Executive staff 2, Other staff 2. ***CC*** No.1042573. Began 1988; interdenominational. Magazine: *The Worshipping Heart* (2,000 frequency n/a). Turnover £20,000 to year end Dec 02.

Radius (The Religious Drama Society of Great Britain), Noda House, 58 Lincoln Road, Peterborough PE1 2RZ
☎01733 565 613
E: office@radius.org.uk
Web: www.radius.org.uk
Supporting religious drama production for Christian understanding through training, advice, play supplies, lending library.
Coordinator: Name not supplied. ***CC*** No.214943. Began 1929 ecumenical. Magazine: *Radius Performing* (Circulation n/a quarterly). Turnover £2[illegible],000 to year end Dec 02.

Riding Lights Theatre Company, Friargate Theatre, Lower Friargate, York YO1 9SL
☎01904 655 317 🖷01904 651 [illegible]32
E: info@rltc.org
Web: www.ridinglights.org
Professional Christian theatre company; community theatre available to any venue; workshops, books.
Artistic Director: Mr Paul Burbridge. *General Manager:* Jonathan Brown. Executive staff 4, Other staff 13. ***CC*** No.1070142. Began 1977; non-denominational. No magazine. Turnover £500,000 to year end Dec [illegible]4.

†Rodgers Classical Organs, Atlantic Close, Swansea SA7 9FJ
☎01792 515 033 M: 079[illegible]7 437[illegible]48
🖷01792 515 048
E: info@rodgersinstruments.co.uk
Web: www.rodgersinstruments.co.uk
Supplying and marketing classical electronic musical instruments to churches and schools.
Divisional Manager: Mr Sean Montgomery. Executive staff 20, Other staff 40. Began 1958; non-denominational. No magazine. Turnover n/a.

Robin J S Rust, 70 Greenways, Fleet GU52 7XD
☎01252 617 908
Pipe organ builders undertaking tuning, maintenance, cleaning, rebuilds to all types of action.
Proprietor: Mr Robin J S Rust. Executive staff 1, Other staff 2. Began 1960; non-denominational. No magazine. Turnover £60,000 to year end Apr 05.

Shorehill Arts, Thatched Cottage, Otford Hills, Sevenoaks TN15 6XL
☎01959 523 740
E: nickpage@cnet.org
Web: www.shorehillarts.co.uk
Production, presentation and consultancy in public events. Guest appearances of Christian performers for outreach events.
Proprietor: Mr Nick Page. No full-time staff. Began 1989; non-denominational. Incorporating Sound Supplement. No magazine. Turnover £43,000 to year end Aug 04.

Songs of Fellowship Arrangements Service, 3 Tapton House Road, Sheffield S10 5BY
☎0845 890 4452
E: sofas@peakmusic.co.uk
Web: www.peakmusic.co.uk
Sheet music arrangement of Christian songs and hymns for choirs and instrumentalists.
Managing Director: Ruth Milsom. Executive staff 1, Other staff 1. Began 1981; interdenominational. No magazine. Turnover n/a.

Sovereign Music UK, PO Box 356, Leighton Buzzard LU7 3WP
☎01525 385 578 🖷01525 372 743
E: sovereignmusic@aol.com
Representing Sovereign Lifestyle Music, Restoration Music, Christian Music Ministries, Integrity Music, Deep Blue Publishing.
Managing Director: Mr Robert Lamont. Executive staff 2, Other staff 1. Began 1981; interdenominational. No magazine. Turnover n/a.

Spirit Christian Distribution, Meadow House, Kingcombe Road, Toller Porcorum, Dorchester DT2 0DG
☎01300 321 564/565
M: 0788- 267 960
🖷01300 321 565
E: info@spiritmusic.co.uk
Web: www.spiritmusic.co.uk
Distributing contemporary Christian music, CDs, videos, clothing, audio books.
Partners: Mr & Mrs Rob & Karen Hillman. Executive staff 2, Other staff 2. Began 1995; non-denominational. (Previously Spirit Music). No magazine. Turnover n/a.

†Spirit Enterprises, 61 Lilford Road, Camberwell, London SE5 9HY
☎020 7738 7678 M: 07930 640 407
🖷020 7738 4040
E: jjatspirit@aol.com
Distributing Christian music and books.
Director: Ms Jennifer James. Executive staff 1 Began 1991; interdenominational. (Previously Spirit). No magazine. Turnover n/a.

Stage Lighting Services, 11 Gedling Road, Carlton, Nottingham NG4 3EX
☎0115 961 9988 🖷0115 956 1966
E: spotlight@stagelightingservices.co.uk
Web: www.stagelightingservices.co.uk
Hiring and selling theatrical lighting and sound equipment to churches, schools and drama groups.
Proprietor: Mr Simon Warren. Executive staff 1. Began 1994; interdenominational. No magazine. Turnover £20,000 to year end Mar 02.

***Storm Ministries**, Pound Cottage, 19 Ardsheal Road, Worthing BN14 7RN
☎01903 201 234
M: 07810 522 307
E: ginnycassell@hotmail.com
Web: www.stormministries.org.uk
Training all-age teams in Christianity and performing arts; training workshops, outreach, mission.
Director: Rev Ginny Cassell. No full-time staff. ***CC*** No.1088727. Began 1996; interdenominational. (Previously TSS). No magazine. Turnover £20,000 to year end Oct 05.

Synergy Audio, The Old Bakery, Framlingham, Woodbridge IP13 9DT
☎01394 460 099
M: 07850 730 319
🖷01728 724 207
E: info@synergyaudio.co.uk
Web: www.synergyaudio.co.uk
Providing professional audio equipment for hire and sale; installation; tours and festivals.
Managing Director: Mr Rob Quin. *Technical Manager:* Mr Mark Isbister. Executive staff 1, Other staff 2. Began n/a; Baptist. No magazine. Turnover £300,000 to year end Apr 05.

MJ Syson, 6 Langham Road, Milton, Stoke-on-Trent ST2 7DP
☎01782 545 945
🖷01782 545 945
E: msyson@ukonline.co.uk
Web: www.musiclink.co.uk/piano/syson.html
Piano tuning and repair for churches and others.
Proprietor: Mr Michael Syson. Executive staff 1. Began 1981; non-denominational. No magazine. Turnover n/a.

***Thankyou Music**, PO Box 75, Eastbourne BN23 6NW
☎01323 437 700
🖷01323 411 970
E: slockhart@kingsway.co.uk or pjohnson@kingsway.co.uk
Web: www.kingswaysongs.com
Publishing of Christian songs.
Copyright Administration Manager: Mrs Sue Lockhart. *Song Publishing Manager:* Phil Johnson. Executive staff 3, Other staff n/a. ***CC*** No.265612. Began n/a; interdenominational. (Previously Kingsway's Thankyou Music). No magazine. Turnover included in Kingsway.

Vineyard Records UK, 252 Cottingham Road, Hull HU6 8QA
☎0870 120 0553 🖷01482 446 259
E: chris.whitelock@vineyardrecords.co.uk
Web: www.vineyardrecords.co.uk
Documenting, modelling and imparting worship to the church through recordings, training events, resource materials.
General Manager: Mr Chris Whitelock. Executive staff 2, Admin staff 4. ***CC*** No.1087771. Began 1987; Vineyard Churches UK. (Previously Vineyard Music). Magazine: *Equipped* (Circulation n/a quarterly). Turnover n/a.

Viscount (Church) Organs Ltd, 5 Caxton Way, Watford WD18 8UA
☎01923 247 437 🖷01923 249 345
E: sales@viscount-organs.co.uk
Web: www.viscount-organs.co.uk or www.viscount.it
Supplying 'pipeless' / digital, classically-voiced organs to churches, and instruments for the organist's home.
Managing Director: Mr D A Cuttill. Executive staff 3. Began 1976; non-denominational. No magazine. Turnover £700,000 to year end Sep 02.

†Visiting Speakers, 13 Leopold Street, Southsea PO5 4BX
M: 07773 873 167
Providing disco, sound and lighting, Christian engineers.
Leader: Rev Matt Troke. Executive staff 4. Began 1993; interdenominational. (Previously Him 'N' Us Ministries). No magazine. Turnover n/a.

***VM Music**, PO Box 51, East Grinstead RH19 3FQ
☎01342 410 696 🖷01342 410 696
E: info@vmmusic.com
Web: www.vinesong.com
Designing, producing, marketing, distributing Christian music in audio and video format. Predominantly Vinesong.
General Manager: Mr Geoff Tompkins. Executive staff 3, Other staff 6. ***CC*** No.1046242. Began 1998; non-denominational. No magazine. Turnover n/a.

Winsome Music, Chycoll, Sancreed, Penzance TR20 8QY
☎01736 811 036 M: 07754 122 352
E: info@winsome-music.com
Web: www.winsome-music.com
Providing professional worship and music resources with residential recording facilities in west Cornwall.
Managing Director: Mr David Ceredig-Evans. Executive staff 1. Began 1997; non-denominational. No magazine. Turnover £1,000 to year end Apr 03.

NEWSPAPERS & PERIODICALS

By Frequency and Circulation in 2005
Publications which did not supply this information are not listed here

Name	Circulation
Weekly	
The Universe	55,000
The War Cry	53,000
Church Times	31,000
Catholic Times	26,500
The Tablet	22,100
Catholic Herald	22,000
Methodist Recorder	22,000
Kids Alive!	20,000
Salvationist	20,000
Scottish Catholic Observer	18,000
The Church of England Newspaper	8,200
Baptist Times	8,000
Church of Ireland Gazette	5,000
Fortnightly	
Messenger	12,000
Monthly	
The Sign	61,000
Challenge Newsline	60,000
The Good News	55,000
Inspire	50,000
News Special	50,000
Life & Work	45,569
UK Focus	40,000
Home Words	32,000
Joy Magazine	30,000
Protestant Truth	25,000
News Extra	20,000
News Today	18,000
Direction Magazine	16,500
Christianity	16,000
Reform	13,500
The Presbyterian Herald	13,000
The Officer	12,500
Woman Alive	10,000
Evangelical Times	9,500
Youthwork	8,000
Evangelicals Now	7,000
Expository Times	6,000
Inspires	5,000
The Banner of Truth	5,600
Cheering Words Magazine	4,500
The Briefing	3,500
Christian Marketplace	2,500
The Instructor	2,300
Needed Truth	2,000
Gospel Standard	1,750
Prophetic Witness	1,500
Y Llan	800
Eleven per Year	
Priests & People	9,000
Grace Magazine	2,000
Ten per year	
Plus/Eagles Wings	9,000
Reachout	8,000
Third Way	5,000
Every two months	
New Life Newspaper	40,000
idea	38,000
The Trinitarian	20,000
Decision Magazine	15,000
Enough	15,000
The Upper Room	8,520
Goodnews	8,000
Prophecy Today	8,000
Church Building	7,500
Library of Lives The Journal	5,000
The Reformer	5,000
Theology	4,200
Quadrant	2,600
Bound Together	3,000
Protestant Truth	3,000
The Evangelical Magazine of Wales	1,800
The Young Reformer	1,600
Gwyliedydd [= Sentinel]	1,000
Orthodox Outlook	1,000
The Gospel Magazine	800
Biblical Archaeology Review	275
Quarterly	
The Messenger	84,000
Share It!	55,000
Nota Bene (European Theological Media)	30,000
Maintenance and Equipment News for Churches and Schools	21,000
Focus	20,000
Just Right Magazine	18,000
Precious Seed Magazine	14,500
All the World	13,000
EWCH	11,000
The Reader	10,000
Sword and Trowel	6,500
The Flame	4,000
The Chesterton Review	3,000
Communio	3,000
Crown & Commonwealth	2,500
New Testament Studies	2,000
Scottish Journal of Theology	1,750
Transformation	1,400
Epworth Review	1,330
The Christian Counsellor	1,200
Churchman (Journal of Anglican Theology)	1,000
Evangelical Quarterly	1,000
The Heythrop Journal	1,000
Review of Theological Literature	1,000
Anvil	900
Evangelical Review of Theology	800
Y Cylchgrawn Efengylaidd	800
Christian History Magazine	300
Orthodox England	300
Areopagus	150
Five per year	
Journal for the Study of the New Testament	1,300
Every four months	
Pro-Life Times	130,000
Country Way	4,000
Church Observer	3,500
The Overcomer	3,500
Ethics and Medicine	1,300
Evangel	600
Studies in Christian Ethics	600
Feminist Theology	500
Baptismal Integrity	500
Journal for the Study of the Pseudepigrapha	400
Theology and Sexuality	400
ACC–UK	200
Half-yearly	
Alpha News	200,000
Science and Christian Belief	2,000
Journal of Theological Studies	1,300
Rutherford Journal of Church and Ministry	1,000
Scottish Bulletin of Evangelical Theology	800
Journal of Education and Christian Belief	600
European Journal of Theology	500
Journal of Pentecostal Theology	500
Black Theology in Britain	350
Ecotheology	300
Quaker Studies	300
British Journal of Theological Education	200
International Congregational Journal	100
Annually	
Veritasse Magazine	18,000
Currents in Research: Biblical Studies	600
Reformed Theological Journal	450
Journal of the European Pentecostal Theological Association	350
The Merton Annual: Studies in Culture, Spirituality and Social Concerns	350
Journal of Greco-Roman Christianity and Judaism	50
Irregularly	
Partnership Publications	450
Internet	
Christian Today	
The Good Bookstall	
Parish Pump	
Independent Catholic News	
Ship of Fools	

NEWSPAPER & PERIODICALS

ACC-UK, Diocesan Office, 42 High Street, Lydd, Romney Marsh TN29 9AN
☎01797 321 704 📠01797 321 704
Web: www.anglicancatholic.org.uk
Editor: Very Rev Damien Mead. No full-time staff. Began 2000; Anglican Catholic Church. Turnover £500 to year end Dec 02.

All the World, Salvation Army, International Headquarters, 101 Queen Victoria Street, London EC4P 4EP
☎020 7332 8084 📠020 7332 8076
E: kevin_sims@salvationarmy.org or allworld@salvationarmy.org
Web: www.salvationarmy.org
Editor: Mr Kevin Sims. Executive staff 1. ***CC*** No.2538134. Began 1884; Salvation Army. Turnover n/a.

Alpha News, Holy Trinity Brompton Church, Brompton Road, London SW7 1JA
☎0845 644 7544 📠020 7052 0207
E: communications@alpha.org
Web: www.alphacourse.org
Multi-cultural.
Editor: Mark Elsdon Dew. Executive staff 6. ***CC*** Began 1993; interdenominational. Turnover included in Alpha Course.

***Anvil**, Wycliffe Hall, Oxford OX2 6PW
☎01865 274 760 📠01865 274 215
E: editor@anviljournal.co.uk
Web: www.anviljournal.co.uk
Anglican evangelical journal for theology and mission.
Editor: Rev Dr A Goddard. No full-time staff. ***CC*** No.1013559. Began 1984; Anglican. Turnover £15,527 to year end Dec 05.

Areopagus, 91 Carbeile Road, Torpoint PL11 2HR
☎No telephone 📠03701 346 384
E: editor@areopagus.org.uk
Web: www.areopagus.org.uk
Christian writers' magazine.
Editor: Mr Julian Barritt. No paid staff. Began 1990; interdenominational. Turnover £1,500 to year end Dec 05.

The Banner of Truth, The Grey House, 3 Murrayfield Road, Edinburgh EH12 6EL
☎0131 337 7310 📠0131 346 7484
E: info@banneroftruth.cc.uk
Web: www.banneroftruth.co.uk
Editor: Walter J Chantry. *General Manager:* Mr John Rawlinson. Executive staff 4, Other staff 7. ***CC*** No.235652. Began 1955; non-denominational. Turnover n/a.

Baptist Times, 129 Broadway, Didcot OX11 8XB
☎01235 517 670 📠01235 517 678
E: editor@baptisttimes.co.uk
Web: www.baptisttimes.co.uk
Editor: Mr Mark Woods. Executive staff 4. Began 1855; owned by Baptist Union but non-denominational. Turnover n/a.

Biblical Archaeology Review, Paternoster Periodicals, PO Box 300, Carlisle CA3 0QS
☎UK 0800 195 7969 📠01228 51 49 49
E: pp@stl.org
Web: www.authenticmedia.co.uk/paternoster
Publisher: Mr Mark Finnie. No full-time staff. Began 1975; interdenominational. Turnover n/a.
Editor: Mr Hershel Shanks, 4710 41st Street NW, Washington DC 20016 USA
☎001 202 364 3300 📠001 202 364 2636

Black Theology: An International Journal, Equinox Publishing, Taylor and Francis Group, 2 Park Square, Milton Park, Abingdon OX14 4RN
☎020 7017 6000 📠020 7017 6699
Web: www.tandf.co.uk/journals
Publisher: Name not supplied. No full-time staff. Began n/a; non-denominational. (Previously Black Theology In Britain). Turnover n/a.

†Bound Together, 367 Warwick Road, Carlisle CA1 2BS
☎01228 594 239
E: happy@bound-together.org.uk
Web: www.bound-together.org.uk
For Cumbria and the Borders.
Editor: Mr Leslie Irving. Admin staff 1. Began 1994; interdenominational. Part of Happy to Help Ministries. Turnover n/a.

***The Briefing**, The Good Book Company, Elm House, 37 Elm Road, New Malden KT3 3HB
☎08452 250 880 📠08452 250 990
E: editor@thegoodbook.co.uk
Web: www.thegoodbook.co.uk
UK Publisher: Mr Tim Thornborough. Executive staff 3. Began 1987; non-denominational. Turnover n/a.

British Church Newspaper, Kingswood House, Pilcorn Street, Wedmore BS28 4AW
☎01934 712 520 📠01934 710 521
E: nama@kpws.demon.co.uk
Fortnightly Protestant newspaper with UK and worldwide news, features, comment, letters, book reviews.
Hon Editor: Dr Napier Malcolm. Executive staff 1, Admin staff 1. Began 2002; interdenominational. Turnover n/a.

Catholic Herald, Herald House, 15 Lambs Passage, Bunhill Row, London EC1Y 8TQ
☎020 7588 3101 📠020 7256 9728
E: editorial@catholicherald.co.uk
Web: www.catholicherald.co.uk
Editor: Dr William Oddie. Executive staff 2, Other staff 12. Began 1885; Roman Catholic. Turnover n/a.

Catholic Times, 1st Floor, St James Court, St James Buildings, Oxford Street, Manchester M1 6FP
☎0161 236 8856 📠0161 237 5590
E: kevin.flaherty@the-universe.net
Web: www.totalcatholic.com
Editor: Mr Kevin Flaherty. Executive staff 5. Began 1892; Roman Catholic. Turnover n/a.

***Challenge Newsline**, 8 St John's Parade, Alinora Crescent, Goring-by-Sea, Worthing BN12 4HJ
☎0845 166 8463 📠0845 166 8459
E: challenge@veritecm.com
Web: www.challengenewsline.com
Evangelistic newspaper for personal and local contact. New format available online.
Editor: Mrs Debbie Bunn. ***CC*** No.270162. Began 1958; interdenominational. (Previously Challenge). Turnover £75,000 to year end Sept 05.

M

Cheering Words Magazine, 22 Victoria Road, Stamford PE9 1HB
☎01780 763 780
Short articles, topical, historical, poetry, youth page with questions: KJV basis throughout.
Editor & Publisher: Mr D Oldham. Executive staff 1. Began 1851; non-denominational and Reformed. Turnover £11,500 to year end Dec 00.

The Christian Counsellor, PO Box 2667, Eastbourne BN21 1RY
☎01792 371 491 🖷01792 371 491
E: TCC@theway.co.uk
Web: www.christiancounsellor.com
For Christians involved in pastoral care, counselling and spiritual direction. Previously published by CWR.
Editor: Helena Wilkinson. No full-time staff. Began n/a; interdenominational. Publisher Roger Penberthy Publishing Ltd. Turnover n/a.

Christian History Magazine, Paternoster Periodicals, PO Box 300, Carlisle CA3 0QS
☎0800 195 7969 🖷+(0) 1228 51 49 49
E: pp@stl.org
Web: www.authenticmedia.co.uk/paternoster
Publisher: Mr Mark Finnie. No full-time staff. Began 1970; non-denominational. Turnover n/a.
Editor: Mark Galli, Christianity Today Inc, 465 Gundersen Drive, Carol Stream, IL 60188, USA
☎00 1 630 260 6200 🖷 00 1 630 260 0114

***Christian Marketplace**, CCP, Broadway House, The Broadway, Crowborough TN6 1HQ
☎01892 652 364 🖷01892 663 329
E: christianmarketplace@premier.org.uk
Web: www.christianmarketplace.org.uk
Magazine resourcing retailers and suppliers of Christian products around the world.
Editorial Director: Mr John Buckeridge. *Advertising Sales:* Fiona Grunwell. Executive staff 2, Other staff n/a. Began 2001; interdenominational. Turnover n/a.

***Christian Today**, Partnership House, 157 Waterloo Road, London SE1 8XA
☎020 7620 0210 🖷020 7401 8257
E: info@christiantoday.com
Independent online newspaper updated daily; serving Christian communities with UK and world new.
Executive Director: Mr Andrew Clark. Executive staff 5, Other staff 12. Began 2000; interdenominational. Turnover n/a.

***Christianity**, CCP, PO Box 17911, London SW1P 4YX
☎020 7316 1450 🖷020 7316 1453
E: ccp@premier.org.uk
Web: www.christianitymagazine.co.uk
Examining real life, real faith - in the real world.
Senior Editor: Mr John Buckeridge. Executive staff 1, Other staff 12. Began 2000; interdenominational. (Previously Christianity + Renewal. Turnover n/a.

†Church Building, 1st Floor, St James's Buildings, Oxford Street, Manchester M1 6FP
☎0161 236 8856 🖷0161 236 8892
E: normanl@the-universe.net
Editor: Mr Norman Lawton. Executive staff 1, Other staff 7. Began 1984; non-denominational. Turnover n/a.

†Church Observer, Church Union, Faith House, 7 Tufton Street, London SW1P 3QN
☎020 7222 6952 🖷020 7976 7180
E: churchunion@care4free.net
Web: www.churchunion.care4free.net
Editor: Mrs Jenny Miller. Executive staff 1. Began 1879; Anglican. Turnover n/a.

The Church of England Newspaper, Fourth Floor, Central House, 142 Central Street, London EC1V 8AR
☎020 7417 5800 M: 07941 041 959
🖷020 7216 6410
E: cen@churchnewspaper.com
Web: www.churchnewspaper.com
Editor: Mr Colin Blakely. Executive staff 1, Other staff 5. Began 1828; Anglican. Turnover n/a.

†Church of Ireland Gazette, 3 Wallace Avenue, Lisburn BT27 4AA
☎028 9267 5743 🖷028 9266 7580
E: gazette@ireland.anglican.org
Web: www.gazette.ireland.anglican.org
Editor: Rev Canon Ain Ellis. No full-time staff. Began 1856; Church of Ireland. Turnover n/a.

Church Times, 33 Upper Street, London N1 0PN
☎020 7359 4570
🖷020 7226 3051/3073
E: editor@churchtimes.co.uk
Web: www.churchtimes.co.uk
Editor: Mr Paul Handley. *Deputy Editor:* Mr Glyn Paflin. *Advertisement Manager:* Mr Stephen Dutton. Executive staff 3, Other staff 19. ***CC*** No.270060. Began 1861; Anglican. Turnover £1,777,428 to year end Sep 00.

Churchman (Journal of Anglican Theology), Church Society, Dean Wace House, 16 Rosslyn Road, Watford WD18 0NY
☎01923 235 111 🖷01923 800 362
E: churchman@churchsociety.org
Web: www.churchsociety.org
Extensive book reviews.
Editor: Rev Prof Gerald L Bray. Other staff 2. Began 1878; Anglican. Turnover n/a.

Communio, Sage Publications Ltd, 1 Oliver's Yard, 55 City Road, London EC1Y 1SP
☎020 7324 8500 🖷020 7324 8600
E: market@sagepub.co.uk
Web: www.sagepub.co.uk
International Catholic journal centred on the theological renewal in 'creative fidelity' to the Church.
Editor: Mr David L Schindler. Staff n/a. Began 1972; Roman Catholic. Turnover n/a.

Country Way, Arthur Rank Centre, Stoneleigh Park, Kenilworth CV8 2LZ
☎024 7685 3073 🖷024 [illegible]641 48[illegible]8
E: jillh@rase.org.uk
Web: www.arthurrankcentre.org.uk
Ecumenical publication for rural churches.
Editor: Dr Jill Hopkinson. No paid staff. ***CC*** No.209961. Began 1992; ecumenical. Turnover n/a.

Crown and Commonwealth, 121 Low Etherley, Bishop Auckland DL14 0HF
☎01388 834 395 🖷0138[illegible] 835 [illegible]7
E: admin@britishisrael.co.uk
Web: www.britishisrael.co.uk
Editor: Mr Matthew J Browning. Executive staff 1, Admin staff 2. Began 1981; non-denominational. (Previously Wake Up!). Published by The British-Israel-World Foundation (BIWF). Turnover £2[illegible] 000 to year end Jun 98.

Cultural Encounters, Paternoster Periodicals, PO Box 300, Carlisle CA3 0QS
☎0800 195 7969 🖷0122[illegible] 514 [illegible]9
E: pp@stl.org.uk
Web: www.authenticmedia.co.uk/paternoster
Publisher: Mr Mark Finnie. No full-time staff. Began 2005; interdenominational. Turnover n/a.
Editor: Paul L Metzger, Multnomah Biblical Seminary, 8435 NE Glisan Street, Portland, OR 97220, USA
E: culturalencouners@multnomah.edu
☎00 1 503 251 6766

Currents in Biblical Research, Sage Publications Ltd, 1 Oliver's Yard, 55 City Road, London EC1Y 1SP
☎020 7324 8500 🖷020 7[illegible]24 86[illegible]0
E: market@sagepub.co.uk
Web: www.sagepub.co.uk
Editor: Alan J Hauser. No full-time staff. Began 1993; non-denominational. Turnover n/a.

Y Cylchgrawn Efengylaidd, Evangelical Movement of Wales, Bryntirion, Bridgend CF31 4DX
☎01656 655 886 🖷01656 665 9[illegible]9
E: swyddfa@mudiad-efengylaidd.org
Web: www.emw.org.uk
Editor: Robert Rhys. Executive staff 1, Other staff 2. ***CC*** No 222[illegible]07. Began 1948; non-denominational. Turnover n/a.

***Decision Magazine**, PO Box 2032, Woodford Green IG9 5AP
☎020 8559 0342 🖷020 8502 906[illegible]
E: ukoffice@bgea.org
Web: www.billygraham.org
Official magazine of the Billy Graham Evangelistic Association, British edition.
Director: Miss Jean Wilson. Executive staff 1, Admin staff 1. ***CC*** No 233[illegible]81. Began 1960; interdenominational. Turnover included in Samaritan's Purse

For circulation see list on page [illegible]46

***Direction Magazine**, New Life Publishing, PO Box 777, Nottingham NG11 6ZZ
☎0115 921 7280 🖷0115 984 5251
E: direction@newlifepublishing.co.uk
Web: www.newlifepublishing.co.uk/direction
Official monthly publication of Elim Pentecostal Church.
Editor in Chief: Mr John Glass. Executive staff 2, Other staff 5. **CC** No.251549. Began 1989; Pentecostal. (Previously Direction) Turnover n/a.

Ecotheology: The Journal of Religion, Nature and the Environment, Department of Theology and Religious Studies, University College Chester, Parkgate Road, Chester CH1 4BJ
E: c.deane-drummond@chester.ac.uk
Editor: Celia Deane-Drummond. No full-time staff. Began 1978; non-denominational. (Previously Theology in Green). Relaunched 1996. Turnover n/a.

English Churchman & St James's Chronicle, 64 Roley Road, Worthing BN11 5NH
☎01903 505 555 🖷01903 600 019
E: englishchurchman@aol.com
Hon Editor: Rev P. Ratcliff. *Office Manager:* Mr T J Evans. Admin staff 1. **CC** No.249957. Began 1761 St James's Chronicle; 1843 English Churchman; Anglican. Turnover n/a.

Epworth Review, 4 John Wesley Road, Werrington, Peterborough PE4 6ZP
☎01733 325 002 🖷01733 384 180
E: sales@mph.org.uk
Web: www.mph.org.uk
Theological journal containing scholarly articles by leading names in academic and pastoral fields
Editor: Revd Dr Angela Shier-Jones. No full-time staff. Began 1973; Methodist. Turnover n/a.

Ethics and Medicine, Paternoster Periodicals, PO Box 300, Carlisle CA3 0QS
☎01228 512 512 🖷01228 593 388
E: info@authenticmedia.co.uk
Web: www.authenticmedia.co.uk/paternoster
Publisher: Mr Mark Finnie. No full-time staff. Began 1983; interdenominational. Turnover n/a.
Editor: C Ben Mitchell, Southern Baptist Theological Seminary, 2825 Lexington Road, Louisville KY 40280, USA
E: c.benmitchell.76041.2412@compuserve.com
☎001 502 897 4011 🖷001 502 897 4056

European Journal of Theology, Paternoster Periodicals, PO Box 300, Carlisle CA3 0QS
☎0800 195 7969 🖷 01228 514 949
E: pp@stl.org
Web: www.authenticmedia.co.uk/paternoster
Publisher: Mr Mark Finnie. No full-time staff. Began 1992; interdenominational. Turnover n/a.
Editor: Mr Mark Elliott, St Mary's College, University of St Andrews, St Andrews KY16 9JU
E: mwe1@st-andrews.ac.uk
☎01334 462 825

Evangel, Paternoster Periodicals, PO Box 300, Carlisle CA3 0QS
☎01228 512 512 🖷01228 593 388
E: info@authenticmedia.co.uk
Web: www.authenticmedia.co.uk/paternoster
Publisher: Mr Mark Finnie. No full-time staff. Began 1982; interdenominational. Turnover n/a.
Editor: Stephen Dray, 1 Weybridge Walk, North Shoebury, Southend-on-Sea SS3 8YJ
☎01702 300 164
E: stephenpauldray@yahoo.co.uk

The Evangelical Magazine of Wales, Evangelical Movement of Wales, Bryntirion, Bridgend CF31 4DX
☎01656 655 886 🖷01656 665 919
E: office@emw.org.uk
Web: www.emw.org.uk
Chairman of Editorial Board: Rev Spencer Cunnah. Staff 1. **CC** No.222407. Began 1955; non-denominational. Turnover n/a.

Evangelical Quarterly, Paternoster Periodicals, PO Box 300, Carlisle CA3 0QS
☎01228 512 512 🖷01228 593 388
E: info@authenticmedia.co.uk
Web: www.authenticmedia.co.uk/paternoster
Publisher: Mr Mark Finnie. No full-time staff. Began 1929; interdenominational. Turnover n/a.
Editor: Professor I Howard Marshall, Kings College, Old Aberdeen Aberdeen AB24 3UB
E: i.h.marshall@abdn.ac.uk
☎01224 272 388

Evangelical Review of Theology, Paternoster Periodicals, PO Box 300, Carlisle CA3 0QS
☎01228 512 512 🖷01228 593 388
E: info@authenticmedia.co.uk
Web: www.authenticmedia.co.uk/paternoster
Publisher: Mr Mark Finnie. No full-time staff. Began 1977; interdenominational. Turnover n/a.
Editor: Bruce J Nicholls, 73 Kohimarama Road, Auckland 1005 New Zealand
E: bknichol@ihug.co.nz
☎00 64 9 528 6845 🖷00 64 9 528 6845

Evangelical Times, Faverdale North Industrial Estate, Darlington DL3 0PH
☎01325 380 232 🖷01325 466 153
E: theeditors@evangelicaltimes.org
Web: www.evangelicaltimes.org
News and comment for today's churches.
Business Manager: Mr A L Gosling. *Editors:* Prof E H Andrews, Rev Roger Fay. Executive staff 1. **CC** No.258927. Began 1967; non-denominational. (Previously Evangelical Times Ltd). Turnover £125,000 to year end Dec 98.

Evangelicals Now, 14 Silverleigh Road, Thornton Heath CR7 6DU
☎020 8689 6252 🖷020 8665 0994
E: editor@e-n.org.uk
Web: www.e-n.org.uk
Christian newspaper with features, UK and world news, comment and reviews.
Managing Editor: Dr John E Benton. Executive staff 1, Other staff 3. **CC** No.296794. Began 1986; non-denominational. Turnover n/a.

The Expository Times, Sage Publications Ltd, 1 Oliver's Yard, 55 City Road, London EC1Y 1SP
☎020 7324 8500 🖷020 7324 8600
E: market@sagepub.co.uk
Web: www.sagepub.co.uk
Editors: Paul Foster, John Riches, Karen Wenellok. Staff n/a. Began 1889; non-denominational. Turnover n/a.

†Faith Magazine, Suite 209b, The Big Peg, 120 Vyse Street, The Jewellery Quarter, Birmingham B18 6NF
☎0121 689 4884 🖷0121 689 4838
Web: www.faithmagazine.co.uk
Editor: Mr Derrick Dunkley. Executive staff 1, Other staff 3. Began 2000; non-denominational. Turnover n/a.

For circulation see list on page 246

Feminist Theology, Sage Publications Ltd, 1 Oliver's Yard, 55 City Road, London EC1Y 1SP
☎020 7324 8500
🖷020 7324 8600
E: market@sagepub.co.uk
Web: www.sagepub.co.uk
Editors: Lisa Isherwood, Janet Wootton. *Julie Claque:* Claque, Julie, Lillalou Hughes. No full-time staff. Began 1992; non-denominational. Turnover n/a.

Fieldwork in Religion, Equinox Publishing, Taylor and Francis Group, 2 Park Square, Milton Park, Abingdon OX14 4RN
☎020 7017 6000
🖷020 7017 6699
Web: www.equinox.com/journals
Covering anthropology, ethonography, sociology, cultural studies, psychology of all religions.
Publisher: Name not supplied. No full-time staff. Began n/a. Turnover n/a.
Editors: Professor Christopher Partridge, Professor Ron Geaves, Department of Theology & Religious Studies, University of Chester, Parkgate Road, Chester CH1 4BJ
☎01244 375 444
E: c.partridge@chester.ac.uk or r.geaves@chester.ac.uk
Web: www.chester.ac.uk/trs

The Flame, 5 Green Park Avenue, Caston, Scarborough YO11 3RY
☎01723 584 474
M: 07901 925 515
E: armistead@surefish.co.uk
Devoted to teaching scriptural holiness for today.
Editor: Major Norman Armistead. Executive staff 3. ***CC*** No.279983. Began 1935; Independent. Turnover £11,600 to year end Dec 04.

Focus, The Stanborough Press Ltd, Alma Park, Grantham NG31 9SL
☎01476 591 700
🖷01476 577 144
E: editordnm@aol.com
Editor: Dr David Marshall. Staff included in The Stanborough Press. ***CC*** No.235245. Began 1884; Seventh-day Adventist. Turnover included in The Stanborough Press.

The Good News, The Forge, Station Road, Newton le Willows, Bedale DL8 1SP
☎01677 450 518 🖷01677 450 525
E: editor@thegoodnews.co.uk
Web: www.thegoodnews.co.uk
National Christian news and features for the UK online Christian community.
Publisher/Editor: Mr Howard Dobson. No full-time staff. Began 1994; interdenominational. Turnover n/a.

Good News, 11 Pickford Road, Bournemouth BH9 2RR
☎01202 522 177 🖷01202 522 177
E: goodnews@pepr.co.uk
Evangelistic newspaper: a literature mission to the UK.
Editor: Paul Eddy. Staff n/a. ***CC*** No.1075894. Began 2001; interdenominational. Turnover n/a.
Distribution 21 Holmewood Crescent, Holme, Peterborough PE7 3PY
☎01487 831 888 🖷 01487 831 888

***Goodnews**, Allen Hall, 28 Beaufort Street, London SW3 5AA
☎020 7352 5298 🖷020 7351 4486
E: ccruk@onetel.com
Information, teaching and testimonies about charismatic renewal in the Roman Catholic church.
Editor: Miss Kristina Cooper. Executive staff 1, Other staff 1. ***CC*** No.277425. Began 1979; Roman Catholic/Charismatic. Part of World Wide Catholic Charismatic Movements. Turnover n/a.

The Gospel Magazine, 15 Bridge Street, Knighton LD7 1BT
☎01547 528 815/01323 442 996
M: 07976 358 611
E: edward@revmalcolm.freeserve.co.uk
Web: www.gospelmagazine.org.uk
Upholding free Grace; remaining completely faithful to original purposes set out in January 1766 preface.
Hon Secretary: Mr Peter King. *Editor:* Rt Rev Edward Malcolm. No full-time staff. Began 1766; non-denominational. Turnover n/a.

Gospel Standard, 12b Roundwood Lane, Harpenden AL5 3DD
☎01582 765 448 🖷01582 469 148
Editor: Mr B A Ramsbottom. Executive staff 1, Other staff 1. ***CC*** No.209373. Began 1835; Strict Baptist. Turnover n/a.

Grace Magazine, 4 Beechwood Road, Caterham CR3 6RF
☎01883 348 893
E: editor@gracemagazine.org.uk
Web: www.gracemagazine.org.uk
Reformed Baptist magazine for all Christians.
Editor: Tim Curnow. All voluntary staff. ***CC*** No.277106. Began 1970 but 1833 as *Gospel Herald*. Turnover n/a.

†**Gwyliedydd [= Sentinel]**, Hafan, 1 Plas Newydd, Llandudno LL30 1GD
☎01766 831 104
Editor: Mr Aled Morgan. No full-time staff. Began 1809; Methodist. Turnover n/a.

†**The Heythrop Journal**, Heythrop College, Kensington Square, London W8 5H[illegible]
☎020 7795 6600/42[illegible]9 (editorial)
🖷020 7795 4200
Editor: Mr Michael Walsh. No full-time staff. Began 1960; ecumenical. Turnover n/a.
Publishing: Blackwell Publishers, [illegible]600 Garsington Road, Oxford OX4 2DQ

Holy Land Studies: A Multidiscovery Journal, Edinburgh University Press, 22 George Square, Edinburgh EH8 9LF
☎0131 650 4218
🖷0131 662 0053
E: marketing@eup.ed.ac.uk
Web: www.eup.ed.ac.uk
Editor: Nur Masalha. No full-time staff. Began n/a; non-denominational. Turnover n/a.

Home Words, G. J. Palmer & Sons Ltd, St Mary's Works, St Mary's Plain, Norwich NR3 3BH
Monthly parish magazine inset.
Editor: Rev Terence Handley-MacMath. *Administrator:* Mr Clive Edwards. Executive staff 2, Other staff [illegible]. ***CC*** No.270[illegible]60. Began 1870; Anglican. Part of Hymns Ancient & Modern group. Turnover £4,000,000 to year end Dec 04.
Subscriptions Office: G J Palmer & Sons Ltd, 16 Blyburgate, Beccles NR34 [illegible]B
☎01502 711 171
🖷 01502 711 585
E: jennyp@scm-canterburypress.co.uk

***idea**, Evangelical Alliance Developments Ltd, Whitefield House, 18[illegible] Kennington Park Road, London SE11 4BT
☎020 7207 2118
🖷020 7207 2150
E: idea@eauk.org or advertising@eauk.org
Web: www.eauk.org
Editor: To be appointed. Staff included in Evangelical Alliance. ***CC*** No.123[illegible]48. Began n/a; interdenominational. Turnover included in Evangelical Alliance.

Independent Catholic News, [illegible]47a Leighton Road, London NW5 2RB
☎020 7267 3616
🖷020 7267 3616
E: news@indcatholicnews.com
Web: www.indcatholicnews.com
Daily on-line catholic news service run by volunteers.
Editor: Jo Siedlecka. Executive staff 1. ***CC*** No.233699. Began 2000; Roman Catholic. Turnover n/a.

The Innes Review, Edinburgh University Press, 22 George Square, Edinburgh EH8 9LF
☎0131 650 4218
🖷0131 662 0053
E: marketing@eup.ed.ac.uk
Web: www.eup.ed.ac.uk
Editor: Name not supplied. No full-time staff. Began n/a; non-denominational. Turnover n/a.

For circulation see list on page [illegible]46

***Inspire**, Christian Publishing and Outreach, Garcia Estate, Canterbury Road, Worthing BN13 1BW
☎01903 264 556 Advertising 01903 604 342 ISDN 01903 537 308 Advertis
E: editor@inspiremagazine.org.uk
Web: www.inspiremagazine.org.uk
Free to churches.
Editor: Mr Russ Bravo. Executive staff 5, Other staff 28. Began 2006; interdenominational. Turnover n/a.

Inspires, 21 Grosvenor Crescent, Edinburgh EH12 5EE
☎0131 225 6357 📠0131 346 7247
E: inspires@scotland.anglican.org
Church magazine.
Editors: Mr Cliff Piper, Lorna Finley. No full-time staff. **CC** No.SCO 00161. Began 2005; Scottish Episcopal. (Previously The Scottish Episcopalian). Turnover n/a.

†**The Instructor**, Free Church Manse, Kilberry Road, Tarbert PA29 6XX
☎01880 820 134
E: ihowat@aol.com
For primary school aged-children.
Editor: Mrs Irene Howat. Executive staff 1. **CC** No.SCO 12925. Began 1904; Free Church of Scotland. Turnover n/a.

International Congregational Journal, Congregational Press, The Congregational Centre, 8 Castle Gate, Nottingham NG1 7AS
☎0115 911 1460 📠0115 911 1462
E: admin@congregational.org.uk
Editor: Janet Wootton. No full-time staff. Began 2001 non-denominational. Turnover n/a.

International Journal for the Study of the Christian Church, Equinox Publishing, Taylor and Francis Group, 2 Park Square, Milton Park, Abingdon OX14 4RN
☎020 7017 6000 📠020 7017 6699
Web: www.tandf.co.uk/journals
Editor: Paul Avis. No full-time staff. Began n/a; non-denominational. Turnover n/a.

Journal for the Study of the Historical Jesus, Sage Publications Ltd, 1 Oliver's Yard, 55 City Road, London EC1Y 1SP
☎020 7324 8500 📠020 7324 8600
E: market@sagepub.co.uk
Web: www.sagepub.co.uk
Editor: Robert L Webb. No full-time staff. Began n/a; non-denominational. Turnover n/a.

Journal for the Study of the New Testament, Sage Publications Ltd, 1 Oliver's Yard, 55 City Road, London EC1Y 1SP
☎020 7324 8500 📠020 7324 8600
E: market@sagepub.co.uk
Web: www.sagepub.co.uk
Editor: David G Horrell. No full-time staff. Began 1978; non-denominational. Turnover n/a.

Journal for the Study of the Old Testament, Sage Publications Ltd, 1 Oliver's Yard, 55 City Road, London EC1Y 1SP
☎020 7324 8500 📠020 7324 8600
E: market@sagepub.co.uk
Web: www.sagepub.co.uk
Editors: John Jarrick and, Keith W Whitelam. No full-time staff. Began 1976; non-denominational. Turnover n/a.

Journal for the Study of the Pseudepigrapha, Sage Publications Ltd, 1 Oliver's Yard, 55 City Road, London EC1Y 1SP
☎020 7324 8500 📠020 7324 8600
E: market@sagepub.co.uk
Web: www.sagepub.co.uk
Editors: James R Mueller, Loren Struckenbruck, Robert Hayward. No full-time staff. Began 1987; non-denominational. Turnover n/a.

Journal of Adult Theological Education, Cambridge Theological Federation, Wesley House, Jesus Lane, Cambridge CB5 8BQ
☎01223 741 047 📠01223 321 177
E: cpww2@cam.ac.uk
Web: www.theofed.cam.ac.uk/paternoster
UK Editorial: Zoe Bennett. *Editor:* Rev R E Y Wickett. No full-time staff. Began 2001; non-denominational. (Previously British Journal of Theological Education). Published by Equinox Publishing. Turnover n/a.

Journal of Education and Christian Belief, Paternoster Publishing, PO Box 300, Carlisle CA3 0QS
☎01228 512 512 📠01228 593 388
E: info@authenticmedia.co.uk
Web: www.authenticmedia.co.uk
Publisher: Mr Mark Finnie. No full-time staff. Began 1968; interdenominational. (Previously Spectrum). Turnover n/a.
Editor: John Shortt, The Old Lace Mill, Frederick Road, Stapleford, Nottingham NG9 8FN
E: admin@stapleford-centre.org
☎0115 939 6270 📠 0115 939 2076

Journal of Greco-Roman Christianity and Judaism, Sheffield Phoenix Press, Department of Biblical Studies, University of Sheffield, Sheffield S10 2TN
☎0114 222 0505 📠0114 222 0500
E: phoenix.bibs@sheffield.ac.uk
Web: www.sheffieldphoenix.com
Editors: Stanley E Porter, Matthew Brook O'Donnell, Wendy J Porter. No full-time staff. Began 2001; non-denominational. Turnover n/a.

Journal of Pentecostal Theology, Sage Publications Ltd, 1 Oliver's Yard, 55 City Road, London EC1Y 1SP
☎020 7324 8500 📠020 7324 8600
E: market@sagepub.co.uk
Web: www.sagepub.co.uk
Editors: Mr Rickie D Moore, John Christopher Thomas, Stephen J Land. No full-time staff. Began 1992; Pentecostal. Turnover n/a.

Journal of Theological Studies, Oxford University Press, Walton Street, Oxford OX2 6DP
☎01865 267 679
Editors: Dr G Gould, Prof J Barton. No full-time staff. Began 1899; non-denominational. Turnover n/a.

Journal of the European Pentecostal Theological Association, Regents Theological College, London Road, Nantwich CW5 6LW
☎01270 615 405 📠01270 610 013
E: keith.warrington@regents-tc.ac.uk
Web: www.epta.nu
Special reference to Pentecostal and charismatic issues.
Editor: Rev Dr Keith Warrington. No full-time staff. Began 1983; Pentecostal. (Previously Epta Bulletin). Turnover n/a.

Joy Magazine, PO Box 777, Nottingham NG11 6ZZ
☎0115 921 7280 📠0115 984 5251
E: joy@newlifepublishing.co.uk
Web: www.newlifepublishing.co.uk/joy
The official monthly publication of Assemblies of God, which has over 600 UK churches.
Editor: Mr Peter Wreford. Executive staff 2, Other staff 5. ***CC*** Began 1994; Assemblies of God. (Previously Redemption). Turnover n/a.

Just Right Magazine, 96 High Street, Guildford GU1 3HE
☎0845 450 4748 📠 01483 565 475
E: info@jubileeaction.co.uk
Web: www.jubileeaction.co.uk
Editor: Danny Smith. Executive staff 1, Admin staff 4. ***CC*** No.1013587. Began 2001; non-denominational. Turnover n/a. Informing and inspiring action on human rights.

Kids Alive!, The Salvation Army, UK Territorial Headquarters, 101 Newington Causeway, London SE1 6BN
☎020 7367 4910 📠020 7367 4710
E: kidsalive@salvationarmy.org.uk
Web: www.salvationarmy.org.uk
weekly comic for children aged 7 to 12.
Editor: Major Justin Reeves. Executive staff 1, Other staff 2. Began 1996; Salvation Army. (Previously Young Soldier). Turnover n/a.

Library of Lives: The Journal, Rayleigh House, 32 High Street, Bookham, Leatherhead KT23 4AG
☎01372 459 413
E: admin@pioneer.org.uk
Web: www.pioneer.org.uk
Editor: Mr Gerald Coates. Executive staff 4. ***CC*** No.327160. Began 1982; Pioneer. (Previously Compass Magazine). Turnover included in Pioneer Trust.

Life & Work, 121 George Street, Edinburgh EH2 4YN
☎0131 225 5722 📠0131 240 2207
E: magazine@lifeandwork.org
Editor: Lynne McNeil. Executive staff 2, Other staff 2. ***CC*** Began 1879; Church of Scotland. Turnover n/a.

M

For circulation see list on page 246

†Y Llan, 12 Neville Place, Glanyrafon, Cardiff CF11 6EP
☎029 2066 7344 🖷029 2066 7344
E: hendrikhaye@churchinwales.org.uk
Editor: Mr Tim Sanders. Executive staff 1, Other staff 4. Began 1881; Church in Wales. (Previously Welsh Church Life). Turnover n/a.

Maintenance and Equipment News for Churches and Schools, PO Box 249, Ascot SL5 0BZ
☎01344 459 528 🖷01344 862 569
E: crownwood@btconnect.com
Web: www.cwponline.co.uk
Free magazine for full time clergy, treasurers etc detailing companies offering building and refurbishment services.
Editor: Mrs Christine Stevens. Executive staff 2. Began 1959; non-denominational. Turnover n/a.

Maria, Centre for Marian Studies, Department of Theology and Religious Stu, University of Wales, Lampeter SA48 7ED
☎01570 424 872
E: s.boss@lamp.ac.uk
Web: www.lamp.ac.uk/ims
Marian studies.
Editors: Sarah Jane Boss, Simon Coleman, Philip Endean SJ & Christopher Maunder. No full-time staff. Began 1999; non-denominational. Turnover n/a.

M

Messenger, The Stanborough Press Ltd, Alma Park, Grantham NG31 9SL
☎01476 591 700 🖷01476 771 44
Editor: Dr David Marshall. Staff included in The Stanborough Press. ***CC*** No.235245. Began 1884; Seventh-day Adventist. Turnover included in Stanborough Press.

The Messenger, 18 Ventnor Avenue, Sale M33 6LA
☎0161 976 6450
E: george.croston@tesco.net
Bible studies, poetry and testimony.
Editor: Pastor George Carl Croston. No full-time staff. Began 1986; non-denominational. Turnover £1,500 to year end Dec 00.

Methodist Recorder, 122 Golden Lane, London EC1Y 0TL
☎020 7251 8414 🖷020 7608 3490 or Advertising: 020 7251 8600
E: editorial@methodistrecorder.co.uk or ads@methodistrecorder.co.uk
Web: www.methodistrecorder.co.uk
National weekly newspaper with news, analysis, features, reviews and resources.
Managing Editor: Ms M Sleight. Executive staff 1, Other staff 6. Began 1861; Methodist. Turnover £11,500,000 to year end Dec 04.

Needed Truth, Hayes Press, Essex Road, Leicester LE4 9EE
☎0116 294 9949
E: info@hayespress.org
Web: www.hayespress.org
Teaching of the Word of God.
Editor: Mr R Fisher. included in Hayes Press. ***CC*** No.242257. Began 1888; non-denominational. Turnover staff included in Hayes Press.

New Life Newspaper, PO Box 777, Nottingham NG11 6ZZ
☎0115 921 7280 🖷0115 984 5251
E: info@newlifenewspaper.co.uk
Web: www.newlifepublishing.co.uk
Evangelistic monthly newspaper bringing the Good News to communities.
Editor: Mr Peter Wreford. Executive staff 2, Other staff 5. Began 1982; non-denominational. Turnover n/a.

New Testament Studies, Department of Theology, King's College, Strand, London WC2R 2LS
☎020 7848 2336 🖷020 7848 2255
E: judith.lieu@kcl.ac.uk
Web: uk.cambridge.org/journals/nts.htm
Academic journal covering New Testament and early Christianity; English, French and German articles.
Editor: Prof Judith Lieu. No full-time staff. Began 1947; interdenominational. Turnover n/a.

News Extra, Appleford House, Appleford, Abingdon OX14 4PB
☎01235 848 319
Church magazine insert.
Editor: Mr Gervase Duffield. No full-time staff. Began 1965; evangelical. Turnover n/a.

***News Special**, Paternoster Periodicals, PO Box 300, Kingstown Broadway, Carlisle CA3 0QS
☎01228 512 512 🖷01228 593 388
E: info@authenticmedia.co.uk
Web: www.authenticmedia.co.uk/paternoster
Outreach newspaper.
Editor: Mrs Debbie Bunn. No full-time staff. ***CC*** No.270162. Began 1968; interdenominational. Turnover n/a.

News Today, Appleford House, Appleford, Abingdon OX14 4PB
☎01235 848 319
Church magazine outset.
Editor: Mr Gervase Duffield. Executive staff 1. Began 1980; evangelical. Turnover n/a.

Nota Bene (European Theological Media), Paternoster Periodicals, PO Box 300, Carlisle CA3 0QS
☎01228 512 512 🖷01228 593 388
E: info@authenticmedia.co.uk
Web: www.authenticmedia.co.uk/paternoster
Publisher: Mr Mark Finnie. No full-time staff. ***CC*** No.270162. Began n/a; interdenominational. Turnover n/a.

The Officer, The Salvation Army, International Headquarters, 101 Queen Victoria Street, London EC4P 4EP
☎020 7332 8065 🖷020 7332 8076
E: charles_king@salvationarmy.org
Web: www.salvationarmy.org.uk
Editor: Major Charles King. Executive staff 2. Began 1893; Salvation Army. Turnover n/a.

Orthodox England, Seeking House, 12 Garfield Road, Felixstowe IP11 7PU
☎01394 273 820
E: frandrew@edmund.felix.t[illegible]
Web: www.orthodoxengland.org.uk
Distributing Orthodox reading and pastoral care material to English-speaking Orthodox Christians.
Editor: Fr Andrew Phillips. No paid staff. ***CC*** No.1081707. Began 1997; Orthodox. Turnover £2,500 to year end Aug 05.

†Orthodox Outlook, PO Box 142, Oswestry SY10 8WH
☎01691 680 557 🖷01691 680 [illegible]7
E: orthodox.outlook@virgin.net
News, theology and teaching of the Orthodox Church worldwide.
Editor: Michael Ward. Executive staff. Began 1986; Orthodox. Turnover £[illegible]00 to year end Dec 02.

The Overcomer, 10 Bydemill Gardens, Highworth, Swindon SN6 7B[illegible]
☎01793 763 141
E: 106345.3433@compuserve.com
Editor: Michael C Metcalfe. No full-time staff. ***CC*** No.256633. Began 1909; interdenominational. Turnover £20,500 to year end Dec 05.

Parish Pump, PO Box 236, Macclesfield SK10 4GJ
☎No telephone 🖷01625 585 442
E: enquiries@parishpump.co.uk
Web: www.parishpump.co.uk
Internet-based editorial and graphic resource site for church magazine editors.
Editor: Anne Coomes. *Graphics:* Rev [illegible]ffy Davies. No full-time staff. Began 1999; interdenominational. Turnover £75,[illegible]00 to year end Dec 05.

Partnership Publications World Action Ministries, PO Box 789, Sutton Coldfield B73 7RT
☎0121 355 8333 🖷0121 355 383[illegible]
E: worldactmin@aol.com
Publisher: Mr Philip B South. No full-time staff. Began 1964; interdenominational. Turnover n/a.
Editor: Dr Neil Summerton, Abbey Court, Cove, Tiverton EX16 7RT
☎01398 331 105
E: neil.summerton@ruralinternet.co.uk

***Plus/Eagles Wings**, Hayes Press, Essex Road, Leicester LE4 9EE
☎0116 294 9949
E: pew@hayespress.org
Web: www.hayespress.org
Monthly Bible-based comic for individuals or youth groups aged 6 to 10.
Editor: K S Hickling. No full-time staff. ***CC*** No.242257. Began 1972; interdenominational. Turnover n/a.

For circulation see list on page 2[illegible]

Political Theology, Equinox Publishing Ltd, Unit Six, The Village, 101 Amies Street, London SW11 2JW
☎020 7350 2836
Web: www.equinoxpub.com
No full-time staff. Began 1999; non-denominational. Turnover n/a.
Editors: Graeme Smith, Julie Clague, St Michael's College, Llandaff, Cardiff CF5 2YJ
E: gs@stmichaels.ac.uk
☎029 2056 3379 Fax 029 2083 8008

Precious Seed Magazine, 5 Turnham Green, Penylan, Cardiff CF23 9DL
☎029 2049 2346
E: info@precioussseed.org
Web: www.preciousseed.org
Treasurer: Mr Michael Jones. No full-time staff. **CC** No.326157. Began 1945; interdenominational. Turnover n/a.

The Presbyterian Herald, Church House, Fisherwick Place, Belfast BT1 6DW
☎028 9032 2284
Fax 028 9041 7307
E: herald@presbyterianireland.org
Web: www.presbyterianireland.org
Official magazine of the Prebyterian Church in Ireland.
Editor: Rev Arthur Clarke. Executive staff 4. **CC** Began 1943; Presbyterian Church in Ireland. Turnover n/a.

†Priests & People, Blackfriars, 64 St Giles, Oxford OX1 3LY
☎01865 514 845
Fax 01865 515 119
Web: www.thetablet.co.uk/p&p.htm
Journal of pastoral theology for clergy and laity, especially those in parish and school.
Editor: Rev David Sanders. Executive staff 2. Began 1931; Roman Catholic. Turnover n/a.

***Pro-Life Times**, Society for the Protection of Unborn Children (SPUC), Phyllis Bowman House, 5 St Matthew Street, Westminster, London SW1P 2JT
☎020 7222 5845
Fax 020 7222 0630
E: prolifetimes@spuc.org.uk
Web: www.spuc.org.uk
Editor: Mr John Smeaton. Executive staff 1. Began 1967; non-denominational. (Previously Human Concern). Turnover included in SPUC.

Prophecy Today, Workspace House, 28 Maxwell Road, Peterborough PE2 7JE
☎01733 2329 090
E: editorial@prophecytoday.co.uk
Web: www.prophecytoday.co.uk
Seeking to apply biblical insights to contemporary issues.
Editor: Rev David Andrew. *Founder:* Dr Clifford Hill. Executive staff 1, Other staff 2. **CC** No.326533. Began 1984; interdenominational. Owned by Present Day Publishing Ltd. Turnover £158,000 to year end Mar 03.

†Prophetic Witness, Prophetic Witness Movement International, PO Box 109, Leyland, Preston PR25 1WB
☎01772 452 846
Fax 01772 452 846
E: colin.lenoury@virgin.net
Web: www.pwmi.org
Proclaiming Christ's return.
Editor: Rev Glyn Taylor. Executive staff 1. **CC** No.228941. Began 1917; interdenominational. (Previously Your Tomorrow). Turnover n/a.

Protestant Truth, 184 Fleet Street, London EC4A 2HJ
☎020 7405 4960
E: ptslondon@btconnect.com
Web: www.protestant-truth.org
Furtherance of Christ's Gospel and the promotion of the Protestant Reformed religion and faith.
Editor: Rev G J Murray. Executive staff 1, Other staff 1. **CC** No.248505. Began 1846; interdenominational. Turnover n/a.

Quadrant, Christian Research, Vision Building, Footscray Road, Eltham, London SE9 2TZ
☎020 8294 1989
Fax 020 8294 0014
E: admin@christian-research.org.uk
Web: www.christian-research.org.uk
Joint Editors: Dr Peter Brierley, Heather Wraight. No full-time staff. **CC** No.1017701. Began 1993; interdenominational. (Previously LandMARC). Turnover included in Christian Research.

M

Newspaper & Periodicals

Quaker Studies, Woodbrooke, 1046 Bristol Road, Birmingham B29 6LJ
☎0121 472 5171 📠0121 472 5173
E: enquiries@woodbrooke.org.uk
Web: www.woodbrooke.org.uk
Editor: Ben P Dandelion. No full-time staff. Began 2001; Religious Society of Friends. Turnover n/a.

Reachout, Board of Mission in Ireland, Church House, Fisherwick Place, Belfast BT1 6DW
☎028 9032 2284 📠028 9041 7305
E: bmi@presbyterianireland.org
Web: www.presbyterianireland.org/bmi
Editor: Mr Robin Fairbairn. Executive staff 1, Other staff 4. Began 1710; Presbyterian. (Previously Christian Irishman). Turnover included in Irish Mission.

The Reader, Church House, Great Smith Street, London SW1P 3NZ
☎020 7898 1415 📠020 7898 1421
E: nigel@gt-corby.demon.co.uk
Web: www.thereader@c-of-e.org.uk
Chairman, Editorial Committee: Nigel Holmes. No full-time staff. Began 1904; Anglican. (Previously The Reader and Lay Worker). Turnover n/a.

Reform, 86 Tavistock Place, London WC1H 9RT
☎020 7916 2020 / 8630
📠020 7916 2021
E: reform@urc.org.uk
Web: www.urc.org.uk
Editor: Rev David Lawrence. Executive staff 1, Other staff 1. Began 1972; United Reformed. Turnover n/a.

Reformation and Renaissance Review, Equinox Publishing Ltd, Unit Six, The Village, 101 Amies Street, London SW11 2JW
☎020 7350 2836
E: I.Hazlett@arts.gla.ac.uk
Web: www.equinoxpub.com
Editor: Professor I Hazlett. No full-time staff. Began 1999; non-denominational. Journal of the Society for Reformation Studies. Turnover n/a.

Reformed Theological Journal, 429 Cregagh Road, Belfast BT6 0LG
☎028 9079 5454
E: rti@rpc.org
Web: www.rpc.org/college/rtj
Joint Editors: Prof Edward Donnelly, Rev C Knox Hyndman, Prof David McKay. No full-time staff. Began 1985; Reformed Presbyterian Church of Ireland. Turnover n/a.

†**The Reformer**, 77 Ampthill Road, Flitwick, Bedford MK45 1BD
☎01525 712 348 📠01525 712 348
General Secretary & Editor: Dr Stephen J Scott-Pearson. Executive staff 2, Other staff 3. ***CC*** Began 1845; interdenominational. Turnover n/a.

Rutherford Journal of Church and Ministry, 17 Claremont Park, Edinburgh EH6 7PJ
☎0131 554 1206 📠0131 555 1002
E: info@rutherfordhouse.org.uk
Web: www.rutherfordhouse.org.uk
Editor: Rev Dr Robert Fyall. No full-time staff. ***CC*** No.SCO 15111. Began 1994; interdenominational. Turnover n/a.

Salvationist, The Salvation Army, UK Territorial Headquarters, 101 Newington Causeway, London SE1 6BN
☎020 7367 4890 📠020 7367 4710
E: salvationist@salvationarmy.org.uk
Web: www.salvationarmy.org.uk/salvationist
Editor: Captain Dean Pallant. Executive staff 2, Other staff 6. Began 1986; Salvation Army. Turnover n/a.

Science and Christian Belief, Paternoster Periodicals, PO Box 300, Carlisle CA3 0QS
☎01228 512 512 📠01228 593 388
E: info@authenticmedia.co.uk
Web: www.authenticmedia.co.uk/paternoster
Publisher: Mr Mark Finnie. No full-time staff. Began 1989; interdenominational. Turnover n/a.
Editor: Denis Alexander, 77 Beaumont Road, Cambridge CB1 4PX
☎01223 246 696 📠 01223 246 696

Scottish Bulletin of Evangelical Theology, 17 Claremont Park, Edinburgh EH6 7PJ
☎0131 554 1206 📠0131 555 1002
E: info@rutherfordhouse.com
Web: www.rutherfordhouse.org.uk
Editor: Dr Alistair Wilson. No full-time staff. Began 1983; interdenominational. Turnover n/a.

†**Scottish Catholic Observer**, 19 Waterloo Street, Glasgow G2 6BT
☎0141 221 4956 📠0141 221 4546
E: info@scottishcatholicobserver.com
Web: www.scottishcatholicobserver.com
Editor: Mr H Conroy. Executive staff 1, Other staff 14. Began 1885; Roman Catholic. Turnover n/a.

Scottish Journal of Theology, Cambridge University Press, Edinburgh Building, Shaftesbury Road, Cambridge CB2 2RU
☎01223 325 586 📠01223 246 151
Web: www.journals.cambridge.org
Historical and systematic theology, including articles on biblical and applied theology.
Editor: Dr I Torrance. No full-time staff. Began 1948; interdenominational. Turnover n/a.

***Share It!**, Church Army, Marlowe House, 109 Station Road, Sidcup DA15 7AD
☎020 8309 3516 M: 07958 997 455
📠020 8309 3500
E: info@churcharmy.org.uk
Web: www.churcharmy.org.uk
Communications Manager: Mr David Coleman. *Publications and New Media Officer:* Niall Donnelly. Staff included in Church Army. ***CC*** No.226226. Began 1882; Anglican. Turnover included in Church Army.

Ship of Fools, 14 Hillcrest Road, London W3 9RZ
☎020 8993 3936 M: 078[illegible]8 297 [illegible]46
📠020 8752 0949
E: editor@ship-of-fools.com
Web: www.shipoffools.com
Internet magazine and online community: humour, satire, comment and discussion about Christianity in today's world.
Editor: Mr Steve Goddard. No full-time staff. Began 1998; ecumenical. Turnover n/a.

The Sign, G J Palmer & Sons Ltd, St Mary's Works, St Mary's Plain, Norwich NR3 [illegible]BH
Monthly parish magazine inset.
Editor: Rev Terence Handley-MacMath. Executive staff 2, Other staff 3. ***CC*** No.270060. Began 19[illegible]5; Anglican. Part of Hymns Ancient & Modern group. Turnover £4,000,000 to year end Dec [illegible].
Subscriptions: G J Palmer & Sons Ltd, 16 Blyburgate, Beccles NR3[illegible] 9TB
☎01502 711 231 📠 0150[illegible] 711 [illegible]35
E: Jennyp@scm-canterburypress.co.uk

Studies in Christian Ethics, Sage Publications Ltd, 1 Oliver's Yard, 5[illegible] City Road, London EC1Y 1SP
☎020 7324 8500 📠020 7[illegible]24 86[illegible]0
E: market@sagepub.co.uk
Web: www.sagepub.co.uk
Examining important themes in contemporary Christian ethics, with contributions from leading moral theologians.
Editor: Susan Frank Parsons. No full-time staff. Began 1988; non-denominational. Turnover n/a.

Sword and Trowel, Metropolitan Tabernacle, Elephant and Castle, London SE1 [illegible]SD
☎020 7735 7076 📠020 7[illegible]35 79[illegible]
E: swordtrowel@metropolitantabernacle.org
Web: www.metropolitantabernacle.org
Editor: Dr Peter Masters. No full-time staff. ***CC*** Began 1865; non-denominational. Turnover n/a.

The Tablet, The Tablet Publishing Co Ltd, 1 King Street Cloisters, Clifton Walk, London W6 0QZ
☎020 8748 8484 📠020 8748 155[illegible]
E: thetablet@thetablet.co.uk
Web: www.thetablet.co.uk
International Catholic weekly offering church news and articles on religion, politics, social issues and the arts.
Editor: Ms Catherine Pepinster. *Publisher:* Mr Ignatius Kusiak. Executive staff 2, Other staff n/a. Began 1840; Roman Catholic. Turnover n/a.

Theology, 36 Causton Street, London SW1P 4ST
☎020 7592 3900 📠020 75[illegible]2 39[illegible]
E: theology@spck.org.uk
Web: www.spck.org.uk
Editor: Dr William Jacob. No full-time staff. ***CC*** No.231144. Began 1[illegible]20; non-denominational. Turnover included in SPCK.

For circulation see list on page [illegible]46

Theology and Sexuality, Sage Publications Ltd, 1 Oliver's Yard, 55 City Road, London EC1Y 1SP
☎020 7324 8500
🖷020 7324 8600
E: market@sagepub.co.uk
Web: www.sagepub.co.uk
Editors: Elizabeth Stuart, Heather Walton. No full-time staff. Began 1994; interdenominational. Turnover n/a.

Third Way, St Peter's, Sumner Road, Harrow HA1 4BX
☎020 8423 8494
🖷020 8423 5367
E: editor@thirdway.org.uk
Web: www.thirdway.org.uk
Editor: Mr Simon Jones. Executive staff 2. ***CC*** No.327969. Began 1977; non-denominational. Turnover n/a.

Transformation, Paternoster Periodicals, PO Box 300, Carlisle CA3 0QS
☎01228 512 512
🖷01228 593 388
E: info@authenticmedia.co.uk
Web: www.authenticmedia.co.uk
Publisher: Mr Mark Finnie. No full-time staff. Began 1984; interdenominational. Turnover n/a.
Editors: Kwame Bediako, Vinay Samuel, René Padilla, Ronald Sider, Chris Sugden, St Philip and St James Church, PO Box 70, Woodstock Road, Oxford OX2 6HB
web: www.culturalencounters.org
E: ocms@ocms.ac.uk
☎01865 556 071 M: 07808 297 043 🖷 01865 510 823

The Trinitarian, The Diocesan Office, 42 High Street, Lydd, Romney Marsh TN29 9AN
☎01797 321 704
🖷01797 321 704
Editor: John Omwake. Executive staff 1, Other staff n/a. Began 1979; Anglican Catholic. Turnover n/a.

†Ulster Christian Magazine, INC Publishing, Regus House, 33 Clarendon Dock, Laganside, Belfast BT1 3BG
☎028 9051 1234
🖷028 9051 1677
E: info@theincgroup.com
Editor: Keith Giles. Executive staff 1, Other staff 12. Began 1995; evangelical. Turnover n/a.

The Universe, Gabriel Communications Ltd, First Floor, St James's Buildings, Oxford Street, Manchester M1 6FP
☎0161 236 8856
🖷0161 236 8530
E: newsdesk@the-universe.net
Web: www.demon.co.uk/gabcom/
Editorial Director: Mr Joseph Kelly. Executive staff 4, Other staff 56. Began 1860; Roman Catholic. Turnover n/a.

The Upper Room, MPH, 4 John Wesley Road, Werrington, Peterborough PE4 6ZP
☎01733 325 002
🖷01733 384 180
E: susan@mph.org.uk
Web: www.mph.org.uk
Daily devotional guide with a worldwide readership.
Editor: Susan Hibbins. No full-time staff. Began 1985; ecumenical. Turnover n/a.

Veritasse Magazine, PO Box 325, Witney OX28 1ZP
☎0845 123 5884
🖷01993 708 844
E: info@veritasse.co.uk
Web: www.veritasse.co.uk
Christian arts magazine.
Business Manager: Aidan Meller. Executive staff 2, Other staff 5. Began 1998; non-denominational. Turnover n/a.

The War Cry, The Salvation Army, UK Territorial Headquarters, 101 Newington Causeway, London SE1 6BN
☎020 7367 4900
🖷020 7367 4710
E: warcry@salvationarmy.org.uk
Web: www.salvationarmy.org.uk/warcry
Presenting positive Christian lifestyle and comment to un-churched readership.
Editor: Major Nigel Bovey. Executive staff 2, Other staff 4. Began 1879; Salvation Army. Turnover n/a.

***Woman Alive**, Christian Publishing and Outreach, Garcia Estate, Canterbury Road, Worthing BN13 1BW
☎01903 264 556
☎Advertising 01903 604 342
E: womanalive@cpo.org.uk or advertising@christianmedia.org.uk
Web: www.womanalive.co.uk
Editor: Jackie Stead. Executive staff 1. Began 1982; interdenominational. Turnover n/a.

†The Young Reformer, 77 Ampthill Road, Flitwick, Bedford MK45 1BD
☎01525 712 348
🖷01525 712 348
Editor: Dr Stephen J Scott-Pearson. No full-time staff. ***CC*** Began n/a; interdenominational. Part of The Protestant Alliance. Turnover n/a.

Youthwork, CCP, PO Box 17911, London SW1P 4YX
☎020 7316 1450
🖷020 7316 1453
E: youthwork@premier.org.uk
Web: www.youthwork.co.uk
Ideas, resources and guidance for Christians in youth ministry. Co-sponsors of Youthwork: The Conference.
Editor: Mr Martin Saunders. Executive staff 2, Other staff 12. Began 1992; interdenominational. Turnover n/a.

VIDEO, FILM & CASSETTE LIBRARIES & SUPPLIERS

***1904 Ltd**, 6 College Street, Ammanford SA18 3AF
☎01269 596 939 🖷01269 597 355
E: admin@1904revival.com
Web: www.1904revival.com
Producing and distributing films and books; presentations on Welsh Revival in 1904.
Director: Mr E O Jones. Executive staff 3, Admin staff 1. Began 2002; interdenominational. No magazine. Turnover n/a.

Audio Visual Ministries, PO Box 1, Newcastle BT33 0BF
☎028 4376 8007 M: 07801 474 630
🖷028 4376 8007
E: avmuk@aol.com
Web: www.avmworld.co.uk or www.audiochristian.com
Teaching by audio and video tapes and CDs.
Principal: Mr K Gerner. Executive staff 1, Other staff n/a. ***CC*** No.XN 88288. Began 1969; interdenominational. No magazine. Turnover n/a.

***Chichester Christian Fellowship (Tapes)**, 30 Crescent Road, Bognor Regis PO21 1QG
☎01243 862 621 🖷01243 862 621
E: sales@ccftapes.co.uk
Web: www.ccftapes.co.uk
Distributing Christian audio and video Bible study tapes; principally work of the late Roger Price.
Manager: Mr Ralph Page. Executive staff 1, Other staff 1. ***CC*** No.276242. Began 1970; non-denominational. No magazine. Turnover £22,000 to year end Mar 98.

Evangelical Films, Danbury Common Old Mission, The Common, Danbury, Chelmsford CM3 4EE
☎01245 226 642 / 227 880
M 07860 340 107 🖷01245 226 642
E: evan.films@btopenworld.com
Web: www.evangelicalfilms.org.uk
Christian DVD, video and 16mm/35mm film distribution, sales and hire. Video projector and screen sales.
Administrator: Mr Christopher G Bryant. Admin staff 2, Other staff 2. ***CC*** No.270736. Began 1967; interdenominational. No magazine. Turnover n/a.

†Good News Video Centre, 21 St Leonards Road, Charminster, Bournemouth BH8 8QL
☎01202 515 825
Video and audio tape library, free loan of tapes; 2,000 tapes.
General Managers: Mr & Mrs A Absolom. Executive staff 2. ***CC*** No.291650. Began 1985; non-denominational. No magazine. Turnover n/a.

***Good Shepherd Ministries International (UK)**, The Old Bakery, Ashley Gardens, Rusthall, Tunbridge Wells TN4 8TU
☎01892 549 141
🖷01892 529 500
E: uk@isom.org
Web: www.isom.org
Supplying International Curriculum as bilingual video/VCD Bible course in over 60 languages.
Contact: Mrs R Hopkinson. Admin staff 1. ***CC*** No.266445. Began 1970; non-denominational. (Previously CHR-IMM). No magazine. Turnover £40,000 to year end Dec 01.

Grace To You, Europe, 2 Caxton House, Wellesley Road, Ashford TN24 8ET
☎01233 662 262
🖷01233 638 810
E: info@gty.org.uk
Web: www.gty.org.uk
Distributing the audio and video teaching materials of Dr John MacArthur; daily radio broadcast.
European Director: Mr Anthony M Ruston. Executive staff 2, Other staff 5. Began 1990; interdenominational. No magazine. Turnover n/a.

The Martyn Lloyd-Jones Recordings Trust, 2 Caxton House, Wellesley Road, Ashford TN24 8ET
☎01233 662 262
🖷01233 638 810
E: info@mlj.org.uk
Web: www.mlj.org.uk
Reproducing and distributing the sermons of Dr Martyn Lloyd-Jones.
Administrator: Mr Anthony M Ruston. Executive staff 2, Other staff 5. ***CC*** No.286003. Began 1982; non-denominational. No magazine. Turnover n/a.

Storykeepers, 26 St James' Street, South Petherton TA13 5BS
☎01460 242 405
M 07802 278 101
E: info@coadmedia.co.uk
Web: www.storykeepers.com
Offering the Gospel in video/DVD format to churches and schools.
Director: Mr Ross Coad. Executive staff 1. Began 1996; non-denominational. (Previously Columba Scheme). No Magazine. Turnover n/a.

†Trinity Vision, Wraxall, Bristol BS48 1PG
☎01275 851 555
🖷01275 851 550
E: info@trinityvision.org
Web: www.trinityvision.org
Promoting and distributing British and overseas Christian visual media resources.
Director: Mr Malcolm Turner. No full-time staff. ***CC*** Began 2003; non-denominational. No magazine. Turnover n/a.

***Video Bible Teaching Ministry**, 2 Warren Field, Epping CM16 7BA
☎01992 579 226
E: gstirrup@tiscali.co.uk
Providing Bible teaching on videotape specifically for homegroups or small churches.
Coordinator: Rev George Stirrup. Executive staff 1. Began 1989; interdenominational. No magazine. Turnover n/a.

OVERSEAS

O

EVANGELISTIC AGENCIES

***3P Ministries**, PO Box 43623, London SE22 0WU
☎No telephone
E: admin@3pministries.org
Web: www.3pministries.org
Promoting church planting, prayer networks alongside national believers in nations where they suffer persecution.
Director: Dr S F Nash. Executive staff 1, Other staff 1. ***CC*** No.1097597. Began 2002; non-denominational. No magazine. Turnover £50,000 to year end Dec 04.

†L'Abri Fellowship, The Manor House, Greatham, Liss GU33 6HF
☎01420 538 436
Fax 01420 538 432
E: enquiries@englishlabri.org
Web: www.englishlabri.org
Residential study centres in Europe, USA; distributing talks by Francis Schaeffer and other L'Abri staff.
Director: Rev Ranald Macaulay. *Coordinator:* Mr Andrew Fellows. Executive staff 10, Other staff 1. ***CC*** No.237618. Began 1971; interdenominational. No magazine. Turnover £120,000 to year end Dec 98.

***AE Evangelistic Enterprise Ltd**, Victoria House, Victoria Road, Buckhurst Hill IG9 5EX
☎020 8559 2422
Fax 020 8502 9062
E: info@africanenterprise.co.uk
Supporting evangelistic and relief work in Africa.
Company Secretary: Miss Jean Wilson. No full-time staff. ***CC*** No.278704. Began 1977; interdenominational. Magazine: *Out of Africa* (Circulation n/a quarterly). Turnover £130,000 to year end Dec 04.

The Bible Land Mission, PO Box 196, Aberdeen AB15 9HZ
☎01224 734 710
M: 07803 296 279
Fax 01224 734 710
Undertaking church work in Lebanon; Bible students, radio and television.
Secretary: Mr George McRobb. Executive staff 1. ***CC*** No.253884. Began 1967; interdenominational. Magazine: *Evangelist* (1,000 quarterly (internationally)). Turnover £8,000 to year end Sep 05.

Bible Voice, PO Box 22, Kirkby Stephen CA17 4LE
☎01768 372 656
Fax 01768 372 408
E: uk@biblevoice.org
Web: www.biblevoice.org
Global shortwave and FM radio ministry.
Director: Mr Martin Thompson. Executive staff 2. ***CC*** No.327348. Began 1981, re-formed 2002; interdenominational. (Previously High Adventure Ministries). No magazine. Turnover n/a.

Blythswood Care, Deephaven, Evanton, Dingwall IV16 9XJ
☎01349 830 777 Fax 01349 830 477
E: info@blythswood.org
Web: www.blythswood.org
International aid, disaster relief, child poverty aid, social care, Gospel mission; Eastern Europe, Africa, UK.
Chief Executive: James Campbell. Executive staff 6, Other staff 72. ***CC*** No.SCO 21848. Began 1966; Protestant. Magazine: *Blythswood News* (60,000 half-yearly). Turnover £5,348,473 to year end Dec 02.

***Christ for All Nations**, Highway House, 250 Coombs Road, Halesowen B62 8AA
☎0121 602 2000 Fax 0121 602 7003
E: info@cfan.org.uk
Web: www.cfan.org
Spreading the Christian Gospel throughout the world especially Africa.
UK Administrator: Mr Mark Oakes. Executive staff 4, Other staff 8. ***CC*** No.327522. Began 1974, UK office opened in 1984, head office in Frankfurt; interdenominational. No magazine. Turnover n/a.

†*Connections Trust, 93 Acre Lane, Brixton, London SW2 5TU
☎020 7924 9700 Fax 020 7924 9800
E: connuk@aol.com
Web: www.connectionsuk.org
Pioneer evangelism, relief, church planting, outreach to Muslims and immigrants, training leaders; Bible School.
Director: Name not supplied. Admin staff 6. ***CC*** No.1017593. Began n/a; non-denominational. Magazine: *Connectoscope* (1,000 quarterly). Turnover £91,000 to year end Apr 02.

Day of Salvation Ministries, International Gospel Centre, Ranelagh Road, Malvern WR14 1BQ
☎01684 568 241 M: 07951 110 770
Fax 01684 568 241
E: gordon.leveratt@talk21.com
Web: www.dofs.org.uk
Reaching out with the Gospel; crusade evangelism overseas in India and Africa (9000-seat tent).
Evangelist: Mr Gordon Leveratt. Executive staff 2. ***CC*** No.1037693. Began 1992; non-denominational. No magazine. Turnover £72,000 to year end Oct 04.

†Dovetales International Trust, Gospel Mission, Maygate, Westwood, Oldham OL9 6TR
☎0161 652 4060
E: admin@dovetales.org
Medical, educational and vocational training mainly in India, Romania, Moldova; also UK.
Contacts: Mr & Mrs W E & J A Heap, Marcus Heap. No full-time staff. ***CC*** No.1016673. Began 1993; interdenominational. No magazine. Turnover n/a.

***Elam Ministries**, Grenville, Grenville Road, Shackleford, Godalming GU8 6AX
☎01483 427 778 Fax 01483 427 [illegible]07
E: info@elam.com
Web: www.elam.com
Relieving poverty; advancing education; furtherance of the Christian faith.
Executive Director Rev Samuel Yeghnazar. Executive staff 6, Other staff 7. ***CC*** No.281457. Began 198[illegible]; non-denominational. Magazines: *Elam News* (Circulation n/a quarterly), *Kalameh* (Circulation n/a quarterly). Turnover n/a.

***Eurovangelism**, PO Box 50, Kingswood, Bristol BS15 1EX
☎0117 961 5161 Fax 0117 935 2[illegible]27
E: office@eurovangelism.org.uk
Web: www.eurovangelism.org.uk
Helping Christian nationals in Eastern Europe share the Gospel by word and deed.
Secretary: Mr David Roderick. Executive staff 2, Other staff 5. ***CC*** No.24[illegible]488. Began 1966; interdenominational. Magazine: *Euro News* (5,000 every two months). Turnover £1,030,450 to year end Mar 00.

Eurovision Mission to Europe, 41 Healds Road, Dewsbury WF13 4HU
☎01924 453 693 Fax 01924 465 [illegible]26
E: office@euro-vision.org.uk
Web: www.propheticvision.org.uk
Holding evangelistic crusades in Russia, Ukraine, Bulgaria and Europe. Weekly TV broadcasts in Ukraine/Russia.
President: Rev David Hathaway. Executive staff 3, Other staff 9. ***CC*** No.101[illegible]288. Began 1992; interdenominational. Magazine: *Prophetic Vision* (1[illegible]0,000 quarterly). Turnover £1,000,000 [UK only] to year end Dec 99.

***Every Home for Christ**, PO Box 391, Winchester SO23 0XZ
☎01794 388 088
E: admin@ehcuk.com
Web: www.ehcuk.com
Specialising in home-to-home evangelism, humanitarian projects overseas; leading schools of prayer.
Contact: Mrs Faith Armstrong. Admin staff 1. ***CC*** No.286042. Began 1[illegible]82; interdenominational. Magazine: *Every Home for Christ* (1,500 monthly). Turnover £73,000 to year end Dec 04.

***Fountain of Wisdom Ministries**, The Old Church Hall, Rear of Station Parade, Virginia Water GU25 4AB
☎01344 844 172
E: admin@fowm.org
Web: www.fowm.org
Raising disciples for Christ in every nation of the earth.
Founder: Rev Kola Ewuosho. Executive staff 2, Admin staff 2. ***CC*** No.1088[illegible]29. Began 2000; interdenominational. Magazine: *Wisdom Digest* ([illegible],000 quarterly). Turnover n/a.

***Friends of Indian Evangelical Mission**, 5 Stenton Close, Abingdon OX14 5LN
☎01235 527 098
E: philip@gbm.org.uk
Financing missionary projects for the Indian Evangelical Mission in India; providing prayer support.
Honorary Treasurer: Mr Philip A Grist. Other staff n/a. ***CC*** No.1084875. Began 1989; interdenominational. No magazine. Turnover £20,000 to year end Mar 05.

***Fulani Ministries**, PO Box 5318, Christchurch BH23 1ZX
☎0845 257 0831 M: 07966 288 517
🖷01202 615 514
E: info@fulaniministries.org
Web: www.fulaniministries.org
Evangelism, education, relief of poverty, radio broadcasts, literacy, community development among Fulani people in Africa.
Evangelist: Mr Diallo Boureima. No paid staff. ***CC*** No.1096807. Began 1999; interdenominational. No magazine. Turnover £2,000 to year end Apr 03.

***Peter Gammons Ministries International**, PO Box 4, Ramsey, Huntingdon PE26 1SW
☎01487 710 515 🖷01487 710 515
E: info@pgmi.org
Web: www.pgmi.org
Evangelism, leadership training and Gospel radio broadcasting in UK and 40 other countries.
International Director: Dr Peter J Gammons. Executive staff 6, Other staff 32. ***CC*** No.298954. Began 1976; interdenominational. (Previously Reach Out Ministries International). Magazine: *Breakthrough!* (10,000 every two months). Turnover n/a.

Ghana Christian Support Group, 22 Ling's Coppice, London SE21 8SY
☎020 8670 5480 🖷020 8771 0959
E: p.stevenson@spurgeons.ac.uk
Supporting theological education, Christian mission and community development projects in Ghana.
Chair of Trustees: Rev Peter K Stevenson. No full-time staff. ***CC*** No.1054905. Began 1994; Baptist. No magazine. Turnover £10,000 to year end Dec 00.

†Gospel For Asia, PO Box 166, York YO10 5WA
☎01904 643 233 🖷01904 675 335
E: infouk@gfa.org
Web: www.gfa.org
Planting churches among the most unreached people of Asia.
UK Representative: Miss Gretchen Carter. Executive staff 3, Admin staff 3. Began n/a. Magazine: *Send!* (5,000 quarterly). Turnover n/a.

***Haggai Institute for Advanced Leadership Training Ltd**, 1a Queen Victoria Street, Belfast BT5 5BG
☎028 9045 2022 🖷028 9045 2275
E: hiuk@haggai-institute.com
Web: www.haggai.co.uk
Non-Western leaders equipping other non-Western leaders to effectively reach their own people with the Gospel.
Office Manager: Iris Ashbridge. Executive staff 1. ***CC*** No.327623. Began 1969; interdenominational. Magazine: *Leaders for Today* (Circulation n/a quarterly). Turnover n/a.

Hallelujah Ministries, 100 School Road, Wales, Sheffield S26 5QJ
☎01909 770 996
🖷01909 770 360
E: alanandstephani@ywclub.net
Preaching the Gospel in many nations; tape ministry in prisons; aid to Uganda.
Administrators: Mr & Mrs Alan & Stephani Bidwell. Executive staff 3. ***CC*** No.1025529. Began 1993; interdenominational. No magazine. Turnover £55,179 to year end Dec 04.

Harvest Fields Commissioning International, PO Box 740, Hemel Hempstead HP1 3RH
☎No telephone
E: info@hfci.net
Web: www.hfci.net
Church leadership training and church development including missions in UK, Americas, Eastern and Western Europe.
International Director: Rev David Sullivan. Executive staff 2, Other staff 1. ***CC*** No.1099460. Began 2003; non-denominational. Magazine: *Midnight Oil* (2,000 frequency n/a). Turnover n/a.

***Hope Now Ltd**, Malvern Centre, Malvern Road, Southampton SO16 6PY
☎023 8078 0720
🖷023 8051 0680
E: info@hopenow.org.uk
Web: www.hopenow.org.uk
Working in Ukraine and South Africa to bring the news of Jesus Christ to poor and needy people.
Founder: Rev Vic Jackopson. *Office Manager:* Mr Jonathan Budgell. Executive staff 1, Other staff 4. ***CC*** No.1072038. Began 1985; interdenominational. No magazine. Turnover £500,000 to year end Dec 04.

***Inn Christian Ministries**, PO Box 197, Gillingham ME7 4HF
☎01634 300 325
M: 07712 271 598
🖷01634 300 325
E: inncm@inn.org.uk
Web: www.inn.org.uk
Evangelism with church planting overseas; cross-cultural partnership in mission; resourcing churches locally, nationally and internationally.
Director: Mr Peter Marchand. Executive staff 1, Other staff 3. ***CC*** No.1009911. Began 1989; interdenominational. Magazine: *Inn-News* (Circulation n/a every four months). Turnover £25,000 to year end Feb 03.

The International Messianic Jewish Alliance, 36 Clydesdale Close, Borehamwood WD6 2SD
☎020 8236 0995
🖷020 8236 0995
E: DrRF1997@ntlworld.com
Spiritual and temporal care of Jewish believers in Messiah Yeshua.
Secretary for Europe: Dr Ruth Fleischer. Executive staff 3. ***CC*** No.231016. Began 1925; interdenominational. Headquarters, USA. No magazine. Turnover n/a.

***The International Miners' Mission**, 53 High Street, Kimpton, Hitchin SG4 8PU
☎01438 833 048
E: imm@niall.com
Web: www.minersmission.com
Making known the saving truths of the Christian Gospel to miners and their families.
Hon General Secretary: Mr David R Shillitoe. No full-time staff. ***CC*** No.221853. Began 1906; interdenominational. Magazine: *The Safety Lamp* (400 frequency n/a). Turnover £28,500 to year end Dec 04.

†*Jesus is the Answer International Mission, 12 High Street, Camelford PL32 9PQ
☎01840 212 620
🖷01840 212 620
E: soulsharb@aol.com
Evangelising unreached areas (priority Europe) by crusades, training, printing, church planting, relief; Bible School ministry.
President/Administrator: Rev David Flanders. Admin staff 1, Other staff 2. Began 1981; Assemblies of God. Magazine: *Jam News* (100 every two months). Turnover n/a.

†London Steward Church, Farm Road, Morden SM4 6RB
☎020 8647 2723
M: 07878 232 752
🖷020 8647 3721
E: stewardlee@daum.net
Mission to India and UK; also local Korean congregation.
Director: Rev Ho Keun Lee. Executive staff 2, Serving missionaries 2, Admin staff 3. ***CC*** No.1078377. Began n/a; Presbyterian. No magazine. Turnover £50,000 to year end Dec 02.

Mission of Compassion, 1 Locke Grove, Dalziel Park, Motherwell ML1 5ES
☎01698 861 166
🖷01698 824 601
E: laveresoper@missionof compassion.org
Web: www.missionofcompassion.org
Sending and receiving teams, mission in Eastern Europe; Bible schools, healing crusades.
President: Rev LaVere Soper. Executive staff 2. ***CC*** Began 1984; interdenominational. (Previously Latter Rain Ministries). No magazine. Turnover n/a.

†**Mission Relax**, 90 Gordon Road, Ilford IG1 1SL
☎020 8636 1633 🖷020 8636 9994
E: aggreykimambo@hotmail.com
Preparing revival seminars and Gospel crusades in the cities and towns of Africa.
Director: Rev Aggrey Kimambo. Executive staff 3, Admin staff 1. Began 1990; interdenominational. No magazine. Turnover n/a.

Mission Without Borders (UK) Ltd, 258 Belsize Road, London NW6 4BT
☎020 7316 1845 🖷020 7316 1893
E: info_uk@mwbi.org
Web: www.mwbuk.org
Providing material and spiritual aid to Christians in Eastern Europe and China.
Director: Rev Harry Graham. Executive staff 2, Other staff n/a. ***CC*** No.270659. Began 1960; interdenominational. No magazine. Turnover £2,412,000 to year end Dec 04.

***Nations Trust**, International Centre, 2a Glanmor Road, Llanelli SA15 2LU
☎01554 778 035 🖷01554 777 989
E: office@nations.org.uk
Web: www.nations.org.uk
A community of nations in training together for the evangelisation of the world.
Administration Director: Mr Steve Coupe. Executive staff 7, Admin staff 6, Other staff 10. ***CC*** No.1069419. Began 1998; interdenominational. Turnover £64,000 to year end Feb 05.
Also at: Robert Chiogwin, PO Box 6220, Wellingborough NN8 3YU
E: ebcftn@lineone.net
☎01933 223 454 🖷 01933 223 454

Operation Rescue, 21 Law Cliff Road, Great Barr, Birmingham B42 1LP
☎0121 358 6019
E: norman.f.smith@talk21.com
Evangelism to many countries; providing for spiritual and physical needs.
Missionary Evangelist: Rev Norman F Smith. Executive staff 2, Other staff 1. Began 1968; interdenominational. Linked with Zion Teaching Ministry. No magazine. Turnover n/a.

* **Derek Prince Ministries - UK**, Kingsfield, Hadrian Way, Baldock SG7 6AN
☎01462 492 100 🖷01462 492 102
E: enquiries@dpmuk.org
Web: www.dpmuk.org
Supplying Bible teaching resources: books, audios, CDs, videos, radio/TV broadcasting, youth materials.
Director: Mr Neil Cornick. Executive staff 3, Other staff 8. ***CC*** No.327763. Began 1983; interdenominational. Magazine: *Proclamation* (Circulation n/a quarterly). Turnover £784,000 to year end Mar 00.

Romanian Aid Fund, 29 Martlet Avenue, Disley, Stockport SK12 2JH
☎01663 763 971
E: info@romaf.org
Web: www.romaf.org
Encouraging indigenous evangelical Christian work in Romania by supporting churches, pastors and Christian workers.
Secretary: Mrs Pauline Lucas. No full-time staff. ***CC*** No.285160. Began 1970; interdenominational. Magazine: *Romanian Aid Fund Bulletin* (1,000 quarterly). Turnover £48,000 to year end May 05.

†***Seacare**, 30 Kimbolton Close, Lee, London SE12 0JJ
☎020 8851 0443 🖷020 8851 0443
E: vitsea1@aol.com
Evangelism, training, relief work in UK and overseas; mission ship 'Redeemer'.
Director: Mr Maurice Vitty. Executive staff 2, Other staff 1. ***CC*** No.287071. Began 1981; interdenominational. Also known as CCP Trust. No magazine. Turnover £10,000 to year end Apr 02.

***Soapbox Communications Trust**, PO Box 169, Cranleigh Road, Cranleigh GU6 7WX
☎01483 268 467 M: 07739 966 805
E: admin@soapboxtrust.com
Web: www.soapboxtrust.com
Short-term projects in developing countries, prison work, worship ministry support, childcare programme.
Operations Director: John Russell. *Project Officers:* Shaun & Kathy Murphy. Executive staff 3, Other staff 1. ***CC*** No.1088937. Began 1987; interdenominational. (Previously Soapbox Expeditions). Magazine: *Soapbox News Update* (Circulation n/a half-yearly). Turnover £323,000 to year end Dec 04.

†**Steward Mission**, 66 Blenhein Gardens, Wallington SM6 9PS
☎020 8647 2723 🖷020 8647 3721
Mission in India, Africa and Korea.
Pastor-in-Charge: Rev Joshua Lee. Admin staff 2. Began 1997; Presbyterian. No magazine. Turnover £30,000 to year end Mar 01.

Ukraine Christian Ministries, Heathside, Milland, Liphook GU30 7LU
☎01428 741 617 🖷01428 741 617
E: info@ucm.org.uk
Evangelism, church planting, Bible teaching, training, distributing literature and humanitarian aid.
Director: Rev John David Hendy. Executive staff 3, Other staff 5. ***CC*** No.1061221. Began 1996; interdenominational. Magazine: *In Touch* (1,000 every four months), *Prayer Diary* (Circulation n/a every two months). Turnover £79,377 to year end Mar 04.

***Vinesong**, PO Box 51, East Grinstead RH19 3FQ
☎01342 410 696 🖷01342 410 [illegible]96
E: info@vinesong.com
Web: www.vinesong.com
Music team taking the Gospel to the world using praise and worship.
International Ministry Coordinator: Mr Chris Woolley. Executive staff 1, Admin staff 3, Music team 6. ***CC*** No.104[illegible]246. Began n/a; interdenominational. No magazine. Turnover n/a.

Voice of Renewal UK, 28 Cedar Avenue, Nuthall, Nottingham NG16 1AF
☎0115 927 3816
E: georgjesze@aol.com
Web: www.voice-of-renewal.com
Interpreting evangelism, teaching, CDs, cassettes, women's gathering, books; Europe, Russia, Romania, USA.
Directors: Rev George and Rev Helen Jesze. No full-time staff. ***CC*** No.3[illegible]377. Began 1974; interdenominational. Magazine: *Voice of Renewal International* (1,000 quarterly). Turnover n/a.

***Watchmen International**, [illegible]3 Hadleigh Road, Frinton-on-Sea CO13 9HQ
☎01255 852 640
E: hcshelbourne@onetel.com
Bible teaching to indigenous churches in central and East Africa with Pentecostal end-times emphasis.
International Director: Mr Hugh Shelbourne. Other staff n/a. ***CC*** No.1062[illegible]61. Began 1999; non-denominational. No magazine. Turnover £25,000 to year end Dec 04.

World Outreach Bible Academy, 21 Law Cliff Road, Great Barr, Birmingham B42 1LP
☎0121 358 6019 M: 079[illegible]1 412 [illegible]47
E: norman.f.smith@talk21.com
Global teaching ministry providing Bible Study notes worldwide.
Missionary Evangelist: Rev Norman F Smith. Executive staff 2, Admin staff 1, Other staff 1. Began 1998; interdenominational. Linked with Operation Rescue and Teaching Ministries. No magazine. Turnover n/a.

O

LITERATURE PRODUCERS & DISTRIBUTORS

Africa Christian Press, 50 Loxwood Avenue, Worthing BN14 7RA
☎01903 232 208
Publishing books mainly by African authors for the African continent.
UK Representative: Mr Donald Banks. Admin staff 1, Other staff 1. ***CC*** No.243254. Began 1964; interdenominational. No magazine. Turnover n/a.

***Book Aid**, Bromley House, Kangley Bridge Road, Sydenham, London SE26 5AQ
☎020 8778 2145 🖷020 8778 2265
E: office@book-aid.org
Web: www.book-aid.org
Sending new and second-hand Christian books and Bibles to 'book famine' areas overseas. Collecting centres - see Page 93.
International Coordinator: Mr Bob Hiley. Executive staff 5, Other staff 20. ***CC*** No.1039484. Began 1987; interdenominational. Magazine: *Book Aid Update* (3 000 occasionally). Turnover £150,000 to year end Dec 04.

***Christian Publishing & Outreach**, Garcia Estate, Canterbury Road, Worthing BN13 1BW
☎01903 264 556/263 354 (sales)
🖷01903 830 066
E: enquiries@cpo.org.uk
Web: www.cpo-org.uk
Printing and publishing evangelistic resources for use overseas; CPO Project Fund supports agencies.
Chief Executive: Paul Slide. *Director of Production:* Mike Axell. Executive staff 4, Other staff 41. ***CC*** No.221462. Began 1957; non-denominational. No magazine. Turnover £2,400,000 to year end Apr 02.

***East European Literature Advisory Committee**, 68 Suilven Way, Inverness IV3 8PD
☎01463 236 354 M: 07808 938 753
🖷01463 242 030
E: eelac@cali.co.uk
Cooperating with East Europeans and former USSR evangelicals to develop indigenous, self-supporting publishing houses.
General Secretary: Dr Colin MacPherson. Executive staff 3. ***CC*** No.327179. Began 1986; non-denominational. No magazine. Turnover n/a.

Emmaus Bible School UK, Carlett Boulevard, Eastham, Wirral CH62 8BZ
☎0151 327 1172/6153/7373
🖷0151 327 1592
E: info@emmausuk.org.uk
Web: www.emmausuk.org.uk
Offering studies in over 120 languages used by missionaries and missions worldwide. 112 English studies.
UK Director: Mr David A Thompson. Executive staff 1, Other staff 7. ***CC*** No.267322. Began 1951; interdenominational. Magazine: *By the Way* (2,000 quarterly). Turnover £215,000 to year end Dec 05.

The Emmaus Road Trust, 68 Suilven Way, Inverness IV3 8PD
☎01463 236 354 M: 07808 938 753
🖷01463 242 030
E: ert@cali.co.uk
Supporting literature projects worldwide, particularly indigenous publishing. No unsolicited requests.
Trustee: Dr Colin MacPherson. Executive Staff 1. ***CC*** No.SCO 26006. Began 1996; non-denominational. No magazine. Turnover £26,500 to year end Mar 05.

Feed the Minds, 36 Causton Street, London SW1P 4ST
☎020 7592 3900/0845 121 2102
🖷020 7592 3939
E: info@feedtheminds.org
Web: www.feedtheminds.org
Transforming lives in developing countries through projects that educate, build peace, understanding and prevent HIV/AIDS.
Director: Rachel Searle. Executive staff 2, Other staff 5. ***CC*** No.291333. Began 1963; interdenominational. Magazine: *Connect* (7,500 every six months). Turnover £831,984 to year end Apr 05.

***Gospel Printing Mission**, 46 Roxy Avenue, Chadwell Heath, Romford RM6 4AY
☎020 8597 2140
Publishing and printing tracts and booklets in 40 languages for 80 countries worldwide.
General Director: Rev David W Cotton. Executive staff 2, Other staff 15. ***CC*** No.267903. Began 1960; non-denominational. Magazine: *GPM Review/Prayer News* (2,000 quarterly). Turnover £29,836 [donation income] to year end Dec 04.

***Institute for Bible Translation**, PO Box 6481, Colchester CO4 3AF
☎No telephone
E: ibtuk@ibtnet.org
Web: www.ibtnet.org
Translating and printing the Bible in 80 languages spoken in former Soviet Union.
Secretary: Prof Richard H Williams. No full-time staff. ***CC*** Began 2001; interdenominational. Magazine: *Translator's News* (Circulation n/a quarterly). Turnover n/a.

***Langham Literature**, PO Box 296, Carlisle CA3 9WZ
☎01228 592 033 🖷01228 380 441
E: literature@langhampartnership.org
Web: www.langhampartnership.org
Creating and supplying Christian books to theological colleges, students and pastors in the majority world.
International Programme Director: Mr Pieter Kwant. Executive staff 1, Other staff 3. ***CC*** No.1092233. Began 1971; evangelical. (Previously Evangelical Literature Trust). Part of Langham Partnership International. No magazine. Turnover n/a.

***Lifewords**, Radstock House, 5 Eccleston Street, London SW1W 9LZ
☎020 7730 2155 🖷020 7730 0240
E: uk@lifewords.info
Web: www.lifewords.info
Equipping people to use the Bible effectively, and engage with it through creative, contemporaty resources.
International Director: Mr Neil Crosbie. UK staff 32. ***CC*** No.219055. Began 1888; non-denominational. (Previously Scripture Gift Mission). Magazine: *Interact* (32,000 quarterly). Turnover £2,700,000 to year end Dec 02.

†**Literature Ministry to Poland**, Chapelhouse, 40 Market Street, Southport PR8 1HJ
☎01704 560 698 🖷01704 560 728
E: maciek@gbmlit.mersinet.co.uk
Helping to provide Bible-based literature in the Polish language.
Administrator: Mr M M Stolarski. No full-time staff. Began 1982; Grace Baptist. No magazine. Turnover £1,000 to year end Dec 02.

Manna Publications (UK), 4 Sealey Close, Willington, Derby DE65 6EP
☎01283 702 143
E: pandpskinner@onetel.com
Web: www.mannapublications.org.uk
Providing easy-to-read and translate Bible commentaries in worldwide English for self-publishing overseas.
Director: Mr Peter Skinner. Executive staff 3. Began 2000; non-denominational. Turnover £6,000 to year end Sep 05.

***Media Associates International**, European Office, Mayfield House, 256 Banbury Road, Oxford OX2 7DH
☎01865 302 759 🖷 01865 302 757
E: maieurope@aol.com
Web: www.littworld.org
Supporting Christian writing and publishing programmes in Africa, Asia, Latin America and Central Europe.
Hon Chair of Trustees: Mr Nicholas Gray. *Hon Secretary of Trustees:* Mrs Pat Alexander. *Hon Treasurer to Trustees:* Mr Graham Wilson. No paid staff. ***CC*** No.328568. Began 1985; interdenominational. Magazine: *Profile* (3,000 quarterly). Turnover n/a.

***Mission India**, 4 Alma Road, Orpington BR5 4PT
☎01689 605 421
E: peterj.honour@ntlworld.com
Web: www.missionindia.org
Working in partnership with churches throughout India; children's Bible clubs; literacy programmes; church planter training.
Director: Mr Peter Honour. Executive staff 1. ***CC*** No.1076598. Began 1999; non-denominational. Turnover £160,000 to year end Mar 05.

***No Frontiers (Literature Outreach) Ltd**, 26 Lottbridge Drove, Eastbourne BN23 6NT
☎01323 437 723 M: 07764 391 033
🖷01323 411 970
E: office@nofrontiers.org
Web: www.nofrontiers.org
Providing foreign language Bibles and Christian literature in 140 languages; distribution worldwide.
Administrator: Mr Allistair Graham. Executive staff 1, Other staff 1. ***CC*** No.1022425. Began 1992; interdenominational. Magazine: *Breaking Through* (3,500 every four months). Turnover £85,000 to year end Dec 04.

Revival Movement Association, 2 Clara Street, Belfast BT5 5GB
☎028 9045 5026 🖷028 9045 5026
E: adamssamuel@compuserve.com
Web: www.revivalmovement.org
Publishing Gospel tracts and booklets in 80 languages sent free to over 110 countries.
Mission Directors: Mr Samuel Adams, Mr Clive Allen. Executive staff 4, Other staff 15. ***CC*** No.XN 48143. Began 1960; interdenominational. Also known as Every Home Crusade. Magazine: *Good News* (5,000 monthly). Turnover £1,100,000 to year end Dec 04.

***The Rushworth Enterprise Ltd**, 2 Dimple Lane, Crich, Matlock DE4 5BQ
☎01773 857 313 🖷01773 856 062
E: rushworth.lit@virgin.net
Web: www.rushworth.org.uk
Publishing and donating Christian study books to pastors in the third world.
General Secretary: Miss Catherine S Cheetham. *Founder:* Rev David Rushworth-Smith. Executive staff 3. ***CC*** No.241364. Began 1953; non-denominational. Magazine: *Rushworth News* (1,000 seasonally). Turnover £34,000 [excluding second-hand books] to year end Mar 05.

Society for Promoting Christian Knowledge (SPCK), 36 Causton Street, London SW1P 4ST
☎020 7592 3900 🖷020 7592 3939
E: spck@spck.org.uk
Web: www.spck.org.uk
Specialising in Christian communications and education; grants to support education and communication projects worldwide.
General Secretary: Mr Simon Kingston. Executive staff 6, Other staff 250. ***CC*** Began 1698; interdenominational but historically Anglican. Magazine: *Theology* (3,000 every two months). Turnover n/a.

***SOON Ministries**, 44 Twyford Road, Willington, Derby DE65 6BN
☎01283 702 334 🖷01283 702 334
E: office@soon.org.uk
Web: web-evangelism.com/resources/free-papers.php
Evangelistic papers in easy English, French, Fula, Portuguese, Swahili; evangelistic Bible correspondence course; web evangelism training.
Team Leader: Mr Basil Aiken. Executive staff 13. ***CC*** No.237005. Began 1960; interdenominational. Incorporating Soon, Bientôt, Cedo and Upesi. Magazine: *Prayer Digest* (5,000 frequency n/a). Turnover £80,000 to year end Apr 05.

***Sovereign World Trust**, PO Box 777, Tonbridge TN11 0ZS
☎01732 851 150 🖷01732 851 077
E: mike@sovereignworldtrust.com
Web: www.sovereignworldtrust.com
Sending new Christian books to pastors, leaders, colleges and libraries in developing nations.
Founder & Foreign Rights: Mrs Jan Mungeam. Executive staff 1, Other staff 3. ***CC*** No.327284. Began 1986; non-denominational. No magazine. Turnover £189,000 to year end Dec 02.

Translation Trust, PO Box [illegible]017, Lessingham, Norwich NR12 0WA
☎01692 584 900
E: translation_trust@btopenworld.com
Publishing and distribution of Scripture and other Christian books in modern Turkish and Turkic languages.
Director: Mr Gerry Davey. Executive staff 1. ***CC*** No.326789. Began 1984; non-denominational. No magazine. Turnover n/a.

United Society for Christian Literature, 36 Causton Street, London SW1P 4ST
☎020 7592 3900/0845 121 2102
🖷020 7592 3939
E: info@feedtheminds.org
Web: www.feedtheminds.org
Transforming lives in developing countries through projects that educate, build peace, understand and prevent HIV/AIDS.
General Secretary: Rachel Searle. ***CC*** No.226512. Began 1799; interdenominational. In partnership with Feed The Minds and SPCK. No magazine. Turnover £137,004 to year end Apr 05.

O

UK MISSION AGENCIES AND MISSION WORKERS

Information about UK Mission Agencies and Mission Workers is contained in the following four lists and two categories. The two categories, *Mission Sending Churches (Direct)* and *Mission Agencies,* are both on Page 282. They are preceded by lists showing how many mission workers each agency has and where they are working. List 2 on Page 265 identifies by country and denominational grouping where agencies have UK mission workers. List 3 on Page 270 gives the location and numbers of service by agency and direct sending churches. In order to save space, abbreviations have been used for agency names, and these are in List 1 below. List 4 on Page 277 shows the numbers of staff in each agency and the type of work they undertake. These numbers will be analysed in *Religious Trends* No 7, 2008/2009, Section 3, when published.

1. ABBREVIATIONS OF AGENCIES

Mission Agencies (Anglican) = A in list 2

C	Crosslinks
CMJ	Church's Ministry Among Jewish People
CMS	Church Mission Society
CMSI	Church Missionary Society Ireland (CMS Ireland)
ICS	Intercontinental Church Society
MM	Melanesian Mission
MS	The Missions to Seamen
OXM	Oxford Mission
PNG	Papua New Guinea Church Partnership
SAMS	South American Mission Society
SOMA	Sharing of Ministries Abroad
SSF	Society of St Francis
USPG	United Society for the Propagation of the Gospel

Direct Sending Churches = CH in list 2

ANC	All Nations Church
BCC	Basingstoke Community Church
BHCF	Biggin Hill Christian Fellowship
CCF	Coventry Christian Fellowship
EOS	Echoes of Service
HCF	Hollybush Christian Fellowship
ICF	Ichthus Christian Fellowship

Mission Agencies (Interdenominational) = I in list 2

A	Agapé
ACCT	Accts Military Ministries International
ACT	Action International Ministries (UK)
AEF	Africa Evangelical Fellowship
AEM	Albanian Evangelical Mission
AGM	Acre Gospel Mission
AIM	Africa Inland Mission International
AM	Antioch Mission UK
AP	Action Partners Ministries
AWM	Arab World Ministries
BCM	BCM International
BEM	Belgian Evangelical Mission
BIS	British & International Sailors' Society
CEF	Child Evangelism Fellowship
CIA	Christians in Action
CLC	CLC (Christian Literature Crusade)
CMA	The Christian and Missionary Alliance
CT	Carrot Tops
CWI	Christian Witness to Israel
DF	Dohnavur Fellowship
EAB	Evangelical Action (Brazil)
ECM	European Christian Mission (Britain)
EI	Emmanuel International
EMF	European Missionary Fellowship
EMMS	EMMS International
F	Frontiers
FEBA	Feba
FMT	France Mission Trust
GMSA	Gospel Mission of South America
GNF	Gorakhpur Nurseries Fellowship
GO	Global Outreach UK
GTNM	Go To The Nations Ministry
HCJB	HCJB-UK
IFES	International Fellowship of Evangelical Students
INF	International Nepal Fellowship
IS	INTERSERVE
ISI	INTERSERVE Ireland
ISS	INTERSERVE Scotland
IT	International Teams UK
JT	Janz Team UK
JCL	Japan Christian Link
JM	Japan Mission
LL	Latin Link UK
LM	The Leprosy Mission
LMI	The Leprosy Mission (International Office)
LMNI	The Leprosy Mission Northern Ireland
LMS	The Leprosy Mission Scotland
LRI	Language Recordings UK
LI	Lightforce International
MAF	Mission Aviation Fellowship
MECO	Middle East Christian Outreach
MEM	Middle East Media
QIF	Mission Africa (Qua Iboe Fellowship)
MMG	Mission to Military Garrisons Inc
MT	The Messianic Testimony
N	The Navigators
NTM	New Tribes Mission
NTMU	New Testament Missionary Union
NWFF	North West Frontier Fellowship
OM	Operation Mobilisation
OMF	OMF International (UK)
OMS	OMS International
PEI	People International
RSMT	Red Sea Mission Team
SAUB	Servants to Asia's Urban Poor
SC	SAO Cambodia
SAT	SAT-7 Trust
SCFS	Seamen's Christian Friend Society
SCI	Sharing Christ Internationally
SCM	Siloam Christian Ministries
SDM	Sahara Desert Mission
SGM	Spanish Gospel Mission
SI	Signpost International
SIM	SIM UK (Society for International Ministries)
TF	Tearfund
TWR	Trans World Radio
UFM	UFM Worldwide
WBT	Wycliffe Bible Translators
WEC	WEC International
WGM	World Gospel Mission
WH	World Horizons (Britain)
WIN	World in Need
WO	World Outreach
YWAM	Youth With A Mission UK
ZMI	Zambesi Mission

Mission Agencies (Other Denominational) = O in list 2

ACMM	Apostolic Church Missionary Movement
AGWM	Assemblies of God World Ministries
BM	Baptist Missions
BMS	BMS, Baptist Missionary Society
CAM	Central African Missions
CSB	Church of Scotland World Mission Council
EIM	Elim International Missions
FCS	Free Church of Scotland International Missions Board
FOI	Focus on Israel
FPCS	Free Presbyterian Church of Scotland Mission Committee
FPCU	Free Presbyterian Church of Ulster Mission Board
GBM	Grace Baptist Mission
JGNM	Japan Good News Ministries
MPM	Maranatha Pentecostal Mission
MCWCO	Methodist Church World Church Office
PCI	Presbyterian Church in Ireland Overseas Board
PCW	Presbyterian Church of Wales Mission Board
SA	Salvation Army
UICR	United Reformed Church International Relations
WAM	World-Wide Advent Missions

UK Mission Agencies and Mission Workers

Mission Agencies (Roman Catholic) = RC in list 2

Roman Catholics distinguish between Mission Agencies (whose main thrust is directed towards countries overseas) and Mission-Sending Societies (whose activity is mostly in UK, but who either send some personnel overseas or support overseas personnel from their province). The two are integrated in the following lists and the category entries.

The abbreviations are the initials used by the Agencies themselves, except where differentiation required additional letters.

Agencies in Abbreviation Order

AA	Assumptionists Fathers and Brothers
BS	Sisters of the Good Saviour (Bon Sauveur)
CFC	Congregation of Christian Brothers
CHS	Crusade of the Holy Spirit
CJ	Congregation of Josephites
CLM	Columban Lay Missionaries
CMF	Claretian Missionaries
CMS	Comboni Missionary Sisters (Verona Sisters)
CP	Sisters of the Cross and Passion
CSSP	Holy Ghost Fathers
CSSR	Redemptorists
DC	Daughters of Charity of St Vincent de Paul
DHM	Daughters of the Heart of Mary
DHS	Daughters of the Holy Spirit
DJ	Daughters of Jesus
DMJ	Daughters of Mary and Joseph
FCJ	Faithful Companions of Jesus
FD	Fidei Donum Priests
FMA	Salesian Sisters of St John Bosco
FMDM	Franciscan Missionaries of the Divine Motherhood
FMM	Franciscan Missionaries of Mary
FMS	Marist Brothers
FMSA	Franciscan Missionary Sisters for Africa
FMSJ	Franciscan Missionary Sisters of St Joseph
FSC	De La Salle Brothers
FSM	Franciscan Minoresses
FSP	Daughters of St Paul
HFB	Sisters of the Holy Family of Bordeaux
HHS	Helpers of the Holy Souls
IBVM	Institute of the Blessed Virgin Mary (see Congregation of Josephites CJ)
IC	Institute of Charity (Rosminian Fathers & Brothers)
IMC	Consolata Fathers
JM	Sisters of Our Lady of the Apostles
JOS	St Joseph's Hospice Association (Jospice International)
LSU	Congregation of La Sainte Union des Sacré-Coeurs
MAFR	Missionaries of Africa (White Fathers)
MC	Consolata Missionary Sisters
MCCJ	Comboni Missionaries
MCH	Missionaries of Charity
MHM	Mill Hill Missionaries (St Joseph's Missionary Society, Mill Hill)
MHM	Associates of Mill Hill Missionaries
MHMJ	St Joseph's Missionary Society, Mill Hill (see MHM)
MMM	Medical Missionaries of Mary
MMS	Medical Mission Sisters (Society of Catholic Medical Missionaries)
MSHR	Missionary Sisters of the Holy Rosary (MSHR)
MSOLA	Missionary Sisters of Our Lady of Africa (White Sisters)
MSSC	Missionary Society of St Columban
MSSPC	Sisters of St Peter Claver
OAR	Augustinian Recollects
OFMCap	Capuchin Franciscans (Order of Friars Minor Capuchin)
OFMCon	Franciscan Conventuals
OH	Hospitaller Order of St John of God
OLA	Missionary Sisters of Our Lady of Apostles
OLC	Sisters of Our Lady of Charity
OLF	Sisters of Our Lady of Fidelity
OMI	Oblates of Mary Immaculate
OP	Dominicans
OPC	Dominican Sisters of St Catherine of Siena of Oakford
OPZ	Dominican Sisters of Zimbabwe
OSA	Augustinians
OSB	Benedictines (incorporating English Benedictine Congegations and Grace & Compassion Benedictines)
OSF/MH	Franciscan Sisters of Mill Hill
OSM	Servite Friars
OSU	Ursulines of the Roman Union
RA	Religious of the Assumption
RGS	Our Lady of Charity of the Good Shepherd
RHF	Sisters of the Holy Family (St Emilie de Rodat)
RJM	Religious of Jesus and Mary
RLR	Sisters of La Retraite
RNDM	Congregation of Our Lady of the Missions
RSCJ	Sacred Hearts Community
RSM	Institute of Our Lady of Mercy
RSMU	Mercy Sisters of the Union of Great Britain
SAC	Pallottine Missionary Sisters
SC	Brothers of the Sacred Heart
SCE	Sisters of Charity of Our Lady of Evron
SCI	Sisters of Christian Instruction (St Gildas)
SCJB	Sacred Heart Fathers (Betharram)
SCJD	Sacred Heart Fathers (Dehonians)
SCS	Sisters of Christ
SDB	Salesian Fathers and Brothers
SdeC	Sisters of Charity of St Jeanne Antide Thouret
SDS	Society of the Divine Saviour (Salvatorians)
SHCJ	Society of the Holy Child Jesus
SJ	Society of Jesus
SJA	Sisters of St Joseph of the Apparition
SJC	Sisters of St Joseph of Cluny
SM	Society of Mary
SMA	Society of African Missions
SMM	Montfort Fathers
SMM/SRS	Montfort Sisters, La Sagesse (Daughters of Wisdom)
SMR	Society of Marie Reparatrice
SP	Sisters of Providence, Rosminians
SPC	Sisters of Charity of St Paul
SPS	St Patrick's Missionary Society
SSC	Sisters of St Clare
SSCL	Missionary Sisters of St Columban
SSHJM	Sisters of the Sacred Heart of Jesus and Mary
SSJA	Sisters of St Joseph of Annecy
SSMMP	Sisters of St Marie Madeleine Postel
SSMN	Sisters of St Mary of Namur
SSMND	Sisters of Notre Dame de Namur
SSPS	Missionary Sisters Servants of the Holy Spirit
VMM	Volunteer Missionary Movement

Abbreviations in Agencies Order

AMHM	Associates of Mill Hill Missionaries
HFB	Association of the Holy Family of Bordeaux
AA	Assumptionists Fathers and Brothers
OAR	Augustinian Recollects
OSA	Augustinians
SC	Brothers of the Sacred Heart
OFMCap	Capuchin Franciscans (Order of Friars Minor Capuchin)
CMF	Claretian Missionaries
CLM	Columban Lay Missionaries
MCCJ	Comboni Missionaries
CMS	Comboni Missionary Sisters (Verona Sisters)
CFC	Congregation of Christian Brothers
CJO	Congregation of Josephites
LSU	Congregation of La Sainte Union des Sacré-Coeurs
RNDM	Congregation of Our Lady of the Missions
IMC	Consolata Fathers
MC	Consolata Missionary Sisters
CHS	Crusade of the Holy Spirit
DC	Daughters of Charity of St Vincent de Paul
DJ	Daughters of Jesus
DMJ	Daughters of Mary and Joseph
DHM	Daughters of the Heart of Mary
DHS	Daughters of the Holy Spirit
FSC	De La Salle Brothers
OPC	Dominican Sisters of St Catherine of Siena of Oakford
OPZ	Dominican Sisters of Zimbabwe
OP	Dominicans
FCJ	Faithful Companions of Jesus
FD	Fidei Donum Priests
OFMCon	Franciscan Conventuals
FSM	Franciscan Minoresses
FMM	Franciscan Missionaries of Mary

FMDM Franciscan Missionaries of the Divine Motherhood
FMSA Franciscan Missionary Sisters for Africa
FMSJ Franciscan Missionary Sisters of St Joseph
OSF/MH Franciscan Sisters of Mill Hill
HHS Helpers of the Holy Souls
CSSP Holy Ghost Fathers
OH Hospitaller Order of St John of God
IC Institute of Charity (Rosminian Fathers & Brothers)

RSM Institute of Our Lady of Mercy
FMS Marist Brothers
MMM Medical Missionaries of Mary
RSMU Mercy Sisters of the Union of Great Britain
MHM Mill Hill Missionaries
MAFR Missionaries of Africa (White Fathers)
MCH Missionaries of Charity
MSOLA Missionary Sisters of Our Lady of Africa (White Sisters)
OLA Missionary Sisters of Our Lady of Apostles
SSCL Missionary Sisters of St Columban

MSHR Missionary Sisters of the Holy Rosary
SSPS Missionary Sisters Servants of the Holy Spirit
MSSC Missionary Society of St Columban
SMM Montfort Fathers
SMM/SRS Montfort Sisters, La Sagesse (Daughters of Wisdom)
OMI Oblates of Mary Immaculate
RGS Our Lady of Charity of the Good Shepherd
SAC Pallottine Missionary Sisters
CSSR Redemptorists
RJM Religious of Jesus and Mary

RA Religious of the Assumption
SCJB Sacred Heart Fathers (Betharram)
SCJD Sacred Heart Fathers (Dehonians)
RSCJ Sacred Hearts Community
JOS St Joseph's Hospice Association (Jospice International)
MHMJ St Joseph's Missionary Society, Mill Hill
(see Mill Hill Missionaries)
SPS St Patrick's Missionary Society
SDB Salesian Fathers and Brothers

FMA Salesian Sisters of St John Bosco
OSM Servite Friars

SCE Sisters of Charity of Our Lady of Evron
SdeC Sisters of Charity of St Jeanne Antide Thouret
SPC Sisters of Charity of St Paul
SCS Sisters of Christ
SCI Sisters of Christian Instruction (St Gildas)
RLR Sisters of La Retraite
SSMND Sisters of Notre Dame de Namur
OLC Sisters of Our Lady of Charity
OLF Sisters of Our Lady of Fidelity
JM Sisters of Our Lady of the Apostles

SP Sisters of Providence, Rosminians
SSC Sisters of St Clare
SSJA Sisters of St Joseph of Annecy
SJC Sisters of St Joseph of Cluny
SJA Sisters of St Joseph of the Apparition
SSMMP Sisters of St Marie Madeleine Postel
SSMN Sisters of St Mary of Namur
MSSPC Sisters of St Peter Claver
CP Sisters of the Cross and Passion
BS Sisters of the Good Saviour (Bon Sauveur)

HFB Sisters of the Holy Family of Bordeaux
RHF Sisters of the Holy Family (St Emilie de Rodat)
SSHJM Sisters of the Sacred Heart of Jesus and Mary
SMA Society of African Missions
SJ Society of Jesus
SMR Society of Marie Reparatrice
SM Society of Mary
SHCJ Society of the Holy Child Jesus
RSCJ Society of the Sacred Heart
SDS Society of the Divine Saviour (Salvatorians)

OSU Ursuline Sisters
VMM Volunteer Missionary Movement
SX Xaverian Missionary Fathers

2. LOCATION OF SERVICE BY COUNTRY

Only those countries in which UK mission workers are specifically known to be working are included in this list. The total number shown for each agency corresponds to that shown in brackets after each country in column two of the list **Location of Service by Agency** on Page 270.

Country/ Region	Denomin-ation	Agencies working in country (excluding Associates)	Total personnel per Denom	Grand Total
Afghanistan	I	TF(6)	6	6
Africa	I	WH(12)	12	12
Albania	CH	EOS(2)	2	
	I	AEM(5), ECM(2), LI(1), OM(1), WEC(1), YWAM(3)	13	
	O	BMS(26), EIM(2)	28	43
Algeria	RC	MAFR(1)	1	1
Angola	CH	EOS(2)	2	
	O	BMS(3)	3	5
Arab World	I	ISS(3)	3	3
Argentina	CH	ANC(1), EOS(8)	9	
	A	SAMS(4), USPG(4)	8	
	I	LL(13), YWAM(4)	17	
	O	MCWCO(1), SA(1)	2	
	RC	CHS(1), FCJ(2), CSSP(1)	4	40
Asia	I	OMF(40)	40	40
Australia	I	NTM(4), YWAM(5)	9	
	O	CWI(1), EIM(2), FPCU(5), WAM(1)	9	
	RC	FMM(1), MSSC(1), SMA(1)	3	21
Austria	CH	EOS(1)	1	
	I	ECM(4), IFES(2), IT(5), OM(4)	15	
	O	AGWM(3), GBM(1)	4	20
Austria & Europe	I	TWR(1)	1	1
Azerbaijan	CH	ICF(6)	6	6
Bahamas	CH	EOS(2)	2	
	O	CSB(2)	2	4
Bangladesh	A	CMS(3), USPG(5)	8	
	I	IS(8), LM(1), LMI(1), LMS(2), MAF(1), OM(4), SIM(2)	19	
	O	BMS(4), MCWCO(4)	8	35
Barbados	CH	OP(2)	2	
	RC	SJ(1)	1	3
Belgium	CH	EOS(1)	1	
	A	ICS(5)	5	
	I	BEM(16), EMF(1), IFES(4), OM(3), YWAM(2)	26	
	O	BMS(4), CSB(1), EIM(10)	15	47
Belize	A	USPG(4)	4	
	RC	CMF(2)	2	6
Benin	I	SIM(2)	2	2
Bermuda	O	CSB(1)	1	1
Bolivia	CH	EOS(6)	6	
	I	IT(1), LL(18), NTM(1), SIM(7), YWAM(5)	32	
	RC	FD(1)	1	39
Botswana	CH	EOS(5)	5	
	O	EIM(1)	1	
	RC	CP(2)	2	8

O

Country/ Region	Denomin-ation	Agencies working in country (excluding Associates)	Total personnel per Denom	Grand Total
Brazil	CH	BCC(2), EOS(17), ICF(1)	20	
	A	ICS(1), SAMS(4), USPG(2)	7	
	I	AGM(8), ACT(2), EAB(4), LL(18), NTM(3), UFM(22), WEC(5), WBT(12), YWAM(3)	77	
	O	AGWM(1), BMS(19), GBM(2), PCI(1), SA(6)	29	
	RC	MCCJ(1), FD(1)	2	135
Bulgaria	CH	ICF(3)	3	
	I	UFM(1)	1	
	O	BMS(5), MCWCO(2)	7	11
Burkina Faso	I	QIF(2), SIM(4), WEC(4), WBT(16), WH(1)	27	
	RC	SCI(1), MAFR(1)	2	29
Burma	CH	HCF(2)	2	2
Burundi	I	GLO(2), TF(5)	3	3
Cambodia	A	CMS(2)	2	
	I	NTM(2), OMF(21), SC(9), TF(1), UFM(1), WAM(2), WEC(1), WH(6), YWAM(4)	47	49
Cameroon	I	AP(2), UFM(2), WBT(8),	12	
	RC	LSU(1), MHM(3), SCS(3), SM(1), OSU(1)	9	21
Canada	I	EI(23), FPCU(18), IT(1), N(2), NTM(5), OM(1), UFM(2), WEC(2), WBT(7), YWAM(2)	63	
	O	AGWM(2)	2	65
Canary Islands	I	AGM(2)	2	2
Cape Verde Islands	I	WBT(2)	2	2
Caribbean	O	MCWCO(3), SA(2)	5	5
Central African Republic	I	WBT(6)	6	6
Central Asia	A	CMS(9)	9	
	I	F(29), IS(20), ISI(4), ISS(9), PEI(17), YWAM(10)	89	98
Chad	I	AIM(6), QIF(2), MAF(2), WEC(6), WBT(5),	21	21
Chile	A	ICS(1), SAMS(6), USPG(3)	10	
	O	ACMM(2), MCWCO(3)	5	
	RC	CLM(1), DJ(1), MSSC(1)	3	18
China	CH	ICF(2)	2	
	A	CMS(3), USPG(14)	17	
	I	FT(2), IS(7), WH(2), WBT(7)	18	
	O	PCI(1), PCW(3)	4	41
Colombia	CH	EOS(2)	2	
	I	FCS(2), IT(1), LL(4), NTM(2), OMS(2)	11	
	O	AGWM(1), GBM(2)	3	
	RC	SSHJM(1)	1	17
Congo	CH	EOS(5)	5	
	A	CMS(4)	4	
	I	AIM(2), TF(2), UFM(1), WEC(3)	8	
	O	BMS(6), CAM(10), EIM(2), SA(1)	19	
	RC	MHM(1), MSOLA(1)	2	38
Costa Rica	I	LL(4)	4	
	O	SA(2)	2	6
Cote d'Ivoire	CH	HCF(1)	1	
	I	NTM(2), SIM(2), UFM(4), WBT(2)	10	
	RC	SCE(1)	1	12
Croatia	I	ECM(3)	3	3
Cuba	I	LL(1)	1	1
Cyprus	CH	EOS(2), ICF(2)	4	
	A	CMS(1), ICS(1), MS(2)	4	
	I	AWM(2), FEBA(4), IFES(1), MMG(4), SAT(2), YWAM(6)	19	27
Czech Republic	CH	BCC(2)	2	
	A	ICS(1)	1	
	I	HCJB(2), IFES(2), OM(4)	8	
	O	PCI(1), SA(6), UICR(1)	8	19
Denmark	CH	EOS(2)	2	2
Djibouti	I	RSMT(2)	2	2
East Asia	I	N(1)	1	
	O	GBM(2)	2	3
Eastern Europe	CH	EOS(2)	2	2
Ecuador	A	SAMS(1)	1	
	I	HCJB(3), LL(12), OMS(2), SIM(2)	19	
	O	BMS(9)	9	
	RC	FD(3), MHM(1)	4	33
Egypt	CH	ICF(2)	2	
	A	CMS(6), CMSI(2), ICS(1), USPG(1)	10	
	I	AP(1), TF(1)	2	
	O	CSB(1)	1	15
El Salvador	RC	SSC(2), SSHJM(1)	3	3
Eritrea	A	USPG(2)	2	
	RC	CMSV(1), MCCJ(1)	2	4
Ethiopia	A	C(3)	3	
	I	MAF(1), N(2), SIM(9), WBT(5)	17	
	RC	DC(1), FMM(1), MCH(1)	3	23
Europe	I	IS(2), WBT(23)	25	25
Falkland Islands	A	ICS(2), SMA(1)	3	
	I	MMG(3)	3	6
Far East	I	WBT(6)	6	
	O	AGWM(6)	6	12
Fiji	O	MCWCO(1)	1	
	RC	MSSC(1)	1	2
France	CH	BCC(2), EOS(54), ICF(14)	70	
	A	C(4), ICS(20), MS(4)	28	
	I	AWM(13), CLC(1), ECM(4), EMF(2 FMT(18), IFES(11), MT(2), N(5),OM(5), UFM(6), WEC(10), WH(5), YWAM(4	87	
	O	BM(2), BMS(13), CSB(1), EIM(10), GBM(1), PCI(4)	31	216
Gabon	I	GO(1), WBT(3)	4	4
Gambia	A	CMS(1), C(2)	3	
	I	WEC(10), YWAM(2)	12	
	O	MCWCO(3)	3	
	RC	SSJA(1)	1	19
Georgia	A	CMS(2)	2	2
Germany	CH	EOS(1)	1	
	A	ICS(3)	3	
	I	JT(2), OM(16), YWAM(1)	19	
	O	FPCU(2), MCWCO(5)	7	30
Ghana	A	CMS(2)	2	
	I	SIM(3), WEC(1), WBT(11)	15	
	O	AGWM(3), EIM(2), MCWCO(2), SA(4	11	
	RC	CFC(1), DMJ(1), CSSP(1), SCI(1), SHCJ(1), MAFR(3)	8	36
Gibraltar	I	HCJB(3), WH(2)	5	
	O	CSB(1)	1	6
Greece	A	ICS(1)	1	
	I	EMF(1), IFES(2), OM(1), WEC(2), YWAM(3)	9	10

Country/ Region	Denomin-ation	Agencies working in country (excluding Associates)	Total personnel per Denom	Grand Total
Greenland	CH	EOS(2)	2	
	I	NTM(1)	1	3
Grenada	RC	OP(2)	2	2
Guatemala	I	LL(3)	3	
	RC	VMM(1)	1	4
Guinea	I	NTM(3)	3	
	O	BMS(5)	5	8
Guinea-Bissau	I	WEC(3)	3	3
Gulf	A	CMS(2)	2	2
Guyana	A	USPG(1)	1	
	RC	SJ(6)	6	7
Haiti		OMS(1)	1	1
Honduras		TF(2)	2	
	O	EIM(6), MCWCO(1)	7	
	RC	JOS(1)	1	10
Hong Kong	I	OMS(1)	1	
	O	EIM(1)	1	
	RC	SDB(1)	1	3
Hong Kong & Macao	I	OMF(2)	2	2
Hungary	A	CMS(2)	2	
		OM(3), YWAM(3)	6	
	O	BMS(1), CSB(2)	3	11
India	CH	ANC(1), EOS(12)	13	
	A	CMS(3), C(2), USPG(6)	11	
	I	CIA(1), GNF(2), IS(17), LMI(1), SIM(6), TF(2), WH(2)	31	
	O	AGWM(2), BMS(4), FPCU(2), PCI(3)	11	
	RC	FSC(1), FMM(1), OFM(1), IC(1), MHM(1), MCH(1)	6	72
Indian Ocean/ Islands	I	AIM(9)	9	9
Indonesia	A	CMS(4)	4	
	I	NTM(3), OMF(7), OMS(3), UFM(1) WBT(6)	20	
	O	PCI(1)	1	
	RC	FCJ(1)	1	26
Ireland, Republic of	CH	EOS(18)	18	
	I	ECM(1), OM(1), SCFS(2), UFM(4)	8	
	O	BM(21), FPCU(2)	23	49
Irian Jaya	I	UFM(1)	1	1
Israel	CH	HCF(1)	1	
	A	CMJ(8)	8	
	I	FOI(3), MT(2), WH(2)	7	
	O	CSB(4)	4	
	RC	AA(1), FSC(1), FMM(1)	3	23
Italy	CH	EOS(21)	21	
	I	CLC(3), ECM(2), EMF(1), IFES(3), UFM(2), WEC(1), YWAM(2)	14	
	O	AGWM(2), BMS(6), CSB(1), MCWCO(2), SA(4)	15	50
Jamaica	CH	EOS(2)	2	
	O	AGWM(4), BMS(2), CSB(3), FPCU(2), PCI(1)	12	14
Japan	A	CMS(1), EOS(14), MS(4), USPG(3)	22	
	I	JCL(6), JM(3), OMF(33), WEC(4), WH(3)	49	
	O	AGWM(2), JGNM(1), MCWCO(3)	6	
	RC	SM(1), SJ(1)	2	79
Jordan	A	CMS(4), MS(1)	5	5
Kazakhstan	I	OM(1)	1	1
Kenya	CH	EOS(4)	4	
	A	CMS(12), CMSI(4), C(9), MS(2)	27	
	I	AIM(28), FEBA(1), LI(2), MAF(9), SIM(8), TF(6), WBT(31)	85	
	O	AGWM(6), CSB(3), FPCS(7), FPCU(5), GBM(6), MCWCO(7), PCI(10), SA(3), WAM(1)	48	
	RC	RA(2), RNDM(1), DC(1), FD(3), OFM(1), FMSJ(3), RSM(4), IC(1), MHM(3), MSOLA(1), SPS(1), RSCJ(1), OLC(1), SSMND(1), VMM(3)	27	191
Kenya & Sudan	I	AP(1)	1	1
Korea	CH	EOS(2)	2	
	A	MS(1)	1	
	I	OMF(1)	1	4
Kosovo	I	ECM(2)	2	
	O	BMS(1), EIM(4)	5	7
Kyrgystan	CH	ANC(2)	2	
	I	TF(1)	1	3
Latvia	O	ACMM(2), GBM(2), SA(3)	7	7
Lebanon	CH	EOS(8), ICF(2)	10	
	A	CMS(2)	2	
	O	BMS(4), CSB(1)	5	
	RC	RSMU(1)	1	18
Lesotho	CH	EOS(2)	2	
	I	AIM(1)	1	3
Liberia	I	TF(1)	1	
	O	SA(2)	2	
	RC	SMA(1)	1	4
Lithuania	I	IFES(1)	1	1
Luxemburg	O	AGWM(2)	2	2
Macedonia	CH	EOS(1)	1	
	O	GBM(2)	2	3
Macao	RC	SDB(1)	1	1
Madagascar	A	CMS(2), USPG(1)	3	
	I	AIM(7), MAF(1), UICR(2)	10	13
Malawi	CH	EOS(6)	6	
	A	USPG(6)	6	
	I	EI(8), N(3), SIM(9), ZMI(5), YWAM(1)	26	
	O	ACMM(2), CSB(5), EIM(2), PCI(17), SA(2)	28	
	RC	RNDM(1), MMM(1), SMM(1)	3	69
Malawi & Togo	A	C(2)	2	2
Malaysia	CH	EOS(1)	1	
	I	OMF(12), OM(1), WBT(2), YWAM(1)	16	
	O	AGWM(1), MCWCO(2), SA(1)	4	
	RC	MHM(1)	1	22
Mali	I	N(2), RSMT(2), WH(1), WBT(8), YWAM(4)	17	17
Malta	I	HCJB(1)	1	
	O	AGWM(2)	2	3
Mauritania	CH	ICF(1)	1	1
Melanesia	A	MM(2)	2	2
Mexico	CH	BHCF(2), EOS(3)	5	
	I	LL(3), NTM(3), OMS(8), WEC(1), WBT(3)	18	23
Middle East	A	CMS(2)	2	
	I	AWM(22), F(11), IS(9), ISI(2), MECO(43), OM(32), YWAM(1)	120	
	O	WAM(5)	5	127
Moldova	I	OM(2)	2	2
Mongolia	I	IS(8), MAF(1), OMF(7), UFM(2)	18	18

UK Mission Agencies and Mission Workers

Country/ Region	Denomin-ation	Societies working in country (excluding Associates)	Total personnel per Denom	Grand Total
Morocco	A	ICS(1)	1	1
Mozambique	A	C(2)	2	
	CH	BCC(2)	2	
	I	AIM(9), NTM(7), OMS(2), SIM(5), WO(2), WBT(4), YWAM(2), ZMI(2),	33	
	O	ACMM(2), AGWM(1), EIM(2)	5	42
Namibia(4)	I	A(2), SIM(4), YWAM(2)	8	
	RC	CFC(2), SDB(1)	3	11
Near East	I	F(7)	7	7
Nepal	CH	HCF(2)	2	
	A	CMS(6), CMSI(5)	11	
	I	INF(29), IS(20), ISI(9), ISS(3), LMI(2), LMS(2), OM(6), TF(1)	72	
	O	BMS(19), CSB(2), MCWCO(6)	27	112
Netherlands	A	ICS(12), MS(4)	16	
	I	OMF(2), WEC(5), YWAM(2)	9	
	O	CSB(2)	2	27
Netherlands Antilles	A	ICS(1)	1	1
New Caledonia	CH	EOS(2)	2	2
New Zealand	A	MS(1)	1	
	I	OM(3), WEC(5), YWAM(6)	14	
	RC	MHM(5), SJC(1)	6	21
Niger	I	SIM(11), WH(2), WBT(2)	15	15
Nigeria	A	CMS(6)	6	
	I	AP(5), LM(1), LMI(1), MCWCO(3), N(2), QIF(12), SIM(5), WBT(7), YWAM(1)	37	
	RC	OAR(1), OSA(1), DHS(4), FSC(1), FMDM(2), CSSP(3), MMM(1), SMA(1), SSMND(4)	18	61
North Africa	A	C(5)	5	
	I	AWM(19), F(21), IS(2), YWAM(4)	46	
	O	AGWM(2), BMS(17)	19	70
Norway	CH	EOS(2)	2	
	I	EMF(1)	1	3
Pakistan	CH	EOS(5)	5	
	A	CMS(7), USPG(1)	8	
	I	IS(9), ISS(2), OM(2), SIM(5), TF(3)	21	
	O	AGWM(4), SA(1)	5	
	RC	MHM(3), HFB(1)	4	43
Panama	I	NTM(8)	8	8
Papua Newa Guinea	A	PNG(10)	10	
	I	MAF(1), NTM(22), UFM(9), WBT(20)	52	
	RC	OFMCap(1), RNDM(1), CP(1)	3	65
Paraguay	A	SAMS(15)	15	
	I	YWAM(2)	2	
	O	BMS(2), SA(1)	3	20
Peru	CH	EOS(2)	2	
	A	SAMS(2), USPG(2)	4	
	I	FCS(10), LL(20), SIM(11), UFM(4)	45	
	O	AGWM(3), BM(13), BMS(14), GBM(2)	32	
	RC	OSB(3), FSC(2), FD(9), RSM(3), MSSC(2), JOS(1), SDB(1), SCE(1), SSMND(2)	24	107
Philippines	CH	EOS(2), HCF(2)	4	
	A	CMS(2)	2	
	I	ACT(3), FEBA(2), NTM(3), OMF(15), OMS(2), SI(2), WBT(5), YWAM(5)	37	
	O	AGWM(3), EIM(4), GBM(5), SA(1)	13	
	RC	SCJ(1), FCJ(2), MHM(1), SSCL(1), HFB(1), SSHJM(1)	7	63
Poland	I	ECM(2), N(7)	9	
	O	EIM(2)	2	11
Portugal	CH	EOS(2)	2	
	A	ICS(1)	1	
	I	AGM(4), BCM(2), ECM(2), UFM(1), WEC(1)	10	
	O	BMS(2), CSB(1), SA(1)	4	17
Romania	A	CMS(3)	3	
	I	AIM(1), IT(3), JT(2), YWAM(2)	8	
	O	PCI(3)	3	14
Russia	A	CMS(3)	3	
	I	A(6), IFES(8), MT(2), NTM(1), OM(9), YWAM(1)	27	
	O	MCWCO(1), SA(1)	2	32
Rwanda	CH	EOS(4)	4	
	A	CMS(3)	3	
	I	AIM(2), YWAM(1)	3	
	O	SA(2)	2	
	RC	MMM(1), SSMN(2)	3	15
St Helena	A	USPG(2)	2	2
Senegal	I	AP(1), NTM(2), WEC(8), WBT(18)	29	
	RC	SSJA(1)	1	30
Serbia	CH	EOS(2)	2	
	A	C(2)	2	
	I	N(4)	4	8
Sierra Leone	I	TF(5), UFM(2), WEC(2)	9	
	RC	CFC(1)	1	10
Singapore	A	CMS(3), MS(1)	4	
	I	OMF(12)	12	
	O	SA(2)	2	18
Solomon Islands	O	MCWCO(2)	2	
	RC	SM(1)	1	3
South Africa	CH	EOS(12)	12	
	A	CMS(2), C(6), USPG(13)	21	
	I	AIM(1), FCS(8), MT(2), MAF(1), OM(10), SIM(11), WEC(2), YWAM(7)	42	
	O	ACMM(2), CSB(2), EIM(2), MCWCO(1), SA(2)	9	
	RC	OPC(1), OP(1), FD(1), FMM(5), OFM(1), MHM(3), CSSR(2), SDB(8), SPC(3), SJ(5), HFB(2), SSMMP(1), SSMND(2), OSJ(1)	36	120
South Asia	I	F(1), YWAM(16)	17	17
South Central Asia	O	BMS(13)	13	13
South East Asia	A	C(4)	4	
	I	F(7), IS(3), UFM(2)	12	16
Spain	CH	BCC(2), EOS(12)	14	
	A	ICS(2)	2	
	I	AWM(2), ECM(17), EMF(3), IFES(2), LL(2), NTMU(1), OMS(4), OM(2), SGM(8), UFM(7), WEC(6), WH(8), YWAM(2)	64	
	O	AGWM(11), BM(2), BMS(4), EIM(8), FPCU(5), GBM(4), PCI(2)	36	116
Sri Lanka	A	CMS(3), USPG(1)	4	
	I	OM(4)	4	
	O	BMS(1), CSB(1), MCWCO(3)	5	
	RC	FMM(1)	1	14
Sudan	A	CMS(9), CMSI(2)	11	
	I	A(2), AP(4), AIM(2), EI(4), LMI(1), LMS(1), SIM(13), WBT(20)	47	
	RC	MCCJ(1), SdeC(1), MAFR(1), VMM(1)	4	62
Swaziland	RC	OSM(1)	1	1
Sweden	I	YWAM(2)	2	2
Switzerland	A	ICS(4)	4	
	I	LL(1), WEC(1), WBT(2), YWAM(7)	11	
	O	AGWM(2), CSB(1)	3	18

Country/ Region	Denomin-ation	Agencies working in country (excluding Associates)	Total personnel per Denom	Grand Total
Syria	RC	RJM(1)	1	1
Taiwan	A	CMS(1)	1	
	I	OMF(11), WEC(1), YWAM(1)	13	
	O	AGWM(2), PCW(1)	3	
	RC	OSU(1)	1	18
Tajikistan	CH	BHCF(3)	3	
	I	OM(2), TF(1), WH(3)	6	9
Tanzania	CH	EOS(10)	10	
	A	CMS(12), C(14), MS(1), USPG(5)	32	
	I	AIM(10), EI(9), MAF(7), N(2), WBT(5), YWAM(1)	34	
	O	EIM(2), SA(5)	7	
	RC	LSU(2), MMM(1), RA(1), SDB(1), SDS(2), SP(3), MAFR(7), VMM(7)	24	107
Thailand	CH	EOS(6), HCF(1), ICF(2)	9	
	A	CMS(4), MS(1)	5	
	I	ISI(2), LRI(2), NTM(5), OMF(18), WEC(10), YWAM(3)	40	
	O	AGWM(2), BMS(7), CSB(2)	11	65
Togo & Benin	I	WBT(8)	8	8
Tonga	I	YWAM(1)	1	
	O	MCWCO(2)	2	
	RC	SM(1)	1	4
Trinidad & Tobago	A	USPG(2)	2	2
Tunisia	A	ICS(1)	1	1
Turkey	CH	ICF(2)	2	
	I	IFES(2), OM(11)	13	15
Uganda	CH	BCC(4), ICF(2)	6	
	A	CMS(20), CMSI(9), C(2)	31	
	I	AIM(9), EI(10), LI(2), MAF(3), YWAM(5)	29	
	O	AGWM(1), BMS(10)	11	
	RC	CMSV(1), MCCJ(2), MHM(1), SMM(1), OSM(1), MAFR(3), VMM(6)	15	92
Ukraine	A	ICS(2)	2	
	I	IFES(1), OM(1), YWAM(1)	3	
	O	EIM(1)	1	6
United Arab Emirates	A	MS(1)	1	1
United Kingdom (*not* including Executive or Home staff)	A	CMS(33), CMSI(1), CMJ(6), C(17), SAMS(2)	59	
	I	A(64), AP(2), AIM(2), AWM(17), BCM(11), CWI(4), CIA(4), CLC(46), FPCU(26), F(4), GO(13), HCJB(2), IT(9), IS(39), JCL(1), LL(2), MM(2), MT(7), MMG(5), N(93), OMF(14), OM(32), RSMT(2), SCFS(15), SIM(6), UFM(5), USPG(1), WEC(24), WH(3), WO(2), WBT(40), YWAM(153)	650	
	O	AGWM(5), BM(5), EOS(12), FPCS(8), GBM(9), PCI(2), PCW(21), SA(7), WAM(15)	84	
	RC	RA(1)	1	794
USA	I	CIA(2), N(4), NTM(4), OMF(3), OM(10), WH(1), WBT(11), YWAM(9)	44	
	O	FPCU(28), WAM(2)	30	74
Uruguay	I	OM(1)	1	1
Uzbekistan	I	OM(3), WH(2)	5	5
Venezuela	CH	EOS(1)	1	
	A	USPG(2)	2	
	I	NTM(4)	4	7
Vietnam	I	WH(2)	2	2
Windward Islands	A	USPG(1)		1
Zambia	CH	EOS(50)	50	
	A	CMSI(2), USPG(6)	8	
	I	SIM(9), UICR(1)	10	
	O	CAM(4), CSB(4), MCWCO(5), SA(6)	19	
	RC	CFC(1), SC(1), OFMCon(2), FMDM(10), SJ(20), SSHJM(1), MAFR(4), VMM(1)	40	127
Zimbabwe	CH	EOS(2)	2	
	A	C(2), USPG(11)	13	
	I	SIM(6), YWAM(1)	7	
	O	AGWM(2), EIM(5), FPCS(8), MCWCO(2), SA(10)	27	
	RC	CJ(1), OPZ(2), FMDM(5), RSMU(1), CSSR(1), SSMND(3)	13	62
Ships	I	OM(63)	63	63
Short-term Overseas	I	MAF(2)	2	2
Limited Access/ Special Ministries/ Undisclosed/ Other	CH	EOS(30)	30	
	I	AIM(3), ISS(1), NTM(1)	5	35

3. LOCATION OF SERVICE BY AGENCY OR CHURCH
(INCORPORATING *DIRECT SENDING CHURCHES,* PREVIOUSLY UNDER LIST 5)

UK Mission Workers = all UK mission workers serving overseas and in UK, *excluding* associates, office staff and retired personnel, and *including* UK executive and home staff and secondments.

Other Countries = countries in which the agency or church is involved but where none of their UK mission workers are currently serving.

† denotes data carried over from the previous edition. * denotes 2005 data from *Religious Trends* no 5.
All other data has been updated for this edition

Agency	Countries with UK Mission Workers	UK Mission Workers	Other Countries	Mission Workers World-wide
Accts Military Ministries International	UKHome(7)	7	Burkina Faso, Germany, Kenya, Nigeria, Norway, Poland, Zimbabwe	14
Acre Gospel Mission*	Brazil(8), Lanzarote(2), Portugal(4), UKHome(1)	15		
Action International Ministries (UK)	Brazil(2), Philippines(3), UKHome(2)	7	Brazil, Cambodia, Colombia, Ecuador, Honduras, India, Malawi, Mexico, Portugal, Sri Lanka, Uganda, Zambia	[illegible]220
Action Partners Ministries	Cameroon(2), Egypt(1), Kenya & Sudan(1), Nigeria(5), Senegal(1), Sudan(4), UK(2), UKHome(2)	18		n/a
Agapé	Namibia(2), Russia(6), Sudan(2), UK(66), UKHome(34)	110	150 countries worldwide	22[illegible]00
AIM International*	Chad(6), Congo(2), Indian Ocean(9), Kenya (28), Lesotho(1), Madagascar(7), Mozambique(9), Romania (1), Rwanda(2), South Africa(1), Sudan(2), Tanzania(10), Uganda(9), UK(2), UKHome(16), Other/Specialized(3)	108		[illegible]00
Albanian Evangelical Mission	Albania(5), UKHome(2)	7	Kosovo	n/a
All Nations Church*	Argentina(1), India(1), Kyrgystan(2)	4		4
Apostolic Church Missionary Movement	Chile(2), Latvia(2), Malawi(2), Mozambique(2), South Africa(2), UKHome(3)	13	Angola, Brazil, India, Namibia, Pakistan, Sri Lanka	
Arab World Ministries	Cyprus(2), France(13), Middle East(22), North Africa(19), Spain(2), UK(17), UKHome(6)	81		[illegible]00
Assemblies of God World Ministries	Austria(3), Brazil(1), Canada(2), Colombia(1), Far East(6), Ghana(3), India(2), Italy(2), Jamaica(4), Japan(2), Kenya(6), Luxemburg(2), Malaysia(1), Malta(2), Mozambique(1), North Africa(2), Pakistan(4), Peru(3), Philippines(3), Spain(11), Switzerland(2), Taiwan(2), Thailand(2), Uganda(1), UK(5), UKHome(19), Zimbabwe(2)	94	Bosnia, Bulgaria, Burkina Faso, China, Croatia, Egypt, Ethiopia, Hungary, Iraq, Jordan, Macedonia, Mexico, Nigeria, Serbia & Montenegro, Romania, Sri Lanka, Uganda, Zimbabwe.	[illegible]9
Assumptionist Fathers and Brothers	Israel(1)	1		n/a
Augustinian Recollects	Nigeria(1)	1		n/a
Augustinians	Nigeria(1)	1		n/a
Baptist Missions*	France(2), Ireland, Republic of(21), Peru(13), Spain(2), UK(5), UKHome(1)	44		[illegible]7
Basingstoke Community Church*	Brazil(2), Czech Republic(2), France(2), Mozambique(2), Spain(2), Uganda(4)	14		[illegible]4
BCM International	Portugal(2), UK(11), UKHome(1)	14		7[illegible]0
Belgian Evangelical Mission	Belgium(16), UKHome(2)	18		1[illegible]
Benedictines (English Benedictine Congregation)	Peru(3)	3		n/a
BMS World Mission	Albania(26), Angola(3), Bangladesh(4), Belgium(4), Brazil(19), Bulgaria(5), Congo(6), Ecuador(9), France(13), Guinea(5), Hungary(1), India(4), Italy(6), Jamaica(2), Kosovo(1), Lebanon(4), Nepal(19), North Africa(17), Paraguay(2), Peru(1), Portugal(2), Spain(4), South Central Asia(13), Sri Lanka(1), Thailand(7), Uganda(10), UKHome(26)	216	Bosnia, Croatia, Indonesia, Latvia, Lebanon, Poland, South Africa, Zimbabwe	n/a
Biggin Hill Christian Fellowship	Mexico(2), Tajikistan(3)	5		[illegible]
British and International Sailors' Society	UKHome(5)	5	American Samoa, Australia, Belgium, Bermuda, Brazil, Canada, Ghana, India, Indian Ocean, Indonesia, Jamaica, Madagascar, Mali, Netherlands Antilles, New Zealand, Philippines, Russia, South Africa, Sri Lanka, Ukraine, USA	[illegible]
Brothers of the Sacred Heart	Zambia(1)	1		5[illegible]
Capuchin Franciscans	Papua New Guinea(1)	1		2,00[illegible]
Central African Missions	Congo(10), Zambia(4)	14	Ethiopia	1[illegible]
Child Evangelism Fellowship	UKHome(13)	13		1,90[illegible]
Christian and Missionary Alliance†	Colombia(1), France(1), UK(2), UKHome(5)	9	Balkans, Poland	n/a
Christian Witness to Israel*	Australia(1), UK(4), UKHome(1)	6	Bulgaria, Hungary, Israel, New Zealand	1
Christians in Action	India(1), UK(4), USA(2)	7	Ghana, Macau, Sierra Leone	5

Agency	Countries with UK Mission Workers	UK Mission Workers	Other Countries	Mission Workers World-wide
Church Mission Society*	Bangladesh(3), Cambodia(2), Central Asia(9), China(3), Congo (4), Cyprus(1), Egypt(6), (Gambia (1), Ghana(2), Gulf(2), Hungary(2), India(3), Indonesia(4), Georgia(2), Japan(1), Jordan(4), Kenya(12), Lebanon(2), Madagascar(2), Middle East(2), Nepal(6), Nigeria(6), Pakistan(7), Philippines(2), Romania(3), Russia(3), Rwanda(3), Singapore(3), South Africa(2), Sri Lanka(3), Sudan(9), Taiwan(1), Tanzania(12), Thailand(4), Uganda(20), UK(33), UKHome(36)	220		200
Church Mission Society Ireland	Egypt(2), Kenya(4), Nepal(5), Uganda(9), Sudan(2), UK(1), UKHome(4), Zambia(2)	29	India	n/a
Church of Scotland World Mission Council (formerly Church of Scotland Board of World Mission)	Bahamas(2), Belgium(1), Bermuda(1), Egypt(1), France(1), Gibraltar(1), Hungary(2), Israel(4), Italy(1), Jamaica(3), Kenya(3), Lebanon(1), Malawi(5), Nepal(2), Netherlands(2), Portugal(1), South Africa(2), Sri Lanka(1), Switzerland(1), Thailand(2), UKHome(6), Zambia(4)	47		41
Church's Ministry Among Jewish People*	Israel(8), UK(3), UKHome(3)	14	Ukraine	22
Claretian Missionaries	Belize(2)	2		3,000†
CLC	France(1), Italy(3), UK(46), UKHome(7)	57		650
Columban Lay Missionaries	Chile(1)	1		70
Comboni Missionaries	Brazil(1), Eritrea(1), Sudan(1), Uganda(2)	5		
Comboni Missionary Sisters	Eritrea(1), Uganda(1)	2		57
Congregation of Christian Brothers	Ghana(1), Namibia(2), Sierra Leone(1), Zambia(1)	5		10
Congregation of Josephites	Zimbabwe(1)	1		n/a
Congregation of La Sainte Union des Sacré-Coeurs	Cameroon(1), Tanzania(2)	3		24
Congregation of Our Lady of the Missions	Kenya(1), Malawi(1), Papua New Guinea(1)	3		960†
Crosslinks	Ethiopia(3), France(4), Gambia(2), India(2), Kenya(9), Malawi & Togo(2), Mozambique(2), North Africa (5), Serbia(2), South Africa(6), South East Asia(4), Tanzania(14), Uganda(2), UK(17), UKHome(7), Zimbabwe(2)	83		67
Crusade of the Holy Spirit	Argentina(1)	1		30
Daughters of Charity of St Vincent de Paul	Ethiopia(1), Kenya(1)	2		24,000†
Daughters of Jesus	Chile(1)	1		100†
Daughters of Mary and Joseph	Ghana(1)	1		85,000†
Daughters of the Holy Spirit	Nigeria(4)	4		30†
Daughters of Mary Help of Christians (Salesian Sisters of St John Bosco)*	Australia(1), Ethiopia(2), Kenya(1), Zambia(1)	5		3,500
De La Salle Brothers	India(1), Israel(1), Nigeria(1), Peru(2)	5		2,000†
Dominican Sisters of St Catherine of Siena of Oakford	South Africa(1)	1		190
Dominican Sisters of Zimbabwe	Zimbabwe(2)	2		374
Dominicans	Barbados(2), Grenada(2), South Africa(1)	5		7,000†
Echoes of Service	Albania(2), Angola(2), Argentina(8), Austria(1), Bahamas(2), Belgium(1), Bolivia(6), Botswana(5), Brazil(17), Colombia(2), Congo(5), Denmark(2), Eastern Europe(2), France(54), Germany(1), Greenland(2), India(12), Ireland(18), Italy(21), Japan(14), Kenya(4), Lebanon(8), Lesotho(2), Macedonia(1), Malawi(6), Malaysia(1), Mexico(3), New Caledonia(2), Norway(2), Pakistan(5), Peru(2), Philippines(2), Portugal(2), Rwanda(4), Serbia(2), South Africa(12), Spain(12), Tanzania(10), UK(12), UKHome(2), Venezuela(1), Zambia(50), Zimbabwe(2), Other(30)	368		
Elim International Missions†	Albania(2), Australia(2), Belgium(10), Botswana(1), Congo(2), France(10), Ghana(2), Honduras(6), Hong Kong(1), Kosovo(4), Malawi(2), Mozambique(2), Philippines(4), Poland(2), South Africa(2), Spain(8), Tanzania(2), UKHome(4), Ukraine(1), Zimbabwe(5)	72	Brazil, Burundi, Greece, Guyana, India, Italy, Kenya, Nigeria, Papua New Guinea, Rwanda, Uganda	120
Emmanuel International	Canada(23), Malawi(8), Sudan(4), Tanzania(9), Uganda(10) UKHome(1)	55		15

UK Mission Agencies and Mission Workers

Agency	Countries with UK Mission Workers	UK Mission Workers	Other Countries	Mission Workers World-wide
European Christian Mission	Albania(2), Austria(4), Croatia(3), France(4), Ireland, Republic of(1), Italy(2), Kosovo(2), Poland(2), Portugal(2), Spain(17), UKHome(6)	45		160
European Missionary Fellowship	Belgium(1), France(2), Greece(1), Italy(1), Norway(1), Spain(3), UKHome(4)	13	Belarus, Czech Republic, Germany, Poland, Portugal, Romania, Switzerland, Ukraine	85
Evangelical Action (Brazil)	Brazil(4), UKHome(1)	5		4
Faithful Companions of Jesus	Argentina(2), Indonesia(1), Philippines(2)	5		20†
Feba	Cyprus(4), Kenya(1), Philippines(2), UKHome(10)	17	Ethiopia, Malawi, South Africa	n/a
Fidei Donum Priests	Bolivia(1), Brazil(1), Ecuador(3), Kenya(3), Peru(9), South Africa(1)	18		n/a
Focus on Israel*	Israel(3), UKHome(8)	11		3
France Mission Trust	France(18), UKHome(2)	20		130
Franciscan Conventuals	Zambia(2)	2		n/a
Franciscan Fathers and Brothers (Minoresses)	India(1), Kenya(1), South Africa(1)	3		60
Franciscan Missionaries of Mary	Austria(1), Ethiopia(1), India(1), Israel(1), South Africa(5), Sri Lanka(1)	10		9,[illegible]0†
Franciscan Missionaries of the Divine Motherhood	Nigeria(2), Zambia(10), Zimbabwe(5)	17		[illegible]20†
Franciscan Missionary Sisters of St Joseph	Kenya(3)	3		[illegible]5†
Free Church of Scotland International Missions Board	Colombia(2), Peru(10),South Africa(8), UKHome(1)	21	Central Asia, India	22
Free Presbyterian Church of Scotland Mission Committee†	Kenya(7), UK(8), Zimbabwe(8)	23	none	41
Free Presbyterian Church of Ulster Mission Board†	Australia(5), Canada(18), Germany(2), India(2), Ireland, Republic of(2), Jamaica(2), Kenya(5), Spain(5), UK(26), UKHome(1), USA(28)	96	Cameroon, South Africa	[illegible]60
Frontiers	Central Asia(29), Middle East(18), North Africa(21), South and SE Asia(8), UK(4), UKHome(3)	83		[illegible]96
Frontline Trust	China(2), UKHome(1)	3		2
Global Outreach UK	Gabon(1), UK(13), UKHome(1)	15		[illegible]00
Go to the Nations Link	UKHome(27)	27	France, Germany, India, Ireland, Japan, Portugal, Spain	[illegible]45
Gorakhpur Nurseries Fellowship	India(2), UKHome(2)	4		[illegible]/a
Grace Baptist Mission	Austria(1), Brazil(2), Colombia(2), East Asia(2), France(1), Kenya(6), Latvia(2), Macedonia(2), Peru(4), Philippines(5), Spain(4), UK(9), UKHome(7)	47		[illegible]50
Great Lakes Outreach	Burundi(2)	2		2
HCJB-UK	Czech Republic(2), Ecuador(3), Gibraltar(3), Malta(1), UK(2), UKHome(3)	14		[illegible]0
Hollybush Christian Fellowship	Israel(1), Ivory Coast(1), Philippines(2), Thailand(1), Burma(2), Nepal(2)	9		[illegible]9
Holy Ghost Fathers	Australia(1), Nigeria(3), Ghana(1)	5		3,0[illegible]†
Ichthus Christian Fellowship*	Azerbaijan(6), Brazil(1), Bulgaria(3), China(2), Cyprus(2), Egypt(2), France(14), Lebanon(2), Mauritania(1), Thailand(2), Turkey(2), Uganda(2)	39	Nepal	[illegible]
Institute of Charity	India(1), Kenya(1)	2		[illegible]
Institute of Our Lady of Mercy	Kenya(4), Peru(3)	7		[illegible]
Intercontinental Church Society	Belgium(5), Brazil(1), Chile(1), Cyprus(1), Czech Republic(1), Egypt(1), Falklands Islands(2), France(20), Germany(3), Greece(1), Morocco(1), Netherlands(12), Netherlands Antilles(1), Portugal(1), Spain(2), Switzerland(4), Tunisia(1), Ukraine(2)	60		[illegible]
International Fellowship of Evangelical Students	Austria(2), Belgium(4), Cyprus(1), Czech Republic(2), France(11), Greece(2), Italy(3), Lithuania(1), Russia(8), Spain(2), Turkey(3), UKHome(6), Ukraine(1)	46		18[illegible]
International Nepal Fellowship	Nepal(29)	29		n[illegible]
International Teams UK†	Austria(5), Bolivia(1), Canada(1), Colombia(1), Romania(3), UK(9)	20	n/a	n[illegible]

Agency	Countries with UK Mission Workers	UK Mission Workers	Other Countries	Mission Workers World-wide
Interserve	Bangladesh(8), Central Asia(20), China(7), India(17), Middle East(9), Mongolia(8), Nepal(20), North Africa(2), Pakistan(9), Europe(2), South East Asia(3), UK(39), UKHome(8)	152		650
Ireland	Central Asia(4), Middle East(2), Nepal(9), Thailand(2), UKHome(2)	19		17
Scotland*	Arab Nations(3), Central Asia(9), Nepal(3), Pakistan(2), UKHome(4), Various(1)	22		n/a
Janz Team UK	Germany(2), Romania(2), UKHome(2)	6		7
Japan Christian Link	Japan(3), UK(1), UKHome(1)	5		12
Japan Good News Ministries	Japan(1), UKHome(1)	2		2
Japan Mission	Japan(3)	3		14
Language Recordings UK	Thailand(2), UKHome(4)	6		n/a
Latin Link	Argentina(13), Bolivia(18), Brazil(18), Colombia(4), Costa Rica(4), Cuba(1), Ecuador(12), Guatemala(3), Mexico(3), Peru(20), Spain(2), Switzerland(1), UK(2), UKHome(8)	109		135
Leprosy Mission	Bangladesh(1), Nigeria(1), UKHome(18)	20		36
International Office	Bangladesh(1), India(1), Nepal(2), Nigeria(1), Sudan(1), UKHome(4)	10		29
Northern Ireland*	UKHome(3)	3		3
Scotland	Bangladesh(2), Nepal(2), Sudan(1), UKHome(2)	7		7
Lightforce International	Albania(1), Kenya(2), Uganda(2), UKHome(1)	6	India, Serbia, Sudan	n/a
Medical Missionaries of Mary	Malawi(1), Nigeria(1), Rwanda(1), Tanzania(2)	5		119†
Melanesian Mission	Melanesia(2), UK(2), UKHome(1)	5	Pacific Islands	4
Mercy Sisters of the Union of Great Britain	Lebanon(1), Zimbabwe(1)	2		49†
Messianic Testimony	France(2), Israel(2), Russia(1), South Africa(1), UK(7), UKHome(1)	14	Belgium, Germany	20
Methodist Church World Office	Argentina(1), Bangladesh(4), Bulgaria(2), Caribbean(3), Chile(3), Fiji(1), Gambia(3), Germany(5), Ghana(2), Honduras(1), Italy(2), Japan(3), Kenya(7), Malaysia(2), Nepal(6), Nigeria(3), Russia(1), Solomon Islands(2), South Africa(1), Sri Lanka(3), Tonga(2), UKHome(6), Zambia(5), Zimbabwe(2)	70	Belgium, Bolivia, Brazil, Cameroon, Colombia, Cote d'Ivoire, Cuba, Ecuador, Estonia, Haiti, India, Indonesia, Jamaica, Latvia, Leeward Islands, Macedonia, Mexico, Myanmar, Pakistan, Panama, Portugal, Samoa, Serbia, Sierra Leone, Spain, Togo, Ukraine, Uruguay	93
Middle East Christian Outreach	Middle East(43), UKHome(5)	48		n/a
Middle East Media	UKHome(5)	5		n/a
Mill Hill Missionaries	Cameroon(3), Congo(1), Ecuador(1), India(1), Kenya(3), Malaysia(1), New Zealand(5), Pakistan(3), Philippines(1), South Africa(3), Uganda(4)	26		n/a
Mission Africa (Qua Iboe Fellowship)	Burkina Faso(2), Chad(2), Nigeria(12), UKHome(3)	19		19
Mission Aviation Fellowship UK*	Bangladesh(1), Ethiopia(1), Chad(2), Kenya(9), Madagascar(1), Mongolia(1), Papua New Guinea(1), South Africa(1), Tanzania(7), Uganda(3), UKHome(13), Other/short-tem(2)	42		58
Mission to Military Garrisons Inc†	Cyprus(4), Falkland Islands(3), UK(5), UKHome(1)	13	n/a	13
Mission to Seafarers	Cyprus(2), France(4), Japan(4), Jordan(1), Kenya(2), Korea(1), Netherlands(4), New Zealand(1), Singapore(1), Tanzania(1), Thailand(1), United Arab Emirates(1), UK(17)	40		n/a
Missionaries of Africa (White Fathers)	Algeria(1), Burkina Faso(1), Ghana(3), Sudan(1), Tanzania(7), Uganda(3), Zambia(4)	20		1,850†
Missionaries of Charity	Ethiopia(1), India(1)	2		n/a
Missionary Sisters of Our Lady of Africa	Congo(1), Kenya(1)	2		1,080†
Missionary Sisters of St Columban	Philippines(1)	1		209†
Missionary Society of St Columban	Australia(1), Chile(1), Fiji(1), Peru(2)	5		770†
Montfort Fathers	Malawi(1), Uganda(1)	2		2,000†
Navigators	Canada(2), Ethiopia(2), East Asia(1), France(5), Malawi(3), Mali(2), Nigeria(4), Peru(2), Poland(7), Serbia(4), Tanzania(2), UK(93), UKHome(8), USA(4)	139	100+ countries worldwide	3,800†

UK Mission Agencies and Mission Workers

Agency	Countries with UK Mission Workers	UK Mission Workers	Other Countries	Mission Workers World-wide
New Foundations Medical Charity	Nigeria(11), UKHome(1)	12		n/a
New Testament Missionary Union	Spain(1)	1	Argentina, Bolivia, Brazil, Mexico, Nigeria, Paraguay, Puerto Rico, USA	47
New Tribes Mission	Australia(4), Bolivia(1), Brazil(3), Cambodia(2), Canada(5), Colombia(2), Greenland(1), Guinea(3), Indonesia(3), Ivory Coast(2), Mexico(3), Mozambique(7), Panama(8), Papua New Guinea(22), Philippines(3), Russia(1), Senegal(2), Thailand(5), UKHome(21), USA(4), Venezuela(4), Other(1)	107		[illegible]14†
OMF International (UK)	Asia(40), Cambodia(21), Hong Kong(2), Indonesia(7), Japan(33), Korea(1), Malaysia(12), Mongolia(7), Netherlands(2), Philippines(15), Singapore(12), Taiwan(11), Thailand(18), UK(14), UKHome(14), USA(3)	212		[illegible]300
OMS International	Colombia(2), Ecuador(2), Haiti(1), Hong Kong(1), Indonesia(3), Mexico(8), Mozambique(2), Philippines(2), Spain(4), UKHome(12)	37		450
Operation Mobilisation	Albania(1), Austria(4), Bangladesh(4), Belgium(3), Canada(1), Czech Republic(4), France(6), Germany(16), Greece(1), Hungary(3), Ireland, Republic of(1), Kazakhstan(1), Malaysia(1), Middle East(32), Moldova(2), Nepal(6), New Zealand(3), Pakistan(2), Russia(9), Spain(2), Sri Lanka(4), South Africa(10), Tajikistan(2), Turkey(11), UK(32), UKHome(64), Ukraine(1), Uruguay(1), USA(10), Uzbekistan(3), OM Ships(63)	303		[illegible]750
Our Lady of Charity of the Good Shepherd†	n/a	27		[illegible]00
Oxford Mission	UKHome(1)	1	Bangladesh	17
People International	Central Asia(17)	19		n/a
Papua New Guinea Church Partnership*	Papua New Guinea(10), UKHome(1)	11		n/a
People International	Central Asia(17), UKHome(2)	19		11
Presbyterian Church in Ireland Overseas Mission Board*	Brazil(1), Czech Republic(1), China(1), France(4), India(3), Indonesia(1), Jamaica(1), Kenya(10), Malawi(17), Romania (3), Spain(2), UK(2), UKHome(3)	49		44
Presbyterian Church of Wales Mission Board	China(3), Taiwan(1), UK(21), UKHome(22)	47		[illegible]24
Red Sea Mission Team	Djibouti(2), Mali(2), UK(2), UKHome(1)	7		[illegible]78
Redemptorists	South Africa(2), Zimbabwe(1)	3		[illegible]†
Religious of Jesus and Mary	Syria(1)	1		n/a
Religious of the Assumption†	Kenya(1), Tanzania(1), UK(1)	3	30+ Countries	n/a
Sahara Desert Mission	None	0	Niger	4
St Joseph's Hospice Association	Honduras(1), Peru(1)	2		n/a
St Patrick's Missionary Society	Kenya(1)	1		n/a
Salesian Fathers and Brothers	Hong Kong(1), Macau(1), Namibia(1), Peru(1), South Africa(8), Tanzania(1)	13		3[illegible]†
Salvation Army International*	Argentina(1), Brazil(6), Caribbean(2), Congo Kinshasa(1), Costa Rica(2), Czech Republic(6), Ghana(4), Italy(4), Kenya(3), Latvia(3), Liberia(2), Malawi(2), Malaysia(1), Pakistan(3), Paraguay(1), Philippines(1), Portugal(1), Russia(1), Rwanda(2), Singapore(2), South Africa(2), Tanzania(5), UK(7), UKHome(4), Zambia(6), Zimbabwe(10)	82	Belize, Colombia, Cuba, El Salvador, Guatemala, Panama, Nigeria, Southern Africa, Venezuela, Zimbabwe	[illegible]0
SAO Cambodia	Cambodia(9), UKHome(2)	11		[illegible]
SAT-7	Cyprus(2), UKHome(1)	3	Cyprus, Egypt, Lebanon	[illegible]
Seamen's Christian Friend Society	Ireland, Republic of(2), UK(15), UKHome(2)	19	Australia, Germany, Ghana, Netherlands, Philippines, St Lucia	[illegible]
Servants to Asia's Urban Poor†	n/a	1	Cambodia, India, Nepal, Phjlippines, Thailand	[illegible]
Servite Friars	Swaziland(2), Uganda(1)	3		[illegible]
Signpost International	Philippines(2), UKHome(7)	9	Rwanda	
SIM UK*	Bangladesh(2), Benin(3), Bolivia(7), Burkina Faso(4), Cote d'Ivoire(2), Ecuador(2), Ethiopia(9), Ghana(3), India(6), Kenya(8), Malawi(9), Mozambique(5), Namibia(4), Niger(11), Nigeria(5), Pakistan(5), Peru(11), South Africa(11), Sudan(3), UK(6), UKHome(9), Zambia(9), Zimbabwe(6),	140		15[illegible]

Agency	Countries with UK Mission Workers	UK Mission Workers	Other Countries	Mission Workers World-wide
Sisters of Charity of Our Lady of Evron	Cote d'Ivoire(1), Peru(1)	2		n/a
Sisters of Charity of St Jeanne Antide Thouret	Sudan(1)	1		n/a
Sisters of Charity of St Paul	South Africa(3)	3		278†
Sisters of Christ	Cameroon(3)	3		20†
Sisters of Christian Instruction (St Gildas)	Burkina Faso(1), Ghana(1)	2		23†
Sisters of Notre Dame de Namur	Kenya(1), Nigeria(4), Peru(2), South Africa(2), Zimbabwe(3)	12		50†
Sisters of Our Lady of Charity	Kenya(1)	1		n/a
Sisters of Providence, Rosminians	Tanzania(3)	3		n/a
Sisters of St Clare	El Salvador(2)	2		n/a
Sisters of St Joseph of Annecy	Senegal(1), Gambia(1)	2		n/a
Sisters of St Joseph of Cluny	New Zealand(1)	1		n/a
Sisters of St Marie Madeleine Postel	South Africa(1)	1		n/a
Sisters of St Mary of Namur	Rwanda(2)	2		n/a
Sisters of the Cross and Passion	Botswana(2), Papua New Guinea(1)	3		70†
Sisters of the Holy Family of Bordeaux	Pakistan(1), Philippines(1), South Africa(2)	4		60†
Sisters of the Sacred Heart of Jesus and Mary	Colombia(1), El Salvador(1), Philippines(1), Zambia(2)	5		62†
Society of African Missions	Australia(1), Falkland Islands(1), Liberia(1), Nigeria(1)	4		n/a
Society of Jesus	Barbados(1), Guyana(6), Japan(1), South Africa(5), Zimbabwe(20)	33		n/a
Society of Mary	Cameroon(1), Japan(1), Solomon Islands(1), Tonga(1)	4		230†
Society of the Divine Saviour	Tanzania(2)	2		n/a
Society of the Holy Child Jesus	Ghana(1)	1		n/a
Society of the Sacred Heart	Kenya(1)	1		140†
South American Mission Society	Argentina(4), Brazil(3), Chile(6), Ecuador(1), Paraguay(15), Peru(2), UK(2), UKHome(14)	47		50
Spanish Gospel Mission	Spain(8), UKHome(1)	9		16
Tearfund*	Afghanistan(6), Burundi(5), Cambodia(1), Congo(2), Egypt(1), Honduras(2), India(2), Kenya(6), Kyrgyzstan(1), Liberia(1), Nepal(1), Pakistan(3), Sierra Leone(5), Tajikistan(1), UKHome(44)	81	Angola, Brazil, Burkina Faso, Colombia, Ethiopia, Honduras, Malawi, Nigeria, Pakistan, Philippines, Rwanda, Sudan,	909
Trans World Radio*	Austria/Europe(2), UKHome(4)	6	China/Singapore, Indonesia, Kenya, Middle East, South Africa	11,500
UFM Worldwide	Brazil(22), Bulgaria(1), Cambodia(1), Cameroon(2), Canada(2), Congo(1), Cote d'Ivoire(4), France(6), Iran Jaya(1), Ireland(4), Italy(2), Java(1), Mongolia(2), Papua New Guinea(9), Peru(4), Portugal(2), Sierra Leone(2), Spain(7), South East Asia(2), UK(5), UKHome(6)	86		90
United Reformed Church (International Relations)	Czech Republic(1), Madagascar(2), Zambia(1), UKHome(2)	6		n/a
United Society for the Propagation of the Gospel†	Argentina(4), Bangladesh(5), Belize(4), Brazil(2), Chile(3), China(14), Egypt(1), Eritrea(2), Guyana(1), India(6), Japan(3), Madagascar(1), Malawi(6), Pakistan(1), Peru(2), South Africa(13), Sri Lanka(1), St Helena(2), Tanzania(5), Trinidad & Tobago(2), UK(1), UKHome(34), Venezuela(2), Windward Islands(1), Zambia(6), Zimbabwe(11)	133	None	144
Ursuline Sisters	Cameroon(1), South Africa(1), Taiwan(1)	3		n/a
Volunteer Missionary Movement	Guatemala(1), Kenya(3), Sudan(1), Tanzania(7), Uganda(6), Zambia(1), UKHome(2)	21		n/a
WEC International	Albania(1), Brazil(5), Burkina Faso(4), Cambodia(1), Canada(2), Chad(6), Congo(3), France(10), Gambia(10), Ghana(1), Greece(2), Guinea-Bissau(3), Italy(2), Japan(4), Mexico(1), Netherlands(5), New Zealand(5), Portugal(1), Senegal(8), Sierra Leone(2), South Africa(2), Spain(6), Switzerland(1), Taiwan(1), Thailand(10), UK(24), UKHome(80)	200		1,719

UK Mission Agencies and Mission Workers

Agency	Countries with UK Mission Workers	UK Mission Workers	Other Countries	Mission Workers Worldwide
World Gospel Mission†	Kenya(2), UKHome(6)	8		n/a
World Horizons	Africa(12), Burkina Faso(1), Cambodia(6), China(2), France(5), Gibraltar(2), India(2), Israel(2), Japan(3), Mali(1), Niger(2), Spain(8), Tajikistan(3), UK(3), UKHome(4), USA(1), Uzbekistan(2), Vietnam(2)	63		250
World Outreach	Mozambique(2), UK(2), UKHome(1)	5	100+ countries	250
World-Wide Advent Missions	Australia(1) Cambodia(2), Kenya(1), Middle East(5), UK(15), UKHome(2), USA(2)	28	Worldwide	982
Wycliffe Bible Translators	Brazil(12), Burkina Faso(16), Cameroon(8), Canada(7), Cape Verde Islands(2), Central African Republic(6), Chad(5), China(7), Cote d'Ivoire(2), Ethiopia(5), Europe(23), Far East(6), Gabon(3), Ghana(11), Indonesia(6), Kenya(31), Malaysia(2), Mali(8), Mexico(3), Mozambique(4), Niger(2), Nigeria(7), Papua New Guinea(20), Philippines(5), Senegal(18), Sudan(20), Switzerland(2), Tanzania(5), Togo & Benin(8), USA(11), UK(40)	305		5,600
YWAM	Albania(3), Argentina(4), Australia(5), Belgium(2), Bolivia(5), Brazil(3), Cambodia(4), Canada(2), Central Asia(10), Cyprus(6), France(4), Gambia(2), Germany(1), Greece(2), Hungary(3), Italy(2), Malaysia(1), Malawi(1), Mali(4), Middle East(1), Mozambique(2), Namibia(2), Netherlands(2), New Zealand(6), Nigeria(1), North Africa(4), Paraguay(2), Philippines(5), Romania(2), Russia(1), Rwanda(1), South Africa(7), South Asia(16), Spain(2), Sweden(3), Switzerland(7), Tanzania(1), Taiwan(1), Thailand(3), Tonga(1), Uganda(5), UK(153), UKHome(77), Ukraine(1), USA(9), Zimbabwe(1)	380		[illegible],800
Zambezi Mission	Malawi(5), Mozambique(2), UKHome(3)	10		10
Total of All UK Mission Workers		**6,008**		

4. PERSONNEL BY AGENCY AND DENOMINATION

Numbers of personnel were requested as at 30th December 2005, for all UK personnel, both overseas and in UK, broken down as defined below.

These figures relate to UK personnel only, but as many agencies have non-UK members both in the UK and elsewhere, the total given in the final column does not show the total size of a particular society. That may be found in the final column of Table 3 *Location of Service by Agency* on Page 270.

Abbreviations used are as follows:

OMW UK mission workers serving overseas
CCU Cross-culture in UK
OCU Own-culture in UK
SEC Secondments, that is mission workers lent to other agencies but supported by their primary agency. It does not include mission workers seconded from other agencies, since these are included in their primary agency.
UKE UK executive staff. Usually those home staff who may be regarded as full mission members.
HUC UK Home staff, ie UK staff not located at mission headquarters.
SUK Total of preceding columns, ie total of Serving UK Mission Workers.
UKO UK Office staff. Mainly clerical staff, who are often not full mission members. The distinction between Home staff and Office staff is sometimes not possible.
ASS Associates. Qualification for associate membership varies with agencies, and was not defined on the questionnaire. It includes only those working abroad, who are often not financially dependent on the agency.
RET Retired personnel. Includes only those who are at least partly financially dependent on the agency.
Total UK The total of all UK personnel serving with the agency.

A zero in a particular category of personnel for an agency usually indicates that the agency has no personnel in that category. It may occasionally mean that information was not available.

	OMW	CCU	OCU	SEC	UKE	HUC	SUK	UKO	ASS	RET	Total UK
Anglican											
Church Mission Society	151	18	11	4	10	26	**220**	**68**	**40**	**320**	**648**
Church Mission Society Ireland	24	0	1	0	4	0	**29**	4	0	0	**33**
Church's Ministry Among Jewish People	8	3	0	0	1	2	**14**	4	2	8	**28**
Crosslinks	60	9	7	1	5	2	**84**	12	24	0	**120**
Intercontinental Church Society	61	0	0	0	0	0	**61**	9	0	0	**70**
Melanesian Mission	2	2	0	0	1	0	**5**	0	0	0	**5**
Mission to Seafarers	23	0	0	0	6	11	**40**	0	0	5	**45**
Oxford Mission	0	0	0	0	1	0	**1**	0	0	0	**1**
Papua New Guinea Church Partnership	10	0	0	0	1	0	**11**	0	10	0	**21**
South American Mission Society	31	2	0	0	6	8	**47**	5	24	0	**76**
United Society for the Propagation of the Gospel	99	0	0	0	9	25	**133**	0	0	0	**133**
Baptist											
BMS World Mission	188	0	0	0	18	10	**216**	31	0	0	**247**
Baptist Missions	38	0	5	0	1	0	**44**	1	0	0	**45**
Grace Baptist Mission	31	5	1	3	3	4	**47**	3	6	5	**61**
Roman Catholic											
Assumptionist Fathers and Brothers	1	0	0	0	0	0	**1**	0	0	0	**1**
Augustinian Recollects	1	0	0	0	0	0	**1**	0	0	0	**1**
Augustinians	1	0	0	0	0	0	**1**	0	0	0	**1**
Benedictines	3	0	0	0	0	0	**3**	0	0	0	**3**
Brothers of the Sacred Heart	1	0	0	0	0	0	**1**	0	0	0	**1**
Capuchin Franciscans	1	0	0	0	0	0	**1**	0	0	0	**1**
Claretian Missionaries	2	0	0	0	0	0	**2**	0	0	0	**2**
Columban Lay Missionaries	1	0	0	0	0	0	**1**	0	0	0	**1**
Comboni Missionaries	5	0	0	0	0	0	**5**	0	0	0	**5**
Comboni Missionary Sisters	2	0	0	0	0	0	**2**	0	0	0	**2**
Congregation of Christian Brothers	5	0	0	0	0	0	**5**	0	0	0	**5**
Congregation of Josephites	1	0	0	0	0	0	**1**	0	0	0	**1**

UK Mission Agencies and Mission Workers

	OMW	CCU	OCU	SEC	UKE	HUC	SUK	UKO	ASS	PET	Total UK
Congregation of La Sainte Union des Sacré-Coeurs	3	0	0	0	0	0	**3**	0	0	0	**3**
Congregation of Our Lady of the Missions	3	0	0	0	0	0	**3**	0	0	0	**3**
Crusade of the Holy Spirit	1	0	0	0	0	0	**1**	0	0	0	**1**
Daughters of Charity of St Vincent de Paul	2	0	0	0	0	0	**2**	0	0	0	**2**
Daughters of Jesus	1	0	0	0	0	0	**1**	0	0	0	**1**
Daughters of Mary and Joseph	1	0	0	0	0	0	**1**	0	0	0	**1**
Daughters of Mary Help of Christians	5	0	0	0	0	0	**5**	0	0	0	**5**
Daughters of the Holy Spirit	4	0	0	0	0	0	**4**	0	0	0	**4**
De La Salle Brothers	5	0	0	0	0	0	**5**	0	0	0	**5**
Dominican Sisters of St Catherine of Siena of Oakford	1	0	0	0	0	0	**1**	0	0	0	**1**
Dominican Sisters of Zimbabwe	2	0	0	0	0	0	**2**	0	0	0	**2**
Dominicans	5	0	0	0	0	0	**5**	0	0	0	**5**
Faithful Companions of Jesus	5	0	0	0	0	0	**5**	0	0	0	**5**
Fidei Donum Priests	18	0	0	0	0	0	**18**	0	0	0	**18**
Franciscan Conventuals	2	0	0	0	0	0	**2**	0	0	0	**2**
Franciscan Fathers and Brothers	3	0	0	0	0	0	**3**	0	0	0	**3**
Franciscan Missionaries of Mary	10	0	0	0	0	0	**10**	0	0	0	**10**
Franciscan Missionaries of the Divine Motherhood	17	0	0	0	0	0	**17**	0	0	0	**17**
Franciscan Missionary Sisters of St Joseph	3	0	0	0	0	0	**3**	0	0	0	**3**
Holy Ghost Fathers	5	0	0	0	0	0	**5**	0	0	0	**5**
Institute of Charity	2	0	0	0	0	0	**2**	0	0	0	**2**
Medical Missionaries of Mary	5	0	0	0	0	0	**5**	0	0	0	**5**
Mercy Sisters of the Union of Great Britain	2	0	0	0	0	0	**2**	0	0	0	**2**
Mill Hill Missionaries	26	0	0	0	0	0	**26**	0	0	0	**26**
Missionaries of Africa (White Fathers)	20	0	0	0	0	0	**20**	0	0	0	**20**
Missionaries of Charity	2	0	0	0	0	0	**2**	0	0	0	**2**
Missionary Sisters of Our Lady of Africa	2	0	0	0	0	0	**2**	0	0	0	**2**
Missionary Sisters of St Columban	1	0	0	0	0	0	**1**	0	0	0	**1**
Missionary Society of St Columban	5	0	0	0	0	0	**5**	0	0	0	**5**
Montfort Fathers	2	0	0	0	0	0	**2**	0	0	0	**2**
Our Lady of Charity of the Good Shepherd	0	20	0	0	5	2	**27**	2	0	80	**109**
Redemptorists	3	0	0	0	0	0	**3**	0	0	0	**3**
Religious of Jesus and Mary	1	0	0	0	0	0	**1**	0	0	0	**1**
Religious of the Assumption	2	1	0	0	0	0	**3**	0	0	0	**3**
St Joseph's Hospice Association	2	0	0	0	0	0	**2**	0	0	0	**2**
St Patrick's Missionary Society	1	0	0	0	0	0	**1**	0	0	0	**1**
Salesian Fathers and Brothers	13	0	0	0	0	0	**13**	0	0	0	**13**
Servite Friars	3	0	0	0	0	0	**3**	0	0	0	**3**
Sisters of Charity of Our Lady of Evron	2	0	0	0	0	0	**2**	0	0	0	**2**
Sisters of Charity of St Jeanne Antide Thouret	1	0	0	0	0	0	**1**	0	0	0	**1**
Sisters of Charity of St Paul	3	0	0	0	0	0	**3**	0	0	0	**3**
Sisters of Christ	3	0	0	0	0	0	**3**	0	0	0	**3**
Sisters of Christian Instruction	2	0	0	0	0	0	**2**	0	0	0	**2**
Sisters of Notre Dame de Namur	12	0	0	0	0	0	**12**	0	0	0	**12**
Sisters of Our Lady of Charity	1	0	0	0	0	0	**1**	0	0	0	**1**
Sisters of Providence, Rosminians	3	0	0	0	0	0	**3**	0	0	0	**3**
Sisters of St Clare	2	0	0	0	0	0	**2**	0	0	0	**2**
Sisters of St Joseph Annecy	2	0	0	0	0	0	**2**	0	0	0	**2**

	OMW	CCU	OCU	SEC	UKE	HUC	SUK	UKO	ASS	RET	Total UK
Sisters of St Joseph of Cluny	1	0	0	0	0	0	**1**	0	0	0	**1**
Sisters of St Marie Madeleine Postel	1	0	0	0	0	0	**1**	0	0	0	**1**
Sisters of St Mary of Namur	2	0	0	0	0	0	**2**	0	0	0	**2**
Sisters of the Cross and Passion	3	0	0	0	0	0	**3**	0	0	0	**3**
Sisters of the Holy Family of Bordeaux	4	0	0	0	0	0	**4**	0	0	0	**4**
Sisters of the Sacred Heart of Jesus and Mary	5	0	0	0	0	0	**5**	0	0	0	**5**
Society of African Missions	4	0	0	0	0	0	**4**	0	0	0	**4**
Society of Mary	4	0	0	0	0	0	**4**	0	0	0	**4**
Society of the Divine Saviour	2	0	0	0	0	0	**2**	0	0	0	**2**
Society of the Holy Child Jesus	5	0	0	0	0	0	**5**	0	0	0	**5**
Society of the Sacred Heart	1	0	0	0	0	0	**1**	0	0	0	**1**
Ursuline Sisters	3	0	0	0	0	0	**3**	0	0		**3**
Volunteer Missionary Movement	19	0	0	0	2	0	**21**	0	0	0	**21**
Direct Sending Churches											
All Nations Church	4	0	0	0	0	0	**4**	0	0	0	**4**
Basingstoke Community Church	14	0	0	0	0	0	**14**	0	0	0	**14**
Biggin Hill Christian Fellowship	5	0	0	0	5	0	**5**	0	0	0	**5**
Echoes of Service	354	4	0	8	2	0	**368**	8	0	0	**376**
Hollybush Christian Fellowship	9	0	0	0	0	0	**9**	0	0	0	**9**
Ichthus Christian Fellowship	9	0	0	0	0	0	**9**	0	0	0	**9**
Interdenominational/Non-denominational											
Acts Military Ministries International	0	0	0	0	7	0	**7**	1	0	0	**8**
Acre Gospel Mission	14	0	0	0	1	0	**15**	0	0	0	**15**
Action International Ministries (UK)	5	0	0	0	2	0	**7**	4	3	0	**14**
Agapé	10	9	57	0	6	28	**110**	22	28	0	**160**
AIM International	90	2	0	0	5	11	**108**	7	0	0	**115**
Albania Evangelical Mission	5	0	0	0	1	1	**7**	0	0	0	**7**
Arab World Ministries	58	4	13	0	5	1	**81**	8	0	31	**120**
BCM International	2	0	11	0	0	1	**14**	0	0	0	**14**
Belgian Evangelical Mission	16	0	0	0	2	0	**18**	0	0	0	**18**
British & International Sailors' Society	0	0	0	0	0	5	**5**	37	0	6	**48**
Child Evangelical Fellowship	0	0	0	0	2	11	**13**	3	0	0	**16**
Christian and Missionary Alliance	4	0	4	0	1	0	**9**	0	14	0	**23**
Christian Witness to Israel	1	4	0	0	1	0	**6**	6	0	0	**12**
Christians in Action	3	0	2	2	0	0	**7**	2	0	0	**9**
CLC	4	0	46	0	7	0	**57**	1	0	26	**84**
Emmanuel International	54	0	0	0	1	0	**55**	3	0	0	**58**
European Christian Mission	39	0	0	0	3	3	**45**	5	2	2	**54**
European Missionary Fellowship	9	0	0	0	2	2	**3**	2	0	8	**23**
Evangelical Action (Brazil)	4	0	0	0	0	1	**5**	0	0	0	**5**
Feba	7	0	0	0	8	2	**17**	26	0	0	**43**
France Mission Trust	18	0	0	0	2	0	**20**	1	0	0	**21**
Frontiers	78	0	0	4	3	0	**85**	15	0	0	**100**
Frontline Trust	2	0	0	0	1	0	**3**	1	0	0	**4**
Global Outreach UK	14	13	0	0	1	0	**28**	1	0	0	**29**
Go to the Nations Link	0	0	0	0	2	25	**27**	0	0	0	**27**
Gorakhpur Nurseries Fellowship	2	0	0	0	0	2	**4**	0	0	1	**5**
Great Lakes Outreach	2	0	0	0	0	0	**2**	1	0	0	**3**
HCJB-UK	9	0	2	0	1	2	**14**	5	0	0	**19**
International Fellowship of Evangelical Students	41	0	0	0	4	2	**46**	18	0	0	**64**

UK Mission Agencies and Mission Workers

	OMW	CCU	OCU	SEC	UKE	HUC	SUK	UKO	ASS	FET	Total UK
International Nepal Fellowship	29	0	0	0	0	0	**29**	6	0	0	**35**
International Teams UK	11	9	0	0	0	0	**20**	0	0	0	**20**
Interserve	105	33	6	0	6	2	**152**	16	0	0	**168**
Ireland	17	0	0	0	1	1	**19**	3	0	0	**22**
Scotland	18	0	0	0	0	4	**22**	0	0	0	**22**
Janz Team UK	4	0	0	0	1	1	**6**	1	0	0	**7**
Japan Christian Link	3	0	1	0	1	0	**5**	0	3	4	**12**
Japan Good News Ministries	1	0	0	0	1	0	**2**	0	0	0	**2**
Japan Mission	3	0	0	0	0	0	**3**	1	0	0	**4**
Language Recordings UK	2	0	0	0	2	2	**6**	0	0	0	**6**
Latin Link	99	0	2	0	4	4	**109**	11	0	0	**120**
The Leprosy Mission	2	0	0	0	3	15	**20**	18	0	0	**38**
International Office	6	0	0	0	4	0	**10**	18	6	0	**34**
Northern Ireland	0	0	0	0	3	0	**3**	2	0	0	**5**
Scotland	5	0	0	0	1	1	**7**	4	0	0	**11**
Lightforce International	5	0	0	0	1	0	**6**	1	0	0	**7**
The Messianic Testimony	12	3	4	0	1	0	**20**	2	0	6	**28**
Middle East Christian Outreach	43	0	0	0	3	2	**48**	2	0	0	**50**
Middle East Media	0	0	0	0	3	2	**5**	1	0	0	**6**
Mission Africa (Qua Iboe Fellowship)	16	0	0	0	2	1	**19**	4	0	0	**23**
Mission Aviation Fellowship UK	29	0	0	0	5	8	**42**	36	0	2	**80**
Mission to Military Garrisons Inc	7	0	5	0	1	0	**13**	1	0	0	**14**
The Navigators	38	11	82	0	8	0	**139**	0	0	0	**139**
New Foundations Medical Charity	11	0	0	0	1	0	**12**	0	0	0	**12**
New Testament Missionary Union	1	0	0	0	0	0	**1**	1	1	0	**3**
New Tribes Mission	86	0	0	0	4	17	**107**	8	0	2	**117**
OMF International (UK)	184	6	1	7	8	6	**212**	28	0	68	**308**
OMS International	25	0	0	0	2	10	**37**	7	0	4	**48**
Operation Mobilisation	207	13	19	0	32	32	**303**	31	3	6	**343**
People International	17	0	0	0	1	1	**19**	2	0	0	**21**
Red Sea Mission Team	4	2	0	0	1	0	**7**	0	5	0	**12**
Sahara Dessert Mission	0	0	0	0	0	0	**0**	0	4	0	**4**
SAO Cambodia	9	0	0	0	2	0	**11**	1	4	0	**16**
SAT-7	2	0	0	0	1	0	**3**	2	14	0	**19**
Seamen's Christian Friend Society	2	15	0	0	2	0	**19**	2	0	4	**25**
Servants to Asia's Poor	0	0	0	0	0	1	**1**	0	0	0	**1**
Signpost International	2	0	0	0	7	0	**9**	7	0	0	**16**
SIM UK	125	6	0	0	5	4	**140**	0	7	7	**154**
Spanish Gospel Mission	8	0	0	0	1	0	**9**	1	0	0	**10**
Tearfund	37	0	0	0	11	33	**81**	235	0	0	**316**
Trans World Radio	2	0	0	0	1	3	**6**	9	0	0	**15**
UFM Worldwide	75	0	0	5	2	4	**86**	6	0	0	**92**
WEC International	96	10	5	9	4	76	**200**	30	0	0	**230**
World Gospel Mission	2	0	0	0	0	6	**8**	2	0	4	**14**
World Horizons	56	0	1	2	4	0	**63**	28	0	0	**91**
World Outreach	2	2	0	0	1	0	**5**	0	0	0	**5**
Wycliffe Bible Translators	265	0	0	0	20	20	**305**	32	0	15	**352**
Youth with a Mission	150	49	101	3	26	51	**380**	0	0	0	**380**
Zambesi Mission	7	0	0	0	1	2	**10**	1	1	0	**12**
Methodist											
Methodist Church World Office	64	0	0	0	6	0	**70**	8	0	0	**78**
Pentecostal											
Apostolic Church Missionary Movement	10	0	0	0	1	2	**13**	0	0	0	**13**

	OMW	CCU	OCU	SEC	UKE	HUC	SUK	UKO	ASS	RET	Total UK
Assemblies of God World Ministries	70	1	0	4	19	0	**94**	1	4	0	**99**
Central African Missions	14	0	0	0	0	0	**14**	2	0	0	**16**
Elim International Missions	71	0	0	0	1	0	**72**	2	0	0	**74**
Focus on Israel	3	0	0	0	8	0	**11**	1	0	0	**12**
Presbyterian											
Church of Scotland World Mission Council	41	0	0	0	6	0	**47**	8	0	20	**75**
Free Church of Scotland International Missions Board	20	0	0	0	1	0	**21**	0	0	0	**21**
Free Presbyterian Church of Scotland Mission Committee	15	0	0	0	8	0	**23**	0	15	3	**41**
Free Presbyterian Church of Ulster Mission Board	69	26	0	0	1	0	**96**	1	0	0	**97**
Presbyterian Church in Ireland Overseas Board	44	0	0	2	3	0	**49**	5	0	0	**54**
Presbyterian Church of Wales Mission Board	4	3	18	0	1	21	**47**	1	0	0	**48**
Salvation Army											
Salvation Army International	71	0	3	4	2	2	**82**	7	0	0	**89**
Seventh-day Adventists											
World-Wide Advent Missions	11	0	0	15	2	0	**28**	6	0	0	**34**
United Reformed Church											
United Reformed Church International Relations	4	0	0	0	2	0	**6**	0	0	0	**6**

MISSION SENDING CHURCHES (DIRECT)

***All Nations Church**, Bonneville Centre, 12 Poynders Road, London SW4 8NY
☎020 8673 0639 🖷020 8673 0639
E: office@allnationsbc.plus.com
Web: www.allnationschurch.co.uk
Evangelism, church planting in Balham, Brixton and Clapham, and overseas in India, Africa, Bangladesh.
Team Leader: Rev Les Ball. Executive staff 2, Other staff 3, Serving missionaries 4. ***CC*** No.249703. Began 1958; Baptist. No magazine. Turnover £200,000 to year end Dec 04.

***Basingstoke Community Churches**, The Centre, 18 Winchester Street, Basingstoke RG21 7DY
☎01256 812 708 🖷01256 300 149
E: office@bccnet.org.uk
Web: www.bccnet.org.uk
Local churches sending their own people with an Antioch call to go to the nations.
Church Adminstrator: Mr Mike Poulton. *Chairman of Area Council:* Mr Phil Norris. Serving missionaries 14. ***CC*** No.1067316. Began 1861; re-formed 1978; Salt & Light Ministries. No magazine. Turnover £871,973 to year end Mar 00.

†*Biggin Hill Christian Fellowship, Main Road, Biggin Hill, Westerham TN16 3BA
☎01959 571 667 🖷01959 570 215
E: info@bhcf.org.uk
Web: www.bhcf.org.uk
Senior Pastor: Mr Gareth Wales. Serving missionaries 5. ***CC*** Began n/a; Baptist/New Frontiers. No magazine. Turnover £160,000 to year end Dec 00.

†*Coventry Christian Fellowship, 70 David Road, Coventry CV1 2BW
☎024 7622 6309
Leader: Mr John Patterson. Serving missionaries 10. ***CC*** No.510955. Began 1977; non-denominational. No magazine. Turnover n/a.

***Echoes of Service**, 124 Wells Road, Bath BA2 3AH
☎01225 310 893 / 480 635
🖷01225 480 134
E: echoes@echoes.org.uk or echoes_of_service@msn.com
Web: www.echoes.org.uk
Managing Editor: John H Burness. *Advisory Editor:* Andrew J Street. Executive staff 2, Serving missionaries 352. ***CC*** No.234556. Began 1872 (first issue of magazine); Christian Brethren). Magazine: *Echoes* (7,000 monthly). Turnover £3,500,000 to year end Dec 00

***Hollybush Christian Fellowship**, Newsham, Thirsk YO7 4DH
☎01845 587 386
M: 07974 256 379
🖷01845 587 103
E: HollybushCF@aol.com
Web: www.hollybushchristianfellowship.com
Resourcing the church through mission.
Associate Pastor: Mr Andy Newlove. *Administrator:* Mrs Tracey Newlove. Serving missionaries 1, Short-term missionaries 9. ***CC*** Began 1967; non-denominational. No magazine. Turnover £120,000 to year end Dec 02.

***Ichthus Christian Fellowship**, 7 Greenwich Quay, Clarence Road, Greenwich, London SE8 3EY
☎020 8694 7171 🖷020 8694 7172
E: admin@ichthus.org.uk
Web: www.ichthus.org.uk
Leader: Mr Roger Forster. Serving missionaries 40. ***CC*** No.1099412. Began 1974; non-denominational. No magazine. Turnover n/a.

Lifeline Network International, Lifeline House, Neville Road, Dagenham RM8 3QS
☎020 8597 2900 🖷020 8597 1990
E: lni@lifelinenetwork.org
Web: www.lifelinenetwork.org
Team Leader: Mr John Singleton. *UK Coordinator:* Miss A McIntyre. Executive staff 1, Serving missionaries n/a. ***CC*** No.1062615. Began 1981; non-denominational. (Previously Community Resources). Magazine: *Network News*(Circulation & frequency n/a). Turnover n/a.

MISSION AGENCIES

For other Roman Catholic Orders see Religious Orders (Roman Catholic) on Page 190, Retreat Houses on Page 72.

Accts Military Ministries International, Havelock House, Barrack Road, Aldershot GU11 3NP
☎01252 311 222
🖷01252 350 722
E: headoffice@acctsmmi.com
Web: www.acctsmmi.com
Serving Christians and chaplaincies in the military worldwide, including evangelism.
Hon Executive Chairman: Major Homfray Vines. *Home Director:* Lt Col Mike Paterson OBE. Executive staff 7, Currently no UK missionaries serving overseas. ***CC*** No.284203. Began 1974; interdenominational. No magazine. Turnover £180,000 to year end Mar 05.

†Acre Gospel Mission, 33 Ravensdene Park, Belfast BT6 0DA
☎028 9064 2638
🖷028 9049 2358
E: info@acremission.co.uk
Web: www.acremission.co.uk
Church planting in Brazil, Portugal and Lanzarote.
President: Dr T H Geddis. *Coordinator:* Stephen Smith. Executive staff 1, Serving missionaries 14. ***CC*** No.XN 47625. Began 1937; interdenominational. Magazine: *Insight* (6,000 quarterly). Turnover £245,718 to year end Dec 01.

***Action International Ministries (UK)**, PO Box 144, Wallasey CH44 5WE
☎0151 630 2451
E: actionuk@btinternet.com
Web: www.actionuk.org
Reaching urban poor of the world through evangelism, discipleship, social development projects especially amongst street children.
UK Director: Mr Ingo Abraham. Executive staff 1, Serving missionaries 5, Other staff 4. ***CC*** No.1058661. Began 1988; interdenominational. (Previously ACTION UK). Magazines: *ACTIONPOINT* (1,500 quarterly), *Street Children* (1,500 every two months). Turnover n/a.

For further information see lists on Pages 263 - 281

***Action Partners**, Bawtry Hall, Bawtry, Doncaster DN10 6JH
☎01302 710 750 🖷01302 719 399
E: info@actionpartners.org.uk
Web: www.actionpartners.org.uk
Mobilising teams, initiating church planting and resourcing cross-cultural witness; UK and abroad.
Director: Mr Gerard Pontier. Executive staff 1, Serving missionaries 16, Admin staff 4. ***CC*** No.1037154. Began 1904; interdenominational. (Previously The Sudan United Mission (SUM)). Magazine: *Interface* (3,000 every four months). Turnover £558,000 to year end Dec 04.

***Agapé**, Fairgate House, Kings Road, Tyseley, Birmingham B11 2AA
☎0121 765 4404 🖷0121 765 4065
E: info@agape.org.uk
Web: www.agape.org.uk
Evangelism and discipleship in different segments of society: schools, universities, businesses, sports, arts, family life.
National Director: Mr David Wilson. Staff 110. Serving missionaries 76. ***CC*** No.258421 Began 1967; interdenominational. Part of Campus Crusade for Christ International. Magazine: *Move* (12,000 every six months). Turnover £2,500,000 to year end Jun 05.

***AIM International**, Halifax Place, Nottingham NG1 1QN
☎0115 983 8120
E: uk@aimeurope.net
Web: www.aimeurope.net
Church planting in unevangelised areas and helping churches grow, assisting church development projects.
UK Director: Rev John Brand. *International Director:* Rev Lanny Arensen. *Overseas Personnel Director:* Mr Bill Rettie. Executive staff 5, Serving missionaries 92, Other staff 19. ***CC*** No.1096364. Began 1895; interdenominational. (Previously Africa Inland Mission International). Magazine: *The African Connection* (5,000 quarterly). Turnover £2,324,325 to year end Dec 04.
Northern England: 21 Serpentine Road, Kendal LA9 4PF
E: northengland@aimeurope.net
☎01539 738 818
Ireland: 279 Woodstock Road, Belfast BT6 8PR
E: ireland@aimeurope.net
☎028 9045 3497
Scotland: 265 St Vincent Street, Glasgow G2 7LA
E: scotland@aimeurope.net
☎0141 221 4541

Albanian Evangelical Mission, 29 Bridge Street, Penybryn, Wrexham LL13 7HP
☎01978 290 138
E: office@aemission.org
Web: www.aemission.org
Church planting, orphanage work, training Christian workers, literature publication in Albania; conferences, prayer in UK.
Director: David M Young. *Treasurer & Hon Assistant Director:* David J Hickman. Executive staff 2, Serving missionaries 5. ***CC*** No.1036807. Began 1986; interdenominational. No magazine. Turnover £142,000 to year end Mar 03.

***Apostolic Church Missionary Movement**, 17 Tawe Business Village, Phoenix Way, Enterprise Park, Swansea SA7 9LA
☎01792 790 300 🖷01792 790 363
E: admin@apostolic-church.org
Web: www.apostolic-church.org
Chairman, Overseas Board: Rev Peter Vincent. *Administrator:* Rev Andrew Saunders. Executive staff 7, Serving missionaries 10, Admin staff 2. ***CC*** No.284789. Began 1922; Apostolic. Magazine: *Christian Lifestyle* (1,200 quarterly). Turnover £1,458,446 to year end Mar 03.

***Arab World Ministries**, PO Box 51, Loughborough LE11 0ZQ
☎01509 239 525 🖷01509 264 820
E: awmuk@awm.org
Web: www.awmuk.org
Building Christ's Church among Muslims of the Arab world.
National Director: Mr Michael Thomas. *Promotion Managers:* Mr Andrew Reed and Alex Ison. *Member Care Manager:* Mr Alasdair McLaren. Executive staff 5, Serving missionaries 75, Other staff 9. ***CC*** No.1059106. Began 1881; interdenominational. Magazine: *Frontline* (8,500 ten times a year). Turnover £1,500,000 to year end Dec 04.
Northern Ireland: PO Box 1010, Ballymena BT42 1WZ
E: eawm_ireland@a2bmail.net
☎028 2587 1010
International Office PO Box 4006, Worthing BN13 1AP
☎01903 215 234 🖷01903 215 456
E: reception@wornet.org

***Assemblies of God World Ministries**, PO Box 7634, Nottingham NG11 6ZY
☎0115 921 7272 🖷0115 921 7273
E: worldministries@aog.org.uk
Web: www.worldministries.org.uk
General Director: Rev J R Hibbert. Executive staff 19, Serving missionaries 76, Other staff 12. ***CC*** No.1032245. Began 1909; Assemblies of God. Magazine: *CoMission* (4,000 quarterly). Turnover n/a.

Associates of Mill Hill Missionaries, St Joseph's College, Lawrence Street, Mill Hill, London NW7 4JX
☎020 8959 3222 🖷020 8959 8493
E: mhmgc@lineone.net
Web: www.millhillmissionaries.org
Taking the Gospel to the marginalised, crossing economic, cultural and religious boundaries.
Coordinator: Brother Jos Boerkamp MHM. Executive staff 1, Currently no UK missionaries serving overseas. Lay associates 15. ***CC*** No.220690. Began 1970, Mill Hill Society founded 1866; Roman Catholic. Lay arm of St Joseph's Missionary Society, Mill Hill. No magazine. Turnover n/a.

Assumptionists Fathers and Brothers, 16 Nightingale Road, Hitchin SG5 1QS
☎01462 457 673 🖷01462 459 126
E: assumptionists@freeuk.com
Provincial Superior: Rev Robert Henshaw. Serving missionaries 1, Community n/a. ***CC*** Began n/a; Roman Catholic. No magazine. Turnover n/a.

Augustinian Recollects, 18 Cheniston Gardens, Kensington, London W8 6TQ
☎020 7937 7681 🖷020 7937 7681
Web: www.btinternet.com/~augustinian.recollects/
Vicar Provincial: Rev Dennis Caddle. *Prior General:* Rev Javier Guerra. Community 18. Serving missionaries 1. ***CC*** Began 1932; Roman Catholic. Magazine: *Friends Letter* (8,000 seven times a year). Turnover n/a.

Augustinians, Austin Friars, 15 Dorville Crescent, London W6 0HH
☎020 8748 1529 🖷020 8748 1529
E: augprov.engscot@btinternet.com
Web: www.augustinians.co.uk
Education, secondary and tertiary; pastoral work; spiritual direction; clerical formation.
Provincial Superior: Rev David Middleton. Community 30, Serving missionaries 1. ***CC*** No.233010. Began 1244; Roman Catholic. No magazine. Turnover n/a.

†Baptist Missions, The Baptist Centre, 19 Hillsborough Road, Craigavon BT67 0HG
☎028 9261 9267 🖷028 9261 0150
E: bm@thebaptistcentre.org
Missions Secretary: Rev Derek Baxter. Executive staff 1, Serving missionaries 43, Other staff 2. ***CC*** Began 1888; Baptist. Magazine: *Info-Mission* - in *The Irish Baptist* (3,000 monthly). Turnover £630,000 to year end Dec 02.

BCM International, 39a Swiss Road, Weston-super-Mare BS23 3AY
☎01934 413 484 🖷01934 413 484
E: bcmuk@aol.com
Web: www.bcm.org.uk
Mobilising, training and assisting local churches to reach children with the Gospel.
UK Director: Rev Bert Weenink. *Financial Secretary:* Mr Joe Dukes. Executive staff 2, Serving missionaries 13. ***CC*** No.1044539. Began 1936; interdenominational. Magazine: *Newslink* (800 every four months). Turnover £118,733 to year end Dec 04.

***Belgian Evangelical Mission**, 137 Lyndhurst Avenue, Whitton, Twickenham TW2 6BH
☎020 8894 0912
E: bemuk@b-e-m.org
Web: www.b-e-m.org
Evangelism and church planting in Belgium.
British Coordinators: Mr & Mrs Brian & Carol Stockman. *Director, France:* Mr Eric Zander. *Director, Flemish:* Mr Wilfred Goossens. Executive staff 2, Serving missionaries 16. ***CC*** No.247192. Began 1919; interdenominational. Magazine: *Spotlight Belgium* (2,500 quarterly). Turnover £178,696 to year end Jan 05.

***BMS World Mission**, PO Box 49, 129 Broadway, Didcot OX11 8XA
☎01235 517 700 🖷01235 517 601
E: mail@bmsworldmission.org
Web: www.bmsworldmission.org
Sharing life in all its fullness with the world's peoples.
General Director: Rev Dr Alistair Brown. *Director for Mission:* Rev David Kerrigan. *Director of Communications:* Mr Mark Craig. Executive staff 5, Serving missionaries 188, Other staff 70. ***CC*** No.233782. Began 1792; Baptist. (Previously Baptist Missionary Society). Magazine: *World Mission* (15,500 every two months). Turnover £6,900,000 to year end Oct 05.

British & International Sailors' Society, 350 Shirley Road, Southampton SO15 3HY
☎023 8051 5950 🖷023 8051 5951
E: chaplains@biss.org.uk
Web: www.biss.org.uk
Caring for merchant seafarers and their dependants.
General Secretary: Mr Alan Smith. *Principal Chaplain:* Rev David Potterton. Executive staff 5, Currently no UK missionaries serving overseas, Other staff 131. ***CC*** No.237778. Began 1818; interdenominational. Magazine: *Chart & Compass* (45,000 half-yearly). Turnover £3,834,000 to year end Dec 01.

Brothers of the Sacred Heart, Watling House, 8 King Harry Lane, St Albans AL3 4AW
☎01727 861 969
Head Brother: Br Donald Tardif. Community 8, Serving missionaries 1. ***CC*** No.231733. Began 1955; Roman Catholic. No magazine. Turnover n/a.

Capuchin Franciscans (Order of Friars Minor Capuchin), Provincial Curia, Franciscan Friary, Carlton Road, Erith DA8 1DN
☎01322 444 963 🖷01322 438 361
E: capcuriagb@0800dial.com
Web: www.capuchin-franciscans-gb.org.uk
Provincial Minister: Br Anthony McDowell. Community 36, Serving missionaries 1. ***CC*** No.231143. Began 1873; Roman Catholic. No magazine. Turnover n/a.

***Central African Missions**, 355 Blackpool Road, Preston PR2 3AB
☎01772 717 830 🖷01772 719 322
E: admin@camafrica.fsnet.co.uk
Web: www.camafrica.org
UK Administrator: Rev Ivor D Pepper. *UK Director:* Mr David Garrard. Executive staff 2, Serving missionaries 14, Other staff 1. ***CC*** No.1049246. Began 1915; Pentecostal. (Previously Zaire Evangelistic Mission & Congo Evangelistic Mission). Magazine: *Contact* (3,200 monthly). Turnover £392,469 to year end Sep 04.

Child Evangelism Fellowship of Britain, 478 Victoria Road, Glasgow G42 8YJ
☎0141 423 8188 🖷0141 422 2272
E: enquiries@cefbritain.org
Web: www.cefbritain.org
Working in the UK and worldwide in over 150 countries.
National Chairman: Mr Ron McLean. *National Directors:* Mr & Mrs Raymond Barr. Executive staff 6, Currently no UK missionaries serving overseas, Other staff 4. ***CC*** No.235080. Began 1956; non-denominational. Magazine: *Teach Kids!* (35,000 every two months). Turnover n/a.

Christian and Missionary Alliance, 59 Crighton, Oxclose, Washington NE38 0LD
☎Number not supplied
Facilitating mission-minded church planting in UK and overseas; short and long term missionary sending.
Director: Rev Chris Williams. Executive staff 1, Serving missionaries 4, Other staff 4. ***CC*** No.802990. Began 1973; interdenominational. No magazine. Turnover £104,787 to year end Jan 00.

***Christian Witness to Israel**, 166 Main Road, Sundridge, Sevenoaks TN14 6EL
☎01959 565 955 🖷01959 565 966
E: hq@cwi.org.uk
Web: www.cwi.org.uk or www.shalom.org.uk
Proclaiming the Gospel "to the Jew first".
General Secretary: Mr Mike Moore. *Office Manager:* Mr Andrew Quinney. *Chairman of Council:* Mr Rodney Lissenden. Executive staff 1, Serving missionaries 5, Other staff 5. ***CC*** No.271323. Began 1842; interdenominational. Magazine: *CWI Herald* (15,000 quarterly). Turnover £631,250 to year end Mar 05.

***Christians in Action**, 67 Melfort Road, Thornton Heath CR7 7RT
☎020 8684 1603 🖷020 8684 1603
E: christiansinaction@blueyonder.co.uk
Discipling the nations through practical training and church planting both at home and abroad.
UK Director: Rev Freddie C Roberson Jr. *International President, USA:* Rev Dave Konold. Executive staff 1, Serving missionaries 7, Other staff 2. ***CC*** No.257785. Began 1965; interdenominational. No magazine. Turnover £113,000 to year end Mar 05.

***Church Mission Society**, Partnership House, 157 Waterloo Road, London SE1 8UU
☎020 7928 8681 🖷020 7401 3215
E: info@cms-uk.org
Web: www.cms-uk.org
Working in partnership with local churches in leadership training, community development, health care and teaching.
General Secretary: Rev Canon Tim Dakin. *International Mission Director:* Rev Canon Mark Oxbrow. *Head of Communications:* John Martin. Executive staff 55, Serving missionaries 184. ***CC*** No.220297. Began 1799; Anglican. (Previously Church Missionary Society). Magazine: *Yes* (25,000 every four months). Turnover £7,900,000 to year end Jan 05.

Church Mission Society Ireland (CMS Ireland), Church of Ireland House, 61 Donegall Street, Belfast BT1 2QH
☎028 9032 4581
🖷028 9032 1756
E: belfastoffice@cmsireland.org
Web: www.cmsireland.org or www.youth.cmsireland.org
Partnership with Anglican dioceses in 15 countries, working in evangelism, church growth and development programmes.
General Secretary: Rev Canon Cecil H Wilson. *Youth Officer:* Miss Sulie Currie. *Mission Development Officer:* Mr Brian Lavery. Executive staff [illegible], Serving missionaries 25, Admin staff 3. ***CC*** No.XN 48809. Began 1814; Anglican. (Previously Church Missionary Society Ireland (Name Changed 2004)). Incorporating Mid Africa Ministry, Ireland. Magazine: *InMission* (5 000 quarterly). Turnover £1,237,000 to year end Oct 04.

Church of Scotland World Mission Council, 121 George Street, Edinburgh EH2 4YN
☎0131 225 5722
🖷0131 226 6121
E: info@world-mission.org
Web: www.world-mission.org
Council Secretary: Rev Prof Kenneth R Ross. *Personnel Manager:* Miss Sheila Ballantyne. Executive staff 6, Serving missionaries 41, Other staff 8. ***CC*** Began 1796; Church of Scotland. (Previously Church of Scotland Board of World Mission). Magazine *Insight* (Circulation & frequency n/a). Turnover n/a.

***Church's Ministry Among Jewish People**, 30c Clarence Road, St Albans AL1 4JJ
☎01727 833 114
🖷01727 848 312
E: enquiries@cmj.org.uk
Web: www.cmj.org.uk
Seeking to lead Jewish people to faith in Jesus the Messiah.
General Director: Rev Tony Higton. Executive staff 1, Serving missionaries 1[illegible], Other staff 5. ***CC*** No.223519. Began 1809; Anglican. Magazine: *Shalom* (3,500 every four months). Turnover £643,000 to year end Dec 02.

Claretian Missionaries, 68 Grange Park Road, Leyton, London E10 5ES
☎020 8539 2908
🖷020 8928 1057
E: provincial@claret.org.uk
Web: www.claret.org.uk
Provincial Superior: Rev Christopher Cutler. *Superior General, Italy:* Rev Aquilino Bocos. Executive staff 1[illegible], Serving missionaries 2. ***CC*** No.234026. Began 1849; Roman Catholic. Magazine: *New Tidings* (2,000 every four months). Turnover n/a.

For further information see lists on Pages 263 - 281

***CLC (Christian Literature Crusade)**, Shawton House, 792 Hagley Road West, Oldbury B68 0PJ
☎0121 422 5755
🖷0121 423 2298
E: clcukr@aol.com
Web: www.clc.org.uk
Making evangelical literature available so that people may come to faith and maturity in Christ.
UK National Leader: Mr Guy Cornell. *International Leader, UK:* Mr Neil Wardrope. Serving missionaries 50. ***CC*** No.1015793. Began 1941; interdenominational. Magazine: *CLC World* (6,000 every two months). Turnover n/a.

†COI International Christian Outreach, Shaftesbury Christian Centre, Christy's Lane, Shaftesbury SP7 8PH
☎01747 858 588
M: 07905 218 502
🖷01747 858 588
E: coi@waitrose.com
Facilitating short-term missions and teaching English as a means of sharing the Gospel.
UK Director: Mr Andrew White. Executive staff 1, Serving missionaries 36. Began 1999; non-denominational. No magazine. Turnover n/a.

Columban Lay Missionaries, 66 Newland Road, Silvertown, London E16 2HN
☎020 7059 0253
E: info@laymission.freeserve.co.uk
Web: www.columban.org
Pastoral work in Roman Catholic communities in Asia and Latin America.
Coordinator: Ms Susie Brouard. Executive staff 1, Serving missionaries 2, Other staff 2. ***CC*** No.221594. Began 1982; Roman Catholic. Magazine: *Far East* (40,000 monthly, worldwide). Turnover £60,000 to year end Mar 99.

Comboni Missionaries (Verona Fathers), London Road, Sunningdale, Ascot SL5 0JY
☎01344 621 267
🖷01344 621 351
E: veronaf@globalnet.co.uk
Web: www.comboni.org.uk
Evangelism among disadvantaged people.
Provincial Superior: Rev Martin Devenish. Serving missionaries 5, Other staff 18. ***CC*** No.220240. Began 1867; Roman Catholic. Magazine: *Comboni Missions* (17,000 quarterly). Turnover n/a.

Comboni Missionary Sisters (Verona Sisters), 26 Blackboy Lane, London N15 3AR
☎020 8809 2893
🖷020 8809 2893
E: cmsprovlondon@aol.com
Provincial Superior: Sr Johann Macleod. Serving missionaries 2, Home staff 9. ***CC*** No.214864. Began 1872; Roman Catholic. No magazine. Turnover n/a.

Congregation of Christian Brothers, Woodeaves, Hale Barns, Altrincham WA15 0HF
☎0161 904 0786 🖷0161 903 9182
E: pgg.cfc@virgin.net
Web: www.christianbrothers.org.uk
Working in 32 countries on all five continents principally among poor and marginalized people.
English Province Leader: Br Patrick G Gordon. *Congregation Leader:* Br Philip Pinto. Serving missionaries 5. ***CC*** Began 1802; Roman Catholic. No magazine. Turnover n/a.

Congregation of Josephites, St George's College, Weybridge Road, Addlestone KT15 2QS
☎01932 839 452/470 🖷01932 842 268
Provincial Superior: Rev Paul Connor. Community n/a, Serving missionaries 1. ***CC*** No.312071. Began 1929; Roman Catholic. No magazine. Turnover £100,000 to year end Dec 98.

Congregation of La Sainte Union des Sacré-Coeurs, 53 Croftdown Road, London NW5 1EL
☎020 7482 7225 🖷020 7284 4760
Provincial Superior: Sr Evelyn Treacy. *Superior General, Italy:* Sr Carol Regan. Community n/a, Serving missionaries 3. ***CC*** No.233872. Began 1859; Roman Catholic. No magazine. Turnover n/a.

Congregation of Our Lady of the Missions, 108 Spencer Road, Wealdstone, Harrow HA3 7AR
☎020 8861 4174 🖷020 8424 2133
E: rndmsec@aol.com
Provincial Superior: Sr Margaret McKeown. *Superior General, Italy:* Sr Maureen McBride. Community n/a, Serving missionaries 3, ***CC*** Began 1870; Roman Catholic. No magazine. Turnover n/a.

Consolata Missionary Sisters, 13 The Avenue, London E11 2EE
☎020 8989 6186 🖷020 7837 2256
E: mc.london@mdcuk.freeserve.co.uk
Provincial Superior: Sr Celestia Quaranta. Community n/a, Currently no UK missionaries serving overseas. ***CC*** No.263229. Began 1910; Roman Catholic. No magazine. Turnover n/a.

***Crosslinks**, 251 Lewisham Way, London SE4 1XF
☎020 8691 6111 🖷020 8694 8023
E: info@crosslinks.org
Web: www.crosslinks.org
Evangelical agency taking God's word to God's world.
General Secretary: Rev Canon Andrew Lines. *President:* Rev Dr Chris Wright. Executive staff 5, Serving missionaries 75, Other staff 19. ***CC*** No.249986. Began 1922; Anglican. Magazine: *The Crosslinks Magazine* (10,000 quarterly). Turnover £2,323,000 to year end Dec 04.
Ireland: *Irish Coordinator:* To be appointed, 32 Montgomery Road, Belfast BT5 4NH
E: belfast@crosslinks.org
☎028 9079 6028 🖷 028 9079 2737

Crusade of the Holy Spirit, 464 Chester Road, Sutton Coldfield B73 5BP
☎0121 384 4280 🖷0121 328 8148
Missionary association providing education of priests and parish work in South America.
General Director: Rev Bernard Kelly. Community n/a, Serving missionaries 1. ***CC*** No.257147. Began 1966; Roman Catholic. No magazine. Turnover n/a.

Daughters of Charity of St Vincent de Paul, Provincial House, The Ridgeway, Mill Hill, London NW7 1EH
☎020 8906 3777 🖷020 8201 0542
E: londondc@aol.com
Web: www.daughtersofcharity.org.uk
Service/ministry among people suffering from various forms of poverty or handicap; 85 countries worldwide.
Provincial Superior: Sr Sarah King-Turner. Community n/a, Serving missionaries 2. ***CC*** No.236803. Began 1847; Roman Catholic. No magazine. Turnover n/a.

Daughters of Jesus, Brook House, 95a Uxbridge Road, Rickmansworth WD3 7DJ
☎01923 771 566 🖷01923 775 048
Provincial: Sr Teresa McMenamin. Community n/a, Serving missionaries 1. ***CC*** No.234925. Began 1904; Roman Catholic. No magazine. Turnover n/a.

Daughters of Mary and Joseph, 55 Fitzjames Avenue, Croydon CR0 5DN
☎020 8654 8041 🖷020 8655 4337
Provincial Superior: Sr Felicé Wright. Community n/a, Serving missionaries 1. ***CC*** No.232421. Began 1869; Roman Catholic. No magazine. Turnover n/a.

Daughters of St Paul, Middle Green, Slough SL3 6BS
☎01753 577 629 🖷01753 511 809
E: slough@pauline-uk.org
Web: www.pauline-uk.org
Provincial Superior: Sr Mary Connell. *Sister-in-charge:* Sr Rina Risitano. Community n/a. Currently no UK missionaries serving overseas. ***CC*** No.296042. Began 1955; Roman Catholic. No magazine. Turnover n/a.

Daughters of the Holy Spirit, 103 Harleston Road, Northampton NN5 7AQ
☎01604 587 423 🖷01604 587 423
E: provincial.office@virgin.net
Provincial Superior: Sr Regina Bond. *Superior General, France:* Sr Agnes Stephan. Serving missionaries 4, Community n/a. ***CC*** No.234520. Began 1902; Roman Catholic. No magazine. Turnover n/a.

Daughters of Wisdom (La Sagesse), 10 The Abbey, Romsey SO51 8EL
☎01794 516 129 🖷01794 518 702
E: provincial.house@southampton-net. co.uk
Provincial Superior: Sr Maureen Seddon. Community n/a, Currently no UK missionaries serving overseas. ***CC*** No.234184. Began 1891; Roman Catholic. (Previously Montfort Sisters, La Sagesse (Daughters of Wisdom)). No magazine. Turnover n/a.

For further information see lists on Pages 263 - 281

De La Salle Brothers, 140 Banbury Road, Oxford OX2 7BP
☎01865 311 332 🖷01865 554 356
E: ldwpuk@hotmail.com
Web: www.delasalle.org.uk
Provincial Superior: Br Sean Sellors. Community 80, Serving missionaries 5. ***CC*** No.232632. Began 1855; Roman Catholic. No magazine. Turnover n/a.

Dominican Sisters of St Catherine of Siena of Oakford, Dominican Convent, 34 Love Lane, Pinner HA5 3EX
☎020 7242 0240 🖷020 7905 4786
E: dominican.pinner@lineone.net
Teaching, nursing and residential homes for elderly people; clinics in Africa.
Provincial Superior: Sr Mary O'Rourke. Community n/a, Serving missionaries 1. ***CC*** No.233474. Began n/a; Roman Catholic. No magazine. Turnover n/a.

Dominican Sisters of Zimbabwe, 38 Hyde Vale, Greenwich, London SE10 8QH
☎020 8692 3382
E: sisters@dominican.fsnet.co.uk
Teaching, nursing, counselling, parish and social work.
Delegation Superior: Sr Martha Stilger. Community n/a, Serving missionaries 2. ***CC*** No.231237. Began 1890; Roman Catholic. No magazine. Turnover n/a.

Dominicans, St Dominic's Priory, Southampton Road, London NW5 4LB
☎020 7485 2760 🖷020 7485 2760
Web: www.english.op.org
Pastoral work in the West Indies, some teaching in the regional seminary.
Prior Provincial: Very Rev Allan White. *Master General, Italy:* Rev Timothy Radcliffe. Community n/a, Serving missionaries 5. ***CC*** No.231192. Began 1221; Roman Catholic. Magazine: *New Blackfriars* (Circulation n/a monthly). Turnover n/a.

O

***Eastern European Outreach**, PO Box 399, Margate CT9 2WE
☎0800 298 0126 or 01256 896 596
🖷01843 232 335
E: info@eeouk.org
Web: www.eeouk.org
Evangelism, child-sponsorship, relief goods, building, medical, youth camps, educational help worldwide, especially Eastern Europe.
International Supervisor: Rev Helen Jesze. Executive staff 1, Serving missionaries n/a. ***CC*** No.290643. Began 1984; interdenominational. Turnover n/a.

†*Elim International Missions, PO Box 38, Cheltenham GL50 3HN
☎01242 519 904 🖷01242 222 279
E: kcooper@elimhq.com
Web: www.elim.org.co.uk
International Missions Director: Rev Chris Jones. Executive staff 1, Serving missionaries 68, Other staff 6. ***CC*** No.251549. Began 1930; Elim Pentecostal. Magazine: *Direction* (24,000 monthly). Turnover £982,000 to year end Dec 00.

***Emmanuel International UK**, PO Box 58, Chichester PO19 8PR
☎01243 537 040 🖷01243 537 040
E: info@eiuk.org.uk
Web: www.eiuk.org.uk
Encouraging, strengthening and assisting churches worldwide; practical help, meeting spiritual need; short and long term.
UK Director: Rev David Bendell. *Manager:* Rev Steve Flashman. Executive staff 1, Serving missionaries 54, Other staff 3. ***CC*** No.289036. Began 1984; interdenominational. Magazine: *BushNet* (3,500 frequency n/a). Turnover £250,000 to year end Sep 03.

English Benedictine Congregation, Belmont Abbey, Hereford HR2 9RZ
☎01432 374 718 🖷01432 374 711
E: abbot@belmontabbey.org.uk
Web: www.belmontabbey.org.uk
Abbot: Rt Rev Paul Stonham. Community n/a, Serving missionaries 3. ***CC*** No.226277. Began n/a; Roman Catholic. No magazine. Turnover n/a.

***European Christian Mission**, 50 Billing Road, Northampton NN1 5DB
☎01604 621 092 🖷01604 620 594
E: ecm.gb@ecmi.org
Web: www.ecmbritain.org or www.prayforeurope.com
Planting and developing churches which evangelise and disciple the peoples of Europe.
British Director: Mr Richard Tiplady. *Business Manager:* Mr Nigel Bond. *Personnel Officer:* Mrs Angela Richards. Executive staff 3, Serving missionaries 39, Other staff 7. ***CC*** No.1064037. Began 1904; interdenominational. Magazine: *Europe's Millions* (7,500 quarterly). Turnover £850,000 to year end Dec 04.
International Office: *International Director:* Mr Ernie Addicott, PO Box 12569, Lapworth, Solihull B93 3AE
E: ecm.int@ecmi.org
☎01564 784 282
Ireland: St. Enoch's Church, 31 Carlisle Circus, Belfast BT14 6AT
☎028 9023 8888 🖷 028 9023 8833

European Missionary Fellowship, Guessens, 6 Codicote Road, Welwyn AL6 9NB
☎01438 716 398 🖷01438 715 942
E: hq@emf-welwyn.org
Web: emf-welwyn.org
Evangelism, church planting, publishing Christian literature, providing theological training.
Director: Rev Daniel Webber. *Assistant Director:* Rev Martin Leech. Executive staff 2, Serving missionaries 9, Other staff 4. ***CC*** No.1071823. Began 1959; interdenominational. Magazine: *Vision of Europe* (10,000 quarterly). Turnover £511,184 to year end Dec 04.

Evangelical Action (Brazil), 6 The Glade, Langley, Southampton SO45 1ZP
☎023 8089 1021
E: benbj@tiscali.co.uk
Web: www.eabrazil.com
Advancing the Christian religion in north-east Brazil; Christian charitable work.
Treasurer: Mrs B J Gough. Serving missionaries 4, Other staff 1. ***CC*** No.277[illegible]35. Began 1938; interdenominational. (Previously Gospel to Brazil Faith Mission). Magazine: *In Touch* (500 every two months). Turnover £119,000 to year end Jun 05.

Faithful Companions of Jesus, 24 Singleton Road, Salford M7 4WL
☎0161 792 2267 🖷0161 708 968[illegible]
E: jograingerfcj@aol.com
Web: www.fcjsisters.org
Provincial Superior: Sr Jo Grainger. Community n/a, Serving missionaries 5. ***CC*** No.239285. Began 18[illegible]; Roman Catholic. No magazine. Turnover £1,106,871 to year end Dec [illegible].

***Feba**, Ivy Arch Road, Worthing BN14 8BX
☎01903 237 281 🖷01903 205 294
E: info@feba.org.uk
Web: www.feba.org.uk
Evangelical radio mission broadcasting to over 40 countries.
Chief Executive: Mr John Bartlett. *Director for Resources:* Mr Dave Mason. Executive staff 8, Serving missionaries 7, Other Staff 28. ***CC*** No.257343. Began 1968; interdenominational. (Previously FEBA Radio). Magazine: *Threshold* (21,000 quarterly). Turnover £2,915,170 to year end Sep 04.

Fidei Donum Priests, St Margaret Mary, Pilch Lane, Knotty Ash, Liverpool L14 0JG
☎0151 228 1332 🖷0151 259 5019
E: smmp@mersinet.co.uk
Contact Person: Rev Gerry Proctor. Community n/a, Serving missionaries 18. Began 1957; Roman Catholic. No magazine. Turnover n/a.

†*Focus on Israel, 29 Clarendon Road, Leytonstone, London E11 1BZ
☎020 8556 3229 🖷020 8532 8584
E: foi@wyrecompute.com
Chairman: Rev M Tilley. Executive staff 2, Serving missionaries 3. ***CC*** No.803140. Began 1931; Pentecostal. (Previously Pentecostal Jewish Mission). Magazine: *Focus on Israel* (2,500 every two months). Turnover n/a.

***France Mission Trust**, The Old Chapel, Chapel Lane, Minchinhampton, Stroud GL6 9DL
☎01453 884 454 🖷01453 884 454
E: fmtrust@france-mission.org
Web: www.france-mission.org
Church planting: 50 churches in ten regions of France. Church growth through multiplication.
British Director: Mr Peter H Farley. *President of French Committee, France:* Mr David Rowley. Executive staff 3, Serving missionaries 18, Other staff 1. ***CC*** No.267979. Began 1974; interdenominational. Magazine: *Action Missionnaire* (8,000 quarterly). Turnover £248,000 to year end Dec 04.

For further information see lists on Pages 263 - 281

Franciscan Conventuals, 26 Cornwall Road, Waterloo, London SE1 8AY
☎020 7928 8897 🖷020 7928 2887
Provincial Superior: Fr Bead. Community 2, Serving missionaries 2. ***CC*** No.249881. Began 1224; Roman Catholic. Magazine: *Crusader* (15,000 monthly). Turnover n/a.

Franciscan Minoresses, Dalby Road, Melton Mowbray LE13 0BP
☎01664 562 422
Provincial Superior: Sr Columba Redmond. Community n/a, Serving missionaries 3. ***CC*** No.232532. Began n/a; Roman Catholic. No magazine. Turnover n/a.

Franciscan Missionaries of Mary, 5 Vaughan Avenue, London W6 0XS
☎020 8748 4077 🖷020 8741 9618
E: provsecuk@aol.com
Web: www.fmm.org
Pastoral work, care of sick and elderly people, retreats, counselling, school governors.
Provincial: Name not supplied. *Superior General, Italy:* Sr Christian Megbne. Home staff 105, Serving missionaries 10. ***CC*** Began 1901; Roman Catholic. No magazine. Turnover n/a.

Franciscan Missionaries of the Divine Motherhood, 19 West Side, Clapham Common, London SW4 9AL
☎020 7350 1790 🖷020 7350 1798
E: janebertelsen@hotmail.com
Health care and pastoral care, especially of poor and deprived people.
Regional Leader: Sr Jane Bertelsen. Home staff 113, Serving missionaries 17. ***CC*** No.232098. Began 1887; Roman Catholic. Magazine: *The Voice* (2,000 half-yearly). Turnover n/a.

Franciscan Missionary Sisters of St Joseph, St Joseph's Convent, Greenleach Lane, Worsley, Manchester M28 2TS
☎0161 794 1062 🖷0161 794 6420
E: fmsj@aol.com
Building up communities through religious, medical, social, educational, pastoral work among poor and marginalised people.
Superior General: Sr Joan O'Gorman. Home staff 40, Serving missionaries 3. ***CC*** No.232533. Began 1883; Roman Catholic. No magazine. Turnover n/a.

Franciscan Sisters of Mill Hill, St Francis Cottage, The Ridgeway, Mill Hill, London NW7 4HX
☎020 8959 4854 🖷020 8906 9370
Superior General: Sr Margaret Macavoy. Community n/a, Currently no UK missionaries serving overseas. ***CC*** No.232494. Began 1868; Roman Catholic. No magazine. Turnover n/a.

***Free Church of Scotland International Missions Board**, Free Church Offices, The Mound, Edinburgh EH1 2LS
☎0131 226 5286 🖷0131 220 0597
E: calum@freechurchofscotland.org.uk
Web: www.freechurch.org
Secretary: Mr Calum Ferguson. Executive staff 1, Serving missionaries 20. ***CC*** No.SCO 12925. Began 1843. (Previously Free Church of Scotland Overseas Missions Board). Magazine: *From the Frontiers* (5,000 annually). Turnover £375,000 to year end Dec 04.

Free Presbyterian Church of Scotland Mission Committee, Free Presbyterian Manse, Raasay, Kyle IV40 8PB
☎01478 660 216 M: 07715 087 953
🖷01478 660 358
E: JMacL265@aol.com
Web: www.fpchurch.org.uk
Preaching the Gospel with medical (hospital) and educational (secondary school) work as handmaids.
Clerk to Committee: Rev James R Tallach. *Clerk of Synod:* Rev John MacLeod. Executive staff 7, Serving missionaries 23. ***CC*** No.SCO 03545. Began n/a; Free Presbyterian Church of Scotland. No magazine. Turnover £500,000 to year end Dec 98.

†Free Presbyterian Church of Ulster Mission Board, Carginagh Road, Kilkeel, Newry BT34 4NE
☎028 4176 5574 🖷028 4176 5574
E: fpcmisson@aol.com
Web: www.fpcmission.org
Chairman: Rev David McIlveen. *Secretary:* Rev Ron Johnston. Executive staff 1, Serving missionaries 96. Began 1978; Free Presbyterian Church of Ulster. Magazine: *Missionary Newsletter* (4,000 every four months). Turnover n/a.

Friends of Peru, Worth Abbey, Paddockhurst Road, Crawley RH10 4SB
☎01342 710 328
M: 07941 460 721
🖷01342 710 311
E: alexandercf@ukonline.co.uk
Working for the relief of poverty and sickness through sustainable development and formation projects.
Abbot: Rt Rev Christopher Samison. Community 25. Currently no UK missionaries serving overseas. ***CC*** No.1093913. Began 1976; Roman Catholic. (Previously English Benedictine Congregation, Worth Abbey). No magazine. Turnover n/a.

***Frontiers**, PO Box 600, Hemel Hempstead HP3 9UG
☎01442 254 540
🖷01442 236 898
E: info@frontiers.org.uk
Web: www.frontiers.org.uk
Partnering to see God's kingdom come in Muslim lives and communities.
British Director: Mr Alan Stevens. Executive staff 5, Serving missionaries 80, Other staff 5. ***CC*** No.1012566. Began 1991; interdenominational. Magazine: *Connected* (4,200 quarterly). Turnover £676,000 to year end Dec 04.
Also at: *International Director:* Dr Rick Love, PO Box 4, High Wycombe HP14 3YX
☎01494 484 391
🖷 01494 485 917

***Frontline Trust (China)**, 16 Battlehill Road, Portadown, Craigavan BT62 4ER
☎028 3835 4503
M: 07793 683 253
🖷028 3835 4503
Creating Bible teaching in Mandarin and minority Chinese languages.
Managing Director: Mr Glenn Robinson. Executive staff 2, Serving missionaries 2. ***CC*** No.XR 30895. Began 1999; interdenominational. Turnover £30,000 to year end Mar 03.

***Global Outreach UK**, 108 Sweetbriar Lane, Exeter EX1 3AR
☎01392 259 673 🖷01392 491 176
E: davecgom@aol.com
Web: www.globaloutreachmission.com
Evangelism through Church-based ministries; radio; medical; Jewish ministries in 40 countries.
UK Secretary: Rev David T Cole. *President, USA:* Dr Brian Albrecht. Executive staff 1, Serving missionaries 14. ***CC*** No.281583. Began 1980; interdenominational. Magazine: *Global Times* (10,000 every two months). Turnover £8,339 to year end Aug 04.

***Gorakhpur Nurseries Fellowship**, 37 Thetford Road, New Malden KT3 3DP
☎020 8942 0270
Children's home.
Hon Secretary: Mrs Joy Devis. *Leader India:* Miss Irene Rudling. Serving missionaries 2. Began 1908; interdenominational. Magazine: *Newsletter* (1,000 every four months). Turnover £12,000 to year end Apr 00.

Grace and Compassion Benedictines, St Benedict's, 1 Manor Road, Kemp Town, Brighton BN2 5EA
☎01273 680 720 🖷01273 680 527
E: osb@graceandcompassion.co.uk
Web: www.graceandcompassion benedictines.org
Caring for the frail elderly in England; hospitals, clinics, farms in India, Kenya, Sri Lanka.
Prioress General: Mother Mary Garson. Community 220, Serving missionaries 3. ***CC*** No.1056064. Began 1954; Roman Catholic. Magazine: *Our Lady's Newsletter* (6,000 quarterly). Turnover n/a.

Grace Baptist Mission, 12 Abbey Close, Abingdon OX14 3JD
☎01235 520 147 🖷01235 559 796
E: infodesk@gbm.org.uk
Web: www.gbm.org.uk
Helping churches to support and care for their missionaries worldwide.
Coordinator of Missions: Mr David Higham. *Coordinator of Administration:* Mr John McDonald. *Financial Secretary:* Mr Andrew Sadler. Executive staff 3, Serving missionaries 40, Other staff 2. ***CC*** No.263133. Began 1861; Grace Baptist. Magazine: *The Herald* (6,500 quarterly). Turnover £650,000 to year end Dec 04.

Great Lakes Outreach, 21 Raymond Road, Maidenhead SL6 6DF
☎01628 634 246
E: simon@greatlakesoutreach.org
Web: www.greatlakesoutreach.org
Working with orphans, street children, AIDS victims, students, and evangelists in Burundi.
International Co-ordinator: Mr Simon Guillebaud. Admin staff 1, Serving missionaries 2. ***CC*** No.1097267. Began 2003; interdenominational. Turnover £150,000 to year end Dec 04.

***HCJB-UK**, 131 Grattan Road, Bradford BD1 2HS
☎01274 721 810 🖷01274 514 960
E: airwave@hcjb.org.uk
Web: www.hcjb.org.uk
Radio, medical and training ministries.
Executive Director, UK: Colin Lowther. *President, USA:* Dave Johnson. Executive staff 3, Other staff 1, Serving missionaries 11. ***CC*** No.263449. Began 1931; interdenominational. Magazine: *Wavelength* (3,500 every four months). Turnover £366,283 to year end Aug 04.

***Heartlink**, PO Box 3762, Coventry CV2 1XH
☎024 7666 3322 🖷024 7666 3322
E: Hlinktrust@aol.com
Web: www.heart-link.org.uk
Evangelism, medical care and support, training, church planting especially in India (Bihar), Albania and UK.
Executive Officer: Mr Les Wade. Executive staff 1. Currently no UK missionaries serving overseas. ***CC*** No.1059838. Began 1996; non-denominational. (Previously All India Mission). Magazine: *Heartlink and India Today* (800 quarterly). Turnover £36,000 to year end Sept 05.

Helpers of the Holy Souls, 32 St Agnes Road, Liverpool L36 5TA
☎01514 807 904 🖷01514 810 072
Provincial Superior: Sr Elizabeth Kelly. Community n/a, Currently no UK missionaries serving overseas. ***CC*** No.240876. Began 1873; Roman Catholic. No magazine. Turnover n/a.

Holy Ghost Fathers, 26 Eastbury Avenue, Northwood HA6 3LN
☎01923 825 615 🖷01923 836 975
E: spiritans.uk@virgin.net
Provincial Superior: Rev John McFadden. Community 32, Serving missionaries 5. ***CC*** No.227350. Began 1703; Roman Catholic. Magazine: *Missionwide* (5,000 quarterly). Turnover n/a.

Hospitaller Order of St John of God, St John of God Hospital, Scorton, Richmond DL10 6EB
☎01748 811 535 🖷01748 818 194
E: information@hospitaller.org.uk
Web: www.hospitaller.co.uk
Provincial Superior: Br John Martin. Community n/a. Currently no UK missionaries serving overseas. ***CC*** Began 1572; Roman Catholic. No magazine. Turnover £2,300,000 to year end Dec 02.

Institute of Charity (Rosminian Fathers & Brothers), 383 Fosse Way, Ratcliffe on the Wreake, Leicester LE7 4SG
☎01509 817 048 🖷01509 817 048
E: aa.belsito@hotmail.com
Mission station orphanage and leprosy work.
Rector of College: Fr Antonio Belsito. Community n/a, Serving missionaries 2. ***CC*** Began 1828; Roman Catholic. No magazine. Turnover n/a.

Institute of Our Lady of Mercy, Convent of Mercy, Cemetery Road, Yeadon, Leeds LS19 7UR
☎0113 250 0253 🖷0113 250 0241
E: ilom@zetnet.co.uk
Superior General: Sr Patricia Bell. Community n/a, Serving missionaries 7. ***CC*** Began 1839; Roman Catholic. No magazine. Turnover n/a.

Interchristian Fellowships Evangelical Mission (IcFEM), Kolmio, Wallace Fields, Epsom KT17 3AS
☎020 8394 2464
E: office@icfem-mission.org
Web: www.icfem-mission.org
Supporting IcFEM-Kenya in Gospel outreach, community social and economic development in rural Western Kenya.
Administrator: Mr David Goodman. Admin staff 1. ***CC*** No.1107038. Began 2004; non-denominational. No magazine. Turnover £100,000 to year end Mar 05.

***Intercontinental Church Society**, 1 Athena Drive, Tachbrook Park, Warwick CV34 6NL
☎01926 430 347 🖷01926 888 092
E: enquiries@ics-uk.org
Web: www.ics-uk.org
Planting and resourcing English-language Anglican Churches abroad, especially by recruitment and outreach to holidaymakers.
Communications Manager: Mr David Healey. *Seasonal Ministries Manager:* Mr Trevor Letchford. Executive staff 9, Serving missionaries 61. ***CC*** No.1072584. Began 1823; Anglican. Magazine: *ICS News* (4,500 quarterly), *Directory of English Speaking Churches Abroad* (750 annually). Turnover £590,000 to year end Dec 04

***International Fellowship of Evangelical Students (IFES Trust, International Office)**, 321 Banbury Road, Oxford OX2 7Z[illegible]
☎01865 292 555 🖷01865 292 556
E: info@ifesworld.org
Web: www.ifesworld.org
Working to establish a clear witness to Christ in the world's universities; 150 countries.
General Secretary: Mr Lindsay Brown. *Head of Advancement:* Mrs Deborah Lake. *Head of External Relations:* Miss Julia Cameron. Executive staff 15, Other staff 140, Serving missionaries 36. ***CC*** No.247919. Began 1947; interdenominational. Magazine: *Special Report* (40,000 annually, worldwide). Turnover £3,200,000 to year end Dec 04.

***International Nepal Fellowship**, 69 Wentworth Road, Harborne, Birmingham B17 9SS
☎0121 427 8833 🖷0121 428 3110
E: ukoffice@inf.org.uk
Web: www.inf.org
UK Director: John Reynolds. *International Director, Nepal:* Steve Aisthorpe. *Chairman:* Andrew Gammie. Executive staff 1, Serving missionaries 29, Other staff 5. ***CC*** No.1047178. Began 1940; interdenominational. Magazine: *Today in Nepal* (2,000 quarterly). Turnover £1,500,000 to year end Jul 05.

For further information see lists on Pages 263 - 281

***International Teams UK**, PO Box 11, Brecon LD3 9WJ
☎01874 611 995 🖷01874 611 799
E: uk@iteams.org
Web: www.iteams.org
An international, non denominational mission organisation, serving in 57 Countries, with a wide variety of ministry opportunities.
Director: Mr Anthony Jones. Executive staff 1, Other staff 7, Serving missionaries 20. **CC** No.1089864. Began 1960; interdenominational. Magazine: *Talkabout IT* (Circulation n/a quarterly). Turnover £230,000 to year end Dec 00.

***Interserve**, 325 Kennington Road, London SE11 4QH
☎020 7735 8227 🖷020 7587 5362
E: enquiries@isewi.org
Web: www.interserveonline.org.uk
Enabling churches to be involved in cross-cultural mission in Asia, Middle East, Britain.
National Director: Mr Richard Clark. *International Director:* Dr Paul Bendor-Samuel. *Personnel Director:* Miss Ruth Millson. Executive staff 6, Serving missionaries 144, Other staff 16. **CC** No.1020758. Began 1852; interdenominational. Magazine: *GO* (11,000 quarterly). Turnover £2,394,000 to year end Dec 04.
Ireland, 14 Glencregagh Court, Belfast BT6 0PA
☎028 9040 2211 🖷028 9040 1298
E: info@isire.org
Web: www.isire.org
National Director: Mr Merrill Morrow. *Chair of Council:* Mrs Maggi Holmes. Executive staff 1, Serving missionaries 17, Other staff 4. **CC** No.16632. Began 1852; interdenominational. Magazine: *Irish Insight* (1,500 quarterly), *GO* (1,500 quarterly). Turnover £296,000 to year end Dec 04.
Scotland, 12 Elm Avenue, Lenzie, Glasgow G66 4HJ
☎0141 578 0207 🖷0141 578 0208
E: info@isscot.org
Web: www.interservescotland.org.uk
National Director: Mr John Jackson. *Assistant Director - Personnel:* Miss Maggie Hobbs. Executive staff 2, Serving missionaries 18, Other staff 2. **CC** No.SCO 05316. Began 1852; interdenominational. Magazine: *GO* (2,000 quarterly). Turnover £365,000 to year end Dec 02.

***Janz Team**, 129 Whippendell Road, Watford WD18 7NH
M: 07939 217 824
E: rsanderson@janzteam.com
Web: www.janzteamuk.org
Creative evangelism - English language camps; Christian education - Black Forest Academy; compassionate empowerment - relief/development programmes.
National Director: Mr Robin Sanderson. Executive staff 1. Serving missionaries 4. **CC** No.1090648. Began 2002; non-denominational. No magazine. Turnover £102,000 to year end Jun 05.

***Japan Christian Link**, PO Box 68, Sevenoaks TN13 2ZY
☎01732 455 453 🖷01732 455 453
E: info@jclglobal.org
Web: www.jclglobal.org
Working to bring the Gospel to Japanese worldwide through full-time workers and part-time volunteers.
Director: Mr Selvan Anketell. Executive staff 1, Serving missionaries 4, Other staff 1. **CC** No.213834. Began 1903; interdenominational. (Previously Japan Evangelistic Band). Magazine: *JCL News* (1,800 half-yearly). Turnover £145,192 to year end Dec 04.

Japan Good News Ministries, 36 Suffolk Road, North Harrow, Harrow HA2 7QQ
☎020 8427 0131 🖷020 8861 3137
E: jgnm@faithmedia.jp
Evangelism, church planting, pastors' seminars, crusades, cell groups, children's ministry, television and media.
Treasurer (UK): Mr George Smith. *Director, Japan:* Donald R Thompson. Executive staff 1, Serving missionaries 1, Other staff 2. Began 1970; Full Gospel. Magazine: *Hour of Evangelism* (Circulation n/a quarterly). Turnover £7,680 to year end Dec 98.

Japan Mission, 56 Warrenside Close, Blackburn BB1 9PF
☎01254 720 269
E: uk@japanmission.org
Web: www.japanmission.org
Supporting existing evangelical churches in Japan; teaching English; full-time workers from overseas and Japan.
Secretary: Mrs S Oliver. *Co-founder (with his wife), Japan:* Mr N Verwey. Admin staff 6, Serving missionaries 3, Other staff 11. **CC** No.252768. Began 1957; interdenominational. Turnover £31,646 to year end Mar 02.

***Language Recordings UK**, PO Box 197, High Wycombe HP14 3YY
☎01494 485 414
🖷01494 485 414
E: lrukoffice@aol.com
Web: www.languagerecordingsuk.co.uk
Producing culturally relevant Gospel messages on cassette in storytelling form in people's mother tongue.
Director: Mr Jim McKechnie. Executive staff 2, Serving missionaries 2. **CC** No.266476. Began 1955; interdenominational. Magazine: *The Messenger* (1,200 every two months). Turnover £57,532 to year end June 02.

***Latin Link**, 175 Tower Bridge Road, London SE1 2AB
☎020 7939 9000
🖷020 7939 9015
E: info@latinlink.org
Web: www.latinlink.org
International fellowship from many churches focused on Latin America and committed to world mission.
International Team Leader: Mr Marcel Dürst. *Team Leader in Britain & Ireland:* Mr Alan Tower. Executive staff 4, Serving missionaries 101, Other staff 16. **CC** No.1020826. Began 1908; interdenominational. Magazine: *Latinfile* (7,500 every four months). Turnover £1,979,852 to year end Mar 05.

O

***The Leprosy Mission, England and Wales Office**, Goldhay Way, Orton Goldhay, Peterborough PE2 5GZ
☎01733 370 505 🖷01733 404 880
E: post@tlmew.org.uk
Web: www.leprosymission.org.uk
Curing people and providing care after cure, reconstructive surgery, rehabilitation and training to leprosy sufferers.
National Director: Mr Warren Lancaster. *Director of Finance and Administration:* Mr Keith Nicholson. Executive staff 3, Serving missionaries 2, Other staff 34. ***CC*** No.1050327. Began 1874; interdenominational. Magazine: *New Day* (128,760 half-yearly). Turnover £4,764,489 to year end Dec 04.
International Office, 80 Windmill Road, Brentford TW8 0QH
☎020 8326 6767 🖷020 8326 6777
E: friends@tlmint.org
Web: www.leprosymission.org
General Director: Mr Geoff Warne. *International Chairman:* Dr John Clement. *Hon Treasurer:* Miss Christine Osman. Executive staff 4, Serving missionaries 6, Other staff 17. ***CC*** No.1076356. Began 1874; interdenominational. No magazine. Turnover n/a.
Northern Ireland, 2a Queen Road, Lisburn BT27 4TZ
☎028 9038 1937 🖷028 9038 1842
E: info@tlm-ni.org
Web: www.tlm-ni.org
Executive Director: Mr Colin Ferguson. *Deputy Director:* Rev Tom Robinson. Executive staff 2. ***CC*** No.XR 11501. Began n/a; interdenominational. Magazine: *In Touch Northern Ireland* (6,500 half-yearly). Turnover £480,000 to year end Dec 00.
Scotland, Suite 2, Earlsgate Lodge, Livilands Way, Stirling FK8 2BG
☎01786 449 266 🖷01786 449 766
E: contactus@tlmscotland.org.uk
Web: www.tlmscotland.org.uk
Executive Director: Ms Linda Todd. *Area Coordinator (South and Central Scotland):* Mr Stuart McAra. *Area Coordinator (North of Scotland):* Mr Jim Clark. Executive staff 1, Serving missionaries 5, Other Staff 6. ***CC*** No.SCO 22411. Began 1874; interdenominational. Magazine: *New Day* (3,500 half-yearly). Turnover £788,577 to year end Dec 04.

Lightforce International, Christian Centre, Strudwick Drive, Oldbrook, Milton Keynes MK6 2TG
☎01908 670 655 M: 07899 998 801
🖷01908 553 077
E: mission@lightforce.org.uk
Web: www.lightforce.org.uk
Taking good news to the poor and practical help to people in need.
International Director: Rev George R Ridley. Executive staff 1, Admin staff 2, Serving missionaries 5. ***CC*** No.1050871. Began 1991; non-denominational. No magazine. Turnover £250,000 to year end Dec 04.

Medical Missionaries of Mary, 2 Denbigh Road, Ealing, London W13 8PX
☎020 8998 1725
E: mmmealing@ukonline.co.uk
Web: www.medical-missionaries.com
Offering a healing service to disadvantaged people in Africa, especially mothers and children.
Regional Representative: Sr Maureen Clarke. Community 14, Serving missionaries 5. ***CC*** No.293494. Began n/a; Roman Catholic. No magazine. Turnover n/a.

Melanesian Mission, 15 Covell Close, Bury St Edmunds IP33 2HU
☎01284 701 988
E: david.friswell@btconnect.com
Supporting the Church of Melanesia, caring for visiting Melanesians, encouraging links financially, prayerfully and administratively.
Executive Officer: Mr David Friswell. *Commissary:* Rev Cannon D Probets. Executive staff 1, Serving missionaries 3. ***CC*** No.1104551. Began 1848; Anglican. Magazine: *Melanesia News* (1,500 half-yearly). Turnover £70,000 to year end Mar 04.

***Mercy Ships UK**, The Lighthouse, 12 Meadway Court, Stevenage SG1 2EF
☎01438 727 800/0870 870 447
🖷01438 721 900
E: info@mercyships.org.uk
Web: www.mercyships.org.uk
Bringing hope and healing to the world's poor primarily through a fleet of hospital ships.
Executive Director: Mrs Judy Polkinhorn. Admin staff 18. Serving missionaries n/a. ***CC*** No.1053055. Began 1978; interdenominational. Magazine: *Mercy* (80,000 quarterly). Turnover £4,300,000 to year end Dec 04.

Mercy Sisters of the Union of Great Britain, Mercy Union Generalate, St Edwards Convent, 11 Harewood Avenue, London NW1 6LD
☎020 7402 7785 🖷020 7224 8551
E: rsmgeneral@aol.com
Congregational Leader: Sr Evelyn Gallagher. Community n/a, Serving missionaries 2. ***CC*** No.288158. Began 1846; Roman Catholic. No magazine. Turnover n/a.

***The Messianic Testimony**, 93 Axe Street, Barking IG11 7LZ
☎020 8594 3072 🖷020 8594 0993
E: tmt@tmtestimony.org.uk
Web: www.tmtestimony.org.uk
Sharing the Gospel with Jewish people, teaching God's purposes for Israel to the church.
Director: Rev Colin Leyshon. *Evangelism Director:* Mr Tom Mayr-Lori. Executive staff 1, Serving missionaries 13, Other staff 2. ***CC*** No.274750. Began 1973; interdenominational. (Previously The Mildmay Mission to the Jews and The Hebrew Christian Testimony to Israel). Magazine: *The Messianic Testimony* (5,000 quarterly). Turnover £441,608 to year end Dec 01.

Methodist Church World Church Office, Methodist Church House, 25 Marylebone Road, London NW1 5JR
☎020 7486 5502 🖷020 7467 5285
E: WCO.leader@methodistchurch.org.uk
Web: www.methodist.org.uk
Working in partnership with overseas churches, theological and ecumenical institutions; sharing resources for mission, service.
Team Leader: Mr Michael King. Executive staff 9, Admin staff 14, Serving mission partners 64. Began n/a; Methodist. Magazines: *Mission Matters* (32,000 quarterly), *Rainbow and Fun* (42,000 every four months (for children)). Turnover £4,660,000 to year end Aug 04.

***Middle East Christian Outreach**, 22 Culverden Park Road, Tunbridge Wells TN4 9RA
☎01892 521 541 🖷01892 549 745
E: info@twoffice.co.uk
Web: www.aboutmeco.org
Serving the church in the Arab world.
UK Director: Rev John Carrick. Executive staff 2, Serving missionaries 43, Other staff 3. ***CC*** No.272327. Began 1976; interdenominational. Magazine: *Crossroads* (5,500 quarterly). Turnover £441,801 to year end Mar 05.

***Middle East Media**, PO Box 826, High Wycombe HP10 9WQ
☎0870 162 1826 🖷01306 881 179
E: ukoffice@mem-eu.org
Web: www.mem.org
Serving people in the Middle East, primarily through media ministries.
UK Director: To be appointed. Executive staff 4, Currently no UK missionaries serving overseas. ***CC*** No.271373. Began 1975; interdenominational. Magazine: *Memo* (3,000 every two months). Turnover £700,000 to year end Dec 00.

Mill Hill Missionaries, St Michael's, 40 George Leigh Street, Ancoats, Manchester M4 5DG
☎0161 278 0775 🖷0161 950 8697
E: regional@millhill17.freeserve.co.uk
Web: www.millhillmissionaries.org
Superior: Rev Liam Armour MHM. *Superior:* Rev Morris Crean. Community n/a, Serving missionaries 26. ***CC*** No.220690. Began n/a; Roman Catholic. No magazine. Turnover n/a.

***Mission Africa**, 14 Glencregagh Court, Belfast BT6 0PA
☎028 9040 2850 🖷028 9079 9190
E: jcardoo.qif@ukonline.co.uk
Web: www.missionafrica.org.uk
Chief Executive: Rev John F Cardoo. *Senior Executive:* Rev Paul Bailie. Executive staff 3, Serving missionaries 16, Other staff 8. ***CC*** No.XN 45493. Began 1887; interdenominational. (Previously Qua Iboe Fellowship). Magazine *Dispatch* (3,700 every four months). Turnover £320,000 to year end Dec 02.
Scotland: 44 Quarry Drive, Kilmacolm PA13 4QA
☎01505 873 731

For further information see lists on Pages 263 - 281

***Mission Aviation Fellowship**, Castle House, Castle Hill Avenue, Folkestone CT20 2TN
☎01303 850 950 🖷01303 852 800
E: supporter.relations@maf-uk.org
Web: www.maf-uk.org
Flying light aircraft to help remote communities in the developing world.
Chief Executive, MAF UK: Ruth Whitaker. *Chief Executive, MAF Operations:* Mr Chris Lukkien. Executive staff 5, Serving missionaries 30, Other staff 46. ***CC*** No.1064598. Began 1945; interdenominational. Magazine: *MAF News* (61,000 quarterly). Turnover £8,648,000 to year end Dec 05.

Mission to Military Garrisons Inc, Challenge House, 29 Canal Street, Glasgow G4 0AD
☎0141 333 0703 🖷0141 331 0563
E: mmg@wclauson.freeserve.co.uk
Web: www.mmg-online.co.uk
Secretary & Treasurer: Mr William J Clauson. Executive staff 1, Serving missionaries 12, Other staff 1. ***CC*** No.SCO 05038. Began 1883; interdenominational. Magazine: *MMG News* (1 250 quarterly). Turnover £500,000 to year end Jan 03.

The Mission to Seafarers, St Michael Paternoster Royal, College Hill, London EC4R 2RL
☎020 7248 5202 🖷020 7248 4761
E: general@missiontoseafarers.org
Web: www.missiontoseafarers.org
Caring for the welfare of seafarers in ports around the world.
Secretary General. Rev Canon Bill Christianson. *Ministry Secretary:* Rev Tom Heffer. *Justice & Welfare Secretary:* Rev Canon Ken Peters. Executive staff 7, Serving missionaries 40, Other staff 25. ***CC*** No.212432. Began 1856; Anglican. Magazine: *Flying Angel News* (18,000 every four months), *The Sea* (26,500 every two months). Turnover £4,804,000 to year end Dec 01.

Missionaries of Africa (White Fathers), 42 Stormont Road, London N6 4NP
☎020 8348 7799 / 8340 5036
🖷020 8347 8147
E: mafrgb@ukonline.co.uk
Web: www.thewhitefathers.org.uk
Liberation and emancipation of African peoples wherever they are.
Provincial Superior: Rev Peter Smith. *Superior General, Italy:* Rev François Richard. Community 48, Serving missionaries 20. ***CC*** No.233302. Began 1868; Roman Catholic. Magazine: *White Fathers/White Sisters* (37,500 every two months). Turnover n/a.

Missionaries of Charity of Mother Teresa of Calcutta Trust 177 Bravington Road, London W9 3AR
☎020 8960 2644
Provincial Superior: Sr Lawrence. Community 10, Serving missionaries 2, Community 67. ***CC*** No.1073795. Began n/a; Roman Catholic. No magazine. Turnover n/a.

Missionary Sisters of Our Lady of Africa (White Sisters), 25 Waldemar Avenue Ealing, London W13 9PZ
☎020 8567 6980/6583
🖷020 8579 7822
E: msolatreuk@aol.com
Provincial Superior: Sr Marion Carabott. *Superior General, Italy:* Sr Marie Macdorald. Community 26, Serving missionaries 2. ***CC*** No.228983. Began 1869; Roman Catholic. Magazine: *White Fathers/White Sisters* (37,500 every two months). Turnover n/a.

Missionary Sisters of St Columban, 53 Thornhill Road, Birmingham B21 9BT
☎0121 515 2043 🖷0121 551 2896
E: colclt@aol.com
Regional Superior: Sr Kathleen Geaney. Community 15, Serving missionaries 1, Home staff 3. Began n/a; Roman Catholic. No magazine. Turnover n/a.

Missionary Sisters Servants of the Holy Spirit, 14 Nye Cliff Road, The Pitchens, Birmingham B20 3TB
☎0121 515 2341
E: bham.ssps@virgin.net
Provincial Superior: Sr Mary Hudson. *Superior General, Italy:* Sr Agada Brand. Community 6. Currently no UK missionaries serving overseas ***CC*** Began 1889; Roman Catholic. No magazine. Turnover n/a.

Missionary Society of St Columban, Widney Manor Road, Knowle, Solihull B93 9AB
☎01564 772 096 🖷01564 770 500
Web: www.columbans.co.uk
Working worldwide in pastoral, education and health projects.
Regional Director: Rev Bernard McDermott. *Superior General, Republic of Ireland:* Fr Brendan O'Sullivan. Home staff 6, Serving missionaries 5. ***CC*** No.221594. Began 1935; Roman Catholic. Magazine: *The Far East* (69,000 eight times a year). Turnover n/a.

Montfort Fathers, 28 Burbo Bank Road, Blundellsands, Liverpool L23 6TH
☎0151 287 6862 🖷0151 287 0410
Provincial Superior: Rev Frederick Scragg. Community n/a, Serving missionaries 2. ***CC*** No.241963. Began 1712; Roman Catholic. No magazine. Turnover n/a.

***The Navigators**, Turner House, 54 The Avenue, Southampton SO17 1XQ
☎023 8055 8800
E: info@navigators.co.uk
Web: www.navigators.co.uk
National Director: Mr Dirk van Zuylen. *National Administrator:* Mr Simon Lexton. *General Director, USA:* Mr Mike Treneer. Executive staff 4, Serving missionaries 131, Other staff 3. ***CC*** No.1099148. Began 1955; interdenominational. Magazines: *20/20 Vision* (Circulation n/a quarterly), *Harvest* (Circulation n/a quarterly). Turnover £1,155,738 to year end Aug 00.

New Foundations Medical Charity, 88 Hartington Grove, Cambridge CB1 7UB
☎01223 710 488
E: david.donovan@nhs.net
Web: www.newfoundations.org.uk
Medical mission to the people of the Niger Delta, Nigeria.
Co-Founder / Director: Dr David Donovan. Executive staff 1, Serving missionaries 11. ***CC*** No.1100698. Began 2003; interdenominational. No magazine. Turnover £40,000 to year end Apr 05.

New Testament Missionary Union, 3 Knottingley Drive, Great Sutton, Ellesmere Port CH66 4XF
☎0151 339 9180 🖷0151 339 9180
E: ARob050572@aol.com
Evangelism and church planting following the New Testament pattern.
Secretary & Treasurer: Mr Albert S Robinson. Admin staff 2, Serving missionaries 1. ***CC*** No.282565. Began 1902; interdenominational. Magazine: *Pressing On* (1,000 quarterly). Turnover £19,000 to year end Dec 04.

New Tribes Mission, North Cotes, Grimsby DN36 5XU
☎01472 387 700 🖷01472 387 707
E: info@ntm.org.uk
Web: www.ntm.org.uk
Church planting, evangelism and Bible translation amongst unreached ethnic groups; national training programmes.
UK Chairman: Frank Brearley. *Director of Biblical Studies:* Joseph Bailie. *Director of Cross Cultural Communication Studies:* Dr Colin Lamb. Home Staff 51, Serving missionaries 86. ***CC*** No.278627. Began 1980; interdenominational. Magazines: *NTM Link* (5,000 quarterly, UK), *NTM@Work* (40,000 every two months, international). Turnover £1,429,625 to year end Dec 05.

Oblates of Mary Immaculate, St Teresa's Presbytery, Sedgemoor Road, Norris Green, Liverpool L11 3BW
☎0151 226 1354 🖷01512 702 665
E: oblate@noms3.freeserve.co.uk
Provincial: Very Rev Edward Quinn. Community 3. Currently no UK missionaries serving overseas Began 1816; Roman Catholic. No magazine. Turnover n/a.

***OMF International (UK)**, Station Approach, Borough Green, Sevenoaks TN15 8BG
☎01732 887 299 🖷01732 887 224
E: omf@omf.org.uk
Web: www.omf.org.uk
Serving East Asia's peoples through evangelism, church planting, professional skills, community projects and short-term opportunities.
National Director: Mr Chris Wigram. *International Director, Singapore:* Dr Patrick Fung. Executive staff 8, Serving missionaries 198, Other staff 34. ***CC*** No.1086040. Began 1865; interdenominational. Magazine: *East Asia's Billions* (14,500 quarterly). Turnover £4,329,079 to year end Dec 04. **Continued over:**

For further information see lists on Pages 263 - 281

East/South East England Regional Office: *Regional Director:* Mr Keith Wood, Danehurst, The Avenue, Bushey, Watford WD23 2LL
E: east@omf.org.uk
☎01923 247 382 M: 07977 013 853
North England & North Wales Office: *Regional Director:* David Robinson, 440 Parrs Wood Road, Manchester M20 5GP
E: north@omf.org.uk
☎0161 434 3883 🖷 0161 434 3883
West England & South Wales Office: *Regional Directors:* Martin & Alison Clarkson Webb, 174 Redland Road, Bristol BS6 6YG
E: west@omf.org.uk
☎0117 973 7490 🖷 0117 973 7490
Ireland Regional Office: *Regional Director:* Wilson McMahon, 53 Wellington Park, Belfast BT9 6DP
E: ireland@omf.org.uk
☎028 9038 1995 🖷 028 9068 3472
Scotland Regional Office: *Regional Director:* Phil Steed, Lechler House, 25 Abbey Drive, Glasgow G14 9JP
E: scotland@omf.org.uk
☎0141 959 4180 🖷 0141 959 4180

***OMS International**, 1 Sandileigh Avenue, Didsbury, Manchester M20 3LN
☎0161 283 7992 🖷0161 283 8981
E: info@omsinternational.co.uk
Web: www.omsinternational.co.uk
Evangelism, training national believers, planting churches; partnering national church groups.
UK Director: Mr Michael Berkeley. *International President, USA:* Dr David Long. *Finance Officer:* Mr Stephen Davison. Executive staff 2, Serving missionaries 25, Other staff 9. ***CC*** No.245124. Began 1901; interdenominational. Magazine: *OMS Outreach* (2,500 quarterly). Turnover £708,691 to year end Sep 01.

***Operation Mobilisation**, The Quinta, Weston Rhyn, Oswestry SY10 7LT
☎0845 450 7800 🖷01691 778 378
E: info@uk.om.org
Web: www.uk.om.org
Mobilizing people to share the knowledge of Jesus and His compassion with each generation.
UK Director: Mr Gary Sloan. *Director of Human Resources:* Mr Mike Wheate. *Director of Marketing and Communications:* Mr Derek Paterson. Staff in UK 101, Serving missionaries 239. ***CC*** No.1008196. Began 1962; interdenominational. Magazine: *Global* (26,000 monthly). Turnover £9,257,000 to year end Dec 04.
Also at: *UK Director:* Rev Peter Nicoll, International Office, PO Box 27, Carlisle CA1 2HG
☎01228 615 100

Our Lady of Charity of the Good Shepherd, Good Shepherd Provincialate, 61 East End Road, London N2 0SF
☎020 8346 8100 🖷020 8343 0970
Provincial Superior: Sr Olivia Ward. *Superior General, Italy:* Sr M G Cadena. Community n/a, Serving missionaries 27. ***CC*** No.234880. Began 1835; Roman Catholic. No magazine. Turnover n/a.

Oxford Mission, PO Box 86, Romsey SO51 8YD
☎01794 515 004 🖷01794 515 004
E: oxfordmission@aol.com
Web: www.oxford-mission.org
Working for the education and welfare of children; one centre in India, two in Bangladesh.
General Secretary: Mrs Mary K Marsh. Executive staff 1. Currently no UK missionaries serving overseas ***CC*** No.211618. Began 1880; Anglican. Magazine: *Oxford Mission News* (1,600 half-yearly). Turnover £244,656 to year end Dec 04.

Pallottine Fathers, 358 Greenford Road, Greenford UB6 9AN
☎020 8578 1363 🖷020 8813 2230
Provincial Superior: Rev George Ranahan. Community n/a. Currently no UK missionaries serving overseas Began n/a; Roman Catholic. No magazine. Turnover n/a.

Pallottine Missionary Sisters, 52 Park Mount Drive, Macclesfield SK11 8NT
☎01625 616 459 🖷01625 869 080
Provincial Superior: Sr Marie Keegan. Community n/a, Currently no UK missionaries serving overseas. ***CC*** No.234185. Began 1909; Roman Catholic. No magazine. Turnover n/a.

Papua New Guinea Church Partnership, St Mary Abbots Hall, Vicarage Gate, London W8 4HN
☎020 7937 5794 M: 07801 481 359
🖷020 7937 4159
E: pngcpluxton@aol.com
Web: hometown.aol.co.uk/pngcpluxton/PNGChurchPartnership
Supporting the Anglican Church of PNG by prayer, finance, and recruiting for training posts.
General Secretary: Mrs Chris Luxton. Executive staff 1, Serving missionaries 10. ***CC*** No.249446. Began 1891; Anglican. Magazine: *Family Magazine* (Circulation n/a every four months). Turnover £130,000 to year end Dec 03.

Passionists, 12 Belgrave Road, Liverpool L17 7AG
☎0151 727 2024 🖷0151 222 1207
E: npostlethwaite@ukonline.co.uk
Provincial Superior: Rev Nicholas Postlethwaite. Community n/a, Currently no UK missionaries serving overseas. ***CC*** Began 1720; Roman Catholic. No magazine. Turnover n/a.

***People International**, PO Box 310, Tunbridge Wells TN1 1WT
☎01892 545 509 🖷01892 545 520
E: uk@peopleintl.org
Web: www.peopleintl.org
Bringing Christ's love to the Muslim peoples of Central Asia.
UK Director: Name withheld. *International Director:* To be appointed. Executive staff 1, Serving missionaries 17, Other staff 3. ***CC*** No.280036. Began 1979; interdenominational. Magazine: *SCAN* (10,000 annually), *People International News Update* (6,000 half-yearly). Turnover £389,072 to year end Dec 04.

***Presbyterian Church in Ireland Board of Mission Overseas**, Church House, Fisherwick Place, Belfast BT1 6DW
☎028 9032 2284 🖷028 [illegible]041 7[illegible]06
E: overseas@presbyterianireland.org
Web: www.presbyterianireland.org
Executive Officer & Secretary: Rev Uel Marrs. *Education for Mission/Asia Secretary:* Mr Nigel Eves. *Personnel Officer (Overseas):* Miss Helen Johnston. Executive staff 3, Serving missionaries 46, Other staff 5. ***CC*** No.XN 4[illegible]376. Began 1840; Presbyterian. Magazine: *Wider World* (24,000 quarterly). Turnover £1,690,000 to year end Dec 04.

Presbyterian Church of Wales Mission Board, Tabernacle Chapel 81 Merthyr Road, Whitchurch, Cardiff CF14 1D[illegible]
☎029 2062 7465 M: 079[illegible]6 145 [illegible]22
🖷 029 2061 6188
E: dafydd@ebcpcw.org.uk
Web: www.ebcpcw.org uk
Mission and evangelism in Wales and in partnership with 30 other churches worldwide through CWM.
Mission Secretary: Rev D A Jones. Executive staff 1, Serving missionaries 25, Other staff 2. ***CC*** Began 18[illegible]0; Presbyterian. Magazine: *Treasury* (1,[illegible]0 monthly), *Y Goleuad* (1,800 weekly). Turnover £350,000 to year end Dec [illegible]2.

***Red Sea Mission Team**, PO Box [illegible]04, Sevenoaks TN13 9EL
☎01732 885 688 🖷01732 885 6[illegible]3
E: postbox@rsmt.co.uk
Web: www.rsmt.com
UK Director: Captain Glenn Ta[illegible]io. *International Team Leader, UK:* Laurence Epp. Executive staff 1, Serving missionaries 6, Other staff 1. ***CC*** No.232[illegible]03. Began 1951; interdenominational. Magazine: *Islam Shall Hear* (1,500 frequency n/a). Turnover £180,000 to year end Mar [illegible]4.
International Team *Director:* Mr Laurence Epp, 66 Park Hill, Moseley, Birmingham B13 8DS
☎ 0121 449 2290
E: offfice@ithbirmingham.co.uk

Redemptorists, St Mary's Church, Clapham, London SW4 7AP
☎020 7622 2793 🖷020 7627 315[illegible]
E: jtrenchard@aol.com
Web: www.redemptorists biz
Provincial Superior: Rev John Trenchard. *Superior General, Italy:* Rev Joseph Tobin. Community 70, Serving missionaries [illegible]3. ***CC*** No.252041. Began 17[illegible]; Roman Catholic. No magazine. Turnover n/a.

Religious of Jesus and Mary, [illegible]20 Woodbridge Road, Ipswich IP4 [illegible]BD
☎01473 713 162 🖷01473 7[illegible]7 297
Education in schools; pastoral activities in parishes.
Provincial Superior: Sr Judith Mary Cuff. Community 50, Serving missionaries [illegible]. ***CC*** No.247358. Began n/a; Roman Catholic. No magazine. Turnover n/a.

For further information see lists on Pages [illegible]63 - 2[illegible]

†Religious of the Assumption, 23 Kensington Square, London W8 5HN
☎020 7351 ‑742
📠020 7361 4710
E: relassump@aol.com
Web: www.assumptionreligious.org
Provincial Superior: Sr Christine Charlwood. *Superior General, France:* Sr Cristina, Conzalez. Community n/a, Serving missionaries 3. ***CC*** Began 1839; Roman Catholic. No magazine. Turnover n/a.

Sacred Heart Fathers (Betharram), St Joseph's, Mather Lane, Leigh WN7 2PR
☎01942 673 517
📠01942 269 094
Provincial Superior: Rev Austin Hughes. Community n/a. Currently no UK missionaries serving overseas Began n/a; Roman Catholic. No magazine. Turnover n/a.

†Sacred Heart Fathers (Dehonians), St Joseph's Retreat & Conference Centre, Tilston Road, Malpas SY14 7DD
☎01948 860 416
📠01948 860 619
E: scj@malpas2000.freeserve.co.uk
Web: www.malpas2000@freeserve.co.uk
Provincial Superior: Rev Michael Walshe. Community n/a, Currently no UK missionaries serving overseas. ***CC*** Began 1936; Roman Catholic. Magazine: *Contact* (5,000 every four months). Turnover n/a.

Sacred Hearts Community, 372 Uxbridge Road, Ealing, London W5 3LH
☎020 8992 5941
Provincial Superintendent: Fr Michael Foley. Community n/a. Currently no UK missionaries serving overseas ***CC*** Began 1954; Roman Catholic. No magazine. Turnover n/a.

Sahara Desert Mission, 82 Leconfield Road, Loughborough LE11 3SQ
☎01509 267 583
📠01509 267 583
Hon Secretary: Mr J R Hall. *Superintendent, Niger:* Rev S Baggott. Currently no UK missionaries serving overseas, Other staff 2. Began 1953; interdenominational. Magazine: *Streams in The Desert* (1,000 every four months). Turnover £33,000 to year end Feb 03.

St Joseph's Hospice Association (Jospice International), St Joseph's Hospice, Ince Road, Liverpool L23 4UE
☎0151 9 243 812
📠0151 9 326 020
E: patmurphy@jospice.org.uk
Web: www.jospice.org.uk
Caring for terminal and chronic sick without charge.
General Manager: Mr Keith Cawdron. *Director Clinical Care:* Julie Baden. Executive staff 3, Serving missionaries 2, Other staff 120. ***CC*** No.250778. Began 1966; Roman Catholic. No magazine. Turnover £2,000,000 to year end Apr 03.

St Joseph's Missionary Society, Mill Hill, St Joseph's College, Lawrence Street, Mill Hill, London NW7 4JX
☎020 8959 3222 📠020 8959 8493
E: mhmgc@lineone.net
Web: www.millhillmissionaries.org
Superior: Fr Jack Hetson. Home staff 93, Serving missionaries n/a, Community 50. ***CC*** Began 1866; Roman Catholic. Magazine: *Missions and Missionaries* (200,000 every two months). Turnover n/a.

St Patrick's Missionary Society, 20 Beauchamp Road, East Molesey KT8 0PA
☎020 8979 1890 📠020 8941 8221
E: spsuk@aol.com
Web: www.spms.org
Superior: Rev Tom Ryan. *Superior General Republic of Ireland:* Rev Seamus O'Neill. Home staff 1, Serving missionaries 1. ***CC*** No.269640. Began 1970; Roman Catholic. Magazine: *Africa* (30,000 nine times a year). Turnover n/a.

Salesian Fathers and Brothers, 266 Wellington Road North, Stockport SK4 2QR
☎0161 431 6633 📠0161 443 2378
E: provincial@salesians.org.uk
Web: www.salesians.org.uk
Evangelising and educating to the faith young and working class people.
Provincial Superior: Rev Francis Preston. *Rector Major, Italy:* Rev Pascual Chavez. Community n/a, Serving missionaries 13. ***CC*** No.233779. Began 1887; Roman Catholic. Magazine: *Don Bosco Today* (10,000 quarterly). Turnover n/a.

Salvation Army International.
See page 305.

* **SAO Cambodia**, Bawtry Hall, Bawtry, Doncaster DN10 6JH
☎01302 714 004 📠01302 710 027
E: admin@saocambodia.org
Web: www.saocambodia.org
Promoting the Christian faith and relieving poverty and distress among Cambodian people.
Operations Director: Mr Ivor Greer. *Executive Director, Cambodia:* Mr Geoff Collett. Executive staff 2, Serving missionaries 9, Other staff 1. ***CC*** No.293382. Began 1973; interdenominational. (Previously Southeast Asian Outreach). Magazine: *Vision* (1,800 quarterly). Turnover £324,000 to year end Sept 04.

SAT-7 Trust, The Coach House, 43 New Road, Chippenham SN15 1HL
☎01249 765 865 📠01249 765 865
E: admin@sat7trust.org
Web: www.sat7trust.org
Arabic Christian television, making God's love visible in the Middle East.
Executive Director, Great Britain & Ireland: Mrs Sonia Home. *Administrator:* Miss Kathy Flesher. Executive staff 1, Serving missionaries 2, Other staff 2 ***CC*** No.1060612. Began 1997; interdenominational. Magazine: *Uplink* (2,000 quarterly). Turnover £650,000 to year end Dec 04.

***Seamen's Christian Friend Society**, 48 South Street, Alderley Edge SK9 7ES
☎01625 590 010 📠01625 585 442
E: headquarters@scfs.org
Web: www.scfs.org
Cross-cultural evangelism to seafarers carried out by missionaries employed in ports around the world.
Director: Mr Michael J Wilson. *Administrator:* Mr J C Gordon Pickering. Executive staff 2, Serving missionaries 17, Other staff 1. ***CC*** No.209133. Began 1846; interdenominational. Magazine: *The Helmsman* (10,000 quarterly). Turnover £250,000 to year end Dec 04.

***Servants to Asia's Urban Poor**, 30 Osborne Road, Coventry CV5 6DY
☎024 7672 1093
E: uk@servantsasia.org
Web: www.servantsasia.org
Living and participating with the poor in evangelism and community development in Asia's urban slums.
UK Coordinator: Mrs Helen Sidebotham. No full-time staff, Serving missionaries 1. ***CC*** No.1031973. Began 1992; interdenominational. No magazine. Turnover £16,313 to year end Dec 04.

Servite Friars, St Mary's Priory, 264 Fulham Road, London SW10 9EL
☎020 7352 6965 📠020 7351 9749
Prior Provincial: Rev Patrick Ryall. Community n/a, Serving missionaries 3. ***CC*** Began 1864; Roman Catholic. Magazine: *Servite Missions* (10,000 annually). Turnover n/a.

Sharing Christ Internationally, PO Box 351, London W10 5GB
☎01274 598 138
E: clarsciimf@blueyonder.co.uk
Supporting the translation of the Bible and other Christian books in Mongolian including in Braille.
Contact point: Mr D J Clarke. *Field Director, Mongolia:* Mr John Gibbens. Executive staff 2, Currently no UK missionaries serving overseas. ***CC*** No.328110. Began 1986; interdenominational. Magazine: *Focus on Mongolia* (1,300 quarterly). Turnover £23,171 to year end Jun 02.

Signpost International, The Mark Henderson Centre, Ann Street, Dundee DD3 7TH
☎01382 660 072 📠01382 666 681
E: enquiries@signpost-international.org
Web: www.signpost-international.org
Sharing the Gospel in word and action to families and children at risk; UK / worldwide.
International Director: Captain Kerry Dixon. *Head of Mission:* Rev Hugh Henderson. Executive staff 6, Serving missionaries 2, Admin staff 6. ***CC*** No.1057437. Began 1992; interdenominational. Magazine: *Signpost International* (4,500 half-yearly). Turnover £650,000 to year end Mar 05.

***SIM UK (Serving in Mission)**, Wetheringsett Manor, Wetheringsett, Stowmarket IP14 5QX
☎01449 766 464 🖷01449 767 148
E: postmast@sim.co.uk
Web: www.sim.co.uk
Working in Africa, Asia and South America.
Director, UK & North Europe: Mr Keith Walker. *International Director, USA:* Mr Malcolm McGregor. *Associate Director:* Mr Will Elphick. Executive staff 2, Serving missionaries 131, Other staff 20. ***CC*** No.219763. Began 1889; interdenominational. Incorporating Africa Evangelical Fellowship. Magazine: *Mission Together* (7,500 every four months). Turnover £3,200,000 to year end Sep 04.
Ireland: SIM Ireland, 285a Woodstock Road, Belfast BT6 8PR
☎028 9045 1451
Scotland: SIM Scotland, 110 St James Road, Glasgow G4 0PS
☎01475 520 474

***Sisters of Charity of Jesus and Mary**, 108 Spring Road, Letchworth SG6 3SL
☎01462 675 694 🖷01462 623 862
E: helen@scjm.org
Caring for elderly people with disabilities, chaplaincy, nursing, education, parish work.
Provincial Superior: Sr Helen O'Brien. Community 38. Currently no UK missionaries serving overseas ***CC*** No.251262. Began 1802; Roman Catholic. No magazine. Turnover n/a.

Sisters of Charity of Our Lady of Evron, Emmaus, Sudell Street, Collyhurst, Manchester M4 4JG
☎0161 834 8828 🖷0161 833 3674
Provincial Superior: Sr Mary Linnane. Community n/a, Serving missionaries 2. Began n/a; Roman Catholic. No magazine. Turnover n/a.

Sisters of Charity of St Jeanne Antide Thouret, 53 Bethune Road, Stoke Newington, London N16 5EE
☎020 8802 3430 🖷020 8800 5182
Regional Superior: Sr Mary Bernadette Hunston. Community n/a, Serving missionaries 1. ***CC*** No.246712. Began 1903; Roman Catholic. No magazine. Turnover n/a.

Sisters of Charity of St Paul, 94 Selly Park, Birmingham B29 7LL
☎0121 415 6103 🖷0121 414 1063
E: secretary@sellypark.org
Web: www.sellypark.org
Superior General: Sr Thérèse Browne. Community n/a, Serving missionaries 3. ***CC*** No.211200. Began 1847; Roman Catholic. No magazine. Turnover n/a.

Sisters of Christ, 9 Lower Road, Bedhampton, Havant PO9 3LH
☎023 9247 5112 🖷023 9248 1556
Working with disadvantaged people.
Contact: Sister Superior. Community 25, Serving missionaries 3. ***CC*** No.294746. Began n/a; Roman Catholic. No magazine. Turnover n/a.

Sisters of Christian Instruction (St Gildas), Summerhill, Leecroft Road, Barnet EN5 2TH
☎020 8449 2690 🖷020 8449 2690
E: stgildas@talk21.com
Regional Superior: Sr Paula O'Leary. Community n/a, Serving missionaries 2. ***CC*** No.265715. Began 1903; Roman Catholic. No magazine. Turnover n/a.

Sisters of La Retraite, Emmaus House, Clifton Hill, Bristol BS8 4PD
☎0117 907 9955 🖷0117 377 1769
E: annemmaus@compuserve.com
Provincial: Sr Ann O'Sullivan. Community n/a, Currently no UK missionaries serving overseas. ***CC*** No.266160. Began 1880; Roman Catholic. No magazine. Turnover n/a.

Sisters of Notre Dame de Namur, Lancaster House, Lancaster Lane, Parbold, Wigan WN8 7HT
☎01257 465 000 🖷01257 464 544
E: ukprov@aol.com
Provincial Moderator: Sr Kathleen McGhee. Community n/a, Serving missionaries 8. ***CC*** No.232411. Began 1804; Roman Catholic. No magazine. Turnover n/a.

Sisters of Our Lady of Charity, Fairlight, The Avenue, Ascot SL5 7LY
☎01344 876 447 🖷01344 876 447
E: charlotte@olc.ndo.co.uk
Provincial Superior: Sr Charlotte Cassidy. Community n/a, Serving missionaries 1. ***CC*** Began 1641; Roman Catholic. No magazine. Turnover n/a.

Sisters of Our Lady of Fidelity, Virgo Fidelis Convent, Central Hill, Upper Norwood, London SE19 1RS
☎020 8670 2506 🖷020 8761 7459
Clinic, nutritional centre and training.
Mother Superior: Sr Bernadette. Community 10. Currently no UK missionaries serving overseas ***CC*** No.245644. Began 1841; Roman Catholic. (Previously Society of the Faithful Virgin). No magazine. Turnover n/a.

Sisters of Providence, Rosminians, The Convent, Park Road, Loughborough LE11 2EF
☎01509 260 621 🖷01509 267 059
E: rosminiansisters@talk21.com
Councillor: Sr M Bernardine Shaw. Community n/a, Serving missionaries 3. ***CC*** No.229120. Began 1843; Roman Catholic. No magazine. Turnover n/a.

Sisters of St Clare, St Clare's Convent, 15 Glyndebourne Gardens, Corby NN18 0QA
☎01536 741 425 🖷01536 743 573
Regional Superior: Sr Stephanie Davidson. Community n/a, Serving missionaries 2. ***CC*** No.247380. Began 1212; Roman Catholic. No magazine. Turnover n/a.

Sisters of St Joseph of Annecy, St Joseph's House, Llantarnam Abbey, Cwmbran NP44 3YJ
☎01633 483 232 🖷01633 872 [illegible]35
Web: www.geocities.com/s[illegible]jannec[illegible]1
Provincial Superior: Sr Alice Mary Brennan. Community 40, Serving missionaries 2. ***CC*** No.232[illegible]35. Began [illegible]650; Roman Catholic. No magazine. Turnover n/a.

Sisters of St Joseph of Cluny St Joseph's Convent, Lichfield Road, Stafford ST17 4LG
☎01785 251 577 🖷01785 223 [illegible]36
Superior: Sr Teresa Cunniffe. Community 19, Serving missionaries 1. ***CC*** No.237340. Began 1903; Roman Catholic. No magazine. Turnover n/a.

Sisters of St Marie Madeleine Postel, 236 Alcester Road South, Kings Heath, Birmingham B14 6DR
☎0121 444 7463
Education, nursing, pastoral ministry and evangelisation.
Provincial Superior: Sr Frances [illegible]an. Community n/a, Serving missionaries 1. ***CC*** No.264529. Began 1894; Roman Catholic. No magazine. Turnover n/a.

Sisters of St Mary of Namur, [illegible]7 Cornwall Crescent, London W11 [illegible]PJ
☎020 7727 4208 / 7221 4[illegible]50
🖷020 7221 3382
E: louise@ssmnbrit.demon.co.uk
Provincial Superior: Sr Louise Swanson. Community 27, Serving missionaries 2. ***CC*** No.232842. Began 18[illegible]6; Roman Catholic. No magazine. Turnover n/a.

***Sisters of St Peter Claver** 70 The Avenue, Beckenham BR3 2ES
☎020 8650 5744 🖷020 86[illegible]8 535[illegible]
Provincial Superior: Sr Monica Daly. Community 3. Currently no UK missionaries serving overseas ***CC*** No.10489[illegible]6. Began n/a; Roman Catholic. No magazine. Turnover £200,000 to year end Dec 02.

Sisters of the Cross and Passion, Cross and Passion Convent, Boarshaw Road, Middleton, Manchester M24 2PF
☎0161 655 3184 🖷0161 653 3666
Provincial Superior: Sr Moya Cleary. Community n/a, Serving missionaries 3. Began 1852; Roman Catholic. No magazine. Turnover n/a.

Sisters of the Good Saviour (Bon Sauveur), Brynhyfryd, Longford Road, Holyhead LL65 1TR
☎01407 762 084
Contact: Sr Sylvia Healy. Community [illegible] Currently no UK missionaries serving overseas. ***CC*** No.225925. Began 190[illegible] Roman Catholic. No magazine. Turnover n/a.

For further information see lists on Pages 263 - 28[illegible]

O

Sisters of the Holy Family of Bordeaux, 2 Aberdare Gardens, London NW6 3PX
☎020 7624 7573
🖷020 7625 8984
E: hfb.provincial@virgin.net
Web: www.holyfamilybordeaux.org
Provincial Superior: Sr Kate Cuskelly. Community 154, Serving missionaries 4. ***CC*** No.232633. Began 1820; Roman Catholic. No magazine. Turnover n/a.

Sisters of the Holy Family (St Emilie de Rodat), 36 Albert Square, South Lambeth, London SW8 1BZ
☎020 7782 2016
🖷020 7735 6568
E: marion@hfe.demon.co.uk
International congregation.
Provincial Superior: Sr Marion Daly. *Superior General, France:* Sr Magdelena Leon. Community n/a. Currently no UK missionaries serving overseas ***CC*** Began 1904; Roman Catholic. No magazine. Turnover n/a.

Sisters of the Sacred Heart of Jesus and Mary, 803 Chigwell Road, Woodford Green IG8 8AU
☎020 8504 1624
🖷020 8559 2149
E: shjmgensec@aol.com
Superior General: Sr Catherine Collins. Community n/a, Serving missionaries 5. ***CC*** No.287232. Began 1903; Roman Catholic. No magazine. Turnover n/a.

Society of African Missions, 378 Upper Brook Street, Manchester M13 0EP
☎0161 224 4949
🖷0161 248 0241
E: thomasjryan@compuserve.com
Provincial Superior: Rev Tom Ryan. *Superior General, Italy:* Very Rev K O'Reilly. Home staff 10, Serving missionaries 4. ***CC*** No.232541. Began 1923; Roman Catholic. Magazine: *Mission News* (25,000 quarterly). Turnover n/a.

Society of Jesus, 114 Mount Street, London W1K 3AH
☎020 7499 0285
🖷020 7408 7111
E: curia@gbsj.org
Web: www.jesuit.co.uk
Provincial Superior: Rev David Smolira. *Superior General, Italy:* Rev Peter H Kolvenbach. Community n/a, Serving missionaries 33. ***CC*** No.230165. Began 1540; Roman Catholic. Magazine: *Jesuits & Friends* (12,000 every four months). Turnover n/a.

Society of Marie Reparatrice, 115 The Ridgway, Wimbledon, London SW19 4RB
☎020 8946 1088
🖷020 8947 9820
E: retreathouse.wim@smr.org
Welcoming groups and individuals who desire prayer and quiet reflection.
Provincial Superior: Sr Maureen Peart. Community 5. Currently no UK missionaries serving overseas. Began n/a; Roman Catholic. No magazine. Turnover n/a.

Society of Mary, Provincial House, 3 Hamilton Road, Sidcup DA15 7HB
☎020 8300 5339 🖷020 8300 9733
Web: freespace.virgin.net/marist.sidcup
Provincial Superior: Rev Clive Birch. Community n/a, Serving missionaries 4. ***CC*** No.235412. Began 1836; Roman Catholic. No magazine. Turnover n/a.

Society of the Divine Saviour (Salvatorians), 129 Spencer Road, Harrow Weald, Harrow HA3 7BJ
☎020 8426 0495 🖷020 8426 0972
Provincial: Rev Desmond Cantwell. Serving missionaries 2. ***CC*** No.231410. Began 1901; Roman Catholic. No magazine. Turnover n/a.

Society of the Holy Child Jesus, 10 Holland Villas Road, London W14 8BP
☎020 7603 2133 🖷020 7602 7304
E: europeanprovince@shcj.org
Web: www.shcj.org
Provincial Superior: Sr Louise Frey. Community n/a, Serving missionaries 1. ***CC*** No.223035. Began 1846; Roman Catholic. No magazine. Turnover n/a.

Society of the Sacred Heart, 3 Bute Gardens, London W6 7DR
☎020 8748 9353 🖷020 8748 6814
E: sshprovincial@aol.com
Provincial Superior: Sr Mary Hinde. *Superior General, Italy:* Sr Clare Pratt. Community n/a, Serving missionaries 1. ***CC*** No.227848. Began 1842; Roman Catholic. No magazine. Turnover n/a.

SOMA (Sharing of Ministries Abroad), PO Box 6002, Heath and Reach, Leighton Buzzard LU7 0ZA
☎01525 237 953 🖷01525 237 954
E: info@somauk.org
Web: www.somauk.org
Assisting renewal of the Anglican Communion by training and sending teams on short-term missions.
National Director: Rev Don Brewin. Executive staff 1, Other staff 2, Serving missionaries n/a. ***CC*** No.279759. Began 1979; Anglican. Magazine: *Sharing* (3,000 every four months). Turnover £130,000 to year end Jan 05.

***South American Mission Society**, Allen Gardiner Cottage, Pembury Road, Tunbridge Wells TN2 3QU
☎020 8506 0973 🖷01892 525 797
E: gensec@samsgb.org
Web: www.samsgb.org
General Secretary: Rev Canon John Sutton. *Financial and Administrative Secretary:* Mr Philip Tadman. Executive staff 3, Serving missionaries 33, Associates 28. ***CC*** No.221328. Began 1844; Anglican. Magazine: *Share* (9,000 quarterly). Turnover £1,564,307 to year end Dec 04.

Spanish Gospel Mission, 70 Butts Road, Barton-upon-Humber DN18 5JH
☎01652 661 340
E: office@spanish-gospel-mission.org.uk
Web: www.spanish-gospel-mission.org.uk
Propagating the Protestant evangelical faith in Spain and encouraging Christians to support the work.
Home Secretary: Rev David M Stevens. *Secretary of Field Council Spain:* Sr Manolo Valero. Executive staff 1, Serving missionaries 8. ***CC*** No.1017224. Began 1913; interdenominational. Magazine: *Spotlight on Spain* (3,250 half-yearly). Turnover £120,000 to year end Dec 04.

***Tearfund**, 100 Church Road, Teddington TW11 8QE
☎020 8977 9144 🖷020 8943 3594
E: enquiry@tearfund.org
Web: www.tearfund.org
Evangelical Christian relief and development charity working for physical/spiritual transformation in poor communities worldwide.
Chief Executive: Mr Matthew Frost. *Deputy Chief Executive:* Mr Graham Fairbairn. *Director of Finance:* Mr Richard Gough. Executive staff 11, Staff serving overseas 37, Other staff 268. ***CC*** No.265464. Began 1968; interdenominational. Magazine: *Tear Times* (224,000 quarterly). Turnover £53,025,000 to year end Mar 05.

***Trans World Radio Ltd**, PO Box 606, Altrincham WA14 2YS
☎0161 923 0272
E: info@twr.org.uk
Web: www.twr.org.uk
Working in over 50 countries worldwide through direct involvement or cooperation with TWR Partners.
Chief Executive: Rev Dr Russell Farnworth. Executive staff 1, Serving missionaries 2, Other staff 11. ***CC*** No.233363. Began 1963; interdenominational. Magazine: *Listening World* (30,000 quarterly). Turnover £1,000,000 to year end Dec 99.

***UFM Worldwide**, 145 Faringdon Road, Swindon SN1 5DL
☎01793 610 515 🖷01793 432 255
E: ufm@ufm.org.uk
Web: www.ufm.org.uk
Evangelical mission committed to pioneer evangelism and church planting worldwide in partnership with local churches.
Director: Peter Milsom. Executive staff 2, Serving missionaries 80, Other staff 10. ***CC*** No.219946. Began 1931; interdenominational. Magazine: *4 Corners* (9,000 every four months). Turnover n/a
Ireland: Howard Buildings, 28 Howard Street, Belfast BT1 6PD
☎028 9023 2404
Scotland: 11 Newton Place, Glasgow G3 7PR
☎0141 353 0666

United Reformed Church International Relations
See United Reformed Church headquarters on page 177.

For further information see lists on Pages 2[illegible]3 - 28[illegible]

United Society for the Propagation of the Gospel, Partnership House, 157 Waterloo Road, London SE1 8XA
☎020 7803 3422 🖷020 7928 2371
E: enquiries@uspg.org.uk
Web: www.uspg.org.uk
General Secretary: Rt Rev Michael Doe. *Chair of Governors:* Rev Alan Moses. *Central Services Director & Deputy General Secretary:* Mr Michael Hart. Executive staff 9, Serving missionaries 99, Other staff 44. CC No.234518. Began 1701; Anglican. Joint programmes of Anglican and Methodist Church. Magazine: *TransMission* (25,000 quarterly). Turnover £4,753,000 to year end Dec 05. Enabling people to grow spiritually, to thrive physically, to have a voice in an unjust world.

Ursuline Sisters, 28 Mansel Road, Wimbledon, London SW19 4AA
☎020 8946 8191 🖷020 8946 4569
E: ursprov@aol.com
Provincial: Sister Anne Benyon. Community 65, Serving missionaries 5. ***CC*** No.245651 Began 1535; Roman Catholic. No magazine. Turnover n/a.

Volunteer Missionary Movement, Hope Park, Liverpool L16 9JD
☎0151 291 3438 🖷0151 291 3298
E: vmm@hope.ac.uk
Partnering with local communities to address causes and symptoms of hunger, poverty, disease and injustice.
Regional Coordinator: Mr Cliff Jenkinson. Executive staff 2, Serving missionaries 19, Other staff 2. ***CC*** No.314104. Began 1969; interdenominational. Magazine: *VMM Newsletter* (2,000 every four months). Turnover £130,000 to year end Dec 97.

***WEC International**, Bulstrode, Oxford Road, Gerrards Cross SL9 8SZ
☎01753 884 631 🖷01753 278 166
E: info@uk.wec-int.org
Web: www.wec-int.org
Working to see Christ loved and worshipped by the remaining unevangelised peoples of the world.
UK Directors: Mr & Mrs Stuart & Jean Moulds. *Deputy UK Directors:* Mr & Mrs David & Margie Whitehorn. *International Directors, UK:* Mr & Mrs Trevor & Jenny Kallmier. Admin staff 30, Serving missionaries 196. ***CC*** No.237005. Began 1913; interdenominational. Magazine: *Worldwide* (5,100 every two months). Turnover £2,841,000 [excluding designated donations] to year end Mar 05.
Scottish Headquarters: *Scottish Coordinators:* Mr & Mrs Wilf & Pat Urquhart, International Christian College, 110 St James Road, Glasgow G4 0PS
E: scotland@uk.wec-int.org
M: 07922 163 700
Ireland Headquarters: *National Coordinators:* Mr & Mrs John & Ruth Hamilton, 35 Seagoe Road, Portadown, Craigavon BT63 5HW
E: johnandruth.hamilton@btinternet. com
☎028 3833 6725

†World Gospel Mission, 8 Beechcroft, Dollingstown, Craigavon BT66 7GL
☎028 3832 8197 M: 07879 420 443
🖷028 3832 8197
E: tommy@tommyanderson.freeserve.co.uk
Web: www.wgm.org
Director: Mr Tommy Anderson. *President, USA:* Rev Hebert Harriman. Executive staff 6, Serving missionaries 2, Other staff 2. ***CC*** No.274142. Began 1910; interdenominational. Magazine: *Call To Prayer* (800 every two months). Turnover £27,500 to year end Dec 02.

***World Horizons UK**, Centre for the Nations, North Dock, Llanelli SA15 2LF
☎01554 750 005 🖷01554 773 304
E: enquiries@worldhorizons.co.uk
Web: www.worldhorizons.co.uk
Prayer-based, pioneering, prophetic and pastoral mission movement for places/people not yet reached.
UK Director: Mr Tim Morris. *Team Leaders:* Mr Graham Davies, Mr Robert Snowdon. Executive staff 4, Serving missionaries 57, Other staff 25. ***CC*** No.513524. Began 1976; interdenominational. No magazine. Turnover £150,000 to year end Jan 02.

***World Outreach**, World Outreach, PO Box 7973, Reading RG6 5WY
☎0118 967 3355
E: mission@wouk.org
Web: www.wouk.org
Training church leaders, church planting among unreached, reaching children, facilitating non-western missionaries, humanitarian relief.
UK Director: Dr Michael Cross. *International Director, Singapore:* Rev John Elliott. Executive staff 1, Serving missionaries 4, Other staff 2 ***CC*** No.1101264. Began 1932; interdenominational. Magazine: *Nations* (11,000 quarterly). Turnover £493,155 to year end Dec 99.

World-Wide Advent Missions
Contact Seventh-day Adventist headquarters on page 176.

***Wycliffe Bible Translators**, Wycliffe Centre, Horsleys Green, High Wycombe HP14 3XL
☎01494 682 268 🖷01494 682 300
E: askus@wycliffe.org
Web: www.wycliffe.org.uk
Translating and distributing Scriptures in minority languages with related literacy and language development.
Executive Officer: Mr Geoff Knott. Executive staff 17, Serving missionaries 305, Other staff 32. ***CC*** No.251233. Began 1954; interdenominational. Magazine: *Words for Life* (12,500 quarterly). Turnover £5,945,260 to year end Sep 04.
Scotland: *Scottish Director:* Mr David Gilchrist, 129 High Street, Linlithgow EH49 7EJ
E: scotland_uk@wycliffe.org
☎01506 840 500
Northern Ireland: *Northern Ireland Director:* Mr John Hamilton, 342 Beersbridge Road, Belfast BT5 5DY
E: nireland_uk@wycliffe.org
☎028 9046 9905

Xaverian Missionary Fathers, St Francis Xavier Centre, Calder Avenue, Coatbridge ML5 4JS
☎01236 606 364 🖷01236 606 365
E: coatbridge@xavs.org
Provincial Superior: Rev Tom Welsh. Home staff 9. Currently no UK missionaries serving overseas. ***CC*** No.35191. Began 1895; Roman Catholic. Magazine: *Xaverian Way* (5,000 every two months). Turnover n/a.

***Youth With A Mission (YWAM) - England**, Highfield Oval, Ambrose Lane, Harpenden AL5 4BX
☎01582 463 216 🖷01582 463 213
E: enquiries@oval.com
Web: www.ywam-england.com
Training and mercy ministries.
Director (England): Mr Donovan Palmer. *Europe, Middle East & Africa Director:* Mr Lynn Green. Executive staff 25, Serving missionaries 303. ***CC*** No.264078. Began 1972; interdenominational. Magazine: *Advance* (1,600 quarterly). Turnover £2,500,000 to year end Dec 04.
Northern Ireland: *Director Northern Ireland:* Mr Mike Oman, 45 Closkelt Road, Ballyward, Castlewellan BT31 9QF
E: niywam@aol.com
☎028 4067 1919
Scotland: *Director Scotland:* Mr Andy Hall, The Seamill Missionary Training Centre, 9 Glenbryde Road, Seamill, West Kilbride KA23 9NJ
E: seamill@ywamscotland.org
☎01294 829 400 🖷 01294 829 312
Wales: *Director Wales:* Mr Mark Vening, PO Box 5, Llangollen LL20 8ZG
E: north-wales@ywam.co.uk

***Zambesi Mission**, 80 Sir Douglas Park, Stockton-on-Tees TS17 0JZ
☎01642 763 681
E: j.hasnip@zambesimission.org
Web: www.zambesimission.org
Supporting, supplying and strengthening the national church in Malawi and northen Mozambique.
Director: Mr Jim Hasnip. *Hon Treasurer:* Mr Colin Stonelake. Executive staff 1, Serving missionaries 7. ***CC*** No.1078673. Began 1892; interdenominational. Magazine: *In Prayer* (2,000 quarterly), *Update* (2,000 quarterly). Turnover £254,000 to year end Dec 04.

MISSION SUPPORT ORGANISATIONS

***African Pastor's Fellowship**, 2 Binley Avenue, Binley, Coventry CV3 2EE
☎024 7644 8068 📠024 7644 8068
E: africanpastors@aol.com
Web: www.africanpastors.org
Providing training and practical support for church leaders and their dependants in Africa.
Director: Rev Ralph Hanger. Executive staff 1, Other staff 2. ***CC*** No.282756. Began 1974; interdenominational. Magazine: *Information Sheet* (1,500 monthly). Turnover £125,000 to year end Dec 04.

Aid to the Church in Need, 1 Times Square, Sutton SM1 1LF
☎020 8642 8668 📠020 8661 6293
E: acn@acnuk.org
Web: www.acnuk.org
Pastoral aid agency of the Roman Catholic Church wherever she is in need.
National Director: Mr Neville Kyrke-Smith. Executive staff 5, Other staff 21. ***CC*** No.1097984. Began 1973; Roman Catholic. Magazine: *Mirror* (50,000 every six weeks). Turnover £4,990,000 to year end Dec 04.

***AsiaLink**, 2 Kingswood Close, Lytham St Annes FY8 4RE
☎01253 733 801 📠01253 733 770
E: talk2us@asialink.org.uk
Web: www.asialink.org.uk
Encouraging and supporting the Asian church in its mission to unreached peoples.
Executive Director (Operations): Colin Dudgeon. Executive staff 4, Other staff 3. ***CC*** No.327165. Began 1982; interdenominational. Magazine: *Asialink - the Magazine* (3,500 quarterly). Turnover n/a.

The Asian Christian Development Programme, 18 Woodville Road, Brierfield, Nelson BB9 5RW
☎01282 613 094 📠01282 613 094
E: tacdp@onetel.net.uk
Supporting Christian workers, developing the Christian community and Church in Pakistan and Asia.
Trustee/International Director: Rev David L White. Executive staff 4. Began 1990; interdenominational. No magazine. Turnover £9,000 to year end Dec 98.

†Asian Outreach UK, Christians Alive, Lancaster Church Offices, 1 The Barracks, White Cross, South Road, Lancaster LA1 4XD
☎01524 845 544
E: agorman@fish.co.uk
Serving the church in Asia by every means possible. Affiliated to AO International in Hong Kong.
Executive Director: Mrs Ann Borman. No full-time staff. ***CC*** No.1088419. Began n/a; interdenominational. Turnover £10,000 to year end Dec 02.

***Assist Europe**, Fountains Building, Upper Northgate Street, Chester CH1 4EF
M: 07722 813 230 📠 01782 641 121
E: assisteurope@yahoo.co.uk
Web: www.assisteurope.net
Director: Mr Peter Wooding. No full-time staff. ***CC*** No.328309. Began 1989; interdenominational. No magazine. Turnover £10,000 to year end Dec 02. Supporting comfort and reconciliation centre in Beslan, Russia, and special needs orphanage in Vladikavkaz.

***Bethany Ministries**, 1 Ashby Road, Packington, Ashby-de-la-Zouch LE65 1TD
☎01530 564 412 M 07970 147 207
📠01530 564 417
E: robertwawildgoose@btinternet.com
Organising itineraries of visiting overseas ministries, support of UK missionaries abroad and musical events.
Chairman: Rev Robert W A Wildgoose. No full-time staff. ***CC*** No.701425. Began 1984; interdenominational. No magazine. Turnover £14,300 to year end Apr 05.

BibleLands, PO Box 50, High Wycombe HP15 7QU
☎01494 897 950 📠01494 897 951
E: info@biblelands.co.uk
Web: www.biblelands.org.uk
Supporting Christians in Bible lands: education, social/medical care, special needs, training, refugees.
Director: Nigel Edward-Few. *Head of Overseas Programmes:* Mo Burnley. *Head of Finance:* Rev Nick Plant. Executive staff 4, Other staff 14. ***CC*** No.1076329. Began 1854; non-denominational. (Previously The Bible Lands Society). Magazine: *The Star in the East* (30,000 half-yearly). Turnover £3,106,177 to year end Apr 05.

***Brass Tacks**, 17 Osborne Avenue, Wallasey CH45 1JD
☎0151 630 1182
E: brasstacksuk@aol.com
Web: www.brass-tacks.org.uk
Providing practical and technical service to missionaries overseas using volunteer workers.
Executive Director: Mr Colin Breeze. Executive staff 1, Admin staff 3. ***CC*** No.2216281. Began 1986; Open Brethren. Magazine: *Brass Tacks News* (5,000 every four months). Turnover £90,000 to year end Apr 04.

Bridgebuilders International Charitable Trust, 30 Farley Copse, Bracknell RG42 1PF
☎01344 484 235 📠01344 484 219
E: bict@4keys.co.uk
Web: www.4keys.co.uk/bict
Encouraging, challenging and guiding individuals, groups and churches.
Director: Mr Richard Emery. Executive staff 1. ***CC*** No.1043086. Began 1995; interdenominational. No magazine. Turnover n/a.

***Cambodian Communities Out of Crisis**, PO Box 7591, Loughborough LE12 9WN
☎01509 507 402 M 07968 778 990
📠01509 507 402
E: info@cambcomm.org.uk
Web: www.cambcomm.org.uk
Equipping the Cambodian Church for ministry and expressing Jesus Christ's love for the Cambodian people.
Director: Rev Ross Rennie. Executive staff 1. ***CC*** No.1062205. Began 1994; non-denominational. Magazine: *The Cambodian Herald*(Circulation & frequency n/a). Turnover £10,000 to year end Dec 03.

Roman Catholic Bishops' Conference Department of Mission and Unity, 39 Eccleston Square, London SW1V 1BX
☎020 7901 4842 📠020 7901 4821
E: misunity@cbcew.org.uk
Web: www.catholic-aw.org.uk
Encouraging Christian unity, relationships with other faiths, home and overseas mission.
Chairman: Rt Rev Crispian Hollis. *Secretary:* To be appointed. Executive staff 2. ***CC*** No.257239. Began 1984; Roman Catholic. No magazine. Turnover n/a.
Note: Each Diocese has an Officer for this area of ministry. Contact them via the appropriate Curial Office.

Catholic Missionary Union of England and Wales, 8 King Harry Lane St Albans AL3 4AW
☎01727 861 463
E: llabbesc@hotmail.com
Web: www.cmu.org.uk
Forum where all missionary activity and interests come together.
Secretary: Br Leo Labbe. Executive staff 2, Other staff 1. ***CC*** No.257239. Began 1971; Roman Catholic. Magazine: *Focus* (750 quarterly). Turnover n/a.

†*CEDARS (Charity Equipment for Development & Relief Services), Bulstrode, Oxford Road, Gerrards Cross SL9 8SZ
☎01753 886 105 📠01753 889 378
E: unimatco@aol.com
Web: www.unimatco.co.uk
Freight forwarding for Christians overseas; funding for aid equipment for missions.
Director: Mrs Brenda Chudley. Executive staff 1, Other staff 1. ***CC*** No.1[illegible]77217. Began 1981; interdenominational. No magazine. Turnover n/a.

Morris Cerullo World Evangelism Society of Great Britain, PO Box 27[illegible], Hemel Hempstead HP2 7DH
☎01442 232 432 📠01442 288 494
E: englandoffice@mcwe.co.uk
Web: www.mcwe.com
Evangelising and training nationals worldwide.
European Director: Mr Julian Richards. Executive staff 4, Other staff 3. ***CC*** Began 1961; interdenominational. No magazine. Turnover n/a.

Chinese Church Support Ministries, PO Box 73, Bury BL9 7FW
☎0161 763 1500 M: 07711 528 881
🖷0161 763 1555
E: ccsm01@nildram.co.uk
Web: www.am-ccsm.org
China ministries short term teams; radio, literature tapes, sending professionals, mission outreach to students.
UK Director: Mr Ian Robertson. Executive staff 2, Other staff 5. **CC** No.327709. Began 1987; interdenominational. Magazine: *China Challenge* (3,500 monthly). Turnover £400,000 to year end Dec 05.

Christian International Relief Mission (CIRM), 44a Whittington Road, Stourbridge DY8 3DD
☎01384 390 152 🖷01384 393 871
E: cirmmissionuk@aol.com
Promoting church planting, evangelism, discipleship and social projects/ programmes worldwide.
Director: Mr Stephen Methuen. Executive staff 2, Other staff 2. **CC** No.1044410. Began 1958; interdenominational. Magazine: *CIRM News* (2,000 quarterly). Turnover £[illegible]6,500 to year end Jun 01.

Christian Resource Ministries, The Bible Shop, 168 King Street, Castle Douglas DG7 1DA
☎01556 504 416 🖷01556 504 416
Church planting in remote villages in Malawi, Mozambique, India; Bible distribution, orphanage, financing water boreholes.
International Fowarding Agent: Mr Jim Figgis. Staff n/a. **CC** No.SCO 30806. Began 1997; non-denominational. No magazine. Turnover £33,000 to year end Nov 04.

***Christian Solidarity Worldwide**, PO Box 99, New Malden KT3 3YF
☎020 8942 8810 🖷020 8942 8821
E: admin@csw.org.uk
Web www.csw.org.uk
Research and advocacy organisation helping persecuted Christians globally through campaigning, prayer.
Chief Executive: Mr Mervyn Thomas. *National Director:* Rev Stuart Windsor. Executive staff 2, Other staff 21. **CC** No.281836. Began 1979; interdenominational. Magazine: *Response* (20,000 every two months). Turnover £1,331,000 to year end Dec 04.

***Christian Vision**, PO Box 3040, West Bromwich B70 0EJ
☎0121 522 6087 🖷0121 522 6083
E: adminuk@christianvision.com
Web: www.christianvision.org
Supporting evangelism, leadership training, church planting programmes through nationals and media.
Director of Operations: Mr Terry Bennett. Executive staff 5, Other staff 20. **CC** No.1031031. Began 1988; Anglican. No magazine. Turnover n/a.

Christian Visual Aids Team, 68 Church Crescent, Muswell Hill Road, London N10 3NE
☎020 8883 4590
Missionary and church support ministry for film and filmstrip loan/hire; projector service in the UK only.
Hon Organising Secretary: Mr K E E Ponder. No paid staff. Began 1952; interdenominational. No magazine. Turnover n/a.

Christians Aware, 2 Saxby Street, Leicester LE2 0ND
☎0116 254 0770 🖷0116 254 0770
E: barbarabutler@christiansaware.co.uk
Web: www.christiansaware.co.uk
Developing international multi-cultural understanding, friendship and encounter by conferences, overseas visits and publications.
Executive Secretary: Mrs Barbara Butler. Executive staff 1. **CC** No.328322. Began 1977; ecumenical. Magazine: *Ecumenical Magazine* (1,200 quarterly). Turnover £80,000 to year end Sep 04.

Christians in Health Care, 11 Grove Road, Northwood HA6 2AP
☎01923 825 634 M: 07979 811 140
🖷01923 836 401
E: howard@lyons.co.uk
Web: www.christian-healthcare.org.uk
Specialist management consultants for medical-oriented missions; resource for missions and individuals in overseas healthcare.
Director: Mr Howard Lyons. No full-time staff. **CC** No.328018. Began 1989; interdenominational. Linked with MMA HealthServe. Magazine: *Among All Nations* (5,000 quarterly (published with MMA)). Turnover £7,500 to year end Dec 02.

Council for World Mission, Ipalo House, 32 Great Peter Street, London SW1P 2DB
☎020 7222 4214 🖷020 7233 1747
E: council@cwmission.org.uk
Web: www.cwmission.org.uk
Coordinating missionary activity of 31 churches worldwide, assisting them in sending and receiving personnel.
General Secretary: Rev Dr Des van der Water. *Secretary for Personnel Resources:* Rev Andrew Williams. *Secretary for Administration:* Mr Andrew Johnston. Executive staff 6, Other staff 18. **CC** No.1097842. Began 1795; reformed 1977 as an international and ecumenical body. Magazine: *Inside Out* (6,000 every two months). Turnover £5,000,000 to year end Dec 01.

DAI UK, 36 Deerbrook, Springfield Road, Ashford TW15 2LR
☎01784 245 602
E: jrogers@daintl.org
Web: www.daintl.org
Providing leadership development courses and management consultancy to enhance the effectiveness of Christian leaders worldwide.
Senior Consultant: Mr John Rogers. Executive staff 1. Began 2006; interdenominational. Part of DAI International. No magazine. Turnover: first year of operation.

The David House Fellowship, 78 Woodville Road, Cardiff CF24 4ED
☎029 2039 9119
E: dhf@btclick.com
Establishing and advancing the Christian Gospel of Jesus Christ among Jews.
Director: Mr Kenneth J Price. Executive staff 1, Other staff 1. **CC** No.267077. Began 1974; interdenominational. Magazine: *The Vineyard* (28,000 monthly). Turnover £100,000 to year end Jan 98.

†L'Eau Vive UK Trust, 172 Wier Road, London SW12 0NP
☎020 8675 2943
Supporting Christian outreach and training in France, especially among young people; church planting.
Trustee: Mr David Woods. No full-time staff. **CC** Began 1980; interdenominational. No magazine. Turnover n/a.

***ECHO International Health Services**, 1 New Street, Leamington Spa CV31 1HP
☎01926 315 301
🖷01926 885 786
E: echo@cord.org.uk
Providing financial support to health care institutions mainly in Sub-Saharan Africa and health care initiatives.
Chair of Trustees: Mr Ron Irwin. *Secretary to Trustees:* Mr Martin Lee. No full-time staff. Began 1966; non-denominational. No magazine. Turnover £100,400 to year end Dec 04.

Echoes of Service, 124 Wells Road, Bath BA2 3AH
☎01225 310 893 / 480 635
🖷01225 480 134
E: echoes@echoes.org.uk or echoes_of_service@msn.com
Web: www.echoes.org.uk
Missionary support group for Assembly missionaries; publishing news, forwarding gifts, caring for missionaries.
Managing Editor: John H Burness. Executive staff 2, Other staff 8. **CC** Began 1872; Christian Brethren. Magazine: *Echoes* (7,000 monthly). Turnover £3,500,000 to year end Dec 00.

Egypt Diocesan Association, The Horseshoes, The Green, Gressenhall, Dereham NR20 4DT
☎01362 860 302
🖷01362 860 302
E: elspeth.mackinlay@tesco.net
Web: eda-egypt.org.uk
Support for the Diocese of Egypt in prayer and finance.
Secretary: Mrs Elspeth Mackinlay. Staff n/a. **CC** No.209145. Began n/a; Anglican. No magazine. Turnover n/a.

***EMMS International (operating as Emmanuel Healthcare)**, 7 Washington Lane, Edinburgh EH11 2HA
☎0131 313 3828 🖷0131 313 4662
E: info@emms.org
Web: www.emms.org
Medical mission to the world community.
Chief Executive: Mr Robin G K Arnott. *Finance Officer:* Miss Barbara Hunt. Executive staff 1, Other staff 6. ***CC*** No.SCO 32327. Began 1841, merged with EHA (UK) in 2004; interdenominational. (Previously Edinburgh Medical Missionary Society). Magazine: *The Healing Hand* (4,000 every four months). Turnover £938,000 to year end Dec 04.

Encourage International Group, 20 Briarside Road, Brentry, Bristol BS10 6JA
☎0117 950 8334 🖷0870 132 9762
E:info@encourage-international.co.uk
Web: www.encourage-international.co.uk
Encouraging church planting through friendship, standing alongside missionaries.
International Director: Rev Alastair K C Dickson. Executive staff 1, Admin staff 1. Began 1988; interdenominational. No magazine. Turnover £25,000 to year end Aug 02.

†*Europe Now, PO Box 168, Bristol BS9 2YE
☎0117 914 9007 🖷0117 914 9007
E: en@oaci.org
Web: www.oaci.org/branches/europenow/
Equipping the church to proclaim the Gospel in mainland Europe.
Contact: Mr Steve Poulard. Executive staff 2, Other staff 1. ***CC*** No.1051283. Began 1995; non-denominational. No magazine. Turnover £44,000 to year end Dec 01.

***European Partners in Christ (EPIC)**, PO Box 15, Hadleigh, Ipswich IP7 7BE
☎01449 741 585 🖷01449 741 585
E: epic1996@aol.com
Web: www.epic-churches.org
Establishing partnership between churches in Eastern Europe and the UK also providing support for pastors.
Director: Miss Chris Fox. Admin staff 1. ***CC*** No.1057592. Began 1996; interdenominational. No magazine. Turnover £95,000 to year end Jul 05.

†Experience Exchange Programme, Methodist Church, 25 Marylebone Road, London NW1 5JR
☎020 7486 5502 🖷020 7467 5283
E: eep@methodistchurch.org.uk
Web: www.methodist.org.uk
Providing opportunities to share in mission situations overseas (6-12 months). Self-funded/voluntary.
Programme Officer: Mr Habib Nader. Executive staff 1, Other staff 4. ***CC*** No.234518. Began 1978; Anglican and Methodist. (Previously Short Term Experience Programmes & Experience Exchange). Joint programmes of Anglican and Methodist Church. No magazine. Turnover £100,000 to year end Dec 99.

***FEBC - Far East Broadcasting International**, UK Office, 1 Hazelwood Road, Callington PL17 7EU
☎01579 383 111 M: 07740 192 268
E: fgray@febi.org
Web: www.febc.org
Missionary radio broadcasting throughout East and Southeast Asia, Russia and CIS.
International Programme Director: Mr Frank Gray. Admin staff 3. Began 1991; interdenominational. Magazine: *The Broadcaster* (Circulation n/a quarterly (published in USA)). Turnover £50,000 to year end Jun 00.

***FFM**, PO Box 5864, Basildon SS13 3FF
☎01268 552 895
E: admin@ffm.org.uk
Challenging the church to pray for the Muslim world; literature work; inter-mission fellowship; annual conference.
Chairman: Mr Malcolm Steer. Full-time Staff 1. ***CC*** No.77687. Began 1915; interdenominational. Fellowship of Faith for the Muslims. No magazine. Turnover £31,939 to year end Dec 04.

†Freight Services International Ltd, Unit 8 Chester Park, Alfreton Road, Derby DE21 4AB
☎01332 347 48 🖷01332 293 549
E: fsiltd@aol.com
Web: www.fsiltd.com
Providing airfreight and seafreight services for churches, mission organisations and charities.
Managing Director: Mr Les Church. Executive staff 2, Other staff 2. Began 1998; non-denominational. No magazine. Turnover £300,000 to year end Aug 02.

Friends of Ludhiana, 157 Waterloo Road, London SE1 8UU
☎020 7928 1173
E: foluk@charis.co.uk
Web: www.friendsofludhiana.org.uk
Supporting the work of the Christian Medical College and Hospital in Ludhiana, Punjab, North India.
Executive Officer: Miss Heather Smith. Executive staff 1. ***CC*** No.314148. Began 1894; interdenominational. Magazine: *News Bulletin* (Circulation n/a quarterly). Turnover £120,600 to year end Dec 04.

Friends of the Church in China, Pin Mill, Chelmondiston, Ipswich IP9 1JN
☎01473 780 051
E: simon@rosemarybrown.freeserve.co.uk
Web: www.thefcc.org
Promoting contact, friendship, encouragement and understanding between Christians in Britain and Ireland and China.
Secretary: Canon Simon Brown. *Chairman:* Rev John Pritchard. No full-time staff. ***CC*** No.1004221. Began 1984; ecumenical. Magazine: *Newsletter* (550 every four months). Turnover £16,000 to year end Aug 05.

Friends of the Church in India, 15 Gorselands, Sedlescombe, Battle TN33 0PT
☎01424 870 431 M: 07761 838 083
E: msmith15@fish.co.uk
Web: www.f-c-i.org.uk
Encouraging prayerful interest in the life, work and mission of churches in India.
Secretary: Mrs Margaret Smith. No full-time staff. ***CC*** No.1042850. Began 1992; interdenominational. Magazine: *Pilgrim* (700 half-yearly). Turnover £6,523 to year end Mar 02.

Friends of Vellore, Flempton Hall, Bury Road, Flempton, Bury St Edmunds IP28 6EG
☎01284 728 453
E: friendsofvellore@flemphall.cilara.uk
Web: fovuk.tripod.com/home.html
Supporting medical work in Vellore, South India through a Christian Medical College Hospital and outreach.
Director: Mr Richard Smith. Executive staff 1. ***CC*** No.209168. Began 1940; interdenominational. Magazine: *Vellore Newsletter* (2,000 half-yearly). Turnover £100,000 to year end Dec 04.

Garden Tomb (Jerusalem) Association, South Hall, Merrow Grange, Horseshoe Lane East, Guildford GU1 2QW
☎01483 505 464 🖷01483 450 689
E: mail@gardentomb.com
Web: www.gardentomb.com
Maintaining the tomb and garden believed to be the garden of Joseph of Arimathea
General Secretary: Mr Peter G L Wells. Executive staff 1. ***CC*** No.1004062. Began 1893; interdenominational. No magazine. Turnover n/a.

The Girls' Brigade International, Challenge House, 29 Canal Street, Glasgow G4 0AD
☎0141 332 9696 🖷0141 332 9696
E: hq@gbic.org
Web: www.gbic.org
Youth-service movement operating in over 60 countries.
Vice President: Miss Sheena MacFarlane OBE. Executive staff 1, Other staff 2. ***CC*** Began 1893; interdenominational. No magazine. Turnover £100,000 to year end Dec 98.

Global Mission Network, CTBI, Bastille Court, 2 Paris Garden, London SE1 8ND
☎020 7654 7254 🖷020 7654 7222
E: ccom@ctbi.org.uk
Web: www.ctbi.org.uk
As part of CTBI, relating the churches' commitments to mission in Britain and Ireland with those in the wider world.
Secretary: Canon Janice Price. Executive staff 3, Other staff 1. ***CC*** No.259688. Began 1990; interdenominational. (Previously Churches' Commission on Mission). A commission of Churches Together in Britain and Ireland. Magazine: *Connections* (500 every four months). Turnover n/a.

For member organisations see list on page 22

***Go To The Nations Link**, 21 Hogshill Lane, Cobham KT11 2AG
☎01932 589 257 M: 07962 317 776
E: info@gonations.org
Web: www.gonations.org
Facilitating missionary relationships between churches in Brazil, UK and Europe to reach other nations together.
European Contact: Mr Stuart Lindsell. No full-time staff. ***CC*** No.1062124. Began 1993; interdenominational. (Previously Go To The Nations Ministry). Magazine: *What's Going On?* (1,000 quarterly). Turnover £10,000 to year end Dec 02.

Hope in Action/ Gobaith mewn Gweithrediad, 32 Garth Drive, Liverpool L18 6HW
☎0151 724 1989 🖷0151 724 5691
E: be@garthdrive.fsnet.co.uk
Web: www.lordsdaywales.co.uk
Assisting African countries in education and propagating the Gospel, especially Kenya.
Founders: Rev Prof D Ben Rees, Mr Hefin E Rees. No full-time staff. ***CC*** Began 1987; interdenominational. (Previously Faith in Action). Magazine: *Hope* (Circulation n/a annually). Turnover £1,500 to year end Dec 00.

Horizons International, 13 Victory Grove, Audenshaw, Manchester M34 5XA
☎0161 301 1162 🖷0161 301 1162
E: horizonsmission@aol.com
Web: www.horizonsinternational.org.uk
Working with national leaders; Eastern/Central Europe, South America, Africa; providing training, relief, literature, support.
Executive Director: Rev Colin Carson. *Director:* Mrs Judith Carson. Executive staff 2, Admin staff 1. ***CC*** No.1086929. Began 1998; interdenominational. No magazine. Turnover n/a.

ICC Missions, 4-5 Regency Mews, Silverdale Road, Eastbourne BN20 7AB
☎01323 643 341 🖷01323 649 240
E: info@icc.org.uk
Suppling a variety of resources in the Ukraine to help people in their Christian faith.
Chief Executive Director: Mr Peter Martin. Executive staff 2, Other staff 40. ***CC*** No.1079801. Began 1976; interdenominational. No magazine. Turnover n/a.

ICCOWE (International Charismatic Consultation on World Evangelisation), 36a Tutbury Avenue, Coventry CV4 7BJ
☎024 7669 6410 🖷024 7669 6377
E: office@iccowe.com
Web: www.iccowe.com
Furthering spiritual renewal, unity in Christ and evangelisation through international meetings and conferences.
Chairman: Mr Charles Whitehead. Admin staff 2. ***CC*** No.1003378. Began 1989; interdenominational. No magazine. Turnover £9,000 to year end Mar 02.

Ichthus Motor Mission Ltd, Grove Close, Forest Hill, London SE23 1AS
☎020 8291 5144 🖷020 8291 0273
E: enquiries@ichthusmotormission.com
Web: www.ichthusmotormission.com
Supplying motor vehicles to missionaries home on furlough or deputation.
Chairman: Mr M Beard. All voluntary staff. ***CC*** No.1028735. Began 1981; non-denominational. No magazine. Turnover £150,000 to year end Dec 95.

IDWAL (Inter-Diocesan West Africa Link), The Vicarage, Cot Lane, Chidham, Chichester PO18 8TA
☎01243 573 147
E: davidcpain@hotmail.com
Anglican friendship link between Dioceses of Guildford, Chichester and Portsmouth, and Provinces of Nigeria and West Africa.
Secretary: Rev Canon David Pain. All voluntary staff. Began 1964; Anglican. No magazine. Turnover n/a.
World Mission Officer: Rev Mark Payne, The Vicarage, Scaynes Hill, Haywards Heath RH17 7PB
☎01444 831 265

India Link Ministries, PO Box 5884, Basildon SS13 3AJ
☎01268 552 895 M: 07786 872 318
E: admin@indialink.org.uk
Web: www.indialink.org.uk
Assisting full-time Christian workers in India by partnership, practical aid, literature and Bible teaching/training.
Director: Mr Paul Barnes. No full-time staff. ***CC*** No.1063882. Began 1996; interdenominational. No magazine. Turnover £93,000 to year end Dec 04.

Indian Evangelical Team (UK), 27 Eynsford Rise, Eynsford, Dartford DA4 0HS
☎01322 865 059
E: voyagerministries@ukonline.co.uk
Web: eynsfordbaptist.co.uk
Representing Indian Evangelical Team in the UK; collecting funds, deputation work.
Director: Rev John Saunders. Executive staff 1. Began 2000; interdenominational. Magazine: *Faith Today* (10,000 worldwide). Turnover £6,350 to year end Mar 05.

***The Inter-National Needs Network**, 111b South End, Croydon CR0 1BJ
☎020 8688 3939 🖷020 8688 3939
E: inuk@ineeds.org.uk
Web: www.ineeds.org.uk
Supporting national workers worldwide; orphan sponsorship, relief, social projects; training centres, evangelism, missions.
National Director: Mr Peter Staley. Executive staff 1, Other staff 2. ***CC*** No.1010597. Began 1976; non-denominational. Magazine: *UK Update* (1,500 quarterly). Turnover £250,000 to year end Dec 04.

***InterHealth**, Partnership House, 157 Waterloo Road, London SE1 8US
☎020 7902 9000 🖷020 7902 9091
E: info@interhealth.org.uk
Web: www.interhealth.org.uk
Providing comprehensive healthcare services, supplies, advice to missions, aid agencies, GAP year organisations, voluntary sector.
Executive Director: David White. *Director of Health Care:* Dr Ted Lankester. *Marketing & Client Services:* Sarah Marfleet. Clinical Staff 13, Support Staff 13. ***CC*** No.1103935. Began 1989; interdenominational. No magazine. Turnover £1,500,000 to year end Sep 02.

The Jerusalem and the Middle East Church Association, 1 Hart House, The Hart, Farnham GU9 7HJ
☎01252 726 994 🖷01252 735 558
E: secretary@jmeca.eclipse.co.uk
Web: www.jmeca.org.uk
Enabling organisation serving the Anglican province of the Episcopal Church in Jerusalem and Middle East.
Secretary: Mrs Mary Knight. Executive staff 1. ***CC*** No.248799. Began 1887; Anglican. Magazine: *Bible Lands* (3,500 half-yearly). Turnover n/a.

†Jesuit Missions, 11 Edge Hill, Wimbledon, London SW19 4LR
☎020 8946 0466 🖷020 8946 2292
E: director@jesuitmissions.org.uk
Supporting Jesuits working in Guyana, Zimbabwe and South Africa.
Director: Mr Anthony E Montfort. *Assistant Director:* Mr Alan Fernandes. Executive staff 1, Other staff 2. ***CC*** No.230165. Began 1896; Roman Catholic. Magazine: *Jesuits and Friends* (28,000 every four months). Turnover £1,000,000 to year end Sep 98.

***Jian Hua Foundation**, 18 Birch Avenue, Carlton, Nottingham NG4 1EJ
☎0115 911 5654 M: 07711 361 637
🖷0115 911 1990
E: doug.plummer@jhf-china.org
Web: www.jhf-hk.org
An association of Christian professionals committed to service in China.
Coordinator for Europe: Doug Plummer. Executive staff 1, No other full-time staff. ***CC*** No.327925. Began 1982; interdenominational. No magazine. Turnover £80,000 to year end Dec 00.

†*Keston Institute, 38 St Aldate's, Oxford OX1 1BN
☎01865 792 929 🖷01865 240 042
E: keston.institute@keston.org
Web: www.keston.org
Monitoring freedom of religion and researching religious affairs in Communist and post-Communist countries.
Director: Dr Davorin Peterlin. *Research Director:* Dr Philip Walters. Executive staff 3, Other staff 3. ***CC*** No.314103. Began 1970; interdenominational. Journal: *Religion, State and Society* (Circulation n/a quarterly). Turnover £523,000 to year end Mar 02.

O

Kisumu Children's Trust, 4 The Cedars, Evercreech, Shepton Mallet BA4 6LG
☎01749 830 330
E: info@kisumuchildren.org.uk
Web: www.kisumuchildren.org.uk
Changing the lives of 60 orphaned children by providing loving, caring, educational Christian environment; Kenya.
Executive Secretary: Mr Michael Dare. Executive staff 1. ***CC*** No.1091477. Began 1994; interdenominational. (Previously Cherry Brierley Children's Home). Magazine: *Kisumu Children* (320 every four months). Turnover £38,000 to year end Dec 05.

***The Langham Partnership International**, 19 Whitfield Place, London W1T 5JX
☎020 7209 0915
🖷020 7209 0915
E: ian@langhampartnership.org
Web: www.langhampartnership.org
Supporting pastors, teachers and seminaries in developing world through literature, doctoral scholarships and preaching seminars.
International Ministries Director: Rev Dr Chris Wright. *Executive Director:* Ian Buchanan. Executive staff 5, Other staff 8. ***CC*** No.1092233. Began 1975; non-denominational. (Previously Langham Trust, Evangelical Literature Trust). Magazine: *Langham Partnership News* (1,500 every four months). Turnover £795,186 to year end Dec 04.

Life Changing Ministries International, PO Box 106, Colwyn Bay LL28 4XJ
☎01492 544 394
M: 07950 208 281
🖷01492 545 211
E: lcmi1@aol.com
Web: www.sonsofgod.co.uk
UK and overseas short term missions equipping nationals with the "Sons of God" vision.
Director: Rev David P Griffiths. Executive staff 1. ***CC*** No.1065192. Began 1996; non-denominational. Magazine: *Revival News* (Circulation & frequency n/a). Turnover £38,827 to year end Apr 04.

***Links International**, PO Box 198, Littlehampton BN16 3UQ
☎01903 778 515 🖷01903 778 516
E: office@linksinternational.org.uk
Web: www.linksinternational.org.uk
Joining together to serve the church around the world.
Directors: Mr Norman Barnes, Mr Rich Hubbard. Executive staff 2, Other staff 2. ***CC*** No.327000. Began 1982; in association with Pioneer. Magazine: *Links* (3,500 every four months). Turnover £545,000 to year end Dec 04.

LMI-Logos Ministries International, PO Box 1131, Belfast BT5 4UD
☎028 9045 8362 M: 07802 844 610
🖷028 9045 8362
E: info@logosministries.org.uk
Web: www.logos.ministries.org.uk
Motivating people into mission; providing information on missions and job opportunities both home and overseas.
Director: Rev Thomas McClean. Executive staff 4, Other staff 8. ***CC*** No.N 46135. Began 1977; interdenominational. (Previously Logos Ministries). Magazine: *Edge* (3,000 quarterly). Turnover £163,000 to year end Dec 02.

Manna Ministries Europe, West House Cottage, 21 Broadway, Chilton Polden, Bridgwater TA7 9DR
☎01278 722 310 M: 07941 650 207
🖷01278 723 357
E:davidoram@westhouse.freeserve.co.uk
Supporting workers in overseas locations; contributing funds to meet needs as made known.
Chief Executive: Rev David E J Oram. Executive staff 1. ***CC*** No.1090460. Began 1997; non-denominational. Magazine: *Macedonian Quarterly* (400 quarterly). Turnover £50,000 to year end Dec 02.

***Henry Martyn Trust**, Henry Martyn Centre, Westminster College, Cambridge CB3 0AA
☎01223 741 088 🖷01223 741 089
E: pk262@cam.ac.uk
Web: www.martynmission.cam.ac.uk
Promoting world mission through academic resources and vocational advice, particularly to students of Cambridge University.
Centre Director: Dr Brian Stanley. Executive staff 2, Other staff 5. ***CC*** No.266612. Began 1887; ecumenical. No magazine. Turnover n/a.

MasterServe, Thames House, 63 Kingston Road, New Malden KT3 3PB
☎020 8942 9442 🖷020 8949 4398
E: masterserve@mastersun.co.uk
Web: www.mastersun.co.uk
Supporting churches and missionary work in tourist areas.
Director: Mr Gordon Miller. Executive staff 1. ***CC*** No.1050931. Began 1997; non-denominational. Linked to MasterSun. No magazine. Turnover £620,000 to year end Dec 04.

***Medical Service Ministries**, PO Box 13, Newton Abbot TQ13 8WZ
☎01647 440 113
🖷08701 315 594
E: resources.msm@btopenworld.com
Web: www.preachandheal.org.uk
Providing funding for personal and community health care training for Christian missionary workers.
Secretary: Mr Lionel Holmes. Executive staff 1. ***CC*** No.234037. Began 1903; interdenominational. (Previously Missionary School of Medicine). No magazine. Turnover £12,000 to year end Sept 05.

Middle East Concern, PO Box 2, Loughborough LE11 3BG
☎01509 239 400
🖷0870 134 8312
E: office@meconcern.org
Collaborative effort addressing persecution of Christians in the Middle East and North Africa.
Director: Mr Daniel Hofman. Executive staff 2, Admin staff 1. Began 1991; non-denominational. No magazine. Turnover n/a.

Mildmay International, 1 Nelson Mews, Southend-on-Sea SS1 1AL
☎01702 394 450
🖷01702 394 454
E: mildint@mildmay.org
Web: www.mildmay.org
Consultancy and training in palliative HIV/AIDS care worldwide.
Chief Executive: Dr Veronica Moss. *Director of International Development:* Mr Graham Blois. *Director of Education and Programme Design:* Catherine M O'Keeffe. Executive staff 3, Staff 360. ***CC*** No.292058. Began 1996; interdenominational. Magazine: *Highlights* (Circulation n/a every four months). Turnover £8,000,000 to year end Apr 05.

Mission and Public Affairs Division (Archbishops' Council), Church House, Great Smith Street, Westminster, London SW1P 3NZ
☎020 7898 1469
🖷020 7898 1431
E: john.clark@c-of-e.org.uk
Web: www.c-of-e.anglican.org or www.evangelism.uk.net
Mission, evangelism, inter-faith relations, world mission, social policy, family life, environment, international relations, hospital chaplaincy.
Director: Mr John Clark. Executive staff 14, Other staff 13. ***CC*** Began 2003; Anglican. No magazine. Turnover n/a.

Note: each Diocese has a range of Mission and Evangelism Officers. Contact them via the appropriate Diocesan Office. See pages 155-162.

Mission Supplies Ltd, c/o Brooklands International Freight Services Ltd, Airport House, King's Mill Lane, South Nutfield, Redhill RH1 5JY
☎01737 824 059
🖷01737 823 634
E: tony@bifs.net
Web: www.bifs.net
Supplying/packing/freighting everything required by relief agencies, missionary societies, missionaries overseas; VAT-free sales.
Managing Director: Mr Tony Barnes. Executive staff 1. Other staff 10. Began 1982; interdenominational. Linked to International Supplies. No magazine. Turnover £1,250,000 to year end Dec 04.

Missionaries' Children's Fund, Stewards Company Ltd, 124 Wells Road, Bath BA2 3AH
☎01225 427 236 🖷01225 427 278
E: mcf@stewards.co.uk
Supporting missionary families with educational expenses of children (those commended by UK Assemblies).
Administrator: Stewards Company Ltd. No full-time staff. **CC** No.220204. Began 1966; Christian Brethren. No magazine. Turnover £80,721 to year end Apr 04.

Missionary Ventures, Champness Hall, Drake Street, Rochdale OL16 1PB
☎01706 639 333 🖷01706 642 333
E: info@mvgb.org.uk
Web: www.mvgb.org.uk
Facilitating indigenous pastors through sponsorship and short-term evangelistic, medical, construction, teaching teams; Bible schools.
Director: Mr Robert Carter. *Executive Overseer:* Rev Luther L Meier. Executive staff 4, Other staff 3. **CC** No.1067612. Began 1995; non-denominational. (Previously Missionary Ventures Europe). Magazine: *MVGB Update* (400 quarterly). Turnover £175,000 to year end Dec 05.

*__Missions Mobilisation Network__, 39 Honor Oak Road, Forest Hill, London SE23 3SH
☎020 8699 6077 🖷020 8699 7160
E: info@missionsmobilisation.org
Web: www.missionsmobilisation.org
Resourcing mission mobilisers to significantly increase the missionary workforce worldwide, especially among unreached peoples.
Chief Administrator: Name not supplied. Executive staff 1, Other staff 3. **CC** No.1008196. Began 1993; interdenominational. (Previously AD 2000 and Beyond Movement). A network of World Evangelical Alliance Mission Commission. No magazine. Turnover n/a.

Moravian Missions (London Association in Aid of Moravian Missions), Moravian Church House, 5 Muswell Hill, London N10 3TJ
☎020 8883 3409 🖷020 8365 3371
E: office@moravian.org.uk
Supporting British Moravian Church in its partnership with Moravian Church overseas, in South Asia, Tanzania, Jamaica.
Secretary: Rev David Newman. No full-time staff. **CC** Began 1817; interdenominational. Magazine: *News and Views* (400 annually). Turnover £45,000 to year end Apr 00.

Network for Anglicans in Mission and Evangelism, PO Box 70, Oxford OX2 6HB
☎01865 556 071 🖷01865 510 823
E: ocms@ocms.ac.uk
Web: www.anglicanmission.net
Global activist network of Anglican bishops and dioceses to develop the church's capacity for mission.
International Co-ordinator: Rev Canon Dr Vinay Samuel. No full-time staff. Began 1998; Anglican. No magazine. Turnover n/a.

*__Next Level International__, PO Box 1317, Bedworth CV12 9ZS
☎024 7664 3415 🖷024 7664 3503
E: info@nlieurope.com
Web: www.nlieurope.com
Church planting, leadership development, short-term missions in Europe.
Executive Director: Rev Ian Green. Executive staff 4, Other staff 15. **CC** No.1034023. Began 1991; interdenominational. (Previously Youth Ministries International). No magazine. Turnover £498,000 to year end Dec 04.

†**The North Eastern Caribbean and Aruba Association**, 77 Hangleton Way, Hove BN3 8AF
☎01273 249 074
Supporting the work of North Eastern Caribbean and Aruba Diocese.
Chairman: Rev Canon Robert Eke. All voluntary staff. **CC** Began 1906; Anglican. No magazine. Turnover £2,000 to year end Dec 02.

NorthStar UK, 37 Balmoral Crescent, Dronfield Woodhouse, Dronfield S18 8ZY
☎01246 410 122 🖷01246 410 122
E: info@northstaruk.org
Web: www.northstaruk.org
Providing on-line educational support for secondary school students up to GCSE and IGCSE level.
Administrator: Julie Thompson. No full-time staff. **CC** No.1003691. Began 1989; non-denominational. (Previously Veritas Trust). No magazine. Turnover £70,000 to year end Jul 04.

Northwood Missionary Auctions, FREEPOST, Northwood HA6 1AU
☎01923 836 634 🖷01923 829 472
E: info@nmauctions.org.uk
Web: www.nmauctions.org.uk
Holding regular auctions; receiving items from donors or legacies; benefit to nominated Christian organisations.
Chairman: Mr Howard White. No full-time staff. **CC** No.290227. Began 1969; interdenominational. No magazine. Turnover £48,000 to year end Aug 02.

*__Novi Most International__, Bushell House, 118 Broad Street, Chesham HP5 3ED
☎01494 793 242 🖷01494 793 771
E: chesham@novimost.org
Web: www.novimost.org
Ministering to traumatised young people of Bosnia Herzegovina: relational youth/children's work, camps, evangelism, relief.
Director: Mr Paul H Brooks. Executive staff 5. **CC** No.1043501. Began 1993; non-denominational. Magazine: *New Bridge* (Circulation n/a quarterly). Turnover £260,000 to year end Sep 00.

***OC Team**, Overseas House, New Road, Colston Bassett, Nottingham NG12 3FQ
☎01949 818 18 🖷01949 811 18
E: mail@octeam.com
Web: www.octeam.com
Sponsoring the training of Christian leaders in developing nations through evangelical theological education.
Executive Director: Rev Frederick Connell. *Administrator:* Mr Lance Eames. Executive staff 1, Admin staff 1. ***CC*** No.1080220. Began 1999; interdenominational. No magazine. Turnover £259,042 to year end Sep 01.

***Open Doors UK & Ireland**, PO Box 129, Witney OX29 6WN
☎01993 885 400 🖷01993 885 401
E: info@opendoorsuk.org
Web: www.opendoorsuk.org
Serving persecuted Christians worldwide through Bibles / literature, leadership training, Scripture-based literacy programmes and livelihood projects.
Regional Director: Mr Peter Cowell. *Supporter Relations Director:* Mr Paul Tew. *Supporter Services Director:* Mr Peter Wilson. Executive staff 3, Office staff 15. ***CC*** No.260600. Began 1970; interdenominational. (Previously Open Doors UK). Magazine: *Open Doors* (25,000 monthly). Turnover £3,400,000 to year end Dec 02.

The Order of Mission (TOM), St Thomas Church, Philadelphia Campus, Gilpin Street, Sheffield S6 3BL
☎0114 241 9560 🖷0114 278 9600
E: admin@missionorder.org
Web: www.missionorder.org
Identifying, training, discipling and releasing missional leaders to develop new expressions of church.
Superior: Rev Mike Breen. *Administrator:* Mrs Rowan Holt. Staff 2. ***CC*** Began 2003; interdenominational. No magazine. Turnover n/a

***OSCAR**, Wootton House, Horton Road, Gloucester GL1 3PT
☎0845 257 6315 M 07866 366 657
🖷07092 294 537
E: info@oscar.org.uk
Web: www.oscar.org.uk
Providing information, advice and resources for those interested or involved in world mission.
Director: Mr Mike Frith. Executive staff 1. ***CC*** No.1093265. Began 2000; non-denominational. No magazine. Turnover £6,151 to year end Aug 02.

Partnership for World Mission, Partnership House, 157 Waterloo Road, London SE1 8XA
☎020 7803 3200 🖷020 7633 0185
E: stephen.lyon@c-of-e.org.uk
Web: www.pwm-web.org.uk
Coordinating body for world mission work of mission agencies and Archbishops' Council of Church of England.
Partnership Secretary: Mr Stephen Lyon. Executive staff 1, Other staff 1. Began 1978; Anglican. No magazine. Turnover n/a.

For member organisations see list on page 22.

Pontifical Missionary Societies, 23 Eccleston Square, London SW1V 1NU
☎020 7821 9755 🖷020 7630 8466
E: director@missio.org.uk
Web: www.missio.org.uk
Raising funds to support the Catholic Church in mission territories and mission education.
National Director: Rev John Dale. Executive staff 1, Other staff 10. ***CC*** No.1056651. Began 1833; Roman Catholic. Incorporating Association for the Propagation of the Faith, Missionary Union, Society of St Peter the Apostle, Society of the Holy Childhood. Magazines: *Mission Outlook* (2,300 quarterly), *Mission Together* (120,000 frequency n/a), *Mission Today* (206,000 quarterly). Turnover £4,200,000 to year end Dec 04.

†Portable Recording Ministries, Newton Lodge, Cynwyl Elfed, Carmarthen SA33 6SP
☎01267 281 252 🖷01267 281 252
Teaching the use of cassette communication for church planting and growth.
Hon Treasurer: Mr Alan Lansdown. No full-time staff. Began 1983; interdenominational. No magazine. Turnover £1,200 to year end Mar 03.

***Radstock Ministries**, 2a Argyle Street, Mexborough S64 9BW
☎01709 582 345 🖷01709 582 345
E: info@radstock.org
Web: www.radstock.org
Helping to connect churches worldwide to make mission their priority.
UK Co-ordinator: Mrs Katy Jones Parry. *Administrator:* Mrs Ruth Bellerby. Executive staff 12, Other staff 10. ***CC*** No.326879. Began 1984; non-denominational. Magazine: *Rapport* (3,000 every two months). Turnover £150,000 to year end Dec 04.

The Raven Trust, Bay Villa, Strachur, Cairndow PA27 8DE
☎01369 860 436 🖷01369 860 436
E: strachur@aol.com
Web: www.theraventrust.org
Training, funding, resourcing, shipping, installing goods and equipment to Christians in mission worldwide; networking.
Chairman: Mr John Challis. Executive staff 1, Admin staff 1. ***CC*** No.SCO 30260. Began 2000; non-denominational. No magazine. Turnover £52,000 to year end Dec 04.

Redbourn Missionary Trust, 35 Lemsford Road, St Albans AL1 3PP
☎01727 852 019
E: carolann_evershed@yahoo.co.uk
Five houses for missionaries on furlough; five retirement flats for retired missionaries.
Hon Secretary: Mrs Carol Evershed. No full-time staff. ***CC*** No.251960. Began 1968; evangelical. No magazine. Turnover £25,000 to year end Sep 02.

***Release International**, PO Box 54, Orpington BR5 9RT
☎01689 823 491 🖷01689 834 647
E: info@releaseinternational.org
Web: www.releaseinternational.org
Serving persecuted Christians: supporting pastors and families; supplying Christian literature and Bibles; working for justice.
UK Director: Mr Colin King. *Operations Director:* Mr Chris Badley. Executive staff 4, Other staff 16. ***CC*** No.280[illegible]77. Began 1968; interdenominational. (Previously Christian Mission to the Communist World). Magazine: *Witness* (18,000 every two months). Turnover £1,062,000 to year end Dec 04.

RURCON (Rural and Urban Resources, Counselling, Outreach and Networking), Springvale Orchard Close, Shaldon, Teignmouth TQ14 0HF
☎01626 873 159 🖷01626 873 159
E: john@wibbs.fsnet.co.uk
African team of Christian development leaders counselling and training churches, organisations and individuals in sub-Saharan Africa.
Communications Unit Coordinator: Dr John Wibberley. Executive staff 3, Other staff 7. ***CC*** No.275581. Began 1971; interdenominational. Magazines: *RURCON Newsletter* (3,000 quarterly), *Friends of RURCON* (450 quarterly). Turnover £75,000 to year end Dec 02.

Russian Ministries (Peter Deyneka), 24 Birchgrove, Cobham KT11 2HR
☎01932 867 086
Web: www.russianministries.org
Evangelism and church planting in the former USSR through strategic ministry development, global Christian partnerships.
Chairman, British Advisory Council: Mr Ian S Bull. Admin staff 1. Began 1991; interdenominational. Magazine: *Network* (8,000 quarterly worldwide). Turnover n/a.

St Francis Leprosy Guild, 73 St Charles Square, London W10 6EJ
☎020 8969 1345 🖷020 8969 3272
E: enquiries@stfrancisleprosy.org
Web: www.stfrancisleprosy.org
Collecting funds to help care for leprosy sufferers abroad.
Hon Secretary: Sr Eleanor Marshall. Executive staff 1. ***CC*** No.208741. Began 1895; Roman Catholic. No magazine. Turnover £370,000 to year end Dec 04.

***The Salvation Army**, International Headquarters, 101 Queen Victoria Street, London EC4P 4EP
☎020 7332 0101
E: the_general@salvationarmy.org
Web: www.salvationarmy.org
Working in 110 countries.
International Leader: General Shaw Clifton. *Chief of Staff:* Commissioner Robin Dunster. *Territorial Commander, UK Territory:* Commissioner John Matear. Executive staff 28, UK staff included in UK Headquarters. **CC** No.214779. Began 1865; Salvation Army. Turnover n/a.

Scottish Episcopal Church Mission Association (Links), 21 Grosvenor Crescent, Edinburgh EH12 5EE
☎0131 225 6357 🖷0131 346 7247
E: secma@surefish.co.uk
Supporting mission outreach overseas and raising awareness at home.
Provincial Secretary: Miss Jinty Kerr. No full-time staff. **CC** No.SCO 02555. Began 1875; Scottish Episcopal Church. (Previously Church Women's Missionary Association). Magazine: *Links* (2,200 half-yearly). Turnover £18,000 to year end Dec 99.

Sedgley International Christian Ministries, PO Box 1216, Dudley DY3 1GW
☎01902 670 444 M: 07956 444 628
E: info@sicm.org
Web: www.sicm.org
Overseas missions opportunities, short and long term; working mainly in Africa.
Director: Rev Stewart R Bloor. Executive staff 4, Other staff 9. **CC** No.1057488. Began 1992; interdenominational. No magazine. Turnover £47,000 to year end Dec 02

†**Seed, Bible Mission International**, PO Box 3, Skelton, Saltburn-by-the-Sea TS12 3YT
☎01287 659 410 🖷01287 659 410
E: bmi@seeduk.com
Web: www.seedbmi.co.uk
Supplying Bibles free.
Executive Director: Mr Tony John. Executive staff 3. **CC** No.1068968. Began 1985; non-denominational. Magazine: *New Update* (5,000 every two months). Turnover £60,000 to year end Aug 98.

SEN UK, 3 Springfield Road, Hinckley LE10 1AN
☎01455 446 899
E: tim.oglesby@ntlworld.com
Web: www.citygate.org
Demonstrating historic biblical Christianity in Central European cultures; study centre, research for missions, publishing, evangelism.
Executive Officer: Mrs Judi Oglesby. **CC** No.327237. Began 1984; non-denominational. (Previously Central European Missionary Fellowship, Central European Foundation). Magazine: *The City Gate* (3,000 every four months). Turnover £38,000 to year end Dec 05.

***Servants Fellowship International**, The Old Rectory, River Street, Pewsey SN5 5DB
☎01672 564 938 🖷01672 565 030
Cross-cultural urban mission; training.
Director: Dr Patrick Sookhdeo. Executive staff 2, Other staff 6. **CC** No.280859. Began 1975; interdenominational. No magazine. Turnover n/a.

***Share Trust**, 58 Slimmons Drive, St Albans AL4 9AP
☎01727 862 935 🖷01727 862 935
E: admin@sharetrust.org
Web: www.sharetrust.org
Encouraging new Christian initiatives.
Director: Mr John Barron. Executive staff 2. **CC** No.801625. Began 1989; interdenominational. No magazine. Turnover n/a.

Shunem Trust, 4 Tinkers Drive, Winslow, Buckingham MK18 3RD
☎01296 715 341
Providing accommodation for needy missionaries and other Christian workers on home leave.
Administrator: Mr Philip King. No full-time staff. **CC** No.276109. Began 1978; interdenominational. No magazine. Turnover £2,500 to year end Apr 00.

***Sierra Leone Mission**, 44 Eastern Avenue, Shoreham-by-Sea BN43 6PD
☎01273 453 480
E: ben.quant@ntlworld.com
Web: www.cofhconnexion.org.uk
Providing spiritual, financial and material support for ministers, teachers, churches, schools in Sierra Leone.
Contact Person: Rev Ben Quant. Other staff n/a. **CC** No.232674. Began 1841; Countess of Huntingdon's Connexion. Magazine: *Voice* (750 quarterly). Turnover £12,500 to year end June 00.

Siloam Christian Ministries, Clent House, 25 Beauchamp Avenue, Leamington Spa CV32 5RG
☎01926 335 037 🖷01926 431 193
E: siloam.c.min.uk@zetnet.co.uk
Web: www.siloam.org.uk
Assisting national churches and independent missionaries worldwide; education, social work, medical aid.
Directors: Mr Richard Norton, Mr John Eld. *Company Secretary:* Mrs Annette C Roberts. Executive staff 2, Other staff 2. **CC** No.327396. Began 1982; interdenominational. Magazine: *Siloam News* (5,000 monthly). Turnover £1,308,484 to year end Dec 04.

Slav Lands Christian Fellowship, 28 Hayesford Park Drive, Bromley BR2 9DB
☎020 8402 0695 🖷020 8402 0695
Supporting Russian missionaries in Siberia and sending help to poor Christian families.
Secretary: Mr R J Weil. Executive staff 1. **CC** No.1037023. Began 1959; interdenominational. Magazine: *Slavonia* (700 half-yearly). Turnover £40,000 to year end Apr 03.

Slavic Gospel Association (British Section) Ltd, 37a The Goffs, Eastbourne BN21 1HF
☎01323 725 583
🖷01323 739 724
E: office@sga.org.uk
Web: www.sga.org.uk
Biblical leadership training, leadership support, Bible Student sponsorship, Christian literature, crisis response in Eastern Europe.
General Director: Mr William Smylie. Executive staff 7, Office staff 3. **CC** No.258253. Began 1934; interdenominational. Magazine: *Breakthrough* (12,000 quarterly). Turnover £900,000 to year end Dec 05.

***Smile International**, PO Box 3, Orpington BR5 1WZ
☎01689 870 932
🖷01689 823 213
E: info@smileinternational.org
Web: www.smileinternational.org
A mission and humanitarian aid organisation; Africa, Asia and Europe.
Director: Rev Clive Doubleday. Admin staff 1. **CC** No.1079730. Began 1989; Baptist. No magazine. Turnover n/a.

†**Society of St John the Divine (Natal) English Association**, 7 Hewgate Court, Henley-on-Thames RG9 1BD
☎01491 578 885
Supporting sisters in South African convent. No unsolicited requests.
Joint Secretaries: Mr & Mrs J E Coffee. No full-time staff. Began 1911; Anglican. No magazine. Turnover n/a.

Spatial Post, Spatial House, Willow Farm Business Park, Castle Donington, Derby DE74 2TW
☎01332 815 405
🖷01332 812 409
E: info@the-spatial-group.com
Web: www.the-spatial-group.com
International and UK mailing company.
Postal Manager: Mr Ron O'Meara. Executive staff 1, Other staff 80. Began 1984; non-denominational. No magazine. Turnover n/a.

SPCK Worldwide (Society for Promoting Christian Knowledge), 36 Causton Street, London SW1P 4ST
☎020 7592 3900
🖷020 7643 0391
E: spckww@spck.org.uk
Grants to support Christian literature/communication work in over 75 countries each year.
Director: Ms Sue Parks. Executive staff 1, Other staff 3. **CC** Began 1698; interdenominational but historically Anglican. No magazine. Turnover n/a.

The Spring Project, PO Box 20, Morpeth NE61 3YP
☎01670 505 622 Ⓜ: 07799 413 095 🖷01670 505 622
E: info@springproject.org.uk
Web: www.springproject.org.uk
Making wind-up clockwork radios available to churches and missionaries in remote areas of the world.
Trustee: Mr Richard Hubbard. No full-time staff. ***CC*** No.1067992. Began 1997; non-denominational. No magazine. Turnover £2,000 to year end Mar 05.

Stamps for Christian Missions, PO Box 5798, Milton Keynes MK10 1BP
☎01908 235 519 Ⓜ: 07732 657 716 🖷01908 672 260
E: sfcm@usa.com
Web: www.s4cm.org.uk
Collecting and preparing postage stamps for sale to dealer trade and stamp collectors.
Executive Director: Rev Arthur Rowley. Executive staff 3. Began 1987; interdenominational. No magazine. Turnover n/a.

***Stamps for Evangelism**, 11 St John's Drive, Chaddesden, Derby DE21 6SD
☎01332 663 270 🖷01332 663 270
E: peter.bysh@ntlworls.com
Web: www.stampsforevangelism.co.uk
Making gifts of money to those engaged in evangelism from selling used postage stamps.
Secretary: Mr Peter Bysh. No full-time staff. Began 1966; non-denominational. No magazine. Turnover £14,603 to year end Dec 04.

***Supplyline**, 13 Paget Road, Wolverhampton WV6 0DS
☎01902 423 919
E: supplyline@blueyonder.co.uk
Web: www.supplyline.org.uk
Christian partnership with West Africa.
Director: Mr Jamie Handscomb. Executive staff 1. ***CC*** No.1010354. Began 1965; interdenominational. Part of Anvil Trust since 1999. Magazine: *Supplyline News* (250 every four months). Turnover included in Anvil Trust.

†Survive - MIVA, 5 Park Vale Road, Aintree, Liverpool L9 2DG
☎0151 523 3878 🖷0151 523 3841
E: info@survive-miva.org
Web: www.survive-miva.org
Providing essential transport to missionaries working in the developing world.
Director: Mr Simon Foran. Executive staff 1, Other staff 3. ***CC*** No.268745. Began 1974; Roman Catholic. Magazine: *Awareness* (15,000 half-yearly). Turnover £620,000 to year end Dec 02.

***TASK (Training and Advice for Service in the Kingdom)**, 13 School Road, Bradenham, Thetford IP25 7QU
☎01760 440 200
E: enquiries@taskgb.co.uk
Web: www.taskgb.co.uk
Advising and training Christians to work effectively in secular and cross-cultural positions overseas.
Director: Mr Roger G Wells. Network of mentors 8. ***CC*** No.1068212. Began 1994; interdenominational. No magazine. Turnover £6,000 to year end Oct 05.

***Tearcraft (Tearfund Trading)**, 100 Church Road, Teddington TW11 8QE
☎020 8977 9144 🖷020 8943 3594
E: enquiry@tearfund.org
Web: www.tearfund.org
Bringing Christian help and hope to Third World craft producers by selling their goods.
Director of Finance: Mr Richard Gough. Executive staff 1, Other staff 7. ***CC*** No.265464. Began 1975; interdenominational. No magazine. Turnover £1,424,000 to year end Mar 05.

***Tools With a Mission**, Unit B, 2 Bailey Close, Hadleigh Road Industrial Estate, Ipswich IP2 0UD
☎01473 210 220 🖷01473 210 293
E: twamhq@twam.co.uk
Supply of tools and tool kits to third world and other countries via vocational training centres.
Administrative Secretary: Mr M Humphries. Executive staff 3, Other staff 30. ***CC*** No.1076983. Began 1983; interdenominational. Magazine: *TWAM News* (5,000 every four months). Turnover n/a.

***The Toybox Charity**, 13 Hill Avenue, Amersham HP6 5BD
☎01494 432 591 🖷01494 432 593
E: info@toybox.org
Web: www.toybox.org
Promoting awareness of the plight of street children in Latin America; helping in practical ways.
Chief Executive: Mr Andy Stockbridge. Other staff 12. ***CC*** No.1084243. Began 1992; non-denominational. No magazine. Turnover £1,720,000 to year end Mar 05.

†Unimatco Ltd, Bulstrode, Oxford Road, Gerrards Cross SL9 8SZ
☎01753 886 105 🖷01753 889 378
E: unimatco@aol.com
Web: www.unimatco.co.uk
Land Rover export specialist.
Director: Mr John Chudley. Executive staff 1, Other staff 3. Began 1976; interdenominational. No magazine. Turnover n/a.

Vision for Missions Training, PO Box 51, Torquay TQ2 6HN
☎01803 323 225
E: rms_lkt@btopenworld.com
Teaching Romanians to a high level of theological education.
British Director: Mr Les Tidball. Executive staff 1, Other staff 1. ***CC*** No.327724. Began 1987; interdenominational. (Previously Romanian Missionary Society). Magazine: *RMS Review* (800 quarterly). Turnover £80,000 to year end Dec 04.

***Viva Network**, PO Box 633, Oxford OX2 9PT
☎01865 320 100 🖷01865 320 101
E: info@viva.org
Web: www.viva.org
Helping 'children at risk' by working together linking and enhancing the Christian response.
International Director: Mr Patrick McDonald. *General Manager:* Mr Brian Wilkinson. Executive staff 4, Admin staff 3, Other staff 13. ***CC*** No.1053389. Began 1996; non-denominational. Magazine: *Reaching Children at Risk* (1,000 quarterly). Turnover £450,000 to year end Mar 03.

†Waldensian Church Missions, 21 de Freville Avenue, Cambridge CB4 1HW
☎01223 315 753 🖷01223 562 2505
E: erica.scroppo@ntlworld.com
Supporting Waldensian work in Italy; encouraging interest in UK through tours, meetings and literature.
Executive Secretary: Mrs Erica Scroppo-Newbury. No full-time staff. ***CC*** Began 1825; non-denominational. Magazine: *Waldensian Review* (900 half-yearly). Turnover £9,687 to year end Dec 98.

***Wallington Missionary Mart and Auctions**, 105 Stafford Road, Wallington SM6 9AP
☎020 8669 3495
Auctions 020 8647 8437
E: auction@wallingtonmissionary.org.uk
Web: www.wallingtonmissionary.org.uk
Warehouse, selling second-hand donated household items to raise funds for missionary work overseas; auctions.
President: Mr Stephen Crawley. *Secretary:* Brian Chapman. Admin staff 5. ***CC*** No.289030. Began 1965; non-denominational. No magazine. Turnover £261,408 to year end Dec 04.

†*WMA-UK, PO Box 436, Reading RG1 1FW
☎No telephone
E: glennschwartz@msn.com
Web: www.wmausa.org
Conducting seminars and consultations primarily in Africa on dependancy and self-reliance for mission-established institutions.
Executive Director: Rev Glenn Schwartz. Executive staff 1, Other staff 1. ***CC*** No.1029198. Began 1993; interdenominational. No magazine. Turnover £2,000 to year end Dec 00.

Workaid, Unit 2b, St Georges Industrial Estate, White Lion Road, Amersham HP7 9JQ
☎01494 765 506 🖷01494 765 507
E: admin@workaid.org
Web: www.workaid.org
Collecting and refurbishing tools and sewing machines to send to training centres mainly in East Africa.
Chairman: Sylvia Parrott. *Administrator:* Mr Ray Richards. Admin staff 1. ***CC*** No.1041574. Began 1986; interdenominational. Magazine: *Workaid World* (5,000 every four months). Turnover £120,000 to year end Dec 02.

***World Association for Christian Communication**, 357 Kennington Lane, Vauxhall, London SE11 5QY
☎020 7735 1362
🖷020 7735 0340
E: info@wacc.org.uk
Web: www.wacc.org.uk
Seeking to promote human dignity, justice and peace, and the democratisation of communication.
General Secretary: Rev Randy Naylor. *President:* Dr Musimbi Kanyoro. Executive staff 11, Other staff 10. ***CC*** No.296073. Began 1975. Magazines: *Media Gender Monitor* (3,304 half-yearly, bulletin), *Media Development* (1,834 quarterly, journal). Turnover £1,546,896 to year end Dec 02.

World Christian Ministries, PO Box 300, Paignton TQ4 6XW
☎01803 563 681 M: 07793 805 498
🖷01803 665 166
E: admin@wcm-online.co.uk
Web: www.wcm-online.co.uk
Relieving poverty and sickness, advancing Christianity in developing countries, through sponsorship programmes and donations.
Director: Mr Andrew David. Executive staff 5. ***CC*** No.1001691. Began 1988; Assemblies of God. No magazine. Turnover £380,000 to year end Aug 05.

World Mission Consultancy
Wootton House, Horton Road, Gloucester GL1 3PT
☎0845 257 6315
M: 07866 366 657
🖷07092 254 537
E: info@worldmission.co.uk
Web: www.worldmission.co.uk
Providing consultancy, advice and training to organisations and churches engaged in world mission.
Director: Mr Mike Frith. No full-time staff. Began 2003; non-denominational. No magazine. Turnover n/a.

***WorldShare**, Bawtry Hall, Bawtry, Doncaster DN10 6JH
☎01302 710 273
🖷01302 710 027
E: info@worldshare.abel.co.uk
Web: www.worldshare.org.uk
Resourcing indigenous Christian organisations to fulfil their God-given calling to holistic evangelism and Bible teaching.
Chief Executive: Mr John Rose. *Stewardship Officer:* Mr Simon Garrett. Executive staff 1, Other staff 6. ***CC*** No.803575. Began 1943; interdenominational. Magazine: *Window* (5,500 quarterly). Turnover £577,000 to year end Jun 02.

***Wycliffe Associates (UK)**, 7 Conwy Street, Rhyl LL18 3ET
☎01745 343 300
E: info@wa-uk.org
Web: www.wycliffeassociates.com
Using people's gifts at home to serve missionaries of Wycliffe Bible Translators and other missions.
Directors: David & Rachel Landin. Executive staff 2, Admin staff 2. ***CC*** No.1007772. Began 1989; interdenominational. Magazine: *Help!* (1,200 every four months). Turnover £65,570 to year end Nov 03.

RELIEF & DEVELOPMENT ORGANISATIONS

Act 4 Africa, 17 Seamon Road, Altrincham WA14 4ND
☎0161 941 2161
E: admin@act4africa.co.uk
Web: www.act4africa.org.uk
Delivering HIV/AIDS prevention programmes in Africa using drama and sport as a communication tool.
Project Director: Mr M Smedley. Executive staff 2, Other staff 1. ***CC*** No.1092074. Began 2000; interdenominational. No magazine. Turnover £55,000 to year end Aug 04.

Action Around Bethlehem Children with Disability (ABCD), 16a Park View Road, London N3 2JB
☎020 8343 4246 🖷020 8343 4048
E: bethlehem@btconnect.com
Web: www.abcdbethlehem.org.uk
Sponsoring rehabilitation programmes to disabled children in Palestine and supporting their families.
Founder, Trustee: Mrs Val Jourdan. *Director:* Georgina Mortimer. All voluntary staff. ***CC*** No.1097623. Began 1985; interdenominational. Magazine: *ABCD Newsletter* (2,000 annually). Turnover £135,000 to year end Mar 04.

Action by Christians Against Torture, 3 Southfield, Saltash PL12 4LX
☎01752 210 389
E: acatuk2004@yahoo.com
Web: www.acatuk.org.uk
Campaigning, information and prayer for worldwide abolition of torture; prisoner support scheme.
Information Officers: Mr & Mrs Terry & Eleanor Newland. Admin staff 2. ***CC*** No.1072628. Began 1984; interdenominational. Affiliated to the International Federation of Action by Christians for the Abolition of Torture. No magazine. Turnover n/a.

***Adopt-A-Child**, PO Box 5589, Inverness IV2 7WG
☎01463 792 600
E: info@adopt-a-child.org.uk
Web: www.adopt-a-child.com
Sharing the whole Gospel with children in need through sponsored feeding programmes and other ministries.
International Sponsorship Coordinator: Mr Paul Cocking. *UK & Ireland Coordinator:* Miss Jenny Dougal. Admin staff 2. ***CC*** No.SCO 29685. Began 1993; interdenominational. No magazine. Turnover £530,992 to year end Dec 04.

Adventist Development and Relief Agency (ADRA-UK), Stanborough Park, Watford WD25 9JZ
☎01923 681 723 🖷01923 681 723
E: director@adra.org.uk
Web: www.adra.org.uk
Providing assistance for disaster relief and humanitarian work in developing countries.
Director: Mr Mark Castellino. Executive staff 1, Other staff 3. ***CC*** No.1074937. Began 1989; Seventh-day Adventist. No magazine. Turnover £3,000,000 to year end Dec 04.

†*Africa, 54a Church Road, Burgess Hill RH15 9AE
☎01444 254 443 🖷01444 254 443
E: africa@tinyonline.co.uk
Providing sponsorship for educational and medical needs for AIDS orphans and destitute children; feeding programmes.
Founder Directors: Mr & Mrs Willard. Admin staff 3. ***CC*** No.1079952. Began 1998; interdenominational. No magazine. Turnover £30,000 to year end Aug 00.

***Aid to Romania**, 19 Crancott Close, Houghton Conquest, Bedford MK45 3ND
☎01234 741 021 🖷01234 350 544
E: jhammond@callnetuk.com
Medical relief and evangelism; Africa, Romania.
UK Operations Manager: Mr J Hammond. Executive staff 3. ***CC*** No.1020084. Began 1991; non-denominational. No magazine. Turnover n/a.

Amos Trust, All Hallows on the Wall, 83 London Wall, London EC2M 5ND
☎020 7588 2638 🖷020 7588 2663
E: info@amostrust.org
Web: www.amostrust.org
Promoting justice and development through music, education and projects worldwide; also supporting Garth Hewitt's ministry.
Director: Rev Garth Hewitt. *Office Manager:* Clare Dowding. Executive staff 2, Other staff 2. ***CC*** No.292592. Began 1985; interdenominational. No magazine. Turnover £333,811 to year end Mar 04.

***Association of Christian Resource Organisations Serving Sudan (UK)**, 5 Elm Park Way, York YO31 1DX
☎01904 423 277
Facilitating relief of poverty and advancement of Christianity in Africa, mainly in Sudan, Kenya . No financial requests.
Contact: Mr Ian Anderson. No full-time staff. ***CC*** No.1069973. Began 1998; non-denominational. Known as ACROSS (UK). No magazine. Turnover £25,384 to year end Jun 05.

Assumption Lay Volunteer Programme, 23 Kensington Square, London W8 5HN
☎020 7361 4752 🖷020 7361 4757
E: alvpcoordinator@hotmail.co.uk
Web: www.alvp.org.uk
Volunteer opportunities for young people in development projects around the world.
Volunteer Co-ordinator: Miss Caroline Burns. Executive Staff 2. ***CC*** No.233084. Began 1998; Roman Catholic. No magazine. Turnover £50,000 to year end Apr 05.

***Barnabas Fund**, The Old Rectory, River Street, Pewsey SN9 5DB
☎01672 564 938 🖷01672 565 030
E: info@barnabasfund.org
Web: www.barnabasfund.org
Providing financial assistance to and prayer information about suffering Christians in the Muslim world.
Director: Dr Patrick Sookhdeo. Executive staff 2, Other staff 18. ***CC*** No.1092935. Began 1993; interdenominational. Magazine: *Barnabas Aid* (10,000 every two months). Turnover n/a.

†**The Bethany Children's Trust**, Community Church, Werter Road, Putney, London SW15 2LJ
☎020 8785 7736 🖷020 8785 7736
E: admin@bethanychildrenstrust.org.uk
Web: bethanychildrenstrust.org.uk
Supporting Christian projects worldwide which care for vulnerable children, through advocacy and action.
Director: Mrs Susie Howe. Executive staff 1, Other staff 3. ***CC*** No.1073817. Began 1998; interdenominational. No magazine. Turnover n/a.

***Breadline**, 84 Liverpool Road, Walmer, Deal CT14 7PS
☎01304 380 597
E: brianpile@breadline-international.org
Web: www.breadline-international.org
Supporting, evangelism, ministry building, advocacy, relieving poverty, community development through local partners; Eastern Europe and Siberia.
Director: Mr Brian Pile. Executive staff 1. ***CC*** No.1066061. Began 1995; interdenominational. Magazine: *Breadline Update* (5,000 annually). Turnover £87,000 to year end Dec 04.

†**Bridges for Peace**, Victoria House, Victoria Road, Buckhurst Hill IG9 5EX
☎020 8559 2479 🖷020 8502 9062
E: info@bridgesforpeace.co.uk
Web: www.bridgesforpeace.com
Working to build Christian-Jewish understanding and support for the people and land of Israel.
Administrator: Miss Jean Wilson. No full-time staff. ***CC*** No.1014411. Began 1991; non-denominational. Magazine: *Dispatch from Jerusalem* (2,200 every two months). Turnover £174,690 to year end Dec 02.

British Eastern Aid Doorways, 8 Latchford Lane, Shrewsbury SY1 4YG
☎01743 465 079 🖷01743 465 079
E: breadtrust@connectfree.co.uk
Web: www.breadtrust.com
Assisting local churches in the former Soviet Union to help needy people in their areas.
Secretary: Mrs Beryl Green. Executive staff 3. ***CC*** No.1064603. Began 1997; interdenominational. Magazine: *Breadlines* (1,000 quarterly). Turnover £25,000 to year end Mar 00.

***Care & Compassion**, 23 Glen Crescent, Darvel KA17 0BG
☎01560 323 206
E: dindo@carecompassion.fsnet.co.uk
Web: www.care-compassion.org.uk
Helping children at risk in Brazil, offering food, love and bringing them to Christ.
Secretary: Miss Christine Blake. Executive staff 2. ***CC*** No.SCO 18368. Began 1988; interdenominational. (Previously PAM Mission). No magazine. Turnover n/a.

***Care and Relief for the Young (CRY)**, Sovereign Place, Upper Northam Close, Hedge End, Southampton SO30 4BB
☎01489 788 300 M: 07775 744 187
🖷01489 790 750
E: ukoffice@cry.org.uk
Web: www.cry.org.uk
Rescuing and restoring young lives broken by poverty, oppression, exclusion and abuse.
Chief Executive Officer: Mr David Farndale. *Chairman:* Mr Martyn Dunsford. Executive staff 1, Other staff 7. ***CC*** No.1011513. Began 1992; non-denominational. Magazine: *Cry News* (3,000 quarterly). Turnover £451,000 to year end Dec 04.

Carrot Tops, Green Pastures, Buxhall, Stowmarket IP14 3DX
☎01449 736 628 🖷01449 737 677
E: jangreen@buxhall.co.uk
Hostel for polio-affected children, facilitating medical care and operations in India.
Correspondent/Trustee: Mrs Jan Green. Executive staff 3. ***CC*** No.1016820. Began 1984; interdenominational. (Previously Project India). Magazine: *Carrot Tops* (200 quarterly). Turnover £15,000 to year end Mar 04.

Catholic Agency for Overseas Development (CAFOD), Romero Close, Stockwell Road, London SW9 9TY
☎020 7733 7900 🖷020 7274 9630
E: hq@cafod.org.uk
Web: www.cafod.org.uk
Official overseas development and relief agency of the Catholic Church in England and Wales.
Director: Mr Chris Bain. Executive staff 8, Other staff 170. ***CC*** No.285776. Began 1962; Roman Catholic. Magazine: *Side by Side* (120,000 half-yearly). Turnover £47,000,000 to year end Mar 05.

†**Catholic Institute for International Relations**, Unit 3, Canonbury Yard, 190a New North Road, London N1 7BJ
☎020 7354 0883 🖷020 7359 0017
Web: www.ciir.org
Promoting justice and development in the developing world; sending skilled workers overseas; publishing, analysis, advocacy.
Executive Director: Miss Christine Allen. Executive staff 4, Other staff 35. ***CC*** No.294329. Began 1940; Roman Catholic. Magazine: *Interact* (3,500 every three months). Turnover £4,400,000 to year end Mar 02.

***Centre for Legal Aid Assistance**, PO Box 81, Southall UB2 5YQ
☎07000 780 466 M: 07951 676 430
🖷020 8867 7422
E: claasuk@aol.com
Web: www.cltf.org.uk
Supporting persecuted Christians in Pakistan and elsewhere through advocacy lobbying, campaigning legal aid and shelter.
Coordinator: Mr Nasir Saeed. Executive staff 1, Admin staff 1. Began 1998; interdenominational. Also known as CLAAS. No magazine. Turnover £30,000 to year end Mar 03.

CFR Footprints, Barnes Close, Chadwick, Bromsgrove B61 0RA
☎01562 710 231 🖷01562 710 278
E: fowle@ukonline.co.uk
Web: www.cfrbarnesclose.co.uk
Reconciliation in Croatia and surrounding areas; healing the hurts of war.
Director: Rev Clive Fowle. Executive staff 1. ***CC*** No.295113. Began 2005; non-denominational. Turnover £10,000 to year end Dec 05.

ChildAid to Russia and the Republics, PO Box 200, Bromley BR1 1QF
☎020 8460 6046 🖷020 8466 1244
E: info@childaidrr.org.uk
Web: www.childaidrr.org.uk
Christian projects in Russia and FSU transforming lives of street children, orphans, children with disabilities.
Chief Executive: Ms Carolearne Clarke. *Support Manager:* Ms Lois Clarkson. Other staff 4. ***CC*** No.281099. Began 1973; interdenominational. Previously Aid to Russia and the Republics. No magazine. Turnover £410,513 to year end Mar 05.

Children in Distress, Unit 36/38, Ladywell Business Centre, 94 Duke Street, Glasgow G4 0JW
☎0141 559 5690 📠0141 559 5694
E: admin@childrenindistress.org.uk
Web: www.children-in-distress.org
Hospice and community care for children in Romania and Bulgaria.
Director: Dermot Lamb. Executive staff 1, Other staff 5. **CC** No.1001327. Began 1990; interdenominational. Magazine: *Vision* (13,000 half-yearly). Turnover £769,000 to year end Oct 04.

Christian African Relief Trust, PO Box 554, Huddersfield HD1 9ZQ
☎01484 423 453 📠01484 423 453
E: cart@glennet.demon.co.uk
Web: www.cartyorkshire.co.uk
Voluntary organisation sending relief supplies, sponsoring education, supplying fresh water to recognised NGOs in Africa.
Secretary: Mr G R Dawson. *Treasurer:* Mr A F Sims. Volunteers 80. **CC** No.803686. Began 1984; interdenominational. No magazine. Turnover £130,000 to year end Mar 05.

Christian Aid, PO Box 100, London SE1 7RT
☎020 7620 4444 📠020 7620 0719
E: info@christian-aid.org
Web: www.christian-aid.org.uk
Exposing the scandal of poverty, working to eradicate it through local partners, ecumenical networks.
Director: Daleep Mukarji. Executive staff 1, Other staff 500. **CC** No.1105851. Began 1945; interdenominational. Magazine: *Christian Aid News* (300,000 every four months). Turnover £71,000,000 to year end Dec 05.

***Christian Blind Mission**, Vision House, 7 Oakington Business Park, Oakington, Cambridge CB4 5DQ
☎01223 425 161 📠01223 425 455
E: cbm@cbmuk.org.uk
Web: www.cbmuk.org.uk
Showing Christ's love by preventing and curing blindness in the developing world.
UK National Director: Dr William McAllister. *Assistant Director:* Mr Martin Carter. *Public Relations Manager:* Ms Lindsey Brown. Executive staff 5, Other staff 17. **CC** No.1058162. Began 1996; ecumenical. Magazine: *Light* (Circulation n/a every two months). Turnover £3,488,948 to year end Dec 02.

Christian Community Ministries, 105 Runcorn Road, Barnton, Northwich CW8 4EX
☎01606 782 244 📠01606 782 244
E: maxkeelty.ccm@tesco.net
Web: www.ccm-international.org.uk
Providing finance and support to Emanuel Children's Home, Romania; sponsorship of daughter charity, CCM Romania.
Chairman & Overseas Mission Director: Mr Maxwell Keelty. Executive staff 1. **CC** No.1020071. Began 1992; interdenominational. Magazine: *Newsletter* (2,000 every two months). Turnover £63,000 to year end Dec 02.

Christian Compassion Ministries UK, 34 Woodland Rise, Welwyn Garden City AL8 7LF
☎01707 325 345
E: pat.goodrich@ntlworld.com
Relief of street children and indigent families in Manila, Philippines.
Hon Secretary: Mrs Pat Goodrich. Admin staff 1. **CC** No.1084104. Began 2001; Reformed Baptist. No magazine. Turnover £93,000 to year end Dec 04.

Christian Engineers in Development, 37 Kidmore End Road, Emmer Green, Reading RG30 2EB
☎01223 327 448
E: treasurer@ced.org.uk
Web: www.ced.org.uk
Professional engineering services in partnership with churches and community groups in developing countries.
Treasurer: W R Harper. No UK full-time staff. **CC** No.293734. Began 1985; interdenominational. Magazine: *CED Newsletter* (150 quarterly). Turnover £91,500 to year end Mar 04.

†**Christian Forum in Support of Persecuted Religious Minorities Worldwide**, c/o USPG, Partnership House, 157 Waterloo Road, London SE1 1UJ
☎020 7803 3439
E: clare@uspg.org.uk
Web: www.sufferingandhope.org
Providing support and advocacy for religious minorities suffering persecution or discrimination.
Secretary: Mrs Clare Amos. No full-time staff. Began 1999; interdenominational. Working with USPG. No magazine. Turnover £1,000 to year end Aug 02.

***Christian Hope International**, Hope House, Elms Industrial Estate, Church Road, Romford RM3 0JU
☎01708 377 795 M: 07740 681 005
📠01708 371 332
E: vbull@btinernet.com
Web: www.christianhope.org.uk
Aid agency working through the church worldwide.
Director of Operations: Mr Victor Bull. Executive staff 1, Admin staff 2. **CC** No.1061526. Began 1994; interdenominational. (Previously Containers of Hope). Magazine: *Hope Magazine* (5,000 quarterly). Turnover £150,000 to year end Mar 03.

Christian Partners in Africa, Stonebow House, 1 Silver Street, Lincoln LN2 1DY
☎01522 544 830 📠01522 544 949
E: office@cpafrica.org.uk
Web: www.cpafrica.org.uk
Working alongside some of the poorest people in Africa to facilitate community-led development projects.
Directors: Mr Christopher Shelbourne, Mr Paul Quincey. Executive staff 5, Admin staff 2, Other staff 5. **CC** No.1043695. Began 1995; non-denominational. No magazine. Turnover £225,000 to year end Dec 04.

***Church Relief International**, The King's Centre, Osney Mead, Oxford OX2 0ES
☎01865 297 440 📠01865 297 401
E: european@saltlight.org
Web: www.saltlight.org
Relief projects in third world; medical, educational, orphanages.
Director: Rev Stephen P Thomas. No full-time staff. **CC** No.1071600. Began 1986; Salt and Light Ministries. No magazine. Turnover £190,000 to year end July 04.

Cleaford Christian Trust, 46 Hazell Road, Farnham GU9 7BP
☎0845 124 9402 M: 07713 322 290
📠01252 717 137
E: cleaver@cleaford.co.uk
Web: www.cleafordchristiantrust.org.uk
Supporting church ministry in Romania to churches, schools, hospitals, poor people; Christian camp.
Chairman: Mr Angus Cleaver. Executive staff 2. **CC** No.1039861. Began 1994; interdenominational. No magazine. Turnover £35,000 to year end Dec 02.

***Compassion**, 43 High Street, Weybridge KT13 8BB
☎01932 836 490 📠01932 831 275
E: info@ukpc.ci.org
Web: www.compassionuk.org
Child sponsorship ministry addressing spiritual, physical, economic and social needs of children in 24 countries.
Director of Operations: Mr Richard Atterton. *Executive Director:* Mr Ian Hamilton. *Sponsor Relations Director:* Mrs Ginny Sharman. **CC** No.1077216. Began 1999; non-denominational. Magazine: *Childlink* (25,000 quarterly). Turnover £6,000,000 to year end Jun 05.

***CORD (Christian Outreach - Relief and Development)**, 1 New Street, Leamington Spa CV31 1HP
☎01926 315 301 M: 07713 594 506
📠01926 885 786
E: info@cord.org.uk
Web: www.cord.org.uk
Relief and development work among refugees in areas of conflict.
Director: Mr Michael Godfrey. *HR Manager:* Mrs Vanessa Tyler. *Head of Fundraising and Communications:* Mr Richard Dickson. Executive staff 5, Other UK staff 11. **CC** No.1070684. Began 1967; non-denominational. (Previously Christian Outreach). Magazine: *Compassion in Action* (6,000 every two months). Turnover £1,996,000 to year end Dec 04.

Dentaid, Giles Lane, Landford, Salisbury SP5 2BG
☎01794 324 249 📠01794 323 871
E: info@dentaid.org
Web: www.dentaid.org
Improving the oral health of disadvantaged communities around the world.
Chief Executive: Luke Wordley. *Dental Executive:* Dr Jenny Wordley. Executive staff 3, Other staff 4. **CC** No.1075826. Began 1996; non-denominational. Magazine: *Extractions* (3,000 every two months). Turnover £144,000 to year end Mar 02.

Dohnavur Fellowship, 80 Windmill Road, Brentford TW8 0QH
☎020 8569 8952 🖷020 8569 8952
E: dohnavur.inuk@tiscali.co.uk
Web: www.dohnavurfellowship.org
Children's home, school, hospital in India.
Secretary for Great Britain: Miss Tahany Hanna. *Co-leaders, India:* Miss Sura Carunia, Miss Anihala Carunia. Admin staff 1. ***CC*** No.232510. Began 1901; interdenominational. Magazine: *Dust of Gold* (1,700 quarterly). Turnover £187,481 to year end Apr 05.

East Gate Trust, Carey House, Brecklands Green, North Pickenham, Swaffham PE37 8LG
☎01760 440 561 M: 07742 219 756
🖷01760 440 561
E: peter@eastgate.org.uk
Web: www.eastgate.org.uk
In-house and itinerant teaching, preaching, pastoral care for leaders; healing and wholeness ministry; day retreats.
Director: Mr Peter Gillett. Executive staff 3, Admin staff 1. ***CC*** No.1009279. Began n/a; non-denominational. (Previously Pickenham Ministries). No magazine. Turnover £9,000 to year end Sep 02.

Ebenezer Aid Fund, Ebenezer House, 5a Poole Road, Bournemouth BH2 5QJ
☎01202 294 455 🖷01202 295 550
E: enquiries@ebenezer-ef.org
Web: www.operation-exodus.org
Providing humanitarian aid to poor and needy communities within the former Soviet Union.
UK Administrator: Name not supplied. Executive staff 2. ***CC*** No.1058068. Began 1991; non-denominational. Magazine: *Ebenezer Bulletin* (7,000 quarterly). Turnover £140,000 to year end Dec 04.

The Epiphany Trust, St David's, Park Road South, Newton-le-Willows WA12 8EY
☎01925 220 999 M: 07968 741 626
🖷 01942 261 249
Email: bill@epiphany.org.uk
Web: www.epiphany.org.uk
Director: Mr Bill Hampson. *Chairman:* Dr Robert Song. Executive staff 3. ***CC*** No.1006653. Began 1990; interdenominational. (Previously Movement for Christian Democracy Trust) No magazine. Turnover £200,000 to year end Jul 04. Education, specifically political; relief and aid work for children in Eastern Europe and Asia.

†Every Child, 4 Bath Place, Rivington Street, London EC2A 3DR
☎020 7749 2468 🖷020 7729 8339
E: gen@everychild.org.uk
Web: www.everychild.org.uk
Assisting needy children in developing countries through one-to-one sponsorship, direct marketing and grants.
Chief Executive: Mr Robert Pritchett. *Director of Fundraising:* Ms Katrina Lawson. *Director of Finance and IT:* Miss Lindy Jordan. Executive staff 4, Other staff 40. ***CC*** No.287545. Began 1983, Merged with European Children's Trust 2001; non-denominational. (Previously The Christian Children's Fund of Great Britain). Magazine: *Childworld GB* (19,000 quarterly). Turnover £7,450,000 to year end June 03.

***Food for the Hungry - UK**, 44 Copperfield Road, Bassett, Southampton SO16 3NX
☎023 8090 2327 🖷023 8090 2327
E: uk@fhi.net
Web: www.uk.fhi.net
Facilitating emergency relief and sustainable development to meet physical and spiritual needs of the poor.
Executive Officer: Mr Doug Wakeling. Executive staff 1. ***CC*** No.328273. Began 1989; interdenominational. No magazine. Turnover £130,000 to year end Dec 04.

†Friends of TREAD, 41 Albany Road, St Leonards-on-Sea TN38 0LJ
☎01424 421 760 M: 07973 283 117
🖷01424 421 760
E: treaduk@hotmail.com
Web: www.friendoftread.org
Giving hope and a new future to needy Indian children.
Founder/Trustee: Mr David Owen. Executive staff 1. ***CC*** No.1081400. Began 2000; non-denominational. Trinity Rural Educational Association for Development. No magazine. Turnover £37,449 to year end Mar 03.

***Global Care**, Global Care House, 2 Dugdale Road, Coventry CV6 1PB
☎024 7660 1800 🖷024 7660 1444
E: hq@globalcare.org.uk
Web: www.globalcare.org.uk
Working internationally for needy children, through relief, development, education and childcare programmes.
Chief Executive: Mr Ron Newby. Executive staff 4, Other staff 12. ***CC*** No.1054008. Began 1983; interdenominational. No magazine. Turnover £1,200,000 to year end Mar 05.

Habitat for Humanity Great Britain, 11 Parsons Street, Banbury OX16 5LW
☎01295 264 240 🖷01295 264 230
E: enquiries@hfhgb.org
Web: www.habitatforhumanity.org.uk
International Christian housing charity that builds houses with volunteers and families living in poverty.
National Director: Mr Ian Walkden. Executive staff 2, Other staff 11. ***CC*** No.1043641. Began 1995; interdenominational. Magazine: *Newsletter* (18,000 every four months). Turnover £2,500,000 to year end Jul 05.

***Hand in Hand**, Springfield Lyons House, Chelmsford Business Park, Chelmsford CM2 5TH
☎01245 236 561
🖷01245 236 660
E: info@hihand.org
Web: www.hihand.org
Supporting children, adults and organisations in need or hardship in selected parts of the world.
Development Manager: Mr Clive Pickett. Staff 1. ***CC*** No.1069976. Began 1998; interdenominational. No magazine. Turnover £66,000 to year end Jun 02.

Help International, Nettle Hill, Brinklow Road, Ansty, Coventry CV7 9JL
☎024 7660 2777
🖷024 7660 3276
E: info@helpinternational.org.uk
Web: www.helpinternational.org.uk
Assisting mission and providing relief and development in impoverished countries worldwide.
Co-ordinating Director: Mrs Sally Marcutt. Executive staff 1, Admin staff 1. ***CC*** No.327645. Began 1986. Magazine: *Together* (Circulation n/a quarterly). Turnover £300,000 to year end Dec 98.

†*Holy Ground Mission in Faith, 1 Farrow Close, Dodworth, Barnsley S75 3TL
☎01226 200 133
M: 07803 249 714
🖷01226 203 291
Furthering the Christian Gospel; providing palliative / hospital care; distributing humanitarian aid to war victims in Bosnia.
Foundation Missionary: Mrs Jacqueline Ryalls. Executive staff 6, Other staff 13. ***CC*** No.1096594. Began 1992; interdenominational. No magazine. Turnover £50,000 to year end Mar 03.

Hope of Lugazi, 6 Cedar Close, Worthing BN13 2HZ
☎01903 694 433
E: johnray@onetel.com
Operating sponsorship scheme for young people's education in Uganda.
Contacts: John & Christine Ray. Executive staff 1. Began n/a. No magazine. Turnover n/a.

Hospice of Hope Romania, 28a High Street, Otford, Sevenoaks TN14 5PQ
☎01959 525 110
🖷10959 525 013
E: office@hospiceofhope.co.uk
Web: www.hospiceofhope.co.uk
Supporting Hospice Casa Sperantei Brasov and the development of hospice care in south-east Europe.
UK Coordinator: Mr John Hardley. *Director, Romania:* Mr Graham Perolls. Executive staff 1, Other staff 1. ***CC*** No.1088475. Began 2001; non-denominational. No magazine. Turnover £500,000 to year end Dec 04.

†The Hoveraid Trust, 101a High Street, Gosport PO12 1DS
☎023 9251 0593 🖷023 9250 2302
Web: www.hoveraid.co.uk
Developing appropriate technology hovercraft for use by missions and relief agencies in developing countries.
Chairman: Mr Nigel Pool. No full-time staff. **CC** No.1005977. Began 1991; interdenominational. No magazine. Turnover £24,862 to year end Mar 02.

Incare, Assemblies of God, PO Box 7634, Nottingham NG11 6ZY
☎0115 921 7272 🖷0115 921 7273
E: info@aog.org.uk
Web: www.aog.org.uk
International care, relief and social concern department of Assemblies of God.
Director: Name not supplied. Executive staff 1, Other staff 1. Began 1984; Assemblies of God. No magazine. Turnover n/a
Also at: *National Care Coordinator:* Mr Harry Wake, 31 Ryeburn Way, Wellingborough NN8 3AH
E: harry.j.wake@btconnect.com
☎01933 229 598

†India Ministries Fellowship, 8 Blinkbonny Cresent, Edinburgh EH4 3NB
☎0131 332 3364
E: graham@dickson22.fsnet.co.uk
Web: www.littlemistymusic.co.uk/imf
Working in partnership with Indian Christians to provide care, education and training for destitute children.
Chairman: Rev Malcolm Duff. No full-time staff. **CC** No.SCO 10146. Began 1984; interdenominational. No magazine. Turnover £30,000 to year end Dec 00.

International Care and Relief (ICR), 27 Church Road, Tunbridge Wells TN1 1HT
☎01892 519 619 🖷01892 529 029
E: hq@icrcharity.com
Web: www.icrcharity.org.uk
Enabling young people and communities to tackle underlying causes of poverty and affect their future.
Chief Executive: Mr Susanne Niedrum. Executive staff 1, Other staff 13. **CC** No.298316. Began 1978; interdenominational. (Previously International Christian Relief). Magazine: *Habari* (10,000 quarterly). Turnover £1,600,000 to year end Mar 03.

***International China Concern**, PO Box 20, Morpeth NE61 3YP
☎01670 505 622 M: 07799 413 095
🖷01670 505 622
E: info@intlchinaconcern.org
Web: www.intlchinaconcern.org
Bringing hope, opportunity and love to China's abandoned and orphaned children.
Chairman of Trustees: Mr Richard Hubbard. No full-time staff. **CC** No.1058349. Began 1998; non-denominational. No magazine. Turnover £100,000 to year end Aug 05.

International Fellowship for the Handicapped, 11 Coastguard Square, Barden Road, Eastbourne BN22 7EE
☎01323 638 744 🖷01323 638 744
E: martyn@msrelf.freeserve.co.uk
Encouraging evangelisation and integration of people with handicaps causing them to be socially excluded; worldwide.
Secretary: Mr Martyn J Relf. No full-time staff. **CC** No.1087581. Began 1989; non-denominational. No magazine. Turnover £10,000 to year end Mar 05.
Administrator: Mrs Sylvia Cronin, 16 Beacon Hill, Bexhill-on-Sea TN39 5DF
☎01424 219 425 🖷01424 219 425

International Justice Mission - UK, 14 Hurst Way, Sevenoaks TN13 1QN
☎01732 741 581 🖷01732 459 918
E: rogerhm@attglobal.net
Web: www.spearbooks.com
Seeking justice for victims of abuse around the world; short and long-term efforts.
Director: Mr Roger Malstead. Executive staff 1, Other staff 1. Began 2001; interdenominational. No magazine. Turnover n/a.

The International Order of St George, 24 Weston Road, Strood, Rochester ME2 3EZ
☎01634 725 143 M: 07761 001 273
Web: www.orderofstgeorge.org
To vanquish the dragons of want poverty and injustice in ancient Hungarian order of chivalry.
CC No.1095339. Began n/a.
Director: Name not supplied. Staff n/a. Interdenominational. No magazine. Previously St Lazarus Trust. Turnover n/a

***Jabez**, Byways, Shuckburgh Road, Priors Marston, Southam CV47 7RS
☎0845 644 6444 🖷0845 644 6333
E: mail@jabez.org
Web: www.jabez.org
Supporting the education and development of young Christian leaders in developing countries.
Chief Executive: Mr Robert Chambers. Executive staff 1. **CC** No.1100901. Began 2003; non-denominational. No magazine. Turnover £50,000 to year end Apr 05.

***Jubilee Action**, 96 High Street, Guildford GU1 3HE
☎0845 450 4748 🖷 01483 565 475
E: info@jubileeaction.co.uk
Web: www.jubileeaction.co.uk
Director: Mr Danny Smith. Executive staff 1, Other staff 4. **CC** No.1013587. Began 1992; non-denominational. Magazine: *Just Right* (20,000 quarterly). Turnover £950,000 to year end Apr 05. Action on children's rights issues, religious liberty; supporting long-term aid and combating poverty.
Parliamentary Office *Researcher & Parliamentary Officer:* Mr Wilfred Wong, Room LG6, Norman Shaw North, Victoria Embankment, London SW1A 2HZ
☎020 7219 5129 🖷 020 7219 5129

***Kingscare**, The King's Centre, High Street, Aldershot GU11 1DJ
☎01252 333 233 🖷01252 310 814
E: info@kingscare.org
Web: www.kingscare.org
Showing the love of God in a practical and caring way in developing countries.
Director: Mr George Dowdell. *Chairman of Trustees:* Mr Jeff Fisher. Executive staff 1, Other staff 2. **CC** No.1072613. Began 1988; non-denominational. No magazine. Turnover £448,000 to year end Dec 04.

†Lifespring International, New Life Christian Centre, Cairo New Road, Croydon CR0 1XP
☎ M 07711 345 231
E: arthurh@nlsm.freeserve.co.uk
Web: www.lifespringinternational.org
Making social and educational provision for deprived children in Africa.
Chairman: Rev Arthur Hibbert. Executive staff 7, Other staff 18. **CC** Began 2002; interdenominational. No magazine. Turnover £44,967 to year end Apr 03.

***Link Romania**, Link House, Park Road, Worthing BN11 2AN
☎01903 529 333 🖷01903 529 007
E: info@linkromania.co.uk
Web: www.linkromania.co.uk
Helping to rebuild lives and communities in Romania; agricultural development, transport service, charity development.
Directors: Roger Gale, Chris Chatfield, Tony Hayes. Executive staff 1, Other staff 4. **CC** No.1069722. Began 1990; interdenominational. (Previously Link Romania/Partnership for Growth). Magazine: *Newslink* (3,500 quarterly). Turnover £1,000,000 to year end Apr 05.

***David Livingstone International**, The Mount, Western Gardens Road, Combe Martin, Ilfracombe EX34 7UY
☎No telephone 🖷01271 883 287
E: david_livingstone_international@yahoo.co.uk
Web: www.livingstone.com
Providing emergency food, medical shipments; operating orphanages, hospitals, schools; sponsoring children's homes; Bible teaching.
Executive Director: Rev G Cozens. *Secretary/Treasurer:* Mrs Barbara Cozens. No paid staff. **CC** No.53789. Began 1974; non-denominational. No magazine. Turnover n/a.

***Love Russia**, Falcon House, 3 Castle Road, Newport PO30 1DT
☎01983 530 262 🖷01983 530 520
E: love.russia@ukonline.co.uk
Web: www.loverussia.org
Providing spiritual and humanitarian aid to orphans and others in need in Russia.
Director: Mr Alex Cooke. *UK Coordinator:* Mrs Jacqui Cooke. Executive staff 2, Admin staff 3. **CC** No.1092154. Began 1993; non-denominational. Magazine: *Love Russia News* (5,000 quarterly). Turnover £309,000 to year end Jun 02.

Malawi Orphan Fund, 22 Bitteswell Road, Lutterworth LE17 4EZ
☎01455 550 813
E: homeofhope@onetel.com
Web: www.homeofhope.tk
Support Christian orphan care and education at Mchinji orphanage and elsewhere in Malawi.
Chairman: Mr Martin Lowdon. No other staff. ***CC*** No.1110640. Began 2005; non-denominational. No magazine. Turnover £10,000 to year end Feb 06.

Father Marek Sujkowski Children's Aid to Ukraine, Romania and Poland, 48 Achilles Road, London NW6 1EA
☎020 7794 7891 🖷020 7431 5265
Sending medicines and hospital supplies to children's hospitals in Eastern Europe.
Trustees: Mr & Mrs C Kyriakides. Executive staff 1, Other staff n/a. ***CC*** No.1031451. Began 1994; ecumenical. (Previously Children's Aid to Ukraine, Romania and Poland). No magazine. Turnover n/a.

Medair UK, Unit 3, Taylors Yard, 67 Alderbrook Road, London SW12 8AD
☎020 8772 0100 🖷020 8772 0101
E: united.kingdom@medair.org
Web: www.medair.org
Responding to humanitarian emergencies and forgotten crises with a Christian presence and qualified technical assistance.
National Coordinator: Jennifer Matthews. Executive staff 8, Other staff 100. ***CC*** No.1056731. Began 1996; non-denominational. Magazine: *MEDAIR News* (2,500 quarterly). Turnover £4,068,000 to year end Dec 04.

Mercy Trucks, PO Box 73, Hexham NE47 0YT
☎0870 126 9120
E: roydixon@mercytrucks.org
Web: www.mercytrucks.org
Providing a platform enabling people to undertake overseas missionary work including relief and development.
Director: Mr Roy Dixon. Executive staff 3, Admin staff 2, Serving missionaries 30. ***CC*** No.1087704. Began 1998; interdenominational. No magazine. Turnover £5,000 to year end May 04.

Methodist Relief and Development Fund, Methodist Church House, 25 Marylebone Road, London NW1 5JR
☎020 7467 5132 🖷020 7467 5233
E: mrdf@methodistchurch.org.uk
Web: www.mrdf.org.uk
Relief and development overseas through Methodist, ecumenical and secular channels; development education in UK.
Team Leader: Kirsty Smith. Executive staff 1, Other staff 6. ***CC*** No.291691. Began 1946; Methodist. Magazine: *Funds in Focus* (10,000 quarterly). Turnover £1,200,000 to year end Aug 02.

Micah Network, PO Box 731, Woking GU21 4XW
☎01483 760 156
E: ukinfo@micahnetwork.org
Web: www.micahnetwork.org
Global network of agencies and churches in Christian relief, development and justice ministries.
Secretary: Dr David Boul. Exective staff 1. ***CC*** No.1103048. Began 2000; non-denominational. No magazine. Turnover £67,000 to year end Dec 04.

***Mission to Eastern Europe**, 67 Lugsdale Road, Widnes WA8 6BG
☎0151 420 1838
M: 07775 747 123
E: john@mission-romania.org.uk
Web: www.mission-romania.org.uk
Providing aid and Christian literature to Romania; building work in churches, hospitals, orphanages, children's clinics.
Mission Director: Mr John Rushworth. Admin staff 2, Other staff 6. ***CC*** No.1048423. Began 1990; interdenominational. No magazine. Turnover £31,000 to year end Dec 02.

Nepal Leprosy Trust, 10a The Vineyard, Richmond TW10 6AQ
☎020 8332 9023
🖷020 8948 2703
E: info@nlt.org.uk
Web: www.blt.org.uk
Income-generation, social welfare, and health care projects in Nepal.
General Manager: Miss Ruth Odell. Executive staff 3. ***CC*** No.1081952. Began 1972; interdenominational. Magazine: *NLT News* (700 quarterly). Turnover £327,032 to year end Dec 04.

†**The New Hope Trust**, Faith Acres, Peterhead AB42 3DQ
☎0845 230 4673
🖷01779 838 548
E: aid@newhopetrust.org
Providing aid, mainly to Eastern Europe.
Managing Director: Wendy Smith. Executive staff 2, Admin staff 4. ***CC*** No.276520. Began 1990; interdenominational. No magazine. Turnover n/a.

***Open Hands International**, PO Box 525, Stockport SK3 8WX
☎0161 236 8222
E: andrew.belfield@ukonline.co.uk
Discovering purpose in people's lives by providing accommodation, education; primarily with deprived children.
Founding Director: Mr Andrew Belfield. Executive staff 3. ***CC*** No.10710[illegible]1. Began 1998; interdenominational. No magazine. Turnover £80,000 to year end Apr 03.

Operation Agri, 361 Firs Lane, Palmers Green, London N13 5LX
☎020 8803 0113
E: admin@operationagri.org.uk
Web: www.operationagri.org.uk
Supporting church-based rural and urban development in almost 20 countries worldwide.
Contact Person: Dr Malcolm Drummond. *Treasurer:* Mr Michael Putnam. No full-time staff. ***CC*** No.106934[illegible]. Began 1961; Baptist. Magazine: *Outreach Abroad* (5,000 quarterly). Turnover £265,000 to year end Oct 04.

Opportunity International UK, Angel Court, 81 St Clements, Oxford OX4 1AW
☎01865 725 304 🖷01865 2[illegible]5 161
E: impact@opportunity.org.uk
Web: www.opportunity.org.uk
Business development and job creation through micro-credit to poor people in developing contries.
Director: Mr David Coates. Executive staff 1, Other staff 7. ***CC*** No.11[illegible]7713. Began 1992; interdenominational. (Previously Opportunity Trust). No magazine. Turnover £2,090,000 to year end Dec 04.

***The Philippine Community Fund**, PO Box 294, Hedge End, Southampton SO30 2YD
☎01489 790 219 Ⓜ: 07950 132 684
E: info@p-c-f.org
Web: www.p-c-f.org
Serving waste-picker communities in dump sites, through Christian education, feeding, medical, employment.
Chief Executive Officer: Mrs Jane Walker. *Fundraising and Development Manager:* Mrs Andrea Booker. Other staff 2, Serving missionaries 1. ***CC*** No.1091581. Began 2002; non-denominational. Turnover £150,000 to year end Apr 05.

Praise Valley Foundation (UK), 19 Zetland Street, Poplar, London E14 6PR
☎020 7537 9155 Fax 020 7537 9155
E: info@praisevalley.com
Web: www.praisevalley.com
Relieving hardship in the name of Jesus in Africa and around the world.
Chairman: Rev Gilbert Amartey. No full-time staff. ***CC*** No.1092686. Began 2000; non-denominational. No magazine. Turnover £17,000 to year end Mar 03.

Romania Concern, Barnes Close, Malthouse Lane, Chadwich, Bromsgrove B61 0RA
☎01562 710 231 Fax 01562 710 278
E: cfrenquiry@aol.com
Web: www.cfrbarnesclose.co.uk
Ecumenical network providing aid for projects, courses on reconciliation, twinning and exchanges.
Contact: Rev John Johansen-Berg. Executive staff 2, Other staff 4. ***CC*** No.295113. Began 1984; ecumenical. Linked to Community for Reconciliation. No magazine. Turnover n/a.

***ROPE**, Fairway House, Rear 64/66 High Street, Great Missenden HP16 0AN
☎01494 866 724 Fax 01494 864 679
E: office@rope.org.uk
Web: www.rope.org.uk
Helping the poor at grass-roots level in 80 countries through practical, sustainable direct action.
Chief Executive: Mr Andrew Jong. *Company Secretary:* Mrs Sylvia Cook. All voluntary staff. ***CC*** No.1069608. Began 1991; interdenominational. Magazine: *PressRelief* (6,000 quarterly). Turnover £440,000 to year end Apr 04.

St Andrew's Evangelical Mission (Peru), 126 Ealing Road, Brentford TW8 0LD
☎020 8840 9066 Fax 020 8840 9066
Christian children's orphanage caring for disabled, orphaned and abandoned children at Chosica, Lima, Peru.
Honorary General Secretary: Mr Raymond G H Spencer. Executive staff 1, Admin staff 1, Serving missionaries 2. ***CC*** No.290252. Began 1983; interdenominational. No magazine. Turnover £87,844 to year end Dec 04.

***Samaritan's Purse International**, Victoria House, Victoria Road, Buckhurst Hill IG9 5EX
☎020 8559 2044
Fax 020 8502 9062
E: london@samaritans-purse.org.uk
Web: www.samaritanspurse.uk.com
Worldwide Christian service agency.
General Manager: Mr Simon Barrington. Executive staff 1, Other staff 16. ***CC*** No.1001349. Began 1989; interdenominational. Incorporating Operation Christmas Child. No magazine. Turnover £20,929,988 to year end Dec 02.

†Scottish Catholic International Aid Fund (SCIAF), 19 Park Circus, Glasgow G3 6BE
☎0141 354 5555
Fax 0141 354 5533
E: sciaf@sciaf.org.uk
Web: www.sciaf.org.uk
Supporting relief and development projects in the Third World; development education in Scotland.
Chief Executive: Mr Paul Chitnis. *President:* Rt Rev John Mone. Executive staff 14, Other staff 13. ***CC*** No.SCO 12302. Began 1965; Roman Catholic. Magazine: *The Review*(Circulation & frequency n/a). Turnover £4,000,000 to year end Dec 02.

†Send A Cow, Unit 4, Priston Mill, Priston, Bath BA2 9EQ
☎01225 447 041
Fax 01225 317 627
E: admin@sendacow.org.uk
Web: www.sendacow.org.uk
Operating self-help livestock projects for needy communities in East Africa to improve income and nutrition.
UK General Manager: Mr Martin Geake. *Fundraising Manager:* Ms Jenny Clarke. Executive staff 4, Other staff 6. ***CC*** No.299717. Began 1988; non-denominational. Magazine: *Lifeline* (19,000 quarterly). Turnover £1,500,000 to year end Mar 03.

S.H.A.R.E. (Social, Health, Assistance, Reconciliation and Education), 69 Liverpool Old Road, Much Hoole, Preston PR4 4RB
☎0772 612 267
E: steven.hughes24@btinternet.com
Web: www.ascensium.ro
Establishing and networking health promotion and related projects; ecumenical centre for reconciliation.
Administrator: Mrs Jayne Crooks. Admin staff 1, Other staff 1. ***CC*** No.1002326. Began 1990; ecumenical. (Previously Hawkesley Christian Romania Trust). Magazine: *Newsletter* (300 quarterly). Turnover £27,000 to year end Mar 00.

The Smiles Foundation, PO Box HK70, Leeds LS11 6YR
☎0113 276 5060
Fax 0113 276 5060
E: info@thesmilesfoundation.org
Web: www.thesmilesfoundation.org
Supporting a range of community based projects in Romania and Armenia.
Director: Dann Wilson. Executive staff 1, Other staff n/a. ***CC*** No.108[illegible]961. Began n/a; interdenominational. (Previously [illegible]ia). No magazine. Turnover n/a.

Society for the Protection of African Children, 168 King Street, Castle Douglas DG7 1DA
☎01556 504 416
Fax 01556 504 416
Supporting child welfare projects and education in Africa.
Director: Mr Jim Figgis. No other staff. Began 2003; non-denominational. No magazine. Turnover £4,805 to year end May 05.

Starfish Asia Fund, 32 Beckham Lane, Beckenham BR3 4RE
☎020 8402 1914
Fax 020 8402 1914
E: mike@starfishasia.com
Web: www.starfishasia.com
Partnership with national Christians to tackle poverty in Pakistan through education, medical provision, direct action.
Director: Mr Michael Wakely. Executive staff 1. ***CC*** No.10996[illegible]2. Began 2003; non-denominational. No magazine. Turnover £55,000 to year end Mar 05.

Streams in the Desert, 27 Pirelli Way, Eastleigh SO50 5GE
☎023 8064 7199
Fax 023 8064 7199
E: streams@streamsinthedesert.org.uk
Web: www.streamsinthedesert.org.uk
Providing housing for elderly new immigrants in Israel; teaching biblical basis of work.
Coordinator: Miss Helen J Mears. Paid Staff 1, Voluntary Staff 2. ***CC*** No.1043034. Began 1994; non-denominational. Magazine: *Streams Update* (Circulation n/a quarterly). Turnover n/a.

***Teachers for China/Caring for China's Children/Health for China**, The Longcroft, Storeton Lane, Barnston, Heswall, Wirral CH61 1EU
☎0151 648 5605
E: lynda@leelyn.freeserve.co.uk
Web: www.tfc-cfcc.org
Placing and supporting Christian TEFL teachers; running 3 childcare centres; developing health and community work.
International Director: Mr Cyril Thomas. *UK Director:* Mr David Newbery. Executive staff 2, Admin staff 7. **CC** No.1007[illegible]34. Began 1991; non-denominational. No magazine. Turnover £150,000 to year end Dec 00.

***Tearfund**, 100 Church Road, Teddington TW11 8QE
☎020 8977 9144 Fax 020 8943 3594
E: enquiry@tearfund.org
Web: www.tearfund.org
Evangelical Christian relief and development charity working with communities in need around the world.
Chief Executive: Mr Matthew Frost. *Deputy Chief Executive:* Mr Graham Fairbairn. *Director of Finance:* Mr Richard Gough. Executive staff 10, Staff serving overseas 122, Other staff 335. ***CC*** No.265464. Began 1968; interdenominational. Magazine: *Tear Times* (224,000 quarterly). Turnover £53,025,000 to year end Mar 05.

***Teso Development Trust**, 24 Sandhurst Avenue, Stourbridge DY9 0XL
☎01384 829 580 Fax 01384 829 580
E: david@drwatts.freeserve.co.uk
Web: www.teso.org.uk
Providing relief and development aid to Teso people in Uganda; working with the churches.
Administrator: Mr Dave Watts. Executive staff 1. ***CC*** No.1005139. Began 1989; non-denominational. Magazine: *Teso Newsletter* (500 quarterly). Turnover £83,000 to year end Mar 05.

Therapy in Romania, 30 Millfields Avenue, Rugby CV21 4HJ
☎UK: 07885 823 046 Romania: 0746 463 345 Fax: UK: 01788 547 516
E: rogerday@3-cp.fsnet.co.uk
Web: therapyinromania.org.uk
Coordinator: Mr Roger Day. Executive staff 2. Began 1995; non-denominational. (Previously Professional Counselling Services) No magazine. Turnover £25,000 to year end May 05. Psychotherapy and play-therapy training and consultancy to charities, churches and statutory organisations in Romania.

†To Russia With Love, PO Box 365, Swansea SA2 0YX
☎01792 201 449
E: info@torussiawithlove.freeserve.co.uk
Web: www.torussiawithlove.org.uk
Providing spiritual and humanitarian aid in partnership with churches in the former Soviet Union.
Chairman: Mr Mike Lewis. No full-time staff. ***CC*** No.1019532. Began 1993; non-denominational. No magazine. Turnover £6,200 to year end Sep 02.

Traidcraft plc, Kingsway, Team Valley Trading Estate, Gateshead NE11 0NE
☎0191 491 0591 Fax 0191 497 6562
E: comms@traidcraft.co.uk
Web: www.traidcraft.co.uk
Direct sales and mail order business giving market opportunities to producers in 30 developing countries.
Chief Executive: Mr Paul Chandler. *Board Chairman:* Mr David Nussbaum. *Public Relations Manager:* Mr Peter Collins. Executive staff 5, Other staff 38. ***CC*** No.1048752. Began 1981; non-denominational. Magazine: *Annual report* (15,000 annually). Turnover £2,500,000 to year end Mar 03.

UNAFRAID (United Africa Aid), Barnes Close, Malthouse Lane, Chadwich, Bromsgrove B61 0RA
☎01562 710 231 Fax 01562 710 278
E: johnjoberg@tiscali.co.uk
Web: www.cfrbarnesclose.co.uk
Conflict resolution and peacebuilding courses, mainly East Africa; project support; partnership with African organisations.
Contact: Rev John Johansen-Berg. No full-time staff. ***CC*** No.295113. Began 1984; ecumenical. Linked to Community for Reconciliation. No magazine. Turnover n/a.

Voice for Change UK, PO Box 92, Dereham NR20 4WD
☎0845 130 3832 M 07968 120 870
Fax 01362 686 208
E: voiceforchangeuk@dovetrust.com
Web: www.voiceforchange.org
Providing homes and social care for children; taking short-term teams to southern Brazil.
Trustee: Mr Neil Green. No full-time staff. ***CC*** No.1087066. Began 2000; non-denominational. No magazine. Turnover £25,000 to year end Mar 02. .

***World Emergency Relief**, 20 York Buildings, London WC2 6JU
☎0870 429 2129 M: 07710 701 118
Fax 020 7839 8202
E: alex@wer-uk.org or info@wer-uk.org
Web: www.wer-uk.org
Linking with overseas charities, agencies and churches, identifing relief and development needs, delivering cost effective aid.
Chief Executive Officer: Rev Joel MacCollam. *Director of Operations:* Mr Alex D Haxton. *Business Manager:* Mr Mark Plummer. Executive staff 3, Admin staff 5. ***CC*** No.1045572. Began 1994; interdenominational. No magazine. Turnover £34,801,105 to year end Mar 05.

***World in Need**, PO Box 109, Crowborough TN6 2ZN
☎01892 669 834 Fax 01892 669 894
E: info@winint.org
Web: www.winint.org or www.restoredlives.co.uk
Empowering overseas people to do their own mission and development work.
International Director: Mr Ron George. Executive staff 1, Admin staff 5, Other staff 30. ***CC*** No.800940. Began 1991; interdenominational. A division of Leadership Training Resources. Magazine: *WIN News* (Circulation & frequency n/a). Turnover n/a.

***World Vision UK**, World Vision House, Opal Drive, Fox Milne, Milton Keynes MK15 0ZR
☎01908 841 000 Fax 01908 841 025
E: info@worldvision.org.uk
Web: www.worldvision.org.uk
Humanitarian aid agency serving the poor in over 40 countries
Chief Executive: Mr Charles Badenoch. *Churches Team Leader:* Mr Bruce Thomson. *Human Resources Director:* Mr Richard Marshall. Executive staff 6, Other staff 220. ***CC*** No.285908. Began 1979; interdenominational. Magazine: *Insight* (100,000 half-yearly). Turnover £49,157,000 to year end Sep 05.

O

O

SERVICES

ADDICTIONS & REHABILITATION CENTRES

See also Residential Homes for Disadvantaged People on Page 59, Social Service & Welfare Organisations on Page 387.

***Adullam Homes Housing Association,** Gordana House, The Mount, Shelton, Shrewsbury SY3 8BH
☎01743 365 050 🖷01743 365 070
E: lwatts@adullam.org.uk
Web: www.adullam.org.uk
Drug/alcohol dependency rehabilitation service for 20 people aged 18 to 60.
Service Manager: To be appointed. *Admissions:* Samantha Slater. Executive staff 2, Other staff n/a. ***CC*** No.326743. Began 1970; interdenominational. Magazine: *Lifebuilder* (5,000 yearly). Turnover £200,000 to year end Apr 00.

***Beechwood House,** 69 Old Perth Road, Inverness IV2 3JH
☎01463 711 355 🖷01463 711 544
Web: www.crossreach.org.uk
Residential accommodation: 15 rehabilitation beds, 4 support beds, 4 designated places.
Unit Manager: Mrs Cathy Cairns. Admin staff 1, Other staff 26. ***CC*** No.SCO 24366. Began 1991; Church of Scotland. No magazine. Turnover n/a.

†*BETEL of Britain, Windmill House, Weatheroak Hill, Alvechurch, Birmingham B48 7EA
☎01564 822 356 🖷01564 824 929
E: info@betel.charis.co.uk
Free Christian residence, helping restore alcoholics, drug addicts, homeless and desperately needy people. 130 places.
Directors: Kent and Mary Alice Martin. Executive staff 2, Other staff n/a. ***CC*** No.1081462. Began 1996; interdenominational. A WEC International ministry. No magazine. Turnover n/a.

Castle Craig Hospital, Castle Craig, Blyth Bridge, West Linton EH46 7DH
☎01721 722 763 🖷01721 752 662
Residential treatment for alcoholism and other addictions; detoxification and emergency care; specialist medical supervision. 94 beds.
Medical Director: Dr Margaret McCann. Executive staff 4, Other staff 55. Began 1988; non-denominational. No magazine. Turnover £2,200,000 to year end Dec 04.

Charis Alcohol and Drug Therapy Unit, 31 Mile End Road, London E1 4TP
☎020 7790 6278 🖷020 7702 8251
E: charis@thmission.f9.co.uk
Residential alcohol and drug therapy unit for men; homeless, potentially homeless receiving benefits.
Director: Mr Andrew Bannell. Executive staff 2, Other staff 11. ***CC*** No.259535. Began 1870; non-denominational. (Also known as The F N Charrington Tower Hamlets Mission). No magazine. Turnover £350,000 to year end Mar 02.

***Crisis Centre Ministries,** 12 City Road, St Pauls, Bristol BS2 8TP
☎0117 942 3088
E: admin@crisis-centre.org.uk
Web: www.crisis-centre.org.uk
Serving people with life-disrupting problems such as addiction, homelessness and unemployment.
General Manager: Paul Hazelden. Executive staff 4, Volunteers staff 60. ***CC*** No.298528. Began 1984; non-denominational. No magazine. Turnover £117,000 to year end Mar 05.

***Daybreak Drug Project,** St Luke's Daybreak Centre, Dagenham Road, Dagenham RM10 7UP
☎020 8595 2010 🖷020 8592 1899
E: office@daybreakdrugproject.org.uk
Web: www.daybreakdrugproject.org.uk
Promoting the care and rehabilitation of persons affected by drug misuse.
Manager: Mrs Rita Pennington. *Administrator:* To be appointed. Executive staff 1, Admin staff 5, Other staff 12. ***CC*** No.801027. Began 1985; non-denominational. Magazine: *Drugs And You!* (250 every two months). Turnover £400,000 to year end Mar 05.

Fewster House Alcoholism Rehabilitation Unit, 10 Terrace Road, Greenock PA15 1DJ
☎01475 721 572
Care for 4 men.
Officer-in-Charge: Centre Manager. Executive staff 3. ***CC*** Began n/a; Salvation Army. No magazine. Turnover n/a.

***Gilead Foundations,** Risdon Farm, Okehampton EX20 3AJ
☎01837 851 240 🖷01837 851 520
E: gilead.foundations@ukonline.co.uk
Web: www.gilead.org.uk
Unlocking people; releasing potential; residential Christian training and work. Two centres.
General Manager: Pastor Ian Samuel. Executive staff 9, Other staff 14. ***CC*** No.1002909. Began 1988; non-denominational. No magazine. Turnover £200,000 to year end Apr 03.

Gloucester House, 6 High Street, Highworth, Swindon SN6 7AG
☎01793 762 365 🖷01793 765 022
E: david.day@salvationarmy.org.uk
Unregistered residential rehabilitation centre for 15 men with severe alcohol/drug dependencies; also day programme.
Unit Manager: Mr David Day. Executive staff 3, Admin staff 1, Other staff 10. ***CC*** Began 1959; Salvation Army. No magazine. Turnover n/a.

Halfway House: 214 Windrush, Highworth, Swindon SN6 6HX
Accommodation for 3 men

Greig House Social Services Centre, 20 Garford Street, London E14 [illegible]JG
☎020 7987 5658 🖷020 7[illegible]36 16[illegible]
Residential addiction services for 17 men and women.
Officer-in-Charge: Centre Manager. Staff 31. Began 2000; Salvation Army. No magazine. Turnover n/a.

***The Hebron Trust,** Hebron House, 12 Stanley Avenue, Norwich NR7 0BE
☎01603 439 905 🖷01603 [illegible]00 79[illegible]
E: philippa@hebrontrust.co.uk
Web: www.hebrontrust.com
Residential treatment and care for women with substance misuse problems.
Director: Steve Seedall. *Administrator:* Ms Philippa Morris. Executive staff 1, Other staff 13. ***CC*** No.102009[illegible]. Began 19[illegible]3; interdenominational. No magazine. Turnover £500,000 to year end Mar 05.

Helping Hand, 29 Ripon Road, Blackpool FY1 4DY
☎01253 621 366 🖷01253 621 599
E: hhblackpoolaspire@yahoo.co.uk
Meeting the physical, psychological, spiritual and social needs of those addicted to drugs or alcohol.
Director: Name not supplied. Other staff 2. ***CC*** No.3204385. Began 1[illegible]96; interdenominational. No magazine. Turnover £25,000 to year end Mar 05.

Hope House Project, Stonham Housing Association, 36 Moor Street, Luton LU[illegible] 1HA
☎01582 722 673 🖷01582 48[illegible] 240
E: mary.ryan@homegroup.org.uk
Housing for 8 men and women with substance abuse problems.
Team Manager: Mary Ryan. Executive staff 3, Other staff 2, Project workers 3. ***CC*** Began 1979; non-denominational. No magazine. Turnover n/a.

***ISAAC (International Substance Abuse And Addiction Coalition),** 21a Woodlands Avenue, Burghfield Common, Reading RG7 3HU
☎0118 983 6684 M: 0778[illegible] 51[illegible] 402
🖷0118 927 2070
E: davidpisaac@aol.com
Web: www.isaacinternational.com
Supporting and encouraging Christians in the addiction arena through training and networking around the world.
General Secretary: Mr David Partington. Executive staff 2. ***CC*** No.10[illegible]1548. Began 1997; interdenominational. No magazine. Turnover £83,000 to year end Mar 04.

Kaleidoscope Project, 28-46 Cromwell Road, Kingston upon Thames KT2 6RN
☎020 8549 2681 🖷020 8547 0228
🄴 info@kaleidoscopeproject.org.uk
Web: www.kaleidoscopeproject.org.uk
Counselling, accommodation, medical and specialist drug help, educational/social facilities for young people in need.
Director: Mr Benn Keaveney. Executive staff 1, Other staff n/a. ***CC*** Began 1968; Baptist. No magazine. Turnover n/a.

Kenward Trust, Kenward House, Yalding, Maidstone ME18 6AH
☎01622 814 187 🖷01622 815 805
🄴 enquiry@kenwardtrust.org.uk
Web: www.kenwardtrust.org.uk
Communities for the care of men and women with alcohol and other drug problems.
Director: Mr Godfrey Featherstone. *Deputy Director:* Mrs Jean Park. *Director of Residential Projects:* Mr David Park. Executive staff 5, Other staff 64. ***CC*** No.265394. Began 1968; interdenominational. No magazine. Turnover £2,000,000 to year end Mar 05.

Kingswell Centre, 9 Arthur Street, Oswestry SY11 1JN
☎01691 655 126 🖷01691 654 064
🄴: office@kingswellcentre.co.uk
Web: www.kingswellcentre.org.uk
Family support for drug/alcohol problems and drop-in centre.
Centre Manager: Sarah O'Connoll. Executive staff 3, Admin staff 4. ***CC*** No.1104474. Began 1984; interdenominational. In partnership with Spurgeon's Child Care. No magazine. Turnover £70,000 to year end Feb 04.

***Life For The World Trust,** Micklefield Christian Centre, Buckingham Drive, High Wycombe HP13 7YB
☎01225 426 265
🄴: info@lftw.org
Web: www.lftw.org
Equipping church and community to give help and hope to victims of drug abuse and addiction.
Executive Director: Peter Smith. Executive staff 2, Other staff 4. ***CC*** No.1038410. Began 1967; non-denominational. Magazine: *Release* (1,000 quarterly). Turnover £200,000 to year end May 03.
Also at: Genesis Centre, 6 Green Park Road, Bath BA1 1XE

The Living Room, 8 The Glebe, Chells Way, Stevenage SG2 0DJ
☎01438 355 649 🖷01438 360 098
🄴: enquiries@thelivingroom.me.uk
Web: www.thelivingroom.me.uk
Daytime treatment for all kinds of addiction.
Director: Mrs Janis Feely. *Development Manager:* Mr Simon Bloomfield. Executive staff 4, Other staff 4. ***CC*** No.1080634. Began 2000; interdenominational. No magazine. Turnover n/a.

***Malta House,** 1 Malta Terrace, Edinburgh EH4 1HR
☎0131 332 3217 🖷0131 315 2313
Web: www.crossreach.org.uk
Offering 24-week rehabilitation programme for those with alcohol or drug dependency.
Unit Manager: James Stevely. Admin staff 1, Other staff 7. ***CC*** No.SCO 24366. Began n/a; Church of Scotland. No magazine. Turnover £350,000 to year end Mar 03.

***The Matthew Project,** 24 Pottergate, Norwich NR2 1DX
☎01603 626 123/764 754 (24-hour helpline) 🖷01603 630 411
🄴: thematthewproject@btinternet.com
Web: www.matthewproject.org
Counselling, advice, information and support for drug users, their families or friends. Education and prevention.
Director: Mr Julian Bryant. Executive staff 1, Other staff 52. ***CC*** No.285256. Began 1982; non-denominational. Magazine: *Report* (600 annually). Turnover £100,000 to year end Mar 05.

***Mission Vision,** 29 West Cliff, Preston PR1 8HX
☎01772 884 458 🖷01772 251 765
🄴: info@missionvision.org.uk
Web: www.missionvision.org.uk
Residential accommodation for those with alcohol or drug dependency.
Centre Manager: Zena Ridyard. Executive staff 1, Other staff 4. ***CC*** Began 1990; interdenominational. (Previously Lydia House Trust). No magazine. Turnover n/a.

MR Associates, 19 Wemyss Court, Leapmoor Drive, Wemyss Bay PA18 6BF
☎01475 522 962 🄼: 07967 963 806
🄴: info@mrassociates.org.uk
Web: www.mrassociates.org.uk
Advisors to drug and alcohol services, specialising in housing benefit, supporting people and care commission issues.
Supported Housing Advisor: Mr Mark Rodgers. Executive staff 2, Admin staff 1. Began 2000; interdenominational. No magazine. Turnover n/a

***The Nehemiah Project,** 47 Tooting Bec Gardens, Streatham, London SW16 1RF
☎020 8769 3444 🖷020 8773 7419
🄴: enquiries@nehemiahproject.org.uk
Web: www.nehemiahproject.org.uk
Providing rehabilitation for drug and alcohol addicts along with vocational training and move-on accommodation.
Chief Operating Officer: Mr Wendell Smith. Executive staff 4, Other staff 13. ***CC*** No.1058536. Began 1997; non-denominational. No magazine. Turnover £300,000 to year end Dec 02.

†Peniel Christian Centre, Halterburn, Kirk Yetholm, Kelso TD5 8PP
☎01573 420 639
Providing residential rehabilitation for 13 people.
Trustee: Mr Duncan Francis. Executive staff 1, Other staff 2. ***CC*** No.SCO 26038. Began 1969; interdenominational. No magazine. Turnover n/a.

***Rainbow House,** 52 Queen Mary Avenue, Crosshill, Glasgow G42 8DT
☎0141 423 2736
Providing residential drug and alcohol rehabilitation.
Unit Manager: Vic Walker. Executive staff 1, Other staff 13. ***CC*** No.SCO 24366. Began n/a; Church of Scotland. No magazine. Turnover n/a.

***Rankeillor Initiative,** Simpson House, 52 Queen Street, Edinburgh EH2 4NS
☎0131 225 4901
Supported accommodation and home support service for adults with addiction problems.
Unit Manager: Mr David Flett. Admin staff 1, Other staff 3. ***CC*** No.SCO 24366. Began n/a; Church of Scotland. No magazine. Turnover n/a.

Remar Association UK, PO Box 82, Sheffield S1 2XT
☎Number not supplied
Web: www.remar.org
Rehabilitating drug addicts, alcoholics and ex-offenders and the promotion of Christian faith; 57 offices worldwide.
Director and Trustee: To be appointed. *Manager and Pastor:* Mr Joaquin Munt. All voluntary staff. ***CC*** No.1010448. Began 1992; non-denominational. No magazine. Turnover £900,000 to year end Mar 99.
London office ☎020 8558 1660
🖷 0208 558 1660
🄴: remarlondon@btconnect.com

S

Rhoserchan, Capel Seion, Aberystwyth SY23 4ED
☎01970 611 127 🖷01970 625 447
E: enquires@rhoserchan.org.uk
Providing residential rehabilitation for people with an addictive illness.
Manager: Graeme Menzi. Admin 2, Other staff 4, Counsellors 4. ***CC*** No.1015750. Began 1984; non-denominational. No magazine. Turnover £306,482 to year end Mar 05.

***Ronachan House,** Clachan, Tarbert PA29 6XW
☎01880 740 252
Web: www.crossreach.org.uk
Providing residential alcohol and drug rehabilitation for 20 people.
Unit Manager: Shiela Moir. Executive staff 1, Admin staff 1, Other staff 8. ***CC*** No.SCO 24366. Began n/a; Church of Scotland. No magazine. Turnover n/a.

Spitalfields Crypt Trust, Acorn House, 116 Shoreditch High Street, London E1 6JN
☎020 7613 5588/613 3055 (Acorn House) 🖷020 7613 4427
E: janice.sct@virgin.net
Web: www.sct.org.uk
Providing rehabilitation, training for alcoholics, homeless and other vulnerable people; 5 charity shops.
Director: Mr Graham P Marshall. Executive staff 3, Other staff 36. ***CC*** No.1075947. Began 1965; interdenominational. Magazine: *The Crypt* (1,100 quarterly). Turnover £1,175,826 to year end Mar 05.

†Team Challenge Trust, Woodhead, Fyvie, Turriff AB53 8LS
☎01651 891 627 🖷01651 892 015
E: tcsunnybrae@tiscali.co.uk
Supported accommodation for young men with substance misuse problems.
Manager: Name not supplied. Executive staff 10. ***CC*** No.SCO 04829. Began 1982; interdenominational. (Previously Sunnybrae Christian Trust). No magazine. Turnover £150,000 to year end May 98.

***Teen Challenge UK,** 52 Penygroes Road, Gorslas, Llanelli SA14 7LA
☎01269 844 168 🖷01269 832 615
E: info@teenchallenge.co.uk
10 residential/discipleship drug rehabilitation centres for men and women aged 18 to 35.
Exeutive Director: Rev John E J Macey. Executive staff 9, Other staff 80. ***CC*** No.298900. Began 1968; non-denominational. No magazine. Turnover n/a.

†*Victory Outreach UK HQ, The Bush Hotel, High Street, Abertillery NP13 1DD
☎01495 212 516 🖷01495 212 571
Providing Christian homes for young people in need, ex-offenders, homeless, drug-dependants, alcoholics and abused.
Directors: Rev David Sansome, Mrs Dinah Sansome MBE. Admin staff 2, Other staff 7. ***CC*** No.291611. Began 1984; interdenominational. No magazine. Turnover n/a.

Willowdene Farm Rehabilitation, Training and Mission Centre, Chorley, Bridgnorth WV16 6PP
☎01746 718 658 🖷01746 718 039
E: info@willowdenefarm.org.uk
Web: www.willowdenefarm.org.uk
Stimulating, promoting and encouraging a substance-free lifestyle in a working society; training, mission; residential.
Director: Mr John Home. Executive staff 2, Other staff 8. Began 1988; interdenominational. No magazine. Turnover £320,000 to year end Dec 00.

***Yeldall Christian Centres,** Yeldall Manor, Hare Hatch, Reading RG10 8XR
☎0118 940 1093 🖷0118 940 4852
E: yeldall@aol.com
Web: www.yeldall.org.uk
Drug/alcohol rehabilitation for men; homeless hostels; employment training; supported employment.
Chief Executive Officer: Peter Emms. *Director, Residential Rehabilitation:* Ken Wiltshire. *Directors, Yeldall Homeless Projects:* Steve Hedley. Executive staff 4, Other staff 45. ***CC*** No.1000[illegible]38 (Yeldall Christian Centres), 10[illegible]268[illegible] (Bridges International). Began 1977; non-denominational. (Previously Yeldall Bridges). No magazine. Turnover £1,372,071 to year end Mar 04.

ANIMAL WELFARE AGENCIES

Anglican Society for the Welfare of Animals, PO Box 7193, Hook RG27 8GT
☎01252 843 093 🖷01252 843 093
E: AngSocWelAnimals@aol.com
Web: www.aswa.org.uk
Prayer, study and action on behalf of animals; educational assistance with animal blessing services.
Organising Secretary: Mrs Samantha Chandler. No full-time staff. ***CC*** No.1087270. Began 1972; Anglican. Magazine: *The Bulletin* (600 half-yearly). Turnover n/a.

Catholic Concern for Animals, 15 Rosehip Way, Bishops Cleeve, Cheltenham GL52 8WP
☎01242 677 423
E: deborahjark@aol.com
Web: www.catholic-animals.org
Influencing society and churches into becoming more compassionate towards and better informed about animal creation.
General Secretary: Miss Deborah Jones. Executive staff 1, No other paid staff. ***CC*** No.231022. Began 1929; ecumenical. (Previously The Catholic Study Circle for Animal Welfare). Magazine: *The Ark* (2,500 every four months). Turnover £12,000 to year end Mar 03.

Christian Animal Rights Education (CARE), PO Box 407, Sheffield S1 1E[illegible]
☎No telephone
Campaigning against vivisection, factory farming and all cruelty, through prayer, videos, books, demonstrations.
Organiser: Mr White. Executive staff [illegible]. Began 1987; non-denominational. No magazine. Turnover £35,000 to year end Dec 05.

Fellowship of Life, 43 Brachmely[illegible] Bethesda, Bangor LL57 3RD
☎No telephone
Establishing cruelty-free, green living as a Christian way of life, through the publication of literature.
Hon Secretary: Mrs Claire Harra[illegible]. No full time staff. Began 1973; ecumenical. Magazine: *Newsletter* (800 annually). Turnover £450 to year end Jan 02.

S

Additional Curates Society, Gordon Browning House, 8 Spitfire Road, Birmingham B24 9PB
☎0121 382 5533 ℻0121 382 6999
E: acsb24@aol.com
Giving grants to parishes to help pay costs of curates and encouraging vocations.
Secretary: Rev Stephen Leach. Executive staff 1, Other staff 3. **CC** No.209448. Began 1837; Anglican. Magazine: *Good News* (13,000 half-yearly). Turnover n/a.

All Saints Educational Trust, St Katharine Cree Church, 86 Leadenhall Street, London EC3A 3DH
☎020 7283 4485 ℻020 7621 9758
E: enquiries@aset.org.uk
Web: www.aset.org.uk
Supporting teachers/intending RE teachers/dietitians to obtain/further qualifications; corporate awards for educational projects.
Clerk: Mr Stephen Harrow FKC. No full-time staff. **CC** No.312934. Began 1979; Anglican. No magazine. Turnover £430,000 to year end July 05.

†Frances Ashton's Charity, Charities Aid Foundation, Kings Hill, West Malling ME19 4TA
☎01732 520 081
Giving annual grants to Church of England clergy and widows in need.
Receiver: Mrs Barbara Davis. Executive staff 2. **CC** No.200162. Began 1747; Anglican. No magazine. Turnover £45,000 to year end Dec 02.

Catholic Clothing Guild, 3 Spring Way, Sible Hedingham, Halstead CO9 3SB
☎01787 460 234
Supplying new, useful and warm clothing to those in real need; mainly children..
Hon Secretary: Mrs F Ripper. All voluntary staff. **CC** No.277952. Began 1886; Roman Catholic but serving all. (Previously Catholic Needlework Guild). No magazine. Turnover n/a.

Catholic Council for Polish Welfare, 240 King Street, London W6 0RF
☎020 8992 3328 ℻020 8563 0206
Assisting people of Polish origin not covered by other welfare bodies.
Hon Secretary: Mr Olgierd M Stepan KCSG. All voluntary staff. **CC** Began 1942; Roman Catholic but serving all. No magazine. Turnover £1,000 to year end June 05.

Christian Workers Relief Fund, PO Box 2880, Bath BA2 6WR
☎01225 427 236 ℻01225 427 278
Providing support for retired, infirm and needy evangelists and Bible teachers from the Christian Brethren.
Treasurer: Miss Rachel Daws. No full-time staff. **CC** No.234676. Began 1961; Christian Brethren. (Previously Home Workers Fund). No magazine. Turnover £104,000 to year end Dec 04.

Church Commissioners, 1 Millbank, London SW1P 3JZ
☎020 7898 1000 ℻020 7898 1001
E: commissioners.enquiry@c-of-e.org.uk
Web: www.cofe.anglican.org
Principally management of funds to support the Church of England's ministry.
First Church Estates Commissioner: Mr Andreas Whittam Smith. *Second Church Estates Commissioner:* Sir Stuart Bell MP. *Secretary:* Mr Andrew Brown. Executive staff 2, Full-time staff 257. **CC** Began 1948; Anglican. No magazine. Turnover £145,000,000 to year end Dec 97.

Church Housing Trust, PO Box 50296, London EC1P 1WF
☎020 7269 1630 ℻020 7404 2562
E: info@cht.dircon.co.uk
Web: www.churchhousingtrust.org.uk
Charitable support for people in housing need through English Churches Housing Group.
Chief Executive: Jan Bunstead. *Trust Executive:* Sally Isaacs. Executive staff 2, Other staff 4. **CC** No.802801. Began 1984; Anglican. No magazine. Turnover £700,000 to year end Mar 02.

Church Schoolmasters' and Schoolmistresses' Benevolent Institution, Glen Arun, 9 Athelstan Way, Horsham RH13 6HA
☎01403 253 881 ℻01403 253 881
E: glenarun@hotmail.com
Providing nursing and residential accommodation; grants for retired Anglican teachers, widows, orphans and dependants.
Administrator: Mr P G Gooch. Executive staff 2, Other staff 48. **CC** No.207236. Began 1857; Anglican. No magazine. Turnover n/a.

Church Urban Fund, Great Smith Street, London SW1P 3NZ
☎020 7898 1647 ℻020 7898 1601
E: enquiries@cuf.org.uk
Web: www.cuf.org.uk
Supporting local faith-based social action in the poorest areas of England.
Chief Executive: Ms Fran Beckett. Executive staff 1, Other staff n/a. **CC** No.297483. Began 1987; Anglican. Magazine: *City Lights* (23,000 every four months). Turnover £2,360,000 to year end Dec 99.

Corporation of the Sons of the Clergy, 1 Dean Trench Street, Westminster, London SW1P 3HB
☎020 7799 3696 ℻020 7222 3468
E: registrar@sonsoftheclergy.org.uk
Web: www.sonsoftheclergy.org.uk
Making grants to Anglican clergy and their dependants.
Registrar: Mr R A M Welsford. *Deputy Registrar:* Mr I K H Baker. Executive staff 2, Other staff 5. **CC** No.207736. Began 1655; Anglican. Trustee for the Clergy Orphan Corporation. No magazine. Turnover £1,620,000 to year end Dec 04.

The Ecumenical Preceptory of the Holy Trinity, 48 Rossmore Court, Park Road, London NW1 6XY
☎020 7706 2812 ℻020 7706 3725
Providing and maintaining, by endowments, ecumenical churches and chapels, libraries and educational facilities.
Trustee: Dr F M S Muller. No full-time staff. **CC** No.801437. Began 1989; ecumenical. No magazine. Turnover £10,000 to year end Dec 00.

The Friends of the Clergy Corporation, 27 Medway Street, London SW1P 2BD
☎020 7222 2288 ℻020 7976 0573
E: focc@btinternet.com
Providing financial help, retirement accommodation for clergy of Anglican communion and dependants.
Acting Secretary: Ms Jennifer Ringwood. Executive staff 1, Other staff 3. **CC** No.264724. Began 1849; Anglican. No magazine. Turnover £1,116,612 to year end Jan 05.

Gospel Advocate Relief Fund, 10 Ryefield Court, Eastbourne BN21 2XJ
☎01323 507 168 M: 07904 240 216
E: secretary@garf.org.uk
Web: www.garf.org.uk
Providing quarterly grants to preachers on very meagre salaries who uphold doctrines of free grace.
Hon Secretary: Mr David Cottington. No paid staff. **CC** No.209606. Began 1878; non-denominational. No magazine. Turnover £20,000 to year end Mar 05.

Haddon House Trust, 46 Prince of Wales Road, Westbourne, Bournemouth BH4 9HF
☎01202 762 848
Supporting financially the evangelical movement and those churches and people working in it.
Director: Mrs Honor Beesley. No full-time staff. ***CC*** Began 1976; interdenominational. No magazine. Turnover n/a.

***The Harvesters Trust,** 82 St Andrews Road South, Lytham St Annes FY8 1PS
☎01253 728 458 M: 07932 894 260
E: info@harvesters-trust.org.uk
Web: www.harvesters-trust.org.uk
Grant-making trust to advance the Christian religion and relieve persons in distress worldwide.
Chairman: Mr Michael Wood. No full-time staff. ***CC*** No.1031741. Began 1993; non-denominational. No magazine. Turnover £12,000 to year end Apr 02.

†HCPT The Pilgrimage Trust, Oakfield Park, 32 Bilton Road, Rugby CV22 7HQ
☎01788 564 646 Minicom 01788 564 642
Fax 01737 353 008
E: hq@hcpt.org.uk
Web: www.hcpt.org.uk
Taking children and adults with disabilities on holiday and pilgrimage to Lourdes.
Chief Executive: Mr R A Mills. Executive staff 9, Other staff 2. ***CC*** No.281074. Began n/a; HCPT (1956) and HH Trust (1971) merged in 1980; interdenominational. (Previously Handicapped Children's Pilgrimage Trust & Hosanna House Trust). Magazine: *Trust News* (35,000 quarterly). Turnover £3,500,000 to year end Oct 00.

Historic Churches Preservation Trust, 31 Newbury Street, London EC1A 7HU
☎020 7600 6090 Fax 020 7796 2442
E: info@historicchurches.org.uk
Web: www.historicchurches.org.uk
Assisting eligible churches of all recognised Christian denominations with essential fabric repairs.
Assistant director: James Blott. Executive staff 5. ***CC*** No.207402. Began 1953; non-denominational. No magazine. Turnover £1,500,000 to year end Dec 01.

Rebecca Hussey's Book Charity, 36 Causton Street, London SW1P 4ST
☎020 7592 3900 Fax 020 7592 3939
Giving grants to certain institutions for purchase of Christian books.
Clerk to the Trustees: Sue Knight. No full-time staff. ***CC*** No.207101. Began 1862; non-denominational. No magazine. Turnover £6,700 to year end Dec 00.

The Keswick Hall Trustees, School of Education & Lifelong Learning, University of East Anglia, Norwich NR4 7TJ
☎01603 592 632 Fax 01603 593 446
E: khrec@uea.ac.uk
Limited grants to support RE in schools through teachers' initial and in-service training and research.
Executive Secretary: Mr Jonathan Davis. Executive staff 1, Other staff 1. ***CC*** No.311246. Began 1981; Anglican. No magazine. Turnover £160,000 to year end Apr 05.

King Edward Orthodox Trust Company Ltd, St Edward Brotherhood, St Cyprian's Avenue, Brookwood, Woking GU24 0BL
☎01483 487 763 Fax 01483 487 763
E: theshepherd@mac.com
Providing properties to further the mission of Orthodox Christians; maintaining shrine of St Edward; cemetery.
Chairman: Very Rev Archimandrite Alexis. No full-time staff. ***CC*** No.284929/0. Began 1981; Orthodox. (Previously Orthodox Trust Company Ltd). No magazine. Turnover £8,000 to year end Dec 00.

The Leaders of Worship and Preachers Trust (LWPT), 89 High Street, Rickmansworth WD3 1EF
☎01923 776 856 Fax 01923 710 075
E: lwptoffice@lwpt.org.uk
Web: www.lwpt.org.uk
Financial assistance to necessitous preachers/ leaders of worship; also for training, development.
General Secretary: Mr Godfrey Talford. Executive staff 1, Other staff 4. ***CC*** No.1107967. Began 1849; Methodist and Wesleyan Reform Union. (Previously Methodist Local Preachers Mutual Aid Association (LPMA)). Magazine: *Ichthus* (23,000 quarterly). Turnover £879,567 to year end Aug 05.

The Graham Leavers Memorial Trust, 1 Hall Close, Henham, Bishop's Stortford CM22 6AU
☎01279 850 374
E: lmpeake1@hotmail.com
Giving small grants to individuals aged 7 to 19, from deprived UK homes attend Christian activities.
Secretary: Mrs Linda Peake. All voluntary staff. ***CC*** No.279885. Began 1979; Baptist, but open to all. No overseas applications. No magazine. Turnover n/a

National Society for Promoting Religious Education, Church House, Great Smith Street, London SW1P 3NZ
☎020 7898 1501 Fax 020 7898 1520
E: john.hall@c-of-e.org.uk
Web: www.natsoc.org.uk or www.churchschools.co.uk
Supporting church schools, RE and parish education; producing resources; training courses, archives.
General Secretary: Rev Canon John Hall. *Deputy Secretary:* Mr Nick McKenney. Executive staff 4, Other staff 3. ***CC*** No.313070. Began 1811; Anglican. Magazine: *NS News* (5,000 every four months). Turnover n/a.

The Open Churches Trust, 22 Tower Street, London WC2H 9TW
☎020 7240 0880 Fax 020 7240 120[illegible]
E: oct@reallyuseful.co.uk
Web: www.openchurchestrust.org.uk
Opening locked places of worship to the puplic.
Administrator: Brigadier Adam Gurdon. Executive staff 1, Admin staff 1. ***CC*** No.1045248. Began 1994; ecumenical. No magazine. Turnover £50,000 to year end Apr 02.

The Ouseley Trust, 127 Coleherne Court, London SW5 0EB
☎020 7373 1950 Fax 020 734[illegible] 0043
E: 106200.1023@compuserve.com
Making grants to promote and maintain a high standard of choral service
Clerk to the Trustees: Mr Martin Williams. *Chairman:* Mr C J Robinson. No full-time staff. ***CC*** No.252716. Began 198[illegible]; Church of England, Church in Wales, Church of Ireland. No magazine. Turnover £140,000 to year end Dec 03.

Partis College, Violet Wills Wing, Newbridge Hill, Bath BA1 3QD
☎01225 421 532 🖷01225 421 567
E: partiscol@aol.com
Providing a home for retired and poor Anglican ladies.
Bursar: Bob Siderfin. Executive staff 1, Chaplain 1. **CC** No.200606. Began 1825; Anglican. No magazine. Turnover £75,000 to year end Dec 02.

The Payne Charitable Trust, 1st Floor, Costhorne House, The Broadway, Abergele LL22 7DD
☎01745 825 779 🖷01745 833 161
Giving grants for the furtherance of the Gospel.
Secretary: Mr John Payne. Executive staff 1, Other staff 1. **CC** No.241816. Began n/a; non-denominational. No magazine. Turnover n/a.

Queen Victoria Clergy Fund, Church House, Great Smith Street, London SW1P 3AZ
☎020 7898 1310 🖷020 7898 1321
E: colin.menzies@c-of-e.org.uk
Assisting (through the dioceses) Church of England clergy in financial need.
Secretary: Mr Colin Menzies. No full-time staff. **CC** No.213258. Began 1897; Anglican. No magazine. Turnover £122,200 to year end June 04.

Queen's Hall Help, Wigan, 160 Gidlow Lane, Wigan WN6 7EA
☎01942 324 883
E: shop@queenshall.ukfreedom.com
Redistributing unwanted household furniture and clothing to those most in need in the community.
Administrator: Manageress. Executive staff 1. **CC** No.506518. Began 1970; Methodist. (Previously Wigan Help Committee, Queen's Hall). No magazine. Turnover n/a.

The Revd Dr George Richards' Charity, 38 Thomas More House, Barbican, London EC2Y 8BU
☎020 7588 5583
Providing financial assistance for Anglican clergy retired early through ill health; also widows and dependants.
Secretary: Dr P D Simmons. No full-time staff. **CC** No.246965. Began 1837; Anglican. (Previously Dr George Richards' Charity). No magazine. Turnover £20,000 to year end Dec 02.

The St Barnabas Society, 4 First Turn, Wolvercote, Oxford OX2 8AH
☎01865 513 377 🖷01865 516 542
E: secretary@stbarnabassociety.org.uk
Web: www.stbarnabassociety.org.uk
Assisting needy clergy and religious who have been received into the Catholic church.
Secretary: Rev Robin Sanders. Executive staff 1, Admin staff 2, Other staff 4. **CC** No.1009910. Began 1992; Roman Catholic. Magazine: *St Barnabas Society News* (9,000 annually). Turnover £320,950 to year end May 04.

***Scriptural Knowledge Institution,** Müller House, 7 Cotham Park, Bristol BS6 6DA
☎01179 244 918
🖷0117 924 4855
E: admin@mullers.org
Web: www.mullers.org
Providing prayer, encouragement and support for missionaries working at home and abroad.
Chief Executive: Mr Julian Marsh. Executive staff 1, Other staff 2. **CC** No.202652. Began 1834; interdenominational. Part of the George Müller Foundation. Magazine: *Report on the Work* (4,000 annually). Turnover £1,230,000 to year end Feb 05.

Shared Interest, 2 Cathedral Square, Groat Market, Newcastle upon Tyne NE1 1EH
☎0191 233 9100
🖷0191 233 9110
E: post@shared-interest.com
Web: www.shared-interest.com
Cooperative investment society; people investing in Fair Trade to support disadvantaged producers in developing world.
Managing Director: To be appointed. *Finance Director & Company Secretary:* Mr Stuart Raistrick. Executive staff 5, Other staff 13. Began 1990; ecumenical. Magazine: *Quarterly Return* (11,000 quarterly). Turnover £17,700,000 to year end Sep 02.

Society for Relief of Poor Clergymen, c/o CPAS, Athena Drive, Tachbrook Park, Warwick CV34 6NG
☎01926 458 458
🖷01926 458 459
Helping evangelical Anglican clergy in times of financial need caused by illness or bereavement.
Hon Chairman: Rev Canon John Moore. *Secretary:* Mrs Jo King. No full-time staff. **CC** No.232634. Began 1788; Anglican. No magazine. Turnover £20,000 to year end Dec 99.

The Society of St Vincent de Paul, 546 Sauchiehall Street, Glasgow G2 3NG
☎0141 332 7752
🖷0141 332 6775
E: svdp.scotland@btconnect.com
Alleviating all forms of poverty through personal contact, financial and other assistance.
National Secretary (Scotland): Ms Eileen Lauter. Executive staff 1, Other staff n/a. **CC** No.SCO 06326. Began national 1845; international 1833; Roman Catholic. Magazine: *Scottish Ozanam News* (1,750 quarterly). Turnover n/a.

Strict Baptist Pension Fund, 82 Selwyn Drive, Stockton-on-Tees TS19 8XF
☎01642 587 664
E: philip.tait@lineone.net
Giving grants to retired pastors.
Secretary: Rev Philip Tait. No full-time staff. **CC** No.250195. Began 1931; Grace Baptist. No magazine. Turnover £5,295 to year end Dec 04.

S

Strict Baptist Trust, 82 Selwyn Drive, Stockton-on-Tees TS19 8XF
☎01642 587 664
E: philip.tait@lineone.net
Augmenting stipends of pastors in small churches.
Secretary: Rev Philip Tait. No full-time staff. **CC** No.250485. Began 1930; Grace Baptist. No magazine. Turnover £7,235 to year end Dec 04.

Alpha Land Solutions, Alpha House, 184 Bath Road, Longwell Green, Bristol BS30 9DB
M: 07969 256 424
E: growingchurches@alphalandsolutions.com
Web: www.alphalandsolutions.com
Making the cost of an expanding building programme affordable by buying/selling land/property anywhere.
Director: Mr Andy Lampard. Executive staff 1, Other staff n/a. Began 2006; non-denominational. No magazine. Turnover: first year of operation.

Biscoe Craig Hall, 5 Staple Inn, London WC1V 7QU
☎020 7242 4321 🖷020 7242 4327
E: info@biscoecraighall.co.uk
Providing architecture, surveying and planning supervisor services.
Partner: Mr Robert Stibbards. Executive staff 6, Other staff 4. Began 1963; inter-denominational. (Previously Craig Hall & Rutley). No magazine. Turnover n/a.

Byrom Clark Roberts Ltd, Main Office, Washbrook House, Talbot Road, Old Trafford, Manchester M32 0FP
☎0161 875 0600 🖷0161 875 0601
E: awhawksworth@bcr.uk.com
Web: www.bcr.uk.com
Providing architectural, building surveying, structural and civil engineering, project management and forensic services.
Chairman: Mr Alex E H Roberts. *Managing Director:* Mr Andrew W Hawksworth. Executive staff 7, Other staff 45. Began 1925; non-denominational. No magazine. Turnover £2,150,000 to year end June 05.
Also at: 2 Heritage Court, Lower Bridge Street, Chester CH1 1RD
E: ajsears@bcr.uk.com
☎01244 348 849
🖷 01244 320 783
And: 53 The Calls, Leeds LS2 7EY
E: dagoud@bcr.uk.com
☎0113 388 8000
🖷 0113 388 8001
And: Jubilee House, West Bar Green, Sheffield S1 2BT
E: alexroberts@bcr.uk.com
☎0114 275 7879
🖷 0114 272 8954

The Cathedrals Fabric Commission for England, Church House, Great Smith Street, London SW1P 3NZ
☎020 7898 1863 🖷020 7898 1881
E: paulagriffiths@c-of-e.org.uk
Web: www.cofe.anglican.uk
Statutory body controlling and advising on alterations to cathedral churches, contents and precincts.
Secretary: Ms Paula Griffiths. Executive staff 3, Other staff 1. ***CC*** Began 1991; Anglican. (Previously Cathedrals Advisory Commission for England). No magazine. Turnover n/a.

The Church Notice Board Company, The Workshop, Winnington Avenue, Northwich CW8 4EE
☎ 01606 871 188 🖷01606 871 199
E: info@churchnoticeboards.co.uk
Web: www.churchnoticeboards.co.uk
Suppliers of maintenance free aluminium and traditional oak notice boards.
Director: Mr Simon Johnson. Executive staff 3, Admin staff 1, Other staff 2. Began n/a; non-denominational. No magazine. Turnover £300,000 to year end Mar 05.

Church Restoration Co (UK) Ltd, 384 Green Lane, London SE9 3TQ
☎020 8851 3980 🖷020 8265 6352
E: churchrestorationltd@hotmail.com
Church restoration, decoration, renovation-cleaning of masonry, roofing, stained glass work.
Manager: Mr Daniel Hussey. Executive staff 2. Began 1995; non-denominational. (Previously Mayfair (UK) Ltd). No magazine. Turnover £400,000 to year end Dec 04.

Churches Tourism Network Wales (CTNW), 4 Church View Close, Llandough, Penarth CF64 2NN
☎029 2071 0014 M: 07815 062 040
E: john@ctnw.fsnet.co.uk
Web: www.ctnw.co.uk
Working with all Christian churches in Wales to develop buildings as a tool for mission.
Company Secretary: Mr John Winton. Executive staff 1. ***CC*** No.1090957. Began 2001; ecumenical. No magazine. Turnover n/a.

Council for the Care of Churches (General Synod), Church House, Great Smith Street, London SW1P 3NZ
☎020 7898 1886
🖷020 7898 1881
E: enquiries@ccc.c-of-e.org.uk
Web: www.cofe.anglican.org
Advising on care of churches/furnishings; coordinating Diocesan Advisory committees; statutory responsibilities; awarding grants; publications.
Secretary: Paula Griffiths. Executive staff 14, Other staff 2. ***CC*** Began 1921 Anglican. No magazine. Turnover n/a.

***CPL Chartered Architects (Church Projects Ltd),** 33 Darley Road, Eastbourne BN20 7UT
☎01323 416 900
🖷01323 416 378
E: admin@cplarchitects.co.uk
Web: www.cplarchitects.co.uk
Specialist church architects.
Managing director: Mr Derek Foster Kemp. Executive staff 6. Began 1990; non-denominational. No magazine. Turnover n/a.

Easthope Stained Glass Studios, 7[illegible] The Bayle, Folkestone CT20 1SJ
☎01303 850 502
M: 07814 580 753
🖷01303 850 502
E: nick@easthopestudios.co.uk
Web: www.easthopestudios.co.uk
New commissions, restoration and conservation of stained glass and leaded light windows.
Principal: Mr Nick Easthope. Staff 2. Began 1957; non-denominational. No magazine. Turnover n/a.

Ecclesiastical Property Solutions, The Garden House, Holme Place, Oakford, Tiverton EX16 9DH
☎01398 351 581 M: 07960 726 [illegible]17
E: andrew@abetterview.co.uk
Web: www.abetterview.co.uk
Christian vocation and professional property expertise, enabling Churches to have property that serves the mission.
Director: Rev Andrew Mottram. Other staff n/a. Began n/a; non-denominational. Turnover n/a.

S

D G J Flett Chartered Architect, Ardcraig, Barkhead Grove, Dalmeny, South Queensferry EH30 9JZ
☎0131 331 3310
📠0131 331 3310
E: dgj.flett@uk.iccc.net
Architect to churches and community groups; church consultant on vision, structure, restoration and development.
Architect/Principal: Mr Douglas G J Flett. Executive staff 1, Other staff 1. Began 1981; non-denominational. No magazine. Turnover n/a.

Grace Architects, One High Street, Chelmsford CM1 1BE
☎01245 258 600
📠01245 258 601
E: info@gracearchitects.co.uk
Web: www.gracearchitects.co.uk
Designing and maintaining churches, schools, residential and community facilities, working with historic buildings.
Directors: Mr Richard J Naylor, Mr John Quinlan. Executive staff 6, Other staff 2. Began 1953; interdenominational. (Previously KC White Partnership). No magazine. Turnover £195,000 to year end Apr 03.

Historic Chapels Trust, St George's German Lutheran Church, 55 Alie Street, London E1 8EB
☎020 7481 0533
📠020 7488 3756
E: chapels@hct.org.uk
Web: www.hct.org.uk
Acquiring, repairing, regenerating disused places of worship of outstanding architectural and historic interest.
Director: Dr Jennifer Freeman. *Chairman:* Rt Hon Alan Beith MP. Executive staff 1, Other staff 5. **CC** No.1017321. Began 1993; Non-denominational. No magazine. Turnover £1,000,000 to year end Mar 05.

i58 Architecture Ltd, Cedar House, 9 Beresford Road, St Albans AL1 5NW
☎01727 753 541
📠01727 762 355
E: info@i58.co.uk
Web: www.i58.co.uk
Providing architectural services for construction of new churches, conversion of old buildings into churches.
Director: Mr Frank H Ferrett. Executive staff 3, Admin staff 1. Began 2005; non-denominational. No magazine. Turnover first year of operation.

JBKS Architects, The Old Coach House, Adwell, Thame OX9 7DQ
☎01844 281 281
📠01844 281 813
E: architects@jbks.co.uk
Web: www.jbks.co.uk
Specialist church architects: quinquennials, new churches, re-ordering, lighting, heating, church development, budget control, project management.
Directors: Mr Kelvin Sampson, Mr Jeremy Bell. Executive staff 4, Admin staff 2. Began 2004; non-denominational. Turnover £150,000 to year end Jun 05.

Keystone Initiatives, 35 Catherine Street, Salisbury SP1 2DQ
☎01722 335 306
📠01722 411 038
E: enquiries@sarumarchitects.co.uk
Web: www.keystone-initiatives.com
Helping churches make best use of premises to help serve their mission and service.
Administrator: Mr Luke Butland. Executive staff 8, Admin staff 1. Began 1993; ecumenical. No magazine. Turnover n/a.

Glyn Leaman Architects, 35 Oakfield Road, Clifton, Bristol BS8 2AT
☎0117 923 8617
📠0117 974 2781
E: glyn.leaman@btconnect.com
Quinquennial inspections, repairs, re-ordering, new buildings, landscape design.
Principal: Mr Glyn Leaman. Executive staff 1, Other staff 2. Began 1983; non-denominational. No magazine. Turnover n/a.

The Living Stones Consultancy, Quoin House, 11 East Park, Crawley RH10 6AN
☎01293 431 899
📠01293 431 899
E: info@living-stones.org.uk
Web: www.living-stones.org.uk
Advising churches in total stewardship of buildings and resources for worship and service to the community.
South England Field Worker: Graham Ball. Executive staff 2. **CC** No.269319. Began 1975; interdenominational. (Previously Church and Community Trust). Magazine: *Living Stones* (5,000 periodically). Turnover £10,000 to year end Apr 03.

Bob Massey Associates (Consulting Engineers), 9 Worral Avenue, Arnold, Nottingham NG5 7GN
☎0115 967 3969
📠0115 967 3969
E: bm.associates@virgin.net
Web: www.bobmasseyassociates.co.uk
Consulting engineers for large or small theatre/visual arts projects for churches and architects.
Principal Consulting Engineer: Mr Bob Massey. Executive staff 2, Other staff 5. Began 1989; interdenominational. No magazine. Turnover n/a.

M.J.T. Associates, 2 Parish Lane, London SE20 7LH
☎020 8776 7997
📠020 8776 7220
E: martyn@mjtassociates.freeserve.co.uk
Web: www.mjtassociates.freeserve.co.uk
Building cost control, quantity surveying, planning supervision and project coordination for churches and charities.
Proprietor: Mr Martyn Tickner. Executive staff 1, Other staff n/a. Began 1984; non-denominational. No magazine. Turnover £80,000 to year end Nov 04.

S

Pastoral Reorganization Advisory Service, 18 West Avenue, Clarendon Park, Leicester LE2 1TR
☎0116 270 2901
Providing comprehensive independent advisory service specialising in church redundancy matters; reviews, appeals and post-closure.
Practitioner: Mr David Gillman. Executive staff 1, Other staff 1. Began 1984; interdenominational. No magazine. Turnover n/a.

PDG Architects, Toll Bar House, Shrewsbury Avenue, Peterborough PE2 7BX
☎01733 371 000 🖷01733 370 666
E: design@pdgarchitects.co.uk
Web: www.pdgarchitects.co.uk
Providing architectural services to private and public sector clients including churches and community groups.
Partner: Mr Paul T D Hutchings. Executive Staff 4, Technical Staff 3, Admin Staff 2. Began 1988; non-denominational. (Previously Peterborough Design Group). No magazine. Turnover £400,000 to year end Sep 04.

People and Places Architects Ltd, The Design Studio, 2 Delacourt Road, Blackheath, London SE3 8XA
☎020 8269 2888 🖷020 8269 0888
E: admin@peopleandplaces.uk.com
Web: www.peopleandplacesarchitects.com
Providing a sense of belonging when places clothe people, people the life of God.
Managing Director: Mr Raymond Hall. Staff n/a. ***CC*** No.1013750. Began 1973; non-denominational. (Previously New Wineskins). No magazine. Turnover n/a.

Christopher Rayner Architects, Apple Cross House, 52 The Rise, Sevenoaks TN13 1RN
☎01732 461 806
🖷01732 461 824
Architects working with churches and religious bodies, guided by Christian belief.
Principal: Mr Christopher Rayner. Executive staff 1, Other staff 3. Began 1991; Anglican. No magazine. Turnover £70,000 to year end Dec 04.

Save Our Parsonages, Flat 2, 12 Bloomsbury Street, London WC1B 3QA
☎020 7636 4884
E: ajsjennings@hotmail.com
Web: www.saveourparsonages.co.uk
Support group for the traditional parsonage in church use.
Director: Mr Anthony Jennings. No full-time staff. Began 1994; Anglican. No magazine. Turnover £1,000 to year end Nov 04.

SDA Architects Ltd, The Courtyard, Swillington Lane, Hollinthorpe, Leeds LS26 8BZ
☎0113 232 0222
M: 07803 265 528
🖷0113 232 0777
E: mail@sdapartnership.com
Web: www.sdapartnership.com
Nationwide service delivering handcrafted design, traditional to modern, contemporary; cost control. Offices London, Leeds.
Director: Pete Ford. Executive staff 4, Other staff 30. Began 1994; non-denominational. (Previously Stocks Design Build Ltd). No magazine. Turnover n/a.

†Steve Sherriff Stained Glass, 10 Brackenhill Road, Wimborne BH21 [illegible]LT
☎01202 882 208 M: 079[illegible]1 74[illegible] 453
🖷01202 882 208
E: ssherriff@yahoo.com
Web: www.lead-windows.co.uk
Designing, repairing, restoring historical churchglass leaded lights, their frames and associated work.
Proprietor: Mr Steve Sherriff. *Partner:* Mr Aran Sherriff. Executive staff 1, Admin staff 1, Other staff 4. Began n/a. No magazine. Turnover n/a.

Stone Ecclesiastical, The Cart Shed, Manor Farm, Aust, Bristol BS35 4A[illegible]
☎01454 631 049 🖷01454 631 [illegible]50
E: contact@stone-ecclesiastical.co.uk
Web: www.stone-ecclesiastical.co.uk
Ecclesiastical designers, surveyers and project managers, providing multi-disciplinary advice to churches nationwide.
Managing Director: Mr Michael S[illegible]tter. Executive staff 3, Other staff 1. Began n/a; non-denominational. No magazine. Turnover £200,000 to year end Jan 03.

Whitechapel Bell Foundry, 34 Whitechapel Road, London E1 1DY
☎020 7247 2599 🖷020 7[illegible]75 1[illegible]9
E: bells@whitechapelbellfoundry.co.uk
Web: www.whitechapelbellfoundry.co.uk
Bell founders, bell hangers, musical handbells, handbell music and accessories, clock bells.
Directors: Mr & Mrs Alan & Kathryn Hughes. Executive staff 2, Other staff 25. Began 1420; non-denominational. No magazine. Turnover n/a.

BUSINESS SERVICES

**For computer entries see Computer, IT Services & Web Listings on Page 216.
See also Design, Layout & Editorial Services on Page 219.
Marketing & Fundraising Services on Page 360.**

S

Blackbourn Andrews Solicitors, 12 Belmont, Shrewsbury SY1 1TE
☎01743 233 255 M: 07811 102 507
🖷01743 233 117
E: rob@ba-law.co.uk
Web: www.ba-law.co.uk
Providing legal and business support advice to businesses and charities.
Partner/Directors: Mr Rob Andrews, Mr Nick Blackbourn. Executive staff 3, Admin staff 1. Began 2003; non-denominational. No magazine. Turnover £200,000 to year end Mar 05.

†Bristol Christian Resource Centre, 4 Greenlands Way, Bristol BS10 7PR
☎0117 950 7355 🖷0117 950 7355
Resource centre and mailing service to 25,000 church leaders in UK and Channel Islands.
Trustee: Mr Michael P J Simmons. Executive staff 4, Other staff 8. ***CC*** No.1011132. Began 1983; non-denominational. No magazine. Turnover £14,696 to year end Mar 02.

***Fiona Bruce & Co Solicitors,** Justice House, 3 Grappenhall Road, Stockton Heath, Warrington WA4 2AH
☎01925 263 273 🖷01925 217 0[illegible]
E: rbruce@fionabruce.co.uk
Web: www.fionabruce.co.uk
Advising individuals, businesses, churches and charities on all aspects of the law.
Practice Development Manager: Mr Richard Bruce. *Managing Partner:* Mrs Fiona Bruce. *Head of Family Law:* Mr Stephen Hayes. Executive staff 12, Admin staff [illegible]8. Began 1988; non-denominational. No magazine. Turnover £1,000,000 to year end Mar 06.

Business Transformations Ltd, 87 Hayclose Road, Kendal LA9 7NF
☎01539 741 884 M: 07766 600 737
📠01539 741 884
E: jonfi.brook@btopenworld.com
Web: business-transformations.co.uk
Working sensitively with churches, charities and businesses, to help plan and deliver purpose-driven change.
Managing Director: Mr Jonathan Brook. Executive staff 1, Other staff 1. Began 2002; non-denominational. No magazine. Turnover n/a.

The Cartridge Family, The Rural Business Centre, Winterbourne Whitechurch, Blandford Forum DT11 9AW
☎01258 880 050 / 0800 980 9399
📠01258 881 448
E: enquiries@thecartridgefamily.co.uk
Web: www.thecartridgefamily.co.uk
Fundraising for Christian and charity groups by recycling empty inkjet and laser cartridges. No unsolicited requests.
Contact: Mr Graham Burton. Executive staff 2, Other staff 4. Began 1998; Anglican. (Previously Eleventh Hour). No magazine. Turnover £100,000 to year end Dec 04.

***Charity Logistics,** Charles House, 4th Floor, 375 Kensington High Street, London W14 8QH
☎0845 1303 845 📠0845 1303 895
E: enquiries@charitylogistics.org
Web: www.charitylogistics.org
Helping charities to increase capacity; advising churches on social action.
Charity Services Manager: Miss Lisa Brook. Executive staff 1, Admin staff 15, Other staff 4. ***CC*** No.1056801. Began 1996; non-denominational. Other offices: Birmingham, Sheffield, Swansea. No magazine. Turnover £700,000 to year end Mar 00.

Christian Information Network, 53 King Street, Nairn IV12 4NP
☎01667 459 955
E: iain@fairweather.co.uk
Web: www.cin.co.uk
Directory of Christian organisations and churches.
Website Manager: Mr Iain Fairweather. Executive staff 1. Began 1994; non-denominational. No magazine. Turnover n/a.

***Anthony Collins Solicitors,** 134 Edmund Street, Birmingham B3 2ES
☎0121 200 3242 📠0121 212 7442
E: phil.watts@anthonycollins.com
Web: www.anthonycollins.com
Providing a wide range of private and corporate legal services, especially to charities and churches.
Senior Partners: Miss Romaine Thompson, Mr Ian McQuay. Partners 20, Other staff 210. Began 1973; non-denominational. No magazine. Turnover n/a.

Ellis-Fermor & Negus, 5 Market Place, Ripley DE5 3BS
☎01773 744 744 📠01773 570 047
E: info@ellis-fermor.co.uk
Web: www.ellis-fermor.co.uk
Providing legal services for the Christian community.
Senior Partner: Mr Michael S Cobbett. *Partner:* Mrs Sarah J Slack. *Practice Administrator:* Mr Michael E Amos. Executive staff 16, Other staff 49. Began 1893; non-denominational. Member of the Association of Christian Law Firms. Magazine: *Newsletter* (Circulation n/a quarterly). Turnover £2,000,000 to year end Apr 05.
Also at: 35 Derby Road, Long Eaton, Nottingham NG10 1LU
E: longeaton@ellis-fermor.co.uk
☎0115 972 5222 📠0115 946 1152
And: 2 Devonshire Avenue, Beeston, Nottingham NG9 1BS
E: beeston@ellis-fermor.co.uk
☎0115 922 1591 📠0115 925 9341

MR Associates, 19 Wemyss Court, Leapmoor Drive, Wemyss Bay PA18 6BF
☎01475 522 962 M: 07967 963 806
E: info@mrassociates.org.uk
Web: www.mrassociates.org.uk
Offering specialist advice and assistance for accommodation-based schemes providing support to vulnerable adults in the UK.
Supported Housing Advisor: Mr Mark Rodgers. Executive staff 2, Admin staff 1. Began 2000; interdenominational. No magazine. Turnover n/a.

My Father's Business, 12 Stable Lane, Seer Green, Beaconsfield HP9 2YT
☎01494 673 407 M: 07931 773 013
📠01494 673 840
E: barry@myfathersbusiness.co.uk
Web: www.myfathersbusiness.co.uk
Interim management services.
Principal Consultant: Mr Barry Richardson. Executive staff 1. Began n/a; Baptist. No magazine. Turnover £40,000 to year end Mar 01.

†NCA Practical Business Support, 2 St Martin's Cottages, St Martin's Road, Bilborough, Nottingham NG5 1FN
☎0115 929 1024 📠0115 929 1024
Working with businesses where people matter, with marketing, research, managing projects, business development, managing change.
Proprietor: Mrs Nicky Webb. Executive staff 1, Other staff 3. Began 1994; ecumenical. No magazine. Turnover n/a.

†Pearce Legal (Solicitors), Centre Court, 1301 Stratford Road, Hall Green, Birmingham B28 9HH
☎0121 777 9099 📠0121 777 9210
E: enquiries@pearcelegal.co.uk
Web: www.pearcelegal.co.uk
Solicitors offering full range of legal services to private and business clients and charitable organisations.
Senior Partner: Mr Graham Pearce. Executive staff 1, Other staff 5. Began 1981; non-denominational. No magazine. Turnover n/a.

***Reprotec Office Solutions Ltd,** Reprotec House, 7 Churchill Park, Colwick, Nottingham NG4 2HF
☎0115 940 0900 📠0115 940 4101
E: kevin@reprotec.uk.com
Web: www.reprotec.uk.com
Supplying digital photocopiers, colour copiers and printers to churches, businesses, Christian organisations throughout the UK.
Managing Director: Mr Kevin Lock. Executive staff 1, Other staff 20. Began 1981; interdenominational. (Previously Reprotec (Business Services) Ltd). No magazine. Turnover £198,000 to year end Dec 04.

S

Maurice Rowlandson Consultancy, 16 Squires Copse, Peatmoor, Swindon SN5 5HB
☎01793 871 006 M: 07860 300 174
E: mauricerow@btinternet.com
Web: www.mauricemarilyn.com
Consultant on administration to Christian organisations and charities.
Principal: Mr Maurice L Rowlandson. Executive staff 1, Other staff 1. Began 1987; interdenominational. No magazine. Turnover £25,000 to year end Mar 04.

***Stewardship,** PO Box 99, Loughton IG10 3QJ
☎020 8502 5600 Fax 020 8502 5333
E: enquiries@stewardship.org
Web: www.stewardship.org.uk
Christian giving agency and provider of services helping churches/charities with legal and financial administration.
Chief Executive: Mr David C Jones. Executive staff 4, Other staff 32. ***CC*** No.234714. Began 2004 merger of Sovereign Giving with Stewardship Services Trust. Magazine: *Stewardship* (28,000 three times a year). Turnover £30,600,000 to year end Sept 04.

John Truscott, 69 Sandridge Road, St Albans AL1 4AG
☎01727 832 176 Fax 01727 832 176
E: john@john-truscott.co.uk
Web: www.john-truscott.co.uk
Advice and training in organisation and people skills to churches, ministers and mission agencies.
Church Consultant & Trainer: Mr John Truscott. Executive staff 1. Began 1999; interdenominational. No magazine. Turnover n/a.

Unigraph (UK) Ltd, Unigraph House, Pitsmoor Road, Sheffield S3 9AS
☎0114 275 2801 Fax 0114 275 9769
E: sales@unigraph.uk.com
Web: www.unigraph.uk.com
Supplying stationery, duplicating, copying and OHP products; print contractors; operators of national church copier scheme.
Managing Director: Mr Stephen Hunter. *Sales Director:* Mr S Ellis. *Company Accountant:* Mr P J Homewood. Executive staff 5, Other staff 15. Began 1966; interdenominational. No magazine. Turnover £2,000,000 to year end July 04.

Wellers Solicitors, Tenison House, Tweedy Road, Bromley BR1 3NF
☎020 8464 4242
Fax 020 8464 6033
E: law@wellers.net
Web: www.wellers.net
Providing a full range of legal services; local firm with a City office.
Partners: Mr Paul Martin, Mr Tony Summers, Mr Stephen Scott. Executive staff 16, Admin staff 19. Began 1[illegible]31; non-denominational. No magazine. Turnover £500,000 to year end Sep 05.

***World Action Ministries** PO Box [illegible]9, Sutton Coldfield B73 5FX
☎0121 355 8333
Fax 0121 355 3833
E: worldactmin@aol.com
Web: www.worldactionministries.org.[illegible]
Providing administration and financial management for Christian organisations.
Executive Director: Mr Philip B Smith. *Financial Director:* Miss Jennifer Beardsmore. Executive staff 2. ***CC*** No.295793. Began 1986 interdenominational. No magazine. Turnover £120,000 to year end Dec 04.

CHILDREN'S CARE & ADOPTION SOCIETIES

See also Youth and Children's Organisations on Page 397.

Adoption Matters, 14 Liverpool Road, Chester CH2 1AE
☎01244 390 938
Fax 01244 390 067
E: info@adoptionmatters.org
Web: www.adoptionmatters.org
Providing a comprehensive service to all whose lives are touched by adoption.
Chief Executive: Mr Norman G Goodwin. *Support Services and Office Manager:* Mrs Valerie Johnson. *Social Work Team Leader:* Ms Ann Davison. Executive staff 4, Other staff 25. ***CC*** No.512892. Began 1955; interdenominational. (Previously Chester Diocesan Adoption Services). No magazine. Turnover £1,600,000 to year end Mar 03.

†***The Agapé Trust,** Blatchington Haven, 490 The Ridge, Hastings TN34 2RY
☎01424 757 960
E: agape-trust-hp@tiscali.co.uk
Offering lifecare and short-stay respite/shared care to young people with profound learning disabilities/complex needs.
Project Manager: Dr Peter Frost. *Administrator:* Lesley Downes. Executive staff 1, Other staff 30. ***CC*** No.1011416. Began 1992; non-denominational. No magazine. Turnover £800,000 to year end Apr 02.

Barcombe and Lewis Project: The Willows, Dean's Meadow, Barcombe, Lewes BN8 5DX
☎01273 400 752

Blackburn Diocesan Adoption Agency St Mary's House, Cathedral Close, Blackburn BB1 5AA
☎01254 577 59
M: 07801 794 656
Fax 01254 670 810
E: adoptionagency@btconnect.com
Web: www.bdaa.org.uk
Providing a comprehensive adoption service for all parties involved in all aspects of adoption.
Director: Mr Brian Williams. *Deputy Director:* Mrs Gwen Laird. Executive staff [illegible], Other staff 2. ***CC*** No.10330[illegible]. Began 1948; Anglican. No magazine. Turnover £280,000 to year end Dec 00.

Catholic Caring Services (Diocese of Lancaster) Ltd, 218 Tulketh Road, Preston PR2 1ES
☎01772 732 313 ℻01772 768 726
E: info@catholiccaringservices.org.uk
Web: www.catholiccaringservices.org.uk
Working with children in need, people with disabilities, marginalised communities to make a positive difference.
Director: Mr James Cullen. Executive staff 1, Other staff 150. ***CC*** No.326021. Began 1934; Roman Catholic. (Previously Catholic Caring Services (Diocese of Lancaster)). No magazine. Turnover £3,500,000 to year end Dec 05.

Catholic Children's Rescue Society (Diocese of Salford), 390 Parrs Wood Road, Didsbury, Manchester M20 5NA
☎0161 445 7741 ℻0161 445 7769
E: info@ccrs.org.co.uk
Web: www.ccrs.org.uk
Residential care of children, young pregnant homeless women, young men; preventive social work, adoption, fostering.
Director: Ms Kathy Batt. *Head of Children and Family services:* Mrs Susan Bunch. Executive staff 6, Other staff 150. ***CC*** No.239172. Began 1886; Roman Catholic. No magazine. Turnover £2,700,000 to year end Mar 04.
Other centres: Rochdale, Blackburn and Bolton

Catholic Children's Society (Dioceses of Arundel and Brighton, Portsmouth and Southwark), 49 Russell Hill Road, Purley CR8 2XB
☎020 8668 2181 ℻020 8763 2274
E: info@cathchild.org
Web: www.cathchild.org
Working with families through adoption including special needs, fostering, counselling and community and homelessness projects.
Director: Mr T Connor. *Deputy Director:* Mrs Anne Burnage. *Publicity and Fundraising Manager:* Mr Adrian Thacker. Executive staff 5, Other staff 170. ***CC*** No.252256. Began 1887; Roman Catholic. Magazine: *Child* (44,000 half-yearly). Turnover £4,346,083 to year end Mar 00.

Catholic Children's Society (Diocese of Brentwood), Child Care House, Little Wheatley Chase, Rayleigh SS6 9EH
☎01268 784 544 ℻01268 784 540
E: director.childcarebccs@virgin.net
Web: www.bccs.org.uk
Working with children and families who need care and support irrespective of race or religion.
Director: Mr Frank Maguire. *Deputy Director:* Eileen Campling. *Chair of Trustees:* Miss Collette Kelly. Admin staff 4, Other staff 12. ***CC*** No.1000661. Began 1984; Roman Catholic. No magazine. Turnover £470,000 to year end Mar 03.

Catholic Children's Society (Diocese of Clifton), 162 Pennywell Road, Easton, Bristol BS5 0TX
☎08451 220 077 ℻0117 935 0078
Adoption agency; social work support to families; adoption counselling and parenting project.
Director: Ms J Ball. Admin staff 5, Social workers 7. ***CC*** No.286814. Began 1904; Roman Catholic but serving all. No magazine. Turnover n/a.

Catholic Children's Society (Diocese of Nottingham), 7 Colwick Road, West Bridgford, Nottingham NG2 5FR
☎0115 955 8811 ℻0115 955 8822
E: enquiries@ccsnotts.co.uk
Web: www.families-are-best.co.uk
Adoption and adoption support services, specialising in sibling groups and black children of all ages.
Director: Ms Margaret Dight. *Deputy Director:* Mr Graham Pellew. Executive staff 2, Other staff 14. ***CC*** No.213692. Began 1948; Roman Catholic. Magazine: *Connections* (3,000 half-yearly). Turnover £759,000 to year end Mar 03.

†Catholic Children's Society (Diocese of Shrewsbury), St Paul's House, Farm Field Drive, Beechwood, Prenton CH43 7ZT
☎01516 521 281 ℻01516 525 002
E: info@cathchildsoc.org.uk
Web: www.cathchildsoc.org.uk
Social and community work agency for disadvantaged children and families; helping build strong supportive communities.
Director: Mr Ged Edwards. *Social Awareness & Appeals Manager:* Mr Peter Gordon. Executive staff 1, Other staff 23. ***CC*** No.509793. Began 1889; Roman Catholic. No magazine. Turnover £316,000 to year end Mar 02.

Catholic Children's Society (Diocese of Westminster), 73 St Charles Square, London W10 6EJ
☎020 8969 5305 ℻020 8960 1464
E: rosemaryk@cathchild.org.uk
Web: www.cathchild.org.uk
Helping children and families through counselling, family centres, adoption, psychotherapy, irrespective of race or creed.
Director: Mr Jim Richards. *Deputy Director:* Ms Rosemary Keenan. *Appeals Manager:* Ms Patricia Hatton. Executive staff 5, Admin staff 10, Social work staff 37. ***CC*** No.210920. Began 1859; Roman Catholic. (Previously Crusade of Rescue). Magazine: *Network* (6,000 half-yearly). Turnover £2,500,000 to year end Dec 05.

The Children's Society, Edward Rudolf House, Margery Street, London WC1X 0JL
☎0845 300 1128 ℻020 7841 4500
E: info@childrenssociety.org.uk
Web: www.childrenssociety.org.uk
Working with children, young people and families whose circumstances make them particularly vulnerable.
Chief Executive: Mr Bob Reitemeier. Executive staff 5, Other staff 1,400. ***CC*** No.221124. Began 1881; Anglican. Magazine: *Bright Futures* (350,000 annually). Turnover £40,000,000 to year end Mar 02.

***Churches' Child Protection Advisory Service,** PO Box 133, Swanley BR8 7UQ
☎0845 120 4550 / 0845 120 4551 (24-hour helpline) ℻0845 120 4552
E: info@ccpas.co.uk
Web: www.ccpas.co.uk
Training, resources, advice and support in all areas of child protection and good working practice.
Director: Mr David Pearson. Executive staff 5, Other staff 11. ***CC*** No.1004490. Began 1977; non-denominational. Working name of PCCA Christian Child Care. Magazines: *Caring* (17,500 quarterly), *PCCA Bulletin* (16,000 every four months). Turnover £433,000 to year end Mar 05.

The Exodus Project, 34 Eldon Street, Barnsley S70 2EL
☎01226 786 300 M: 07840 463 642
℻01226 786 300
E: theexodusproject@msn.com
Working with disadvantaged children through provision of activity clubs and weekend holidays.
Development Manager: Mr Martin Sawdon. Executive staff 1, No other full-time staff. ***CC*** No.1092985. Began 2001; interdenominational. No magazine. Turnover £60,000 to year end Mar 04.

***Fegans,** 160 St James Road, Tunbridge Wells TN1 2HE
☎01892 538 288 ℻01892 515 793
E: info@fegans.org.uk
Web: www.fegans.org.uk
Emotional support and counselling in schools; pre-school day-care provision; counselling service; community-based family support.
Chief Executive: Mr David Walles. *Senior Social Worker:* Mary Dicker. Executive staff 3, Other staff 34. ***CC*** No.209930. Began 1870; interdenominational. Magazine: *Focus* (3,500 half-yearly). Turnover £330,000 to year end Dec 04.
Also at: 10 High Street, Heathfield TN21 8LS
☎01435 862 975
And: 160 Margate Road, Ramsgate CT12 6AA
☎01843 587 000

The Haven Community Home, Springfield Road, Sydenham, London SE26 6HG
☎020 8659 4033/4034 ℻020 8676 7871
Accommodating 24 children.
Officer-in-Charge: Centre Manager. Admin staff 1, Other staff n/a. ***CC*** Began n/a; Salvation Army. No magazine. Turnover n/a.

Marshfield Children's Home, 79 Albert Road, Southport PR9 9LN
☎01704 538 643 M: 07711 799 778 (Duty Officer) ℻01704 542 030
An assisted home for up to 20 children; special needs, mainstream and respite; day nursery.
Officer-in-Charge: Centre Manager. Executive staff 3, Other staff 30. ***CC*** Began n/a; Salvation Army. No magazine. Turnover n/a.

Children's Care & Adoption Societies

***Mill Grove,** 10 Crescent Road, South Woodford, London E18 1JB
☎020 8504 2702
E: millgrove@btinternet.com
Supporting, caring for children and families through Christian extended family network, rooted in family home.
Director: Dr Keith White. *Assistant Director:* Mrs Ruth White. Executive staff 2, Other staff 8. ***CC*** No.1078661. Began 1899; non-denominational. Magazine: *Links* (2,500 annually). Turnover £174,000 to year end Dec 01.

***The Müller Homes for Children,** 7 Cotham Park, Bristol BS6 6DA
☎0117 924 5001 🖷0117 924 4855
E: admin@mullers.org
Web: www.mullers.org
Helping churches to be more effective in working with children, families and young people.
Chief Executive: Mr J P Marsh. Executive staff 1, Other staff 35. ***CC*** No.1066832. Began 1836; interdenominational. Part of the George Müller Foundation. No magazine. Turnover £662,000 to year end Feb 05.

NCH, 85 Highbury Park, London N5 1UD
☎020 7704 7000 🖷020 7226 2537
Web: www.nch.org.uk
Nearly 550 projects helping 140,000 vulnerable and excluded children, young people and their families.
Chief Executive: Clare Tickell. *Pastoral Director:* Rev W M Lynn. Other staff 6000. ***CC*** No.1097940. Began 1869; Methodist. (Previously NCH Action for Children). Magazine: *Children Today*(Circulation & frequency n/a). Turnover n/a.
Eastern Regional Office 1 Carisbrooke Court, Buckingway Business Park, Swavesey, Cambridge CB4 5UG
☎01954 233 920 🖷 01854 233 939
London Regional Office Turner House, 22 Lucerne Road, London N5 1TZ
☎020 7704 7070 🖷 020 7704 7080
North East Regional Office 12 Granby Road, Harrogate HG1 4ST
☎01423 524 286 🖷 01423 501 987
North West Regional Office Aquila House, Delta Crescent, Westbrook, Warrington WA5 7NR
☎01925 715 380 🖷 01925 715 381
South East Regional Office 158 Crawley Road, Roffey, Horsham RH12 4EU
☎01403 225 900 🖷 01403 225 911
South West Regional Office Horner Court, 637 Gloucester Road, Horfield, Bristol BS7 0BJ
☎0117 935 4440 🖷 0117 951 2470
West Midlands Regional Office Princess Alice Drive, Chester Road North, Sutton Coldfield B73 6RD
☎0121 355 4615 🖷 0121 354 4717
NCH Cymru Office St David's Court, 68a Cowbridge Road East, Cardiff CF11 9DN
☎029 2022 2127 🖷 029 2022 9952
NCH Northern Ireland 10 Heron Road, Belfast BT3 9LE
E: nioffice@nch.org.uk
☎028 9046 0500 🖷 028 9045 9169
NCH Scotland Office, City Park, 368 Alexandra Parade, Glasgow G31 3AU
☎0141 550 9010/0845 601 2810 (helpline) 🖷 0141 550 9088

The Orange Grove Foster Care Agency, Upper Interfields, Leigh Sinton Road, Malvern WR14 1UT
☎01886 833 860 🖷01886 833 280
E: enquiries@theorangegrove.co.uk
Web: www.theorangegrove.co.uk
Independent foster care agency providing short and long-term foster care with experienced foster carers.
Executive Director: Mr Gordon Stopani. *Director of Child Care:* Mrs Nicci Willock. Executive staff 3, Other staff n/a. ***CC*** Began 1996; non-denominational. (Previously Children's Family Trust). No magazine. Turnover £5,000,000 to year end Dec 04.

***PCCA Christian Child Care,** PO Box 133, Swanley BR8 7UQ
☎0845 120 4550/0845 120 4551 (24-hour helpline) 🖷0845 120 4552
Web: www.pcca.co.uk
Training, resources advice and support in all areas of child protection and good working practice.
Director: Mr David Pearson. Executive staff 5, Other staff 11. ***CC*** No.1004490. Began 1977; non-denominational. (Previously Pentecostal Child Care Association). Magazines: *Caring* (17,500 quarterly), *PCCA Bulletin* (16,000 every four months). Turnover £433,000 to year end Mar 05.

†St David's Children Society, Bishop Brown House, Durham Street, Grangetown, Cardiff CF11 6PB
☎029 2066 7007 🖷029 2039 4344
E: stdavidscs@aol.com
Web: www.adoptionofwales.co.uk
Adoption and pastoral care in schools.
Director: Mr G Cooney. Executive staff 2, Other staff 5. ***CC*** No.509163. Began n/a; Roman Catholic. (Previously Catholic Children and Family Care Society - Wales). No magazine. Turnover n/a.

St Francis Children's Society (Diocese of Northampton), Collis House, 48 Newport Road, Woolstone, Milton Keynes MK15 0AA
☎01908 572 700
🖷01908 572 701
E: enquiries@sfcs.org.uk
Web: www.sfcs.org.uk
Registered adoption and fostering agency.
Co-Directors: Mr Richard Gordon, Christine Smith. Executive staff 2, Social workers 10. ***CC*** No.211670. Began 1[illegible]59; Roman Catholic. No magazine. Turnover £621,642 to year end Mar 05.

†St Michael's Fellowship Herne Hill, 46 Herne Hill, London SE24 9QP
☎020 7738 4242
🖷020 7738 4242
E: fortysix@zetnet.co.uk
Residential family assessment centre.
Project Manager: Ms Alison Edwards. Executive staff 1, Other staff 6. ***CC*** No.1035820. Began 1992; interdenominational. No magazine. Turnover n/a.

***Spurgeon's Child Care,** 74 Wellingborough Road, Rushden NN10 9TY
☎01933 412 412
🖷01933 412 010
E: scc@spurgeons.org
Web: www.spurgeonschildcare.org
Supporting children, young people, families, through local authority and church-based partnerships, international locations.
Chief Executive: Mr Tim Jeffery. *Executive Director of Operations:* Garry Johnson. *Executive Director of Support Services:* Philip Rolfe. Executive staff 3, Other staff 857. ***CC*** No.1081182. Began 1867; interdenominational. Magazine: *Open House* (8,000 every four months). Turnover £12,295,000 to year end Mar 05.

YMCA, Sheffield, 7 Broomgrove Road, Sheffield S10 2LW
☎0114 268 9930
🖷0114 268 9931
E: david@sheffieldymca.org.uk
Web: www.sheffieldymca.org.uk
Providing children's services and youth and community programmes.
Chief Executive: Mr David Reynolds. *Company Secretary:* Mr Neville Chambers. Staff 14. ***CC*** No.243410. Began 1855; interdenominational. No magazine. Turnover n/a.

S

COUNSELLING ORGANISATIONS

See also Information and Telephone Organisations on Page 358.
For career counselling see Personnel Consultancy and Placement on Page 367.
For marriage counselling see Marriage Ministries on Page 366.
For family issues see Family Care & Support Ministries on Page 341.

Acorn Pregnancy Counselling Centre, 8 Stanford Square, Warwick Street, Worthing BN11 3EZ
☎01903 823 893
E: acornpcc@btconnect.com
Web: www.acornpcc.org.uk
Offering free pregnancy testing; pregnancy and post-abortion counselling; giving talks to Year 11 pupils.
Chair: Dr Robert Fergeson. Admin staff 1. ***CC*** No.1061813. Began 1995; interdenominational. No magazine. Turnover £10,000 to year end Feb 03.

Tom Allan Centre, 23 Elmbank Street, Glasgow G2 4PB
☎0141 221 1535 🖷0141 248 8452
E: tomallan@crossreach.org.uk
Web: tom-allan.org.uk
Counselling personal, emotional, marital and family problems; training in related subjects.
Manager: Mrs Dorothy Smith. Executive staff 3. Began 1962; Church of Scotland. No magazine. Turnover n/a.

***Alternatives Pregnancy Centre,** 48 Huntly Street, Inverness IV3 5HR
☎01463 713 999
E: cfl.scot@btopenworld.com
Advising senior pupils in schools.
Administrator: Mrs Catherine MacInnes. Admin staff 1, No other paid staff. ***CC*** No.SCO 20756. Began 1992; interdenominational. (Previously Inverness Crisis Pregnancy Centre). Member of Care Centres Network. Magazine: *Life Issues* (3,000 every two months). Turnover £16,484 to year end Jul 05.

***Alternatives Pregnancy Counselling Centre,** City Gate Centre, 84 London Road, Brighton BN1 4JF
☎01273 687 687
E: alternativesbtn@aol.com
Providing free pregnancy testing, confidential counselling, ongoing support and post-abortion counselling.
Centre Manager: Mrs Christine Liddiard. Executive staff 1, Other paid staff 2. ***CC*** No.1059942. Began 1991; evangelical. No magazine. Turnover £12,000 to year end Dec 02.

Associates in Christian Training, 2 Glasgow Road, Camelon, Falkirk FK1 4HJ
☎01324 630 643/0845 658 0045 (helpline) 🖷01324 628 583
E: crossline.central@virgin.net
Web: www.crosslinecentral.org
Providing training in Christian counselling and pastoral care in pastoral and community settings.
Chairman: Mr Norman Aitken. No full-time staff. ***CC*** No.SCO 22489. Began 1993; interdenominational. (Previously Crossline Scotland). No magazine. Turnover n/a.

Association of Christian Counsellors, 29 Momus Boulevard, Coventry CV2 5NA
☎0845 124 9569/9570
🖷0845 124 9571
E: office@acc-uk.org
Web: www.acc-uk.org
National professional organisation accrediting Christian counsellors and training organisations.
Chief Executive: Mr David Depledge. *Director of Professional Standards:* Mr John Nightingale. Executive staff 2, Other staff 5. ***CC*** No.1018559. Began 1991; interdenominational. Magazine: *Accord* (4,000 quarterly). Turnover £300,000 to year end Dec 02.

***Cardiff Christian Healing Ministry,** Woodvale Christian Centre, Crwys Road, Cathays, Cardiff CF24 4ND
☎029 2019 0113
E: info@cardiffchristianhealing.org.uk
Web: www.cardiffchristianhealing.co.uk
Offering counselling and prayer ministry for individuals; also counselling and prayer ministry training.
Director: Mrs Linda Alexander. Executive staff 4, Other staff 10. ***CC*** No.1066427. Began 1995; non-denominational. No magazine. Turnover £10,750 to year end Apr 04.

***Cardiff Concern Christian Counselling Service,** Regal House, Gelligaer Lane, Cathays, Cardiff CF14 3JS
☎029 2022 2557/2066 4410 (counselling)
E: cardiffconcern@btinternet.com
Providing a counselling service to the community around Cardiff and Glamorgan; training in Christian counselling.
Administrator: Mrs Jenny Lewis. ***CC*** No.1007504. Began 1990; interdenominational. No magazine. Turnover £12,000 to year end Dec 04.

Care in Crisis, 39 Union Street, Lurgan, Craigavon BT66 8DY
☎028 3832 9900 🖷028 3832 9900
E: info@careincrisis.org.uk
Web: www.careincrisis.org.uk
Crisis pregnancy, relationships and bereavement counselling; divorce/separation group therapy; abstinence-centred sex education programme.
Director: Mrs M Lee. *Chairman:* Dr David Rogers. Executive staff 3. ***CC*** No.XR 1098. Began 1994; interdenominational. No magazine. Turnover £40,000 to year end Mar 03.

†Cenacle Retreat and Conference Centre, Unit 10, St Wilfrid's Enterprise Centre, Royce Road, Hulme, Manchester M15 5BJ
☎0161 226 2332
Spiritual guidance and counselling; prayer cards and prayer line facility.
Warden: Name not supplied. Community 2. ***CC*** No.232928. Began 1888; Roman Catholic but open to all. No magazine. Turnover n/a.

Centre for Health and Pastoral Care, Holy Rood House, 10 Sowerby Road, Sowerby, Thirsk YO7 1HX
☎01845 522 580
🖷01845 527 300
E: holyroodhouse@centrethirsk.fsnet.co.uk
Web: www.holyroodhouse.freeuk.com
Therapeutic community and team affiliated to BAC; creative arts, massage, counselling, retreat training.
Directors: Revs Stanley & Elizabeth Baxter. Executive staff 4, Other staff 12. ***CC*** No.511151. Began 1982; ecumenical. (Previously North of England Christian Healing Trust). No magazine. Turnover £110,000 to year end Dec 02.

Cephas, 42 Hyde Park Avenue, Wollaston, Stourbridge DY8 3NE
☎01384 393 852
M: 07958 782 392
🖷01384 393 852
E: charity@cephastrust.org
Web: www.cephastrust.org
Restoring and rebuilding broken lives through encouragement, healing, teaching.
Pastoral Director: Pastor Jim Wilson. No full-time staff. ***CC*** No.1009248. Began 1991; interdenominational. No magazine. Turnover £9,000 to year end Dec 02.

Choices, 43 St Marys Road, Ealing, London W5 5RG
☎020 8840 8034
E: choices@fish.co.uk
Web: www.choices-ealing.org
Providing crisis pregnancy counselling, free pregnancy testing and post-abortion counselling.
Counsellor: Dr Janet Hereward. No paid staff. ***CC*** No.1076758. Began 1999; non-denominational. No magazine. Turnover £13,500 to year end Sep 02.

Christian Counselling Service, 12 Ellesmere Road, Colwyn Bay LL29 8RP
☎01492 530 528
🖷01492 534 558
E: christianresourcesint@yahoo.com
Offering biblically-based counselling, healing and deliverance; courses available.
Chief Executive: Ms Esther Wintringham. Executive staff 2, Other staff 2. Began 1993; Free evangelical. Magazine: *Forerunner* (Circulation & frequency n/a). Turnover n/a.

S

Counselling Organisations

†***Christian Fellowship Ministry,** The Lighthouse Centre, 34 Yarm Road, Stockton-on-Tees TS18 3NG
☎01642 611 497
🖷01642 611 497
E: Lighthouse@CFMstockton.freeserve.co.uk
Counselling, training, and outreach ministry community and pastoral emphasis; UK and worldwide; ACC affiliated.
Hon Directors: Mr Gordon Clarke, Mr John Clarke. All voluntary staff. ***CC*** No.328335. Began 1983; ecumenical. No magazine. Turnover £10,000 to year end Apr 03.

***Christian Guidelines,** 66 Newtownards Road, Bangor BT20 4DR
☎028 9146 8846
🖷028 9147 0060
E: admin@cguidelines.org.uk
Web: wwwcguidelines.org.uk
Training, counselling, pastoral care, mentoring and leadership support.
Chief Executive Officer: Rev Gary Haire. Executive staff 2, No other full-time paid staff. ***CC*** No.XR 2927. Began 1994; interdenominational. Magazine: *Guide to Guidelines* (2,000 annually). Turnover £144,000 to year end May 05.

Christian Prayer Ministries, 9 West Drive, Bonehill, Tamworth B78 3HR
☎01827 287 701
E: hugh.baker1@tesco.net
Web: www.cpm-uk.org
Ministering deep prayer to Christians wanting deeper holiness in their lives.
Chairman of Executive: Rev Hugh Baker. Admin staff 1. ***CC*** No.1090856. Began 2000; non-denominational. No magazine. Turnover £8,500 to year end Dec 04.

Churches' Ministerial Counselling Service, c/o Baptist House, PO Box 44, 129 Broadway, Didcot OX11 8RT
☎01235 517 705
🖷01235 517 750
E: admin@cmcs.org.uk
Web: www.cmcs.org.uk
Providing confidential, financially supported counselling to ministers and adult family members; mainly for Free Churches.
Administrator: Rev Ian Millgate. Admin staff 1. Began 1996; interdenominational. No magazine. Turnover £40,000 to year end Dec 02.

The Claybury Trust, The Pixmore Center, Pixmore Avenue, Letchworth SG6 1JG
☎0845 434 0021
🖷0845 434 0023
E: info@claybury.com
Web: www.claybury.com
Offering encouragement, healing, resources to benefit church leaders in their lives and relationships.
Director: Rev Colin D Buckland. Executive staff 2. ***CC*** No.1072978. Began 1993; non-denominational. No magazine. Turnover n/a.

The Cogwheel Trust, 1 Portugal Place, Cambridge CB5 8AF
☎01223 464 385 🖷01223 464 385
E: cwt@btconnect.com
Counselling service for individuals, couples and families covering a wide range of issues.
Director: Mr Ben Palmer. Executive staff 2, Counsellors 18. ***CC*** No.299228. Began 1988; non-denominational. No magazine. Turnover £82,510 to year end Dec 04.

Compass, 25 Hope Street, Liverpool L1 9BQ
☎0151 708 6688 🖷0151 707 8728
Counselling for those with emotional problems; training in counselling; supervision for pastoral work.
Director: Brenda Dunn. *Assistant Director:* Angela Ross. Executive staff 2, Other staff 7. ***CC*** No.700335. Began 1978; interdenominational. Counselling on Merseyside Pastoral and Supporting Service. No magazine. Turnover £190,000 to year end Dec 02.

Connect Christian Counselling Service, 8 Portesbery Road, Camberley GU15 3TA
☎0127 624 210 🖷0127 622 311
E: connect.office@btconnect.com
Web: www.connectcounselling.org.uk
Offering professional counselling within a Christian ethos for individuals, couples and families; training: introductory/ongoing.
Director: Cathie Russell. Executive staff 2, Other staff 2. ***CC*** No.1042852. Began 1994; non-denominational. Magazine: *Connections* (2,000 half-yearly). Turnover £78,000 to year end Mar 05.

Cornerstone, 23 Hazellville Road, London N19 3NF
☎020 7372 8901
E: cornerstone-london@yahoo.com
Web: www.cornerstonelondon.co.uk
Network of Christian counsellors and psychotherapists working in the London area; professional fees apply.
Coordinator: Ms Elizabeth O'Donohoe. No full-time staff. Began 1990; interdenominational. No magazine. Turnover n/a.

†**Counsel For Life (Personal Wholeness Trust),** 10 The Broadway, Woodford Green IG8 0HL
☎020 8491 0222 🖷020 8505 8426
E: pwtcfl@aol.com
Web: www.cfl.uk.com
Professional care and counselling for individuals and couples, based on Christian beliefs and values.
Executive Director: Rev David Blackledge. *Administrator:* Mrs Natalie Grant. Executive staff 2, Other staff 10. ***CC*** No.1000837. Began 1989; non-denominational. No magazine. Turnover £37,220 to year end Mar 03.

***Counselling & Prayer Trust,** The Courtyard, Fulham Palace, Bishop's Avenue, London SW6 6EA
☎020 7384 9212 🖷020 7384 9213
E: admin@counsellingpray.org
Web: www.counsellingpray.org
Professional counselling and counselling training: individual, couples, parents, children and group therapy; mood management groups.
Principal: Rev Agnes Sullivan. Executive staff 1, Counsellors 10. ***CC*** No.1027526. Began 1993; non-denominational. No magazine. Turnover £40,000 to year end Dec 02.

Counselling Associates, 157 Hoo Road, Kidderminster DY10 1LF
☎01562 755 338
E: andy@counsellingassociates.org
Web: www.counsellingassociates.org
BACP accredited counsellors providing personal counselling and related services; individuals, organisations; locations in England and Wales.
Contact: Mr Andrew Stanton. Executive staff 1, Counselling staff 7. Began 1987; non-denominational. No magazine. Turnover n/a.

Courage UK, PO Box 748, Guildford GU1 2ZY
☎01483 301 411
E: office@courage.org.uk
Web: www.courage.org.uk
Spiritual direction, retreats, discipleship groups for people experiencing conflict between their Christian faith and homosexuality.
Director: Mr Jeremy Marks. Executive staff 1, Other staff 1. Began 1988; interdenominational. No magazine. Turnover £60,000 to year end Aug 02.

***Credit Action,** Howard House, The Point, Weaver Road, Lincoln LN6 3QN
☎01522 699 777 🖷01522 697 703
E: office@creditaction.org.uk
Web: www.creditaction.org.uk
Teaching all aspects of personal money management through preaching, seminars and books using biblical principles.
National Director: Mr Keith Tondeur. Executive staff 2, Other staff 4. ***CC*** No.1106941. Began 1988; non-denominational. No magazine. Turnover £423,000 to year end Mar 05.

***Crossline Central,** 2 Glasgow Road, Camelon, Falkirk FK1 4HJ
☎01324 630 643 Helpline 0845 658 0045
E: crossline.central@virgin.net
Web: www.crosslinecentral.org
Confidential helpline and counselling referral service for anyone in crisis or turmoil or personal emotional difficulties.
Coordinator: Mrs Isobel Brownlee. *Chairman:* Mr N Aitken. No full-time staff. ***CC*** No.SCO 23661. Began 1995; interdenominational. No magazine. Turnover n/a.

Crossline Christian Centre, 5 Heavitree Road, Exeter EX1 2LD
☎01363 384 555/433 333(24-hour listening) M: 07866 672 299
🖷01363 384 555
E: brianwarren@waitrose.com
Counselling by appointment, evening soup kitchen.
Secretary: Mr Brian Warren. All voluntary staff. **CC** No.281168. Began 1977; non-denominational. No magazine. Turnover n/a.

Crossline Edinburgh, 9 Pilrig Street, Edinburgh EH6 5AH
☎0131 554 6140/0845 658 0045 (helpline)
🖷0131 467 0010
E: post@ecm.org.uk
Web: www.ecm.org.uk
Providing a Christian telephone helpline, befriending face-to-face counselling and prayer ministry.
Coordinator: Bill Staig. Executive staff 1. Began 1990; interdenominational. A ministry of Edinburgh City Mission. No magazine. Turnover n/a.

***Crossline (Plymouth City Mission),** 37 Grenville Road, Plymouth PL4 9PY
☎01752 564 243/666 777 (24-hour helpline) 🖷01752 664 243
E: crossline-plymouth@tiscali.co.uk
Web: www.crossline-plymouth.co.uk
Providing helplines, counselling; training.
Director: Mrs K McGuiness. Executive staff 1, Other staff 2. **CC** No.251197. Began 1974; interdenominational. No magazine. Turnover £18,000 to year end Apr 05.

***Crossroads Christian Counselling Service,** 144 Roman Road, London E2 0RY
☎020 8981 8388 🖷020 8981 6778
E: cccs@btconnect.com
Counselling for individuals aged over 16 and families resident in Tower Hamlets.
Development Manager: Marcie Haley. Executive staff 3, Admin staff 1, Counsellors 11. **CC** No.1043304. Began 1994; ecumenical. No magazine. £100,000 to year end Dec 04.

†CURA, Colmcille House, 1a Miller Street, Londonderry BT48 6SU
☎028 7126 8467 🖷028 7126 8467
Confidential telephone information, counselling and referral service for pregnant women.
Hon Secretary: Sue Nelis. All voluntary staff. **CC** Began 1977; Roman Catholic. No magazine. Turnover £40,000 to year end Dec 02.

***CWR (Crusade for World Revival),** Waverley Abbey House, Waverley Lane, Farnham GU9 8EP
☎01252 784 731 🖷01252 784 734
E: mail@cwr.org.uk
Web: www.cwr.org.uk/waverley
Providing training in biblical pastoral care and counselling; counselling referrals.
Chief Executive: Mr Mick Brooks. *Head of Counselling Training:* Mr Nigel James. *Business Manager:* Mr Eddie Olliffe. Executive staff 6, Other staff 46. **CC** No.294387. Began 1987; interdenominational. No magazine. Turnover £2,557,000 to year end Dec 04.

Deep Release Ltd, 122 Hunter Avenue, Shenfield, Brentwood CM15 8PG
☎01277 226 121
E: dr.ltd@btinternet.com
Web: www.deeprelease.org.uk
Christian counselling, creative therapy, life-coaching; training in deep release, communication skills, group work.
Directors: Dr Chris & Pauline Andrew. Executive staff 2, Admin staff 1. Began 1994; interdenominational. No magazine. Turnover £30,000 to year end Dec 05.

†DialogCentre UK Trust, BM DialogCentre, London WC1N 3XX
☎01235 200 404 🖷01235 200 404
Research, re-evaluation and rehabilitation counselling, public information and counsellor training about new religions.
National Director: Mr Richard Howard. All voluntary staff. **CC** No.1080175. Began 1985; interdenominational. No magazine. Turnover n/a.

***Edinburgh International Health Centre,** Elphinstone Wing, Carberry, Musselburgh EH21 8PW
☎0131 653 6767 M: 07710 276 208
🖷0131 653 3646
E: admin@eihc.org
Web: www.eihc.org
Out-patient medical care, debriefing assessment, counselling, retreats for missionaries, agency volunteers, UK Christian workers.
Medical Director: Dr Michael Jones. *Director Psychiatric Services:* Mrs Elizabeth Jones. Executive staff 4, Other staff 6. **CC** No.SCO 00948. Began 1983; interdenominational. (Previously Care for Mission). No magazine. Turnover £110,811 to year end Apr 05.

Exodus Counselling, Guy Chester Centre, Pages Lane, Muswell Hill, London N10 1PR
☎020 8883 4411
E: vacounselling@aol.com
Web: www.exodus-counselling.org.uk
Professional counselling service for North London which explicitly values the beliefs of the Christian faith.
Director: Mrs Victoria Alexander. No full-time paid staff. **CC** No.1060107. Began 1996; ecumenical. No magazine. Turnover £5,000 to year end Dec 04.

***Family Life Foundation,** 3 Queen Street, Carrickfergus BT38 8AP
☎028 9336 8899
E: info@familylifefoundation.org.uk
Web: www.familylifefoundation.org.uk
Caring for families through Christian Caring Initiatives programme, counselling, training, Family Care-in-Cancer project.
Director: Rev Roy Kerr. Executive staff 1, Other staff 1. **CC** No.XR 16542. Began 1995; interdenominational. No magazine. Turnover £20,000 to year end Mar 05.

The Five Gables Counselling Service, 843 Decoy Drive, Hampden Park, Eastbourne BN22 0AD
☎01323 509 002 🖷01323 509 002
Providing counselling.

020 7384 9212

COUNSELLING & PRAYER TRUST
CPT

- **Individual Counselling**
- **Couples Counselling**
- **Psychotherapy Groups**
- **Mood Management Groups**

Counselling & Prayer Trust

The Courtyard, Fulham Palace,
Bishop's Avenue, London SW6 6EA
admin@counsellingpray.org

Administrator: Mrs R Heptinstall. Admin staff 1. Began n/a; interdenominational. No magazine. Turnover n/a.

Focus Counselling, The Crypt, St Michael's Church, Broad Street, Bath BA1 5LJ
☎01225 330 096
E: focusbath@yahoo.co.uk
Delivering a professional, confidential counselling service.
Director: Mrs Jan Douglas-Bate. Admin staff 1, Other staff 1. **CC** Began 1999; ecumenical. No magazine. Turnover £12,000 to year end Apr 02.

Foundation Ministries, The Armagh Pastoral Centre, 7a Russell Street, Armagh BT61 9AA
☎028 3752 5282
Ministry of counselling and evangelism offering help to anxious, suicidal, guilty, lonely, fearful people.
Director: Eleanor Burton. *Counsellor:* David Bird. Executive staff 1. **CC** No.45237A. Began 1979; interdenominational. No magazine. Turnover £24,500 to year end Dec 02.

Freshfields Charitable Trust, 1 Forest Drive East, Leytonstone, London E11 1JX
☎020 8539 8002 🖷020 8539 8002
E: freshfieldscharity@supanet.com
Prayer, counselling and healing ministry; training for that ministry.
Trustee: Mrs Jill Lawrence. Executive staff 1, No other full-time staff. **CC** No.1015521. Began 1992; Anglican. No magazine. Turnover £19,248 to year end Dec 02.

Green Pastures Christian Centre of Pastoral Care and Healing, 17 Burton Road, Branksome Park, Poole BH13 6DT
☎01202 764 776 🖷01202 768 144
E: admin@green-pastures.org
Web: www.green-pastures.org
Short-term residential therapeutic environment for personal growth, healing, fellowship, counselling, spiritual direction, creativity, hands-on therapies.
Pastoral Director: Rev Colin Norris. *Centre Manager:* Audri Coleman. Executive staff 1, Other staff 10. **CC** No.1090568. Began 1955; interdenominational. Magazine: *Update* (3,000 quarterly). Turnover n/a.

***Growing Through,** 3 Grange Road, Erdington, Birmingham B24 0DG
☎0121 681 6855 🖷0121 681 6855
E: information@growing-through.org.uk
Web: www.growing-through.org
Offering support groups for children, teens and adults experiencing significant loss through death or divorce.
General Secretary: Mr Dale Erickson. Executive staff 2, Other staff 4. ***CC*** No.1059743. Began 1995; interdenominational. No magazine. Turnover £52,600 to year end Dec 04.

†*Help Counselling Service, Bridge House, Stallard Street, Trowbridge SN15 3DZ
☎01225 767 459 🖷01225 776 313
Free confidential counselling for anyone in west Wiltshire with any personal or family problems.
Service Manager: Mr David Thompson. Executive staff 1, Other staff 2. ***CC*** No.776313. Began 1983; interdenominational. (Previously Help Trowbridge Project). No magazine. Turnover £26,500 to year end Mar 03.

***Hope (Counselling and Support),** 33 High Street, Aldershot GU11 1BH
☎01252 350 466 🖷01252 310 814
E: info@hope-counselling.org.uk
Web: www.hope-counselling.org.uk
Director: Mr Roderic Homberger. Counselling staff 5. Began 1994; non-denominational. No magazine. Turnover n/a.

†IGWIT, Wholeness Workshops, Grappenhall Youth and Community Centre, Bell House, Grappenhall, Warrington WA4 2SG
☎01925 453 941 M: 07753 498 277
E: claire@igwit.freeserve.co.uk
Wholeness workshops, counselling, coaching and personal development encouraging inner healing, balance and shalom.
Counsellor & Life Coach: Claire Book. Executive staff 1, No other staff. Began 1979; non-denominational. IGWIT - In God we implicitly trust. No magazine. Turnover n/a.

Institute of Counselling, 6 Dixon Street, Glasgow G1 4AX
☎0141 204 2230 🖷0141 221 2841
E: admin@instituteofcounselling.org.uk
Web: www.instituteofcounselling.org.uk
Diploma in clinical and pastoral counselling skills, home study training; mail order books. University accredited.
Chief Executive: Rev Neil Morrison. Executive staff 12, Other staff 45. Began 1985; interdenominational. Magazine: *The Living Document* (600 every four months). Turnover £400,000 to year end Dec 00.

***Into the Light,** Manna Counselling Service, 23 Mitcham Lane, London SW16 6LQ
☎No telephone
E: info@intothelight.org.uk
Web: www.intothelight.org.uk
Offering counselling, support, training for people who have experienced sexual abuse or who support them.
Founder, Trainer, Counsellor: Mrs Rebecca Mitchell. Executive staff 1. Began 1993; interdenominational. Part of Streatham Baptist church. No magazine. Turnover £1,000 to year end Sep 05.

Key Counselling Services Limited, 12 Davies Close, Rainham RM13 9LJ
☎01708 522 293 🖷01708 551 547
E: admin@keycounselling.org.uk
Web: www.keycounselling.org.uk
Caring, confidential counselling provided by professionally trained counsellors.
Administrator: Mr David Fowler. Executive staff 2, Other staff 3. ***CC*** No.1069652. Began 1997; non-denominational. No magazine. Turnover £5,000 to year end Jul 05.

***Kings Communications,** PO Box 129, High Wycombe HP13 7WP
☎01494 512 441
E: ukoffice@kingscommunications.com
Web: www.kingscommunications.com
Professional Christian counselling; coaching and consultancy training programmes and development for churches organisations and individuals.
Directors: Andy and Dot Croall. Executive staff 3, Other staff 8. Began 1988; non-denominational. No magazine. Turnover £45,000 to year end July 02.

The Light House Christian Care Ministry, 1a Argyll Street, Coventry CV2 4FJ
☎024 7644 0095 🖷024 7645 1141
E: christian.counsel@zetnet.co.uk
Web: lighthousechristian.care.co.uk
General counselling service available to all; training in counselling to Level 3.
Office Manager: Miss Lynne Kirby. Other staff 6. ***CC*** No.1064132. Began 1986; interdenominational. No magazine. Turnover £90,000 to year end Mar 05.

***Lighthouse Centre,** Mac Murdo House, 79 Springfield Road, Chelmsford CM2 6JG
☎01245 494 838 🖷01245 495 427
E: enquiries.lighthouse@virgin.net
Web: www.lighthouseft.org.uk
Pregnancy, post-abortion and miscarriage counselling; free pregnancy testing; practical help.
Chairman: Mr Chris Blowers. Executive staff 3, Other staff 9. ***CC*** No.803069. Began 1989; interdenominational. (Previously Lighthouse Family Trust). ACC, Care for Life affiliated. No magazine. Turnover £12,000 to year end Sep 98.

Listening Post (Christian Counselling Service), YMCA Building, Sebert Street, Gloucester GL1 3BS
☎01452 383 820 🖷01452 412 379
E: lpostcounselling@tesco.net
Web: www.listeningpost.org.uk
Counselling Christians and non-Christians; counselling and related training for Christians and non-Christians; BACP standards.
Director: Mrs Sheila Appleton. Executive staff 2, Other staff 3. ***CC*** No.1013442. Began 1991; ecumenical. No magazine. Turnover £50,000 to year end Mar 05.
Also at: YMCA Building, Vittoria Walk, Cheltenham GL50 1TP
☎01242 256 060
And: Northcote House, Middle Street, Stroud GL5 1DZ
☎01453 750 123
And: 77 Barton Street, Tewkesbury GL20 5PY
☎01452 383 820

***Living Waters Discipleship & Healing Trust,** PO Box 1530, London SW1W [illegible]
☎020 7630 1044 🖷020 7630 10[illegible]
E: lw1uk@aol.com
Web: www.living-waters-uk.com
Healing and discipleship church-based programmes and conferences for Christians struggling with gender and relationship issues.
Director: Dr Lisa Guinness. Executive staff 1, Admin staff 1. ***CC*** No.[illegible]. Began 1991; interdenominational. No magazine. Turnover £120,000 to year end Dec [illegible]4.

***Manna Counselling Service,** 23 Mitcham Lane, Streatham, London SW16 6LQ
☎020 8769 1718 🖷020 87[illegible]9 171[illegible]
E: manna_counselling@lineone.net
Counselling service mainly for individuals; information service; training for local churches.
Counselling Service Leader: Katrina Redpath. Executive staff 1, Other staff 1. ***CC*** No.1094314. Began 19[illegible]1; interdenominational. Part of Streatham Baptist Church. No magazine. Turnover n/a.

Manna House Counselling Service, The Manna House, St Giles Street, Northampton NN1 1JW
☎01604 633 304 🖷01604 [illegible]35 49[illegible]
E: mhcs@mannahouse.org.uk
Web: www.mannahouse.org.uk
Providing Christian counselling to the community; offering training courses locally, nationally and internationally; ACC accredited.
Director: Mr John Nightingale. Executive staff 1, Other staff 4. ***CC*** No.28635[illegible]. Began 1985; interdenominational. ACC accredited. No magazine. Turnover £138,000 to year end Sep 04.

Maroa Christian Counselling International, Glyndon Community Centre, Raglan Road, Plumstead, London SE18 [illegible]LB
☎020 8855 5759 M: 07837 [illegible]68 98[illegible]
🖷020 8855 5759
E: radeosun@maroa.org.uk
Web: www.maroa.org.uk
Counselling in all areas of need except addictions.
Director: Pastor Rebecca Adeosun. Executive staff 3, Admin staff 1. ***CC*** No.1080015. Began 2000; Baptist. (Previously Pentecostal Redeemed Ministries). No magazine. Turnover n/a.

My Father's Business, 12 Stable Lane, Seer Green, Beaconsfield HP9 2[illegible]T
☎01494 673 407 M: 07931 7[illegible]3 013
🖷01494 673 840
E: barry@myfathersbusiness.co.uk
Web: www.myfathersbusiness.co.uk
Interim management services.
Principal Consultant: Mr Barry Richardson. Executive staff 1. Began n/a; Baptist. No magazine. Turnover £40,000 to year end Mar 01.

Network Counselling and Training, College Park Drive, Henbury Road, Henbury, Bristol BS10 7QD
☎0117 950 7271 ℻0117 950 7272
Ⓔ: info@network.org.uk
Web: www.network.org.uk
Offering general counselling; externally validated (University of Gloucestershire) counsellor training within a Christian context.
Acting Director: Mary Barrett. *Head of Training:* Kay Steele. Executive staff 2, Other staff 6, Counsellors 80. ***CC*** No.292801. Began 1986; non-denominational. Member of BACP. Magazine: *Support* (1,200 every four months). Turnover £100,000 to year end Jun 04.

†**New Beginnings,** 19 Chedworth Crescent, Paulsgrove, Portsmouth PO6 4ER
☎023 9238 7813 Ⓜ: 07930 676 056
Ⓔ: b.troke@btopenworld.com
Counselling adult survivors of child abuse; support for families; seminars.
Founder: Mrs Becky Troke. No full-time paid staff. Began 1988; interdenominational. No magazine. Turnover £1,500 to year end Apr 02.

New Door: Christian Care and Support, Oliver Bird Hall (rear of), Church Hill Road, Solihull B91 3RQ
☎0121 704 2355
Christian care and support through listening sessions by appointment.
Chairman: Mrs Anne Rock. No paid staff. Began 1987; interdenominational. No magazine. Turnover £300 to year end Mar 05.

Number 21 Counselling Service, 21 Rutland Square, Edinburgh EH1 2BB
☎0131 221 9377 ℻0131 221 9399
Ⓔ: staff@number21.bosr.org.uk
Counselling service for general public: one-to-one, couples and groups; art therapy department.
Manager: Mr Jonathan Wood. Executive staff 2, Admin staff 2. ***CC*** No.SCO 11353. Began n/a; Church of Scotland. (Previously Simpson House). No magazine. Turnover n/a.

***The Olive Tree Centre,** PO Box 2018, Rayleigh SS6 7FD
☎01268 779 900
Ⓔ: enquiries@olivetreecentre.org.uk
Web: www.olivetreecentre.org.uk
Providing Christian counselling to those suffering spiritually and psychologically; training those involved.
Director: Mr Sydney Platt. Executive staff 1, No other paid staff. ***CC*** No.1075617. Began 1996; non-denominational. No magazine. Turnover £13,240 to year end Jul 02.

†**Orpington Christian Counselling Service,** 8 Northolme Rise, Orpington BR6 9RF
☎01689 821 622
Providing counselling through varying circumstances; training in counselling skills, supervision offered.
Director: Mrs Sheila Simmons. All voluntary staff. ***CC*** No.1042634. Began 1986; interdenominational. No magazine. Turnover n/a.

The Oxford Christian Institute for Counselling, First Floor Offices, 119 London Road, Headington, Oxford OX3 9HZ
☎01865 308 889
Ⓔ: counselling@ocic.org.uk
Web: www.ocic.org.uk
Providing counselling, supervision, training and consultation.
Director: Mr Giles Charrington. Executive staff 1, Other staff 2. ***CC*** No.291819. Began 1985; ecumenical. (Previously Oxford Health Living Centre (OCIC)). No magazine. Turnover £48,000 to year end June 00.

***REACH Merseyside,** 85a Allerton Road, Liverpool L18 2DA
☎0151 737 2121 ℻0151 737 2185
Ⓔ: reach@reachuk.co.uk
Web: www.reachuk.co.uk
Christian counselling in Liverpool, Wirral, Manchester, Chester and Southport; training across the North West.
Co-ordinator: Andy Bond. Executive staff 1, Other staff 2, Volunteers 25. ***CC*** No.701330. Began 1986; interdenominational. No magazine. Turnover £40,000 to year end Sep 04.

St Marylebone Healing and Counselling Centre, St Marylebone Church, 17 Marylebone Road, London NW1 5LT
☎020 7935 5066 ℻020 7935 5493
Ⓔ: healing@stmarylebone.org
Web: www.stmarylebone.org.uk
Psychodynamic counselling and psychotherapy, spiritual direction, healing prayer; courses/conferences on Christian and psychotherapeutic understanding.
Director: Rev Chris MacKenna. Executive staff 1, Other staff 21. ***CC*** Began 1987; non-denominational. (Previously St Marylebone Centre for Healing and Counselling). No magazine. Turnover n/a.

Salvation Army Counselling Service, 1 Water Lane, Stratford, London E15 4LU
☎020 8536 5480 ℻020 8536 5489
Ⓔ: counselling@salvationarmy.org.uk
Web: www.salvationarmy.org.uk/counselling
Professional counselling service; referrals from general public, churches, other agencies. BACP Code of Ethics and Practice.
Head of Counselling Service: Major Phil Packman. Executive staff 1, Admin staff 1, Counsellors 5. Began 1972; Salvation Army. No magazine. Turnover n/a.

Sevenoaks Christian Counselling Service, The Bridge, Littlecourt Road, Sevenoaks TN13 2JG
☎01732 450 118
Web: www.sevenoakscounselling.org.uk
Professional counselling, supervision and training offered to all irrespective of religious or sexual orientation.
Director of Counselling: Maureen King. Executive staff 1, Other staff 14. ***CC*** No.288191. Began 1983; interdenominational. No magazine. Turnover n/a.

Sozo Ministries International, Sozo House, Alma Road, Romsey SO51 8ED
☎01794 522 511 ℻01794 522 577
Ⓔ: Ⓔ@sozo.org
Web: www.sozo.org
Preaching salvation, healing and deliverance to the church and to the world.
Director: Mrs Marion Daniel. Executive staff 6, Other staff 2. ***CC*** No.1042420. Began 1983; non-denominational. No magazine. Turnover n/a.

Stockport Christian Counselling, The Town House, Hope Terrace, Thomson Street, Stockport SK3 9DU
☎0161 428 7388
Web: www.stockportchristiancounselling.org
Providing counselling service to the churches and the community; also drop-in listening service.
Administrator: Name not supplied. All voluntary staff. ***CC*** No.1025437. Began 1991; interdenominational. No magazine. Turnover £4,000 to year end July 00.

Stroud Pregnancy Care Centre, The Cross, Nelson Street, Stroud GL5 2HL
☎01453 757 643
Web: www.stroud-pregnancy-helpline. org.uk
Providing free pregnancy test, counselling, support and information about pregnancies and abortion; resources for schools/churches.
Coordinator: Mrs Rachel Coysh. Executive staff 1. ***CC*** No.1039328. Began 1987; non-denominational. No magazine. Turnover £6,000 to year end Mar 03.

†**Support Group & Counselling Service,** PO Box 30, Potters Bar EN6 3JD
☎01707 659 996 Ⓜ 07946 739 206
Counselling people with stress and other mental problems.
Manager: Mr Daniel Lim. No full-time paid staff. Began 1992; interdenominational. No magazine. Turnover n/a.

***True Freedom Trust,** PO Box 13, Prenton CH43 6YB
☎0151 653 0773 ℻0151 653 7036
Ⓔ: info@truefreedomtrust.co.uk
Web: www.truefreedomtrust.co.uk
Christian counselling, support and teaching on homosexuality and related issues.
Director: Mr Martin Hallett. *Co-Director:* Rev Martin Daly. Executive staff 4, Other staff 3. ***CC*** No.513863. Began 1977, merged with Turnabout 1991; interdenominational. magazine: *TFT Newsletter* (1,500 quarterly). Turnover £129,000 to year end Apr 05.

†***U-Turn Anglia Trust,** PO Box 138, Witnesham, Ipswich IP6 9EP
☎01473 785 129
Web: www.u-turnanglia.fsnet.co.uk
Christian counselling ministry to homosexual men and women seeking healing; assisting church understanding; ACC accredited.
Director: Rev George A Harvey. Executive staff 3. ***CC*** No.1004424. Began 1987; interdenominational. ACC accredited. Magazine: *U-Turn Anglia Newsletter* (300 every four months). Turnover n/a.

***Valley Counselling Service & Debt Advice Centre,** New Life Church, Danesford Community Centre, West Road, Congleton CW12 4EY
☎01260 297 961 (counselling) 274 380 (debt advice) M: 07891 060 447
Fax 01260 297 961
E: valleycounselling@nlchurch.org.uk or debtadvice@nlchurch.org.uk
Providing counselling service, debt advice and budgeting skills to the general public; education for schools.
Counselling Coordinator: Mrs Rachel Lees. *Debt Advice Centre Trustee:* Mr Mike Bright. Counselling staff 2, Debt Advisers 2. ***CC*** No.514539. Began 1998; non-denominational. No magazine. Turnover n/a.

†*Vine Care Pregnancy Crisis Centre, 193 Crumlin Road, Belfast BT14 7DX
☎028 9074 8888
Assisting those who face difficulties or suffering as a result of pregnancy, miscarriage or abortion.
Coordinator: Mrs Pat Kennedy. Executive staff 1, No other full-time staff. ***CC*** No.XR 11516. Began 1995; non-denominational. No magazine. Turnover £10,000 to year end Dec 02.

The Vine Christian Bookshop and Coffee House, 6 Albert Street, Littleborough OL15 8BS
☎01706 374 534 Fax 01706 377 322
E: info@thevinefellowship.co.uk
Web: www.thevinefellowship.co.uk
Also bookshop and coffee shop.
Manager: Mr Geoff Hopcroft. Executive staff 1. ***CC*** No.515709. Began 1981; non-denominational. Turnover £45,000 to year end Mar 00.

***The Well Trust,** 105 High Street, Stourbridge DY8 1EE
☎01384 443 446 Fax 01384 443 636
E: books@thewelltrust.org.uk
Counselling centre, pregnancy crisis service.
Director: Mr Roger Eames. Executive staff 4. ***CC*** No.1100362. Began 1989; interdenominational. No magazine. Turnover n/a.

***Wellspring Christian Trust,** 61 Main Street, Frodsham WA6 7DF
☎01928 735 589
Web: www.wellspringchristiantrust.co.uk
Sharing the love of God through Christian listening ear service, coffee shop, bookshop.
Trustee: Dr Andrew Faraday. Executive staff 1. ***CC*** No.1035086. Began 1992; ecumenical. No magazine. Turnover n/a.

WHCM Bridge Counselling, Bodey House, Church Walk, Basildon SS14 1WW
☎01268 822 800 Fax 01268 822 802
E: bridge@whcm.org.uk
Web: www.whcm.org.uk
Providing professional counselling in a Christian context to individuals, couples, families, children and young people. Branches; Essex, East London.
Director: Stefano Ferraiolo. Executive staff 3, Counselling staff 21, Other staff 5. ***CC*** No.1084940. Began 1983; ecumenical. (Previously Bridge Counselling Services). Registered with UKRC. Part of West Ham Central Mission. No magazine. Turnover £200,000 to year end Mar 05.

WHCM Forrest Counselling, Forrest House, 63 Rowntree Clifford Close, Liddon Road, London E13 8AB
☎020 7473 4060 Fax 020 7473 3467
E: forrest@whcm.org.uk
Web: www.whcm.org.uk
Providing counselling services for individuals, couples, children and young people; supervision.
Director: Maureen Keane. Executive staff 1, Other staff 20. ***CC*** No.1084940. Began n/a; ecumenical. (Previously Forrest House Counselling Centre). Registered with UKRC. Part of West Ham Central Mission. No magazine. Turnover £88,000 to year end Dec 04

WHCM Sycamore Counselling, Sycamore, Sadlers House, 2 Legg Street, Chelmsford CM1 1AH
☎01245 359 353 Fax 01245 264 3[illegible]8
E: sycamore@whcm.org.uk
Web: www.whcm.org.uk
Delivering counselling to children, young people, couples families, individuals; providing counselling training courses to BS[illegible].
Director: Ms Jan Siddle. Executive staff 1, Other staff n/a. ***CC*** No.1084940. Began 1995; Baptist. (Previously Sycamore Counselling and Training). Part of West Ham Central Mission. No magazine. Turnover £200,000 to year end Mar 05.

***Whitchester Christian Guest House and Retreat,** Borthaugh, Hawick TD9 7L[illegible]
☎01450 377 477 Fax 01450 371 0[illegible]
E: enquiries@whitchester.org.uk
Web: www.whitchester.org.uk
Country house; rest; prayer; chapel; library. ACC acredited counsellor available.
Warden: Evelyn Jackson. Executive staff 1, Other staff 4. ***CC*** No.SCO 11[illegible]36. Began 1984; interdenominational. ACC affiliated. No magazine. Turnover £75,000 to year end Jun 05.

CREATION MOVEMENTS

See also Environment Movements on Page 339.

Answers in Genesis, PO Box 8078, Leicester LE21 9AJ
☎0116 270 8400 Fax 0116 270 0110
E: ukinfo@answersingenesis.org
Web: www.answersingenesis.org
Promoting belief in biblical creation through seminars, magazine, books, DVDs, videos and CD roms.
Chief Executive: Dr A J Monty White. *Head of Ministry:* Mrs Irene White. Executive staff 1, Other staff 12. ***CC*** No.1024543. Began 1991; non-denominational. (Previously Creation Science Foundation UK). Magazine: *Creation* (5,000 quarterly). Turnover £542,000 to year end Jun 05.

The Biblical Creation Society, PO Box 22, Rugby CV22 7SY
☎01788 810 633
E: reeves@clara.co.uk
Web: www.biblicalcreation.org.uk
Spreading biblical and scientific opposition to the theory of evolution especially among Christians.
Administrators: Mr Brian Watt, Mrs Elizabeth Reeves. No full-time staff. ***CC*** No.CR 42386. Began 1976; interdenominational. Magazine: *Origins* (600 every four months). Turnover £12,000 to year end Dec 02.

Creation Research, PO Box 1, Ashton-Under-Lyne OL6 9WW
☎0161 282 1111 Fax 0161 282 1111
E: creationresearch@amen.org.uk
Web: www.amen.org.uk/cr or www.creationresearch.net
Encouraging an understanding of the importance of creation throughout the Bible; providing speakers and resources.
UK Coordinator: Mr Randall Hardy. All voluntary staff. ***CC*** No.1103449. Began 1990; non-denominational. No magazine. Turnover £37,000 to year end Jun 04.

***Creation Resources Trust,** PO Box 3237, Yeovil BA22 7WD
☎01935 850 569 Fax 01935 850 569
E: info@crt.org.uk
Web: www.crt.org.uk
Sharing the evidence for biblical creation: literature, books, videos, CDs, seminars and creation days.
Director: Mr Geoff Chapman. Executive staff 1. ***CC*** No.1016666. Began 1[illegible]1; non-denominational. Magazines: *Creation Update* (1,000 quarterly), *Our World* (2,000 quarterly (for children)), *Original View* (2,000 every four months (for teenagers)). Turnover £25,000 to year end Dec 04.

Creation Science Movement, PO Box 888, Portsmouth PO6 2YD
☎023 9229 3988 Fax 023 92[illegible]3 561[illegible]
E: info@csm.org.uk
Web: www.csm.org.uk
Publishing, distributing literature; lecturing on doctrine or creation as opposed to secular evolution; exhibiting.
Hon Secretary & Treasurer: Mrs Jean Rosevear. Other staff 2. ***CC*** No.801[illegible]45. Began 1932; interdenominational. Magazine: *Creation* (Circulation n/a quarterly). Turnover £70,000 to year end Dec 0[illegible]

Daylight Origins Society, 19 Francis Avenue, St Albans AL3 6BL
☎01727 868 427
E: algnevard@hotmail.com
Web: www.theotokos.org.uk
Organising meetings and distributing literature and audio-visuals to inform Catholics on creation science.
Editor & Secretary: Mr Anthony Nevard. No paid staff. Began 1991; Roman Catholic. (Previously CESHE-UK). Magazine: *Daylight* (Circulation n/a half-yearly). Turnover £2,500 to year end Dec 02.

Northants Creation Group, 22 Hinton Road, Northampton NN2 8NX
☎01604 471 626
E: vineyards@ntlworld.com
Organising regular creation science lectures; providing speakers for churches, schools and groups.
Chairman: Mr Lewis Houston. No paid staff. Began 2003; interdenominational. No magazine. Turnover n/a.

DISABILITIES, ORGANISATIONS FOR PEOPLE WITH

See also Social Associations on Page 384.
Social Service & Welfare Organisations on Page 387.
Residential Homes for Disadvantaged People on Page 59.

Ambless Society, Shalom House, Lower Celtic Park, Enniskillen BT74 6HP
☎028 6632 0320/6632 0321(24-hour helpline) M: 07920 793 000
🖷028 6632 0320
Christian medical charity offering compassion and care to accident sufferers, the lonely and the bereaved.
Director Mr John Wood. Executive staff 2, Other staff 5. Began 1984; non-denominational. (Previously I Am Blessed Ministries). Incorporating DAP (Disasters, Accidents involving People). Magazines: *Our Companion Newsletter* (1,800 every two months), *Ambless Careletter* (1,800 half-yearly). Turnover n/a.

Archbishops' Council - Committee for Ministry among Deaf and Disabled People Church House, Great Smith Street, London SW1P 3NZ
☎020 7898 1439 M: 07966 583 106
🖷020 7898 1421
E: philip.maddock@c-of-e.org.uk
Web: www.cofe.anglican.uk
Advice and support of and among deaf people and people with disabilities.
Secretary: Rev Philip Maddock. Executive staff 1. **CC** Began 1929; Anglican. (Previously ABM Committee for Ministry among Deaf People). No magazine. Turnover n/a.

L'Arche, 10 Briggate, Silsden, Keighley BD20 9JT
☎01535 656 186 🖷01535 656 426
E: info@larche.org.uk
Web: www.larche.org.uk
Creating communities where people with learning disabilities and their assistants can live and work together.
General Secretary: John Peet. Executive staff 5, Other staff 204. **CC** No.264166. Began 1974; interdenominational. Magazine: *Letters of L'Arche* (600 frequency n/a). Turnover £4,973,160 to year end Jul 04.
Also at: Bognor Regis Community, 51a Aldwick Road, Bognor Regis PO21 2NJ
E: bognor@larche.org.uk
☎01243 863 426 🖷 01243 840 383
And: Brecon Community, 99 The Struet, Steeple Lane, Brecon LD3 7LS
E: brecon@larche.org.uk
☎01874 624 483 🖷 01874 610 046
And: Kent Community, Little Ewell, Barfrestone, Dover CT15 7JJ
E: kent@larche.org.uk
☎01304 830 930 🖷 01304 832 393
And: Edinburgh Community, 132 Constitution Street, Leith, Edinburgh EH6 6AJ
E: edinburgh@larche.org.uk
☎0131 553 3478 🖷 0131 554 3235
And: Inverness Community, 13 Drummond Crescent, Inverness IV2 4QR
E: inverness@larche.org.uk
☎01463 239 615 🖷 01463 711 089
And: Lambeth Community, 15 Norwood High Street, West Norwood, London SE27 9JU
E: lambeth@larche.org.uk
☎020 8670 6714 🖷 020 8670 0818
And: Liverpool Community, The Ark Workshops, Lockerby Road, Liverpool L7 0HG
E: liverpool@larche.org.uk
☎0151 260 0422
🖷 0151 263 2260/8499
And: Preston Community, 3 Moor Park Avenue, Preston PR1 6AS
E: preston@larche.org.uk
☎01772 251 113 🖷 01772 251 116

Association of Blind Catholics, 58 Oakwood Road, Horley RH6 7BU
☎01293 772 104
Providing Catholic talking newspaper, cassette lending library of religious books; retreats and similar gatherings.
Hon Secretary: Mr Paul Questier. All voluntary staff. **CC** No.259343. Began 1961; Roman Catholic. Magazine: *Catholic Talking Newspaper* (400 monthly (cassette)). Turnover n/a.

***At Home in the Community,** 391 West Road, Newcastle upon Tyne NE15 7PY
☎0191 228 8300
🖷0191 228 8301
Providing advice, support, care, advocacy and housing management for adults with learning disabilities.
Chief Executive: Mr David Crellin. *Chairman:* Sir Donald Curry. Executive staff 3, Staff 55. **CC** No.803280. Began 1990; non-denominational. No magazine. Turnover £1,000,000 to year end Apr 03.

Catholic Handicapped Fellowship, 15 Woodlands Park Drive, Blaydon-on-Tyne NE21 5PQ
☎0191 414 3221 M: 07870 868 463
E: jmair@talk21.com
Web: www.rc.net/uk/national-chf
Providing a forum where leaders of Diocesan Handicapped Groups meet to discuss items of mutual interest.
National Secretary: Mr John Mair. Executive staff 2. **CC** No.208717. Began 1957; Roman Catholic, but open to all. No magazine. Turnover £5,000 to year end Mar 96.

***Christian Deaf Link UK,** Friendship House, 484 Southchurch Road, Southend-on-Sea SS1 2QA
☎01702 613 113 Minicom 01702 613 114 🖷01702 613 113
E: general@cdluk.org
Web: www.deafchristian.org.uk
Enabling deaf people to develop their Christian lives and providing support to churches they attend.
Chairman of Trustees: Mr Laurence Banks. Part-time staff 3. **CC** No.1071830. Began 1998; interdenominational. (Previously London Christian Deaf Link). Magazine: *DeafLink* (500 quarterly). Turnover £61,500 to year end Mar 05.

Christian Outreach to the Handicapped, Fountain House, Conduit Mews, London SE18 7AP
☎020 8316 5389
E: COttHTrust@aol.com
Propagating the Gospel among disabled people. Worldwide outreach.
Principal: Mr Edwin Cross. Executive staff 2. Began 1978; Christian Brethren. No magazine. Turnover £100,000 to year end Dec 05.

†Church Action on Disability, PO Box 10918, Birmingham B29 6WF
☎0870 243 0678
E: coordinator@chaduk.org
Web: www.chaduk.org
Educational campaign addressing attitudes to all forms of disability in churches.
Co-ordinator: To be appointed. No full-time staff. **CC** No.1003716. Began 1987; interdenominational. Magazine: *All People* (1,100 quarterly). Turnover £21,000 to year end Mar 03.

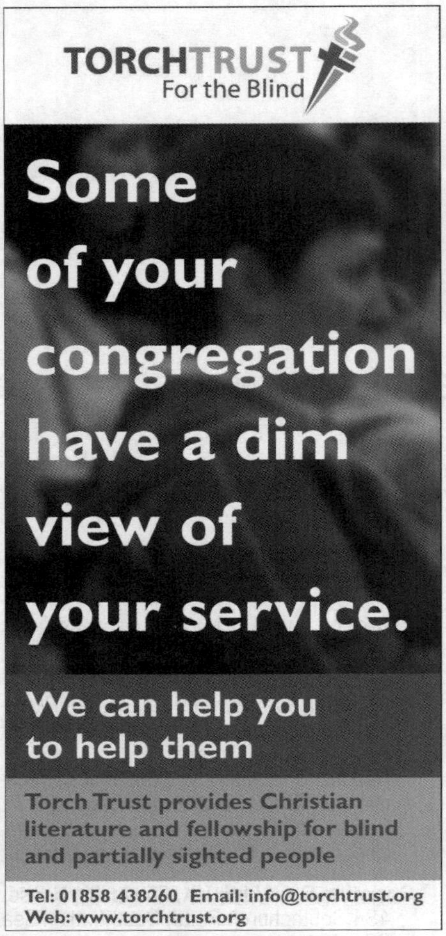

***Compass Braille/Sightlink,** 26 Cross Street, Moretonhampstead, Newton Abbot TQ13 8NL
☎01647 440 101
🖷01647 440 101
E: info@compassbraille.org or info@sightlink.org
Web: www.compassbraille.org or www.sightlink.org
Producing/transcribing multi-language braille Bibles/Christian literature, also giant print; supporting overseas visual impairment ministries.
Chief Executive: Mr Colin Dowling. *Administrator:* Mr Andrew John. Executive staff 1, Other staff 4. ***CC*** No.292625. Began 1985; interdenominational. (Previously Fellowship for the Visually Handicapped). Magazine: *Newscast* (Circulation n/a every four months). Turnover £118,000 to year end Mar 05.

***Compassionate Response,** PO Box 3358, Sheffield S8 0WP
☎0114 296 6274
E: david@compassionateresponse.org
Web: www.compassionateresponse.org
Offering care and compassion, support, training programmes for people with hurts and disabilities.
Director: Rev David Middleton. Executive staff 3, Other staff 3. ***CC*** Began 1994; interdenominational. (Previously Handi *Vangelism UK). No magazine. Turnover £5,000 to year end Dec 04.

***DCF Premier Workshops Trust,** Ruthven Road, Filwood Park, Knowle West, Bristol BS4 1ST
☎0117 985 1188 M: 07816 925 763
🖷0117 985 1188
E: dcfpremier@aol.com
Web: members.aol.com/dcfpremier
Providing a working environment for people with various disabilities; sharing the Gospel with them.
Manager: Mr Peter George Hamar. *Shop Manager:* Mrs Zoe Hamar. Executive staff 1, Other staff 5. ***CC*** No.1059468. Began 1990; interdenominational. (Previously Disabled Christian Fellowship Centre). No magazine. Turnover £10,000 to year end Dec 02.

***Deaf Christian Network (Hands Together),** PO Box 212, Doncaster DN2 5XA
☎029 2061 1798 🖷01302 739 660
E: handstogether@deafcn.freeserve.co.uk
Web: www.handstogether.org.uk
National resource centre providing literature, newsletters, ministry videos in sign language for the deaf.
Administrator: Mr Kenneth R Nuttall. Admin staff 1, Other staff 1. ***CC*** No.253131. Began 1990; interdenominational. No magazine. Turnover n/a.

Efficient Learning, 10 Fairmeadow, Winslow, Buckingham MK18 3JD
☎01296 715 870 M: 07790 271 753
E: eloffice1@aol.com
Web: www.efficientlearning.co.uk
Offering educational assessment, therapy, tuition to adults and children with learning difficulties including dyslexia.
Chief Executive: Mrs Julie Thorpe. Admin staff 3, Other staff 11. ***CC*** No.1101501. Began 2002; interdenominational. (Previously Thame Dyslexia Centre). No magazine. Turnover £40,000 to year end Aug 03.

***Evangelical Concern for People with Disabilities,** 48 Peel Close, Chingford, London E4 6XU
☎020 8281 9682 M: 07956 651 940
🖷020 8281 9682
E: ccpd2002@yahoo.com
Counselling, prayer, integration into church; educating churches; distributing Bibles and cassettes; distributing aid relief worldwide.
Administrator/Coordinator: Pastor Jesse Olu Adeniyi. No paid staff. ***CC*** No.1056174. Began 1994; interdenominational. No magazine. Turnover n/a.

***John Grooms,** 50 Scrutton Street, London EC2A 4XQ
☎020 7452 2000 🖷020 7452 2001
E: charity@johngrooms.org.uk
Web: www.johngrooms.org.uk
Providing care and housing for people with disabilities including holidays, rehabilitation and residential care.
Chief Executive Officer: Rev Michael Shaw. *Head of Marketing:* Mr John Chamberlain. Executive staff 5, Other staff 500. ***CC*** No.212463. Began 1866; interdenominational. Magazine: *Grooms News* (50,000 half-yearly). Turnover £10,000,000 to year end Mar 02.

The Kepplewray Centre, Broughton-in-Furness LA20 6HE
☎01229 716 936 🖷01229 716 [illegible]38
E: stay@kepplewray.org.uk
Web: www.kepplewray.org.uk
Lake District activity, education and holiday centre for disabled and non-disabled people as equal partners.
Project Director: Mr Peter Sanders. *Activity Services Manager:* Mr Andy G[illegible]es. Executive staff 3, Other staff 15. ***CC*** No.101[illegible]762. Began 1993; ecumenical. Magazine: *K News* (Circulation n/a half-yearly). Turnover £450,000 to year end Jun 0[illegible].

Martha Trust, Homemead Lane, Hacklinge, Deal CT14 0PG
☎01304 615 223 🖷01304 615 4[illegible]2
E: contact@marthatrust.org.uk
Web: www.marthatrust.org.uk
Providing residential care and respite care for children and adults with severe learning disabilities.
Chief Executive: Graham Simmons. Executive staff 1, Other staff 80. ***CC*** No.1067885. Began 1982; interdenominational. No magazine. Turnover n/a.

†Ministry to Deaf People, 5 College Square North, Belfast BT1 6AR
☎028 9261 9140
E: ddo@connor.anglican.org
Providing pastoral care for deaf people in Northern Ireland.
Chaplain: Rev William A Murphy. Executive staff 1. ***CC*** Began 1[illegible]88; Church of Ireland. (Previously Mission to Deaf people). No magazine. Turnover n/a.

***Open Ears,** 11 York Avenue, New Milton BH25 6BT
☎01425 615 215
E: admin@openears.org.uk
Web: www.openears.org.uk
Providing fellowship, support for hearing-impaired Christians; conferences; advising churches on pastoral care, loops/equipment.
Administrator: Christine Fitts. Admin staff 1. ***CC*** No.284487. Began 19[illegible]4; interdenominational. (Previously Hard of Hearing Christian Fellowship). Magazine: *Hearing Eye* (350 quarterly). Turnover £17,000 to year end Dec 02.

***PROSPECTS for People with Learning Disabilities,** PO Box 351, Reading RG[illegible]0 4XQ
☎0118 950 8781 🖷0118 9[illegible]9 168[illegible]
E: info@prospects.org.uk
Web: www.prospects.org.uk
Providing residential support, day services, development opportunities and spiritual ministry for people with learning disabilities.
Chief Executive: Mr Paul Ashton. *Director of Operations:* Mrs Jan Groat. *Director of Causeway PROSPECTS:* Mr Tony Phelps-Jones. Executive staff 6, Other staff 61[illegible]. ***CC*** No.1060571. Began 1976; interdenominational. (Previously A Cause for Concern). Magazine: *Better Prospects* (11,000 half-yearly). Turnover £7,850,000 to year end Mar 04.

S

Northern Ireland Office: 37 Movilla Street, Newtownards BT23 7JQ
E: mervynb@prospects-uk.org
☎028 9182 6862 🖷 028 9182 6860

***Michael Roberts Charitable Trust (MRCT),** 49 Bell Street, Sawbridgeworth CM21 9AR
☎01279 724 515 M: 07734 128 430
E: enquiries@mrct.org.uk
Web: www.mrct.org.uk
Working with people with physical and learning disabilities in community outreach and Christian ministry.
Director of Community Services: Mr Gary Knott. Executive staff 1, Other staff 3. ***CC*** No.1065006. Began 1997; non-denominational. Magazine: *Capstone* (500 every four months). Turnover £69,299 to year end Mar 04.

The Royal Association for Deaf People (RAD), Walsingham Road, Colchester CO2 7BP
☎01206 509 509 Text & Minicom 01206 711 260 🖷01206 769 755
E: info@royaldeaf.org.uk
Web: www.royaldeaf.org.uk
Centres for the deaf community, support services, interpreting, training and chaplaincy.

Chief Executive: Mr Tom Fenton. Executive staff 8, Other staff 40. ***CC*** No.1081949. Began 1841; Anglican. No magazine. Turnover £1,500,000 to year end Mar 00.

St Vincent's School for the Deaf, 30 Fullarton Avenue, Tollcross, Glasgow G32 8NJ
☎0141 7782 254 🖷01417 641 482
E: schoolst1@aol.com
School for deaf pupils aged 2 to 18.
Head Teacher: Mrs A Hodos. Executive staff 2, Other staff 14. ***CC*** No.SCO 05129. Began 1911; Roman Catholic. No magazine. Turnover n/a.

***Through The Roof,** PO Box 353, Epsom KT18 5WS
☎01372 749 955
Minicom 01372 737 041
🖷01372 737 040
E: info@throughtheroof.org
Web: www.throughtheroof.org
Information, advice, training, website for churches to be inclusive of disabled people; fellowship groups.
Director: Mr Paul Dicken. Executive staff 2, Other staff 4. ***CC*** No.1087788. Began 1997; non-denominational. UK ministry of Joni Eareckson Tada. Incorporating Disabled Christians Fellowship. Magazine: *The Vital Link* (6,000 quarterly). Turnover £235,000 to year end Sep 02.

***Torch Trust for the Blind,** Torch House, Torch Way, Northampton Road, Market Harborough LE16 9HL
☎01858 438 260
🖷01858 438 275
E: info@torchtrust.org
Web: www.torchtrust.org
Christian literature in Braille, giant print, audio; fellowship, holidays for blind and partially-sighted people.
Chief Executive: Dr Gordon Temple. *Technical Director:* Dr M Townsend. Executive staff 6, Other staff 40. ***CC*** No.1095904. Began 1959; interdenominational. Magazine: *Torch Family News* (8,000 frequency n/a). Turnover £534,000 to year end Sep 04.

***Woods Hills and Tracks,** Moelfre, Llansilin, Oswestry SY10 7QX
☎01691 791 486
🖷01691 791 486
E: woodhillproject@lineone.net
Web: www.pco.powys.org.uk/woodhill
Serving disadvantaged people through therapeutic, environmental and rural amenities including wheelchair access, workshops and retreat.
Chairman: Ms Janet Randell. Admin staff 1, Other staff 1. ***CC*** No.1050270. Began 1995; interdenominational. No magazine. Turnover n/a.

ENVIRONMENT MOVEMENTS

See also Creation Movements on Page 336.

Christian Ecology Link, 3 Bond Street, Lancaster LA1 3ER
☎01524 333 58 🖷01524 338 58
E: info@christian-ecology.org.uk
Web: www.christian-ecology.org.uk
Encouraging Christians and churches to respond to environmental concerns. Sharing Christian insights on green movement.
Correspondent/Information Officer: Miss Laura Deacon. No full-time staff. ***CC*** No.328744. Began 1981; interdenominational. Magazine: *Green Christian* (800 every three months). Turnover n/a.

The Church Energy Trust, PO Box 1039, Newcastle upon Tyne NE99 4TE
☎0870 429 6197 M: 07761 339 469
E: info@churchenergy.co.uk
Web: www.churchenergy.co.uk
Providing environmental and sustainable energy management to the church and community.
Chief Executive: Mr Bob Pritchard. Executive staff 1, Other staff 2. Began 2003; interdenominational. No magazine. Turnover n/a.

†Quaker Green Action, 76 Harpes Road, Oxford OX2 7QL
☎01865 302 907
E: laurie.michaelis@mansfield.oxford. ac.uk
Web: www.quakergreenaction.org.uk
Supporting one another in changing lifestyles and influencing the Religious Society of Friends.
Secretary: Laurie Michaelis. No full-time staff. ***CC*** Began 1986; Religious Society of Friends. (Previously Quaker Green Concern). Magazine: *Earth Quaker* (200 quarterly). Turnover £1,500 to year end Dec 02.

The John Ray Initiative, Room QW212, Francis Close Hall, Swindon Road, Cheltenham GL50 4AZ
☎01242 543 580 🖷01242 542 997
E: jri@glos.ac.uk
Web: www.jri.org.uk
Connecting environment, science, and Christianity.
Administrator: David Thistlethwaite. Other staff 1. ***CC*** No.1067614. Began 1998; interdenominational. No magazine. Turnover £22,000 to year end Aug 05.

***A Rocha International,** 3 Hooper Street, Cambridge CB1 2NZ
☎01387 710 286 🖷01387 710 286
E: international@arocha.org
Web: www.arocha.org
An international conservation organisation working to show God's love for all creation.
International Administrator: Mrs Barbara Mearns. *Directors:* Peter Harris, David Payne. Executive staff 8. ***CC*** No.288634. Began 1983; non-denominational. Magazine: *A Rocha International News* (7,000 quarterly). Turnover £283,000 to year end Dec 04.
A Rocha UK, 13 Avenue Road, Southall UB1 3BL
☎020 8574 5935

ETHNIC MINORITY ASSOCIATIONS

For overseas national church congregations see Denominational Headquarters on Page 148.

***African and Caribbean Evangelical Alliance,** Whitefield House, 186 Kennington Park Road, London SE11 4BT
☎020 7735 7373 🖷020 7735 7275
E: acea@eauk.org
Web: www.aceauk.org
Reflecting black Christian faith in Britain and promoting unity, reconciliation, understanding among all Christians.
Director: Rev Katei Kirby. Executive staff 1, Other staff 3. ***CC*** No.802887. Began 1984; interdenominational. In partnership with Evangelical Alliance. Magazine: *Focus* (3,000 quarterly). Turnover included in Evangelical Alliance.

***Alliance of Asian Christians,** PO Box 1375, Headington, Oxford OX3 0WJ
☎01865 741 400 🖷01865 741 400
E: raj@patelz.net
Supporting and encouraging the contributions of the Asian Christian community.
Executive Secretary: Mr Pradip Sudra. Executive staff 1, Other staff 3. ***CC*** No.1020767. Began 1989; non-denominational. In partnership with Evangelical Alliance. Magazine: *Aaeki Haae* (2,000 half-yearly). Turnover £10,000 to year end Jun 05.

***Anglo-Japanese Christian Ministries (AJCM),** 9 Beaminster Avenue, Stockport SK4 3HU
☎0161 442 4282 🖷0161 442 4282
E: trevor.howard@ajcm.org.uk
Web: www.ajcm.org.uk
Evangelistic and pastoral work amongst Japanese in Greater Manchester; encouraging evangelism of Japanese in UK.
Ministry Directors: Mr & Mrs Trevor & Cheryl Howard. Executive staff 2. ***CC*** No.1008099. Began 1991; interdenominational. No magazine. Turnover £28,000 to year end Apr 04.

†Asian Christian Fellowship, 174 Owen Road, Pennfields, Wolverhampton WV3 0HQ
☎01902 420 418
Church building through evangelism by literature, visitation and other forms of outreach.
Leader: Mr Hari Kaul. Executive staff 5. Began 1973; non-denominational. No magazine. Turnover £15,000 to year end Mar 02.

Asian Concern, Greenside Church, Royal Terrace, Edinburgh EH7 5AD
☎0131 554 3277 M 07818 670 669
🖷0131 554 3277
Sharing God's love with Asians; evangelism by literature, visitation, teaching, hospitality, practical help.
Hon Field Workers: Mr & Mrs Solomon & Angela Daniel. No paid staff. ***CC*** No.SCO 20697. Began 1989; interdenominational. No magazine. Turnover £3,000 to year end Mar 03.
Also at: 2 Carlyle Place, Edinburgh EH7 5SR
☎0131 652 1519

Association of Nigerian Catholics, 8a Battersea Park Road, Battersea, London SW8 4BH
☎020 8317 8364 M: 07861 351 828
🖷020 7627 8438
E: O-Jon30@yahoo.co.uk
Providing welfare, chaplaincy, consultancy services; pilgrimages, retreats.
Chaplain: Rev F E Chukwu. Executive staff 1, Admin staff 1. Began 1990; Roman Catholic. Magazine: *Nigerian Catholic Community Newsletter* (2,500 quarterly). Turnover n/a.

Austrian Catholic Centre, 29 Brook Green, London W6 7BL
☎020 7603 2697 🖷020 7603 2697
E: acclondon@aol.com
Web: www.acclondon.org.uk
Providing hostel, social centre and welfare work for Austrians.
Social Worker in Charge: Anna Ringler. Executive staff 2. ***CC*** No.240896. Began 1955; Roman Catholic. No magazine. Turnover £95,000 to year end Dec 04.

The British Messianic Jewish Alliance, PO Box 607, Harrow HA2 9TF
M: 07753 527 738 🖷020 8864 4400
E: office@bmja.net
Web: www.bmja.net
Spiritual/temporal care of Jewish people believing in Jesus the Messiah and those standing alongside them.
Office Secretary: Mrs D Rodgers. No full-time staff. ***CC*** Began 1866; interdenominational. (Previously The Hebrew Christian Alliance of Great Britain). Magazine: *Chai* (Circulation n/a quarterly). Turnover n/a.

***Chinese Overseas Christian Mission,** 2 Padstow Avenue, Fishermead, Milton Keynes MK6 2ES
☎01908 234 100 🖷01908 234 200
E: cocm@cocm.org.uk
Web: www.cocm.org.uk
Evangelism, church planting, literature, bookroom; ministries for students, restaurant workers, scholars and British-born Chinese.
Director: Miss Mary Wang. *Council Chairman:* Lord Chan of Oxton. Executive staff 1, Other staff n/a. ***CC*** No.232651. Began n/a; interdenominational. Magazines: *COCM Link* (5,000 every two months), *Living Water* (12,000 every two months). Turnover £1,040,000 to year end Dec 04.

Derby Asian Christian Ministry Partnership, St Augustine's Church Office, Upper Dale Road, Derby DE23 8BP
☎01332 270 837 🖷01332 270 837
E: walbrook-epiphany@tiscali.co.uk
Promoting the Gospel by pastoral care and evangelism to Asians in Derbyshire.
Minister: Andrayas Khan. Executive staff 1. Began 1978; ecumenical. Magazine: *CMS Prayer Link* (Circulation n/a quarterly). Turnover £20,000 to year end Dec 02.

Ethiopian Christian Fellowship Church in the UK, 389 Barking Road, Plaistow, London E13 8AL
☎020 7473 4300 🖷020 7473 4[illegible]40
E: info@ecfcuk.org
Web: www.ecfcuk.org
Bringing the Gospel of Jesus Christ to Ethiopians and Eritreans living in the UK and Europe.
Coordinator: Rev Getachew Zegaw. Admin staff 2. ***CC*** No.101[illegible]782. Began 1981; Pentecostal. Magazine: *Yem[illegible]tach* (400 quarterly). Turnover n/a.

***FOI Ministries,** 26 Wensley Road, Reading RG1 6DJ
☎0118 934 1199 🖷0118 934 9[illegible]26
E: foiministries@hotmail.com
Trustee: Rev Laurance Steceford. Admin staff 2. ***CC*** No.3279[illegible]5. Began [illegible]988; non-denominational. No magazine. Turnover £5,000-10,000 to year end Dec 02. Support to Arabic speaking believers in UK, North Africa and Middle East.

***German Catholic Mission (Wynfrid House),** 20 Mulberry Street, London E1 1EH
☎020 7247 6110/5773 🖷 020 7247 0552
Priest-in-Charge: Rev He[illegible]z Me[illegible]och. *Administrator:* Mrs A E Greaves. Executive staff 1, Other staff 3. Began 1[illegible]61; Roman Catholic. No magazine. Turnover n/a. Caring for German Catholics in the UK; providing temporary accommodation, mainly for German youth groups.

German Young Men's Christian Association, 35 Craven Terrace, Lancaster Gate, London W2 3EL
☎020 7723 9276 🖷020 7[illegible]06 28[illegible]
E: y-services@german-ymca.org.uk
Web: www.german-ymca.org.uk
Support services for young people aged 18 plus.
General Secretary: Mr U Maynard. Executive staff 3. ***CC*** No.250118. Began 1[illegible]50; interdenominational. No magazine. Turnover £128,000 to year end Dec 02.

†The Good Neighbour Ltd, Church of God of Prophecy, 47 George Street, Balsall Heath, Birmingham B12 9RG
☎0121 440 7548/440 33[illegible]6 (24-hour Helpline) 🖷0121 440 3336
Faith-based mentoring programme for ex-offenders returning to the community from the criminal justice system.
Project Manager: Rev Pearl Thomas. *Programme Manager:* Dr Richard S[illegible]nt. Executive staff 1, Admin staff 1. ***CC*** No.1083909. Began 19[illegible]8; interdenominational. (Previously Jericho Community Project). No magazine. Turnover £80,[illegible]00 to year end Dec 02.

Polish Institute of Catholic Action, 240 King Street, London W6 0RF
☎020 8563 0206 🖷020 8563 0206
Lay apostolate among people of Polish origin; representation in international Catholic organisations.
General Secretary: Mr Olgierd Stepan KCSG. All voluntary staff. Began 1948; Roman Catholic. Magazine: *Czyn Katolicki-Wiadomosci* (900 quarterly). Turnover £8,500 to year end Mar 00.

The Serve China Trust, 12 Brookside Avenue, Wollaton, Nottingham NG8 2RD
☎0115 928 3290
Providing Scriptures, literature, and encouraging witness to mainland Chinese in Britain
Administrator: Mrs Kum Kew Wells. No full-time staff. **CC** No.1001001. Began 1990; interdenominational. No magazine. Turnover £5,113 to year end Feb 05.

***South Asian Concern,** PO Box 43, Sutton SM2 5WL
☎020 8770 9717 🖷020 8770 9747
E: info@southasianconcern.org
Web: www.southasianconcern.org
Encouraging and equipping Christ's followers to be more effective in mission among South Asian people.
Chairman: Mr Ram Gidoomal. *Vice-Chairman:* Robin Thomson. Admin staff 3, Other staff 4. **CC** No.1002270. Began 1989; interdenominational. Magazine: *Concern* (2,000 quarterly). Turnover £130,000 to year end Dec 05.

Southampton Asian Christian Outreach, International Christian Centre, St Mary's Road, Southampton SO14 0BB
☎023 8043 5455
E: clivethorne@saco.freeserve.co.uk
Web: www.saco.freeserve.co.uk
Support services for young people aged 18 plus.
Senior full-time worker: Mr K S Rajo. Executive staff 2. **CC** No.290183. Began 1984; interdenominational. No magazine. Turnover n/a.

†Turkish Christian Fellowship, Woodberry Down Baptist Church, 190 Varty Road, London N15 6RA
☎020 8802 9637 M: 07751 930 066
🖷020 8802 3323
E: tim.spring@blueyonder.co.uk
Reaching Turkish-speaking people groups with the Gospel; practical help with translation/advice.
Contact Person: Mr T R Spring. staff 8. **CC** No.246010. Began 1992; Baptist. No magazine. Turnover n/a.

†UK Asian Christians Fellowship, 1 Fortis Way, Salendine Nook, Huddersfield HD3 3WW
☎01484 641 282 M: 07802 940 421
E: ukasianchristians@hotmail.com.uk
Raising the awareness of Asian Christians in the UK; promoting the Gospel.
General Secretary: Mr Yaoub Masih. Admin staff 1. **CC** No.1085557. Began 1986; interdenominational. No magazine. Turnover n/a.

The Well, Asian Information & Advice Centre, 48 Albert Road, Glasgow G42 8DN
☎0141 424 5223 🖷0141 422 1722
E: the.well@btinternet.com
Outreach work to Asian communities through advice; support to other Christians wishing to reach Asians.
Community Worker: Mrs Rhoda Yarmahmadi. Executive staff 2. **CC** Began 1994; Church of Scotland. No magazine. Turnover n/a.

FAMILY CARE & SUPPORT AGENCIES

See also Marriage Ministries on Page 366.

Bethany Family Institute, PO Box 2858, Wolverhampton WV3 0XL
☎01902 621 594 🖷01902 621 594
E: elizabethdavies@bethanyfamilyinstitute.com
Web: www.bethanyfamilyinstitute.com
Resourcing family spirituality and ministry through networking, publishing, seminars and developing adult formation.
Co-Director: Ms Elizabeth Davies. Executive staff 2. Began 2000; Roman Catholic. Magazine: *Just Between Us* (200 quarterly). Turnover £4,000 to year end Mar 05.

***Fiona Bruce & Co Solicitors,** Justice House, 3 Grappenhall Road, Stockton Heath, Warrington WA4 2AH
☎01925 263 273 🖷01925 217 077
E: rbruce@fionabruce.co.uk
Web: www.fionabruce.co.uk
Advising families, individuals, businesses, churches and charities on all aspects of the law.
Practice Development Manager: Mr Richard Bruce. *Managing Partner:* Mrs Fiona Bruce. *Head of Family Law:* Mr Stephen Hayes. Executive staff 12, Admin staff 18. Began 1988; non-denominational. No magazine. Turnover £1,000,000 to year end Mar 06.

***Care for the Family,** Garth House, Leon Avenue, Cardiff CF15 7RG
☎029 2081 0800 🖷029 2081 4089
E: mail@cff.org.uk
Web: www.careforthefamily.org.uk
Providing family support nationally through seminars, workshops, resources, special events, media work and advice.
Director: Rev Jonathan Booth. *Executive Director:* Mr Rob Parsons. *Assistant Director:* Mr Bob Jones. Executive staff 6, Other staff 90. **CC** No.1066905. Began 1988; interdenominational. Magazine: *CARE for the Family* (60,000 every four months). Turnover £3,000,000 to year end Dec 04.

†Catholic Children's Society (Dioceses of Arundel and Brighton, Portsmouth and Southwark), 49 Russell Hill Road, Purley CR8 2XB
☎020 8668 2181
🖷020 8763 2274
E: info@cathchild.org
Web: www.cathchild.org
Working with families through adoption including special needs, fostering, counselling and community and homelessness projects.
Director: Mr T Connor. *Deputy Director:* Mrs Anne Burnage. *Publicity and Fundraising Manager:* Mr Michael McLoughlin. Executive staff 5, Other staff 170. **CC** No.233296. Began 1887; Roman Catholic. Magazine: *Child* (42,000 half-yearly). Turnover £4,346,083 to year end Mar 00.

Cheer Trust, 23 Calbourne Road, London SW12 8LW
☎020 8673 1493 🖷020 8265 3775
E: admin@cheertrust.org
Web: www.cheertrust.org
Extending Christian comfort, hope, encouragement and empathy to those parenting alone.
Director: Mrs Cherie Colman. Executive staff 1, Admin staff 1. Began 1997; interdenominational. No magazine. Turnover n/a.

***Christian Family Concern,** 42 South Park Hill Road, South Croydon CR2 7YB
☎020 8688 0251 🖷020 8686 7114
E: info@christianfamilyconcern.org.uk
Web: www.christianfamilyconcern.org.uk
Day-nursery, bedsit schemes for lone parents with young children, young people.
Chief Executive: Mr Leslie Hillier. Executive staff 1, Other staff 30. **CC** No.279962. Began 1893; interdenominational. No magazine. Turnover £540,000 to year end Mar 05.

Church Welfare Association, 15 Marina Court, Alfred Street, Bow, London E3 2BH
☎No telephone
Assisting single mothers and their children through Christian social work organisations by grant aid.
Secretary: Mr D J Boddington. No full-time staff. **CC** No.209992. Began 1851; Anglican. (Previously Church Moral Aid Association). No magazine. Turnover n/a.

Churches Together for Families, Church House, Great Smith Street, London SW1P 3NZ
☎020 7898 1000 🖷020 7898 1431
Web: www.churchesandfamilies.org
Encouraging development of family life education programmes ecumenically and within member denominations.
Secretary: Mrs Sue Burridge. No full-time staff. ***CC*** No.293389. Began 1981; ecumenical. (Previously Family Life Education Ecumenical Project). No magazine. Turnover n/a.

Concern For Family and Womanhood, Springfield House, Chedworth, Cheltenham GL54 4AH
☎01285 720 454
Web: www.cfw.org.uk
Preserving the value of different sex roles and marriage in accordance with the Bible.
Chairman: Mr David W Stayt. No full-time staff. ***CC*** No.291323. Began 1985; interdenominational. No magazine. Turnover £10,000 to year end Apr 00.

***Divorce Care**, 3 Grange Road, Erdington, Birmingham B24 0DG
☎0121 681 6855
Web: www.divorcecare.org
Providing biblically-based support group and church-run programme for people separated or going through divorce.
Representative: Name not supplied. Staff n/a. Began 1994; interdenominational. Linked to Growing Through. No magazine. Turnover n/a.

†Family & Relationships Crisis Centre, 1st Floor Voluntary Resources Centre, 15 New Bedford Road, Luton LU1 1SA
☎01582 724 844 🖷01582 724 890
E: admin@thefrcc.org.uk
Empowering individuals and families broken by family crisis through a range of social action initiatives.

Centre Director: Pastor Trevor Adams. Executive staff 5. ***CC*** No.1081088. Began 1995; non-denominational. (Previously Family Matters). No magazine. Turnover n/a.

†Family Matters Institute, The Park, Moggerhanger, Bedford MK44 3RW
☎01767 641 002 🖷01767 641 515
E: family@familymatters.org.uk
Web: www.the-park.net
Equipping leaders from church, faith community groups to support family life; focus on relationships, parenting.
Joint Directors: Mrs Ladey Adey, Dr Clifford Hill. Executive staff 1, Other staff 1. Began 1998; interdenominational. Part of CCM. No magazine. Turnover £90,000 to year end Mar 03.

Grief Share, 3 Grange Road, Erdington, Brimingham B24 0DG
☎0121 681 6855
Web: www.grief-share.org
Providing biblically-based support group and church-run programme for people going through bereavement.
Representative: Name not supplied. Staff n/a. Began 1994; interdenominational. Linked to Growing Through. No magazine. Turnover n/a.

***Healing and Empowering Lone Parents - HELP,** 2nd Floor, Spencer House, Austin Street, London E2 7NB
☎020 7012 1172 M: 07811 162 841
E: thehelp@btconnect.com
Supporting and helping lone parents.
Director: Ms Triumph Ayo-Isegun. Executive staff 1, Other staff 1. ***CC*** Began 1998; non-denominational. Magazine: *Inspire* (1,000 quarterly). Turnover £15,000 to year end Mar 03.

†*Homeless Families Centre, Gregory House, 48 Mecklenburgh Square, London WC1N 2NU
☎020 7278 3873 🖷020 7278 3873
E: hfc.1@tiscali.co.uk
Web: www.fieldlane.org.uk
Support for homeless families.
Manager: Ms Carol Joseph. Executive staff 1, Other staff 7. ***CC*** No.207493. Began 1985; non-denominational. Supported by The Field Lane Foundation. Magazine: *Inside Lane Newsletter* (Circulation & frequency n/a). Turnover included in Field Lane Foundation.

Father Hudson's Society (Archdiocese of Birmingham), Coventry Road, Coleshill, Birmingham B46 3EB
☎01675 434 000
🖷01675 434 010
E: enquiries@fatherhudsons.org.uk
Web: www.fatherhudsons.org.uk
Improving the quality of life for children, families and adults.
Director: Mr Kevin P Caffrey. *Finance Manager:* Mr Tim Bradford. *Family Placement Manager:* Mrs Lesley Malley. Executive staff 4, Admin staff 12, Other staff 150. ***CC*** No.512992. Began 1902; Roman Catholic, but serving all. (Previously Father Hudson's Homes). Magazine: *Reaching Out* (5,000 quarterly). Turnover £4,500,000 to year end Mar 05.

†St Cuthbert's Care, St Cuthbert's House, West Road, Newcastle upon Tyne NE15 7PY
☎0191 228 0111
🖷0191 228 0177
E: enquiries@stcuthbertscare.org.uk
Web: www.stcuthbertscare.org.uk
Services for children, families in crisis, people with learning disabilities, fostering, post-adoption counselling; family tracing.
Director: Mr Austin Donahoe. *Marketing Manager:* To be appointed. Executive staff 2, Other staff 250. ***CC*** No.512912. Began 1946; Roman Catholic. (Previously Catholic Care North East). Magazine: *Vision* (10,000 annually), *School Vision* (10,000 annually). Turnover £4,000,000 to year end Dec 02.
Also at: St Aidan's Presbytery, Station Road, Ashington NE63 8AD
☎01670 521 496
Also at: 40a Coniscliffe Road, Darlington DL3 7RG
☎01325 463 914

FINANCIAL SERVICES

See also Business Services on Page 326

1 Stop Insurance Consultants Ltd, Unit B2, Mill Green Business Park, Mill Green Road, Mitcham CR4 4HT
☎020 8648 8868 🖷020 8648 8868
E: sales@1stopinsurance.com
Web: www.1stopinsurance.com
Providing personal insurance consultancy for churches, charities, commercial or personal clients.
Partners: Mr Alan Hiscox, Mr Richard Hiscox. Executive staff 4, Other staff 8. Began 1982; Christian Brethren. (Previously Alan Hiscox Financial Services Partnership). No magazine. Turnover £700,000 to year end May 00.

†Allchurches Investment Management Services Ltd, Beaufort House, Brunswick Road, Gloucester GL1 1JZ
☎01452 305 958 🖷01452 311 690
Web: www.ecclesiastical.co.uk
The Amity Fund is an investment fund (OEIC) which avoids areas such as armaments and tobacco.
Chairman: Mr N Sealy. *Directors:* Mr Prescott, Mr Boswell, Mr Yates. Executive staff 2, Other staff n/a. Began 1981; non-denominational. Magazine: *Investment Watch* (Circulation n/a half-yearly). Turnover £1,272,044 to year end Dec 02.

Alpha Insurance Brokers Limited, Unit B4, Spectrum Business Centre, Anthony's Way, Rochester ME2 4NP
☎01634 296 301
🖷01634 296 305
E: alpha@alpha-insurance.com
Specialising in church and business insurance, liability including professional indemnity, household, travel.
Directors: Colin Stutton, Howard Cooke. Executive staff 2, Other staff 4. Began 2002; non-denominational. No magazine. Turnover n/a.

A.T.BELL
INSURANCE BROKERS LTD
Dedicated
an organisation you can rely on
Personal
efficiency, integrity and care
Expert
technology backed by experience
Focused
customer-led, tailored solutions
Trusted
quality cover at the right price
The Insurance Specialist for the
Christian Community
For all your church and charity related insurance needs including conference centres and youth organisations. Also a special home insurance scheme for church members from the specialist with over 30 years' experience.
Insurance in good hands
A.T. Bell Insurance Brokers Ltd
40 Croydon Road, West Wickham, Kent, BR4 9HT
T: (020) 8462 0769 F: (020) 8462 0773 E: insure@atbell.co.uk
www.atbell.co.uk www.freetime-travel-insurance.com
Authorised and Regulated by the Financial Services Authority

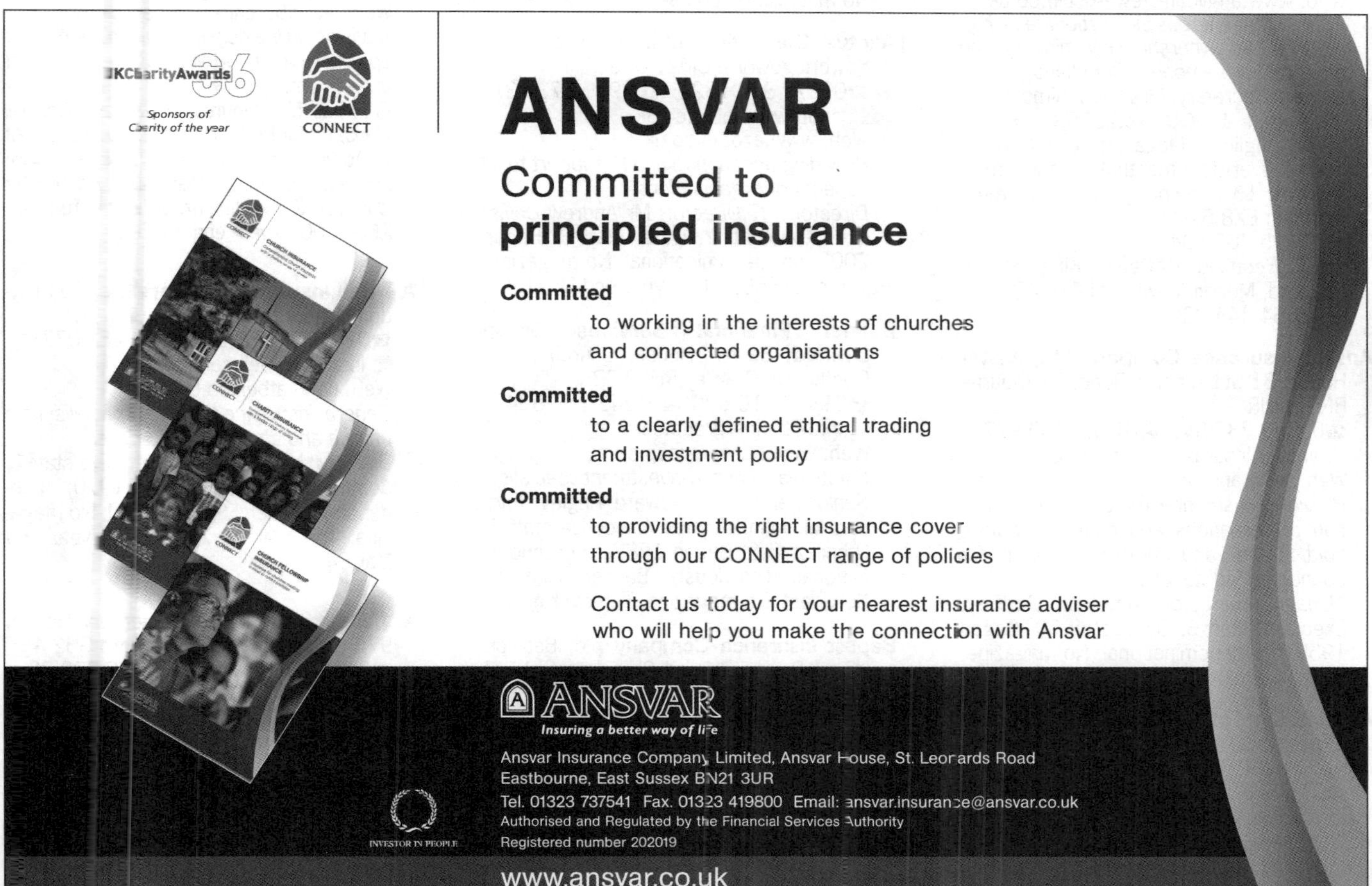
UKCharityAwards 06
Sponsors of
Charity of the year
CONNECT
ANSVAR
Committed to
principled insurance
Committed
to working in the interests of churches and connected organisations
Committed
to a clearly defined ethical trading and investment policy
Committed
to providing the right insurance cover through our CONNECT range of policies
Contact us today for your nearest insurance adviser who will help you make the connection with Ansvar
ANSVAR
Insuring a better way of life
Ansvar Insurance Company Limited, Ansvar House, St. Leonards Road
Eastbourne, East Sussex BN21 3UR
Tel. 01323 737541 Fax. 01323 419800 Email: ansvar.insurance@ansvar.co.uk
Authorised and Regulated by the Financial Services Authority
Registered number 202019
INVESTOR IN PEOPLE
www.ansvar.co.uk

S

Martin Andrews & Associates Ltd, Kings Lodge, London Road, West Kingsdown, Sevenoaks TN15 6AR
☎01474 853 777
E: enquiries@maaltd.co.uk
Web: www.maaltd.co.uk
Independent financial advisers helping people with money issues and general financial planning.
Independent Financial Adviser: Mr Martin Andrews. Executive staff 1, Other staff 2. Began 1996; interdenominational. No magazine. Turnover £160,000 to year end Dec 04.

The Anglican Stewardship Association, 71 Dee Banks, Chester CH3 5UX
☎01244 341 996 🖷01244 400 338
E: enquiries@anglican-stewardship.co.uk
Web: www.anglican-stewardship.co.uk
Promoting generous proportionate giving, responsible ownership, lay ministry and pastoral care amongst Christians.
General Secretary: Mrs Carol Sims. Executive staff 1. **CC** No.235081. Began 1964; Anglican. Magazine: *Link* (Circulation n/a every four months). Turnover n/a.
Also at: 15 Strawberry Hill, Lympstone, Exmouth EX8 5JZ
☎01395 263 804
And: Westfield Cottage, King Street, Scalford, Melton Mowbray LE14 4DW
☎01664 444 239

S

Ansvar Insurance Company Ltd, Ansvar House, 31 St Leonards Road, Eastbourne BN21 3UR
☎01323 737 541 🖷01323 430 977
E: ansvar.insurance@ansvar.co.uk
Web: www.ansvar.co.uk
Providing insurance for churches, Christian organisations and charities; household, travel and motor insurance for connected individuals.
Managing Director: Mr Paul Godfrey. Executive staff 3, Other staff 50. Began 1959; non-denominational. No magazine. Turnover n/a.

Association of Charity Independent Examiners, Bentley Resource Centre, High Street, Bentley, Doncaster DN5 0AA
☎01302 828 338 🖷01302 872 973
E: info@acie.org.uk
Web: www.acie.org.uk
Providing support, training and qualifications for independent examiners of church and charity accounts.
Senior Administrator: Mr Eric Marsden. Executive staff 1, Other staff 1. **CC** No.1077154. Began 1999; non-denominational. Magazine: *Independent Examiner* (525 every four months). Turnover £80,000 to year end Dec 05.

Association of Christian Independent Financial Advisers, c/o Martin Andrews & Associates Ltd, Kings Lodge, London Road, West Kingsdown, Sevenoaks TN15 6AR
☎01474 853 777
E: martin@maaltd.co.uk
Web: www.acifa.org.uk
Providing sound and biblical financial advice to individuals and businesses.
Chairman: Mr Martin Andrews. No full-time staff. Began 1988; interdenominational. No magazine. Turnover n/a.

†Azotus Consulting Ltd, 44 The Crest, Sawbridgeworth CM21 0ES
☎01279 860 182 M: 07970 673 131
E: andrew@azotus.co.uk
Web: www.azotus.co.uk
Providing accounting and IT support to all aspects of organisations.
Director / IT Director: Mr Andrew Davis. Executive staff 2, Other staff 3. Began 2000; non-denominational. No magazine. Turnover £50,000 to year end Nov 03.

Banner Financial Services Group Limited, Banner House, Church Road, Copthorne, Crawley RH10 3RA
☎01342 710 600 🖷01342 712 534
E: info@bannergroup.com
Web: www.bannergroup.com
Estate planning and investment specialist.
Senior Partner: Mr Howard Tingley. *Partner:* Mr John R Jones. Executive staff 2, Other staff 3. Began 1987; interdenominational. (Previously Banner Financial Services). No magazine. Turnover n/a.

Baptist Insurance Company plc, Beaufort House, Brunswick Road, Gloucester GL1 1JZ
☎01452 334 930 🖷01452 302 226
E: enquiries@baptist-ins.com
Web: www.baptist-insurance.co.uk
Church and home insurance for Baptist churches and their members in the UK.
General Manager: To be appointed. *Assistant General Manager:* Mr A J Green. Executive staff 2, Other staff 2. Began 1905; Baptist. No magazine. Turnover £2,600,000 to year end Dec 05.

Baptist Union Corporation Ltd, Baptist House, 129 Broadway, Didcot OX11 8RT
☎01235 517 700 🖷01235 517 7[illegible]5
E: buc.corp@baptist.org.uk
Web: www.baptist.org.uk
Trusteeships of Baptist properties, administering the Baptist Union Loan Fund and covenant scheme.
Manager: Mrs Linda Holder. *Loan Fund Officer:* Mr Rob Bruce. Executive staff 2, Other staff 5. **CC** No.249635. Began 1890; Baptist. No magazine. Turnover £1,409,724 to year end Dec 05.

†Barchester Green Investment, Barchester House, 45 Catherine Street, Salisbury SP1 2DH
☎01722 331 241 🖷01722 414 19[illegible]
E: info@barchestergreen.co.uk
Web: www.barchestergreen.co.uk
Advising on life pensions and investments; specialising in ethical implications of investment.
Principal: Mr Geoffrey W Griffiths. *General Manager:* Mr Rodney Palmer. Executive staff 2, Admin staff 4, Advisors 7. Began 1[illegible]5; non-denominational. Magazine: *Barchester Chronicle* (Circulation n/a annually). Turnover £620,000 to year end Apr 02.

***A T Bell Insurance Brokers Ltd,** 40 Croydon Road, West Wickham BR4 9HT
☎020 8462 0769 🖷020 8462 077[illegible]
E: insure@atbell.co.uk
Web: www.atbell.co.uk
General insurance broking, specialising in church and charity-related risks.
Director: Mr Peter Bell. Executive staff [illegible], Admin staff 9. Began 1970; non-denominational. FSA regulated. No magazine. Turnover £2,706,9[illegible]0 to year end Mar 04.

A J Bennewith & Co, Hitherbury House, 97 Portsmouth Road, Guildford GU2 4[illegible]
☎01483 539 777 M: 07808 093 80[illegible]
🖷01483 576 235
E: tony@bennewith.co.uk
Christian chartered accountancy practice offering audit and independent examination services. Charitable Trust available for fees.
Principal: Mr Tony Bennewith. *Manager:* Mrs Heather Cheesman. Executive staff [illegible], Admin staff 1. Began 1986; non-denominational. No magazine. Turnover £400,000 to year end Sep 05.

***Cansdales**, Bourbon Court, Nightingales Corner, Little Chalfont, Amersham HP7 9QS ☎01494 765 428 🖷01494 541 803 E: david@cansdales.co.uk Web: www.cansdales.co.uk
Chartered accountants, business adviser, registered auditor serving charities, churches, businesses of all sizes and individuals.
Senior Partner: Mr David Stephenson. *Partner:* Mr Nick Evans. *Consultant:* Mr John Clarke. Executive staff 5, Other staff 21. Began 1935; non-denominational. (Previously Cansdales & Co). Magazine: *Spotlight Newsletter* (3,000 occasionally). Turnover £1,100,000 to year end Apr 05.

CCLA Investment Management Ltd, 80 Cheapside, London EC2V 6DZ ☎020 7489 6010 🖷020 7489 6126 E: clientservice@ccla.co.uk Web: www.ccla.co.uk
Providing investment, property fund management services for churches/charities through investment funds and cash management.
Chief Executive Officer: Mr Andrew Gibbs. Executive staff 10, Other staff 80. Began 1987; Anglican. (Previously Central Board of Finance of Church of England Investment Office). Authorised and regulated by the Financial Services Authority. No magazine. Turnover n/a.

Central Finance Board of the Methodist Church, 9 Bunhill Street, London EC2A 4PE ☎020 7496 3630 🖷020 7496 3631 E: admin@cfbmethodistchurch.org.uk
Established under the Methodist Church Funds Act 1960 as investment body of the Methodist Church.
Relationship Manager: Bill Lane. Staff 17. **CC** Began 1960; Methodist. No magazine. Turnover n/a.

Peter Chalk & RPP Taxation Services Ltd, PO Box 6607, Grantham NG31 7NR ☎01476 591 333 M: 07880 745 814 🖷01476 577 733 E: peter@peterchalkcc.co.uk Web: www.peterchalkco.co.uk
Providing specialist clergy taxation services and general personal tax compliance and planning.
Managing Director: Mr Peter Chalk. *Hon Consultant:* Rev Frank Chalk. Executive staff 2, Other staff 3. Began 1987; ecumenical. No magazine. Turnover £180,000 to year end Mar 03.

Christian Ethical Investment Group, 1 St George's Close, Leighton Buzzard LU7 1ZX ☎01525 630 097 E: info@ceig.org Web: www.ceig.org
Promoting debate and the development of vigorous ethical investment policies within all Christian churches.
Chair: Mr Gavin Oldham. *Secretary:* Mr Stephen Dunham. No full-time staff. Began 1988; ecumenical. No magazine. Turnover n/a.

***Christian Insurance Services,** 28 Sutton Street, Durham DH1 4DA ☎0191 384 0934 🖷0191 386 8858 E: sales@christian-insurance.co.uk Web: www.christian-insurance.co.uk
Providing home, motor, personal, travel, commercial insurance for individuals, churches and Christian businesses.
Senior Partner: Mr David McHarry. *Partner:* Mrs Julie Wilson. *Office Manager:* Mr Kevin Wilson. Executive staff 2, Admin staff 5. Began 1994; non-denominational. Regulated by the FSA. No magazine. Turnover £1,600,000 to year end Jun 03.

Christians Against Poverty, Jubilee Mill, North Street, Bradford BD1 4EW ☎01274 760 726 🖷01274 760 745 E: info@capuk.org Web: www.capuk.org
Helping people out of debt, showing God's love in action; debt counselling, budgeting, insolvency services.
Charity Director: Mr John Kirkby. *Operations Director:* Mr Matt Barlow. *Chairman:* Mr Robert Clarkson. Executive staff 6. **CC** No.1097217. Began 1996; non-denominational. Magazine: *Christians Against Poverty News* (20,000 yearly). Turnover £830,000 to year end May 02.

S

Church of England Pensions Board, 29 Great Smith Street, Westminster, London SW1P 3PS
☎020 7898 1800
🖷020 7898 1801
E: enquiries@cepb.c-of-e.org.uk
Pensions, retirement housing for clergy, nursing care home; pension schemes for layworkers.
Secretary: Mr Shaun Farrell. Admin staff 50, Other staff (homes) 240. ***CC*** No.236627. Began 1926; Anglican. No magazine. Turnover n/a.

Church of Scotland General Trustees, 121 George Street, Edinburgh EH2 4YN
☎0131 225 5722
🖷0131 240 2246
E: gentrustees@cofscotland.org.uk
Web: www.churchofscotland.org.uk
Statutory corporation administering trust property and funds, with ancillary duties as directed by General Assembly.
Secretary and Clerk: Mr David D Robertson. *Deputy Secretary:* Mr Tim Parker. Executive staff 4, Admin staff 13. ***CC*** No.SCO 14574. Began 1921; Church of Scotland. No magazine. Turnover n/a.

Church of Scotland Stewardship and Finance Committee, 121 George Street, Edinburgh EH2 4YN
☎0131 225 5722
🖷0131 220 3113
E: stewardship@cofscotland.org.uk
Web: www.churchofscotland.org.uk
Promoting Christian stewardship and providing financial management throughout the Church of Scotland.
General Treasurer: Mr Iain W Grimmond. *Director of Stewardship:* Rev Gordon D. Jamieson. Staff 35. ***CC*** No.SCO 11353. Began n/a; Church of Scotland. (Previously Church of Scotland Board of Stewardship and Finance). No magazine. Turnover n/a.

Congregational & General Insurance plc, Currer House, Currer Street, Bradford BD1 5BA
☎01274 700 700
🖷01274 370 754
E: c&gi@congregational.co.uk
Web: www.congregational.co.uk
General insurance for churches and private houses, including manses.
Marketing Controller: Mr Simon M Dickerson. *Technical Director:* Mr Martin Scott. *Head of Finance:* Mrs Maria Bell. Executive staff 4, Other staff 55. Began 1891; United Reformed / Congregational. No magazine. Turnover £18,830,000 to year end Mar 05.

†Courtiers Financial Services Ltd and Courtiers Investment Services Ltd, 18a Hart Street, Henley-on-Thames RG9 2AU
☎01491 578 368
🖷01491 572 294
E: phillip.manning@courtiers.co.uk
Web: www.courtiers.co.uk
Pensions, investment, ISAs, life assurance, mortgage advice to companies, individuals and charities.
Director: Mr Phillip Manning. Executive staff 2, Other staff 20. Began 1982; non-denominational. Regulated by the PIA. Magazine: *Courtiers Financial Review* (5,500 quarterly). Turnover £1,000,000 to year end Mar 99.

***Credit Action,** Howard House, The Point, Weaver Road, Lincoln LN6 3QN
☎01522 699 777
🖷01522 697 703
E: office@creditaction.org.uk
Web: www.creditaction.org.uk
Teaching all aspects of personal money management through preaching, seminars and books; using biblical principles.
National Director: Mr Keith Tondeur. Executive staff 2, Other staff 4. ***CC*** No.1106941. Began 1988; non-denominational. No magazine. Turnover £423,000 to year end Mar 05.

The Dove Trust, PO Box 92, Dereham NR20 4WD
☎0845 130 3683
🖷01362 686 208
E: keith@dovetrust.com
Web: www.charitygiving.co.uk
Offering one-stop service for tax-efficient giving to charity; Gift Aid, share giving, sponsorship advice.
Trustee: Mr Keith Colman. *Charity & Development Manager:* Mrs Gill Perks. Executive staff 2, Admin staff 1. ***CC*** No.287401. Began 1982; non-denominational. No magazine. Turnover £513,718 to year end Mar 03

†Ecclesiastical Insurance Group plc, Beaufort House, Brunswick Road, Gloucester GL1 1JZ
☎01452 528 533
🖷01452 423 557
Web: www.ecclesiastical.co.uk
Property insurance, life assurance, pensions and unit trusts for churches, charities, commerce and individuals.
Managing Director: Mr G V Doswell. Executive staff 7, Other staff 8[illegible]9. Began 1887; non-denominational. Magazine: *Policy Profile* (Circulation n/a half-yearly). Turnover £[illegible]33,6[illegible]0,000 to year end Dec 02.

Ecumenical Council for Corporate Responsibility (ECCR), PO Box 5[illegible]0, Oxford OX1 1ZL
☎01865 245 349
E: info@eccr.org.uk
Web: www.eccr.org.uk
Research and engagement on the social responsibility of companies, linking values, investments and partners world-wide.
Coordinator: Mr Miles Litvinoff. No full-time staff. Began 1989; ecumenical. Magazine: *ECCR Bulletin* (200 quarterly). Turnover n/a.

S

Epworth Investment Management Limited, 9 Bunhill Street, London EC2A 4PE
☎020 7496 3636 📠020 7496 3637
E: admin@epworthinvestment.co.uk
Providing investment management services to churches and registered UK charities
Relationship Manager: Bill Lane. Staff 17. Began 1995; Methodist but open to all. Regulated by the FSA. Linked to Central Finance Board of the Methodist Church. No magazine. Turnover n/a.

Finance Division of the Archbishops' Council Church House, Great Smith Street, Westminster, London SW1P 3NZ
☎020 7898 1795 📠020 7898 1558
E: gill.laver@c-of-e.org.uk
Web: www.cofe.anglican.uk
Finance and central services Division of the Archbishops' Council of the Church of England
Director of Finance and Central Services: Mrs Gill Laver. Staff 100. ***CC*** Began n/a; Anglican. Magazine: *Annual report* (Circulation n/a annually). Turnover £40,000 to year end Mar 02.
Note: each Diocese has a Secretary and Accountant. Contact them via the appropriate Diocesan Office

***Flowers McEwan Ltd,** The Coach House, 75 Allerton Hill, Chapel Allerton, Leeds LS7 3QB
☎0113 237 1979 M: 07976 432 381
📠0113 237 1118
E: info@flowersmcewan.co.uk
Web: www.flowersmcewan.co.uk
Fee-only financial planning and asset management from a biblically-based perspective.
Directors: Mr David S Flowers, Mr Murray McEwan. Executive staff 2, Other staff 2. Began 2001; interdenominational. (Previously Ronald Blue & Co UK Ltd). Regulated by the FSA. No magazine. Turnover £200,000 to year end Jan 05.

Free from Debt, Bethel, 24 Wilton Drive, Collier Row, Romford RM5 3TJ
☎01708 750 093
E: post@freefromdebt.org.uk
Web: www.freefromdebt.org.uk
Providing debt and insolvency advice and assistance.
Insolvency Practitioner: Mr Mike Reeves. Executive staff 4, Other staff 3. Began 1989; non-denominational. (Previously Debt Solutions). No magazine. Turnover n/a.

David Gee Management Services Ltd, Heathend Court, Wotton-under-Edge GL12 8AS
☎01454 299 445 📠01454 299 443
E: mail@dgms-ltd.co.uk
Independent advice on investment, mortgage and retirement planning; specialist advisors to clergy.
Directors: Mr & Mrs David & Lynne Gee, Samuel Gee. Executive staff 3, Other staff 2. Began 1974; non-denominational. (Previously DGMS partnership). No magazine. Turnover n/a.

Griffin Stone, Moscrop & Co, 41 Welbeck Street, London W1G 8EA
☎020 7935 3793 📠020 7486 8705
E: mail@gsmaccountants.co.uk
Web: www.gsmaccountants.co.uk
Chartered accountants and registered auditors providing a comprehensive service to businesses, charities, trusts, individuals.
Senior Partner: Mr Geoffrey Hill. Partners 5, Other staff 19. Began 1920; inter-denominational. No magazine. Turnover n/a.

†Peter Hannaford & Co, 1556 Stratford Road, Hall Green, Birmingham B28 9HA
☎0121 733 8886 📠0121 733 8887
E: info@PHandCo.co.uk
Web: www.PHandCo.co.uk
Accountants, registered auditors and tax advisors specialising in small and medium-sized businesses and charities.
Principal: Mr Peter J Hannaford. Executive staff 4. Began 1986; non-denominational. No magazine. Turnover n/a.

***Impact Giving UK Trust,** PO Box 140, Unsworth, Bury BL8 9AH
☎0161 796 5682
E: info@impactgiving.org.uk
Web: www.impactgiving.org.uk
Helping individuals to maximise their giving using Gift Aid.
Director: Mr Shane McNicol. Executive staff 1, Other staff 1. ***CC*** No.296834. Began 1986; non-denominational. No magazine. Turnover £1,200,000 to year end Sep 02.

Independent Examiners Ltd, Revelation Centre, Spur Road, Chichester PO19 8PR
☎01243 775 585/537 323 (helpline)
📠01243 775 855
E: support@independentexaminers.co.uk
Web: www.independentexaminers.co.uk
Providing account preparation and examination, Gift Aid, new charity helpline, health check, training.
Director: Mr D F Martin. Executive staff 2, Admin staff 18. Began 1997; interdenominational. Magazine: *The Examiner* (3,000 half-yearly). Turnover n/a.

†Jacob, Cavenagh & Skeet, 5 Robin Hood Lane, Sutton SM1 2SW
☎020 8643 1166 📠020 8643 3467
E: jcs@jcssutton.co.uk
Web: www.jcssutton.co.uk
Assisting family companies and Christian charities with accountancy and taxation matters.
Managing Partner: Mr Andrew Hazael. Executive staff 4, Other staff 45. Began 1927; non-denominational. Magazine: *Journal* (Circulation n/a monthly). Turnover £1,750,000 to year end Mar 03.

S

***Kingdom Bank Ltd**, Ruddington Fields Business Park, Mere Way, Ruddington, Nottingham NG11 6JS
☎0115 921 7250 🖷0115 921 7251
E: info@kingdombank.co.uk
Web: www.kingdombank.co.uk
Deputy Chief Executive: Mr Chris Sheldon. *Director, Savings and Mortgages:* Martin Jessop. *Director, Insurance:* Brian Exall. Executive staff 3, Admin staff 7, Non-executive board 7. ***CC*** Began 1954; Assemblies of God but open to all. (Previously Assemblies of God Property Trust) Turnover £2,129,072 to year end Dec 04. Specialising in ethical savings accounts and mortgage finance for Churches and charities; insurance brokers.

†Kingsworld Walder Ltd, Suite 2, Lansdowne Road, 17 Holdenhurst Road, Bournemouth BH8 8EW
☎01202 467 700 🖷01202 467 736
E: moneymatters@kingsworld.co.uk
Web: www.kingsworld.co.uk
Helping Christians be good stewards; financial, investment, pensions and tax advice; schemes for Christian organisations.
Managing Director: Mr Jeffrey Martina. Executive staff 4, Other staff 10. Began 1979; non-denominational. No magazine. Turnover n/a.

The Kubernesis Partnership, 36 Acomb Wood Drive, York YO24 2XN
☎01904 788 885 🖷01904 339 117
E: info@kubernesis.co.uk
Web: www.kubernesis.co.uk
Training and consultancy in charity finance, charity law and fundraising.
Chief Executive: Dr Gareth G Morgan. Executive staff 2. Began 1979; interdenominational. No magazine. Turnover n/a.

†Linthurst LLP Chartered Tax Advisers, 1st Floor, The Well House, Market Street, Bromsgrove B61 8DA
☎01527 870 748 🖷01527 870 972
E: tax@linthurst.co.uk
Web: www.linthurst.co.uk
Providing business and personal tax advice, including preparation of ministers' tax returns.
Partners: Mr Iain Martin, Mrs Barbara Forbes. Executive staff 2, Admin staff 1. Began 1990; non-denominational. No magazine. Turnover £104,000 to year end Jan 01.

†AA Matthew & Co (Accountants & Business Consultants), 30 Woolley House, Loughborough Road, London SW9 7EH
☎020 7733 1987
M: 07947 384 530
🖷020 7733 1987
E: aamatthew@aol.com
Providing tax and accountancy services to Christian businesses, churches and organisations.
Managing Partner: Mr Matthew Okuboyejo. Executive staff 1, Other staff n/a. Began 2000; non-denominational. No magazine. Turnover n/a.

***Maxco Trust,** 57 Beacon Way, Rickmansworth WD3 7PB
☎01923 350 221
E: maxcotrust@ntlworld.com
Web: www.maxco.btinternet.co.uk
Helping Christians maximise use of tax concessions in giving from capital by gifts, loans, legacies.
Director: Dr P B Cockburn. No full-time staff. ***CC*** No.261238. Began 1970; interdenominational. No magazine. Turnover £3,592,986 to year end Dec 05.

***The Mellor Practice,** 95 North Lane, East Preston, Littlehampton BN16 1HD
☎01903 859 993
M: 07769 593 482
E: laurie.mellor@lighthousetemple.co.uk
Web: www.lighthousetemple.co.uk
Providing independent financial advice.
Senior Practice Executives: Mr & Mrs Laurie & Brenda Mellor. Executive staff 6, Admin staff 2. Began 1992; interdenominational. No magazine. Turnover £110,000 to year end Mar 05.

Methodist Insurance PLC, Brazennose House, Brazennose Street, Manchester M2 5AS
☎0161 833 9696
🖷0161 833 1287
E: enquiries@micmail.com
Web: www.methodist-insurance.co.uk
Insuring of churches, charities, schools, colleges, hotels, houses, shops, weddings, hostels, residential homes.
General Manager: Mr Ian Simpson. Executive staff 4, Other staff 26. Began 1872; Methodist. Magazine: *Methodist Matters* (Circulation & frequency n/a). Turnover £10,200,000 to year end Jun 05.

MMY Accountancy Services, Clarence House, 35 Clarence Street, Market Harborough LE16 7NE
☎01858 432 006
M: 07850 868 833
🖷01858 462 006
Public accountants and taxation advisers serving small/medium sized businesses: accounts, VAT, PAYE, bookkeeping.
Principal: Mr Mans Yousuf. Executive staff 4, Admin staff 1. Began 1977; evangelical. No magazine. Turnover n/a.

The Moss Charitable Trust, 7 Church Road, Parkstone, Poole BH14 8UF
☎01202 730 002
🖷01202 730 002
E: pmalpas@aol.com
Receiving Gift Aid income and legacies and distributing as contributors request. External applications not considered.
Correspondent: Mr Peter D Malpas. Executive staff 1. ***CC*** No.258031. Began 1965; non-denominational. No magazine. Turnover £96,365 to year end Apr 0[illegible]

MR Associates, 19 Wemyss Court, Leapmoor Drive, Wemyss Bay PA18 [illegible]BF
☎01475 522 962 M: 0796[illegible] 963 8[illegible]6
E: info@mrassociates.org.uk
Web: www.mrassociates.org.uk
Offering specialist advice and assistance for accommodation-based schemes providing support to vulnerable adults.Supported Housing Advisor: Mr Mark Rodgers. Executive staff 2, Admin staff 1. Began 2000; interdenominational. No magazine. Turnover n/a.

***Palm Services,** PO Box 199, Bognor Regis PO21 4PB
☎01243 263 717 M: 07815 053 0[illegible]
🖷01243 266 389
E: info@palmservices.org
Web: www.palmservices.org
Providing Gift Aid and related services to the charity sector.
Director: Mr Peter Martin. Executive staff 2. Began 2000; interdenominational. No magazine. Turnover £20,300 to year end Apr 02.

†Paradigm Capital Management Limited, 30 Queen Charlotte Street, Bristol BS[illegible] 4HJ
☎0117 9200 100 🖷0117 9200 101
E: enquiries@paradigmcm.co.uk
Web: www.paradigmcm.co.uk
Serving Christians who are seeking to invest their wealth based on biblical principles.
Managing Director: Mr Barry Horne. *Senior Client Manager:* Mr Richard Chil[illegible] *Business Development Manager:* Mr Ia[illegible] Morrison. Executive staff 3, Admin staff [illegible] Other staff 5. Began 200[illegible]; non-denominational. No magazine. Turnover £500,000 to year end Mar 02.

S

***Quantock Christian Trust,** 9 Rosary Drive, Bridgwater TA6 7JS
☎01278 455 596
E: johnelford@aol.com
Trust for evangelical purposes, receiving Gift Aid income and distributing donors' contributions as requested.
Administrator: Mr John Elford. Executive staff 1, Other staff 1. ***CC*** No.293349. Began 1985; non-denominational. No magazine. Turnover £245,000 to year end Mar 05.

Rechabite Friendly Society, School House, 14 Byrom Street, Manchester M3 4RB
☎0161 832 4821 🖷0161 839 1725
E: enquiries@healthyinvestment.co.uk
Web: www.healthyinvestment.co.uk
Teetotallers and temperate drinkers Friendly Society; alcohol and drug re-education.
Chief Executive: Mr William Turnbull. Executive staff 2, Admin staff 11. Began 1835; interdenominational. (Previously Independent Order of Rechabites). Magazine: *Rechabite News and Views* (5,000 quarterly). Turnover £354,000 to year end Dec 02.

S

Reliance Bank Ltd, Faith House, 23 Lovat Lane, London EC3R 8EB
☎020 7398 5400 🖷020 7398 5401
E: info@reliancebankltd.com
Web: www.reliancebankltd.com
Commercial bank providing full range of services; profits are donated to The Salvation Army.
Managing Director: Mr Gerald Birkett. *Banking Manager:* Mr Michael Meads. Executive staff 20, Others staff n/a. Began 1900; non-denominational. No magazine. Turnover £1,200,000 [taxable profit] to year end Mar 03.

Ross & Co Financial Services, 14 Ludlow Drive, Thame OX9 3XS
☎01844 261 400 🖷01844 261 345
E: mary.ross@rossand.co.uk
All general insurances: household, church, office, motor, travel.
Partner: Mary Ross. Executive staff 2, Other staff 3. Began 1978; interdenominational. No magazine. Turnover n/a.

Solomon's, Elm House, 35 Elm Road, New Malden KT3 3HB
☎08000 736 273
🖷020 8949 5678
E: info@planetsolomons.com
Web: www.planetsolomons.com
Ethical fee-only IFA providing services to individuals, businesses and charities; mortgages, pensions, investments, protection.
Principal: Mr Dominic Thomas. Executive staff 1, Admin staff 3. Began 1999; ecumenical. Turnover n/a.

Southgate Financial Services Ltd, Independence House, 70 Ness Road, Shoeburyness, Southend-on-Sea SS3 9DG
☎01702 298 444
M: 07941 104 114
🖷01702 298 666
E: mail@ifa.cc
Web: www.ifa.cc
Providing fee-based financial and investment planning for private clients.
Managing Director: Mr David Tickett. *Consultant:* Mr Brian Rankin. Executive staff 2, Admin staff 3. Began 1997; non-denominational. No magazine. Turnover £150,000 to year end Aug 05.

†*Caladine Stevens Ltd, 1 The Avenue, Eastbourne BN21 3YA
☎01323 644 579
🖷01323 417 643
E: john@caladine.co.uk
Web: www.caladine.co.uk
Accounts, audits, independent examinations, ministers' tax returns, charity formations and IT consultancy.
Director: Mr John Caladine. *Charity Manager:* Mrs Anne Ford. Executive staff 5, Admin staff 5. Began 1989; interdenominational. No magazine. Turnover £350,000 to year end Mar 05.

***Stewardship,** PO Box 99, Loughton IG10 3QJ
☎0845 262 627 🖷020 8502 5333
E: enquiries@stewardship.org.uk
Web: www.stewardship.org.uk
Giving agency and provider of services helping churches/charities with legal and financial administration.
Chief Executive: Mr David C Jones. Executive staff 4, Other staff 32. ***CC*** No.234714. Began 2004 merger of Sovereign Giving with Stewardship Services; non-denominational. Magazine: *Stewardship* (28,000 three times a year). Turnover £30,600,000 to year end Sept 04.

†Tax Management for Clergy, PO Box 6621, Grantham NG32 3SX
☎01476 514 652 M: 07748 133 791
🖷01476 514 654
E: enquiries@clergytaxuk.com
Web: www.clergytaxuk.com
Providing a nationwide service to clergy of all denominations on tax and financial matters.
Managing Director: Mrs Muriel Moreton. *Director:* Mr Martin Bowler. Executive staff 6, Admin staff 4. Began 2000; interdenominational. No magazine. Turnover £350,000 to year end Mar 03.

Trustees for Methodist Church Purposes, Central Buildings, Oldham Street, Manchester M1 1JQ
☎0161 236 5194
Custodian trustee of Methodist real property and investments.
Secretary: Rev Kenneth E Street. Executive staff 2, Other staff 9. ***CC*** Began 1866; Methodist. No magazine. Turnover n/a.

Wakeling Partnership, 95 Ham Park Road, London E15 4AD
☎020 8519 7978 M: 07956 300 344
E: info@wakelingpartnership.co.uk
Web: wakelingpartnership.co.uk
Providing charity accounts examination and taxation services for Christian workers.
Manager: Mr Mark Wakeling. No full-time staff. Began 1997; non-denominational. No magazine. Turnover £15,000 to year end May 03.

S

Max Willey & Co, 13a Fish Hill, Holt NR25 6HN
☎01263 711 771 🖷01263 711 709
E: max-willey@lineone.net
Solicitors dealing with charity law (including for churches), conveyancing, wills, probate, personal tax.
Proprietor: Mr Max Willey. Executive staff 1, Other staff 2. Began 1993; non-denominational. No magazine. Turnover n/a.

M Wood Insurance Services Ltd, 68 Llandaff Road, Canton, Cardiff CF11 9NL
☎08451 303 035 🖷029 2034 0546
E: enquiries@woodinsurance.co.uk
Web: www.woodinsurance.co.uk
All types of general insurances including special motor and household schemes for Christians.
Managing Director: Mr Michael Wood. Executive staff 1, Other staff 28. Began 1981; non-denominational. (Previously Wood Insurance Group). No magazine. Turnover £5,000,000 to year end Dec 97.
Also at: 115 Oxford Street, Pontycymmer, Bridgend CF32 8DE
☎0845 130 3034

***WRS Limited Insurance Brokers**, Cadman House, Peartree Road, Stanway, Colchester CO3 0NW
☎01206 760 780 🖷01206 760 [illegible]4
E: enquiries@wrsinsurance.co.uk
Web: www.wrsinsurance.co.uk
General insurance brokers offering a personal service to individuals, churches, charities, care homes.
Director: Mr Chris Chapman. *Chairman:* Mr Tony Hughes. Executive staff 2, Other staff 6. Began 1966; non-denominational. Authorised and Regulated by the Financial Services Authority. No magazine. Turnover £2,500,000 to year end Mar [illegible].

FURNISHINGS, FABRIC & CHURCH INTERIORS

See also Buildings & Church Design on Page 324.

Alpha Supplies, 64 London End, Beaconsfield HP9 2JD
☎01494 676 060 M: 07768 517 045
🖷01494 678 181
E: info@alpha-furnishing.co.uk
Web: www.alpha-furnishing.co.uk
Retailing quality furniture for churches, schools.
Managing Director: Mr Phil MacInnes. Executive staff 4, Other staff 6. Began 1997; interdenominational. Turnover £1,500,000 to year end Aug 05.

Avon Silversmiths Ltd, 39 Augusta Street, Hockley, Birmingham B18 6JA
☎0121 604 2121 🖷0121 604 2121
E: des@church-silver.co.uk
Web: www.church-silver.co.uk
Manufacturing church plate, chalices, communion sets, medals, silver and gold jewellery.
Chief Executive: Mr Desmond McCarthy. Executive staff 1, Other staff 5. Began 1994; interdenominational. Turnover n/a.

S

†Yvonne Bell, 44 Oakley Road, Shirley, Southampton SO16 4LG
☎023 8077 3271 🖷023 8077 3271
E: yvonnebell@yvonnebell.co.uk
Illustrating the Gospel by painting vestments, banners, backcloths, altar cloths, icons, pictures.
Artist & Designer: Mrs Yvonne Bell. Artist 1. Began 2004; non-denominational. Turnover n/a.

†Big Tops Ltd, 128 Wilford Lane, West Bridgford, Nottingham NG2 7RL
☎0115 924 9216 🖷0115 924 9218
E: info@bigtops.co.uk
Web: www.bigtops.co.uk
Hiring marquees, big tops, chairs, stage, lights, tables for outreach.
Director: Mr John Rodmell. Executive staff 1, Other staff 3. Began 1984; non-denominational. (Previously Equipment Outreach). Turnover £350,000 to year end Dec 02.

Bolsius (UK) Ltd, PO Box 65, Pershore WR10 2BL
☎0800 1695 126 🖷0800 169 5127
E: roetmond@nl.bopsius.com or kreemers@nl.bolsius.com
Web: www.hoogeland-kristen.nl
Supplying candles of various types.
Sales Manager: Mr Mike Buttery. Executive staff 2. Began 1984; non-denominational. Turnover £3,000,000 to year end Apr 05.

Chancellor's Church Furnishings, Rivernook Farm, Sunnyside, Walton-on-Thames KT12 8ET
☎01932 252 736 M: 07973 139 308
🖷01932 252 736
E: antiquechurch@btconnect.com
Buying and supplying pre-1950 church furniture, fixtures and fittings, from pews to pulpits.
Proprietors: Mr Lawrence Skilling, Mr S Williams. Executive staff 1, Other staff 5. Began 1989; interdenominational. Turnover £250,000 to year end Dec 04.

†James Chase & Son (Furnishings) Ltd, 191 Thornton Road, Bradford BD1 2JT
☎01274 738 282 🖷01274 736 641
E: sales@james-chase.co.uk
Web: www.james-chase.co.uk
Supplying all types of church furniture.
Managing Director: Mr Robert Phillips. Executive staff 1, Other staff 150. Began 1931; non-denominational. Magazine: *Church Furnishings* (10,000 half-yearly). Turnover n/a.

†Christfirst Ltd, Day Lewis House, 324 Bensham Lane, Thornton Heath CR7 7EQ
☎020 8665 6996 M: 07778 804 809
🖷020 8665 6994
E: christfirst@mail.com
Manufacturing and supplying transparent acrylic furnishings for churches, schools, halls and meeting rooms.
Chief Executive: Mr Anthony Martin. Executive staff 1, Admin staff 1, Other staff 2. Began 1997; interdenominational. Turnover n/a.

†Christians in Carpets, 9 St John's Street, Wirksworth, Matlock DE4 4[illegible]R
☎01629 824 815
🖷01629 825 748
E: carpets@steveslater.go-plus.net
Web: www.slatersflooring.co.uk
Retailing and fitting carpet, smooth flooring, curtains and blinds, including for churches.
Contact: Mr Steve Slater. Executive staff 3, Other staff [illegible]. Began 1[illegible]87; interdenominational. Turnover n/a.

The Churches Purchasing Scheme Ltd, Beaufort House, Brunswick Road, Gloucester GL1 1JZ
☎0845 458 4584
🖷01452 383 621
E: sales@cpsonline.co.uk
Web: www.cpsonline.co.uk
Providing goods and services at discounted prices for churches, charities, educational establishments and associated clients.
Manager: Mr Nigel Giffin. Executive staff 3, Other staff 2. Began 19[illegible]4; interdenominational. Turnover n/a.

Christopher Dunphy Ecclesiastical Ltd, Mitre House, Spotland Stadium North Stand, Willbutts Lane, Rochdale OL11 5BE
☎01706 522 702
🖷01706 354 815
E: chris@dunphyheating.co.uk
Web: www.dunphychurchheating.co.uk
Designing, installing, maintaining, repairing, heating systems specifically for churches.
Managing Director: Mr Christopher Dunphy. *Company Secretary:* L[illegible]n Catz. Executive staff 2, Other staff n/a. Began 1972; interdenominational. (Previously Dunphy Ecclesiastical Heating). Turnover £1,750,000 to year end Dec 05.

English County Contracts, Winchester Court, Winchester Road, Brislington, Bristol BS4 3NF
☎ 0117 977 4808 M: 07808 296 201
📠 0117 977 1000
E: englishccltd@btconnect.com
Supplying and fitting church carpets, flooring and fabrics.
Directors: Mr Brian Mogford, Mr Michael Stephens. *Company Secretary:* Mrs Janet Mockford. Executive staff 2, Admin staff 2, Other staff 6. Began 1995; interdenominational. (Previously St Annes Contract Carpeting). Turnover £1,000,000 to year end Dec 02.

Charles Farris Ltd, Quarry Fields Industrial Estate, Mere, Warminster BA12 6LA
☎ 01747 861 839 📠 01747 860 934
E: sales@charlesfarris.co.uk
Web: www.charlesfarris.co.uk
Supplying candles and other requisites for Churches.
Sales Manager: Mr Alan Matthews. Executive staff 4, Other staff 20. Began 1845; non-denominational. Incorporating Ethos Candles. Turnover n/a.

Felix Design Ltd, Unit 15, Tiverton Way, Tiverton Business Park, Tiverton EX16 6SR
☎ 01884 255 420 📠 01884 242 613
E: sales@felixstaging.co.uk
Web: www.felixstaging.co.uk
Manufacturing demountable, custom-built staging rostra for use in churches.
Managing Director: Mr John Felix. Executive staff 3, Admin staff 2, Other staff 10. Began 1983; non-denominational. Turnover n/a.

Fullers Finer Furniture, The Old Coach House, 53b Rear Oxford Street, Weston-Super-Mare BS23 1TR
☎ 01934 618 111 📠 01934 618 112
E: info@fullersfinerfurniture.co.uk
Web: www.fullersfinerfurniture.co.uk
Manufacturing church furniture to clients' requirement; restoration service.
Proprietor: Mr Paul D Fuller. Executive staff 1, Other staff 3. Began 1985; interdenominational. Turnover £87,000 to year end Mar 03.

†Galgorm Group, Galgorm Industrial Estate, Fenaghy Road, Cullybackey, Ballymena BT42 1JQ
☎ 028 2564 3211 📠 028 2564 7614
E: sales@galgormgroup.com
Web www.galgorm.com
Agents for Gopack Ltd, manufacturers of church furniture.
Sales Manager: Mr Brian Mewha. Executive staff 10, Other staff 100. Began n/a; non-denominational. Turnover n/a.

Glasscraft Studios, 2 Robinson Road, High Wycombe HP13 7BL
☎ 01494 813 220 M: 07946 751 775
📠 0871 242 7382
E: bob@glasscraftstudios.co.uk
Web: www.glasscraftstudios.co.uk
Making stained glass; restoring and repairing leaded windows.
Partner: Mr Bob Jackson. Executive staff 1, Other staff 2. Began 1983; non-denominational. (Previously Bob Jackson Glasscraft). Turnover n/a.

†Goddard & Gibbs Studios Ltd, Marlborough House, Cooks Road, London E15 2PW
☎ 020 7531 5680 📠 020 8536 0300
E: sales@goddard.co.uk
Designing and manufacturing stained and decorative glass including conservation-accredited grade 5.
Managing Director: Mr Neil Maurer. *Glass Conservator:* Mr Bard Ibens. Executive staff 5, Other staff 22. Began 1868; non-denominational. Turnover £2,000,000 to year end Dec 00.

†John Hardman Studios, Lightwoods House, Lightwoods Park, Hagley Road West, Warley B67 5DP
☎ 0121 429 7609 📠 0121 420 2316
E: neil@neilphillips.co.uk
Web: www.neilphillips.co.uk
Restoring and conserving stained glass windows and interior church decoration, designing and making new windows.
Manager: Mr David P Williams. Executive staff 3, Other staff 9. Began 1838; non-denominational. Turnover n/a.

†Hayes & Finch Ltd, Hanson Road, Aintree, Liverpool L9 7BP
☎ 0151 523 6303 📠 0151 525 1246
E: sales@hfltd.com
Web: www.hfltd.com
Manufacturing candles; church furnishers and altar wine shippers.
Managing Director: Mr Simon T J Finch. Executive staff 4, Other staff 120. Began 1882; non-denominational. No magazine. Turnover n/a.
Also at: 17 Lower Trinity Street, Deritend, Birmingham B9 4AG
E: birmingham@hfltd.com
☎ 0845 450 5592 📠 0121 753 0022
And: Palace Craig Street, Whifflet, Coatbridge ML5 4RY
☎ 01236 431 116 📠 01236 431 3202
And: Front Street, Kibblesworth, Gateshead NE11 0XB
☎ 0191 410 9213 📠 0191 492 1091
And: Branch Street, Paddock, Huddersfield HD1 4JL
E: huddersfield@hfltd.com
☎ 0845 450 5594 📠 01484 432 854
And: 41 Parkhouse Street, Camberwell, London SE5 7TU
E: london@hfltd.com
☎ 0845 450 5591 📠 020 7252 5806

Juliet Hemingray Church Textiles, The Derwent Business Centre, Clarke Street, Derby DE1 2BU
☎ 01332 366 740 📠 01332 292 817
E: jh@church-textiles.co.uk
Web: www.church-textiles.co.uk
Supplying custom-made stoles, altar frontals, banners, shirts, vestments and general church furnishings.
Director: Mrs Juliet Hemingray. Executive staff 1, Other staff 9. Began 1980; interdenominational. Turnover n/a.

†Henwood Church Supplies, The Bayle, Folkestone CT20 1SQ
☎ 01303 870 652 M: 07836 325 974
E: henwood.churchsupplies@virgin.net
Web: www.henwoodchurchsupplies.co.uk
Manufacturing, restoring and supplying church silver, brassware and communion supplies.
Managing Director: Mr P J Rose. Executive staff 1, Other staff 1. Began 1921; interdenominational. (Previously Henwood Decorative Metal Studios Ltd). No magazine. Turnover £300,000 to year end Mar 03.

†IHS Camping Services Ltd, 10 Melbourne Grove, Bramley, Leeds LS13 3QX
☎ 0113 263 8368 M: 07966 445 973
📠 0113 263 8388
E: ihsoffice@bigfoot.com
Supplying camping equipment for conferences, church holidays and youth events nationwide; also retail mail order.
Director: Mr Marcus Gregg. Executive staff 4. Began 2001; interdenominational. (Previously Intent Hire Services). Turnover £75,000 to year end Nov 02.

J & M Sewing Service, 1 Charlotte Square, Newcastle upon Tyne NE1 4XF
☎ 0191 232 9589 📠 0191 230 1215
E: jandmsewing@btconnect.com
Web: jandmsewing.com
Manufacturing clerical wear and church furnishings for clergy, choirs, readers and vergers.
Administration Manager: Mr Stephen Wroe. *Partners:* Mrs J Davison, Mrs M R Waterston. Executive staff 2, Admin staff 3, Other staff 17. Began 1980; non-denominational. Turnover £750,000 to year end Jan 03.

S

†Just Jayne Sewing, 48 Shearway Business Park, Shearway Road, Folkestone CT19 4RH
☎01303 298 292 🖷01303 298 292
Designing, manufacturing, restoring, repairing vestments, altar frontals, cassocks, surplices, chasubles; choir robes made to measure.
Owner: Miss Jayne Goss. Staff 2. Began n/a; non-denominational. Turnover n/a.

†Kevin Kearney Church Supplies, 7 Skerriffe Road, Cullyhanna, Newry BT35 0JG
☎028 308 615 22 🖷028 308 683 52
E: kevinkearney@religiousarticles.co.uk
Web: www.religiousarticles.co.uk
Religious wholesalers, manufacturers, importers and distributors.
Owner: Mr Kevin Kearney. Executive staff 3. Began 1944; non-denominational. Turnover n/a.

J M Mitchell Church Supplies, Unit 2b, Follifoot Ridge Business Park, Pannal Road, Follifoot, Harrogate HG3 1DP
☎0845 458 8594 🖷0845 458 8596
E: sales@jmchurchsupplies.com
Web: www.jmchurchsupplies.com
Manufacturing/importing church items for trade and retail including silverware, brassware, furniture, communion cups.
Manager & Owner: Mr John Mitchell. Executive staff 1, Other staff 3. Began 1979; non-denominational. Turnover n/a.

Ollerton Hall Decor Services, Ollerton Hall, Knutsford WA16 8SF
☎01565 650 222 🖷01565 754 411
E: sales@ollertonhalldiscountcarpets.co.uk
Web: www.ollertonhalldiscountcarpets.co.uk
Supplying look-alike Wilton carpets, matching pew runners, hassocks, kneelers; nationwide.
Manager: Mrs Suzanne Merrells. Executive staff 1, Other staff 7. Began 1969; interdenominational. Turnover £300,000 to year end Dec 05.

†Pendle Stained Glass Ltd, 39 Burnley Road, Padiham, Burnley BB12 8BY
☎01282 772 449 🖷01282 774 775
E: david@pendlestainedglass.co.uk
Web: www.pendlestainedglass.co.uk
Specialising in design, manufacture, restoration, conservation, protection of stained glass and leaded lights.
Director: Mr David Moore. *Designer & Glass Painter:* Heike Sahner. Executive staff 2, Other staff 10. Began 1989; non-denominational. Turnover £200,000 to year end Sep 00.

Richard & Co - Carrodelta Ltd, The Former County Centre, Bourne Works, High Street, Collingbourne Ducis, Marlborough SN8 3EH
☎01264 850 445 M: 07779 421 083
🖷01264 850 666
E: sales@richardand.co.uk
Web: www.1stforfurniture.com
Supplying contract furniture (new and used) for all areas including receptions, cafés, lounges and dining rooms.
Director: Miss Terri A Dandy. *Administrator:* Mr Paul Jones. Executive staff 2. Began 1956; Anglican. Turnover £450,000 to year end Sep 02.

Rosehill Furniture Group, Brooke Court, Handforth, Wilmslow SK9 3ND
☎0161 485 1717 🖷0161 485 2727
E: sales@rosehill.co.uk
Web: www.rosehill.co.uk
Manufacturing multi-functional seating for churches, public areas, crematoria, village halls, hospitals and education.
Sales Director: Mr Mark McKenzie. Executive staff 6, Other staff 44. Began 1976; interdenominational. Turnover n/a.

St Martin Vestment Ltd, Lutton, Spalding PE12 9LR
☎01406 362 386
E: jcb@johnsplace.force9.co.uk
Producing church robes, banners, altar frontals for all denominations.
Proprietor: Rev David Hill. Executive staff 1, Other staff 4. Began 1973; non-denominational. Turnover £83,000 to year end May 04.

Vanpoulles Ltd, Telford Place, Crawley RH10 1SZ
☎01293 590 100 🖷01293 590 1[illegible]5
E: sales@vanpoulles.co.uk
Web: www.vanpoulles.co.uk
Suppling all church furnishings including candles, textiles, furniture, silver and brassware.
Managing Director: Mr Andrew Appleton. Executive staff 3, Other staff 11. Began 1908; non-denominational. Turnover n/a.

Watts & Co, 7 Tufton Street, Westminster, London SW1P 3QE
☎020 7222 7169 🖷020 7233 1130
E: enquiries@wattsandco.com
Web: www.wattsandco.com
Manufacturing and retailing ecclesiastical vestments, furnishings, textiles, embroidery and church metal work.
Director: Mr D J Gazeley. Executive staff 2, Admin staff 2, Other staff 6. Began 1875; interdenominational. Turnover n/a.

†Whytock & Reid, Sunbury House, Belford Mews, Edinburgh EH4 3DN
☎0131 226 4911 🖷0131 226 4595
Web: www.whytockandreid.com
Cabinet makers, upholsterers, interior design and furnishers supplying church furniture and requisites.
Manager, Church Department: Mr Robert Reid. Executive staff 3, Other staff 24. Began 1807; Protestant. Turnover n/a.

***Frank Wright Mundy & Co Ltd**, Copthorne House, The Broadway, Abergele LL22 7DD
☎01745 827 451 🖷01745 833 161
E: comwine@aol.com
Web: www.frankwrightmundy.com
Producing and supplying non-alcoholic communion wine and communion equipment.
Managing Director: Mr John Payne. Executive staff 3, Other staff 1. Began 1858; non-denominational. Turnover n/a.

HEALTH & HEALING ORGANISATIONS

See also Hospices on Page 46,
Counselling Organisations on Page 331.

***Acorn Christian Healing Foundation**, Whitehill Chase, High Street, Bordon GU35 0AP
☎01420 478 121
📠01420 478 122
E: info@acornchristian.org
Web: www.acornchristian.org
Resourcing the church in its practice of Christian healing, listening and reconciliation.
Director: Rev Dr Russ Parker. *Christian Listener Coordinator:* Rev Andrew Bradley. Executive staff 3, Other staff 16. ***CC*** No.1080011. Began 1983; interdenominational. (Previously Acorn Christian Foundation). Magazine: *Acorn News* (600 quarterly). Turnover £450,000 to year end Mar 05.

***Anorexia and Bulimia Care**, PO Box 173, Letchworth SG6 1XQ
☎01462 423 351
E: anorexiabulimiacare@ntlworld.com
Web: www.anorexiabulimiacare.co.uk
Providing professional training, conference resources, education, support to sufferers of eating disorders and their carers.
Contact: Dr Kate Middleton. Executive staff 2. ***CC*** No.1004468. Began 1989; non-denominational. Magazine: *Lifeline* (Circulation n/a quarterly). Turnover £8,000 to year end Dec 00.

***Breath Ministries**, Weald House, 10a High Street, Tunbridge Wells TN1 1UX
☎01892 512 520
Promoting wholeness through teaching and training; encouraging Christian healing; positive approach to complementary therapies.
Joint Leaders: Rev & Mrs John & Christine Huggett. Executive staff 2. ***CC*** No.1010802. Began 1979; interdenominational. Incorporating PACT. No magazine. Turnover £10,000 to year end Dec 02.

†Burrswood Christian Centre for Healthcare and Ministry, Burrswood, Groombridge, Tunbridge Wells TN3 9PY
☎01892 863 637/863 818 (admissions) 📠01892 863 623
E: admin@burrswood.org.uk
Web: www.burrswood.org.uk
Providing care for short-stay admissions, post-operative, palliative, respite and terminal care. Hydrotherapy, physiotherapy, counselling.
Director: Dr Michael Harper. *Chaplaincy Team Leader:* Mr Steve Clark. Executive staff 12, Other staff 140. ***CC*** No.229261. Began 1948; Anglican. The Dorothy Kerin Trust. Magazine: *Burrswood Newsletter* (4,500 every four months). Turnover £2,000,000 to year end Dec 02.

Calvary Ministries Worldwide, PO Box 372, Welwyn Garden City AL7 4ZL
☎01707 899 727
E: info@calvaryministries.org.uk
Web: www.calvaryministries.org.uk
Healing and restoration ministry for individuals and nations worldwide; also annual tours of Israel.
Leaders: Pastor Isaac Ladipo, Pastor Paul Barfett. No paid staff. Began 2004; non-denominational. No magazine. Turnover n/a.

The Cautley Trust, 95 Seabrook Road, Seabrook, Hythe CT21 5QY
☎01303 230 762 📠01303 237 447
E: cautleyhouse@compuserve.com
Web: www.cautleyhouse.org.uk
Christian centre for healing and wholeness in Canterbury diocese; accommodation, day visitors.
Director: Rev Pat Vowles. Executive staff 1, Other staff 5. ***CC*** No.802861. Began 1990; Anglican. No magazine. Turnover n/a.

Centre for Health and Pastoral Care, Holy Rood House, 10 Sowerby Road, Sowerby, Thirsk YO7 1HX
☎01845 522 580 📠01845 527 300
E: holyroodhouse@centrethirsk.fsnet.co.uk
Web: www.holyroodhouse.freeuk.com
Residential therapeutic centre for counselling retreats, creative; training courses.
Executive Directors: Revs Stanley & Elizabeth Baxter. Executive staff 4, Other staff 16. ***CC*** No.511151. Began 1982; ecumenical. (Previously North of England Christian Healing Trust). No magazine. Turnover £110,000 to year end Dec 05.

†The Christian Fellowship of Healing (Scotland), 6 Morningside Road, Edinburgh EH10 4DD
☎0131 228 6553
Offering prayer to individuals, restoring healing ministry to the Church, fostering links with medical profession.
Chaplain: Rev Jenny Williams. Executive staff 1, Other staff 1. ***CC*** No.SCO 17129. Began 1952; interdenominational. No magazine. Turnover £55,000 to year end Dec 02.

***Christian Healing Mission**, 8 Cambridge Court, 210 Shepherds Bush Road, London W6 7NJ
☎020 7603 8118/7603 0667 (prayer line) 📠020 7603 5224
E: chm@healingmission.org
Web: www.healingmission.org
Working alongside local churches in the ministry of healing and praying with individuals for healing.
Director: Rev John Ryeland. Executive staff 1, Other staff 3. ***CC*** No.1080534. Began 1948; interdenominational. No magazine. Turnover £91,000 to year end Dec 02.

***Crocus Ministries**, Jasmine Cottage, Healey, Ripon HG4 4LH
☎01765 689 559
📠01765 689 559
E: admin@crocusministries.org.uk
Web: www.crocusministries.org.uk
Providing rest, listening ears and intercession for leaders in Christian ministry; 8 centres throughout UK.
Director: Mrs Norma Heasman. Executive staff 4. ***CC*** No.1046184. Began 1995; interdenominational. No magazine. Turnover n/a.

S

Crowhurst Christian Healing Centre, The Old Rectory, Crowhurst, Battle TN33 9AD
☎01424 830 204 🖷01424 830 053
E: crowhurstrectory@btconnect.com
Web: www.crowhursthealing.co.uk
Quiet retreat for healing, rest, renewal through healing ministry of Jesus; teaching and creative courses.
Director: Peter McIntosh. Executive staff 4, Other staff 20. ***CC*** No.208738. Began 1928; Anglican but open to all. Magazine: *Crowhurst* (3,000 quarterly). Turnover £290,000 to year end Mar 04.

Deep End Ministries, 12 Cox Lane, Chessington KT9 1DE
☎020 8255 6786
E: deepend4u@talktalk.net
Teaching that Jesus heals today; through Sky TV, videos and seminars.
Coordinator: Mr Dave Pistol. Executive staff 1, No other staff. Began 1999; non-denominational. No magazine. Turnover n/a.

Divine Healing Fellowship Scotland, Braidwood Road, Crossford, Carluke ML8 5NQ
☎01555 860 716
E: christianhealing@tiscali.co.uk
Divine healing through public services, conferences and retreats, private counselling, prayer ministry; private appointments.
Resident Chaplain: Rev George Fox. Executive staff 3. ***CC*** No.SCO 12091. Began 1972; interdenominational. (Previously Braehead House Christian Healing Center). No magazine. Turnover £17,000 to year end Dec 02.

***Edinburgh International Health Centre**, Elphinstone Wing, Carberry, Musselburgh EH21 8PW
☎0131 653 6767 M: 07710 276 208
🖷0131 653 3646
E: admin@eihc.org
Web: www.eihc.org
Out-patient medical care, debriefing assessment, counselling, retreats; for missionaries, agency volunteers, UK Christian workers.
Medical Director: Dr Michael Jones. *Director Psychiatric Services:* Mrs Elizabeth Jones. Executive staff 4, Other staff 6. ***CC*** No.SCO 00948. Began 1983; interdenominational. (Previously Care for Mission). No magazine. Turnover £110,811 to year end Apr 05.

†***Ellel Ministries**, Ellel Grange, Ellel, Lancaster LA2 0HN
☎01524 751 651 🖷01524 751 738
E: info@grange.ellel.org.uk
Web: www.ellel.org
Centres for training and ministry in Christian healing and discipleship (conferences, schools, courses, retreats, resources).
International Director: Mr Peter Horrobin. *Deputy Director of Ellel Grange:* Mr Ian Coates. Executive staff 7, Other staff 135. ***CC*** No.1041237. Began 1986; non-denominational. No magazine. Turnover £1,674,700 to year end Dec 01.
Also at: Ellel Pierrepont, Frensham, Farnham GU10 3DL
E: info@pierrepont.ellel.org.uk
☎01252 794 060 🖷 01252 794 039
And: Ellel Scotland, Blairmore House, Glass, Huntly AB54 4XH
E: info@scotland.ellel.org.uk
☎01466 700 200 🖷 01466 700 205
And: Glyndley Manor, Stone Cross, Pevensey BN24 5BS
E: info@glyndley.ellel.org.uk
☎01323 440 440 🖷 01323 440 877

Ellenor Foundation, Ellenor Centre, East Hill, Dartford DA1 1SA
☎01322 221 315 🖷01322 626 503
E: head_office@ellenorfoundation.org
Web: www.ellenorfoundation.org
Hospice-at-home care to children and adults of Dartford, Gravesham and Bexley.
Chief Executive: Mrs Carol Stone. *Appeals Manager:* Mrs Linda Trew. *Medical Director:* Dr Nicky King. Executive staff 3, Other staff 35. ***CC*** No.291870. Began 1985; non-denominational. No magazine. Turnover £2,500,000 to year end Dec 05.

***Fit Lives**, 164a Barton Road, Stretford, Manchester M32 8DP
☎0845 130 0552 🖷0870 011 1552
E: admin@fitlives.co.uk
Web: www.fitlives.co.uk
Demonstrating practical caring and support through health and fitness venues.
Director: Rev Andrew Barclay-Watt. Executive staff 1, Other staff 6. ***CC*** No.1062318. Began 1997; interdenominational. (Previously New Life Outreach (NLO)). No magazine. Turnover £34,797 to year end Apr 05.

†**Friends Fellowship of Healing, Claridge House Retreat Centre for Healing**, Dormans Road, DormansLand, Lingfield RH7 6QH
☎01342 832 150 🖷01342 836 730
E: welcome@claridgehouse.freeserve.co.uk
Web: www.claridgehouse.freeserve.co.uk
Providing an environment for rest and renewal; emphasis on spirituality not religion.
Warden: To be appointed. Executive staff 2, Other staff 6. ***CC*** No.228102. Began 1953; Religious Society of Friends. No magazine. Turnover £120,000 to year end Dec 02.

Green Pastures Christian Centre of Pastoral Care and Healing, 17 Burton Road, Branksome Park, Poole BH13 6DT
☎01202 764 776 🖷01202 768 144
E: admin@green-pastures.org
Web: www.green-pastures.org
Short-term residential therapeutic environment for personal growth, healing, fellowship, counselling, spiritual direction, creativity, hands-on therapies.
Pastoral Director: Rev Colin Norris. *Centre Manager:* Audri Coleman. Executive staff 1, Other staff 10. ***CC*** No.1090568. Began 1955; interdenominational. Magazine: *Update* (3,000 quarterly). Turnover n/a.

†**Guideposts Trust Ltd**, Two Rivers, Station Lane, Witney OX28 4BH
☎01993 772 886 🖷01993 778 [illegible]
Web: www.guidepoststrust.org.uk
Providing care through day services centres, outreach projects, housing support service, teaching nursing home.
Chief Executive: Mr Dave McCabe. *General Manager:* Mr Stephen [illegible]aine. Executive staff 5, Other staff 90. ***CC*** No.272619. Began 19[illegible]2; interdenominational. No magazine. Turnover £1,417,508 to year end Mar 03.

†**The Guild of Health Ltd**, St Paul's Church Centre, 3 Rossmore Road, London NW[illegible]NJ
☎020 7723 9680
E: gohealth@freeuk.com
Web: www.gohealth.freeuk.com
Helping people to experience within the fellowship of God's family, freedom and life through prayer and sacraments.
General Secretary: Rev Antonia L[illegible]nn. Executive staff 1. ***CC*** Began 1904; interdenominational. Magazine: *Way of Life* (1,100 quarterly). Turnover n/a.

Harnhill Centre of Christian Healing, Harnhill Manor, Cirencester GL7 5PX
☎01285 850 284 🖷01285 850 51[illegible]
E: office@harnhillcentre.org.uk
Web: harnhillcentre.org.uk
Resource centre for Christian healing offering residential stays, prayer ministry facilities, training courses and healing services.
Warden/Chaplain: Rev Paul Spring[illegible]e. Executive staff 8, Other staff 5. ***CC*** No.292173. Began 1986; Anglican Foundation. Magazine: *Harvest* (Circulation n/a quarterly). Turnover £2[illegible]0,000 to year end June 05.

†**Holton Lee**, East Holton, Holton Heath, Poole BH16 6JN
☎01202 625 562/631 [illegible]63
🖷01202 632 632
E: holton@lds.co.uk
Web: www.lds.co.uk/holtonlee
Short-stay residential accommodation suitable for disabled people: conferences, courses, counselling, retreats, visual arts.
Director: Mr Tony Heaton. Executive staff 2, Other staff 14. ***CC*** No.[illegible]01186[illegible]. Began 1992; non-denominational. Magazine: *Holton Lee Newsletter* (2,000 quarterly). Turnover £300,000 to year end Mar 03.

***InterHealth**, Partnership House, 15[illegible] Waterloo Road, London SE[illegible] 8U[illegible]
☎020 7902 9000 🖷020 7902 9091
E: info@interhealth.org.uk
Web: www.interhealth.org.uk
Providing comprehensive healthcare services, supplies, advice to missions, aid agencies, Gap Year agencies, voluntary sector.
Executive Director: David White. *Director of Health Care:* Dr Ted Lankester. *Marketing & Client Services:* Sarah Marfleet. Clinical Staff 13, Support Staff 13. ***CC*** No.1103935. Began 19[illegible]; interdenominational. No magazine. Turnover £1,500,000 to year end Sep 05.

S

International Community Trust for Health and Education Services (Icthes World Care), West Hurlet House, Glasgow Road, Hurlet, Glasgow G53 7TH
☎0141 881 9633
E: m.mcgavin@icthesworldcare.com
Web: www.icthesworldcare.com
Global health education; producing/sending teaching journals free to 170+ countries; gathering/housing resources.
Executive Director: Dr DD Murray McGavin. Executive staff 1, Other staff 4. **CC** No.1075381. Began 1999; interdenominational. Magazine: *Developing Mental Health* (Circulation n/a half-yearly), *Community Dermatology* (Circulation n/a half-yearly), *Community Ear & Hearing Health* (Circulation n/a half-yearly). Turnover £95,600 to year end Dec 05.

The Linacre Centre for Health Care Ethics, 60 Grove End Road, St John's Wood, London NW8 9NH
☎020 7806 4088 Fax 020 7266 5424
E: admin@linacre.org
Web: www.linacre.org
Defending and developing through education and research traditional medical ethics informed by Catholic teaching; bioethics library.
Director: Dr Helen Watt. *Senior Research Fellow:* Prof Luke Gormally. Research staff 2, Other staff 3. **CC** No.274327. Began 1977; Roman Catholic. No magazine. Turnover £200,000 to year end Dec 02.

†Living Fountains, 10 Hemlock Close, Oakwood, Derby DE21 2NZ
☎0870 748 0427 Fax 0870 748 0427
E: livingfountains@ntlworld.com
Web: www.livingfountains.org
Providing professional alternative health care naturally, nutritional advice, consultation; residential detox centre.
Director: Mrs Emma Biant. Executive staff 2. Began 2003; non-denominational. No magazine. Turnover n/a.

The Maranatha Community, 102 Irlam Road, Flixton, Manchester M41 6JT
☎0161 748 4858 Fax 0161 747 7379
E: info@maranathacommunity.org.uk
Web: www.maranathacommunity.org.uk.
Dispersed interdenominational community of 10,000, committed to Christian unity, healing and renewal.
Community Leader: Mr Dennis Wrigley. Executive staff 1, Other staff 2. **CC** No.327627. Began 1981; ecumenical. Magazine: *Maranatha Newsletter* (6,000 every two months). Turnover £110,000 to year end Dec 00.

†The Matthew Trust, PO Box 604, London SW6 3AG
☎020 7736 5976 Fax 020 7731 6961
E: matthewtrust@ukonline.co.uk
Web: www.matthewtrust.org
Christian mental health reform and caring agency for those in prison and victims of aggression.
Director: Mrs Annabell Thompson. Executive staff 3, Other staff 2. **CC** No.294966. Began 1977; non-denominational. No magazine. Turnover £134,955 to year end Mar 98.

***Mission Care**, 2 Pembroke Road, Bromley BR1 2RU
☎020 8249 1904 Fax 020 8402 8629
E: admin@missioncare.org.uk
Web: www.missioncare.org.uk
Social, health care through care homes for older people, people with disabilities/ mental health problems.
Chief Executive: Mr Colin Bloom. *Groupcare Manager:* Linda Stimson. *Chairman:* Mr Geoff Dean. Executive staff 5, Other staff 500. **CC** No.284967. Began 1904; Bermondsey 1904; Brook Lane 1937; interdenominational. (Previously Bermondsey and Brook Lane Medical Mission). Magazine: *Christmas Letter* (1,500 annually). Turnover £10,000,000 to year end Mar 04.

Nicholaston House, Penmaen, Swansea SA3 2HL
☎01792 371 317 Fax 01792 371 217
E: managers@nicholastonhouse.org
Web: www.nicholastonhouse.org
Offering retreats, prayer ministry, time out, themed breaks, courses for overcoming eating disorders.
Ministry Manager: Mrs Anne Styants. *Training & Development Manager:* Helena Wilkinson. Admin staff 7. **CC** No.1096720. Began 1988; interdenominational. No magazine. Turnover £165,000 to year end Dec 04.

Nissi in Health, PO Box 36252, London SE19 3UW
M: 07957 398 333
E: nissiint@yahoo.co.uk
Web: www.nissiheath.org
Christian health initiatives; currently focusing on AIDS in Africa, especially Swaziland and East Africa.
Medical Director: Dr Naomi Bankole. Executive staff 1, Other staff 1. **CC** No.299242. Began 1987; interdenominational. No magazine. Turnover £2,000 to year end June 05.

Northumbrian Centre of Prayer for Christian Healing, Beggars Roost, 26 Painshawfield Road, Stocksfield NE43 7PF
☎01661 842 364 Fax 01661 844 968
E: centre@christian-healing.com
Web: www.christian-healing.com
Promoting through ministry and teaching the healing ministry of Jesus for the Body of Christ.
Directors: Rev & Mrs David & Karen Vickers. No full-time staff. **CC** No.1064164. Began 1991; interdenominational. No magazine. Turnover £23,000 to year end Aug 02.

***Parakaleo**, PO Box 115, Bromley BR1 2ZA
☎M 07748 662 435
E: parakaleo@btinternet.com
Web: www.parakaleo.co.uk
Focusing on transgender behaviours and sexual wholeness issues.
Coordinator: Mr Keith Tiller. Executive staff 1. Began 1995; interdenominational. No magazine. Turnover £10,000 to year end Sep 05.

***Pennefather Christian Medical Community Trust**, 22a Hanbury Street, London E1 6QR
☎01732 455 425
Supporting Christian medical projects in Tower Hamlets and London's East End.
President: Rev Dr Bill Maxwell. No full-time staff. **CC** Began 1994; interdenominational. (Previously League of Friends of Mildmay Mission Hospital). Magazine: *Bulletin* (400 annually). Turnover n/a.

St Luke's Hospital for the Clergy, 14 Fitzroy Square, London W1T 6AH
☎020 7388 4954 Fax 020 7383 4812
E: stluke@stlukeshospital.org.uk
Web: stlukeshospital.org.uk
Treating and healing Church of England ministering personnel; 22 beds mainly for surgical cases.
Chief Executive: Mr John Cherry. *Director of Finance:* Mr Graham Lloyd. Executive staff 5, Other staff 55. **CC** No.209236. Began 1892; Anglican. Magazine: *Annual Handbook* (12,000 annually). Turnover £2,000,000 to year end Dec 04.

Sozo Ministries International, Sozo House, Alma Road, Romsey SO51 8ED
☎01794 522 511 Fax 01794 522 577
E: E@sozo.org
Web: www.sozo.org
Preaching salvation, healing and deliverance to the church and to the world.
Director: Mrs Marion Daniel. Executive staff 6, Other staff 2. **CC** No.1042420. Began 1983; non-denominational. No magazine. Turnover n/a.

†The Well Christian Healing Centre, PO Box 3407, Leamington Spa CV32 6ZH
☎01926 888 003
E: enquiries@wellhealing.org
Web: www.wellhealing.org
Healing centre.
Director: Mrs Anne Hibbert. Executive staff 5, Admin staff 1. **CC** No.1097443. Began 2003; ecumenical. No magazine. Turnover n/a.

***Wellsprings**, Bawtry Hall, Bawtry, Doncaster DN10 6JH
☎01302 710 020 Fax 01302 710 027
E: info@bawtryhall.co.uk
Web: www.bawtryhall.co.uk
Providing rest and renewal for Christian workers.
Co-ordinator: Mrs Andrea Fairchild. Admin staff 1, Other Staff n/a. **CC** No.225364. Began 1997; interdenominational. No magazine. Turnover n/a.

***Whitchester Christian Guest House and Retreat**, Borthaugh, Hawick TD9 7LN
☎01450 377 477 Fax 01450 371 080
E: enquiries@whitchester.org.uk
Web: www.whitchester.org.uk
Offering care, listening, prayer; daily worship, chapel; library.
Warden: Evelyn Jackson. Executive staff 1, Other staff 4. **CC** No.SCO 011436. Began 1984; interdenominational. ACC affiliated. No magazine. Turnover n/a.

S

INFORMATION & TELEPHONE ORGANISATIONS

See also Counselling Organisations on Page 331, Help Lines on Page 447.

ACB - Association of Christians in Broadcasting, PO Box 6613, South Woodham Ferrers, Chelmsford CM3 5DY
☎01245 322 158 🖷01245 321 957
E: acm@churchesmediacouncil.org.uk
Web: www.churchesmediacouncil.org.uk
Providing support, help, advice for Christians interested or involved in broadcasting.
Director: Andrew Graystone. Executive staff 1. ***CC*** No.297766. Began 1967; interdenominational. Part of Churches' Media Council. Magazine: *Crosstalk* (1,000 quarterly). Turnover £20,000 to year end Dec 05.

Catholic Communications Network, 39 Eccleston Square, London SW1V 1BX
☎020 7901 4800 M: 07891 105 245
🖷020 7901 4820
E: ccn@cbcew.org.uk
Web: www.catholic-ew.org.uk
Press and publications office for Catholic Church in England and Wales.
Head of News: Alexander DesForges. Executive staff 1, Other staff 5. ***CC*** No.257239. Began 1968; Roman Catholic. (Previously Catholic Communications Service). Turnover n/a.

Catholic Enquiry Office, The Chase Centre, 114 West Heath Road, London NW3 7TX
☎020 8458 3316 🖷020 8905 5780
E: info@life4seekers.co.uk
Web: www.life4seekers.co.uk
Advertising through the press and the distribution of free literature for evangelisation.
Director: Mgr Keith Barltrop. Executive staff 3, Other staff 4. ***CC*** No.1097482. Began 1954; Roman Catholic. No magazine. Turnover n/a.

Catholic Press and Media Office, 5 St Vincent Place, Glasgow G1 2DH
☎0141 221 1168 M: 07968 122 291
🖷0141 204 2458
E: mail@scmo.org
Web: www.scmo.org
Providing a service to press, media; information, guidance on activities of Catholic Church in Scotland.
Director: Mr Peter Kearney. Executive staff 1, Other staff 2. ***CC*** No.SCO 00707. Began 1968; Roman Catholic. No magazine. Turnover n/a.

Christian Enquiry Agency, 27 Tavistock Square, London WC1H 9HH
☎020 7387 3659 🖷020 7529 8134
E: enquiry@christianity.org.uk
Web: www.christianity.org.uk
Providing opportunities for people to enquire about the Christian faith and offering information and advice.
Director: Mr Jeff Bonser. Executive staff 1. ***CC*** No.297393. Began 1985; interdenominational. No magazine. Turnover £59,000 to year end Dec 04.
Enquiries about the Christian faith to: FREEPOST WC 2947, South Croydon CR2 8UZ
E: cea@christianity.org.uk

Christian Voice, PO Box 739a, Surbiton KT6 5YA
☎01994 484 544
E: info@christianvoice.org.uk
Web: www.christianvoice.org.uk
Upholding the Christian constitution of the UK; working for Godly government; praying for national repentance.
National Director: Stephen Green. Executive staff 3. Began 1994; non-denominational. Magazine: *Christian Voice* (Circulation n/a ten times a year). Turnover £75,000 to year end Dec 05.

Church in History Information Centre, 757 Borough Road, Birkenhead CH42 6QQ
☎0151 645 7893
Web: www.church-in-history.org
Making available information regarding the involvement of the Church in history.
Director: Mr Dennis Barton. Executive staff 1, No other staff. Began 1985; Roman Catholic. No magazine. Turnover n/a.

Church of Scotland London Advisory Service (COSLAS), Borderline, 7/9 Belgrave Road, London SW1V 1QB
☎020 7881 9246/0845 456 2190 (advice)
🖷0845 456 2199
E: office@borderline-uk.org
Web: www.borderline-uk.org
Assisting homeless and insecurely housed Scots in London; resettlement benefits, identification grants.
Director: Eileen J Ward. *Client Services Manager:* Murdo Maciver. Staff 5. ***CC*** No.208437. Began 1887; Church of Scotland. No magazine. Turnover £250,000 to year end Dec 02.

Communications Department, Church House, Great Smith Street, London SW1P 3NZ
☎020 7898 1326 M: 0777 800 2[illegible]2
🖷020 7222 6672
E: cofecomms@c-of-e.org.uk
Web: www.cofe.anglican.org
Promoting the work of the Church of England in proclaiming the Gospel.
Director of Communications: Mr Peter Crumpler. Executive staff 4, Other staff 3. ***CC*** Began n/a; Anglican. No magazine. Turnover n/a.

Note: Each Diocese has a Communications Officer. Contact them via the appropriate Diocesan Office. See Pages 155 to 162.

Dial-A-Bible-Message Ministry, 74 Scrub Rise, Billericay CM12 9PE
☎01277 626 309/654 455 (24-hour message)
E: trevorargent@lineone.net
Recorded Bible teaching ministry.
Teachers: Mr Trevor Argent, Mr Stan Portch. No full-time staff. Began 198[illegible]; interdenominational. No magazine. Turnover n/a.

Enquiry Centre, Church House, Great Smith Street, London SW1P 3NZ
☎020 7898 1445
E: steve.empson@c-of-e.org.uk
Web: www.cofe.anglican.org
Answering enquiries on matters relating to the Church of England.
Enquiry Centre Officer: Mr Stephen Empson. Executive staff 1, No other staff. Began 1963; Anglican. No magazine. Turnover n/a.

EX C.S. UK, Address withheld
☎01202 576 550 M: 07836 362 825
🖷01202 576 550
E: ex_cs2001@yahoo.com
Providing advice, friendship, support, meetings for former Christian Scientists, whose relations may still be CS.
Coordinator: Kathy. No full-time staff. Began 2002; non-denominational. No magazine. Turnover n/a.

†Fellowship of St Alban & St Sergius, 1 Canterbury Road, Oxford OX2 6LU
☎01865 552 991 📠01865 316 700
E: gensec@sobornost.org
Web: www.sorbosnost.org
Aiding theological understanding between Eastern and Western Christians.
General Secretary: Rev Stephen Platt. Executive staff 1, Other staff 2. ***CC*** No.2451[illegible]2. Began 1928; interdenominational. (Incorporating Eastern Churches Review). Magazine: *Sobornost* (1,300 half-yearly). Turnover £40,000 to year end Mar 94.

***Find a Church** PO Box 364, High Wycombe HP15 7XX
☎01494 718 773 M: 07956 275 917
E: helpdesk@findachurch.co.uk
Web: www.findachurch.co.uk
UK church directory website and supporting ministry.
Director: Mr Lester Peters. Executive staff 2, Admin staff 1. Began 1997; non-denominational. Trading name of UK Church Directory Ltd. No magazine. Turnover £19,000 to year end Dec 04.

Lord's Day Fellowship in Wales/Cymdeithas Dydd yr Arglwydd yng Nghymru, 32 Garth Drive, Liverpool L18 6HW
☎0151 724 1989 📠0151 724 5691
E: ben@garthdrive.fsnet.co.uk
Web: www.lordsdaywales.co.uk
Safeguarding Sunday.
Hon Secretary: Rev Dr D Ben Rees. Began 1937; interdenominational. Magazine: *Inheritance/Etifeddiaeth* (1,500 half-yearly). Turnover £2,000 to year end Dec 04.

***Message The Christian Telephone Service**, PO Box 393, Norwich NR14 6WD
☎01508 528 521
Web: www.nationalmessage.org.uk
Recorded telephone ministry with call-back; providing 24-hour outreach; teaching Christians to witness.
Chairman: Mr Michael Graves. All voluntary staff. ***CC*** No.297409. Began 1969; interdenominational. Magazine: *Ring Round* (1,500 half-yearly). Turnover n/a.

†Methodist Church Media Office, Methodist Church House, 25 Marylebone Road, London NW1 5JR
☎020 7486 5502 📠020 7486 7792
E: mediaoffice@methodistchurch.org.uk
Web: www.methodist.org.uk
Informing all media concerning Methodist work, news and views throughout Britain.
Media Officer: Mr Murray White. Admin staff 1. Began n/a; Methodist. (Previously Methodist Church Press Service). No magazine. Turnover n/a.

†National Council for Christian Standards, 9 Challenger Close, Paddock Wood, Tonbridge TN12 6TZ
☎01892 835 419 M: 07740 258 230
📠01892 835 419
E: davidhilsley@davidhilsley.plus.com
Web: www.amen.org.uk
Upholding and encouraging Christian standards in society, parliament, media, through prayer, petition, campaign information.
Chairman: Jacob Vince. Executive staff 1. ***CC*** No.294803. Began 1986; non-denominational. Magazine: *The Christian Standard* (5,000 half-yearly). Turnover n/a.

The Oriental Orthodox News Service (OONS), 10 Heathwood Gardens, Charlton, London SE7 8EP
☎020 8854 3090 📠020 8244 7888
E: oons-request@uk-christian.net
Web: www.uk-christian.net/oons
Monthly electronic news bulletin on behalf of the Oriental Orthodox Churches.
Director: Fr Sergius Scott. Executive staff 1, Other staff n/a. Began n/a; Orthodox. Magazine: *Ex Oriente Lux* (Circulation online monthly). Turnover n/a.

***Premier Lifeline**, 22 Chapter Street, London SW1P 4NP
☎0845 345 0707 📠020 7233 6706
E: lifeline@premier.org.uk
Web: www.premier.org.uk/lifeline/
Confidential Christian helpline offering emotional, spiritual support, listening ear, prayer advice, information.
Manager: Jonathan Clark. Paid Staff 2. ***CC*** No.287610. Began 1995; interdenominational. Activity of Premier Christian Radio. No magazine. Turnover n/a.

***Rural Christian Information Centre**, Mizpah, Plough Mews, Ledbury HR8 1BX
☎01531 634 113
Reaching rural families nationwide by post, telephone and prayer links; also Christian information service.
Organiser: Mrs Irene D Clegg. No full-time staff. Began 1962; interdenominational. (Previously Farmer's Christian Information Centre). No magazine. Turnover n/a.

St George Orthodox Information Service, The White House, Mettingham, Bungay NR35 1TP
☎01986 896 708 📠01986 896 708
E: stgeorgeois@aol.com
Web: www.sgois.co.uk
Serving the Orthodox Church as public relations office, bookstore and church supplies company.
General Secretary: Mr Andrew Bond. Executive staff 2, Other staff 2. Began 1969; Orthodox. Magazine: *Orthodox News* (3,000 quarterly). Turnover n/a.

TxtaVerse, Olympic House, 196 The Broadway, London SW19 1RY
☎0845 330 5142 📠0845 330 5143
E: contact@txtaverse.com
Web: www.txtaverse.com
Mobile text service delivering daily Bible verses worldwide; profits to the poor.
Director: Mr Stuart McGreevy. Executive staff 1. Began 2003; non-denominational. (Previously Kingdom Business Enterprises). No magazine. Turnover n/a.

S

MARKETING & FUNDRAISING SERVICES

See also Design, Layout & Editorial Services on Page 219, Business Services on Page 326.

Action Planning, Mid-day Court, 30 Brighton Road, Sutton SM2 5BN
☎020 8642 4122
🖷020 8770 2090
E: info@actionplanning.co.uk
Web: www.actionplanning.co.uk
Fundraising and management services to Christian organisations and charities; church capital appeals and feasibility studies.
Principal: Mr David Saint. *Chief Executive:* Judi Stewart. Executive staff 6, Other staff 4. Began 1990; non-denominational. Magazine: *Actionlink* (4,000 every four months). Turnover n/a.

Alpha Fund Raiser, Alpha House, 184 Bath Road, Longwell Green, Bristol BS30 9DB
☎ No telephone
M: 07969 256 424
E: winwin@alphafundraiser.com
Web: www.alphafundraiser.com
Helping supporters save on utility bills by having a sustainable monthly income-stream.
Director: Mr Andy Lampard. Executive staff 1, Other staff n/a. Began 2006; non-denominational. No magazine. Turnover: first year of operation.

Bay Mailing Ltd, 1 Stennack Road, Holmbush, St Austell PL25 3JQ
☎01726 879 239
M: 07987 439 371
🖷01726 879 204
E: info@baymailing.co.uk
Web: www.baymailing.co.uk
Mailing and distributing literature, direct mail; database management, print and production, hand finishing for mailing.
Operations Director: Mr Steve Double. Executive staff 5, Other staff 50. Began 2001; non-denominational. No magazine. Turnover n/a.

Brawn Marketing and Fundraising, Trelowthas Manor Barn, Probus, Truro TR2 4HU
M: 07989 439 371
E: timbrawn@aol.com
Direct mail, including copywriting, campaign management and mailing house; fundraising consultancy.
Managing Director: Mr Tim Brawn. Executive staff 2, Other staff 1. Began 1993; non-denominational. No magazine. Turnover n/a.

Charities Aid Foundation, 25 Kings Hill Avenue, West Malling ME19 4TA
☎01732 520 000
🖷01732 520 001
E: enquiries@cafonline.org
Web: www.cafonline.org
Offering consultancy services to charities banking, investment services, including churches; organisational reviews, training, development.
Manager, Consulting & Development: Mr Mark Scott. Executive staff 2, Admin staff 4, Consultants 6. ***CC*** No.268369. Began 1974; non-denominational. No magazine. Turnover n/a.

Charity Support Services, 49 Oakhurst, Lichfield WS14 9AL
☎01543 268 678
M: 07785 334 077
🖷01543 411 685
E: admin@charitysupportonline.co.uk
Web: www.charitysupportonline.co.uk
Fund rasing; business planning; market research, viability assessment; social enterprise; project development; marketing; public relations; training.
Director: Mr John Wilson. Executive staff 1, Other staff 5. Began 1991; non-denominational. No magazine. Turnover £60,000 to year end Jan 02.

Chown China, Hope Farm, Gwithian Road, Connor Downs, Hayle TR27 5EA
☎01209 713 361/613 153
E: chown@chownchina.co.uk
Web: www.chownchina.co.uk
Manufacturing bone china mugs, plates, thimbles and teatowels for Christian outreach and fund-raising.
Partners: Mr & Mrs John & Heather Chown. Executive Staff 4. Began 1[illegible]7; Methodist/Anglican. No magazine. Turnover £100,000 to year end Ma[illegible] [illegible]5.

†Churches' Advertising Network, The Methodist Centre, 24 School Street, Wolverhampton WV1 4LF
☎01902 422 100
🖷01902 313 301
E: churchads@methodist.acasnet.co.uk
Web: www.churchads.org.uk
Coordinating major advertising initiatives between denominations and regions, and advising churches on religious advertising.
Chairman: Mr Francis Goodwin. No full-time staff. Began 1992; ecumenical. No magazine. Turnover £20,751 to year end Dec 02.

†The Churches' Media Trust, Communications Department, Diocese of Oxford, Church House, North Hinksey, Oxford OX2 0NB
☎01865 208 225
🖷01865 790 470
E: richard.thomas@oxford.anglican.org
Coordinating funding, providing new vision for the churches' work with all areas of the media.
Chair of Trustees: Mark Fudall. No paid staff. ***CC*** Began 1991; interdenominational. Magazine: *Another Voice* (1,000 occasionally). Turnover £27,000 to year end Dec 02.

Cornerstone Vision, 28 Old Park Road, Peverell, Plymouth PL3 4FY
☎01752 225 623
M: 07968 874 503
🖷01752 673 441
E: info@cornerstonevision.com
Web: www.cornerstonevision.com
Providing marketing and fundraising project management, media buying and relations, copywriting design and direct mail.
Partners: Mr Chris Cole, Chris Girdler, Ian Pilkington. Executive staff 6, Other staff 9. Began 1983; interdenominational. (Previously Cornerstone House). No magazine. Turnover £500,000 to year end Apr 04.

S

Craigmyle & Company Ltd, The Grove, Harpenden AL5 1AJ
☎01582 762 441 ℻01582 461 489
E: first@craigmyle.org.uk
Web: www.craigmyle.org.uk
Fundraising services including appeals, feasibility, strategy, recruitment, training, development, mentoring and fundraising clinics.
Director: Mrs Gill Moody. Executive staff 7, Other staff 10. Began 1959; non-denominational. No magazine. Turnover n/a.

The Domain Group, Suite 309, Tea Building, 56 Shoreditch High Street, London E1 6JJ
☎020 7613 7340 ℻020 7613 9308
E: shbutler@thedomain_london.co.uk
Web: www.thedomaingroup.co.uk
Fundraising and advertising for Christian and charity organisations.
UK Partner: Mr Stephen Butler. Executive staff 6, Other staff 20. Began 1994; non-denominational. No magazine. Turnover n/a.

Erne Agency International, Inis Ceithleann House, Lower Celtic Park, Enniskillen BT74 6HP
☎028 6632 3387 ℻028 6632 3387
Marketing, advertising, direct mail, promotions, incentives, public relations for churches, charities and voluntary organisations.
Director: Mr Bill Thompson. Executive staff 4, Other staff 2. Began 1985; non-denominational. No magazine. Turnover n/a.

Felton Fundraising and Appeals, 91 Eastgate Street, North Elmham, Dereham NR20 5HE
☎01362 668 868
E: info@feltonfundraising.co.uk
Web: www.feltonfundraising.co.uk
Offering a dedicated service to church-based projects and charities throughout the UK.
Partners: Richard & Sarah Felton. Executive staff 2, Admin staff 2. Began 1995; non-denominational. (Previously Richard Felton Fundraising and Appeals Consultant). No magazine. Turnover n/a.

Hub Resourcing Limited, 45 Dean Road, Hounslow TW3 2EY
☎020 8755 0657
M: 07956 946 926
E: david.ryde@hubresourcing.com
Web: www.hubresourcing.com
Helping churches, schools and charities achieve business and communications goals: marketing, fundraising, strategy, business development.
Director: Mr David Ryde. Executive staff 2. Began 1994; non-denominational. (Previously DRM Consulting) No magazine. Turnover n/a.

***David Marfleet Ltd**, 7 Concord Close, Paddock Wood, Tonbridge TN12 6UJ
☎01892 834 574
℻01892 834 574
E: david@davidmarfleet.co.uk
Web: www.davidmarfleet.co.uk
Offering fundraising, marketing and development advice for Christian missions and charities.
Consultant: Mr David Marfleet. Executive staff 1, Admin staff 1. Began 20[illegible]3; interdenominational. No magazine. Turnover n/a.

S

***Marketing Strategy & Action Ltd**, Business Innovation Centre, Binley Business Park, Harry Weston Road, Coventry CV3 2TX
☎024 7643 0290
🖷024 7643 0291
E: jerry@strategy-action.com
Web: www.strategy-action.com
Marketing consultancy producing practical, researched marketing plans and feasibility studies, international business development and training.
Director: Mr Jerry Marshall. Executive staff 2, Other staff 4. Began 1987; non-denominational. (Previously Jerry Marshall Associates). No magazine. Turnover £170,000 to year end Dec 04.

The Message Works, Third Floor, Suffolk House (West Entrance), George Street, Croydon CR0 1PE
☎020 8256 6400
🖷020 8256 6401
E: info@the-message-works.com
Web: www.the-message-works.com
Specialising in relationship fundraising and marketing.
Director: Mr Stephen Maxted. Executive staff 1, Other staff 4. Began 2000; interdenominational. (Previously Stephen Maxted and Associates Ltd). No magazine. Turnover n/a.

MR Associates, 19 Wemyss Court, Leapmoor Drive, Wemyss Bay PA18 6BF
☎01475 522 962
M: 07967 963 806
E: info@mrassociates.org.uk
Web: www.mrassociates.org.uk
Specialising in obtaining funding for accommodation-based schemes providing support to vulnerable adults.
Supported Housing Advisor: Mr Mark Rodgers. Executive staff 2, Admin staff 1. Began 2000; interdenominational. No magazine. Turnover n/a.

Oulton-Lee Research Ltd, 40 Fairmount Drive, Loughborough LE11 3JR
☎01509 264 141
M: 07721 992 405
🖷01509 264 141
E: contact@oulton-lee.co.uk
Web: www.oulton-lee.co.uk
Research solutions for marketing problems; questionnaire design, statistical analysis and interpretation; qualitative, especially focus groups.
Managing Director: Sue Garner. Executive staff 1, Other staff 1. Began 1991; non-denominational. (Previously Oulton-Lee Marketing Services Ltd). No magazine. Turnover n/a.

***PRD Associates**, PO Box 151, Stowmarket IP14 2WA
☎01449 721 112
M: 07711 000 050
🖷01449 721 112
E: info@prdassociates.com
Web: www.prdassociates.com
Offering business development; marketing; training in business skills.
Director: Mr Bryan C Hilton. Executive staff 1, Other staff 5. Began 1986; interdenominational. (Previously Professional Resource Development Ltd). No magazine. Turnover n/a.

†Presence Retail Ltd, The Cottage, West Clayton, Chorleywood, Rickmansworth WD3 5EX
☎01923 285 888 🖷01923 285 913
E: cathy.cleveland@presence.uk.com
Creating a faith-based retail business in the major destination shopping centres.
Director: Mr Steve Cardell. Executive staff 2, Admin staff 2. Began 2004; non-denominational. No magazine. Turnover n/a.

†*Ian M Pryce & Associates, 24 Medway Avenue, Oakley, Basingstoke RG23 7DP
☎01256 782 188 🖷01256 782 817
E: pryce1@aol.com
Marketing and market research in Christian, charity and social marketing environments; IT project management.
Partner: Mr Ian Pryce. Executive staff 2. Began 1994; non-denominational. No magazine. Turnover £150,000 to year end Sep 02.

Red & Green Marketing Ltd, 12 Montacute Road, Tunbridge Wells TN2 5QR
☎01892 750 900 🖷01892 750 458
E: info@redandgreenmarketing.com
Web: www.redandgreenmarketing.com
Offering marketing, project management and creative services, charitable and commercial sectors.
Managing Director: Mr Nigel Saunders. *Director:* Roger Hulbert. Executive staff 2, Other staff 7. Began 2001; interdenominational. (Previously Greenleaf Communications Ltd). No magazine. Turnover £900,000 to year end Jun 03.

Sovereign Creative Marketing Ltd, Stanley House, 15 Ladybridge Road, Cheadle Hulme, Cheadle SK8 5BL
☎0161 485 4488 🖷0161 486 1886
E: n.tedford@sovereign.uk.com
Web: www.sovereign.uk.com
Marketing campaigns, advertisement design, media buying, website design/hosting, web marketing campaigns, donor recruitment/development.
Managing Director: Mr Nigel Tedford. *Financial Director:* Mrs Dianne Tedford. Executive staff 2, Other staff 4. Began 1984; interdenominational. No magazine. Turnover £1,000,000 to year end Dec 04.

Support Team Building, 1 Garden House Court, 142 Sandgate Road, Folkestone CT20 2FF
☎01303 253 195
🖷01303 253 195
E: dlongley@fish.co.uk
Helping Christian organisations build strong teams of supporters; copywriting services; address list management consultancy.
Consultant: Mr David Longley. No full-time staff. Began 1985; interdenominational. No magazine. Turnover n/a.

†Tentmakers Ltd, Burstead Cottages, Little Hallingbury, Bishop's Stortford CM22 7QU
☎01279 726 798
🖷01279 723 344
E: sales@ctg.gb.com
Web: www.ctg.gb.com
Returning up to 20% of net invoice value to purchasers of stationery and computer supplies.
Managing Director: Mr Robin Horton. Executive staff 2. Began 1996; interdenominational. No magazine. Turnover n/a.

Graham Waterhouse Consultancy, [illegible]6 Rushyfield Crescent, Romiley, Stockport SK6 4LG
☎0161 494 5607
M: 07821 380 775
🖷0161 494 5607
E: graham.waterhouse@ntlworld.com
Management and fundraising consultancy, training particularly for voluntary organisations and charities.
Proprietor: Mr Graham Waterhouse. Executive staff 2, Admin staff 1. Began 199[illegible]; non-denominational. No magazine. Turnover £54,000 to year end Apr [illegible]2.

S

MARRIAGE MINISTRIES

See also Counselling Organisations on Page 331.
Family Care & Support Ministries on Page 341.

Aquila Care Trust, All Saints Church Old Halls, Chapel Green, Crowborough TN6 1ED
☎01892 665 524 🖷01892 601 359
E: admin@aquilatrust.org
Web: www.aquilatrust.org
Supporting adults experiencing relationship breakdown, separation or divorce.
Chief Executive: Mr Jim Wheeler. Executive staff 2, Admin staff 2. Began 1991; non-denominational. (Previously Oasis). No magazine. Turnover £70,000 to year end Mar 05.

†Association for Marriage Enrichment, 17 Shillington Road, Meppershall, Shefford SG17 5ND
☎01462 813 333
E: ame@care4free.net
Web: www.ame-uk.org.uk
Enabling couples to communicate more effectively, understand each other better and cope with conflict.
Secretaries: Mr & Mrs John & Anne Parsons. No full-time staff. ***CC*** No.327606. Began 1979; non-denominational. No magazine. Turnover £9,800 to year end Dec 02.

Broken Rites, 93 York Road, Teddington TW11 8SL
☎020 8943 4688
E: johannmartin@hotmail.com
Web: www.brokenrites.org
Independent support and action group concerned with the breakdown of clergy marriages.
National Chair: Ms Priscilla Diggle. All voluntary staff. Began 1983; Anglican but serving all. Magazine: *The Rite Lines* (300 every four months). Turnover £7,000 to year end Apr 04.

†Couples for Christ - Living Water Community, 53 St Johns Park, Blackheath, London SE3 7JW
☎020 8853 1719
E: victoriaalexand@aol.com
Helping families live Christ-centred lives, through teaching, prayer and fellowship.
Co-ordinator: Mr Louis Alexander. Executive staff 1, Other staff 3. ***CC*** No.1024147. Began 1988; interdenominational. Magazine: *CFC Newsletter* (500 monthly). Turnover £15,000 to year end Dec 00.

FLAME - Family Life And Marriage Education, Robert Runcie House, 2 Bedford Place, Maidstone ME16 8JB
☎01622 755 014 🖷01622 693 531
E: flame@churchinsociety.org
Web: www.flamefamily.co.uk
Strengthening family life and marriage education; exchanging information and expertise between dioceses.
Co-Chairs: Rev Andrew Body, Rt Rev Anthony Priddis. No full-time staff. ***CC*** No.1001753. Began 1989; Anglican. Magazine: *Newsline* (Circulation n/a every four months). Turnover £8,000 to year end Dec 00.

Marriage Care, Clitherow House, 1 Blythe Mews, Blythe Road, London W14 0NW
☎020 7371 1341/0845 660 6000 (helpline Mon-Fri 11am-3pm)
🖷020 7371 4921
E: angela@marriagecare.org.uk
Web: www.marriagecare.org.uk
Providing relationship counselling for individuals, couples; marriage preparation courses; work in schools; telephone helpline.
Chief Executive: Terry Prendergast. *Director of Finance:* John Yeomans. *Director of Relationship Support Services:* Joseph Mannion. Executive staff 5, Admin staff 4. ***CC*** No.218159. Began 1946; Roman Catholic. (Previously Catholic Marriage Advisory Council). No magazine. Turnover £1,100,000 to year end Mar 05.

Marriage Encounter-Anglican Expression, 5 Holme Road, Bingham, Nottingham NG13 8DZ
☎01949 837 519
E: d-j-gierth@surefish.co.uk
Web: www.marriageencounter.freeserve.co.uk
Providing weekends for married or engaged couples aimed at improving relationships.
Lay Executive Couple: Mr & Mrs Derrick & Jen Gierth. No full-time staff. ***CC*** No.292594. Began 1978; Anglican. No magazine. Turnover £74,000 to year end Jun 02.

***Marriage Encounter-Baptist Expression**, 26 Bellingdon Road, Chesham HP5 2HA
☎01494 782 466
E: billandben26@tiscali.co.uk
Web: www.beofme.org.uk
Encouraging married couples to strengthen and deepen their relationship with each other.
Secretary: Bill & Brenda Reynolds. No full-time staff. Began 1981; Baptist. No magazine. Turnover n/a.

***Marriage Ministries International**, PO Box 1021, Beaconsfield HP9 2WR
☎01494 675 615
E: uk-office@mmi-europe.org
Web: www.mmi-europe.org
Teaching ministry equipping couples with godly and practical tools for marriage, pre-marriage and parenting.
UK National Directors: Mr & Mrs Mike & Lyn Thomas. Executive staff 1, Admin staff 1. ***CC*** No.1051998. Began 1993; interdenominational. No magazine. Turnover £25,000 to year end Mar 03.

***Mission to Marriage: Christian Marriage Ministries**, Allt Goch, Penegoes, Machynlleth SY20 8UW
☎01654 702 656
E: chmarrmin@aol.com
Web: www.christianmarriageministries.co.uk
Public marriage events, relationship events and training for churches and organisations; publication of relationship resources.
Director: Dr Tony Hobbs. Executive staff 3. ***CC*** No.273658. Began 1977; non-denominational. (Previously Mission to Marriage). No magazine. Turnover n/a.

***National Marriage Week**, Futureway Trust, PO Box 6076, Wimborne BH21 [illegible]AL
☎01202 883 887 🖷01202 881 82[illegible]
E: marriageweek@tiscali.co.uk
Web: www.nmw.org.uk
Organising annual church-based event designed to support marriages and create a positive media focus.
Director: Mr Richard Kane. Executive staff 1. ***CC*** No.1034114. Began 1994; evangelical. No magazine. Turnover n/a.

***One Accord**, First Floor, Austen and Co, Market Square, Petworth GU28 0AH
☎01798 345 222 🖷01798 345 22[illegible]
E: admin@oneaccord.org.uk
Web: www.oneaccord.org.uk
Helping teams of couples to become effective in supporting marriage and interpersonal relationships.
General Manager: Mr Andy Taylor. No full-time staff. ***CC*** No.10366[illegible]7. Began 1974; non-denominational. (Previously Marriage Review). No magazine. Turnover £40,650 to year end Mar 05.

Promoting Marriage, 11 Lamborne Close, Sandhurst GU47 8JL
☎01344 779 658
Web: www.promoting-marriage.org.uk
Group of Christian organisations offering marriage preparation and enrichment programmes.
Chairman: Mr & Mrs David Percival. No full-time staff. Began 1990; interdenominational. Linked to Care for the Family. No magazine. Turnover n/a.

***Radiant Life Ministries**, 47 Gloucester Road, Alkrington, Middleton, Manchester M24 1HT
☎0161 653 3040
E: walter-lyn@onet.co.uk
Web: cw.orangenet.co.uk/~radiant
Arranging events for singles, couples, husbands, wives and training in marriage support.
Directors: Rev & Mrs W & L Crick. Executive staff 2. ***CC*** No.100458[illegible]. Began 1991; non-denominational. No magazine. Turnover £4,000 to year end Mar 05.

Scottish Marriage Care, 72 Waterloo Street, Glasgow G2 7DA
☎0141 222 2166 🖷0141 222 2144
E: info@scottishmarriagecare.org
Web: www.scottishmarriagecare.org
Relationship counselling to couples and individuals, courses in relationship skills for couples preparing for marriage.
Chief Executive: Mrs Mary Toner. *Counselling and Training Manager:* Mrs Kathleen Conroy. Executive staff 4, Other staff 9. **CC** No.SCO 18249. Began 1965; Roman Catholic. (Previously Catholic Marriage Advisory Council Scotland). No magazine. Turnover £450,000 to year end Dec 05.

Skills For Living, 8 The Headlands, Heysham, Morecambe LA3 2RX
☎01524 850 121 🖷01524 850 121
E: office@skills.org
Web: www.skills.org
Retreats: personal growth, relationship workshops; church, prison, community, domestic abuse prevention programmes; Kenya ministry; speaking.
Co-Founders: Mr & Mrs Walter & Valerie Acuff. Executive staff 2. Began 1991; non-denominational. No magazine. Turnover £50,000 to year end Dec 04.

Two Agreed, PO Box 118, Cranleigh GU6 7FF
☎01483 272 016
E: enquiries@twoagreed.com
Web: www.twoagreed.com
Equipping couples to build happy and healthy lifestyles on Christian principles; seminars, conferences, workshops.
Directors: David & Maureen Brown. Executive staff 2. Began 2001; Free Church. (Previously The Marriage Agenda). No magazine. Turnover £33,000 to year end Dec 02.

***United Marriage Encounter**, 211 Mottram Road, Stalybridge SK15 2QX
☎0161 338 3035 🖷0161 927 8499
E: graham@leechs.fslife.co.uk
Web: www.ume.org.uk
Weekend residential programme offering encouragement and discovery to strengthen marriages.
Secretaries: Mr & Mrs Graham & Lee Leech. No full-time staff. **CC** No.1065937. Began 1975; interdenominational. Magazine: *Quest* (45 frequency n/a). Turnover £4,000 to year end Dec 04.

Worldwide Marriage Encounter, Little Hollies, Tenbury Road, Clee Hill, Ludlow SY8 3NE
☎01584 891 181
Web: www.wwme.org.uk
Enriching the sacrament of matrimony for couples and the sacrament of holy orders for priests.
Leaders: Mr & Mrs Gary & Kay Johnson. No full-time staff. **CC** No.272318. Began 1972; Roman Catholic. Magazine: *Spirit* (400 quarterly). Turnover n/a.

PERSONNEL CONSULTANCY & PLACEMENT

See also Counselling Organisations on Page 331.

Career Plan Ltd, 37 Great James Street, London WC1N 3HB
☎020 7356 0930 🖷020 7353 5311
E: mail@careerplan-uk.com
Web: www.careerplan-uk.com
Christian-run search and selection practice operating in the not-for-profit sector.
Contact: Mr Anthony Jones. Executive staff 3, Other staff 1. Began 1970; non-denominational. No magazine. Turnover n/a.

Centrepoint Disclosure Service, PO Box 2156, West Bromwich B70 6HA
☎0871 717 7284 🖷0700 396 6292
E: enquiry@centrepointdisclosure.co.uk
Web: centrepointdisclosure.co.uk
Umbrella body offering standard and enhanced disclosures (police checks) for churches and others.
Director: Rev David R Marsh. Executive staff 1, Admin staff 2. Began 2003; non-denominational. No magazine. Turnover n/a.

***Christian Au Pairs**, Berkeley House, 11 Nightingale Crescent, West Horsley, Leatherhead KT24 6PD
☎01483 280 160
E: au.pairs@virgin.net
Web: www.christianaupairs.com
Providing opportunities for Christian young adults to improve English working as au pairs in Christian families.
Directors: Mr & Mrs Mark & Diana Jeffery. Executive staff 2, Other staff 2. Began 1991; interdenominational. No magazine. Turnover n/a.

Christian Connection, PO Box 37355, London N1 9XZ
☎020 7713 8522 🖷020 7713 1902
E: contact@christianconnection.co.uk
Web: www.christianconnection.co.uk
Friendship and matchmaking internet site for UK and Irish Christians.
Managing Director: Ms Jackie Elton. Executive staff 2, Admin staff 1, Other staff 3. Began 2000; interdenominational. Part of Widernet Communications Ltd. No magazine. Turnover n/a.

†***Christian Contact**, 1 The Cherry Trees, High Hoyland, Barnsley S75 4BG
☎No telephone
E: blushford@aol.com
Providing monthly lists and compatibility scheme with marriage and/or friendship in view for those aged over 18.
Organiser: Mr Duncan Bavister. Executive staff 1. Began 1975; interdenominational. No magazine. Turnover n/a.

†***Christian Contact**, PO Box 2114, Ringwood BH24 1GH
☎01425 475 612
E: info@christiancontact.org
Web: www.christiancontact.org.uk
An advice agency for the workplace and for anyone in need.
Director: Mr W J Gammon. No paid staff. **CC** No.1072194. Began 1995; interdenominational. No magazine. Turnover £1,200 to year end Dec 00.

***Christian Friendship Fellowship**, Bawtry Hall Christian Centre, Bawtry, Doncaster DN10 6JH
☎01302 711 007
🖷01302 710 027
E: info@c-f-f.co.uk
Web: www.c-f-f.co.uk
Ministry for unattached Christians; fellowship groups, social events, holidays, penfriends, music groups, UK international.
Chief Executive Officer: Mr Ben Da Costa. Executive staff 1, Other staff 4. **CC** No.327940. Began 1976; interdenominational. Magazine: *News & Views* (1,500 quarterly). Turnover £69,000 to year end Sep 04.

***Christian Vocations (CV)**, St James House, Trinity Road, Dudley DY1 1JB
☎0870 745 4825
🖷01384 233 032
E: info@christianvocations.org
Web: www.christianvocations.org
Releasing God's people into God's work through vocational guidance, teaching and listings of current opportunities.
Executive Director: Mr Paul Lindsay. *Associate Director:* Miss Jo Goode. Executive staff 1, Other staff 6. **CC** No.801806. Began 1985; interdenominational. (Previously Christian Service Centre). Magazines: *Interviews* (3,000 every six months), *STS Directory* (4,500 annually), *Mission Matters* (15,000 annually). Turnover £160,000 to year end Dec 02.

Personnel Consultancy & Placement

Christians Abroad, Room 235, Bon Marché Centre, 241 Ferndale Road, London SW9 8BJ
☎0870 770 7990 🖷0870 770 7991
E: director@cabroad.org.uk
Web: www.cabroad.org.uk
Providing information and advice about work abroad; project management and recruitment for overseas projects.
Director: Rev Philip Wetherell. *Information Officer:* Mr Kevin Cusack. Executive staff 2. ***CC*** No.265867. Began 1973; non-denominational. Also known as World Service Enquiry (www.wse.org.uk). Magazine: *Opportunities Abroad* (Circulation n/a Eleven times a year), *WSE Guide* (25,000 annually). Turnover £200,000 to year end Dec 04.

***Edinburgh International Health Centre**, Elphinstone Wing, Carberry, Musselburgh EH21 8PW
☎0131 653 6767 M: 07710 276 208
🖷0131 653 3646
E: admin@eihc.org
Web: www.eihc.org
Out-patient medical care, debriefing assessment, counselling and retreat for missionaries and UK Christian workers.
Medical Director: Dr Michael Jones. *Director Psychiatric Services:* Mrs Elizabeth Jones. Executive staff 4, Other staff 6. ***CC*** No.SCO 00948. Began 1983; interdenominational. (Previously Care for Mission). No magazine. Turnover £110,811 to year end Apr 05.

***Faith Hope Enterprise Company Ltd**, Lodge Farm, Lodge Lane, Kirk Langley, Ashbourne DE6 4NX
☎01332 824 903 M: 07770 225 332
E: faithhope.ent@btopenworld.com
Providing supported housing, mentoring, coaching, development training, basic skills and social enterprise development.
Director: Mr Carl Taylor. Executive staff 2, Other staff 7. Began 1988; interdenominational. (Previously Third Wave Group Ltd). No magazine. Turnover £150,000 to year end Mar 04.

S

Friends First, PO Box 8377, Harborne, Birmingham B17 9TE
☎0121 427 1286
E: info@friends1st.co.uk
Web: www.friends1st.co.uk
Helping single Christians to find friends and potential partners leading to relationships and marriage.
Coordinator: Ms Katharine Gray. Admin staff 2. Began 2000; interdenominational. No magazine. Turnover n/a.

Integrity HR Consulting Ltd, 2 Prestwold Way, Hasland Hall Park, Chesterfield S41 0YA
☎01246 237 719 M: 07968 550 508
E: steve@integrityhrconsulting.co.uk
Web: www.integrityhrconsulting.co.uk
Human resources consultancy specialising in talent management, attraction acquisition and development of key people.
Managing Director: Mr Steven Jacques. Executive staff 2. Began 2005; non-denominational. No magazine. Turnover £50,000 to year end Mar 06.

International Catholic Society for Girls (ACISJF), 8 Farm Lane, Croydon CR0 8AQ
☎020 8777 8371 M: 07764 672 594
🖷020 8777 8371
E: aupairs@zetnet.co.uk
Web: www.aupairadvice.org.uk
Au pair advisory service in the UK and on the continent.
Organising Secretary: Mrs Andrea Watson. Executive staff 1, Other staff 2. ***CC*** No.275997. Began 1924; Roman Catholic. No magazine. Turnover n/a.

Jesuit Volunteer Community: Britain, 23 New Mount Street, Manchester M4 4DE
☎0161 832 6888 🖷0161 832 6958
E: staff@jvc.u-net.com
Web: www.jesuitvolunteers-uk.org
Offering year of voluntary work, community living and reflective development programme for adults aged 18 to 35.
Contact: Sarah Rogers. Community n/a. ***CC*** No.230165. Began 1987; Roman Catholic. Magazine: *JVC Newsletter* (1,000 half-yearly). Turnover £220,000 to year end Dec 02.

†**Lifewise Coaching**, 9 Timothy Close, Norwich NR1 4NG
☎01603 436 658 🖷01603 700 734
E: john@lifewisecoaching.org
Web: www.lifewisecoaching.org or www.drjohnclements.com
Speaking at men's and business events about personal effectiveness, servant leadership and character development.
Founder: Rev Dr John Clements. Executive staff 2. Began 1986; non-denominational. (Previously Creative Mentors Ltd). No magazine. Turnover £20,000 to year end Mar 02.

MDN Fusion, PO Box 6056, Basingstoke RG22 5YS
☎01256 324 328 M: 07774 820 325
🖷01256 843 673
E: markt@mdnfusion.com
Web: www.mdnfusion.com
People management consultancy including recruitment, training and general human resources development.
Director: Mr Mark Thomas. Executive staff 2, Other staff 3. Began 2003; non-denominational. (Previously Thomas Consultancy). No magazine. Turnover n/a.

***The Network**, PO Box 123, Ludlow SY8 2WU
☎01584 876 116
E: info@singleandchristian.co.uk
Web: www.singleandchristian.co.uk
Holidays for single Christians; self development courses, matching service, internet dating; all ages, all traditions.
Directors: Miss Susan Ashman. Executive staff 1, Other staff 2. Began 1988; non-denominational. (Previously Christian Computer-Link). Magazine: *Christian Single* (1,300 quarterly). Turnover n/a.

New Day Introductions, 15 Greave Close, Rawtenstall, Rossendale BB4 8JT
☎01706 224 049
E: suenewday@aol.com
Web: www.marriageintroductions.co.uk
Arranging nationwide professional marriage introductions for single, widowed and divorced Christians.
Proprietor: Mrs Susan Saxon. Executive staff 2. Began 1990; interdenominational. No magazine. Turnover n/a.

***Partnership Link-up Service**, 2 Blenheim Close, Cambridge CB1 8DU
☎01223 415 757
E: partnership-plus@xalt.co.uk
Web: www.partnershipuk.org
Linking independent evangelical churches with those seeking paid staff positions (pastoral, evangelistic, youth).
Administrator/Secretary: Mr Keith Barnard. Admin staff 1. ***CC*** No.8025[illegible]4. Began 1991; Christian Brethren. Part of Partnership UK. No magazine. Turnover £1,500 to year end Mar 03.

People Matter Trust, 17 Gildredge Road, Eastbourne BN21 4RU
☎01323 431 289
🖷01323 431 289
E: peter@people-matter.org.uk
Web: www.people-matter.org.uk
Job search assistance, CV development and workplace advice service.
Senior Manager: Mr Peter Moore. Support Staff 10. ***CC*** No.1062467. Began 19[illegible]7; ecumenical. No magazine. Turnover £41,000 to year end Oct 04.

Senior Volunteer Network, 9 Brecon Close, Droitwich Spa, Droitwich WR9 0[illegible]B
☎01905 796 313
E: svn.crump@btinternet.com
Web: www.svnet.org
Linking retired Christian teachers with UK and overseas organisations that need their skill and experience.
Director: Mr John Crump. No full-time paid staff. ***CC*** No.106849. Began 1996; non-denominational. No magazine. Turnover £6,000 to year end Mar 03.

†**SIMA (UK) Ltd Management Consultancy**, Clockhouse Barn, Sugworth Lane, Radley, Abingdon OX14 2HX
☎01865 321 123
🖷01865 326 611
E: info@sima.co.uk
Web: www.sima.co.uk
Coaching people and training in coaching to help organisations make productive use of their people.
Managing Director: Dr Nick Isbister. Executive staff 3, Other staff 2. Began 198[illegible]; non-denominational. No magazine. Turnover n/a.

***TASK (Training and Advice for Service in the Kingdom)**, 13 School Road, Bradenham, Thetford IP25 7QU
☎01760 440 200
E: enquiries@taskgb.co.uk
Web: www.taskgb.co.uk
Advising and training Christians to work effectively in secular and cross-cultural positions overseas.
Director: Mr Roger G Wells. Network of mentors 8. ***CC*** No.1068212. Began 1994; interdenominational. No magazine. Turnover £6,000 to year end Oct 05.

TPlacements, 1 Chelsea Embankments, London SW3 4LG
☎020 7352 7494 M: 07913 263 494
E: tplacements@talk21.com
Web: www.tplacements.org.uk
Offering gap years of shorter placements in local Christian charities; worldwide.
Coordinator: Miss Sophia Pain. No full-time staff. Began 2003; interdenominational. Turnover n/a.

Peter Young Consulting Ltd, Mansells, 72 Church Road, Witney OX29 8JF
☎01993 880 529 M: 07788 752 404
🖷01993 880 529
E: pete.y@virgin.net
Leadership coaching, organisational consulting, management training and development within UK and international organisations.
Management Consultant: Mr Peter Young. Executive staff 1. Began 1998; non-denominational. No magazine. Turnover n/a.

PRAYER FELLOWSHIPS

***Christ Intercessors Network**, 30 Woolley House, Loughborough Road, London SW9 7EH
☎020 7733 1987 M: 07947 384 530
🖷020 7733 1987
E: cinsopnet@aol.com
Operating a school of prayer and a prayer centre to win and establish souls.
Senior Minister: Rev Matthew Okuboyejo. Executive staff 1, Admin staff 1. ***CC*** No.1084936. Began 1999; interdenominational. No magazine. Turnover n/a.

Christian Road Safety Association, 7 Goldstone Close, Hove BN3 7PD
☎01273 554 598 🖷01273 554 598
E: crsa1937@msn.com
Web: www.crsa.org.uk
Teaching the Christian concepts of behaviour to all road users through care and prayer.
Hon Organising Secretary: Rev Eric Thorn. Executive staff 1, Other staff 4. ***CC*** No.258938. Began 1937; interdenominational. No magazine. Turnover n/a.

***Crosswinds Prayer Trust**, PO Box 1041, Nailsea, Bristol BS48 4SD
☎01275 852 700 🖷01275 852 700
E: info@crosswinds.co.uk
Web: www.crosswinds.co.uk
Mobilising interdenominational prayer weeks within UK's 124 postcode areas; global intercession through secure internet prayer hub.
National Director: Rev Preb John Simons. Executive staff 2. ***CC*** No.1031629. Began 1994; interdenominational. No magazine. Turnover £7,100 to year end Jun 03.

†**Divine Healing Ministries**, 32 Townsend Street, Belfast BT13 2ES
☎028 9031 1532
Web: www.divinehealing.org.uk
Prayer with laying on of hands, intercession for the sick, prayer for our land.
Pastoral Director: Rev Brother David Jardine. Executive staff 2. ***CC*** No.XN 91984. Began 1993; interdenominational. No magazine. Turnover £20,489 to year end Sep 96.

East Gate Prayer, Carey House, Brecklands Green, North Pickenham, Swaffham PE37 8LG
☎01760 440 561 M: 07742 219 756
🖷01760 440 561
E: peter@eastgate.org.uk
Web: www.eastgate.org.uk
Promoting prayer and intercession; leading prayer initiatives around East Anglia; regular monthly meetings.
Director: Mr Peter Gillett. No full-time staff. ***CC*** No.1009279. Began n/a; interdenominational. (Previously Anglia Prayer). Part of East Gate Trust. No magazine. Turnover n/a.

†**Eden Ministries**, Rose Lodge, Highland Road, Taverham, Norwich NR8 6QP
☎01603 866 212
E: edenmin@clara.co.uk
Teaching and prayer/intercession ministry serving the Church in Norfolk.
Leader: Jill Gower. No full-time staff. Began n/a; Kingdom Faith Church. No magazine. Turnover n/a.

Edinburgh Prayer Network, 3 Little France Mills, Edinburgh EH16 4SF
☎0131 664 9596 M: 07884 125 126
E: morrow@xaltmail.com
Web: www.edinburghprayer.org
Coordinating prayer for the city of Edinburgh.
Coordinator: Mr Tom Morrow. No paid staff. Began 2005; interdenominational. No magazine. Turnover: first year of operation.

The Fellowship of Contemplative Prayer (FCP), 9 All Saints Close, Asfordby, Melton Mowbray LE14 3TF
☎No telephone
E: mj.hall100@virgin.net
Web: www.contemplative-prayer.org.uk
Encouraging and promoting contemplative prayer by teaching, organising prayer groups, quiet days and retreats.
Administrator: Mrs Margaret Hall. All voluntary staff. ***CC*** No.298850. Began 1949; interdenominational. Magazines: *Living Word* (1,000 annually), *Come* (2,000 annually). Turnover £9,000 to year end Apr 05.

The Fellowship of Meditation, Marian Dunlop House, 8 Prince of Wales Road, Dorchester DT1 1PW
☎01305 251 396
E: fellowship.meditation@virgin.net
Web: www.fellowshipofmeditation.org
Teaching and practising Christian contemplative meditation; running gatherings; publishing.
Chair: Mrs Pat Bullamore. Admin staff 2. ***CC*** No.213323. Began 1952; non-denominational. No magazine. Turnover £66,395 to year end Dec 04.

The Guild of the Holy Ghost The Comforter, 2 Norris Gardens, Warblington, Havant PO9 2TT
☎023 9248 2922
E: vichar@supanet.com
Anglican prayer guild; monthly leaflet containing prayers for every day of the week.
Secretary: Mr B deV Hardcastle. No full-time staff. Began 1893; Anglican. No magazine. Turnover n/a.

Inter Prayer, PO Box 136, St Leonards-on-Sea TN37 7NZ
☎01424 850 195 M: 07885 600 903
E: office@interprayer.com
Web: www.interprayer.com
Building partnerships together in prayer across the nations, emphasising reconciliation, revival, transformation and harvest.
Director: Mr Brian Mills. Executive staff 3, International Partners 22. ***CC*** No.1095338. Began 1997; non-denominational. Magazine: *Interprayer News* (500 quarterly). Turnover £16,000 to year end Apr 98.

***Intercessors for Britain**, 14 Orchard Road, Moreton, Wirral CH46 8TS
☎0151 677 6767
Promoting regular and disciplined intercession for the nation.
Director: Mr Raymond Borlase. Executive staff 1, Other staff 2. ***CC*** No.290664. Began 1969; interdenominational. Magazine: *Watchman* (2,000 every four months). Turnover n/a.

S

The Julian Meetings, 32 Alfred Street, Gloucester GL1 4DF
☎No telephone
E: nat.coordinator@julianmeetings.org
Web: www.julianmeetings.org
Fostering the practice and teaching of contemplative prayer in the Christian tradition.
National Coordinator: Deidre Morris. No full-time staff. Began 1973; non-denominational. Magazine: *Julian Meetings Magazine* (Circulation n/a three times a year). Turnover n/a.

†**The League of Prayer**, 69 The Wynding, Bedlington NE22 6HW
☎01670 823 036
E: norryl@fish.co.uk
Promoting prayer for revival and the spread of scriptural holiness in Christian life.
Director: Major Norman Armistead. Executive staff 1. ***CC*** No.1040100. Began 1891; interdenominational. No magazine. Turnover £5,000 to year end Dec 02.

Lighthouse Ministry Prayer Fellowship (MCCPF), 35 Four Acres, Uttlesford, Saffron Walden CB11 3JD
☎Number not supplied
Intercession, literature, cassettes distrubution; UK, Ghana, Malawi, Uganda, Ukraine, Zambia, South America.
Administrator: Mr John E Maddams. No paid staff. Began 1954; interdenominational. (Previously Ministry of Christian Communication Prayer Fellowships (MCCPF)). Magazine: *Lighthouse Ministry(MCCPF) Prayer News* (100 every four months). Turnover £2,860 to year end Jun 00.

The Living Spirituality Network, The Well at Willen, Newport Road, Willen, Milton Keynes MK15 9AA
☎01908 200 675
E: spirituality@ctbi.org.uk
Web: www.living-spirituality.org.uk
Supporting, promoting and facilitating exploration of spirituality within and beyond the traditional churches.
Director: Ms Eley McAinsh. Executive staff 1, No other paid staff. ***CC*** No.259688. Began 2000; ecumenical. (Previously Fellowship of Prayer for Unity, merged with Ecumenical Spirituality Project). Magazine: *Spirituality News* (Circulation n/a quarterly). Turnover n/a.

S

***Lydia Fellowship International**, PO Box 85, Waterlooville PO7 7QU
☎023 9226 7684
E: molly.osborne@ntlworld.com
Prayer fellowship primarily for women.
UK and European Leader: Mrs Molly Osborne. All voluntary staff. Began 1970; non-denominational. No magazine. Turnover n/a.

***Manchester Prayer Network**, Nazarene Theological College, Dene Road, Didsbury, Manchester M20 2GU
☎M: 07762 627 568
E: info@network-ea.org.uk
Web: www.network-ea.org.uk
People and churches praying and working together to see Greater Manchester won for Jesus.
Coordinator: Dr M Hoek. Other staff 1. ***CC*** No.504453. Began 1993; interdenominational. No magazine. Turnover n/a.

***Pray for Scotland**, PO Box 21114, Alloa FK10 3YL
☎01786 823 430
E: admin@prayforscotland.org
Web: www.prayforscotland.org
Networking existing prayer movements in Scotland; issuing calls to pray for nation; seeking revival.
Administrator: Kate Fenn-Tye. Admin staff 1, Other staff 2. ***CC*** No.SC 029844. Began 2002; non-denominational. (Previously Prayer Network for Revival). No magazine. Turnover £20,000 to year end Apr 05.

Prayer at Twelve Fellowship, 17 Villers Road, Woodthorpe, Nottingham NG5 4FB
☎0115 962 2599
E: monkton@surfaid.org
Web: www.prayer12.org.uk
Midday prayer fellowship and support movement for those who are ill or in special need.
Warden: Rev David Monkton. No full-time staff. Began 1975; non-denominational. Magazine: *Twelve* (400 occasionally). Turnover n/a.

***Prayer Expeditions**, 26 Charterhouse Road, Orpington BR6 9EL
☎01689 830 872
E: yvonne.presdee@ntlworld.com
Web: www.prayerexpeditions.org.uk
Praying for UK and Europe by prayer walking, reconciliation and healing the land.
Director: Mr John Presdee. *Secretary:* Mrs Yvonne Presdee. No tull-time staff. ***CC*** No.1057224. Began 1996; interdenominational. No magazine. Turnover £20,000 to year end Dec 05.

***Prayer Fellowship for South Asia**, 28 Musley Lane, Ware SG12 7EW
☎01920 413 572
E: colin@compassbraille.org
Organising prayer for the peoples of South Asia, including in the Indian sub-continent.
Chairman: Mr Colin Dowling. No full-time staff. Began 1940; interdenominational. No magazine. Turnover £800 to year end Dec 04.

Prayer for the City (Glasgow), PO Box 7010, Eaglesham, Glasgow G76 0WF
☎0141 270 9732
E: stevenanderson@btinternet.com
Web: www.pftcglasgow.com
Facilitating unity and encouraging prayer among church leaders and churches in the Glasgow area.
Director: Rev Steven Anderson. No full-time paid staff. ***CC*** No.SCO 32829. Began 1999; non-denominational. No magazine. Turnover £10,000 to year end Dec 05.

***Prayer for the Nations**, PO Box 15027, London SE5 0YS
☎0845 130 9797 M: 07834 356 067
Fax 020 7346 0137
E: info@pfnonline.com
Web: www.prayforthenations.com
Training school of prayer, intercession; UK prayer events; prayer for nation; discipleship training correspondence course.
Founders: Rod & Julie Anderson. Executive staff 2, Other staff 5. ***CC*** No.32[illegible]994. Began 1992; interdenominational. Magazine: *Watchman's Journal* (Circulation n/a occasionally). Turnover £20[illegible],000 to year end Dec 00.

Prayer For The Poor, 2 Piggott House, Sewardstone Road, London E2 9JJ
☎No telephone
E: prayerforthepoor@tesco.net
Praying for the poor and asking God to speak into the problems of poverty.
Director: Mr Mal Grosch. No other staff. Began 1999; ecumenical. No magazine. Turnover n/a.

***Prayer Trust Ministries**, PO Box 10[illegible]22, Rotherhithe, London SE16 5[illegible]H
☎07941 458 679
E: prayertrust@btinternet.com or admin@prayertrust.fsmail.net
Web: www.greaterlondonprayerwall.org or www.prayertrustministries.org
Intercessory and caring ministry for leaders; incorporating the Greater London Prayer Wall.
Coordinator: Rev Grace Komolafe. Admin staff 1. ***CC*** No.106451. Began 1[illegible]97; non-denominational. Magazine: *Mind The Gap* (Circulation n/a quarterly). Turnover n/a.

***Prayer TV**, PO Box 154, Dinas Powys CF64 4WX
☎02920 512 126 Fax 02920 512 4[illegible]
E: admin@prayer.tv
Web: www.prayer.tv
Promoting prayer in Britain and Ireland.
Founder: Mr Carl Brettle. Executive staff 2, Other staff 4. Began 2003; interdenominational. Magazine: *Prayer Magazine* (10,000 quarterly). Turnover £45,0[illegible] to year end Aug 04.

The Quiet Garden Trust, Stoke Park Farm, Park Road, Stoke Poges, Slough SL2 4[illegible]G
☎01753 643 050 Fax 01753 643 08[illegible]
E: quiet.garden@ukonline.co.uk
Web: www.quietgarden.co.uk
Encouraging ministry of hospitality and prayer on occasional basis in local homes, gardens, schools, elsewhere.
Director: Rev Philip D Roderick. Executive staff 1, Other staff 1. ***CC*** No.10385[illegible]8. Began 1992; ecumenical. Magazine: *Quiet Places* (Circulation & frequency n/a). Turnover n/a.

Servants of Christ the King, Well Cottage, The Street, Kilmington, Axminster EX[illegible]3 7RW
☎01297 341 42
E: info@sck.org.uk
Web: www.sck.org.uk
Companies waiting upon God in silence followed by controlled discussion leading to corporate action.
Enquirers' Correspondent: Mrs Sy[illegible]a Wilsdon. No full-time staff. ***CC*** No.249609. Began 1942; interdenominational. Magazine: *SCK Newsletter* (5[illegible] quarterly). Turnover £5,000 to year end Dec 98.

***Telephone Prayer Chain Ministry**, c/o Partick Baptist Church, 19 Crow Road, Glasgow G11 7RT
☎0141 339 9212/9215
🖷0141 332 5152
E: prayerchain@tpcm.org.uk
Activating prayer for our nation, individuals and communities.
UK Leader: Mrs Jessie McFarlane. All voluntary staff. **CC** No.SCO 20478. Began 1931; interdenominational. Magazine: *Chain Link* (1,000 quarterly). Turnover £10,000 to year end Jul 00.

***There is Hope**, 67 Wright Street, Hull HU2 8JD
☎01482 506 606
E: david@hope.karoo.co.uk
Web: www.thereishope.co.uk
Uniting churches in prayer and evangelism.
Director: Mr David Hill. Executive staff 1, Other staff 3. **CC** No.1107542. Began 1985; interdenominational. No magazine. Turnover £20,000 to year end Aug 05.

True Vine Prayer Fellowship, 67 Dovers Park, Bathford, Bath BA1 7UD
☎01225 859 271
Supporting preaching and empowerment of excluded people, including prisoners, youth; lay ministry and creative arts.
Leader: Mr Tom Harper. No full-time paid staff 1. Began 1993; interdenominational. No magazine. Turnover £1,200 to year end Dec 00.

Trumpet Call, St Paul's Vicarage, Lincoln Road, Peterborough PE1 2PA
☎01733 343 746
E: info@trumpetcall.org.uk
Web: www.trumpetcall.org.uk
Gathering, encouraging, teaching intercessors of every denomination to pray for revival.
Chairman: Rev Paul Larcombe. No paid staff. **CC** No.1075520. Began 1996; non-denominational. Magazine: *Prayer Watch Dispatches* (100 every two months). Turnover £3,400 to year end Mar 02.

***Wales Awake**, PO Box 65, Brecon LD3 7XY
☎01874 665 736
E: dudley@walesawake.fsnet.co.uk
Establishing a network of interdenominational prayer groups to pray for revival in Wales.
Director: Mr Dudley Griffiths. Executive staff 1, Admin staff 1. Began 2005; interdenominational. No magazine. Turnover n/a.

†Watchmen Over Britain, 6 Stevenson Road, Doveridge, Ashbourne DE6 5NX
☎01889 568 792
Coordinating prayer groups of Christian men to pray for Britain.
Coordinator: Rev E John Metcalfe. No full-time staff. Began 2001; non-denominational. No magazine. Turnover £600 to year end Mar 03.

†Wholeness Through Christ, Waggon Road, Brightons, Falkirk FK2 0EL
☎01324 714 946 🖷01324 714 946
E: wtcoffice@aol.com
Web: www.wholenessthroughchrist.org
Enabling people to live in a life transforming relationship with Jesus Christ.
Director: To be appointed. Executive staff 2. **CC** No.327055. Began 1971; interdenominational. No magazine. Turnover n/a.

Women's World Day of Prayer, Commercial Road, Tunbridge Wells TN1 2RR
☎01892 541 411 🖷01892 541 745
E: office@wwdp-natcomm.org
Web: www.wwdp-natcomm.org
Organising, training for the Day of Prayer.
Admin Secretary: Mrs Lynda Lynam. Executive staff 1, Other staff 2. **CC** No.233242. Began 1932; interdenominational. Magazine: *Together in Prayer* (13,500 annually). Turnover £291,048 to year end Dec 02.

World Day of Prayer - Scottish Committee, 8 Dovecote View, Kirkintilloch, Glasgow G66 3HY
☎0141 776 1337
E: morag.hannah.wdp@virgin.net
Web: www.wdpscotland.org.uk
Preparing and distributing worship materials, organising and training for the Day of Prayer.
Secretary: Mrs Morag Hannah. No full-time staff. **CC** No.SCO 20446. Began 1930; interdenominational. No magazine. Turnover £68,161 to year end Apr 05.

***World Prayer Centre**, Cornerstone House, 5 Ethel Street, Birmingham B2 4BG
☎0121 633 7393 🖷0121 643 5645
E: office@worldprayer.org.uk
Web: www.worldprayer.org.uk
Encouraging and mobilising Christians to pray for the UK and the world.
Chair of Trustees: Mr Ian Cole. *Staff Contact:* Laurence Sharman. Executive staff 4. **CC** No.1072222. Began 1988; interdenominational. No magazine. Turnover £100,000 to year end Sep 05.

PRINTERS

Agapé Press (UK) Limited, Unit 1D, Kingston Mill, Cobden Street, Pendleton, Salford M6 6WG
☎0161 743 1010 M: 07789 823 095
🖷0161 743 9991
E: info@agape-press.com
Web: www.agape-press.com
Advancing Christian faith through creative communication: print, website design; publishing books, multi-media materials.
Managing Director: Dr Don E Okpalugo. All voluntary staff. **CC** No.1059348. Began 1996; non-denominational. Turnover £15,000 to year end Mar 02.

†Aldridge Print Group, Unit 9, Mitcham Industrial Estate, Streatham Road, Mitcham CR4 2AP
☎020 8239 4141
🖷020 8239 4120
E: info@apgprint.com
Web: www.apgprint.com
Providing printing services to Christian and charitable organisations.
Managing Director: Mr Robert Aldridge. *Operations Director:* Mr Ben Turner. Executive staff 7, Admin staff 25, Other staff 30. Began 1897; non-denominational. Turnover £5,500,000 to year end Apr 03.

Bookprint Creative Services, PO Box 2118, Seaford BN25 9AR
M: 07711 854 371/372
E: bcs@bookprint.co.uk
Web: www.bookprint.co.uk
Book production and design for publishers, Christian organisations and authors; paperbacks, hardbacks, music books, Bibles.
Senior Partner: Mr David Nickalls. Executive staff 2, Other staff 4. Began 1993; non-denominational. Turnover n/a.

Printers

Christian Duplicating Service, 3 Castle Road, Nottingham NG1 6AA
☎0115 947 5311
📠0115 947 5367
E: christianduplicating@tiscali.co.uk
Offset duplicating, colour copying, black and white copying and print finishing services.
Proprietor: Mr Trevor Smith. Executive staff 2, Other staff 1. Began 1966; non-denominational. Turnover £75,000 to year end Dec 00.

Christian Mission Press, 62 Whitby Road, Ruislip HA4 9DP
☎01895 672 161
📠01895 672 161
E: colin.drake@virgin.net
Offering wide range of printing services including full colour; for Christian organisations, churches, individuals.
Master Printer: Mr Colin Drake. Executive staff 2. Began 1987; non-denominational. Turnover n/a.

Christian Printing Services, 54 Roseford Road, Cambridge CB4 2HD
☎01223 322 277
📠01223 322 277
E: cps@christianbooksdirect.co.uk
Printing all types of material from copying to four-colour.
Proprietor: Mr Trevor Hames. Executive staff 2, Other staff 1. ***CC*** No.255001. Began 1992; interdenominational. Turnover £30,000 to year end Apr 05.

***Christian Publishing & Outreach Ltd**, Garcia Estate, Canterbury Road, Worthing BN13 1BW
☎01903 264 556/263 354 (sales)
📠01903 830 066
E: enquiries@cpo.org.uk
Web: www.cpo.org.uk
Providing design, print publishing and fulfilment services.
Chief Executive: Paul Slide. Executive staff 4, Other staff 41. ***CC*** No.221462. Began 1957; non-denominational. (Previously Christian Publicity Organisation). Turnover £2,400,000 to year end Apr 02.

CLS Graphics Ltd, Apex House, 97 High Street, Edenbridge TN8 5AU
☎01732 864 194
📠01732 865 615
E: alanf@clsgraphics.co.uk
Web: www.clsgraphics.co.uk
Providing exhibition and display stands, printing, design and marketing services to Christian and charitable organisations.
Marketing Manager: Mr Alan Franklin. Executive staff 2, Other staff 6. Began 1977; non-denominational. Turnover n/a.

CM Print Ltd, 61 Station Road, Portslade, Brighton BN41 1DF
☎01273 420 983 M: 07850 292 106
📠01273 415 013
E: alan.jarred@cmprint.co.uk
Supplying all types of printing for churches, charities and businesses; nationwide.
Partner: Mr Alan Jarred. Executive staff 2, Other staff 8. Began 1985; non-denominational. Turnover £450,000 to year end Dec 02.

†Creative Solutions, Unit 2, Uplyme Road Business Park, Lyme Regis DT7 3LS
☎01297 444 622 M: 07971 787 742
📠01297 444 690
E: sales@c-s.uk.com
Web: www.c-s.uk.com
Manufacturing banners, bunting, exhibition equipment, display boards, notice boards, A-boards and signage.
Proprietor: Mr Mark Shurey. Executive staff 1, Other staff 1. Began 1998; non-denominational. Turnover £500,000 to year end Dec 02.

***Guerrilla Republic Limited**, 81 Earles Meadow, Horsham RH12 4HR
☎01403 256 225 M: 07775 856 456
📠01403 251 818
E: brian@guerrillarepublic.co.uk
Web: www.guerrillarepublic.co.uk
Producing promotional items: pens, lanyards, wristbands, T-shirts, bags; designing and printing cards, leaflets, booklets.
Proprietor: Mr Brian Abell. Executive staff 1. Began 1991; non-denominational. (Previously Rdi - Revival Digital Imaging). Turnover n/a.

Stanley L Hunt (Printers) Ltd, Midland Road, Rushden NN10 9UA
☎01933 356 226 📠01933 356 613
E: sales@stanleyhunt.co.uk
General printers; suppliers to Christian organisations and institutions for over 85 years.
Managing Director: Mr Andrew M Hunt. Executive staff 6, Other staff 45. Began 1916; non-denominational. Turnover n/a.

†Imprint, Unit 2 & 3 Enterprise Estate, Station Road West, Ash Vale, Aldershot GU12 5QJ
☎01252 547 023 📠01252 376 004
E: info@imprintcolour.co.uk
Web: www.imprintcolour.co.uk
Four-colour printing magazines, newsletters, leaflets, brochures, letterheads, paperback books, calling cards; design, artwork, print finishing.
Proprietors: Mr John & Mr T Reading. Executive staff 2, Other staff 2. Began 1983; non-denominational. Turnover n/a.

Kingsley (Litho) Printers, The Old Blacksmiths, 52 High Street, Ilfracombe EX34 9QB
☎01271 863 131
📠01271 866 646
E: kingsleyprint@hotmail.com
General printers.
Partners: Mr David Lane, Mr Peter M[illegible]nell. Executive staff 2, Other staff 3. Began 1954; Anglican. Turnover £240,000 to year end Jan 99.

MPH, 4 John Wesley Road, Werrington, Peterborough PE4 6ZP
☎01733 325 002
📠01733 384 180
E: chief.exec@mph.org.uk
Web: www.mph.org.uk
Providing printing and mailing services for Christian organisations.
Head of Retail: Mr David Ru[illegible]iger. Executive staff 1, Other staff 28. ***CC*** Began 1750; Methodist. (Previously Methodist Publishing House). Imprints: Epworth, Methodist Publishing House, Inspire. Turnover n/a.

Print by Design Ltd, 16 Castle Street, Bodmin PL31 2DU
☎0845 226 7306
📠0845 226 7307
E: sales@printbydesign.co.uk
Designing and printing books, magazines, leaflets, tracts, stationery, posters, banners.
Director: Mr Peter Walters. Executive staff 2, Admin staff 2. Began 1[illegible]95; interdenominational. Turnover n/a.

Tyndale Press, Tyndale House, Wolla[illegible]on, Lowestoft NR32 2PD
☎01502 561 299
M: 07813 172 440
📠01502 519 180
E: sales@tyndale-press.co.uk
Web: www.tyndale-press.co.uk
Supplying printing nationwide.
Managing Director: Mr Bar[illegible]ie Co[illegible]ey. *Works Manager:* Mr Gordon B[illegible]rden. Executive staff 2, Admin staff 2, Other staff 8. Began 1933; non-denominational. Turnover £480,000 to year end May 02.

Wright's (Sandbach) Ltd, 9 Old Middlewich Road, Sandbach CW11 [illegible]DP
☎01270 762 416
📠01270 760 278
E: andrew@wrightsprinters.com
Web: www.wrightsprinters.com
Nationwide print supplier to Christian organisations.
Directors: Mr G F Galway, Mr D A Sa[illegible]e. Executive staff 2, Other staff 23. Began 1896; interdenominational. Turnover £1,700,000 to year end May 05.

S

PROFESSIONAL CHRISTIAN GROUPS

Actors' Church Union, St Paul's Church, Bedford Street, Covent Garden, London WC2E 9ED
☎020 7240 0344
E: actors_church_union@yahoo.co.uk
Web: www.actorschurchunion.org
Arranging chaplains for each theatre in the UK; providing educational funding for children of actors.
Senior Chaplain: Rev Canon Richard Truss. Staff 1. **CC** No.207315. Began 1899; Anglican. No magazine. Turnover £22,752 to year end Dec 02.

Agricultural Christian Fellowship, Manor Farm, West Haddon, Northampton NN6 7AQ
☎01788 510 866 🖷01788 510 026
E: holmains@pobox.co.uk
Encouraging practical Christian living and developing informed Christian understanding amongst Christians in agriculture. A LCCF group.
Chairman: Dr Peter Carruthers. No full-time staff. **CC** Began 1964; interdenominational. Magazine: *ACF Bulletin* (200 half-yearly). Turnover n/a.

Armed Forces' Christian Union, Havelock House, Barrack Road, Aldershot GU11 3NP
☎01252 311 221 🖷01252 350 722
E: office@afcu.org.uk
Web: www.afcu.org.uk
Christian work in HM Armed Forces.
Executive Secretary: Major (Retd) L R Smith. Executive staff 3, Other staff 3. **CC** No.249636. Began 1851; interdenominational. (Previously Officers Christian Union). Magazine: *Contact* (3,000 quarterly). Turnover £239,000 to year end Dec 04.

***Arts Centre Group**, Menier Chocolate Factory, 51 Southwark Street, London SE1 1RU
☎0845 458 1881 M: 07913 281 918
E: info@artscentregroup.org.uk
Web: www.artscentregroup.org.uk
Supporting Christians working professionally in the arts, media and entertainment.
Administrator: Ms Katy Jones. Executive staff 1. **CC** No.289763. Began 1971; interdenominational. No magazine. Turnover £50,000 to year end Mar 98.

***Association of Bible College Principals**, Redcliffe College, Wotton House, Horton Road, Gloucester GL1 3PT
☎01452 308 097 🖷01452 503 949
Web: www.ukbiblecolleges.com
Co-ordinating activities and fellowship between Bible Colleges.
Secretary: Rev Dr Simon Steer. No full-time staff. Began 1976; interdenominational. No magazine. Turnover £1,000 to year end Mar 97.

Association of Christian Law Firms, 2 Devonshire Avenue, Beeston, Nottingham NG9 1BS
☎0115 922 1591 🖷0115 925 9341
E: s.hale@ellis-fermor.co.uk
Web: www.aclf.org.uk
Encouraging and training for Christian law firms and support of Christian work.
Hon Secretary: Mr Simon Hale. No full-time staff. Began 1990; non-denominational. No magazine. Turnover n/a.

***Association of Christian Teachers**, 94a London Road, St Albans AL1 1NX
☎01727 840 298 🖷01727 848 966
E: act@christian-teachers.org.uk
Web: www.christian-teachers.org.uk
Providing professional and spiritual support to Christians working in schools and colleges in England.
Chief Executive: Mr Rupert Kaye. *Office Manager:* Mrs Carol Horne. Executive staff 1, Other staff 2. **CC** No.295328. Began 1971; non-denominational. Magazine: *ACT Now* (3,000 every four months). Turnover £160,000 to year end Mar 04.

†***Association of Christian Teachers (Scotland)**, Rutherford House, 17 Claremont Park, Edinburgh EH6 7PJ
☎0131 333 4077 🖷0131 335 3993
E: actscotland@tesco.net
Support, resources and prayer for Christian teachers; Christian voice on educational issues in consultations and media.
Chairman: Miss Kirsti Paterson. Staff 1. **CC** No.SCO 09798. Began 1971; interdenominational. Magazine: *Interact* (550 every four months). Turnover £15,612 to year end May 98.

Association of Christian Teachers of Wales, 17 Brynmawr Place, Maesteg, Bridgend CF34 9PB
☎01656 734 118
Upholding Christian ideals and values in education today.
Hon Secretary: Miss J A Miller. No full-time staff. **CC** No.505329. Began 1974; non-denominational. Magazine: *ACTW News* (160 frequency n/a). Turnover £5,000 to year end Aug 05.

Association of Christian Writers, 43 All Saints Close, Edmonton, London N9 9AT
☎020 8884 4348 🖷020 8884 4348
E: admin@christianwriters.org.uk
Web: www.christianwriters.org.uk
Providing encouragement, advice, workshops and forums for Christian writers from beginner to professional.
Administrator: Jenny Kyriacou. No full-time staff. **CC** No.1069839. Began 1969; interdenominational. (Previously Fellowship of Christian Writers). Magazine: *Candle and Keyboard* (1,100 quarterly). Turnover £25,000 to year end Dec 02.

†**Aviation Christian Fellowship**, 5 Stuart House, Plantation Row, Hindhead GU26 6BP
☎01276 709 474
🖷01276 709 474
E: aaacf@lineone.net
Missionary outreach to aviation staff.
General Secretary: Name not supplied. Executive staff 1, Other staff 5. **CC** No.277929. Began 1971; interdenominational. (Previously Airline, Aviation and Aerospace Christian Fellowships). Magazine: *Crossway Outreach Magazine* (20,000 frequency n/a), *Newsline* (2,000 every four months), *Aviation News (Fairford)* (16,000 annually). Turnover n/a.

Baptist Ministers' Fellowship, 13 Wrefords Drive, Exeter EX4 5AU
☎01392 431 097
🖷01392 431 097
E: derek@keenans.org.uk
Promoting fellowship among Baptist ministers in various parts of the world and furthering their interests.
Secretary: Rev Derek J Keenan. No full-time staff. Began 1939; Baptist. Magazine: *The Baptist Ministers' Journal* (1,800 quarterly). Turnover n/a.

British Association of Christians in Psychology (BACIP), c/o Psychology Department, University of East London, London E15 4LZ
☎020 8223 4411
🖷020 8223 4967
E: secretary@bacip.org.uk
Web: www.bacip.org.uk
Association of Christian pychologists, national email network, regional groups, spring residential conference, autumn day conference.
Hon Secretary: Dr Martyn Baker. No full-time staff. Began 1989; interdenominational. (Previously Network of Christians in Psychology (NeCIP)). Magazine: *The Christian Psychologist* (300 half-yearly). Turnover £9,000 to year end Apr 05.

Professional Christian Groups

British Transport Christian Fellowship, 106 Stuart Road, Market Harborough LE16 9PH
☎01858 445 726
E: wjmay106@freeuk.com
Fellowship of Christians associated with transport, predominately rail.
President: Mr John May. No full-time staff. Began 1926; interdenominational. Associated with international Railway Mission. Magazine: *BTCF News* (Circulation n/a every four months). Turnover £8,500 to year end Jul 02.

***Fiona Bruce & Co Solicitors**, Justice House, 3 Grappenhall Road, Stockton Heath, Warrington WA4 2AH
☎01925 263 273 🖷01925 217 077
E: rbruce@fionabruce.co.uk
Web: www.fionabruce.co.uk
Advising individuals, businesses, churches and charities on all aspects of the law.
Practice Development Manager: Mr Richard Bruce. *Managing Partner:* Mrs Fiona Bruce. *Head of Family Law:* Mr Stephen Hayes. Executive staff 12, Admin staff 18. Began 1988; non-denominational. No magazine. Turnover £1,000,000 to year end Mar 06.

Business Men's Fellowship, National Service Centre, 454 Crow Road, Glasgow G11 7DR
☎M 07703 597 311 🖷0141 339 2554
E: agreenwood@bmf-uk.com or nsc@bmf-uk.com
Web: www.bmf-uk.com
Evangelical full gospel laymen's ministry.
Service Centre Coordinator: Mr Andrew Greenwood. Admin staff 1. **CC** No.SCO 25720. Began 1996; interdenominational. Magazine: *Answer* (6,000 quarterly). Turnover n/a.

***Business Study Group**, St. Peters Church, Vere Street, London W1G 0DQ
☎020 7399 9555 🖷020 7399 9556
E: bsg@licc.org.uk
Exploring and applying biblical principles in the business and working world.
Chairman: Mr David Parish. No full-time staff. **CC** Began 1965; non-denominational. No magazine. Turnover n/a.

†***CARE for Education**, Unit 2, The Oakwood Centre, Downley Road, Havant PO9 2NP
☎023 9261 0689 🖷023 9245 4489
E: cfe@care.org.uk or holt@care.org.uk
Web: www.care.org.uk
Equipping parents, governors, teachers and churches to be prayerfully and effectively involved in education.
Director: Mike Simmonds. Executive staff 1, Other staff 3. **CC** No.1066963. Began 1986; interdenominational. (Previously Christians in Education). Magazine: *Education Update* (8,000 half-yearly). Turnover £100,000 to year end Dec 98.

Choir Schools' Association, Wolvesey Palace, College Street, Winchester SO23 9NB
☎01962 890 530 🖷01962 869 978
E: admin@choirschools.org.uk
Web: www.choirschools.org.uk
Publicising the life and educational opportunities of cathedral and collegiate choirs.
Adminstrator: Mrs Susan Rees. Admin staff 1. Began 1921; Anglican and Roman Catholic. Affiliated with the Choir Schools Bursary Trust. Magazine: *Choir Schools Today* (5,000 annually). Turnover n/a.

Christian Academic Network (CAN), 38 De Montfort Street, Leicester LE1 7GP
☎No phone
E: info@c-a-n.org.uk
Web: www.c-a-n.org.uk
Fellowship for academic and administrative staff applying Christian thought to higher education.
Member of Leadership Team: Dr Maurice Manktelow. No full-time staff. **CC** Began 2001; interdenominational. (Previously Association of Christians in Higher Education (ACHE)). A joint partnership of UCCF and Agapé. No magazine. Turnover n/a.

***Christian Booksellers Convention Ltd**, PO Box 148, Uckfield TN22 5GR
☎01825 840 254 🖷01825 840 068
E: cbc@cbcltd.co.uk
Arranging annual event for booksellers and publishers in Great Britain; exhibitions, seminars.
Chairman: Mr Keith Danby. No full-time staff. Began 1975; non-denominational. No magazine. Turnover n/a.

Christian Booksellers Group, Booksellers Association of the United Kingdom & Ireland Limited, Minster House, 272 Vauxhall Bridge Road, London SW1V 1BA
☎020 7802 0802 🖷020 7802 0803
E: john.parke@booksellers.org.uk
Web: www.booksellers.org.uk
Seeking solutions to the problems and fighting for the interests of its members.
Chairman: Mr Steve Mitchell. *Secretary:* Mr John Parke. No full-time staff. Began n/a; non-denominational. No magazine. Turnover n/a.

***Christian Camping International (UK)**, 2 Leon House, Queensway, Bletchley, Milton Keynes MK2 2SS
☎01908 641 641 🖷01908 641 641
E: office@cci.org.uk
Web: www.cci.org.uk and www.ccivenuefinding.org; or www.getaway.org.uk
Resource, training and support association for all in Christian conference, holiday and outdoor centre ministries.
Chief Executive: Mr Jim Hammett. Admin staff 2. **CC** No.326637. Began 1986; non-denominational. Magazine: *Getaway* (700 every four months). Turnover £82,000 to year end Dec 04.

Christian Dance Fellowship of Britain, 14 Brecon Drive, Stourbridge DY8 [illegible]JU
☎01384 379 954
E: jan.cdfb@hotmail.co.uk
Web: www.cdfb.org.uk
Networking Christian dancers; teaching and training dancers of all abilities and styles.
National Coordinator: Jan Dyer. Admin staff 2. **CC** No.1040446. Began 1990; interdenominational. Magazine: *Test of David* (650 half-yearly). Turnover £14,000 to year end May 02.

Christian Dental Fellowship, 44 Pool Road, Hartley Wintney, Hook RG27 [illegible]RD
☎01252 845 991 🖷01252 607 8[illegible]0
E: cdfadmin@btinternet.com
Web: www.cdfuk.org
Fellowship of Christians in the dental profession; supporting dental missionary work. (No advice given)
Secretary: Neil McDonald. No full-time staff. **CC** No.261350. Began 1955; interdenominational. Magazine: *Newsround* (500 quarterly). Turnover £55 000 to year end Sept 04.

Christian Engineers Association, 148 Railway Terrace, Rugby CV21 3HN
☎01788 579 738 🖷01788 546 3[illegible]
E: cea@christiansatwork.org.uk
Study and fellowship group for professional engineers. A UCCF group.
Chairman: Mr John Baden Fuller. No full-time staff. **CC** Began 1981; interdenominational. Associated with Christians at Work. Magazine: *Perspective* (110 half-yearly). Turnover n/a.

Christian Literary Studies Group, 10 Dene Road, Northwood HA6 2AA
☎Number not supplied
E: secretary@clsg.org
Web: www.clsg.org
Promoting a Christian understanding of literature and issues in literary studies. Annual conference in November.
Secretary: Dr Roger Kojecky. No full-time staff. **CC** Began 1978; interdenominational. Magazine: *The Glass* (80 annually). Turnover n/a.

***Christian Medical Fellowship**, 157 Waterloo Road, London SE1 8XN
☎020 7928 4694 🖷020 7620 2453
E: info@cmf.org.uk
Web: www.cmf.org.uk and www.ethicsforschools.org or www.healthserve.org
Fellowship of doctors; evangelism, Christian ethics, literature, student and mission support; international links.
General Secretary: Dr Peter Saunders. *Chief Administrator:* Mr Giles Rawlinson. Executive staff 6, Other staff 15. **CC** No.1039823. Began 1949; interdenominational. Magazine: *Triple Helix - For Today's Christian Doctor* (7,500 quarterly), *Nucleus - Student Journal* (6,000 quarterly). Turnover £1,200,000 to year end Dec 05.

***Christian Police Association**, Bedford Heights, Manton Lane, Bedford MK41 7PG
☎01234 272 865
E: info@cpauk.net
Web: www.cpauk.net
Spiritual welfare of police officers and evangelistic outreach to members of the Police Service.
Executive Director: Mr Don Axcell. Executive staff 1, Other staff 1. **CC** No.220482. Began 1883; interdenominational. Magazine: *On & Off Duty* (2,000 quarterly). Turnover n/a

Christian Students Nurses and Midwives, c/o CMF, 157 Waterloo Road, London SE1 8XN
M: 07941 800 637
E: students@cnm.org.uk
Web: www.cnm.org.uk
Helping nursing and midwifery students in witness, ethical understanding and other related issues.
Coordinator: Steven Fouch. No full-time staff. Began 2001; non-denominational. Magazine: *CNM News* (Circulation n/a quarterly). Turnover £200 to year end Dec 02.

Christian Workplace Forum, Moggerhanger Park, Park Road, Moggerhanger, Bedford MK44 3RW
☎01767 641 005 🖷01767 641 515
E: info@cwf-uk.org
Web: www.cwf-uk.org
Linking Christian workplace associations, supporting students starting work, bringing Christian values and witness to work.
Coordinator: Miss Ros Turner. Executive staff 1. **CC** No.1022698. Began 2004; non-denominational. No magazine. Turnover n/a.

Christianity and History Forum, 1 Trelawny Way, Bembridge PO35 5YE
☎01983 874 218
E: m[illegible]ght1485@aol.com
Web: www.chf-online.org
Promoting Christian thinking and discussion on all areas of history. A UCCF group.
Chairman: Prof John Wolffe. No full-time staff. **CC** Began 1965; interdenominational. (Previously Study Group on Christianity and History). Magazine: *Christianity and History Bulletin* (150 annually). Turnover £1,500 to year end Mar 05.

Christians At Work, 148 Railway Terrace, Rugby CV21 3HN
☎01788 579 738
E: office@christiansatwork.org.uk
Web: www.christiansatwork.org.uk
Encouraging, supporting and equipping workplace ministry and witness.
National Director: Rev J Brian Allenby. Executive staff 1, Other staff 1. **CC** No.254887. Began 1942; non-denominational. No magazine. Turnover £[illegible]1,000 to year end Dec 04.

†*Christians in Business, 241 High Street, Waltham Cross EN8 7BE
☎01992 628 202 🖷01992 632 305
E: info@christiansinbusiness.org
Providing help, support and guidance for Christians in the workplace.
National Director: Mr Martin Higgins. Executive staff 1, Admin staff 1. **CC** No.1072064. Began n/a; interdenominational. No magazine. Turnover n/a.

Christians in Caring Professions, c/o Ty Blaenant Ddu, Hed Myddfai, Felindre, Swansea SA5 7ND
☎0870 909 2006
E: office@cicp.org.uk
Web: www.cicp.org.uk/cicp
Equipping and encouraging Christians to live for Christ in their professional lives.
Administrator: Steve Heatherington. Admin staff 1. **CC** No.288888. Began 1984; non-denominational. No magazine. Turnover £44,000 to year end July 01.

***Christians in Communications (The Post Office and Telecommunications Christian Association)**, 26 Halloughton Road, Southwell NG25 0LR
☎01636 819 195
E: cic@f2s.com
Web: www.ciconline.org.uk
Fellowship of Christians in the communications industries.
General Secretary: Mr Simon Farmer. Executive staff 1, Other staff 1. **CC** No.262642. Began 1887; non-denominational. No magazine. Turnover £16,000 to year end Apr 05.

***Christians in Entertainment**, PO Box 51, Teignmouth TQ14 8WX
☎01737 550 375
E: chris@cieweb.org.uk
Web: www.cieweb.org.uk
Spiritual and emotional support for professionals in the entertainment business and advising individuals and organisations.
Director: Mr Christopher Gidney. Executive staff 1, Other staff 2. **CC** No.801327. Began 1982; interdenominational. No magazine. Turnover £30,000 to year end Dec 05.

†Christians in Finance, 11 Gatehill Road, Northwood HA6 3QF
☎020 7606 8330 🖷020 7606 1204
E: info@christiansinfinance.org
Web: www.christiansinfinance.org
Evangelism, fellowship and support of missionaries in the London financial centre; weekly meetings.
Chairman: Mr Christopher Rogers. No full-time staff. **CC** No.268974. Began 1875; interdenominational. (Previously London Banks' Christian Union). No magazine. Turnover £5,000 to year end Dec 98.

†Christians in Media, Maiden Outdoor Advertising, 128 Buckingham Palace Road, London SW1W 9SA
☎020 7838 4000 🖷020 7838 4078
E: francis.goodwin@maidenoutdoor.co.uk
Association of professionals in advertising who produce campaigns for Christian organisations.
Coordinator: Francis Goodwin. No full-time staff. Began 1995; non-denominational. No magazine. Turnover n/a.

Christians in Politics, PO Box 38539, London SW1P 3YA
☎020 8786 9095
E: mail@christiansinpolitics.fsnet.co.uk
Web: www.christiansinpolitics.org.uk
Encouraging and supporting membership of mainstream political parties and their recognised Christian groups.
Project Manager: Victoria Adamson. Executive staff 1. Began 2002; interdenominational. No magazine. Turnover £8,000 to year end Jul 03.

***Christians in Property**, 143 New Bond Street, London W1S 2TP
☎020 7493 0406 🖷020 7493 0436
E: info@christiansinproperty.org
Web: www.christiansinproperty.org
Communicating the good news of Jesus Christ with surveyors, quantity surveyors, architects and others.
Secretary: Mr Colin Molyneux. No full-time staff. Began 1953; interdenominational. No magazine. Turnover n/a.

†Christians in Road Transport, 37 Langcomb Road, Shirley, Solihull B90 2PN
☎0121 745 1062
Providing Christian fellowship and encouragement for people in the road transport industry; evangelism amongst drivers.
Chair: Mr Graham Leighton. No full-time staff. Began 1997; non-denominational. Magazine: *Talking Diesel* (100 every two months). Turnover £1,000 to year end Nov 98.

***Christians in Science**, 4 Sackville Close, Sevenoaks TN13 3QD
☎01732 451 907 🖷01732 464 253
E: secretary@cis.org.uk
Web: www.cis.org.uk
Exploring God's work in creation; encouraging environmental concern; applying biblical principles to science and technology. A UCCF group.
Secretary: Dr Caroline Berry. No full-time staff. Began 1943; interdenominational. Magazine: *Science and Christian Belief* (800 half-yearly). Turnover n/a.

Professional Christian Groups

Churches Media Council, PO Box 6613, South Woodham Ferrers, Chelmsford CM3 5DY
☎01245 322 158 🖷01245 321 957
E: admin@churchesmediacouncil.org.uk
Web: www.churchesmediacouncil.org.uk
Ecumenical body for the advancement of Christian faith through the media; annual awards, conference.
General Secretary: Andrew Graystone. Executive staff 1. Began 1980; interdenominational. (Previously Churches Advisory Council on Local Broadcasting). See also ACB. Magazine: *Crosstalk* (1,000 quarterly). Turnover £80,000 to year end Dec 05.

Conference of Religious in England and Wales, PO Box 37602, The Ridgeway, Mill Hill, London NW7 4XG
☎020 8201 1860 🖷020 8201 1988
E: gensec@corew.org
Web: www.corew.org
Promoting the welfare of men and women in Religious Orders and Apostolic Institutes.
General Secretary: Connie Burke CoR. Executive staff 1, Other staff 8. ***CC*** No.277024. Began 1959; Roman Catholic with Anglican Associates. No magazine. Turnover n/a.

The Council for Health and Wholeness, 102 Irlam Road, Flixton, Manchester M41 6JT
☎0161 748 4858 🖷0161 747 7379
E: info@maranathacommunity.org.uk
Developing a fuller understanding of the nature of healing amongst professionals in healing ministries.
Medical Director: Dr Linda Stalley. Executive staff 1, Other staff n/a. ***CC*** No.327627. Began n/a; ecumenical. Associated with the Maranatha Community. No magazine. Turnover n/a.

The Ecclesiastical Architects & Surveyors Association, c/o Elden Minns & Co Ltd, 453 Glossop Road, Sheffield S10 2PT
☎0114 266 2458 🖷0114 266 2459
E: eldenminns@aol.com
Web: www.easanet.co.uk
Association of architects and surveyors concerned with repair, re-ordering and re-use of ecclesiastical buildings.
Hon Secretary: Andrew Shepherd. No full-time staff. Began 1872; ecumenical. No magazine. Turnover £20,000 to year end Dec 03.

English Clergy Association, The Old School, Norton Hawkfield, Pensford, Bristol BS39 4HB
☎01275 830 017 🖷01275 830 017
E: masding@breathe.co.uk
Web: www.clergyassoc.co.uk
Upholding the ministry of parish, diocesan, and cathedral clergy within the Established Church; holiday grants.
Chairman: Rev J W Masding. No full-time staff. ***CC*** No.258559. Began 1938; Anglican. Magazine: *Parson and Parish* (600 half-yearly). Turnover £25,000 to year end Dec 04.

Federation of Catholic Priests, The Vicarage, Palace Place, Paignton TQ3 3AQ
☎01803 559 059
E: father_tubbs@compuserve.com
Encouraging mutual support in propagating, maintaining and defending Catholic doctrine and practice.
Secretary General: Rev Preb Brian Tubbs. No full-time staff. ***CC*** Began n/a; Roman Catholic. (Previously Federation of Catholic Priests). Magazine: *ACTA* (Circulation n/a annually). Turnover n/a.

Fellowship of European Broadcasters, 23 The Service Road, Potters Bar EN6 1QA
☎01707 649 910 🖷01707 662 653
E: feb@feb.org
Web: www.feb.org
Fellowship of European Christians involved with broadcasting.
Chairman: Mr Harvey Thomas. No full-time staff. Began 1991; interdenominational. Magazine: *European Update* (6,000 every four months). Turnover n/a.

***Fellowship of European Evangelical Theologians**, Spurgeon's College, 189 South Norwood Hill, London SE25 6DJ
☎020 8653 0850
E: h.lalleman@spurgeons.ac.uk
Promoting evangelical theological research, supporting theologians in Europe by conferences and other contacts.
UK Contact: Dr Hetty Lalleman. *Chair, France:* Professor Henri Blocher. No full-time staff. ***CC*** No.SCO 22952. Began 1976; non-denominational. Magazine: *European Journal of Theology* (500 half-yearly). Turnover n/a.

The Good Gardeners Association, 4 Lisle Place, Wotton-under-Edge GL12 7AZ
☎01453 520 322
E: info@goodgardeners.org.uk
Web: www.goodgardeners.org.uk
Research, education and promotion of organic gardening methods to increase food's nutrition and vitality.
Secretary: Mr Matthew Adams. Executive staff 1. ***CC*** No.255300. Began 1966; Anglican. Magazine: *Newsletter* (500 quarterly). Turnover £14,000 to year end Mar 02.

Guild of Catholic Doctors, 60 Grove End Road, London NW8 9NH
☎020 7266 4246 🖷020 7266 4813
E: office@catholicdoctors.org.uk
Web: www.catholicdoctors.org.uk
Providing facilities to members for prayer, study; upholding Christian moral principles in practice of medicine.
Hon Secretary: Dr John Morewood. No full-time staff. ***CC*** No.1002374. Began 1911; Roman Catholic. Magazine: *Catholic Medical Quarterly* (1,500 quarterly). Turnover £40,000 to year end Oct 98.

***Healthcare Christian Fellowship International (British Isles)**, 38 Lough Moss Park, Carryduff, Belfast BT8 8PD
☎028 9081 4479
E: hcf@hcfni.totalserve.co.uk
Web: www.hcfbi.org.uk
Bringing Christians into fellowship and equipping them to be effective witnesses to staff and patients.
British Isles Promoter: Mrs Ann Silvester. Executive staff 4. ***CC*** Began 1964; non-denominational. (Previously Hospital Christian Fellowship International). No magazine. Turnover n/a
England *Secretary:* Miss Brenda Alexander, 86 Uxbridge Road Hanworth, Feltham TW13 5EH
☎01446 418 272
Channel Islands *Secretary:* Mrs Liz Reed, La Conchée, Le Rues, St Saviours, Guernsey GY7 9FN
☎01481 643 19
Scotland *Secretary:* Mrs Ann Jack, 49 Priestfield Crescent, Edinburgh EH16 5[illegible]H
☎01446 418 272
Wales *Secretary:* Mr Jeff Dyas, 26 Wenvoe Terrace, Barry CF6 8EF

Industrial Christian Fellowship, St Matthews House, 100 George Street, Croydon CR0 1PJ
☎020 8656 1644 🖷020 8656 2074
E: wright@btinternet.com
Web: www.icf-online.org
Helping Christians relate their faith to their daily work.
Information: Mrs A Wright. No full-time staff. ***CC*** Began 1877; ecumenical. (Previously Industry Churches Forum (ICF). Magazine: *Faith in Business Journal* published in association with Ridley Hall, Cambridge (Circulation & frequency n/a). Turnover £37,000 to year end Mar 99.

Institute for British Liberation Theology, 178 Abbeyfield Road, Sheffield S4 7AY
☎0114 243 6688 🖷0114 243 5688
Arranging conferences, research for practitioners in British Liberation Theology, results published by Urban Theology Unit.
Director: Rev Dr John Vincent. *Joint Editors:* Prof Chris Rowland, Rev Dr John Vincent. No full-time staff. Began 1991; ecumenical. Magazine: *British Liberation Theology* series (Circulation n/a half-yearly). Turnover n/a.

***International Christian Chamber of Commerce (AISBL)**, 118 High Street, Staple Hill, Bristol BS16 5HH
☎0845 223 5466 🖷0845 223 5467
E: office@uk.iccc.net
Web: www.uk.iccc.net
Encouraging and equipping Christians for a deeper walk of faith in the marketplace.
Secretary: Mr Roger Ball. Admin staff 1. ***CC*** No.328506. Began 1987; interdenominational. (Registered in UK as Council of Christians in Commerce Ltd) No magazine. Turnover n/a.

S

Lawyers Christian Fellowship, 29 Church Lane, Temple Normanton, Chesterfield S42 5DB
☎01246 855 783
E: admin@lawcf.org
Web: www.lawcf.org
Encouraging educating, equipping Christian lawyers and law students to live out their faith at work.
National Secretary: Mrs Hilary Lyndon. *Chairman:* Mr John Scriven. Admin staff 1, Other staff 2. **CC** No.1017695. Began 1852; interdenominational. Magazine: *The Christian Lawyer* (Circulation & frequency n/a). Turnover n/a.

***Librarians' Christian Fellowship**, 35 Elder Close, Winchester SO22 4LG
☎01962 864 515
E: chair@librarianscf.org.uk
Web: www.librarianscf.org.uk
Organising events and publications helping Christian librarians relate their faith to their work.
Chair: Ms Kirsty Robinson. No full-time staff. Began 1973; non-denominational. Magazine: *Christian Librarian* (500 quarterly). Turnover £7,464 to year end Dec 04.

***Merchant Navy Christian Fellowship**, 48 South Street, Alderley Edge SK9 7ES
☎01625 590 010
℻01625 585 442
E: headquarters@scfs.org
Web: www.scfs.org
Providing pastoral ministry to Christian seafarers worldwide; international network providing hospitality.
Director: Mr Michael J Wilson. Executive staff 1, Other staff 2. **CC** No.209133. Began 1958; interdenominational. No magazine. Turnover £10,000 to year end Dec 04.

Movement of Christian Workers, St Joseph's, Watford Way, London NW4 4TY
☎020 8203 6290
℻020 8203 6291
E: mcworkers@aol.com
Promoting justice based on the values of equality, social justice and solidarity.
Chair: Mrs Mary Foy. Admin staff 1. **CC** No.1023531. Began 1991; ecumenical. Magazine: *MCW Review* (500 quarterly). Turnover £27,000 to year end Dec 02.

National Conference of Priests of England and Wales, Our Lady of Mount Carmel & St Joseph's, 8a Battersea Park Road, London SW8 4BH
☎020 7622 4282
℻020 7978 1800
E: secretary@ncpew.org.uk
Web: www.ncpew.org.uk
Forum for discussion of faith, church needs and priestly ministry.
Executive Secretary: Fr Peter Jenner. No full-time staff. **CC** Began 1970; Roman Catholic. No magazine. Turnover n/a.

Naval Christian Fellowship, Porters Lodge, 1 College Road, HM Naval Base, Portsmouth PO1 3LJ
☎023 9281 4410 ℻023 9281 4420
E: ncf@dial.pipex.com
Web: www.navalcf.org
Evangelical fellowship linking Christians in the Royal Navy, European and other navies.
General Secretary: Cdr J Christopher Mather. Executive staff 1, Other staff 3. **CC** No.256726. Began 1948; interdenominational. No magazine. Turnover £60,000 to year end Mar 03.

Nurses Christian Fellowship International (NCFI), Annandale, 11a Kirkintilloch Road, Lenzie, Glasgow G66 4RW
☎0141 776 0543
E: ncfi-admin@ntlworld.com
Web: www.ncfi.org
Developing Christian beliefs and values in personal and professional life, through teaching and consultancy.
General Director: Mr David Parfitt. Executive staff 1, Other staff 1. **CC** No.258936. Began 1959; interdenominational. Magazine: *Christian Nurse International* (3,000 quarterly). Turnover £80,000 to year end Dec 96.

The Oriental Orthodox Mailing List, 10 Heathwood Gardens, Charlton, London SE7 8EP
☎020 8854 3090 ℻020 8244 7888
E: orthodox@uk-christian.net
Web: www.uk-christian.net/oons
Friendly and scholarly electronic discussion and exchanges for those interested in canonical Oriental Orthodox Churches.
Director: Fr Sergius Scott. Executive staff 1. Began 1998; Orthodox. Magazine: *E-magazine* (via email). Turnover n/a.

People and Places Architects Ltd, The Design Studio, 2 Delacourt Road, Blackheath, London SE3 8XA
☎020 8269 2888 ℻020 8269 0888
E: admin@peopleandplaces.uk.com
Web: www.peopleandplacesarchitects.com
Providing a sense of belonging when places clothe people, people the life of God.
Managing Director: Mr Raymond Hall. Staff n/a. **CC** No.1013750. Began 1973; non-denominational. (Previously New Wineskins). No magazine. Turnover n/a.

***Probation Service Christian Fellowship**, 1 Watchcroft Drive, Buckingham MK18 1GH
☎0870 027 3091 M: 07939 222 467
E: enquries@pscf.org.uk
Web: www.pscf.org.uk
Offering Christian care and concern in the Criminal Justice Services.
Chair: Margaret Gateley. No paid staff. **CC** No.1059037. Began 1954; non-denominational. Magazine: *Probation Service Christian Fellowship Newsletter* (Circulation n/a twice per year). Turnover £5,053 to year end Dec 02.

Religious & Theological Studies Fellowship (RTSF), 38 De Montfort Street, Leicester LE1 7GP
☎0116 255 1700 ℻0116 255 5672
E: rtsf@uccf.org.uk
Web: www.uccf.org.uk/rtsf
Helping students of Theology and Religious Studies in their biblical understanding and training. A UCCF group.
RTSF Co-ordinator: Rev Dr Mike Reeves. Executive staff 3. **CC** Began 1933; non-denominational. Magazines: *From Athens to Jerusalem* (Circulation n/a every four months), *Themelios* (2,000 every four months). Turnover n/a.

Religious Education Council of England & Wales, RE Today, 1020 Bristol Road, Selly Oak, Birmingham B29 6LB
☎0121 472 4242
Web: www.religiouseducationcouncil.org
Providing a forum for the professional and religious institutions concerned with religious education in schools.
Hon Secretary: Dr Brian Gates. No full-time staff. Began 1973; non-denominational. No magazine. Turnover n/a.

Schools Ministry Network, 207 Queensway, Bletchley, Milton Keynes MK2 2EB
☎01908 856 168 ℻01908 856 012
E: info@schoolsministrynetwork.co.uk
Web: www.schoolsministrynetwork.co.uk
Bringing together organisations and individuals committed to maintaining high standards of schools ministry.
Administrator: Mrs Ruth Thomas. No full-time staff. Began 1993; interdenominational. No magazine. Turnover £6,000 to year end Aug 02.

Scottish Evangelical Theology Society, 42 Melville Gardens, Bishopbriggs, Glasgow G64 3YE
☎0141 562 6296
M: 07793 554 979
℻0141 558 1827
E: jk@torrens37.freeserve.co.uk
Web: www.setsonline.org.uk
Promoting serious study of evangelical theology in Scotland amongst ministers and lay people.
Secretary: Rev Dr James Torrens. No full-time staff. **CC** No.SCO 08424. Began n/a; non-denominational. Magazine: *Scottish Bulletin of Evangelical Theology* (700 half-yearly). Turnover £2,700 to year end Dec 00.

***Social Work Christian Fellowship**, c/o Truedata Database Management, 23 Park Road, Ilkeston DE7 5DA
☎0115 932 0643
E: swcf@truedata.org.uk
Web: www.swcf.org.uk
Providing professional, intellectual, spiritual and social support to Christians in social work, care and action.
Membership Secretary: Name not supplied. No full-time staff. **CC** No.278661. Began 1964; interdenominational. Magazine: *The Extra Mile* (Circulation n/a every four months). Turnover n/a.

Student Christian Movement, Unit 308f, The Big Peg, 120 Vyse Street, The Jewellery Quarter, Birmingham B18 6NF
☎0121 200 3355 Ⓜ: 07913 613 499
E: scm@movement.org.uk
Web: www.movement.org.uk
Promoting exploration of faith and its relevance to the contemporary world; groups, conferences, publications.
Coordinator: Liam Purcell. Executive staff 1, Other staff 2. ***CC*** No.241896. Began 1889; ecumenical. Magazine: *Movement* (750 every four months). Turnover £75,000 to year end Aug 00.

Therapy Students Christian Fellowship (TSCF), 38 De Montfort Street, Leicester LE1 7GP
☎0116 255 1700 🖷0116 255 5672
E: tscf@uccf.org.uk
Web: www.uccf.org.uk/tscf
Helping therapy students in witness, ethical understanding and other issues related to their studies. A UCCF group.
Staff Worker: Katy Tuft. Admin staff 1. ***CC*** Began 1952; non-denominational. (Previously Paramedical Students Christian Fellowship). Magazine: *TSCF Magazine* (200 termly). Turnover n/a.

†Transformational Business Network, Nelson House, 271 Kingston Road, Wimbledon, London SW19 3NW
☎0845 330 5142 🖷0845 330 5143
E: info@tbnetwork.org
Web: www.tbnetwork.org
Using business to bring spiritual and physical transformation to the poor.
Chairman: Mr Stuart McGreevy. Admin staff 1, No other paid staff. ***CC*** Began 2003; interdenominational. No magazine. Turnover n/a.

†Tyndale Fellowship for Biblical and Theological Research, Tyndale House, 36 Selwyn Gardens, Cambridge CB3 9BA
☎01223 566 601 🖷01223 566 608
E: dj208@cam.ac.uk
Web: www.tyndale.cam.ac.uk
Fellowship of Christians in biblical and theological research; promoting the faith through careful, scholarly study.
Secretary: Dr Paul Woodbridge. Admin staff 1, Other staff 1. ***CC*** No.273458. Began 1944; non-denominational. Magazine: *Tyndale Bulletin* (1,100 annually). Turnover n/a.

Victoria Institute (Philosophical Society of Great Britain), 15 The Drive, Harlow CM20 3QD
☎01279 422 661 🖷020 8303 04[illegible]5
Web: www.faithandthought.org.uk
Helping the non-specialist relate Christian thought to advancing knowledge and specialisation.
Hon. Treasurer: Rev J D Buxton. No full-time staff. ***CC*** No.285871. Began 1865; non-denominational. Magazines: *Faith and Thought* (Circulation & frequency n/a), *Science and Christian Belief* (800 half-yearly, jointly with Christians in Science). Turnover £7,500 to year end Dec 04.

WACRAL (World Association of Christian Radio Amateurs & Listeners), 10 Grosvenor Avenue, Pontefract WF8 4QU
☎01977 705 395
E: cswl1199g@btinternet.com
Web: www.wacral.org
Promoting Christian friendship and fellowship through the medium of amateur radio.
General Secretary: Shirley Jackson. No full-time staff. Began 1957; interdenominational. Magazine: *WACRAL Annual* ([illegible]00 annually). Turnover £4,970 to year end Dec 01.

PRO-LIFE ORGANISATIONS

***CARE Centres Network**, 1 Winton Square, Basingstoke RG21 8EN
☎01256 477 300/0800 028 2228 (helpline) 🖷01256 477 301
E: ccn@care.org.uk
Web: www.careconfidential.com or www.pregnancy.org.uk
National freephone pregnancy crisis and post-abortion helpline: CAREconfidential; networking 160 independent pregnancy crisis centres.
National Co-ordinator: Mrs Joanna Thompson. Executive staff 1, Other staff 8. ***CC*** No.1066963. Began 1989; interdenominational. A department of CARE. Magazine: *Newsletter*(Circulation & frequency n/a). Turnover included in CARE.

Evangelicals for LIFE, LIFE House, Newbold Terrace, Leamington Spa CV32 4EA
☎01970 880 416 🖷01926 336 497
E: info@lifeuk.org
Web: www.lifeuk.org
Presenting the biblical case against abortion and encouraging evangelicals to work within the LIFE organisation.
Organiser: Dr John R Ling. No full-time staff. Began 1982; interdenominational. No magazine. Turnover n/a.

Human Rights Society, Mariners Hard, Cley, Holt NR25 7RX
☎01263 740 990 🖷01263 740 990
E: human-rights-society@ukgateway.net
Opposing legalisation of euthanasia; providing education material including video; information about hospices, pain relief.

Secretary: Mrs Jennifer J Murray. Executive staff 1. Began 1969; non-denominational. No magazine. Turnover n/a.

***Pregnancy Helpline**, Coverdale Centre, Coverdale Crescent, Manchester M12 4FG
☎0845 330 8466
E: kate@pregnancyhelpline.co.uk
Web: www.pregnancyhelpline.co.uk
Providing free pregnancy tests, confidential counselling for pregnancy and after abortion.
Manager: Mrs Christine Fidler. Part time staff. Began 1994; non-denominational. (Previously IMAGE). Turnover £32,000 to year end Dec 04.

***Society for the Protection of Unborn Children (SPUC)**, Phyllis Bowman House, 5 St Matthew Street, Westminster, London SW1P 2JT
☎020 7222 5845 🖷020 7222 0630
E: information@spuc.org.uk
Web: www.spuc.org.uk
Educating public and parliament about abortion, euthanasia, human embryo experimentation, cloning. Providing speakers, information, counselling.
National Director: Mr John Smeaton. *Evangelicals Development Officer:* Mr Peter Smith. *Evangelicals Chairman:* Mr Alan Thorne. Executive staff 10, Other staff 30. Began 1967; non-denominational. Magazine: *Pro Life Times* (125,000 every two months). Turnover £1,800,000 to year end Feb 03.
Other offices: Belfast, Cardiff, Glasgow, Preston, Stockton

†UK Life League, 7 Kensington High Street, London W8 5NP
☎0870 240 3158 Ⓜ: 07977 195 57[illegible]
🖷0870 240 3159
E: info@uklifeleague.com
Web: www.uklifeleague.com
Pro-woman, pro-child, pro-life group, campaigning on the streets to end abortion.
National Coordinator: Mr James Dowson. *Operational Director:* Miss Anne M Wills. Executive staff 5, Other staff 20. Began 1999; non-denominational. (Previously Precious Life). Magazine: *UK Lifeleague* (5,000 every two months). Turnover £500,000 to year end Feb 03.

United for Life, 22 Moreton Close, Bishops Cleeve, Cheltenham GL52 8AW
☎01242 675 343
E: info@unitedforlife.com
Web: www.unitedforlife.com
Raising awareness of human life issues, providing information, literature for Christian pro-life action and evangelisation.
Coordinator: Grace Mason. All voluntary staff. Began 2003; non-denominational. No magazine. Turnover £1,500 to year end Apr 04.

RECONCILIATION & MEDIATION GROUPS

***The 174 Trust**, Duncairn Complex, Duncairn Avenue, Belfast BT14 6BP
☎028 9074 7114 🖷028 9074 9299
E: info@174trust.org
Web: www.174trust.org
Caring Christian witness, Christian community development, building peace and promoting reconciliation.
Director: Rev Bill Shaw. *Chairperson:* Heather Carey. Executive staff 6, Other staff 30. **CC** No.XN 62669. Began 1983; non-denominational. Magazine: *Trust Times* (500 quarterly). Turnover n/a.

Anglican Pacifist Fellowship, 11 Weavers End, Hanslope, Milton Keynes MK19 7PA
☎01908 510 642
E: ajkempster@aol.com
Web: www.anglicanpeacemaker.org.uk
Witnessing to the pacifist understanding of the Christian faith within the Anglican Communion.
Hon Secretary: Dr Tony Kempster. No full-time staff. **CC** No.209610. Began 1937; Anglican. Magazine: *Anglican Peacemaker* (1,500 every three months). Turnover £17,500 to year end Oct 05.

Association of Interchurch Families, Bastille Court, 2 Paris Garden, London SE1 8ND
☎020 7654 7251 🖷020 7654 7222
E: info@interchurchfamiles.org.uk
Web: www.interchurchfamilies.org.uk
Support network and voice for interchurch families (usually Roman Catholic and another Christian communion).
Executive Officer: Keith Lander. Executive staff 1. **CC** No.283811. Began 1968; interdenominational. Magazine: *Web-based bulletin.* Turnover £733,000 to year end Dec 04.

Baptist Peace Fellowship, 19 Southcot Place, Bath BA2 4PE
☎01225 312 796
E: gma_collins@yahoo.co.uk
Web: www.baptist-peace.org.uk
Keeping issues of peace and justice before the Baptist churches and denomination.
Hon Secretary: G M A Collins. No full-time staff. Began 1932; Baptist. No magazine. Turnover n/a.

Bridge Builders, London Mennonite Centre, 14 Shepherd's Hill, London N6 5AQ
☎0845 450 0214 🖷020 8341 6807
E: bridgebuilders@menno.org.uk
Web: www.menno.org.uk
Offering training workshops on handling conflict, mediation and consultancy services for church-based organisations.
Director: Mr Alastair McKay. Executive staff 1, Other staff 3. Began 1996; Mennonite. No magazine. Turnover n/a.

†Catholic Association for Racial Justice (CARJ), 9 Henry Road, Manor House, London N4 2LH
☎020 8802 8080 🖷020 8211 0808
E: info@carj.co.uk
Web: www.carj.co.uk
Black and white Catholics promoting awareness, understanding and action on issues of racial justice.
Director: Mr Stephen Corriette. Executive staff 1. **CC** No.291601. Began 1984; Roman Catholic. No magazine. Turnover £200,000 to year end Mar 03.

Catholic Peace Action, 7 Putney Bridge Road, London SW18 1HX
☎No telephone
Peace work involving communication with the Ministry of Defence and resistance to nuclear war preparations.
Secretary: Mr Dan Martin. No full-time staff. Began 1982; Roman Catholic but serving all. No magazine. Turnover n/a.

Christian Campaign for Nuclear Disarmament, 162 Holloway Road, London N7 8DQ
☎020 7700 4200 🖷020 7700 2357
E: ccnd@gn.apc.org
Web: www.gn.apc.org/ccnd
Building Christian witness against weapons of mass destruction and militarism, for global peace and justice.
National Co-ordinator: Patricia Pulham. No full-time staff. Began 1960; non-denominational. Magazine: *Ploughshare* (1,000 quarterly). Turnover £11,000 to year end Mar 00.

Christian International Peace Service (CHIPS), 35 Melton Road, Birmingham B14 7DA
☎0121 444 0346
E: office@chipspeace.org
Web: www.chipspeace.org
Christian peacemaking through practical projects in areas of tension worldwide; UK training seminars.
Director: Dr Mark Cuthbert. Executive staff 2. **CC** No.267140. Began 1974; non-denominational. No magazine. Turnover £29,000 to year end Apr 05.

Christian Renewal Centre, 44 Shore Road, Rostrevor, Newry BT34 3ET
☎028 4173 8492 🖷028 4173 8996
E: crcrostrevor@lineone.org
Web: www.crc-rostrevor.org
Residential community committed to prayer, reconciliation and renewal in Ireland; accommodation available.
Leader/Prayer Coordinator: Mr Harry Smith. Community 12. **CC** No.XN48546. Began 1974; interdenominational. House of Prayer for Ireland. Magazines: *Prayer Diary* (700 monthly), *Newsletter* (3,313 half-yearly). Turnover n/a.

Churches' Commission for Racial Justice, CTBI, Bastille Court, 2 Paris Garden, London SE1 8ND
☎020 7654 7254 🖷020 7654 7222
E: ccrj@ctbi.org.uk
Web: www.ctbi.org.uk
Coordinating the work of churches across Britain and Ireland on racial justice issues.
Commission Secretary: Rev Arlington Trotman. *Research & Development Officer:* To be appointed. *Administrator:* Margaret Pattinson. Executive staff 2, Admin staff 1. **CC** No.259688. Began 1992; ecumenical. A Commission of Churches Together in Britain and Ireland. Magazine: *Church and Race* (15,000 every four months). Turnover £350,000 to year end Dec 05.

†Co-operation Ireland, Glendinning House, 6 Murray Street, Belfast BT1 6DN
☎028 9032 1462 🖷028 9089 1000
E: info@cooperationireland.org
Web: www.cooperationireland.org
Advancing mutual understanding and respect by promoting practical co-operation between the peoples of Ireland.
Chief Executive: Mr Tony Kennedy. Executive staff 1, Other staff 50. Began 1979; non-denominational. (Previously Co-operation North). Magazine: *Co-operation Ireland News* (2,500 quarterly). Turnover £3,000,000 to year end Dec 02.

†Cornerstone Community, 445 Springfield Road, Belfast BT12 7DL
☎028 9032 1649 🖷028 9032 7323
E: cornerstone@cornerstonecom.fsnet.co.uk
Web: www.cornerstone.fsnet.co.uk
Reconciliation, peace work, prayer groups, social action; community building.
Development Officer: Mr Bridie Twomey. No full-time staff. **CC** No.NI 20406. Began 1982; ecumenical. Magazine: *Cornerstone Contact* (1,000 every four months). Turnover £90,000 to year end Dec 00.

Corrymeela, 8 Upper Crescent, Belfast BT7 1NT
☎028 9050 8080 🖷028 9050 8070
E: belfast@corrymeela.org
Web: www.corrymeela.org
Dispersed Christian community of reconciliation in Northern Ireland; resource centre, residential centre.
Leader: Mr David Stevens. Staff 32. **CC** No.XN 48052A. Began 1965; interdenominational. Magazine: *Connections* (2,300 quarterly). Turnover £1,320,000 to year end Mar 05.

Corrymeela Link, PO Box 4829, Earley, Reading RG6 1XX
☎0118 926 1062 🖷0118 926 1063
E: reading@corrymeela.org
Web: www.corrymeela.org
Stimulating spiritual and financial support for the Corrymeela Community working for peace in Northern Ireland.
Coordinator: Honor Alleyne. Staff n/a. **CC** No.XN 48052A. Began 1965; ecumenical. Magazine: *Corrymeela* (6,000 quarterly). Turnover n/a.

Reconciliation & Mediation Groups

Council of Christians and Jews, 1st Floor, Cameford House, 87 Albert Embankment, London SE1 7TP
☎020 7820 0090 🖷020 7820 0504
E: cjrelations@ccj.org.uk
Web: www.ccj.org.uk
Promoting good relations between Christians and Jews through dialogue, education, combating discrimination and antisemitism.
Director: Sr Margaret Shepherd. *Education Officer & Deputy Director:* Jane Clements. Executive staff 2, Other staff 5. ***CC*** No.238005. Began 1942. Magazine: *Common Ground* (5,500 every four months). Turnover £165,000 to year end Mar 98.

The Council on Christian Approaches to Defence and Disarmament, 5 Cubitts Meadow, Aylsham Road, Buxton, Norwich NR10 5EF
☎01603 279 939 🖷01603 279 939
E: ccadd@lineone.net
Web: www.lineone.net/~ccadd
Studying problems relating to reconciliation and security within a Christian context.
Adminstrative Secretary: Mrs Liza Hamilton. No full-time staff. ***CC*** No.245130. Began 1963; non-denominational. No magazine. Turnover £10,000 to year end Apr 05.

Cross Group, 6a Cumberland Park, Dundonald, Belfast BT16 2AY
☎028 9087 4750
Providing social support group for those bereaved through violence in Northern Ireland.
Founder: Ms Maura Kiely. No full-time staff. Began 1975; non-denominational. No magazine. Turnover n/a.

Fellowship of Reconciliation, England, St James' Church Centre, Beauchamp Lane, Oxford OX4 3LF
☎01865 748 796
E: office@for.org.uk
Web: www.for.org.uk
Promoting peace/justice through spiritual development, witness and service; reconciling people with God and each other.
Director: Mr Chris Cole. Executive staff 1, Other staff n/a. ***CC*** No.207822. Began 1914; interdenominational. No magazine. Turnover £75,000 to year end Dec 00.

†The Human City Institute, University of Birmingham, Selly Oak Campus, Weoley Park Road, Birmingham B29 6LL
☎0121 415 8354 🖷0121 415 8355
E: hci@humancity.org
Web: www.humancity.org
Bringing religious and secular bodies together to enable Birmingham, Swindon and Bradford to become human cities.
Director: Chauhan Jay. Executive staff 1, Other staff 8. ***CC*** No.1073215. Began 1997; ecumenical. Magazine: *Human City Bulletin* (2,500 quarterly). Turnover £25,000 to year end Dec 00.

International Centre for Reconciliation, Coventry Cathedral, 1 Hill Top, Coventry CV1 5ES
☎024 7652 1201
E: stephen.davis@coventrycathedral.org.uk
Web: www.coventrycathedral.org
Network of groups/individuals working for peace/reconciliation worldwide: supporting Cross of Nails centres.
Director of International Ministry: Dr Stephen Davis. Executive staff 2, Other staff 4. Began 1974; interdenominational. Includes Community of the Cross of Nails. Magazines: *Reconcile* (100,000 frequency n/a), *International Briefing Papers* (Circulation & frequency n/a). Turnover n/a.

Iona Community, Savoy House, 140 Sauchiehall Street, Glasgow G2 3DH
☎0141 332 6343
🖷0141 332 1090
E: ionacomm@iona.org.uk
Web: www.iona.org.uk
Working for peace and social justice, rebuilding community and the renewal of worship.
Leader: Rev Kathy Galloway. *Support Services Manager:* Mr Graham Boyle. *Warden, Iona Abbey:* Rev Richard Sharples. Executive staff 5, Community n/a. ***CC*** No.SCO 03794. Began 1938; ecumenical. Magazine: *The Coracle* (3,500 every two months). Turnover £2,000,000 to year end Dec 05.
Also At: Iona Abbey, Isle of Iona PA76 6SN
☎01681 700 404
🖷 01681 700 460
And: Camas Centre, Bunessan, Isle of Mull PA67 6DX
☎01681 700 367

†Justice and Peace Scotland, 65 Bath Street, Glasgow G2 2BX
☎0141 333 0238
🖷0141 333 0238
E: justice.peace@virgin.net
Advising the Scottish Bishops Conference regarding social justice, international peace, human rights and world development.
Acting Secretary: Mr Tim Duffy. Executive staff 1, Other staff 2. Began 1979; Roman Catholic. Magazine: *Justice & Peace Magazine* (950 monthly). Turnover n/a.

***The Lifeline Expedition**, 58 Geoffrey Road, Brockley, London SE4 1NT
☎020 8694 2220
E: lifeline@fountaingate.co.uk
Web: www.lifelineexpedition.co.uk
Reconciliation journeys; organising March of the Abolitionists for bicentenary of Abolition of Slave Trade, 2007.
Leader: Mr David Pott. Executive staff 1. ***CC*** No.264078. Began 1996; non-denominational. Part of YWAM. No magazine. Turnover n/a.

†Mediation Northern Ireland, 10 Upper Crescent, Belfast BT7 1NT
☎028 9043 8614 🖷028 9031 44[illegible]0
E: joe@mediationnorthernireland.org
Web: www.mediationnorthernireland.org
Offering conflict transformation training and intervention for congregations, leaders, clergy and organisations
Assistant Director: Mr Joe Campbell. Executive staff 2, Admin staff 2, Other staff 8. ***CC*** Began 1991; non-denominational. (Previously Mediation Network). No magazine. Turnover n/a.

Methodist Peace Fellowship, St James' Church Centre, Beauchamp Lane, Oxford OX4 3LF
☎01865 748 796
E: office@for.org.uk
Web: www.for.org.uk
Pacifist witness; sponsorship of young people taking part in peace projects at home and overseas.
President: Rev Dr Kenneth Greet. No full-time staff. ***CC*** Began 1934; Methodist. Part of Fellowship of Reconciliation, England. No magazine. Turnover n/a.
Secretary: Rev Maurice H Wright, 3 Cornwall Drive, Bayston Hill, Shrewsbury SY3 0EP
E: mauriceh@wright.freeserve.co.uk
🖷 01743 873 633

National Justice & Peace Network, 39 Eccleston Square, London SW1V 1E[illegible]
☎020 7901 4864 🖷020 7901 48[illegible]1
E: admin@justice-and-peace.org.uk
Web: www.justice-and-peace.org.uk
Networking in justice and peace issues with dioceses, religious and agencies.
Administrator: Mrs Maureen Matthews. Admin staff 1. Began 1987; Roman Catholic. (Previously National Liaison Committee of Diocesan Justice & Peace Groups). Magazine: *NJPN Newsletter* (3,500 every four months). Turnover £18,000 to year end Dec 00.

†Pax Christi (British Section), St Joseph's, Watford Way, Hendon, London NW4 [illegible]TY
☎020 8203 4884 🖷020 8203 52[illegible]4
E: paxchristi@gn.apc.org
Web: www.paxchristi.org.uk
Promoting peace education and non-violence; campaigning on arms trade, nuclear proliferation.
General Secretary: Ms Patricia Gaffney. Executive staff 1, Other staff 2. Began 1970; Roman Catholic. Magazine: *Just Peace* (2,000 half-yearly). Turnover £95,000 to year end Dec 02.

†The Pilgrims of St Francis, 2 Margaret Street, Derby DE1 3FE
☎01332 383 301
E: barby@barbyr.freeserve.co.uk
Web: www.cdsf.org
International pilgrim movement for peace, social justice and unity amongst the nations, Christians and all.
National Guardian: Rev Canon Shana Barby. All voluntary staff. Began 1[illegible]69; ecumenical. Magazine: *The Way* ([illegible]00 quarterly). Turnover £95,000 to year end Dec 02.

Quaker Peace and Social Witness, Friends House, Euston Road, London NW1 2BJ
☎020 7663 1000 🖷020 7663 1049
E: qpsw@quaker.org.uk
Web: www.quaker.org.uk
Promoting peace and social justice in Britain and overseas; alleviating suffering, seeking positive social change.
General Secretary: Linda Craig. Executive staff 15, Other staff 18. Began 1978; Religious Society of Friends. Magazines: *Quaker News* (15,000 quarterly), *Opportunities for Action* (5,000 every four months). Turnover n/a.

***Resolve - The Christian Mediation and Arbitration Service**, PO Box 122, Brighton BN1 6WX
☎01273 549 512 🖷01273 549 512
E: office@christianmediation.org.uk
Web: www.christianmediation.org.uk
Advising, mediating and/or arbitrating in business and church disputes; teaching biblical response to conflict.
Chairman: Mr Christopher Smyth. Executive staff 1, Other staff n/a. Began 1990; interdenominational. (Previously The Christian Mediation and Arbitration Service). No magazine. Turnover n/a.

Set All Free: Act to End Slavery, Churches Together in England, 27 Tavistock Square, London WC1H 9HH
☎020 7529 8141 🖷020 7529 8134
E: info@setallfree.net
Web: www.setallfree.net
2007 bicentary of abolition of slave trade; remembering the past, applying lessons to the present.
Project Director: Mr Richard Reddie. Executive staff 1, Other staff n/a. ***CC*** No.1005368. Began 2005; ecumenical. Part of Churches Together in England. No magazine. Turnover n/a.

Sisters of Our Lady of Sion, 34 Chepstow Villas, Notting Hill, London W11 2QZ
☎020 8319 1930 🖷020 8319 4570
E: margaret@apcomm.net
Web: www.sistersofsion.org
Promoting relations between Christians and Jews and lessening prejudice between other groups.
Provincial: Sr Margaret Shepherd. Community 41. ***CC*** Began 1858; Roman Catholic. Magazine: *Sidic*. Turnover n/a.

***Youth Action for Peace (Action for Peace Volunteers)**, PO Box 43670, London SE22 0XX

☎08701 657 927
E: action@yap-uk.org
Web: www.yap-uk.org
Participating in an international project as a small step towards peace and intercultural learning.
Secretary: Mr Nigel Watt. Other staff n/a. Began 1961; interdenominational. (Previously Christian Movement for Peace). No magazine. Turnover n/a.

RESEARCH & DEVELOPMENT ORGANISATIONS

Archbishops' Council Research & Statistics, Church House, Great Smith Street, London SW1P 3NZ
☎020 7898 1592 🖷020 7898 1532
E: statistics.unit@c-of-e.org.uk
Web: www.cofe.anglican.uk
Providing research, consultancy and statistical information for the Church of England.
Head of Research & Statistics: Rev Lynda Barley. Executive staff 3, Admin staff 3. Began n/a; Anglican. Magazine: *Church Statistics* (Circulation n/a annually). Turnover n/a.

***The Bethany Trust**, Bethany House, Histon, Cambridge CB4 9HG
☎01223 233 053 M: 07791 346 983
🖷 01223 233 053
E: BethanyTrust@cambridgehealth.org.uk
Supporting medical research of the Cambridge Research Institute regarding new therapeutic proposals from academics.
Founder Trustee: Professor Peter Curtis-Prior. Executive staff 1, Other staff 2. ***CC*** No.1000586. Began 1990; interdenominational. No magazine. Turnover n/a.

†British Teilhard Association, 3 Anthony Road, Largs KA30 8EQ
☎01582 620 145 🖷01582 621 526
E: peterjohncox@lineone.net
Web: www.teilhard.org.uk
Annual conference, study/development of Teilhard de Chardin's evolutionary vision culminating in the cosmic Christ.
Chairman: Professor William Cranston. No full-time staff. ***CC*** No.313682. Began 1965; non-denominational. (Previously Teilhard Centre). No magazine. Turnover n/a.

Christian Institute, PO Box 1, Newcastle upon Tyne NE7 7EF
☎0191 281 5664 🖷0191 281 4272
E: info@christian.org.uk
Web: www.christian.org.uk
Maintaining a Christian influence in a secular world through research, conferences and publications.
Director: Mr Colin J Hart. *Chairman:* Mr John Burn. Executive staff 3, Other staff 13. ***CC*** No.1004774. Began 1991; non-denominational. Magazine: *Institute Update* (Circulation & frequency n/a), *Faith in Education* (Circulation & frequency n/a). Turnover £735,000 to year end Dec 04.

* **Christian Research**, Vision Building, 4 Footscray Road, Eltham, London SE9 2TZ
☎020 8294 1989 🖷020 8294 0014
E: admin@christian-research.org.uk
Web: www.christian-research.org.uk or www.ukchristianhandbook.org.uk
Resource centre for Christian leaders, specialising in research, information dissemination, consultancy and quantitative church data.
Executive Director: Dr Peter Brierley. *Deputy Director:* Heather Wraight. *Business Manager:* Bill Lattimer. Executive staff 3, Other staff 3. ***CC*** No.1017701. Began 1993; interdenominational. (Previously MARC Europe). Magazine: *Quadrant* (2,500 every two months). Turnover £260,000 to year end Dec 05.

For membership organisations see list on page 15.

Christian Social Order, 157 Vicarage Road, London E10 5DU
☎020 8539 3876
🖷020 8539 3876
E: social-owner@smartgroups.com
Web: www.smartgroups.com/vault/social
Promoting Christian social endeavours throughout Europe.
Secretary: Mr Ronald King. Admin staff 1, Other staff n/a. Began 1965; Roman Catholic. Magazine: *The Keys of Peter* (Circulation & frequency n/a). Turnover n/a.

City Vision Ministries, Bemersley House, Gitana Street, Hanley, Stoke-on-Trent ST1 1DY
☎01782 287 654
🖷01782 207 300
E: robert@city-vision.org.uk
Researching past and present to facilitate planning and fuel prayer towards a better future.
Director: Mr Robert J Mountford. Executive staff 1, Admin staff 2. Began 1994; interdenominational. No magazine. Turnover n/a.

Culham Institute, 15 Norham Gardens, Oxford OX2 6PY
☎01865 284 885
🖷01865 284 886
E: enquiries@culham.ac.uk
Web: www.culham.ac.uk
Research, development and information agency in the fields of church schools, collective worship, Religious Education.
Director: Rev Dr John Gay. Executive staff 4. ***CC*** No.309671. Began 1980; Anglican. (Previously Culham College Institute). No magazine. Turnover n/a.

*__Customer Research Technology Ltd__, Business Innovation Centre, Binley Business Park, Harry Weston Road, Binley, Coventry CV3 2TX
☎024 7643 0295 🖷024 7643 0291
E: info@crtbeyondquestion.com
Web: www.crtbeyondquestion.com
Undertaking research for local churches, Christian organisations and secular companies.
Director: Mr Jerry Marshall. Executive staff 3, Other staff 4. Began 2001; non-denominational. (Previously Jerry Marshall Associates). Magazine: *Update* (Circulation & frequency n/a). Turnover £280,000 to year end Dec 04.

Farmington Institute for Christian Studies, Harris Manchester College, Mansfield Road, Oxford OX1 3TD
☎01865 271 965 🖷01865 271 969
E: farmington@hmc.ox.ac.uk
Web: www.farmington.ac.uk
Supporting Christian education; fellowships and bursaries for teachers; publishing papers, arranging seminars and conferences.
Director: Rev Dr Ralph Waller. ***CC*** No.819630. Began 1965; interdenominational. No magazine. Turnover n/a.

†**The Grubb Institute of Behavioural Studies Limited**, Cloudesley Street, London N1 0HU
☎020 7278 8061 🖷020 7278 0728
E: info@grubb.org.uk
Web: www.grubb.org.uk
Advice, research in organisational roles, leadership, cultural change; organisational analysis using psychological, systemic, theological approaches..
Executive Director: Mr Bruce Irvine. Professional staff 6, Other staff 3. ***CC*** No.313460. Began 1969; non-denominational. No magazine. Turnover n/a.

*__The Jubilee Centre__, Jubilee House, 3 Hooper Street, Cambridge CB1 2NZ
☎01223 566 319 🖷01223 566 359
E: info@jubilee-centre.org
Web: www.jubilee-centre.org
Applying biblical research to public policy and contemporary issues.
Chairman: Dr Michael Schluter. *Chief Executive:* Michael Clark. Executive staff 3, Other staff 2. ***CC*** No.288783. Began 1983; non-denominational. Associated with the Relationships Foundation and incorporating Cambridge Papers. Magazine: *Engage* (5,000 quarterly). Turnover £170,000 to year end Aug 05.

Kingdom Trust, 11 William Road, West Bridgford, Nottingham NG2 7QD
☎0115 914 2460 M 07974 768 935
🖷0115 914 2460
E: rkm100@ntlworld.com
Web: www.kingdomtrust.org
Research and consultancy on the relationship between Christianity and culture; ethical approaches to policy making.
Director: Mr Roy McCloughry. Executive staff 1. ***CC*** No.326924. Began 1984; non-denominational. No magazine. Turnover n/a.

The Kuyper Foundation, PO Box 2, Taunton TA1 4ZD
☎01823 665 909 🖷01823 665 721
E: kuyper@kuyper.org
Web: www.kuyper.org
Promoting the renaissance of Christian culture through publishing literature, conferences and audio-visual material.
Director: Stephen C Perks. No full-time staff. ***CC*** No.327537. Began 1987; non-denominational. Magazine: *Christianity and Society* (Circulation n/a half-yearly). Turnover n/a.

†**The Latimer Trust**, 83 Carlton Road, Littleover, Derby DE23 6HE
☎01332 332 256 🖷01332 332 256
Web: www.latimertrust.org
Theological research and writing institution for evangelicals in the Church of England.
Chairman of Council: Rev Dr Mark Burkill. Executive staff 2. ***CC*** No.1084337. Began 1960; Anglican. Magazine: *Latimer Studies* (Circulation n/a irregularly). Turnover n/a.
Publications PO Box 26685, London N14 4XQ
E: secretary@latimertrust.org
☎020 8449 0467 ext 234

*__Men, Women and God__, c/o LICC, St Peter's Church, Vere Street, London W1G 0DQ
☎01483 560 089 🖷01483 560 089
E: menwomenandgod@btinternet.com
Web: www.menwomenandgod.com
Activating and encouraging good practice in gender justice; bulletin issued to share practice and stimulate.
Contact: Mrs Valerie Griffiths. No full-time staff. ***CC*** No.294993. Began 1986; interdenominational. Magazine: *Double Image* (300 half-yearly). Turnover n/a.

MODEM, 24 Rostron Crescent, Formby, Liverpool L37 2ET
☎01704 873 973
Web: www.chrisoc-forum.com
Facilitating communication between management and ministry; encouraging mutual understanding of theory and practice of both.
Secretary: Mr John R Nelson. No full-time staff. ***CC*** No.1048772. Began 1993; non-denominational. Magazine: *MODEM Matters* (600 quarterly). Turnover £6,700 to year end Dec 00.
Membership: *Treasurer:* Peter J Bates, Carselands, Woodmancote, Henfield BN5 9SS
E: peter@bateshouse.freeserve.co.uk
☎01273 493 172 🖷 01273 493 172

Network for Psychological Type & Christian Faith, Centre for Ministry Studies, University of Wales Bangor, Normal Site, Bangor LL57 2PX
☎01248 382 566 🖷01248 383 954
E: practical_theology@bangor.ac.uk
Web: www.bangor.ac.uk/rs/pt/type
Supporting individuals engaged in practice or research using Jungian psychological type theory in Christian contexts.
Network Coordinator: Rev Professor Leslie J Francis. No full-time staff. Began 2002; non-denominational. No magazine. Turnover n/a.

Oulton-Lee Research Ltd, 40 Fairmount Drive, Loughborough LE11 3JR
☎01509 264 141
M: 07721 992 405
🖷01509 264 141
E: contact@oulton-lee.co.uk
Web: www.oulton-lee.co.uk
Research solutions for marketing problems; questionnaire design, statistical analysis and interpretation; qualitative, especially focus groups.
Managing Director: Mrs Sue Garner. Executive staff 1, Other staff 1. Began 19[illegible]1; non-denominational. (Previously Oulton-Lee Marketing Services). No magazine. Turnover n/a.

†**Religious Experience Research Centre**, Department of Theology & Religious Studies, University of Wales, Lampeter SA48 7ED
☎01570 424 821
🖷01570 423 641
E: ahardytrust@lamp.ac.uk
Web: www.alisterhardytrust.org.uk
Researching the varieties of religious experiences; teaching on MA in Religious Experience.
Directors: Prof Paul Badham, Dr Wendy Dossett. Executive staff 2. ***CC*** No.286682. Began 1969; non-denominational. (Previously AH Religious Experience Research Centre). Magazine: *De Numine* (750 occasionally). Turnover £35,000 to year end Dec 02.

Rutherford House, 17 Claremont Park, Edinburgh EH6 7PJ
☎0131 554 1206
🖷0131 555 1002
E: info@rutherfordhouse.org.uk
Web: www.rutherfordhouse.org.uk
Training ministers and elders in pastoral leadership, preaching; publishing study aids; theological library.
Director: Rev Dr Robert Fyall. Executive staff 3, Other staff 3. ***CC*** No.SCO 1511[illegible]. Began 1983; non-denominational. Magazines: *Scottish Bulletin of Evangelical Theology* (800 half-yearly), *Rutherford Journal of Church & Ministry* (700 half-yearly). Turnover £181,000 to year end Dec 04.

Scottish Church History Society, 48 Corbiehill Crescent, Edinburgh EH4 5BD
☎0131 336 4071
E: w.d.graham@btinternet.com
Encouraging interest and research in all aspects of Scottish Church History.
Hon Secretary: Rev William Graham. No paid staff. ***CC*** No.SCO 14412. Began 1927; non-denominational. Magazine: *Records of the Scottish Church History Society* (300 annually). Turnover £3,000 to year end Dec 00.

S

†University of the Holy Land (UK Office), Tangnefedd, Windmill Road, Weald, Sevenoaks TN14 6PJ
☎01732 463 460
E: ukoffice@uhl.ac
Web: www.uhl.ac
Academic research; full-time higher education courses and study tours of the Holy Land; information resource.
UK Director: Mr Ian Mitchell Lambert. Executive staff 1, Other staff 2. Began 1988; interdenominational. (Previously Centre for the Study of Early Christianity). No magazine. Turnover £500 to year end Aug 02.

†The Whitefield Institute, 36 Selwyn Gardens, Cambridge CB3 9BA
☎01223 566 619 🖷01223 566 608
E: whitefield@tyndale.cam.ac.uk
Web: www.whitefield-institute.org.uk
Promoting biblical research in theology, ethics and education. The research wing of UCCF.
Director: To be appointed. Other staff 2. ***CC*** No.273458. Began 1987; non-denominational. Magazine: *Whitefield Briefings* (300 every four months). Turnover £175,000 to year end Apr 00.

SOCIAL ASSOCIATIONS

†Amicus Clergy & Church Workers, 35 King Street, London WC2E 8JG
☎020 7420 8978 🖷020 7420 8989
E: katie.moore@amicustheunion.org
Web: www.amicustheunion.org
Offering information, advice and support on employment issues to clergy and church workers.
Chair of Clergy Section: Rev W F Ward. Executive staff 12. Began 1988; non-denominational. (Previously MSF). Magazine: *Common Ground* (22,000 quarterly). Turnover n/a.

***The Antioch Community**, 49 Manor Drive, Wembley HA9 8EB
☎020 8993 9654
E: trev@antioch.org.uk
Web: www.antioch.org.uk
Non-residential charismatic lay community living out Christian unity in covenant together, practising evangelism.
Senior Leader: Mr T Perry. Executive staff 1, Other staff 3. ***CC*** No.282690. Began 1979; interdenominational. No magazine. Turnover £100,000 to year end Mar 05.

Ashram Community, 178 Abbeyfield Road, Sheffield S4 7AY
☎0114 243 6688
E: ashramcommunity@hotmail.com
Web: www.ashram.org.uk
Voluntary association of radical Christians working in deprived urban areas; also shops, community houses, publications.
Leader: Rev Dr John J Vincent. No full-time staff. ***CC*** No.1099164. Began 1967; ecumenical. Magazine: *ACT* (500 annually). Turnover n/a.
Also at: Ashram Centre and Shop, 347 Glossop Road, Sheffield S10 2HP
☎0114 272 1971
And: Ashram Centre and Shop, 86 Spital Hill, Sheffield S4 7LG
☎0114 270 0971
And: Community House, 75 Rock Street, Sheffield S3 9JB
☎0114 276 1319
And: Community House, 77 Rock Street, Sheffield S3 9JB
☎0114 272 7144
And: Ashram House Centre and Shop, 1 Bowesfield Lane, Stockton-on-Tees TS18 3EG
☎01740 630 475

†The Association for Church Editors, 75 Cymbeline Way, Rugby CV22 6JZ
☎01789 521 468
E: a.jackson@ac-editors.co.uk
Web: www.ac-editors.co.uk
Fostering the highest quality of Christian editorial service to local communities, especially through parish magazines.
Secretary: Mrs Andrea Jackson. No full-time staff. ***CC*** Began 1999; ecumenical. Magazine: *The Ace* (500 every two months). Turnover £2,000 to year end Sep 02.

Association of Church Accountants & Treasurers, Beech House, Pen-y-lan, Cowbridge CF71 7RY
☎01446 775 623
E: norey@acat.uk.com
Web: www.acat.uk.com
Assisting church accountants to fulfil their obligations.
Secretary: R G Norey. No paid staff. ***CC*** No.1072733. Began 1999; ecumenical. No magazine. Turnover £8,681 to year end Mar 05.

Baptist Caravan Fellowship, 36 Cumberland Court, Festing Road, Southsea PO4 0NH
☎023 9281 5609
Web: www.thebcf.org.uk
Holding weekend rallies throughout the country; fostering fellowship among caravanning Christians and supporting small churches.
Publicity: Mr David Marlow. No full-time staff. Began 1968; Baptist. Magazine: *Highway* (160 quarterly). Turnover £10,700 to year end Dec 00.

Boaters Christian Fellowship, Pondside Barn, Canal Road, Thrupp, Kidlington OX5 1JQ
☎01865 841 114
E: bcf@pondside.freeserve.co.uk
Web: www.boaterschristianfellowship.org.uk
Christian witness worship and fellowship for the boating community on the waterways of Britain.
Secretary: Anne Clark. All voluntary staff. ***CC*** No.1101100. Began 1995; interdenominational. Magazine: *The Word* (650 quarterly). Turnover n/a.

Caravanners and Campers Christian Fellowship, 3 The Meadway, Loughton, Milton Keynes MK5 8AN
☎0845 456 1637
🖷0845 456 1637
E: info@cccf.org.uk
Web: www.cccf.org.uk
Evangelical Christian holiday fellowship; weekend and holiday rallies, annual national rally, winter day rallies.
General Secretary: Mr Trevor Giles. All voluntary staff. ***CC*** No.281757. Began 1969; interdenominational. Magazine: *Newsline* (Circulation n/a every two months). Turnover n/a.

†Catenian Association, 8 Chesham Place, London SW1X 8HP
☎020 7235 6671
🖷020 7235 9344
E: catena@dial.pipex.com
Web: www.thecatenianassociation.org
Association for Catholic professional and business people.
Administrator: Mr Hugh Keast. Executive staff 1, Other staff 4. ***CC*** Began 190[illegible]; Roman Catholic. Magazine: *Catena* (11,500 monthly). Turnover n/a.

†Cathedral & Church Shops Association, Wells Cathedral Publications Ltd, The West Cloister, Wells BA5 2PA
☎01749 672 773
🖷01749 676 543
E: shop@wellscathedral.uk.net
Web: www.ccfa.org.uk
Association supporting cathedral and church shops in the UK; annual trade fair, conferences, meetings.
Chair: Jackie Osgodby. *Secretary:* Elizabeth Stafford. No paid staff. Began 1988; interdenominational. No magazine. Turnover £1,000,000 to year end Dec 99.

†Catholic Students Society, Canmore, 24 The Scores, St Andrews KY16 9AS
☎01334 472 179
Social and religious society for Catholic students and others interested.
President: Name not supplied. No full-time staff. Began 1971; Roman Catholic. (Previously Canmore Society). No magazine. Turnover n/a.

S

Central Council of Church Bell Ringers, The Cottage, School Hill, Warnham, Horsham RH12 3QN
☎01403 269 743
E: ihoram@hotmail.com
Web: www.cccbr.org.uk
Promoting ringing of church bells; advising on changing ringing standards.
Hon Secretary: Mr I H Oram. All voluntary staff. ***CC*** No 270036. Began 1890; non-denominational. Magazine: *The Ringing World* (3,500 weekly). Turnover £31,500 to year end Dec 04.

Centre for Christian Democracy, St David's, Park Road South, Newton-Le-Willows WA12 8EY
☎01925 220 999
E: office@mcdpolitics.org
Web: www.mcdpolitics.org
All-party group devoted to promoting Christian inspired values in politics.
Chairman: Richard Tazewell. Executive staff 1. ***CC*** No.1006653. Began 1990; non-denominational. (Previously Movement for Christian Democracy). Magazine: *Christian Politics* (20,000 quarterly). Turnover £35,000 to year end Dec 04.

Changing Attitude, 12 Lavender Gardens, London SW11 1DL
☎020 7738 1305 M: 07770 844 302 🖷020 7738 0584
E: info@changingattitude.org
Web: www.changingattitude.org
Working for lesbian and gay affirmation within the Anglican communion; local groups, conferences.
Director: Rev Colin Coward. Executive staff 1, Admin staff 1. ***CC*** No.1076808. Began 1995; Anglican. No magazine. Turnover n/a.

The Christian Conference Trust, The Hayes Conference Centre, Swanwick, Alfreton DE55 1AU
☎01773 526 000 🖷01773 540 841
E: brian.cupples@cct.org.uk
Web: www.cct.org.uk
Providing facilities for conferences, retreats, meetings at The Hayes and High Leigh Conference Centres.
General Manager. Mr Brian Cupples. *Centre Manager:* Mr Peter Anderson. Executive staff 2. ***CC*** No.1056604. Began 1911; non-denominational. Magazine: *CCT News* (2,000 half-yearly). Turnover n/a.

Christian Guild, Derwent House, Cromford, Matlock DE4 5JG
☎01629 580 550 🖷01629 580 025
E: mail@cgholidays.co.uk
Web: www.christianguild.co.uk
Hotels holidays and conference centres in southern Lakes, North Yorkshire, Wye Valley, Derbyshire Dales, Devon, Cornwall.
Managing Director: Mr Kevin Mantle. Other staff n/a. Began 1910; ecumenical. (Previously Christian Guild Holidays). Owned by Methodist Guild Holidays Ltd. No magazine. Turnover n/a.

Christian Peoples Alliance Party, 7 Storey's Gate, Westminster, London SW1P 3AT
☎020 7976 0003/0845 456 5478
E: info@cpalliance.net
Web: www.cpalliance.net
Political party in the Christian Democratic tradition; running candidates for public office.
President: Mr Peter Flower. Executive staff 1. Began 1999; interdenominational. No magazine. Turnover n/a.

Christian Rambling Club, 10 Primrose Way, Locks Heath, Southampton SO31 6WX
☎01489 582 091
E: membership@crc-net.org.uk
Web: www.crc-net.org.uk
Rambling, hill and fell walking, mountaineering with Christian fellowship and witness.
Membership Secretary: Sue Edwards. No full-time staff. Began 1981; interdenominational. No magazine. Turnover £5,000 to year end Dec 04.

Christian Socialist Movement, Westminster Central Hall, London SW1H 9NH
☎020 7233 3736
E: info@thecsm.org.uk
Web: www.thescm.org.uk
A forum for Christians on the left of politics.
Director: Dr Andrew Bradstock. Other staff n/a. Began 1960; non-denominational. Affiliated to UK Labour Party. Magazines: *The Christian Socialist* (2,500 every four months), *CSM Pamphlet* (2,500 half-yearly). Turnover n/a.

Clergy Correspondence Chess Club, The Rectory, Kippax, Leeds LS25 7HF
☎0113 286 2710
E: brucecarlin@freeuk.com
Enabling clergy to play chess by correspondence or phone.
Secretary: Rev W P Bruce Carlin. No full-time staff. Began 1967; interdenominational. Magazine: *Chess Minister* (60 every four months). Turnover n/a.

Conservative Christian Fellowship, Conservative Central House, 25 Victoria Street, London SW1H 0DL
☎020 7984 8305 🖷020 7222 1135
E: ccf@conservatives.com
Web: www.ccfwebsite.com
Developing Christian contribution to the Conservative Party's life and thinking.
Executive Director: Miss Elizabeth Berridge. Executive staff 2. Began 1990; interdenominational. Magazine: *Conservatism* (1,400 every four months). Turnover n/a.

Council for the Marist Way, 12 Harrow Road, Linthorpe, Middlesbrough TS5 5PD
☎01642 281 408 M: 07733 433 956
E: agnes.mcgrogan@ntlworld.com
Bringing together people who wish to follow the Gospel in the spirit of Mary.
Secretary of the Council: Mrs Agnes McGrogan. No full-time staff. ***CC*** No.235412. Began 1847; Roman Catholic. (Previously Third Order of Mary). No magazine. Turnover n/a.

†The Ecclesiological Society, 143 Leathwaite Road, London SW11 6RW
☎020 7021 9685
E: admin@ecclsoc.org
Web: www.ecclsoc.org
Studying the arts, architecture and liturgy of the Christian Church.
Chairman of Council: Mr Trevor Cooper. No full-time staff. ***CC*** No.210501. Began 1879; non-denominational. Magazine: *Ecclesiology Today* (900 every four months). Turnover £20,000 to year end Dec 01.

The Evangelical Fellowship for Lesbian & Gay Christians, 123 Byron Road, Chelmsford CM2 6HJ
☎01245 252 214
E: info@eflgc.org.uk
Web: www.eflgc.org.uk
Offering affirming support, fellowship to evangelical lesbian and gay Christians through conferences and other resources.
Contact: Sigrid Rutishauser-James. No full-time staff. Began 1979; interdenominational. No magazine. Turnover £11,000 to year end Dec 02.

Families First, 192 New Road, Chilworth, Guildford GU4 8LX
☎01483 454 028
🖷01483 454 028
E: info@families-first.org.uk
Web: www.families-first.org.uk
Upholding the responsibility of parents to reasonably decide how to bring up their children.
Spokeswoman: Mrs Fiona Wyatt. All voluntary staff. Began 1992; non-denominational. (Previously Families for Discipline). Magazine: *Families First* (3,000 occasionally). Turnover n/a.

†Fellowship of Christian Motorcyclists, 8 Butterbur Chase, South Woodham Ferrers, Chelmsford CM3 7AG
☎No telephone
Web: www.fcm-bikers.org.uk
Combining motorcycling activities with Christian fellowship and social events, so witnessing to non-Christians.
Chairman: Ashley John. No full-time staff. Began 1976; non-denominational. Magazine: *Trans-mission* (100 monthly). Turnover £1,500 to year end Dec 98.

***The Fellowship of Evangelists**, 23 Cherry Tree Road, The Bryn, Pontllanfraith, Blackwood NP12 2PY
☎01495 223 255
M: 07960 165 548
🖷01495 226 054
E: ronspillards@btopenworld.com
Encouraging itinerant evangelists in the UK.
Executive Chair: Mr Ron Spillards. No full-time staff. Began 2004; interdenominational. No magazine. Turnover n/a.

International Christian Maritime Association, St Michael Paternoster Royal, College Hill, London EC4R 2RL
☎020 7248 5202 🖷020 7248 4761
E: secgen@missiontoseafarers.org
Web: www.icma.as or www.icma-cpc.as or www.icma-smt.as
Voluntary association of Christian organisations promoting the welfare of seafarers, fishermen and their families.
General Secretary: Rev Dr Juergen Kanz. Executive staff 1. ***CC*** No.1003211. Began 1969; interdenominational. No magazine. Turnover n/a.

***The Keep Sunday Special Campaign**, Jubilee House, 3 Hooper Street, Cambridge CB1 2NZ
☎01223 566 333 🖷01223 566 359
E: kss@r.f.clara.net
Web: www.keepsundayspecial.net
Campaigning to prevent further erosion of Sunday as a day of rest, family activities and worship.
Chairman: Dr Michael Schluter. Executive staff 2, Other staff 2. Began 1984; non-denominational. Linked to Keep Time for Children. No magazine. Turnover £45,000 to year end Aug 04.

Lay Community of St Benedict, PO Box 559, Rickmansworth WD3 7XQ
☎0845 458 2994
E: contact@laybenedictines.org
Web: www.laybenedictines.org
Non-residential community dedicated to Benedictine spirituality as lived out by lay people.
Leader: Michael Woodward. Admin staff 1. ***CC*** No.1100638. Began 2003; Roman Catholic, Benedictine. (Previously Worth Abbey Lay Community). No magazine. Turnover n/a.

Lesbian and Gay Christian Movement (LGCM), Oxford House, Derbyshire Street, London E2 6HG
☎020 7739 1249/8134 (helpline)
🖷020 7739 1249
E: lgcm@lgcm.org.uk
Web: www.lgcm.org.uk
Advocacy and support for lesbian/gay/bisexual Christians and friends through groups, conferences, publications.
General Secretary: Rev Richard Kirker. Executive staff 1. ***CC*** No.1048842. Began 1976; non-denominational. Magazine: *Lesbian & Gay Christian* (2,500 half-yearly). Turnover £115,000 to year end Dec 04.

Liberal Democrat Christian Forum, 4 Cowey Street, London SW1P 3NB
☎020 7799 2170
E: office@christianforum.libdems.org
Web: www.christianforum.libdems.org
Christian fellowship of the Liberal Democrat Party.
LDCF Organiser: Debbie Enever. No full-time staff. Began 1988. Magazine: *Christian Focus* (250 quarterly). Turnover £2,000 to year end Sep 00.

The Living Stones of the Holy Land Trust, 2 Castle Close, London SW19 5NH
☎020 8879 3074
E: info@livingstonesonline.org.uk
Web: www.livingstonesonline.org.uk
Promoting contacts between Christian communities in Britain, the Holy Land and neighbouring countries.
Hon Treasurer: Mr Jamil Bullata. *Chairman:* Rev Deacon Dr Duncan Macpherson. No full-time staff. ***CC*** No.1081204. Began 1986; ecumenical. Magazine: *Living Stones* (1,000 half-yearly). Turnover £106,000 to year end Mar 05.

London Catholic Worker, 14 Deal Street, London E1 5AH
☎Mobile 07985 204 878
E: londoncatholicworker@yahoo.com
Web: www.geocities.com/londoncatholic-worker
Faith-based network exploring anarchism, non-violent resistance, hospitality, community and works of mercy.
Coordinator: Name not supplied. No full-time staff. Began 2000; Roman Catholic but open to all. Magazine: *London Catholic Worker* (500 quarterly). Turnover n/a.

mediawatch-uk, 3 Willow House, Kennington Road, Ashford TN24 0NR
☎01233 633 936 🖷01233 633 836
E: info@mediawatchuk.org
Web: www.mediawatchuk.org
Encouraging involvement in discussion about the effect of broadcasting on the individual/family/society.
Director: Mr John Beyer. Executive staff 2. Began 1965; non-denominational. Magazine: *mediawatch-uk* (6,000 every four months). Turnover n/a.

Methodist Holiday Hotels Ltd, Raven Hall, Ravenscar, Scarborough YO13 0ET
☎01723 870 353 🖷01723 870 072
E: admin@epworth.co.uk
Web: www.epworth.co.uk
Operating holiday hotel in Scarborough; specialist group tour company with a Christian ethos, catering for all denominations.
Managing Director: Mr Clive Rowe-Evans. Executive staff 10, Other staff 56. Began 1922; non-denominational. Trading as Epworth Hotels and Tour Epworth. No magazine. Turnover £1,400,000 to year end Oct 05.

†Order of Christian Unity/Christian Projects, 53 Penerley Road, London SE6 2LH
☎020 7233 4167
Promoting Christian values in the areas of family life, education, medical ethics, the media.
Contact: Mr Andrew Pollock. Admin staff 1. ***CC*** No.266183. Began 1955; ecumenical. Magazine: *Focus* (500 every four months). Turnover £5,000 to year end June 02.

The Order of "On Call Clergy", 41 Ingleborough Way, Leyland, Preston PR25 4ZS
☎01772 436 817 Ⓜ 0788[illegible] 380 [illegible]8
🖷01772 452 578
Web: oncallclergy.org.uk
Clergy on call for all emergencies as non-denominational chaplains.
President: Bishop Michael. Executive staff 5, Serving clergy 37. Began 1999; non-denominational. No magazine. Turnover n/a.

Quest, BM Box 2585, London WC1N 3XX
☎0808 808 0234 (helpline Wed/Fri/Sun 7-10pm)
E: secretary@questgaycatholic.org.uk
Web: www.questgaycatholic.org.uk
Increasing the spiritual and social wellbeing of gay and lesbian Catholics in Britain; free helpline.
Secretary: Name not supplied. All voluntary staff. ***CC*** No.294388. Began 1973; Roman Catholic. Magazine: *Quest Digest* (200 occasional), *Quest Bulletin* (250 quarterly). Turnover n/a.

Retreat Association, The Central Hall, 256 Bermondsey Street, London SE1 3UJ
☎020 7357 7736 🖷020 7357 772[illegible]
E: info@retreats.org.uk
Web: www.retreats.org.uk
Providing information and resources in connection with retreats and spiritual direction.
Executive Officer: Mrs Paddy Lane. Executive staff 1, Other staff 2. ***CC*** No.3287[illegible]6. Began 1989; interdenominational. Comprising Anglican, Baptist, Methodist, Religious Society of Friends, Roman Catholic, United Reformed Church retreat groups. Magazine: *Retreats* (14,000 annually). Turnover £60,000 to year end Mar 00.

RTA (Rural Theology Association), The Vicarage, Rudston, Driffield YO25 4XA
☎01262 420 313
E: stephen.cope@dial.pipex.com
Web: www.rural-theology.org.uk
Encouraging discussions and practical responses to rural Christianity.
Hon Secretary: Rev Stephen Cope. No full-time staff. ***CC*** No.327029. Began 19[illegible]; non-denominational. Magazine: *Rural Theology* (450 half-yearly). Turnover £4,801 to year end Dec 02.

†Sion Centre for Dialogue and Encounter, 17 Chepstow Villas, London W11 3DZ
☎020 7727 3597 🖷020 7313 8281
E: sioncentrecjr@btinternet.com
Understanding and fostering the Church's relationship with the Jewish people; also conference centre facilities.
Contact: Sr Clare Jardine. No paid staff. ***CC*** No.248747. Began 196[illegible]; Roman Catholic. (Previously Study Centre for Christian-Jewish Relations). No magazine. Turnover n/a.

S

†Society for Independent Christian Ministry, 8 Ipswich Road, Westbourne, Bournemouth BH4 9HZ
☎01202 763 609
E: stewart.harrison@tesco.net
Web: www.sicm.fsnet.co.uk
Ministering to people untouched by the traditional work and ministry provided by the denominations.
Secretary: Rev Stewart Harrison. Executive staff 2, Other staff 3. Began 2000; non-denominational. Magazine: *The Living Vine* (100 monthly). Turnover £800 to year end Dec 00.
Also at: *Bishop-in-Charge:* Rt Rev Jonathan Blake, Sunrise, 105 Danson Crescent, Welling DA16 2AS
E: bishop@jonathanblake.freeserve.co.uk
☎020 8303 0461 Office 01322 525 678

†Team R837, 30 Elm Grove, Frinton-on-Sea CO13 0EH
☎01255 850 500 Fax 01255 850 500
E: teamR837@aol.com
Web: www.teamR837.com
Outreach and pastoral support in the international motorsport community.
Organiser: Mr Phil Aiken. No full-time staff. Began 1999; interdenominational. No magazine. Turnover £1,000 to year end Dec 00.

†Toc H, The Stable Block, The Firs, Whitchurch, Aylesbury HP22 4JU
☎01296 642 020 Fax 01296 640 022
E: info@toch.org.uk
Web: www.toch.org.uk
Providing 6 key programmes: Partnership, Vol:tag, In Touch, Talbot Centres, consultancy to charities; international outreach.
Director: Rev Geoff Smith. Executive staff 5, Other staff 50. ***CC*** No.211042. Began 1915; ecumenical. Magazine: *Point Three* (3,000 monthly). Turnover £1,000,000 to year end Mar 02.

Trumpet Call, 102 Irlam Road, Flixton, Manchester M41 6JT
☎0161 748 2948/4858 Fax 0161 748 2948/747 7379
E: trumpet.callbtinternet.com
Web: www.maranathacommunity.org.uk
Maintaining an effective Christian voice for truth, justice and righteousness throughout UK.
Secretary: Maria. Staff n/a. ***CC*** No.327627. Began 1997; ecumenical. Associated with the Maranatha Community. No magazine. Turnover n/a.

***Twenty Thirty**, PO Box 266, Staines TW18 4GP
☎0870 286 3136 M: 07976 877 790
Fax 0870 286 3136
E: TT2030@aol.com
Web: www.twentythirty.org.uk
Serving local churches by providing events for twenties and thirties age range.
Group Coordinator: Mr Barry Mockford. Admin staff 1. ***CC*** No.1031597. Began 1992; interdenominational. No magazine. Turnover £20,000 to year end Dec 04.

United Evangelical Project, 29 Trinity Road, Aston, Birmingham B6 6AJ
☎0121 551 1207 Fax 0121 554 4894
E: enquiries@ueponline.co.uk
Web: www.ueponline.co.uk
Providing support and advice to the local community.
Director: Rev James Herbert. *Chairman:* Rev Robert Pusey. Executive staff 1, Staff 20. ***CC*** No.284543. Began 1976; interdenominational. A Community Care umbrella project. No magazine. Turnover £721,000 to year end Mar 05.
Aston Legal Centre: *Contact:* Mr G Morris
☎0121 523 0965
Prison Link: *Contacts:* Ms L Lewis, Mr P Masih
☎0121 551 1207
Youth Accommodation Project: *Contact:* Miss J Grimes
☎0121 554 0689

WATCH National (Women and the Church), St John's Church, Waterloo Road, London SE1 8TY
☎01763 848 822 Fax 01763 848 774
E: christina@mediamaxima.com
Web: www.watchwomen.com
Providing a national forum for promoting, discussing and monitoring women's ministry in the church.
Chair: Christina Rees. No full time staff. Began 1996; ecumenical. Magazine: *Outlook* (800 half-yearly). Turnover n/a.

SOCIAL SERVICE & WELFARE ORGANISATIONS

See also Counselling Organisations on Page 331, Marriage Ministries on Page 366, Family Care & Support Ministies on Page 341.

†All Souls Clubhouse, 141 Cleveland Street, London W1T 6QG
☎020 7387 1360
Fax 020 7387 2593
E: team@clubhousew1.org
Web: www.clubhouse1.org
Providing for people aged over 60; serving the locality: youth and children's work.
Clubhouse Vicar: Rev Andy Rider. *Centre Administrator:* Ms Cheryl Deja. Executive staff 4, Other staff 9. ***CC*** No.303292. Began 1958; Anglican. No magazine. Turnover £218,337 to year end Dec 02.

†Apostleship of the Sea, Stella Maris Atlantic House, New Strand, Bootle L20 4TQ
☎0151 922 6161 Fax 0151 922 2616
Promoting the spiritual and social welfare of all seafarers.
Port Chaplain: Rev Patrick Harnett. Executive staff 1, Other staff 12. Began 1920; Roman Catholic. Magazine: *The Anchor* (Circulation n/a quarterly). Turnover n/a.

†Apostleship of the Sea (Scotland), Stella Maris Seamen's Centre, 937 Dumbarton Road, Glasgow G14 9UF
☎0141 339 6657 Fax 0141 334 7463
Providing pastoral care of seafarers, tourists and others on the move.
National Director: Mr Leo Gilbert. Executive staff 3. ***CC*** No.SCO 18200. Began 1923; Roman Catholic. No magazine. Turnover £85,000 to year end Dec 94.

Aston-Mansfield, Durning Hall, Earlham Grove, London E7 9AB
☎020 8536 3810 Fax 020 8519 5472
E: ip@aston-mansfield.org.uk
Web: www.aston-mansfield.org.uk
Community development agency, Christian roots, running community centres; outdoor centre; research; East London, Essex.
Chief Executive: Mr Ian Powell. *Company Secretary:* Mr Geoffrey Wheeler. *Community Development Manager:* Ms Caroline Rouse. Executive staff 3, Other staff 60. ***CC*** No.220085. Began 1884; interdenominational. (Previously Mansfield University Settlement). No magazine. Turnover £2,000,000 to year end Dec 00.

†*Barnabus Project, 144 Broomhall Road, Pendelbury, Swinton, Manchester M27 8XG
☎0161 950 6936
Fax 0161 747 7379
E: peter.green57@ntlworld.com
Christian street work with the homeless, prostitutes and drug addicts; Mobile surgery.
Leader: Mr Peter Green. All voluntary staff. ***CC*** Began 1994; interdenominational. (Affiliated to the Maranatha Community). No magazine. Turnover n/a.

***CAHA Christian Alliance Housing Association Ltd**, 2 Exton Street, London SE1 8UE
☎0870 458 4243
Fax 0870 458 4245 / 020 7593 0478
E: mail@caha.org.uk or timf@caha.org.uk
Providing accommodation and support to international students and people of all faiths or none.
Chief Executive: Mr Rob Taylor. Executive staff 6, Admin staff 6. ***CC*** No.293232. Began 1985; interdenominational. (Previously Christian Alliance). No magazine. Turnover £6,000,000 to year end Mar 03.

S

†***The Care Centre**, 97 Monkstown Road, Newtownabbey BT37 0LG
☎028 9086 8059 🖷028 9086 8059
E: carecentre.monkstown@btinternet.com
All-age social provision, facilities and opportunities for volunteering among local churches.
Chair: Mr Alan Taylor. Executive staff 1, Other staff 2. ***CC*** No.XR 29636. Began 1994; interdenominational. No magazine. Turnover £37,000 to year end Mar 03.

Carers Christian Fellowship, 14 Cavie Close, Nine Elms, Swindon SN5 5XD
☎01793 887 068
E: sjones.ccf@ntlworld.com
Web: www.carerschristianfellowship.org.uk
Providing spiritual encouragement to Christians caring at home for relatives with illness or disability.
Co-ordinator: Mrs Sue Jones. All voluntary staff. ***CC*** No.1063112. Began 1994; interdenominational. No magazine. Turnover £4,000 to year end Dec 04.

†**Caring for Life**, Crag House Farm, Smithy Lane, Cookridge, Leeds LS16 7NH
☎0113 230 3600 🖷0113 230 3618
E: info@caringforlife.co.uk
Web: www.caringforlife.co.uk
Sharing the love of Jesus with homeless, disadvantaged and damaged people.
Chief Executive Officer: Pastor Peter Parkinson. *Senior Pastoral Administrator:* Miss Esther Smith. *Pastoral Director:* Mr Jonathan Parkinson. Executive staff 5, Other staff 21. ***CC*** No.519138. Began 1987; interdenominational. No magazine. Turnover £900,000 to year end Jan 93.

CHAT (Churches Housing Action Team) Mid-Devon Ltd, 28 Gold Street, Tiverton EX16 6PY
☎01884 255 606 🖷01884 258 030
E: theoffice@chatmid.co.uk
Working to relieve the need of those who are homeless or threatened with homelessness.
Coordinator: Miss Sally Chapman. Executive staff 1, Admin staff 5. ***CC*** No.1049478. Began 1995; non-denominational. No magazine. Turnover £180,000 to year end Mar 05.

***Christ Church Community Services Ltd**, Parish Office, Christ Church, 2 Quay Road, Bridlington YO15 2AP
☎01262 404 100 🖷01262 404 103
E: info@christchurchbridlington.org
Web: www.christchurchbridlington.org
Providing a wide range of community projects to people in Bridlington area.
Vicar: Rev Jonathan Couper. *Finance Director:* Mr Stuart Anderson. Executive staff 1, Other staff 20. ***CC*** No.1025815. Began 1993; Anglican. No magazine. Turnover £200,000 to year end Dec 02.

***Christian Concern, Crewe**, St Paul's Centre, Hightown, Crewe CW1 3BY
☎01270 586 186
🖷01270 250 683
E: admin@christianconcern.co.uk
Web: christianconcerncrewe.org
Multi-purpose centre: furniture redistribution, supported employment, pregnancy crisis counselling, children's resource services; community/ voluntary engagement.
Director: Rev Rob Wykes. Full-time staff 4, Part-time staff 2, Staff 6. ***CC*** No.1001566. Began 1987; non-denominational. (Previously 3C Teamwork). No magazine. Turnover £134,000 to year end Apr 04.

***Christian Council on Ageing**, Epworth House, Stuart Street, Derby DE1 2EQ
☎01858 432 771
🖷01858 432 771
E: candbhodgson@btinternet.com
National voluntary organisation for the spiritual needs and potential of elderly people.
Chairman: Mr Ray Smith. Admin staff 1. ***CC*** No.289463. Began 1982; interdenominational. Magazine: *Plus* (700 quarterly). Turnover £22,000 to year end Dec 02.

†***Christian Prison Ministries**, PO Box 8806, Carluke ML8 4RJ
☎01698 357 400
🖷01698 357 500
E: anne.mclean@blueyonder.co.uk
Web: www.cpmscotland.org.uk
Prison ministry, primarily evangelism and addictions; also aftercare of ex-prisoners.
Director: Rev Colin Cuthbert. No full-time staff. ***CC*** No.SCO 27020. Began 1997; non-denominational. (Previously Prayer Network for Revival). No magazine. Turnover £18,000 to year end Dec 02.

***Christian Victory Group - I Care Project**, 3rd Floor, 445 Hackney Road, London E2 9DY
☎020 7729 4081
🖷020 7729 4081
E: cvgicare@aol.com
Web: www.cvgicare.org
Providing and promoting community projects to show the love of Christ through practical care.
Administrator: Rev Adegboyega Omooba. *Coordinator:* Rev Olanrewaju Sholola. Executive staff 1, Other staff 10. ***CC*** No.1012692. Began 1992; interdenominational. No magazine. Turnover n/a.

Church Action on Poverty, Central Buildings, Oldham Street, Manchester M1 1JQ
☎0161 236 9321
🖷0161 237 5359
E: info@church-poverty.org.uk
Web: www.church-poverty.org.uk
Tackling the root causes of poverty in the UK; organising Poverty Action Sunday.
National Coordinator: Mr Niall Cooper. *Chairperson:* Ms Anne Forbes. Executive staff 1, Other staff 14. ***CC*** No.1079986. Began 1982; non-denominational. Partner for Debt on our Doorstep. No magazine. Turnover £518,000 to year end Mar 05.

Church in Society, 2 Bedford Place, Maidstone ME16 8JB
☎01622 755 014
🖷01622 693 531
E: office@churchinsociety.org
Web: www.churchinsociety.org
Involving churches in raising awareness, advocacy and action for change in local communities.
Chief Executive: Mr David Grimwood. *Director of Community Ministry:* Ms Jane Winter. *Company Secretary:* Mr Adrian Speller. Executive staff 23, Admin staff 2. ***CC*** No.1091679. Began 2002; Anglican. (Previously Council for Social Aid). Magazine: *Society Matters* (950 quarterly). Turnover £1,400,000 to year end Dec 04.

***CrossReach, Church of Scotland Social Care Council**, Charis House, 47 Milton Road East, Edinburgh EH15 2SR
☎0131 657 2000
🖷0131 657 5000
E: info@crossreach.org.uk
Web: www.crossreach.org.uk
Voluntary social work agency: residential/day care, counselling services, homelessness, mental health, learning disability, offenders.
Director of Social Work: Mr Ian G Manson. Admin staff 64, Other staff 2,200. ***CC*** No.SCO [illegible]. Began 1869; Church of Scotland. (Previously Church of Scotland Board of Social Responsibility). Magazine: *Circle of Care* (45,000 every four months). Turnover £41,180,000 to year end Mar 0[illegible].

***Daventry Contact**, Unit 2 South March, Long March Industrial Estate, Daventry NN11 4PH
☎01327 310 711
Providing training for people with mental illness; furniture collected and delivered.
Chairman: Dr Richard Barrett. Executive staff 1, Other staff 3. ***CC*** No.1002659. Began 1991; ecumenical. No magazine. Turnover n/a.

Farm Crisis Network, Manor Farm, West Haddon, Northampton NN6 7[illegible]
☎01788 510 866/0700 232 632[illegible] (helpline)
🖷01788 511 026
E: mail@fcn.org.uk
Web: www.farmcrisisnetwork.org.uk
Coordinating volunteers from churches and farming community ready to walk with farming families in trouble.
National Coordinator: Mr Christopher Jones. Executive staff 1. ***CC*** No.1095919. Began 1994; interdenominational. No magazine. Turnover n/a.

S

***Field Lane Foundation**, 16 Vine Hill, London EC1R 5EA
☎020 7337 0412 ℻020 7278 4312
E: info@fieldlane.org.uk
Web: www.fieldlane.org.uk
Providing innovative accommodation, care and support for homeless families, older people and people with disabilities.
Chief Executive: Mr Jeremy Lamb. *Fundraising Manager:* Alison Mills. Executive staff 6, Other staff 120. **CC** No.207493. Began 1841; non-denominational. Magazine: *Inside Lane Newsletter* (Circulation & frequency n/a). Turnover £2,005,657 to year end Mar 00.

***Grandma's**, PO Box 1392, London SW6 4EJ
☎020 7610 3904 ℻020 7610 3428
E: headoffice@grandmas.org.uk
Offering practical childcare support for children and families affected by HIV and AIDS; London, Dublin, India.
Project Director: Miss Amanda Williams. Executive staff 2, Other staff 21. **CC** No.800341 Began 1990; non-denominational. No magazine. Turnover £157,000 to year end Dec 00.

†*Help the Aged, 207 Pentonville Road, London N1 9UZ
☎020 7278 1114 ℻020 7278 1116
E: info@helptheaged.org.uk
Web: www.helptheaged.org.uk
Improving the quality of life of older people in the UK and internationally.
Director General: Mr Michael Lake CBE. HQ staff 250, Regional staff 1,000. **CC** No.272786. Began 1962; interdenominational. Magazines: *Help the Aged News* (6,000 every four months), *Adopt a Granny News* (16,000 every four months), *Church Friend Briefing* (3,500 Advent and Pentecost). Turnover £74,930,000 to year end Apr 02.

Housing Justice, 209 Old Marylebone Road, London NW1 5QT
☎020 7723 7273 ℻020 7723 5943
E: info@housingjustice.org.uk
Web: www.housingjustice.org.uk
The voice of the churches in the field of housing and homelessness.
Chief Executive: To be appointed. Executive staff 3, Other staff 10. **CC** No.294665. Began 2003; ecumenical. (Previously Catholic Housing Aid Society). Merger of Churches National Housing Coalition and Catholic Housing Aid Society. Magazine: *Housing Plus - Newsletter* (2,000 every four months). Turnover £820,423 to year end Mar 05.
Also at: Housing Justice Birmingham, The Tower Room, St Catherine's, Bristol Street, Birmingham B5 7BE
☎0121 622 1581
And: Housing Justice Bradford, St Patrick's Centre, Sedgfield Terrace, Bradford BD1 2RU
☎01274 726 790
And: Housing Justice Bristol, 86 Stokes Croft, Bristol BS1 3RH
☎0117 942 6247
And: Housing Justice Croydon, The Old House, 2 Wellesley Court Road, Croydon CR9 1UN
☎020 8688 7900
And: Housing Justice Dewsbury, 8 Empire House, Wakefield Old Road, Dewsbury WF12 8DJ
☎01924 324 990
And: Housing Justice Kirklees, Standard House, 1st Floor, Half Moon Street, Huddersfield HD1 2JF
☎01484 223 922
And: Housing Justice Leeds, 301 Roundhay Road, Leeds LS8 4HT
☎0113 249 2484
And: Housing Justice York, 57 Micklegate, York YO1 6LJ
☎01904 651 570

†JCP Community Business Project Ltd, Edward Road Baptist Church, 196 Edward Road, Balsall Heath, Birmingham B12 9LY
☎0121 440 7919
℻0121 446 5228
E: admin@jcp.org.uk
Web: www.jcp.org.uk
Not-for-profit community business providing paid work for long-term unemployed socially-excluded people.
Project Manager: Mr Ben Parkinson. Executive staff 2, Other staff 6. **CC** No.1037084. Began 1998; interdenominational. No magazine. Turnover £50,000 to year end Dec 02.

Jesus Army Charitable Trust, Jesus Fellowship Central Offices, Nether Heyford, Northampton NN7 3LB
☎0845 166 8172
℻0845 166 8178
E: info@jact.org.uk
Web: www.jact.org.uk
Providing Jesus Centres around the UK for daily worship, friendship and social care for all.
Chair of Trustees: John Campbell. *Coventry Jesus Centre Manager:* Piers Young. *Northampton Jesus Centre Manager:* Stephen Jones. Executive staff 3, Other staff 10. **CC** No.1091912. Began 1997; Jesus Fellowship. No magazine. Turnover £1,200,000 to year end Dec 03.

***The Langley House Trust**, PO Box 181, Witney OX28 6WD
☎01993 774 075
℻01993 772 425
E: info@langleyhousetrust.org
Web: www.langleyhousetrust.org
Providing residential care and rehabilitation for ex-offenders in a Christian environment: 16 projects across England.
Chief Executive: Mr Steve Robinson. *Finance Director:* Mr Ken Brown. *Development Director:* Mr Colin Angus. Executive staff 9, Other staff 270. **CC** No.290059. Began 1958; interdenominational. No magazine. Turnover £6,641,700 to year end Mar 05.

London Diocese Social Justice and Community Ministry Advisors, London Diocesan House, 36 Causton Street, London SW1P 4AU
☎020 7932 1100 ℻020 7932 1112
E: caroll.potter@london.anglican.org
Web: www.london.anglican.org
Advisor of Social Justice: Rev Chris Brice. *Advisor for Community Ministry:* Rev Jack Maple. Executive staff 2, Other staff 2. **CC** No.277173. Began 1889; Anglican. (Previously Caris) Magazine: *Network* (Circulation n/a quarterly). Turnover n/a. Providing social policy and community ministry resources; London-wide collaboration with ecumenical partners.

The Mersey Mission to Seafarers, Colonsay House, 20 Crosby Road South, Waterloo, Liverpool L22 1RQ
☎0151 920 3253 ℻0151 928 0244
E: liverangel@aol.com
Web: www.merseymissiontoseafarers.org
Caring for retired and serving seafarers and their families.
Company Secretary: Captain David Nutman. Executive staff 4, Other staff 11. **CC** No.220793. Began 1855; Anglican. No magazine. Turnover n/a.

MR Associates, 19 Wemyss Court, Leapmoor Drive, Wemyss Bay PA18 6BF
☎01475 522 962 M: 07967 963 806
E: info@mrassociates.org.uk
Web: www.mrassociates.org.uk
Offering specialist advice and assistance for accommodation-based schemes providing support to vulnerable adults.
Supported Housing Advisor: Mr Mark Rodgers. Executive staff 2, Admin staff 1. Began 2000; interdenominational. No magazine. Turnover n/a.

†*Mustard Tree, 66 Wood Street, Glossop SK13 8NL
☎0161 256 1331 ℻0161 256 1616
E: mustard.tree@bigfoot.com
Web: www.mustardtree.co.uk
Meeting the physical, emotional, social and spiritual needs of homeless disadvantaged people and refugees.
Team Leader: Mr Trevor Lee. *Liaison Manager:* Mr Dave Smith. Admin staff 6. **CC** No.1044349. Began 1993; interdenominational. No magazine. Turnover £151,000 to year end Mar 03.

National Christian Alliance on Prostitution, PO Box 37077, London E15 4XR
☎0845 004 4231
E: ncap@ncap.uk.org
Web: www.nsapuk.org
Training and support for churches and teams working with people involved in prostitution.
Director: Mr Mark Wakeling. Part-time Staff 2. **CC** Began 1999; non-denominational. No magazine. Turnover £57,000 to year end Dec 04.

Network Crafts, 18 Lambert Gardens, Shurdington, Cheltenham GL51 4SW
☎01242 862 600
E: alexthom@onetel.com
Helping unwaged, unemployed, retired, single parents by providing workshop with DIY facilities and expert advice.
Chairman: Mr T A Thomson. No full-time staff. ***CC*** No.1023011. Began 1983; interdenominational. (Previously Network). No magazine. Turnover n/a.

†New Assembly of Churches, 15 Oldridge Road, Balham, London SW12 8PL
☎020 8673 0595 📠020 8675 8768
E: rescue@pcul.fsbusiness.co.uk
Rehabilitating young offenders, ex-offenders, those at risk of offending; support for their families.
Chief Executive: Rev Carmel Jones. Executive staff 1, Other staff 5. ***CC*** No.298841. Began 1985; Pentecostal Church of God. No magazine. Turnover £41,000 to year end Sep 02.

†Newham Community Renewal Programme Ltd, 170 Harold Road, Plaistow, London E13 0SE
☎020 8472 2785 📠020 8472 2805
Web: www.nrcp.fsnet.co.uk
Community development in urban areas, including projects for the homeless, unemployed, carers and refugees.
Chief Executive Officer: Rev Canon Ann Easter. Executive staff 12, Other staff 50. ***CC*** No.275796. Began 1971; interdenominational. Magazine: *News for Newham* (300 monthly). Turnover £2,800,000 to year end Mar 02.

PARCHE, The Castle Centre, 39 Church Street, Eastbourne BN21 1HP
☎01323 438 527
E: parcheenquiries@onetel.com
Web: www.parche.org.uk
Providing services and spiritual care to elderly in residential homes, nursing homes and retirement accommodation.
Director: Mrs Buddy Reeve. Admin staff 1. ***CC*** No.1094445. Began 1997; interdenominational. Pastoral Action in Residential Care Homes for the Elderly. No magazine. Turnover £7,000 to year end Apr 05.

***Pecan Ltd**, 121 Peckham High Street, London SE15 5SE
☎020 7732 0007
E: welcome@pecan.org.uk
Web: www.pecan.org.uk
Training for unemployed: job search, ESOL, literacy, IT; ICT Deaf, New Deal; recycled furniture shop.
Chief Executive: Mr Kevin Belcher. *Fundraising & Communications Manager:* Minu Chowdhury-Westlake. Executive staff 2, Other staff 76. ***CC*** No.801819. Began 1989; non-denominational. No magazine. Turnover £3,718,000 to year end Mar 03.

†Pentecostal Youth & Adult Welfare Association, 220 Ellison Road, Streatham, London SW16 5DJ
☎020 8764 2643
Providing advice, representation, information, training and counselling.
General Secretary: Mrs Norma Howard. All voluntary staff. ***CC*** No.287223. Began 1979; interdenominational. No magazine. Turnover n/a.

†*Phoenix Community, The eBase, 85 Bounces Road, London N9 8LD
☎020 8808 8000 📠020 8885 5007
E: info@phoenixcommunity.co.uk
Web: www.phoenixcommunity.org
Working with asylum seekers, vulnerable girls; 5 homes in UK, 1 in Sri Lanka.
Director: Ms Pauline Hawkes. *Manager:* Ms Carla Mayer. Executive staff 2, Other staff 20. Began 2003; Rainbow Foundation. No magazine. Turnover £279,000 to year end Dec 02.

†Prama-Care, 1551 Wimborne Road, Kinson, Bournemouth BH10 7AZ
☎01202 599 199 📠01202 599 200
E: prama@globalnet.co.uk
Web: www.pramacare.co.uk
Undertaking home assistance that a caring relative would do; operating in south-east Dorset. No grants given.
General Manager: Mr Roger A Gregory. *Office Manager:* Jane Harcock. *Chairman:* Dr John Farthing. Executive staff 3, Other staff 200. ***CC*** No.801967. Began 1982; interdenominational. No magazine. Turnover £1,000,000 to year end Apr 00.

Prison Advice & Care Trust, Lincoln House, 1 Brixton Road, London SW9 6DE
☎020 7490 3139/0808 808 2003 (helpline) 📠020 7735 0755
E: info@prisonadvice.org.uk
Web: www.imprisonment.org.uk
Supporting prisoners and their relatives and friends in London and south west England.
Director: Andy Keen-Downs. Executive staff 5, Other staff 43. ***CC*** No.219278. Began 1898; Roman Catholic but open to all. (Previously The Bourne Trust). Magazine: *Fresh Start* (3,000 every four months). Turnover £750,000 to year end Aug 02.

***Prison Fellowship England and Wales**, PO Box 945, Maldon CM9 4EW
☎01621 843 232 📠01621 843 303
E: enquiries@prisonfellowship.org.uk
Web: www.prisonfellowship.org.uk
Mobilising and enabling volunteers from the Christian community to restore all those affected by crime.
Executive Director: Mr Peter A Walker. Executive staff 4, Other staff 11. ***CC*** No.1102254. Began 1979; non-denominational. Magazine: *Prison Fellowship News* (11,000 every four months). Turnover £601,000 to year end Mar 05.

†*Prison Fellowship Northern Ireland, 39 University Street, Belfast BT7 1FY
☎028 9024 3691
📠028 9024 3691
E: info@pfni.org
Web: www.pfni.org
Responding to spiritual, emotional, social and physical needs of prisoners, ex-prisoners and their families.
Executive Director: Mr Robin Scott. Executive staff 1, Other staff 5. ***CC*** No.XN 45576. Began 1981; non-denominational. No magazine. Turnover £100,000 to year end Mar 02.

***Prison Fellowship Scotland**, 110 St James Road, Glasgow G4 0PS
☎0141 522 1288
📠0141 522 1288
E: prisonfellowship@lineone.net
Web: users.colloquium.co.uk/~pfscotland
Supporting work of church and chaplains in serving the needs of prisoners, ex-prisoners and their families.
Chief Executive: Dr Brian Fraser. *Chairman:* Mr Rupert De Klee. Executive staff 1, Other staff 3. ***CC*** No.SC0 02222. Began 1981; interdenominational. Magazine: *Jubilee* (2,000 quarterly) Turnover n/a.

Queen Victoria Seamen's Rest, 121 East India Dock Road, London E14 6DF
☎020 7987 5466 / 4622
📠020 7537 0665
E: personalassistant@qvsr.org.uk
Web: qvsr.org.uk
Ministering to the spiritual needs of seamen; promoting their social and moral welfare.
Chief Executive: Mr Alexander Campbell. Executive staff 6, Other staff 50. ***CC*** No.1106126. Began 1843; Methodist. Seamen's Mission of the Methodist Church. No magazine. Turnover n/a.

Royal National Mission to Deep Sea Fishermen, Mather House, 4000 Parkway, Solent Business Park, Whiteley, Fareham PO15 7FJ
☎01489 566 910
📠01489 566 929
E: enquiries@rnmdsf.org.uk
Web: www.fishermensmission.org.uk
Ministering nationwide to fishermen and their families spiritually, materially, physically.
Mission Secretary: Mr Dan Conley. Executive staff 3, Other staff 130. ***CC*** No.232822. Began 1881; interdenominational. Magazine: *Network* (30,000 half-yearly). Turnover £2,500,000 to year end Oct 98.

S

***RSR (Royal Sailors' Rests)**, Castaway House, 311 Twyford Avenue, Portsmouth PO2 8PE
☎023 9265 0505 🖷023 9265 2929
E: info@rsr.org.uk
Web: www.rsr.org.uk
Evangelism through spiritual, moral and physical care of members of the Royal Navy and their families.
Executive Director: Mr Brian Deverson. Executive staff 2, Other staff 43. ***CC*** No.238748. Began 1876; interdenominational. Magazine: *Ashore and Afloat* (7,200 quarterly). Turnover £745,301 to year end Mar 02.
Also at: Gosport, Helensburgh

†St Hilda's East Community Care Centre, 18 Club Row, London E2 7EY
☎020 7739 8066 🖷020 7729 5172
E: sdhildas@escot.com
Providing advice, social and educational facilities for ethnic groups, the young and elderly people.
Chair of Management Board: Mr Dennis Towmey. Staff 55. ***CC*** No.212208. Began 1889; non-denominational. Magazine: *Annual Report* (1,000 annually). Turnover £900,000 to year end Mar 02.

The Salvation Army Social Services Department, 101 Newington Causeway, London SE1 6BN
☎020 7367 4500 🖷020 7367 4712
E: thq@salvationarmy.org.uk
Web: www.salvationarmy.org.uk
Meeting human need through professional caring services.
Territorial Director of Social Services: Major Ian Harris. Executive staff n/a, Other staff 3,000. ***CC*** No.214779. Began 1884; Salvation Army. (Previously Salvation Army Social Work). Magazine: *Caring Services* (Circulation & frequency n/a). Turnover £42,000,000 to year end Mar 02.
Ireland Division, 12 Station Mews, Sydenham, Belfast BT4 1TL
☎028 9067 5000 🖷 028 9067 5011
E: ireland@salvationarmy.org.uk
Web: www.salvationarmy.org.uk
Divisional Commander: Major David Jackson. *Admin* staff n/a. ***CC*** No.214779. Began 1880; Salvation Army. No magazine. Turnover n/a.
Also at: PO Box 2098, 114 Marlborough Street, Dublin 1, Republic of Ireland
☎00 353 1874 0987
🖷 00 353 1874 7478

Scottish Churches Housing Action, 28 Albany Street, Edinburgh EH1 3QH
☎0131 477 4500 🖷0131 447 2710
E: scotchho@ednet.co.uk
Web: www.churches-housing.org
Motivating Scotland's churches in working towards the elimination of homelessness, through national and local action.
Chief Executive: Mr Alastair Cameron. *Chairman:* Rev Maxwell Craig. Executive Staff 3, Admin Staff 2. ***CC*** No.SCO 22214. Began 1993; interdenominational. Magazine: *Our Homeless Neighbour* (4,000 quarterly). Turnover £173,273 to year end Mar 05.

Set Free, PO Box 62, Kendal LA9 4GF
☎01539 624 837
E: setfreetrust@aol.com
Raising awareness about domestic violence; providing educational resources; supporting and empowering those affected.
Coordinator: Rosemary Campbell. No paid staff. Began 1996; non-denominational. No magazine. Turnover £400 to year end Apr 05.

***The Shaftesbury Society**, 16 Kingston Road, London SW19 1JZ
☎0845 330 6033 🖷020 8239 5580
E: info@shaftesburysociety.org
Web: www.shaftesburysociety.org
Working with disabled people and local communities to achieve social inclusion, empowerment and justice.
Chief Executive: Ms Mary Bishop. Executive staff 8, Other staff 1,400. ***CC*** No.221948. Began 1844; interdenominational. Magazine: *Shaftesbury Changes* (Circulation n/a every four months). Turnover £34,400,000 to year end Mar 05.
London Region: *Regional Manager:* David Eldridge, 27 Hillyard Street, Brixton, London SW9 0NJ
☎020 7840 5840
North and East Region: *Regional Manager:* Ken Tucker, Norman House, Heritage Gate, Newcastle upon Tyne NE1 1NU
☎01332 207 518
South and West Region: *Regional Manager:* Judith Westcott, Crown Chambers, South Street, Andover SP10 2BN
☎01264 361 135

†The Simon Community, PO Box 1187, London NW5 4HW
☎020 7485 6639 🖷020 7482 6305
E: simoncommunity@yahoo.com
Web: www.thesimoncommunity.org.uk
Living and working with London's long-term rough sleepers; residential houses, tea runs.
Community Leader: Brian Robinson. Executive staff 1, Other staff 2. ***CC*** No.283838. Began 1963; non-denominational. Magazine: *Simon Star* (6,000 quarterly). Turnover £200,000 to year end Mar 02.

***South Bristol Christian Centre**, Churchlands Road, Bedminster, Bristol BS3 3PW
☎0117 963 6329 🖷0117 963 6329
Serving the local churches and community through fellowship, training and social programmes.
Manager: Mr D Johnson. Executive staff 1, Other staff 8. ***CC*** No.1026672. Began 1993; interdenominational. Magazine: *Centre Calling* (500 quarterly). Turnover £6,500 to year end Mar 00.

***Southampton Action For Employment (SAFE)**, 364 Hinkler Road, Thornhill, Southampton SO19 6DF
☎023 8042 1001 🖷023 8042 1001
E: info@safe.org.uk
Web: www.safe.org.uk
Pre-employment training/confidence-building programme for long-term unemployed and socially disadvantaged people.
Director: Mr Andy Foreman. *Administrator:* Mrs Lourie Dzikewich. Executive staff 3, Other staff 6. ***CC*** No.1057784. Began 1994; non-denominational. No magazine. Turnover £500,838 to year end Mar 05.

***The Stepping Stones Trust**, Suffolk House, George Street, Croydon CR0 1PE
☎020 8256 6420
🖷020 8680 8077
E: welcome@steppingstonestrust.org.uk
Web: www.steppingstonestrust.org.uk
Providing accommodation and support for ex-offenders.
Chief Executive: Mr Simon Pellew. Executive staff 2, Other staff 11. ***CC*** No.288542. Began 1985; interdenominational. No magazine. Turnover £300,000 to year end Mar 05.

Turnabout Trust, Winters, Shopland Road, Rochford SS4 1LH
☎01702 542 564
🖷01702 542 564
E: tom@turnabout.org.uk
Web: www.turnabout.org.uk
Helping unemployed and disadvantaged people through training, social and spiritual initiatives; also in Nicaragua.
Managing Director: Mr Tom Tyer. Executive staff 1, Other staff 2. ***CC*** No.1062599. Began 1997; non-denominational. No magazine. Turnover n/a.

***Watford New Hope Trust**, 67 Queens Road, Watford WD17 2QN
☎01923 210 680
🖷01923 235 329
E: info@wnht.org
Web: www.watfordnewhope.org.uk
Serving homeless and disadvantaged people: including day centre, resettlement team, night shelter, hostel, social businesses.
Director: Mr Basil Lazenby. Executive staff 2, Other staff n/a. ***CC*** No.1080784. Began 1990; interdenominational. Magazine: *Report* (8,000 annually). Turnover £940,000 to year end Mar 02.

†The Wayside Club for Homeless & Hostel People, 32 Midland Street, Glasgow G1 4PR
☎0141 221 0169
🖷0141 248 1245
E: wayside.daycentre@virgin.net
Meeting place and relief centre for hostel and homeless men; free advice centre.
President: Mr Brian Bonnyman. Executive staff 13, Other staff 7. ***CC*** Began 1932; Roman Catholic. No magazine. Turnover n/a.

S

WHCM Counselling & Support, Sadlers House, 2 Legg Street, Chelmsford CM1 1AH
☎01245 269 335
🖷01245 264 348
E: info@whcm.org.uk
Web: www.whcm.org.uk
Delivering professional counselling services in the fields of mental health care and education.
Chief Executive: Ms Trudy Kilcullen. Executive staff 1, Other staff 96. ***CC*** No.1084940. Began 1905; ecumenical. BACP Accredited. Part of West Ham Central Mission. No magazine. Turnover £800,000 to year end Mar 05.

†***YMCA, City of Belfast**, 58 Knightsbridge Park, Belfast BT9 5EH
☎028 9068 4660 🖷028 9066 6914
E: admin@ymca-bfs.org
Web: www.ymca-bfs.org
Caring for young people, both practically and spiritually; striving for reconciliation in the community.
General Manager: Mr Howard Davey. *Programme Director:* Mr Colin Taylor. Executive staff 3, Other staff 45. ***CC*** Began 1850; interdenominational. No magazine. Turnover £975,827 to year end Mar 97.

†**YMCA, London, West**, 25 St Mary's Road, Ealing, London W5 5RE
☎020 8799 4800 🖷020 8799 4[illegible]0
E: enquiries@londonymca.org
Web: www.westlondonymca.org
Accommodation for students, asylum seekers, homeless, special needs young people, employment training advice and mentoring.
Chief Executive: Clare Scott Booth. *Chaplain:* Rev Michael Johnson. Executive staff 8, Other staff 270. ***CC*** No.105[illegible]93. Began 1877; interdenominational. No magazine. Turnover £8,000,000 to year end Mar 03.
Also at: 14 Bond Street, Ealing, London W5 5AA
☎020 8579 8996 🖷 020 8840 82[illegible]3

SPORTS ORGANISATIONS

Adventure Outreach, Hope House, Blucher Street, Barnsley S70 1AP
☎01226 239 472
E: dave@adventureoutreach.org.uk
Web: www.adventureoutreach.org.uk
Arranging outdoor activities programmes, including leadership courses for youth ministers, camps for youth groups.
Operations Manager: Mr David Thomas. Executive staff 3. ***CC*** No.1093967. Began 2000; non-denominational. No magazine. Turnover n/a.

†***Ambassadors in Sport**, Claremont House, St George's Road, Bolton BL1 2BY
☎01204 363 606 🖷01204 364 040
E: ais@ais-uk.org
Web: www.aisint.org
Making Christ known to the world through football; developing Church football outreach in every community.
Director: Mr Ray D Tucker. *Director of Training:* Mr Dave Oakley. Executive staff 4, Other staff 5. ***CC*** No.1055422. Began 1997; interdenominational. Magazine: *Ambassadors in Sport 'The Goal Post'* (1,500 monthly). Turnover £190,000 to year end Dec 02.

***Christian Surfers UK**, 11 Walnut Close, Nailsea, Bristol BS48 4YH
☎01275 857 834
E: christian.surfersuk@ukgateway.net
Web: www.christiansurfers.org
Being a Christian presence and witness to the surfing population around the UK and Ireland.
National Director: Mr Philip Williams. Admin staff 1. ***CC*** No.1070830. Began 1994; interdenominational. Magazine: *Second Day* (1,000 quarterly). Turnover £40,000 to year end Dec 04.

Christians in Football, National Office, Haven House, 389 London Road, Hemel Hempstead HP3 9AB
☎01442 270 300 🖷01442 270 300
E: go@christiansinfootball.org
Web: www.christiansinfootball.org
National network association for Christian-based football teams and players; international short-term mission tours.
Director: Mr Keith Hammond. No full-time staff. ***CC*** No.1090157. Began n/a; non-denominational. No magazine. Turnover n/a.

***Christians in Sport**, Frampton House, Victoria Road, Bicester OX26 6PB
☎01869 255 630 🖷01869 255 640
E: info@christiansinsport.org.uk
Web: www.christiansinsport.org.uk
Working to see Christian sports people representing Christ and building the church.
General Directors: Mr Graham Daniels, Mr Keith Proctor. Executive staff 7, Other staff 8. ***CC*** No.1086570. Began 1976; interdenominational. Magazine: *Back Pages* (8,000 quarterly). Turnover £528,000 to year end Oct 04.

***The King's Foundation**, The Manor House, Ecclesall Road South, Sheffield S11 9PS
☎0114 281 7100 🖷08700 429 321
E: outreach@kingsfoundation.org
Web: www.kingsfoundation.org
Using sport and sports ministry to reach children across Africa and the UK.
Chief Executive Officer: Mr Richard Holmes. *Chair of Trustees:* Mr David Taylor. Executive staff 5, Admin staff 10. ***CC*** No.1105460. Began 1991; interdenominational. (Previously King's Trust). No magazine. Turnover £2,000,000 to year end Dec 02.

***Mainstream**, 43 West Stockwell Street, Colchester CO1 1HS
☎01206 513 525
Web: www.mainstreamuk.org
Promoting qualified canoeing expertise and training to meet the requirements of Christian centres and camps.
Secretary: Colleen Palmer. No full-time staff. Began 1986; interdenominational. Magazine: *Newsletter* (300 quarterly). Turnover £44,148 to year end Apr 04.

SCORE, PO Box 123, Sale M33 4ZA
☎0161 969 1762 M: 07976 387 9[illegible]7
🖷0161 969 1762
E: jkbscoreuk@aol.com
Web: www.scorechaplaincy.org.uk
UK-wide development, resourcing of club and event sports chaplaincy; training of local church sports ministry.
National Director: Rev John Boyers. *Director of Chaplaincy to Horse-racing:* Rev Graham Locking. Executive staff 3, Admin staff 2. ***CC*** No.1005446. Began 199[illegible]; non-denominational. Magazine: *Scoresheet* (4,000 every four months). Turnover £120,000 to year end Dec 05.

SportsReach, 57 Lancaster Road, Carnforth LA5 9LE
☎01524 730 000 🖷01524 730 000
E: office@sportsreach.org.uk
Web: www.sportsreach.org.uk
Using sport to reach people for Christ through soccer schools, local league and international tours.
Coordinator: Mr Robert Dixon. Executive staff 2, Admin staff 1. ***CC*** No.[illegible]06572[illegible]. Began 1997; non-denominational. No magazine. Turnover £50,000 to year end Dec 04.

***World Sport Ministries**, The Stables, Pickwick Farm, Upper Swainswick, Bath BA1 8BU
☎01225 851 630 🖷01225 851 630
E: info@world-sport-ministries.com
Web: www.world-sport-ministries.com
Planting and developing interdenominational sports ministry teams to reach unsaved through sport in local areas.
Director: Mr Grant Sheppard. Executive staff 1, Admin staff 2. ***CC*** No.1096667. Began 1999; interdenominational. No magazine. Turnover £50,000 to year end Mar 03.

S

Autosave (UK) Ltd, London House, Little London Road, Sheffield S8 0UH
☎0114 255 4040 🖷0114 255 4949
E: helpline@autosave.co.uk
Web: www.autosave.co.uk
Selling new and used cars, mini buses, vans and 4x4 to churches and clergy.
Managing Director: Mrs Jane E Newett. Executive staff 1, Other staff 36. Began 1983; non-denominational. No magazine. Turnover £20,000,000 to year end Mar 03.

C L Ministries, 24 The Street, Capel St Mary, Ipswich IP9 2EE
☎01473 311 128 🖷01473 311 128
E: admin@clministries.org.uk
Web: www.clministries.org.uk
Bible Tours of Israel.
Director: Mr Christopher Hill. Executive staff 1, Admin staff 3. Began 1990; non-denominational. (Previously C L Bible Tours). Magazine: *C L Update* (800 quarterly). Turnover n/a.

***Christian Holiday Handbook**, PO Box 118, Dereham NR19 2WS
☎01362 853 376
E: info@christianholidays.biz
Web: www.christianholidays.biz
Publishing Christian Holiday Handbook.
Coordinator: Mr James Walker. Executive staff 1, Other staff n/a. Began 1988; non-denominational. (Previously Christian Travel Services). No magazine. Turnover n/a.

The Christian Holiday People - Coach Holidays, 10 Bradfield Avenue, Old Roan, Liverpool L10 3JS
☎0151 526 2102
Offering holidays, conferences, coach holidays and self-catering bungalow.
Contact: Mr William Armstrong. Staff n/a. **CC** No.1039170. Began n/a; interdenominational. (Previously Christian Endeavour Coach Holidays Ltd). No magazine. Turnover n/a.

Christian Home Exchange Fellowship (CHEF), Karakorum, Sunnyfield Lane, Up Hatherley, Cheltenham GL51 6JE
☎01242 521 886 🖷01242 694 929
E: peterchef@aol.com
Web: www.christianhomeexchange.net
Making possible inexpensive holidays for Christian families by exchanging their homes by mutual arrangement.
National Organiser: Mr Peter Worsley. No full-time staff. Began 1976; interdenominational. No magazine. Turnover £4,000 to year end Dec 05.

Mike Coles World-Wide Travel, 29 Sydney Road, Exeter EX2 9AH
☎01392 219 499 / 422 090
🖷01392 275 296
E: sales@mike-coles-travel.co.uk
Web: www.mikecolestravel.co.uk
Specialising in low-cost flights for Missionaries and other Christian workers worldwide.
Senior Partner: Mr Mike Coles. Executive staff 2, Other staff 4. Began 1982; interdenominational. No magazine. Turnover £1,500,000 to year end Jun 03.

†**Raymond Cook Christian Tours**, 136 London Road, Leicester LE2 1EN
☎0116 250 7421
🖷0870 832 7119
E: ri@page-moy.co.uk
Arranging Holy Land pilgrimages for group and independent travellers.
Managing Director: Mr Geoff White. Executive staff 1, No other full-time staff. Began 1935; interdenominational. A division of Page & Moy. No magazine. Turnover n/a.

The Flight Bureau, Flight House, 39 Newington Road, Edinburgh EH9 1QW
☎0131 477 7777
🖷0131 477 7888
E: flights@flightbureau.com
Web: www.thinkflights.com
Supplying discounted worldwide air tickets, travel insurance, car hire and accommodation.
Director: Julian Slatter. Executive staff 1, Other staff 6. Began 1990; non-denominational. No magazine. Turnover £2,000,000 to year end Mar 05.

S

Gold Hill Holidays, Hobbit Hollow, Bull Lane, Gerrards Cross SL9 8RZ
☎01753 880 753 🖷01753 880 754
E: E@goldhillholidays.co.uk
Web: www.goldhillholidays.co.uk
Providing outdoor activity holidays: snowsports, mountain-walking, multi-activity; with Christian teaching.
Partners: Mr & Mrs Clive & Ruth Beattie. Executive staff 1, Other staff 2. Began 1986; non-denominational. No magazine. Turnover £300,000 to year end Apr 96.

†Good News Travel Ltd, 65 Moorfield Road, Salford M6 7EY
☎0161 736 5769 🖷0161 736 1561
E: johnogden@btinternet.com
Flight consultants with a ministry of arranging flight itineraries.
Director: Mr John D Ogden. Executive staff 2. Began 1984; non-denominational. No magazine. Turnover £63,000 to year end Aug 99.

†Grace Holidays, The Haven, Canning Road, Colwyn Bay LL29 8EB
☎01492 531 779 M: 07780 982 801
E: info@graceholidays.co.uk
Web: www.graceholidays.co.uk
Providing holidays, tours, booking services.
Proprietor: Mrs Dorothy Warburton. Executive staff 1, Admin staff 1. Began 2003; non-denominational. No magazine. Turnover £7,000 to year end Apr 2004.

†Greencastle Pilgrimage Tours, Portfield House, Daws Road, Hereford HR1 2JJ
☎0870 730 4477 🖷0870 730 8844
E: johnhadler@pilgrimagetours.co.uk
Web: www.pilgrimagetours.co.uk
Organising pilgrimage travel for groups from all denominations to biblical and religious destinations.
Sales Manager: Mr John Hadler. *Managing Director:* Mr Simon Allen. *Director:* Mrs Liz Allen. Executive staff 3, Admin staff 3. Began n/a; non-denominational. No magazine. Turnover £8,000,000 to year end Dec 02.

Ichthus Motor Services, Grove Close, Forest Hill, London SE23 1AS
☎020 8291 1652 🖷020 8291 0273
E: lencarne@hotmail.com
Web: www.ichthuscarsales.com
Carrying out mechanical and body repairs; car sales, MOTs, servicing.
Proprietor: Dr L R Carne. Executive staff 2, Other staff 8. Began 1979; non-denominational. No magazine. Turnover n/a.

Israel Travel Service, 427 Royal Exchange, Old Bank Street, Manchester M2 7EP
☎0161 839 1111/2222 or 0800 0181 839
M: 07957 812 101
E: all@itstravel.co.uk
Web: www.itstravel.co.uk
Pilgrimage tour operator offering tailor-made itineraries to Israel, Middle East, Eastern Mediterranean, world-wide destinations.
Managing Director: Mr Adrian J Cohen. *Director of Operations:* Mrs Hilary Sheldon. *Director of Finance:* Mr David Clayton. Executive staff 3, Other staff 2. Began 1991; non-denominational. No magazine. Turnover £2,000,000 to year end Sep 05.

Key Travel, 28 Britannia St, London WC1X 9JF
☎020 7843 9600 🖷020 7278 8035
E: reservations@keytravel.co.uk
Web: www.keytravel.co.uk
Arranging low-cost airfares for churches, charities, educational establishments, independent travellers; also offices in Manchester, Brussels.
Operations Manager: Ms Corinne Lane. Executive staff 8, Other staff 104. Began 1980; non-denominational. No magazine. Turnover n/a.
Also at: *Operations Manager:* Ms Louise Elgy, 1st Floor, Queen Street, Manchester M2 5HT
E: reservations@keytravel.co.uk
☎0161 819 8900 🖷 0161 839 3893

†Leisure Time Travel, 275 County Road, Walton-on-the-Hill, Liverpool L4 5PQ
☎0151 287 8000 🖷0151 287 8008
E: info@lourdes-pilgrim.com
Web: www.lourdes-pilgrim.com
Operating pilgrimage tours by air and coach.
Proprietor: Mr Michael Langan. Executive staff 4. Began 1988; non-denominational. No magazine. Turnover £100,000 to year end Feb 01.

ISRAEL - HOLY LAND - PALESTINE
EGYPT
JORDAN
SYRIA
LEBANON
TURKEY
GREECE
ITALY
SICILY
Group Planning
for
Pilgrimage ✓
Study Tours ✓
Culture Tours ✓
MARANATHA
Tours
TRAFALGAR HOUSE
HORTON, BERKS SL3 9NU
TEL: 01753-689568
Web: www.maranatha.co.uk
Email: michael@maranatha.co.uk
CHINA - INDIA - RUSSIA

McCabe Pilgrimages, 11 Hillgate Place, Balham Hill, London SW12 9ER
☎020 8675 6828 🖷020 8673 1204
E: alistair@mccabe-travel.co.uk
Web: www.mccabe-travel.co.uk
Specialising in Holy Land pilgrimages and the journeys of St Paul.
Chairman & Managing Director: Mr Alistair McCabe. *Director:* Miss Rosemary Nutt. Executive staff 2, Other staff 2. Began 1982; non-denominational. Magazine: *MET Agenda* (Circulation & frequency n/a). Turnover £2,000,000 to year end Oct 02.

***Maranatha Tours (Euro) Ltd**, Trafalgar House, Horton, Slough SL3 9NU
☎01753 689 568 🖷01753 689 768
E: mail@maranatha.co.uk
Web: www.maranatha.co.uk
Specialising in group tours to the lands of the Bible.
Director: Mr Michael F Hodgson. Executive staff 3, Other staff 5. Began 1978; non-denominational. No magazine. Turnover n/a.

***MasterSki**, Thames House, 63 Kingston Road, New Malden KT3 3PB
☎020 8942 9442 🖷020 8949 4396
E: holidays@mastersun.co.uk
Web: www.mastersun.co.uk
Arranging Christian ski holidays by air in Europe; hotels and chalets.
Managing Director: Mr Bob Fleming. *Directors:* Mrs Jill Fleming, Mr Gordon Miller. Executive staff 6, Other staff 18, Resort staff 20. Began 1984; non-denominational. Magazine: *Unwind* (60,000 quarterly). Turnover included in MasterSun.

***MasterSun**, Thames House, 63 Kingston Road, New Malden KT3 3PB
☎020 8942 9442 🖷020 8949 4396
E: holidays@mastersun.co.uk
Web: www.mastersun.co.uk
Arranging Christian holiday programme using hotels: Greece, Italy, Turkey, France, Israel; cruises to Bible lands.
Managing Director: Mr Bob Fleming. *Directors:* Mrs Jill Fleming, Mr Gordon Miller. Executive staff 6, Office staff 18, Resort staff 80. Began 1988; non-denominational. Magazine: *Unwind* (60,000 quarterly). Turnover £6,000,000 to year end Sep 04.

MIB Travel, 41 Ing Head Terrace, Halifax HX3 7LB
☎01422 202 292/0871 666 0262
M 07947 159 795 🖷0871 666 0263
E: mark@mibtravel.co.uk
Web: www.mibtravel.co.uk
Organising pilgrimages to Holy Land and elsewhere; for groups or individuals; advice for clergy.
Managing Director: Rev Mark Madeley. Executive staff 1, Admin staff 1. Began 2001; non-denominational. No magazine. Turnover £20,000 to year end Nov 04.

North South Travel, Moulsham Mill Centre, Parkway, Chelmsford CM2 7PX
☎01245 608 291 🖷01245 608 291
E: brenda@northsouthtravel.co.uk
Web: www.northsouthtravel.co.uk
Offering discount fares to church groups; profits to projects in the developing world.
Manager: Ms Brenda Skinner. Executive staff 3. ***CC*** No.1040656. Began 1982; non-denominational. No magazine. Turnover n/a.

Oak Hall Expeditions and Skiing, Otford Manor, Otford, Sevenoaks TN15 6XF
☎01732 763 131 🖷01732 763 136
E: office@oakhall.co.uk
Web: www.oakhall.co.uk
Arranging worldwide summer holidays and winter skiing; Bible teaching given by Christian team.
Director: Mr Ian Mayo. Executive staff 1, Other staff n/a. Began 1961; non-denominational. No magazine. Turnover n/a.

Orientours Christian Pilgrimages, 2nd Floor, Sovereign House, 11 Ballards Lane, London N3 1UX
☎020 8371 5216 🖷020 8343 0579
E: sales@peltours.com
Web: www.peltours.com
Organising pilgrim tours to the Holy Land and other religious sites for all denominations.
Managing Director: Mr Stuart Lewis. Executive staff 1, Other staff n/a. Began 1959; interdenominational. (Previously Orientours Pilgrimages). A division of Peltours. No magazine. Turnover n/a.

†Pax Travel Ltd, 152 Kentish Town Road, London NW1 9QB
☎020 7485 3003 🖷020 7485 3006
E: info@paxtravel.co.uk
Web: www.paxtravel.co.uk
Organising pilgrimage and cultural tours.
Managing Director: Mr Philip Dean. *Director of Marketing:* Mr Anthony Burns. Executive staff 9. Began 1978; non-denominational. No magazine. Turnover n/a.

Pilgrim Adventure, Southwinds, Culver Park, Tenby SA70 7ED
☎01834 844 212
E: pilgrim.adventure@virgin.net
Web: www.pilgrim-adventure.org.uk
Christian pilgrimage inspired by the wanderings of the early Celtic saints.
Coordinator: Mr David Gleed. Executive staff 8, Other staff n/a. Began 1987; ecumenical. Magazine: *Shoreline* (Circulation n/a half-yearly). Turnover n/a.

Purpose Holidays, Worthy Park Grove, Abbots Worthy, Winchester SO21 1AN
☎01962 882 082 🖷01962 882 082
Evangelism among British holidaymakers in Spain, France, Italy, Greece and Croatia; training given beforehand.
Director: Rev David Steele. Executive staff 1, Other staff 1. ***CC*** No.326081. Began 1974; interdenominational. No magazine. Turnover n/a.

Rivers Travel, PO Box 54, Barnstaple EX32 9YR
☎01598 710 299
E: alan@rivers.co.uk
Web: www.rivers.co.uk
Discount flights for groups or individuals on ministry or business; insurance and car-hire.
Proprietor: Mr Alan Butler. Executive staff 1, Admin staff 1. Began 1997; non-denominational. Magazine: *Christian Traveller* (500 quarterly E only). Turnover £250,000 to year end Mar 03.

Rosary Pilgrimage Trust Suite 9, Newburn Centre, Dean Street, Swindon SN1 5EW
☎01793 422 714 🖷01793 422 7[illegible]5
E: david@rosarypilg.com
Web: www.rosarypilg.com
Giving each party a uniquely designed pilgrimage, offering a path to sacred rekindling of faith.
General Manager: Mr David Gill. *Deputy Manager:* Mrs Ann Pasqual. Executive staff 1, Admin staff 2. **CC** No.1080[illegible]40. Began 1980; Roman Catholic (Previously Rosary Pilgrimage Apostolate Trust). Turnover £330,000 to year end Apr [illegible]5.

Special Pilgrimages, 55 Queen's Road, Southend-on-Sea SS1 1LT
☎01702 394 000 🖷01702 395 0[illegible]
E: info@special-pilgrimages.co.uk
Web: www.special-pilgrimages.co.uk
Arranging pilgrimages, including to Holy Land, Italy, Spain, Egypt, Jordan, Turkey, Greece, France.
Managing Director: Mr Issa K Tah[illegible]an. Executive staff 1, Other staff 5. Began 1983; interdenominational. No magazine. Turnover n/a.

†Star Tours & Holidays, 50 Vivian Avenue, Hendon NW4 3XH
☎020 8931 8811 🖷020 8931 887[illegible]
E: startours@travelink.uk.com
Web: www.travelink.uk.com/startours.htm
Offering Israel tailor-made tours for Christian, youth, schools and special interest groups.
Executive Manager: Mr Chris Jones. Executive staff 1, Other staff n/a. Began 19[illegible]5; non-denominational. No magazine. Turnover n/a.

Surecar Consultants, 17[illegible] Broad Lane, Coventry CV5 7AP
☎024 7667 3971 M: 07973 [illegible]14 269[illegible]
🖷024 7671 5619
E: stephen.crowter@onetel.net
Web: www.surecar.co.uk
Supplying new and used discount cars to order; most models available.
Senior Partner: Mr Stephen Crowter. Executive staff 2, Other staff n/a. Began 1991; interdenominational. No magazine. Turnover £2,500,000 to year end Dec 0[illegible]

S

Timeline Heritage Tours, 5 Laggots Close, Hinton Waldrist, Faringdon SN7 8RY
☎01865 321 084 M: 07971 692 642
🖷01865 321 084
E: enquiries@toursinbritain.co.uk
Web: www.christiantoursinbritain.co.uk
Increasing awareness of Britain's Christian heritage; tours, themed excursions for groups; Church-based Christian history seminars
Proprietor & Tour Leader: Mr Graham E Hall. Executive staff 1. Began 1994; non-denominational. No magazine. Turnover n/a.

Tours for Churches, 65 London Road, Stapleford, Cambridge CB2 5DG
☎01223 723 420 🖷01223 723 405
E: info@toursforchurches.co.uk
Web: www.toursforchurches.co.uk
Tailor-made pilgrimages and travel worldwide for groups.
General Manager: Mrs Amanda Slater. *Managing Director:* Mr Mark Sanders. Executive staff 20, Admin staff 35. Began 1967; interdenominational. (Previously ETS Tours for Churches). A division of the NST Travel Group plc. No magazine. Turnover £30,000,000 to year end Dec 02.

Trust Vehicle Services, Whatley's Garage, High Street, Horam, Heathfield TN21 0EL
☎01435 812 995 🖷01435 813 337
E: mikewilding@trustvehicles.com
Web: www.trustvehicles.com
Supplying used cars, vans and minibuses; car hire, speciality long-term for missionaries.
Owner: Mr Michael Wilding. *Partner:* Mrs Mary Wilding. Executive staff 2, Other staff 1. Began 1985; Baptist. No magazine. Turnover £230,000 to year end Mar 96.

Venture Abroad, Rayburn House, Parcel Terrace, Derby DE1 1LY
☎01332 342 050 🖷01332 224 960
E: tours@ventureabroad.co.uk
Web: www.ventureabroad.co.uk
Specialising in European and worldwide holidays for youth and church groups.
Director: Mr John Boyden. *Secretary:* Mrs Brenda Boyden. Executive staff 2, Other staff 32. Began 1972; interdenominational. No magazine. Turnover £1,000,000 to year end Dec 02.

†Wind, Sand & Stars Ltd, 6 Tyndale Terrace, London N1 2AT
☎020 7359 7551 🖷020 7359 4936
E: office@windsandstars.co.uk
Web: www.windsandstars.co.uk
Arranging pilgrimages and desert journeys to the Sinai including St Catherine's monastery and Mount Sinai.
Director: Miss Emma Loveridge. Executive staff 2, Other staff 2. Began 1991; non-denominational. No magazine. Turnover n/a.

Worldwide Christian Travel, 36 Coldharbour Road, Redland, Bristol BS6 7NA
☎08454 588 308 🖷08454 588 307
E: info@hadlertours.ltd.uk
Web: www.christian-travel.com
Covering all aspects of travel; groups, individuals; low cost airfares for missionaries, ministers, Christian workers.
Managing Director: Mrs Jocelyn Pimm. *Directors:* Mr Stuart Hadler, Mr Ron Pimm. Executive staff 3, Other staff 3. Began 1967; interdenominational. No magazine. Turnover £2,000,000 to year end Dec 04.

YOUTH & CHILDREN'S ORGANISATIONS

See also Children's Care & Adoption Societies on Page 328.

***ALOVE**, 21 Crown Lane, Morden SM4 5BY
☎020 8288 1202
E: alove@salvationarmy.org.uk
Web: www.salvationarmy.org.uk/alove
Youth work, ministry, ALOVE overseas, The Salvation Army's youth work in the UK and Republic of Ireland.
Director: Mr Russell Rook. Executive staff 3, Admin staff 9. **CC** No.214779. Began 2003; Salvation Army. (Previously Salvation Army Youth Ministry Unit). No magazine. Turnover n/a.

***Amaze**, PO Box 12064, Halesowen B63 3ZN
☎0121 503 0824 M 07946 615 708
🖷0121 503 0824
E: amaze@clara.co.uk
Web: www.amaze.org.uk
Advising on work-related issues and best practice in youth and children's work.
Executive Director: Mrs Claire Lea. Executive staff 1, Admin staff 1. Began 1999; non-denominational. No magazine. Turnover £22,294 to year end Dec 02.

Back 2 School Ministries, 155 Hart Road, Thundersley, Benfleet SS7 3QP
☎01268 743 404 🖷01268 743 404
E: chrisandsuegovus@aol.com
Web: www.back2school.org.uk
Schools work; children's evangelism; holiday clubs and family outreach missions; training in children's work; preaching.
Schools workers: Mr & Mrs Chris & Sue Govus. Executive staff 2. **CC** No 1005205. Began 1991; interdenominational. Magazine: *Back 2 School News* (Circulation n/a termly). Turnover £25,000 to year end Dec 02.

†Baptist Youth (Baptist Union of Ireland), 117 Lisburn Road, Belfast BT9 7AF
☎028 9066 3108 🖷028 9066 3616
E: abcini@aol.com
Web: www.baptistyouth.org
Promoting all aspects of youth and children's work, leadership training and evangelistic outreach.
Baptist Youth Secretary: Mr Jackie Whyte. Executive staff 1, Other staff 1. **CC** No.XN 45793A. Began 1977; Baptist. No magazine. Turnover £80,000 to year end Dec 98.

Bar-N-Bus Trust, Unit 6, 667 High Road, Benfleet SS7 5SF
☎0870 850 3734
E: team@barnbus.org.uk
Web: www.barnbus.org.uk
Reaching out to young people in Benfleet and south-east Essex.
Operations Manager: Mr Stuart Christian. Executive staff 1, Other staff n/a. **CC** No.1055210. Began 1992; interdenominational. No magazine. Turnover £100,000 to year end Apr 05.

***Barnabas Adventure Centres Ltd**, Carroty Wood, Higham Lane, Tonbridge TN11 9QX
☎01732 366 766 🖷01732 366 767
E: headoffice@barnabas.org.uk
Web: www.barnabas.org.uk
Operating 4 youth adventure and conference centres in Scottish Borders, Northamptonshire, Sevenoaks, Tonbridge.
Chief Executive: Mr Graham Carruthers. *Operations Manager:* Mr Mark Blythe. Executive staff 7, Other staff 25. **CC** No.276346. Began 1978; interdenominational. (Previously Barnabas Trust Holiday Centres). Magazine: *Alive* (Circulation & frequency n/a). Turnover £1,171,000 to year end Mar 05.

***Boys' Brigade**, Felden Lodge, Felden Lane, Hemel Hempstead HP3 0BL
☎01442 231 681 🖷01422 235 391
E: enquiries@boys-brigade.org.uk
Web: www.boys-brigade.org.uk
Christian uniformed organisation for boys aged 6 to 18.
Brigade Secretary: Mr Steve Dickinson. Executive staff 6, Office staff 34. **CC** No.305969. Began 1883; interdenominational. Magazine: *Boys' Brigade Gazette* (12,000 every two months). Turnover £2,070,316 to year end Mar 00.
Also at: *Secretary for Northern Ireland:* Mr Alec Hunter MBE, Rathmore House, 126 Glenarm Road, Larne BT40 1DZ
☎028 2827 2794 🖷 028 2827 5150
And: *Secretary for Scotland:* Tom Boyle, Scottish Headquarters, Carronvale House, Carronvale Road, Larbert FK5 3LH
☎01324 562 008 🖷 01324 552 323
And: *Secretary for Wales:* Name not supplied, 80 Woodville Road, Cathays, Cardiff CF24 4ED
☎029 2022 6668

Bristol Youth Bus Project, South Bristol Christian Centre, Churchlands Road, Bedminster, Bristol BS3 3PW
☎0117 963 6329 🖷0117 963 6329
Outreach to children and teenagers in deprived areas using double-decker bus as initial attraction.
Secretary: Mr L Potter. No full-time staff. **CC** No.1012554. Began 1989; non-denominational. No magazine. Turnover £2,060 to year end Aug 00.

S

***Campaigner Ministries**, 6 Eaton Court Road, Colmworth Business Park, Eaton Socon, St Neots PE19 8ER
☎01480 215 622 🖷01480 405 550
E: info@campaigners.org.uk
Web: www.campaigners.org.uk
Church-based evangelistic children's and youth ministry.
Executive Director: Mr John Radcliffe. *Resources Director:* Mr Tony Etherington. Executive staff 3, Other staff 4. ***CC*** No.283171. Began 1922; interdenominational. Magazine: *CNow* (4,500 quarterly). Turnover £372,468 to year end Dec 04.

Catholic Youth Services, 39 Eccleston Square, London SW1V 1BX
☎020 7901 4870 🖷020 7901 4821
E: cys@cbcew.org.uk
Web: www.catholicyouthservices.org.uk
Supporting youth ministry as an agency of the Catholic Bishops' Conference.
Director: Miss Helen Bardy. *Communications:* Paul Hetherington. Executive staff 2, Other staff 1. ***CC*** No.305981. Began 1962; Roman Catholic. Magazine: *CYS News* (Circulation n/a termly). Turnover n/a.

Diocesan Youth Officers:

Arundel and Brighton: Mr Ray Mooney, Tulip Cottage, Old Lane, Tatsfield, Westerham TN16 2LJ
E: dabcec@dabnet.org
☎01293 515 666 M 07904 183 169

Birmingham: Eamonn Corduff, St Joan's House, Coventry Road, Coleshill, Birmingham B46 3ED
☎01675 466 912 🖷 01675 466 909

Brentwood: To be appointed, Cathedral House, 28 Ingrave Road, Brentwood CM15 8AT
☎01277 265 286 🖷 01277 265 261

Cardiff: Rev Canon Robert Reardon, 910 Newport Road, Rumney, Cardiff CF3 4LL
E: r-c-chaplaincy@cardiff.ac.uk
☎029 2036 0044 M: 07774 410 757
🖷 029 2079 3172

Clifton: Miss Mary McGinty, Alexander House, Pennywell Road, Bristol BS5 0TX
☎0117 902 5594 🖷 0117 902 5520

East Anglia: Sr Barbara Brent, Convent of Jesus and Mary, 320 Woodbridge Road, Ipswich IP4 4BD
☎01473 713 162 🖷 01473 727 297

Hallam: Rev Kevan Grady, Hallam CYS, St Charles Street, Attercliffe, Sheffield S9 3WU
E: youthservice@hallam-diocese.com
☎0114 256 6460 🖷 0114 256 2673

Hexham and Newcastle: Fr Dermott Donnelly, Diocese Youth Mission Team (YMT), 16 Arthur Street, Blyth NE24 1EA
☎01670 351 703 🖷 01670 364 873

Lancaster: Miss Anne Kennedy, St Joseph's Presbytery, Slyne Road, Lancaster LA1 2HU
☎01524 848 182 🖷 01524 848 182

Leeds: Anne Emmott, 62 Headingley Lane, Leeds LS6 2BU
☎0113 261 8058 🖷 0113 261 8035

Liverpool: Mr John Biggins, Centre of Evangelisation, Croxteth Drive, Sefton Park, Liverpool L17 1AA
☎0151 522 1042 🖷 0151 522 1060

Menevia: Rev Teyrnon Williams, St Benedict, 41 Pontardawe Road, Clydach, Swansea SA6 5NG
☎01792 842 244

Middlesbrough: Rev Paul Farrer, The Curial Offices, 50a The Avenue, Linthorpe, Middlesbrough TS5 6QT
☎01642 244 775 🖷 01642 851 404

Northampton: Mr Brin Dunsire, Northampton Youth Ministry Office, Ker Anna Centre, Princes Risborough HP27 0JN
☎01844 273 337 🖷 01844 273 337

Nottingham: Rev Paul Newman, The Briars Residential Youth Centre, Crich Common, Matlock DE4 5BW
☎01773 852 044 🖷 01773 852 968

Plymouth: Rebecca Hughes, Newman House, Wonford Road, Exeter EX2 4PF
☎01392 671 324 🖷 01392 761 319

Portsmouth: Miss Julie Meads, Department for Evangelisation Catechesis, Park Place Pastoral Centre, Winchester Road, Wickham, Fareham PO17 5HA
E: youth@portsmouth-dio.org.uk
☎01329 834 677 🖷 01329 833 452

Salford: Miss Theresa Davies, 5 Gerald Road, Pendleton, Salford M6 6DL
E: youth@salforddiocese.org
☎0161 736 1421 🖷 0161 745 9708

Shrewsbury: Rev Anthony Leonard, Dehon House, Welsh Road, Little Sutton, Ellesmere Port CH66 4QP
E: youth@youth-centre.demon.co.uk
☎0151 348 1307 🖷 0151 348 1307

Southwark: Rev John Considene, St Vincent's Centre, Castle Road, Whitstable CT5 2DY
E: jconsidine@lineone.net
☎01227 272 900 🖷 01227 282 384

Westminster: Rev Mgr Vladimir Felzmann, All Saints Pastoral Centre, Shenley Lane, London Colney, St Albans AL2 1AF
E: vladimirf@compuseve.com
☎01727 822 010 🖷 01727 822 927

Children Matter!, 207 Queensway, Bletchley, Milton Keynes MK2 2EB
☎01908 856 125
M: 07785 975 600
🖷01908 856 012
E: info@childrenmatter.net
Web: www.childrenmatter.net
A network for children's ministry in the UK; advocacy for children in the UK church.
Director: Mr Alan Charter. No full-time staff. Began 2004; non-denominational. Magazine: *Children Matter Update* (200 weekly by email). Turnover £8,500 to year end Dec 05.

***Children Worldwide**, Dalesdown, Honeybridge Lane, Dial Post, Horsham RH13 8NX
☎01403 711 032
🖷01403 710 716
E: cwdalesdown@aol.com
Web: www.childrenworldwide.co.uk
Evangelism amongst children and families, camps, training events, resources.
General Directors: Mr Peter Goodall. Executive staff 10, Other staff 50. ***CC*** No.1072626. Began 1975; interdenominational. No magazine. Turnover n/a.

†*Christian Endeavour Union of Great Britain and Ireland, Office 1, Wellesbourne House, Walton Road, Wellesbourne, Warwick CV35 9JB
☎01727 853 297
E: k.f.rankin@ntlworld.com
Training young people for service within the local church.
Hon Secretary: Mr Kenneth Rankin. No paid staff. ***CC*** No.228608. Began 1[illegible]96; interdenominational. Magazines: *Focus* (Circulation & frequency n/a), *Junior Focus* (Circulation & frequency n/a). Turnover n/a.

***Christian Youth Ministries**, 6 Great Colman Street, Ipswich IP4 2[illegible]D
☎01473 216 712
E: ian@c-y-m.org.uk
Web: www.c-y-m.org.uk
Conducting children's and young people's work through schools, residentials, events, training, teaching.
Chief Executive Officer: Mr David Pepper. *Company Secretary:* Mr Ian France. Executive staff 6, No other paid staff. ***CC*** No.1075626. Began 1983; interdenominational. (Previously Ipswich Christian Youth Ministries). Magazine: *CYM Bulletin* (3,500 every four months). Turnover £180,000 to year end Mar 05.

Church Lads' and Church Girls' Brigade, 2 Barnsley Road, Wath-upon-Dearne, Rotherham S63 6PY
☎01709 876 535
🖷01709 878 089
E: generalsecretary@clcgb.org.uk
Web: www.clcgb.org.uk
Uniformed youth organisation for 5 to [illegible] year olds. Fun, faith fellowship in a Christian setting.
General Secretary: Mr A J Reed Screen OBE. Executive staff 1, Other staff 6. ***CC*** No.276821. Began; Church Lads 189[illegible] and Church Girls 1923 merged 1978. Anglican. Magazine: *Report* (1,000 annually). Turnover n/a.

Church of England National Youth Office (Archbishops' Council Education Division), Church House, Great Smith Street, London SW1P 3NZ
☎020 7898 1512
🖷020 7898 1520
E: yvonne.criddle@c-of-e.org.uk or yvonne.criddle@c-of-e.org.uk
Web: www.cofe.anglican.uk
Advising dioceses and General Synod; implementing National Youth Strategy; action in youth and community work.
National Youth Officers: Mr P Ball, Ms Y Criddle. Executive staff 2, Admin staff 1. ***CC*** Began 1970; Anglican. (Previously Church of England Youth Services (General Synod)). No magazine. Turnover n/a.

Note: Youth and Children's Advisers in each diocese can be contacted via the Diocesan Office. See pages 155 to 162

Church of England Youth Council (CEYC), c/o Education Division, Church House, Great Smith Street, London SW1P 3NZ
☎020 7898 1512
E: secretary@ceyc.org
Web: www.ceyc.org
Encouraging young adults to participate fully at all levels in the Anglican Church.
Coordinator: Name not supplied. Staff n/a. Began n/a; Anglican. (Previously Young Adult Network (YAN)). No magazine. Turnover n/a.

†Common Ground Outreach, 11 Ozier Court, Saffron Walden CB11 4BH
☎01799 524 741
E: david.law16@btinternet.com
Web: www.david.law16.btinternet.co.uk/cg.html
Outreach to young people using double decker bus.
Team Leader: Mr Dave Law. No paid staff. Began 1995; interdenominational. No magazine. Turnover £4,000 to year end Dec 02.

CRIBS (Christian Resources in Bexley Schools), 77 Cross Street, Erith DA8 1RB
☎01322 330 730
E: cribs@tiscali.co.uk
School and community-based work with children, young people and teaching staff.
Director: Mr Gordon Raggett. *Administrator:* Mr Ron Jones. Executive staff 1, Other staff 14, Sessional staff 13. **CC** No.327197. Began 1993; interdenominational. No magazine. Turnover £160,000 to year end Apr 03.

***Crusaders/Urban Saints**, Kestin House, 45 Crescent Road, Luton LU2 0AH
☎01582 589 850 ℻01582 721 702
E: @crusaders.org.uk
Web: www.crusaders.org.uk or www.life2themax.net or www.crusadersreunited.org.uk
Youth groups for Christian outreach, supported by training, teaching materials, holidays, centres and specialised resources. **Name change January 07.**
Executive Director: Mr Matt Summerfield. *Fundraising Director:* Mrs Sharon Eason. *Director of National Ministries:* Mr Phil Hulks. Executive staff 10, Other staff 40. **CC** No.223798. Began 1906; interdenominational. Magazine: *Link* (10,000 every four months). Turnover £2,500,000 to year end Dec 02.

CURBS (Children in URBan Situations), 4 Hawksmoor Close, London E6 5SL
M: 07941 336 589
E: info@curbsproject.org.uk
Web: www.curbsproject.org.uk
Providing resources, support and training for children's workers in inner cities and outer urban estates.
Project Leader: Mrs K M Copsey. Executive staff 1. **CC** No.1076902. Began 1996; non-denominational. No magazine. Turnover £25,000 to year end Mar 05.

***CYFA Pathfinder Ventures Ltd**, CPAS, Athena Drive, Tachbrook Park, Warwick CV34 6NG
☎01926 458 456 ℻01926 458 459
E: ventures@cpas.org.uk
Web: www.ventures-online.com
Running residential activities for 8 to 18 year olds; Falcon Camps for children from disadvantaged backgrounds.
Director: David Hart. Executive staff 4. **CC** No.271391. Began 1974; Anglican. Magazine: *Ventures Brochure* (35,000 annually). Turnover £1,500,000 to year end Apr 05.

†DCPA - The Pioneer Association in Down and Connor, Pioneer Information Centre, 511 Ormeau Road, Belfast BT7 3GS
☎028 9049 2424 ℻028 9049 2424
E: info@dcpa.net
Web: www.dcpa.net
Educating and supporting young people who wish to live without alcohol or drugs.
Diocesan President: Mr Brian Jamison. Executive staff 2. **CC** No.XR 4449. Began 1982; Roman Catholic. Magazine: *DCPA News* (1,000 quarterly), *Pioneer Press* (2,000 quarterly). Turnover £15,000 to year end Apr 98.

***The Family Trust**, Old School House, 4 Buckland Road, Maidstone ME16 0SL
☎01622 687 074 ℻01622 664 887
E: admin@familytrust.org.uk
Web: www.familytrust.org.uk
Children's evangelism, primary school assemblies and children's clubs, camps, holiday Bible clubs, training, all-age worship.
Children's Worker: Mr Richard Blackaby. Executive staff 6, Other staff 6. **CC** No.299019. Began 1988; non-denominational. Magazine: *FT Index* (Circulation & frequency n/a). Turnover n/a.

***Fellowship Finders**, Selsdon House, 212 Addington Road, South Croydon CR2 8LD
☎020 8768 3976 ℻020 8768 3976
E: help@finders.uk.net
Web: www.finders.uk.net
Helping Christian young people to find a local church and Christian fellowship.
Administrator: Mrs Rosamund Tolley. Admin staff 1. **CC** No.278027. Began 1979; interdenominational. (Previously Christian Youth Contact Service). Sponsored by The Christian Youth Challenge Trust. No magazine. Turnover n/a.

†The Fellowship of St Nicholas, St Nicholas Centre, 66 London Road, St Leonards-on-Sea TN37 6AS
☎01424 423 683 ℻01424 460 446
E: enquiries@fellowshipofstnicholas.org.uk
Web: www.fellowshipofstnicholas.org.uk
Daycare services for children; playbus after school, holiday playschemes, children's centre, neighbourhood nursery.
Chairman: Mrs Mollie Green. *Services Manager:* Stephanie Edmonds. Admin staff 6, Other staff 32. **CC** No.208446. Began 1939; Anglican. No magazine. Turnover £420,000 to year end Mar 00.

Fellowship of United Reformed Youth (FURY), 86 Tavistock Place, London WC1H 9RT
☎020 7916 2020 ℻020 7916 2021
E: youth@urc.org.uk
Web: www.urc.org.uk
Helping informed choice about the Christian way, in Scotland, England and Wales.
Secretary for Youth Work: To be appointed. Executive staff 1. Began 1972; United Reformed. No magazine. Turnover n/a.

The Forrest Therapeutic Service for Children and Young People, Forrest House, 63 Rowntree Clifford Close, Liddon Road, London E13 8AB
☎020 7473 4060 ℻020 7473 3467
E: forrest@whcm.org.uk
Providing therapy for children in East London schools.
Coordinator: Maureen Keane. Executive staff 1, Other staff n/a. Began n/a; ecumenical. Part of West Ham Central Mission. No magazine. Turnover included in WHCM.

Youth & Children's Organisations

***Frontier Youth Trust**, Unit 208b, The Big Peg, 120 Vyse Street, The Jewellery Quarter, Birmingham B18 6NF
☎0121 687 3505
E: frontier@fyt.org.uk
Web: www.fyt.org.uk
Supporting, training Christians working with disadvantaged young people, mainly in urban/industrial areas.
Chief Executive Officer: Mr David Wiles. Executive staff 1, Other staff 7. ***CC*** No.1059328. Began 1964; interdenominational. Magazine: *FYT Update* (5,000 frequency n/a). Turnover £250,000 to year end Mar 05.

***Fusion**, PO Box 58, Chichester PO19 8UD
☎01243 771 405 🖷01243 531 959
E: info@fusion.uk.com
Web: www.fusion.uk.com
Resourcing Churches involved in student ministry.
Chairman: Roger Ellis. Staff 6. ***CC*** No.1073572. Began 1996; interdenominational. Magazine: *Yes* (Circulation n/a every four months). Turnover £150,000 to year end Aug 03.

GCU (Girl Crusaders' Union), 31 Catherine Place, Westminster, London SW1E 6EJ
☎020 7834 4085 🖷020 7630 1126
E: gcu@gcu.org.uk
Web: www.gcu.org.uk
Running Bible groups and holidays for schoolgirls.
Acting Director: Miss Margaret Norgate. Executive staff 5. ***CC*** No.226487. Began 1915; interdenominational. No magazine. Turnover n/a.

***The Girls' Brigade England and Wales**, PO Box 196, 129 Broadway, Didcot OX11 8XN
☎01235 510 425 🖷01235 510 429
E: admin@girlsbrigadeew.org.uk
Web: www.girlsbrigadeew.org.uk
Varied outreach activities amongst girls and young women leading to evangelism, nurture and Christian discipleship.
National Secretary: Ruth Gilson. Executive staff 5, Other staff 16. ***CC*** No.206655. Began 1893; interdenominational. Magazine: *The View* (5,000 every two months). Turnover n/a.

The Girls' Brigade in Scotland, 11a Woodside Crescent, Charing Cross, Glasgow G3 7UL
☎0141 332 1765 🖷0141 331 2681
E: enquiries@girls-brigade-scotland.org.uk
Web: www.girls-brigade-scotland.org.uk
Offering a programme of informal learning and personal development to girls and young women.
National Director: Mrs Ann Webster. *National Training Officer:* Mrs Sheila Buchan. Executive staff 2, Other staff 9. ***CC*** No.SCO 10980. Began 1893; interdenominational. No magazine. Turnover n/a.

†Global Fellowship, 17a East King Street, Helensburgh G84 7QQ
☎01436 678 087 🖷01436 678 087
E: gf@globalfellowship.net
Web: www.globalfellowship.net
Promoting Christian youth work; liaison and support through autonomous member organisations.
Chief Executive: Mr Tage Kleinbeck. *Executive Assistant:* Miss Caroline Goodfellow. No full-time staff. ***CC*** No.275036. Began 1963; ecumenical. (Previously The World Conference). Magazine: *GF Review* (2,000 annually). Turnover £120,000 to year end Dec 02.

Grove House Centre, 1 Thorpe Avenue, Tonbridge TN10 4PW
☎01732 369 303
Providing all-round ministry to young people.
Leader: Mr William Riley. Executive staff 1. Began 1967; interdenominational. No magazine. Turnover n/a.

GSUS Live, Counties, 30 Haynes Road, Westbury BA13 3HD
☎01373 823 013
E: info@gsuslive.co.uk
Web: www.gsuslive.co.uk
Introducing Jesus to teenagers using mobile classrooms with 3D video and interactive multimedia presentation.
Schools Coordinator: Name not supplied. Executive staff 1, Other staff n/a. Began 2000; non-denominational. Part of Counties. No magazine. Turnover n/a.

†Hertford Youth Together, 52 Cowper Crescent, Bengeo, Hertford SG14 3DZ
☎01992 413 976
E: bp.parker@virgin.net
Providing support, advice, teaching, prayer, finance for Christian youth work in and around Hertford.
Chairperson: Mr Ian Collins. No full-time staff. Began 1992; ecumenical. No magazine. Turnover n/a.

Illusistration, 25 Long Lake Avenue, Tettenhall Wood, Wolverhampton WV6 8EY
M: 07779 608 387
E: mark@illusistration.com
Web: www.illusistration.com
Children's evangelist and all-age communicator using puppets, escapology, Gospel magic to reach families.
All Age Communicator: Mr Mark Harrington. Executive staff 1. Began 2004; non-denominational. No magazine. Turnover n/a.

International Christian Youthworks (ICY), Broadridge Nook, Morchard Bishop, Crediton EX17 6RH
☎01363 877 435 M: 07915 663 542
E: colin@icy.org.uk
Web: www.icy.org.uk
Linking international youth ministries; providing support/accredited courses to trainee youth/schools workers for churches.
Executive and European Director: Mr Colin Piper. Executive staff 2, Other staff 1. Began 2005; non-denominational. No magazine. Turnover n/a.

†*Kingdom Creative, 32 Normandy Road, Worthing BN14 7DX
☎01903 522 627
M: 07973 206 225
🖷01903 522 627
E: jim@kingdomcreative.co.uk
Web: www.kingdomcreative.co.uk
Children's and youth worship production; consultancy in evangelism, children's work, training and all-age worship.
Director: Rev Jim Bailey. Executive staff 2, Other staff 3. ***CC*** No.C[illegible] 107[illegible]87. Began 1989; non-denominational. (Previously Kingdom Kids). No magazine. Turnover n/a.

Link Up Holidays, 112 Carlton Road, Rugby CV22 7PE
☎01788 840 128
E: info@linkupholidays.org.uk
Web: www.linkupholidays.org.uk
Christian activity holidays challenging young people aged 15 to 18 to grow spiritually, physically, mentally.
Chairman: Dr Mark Richmond. No full-time staff. ***CC*** No.1020197. Began 19[illegible]6; interdenominational. No magazine. Turnover £10,000 to year end Dec 04.

Linx Christian Youth Trust, Bank Chambers, 108 Union Street, Torquay TQ2 5[illegible]Y
☎01803 212 111
🖷01803 212 111
E: nigel@linxyouth.net
Operating in secondary schools in Torbay, supporting young people in local churches.
Project Manager: Mr Nigel Taylor. Executive staff 3, Admin staff 1. ***CC*** No.1067449. Began 19[illegible]7; interdenominational. No magazine. Turnover £112,000 to year end Mar 04.

LMI - Logos Ministries International, PO Box 1131, Belfast BT5 4LD
☎028 9045 8362
🖷028 9045 8362
E: info@logosministries.org.uk
Web: www.logosministries.org.uk
Reaching young people with the claims and challenges of Jesus; extensive schools ministry throughout UK.
Director: Rev Thomas McClean. *Mission Director:* Mrs Yvonne McClean. Executive staff 4, Other staff 8. ***CC*** No.X[illegible] 4613[illegible]. Began 1977; interdenominational. (Previously Logos Ministries). Magazine: *Edge* (3,000 quarterly). Turnover £16[illegible],000 to year end Dec 02.

Matrix Trust, 14 Queens Road, Guildford GU1 4JJ
☎01483 595 608
E: info@matrixtrust.com
Web: www.matrixtrust.com
Coordinating youth, schools and student work, and facilitating creative mission to emerging culture.
Director: Mr Ian Nicholson. Executive staff 2, Admin staff 2. ***CC*** No.1081852. Began 2000; interdenominational. (Previously The Warehouse Project). No magazine. Turnover £100,000 to year end Mar 05.

S

†**MAYC (Methodist Association of Youth Clubs)** Methodist Church House, 25 Marylebone Road, London NW1 5JR
☎020 7486 5502 🖷020 7467 5281
E: seatonm@methodistchurch.org.uk
Web: www.mayc.info/
Expressing the church's responsibility to young people everywhere - The Methodist Church serving young people.
National Secretary: Mike Seaton. Executive staff 1, Other staff 3. Began 1945; Methodist. Magazine: *Share* (4,000 every four months). Turnover n/a.

***The Message Trust**, PO Box 151, Manchester M22 4YY
☎0161 946 2300 🖷0161 946 2310
E: info@message.org.uk
Web: www.message.org.uk
Reaching Manchester's young people with the Gospel through words, music, credible events, long-term action.
Chief Executive: Andy Hawthorne. *Office Manager:* Ruth Major. Executive staff 4, Other staff 51. *CC* No.1081467. Began 1993 interdenominational. No magazine. Turnover £1,500,000 to year end Aug 05.

Methodist Church Children's Work, Methodist Church House, 25 Marylebone Road, London NW1 5JF
☎020 7486 5502 🖷020 7467 5281
E: children@methodistchurch.org.uk
Web: www.methodistchildren.org.uk
Coordinating Methodist Church work with children and supporting workers with children in their local churches.
Secretary for Children's Work: Mr Steve Pearce. Executive staff 1, Other Staff 3. Began 1932; Methodist. No magazine. Turnover n/a.

Methodist Church in Ireland Department of Youth and Children's Work, Aldersgate House, Belfast BT7 1NA
☎028 9032 7191
🖷028 9024 1322
E: dycw@irishmethodist.org
Web: www.soulzone.org or www.irishmethodist.org/dycw
Developing work among young people and children.
General Secretary: Rev David Rock. Executive staff 4, Other staff 5. **CC** No.CHY 253. Began 1965; Methodist Church in Ireland. Magazine: *Equip* (700 every four months). Turnover n/a.

Midlands Centre for Youth Ministry, St John's College, Bramcote, Beeston, Nottingham NG9 3DS
☎0115 968 3222
🖷0115 943 6438
E: admin.youth@stjohns-nottm.ac.uk
Web: www.stjohns-nottm.ac.uk
Offering courses and professional qualifications in youth and community work from introductory to Masters level.
Director: Dr Sally Nash. Executive staff 2. **CC** No.1026706. Began 1998; interdenominational. No magazine. Turnover n/a.

Midlands Network of Youth Ministries (MNet), Youth Office, 4 Walmley Road, Sutton Coldfield B76 1QN
☎0121 351 5689
M: 07725 533 336
E: charlie@mnetyouth.org.uk
Web: www.mnetyouth.org.uk
Serving local churches by providing trainee youth/schools workers from ICY with support/accredited training.
Coordinators: Mr & Mrs Charlie & Ruth Morris. Executive staff 1. Began 2005; non-denominational. No magazine. Turnover n/a.

***Northamptonshire Association of Youth Clubs**, Kings Park Conference Centre, Kings Park Road, Northampton NN3 6LL
☎01604 499 699
🖷01604 499 656
E: nayc@nayc.org
Web: www.nayc.org
Providing support services to 150 youth clubs; 'Octopus' after-school project; 4 conference/activity centres.
Chief Executive: Mr John M Whittaker. Executive staff 4, Other staff 3. **CC**. No. 803431. Began 1961; interdenominational. No magazine. Turnover n/a.

S

†One Way UK, Unit 6, Robert Cort Industrial Estate, Britten Road, Reading RG2 0AU
☎0118 975 6303
🖷0118 931 3008
E: info@onewayuk.com
Web: www.onewayuk.com
Specialising in equipping and training children's workers; providing resources.
Director: Mr Harry Barrett. *Administration Director:* Mrs Kath Barrett. Executive staff 3, Other staff 6. Began 1991; Baptist. Magazine: *Creative Ministry Update* (7,000 monthly). Turnover £175,000 to year end Mar 04.

†Oxford Kilburn Club, Christian Holt House, 45 Denmark Road, London NW6 5BP
☎020 7624 6292
🖷020 7372 6598
E: enquiries@okclub.org.uk
Web: www.okclub.org.uk
Working with young people aged 5 to 20 and their families. Accommodation for 12 volunteers.
Chairman: Mr Nick Bent. Executive staff 6, Other staff 8. ***CC*** No.306108. Began 1960; non-denominational. No magazine. Turnover £150,000 to year end Aug 00.

Oxford Youth Works, Church Annex, Jeune Street, Oxford OX4 1BN
☎01865 204 646
E: admin@oxfordyouthworks.co.uk
Web: www.oxfordyouthworks.co.uk
Youth work projects in Oxford Area. BA Hons degree course in youth/community work and applied theology.
Director: Mr Ben Holloway. Staff 14. ***CC*** No.299754. Began 1988; interdenominational. Magazine: *Initiative* (800 half-yearly). Turnover £220,000 to year end Sep 05.

Pact Activity Holidays, PO Box 3727, Brentwood CM13 1AW
☎01442 870 877
🖷01277 263 948
E: pact@activities.org.uk
Web: www.activities.org.uk
Summer ventures for youth combining enjoyable holiday with presentation of the Christian message.
Administrator: Mr J Beavis. Executive staff 1. ***CC*** Began 1956; non-denominational. No magazine. Turnover £60,000 to year end Dec 00.

Pathfinder Fellowship, Bickersteth House, 25 Sheffield Terrace, London W8 7NQ
☎020 7727 5586
E: mary@bickerstethhouse.demon.co.uk
Christian education for young people by means of study meetings, prayer and community life.
Warden and Secretary: Mrs Mary M Mason. Executive staff 1. ***CC*** No.222612. Began 1922; Anglican. No magazine. Turnover £56,000 to year end Dec 02.

Pilots, United Reformed Church, 86 Tavistock Place, London WC1H 9RT
☎020 7916 2020 🖷020 7916 2021
E: pilots@urc.org.uk
Web: www.pilots.org.uk
Non-uniformed ecumenical organisation for children and young people, with emphasis on the world church.
Pilots Development Officer: Mrs Karen Bulley. No full-time staff. Began 1936; United Reformed and Congregational. Magazine: *The Bridge* (Circulation n/a every four months). Turnover n/a.

Powerpack (Heather Thompson), 21a Mountside, Guildford GU2 4JD
☎01483 771 775
E: info@ppcentre.co.uk
Web: www.powerpackministries.co.uk
Training and resourcing children's leaders and churches; leading children's meetings, all-age services; nationwide and abroad.
Director: Miss Heather Thompson. Executive staff 1. ***CC*** No.1050323. Began 1984; Independent. No magazine. Turnover n/a.

***Presbyterian Board of Youth and Children's Ministry**, Church House, Fisherwick Place, Belfast BT1 6DW
☎028 9032 2284 🖷028 9041 7239
E: yac@presbyterianireland.org
Web: www.pciyouth.org or www.pciyac.org
Supporting, encouraging and facilitating congregations in carrying out youth and children's ministry.
Director: Miss Roz Stirling. *Deputy Director:* Rev Ian McKee. Executive staff 4, Other staff 10. ***CC*** Began 1840; Presbyterian Church in Ireland. (Previously Presbyterian Youth Board). Magazine: *Youth in Focus* (2,500 quarterly). Turnover n/a.

†Primary Focus, Mill House, Mill Lane, Cheadle SK8 2NT
☎0161 428 3113 M: 07940 567 046
E: mark@primaryfocus.org.uk
Web: www.primaryfocus.org.uk
Providing support ministry for children, young people and leaders; advice, expertise and other services.
Proprietor: Mr Mark Tomlinson. Executive staff 1. Began 2000; interdenominational. No magazine. Turnover n/a.

Rainbow Ministries Christian Resource, 19 Pondholton Drive, Witham CM8 1QG
☎01376 517 922
E: mail@rainbowministries.org.uk
Web: www.rainbowministries.co.uk
Supplying resources for working with toddlers, children, young teens for church and school.
Director: Rev Alan Bass. Executive staff 1, Other staff 2. Began n/a; interdenominational. No magazine. Turnover n/a.

Rove, PO Box 509, Lydney GL15 5YT
M: 07767 351 194
E: roveuk@hotmail.com
Web: www.rove.org.uk
Teaching drugs/alcohol awareness; sharing the Gospel using a bus, media, friendship evangelism.
Chairman: Mr Gareth B[illegible]rt. Staff n/a. ***CC*** No.1079896. Began 1996; interdenominational. No magazine. Turnover £4[illegible]000 to year end Jun 00.

***The Salmon Youth Centre in Bermondsey**, 43 Old Jamaica Road, London SE16 4TE
☎020 7237 3788 M: 079[illegible] 000 [illegible]07
🖷020 7252 0285
E: info@salmoncentre.co.uk
Web: www.salmoncentre.co.uk
Evangelism within youth work in Bermondsey, south-east London; residential Christian community.
Executive Director: Mr Mark Blu[illegible]ell. *Administration Manager:* Mr Jim G[illegible]ld. Executive staff 2, Other staff 10. ***CC*** No.278979. Began 19[illegible]6; non-denominational. No magazine. Turnover £900,000 to year end Aug 0[illegible].

***The Salvation Army Evangelism Department**, UK Territorial Headquarters, [illegible]01 Newington Causeway, London SE1 6[illegible]N
☎020 7367 4500 🖷020 73[illegible]7 471[illegible]
E: thq@salvationarmy.org.uk or children@salvationarmy.org.uk
Web: www.salvationarmy.org.uk
Supporting, developing and encouraging work among youth and young people.
Evangelism Secretary: Captain Norman Ceo. Executive staff 1, Other staff 9. ***CC*** No.214779. Began 1865; Salvation Army. (Previously The Salvation Army Youth Department and Children's Ministry Unit). No magazine. Turnover n/a.

SAYT - Sevenoaks Area Youth Trust, St Lawrence Vicarage, Stone Street, Seal, Sevenoaks TN15 0LQ
☎01732 761 766 M: 07941 [illegible]88 85[illegible]
🖷0870 162 9893
E: info@sayt.org.uk
Web: www.sayt.org.uk
Supporting church youth work in Sevenoaks; two detached youth workers, schools work.
Chairman and Trustee: Mr Rob Mars[illegible]. Youth workers 2. ***CC*** No.[illegible]09059[illegible]. Began n/a; ecumenical. No magazine. Turnover £50,000 to year end Mar 05.

Schools Outreach, 10 High Street, Bromsgrove B61 8HQ
☎01527 574 404 🖷01527 5[illegible]0 321
E: schoolsoutreach@aol.com
Web: www.schoolsoutreach.org
Employing full-time, school-based pastoral care workers.
Chief Executive: Mr Gordon Bailey. *Company Secretary:* Miss Andrea Bailey. Executive staff 3, Other staff [illegible]0. ***CC*** No.516184. Began 1973; non-denominational. No magazine. Turnover £360,703 to year end Mar 04.

S

***Scottish Crusaders**, Challenge House, 29 Canal Street, Glasgow G4 0AD
☎0141 331 2400 🖷0141 331 2400
E: E@scottishcrusaders.org.uk
Web: www.crusaders.org.uk/scotland
Running youth groups for unchurched young people aged 8 to 18; outdoor centres at Comrie and Tweedsmuir.
Scottish Director: Mr Rob Rawson. *Development Manager:* Mr Billy Kent. Executive staff 3. Other staff 3. **CC** No.SCO 08518. Began 1927; interdenominational. No magazine. Turnover £228,000 to year end Dec 04.

***Soul Survivor**, Unit 2, Paramount Industrial Estate, Sandown Road, Watford WD24 7XF
☎0870 054 3331 🖷0870 054 3334
E: info@soulsurvivor.com
Web: www.soulsurvivor.com
Youth festivals, conferences, roadshows, youth leaders support programme, residential discipleship training courses, schools work.
Director: Mr Mike Pilavachi. *Co-Director:* Ms Liz Biddulph. Executive staff 2, Other staff 20. **CC** No.1080720. Began 1993; interdenominational. No magazine. Turnover £1,500,000 to year end Dec 02.

***South West Youth Ministries (SWYM)**, 14C Pinhoe Road, Exeter EX4 7HJ
☎01392 273 560
E: info@swym.org.uk
Web: www.swym.org.uk
Training and supporting youth workers in south-west England, in partnership with local works.
Director: Mr Paul Friend. *Secretary:* Mrs Rosemary Sowden. Executive staff 11, Admin staff 1. **CC** No.1086877. Began 1997; interdenominational. No magazine. Turnover £216,000 to year end Aug 05.

***Spinnaker Trust Ltd**, 172 High Street, London SE20 7QS
☎020 8778 3181
M: 07850 276 256
E: spinnaker@spinnaker.org.uk
Web: www.spinnaker.org.uk or www.spinnakertrust.org.uk
School assemblies and R E lessons, church children's events and projects, drama and music teams.
Director: Mr Martin Sweet. *Administrator:* Mrs Gill Ashley-Smith. Executive staff 2, Other staff 10, Associate Workers 8. *CC* No.1111351. Began 1986; interdenominational. (Previously Spinnaker Trust). Magazine: *Spinnaker News* (1,500 every four months). Turnover £113,500 to year end April 05.

Teens in Crisis, Unit 6/13, The Mews, Brook Street, Mitcheldean GL17 0SL
☎01594 544 281
🖷01594 544 281
E: tic@teensincrisis.org.uk
Web: www.teensincrisis.org.uk
Crisis prevention, intervention and care through counselling, education and youthwork services.
Chief Executive: Mr Nathan T A Jones. Executive staff 7, Other staff 70. **CC** No.1045429. Began 1993; non-denominational. Magazine: *Focus* (2,000 quarterly). Turnover £150,000 to year end Dec 05.

* **Time For God**, 7 Chester House, Pages Lane, Muswell Hill, London N10 1PR
☎020 8883 1504 🖷020 8365 2471
E: office@timeforgod.com
Web: www.timeforgod.org
Offering gap year experiences for 18 to 25 year olds including youth work, drug rehabilitation; UK, overseas.
Director: Rev David Williamson. Executive staff 7. **CC** No.1101997. Began 1965; interdenominational. (Previously The Time For God Scheme). No magazine. Turnover £200,000 to year end Mar 03.

†**The Two Fat Slugs**, 69 Linacre Avenue, Sprowston, Norwich NR7 8JY
☎01603 403 590
M: 07730 930 784
E: daveABM@aol.com
Web: www.2fatslugs.com
Evangelism through escapology, fire eating and breathing; for missions, street work and youth work.
Evangelist: Mr Dave Townsend. Evangelist 1. Began 1995; interdenominational. No magazine. Turnover n/a.

†**Venturers Norfolk Broads Cruise**, 5 Raymond Avenue, South Woodford, London E18 2HF
☎Mobile 07768 492 900
E: tsmith2020@aol.com
Web: www.venturers.org.uk
Christian sailing holiday for teens every Easter, Norfolk Broads; AALA licensed.
Hon Secretary: Mr T J Smith. No full-time staff. **CC** No.262348. Began 1946; interdenominational. No magazine. Turnover £12,000 to year end Dec 02.

***Viva Network**, PO Box 633, Oxford OX2 0YX
☎01865 320 100 🖷01865 320 101
E: helpdesk@viva.org
Web: www.viva.org
A global network of Christians passionately concerned for children at risk.
International Director: Mr Patrick McDonald. No full-time staff. **CC** No.1053389. Began 2003; interdenominational. (Previously Viva UK). No magazine. Turnover n/a.

***What4**, PO Box 579, Folkestone CT19 4WZ
☎0870 240 6796 M: 07889 524 954
E: info@what4.org.uk
Web: www.what4.org.uk
Mobilising the emerging generation for local and global mission through training, resourcing and going.
National Director: Rev Dave Barker. *Projects Manager:* Mr Ben Stringer. Executive staff 5, Admin staff 6. **CC** No.295567. Began 1994; interdenominational. Magazine: *What 4* (15,000 half-yearly). Turnover £110,000 to year end Mar 05.

Winchester Diocesan Youth and Children, Faith Development Department, Church House, 9 The Close, Winchester SO23 9LS
☎01962 624 779 ext 233
🖷01962 841 815
E: teresa.forward@winchester.anglican.org
Web: www.winchester.anglican.org
Training, resourcing and supporting parishes in delivering youth and children's ministry.
Field Officers: Pete Maidment, Jacqui Lea, Diana Lester. Executive staff 3. **CC** No.249276. Began n/a; Anglican. Magazine: *Youth News* (Circulation n/a quarterly). Turnover n/a.

S

Wise Up, Community Wise, Ocklynge Road, Eastbourne BN21 1PY
☎01323 721 047
E: info@wiseup.info
Web: www.wiseup.info
Working with groups of teenage girls promoting chastity and positive emotional, physical and spiritual health.
Project Leader: Julia Daynes. Executive staff 1, Other staff 4. ***CC*** No.1082841. Began 2001; interdenominational. No magazine. Turnover £31,000 to year end Dec 02.

Word of Life Ministries (UK) Ltd, 172 Main Street, Stenhousemuir, Larbert FK5 3JP
☎01324 559 444 🖷01324 558 535
E: Kelsowoluk@blueyonder.co.uk or wadsworthwoluk@blueyonder.co.uk
Web: www.woluk.org
Serving local churches through children's work, youth evangelism, discipleship; adult missions, residential youth holidays.
Director: Rev David Kelso. *Residential Holidays Director:* Mr Alan Wadsworth. Executive staff 2, Other staff 6. ***CC*** No.283041. Began 1980; interdenominational. No magazine. Turnover n/a.
South-west office 15 Waltham Way, Ivybridge PL21 0YF
☎01752 691 065

†YMCA, England, 640 Forest Road, London E17 3DZ
☎020 8520 5599 🖷020 8509 3190
Web: www.ymca.org.uk
Supporting 160 autonomous local YMCAs helping young people grow in body, mind and spirit.
National Secretary: Angela Sarkis CBE. Executive Staff n/a. ***CC*** No.212810. Began 1844; non-denominational. (Previously National Council of YMCAs). No magazine. Turnover £33,000,000 to year end Mar 02.

YMCA, Hove, 17 Marmion Road, Hove BN3 5FS
☎01273 731 724 🖷01273 715 449
E: info@hoveymca.org.uk
Web: www.hoveymca.org.uk
Youth and community work with a focus on the homeless and excluded young people.
Chief Executive: Mr David Standing. *Chair:* Mr Ian Chisnall. Executive staff 8, Other staff 130. ***CC*** No.1079570. Began 1919; non-denominational. No magazine. Turnover n/a.

†YMCA, Lisburn, 28 Market Square, Lisburn BT28 1AG
☎028 9267 0918 🖷028 9266 7573
E: cl@lisburny.fsnet.co.uk
Web: www.lisburnymca.com
Providing training, education, sports and community activities to young people in the community.
General Secretary: Mrs Claire Hanna. Executive staff 5, Other staff 11. ***CC*** No.LXN 45820. Began 1988; non-denominational. No magazine. Turnover £320,000 to year end Apr 03.

†YMCA, Scotland, 11 Rutland Street, Edinburgh EH1 2AE
☎0131 228 1464 🖷0131 228 5462
E: info@ymcascotland.org
Web: www.ymcascotland.org
Providing programmes and services, especially for young people, to enable growth, development and maturity in Christ.
National General Secretary: Peter Crory. Executive staff 5, Other staff 48. ***CC*** No.SCO 13792. Began 1844; interdenominational. No magazine. Turnover £1,177,382 to year end Mar 03.

Young Christian Workers, St Joseph's, Watford Way, London NW4 4TY
☎020 8203 6290 🖷020 8203 6291
E: ycworkers@aol.com
Web: www.ycwimpact.com
Helping young working people develop their Christian faith and play an active part in society.
National President: Mr Danny Curtin. Executive staff 1, Other staff n/a. ***CC*** No.306149. Began 1937; interdenominational. Magazine: *Real Life* (500 every four months). Turnover £150,000 to year end Mar 03.

Young Friends General Meeting, 1046 Bristol Road, Selly Oak, Birmingham B29 6LJ
☎0121 472 1998 🖷0121 472 1998
E: yfgm@quaker.org.uk
Web: www.yfgm.quaker.org.uk
Organising social and spiritual gatherings for Quakers and enquirers aged 18 to 30.
Coordinator: Ellie Colyer. No full-time staff. ***CC*** No.1064763. Began 1911; Religious Society of Friends. (Previously Young Friends Central Committee). Magazine: *Young Quaker* (270 monthly). Turnover £30,000 to year end Dec 02.

Young Life Holidays, Spring Cottage, Spring Road, Leeds LS6 1AD
☎0113 275 3565 🖷0113 230 4363
E: holidays@younglife.org.uk
Web: www.younglife.org.uk
Evangelistic programme of holidays for young people; promoting Christian discipleship.
Chairman: Mr T Knight. No full-time staff. ***CC*** No.207899. Began 1911; interdenominational. Part of Young Life. No magazine. Turnover £80,000 to year end Dec 05.

Youth Connection, PO Box 266, Staines TW18 4GP
☎0870 286 3136 M 07976 877 790
🖷0870 286 3136
E: youthconnect@aol.com
Web: www.youthconnection.org.uk
Informing youth leaders of what is happening locally, nationally.
Director: Mr Barry Mockford. No full-time staff. ***CC*** No.1031597. Began 1997; interdenominational. (Previously Barry Mockford). No magazine. Turnover £2,000 to year end Dec 04.

***Youth For Christ Northern Ireland**, Manley House, 56 Newforge Lane, Belfast BT9 5NW
☎028 9066 7980 🖷028 9066 7981
E: info@yfcni.org
Web: www.yfcni.org
Evangelising, discipling and mobilising young people through local centres, events, schoolwork, summer and year-out teams.
National Director: Mr Stuart Hamilton. Executive staff 15. ***CC*** No.XN 48776. Began 1947; interdenominational. Magazine: *YFC News* (3,500 monthly). Turnover £415,000 to year end Mar 00.

†Youth Link, 143a University Street, Belfast BT7 1HP
☎028 9032 3217
🖷028 9032 3247
E: info@youthlink.org.uk
Web: www.youthlink.org.uk
Inter-church training and service agency for youth leaders and young people.
Director: Rev Patrick White. Executive staff 4, Other staff 2. ***CC*** Began 1[illegible]43; interdenominational. (Previously The Churches Youth Service Council). No magazine. Turnover n/a.

***Youth With A Mission (YWAM)**, Highfield Oval, Ambrose Lane, Harpenden AL5 4[illegible]X
☎01582 463 216
🖷01582 463 213
E: enquiries@oval.com
Web: www.ywam-england.com
Mobilising youth to fulfil the great commission through evangelism, training and mercy ministries.
Director England: Mr Donovan Palmer. Executive staff 25. ***CC*** No.26407[illegible]. Began 1972; interdenominational. Magazine: *Advance* (1,600 quarterly) Turnover £2,500,000 to year end Aug 0[illegible].
Northern Ireland: *Director Northern Ireland:* Mr Mike Oman, 45 Closkelt Road, Ballyward, Castlewellan BT31 9[illegible]F
E: niywam@aol.com
☎028 4067 1919
Scotland: *Director Scotland:* Mr An[illegible] Hall, The Seamill Missionary Training Centre, 9 Glenbryde Road, Seamill, West Kilbride KA23 9NJ
E: seamill@ywamscotland.org
☎01294 829 400
🖷 01294 829 312
Wales: *Director Wales:* Mark Ve[illegible]ing, PO Box 5, Llangollen LL20 8ZG
E: north-wales@ywam.co.uk

†*YWCA of England & Wales, Clarendon House, 52 Cornmarket Street, Oxford OX1 3EJ
☎01865 304 200
🖷01865 204 805
Web: www.ywca-gb.org
Working with young women aged 11 to 30, enabling them to overcome discrimination and disadvantage.
Joint Presidents: Ms Alison Crookes, Ms Sarah Armstrong. Staff 260. ***CC*** Began 1855; interdenominational. (Previously YWCA of Great Britain). No magazine. Turnover £6,000,000 to year end Mar 02.

†YWCA of Scotland, 7 Randolph Crescent, Edinburgh EH3 7TH
☎No telephone
🖷0131 225 1052
E: info@ywcascotland.org
Providing supported accommodation and welfare services for young women.
Chief Executive: Ms Elaine Samson. Executive staff 1. ***CC*** No.SCO 341[illegible]2. Began 1855; interdenominational. Turnover n/a.

S

TRAINING

T

BIBLE STUDY AGENCIES

See also Bible Distributors & Publishers on Page 84.

***Bible Alive**, Oak Tree Cottage, Haughton, Tarporley CW6 9RN
☎01270 629 323 Ⓜ: 07831 217 148
🖷 01270 625 914
E: ask@bible-alive.co.uk
Web: www.bible-alive.co.uk
Promoting Bible teaching through church seminars and presentations; providing preaching and worship resources.
Director: Nic Willis. Executive staff 1, No other staff. Began 1997; interdenominational. No magazine. Turnover n/a.

Bible Fellowship Union, 5 Simmonds Road, Hucclecote, Gloucester GL3 3WY
☎ No telephone
Publishing Scriptural literature.
Editor: Mr Derrick Nadal. No full-time staff. ***CC*** No.1064607. Began 1946; non-denominational. Magazine: *Bible Study Monthly* (Circulation n/a every two months). Turnover n/a.

Bible Reading Fellowship, First Floor, Elsfield Hall, 15 Elsfield Way, Oxford OX2 8FG
☎ 01865 319 700 🖷 01865 319 701
E: enquiries@brf.org.uk
Web: www.brf.org.uk
Helping people of all ages to encounter the living God through Bible reading and prayer.
Chief Executive Officer: Mr Richard Fisher. Executive staff 1, Other staff 19. ***CC*** No.233280. Began 1922; interdenominational. No magazine. Turnover n/a.

The Big Picture, Downwood, Claverton Down Road, Bath BA2 6DT
☎ 01225 445 595 🖷 01225 445 121
E: ourbestfriend@btinternet.com
Providing a panoramic view of the Bible in word and song.
Director: Mr Robert Hicks. Staff n/a. Began 2003; interdenominational. No magazine. Turnover n/a.

Catholic Biblical Association, PO Box 6201, Edgbaston, Birmingham B16 9LB
☎ 0121 472 3040
Promoting knowledge and love of the Bible; publishing articles which further this aim.
Hon Secretary: Sr M T Roberts MMM. No full-time staff. ***CC*** No.215454. Began 1940; Roman Catholic. Magazine: *Scripture Bulletin* (Circulation n/a half-yearly). Turnover £2,000 to year end Dec 04.

***Christian Women Communicating International in UK**, 24 Hilltop Avenue, Great Glenn, Leicester LE8 9EE
☎ 0116 259 3856
E: info@cwci.uk.com
Web: www.cwci.uk.com
Bible teaching ministry for women through conferences, seminars and Know Your Bible study groups.
Finance Director: Mrs Sharon Jones. Admin staff 1, Other staff 1. ***CC*** No.1002596. Began 1978; interdenominational. Magazine: *Newslink* (3,500 half-yearly). Turnover £14,499 to year end Jun 05.

***Community Bible Study International, UK**, New Welbury Farmhouse, Welbury Park, Hitchin SG5 3BP
☎ 01462 768 627 Ⓜ: 07831 499 858
🖷 01462 763 320
E: veronicaAlvarez@compuserve.com
Web: www.communitybiblestudyuk.com
Offering local classes, UK home study materials, group discussion, teaching; leadership training and support.
Regional Director: Mrs Veronica Alvarez. No full-time staff. ***CC*** No.1044255. Began 1990; non-denominational. In partnership with Community Bible Study International, USA. Magazine: *Newsletter* (550 half-yearly). Turnover £16,000 to year end Aug 00.

†The Concordant Bible Society of Great Britain, New House, Woodside Street, Cinderford GL14 2NL
☎ 01452 421 224
Restoring the original meaning of the Divine Word by the concordant method of translation.
Hon Secretary: Mr David Osgood. No full-time staff. ***CC*** No.281860. Began 1975; interdenominational. No magazine. Turnover n/a.

***CWR (Crusade for World Revival)**, Waverley Abbey House, Waverley Lane, Farnham GU9 8EP
☎ 01252 784 731 🖷 01252 784 734
E: mail@cwr.org.uk
Web: www.cwr.org.uk
Publishing Bible reading notes and other resources; helping people read and understand the Bible; 130 countries.
Chief Executive: Mr Mick Brooks. *Business Manager:* Mr Eddie Oliffe. *Head of Sales & Marketing:* Mr Mike Ashford. Executive staff 6, Other staff 46. ***CC*** No.294387. Began 1965; interdenominational. Magazines: *Every Day with Jesus* (Circulation n/a every two months), *YP's*, *Topz* (Circulation n/a every two months), *Inspiring Women Every Day* (Circulation n/a every two months). Turnover £2,957,000 to year end Dec 04.

***Geared for Growth**, 2 Windermere Road, Carnforth LA5 9AR
☎ 01524 734 797
E: anne@gearedforgrowth.co.uk
Web: www.gearedforgrowth.co.uk
Using Bible studies as tool for evangelism, spiritual and church growth, imparting mission vision.
Ministry Leader: Anne Jenkins. Executive staff 15. ***CC*** No.237005. Began 1970; interdenominational. (Previously The Word Worldwide). A ministry of WEC International. No magazine. Turnover £17,000 to year end Mar 02.

Grow with the Bible
Only contact through Email.
E: mail@grow-with-the-bible.org.uk
Web: www.grow-with-the-bible.org.uk
A joint initiative to encourage regular Bible reading.
Project Coordinator: Name not supplied. No full-time staff. Began 1996; non-denominational. Bible Society, BRF, CWR, Hodder and Stoughton, IBRA, Salvation Army, Scripture Union. No magazine. Turnover n/a.

International Bible Reading Association, 1020 Bristol Road, Selly Oak, Birmingham B29 6LB
☎ 0121 472 4242
🖷 0121 472 7575
E: ibra@christianeducation.org.uk
Web: www.christianeducation.org.uk/ibra.htm
Publishing two different Bible reading notes, 25,000 annually, distributed in [illegible]0 countries.
Chief Executive: Peter Fishpool. Executive staff 1, Other staff 13. ***CC*** No.108699[illegible]. Began 1882; non-denominational. No magazine. Turnover n/a.

***Purley & Andover Christian Trust**, 4 Humberstone Road, Andover SP10 2E[illegible]
☎ 01264 352 587
E: info@bible4today.com
Web: www.bible4today.com
Making the Bible plain by all and every means possible, at home and abroad.
Director: Rev Frank Cooke. Executive staff 1. ***CC*** No.272729. Began 1977; interdenominational. No magazine. Turnover £11,000 to year end Aug 00.

Radio Bible Class (Europe) Trust, PO Box 1[illegible], Carnforth LA5 9ES
☎ 01539 564 149
🖷 01539 564 388
E: england@rbc.org
Web: www.rbc.org.uk
Distributing Bible study resources, booklets, video library, audio tapes.
Regional Director: Mr K Gregory. Executive staff 2, Other staff 9. ***CC*** No.3[illegible]7384. Began 1964; interdenominational. Magazine: *Our Daily Bread* (250,000 quarterly). Turnover n/a.

†Small Group Resources, 1 Hilton Place, Harehills, Leeds LS8 4HE
☎ 0113 237 4974
🖷 0113 237 4964
E: sgr@spark.uk.net
Writing and publishing materials and training leaders for small group learning, growth and Bible exploration.
Partners: Mr Chris Powell, Mr Pete Richardson. No full-time staff. Began 1985; interdenominational. No magazine. Turnover n/a.

Walk Thru the Bible Ministries, Claire Road Business Park, Kirby Cross, Frinton-on-Sea CO13 0LY
☎ 01255 850 600 🖷 01255 850 700
E: walkthru@bible.org.uk
Web: www.bible.org.uk
Providing the 'big picture' of the Bible through seminars, videos, CDs and publications.
Director: Cliff Keeys. Executive staff 1, Other staff 6. **CC** No.299722. Began 1984; interdenominational. Associated with World Teach. No magazine. Turnover £200,000 to year end Dec 02.

***Word of Life**, PO Box 14, Oldham OL1 3WW
☎ 0161 628 4051
🖷 0161 628 4051
E: info@word.org.uk
Web: www.word.org.uk
Publishing and distributing Bible courses for British Muslims in English, Persian, Arabic, Urdu, Bengali and Farsi.
Director: Mr Keith Wood. Executive staff 1. Other staff 3. **CC** No.328492. Began 1988; interdenominational. No magazine. Turnover £20,000 to year end Dec 02.

***Wordplus**, The Kings Centre, King Street, Norwich NR1 1PH
☎ 01603 765 795
🖷 01603 285 265
E: wordplus@kings-norwich.com
Web: www.wordplus.co.uk
Modular training scheme covering basic systematic theology, for use in churches and regions; worldwide.
Director: Goff Hope. Admin staff 1. **CC** No.1083049. Began 1995; interdenominational. No magazine. Turnover n/a.

CONVENTIONS, BIBLE WEEKS, EXHIBITIONS & FESTIVALS

Affinity Events Ltd, PO Box 117, Chepstow NP16 5SX
☎ 0845 0900 183
M: 07778 532 842
🖷 0845 0900 193
E: info@affinityevents.co.uk
Web: www.affinityevents.co.uk
Helping Christians organise conferences, concerts, festivals, youth and other events.
Managing Director: Mr Alan Wallace. Executive staff 3, Admin staff 4. Began 2001; non-denominational. No magazine. Turnover £420,000 to year end Jul 04.

The Apostolic Church International Convention, 17 Tawe Business Village, Phoenix Way, Enterprise Park, Swansea SA7 9LA
☎ 01792 790 300 🖷 01792 790 363
E: admin@apostolic-church.org
Web: www.apostolic-church.org
Annual convention held in Penygroes, Carmarthenshire in August for the deepening of spiritual life.
Administrative Secretary: Mr Andrew Saunders. Admin staff 1, Other staff n/a. **CC** No.284789. Began n/a; Apostolic Church. No magazine. Turnover £1,458,446 to year end Mar 03.

Bible Ventures, PO Box 589, Sharnbrook, Bedford MK44 1ZN
☎ 01234 781 946
M: 07929 341 309
E: howardemmaus@yahoo.co.uk
Web: www.bibleventures.org
Emmaus Road Show, high-tech exhibition visiting schools and churches. CD-Roms and 35mm slides available.
Director: Mr Howard Roberts. Executive staff 4, Other staff 2. **CC** No.327400. Began 1985; interdenominational. (Previously Bible Scene Multimedia). No magazine. Turnover n/a.

T

Bibleworld & Mobile Bibleworld, Bible House, 7 Hampton Terrace, Edinburgh EH12 5XU
☎ 0131 337 9701
🖷 0131 337 0641
E: bibleworld@scottishbiblesociety.org
Web: www.scottishbiblesociety.org
Hi-tech exhibition and mobile experience for late primary/early secondary school children in Scotland.
Educational Exhibition Manager: Mrs Sandra Batt. Admin staff 4, Other staff n/a. ***CC*** No.SCO 10767. Began 1861; interdenominational. The Scottish Bible Society. No magazine. Turnover n/a.

***Bournemouth & Poole Bible Convention**, 73 Northfield Road, Ringwood BH24 1LT
☎ 01425 473 464
Annual Bible convention, four nights in June.
Secretary: Mr Peter Hardy. No paid staff. Began 1950; interdenominational. No magazine. Turnover £1,500 to year end Dec 00.

Carey Conference, 1 The Saddlery, The Chase, Newton Aycliffe DL5 7LY
☎ 01325 310 530
M: 07703 464 971
E: john.rubens@evangelicalpress.org
Web: www.reformation-today.org
Annual national conferences for Reformed Baptist ministers and their families.
Organising Secretary: Mr John Rubens. No full-time staff. ***CC*** No.101700. Began 1970; Baptist. No magazine. Turnover n/a.

†Catholic People's Week, 89 Marlborough Park Avenue, Sidcup DA15 9DY
☎ 020 8300 4432
Web: www.c-p-w.ic24.net
Organising holiday family study weeks in all parts of the country.
Hon Secretary: Mr Ted Monks. No full-time staff. ***CC*** No.241556. Began 1945; Roman Catholic. No magazine. Turnover n/a.

***Christian Resources Exhibitions Ltd**, 2 Forge House, Summerleys Road, Princes Risborough HP27 9DT
☎ 01844 271 476 🖷 01844 344 988
E: cre@resourcex.co.uk
Web: www.creonline.co.uk
Exhibitions of resources for churches and Christians in Belfast, Coventry, Edinburgh, Esher, Exeter, Harrogate, Manchester; Australia.
Chairman: Mr Gospatric Home. Executive staff 8. Began 1985; interdenominational. Magazine: *Exhibitions Handbooks* (Circulation n/a per exhibition). Turnover £700,000 to year end Dec 05.

Church Supplies Exhibitions, Farncombe View, Hungerford Hill, Lambourn, Hungerford RG17 8NP
☎ 01488 710 77 🖷 01488 710 77
E: info@churchsupplies.org.uk
Web: www.churchsuppliesexhibitions.co.uk
Holding exhibitions in Christian venues of resources for the Christian church.
Manager: Mr A Jones. Executive staff 2, Other staff 2. Began 2003; interdenominational. Turnover £40,000 to year end Oct 04.

Epworth Old Rectory, 1 Rectory Street, Epworth, Doncaster DN9 1HX
☎ 01427 872 268
E: curator@epwortholdrectory.org.uk
Web: www.epwortholdrectory.org.uk
John Wesley's boyhood home, built 1709. Guided tours, portraits, Methodist memorabilia, physic garden.
Curator/Warden: Joan Sidaway. Admin staff 1. Began 1954; Methodist. No magazine. Turnover n/a.

†Flames of Fire/Fflamau Tan, 18 Coychurch Road, Pencoed, Bridgend CF35 5NG
☎ 01656 864 476 🖷 01656 864 476
E: enquiries@flamesoffire.co.uk
Web: www.flamesoffire.co.uk
Running Christian family camp/conference to bring people into renewal.
Conference Coordinator: Rev Nicholas Jones. Executive staff 1. ***CC*** No.1053180. Began n/a; Anglican. Part of Anglican Renewal Ministries - Wales. No magazine. Turnover £40,000 to year end Jun 02.

***Focusfest**, 114a Hollywood Road, Belfast BT4 1NU
☎ 028 9047 1100 🖷 028 9047 1190
E: focusfest@emins.com
Major event for women.
Chair Person: Mrs Margaret Ferguson. Admin staff 2. ***CC*** Began 1993; interdenominational. (Previously Feminine Focus). No magazine. Turnover n/a.

Grapevine, 1a Beaumont Fee, Lincoln LN1 1UH
☎ 01522 533 535 🖷 01522 533 636
E: admin@groundlevel.org.uk
Web: www.grapevinecelebration.org.uk
Family celebration camp August Bank Holiday weekend, offering worship, teaching, ministry for all ages.
Operations Manager: Mr Paul Berger. *Team Leader:* Mr Stuart Bell. Executive staff 4, Admin staff 3. ***CC*** No.1001[illegible]99. Began 1982; interdenominational. Part of Ground Level. No magazine. Turnover £400,000 to year end Dec 0[illegible].

Greenbelt Festivals, All Hallows on the Wall, 83 London Wall, London EC2M 5ND
☎ 020 7374 2755 🖷 020 7374 27[illegible]1
E: info@greenbelt.org.uk
Web: www.greenbelt.org.uk
Annual Christian arts festival held August Bank Holiday at Cheltenham Racecourse.
Sales Manager: Ms Beki Bateson. Executive staff 2, Other staff 4. ***CC*** No.28[illegible]372. Began 1974; non-denominational. Partner with Christian Aid. No magazine. Turnover n/a.

ICC Conferences, 4-5 Regency Mews, Silverdale Road, Eastbourne BN20 7A[illegible]
☎ 01323 643 341 🖷 01323 649 24[illegible]
E: info@icc.org.uk
Web: www.icc.org.uk
Providing on-site recording, duplication and sales services at conferences and other events.
Conference Manager: Mr Andy Hooper. Executive staff 2, Other staff 40. ***CC*** No.1079801. Began 1976; interdenominational. No magazine. Turnover included in ICC.

International Ecumenical Fellowship, 59 Old High Street, Headington, Oxford OX3 9HT
☎ 01865 762 247
E: jill@freston.fslife.co.uk
Web: www.iefnet.org or www.uk-ief.co.uk
International ecumenical encounters at the grassroots, especially through eucharistic worship, fellowship, study and conferences.
Hon Secretary: Miss Jill Freston. All voluntary staff. ***CC*** No.272271. Began 196[illegible]; interdenominational. No magazine. Turnover £3,500 to year end Dec 02.

***The Keswick Convention**, Skiddaw Street, Keswick, Cumbria CA12 4BY
☎ 01435 866 034 🖷 01435 865 837
E: info@keswickministries.org
Web: www.keswickministries.org
Bible convention with emphasis on practical, biblical holiness; three weeks in July/August; Lake District.
Operations Manager: Mr Simon Overend. Admin staff 7, Other staff 2. ***CC*** No.1083584. Began 1875; interdenominational. Magazine: *Newsletter* (6,000 half-yearly). Turnover n/a.

Keswick-in-Wales Convention, Carneddau, Highbury Field, Llanyre, Llandrindod Wells LD1 6NF
☎ 01597 822 700 🖷 01445 701 491
E: info@keswickinwales.org.uk
Web: www.keswickinwales.com
Five-day event in Llandrindod Wells for deepening spiritual life; commencing first Monday in August.
Hon Secretary: Mr John W Mitson. No full-time staff. Began 1903; interdenominational. No magazine. Turnover £8,300 to year end Oct 04.

Kingdom Faith Bible Week, Roffey, Faygate, Horsham RH12 4RU
☎ 01293 851 543
🖷 01293 854 610
E: conferences@kingdomfaith.com
Web: www.kingdomfaith.com
Proclaiming the Gospel, renewal and revival; East of England Showground, Peterborough.
Director: Rev Colin Urquhart. Staff n/a. **CC** No.278746. Began 1978; non-denominational. Magazine: *Impact* (Circulation n/a quarterly). Turnover n/a.

Living Water, The Well Christian Centre, Swaffham Road, Ashill, Thetford IP25 7ET
☎ 01760 441 441
🖷 01760 441 441
E: office@living-water.org.uk
Web: www.living-water.org.uk
Annual all-age camping event at Norfolk Showground, Norwich UK; August. National and international speakers.
Events Manager: Mrs Heather Nunn. Executive staff 1. **CC** No.1037997. Began 1994; interdenominational. No magazine. Turnover £160,000 to year end Jun 05.

New Horizon, 12 Killyvally Road, Garvagh, Coleraine BT51 5JZ
☎ 028 2955 7157 🖷 028 2955 7157
E: office@newhorizon.org.uk
Web: www.newhorizon.org.uk
Week of Christian teaching, worship and fellowship for all ages.
Chairman: Rev John Kirkpatrick. *Administrator:* Mrs Shirley Taylor. Admin staff 1. **CC** No.XR 246C/1. Began 1989; interdenominational. No magazine. Turnover £200,000 to year end Dec 04.

New Wine, 4a Ridley Avenue, Ealing, London W13 9XW
☎ 020 8567 6717 🖷 020 8799 3770
E: info@new-wine.org
Web: www.new-wine.org
National and regional conferences for families, church leaders, men, women and those working with children.
Head of Operations: Phil George. Leadership team 7, Other staff 14. **CC** No.1043763. Began 1989; interdenominational. Magazine: *New Wine* (213,500 every four months). Turnover n/a.
New Wine North, 4 Kemp Road, Marple Bridge, Stockport SK6 5BU
☎ 0161 427 2554
E: jean.tripp@new-wine.org
Administrator: Jean Tripp.

***Michael Reid Ministries Conferences**, 49 Coxtie Green Road, Pilgrims Hatch, Brentwood CM14 5PS
☎ 01277 372 996 🖷 01277 375 046
E: info@michaelreidministries.org
Web: www.michaelreidministries.org
Conferences throughout the year; church leaders' seminars held monthly.
Principal: Dr Michael S B Reid. Executive staff 5, Admin staff 10. Began 1977; Pentecostal but open to all. (Previously Peniel Pentecostal Church Conferences). Magazine: *Miracles, Healing, Faith* (Circulation n/a quarterly). Turnover n/a.

Revival Fire Conferences Ltd, PO Box 77, Maidstone ME14 1WF
☎ 0870 901 7777 🖷 0870 902 7777
E: admin@revivalfire.org.uk
Web: www.revivalfire.org.uk
Organising Christian conferences, main event Bible Week at the Kent County Showground, August.
Office Manager: Mrs Helen Bailey. Executive staff 4, Other staff 2. Began 1997; interdenominational. No magazine. Turnover £200,000 to year end Dec 02.

***Spring Harvest**, 14 Horsted Square, Uckfield TN22 1QG
☎ 01825 769 111 🖷 01825 769 141
E: info@springharvest.org
Web: www.springharvest.org
Annual event including teaching, worship, relaxation; equipping the Church for action.
Executive Director: Mr Alan D Johnson. Executive staff 1, Other staff 40. **CC** No.1014540. Began 1979; interdenominational. No magazine. Turnover n/a.

Wigwam Acoustics Ltd, Unit 6, Junction 19, Industrial Estate, Heywood OL10 1NB
☎ Sales 01706 363 400
Hire 01706 363 800
🖷 Sales 01706 363 410
Hire 01706 363 810
E: sales@wigwam.co.uk
Web: www.wigwam.co.uk
Supplying professional sound equipment for hire, sale and installation, consultancy service; sound hire for conferences.
Managing Director: Mr Mike Spratt. Executive staff 4, Other staff 30. Began 1978; non-denominational. No magazine. Turnover £2,300,000 to year end Feb 96.

***Word for Women - Swanwick**, 289 Lordswood Road, Birmingham B17 8PR
☎ 0121 429 3273
E: wearn@tesco.net
Web: wordforwomen.co.uk
Annual conference each September; practical Bible teaching with nationally known speakers; for women of all ages.
Team Leader: Mrs Pat Wearn. No full-time staff. Began 1967; interdenominational. (Previously Swanwick Ladies' Conference). No magazine. Turnover n/a.

***Worldwide Missionary Convention**, 15 Aldergrange Avenue, Newtownards BT23 4FY
☎ 028 9181 7845
E: secretary@worldwidemission.org
Web: worldwidemission.org
Held in Bangor, Northern Ireland; last week in August
Hon Secretary: Mr Eddie Currie. No full-time staff. Began 1937; non-denominational. No magazine. Turnover £170,000 to year end Dec 02.

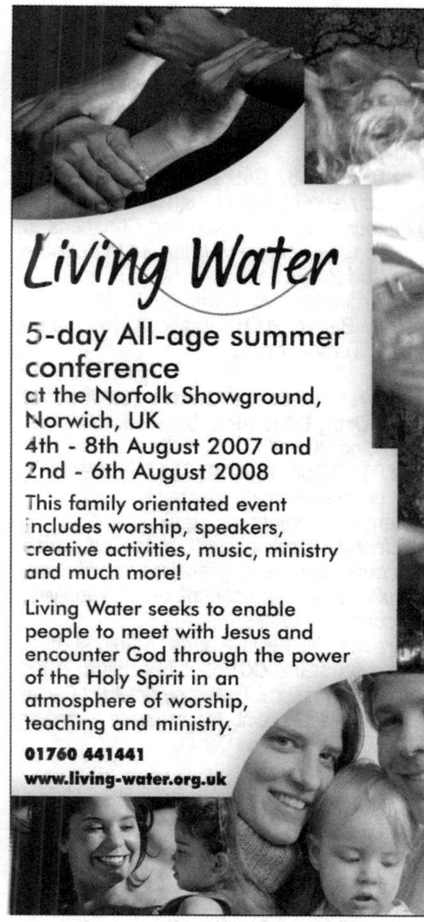

Wye Valley Christian Festival, Gorsley Chapel, Gorsley, Ross-on-Wye HR9 7SE
☎ 01989 720 312
E: festival@gorsleychapel.co.uk
Web: www.gorsleychapel.co.uk
Weekend mini-break for all ages; Bible teaching; seeker friendly events; camping facilities.
Festival Director: Pastor John Lewis. Executive staff 2, Other staff 2. **CC** No.246198. Began 2000; Baptist but open to all. No magazine. Turnover n/a.

Youthwork: The Conference, PO Box 50, Uckfield TN22 1ZG
☎ 0870 060 3327
🖷 0870 060 3328
E: info@youthworkconference.co.uk
Web: www.youthworkconference.co.uk
A weekend event to equip, inspire and resource the church for effective youth work and ministry.
Chairman: Russ Rook. No full-time staff. Began 2003; interdenominational. In partnership with Alove, Oasis Youth Action, Spring Harvest, YFC, Youthwork magazine. Magazine: *Youthwork* (7,500 every two months). Turnover n/a.

T

EDUCATIONAL AGENCIES

Adult Education Team, Bouverie Court, Diocesan Conference & Training Centre, The Lakes, Bedford Road, Northampton NN4 7YD
☎ 01604 887 049 🖷 01604 887 077
E: bouverie@peterborough-diocese.org.uk
Encouraging and equipping Christians in life-long learning and living as the people of God 24/7.
Co-ordinator: Mr Chris Peck. No other staff. Began 2001; Anglican. No magazine. Turnover n/a.

***Amethyst Resource Centre for Alcohol and Drug Education**, 5 Berkeley Avenue, Reading RG1 6EL
☎ 0118 958 9400 🖷 0118 958 9400
E: drugsed@amethyst.org.uk
Web: www.amethyst.org.uk
Offering alcohol and drug education through speakers, literature distribution, multi-media presentations; supplying alcohol-free drinks.
Director: Mr Kevin Woods. Admin staff 1, Education staff 2. ***CC*** No.235564. Began 1832; interdenominational. (Previously Amethyst Centre for Alcohol Concern). No magazine. Turnover £81,000 to year end Dec 02.

***Anvil Trust**, 104 Townend Lane, Deepcar, Sheffield S36 2TS
☎ 0114 288 8816 M: 07881 541 432
🖷 0114 288 8827
E: office@anvil.org.uk
Web: www.anvil.org.uk
Committed to Christian thinking, training and action in Britain and worldwide. See also Workshop, Supplyline.
Programme Coordinator: Mr Noel Moules. Executive staff 2. ***CC*** No.1010354. Began 1983; interdenominational. No magazine. Turnover n/a.

†The Archbishops' Examination in Theology (Lambeth Diploma), St John's House, St John's Wood High Street, London NW8 7NE
☎ 020 7586 3864 🖷 020 7586 3864
Providing opportunity for theological study by examination syllabus or thesis (STh and MA).
Hon Secretary: Rev Dr Anders Bergquist. No full-time staff. Began 1906; Anglican, but open to all. No magazine. Turnover n/a.

Bloxham Project, 29 Leicester Lane, Desford, Leicester LE9 9JJ
☎ 01455 824 089 🖷 01455 824 089
E: admin@bloxhamproject.org.uk
Web: www.bloxhamproject.org.uk
Developing spiritual education, school leadership, pastoral care; network for schools and Dioceses; consultancy, training, resources.
Director: Rev Alison Adams. *Chairman Trustees:* Rt Rev Peter Hullah. Executive staff 1, Admin staff 1. ***CC*** No.271220. Began 1967; ecumenical. Magazine: *Project Papers* (500 termly). Turnover £98,000 to year end Aug 05.

Bridge Pastoral Foundation, The Queen's College, Somerset Road, Edgbaston, Birmingham B15 2QH
☎ 0121 455 7996
E: admin@bridgepastoral.org.uk
Web: www.bridgepastoral.org.uk
Training in Christian pastoral care, pastoral counselling and personal growth.
Executive Director: Name not supplied. Executive staff 8, Other staff 5. ***CC*** No.296816. Began 1962; ecumenical. (Previously Clinical Theology Association). Magazine: *Contact: Interdisciplinary Journal* (600 every four months). Turnover £65,000 to year end Dec 02.

British and Irish Association for Mission Studies, Henry Martyn Centre, Westminster College, Cambridge CB3 0AA
☎ 01223 741 088 🖷 01223 741 089
E: pk262@cam.ac.uk
Web: www.martynmission.cam.ac.uk/biams.htm
Promoting study of the history, theology and practice of Christian mission.
Secretary: Ms Emma Wild Wood. No full-time staff. Began 1990; interdenominational. No magazine. Turnover n/a.

British Israel Bible Truth Fellowship, Manor Barn, Horsington, Templecombe BA8 0ET
☎ 01963 371 137 M 07710 604 777
E: bibtf@classicfm.net
Advancing Christian religion by proclaiming Anglo-Saxon Celtic people descend from biblical Israel and Judah.
General Secretary: Mr Paul Boyd-Lee. Admin staff 1, Other staff n/a. ***CC*** No.272447. Began 1974; interdenominational. Magazine: *Bible Truth* (1,000 every two months). Turnover £21,000 to year end Dec 02.

The British Israel World Federation, 121 Low Etherley, Bishop Auckland DL14 0HA
☎ 01388 834 395 🖷 01388 835 957
E: admin@britishisrael.co.uk
Web: www.britishisrael.co.uk
Studying the biblical prophecies concerning the descendants of the House of Israel.
Secretary: Mr David Aimer. Executive staff 3. ***CC*** No.208079. Began 1919; non-denominational. Magazine: *The Crown & Commonwealth* (2,500 quarterly). Turnover £130,000 to year end Mar 02.

Cambridge Theological Federation, Wesley House, Jesus Lane, Cambridge CB5 8BQ
☎ 01223 741 047 🖷 01223 321 [illegible]77
E: cpww2@cam.ac.uk
Web: www.theofed.cam.ac.uk
Coordinating all that is done together by the member bodies of the Federation.
Executive Officer: Mr Chris Wright. *Director of Postgraduate Studies in Pastoral Theology:* Ms Zoe Bennett. Executive staff 2, Other staff 5. ***CC*** Began 19[illegible]2; ecumenical. (Previously Cambridge Federation of Theological Colleges). No magazine. Turnover £180,000 to year end Aug 04.

Cardiff Adult Christian Education Centre, City Church, Windsor Place, Cardiff CF10 3BZ
☎ 029 2022 5190
🖷 029 2022 5190
E: admin@cityurc.org.uk
Web: www.cityurc.org.uk
Ecumenical study centre for adults.
Administrator: Mr Norman Preston. No full-time staff. ***CC*** No.1019993[illegible]. Began 1961; interdenominational. No magazine. Turnover £2,500 to year end Dec 04.

***CARE (Christian Action Research and Education)**, 53 Romney Street, London SW1P 3RF
☎ 020 7233 0455
🖷 020 7233 0983
E: enquiries@care.org.uk
Web: www.care.org.uk
Transforming society through political lobbying, social initiatives; at grassroots, government, national, international levels.
Chairman: Rev Lyndon Bowring. Executive staff 2, Other staff 60. ***CC*** No.1066963. Began 1983; interdenominational. Magazine: *CARE Prayer Guide* (50,000 quarterly), *CARE Today* (50,000 half-yearly). Turnover n/a.

Roman Catholic Bishops' Conference Department for Catholic Education & Formation, 39 Eccleston Square, London SW1V 1BX
☎ 020 7901 4845
🖷 020 7901 4819
Concerned with theology, Christian and ministerial formation, young people and education.
Chairman: Most Rev Vincent Nichols. No full-time staff. **CC** No.31314[illegible]. Began 1984; Roman Catholic. No magazine. Turnover n/a.

Note Each Diocese has an Officer for this area of ministry. Contact them via the appropriate Curial Office. See pages 151 to 153

Catholic Education Service for England & Wales, 39 Eccleston Square, London SW1V 1BX
☎ 020 7901 4880 🖷 020 7901 4893
E: general@cesew.org.uk
Web: www.cesew.org.uk
Promoting and supporting Catholic education in England and Wales.
Director: Oona Stannard. Executive staff 6, Other staff 5. **CC** No.313147. Began 1905; Roman Catholic. No magazine. Turnover £750,000 to year end Dec 02.

Catholic Independent Schools Conference, Wrigglebank, Mill Lane, Chetnole, Sherborne DT9 6PB
☎ 01935 873 409
Web: catholicindependentschools.org
Promoting Catholic independent education; providing support and an annual conference for Catholic Heads and Governors.
General Secretary: Mrs Mary Head. Executive staff 1, Admin staff 1. **CC** No.1033645. Began 1990; Roman Catholic. (Previously The Nineteen Nineties Group). No magazine. Turnover £109,000 to year end Mar 05.

***Cell UK**, Highfield Oval, Ambrose Lane, Harpenden AL5 4BX
☎ 01582 463 232 🖷 01582 463 305
E: celluk@oval.com
Web: www.celluk.org.uk
Encouraging the development of healthy cells in local churches.
Coordinator: Mr Trevor Withers. Executive staff 1, Other staff 3. **CC** Began 1995; interdenominational. Magazine: *Cell UK Magazine* (1,900 quarterly). Turnover £58,000 to year end Aug 02.

The Centre for the Study of Christianity & Sexuality, Sunnybank House, Holly Green, Upton upon Severn, Worcester WR8 0PG
☎ 01684 594 715 🖷 01684 594 715
E: cscs@revjane.demon.co.uk
Web: www.cscs.co.uk
Promoting dialogue within churches through journal, newsletters, seminars and workshops.
Chair: Rev Jane Fraser. No full-time staff. **CC** No.1070448. Began 1996; interdenominational. (Previously Institute for the Study of Christianity & Sexuality). Magazine: *Theology and Sexuality* (Circulation n/a half-yearly). Turnover £10,000 to year end Apr 01.

Centre for the Study of Implicit Religion & Contemporary Spirituality (CSIRCS), 95 High Street, Winterbourne, Bristol BS36 1RD
☎ 01454 776 518
E: eibailey@csircs.freeserve.co.uk
Web: www.implicitreligion.org
Stimulating study of overall individual and social commitments, in the light of study of religion.
Administrator: Mrs Diane Rix. No full-time staff. **CC** No.326876. Began 1978; non-denominational. Magazine: *Implicit Religion* (200 every four months). Turnover £2,000 to year end Jun 05.

Christian Education, 1020 Bristol Road, Selly Oak, Birmingham B29 6LB
☎ 0121 472 4242 🖷 0121 472 7575
E: enquiries@christianeducation.org.uk
Web: www.christianeducation.org.uk
Developing Christian education in the Church through consultations, training and publications.
Chief Executive: Peter Fishpool. Executive staff 1, Other staff 13. **CC** No.1086990. Began 1803; non-denominational. (Previously National Christian Education Council). No magazine. Turnover n/a.

***Christian Education Europe Ltd.**, Maranatha House, Unit 5, Northford Close, Shrivenham SN6 8HL
☎ 01793 783 783 🖷 01793 783 775
E: info@christian-education.org
Web: www.christian-education.org
Starting, supporting, supplying Christian schools and home educators with Bible-based curriculum and creationist literature.
Executive Director: Mr Arthur Roderick. Executive staff 2, Other staff 10. **CC** Began 1990; interdenominational. Ace Ministries. Magazine: *Accelerator* (1,000 frequency n/a). Turnover n/a.

Christian Educational Resources, Otterhill Farm, Rowtown, Addlestone KT15 1HD
☎ 01932 855 918 🖷 01932 855 918
E: tracyvdb@sermonaudio.com
Web: www.christian-education-uk.co.uk
Importing and distributing curriculum packages for Christian home education.
Proprietor: Mrs T van den Broek. Executive staff 1. Began 1990; evangelical. No magazine. Turnover n/a.

Christian Educator Network, 45 Trafalgar Road, Moseley, Birmingham B13 8BJ
☎ 0121 449 3156 M: 07814 017 804
🖷 0121 449 3156
E: david@isgroves.co.uk
Web: www.cenetwork.org.uk
Education consultancy; enabling Christian training organisations to gain secular accreditation; FE/HE links; networking UK, abroad.
Director: Mr David Isgrove. Executive staff 1. Began 1999; ecumenical. No magazine. Turnover n/a.

Christian Friends of Israel UK, CFI Communications, PO Box 2687, Eastbourne BN22 7LZ
☎ 01323 410 810 🖷 01323 410 211
E: info@cfi.org.uk
Web: cfi.org.uk
Educating Christians about Israel's situation; encouraging prayer; teaching about Jewish roots of Christian faith.
Director: Mr Roy Thurley. *Founder:* Mr Derek White. Executive staff 2, Other staff 10. **CC** No.1101899. Began 1985; interdenominational. No magazine. Turnover £500,000 to year end Dec 04.

Christian Rural Concern, 5 Cedar Court, Addington Road, South Croydon CR2 8RA
☎ 020 8657 0831
E: secretary@cres.org.uk
Web: www.cruc.org.uk
Correspondence courses and local groups addressing rural church and environmental issues from a Christian standpoint.
Course Director: Dr Martin Hodson. No full-time staff. **CC** No.328204. Began 1989; interdenominational. Magazine: *Countrywide Care* (200 half-yearly). Turnover £3,000 to year end June 05.

***The Christian Schools' Trust**, Havering Grange Centre, Havering Road, Romford RM1 4HR
☎ 01708 733 339
E: office@christianschoolstrust.co.uk
Web: www.christianschoolstrust.co.uk
Supporting, encouraging and strengthening independent Christian schools in the UK; developing and promoting Christian education.
Director: Mrs Hilary Reeves. Executive staff 5, Other staff 1. **CC** No.293315. Began 1989; non-denominational. No magazine. Turnover n/a.

†Church of Scotland Board of Parish Education, 21 Young Street, Edinburgh EH2 4HU
☎ 0131 260 3110 🖷 0131 260 3120
E: enquiries@parished.org.uk
Providing Christian education resources; production and training at national, presbytery and congregation levels.
General Secretary: Mr Iain W Whyte. Executive staff 2, Other staff 22. Began 1993; Church of Scotland. No magazine. Turnover £1,000,000 to year end Dec 02.

Church of Scotland Department of Education, 121 George Street, Edinburgh EH2 4YN
☎ 0131 225 5722 🖷 0131 220 3113
E: smleslie@cofscotland.org.uk
Web: www.cofs.org.uk
Church response to government legislation affecting state education; training school chaplains; religious education in schools.
General Secretary: Ms Susan Leslie. Executive staff 1, Admin staff 1. **CC** No.SCO 11353. Began 1827; Church of Scotland. Magazine: *School Chaplaincy Bulletin* (6,500 every two years). Turnover n/a.

Churches Tourism Association, c/o The Churches Conservation Trust, 1 West Smithfield, London EC1A 9EE
☎ 020 7213 0677
E: cshearer@tcct.org.uk
Web: www.churchestourismassociation.org.uk
Educating churches on the mission potential of tourism.
Hon Secretary: Colin Shearer. Executive staff 1. **CC** No.1101254. Began 1991; ecumenical. (Previously National Churches Tourism Group). Magazine: *Faith in Tourism* (250 quarterly). Turnover £5,000 to year end Jun 05. Cont. over

Registered Office: c/o Arthur Rank Centre, Stoneleigh Park, Kenilworth CV8 2LZ

Churches' Criminal Justice Forum, 39 Eccleston Square, London SW1V 1BX
☎ 020 7901 4878
Web: www.ccjf.org.uk
Upholding Christian values in criminal justice, raising awareness in churches, encouraging involvement in practical ways.
Criminal Justice Officer: Mr Francis Davies. Executive staff 2. Began 2002; ecumenical. No magazine. Turnover n/a.

Council on Biblical Manhood & Womanhood, 9 Epsom Road, Leamington Spa CV32 7AR
☎ No telephone
E: info@cbmw.org.uk
Web: www.cbmw.org.uk
Presenting a biblical vision of manhood and womanhood - equal yet different.
UK Agents: Pastor & Mrs Bill & Sharon James. Began 1998; non-denominational. No magazine. Turnover n/a.

Ecumenical Order of Ministry, Barnes Close, Malthouse Lane, Chadwich, Bromsgrove B61 0RA
☎ 01562 710 231 🖷 01562 710 278
E: cfrenquiry@aol.com or editor@e-o-m.co.uk
Web: www.e-o-m.co.uk
Mutual recognition of ministry; fellowship, united service; witness, shared proclamation of faith, symbol of unity.
Company Secretary: Mr David Tubb. Executive staff 2, Other staff 4. ***CC*** No.295113. Began 1990; ecumenical. Administered by Community for Reconciliation. Magazine: *Newslink* (450 quarterly). Turnover n/a.

†Educating for Life, 87 The Street, Hawkinge, Folkestone CT18 7DE
☎ 01303 892 799
E: monica@stringer8.fsnet.co.uk
Web: educatingforlife.net
Supporting and promoting Christ-centred education in independent Christian schools; home education.
Organiser: Rev Monica Stringer. Executive staff 1. Began 2000; interdenominational. No magazine. Turnover n/a.

Education Division (Church of England), Church House, Great Smith Street, London SW1P 3NZ
☎ 020 7898 1501 🖷 020 7898 1520
E: john.hall@c-of-e.org.uk
Web: www.cofe.anglican.uk/about/education
Advising dioceses and the General Synod; taking action in the field of education.
Chief Education Officer: Rev Canon John Hall. Executive staff 9, Other staff 5. Began 1970; Anglican. (Previously Board of Education (Church of England)). Magazine: *ayce* (Circulation n/a half-yearly). Turnover n/a.

Note: each Diocese has a range of training officers for ordained and lay people. Contact them via the appropriate Diocesan Office. See pages 155 to 162.

The European Academy for Christian Homeschooling, Maranatha House, Unit 5, Northford Close, Shrivenham, Swindon SN6 8HL
☎ 01793 783 783 🖷 01793 783 775
E: teach@christian-education.org
Web: www.christian-education.org
Supporting home education families in the UK and missionary families abroad.
Principal: Mr Arthur Roderick. *Pastoral Director:* Mr Neville Downes. Executive staff 2, Other staff 1. ***CC*** No.1045685. Began 1996; interdenominational. (Previously National Christian College for Home Education). Magazine: *At Home* (460 quarterly). Turnover n/a.

***Friendship First**, 2 Knights Close, Burbage, Hinckley LE10 2QN
☎ 0115 921 7272 M: 07815 042 033
E: friendship2101@aol.com
Web: www.friendshipfirst.org
Resourcing and training ordinary Christians to relate the good news to ordinary Muslims.
Consultant: Mr Steve Bell. Executive staff 1, Administrative staff 1. Began 2002; non-denominational. No magazine. Turnover n/a.

***Growing Families International**, Maranatha House, Unit 5 Northford Close, Shrivenham, Swindon SN6 8HL
☎ 01793 783 783 🖷 01793 783 775
E: info@christian-education.org
Web: www.gfi.org
Distributing books, audio and video training courses on biblical parenting; establishing local church groups interdenominationally.
Director: Mr Arthur Roderick. Executive staff 1, Admin staff 2. Began 1997; interdenominational. Supported by Christian Education Europe. No magazine. Turnover n/a.

Hockerill Educational Foundation, 16 Hagsdell Road, Hertford SG13 8AG
☎ 01992 303 053 🖷 01992 425 950
E: hockerill.trust@ntlworld.com
Awards to organisations, teachers or intending teachers especially of religious education in UK schools.
Secretary: Mr Colin Broomfield. Executive staff 1. ***CC*** No.311018. Began 1977; Anglican. No magazine. Turnover £233,731 to year end June 05.

Home Service, 48 Heaton Moor Road, Heaton Moor, Stockport SK4 4NX
☎ 0161 432 3782
E: info@home-service.org
Web: www.home-service.org
National centre for encouragement and support of Christian home education; conferences, contact list, advice, resources.
Secretary: Mrs Ruth Slack. No full-time staff. Began 1992; non-denominational. Magazine: *Home Time* (500 every four months). Turnover £7,000 to year end Dec 04.

***Hope UK**, Unit F, 25 Copperfield Street, London SE1 0EN
☎ 020 7928 0848 (24-hour)
🖷 020 7401 3477
E: a.wilson@hopeuk.org
Web: www.hopeuk.org
Drug awareness presentations, training for church leaders (including youth / children's workers) and voluntary drug educators.
Executive Director: Mr George Rushton. *National Education Coordinator:* Mr Martin Perry. *Training Coordinator:* Ms Sarah Brighton. Executive staff 4, Other staff 1. ***CC*** No.1044475. Began 18[illegible]5; interdenominational. Magazine: *Drug News* (9,000 half-yearly). Turnover £[illegible]60,000 to year end Dec 04.

The Institute for the Study of Christianity and Sexuality, Oxford House, Derbyshire Street, London E2 6HG
☎ 020 7739 1249 🖷 020 7739 124[illegible]
Promoting debate within the churches on human sexuality.
Secretary: Rev Richard Kirker. Executive staff 1. ***CC*** No.327822. Began 198[illegible]; interdenominational. No magazine. Turnover £2,000 to year end Dec 04.

†Institute for Theology and Art, St Mary's College, The University, St Andrews KY16 9JU
☎ 01334 462 850 🖷 01334 462 852
E: itia@st-and.ac.uk
Web: www.thearts.org/ or st-and.ac.uk/institutes/itia
Cambridge University project exploring how different art forms generate new models for doing Christian theology.
Director: Professor Trevor Hart. Executive staff 1, Admin staff 1. ***CC*** Began 1997; non-denominational. Magazine: *Theology Through the Arts - Update* (500 half-yearly). Turnover n/a.
Also at: *Associate Director:* Rev Dr Jeremy Begbie, Ridley Hall Cambridge CB3 9HG
E: jb215@cam.ac.uk
☎ 01223 741 080 🖷 01223 741 081

Institute of Christian Political Thought, PO Box 2, Taunton TA1 4ZD
☎ 01823 665 909 🖷 01823 665 721
E: icpt@kuyper.org
Web: www.kuyper.org
Think-tank dedicated to developing and articulating a distinctively Christian political theory and ethics.
Director: Stephen C Perks. No full-time staff. Began 1994; non-denominational. No magazine. Turnover n/a.

International Association for Reformed Faith and Action, Outwood House, Outwood Lane, Horsforth, Leeds LS18 4HR
☎ 0113 258 9300 🖷 0113 258 1[illegible]09
E: davidhanson@btconnect.com
Christian higher education in the international context of reformational faith and action.
Hon General Secretary: Mr David R Hanson. No full-time staff. ***CC*** No.2719[illegible]7. Began 1958; non-denominational. Agency of WYSOCS. No magazine. Turnover £30,000 to year end Apr 05.

T

***Joshua Generation**, PO Box 498, Walton-on-Thames KT12 1WJ
M: 07092 018 280
E: admin@joshgen.org
Web: www.joshgen.org
Developing leaders to make a transforming contribution to society through mentoring, training, resourcing and consulting.
Director Mr Adam Eakins. *Co-Director:* Mr Matt Stuart. Executive staff 2, Associates 7. **CC** No.1059592. Began 1996; interdenominational. No magazine. Turnover £100,000 to year end Nov 02.

The Leadership Institute, Hilgay Rectory, Church Road, Downham Market PE38 0JL
☎ 01366 382 969
E: tlioffice@aol.com
Web: www.tli.org.uk
Offering courses in developmental leadership training and mentoring for clergy to enable personal growth.
Executive Director: Rev Rob Mackintosh. Executive staff 1, Admin staff 1. **CC** No.1084198. Began 2001; Anglican. No magazine. Turnover n/a.

***Love For Life**, 6 Banbridge Road, Waringstown, Craigavon BT66 7QA
☎ 028 3882 0555
Fax 028 3882 0550
E: info@loveforlife.org.uk
Web: www.loveforlife.org.uk
Abstinence-centred sex and relationship education; schools programme, multimedia presentations; advisory schools support service.
Director: Dr Richard Barr. Development staff 4, Admin staff 3. **CC** No.XR 59713. Began 2000; interdenominational. No magazine. Turnover £250,000 to year end Dec 04.

Maoz UK, 80 Royal Hill, Greenwich, London SE10 8RT
☎ 020 8692 2831
Fax 020 8333 7272
E: maozengland@maozisrael.org
Promoting understanding and prayer concerning Israel's place and purpose in God's kingdom; helping Israeli believers.
Trustee: Dan Delap. No full-time staff. **CC** No.1076084. Began 1995; non-denominational. Magazine: *Maoz Report* (Circulation n/a monthly). Turnover £78,000 to year end Dec 04.

***Henry Martyn Centre**, Westminster College, Cambridge CB3 0AA
☎ 01223 741 088/089
Fax 01223 741 089
E: pk262@cam.ac.uk
Web: www.martynmission.cam.ac.uk
Promoting the academic study of mission and world Christianity.
Henry Martyn Lecturer in Missiology: Dr Brian Stanley. Executive staff 1, Other staff 3. **CC** No.266612. Began 1995; ecumenical. Supported by the Henry Martyn Trust. No magazine. Turnover n/a.

Ministry Today, Central Baptist Church, Victoria Road South, Chelmsford CM1 1LN
☎ 01245 347 095 M: 07966 624 276
Fax 01245 267 203
E: pbeasleymurray@centralbaptist.fs.co.uk
Web: www.ministrytoday.org.uk
Enabling leaders to survive and thrive in pastoral ministry.
Chairman: Rev Dr Paul Beasley-Murray. No full-time staff. **CC** No.1050561. Began 1994; interdenominational. (Previously Richard Baxter Institute for Ministry). Magazine: *Ministry Today* (Circulation n/a e-journal). Turnover n/a.

National Service Committee for Catholic Charismatic Renewal, Allen Hall, 28 Beaufort Street, London SW3 5AA
☎ 020 7352 5298 Fax 020 7351 4486
E: ccruk@onetel.com
Web: www.ccr.org.uk
Promoting charismatic renewal and ecumenical relations; prayer groups; handling enquiries; networking; providing resource materials.
Chairman: Mr Charles Whitehead. Admin staff 2. **CC** No.277425. Began 1979; Roman Catholic. Magazine: *Good News* (6,000 every two months). Turnover n/a.
Also at: PO Box 333, St Albans AL2 1EL
☎ 01727 822 837 Fax 01727 822 837

Network of Adult Theological Educators, Wesley Centre, Westminster Institute of Education, Oxford Brookes University, Harcourt Hill Campus, Oxford OX2 9AT
☎ 01865 488 286
E: alecornu@brookes.ac.uk
Web: www.brookes.ac.uk/schools/wco
Linking individuals at centres of theological education, supporting working groups on issues; conferences, consultations, publications.
Hon Secretary: Alison Le Cornu. No full-time staff. Began 1981; interdenominational. (Previously Association of Adult Theological Education). Magazine: *Journal of Adult Theological Education* (450 half-yearly). Turnover n/a.

The Newman Association, Ashfield, Gate Road, Froncysyllte, Llangollen LL20 7RH
☎ No telephone
E: info@newman.org.uk
Web: www.newman.org.uk
Promoting adult religious formation for Catholic laity through conferences, lecture programmes, journal.
Secretary: Mrs Hanora Birchman. No full-time staff. **CC** No.1006769. Began 1942; Roman Catholic. Member of the Catholic movement Pax Romana. Magazine: *The Newman Journal* (1,000 every four months). Turnover n/a.

NorthStar UK, 37 Balmoral Crescent, Dronfield Woodhouse, Dronfield S18 8ZY
☎ 01246 410 122 Fax 01246 410 122
E: info@northstaruk.org
Web: www.northstaruk.org
Providing on-line educational support for secondary school-aged students up to GCSE and IGCSE level.
Administrator: Julie Thompson. No full-time staff. **CC** No.1003691. Began 1989; non-denominational. (Previously Veritas Trust). No magazine. Turnover £76,240 to year end May 04.

Arthur Rank Centre, Stoneleigh Park, Kenilworth CV8 2LZ
☎ 024 7685 3060 Fax 024 7641 4808
E: arcadmin@rase.org.uk
Web: www.arthurrankcentre.org.uk
Providing focus for the rural church: mission, ministry, agricultural chaplaincy, conservation, ethics, rural community issues.
Director: Rev Dr Gordon Gatward. Executive staff 6, Other staff 6. **CC** No.1104300. Began 1972; ecumenical. Magazine: *Country Way* (4,000 every four months). Turnover n/a.

RE Today Services, 1020 Bristol Road, Selly Oak, Birmingham B29 6LB
☎ 0121 472 4242 Fax 0121 472 7575
E: pamela@retoday.org.uk
Web: www.christianeducation.org.uk
Developing and improving Religious Education in schools.
Director of Professional Services: Mrs Pamela Draycott. Executive staff 9, Other staff 9. **CC** No.1086990. Began n/a; interdenominational. (Previously Christian Education Today Services). Magazine: *RE Today* (5,000 every four months), *British Journal of Religious Education* (2,500 every four months). Turnover n/a.

St Luke's College Foundation, Heathayne, Colyton EX24 6RS
☎ 01297 552 281 Fax 01297 552 281
Making grants for postgraduate studies and research. Applications by 1st May annually.
Director: Prof Michael Bond. Executive staff 1. **CC** No.306606. Began 1978; Anglican. No magazine. Turnover £143,000 to year end July 02.

Scottish Joint Committee on Religious and Moral Education, 6 Clairmont Gardens, Glasgow G3 7LW
☎ 0141 353 3595 Fax 0141 332 2778
Representing teacher organisations, churches, minority faith bodies; developing policy on religious and moral education; Scotland.
Joint Secretary: Mr Lachlan Bradley. No full-time staff. Began n/a; interdenominational. No magazine. Turnover n/a.

†The Scottish Reformation Society, The Magdalen Chapel, 41 Cowgate, Edinburgh EH1 1JR
☎ 0131 220 1450 Fax 0131 220 1450
E: ashbethany41@hotmail.com
Witnessing to the Reformed Faith through publications, lectures, videos, holiday tours; open to visitors.
Secretary: Rev A Sinclair Horne. Executive staff 1. **CC** No.SCO 07756. Began 1850; interdenominational. Magazine: *The Bulwark* (3,500 quarterly). Turnover £30,000 to year end Dec 02.

T

***The Stapleford Centre**, The Old Lace Mill, Frederick Road, Stapleford, Nottingham NG9 8FN
☎ 0115 939 6270
🖷 0115 939 2076
E: admin@stapleford-centre.org
Web: www.stapleford-centre.org
Promoting development in education from a Christian perspective; curriculum resources, training courses and educational research.
Director: Mr Ben Jones. *Educational Projects Manager:* Mrs Alison Farnell. Executive staff 2, Other staff 10. ***CC*** No.1063856. Began 1997; interdenominational. Magazine: *Cracking RE* (Circulation n/a every four months). Turnover £468,000 to year end Aug 02.

Sunday Schools Council for Wales, School of Education, University of Wales Bangor, Normal Site, Bangor LL57 2PX
☎ 01248 382 947
🖷 01248 382 155
E: aled.davies@bangor.ac.uk
Web: www.ysgolsul.com
Developing work of Sunday School and Christian Education in Wales through the Welsh language.
General Secretary: Rev Aled Davies. Executive staff 2, Other staff 4. ***CC*** No.525766. Began 1966; interdenominational. Magazine: *Cysylltiad* (2,000 quarterly). Turnover £150,000 to year end Dec 98.

***TISCA (The Independent Schools Christian Alliance)**, Stocoomb, Netherc-oombe Lane, Sherborne DT9 4BU
☎ 01935 817 582
🖷 01935 817 582
E: tisca@onetel.com
Web: www.tisca.info
Promoting and defending biblical Christian faith, applying it to educational issues in the independent sector.
General Secretary: Mr Mark Greenstock. No full-time staff. ***CC*** No.1047025. Began 1995; interdenominational. Magazine: *TISCA News and Views* (500 termly). Turnover £30,000 to year end Oct 05.

†**UK Directory of Bible Colleges**, Bible College of Wales, Derwen Fawr Road, Sketty, Swansea SA2 8EB
☎ No telephone
E: byfaithmedia@hotmail.com
Web: www.byfaith.co.uk/bcdirectory.htm
Web-based tool to help students find a Bible College in the UK.
Webmaster: Paul Backholer. No full-time staff. Began 2001; interdenominational. No magazine. Turnover n/a.

The Welsh National Centre for Religious Education, University of Wales Bangor, Normal Site, Bangor LL57 2PZ
☎ 01248 382 566 🖷 01248 383 [illegible]54
E: l.j.francis@bangor.ac.uk
Web: www.bangor.ac.uk/rs/pt
Research in and resources for religious education and values education throughout Wales and the UK.
Director: Professor Leslie J Francis. Executive staff 1, Other staff 7. Began 19[illegible]9; non-denominational. Magazine: *RE News / Newyddion AG* (3,500 every four months). Turnover n/a.

Woodard Schools, High Street, Abbots Bromley, Rugeley WS15 3BW
☎ 01283 840 120 🖷 01283 840 89[illegible]
Web: www.woodard.co.uk
Providing and supporting Christian education in Church of England schools.
General Secretary: Name not supplied. Executive staff 1, Other staff n/a. ***CC*** No.314291. Began 1847 Anglican. No magazine. Turnover n/a.

EDUCATIONAL RESOURCE CENTRES

All Saints Resource Centre, 1 All Saints Court, Bristol BS1 1JN
☎ 0117 927 7454 🖷 0117 925 0404
E: allsaints@bristoldiocese.org
Web: www.bristol.anglican.org
Lending religious education resources to schools, churches and individuals.
Resource Administrator: Mrs Joanna Bailey. Admin staff 2. Began 1980; Anglican. No magazine. Turnover n/a.

Archdiocese of Southwark Christian Education Centre, 21 Tooting Bec Road, London SW17 8BS
☎ 020 8672 7684/2422
🖷 020 8672 8894
E: office@cectootingbec.org.uk or bookshop@cectootingbec.org.uk
Web: www.cectootingbec.org.uk
Servicing Christian education and formation of adults in parishes.
Director: Rev John O'Toole. Executive staff 1, Other staff n/a. ***CC*** Began 1967; Roman Catholic. Magazine: *BEC News* (1,000 quarterly). Turnover n/a.

Banbury Area RE Centre, c/o The Methodist Church, Marlborough Road, Banbury OX16 5BZ
☎ No telephone
Organising in-house training for schools, churches, individuals; promoting interfaith understanding.
Centre Manager: Name not supplied. No full-time staff. ***CC*** No.1026363. Began 1978; non-denominational. No magazine. Turnover £1,500 to year end Dec 02.

Bath and Wells Diocesan Education Resource Centre, The Old Deanery, Wells BA5 2UG
☎ 01749 670 777 🖷 01749 674 240
E: education@bathwells.anglican.org or resourcecentre@bathwells.anglican.org
Web: www.bathandwells.org.uk or
Providing resources and support for religious education and worship for churches and schools.
Director of Education: Mr M Evans. Executive staff 1, Other staff 2. ***CC*** No.249398. Began 1981; Anglican. No magazine. Turnover n/a.

Bradford Diocesan Resource Centre, Kadugli House, Elmsley Street, Steeton, Keighley BD20 6SE
☎ 01535 650 531 🖷 01535 650 550
E: resources@kadugli.org.uk
Web: www.bradford.anglican.org.uk
Supplying Christian resources to parishes, schools and the public; hiring equipment.
Development Officer: Uell Kennedy. Executive staff 1, Other staff 11. ***CC*** Began n/a; Anglican. No magazine. Turnover £15,000 to year end Apr 04.

Bristol Methodist District Resource Centre, Wesley College, College Park Drive, Henbury Road, Bristol BS10 7QD
☎ 0117 959 1200 🖷 0117 950 1277
Web: www.wesley-college-bristol.ac.uk
Lending resources to students and members of the Bristol Methodist District.
Resource Centre Assistant: Mrs Julia Traill. No full-time staff. Began 1992; Methodist. No magazine. Turnover n/a.

Carlisle Diocesan Religious Education Resource Centre, West Walls, Carlisle CA3 8UE
☎ 01228 538 086 🖷 01228 815 409
E: dir-educ@carlisle-c-of-e.org or recentre@carlislediocese.org.uk
Lending/selling resources for RE and Christian formation to schools, church groups and voluntary organisations.
Adviser in Religious Education: Rev B J Thomas. Executive staff 1. ***CC*** No.251977. Began 1975; Anglican. No magazine. Turnover £25,000 to year end Dec 96.

Chantmarle Christian Resource Centre, Chantmarle Manor, Frome St Quintin, Dorchester DT2 0HD
☎ 01935 483 201 🖷 01935 838 95
E: resource.centre@chantmarle.co.uk
Web: www.chantmarle.co.uk
Providing resources for seminars, meetings and retreats.
Managing Director: Mr John Glare. Resource centre staff n/a. Began 2005; interdenominational. No magazine. Turnover n/a.

Chelmsford Diocesan Resources Centre, 53 New Street, Chelmsford CM1 1AT
☎ 01245 294 406 🖷 01245 294 477
E: hamor@chelmsford.anglican.org
Web: www.chelmsford.anglican.org
Providing books, out-of-print searches; general sales; support of diocesan staff, parishes, schools.
Resource Centre Manager: Mr Brian Beattie. *Assistant Manager:* Mrs Helen Amor. Executive staff 1, Admin staff 1. ***CC*** No.249505. Began n/a; Anglican. No magazine. Turnover £130,000 to year end Dec 02.

T

***Christian Resources Into Schools**, 85 Barton Road, Comberton, Cambridge CB3 7BT
☎ 01223 262 943 M: 07710 661 003
E: network@cris.org.uk
Web: www.cris.org.uk or www.smsc.org.uk
Helping churches support their local school through the school coordinator network and SMSC online.
Project Manager: Ms Chris Westgarth. Executive staff 1. **CC** No.1092267. Began 2002; interdenominational. No magazine. Turnover £30,000 to year end Mar 03.

***Christians Involved In Derbyshire Schools (CIDS)**, The Saltpot, The Green, Swanwick, Alfreton DE55 1BL
☎ 01773 609 603 🖷 01773 609 603
E: info@valleycids.freeserve.co.uk
Association of Christians with concern for schools in Derbyshire; Christian schools resources centre.
Executive Director: Mrs Dorothy Whitaker. Executive staff 1. Other staff 1. **CC** No.1003799. Began 1988; interdenominational. No magazine. Turnover n/a.

Croydon Religious Education Resource Centre, The Crescent, Croydon CR0 2HN
☎ 020 8689 5343 🖷 020 8689 5343
E: re@crerc.freeserve.co.uk
Web: www.crerc.org.uk
LEA/religious community partnership servicing the RE needs of churches and schools locally.
Resources Officer: Fauzia Ali. Executive staff 1, Other staff n/a. **CC** No.1038238. Began 1980; ecumenical. No magazine. Turnover n/a.

Ekklesia, 21 Tooting Bec Gardens, London SW16 1QY
☎ 020 8769 8163
E: office@ekklesia.co.uk
Web: www.ekklesia.co.uk
Thinktank working to promote radical theological ideas in public life.
Director: Jonathan Bartley. Executive staff 1. **CC** No.1010354. Began 2002; interdenominational. (Previously Ekklesia: A New Way of Thinking). Part of Anvil Trust. No magazine. Turnover included in Anvil Trust.

Gloucester Diocesan Religious Education Resource Centre, 9 College Green, Gloucester GL1 2LX
☎ 01452 385 217 🖷 01452 314 038
E: glosrerc@star.co.uk
Web: www.glosdioc.org.uk
Library, providing resources for religious education for churches and schools.
Manager: Mrs Carolyn Wright. Executive staff 1, Other staff 2. **CC** No.251234. Began 1971; Anglican. No magazine. Turnover n/a.

Guildford Diocesan Education Centre, The Cathedral, Stag Hill, Guildford GU2 7UP
☎ 01483 450 423 🖷 01483 450 424
Web: www.guildford.anglican.org
Supporting parishes and schools by providing consultancy, courses and loaning resource materials.
Director of Education: Mr Derek Holbird. Executive staff 9, Other staff 6. **CC** Began n/a; Anglican. No magazine. Turnover n/a.

Independent Methodist Resource Centre, Fleet Street, Pemberton, Wigan WN5 0DS
☎ 01942 223 526 🖷 01942 227 768
E: resourcentre@imcgb.org.uk
Web: www.imcgb.org.uk
Administration, supplies, resources; also holding independent Methodist Church's archives.
Manager: Mr Andrew M Rigby. Executive staff 1, Other staff 2. **CC** No.254007. Began 1805; Independent Methodist. Magazine: *Connexion* (1,500 monthly). Turnover n/a.

International Community Trust for Health and Education Services (Icthes World Care), West Hurlet House, Glasgow Road, Hurlet, Glasgow G53 7TH
☎ 0141 881 9633
E: m.mcgavin@icthesworldcare.com
Web: www.icthesworldcare.com
Global health education; producing/sending teaching journals free to 170+ countries; gathering/housing resources.
Executive Director: Dr D D Murray McGavin. Executive staff 1, Other staff 4. **CC** No.1075381. Began 1999; interdenominational. Magazine: *Developing Mental Health* (Circulation n/a half-yearly), *Community Dermatology* (Circulation n/a half-yearly), *Community Ear & Hearing Health* (Circulation n/a half-yearly). Turnover £95,600 to year end Dec 05.

***London Mennonite Centre**, 14 Shepherd's Hill, Highgate, London N6 5AQ
☎ 08454 500 214 🖷 020 8341 6807
E: lmc@menno.org.uk
Web: www.menno.org.uk
Offering seminar programme, library, book service and church conflict and mediation service.
Director: Mr Vic Thiessen. Executive staff 3, Other staff 4. **CC** No.227410. Began 1954; Mennonite. No magazine. Turnover £136,000 to year end Dec 04.

The John Newton Project, The Hill Lodge, Warwick Road, Stratford-upon-Avon CV37 0NP
☎ 01789 298 174
E: admin@johnnewton.org
Web: www.johnnewton.org
Working for transformation of society through faith in Jesus Christ, using John Newton's life/works.
Researcher: Miss Marylynn Rouse. No paid staff. **CC** No.212939. Began 2002; interdenominational. (Previously Fact and Faith Films). No magazine. Turnover £3,221 to year end Dec 04.

North East Religious Learning Resources Centre Ltd, Carter House, Pelaw Leazes Lane, Durham DH1 1TB
☎ 0191 375 0586 🖷 0191 375 0586
E: enquiry@resourcescentreonline.co.uk
Web: www.resourcescentreonline.co.uk
Providing resources, training, information and support for schools and churches in the North-East.
Director: Ms K Passmore. Executive staff 8. **CC** No.1055285. Began 1975; ecumenical. (Previously Durham Religious Education Resources Centre). No magazine. Turnover £95,000 to year end Dec 98.

Also at: Church House, St John's Terrace, Percy Main, North Shields NE29 6FS
E: catherine.costigan@resourcescentreonline.co.uk
☎ 0191 270 4161

†The Olive Branch Christian Resource Centre, 1 The Orchard, Harmony Hill, Milnthorpe LA7 7QA
☎ 01539 564 600
🖷 01539 564 600
Free loan of video and audio tapes, audio-visuals, children/youth teaching materials, book library.
Partner: Mr Michael R Cullen. Executive staff 1. Began 1986; interdenominational. No magazine. Turnover n/a.

The RE Centre, Education Development Centre, Church Lane, Princes Plain, Bromley BR2 8LD
☎ 020 8462 8911
🖷 020 8461 6286
E: jan.thompson@bromley.gov.uk
RE resource centre for schools and churches; books for inspection, artefacts on loan.
Associate RE Adviser: Ms Jan Thompson. Executive staff 1. Began 2000; Anglican but open to all. No magazine. Turnover £700 to year end Dec 05.

†St Albans Diocesan Education Centre, Hall Grove, Welwyn Garden City AL7 4PJ
☎ 01707 332 321
🖷 01707 373 089
E: resources@stalbans.anglican.org
Web: www.stalbans.anglican.org
Resources supporting Anglican church schools and voluntary work with children/young people throughout the diocese.
Director of Education: Mr Jon Reynolds. Executive staff 1, Other staff 9. Began 1973; Anglican. No magazine. Turnover n/a.

†St Asaph Diocesan Resource Centre, 20 Rhosnesni Lane, Wrexham LL12 7LY
☎ 01978 265 967/357 713
🖷 01978 290 454
Offering RE resources, photocopying facilities, conference rooms, bookshop.
Manager: Mr J R Nicholas. Executive staff 2, Other staff 4. Began 1978; Anglican. No magazine. Turnover n/a.

***Salt Cellar Ltd (Methodist Resources Centre)**, 11a Church Lane, Oldham OL1 3AR
☎ 0161 628 2426 🖷 0161 620 4007
E: admin@saltcellar.freeserve.co.uk
Web: www.saltcellar.org.uk
Also restaurant, worship area, counselling, youth project, exhibitions, room hire and conference facilities.
Manager: Ms Joan Avison. *Administrator:* Mr Pete Gowers. Executive staff 2, Other staff n/a. Began 1990; Methodist. Magazine: *Oasis* (Circulation n/a quarterly). Turnover £200,000 to year end Dec 02.

Sheffield Christian Education Council, Montgomery Hall, Surrey Street, Sheffield S1 2LG
☎ 0114 272 0455
E: office@scec.org.uk
Web: www.scec.org.uk
Resource centre for churches and Sunday Schools.
Administrator: Mrs Carole Darlow. Admin staff 1, Other staff 5. ***CC*** No.1090172. Began 1812; interdenominational. Magazine: *Spotlight* (1,000 quarterly). Turnover n/a.

Slough & District Religious Studies Centre, Lea Junior School, Grasmere Avenue, Slough SL1 2RW
☎ 01753 822 888 Fax 01753 822 888
E: sloughrscentre@waitrose.com
Web: www.sloughrscentre.org.uk
Resourcing religious education and studies of world religions; loans, advice.
Centre Resources Officer: Mrs J S Osborne. Admin staff 1. ***CC*** No.1064771. Began 1978; non-denominational. No magazine. Turnover n/a.

South Essex Religious Education Centre, St Barnabas Church, Woodfield Road, Hadleigh, Benfleet SS7 2EJ
☎ 01702 552 099/475 169
E: serec@surfaid.org
Web: www.serec.org
Providing library resources: churches - study, training, teaching, worship; assisting schools with RE, Citizenship, PSI.
Administrator: Mrs S Orrock. No paid staff. Began 1975; Anglican but open to all. No magazine. Turnover £2,000 to year end Dec 02.

Suffolk Christian Resource Library, St Nicholas Centre, 4 Cutler Street, Ipswich IP1 1UQ
☎ 01473 298 507 Fax 01473 298 501
E: shirley@stedmundsbury.anglican.org
Web: www.stedmundsbury.anglican.org
Supporting diocese in Christian mission, including other faiths; schools curriculum, loaning resources.
Library Administrator: Ms Shirley Nicholls. Admin staff 2. ***CC*** No.143034. Began n/a; ecumenical. No magazine. Turnover n/a.

†Training Image Resource, The Fold, Sunnyside, Little Asby, Appleby-in-Westmorland CA16 6QE
☎ 01539 623 552
Providing video, audio and publications.
Director: Mr & Mrs Ian & Lilian Stewart. Executive staff 2. Began 1973; independent. (Previously Recording Ministries). No magazine. Turnover n/a.

†Visual Impact Resources, 7 Silverton Drive, Stenson Green, Derby DE24 [illegible]BU
☎ 01332 775 508
E: jemh@visual-impact-resources.co.uk
Visual aids, teaching materials, Bible for children's and youth work.
Evangelist: Mr Jeremy Hudson. Executive staff 2, Other staff 2. Began 1998; non-denominational. No magazine. Turnover n/a.

Winchester Diocesan Resource Centre, Church House, 9 The Close, Winchester SO23 9LS
☎ 01962 624 760 Fax 0196[illegible] 841 8[illegible]5
E: ian.knight@winchester.anglican.org
Web: www.winchester.anglican.org/[illegible]eshome.htm
Providing resources for parishes and schools.
Administrator: Mr Ian Knight. Executive staff 1. Began 1985; Anglican. No magazine. Turnover n/a.

†York Religious Education Centre, Lord Mayor's Walk, York YO31 7EX
☎ 01904 716 858 Fax 01904 612 5[illegible]
E: e.bellett@yorksj.ac.uk
Web: www.yorksj.ac.uk
Courses, resources, loans, consultancy.
Head of Centre: Ms Eileen Bellett. Executive staff 2. Began 1976; interdenominational. No magazine. Turnover n/a.

SCHOOLS, INDEPENDENT CHRISTIAN SECONDARY

By County and Postcode – for location of Postcodes see map on Page 458
Schools which did not supply this information are not listed here

Postcode	Name		Boarding Boys	Boarding Girls	Day Boys	Day Girls	Age Range	Annual Fees Boarding	Annual Fees Day
ENGLAND									
BA10	**Bruton**	King's School	172	72	73	21	13-18	£16,245	£11,995
BA2	**Bath**	Monkton Combe School	170	101	282	167	2-19	£21,306	£8,910
		Prior Park College	67	53	224	166	11-18	£13,485	n/a
BA21	**Yeovil**	The Park School	14	21	103	123	3-18	£11,985	£6,360
BN21	**Eastbourne**	Eastbourne College	185	85	170	81	13-18	£15,465	£9,990
BN6	**Hassocks**	Hurstpierpoint College	111	65	124	48	3-18	£12,030	n/a
CH47	**Wirral**	Kingsmead School	20	14	130	78	3-16	£10,995	£5,490
CM3	**Chelmsford**	New Hall School	-	113	-	285	11-18	£7,250	£11,250
CM15	**Brentwood**	Peniel Academy	n/a	n/a	57	87	5-18	n/a	n/a
CR3	**Caterham**	Woldingham School	-	420	-	140	11-18	£21,240	£[illegible]2,690
		Caterham School	100	48	475	255	11-18	n/a	n/a
GL51	**Cheltenham**	Dean Close School	144	122	106	83	13-18	£5,600	£3,930
GL8	**Tetbury**	Westonbirt School	-	140	-	87	11-18	£20,580	£[illegible]4,280
GU14	**Farnborough**	Farnborough Hill School	-	-	-	500	11-18	n/a	£6,093
IP2	**Ipswich**	St Joseph's College	n/a	n/a	n/a	n/a	3-18	n/a	n/a
KT22	**Leatherhead**	St John's School	117	29	284	21	13-18	£18,210	£12,840
L7	**Liverpool**	Christian Fellowship School	-	-	104	95	4-16	£1,560–£3,050	
LE1	**Leicester**	Leicester Grammar School	-	-	402	296	10-18	n/a	£7,005
LE11	**Loughborough**	Loughborough Grammar School	50	-	90	-	10-18	n/a	n/a
MK17	**Milton Keynes**	Thornton College	-	45	-	267	3-16	£12,825	£5,675
OX15	**Banbury**	Bloxham School	175	50	75	60	11-18	£15,000	n/a
OX3	**Oxford**	Rye St Antony School	-	75	25	325	3-18	£14,025	£3,250
OX7	**Chipping Norton**	Kingham Hill School	140	45	31	15	11-18	£18,711	£12,309
PE3	**Peterborough**	Peterborough High School	-	30	70	290	3-18	£13,155	£[illegible],407
PE37	**Swaffham**	Sacred Heart Convent School	-	28	33	194	3-16	n/a	£[illegible],500
RH10	**Crawley**	Worth School	292	-	152	-	11-18	£21,165	£1[illegible],678
RH17	**Haywards Heath**	Ardingly College	176	116	200	157	3-18	£18,795	£1[illegible],085
S10	**Sheffield**	Birkdale School	-	-	751	49	4-18	n/a	£[illegible]197
SE9	**London**	Eltham College	5	-	730	50	7-18	n/a	£[illegible]525
SL4	**Windsor**	Eton College	1,280	-	-	-	13-18	£16,488	n/a
SL5	**Ascot**	St Mary's School	-	342	-	18	11-18	£17,760	£11,985
ST15	**Stone**	St Dominic's Priory School	-	-	20	300	3-18	£3,967–£6,088	
SW1	**London**	More House School	-	-	-	220	11-18	n/a	£7,590
SW11	**Battersea**	Thames Christian College	n/a	n/a	n/a	n/a	11-18	n/a	n/a
WD3	**Watford**	Royal Masonic School for Girls	-	240	-	500	4-18	£10,090	£3,474
WD6	**Borehamwood**	Aldenham School	131	13	296	5	11-18	£16,770	£11,570
WF16	**Heckmondwike**	The Branch Christian School	-	-	15	13	3-18	n/a	£2,100
WR1	**Worcester**	Royal Grammar School	-	-	869	100	3-18	n/a	£6,714
WR14	**Malvern**	Malvern Girls' College	-	325	-	75	11-18	£18,381	£12,249
YO62	**York**	Ampleforth College	461	33	40	5	13-18	£19,545	n/a
YO7	**York**	Queen Mary's School	-	60	10	180	3-16	n/a	n/a
SCOTLAND									
PH1	**Perth**	Glenalmond College	220	125	30	25	12-18	£17,760	£11,[illegible]85

T

SCHOOLS, INDEPENDENT CHRISTIAN SECONDARY

Aldenham School, Elstree, Borehamwood WD6 3AJ
☎ 01923 858 122 🖷 01923 854 410
E: enquiries@aldenham.com
Web: www.aldenham.com
Boarding and day for boys and girls aged 11 to 18, Nursery, Pre Prep and Prep.
Headmaster: Mr Richard Harman MA (Cantab) PGCE. *Deputy Head:* Mrs D E MacGinty. *Chaplain:* Rev Wealands Bell. Teaching staff 62, Other staff 89. ***CC*** No.298140. Began 1597; Anglican. Affiliated to Bloxham Project. Turnover £8,000,000 to year end Aug 05.

†Ampleforth College, Ampleforth, York YO62 4ER
☎ 01439 766 000 🖷 01439 788 330
E: admin@ampleforth.org.uk
Web: ampleforthcollege.york.sch.uk
Boarding and day for boys and girls aged 13 to 18.
Headmaster: Rev Gabriel Everitt OSB. Teaching staff 69, Other staff 33. Began n/a; Roman Catholic. Affiliated to The Catholic Independent Schools' Conference. Turnover n/a.

†Ardingly College, Haywards Heath RH17 6SQ
☎ 01444 892 577 🖷 01444 892 266
E: head@ardingly.com
Web: www.ardingly.com
Boarding and day for boys and girls aged 3 to 18.
Headmaster: Mr John Franklin BA, MEd Admin. Teaching staff 94, Other staff 150. ***CC*** No.1076456. Began n/a; Anglican. Affiliated to the Woodard Corporation. Turnover n/a.

Birkdale School, 4 Oakholme Road, Sheffield S10 3DH
☎ 0114 266 8408 🖷 0114 267 1947
E: office@birkdale.sheffield.sch.uk
Web: www.birkdaleschool.org.uk
Day, for boys aged 4 to 18, girls aged 16 to 18.
Headmaster: Mr Robert Court MA. Teaching staff 118, Other staff 21. ***CC*** No.2792166. Began 1904; interdenominational. Affiliated to The Independent Schools Christian Alliance and the Bloxham Project. Turnover n/a.

Bloxham School, Bloxham, Banbury OX15 4PE
☎ 01295 720 222 🖷 01295 721 897
E: headmaster@bloxhamschool.com
Web: www.bloxhamschool.com
Boarding and day for boys and girls aged 11 to 18.
Headmaster: Mr Mark Allbrook. Teaching staff 55, Other staff 45. ***CC*** No.3779976. Began 1860; Anglican. Affiliated to the Bloxham Project and Woodard Corporation. Turnover n/a.

The Branch Christian School, 8 Thomas Street, Heckmondwike WF16 0NW
☎ 01924 235 637 🖷 01924 454 750
E: branchsch@aol.com
Using School of Tomorrow curriculum (ACE) for boys and girls aged 3 to 18.
Principal: Mr R Ward. Teaching staff 7, Other staff 2. Began 1994; interdenominational. Turnover n/a.

Caterham School, Harestone Valley Road, Caterham CR3 6YA
☎ 01883 343 028 🖷 01883 347 795
E: enquiries@caterhamschool.co.uk
Web: www.caterhamschool.co.uk
Boarding and day for boys and girls aged 11 to 18; Prep School for boys and girls aged 3 to 11.
Headmaster: Mr Rob Davey MA. *Bursar:* Mr John King. *Chaplain:* Rev Dr Rick Mearkle. Teaching staff 100, Other staff 150. ***CC*** No.1109508. Began 1811; United Reformed. Affiliated to the Bloxham Project and The Independent Schools Christian Alliance. Turnover £7,000 000 to year end Aug 00.

Christian Fellowship School, Overbury Street, Edge Hill, Liverpool L7 3HL
☎ 0151 709 1642 M: 07786 020 059
🖷 0151 709 6164
E: mail@cfschool.org.uk
Web: www.cfschool.org.uk
Providing non-denominational education for boys and girls aged 4 to 16.
Head Teacher: Mr Philip R Williamson. *Bursar:* Mr John Hodge. Executive staff 5, Admin staff 5, Other staff 34. ***CC*** No.1079325. Began 1981; non-denominational. Turnover £376,000 to year end Aug 05.

†Dean Close School, Shelburne Road, Cheltenham GL51 6HE
☎ 01242 258 000 🖷 01242 258 003
E: registrar@deanclose.co.uk
Web: www.deanclose.co.uk
Boarding and day for boys and girls aged 13 to 18.
Headmaster: Rev T M Hastie-Smith BA (Cantab), MA (Oxon). Teaching staff 50, Other staff n/a. ***CC*** No.1086829. Began 1886; evangelical. Affiliated to The Independent Schools Christian Alliance. Turnover n/a.

Eastbourne College, Old Wish Road, Eastbourne BN21 4JX
☎ 01323 452 320 🖷 01323 452 327
E: hmsec@eastbourne-college.co.uk
Web: www.eastbourne-college.co.uk
Boarding and day for boys and girls aged 13 to 18.
Headmaster: Mr Simon Davies MA (Oxon). Teaching staff 76, Other staff 142. ***CC*** No.307071. Began 1867; interdenominational. Affiliated to the Bloxham Project. Turnover n/a.

†Eltham College, Grove Park Road, Mottingham, London SE9 4QF
☎ 020 8857 1455 🖷 020 8857 1913
Web: www.eltham-college.org.uk
Day for boys and some girls aged 7 to 18.
Headmaster: Mr Paul Henderson BA, FRSA. Teaching staff 80, Other staff 50. ***CC*** No.1058438. Began 1841; Baptist and United Reformed but open to all. Affiliated to the Bloxham Project. Turnover n/a.

†Eton College, Windsor SL4 6DT
☎ 01753 671 001 🖷 01753 671 159
Web: www.etoncollege.com
Boarding for boys aged 13 to 18.
Conduct (Senior Chaplain): Rev C W Mitchell-Innes MA (Cantab). *Chaplain:* Rev T D Mullins. Teaching staff 152, Other staff 700. ***CC*** Began 1440; Anglican. Affiliated to the Bloxham Project. Turnover £20,400,000 to year end Dec 00.

†Farnborough Hill School, Farnborough GU14 8AT
☎ 01252 545 197 🖷 01252 513 037
E: devdir@farnborough-hill.org.uk
Web: www.farnborough-hill.org.uk
Day for girls aged 11 to 18.
Headmistress: Miss J Thomas BA (Hons), MA, PGCE. Teaching staff 52, Other staff 30. ***CC*** No.1039443. Began 1889; Roman Catholic. Affiliated to The Catholic Independent Schools' Conference. Turnover n/a.

Glenalmond College, Perth PH1 3RY
☎ 01738 842 056 🖷 01738 842 063
E: registrar@glenalmondcollege.co.uk
Web: www.glenalmondcollege.co.uk
Boarding and day for boys and girls aged 12 to 18.
Warden: Mr Gordon Woods. Teaching staff 40, Other staff 40. ***CC*** No.SCO 06123. Began 1847; Scottish Episcopal. Turnover n/a.

Hurstpierpoint College, College Lane, Hassocks BN6 9JS
☎ 01273 833 636 🖷 01273 835 257
E: info@hppc.co.uk
Web: www.hppc.co.uk
Boarding and day for boys and girls aged 3 to 18.
Headmaster: Mr T J Manly BA MSc. Teaching staff 49, Other staff 21. ***CC*** No.1076498. Began 1849; Anglican. Affiliated to the Woodard Corporation. Turnover n/a.

†King's School, Bruton BA10 0AE
☎ 01749 814 200 🖷 01749 813 426
E: kingshm@kingsbruton.somerset.sch.uk
Web: www.kingsbruton.com
Boarding and day for boys and girls aged 13 to 18.
Headmaster: Mr R I Smyth MA. Teaching staff 41, Other staff n/a. ***CC*** Began n/a; Anglican. Turnover n/a.

T

For further information see list on Page 416

Kingham Hill School, Kingham, Chipping Norton OX7 6TH
☎ 01608 658 999
🖷 01608 658 658
E: admissions@kingham-hill.oxon.sch.uk
Web: www.kingham-hill.oxon.sch.uk
Boarding and day for girls and boys aged 11 to 18. Also vacation accommodation.
Headmaster: Mr Martin Morris. Teaching staff 50, Other staff 50. ***CC*** No.1076618. Began 1886; interdenominational. Member of The Independent Schools Christian Alliance. Turnover n/a.

†Kingsmead School, Bertram Drive, Hoylake, Wirral CH47 0LL
☎ 0151 632 3156
🖷 0151 632 0302
E: kingsmeadschool@compuserve.com
Web: www.kingsmead.wirral.sch.uk
Friendly family school; boarding and day for boys and girls aged 11 to 18.
Headmaster: Mr E H Bradby BA, MA (Oxon), MA (Minnesota), MSc (Oxon). *Bursar:* Mrs L Boyce. *Deputy Head:* Mr Roger Leake. Teaching staff 29, Other staff 6. ***CC*** No.525920. Began 1904; interdenominational. Affiliated to The Independent Schools Christian Alliance. Turnover £1,367,000 to year end Aug 03.

†Leicester Grammar School, 8 Peacock Lane, Leicester LE1 5PX
☎ 0116 222 0400
🖷 0116 291 0505
E: tylerk@leicestergrammar.org.uk
Web: www.leicestergrammar.org.uk
Day for boys and girls aged 10 to 18.
Headmaster: Mr C P M King MA. Teaching staff 69, Other staff 24. ***CC*** Began 1981; Anglican. Affiliated to the Bloxham Project. Turnover £4,432,333 to year end Apr 00.

Loughborough Grammar School, 6 Burton Walks, Loughborough LE11 2DU
☎ 01509 233 233
🖷 01509 218 436
E: admin@loughgs.leics.sch.uk
Web: www.loughs.leics.sch.uk
Boarding and day for boys aged 10 to 18.
Principal: Mr Paul B Fisher MA. Teaching staff 100, Other staff 50. ***CC*** No.1081765. Began 1495. Affiliated to the Bloxham Project. Turnover n/a.

†Malvern Girls' College, Avenue Road, Great Malvern, Malvern WR14 3BA
☎ 01684 892 288
🖷 01684 566 204
E: admin@mgc.worcs.sch.uk
Web: www.mgc.worcs.sch.uk
Boarding and day for girls aged 11 to 18.
Head: Mrs P Leggate BA, MEd, PGCE. Teaching staff 50, Other staff 30. ***CC*** No.527513. Began 1893; Anglican. Affiliated to the Bloxham Project. Turnover n/a.

Monkton Combe School, Monkton Combe, Bath BA2 7HG
☎ 01225 721 102
🖷 01225 721 208
E: admin@monkton.org.uk
Web: www.monktoncombeschool.com
Family-based, boarding and day for boys and girls aged 2 to 19.
Head Master of Senior School: Mr Richard Backhouse MA (Cantab). *Head Master of Junior School:* Mr Chris Stafford. Teaching staff 92, Other staff 45. ***CC*** No.1057185. Began 1868; Anglican but open to all. Affiliated to The Independent Schools Christian Alliance. Turnover n/a.

†More House School, 22 Pont Street, London SW1X 0AA
☎ 020 7235 2855
🖷 020 7259 6782
E: office@morehouse.org.uk
Web: www.morehouse.org.uk
Day for girls aged 11 to 18.
Headmistress: Mrs L Falconer BSc. *Deputy Head:* Mr Shane Fletcher. *Bursar:* Mr John Temple. Teaching staff 31, Other staff 4. ***CC*** No.312737. Began 1953; Roman Catholic. Affiliated to The Catholic Independent Schools' Conference. Turnover £1,400,000 to year end Aug 00.

†New Hall School, Chelmsford CM3 3HT
☎ 01245 467 588
🖷 01245 464 348
E: admin@newhallschool.co.uk
Web: www.newhallschool.co.uk
Boarding and day for girls aged 11 to 18.
Headmistress: Mrs K Jeffrey. Staff 150. ***CC*** No.229288. Began 1798; Roman Catholic. Affiliated to The Catholic Independent Schools' Conference and the Bloxham Project. Turnover n/a.

†The Park School, The Park, Yeovil BA21 4HP
☎ 01935 423 514
🖷 01935 411 257
E: admin@parkschool.com
Web: www.parkschool.com
Boarding and day for boys and girls aged 3 to 18.
Headmaster: Mr Paul W Bate BA, PGCE, Adv Dip MKT. Teaching staff 34, Other staff 37. ***CC*** No.310214. Began 1851; non-denominational. Affiliated to The Independent Schools Christian Alliance. Turnover n/a.

Peniel Academy, Brizes Park, Ongar Road, Kelvedon Hatch, Brentwood CM15 [illegible]DG
☎ 01277 374 123
🖷 01277 373 596
E: penielacademy@peniel.org
Web: www.penielacademy.ac
Day for boys and girls aged [illegible] to 18.
Principal: Dr Michael S B Reid. Teaching staff 26, Other staff 14. Began 1[illegible]82; Pentecostal. Turnover n/a.

†Peterborough High School, Thorpe Road, Peterborough PE3 6JF
☎ 01733 343 357 🖷 0173[illegible] 355 7[illegible]0
Web: www.peterboroughhigh.peterborough.sch.uk
Day and some boarding for girls aged 3 to 18, day for boys aged 3 to 11.
Headmistress: Mrs Sarah Dixon BA (Hons). Teaching staff 40, Other staff 9. ***CC*** No.269667. Began 1895; interdenominational. (Previously Westwood House). Affiliated to the Woodard Corporation. Turnover n/a.

Prior Park College, Ralph Allen Drive, Bath BA2 5AH
☎ 01225 831 000 🖷 01225 [illegible]35 75[illegible]
E: admissions@priorpark.co.uk
Web: www.priorpark.co.uk
Boarding and day for boys and girls aged 11 to 18. Catholic in tradition, ecumenical in spirit.
Headmaster: Dr Giles Mercer MA. *Registrar:* Dr M Ruxton. Teaching staff 7[illegible], Other staff 70. ***CC*** No.2[illegible]124[illegible]. Began n/a; Roman Catholic and interdenominational. Affiliated to The Catholic Independent Schools' Conference and the Bloxham Project. Turnover n/a.

Queen Mary's School, Baldersby Park, Topcliffe, Thirsk YO7 3BZ
☎ 01845 575 000 🖷 01845 5[illegible]5 001
E: admin@queenmarys.org
Web: www.queenmarys.org
Boarding day for girls aged 3 to 16 and a few boys aged 3 to 7.
Headmaster: Mr Robert Mackenzie-Johnston. *Director of Studies:* Mr Paul Nuttall. Teaching staff 30, Other staff 20. ***CC*** No.1098410. Began 19[illegible]5; Anglican. Affiliated to the Woodard Corporation. Turnover £1,500,000 to year end Aug 00.

Royal Grammar School, Upper Tything, Worcester WR1 1HP
☎ 01905 613 391 🖷 01905 72[illegible] 892
E: office@rgsw.org.uk
Web: www.rgsw.org.uk
Day for boys and girls aged 3 to 18.
Headmaster: Mr A R Rattue MA. Teaching staff 85, Other staff 10. ***CC*** No.52[illegible]527. Began 1291; non-denominational. Turnover n/a.

For further information see list on Page 416

†Royal Masonic School for Girls, Rickmansworth Park, Rickmansworth WD3 4HF
☎ 01923 773 168 🖷 01923 896 729
E: enquiries@royalmasonic.herts.sch.uk
Web: www.royalmasonic.herts.sch.uk
Boarding and day for girls aged 4 to 18.
Headmistress: Mrs Diane Rose. *Chaplain:* To be appointed. Teaching staff 80, Other staff 154. **CC** No.276784. Began 1788; Anglican but open to all. Affiliated to the Bloxham Project. Turnover £5,500,000 to year end Dec 00.

Rye St Antony School, Pullens Lane, Oxford OX3 0BY
☎ 01865 762 802 🖷 01865 763 611
E: headmistress@ryestantony.co.uk
Web: www.ryestantony.co.uk
Boarding and day for girls aged 3 to 18, day for boys aged 3 to 8.
Headmistress: Miss Alison Jones BA, PGCE. *Bursar:* Mr Alistair Sinclair. Teaching staff 54, Other staff 45. **CC** No.309685. Began 1930; Roman Catholic. Affiliated to The Catholic Independent Schools Conference. Turnover £2,900,000 to year end Apr 06.

Sacred Heart Convent School, 17 Mangate Street, Swaffham PE37 7QW
☎ 01760 721 330 🖷 01760 725 557
E: info@sacredheartschool.co.uk
Web: www.sacredheartschool.co.uk
Day for girls and some boys, boarding for some girls aged 3 to 16.
Headmistress: Sister Francis Ridler FDC, BEd. Community members 6, Other staff 40. **CC** No.237760. Began 1914; Roman Catholic. Turnover n/a.

St Dominic's Priory School, 21 Station Road, Stone ST15 8EN
☎ 01785 814 181 🖷 01785 819 361
Day for girls aged 3 to 18 and a few boys aged 3 to 11.
Headmaster: Mr Andrew Egan. Teaching staff 32, Other staff 18. **CC** No.271922. Began 1934; Roman Catholic. Affiliated to The Catholic Independent Schools, Conference. Turnover n/a.

St John's School, Leatherhead KT22 8SP
☎ 01372 373 000 🖷 01372 386 606
E: secretary@stjohns.surrey.sch.uk
Web: www.stjohnsleatherhead.co.uk
Boarding and day for boys aged 13 to 18, girls aged 16 to 18.
Headmaster: Mr N J R Haddock MBE MA FRGS. Teaching staff 50, Other staff 50. **CC** No.312064. Began 1851; Anglican. Affiliated to the Bloxham Project. Turnover n/a.

St Joseph's College, Belstead Road, Ipswich IP2 9DR
☎ 01473 690 281 🖷 01473 602 409
E: pubsjcm@ad.com
Web: www.stjos.co.uk
Day, some boarding for boys and girls aged 3 to 18.
Head: Mrs Sian Grant. *Bursar & Clerk to the Governors:* Mr Michael O'Brien. Teaching staff 70, Other staff 20. **CC** No.1051688. Began 1997; Roman Catholic but open to all. Affiliated to The Catholic Independent Schools' Conference. Turnover £3,710,842 to year end Jul 00.

St Mary's School Ascot, St Mary's Road, Ascot SL5 9JF
☎ 01344 623 721 🖷 01344 873 281
E: admissions@st-marys-ascot.co.uk
Web: www.st-marys-ascot.co.uk
Boarding and some day for girls aged 11 to 18.
Headmistress: Mrs Mary Breen BSc, MSc. Teaching staff 75, Other staff 65. **CC** No.290286. Began 1885; Roman Catholic. Affiliated to GSA, The Catholic Independent Schools' Conference and the Bloxham Project. Turnover n/a.

***Thames Christian College**, Wye Street, Battersea, London SW11 2HB
☎ 020 7228 3933 🖷 020 7924 1112
E: info@thameschristiancollege.org.uk
Web: www.thameschristiancollege.org.uk
For boys and girls aged 11 to 18.
Head Teacher: Mr Stephen Holsgrove. *Registrar:* Mrs C Holsgrove. Executive staff 2, Teaching staff 9, Other staff 9. **CC** No.1081666. Began 2000; interdenominational. Turnover £350,000 to year end Aug 05.

Thornton College, Convent of Jesus & Mary, Thornton, Milton Keynes MK17 0HJ
☎ 01280 812 610 🖷 01280 824 042
E: office@thorntoncollege.com
Web: www.thorntoncollege.com
Boarding and day for girls aged 4 to 16; nursery for boys and girls.
Headmistress: Miss A T Williams BEd, Adv Dip Ed. Teaching staff 36, Other staff 49. **CC** No.247358. Began 1917; Roman Catholic but open to all. Affiliated to The Catholic Independent Schools' Conference. Turnover n/a.

Westonbirt School, Tetbury GL8 8QG
☎ 01666 880 333 🖷 01666 880 364
E: office@westonbirt.gloucs.sch.uk
Web: www.westonbirt.gloucs.sch.uk
Boarding and day for girls aged 11 to 18.
Headmistress: Mrs Mary Henderson MA (Hons), PGCE. *Registrar:* Mrs Belinda Holley. *Chaplain:* Rev Philip Dixon. Teaching staff 35, Other staff 64. **CC** No.311715. Began 1928; Anglican. Affiliated to Allied Schools. Turnover £3,000,000 to year end Jul 00.

Woldingham School, Marden Park, Woldingham, Caterham CR3 7YA
☎ 01883 349 431 🖷 01883 348 653
E: registrar@woldingham.surrey.sch.uk
Web: www.woldingham.surrey.sch.uk
Boarding and day for girls aged 11 to 18.
Headmistress: Miss Diana Vernon BA. Teaching staff 85, Other staff 65. **CC** No.291258. Began 1882; Roman Catholic. Affiliated to The Catholic Independent Schools' Conference. Turnover n/a.

Worth School, Paddockhurst Road, Turners Hill, Crawley RH10 4SD
☎ 01342 710 200 🖷 01342 710 201
E: registry@worth.org.uk
Web: www.worthschool.co.uk
Boarding and day for boys aged 11 to 18.
Headmaster: Mr Peter J Armstrong. Teaching staff 66, Other staff 150. **CC** No.1093914. Began 1959; Roman Catholic. Affiliated to The Catholic Independent Schools' Conference. Turnover n/a.

T

TEACHING ENGLISH AS A FOREIGN LANGUAGE SCHOOLS

Central Language School, The Stoneyard Centre, 41b St Andrews Street, Cambridge CB2 3AR
☎ 01223 502 004 🖷 01223 502 004
E: info@central-ls.co.uk
Web: www.central-ls.org.uk
Teaching English as a foreign language to international students in a friendly caring community atmosphere.
Principal: Mrs Elizabeth Giles. Executive staff 2, Admin staff 1. ***CC*** No.1056074. Began 1996; interdenominational. No magazine. Turnover £100,000 to year end Aug 02.

***Christian English Language Centre**, Exchange Buildings, Upper Hinton Road, Bournemouth BH1 2HH
☎ 01202 297 729 🖷 01202 297 460
E: english@celcuk.com
Web: www.celcuk.com
Teaching English to foreign Christians and missionary candidates and equipping them spiritually.
Directors: Mr & Mrs Derek & Jackie White. Executive staff 3, Other staff 8. Began 1977; interdenominational. No magazine. Turnover n/a.

***Functional English**, 5 Chubb Hill Road, Whitby YO21 1JU
☎ 01947 603 933 🖷 01947 820 703
E: office@funenglish.co.uk
Web: www.funenglish.co.uk
Providing English language courses for 75 foreign adults, beginners to advanced. Accredited by the British Council.
Principal: Mr Neil McKelvie. *Director of Studies:* Mr Lindsay Barber. Executive staff 3, Other staff 20. Began 1977; interdenominational. No magazine. Turnover £440,000 to year end Dec 04.

***International Training Network**, PO Box 6335, Christchurch BH23 9BN
☎ 01202 475 956
E: office@itnuk.com
Web: www.itnuk.com
Training teachers of English as a Foreign Language for TESOL; focus on mission.
International Director: Mr Len Grates. Executive staff 3, Other staff 3. ***CC*** No.1048521. Began 1994; interdenominational. No magazine. Turnover £119,000 to year end Dec 02.

***Logos Linguistics**, 2 Beaconsfield Road, Canterbury CT2 7HF
☎ 01227 766 663 🖷 01227 766 663
E: info@logoslinguistics.co.uk
Web: www.logoslinguistics.co.uk
Christian English language home school: outreach, preparing Christians for Bible College/Christian work.
Director: Mr Peter Dufort. Executive staff 2. Began 1992; non-denominational. No magazine. Turnover n/a.

***Olivet English Language School**, 52 Norfolk Square, Brighton BN1 2PA
☎ 01273 325 839 M: 07717 667 666
🖷 01273 325 839
E: info@olivet.co.uk
Web: www.olivet.co.uk
Teaching English to non-English speakers within a Christian ethos; Christian host families.
Director: Angela Starnes. Executive staff 1, Other staff 5. Began 1977; interdenominational. No magazine. Turnover £200,000 to year end Mar 05.

***Regents English Language Centre**, London Road, Nantwich CW5 6LW
☎ 01270 610 800 🖷 0127[illegible] 610 [illegible]3
E: jean@regentsenglish.org.uk
Web: www.regents-english.org.uk
Providing courses for those aged 15 upwards, beginners to advanced; TEFL Teacher Training courses.
Director: Mrs Jean Binns. Executive staff 3, Other staff 5. ***CC*** No 251[illegible]49. Began 1981; interdenominational. No magazine. Turnover £190,000 to year end Jun [illegible]5.

***Southall School of Languages and Missionary Orientation**, Western Road, Southall UB2 5DS
☎ 020 8574 4456 M: 07711 382 9[illegible]5
🖷 020 8606 9699
E: info@sslmo.co.uk
Web: www.sslmo.co.uk
Providing English teaching; cross-cultural evangelism and leadership training for ministry in the UK or overseas.
Director: Pastor Boyd Williams. *Secretary:* Mrs Christine Streets. Executive staff 4, Other staff 14. ***CC*** No.[illegible]068[illegible]6. Began 1989; Baptist. No magazine. Turnover £200,000 to year end Dec 00.

THEOLOGICAL COLLEGES & BIBLE SCHOOLS (FULL-TIME)

By Denomination
Colleges which did not supply any of this information are not listed here
Fees are per annum unless otherwise stated

Name	Places Resident M	Places Resident W	Places Resident M/W	Places Non-Res	Students M	Students W	Course Details	Fees Tuition	Fees Combined	Fees Accom
Anglican										
Church Army, Wilson Carlile College of Evangelism	-	-	45	10	29	12	3 years Dip HE in evangelism studies, Grad Dip, MA	£4,380		£1,82[illegible]
College of the Resurrection	35	0	-	3	n/a	0	3 years undergraduate 1 to 3 years postgraduate	£2,006		n/a
Oak Hill Theological College	-	-	80	80	n/a	n/a	1, 2, 3 or 4 years undergraduate, postgraduate	n/a		n/a
Ridley Hall	-	-	70	40	65	40	2 or 3 years, undergraduate/postgraduate	£5,650		£3,10[illegible]
Ripon College	-	-	70	0	n/a	n/a	2 or 3 years	n/a		n/a
St Chad's College	-	-	310	0	168	142	Undergraduate, postgraduate, PhD	£1,000		£2,18[illegible]
St John's College, Durham with Cranmer Hall	-	-	71	n/a	34	23	1 to 3 years undergraduate	£5,022		£2,51
St John's College, Nottingham	-	-	100	10	60	40	1 to 3 years undergraduate/postgraduate, research		£9,3[illegible]5	
St Michael College	n/a	n/a	-	n/a	n/a	n/a	3 terms, ministerial training	£4,300		£2,64[illegible]
St Stephen's House, Oxford	-	-	50	10	40	10	2/3 years undergraduate/postgraduate, diploma, certificate		Vary according to course	
Trinity College, Bristol	-	-	90	80	63	27	1 to 3 years, Cert, Diplomas, BA, MA, M.Phil, M.Litt, PhD	£4,491		£3,31[illegible]
Trinity College, Carmarthen	n/a	n/a	n/a	n/a	n/a	n/a	3 to 4 years M.Litt, PhD,	£1,050		£2,32[illegible]
Westcott House	-	-	-	60	30	30	2 or 3 years undergraduate		£8,7[illegible]	
Wycliffe Hall	-	-	80	40	88	32	1, 2 or 3 years undergraduate, various postgraduate	£6,246		£4,76[illegible]

Name	Places Resident M	W	M/W	Non-Res	Students M	W	Course Details	Fees Tuition	Combined	Accom.
Anglican / Methodist										
Selly Oak Centre	n/a	n/a	-	-	27	13	Undergraduate Health and Mission, 1 year postgraduate Church management and Women's leadership	n/a		n/a
The Apostolic Church										
The Apostolic School of Ministries	12	12	-	0	n/a	n/a	1 to 3 years n/a	n/a		n/a
Assemblies of God										
Mattersey Hall	60	60	-	40	70	60	1 to 3 years, certificates/diplomas/BA/MTh/PhD	£2,835		£2,325
South London Christian College	-	-	300	-	125	100	3 years, undergraduate, postgraduate, Cert, Dipl, Bth, Mth, MCCP, DMin, ThD		£2,100	
Baptist										
Bristol Baptist College	-	-	16	34	n/a	n/a	1 to 4 years, Cert. Diplomas, BA, MA, M.Phil, M.Litt, PhD	£5,886		n/a
Coleg Gwyr (North Wales Baptist College)	n/a	n/a	n/a	n/a	n/a	n/a	3 years pastoral and ministerial training, theology		n/a	
Northern Baptist College	-	-	30	50	n/a	n/a	1 to 6 years, full and part-time, undergraduate (certificate, diploma, BA), postgraduate (MA, MPhil, PhD)		£5,435	
Regent's Park College	-	-	80	40	n/a	n/a	3 years		£6,900	
Scottish Baptist College	-	-	-	20	n/a	n/a	4 years BD, 2 years diploma, 1 year post-graduate	£2,365		£2,870
South Wales Baptist College	-	-	-	28	n/a	n/a	3 years undergraduate		£4,500	
Southall School of Languages	-	-	-	n/a	-	-	3 to 4 years, MA, BA		variable	
Spurgeon's College	25	25	-	150	n/a	n/a	1,2 or 3 years full and part-time and open learning undergraduate, postgraduate	£2,750		£2,950
Roman Catholic										
Allen Hall	40	0	-	10	30	0	6 years	n/a		n/a
Margaret Beaufort Institute of Theology	0	12	-	18	0	18	2 to 4 years undergraduate BTh, CTM / MA		£3,000	
Franciscan International Study Centre	40	20	-	10	16	7	1 to 6 years	£5,460		£3,520
Institute of St Anselm	-	-	120	0	60	60	7 weeks to 3 years. Certificate diploma, postgraduate courses		£7,000	
Missionary Institute London	n/a	n/a	n/a	n/a	n/a	n/a	1 year diploma, 2 years philosophy, 3 to 4 years theology	£1,750		n/a
Newman College of Higher Education	-	-	1,500	-	-	-	1 to 6 years, undergraduate to postgraduate		Vary according to course	
St Johns Roman Catholic Seminary	60	0	-	60	36	6	3 to 6 years undergraduate (BTh) and postgraduate, Cert.RE		£15,000	
St Mary's, Strawberry Hill	-	-	300	n/a	n/a	n/a	Undergraduate/postgraduate degrees in Theology and Religious Studies. Management Studies with business ethics	n/a		n/a
St Mary's Seminary	90	0	-	0	n/a	0	6 years		£5,040	
Scotus College	28	0	-	3	n/a	0	6 years, diploma, degree in Philosophy, Theology		£2,500	
Ushaw College	-	-	45	0	43	2	3 or 6 years	n/a		n/a
Roman Catholic foundation, but open to all										
Heythrop College (University of London)	n/a	n/a	-	-	n/a	n/a	3 years undergraduate, 1–3 years postgraduate	n/a		n/a
Church of Scotland										
Christ's College, Aberdeen	n/a	n/a	-	100	n/a	n/a	3 or 4 years Tuition as University of Aberdeen fees	n/a		n/a
Church of the Nazarene										
Nazarene Theological College	10	10	-	220	10	10	1 to 4 years, BA Hons Theology, MA/PhD	£2,550		£1,915
Covenant Ministries										
Covenant College	n/a	n/a	-	25	n/a	n/a	1 or 2 years, certificate/diploma	£2,775		£2,800
Elim Pentecostal										
The Elim Pentecostal School of Ministry	-	-	-	-	30	15	1 year ministry course	£1,900		£2,500
Regents Theological College	-	-	100	80	71	30	1 to 3 years full / part-time, undergraduate / postgraduate	£3,450		£2,700
Free Presbyterian										
Whitefield College of the Bible and Theological Hall of the Free Presbyterian Church of Ulster	16	8	-	12	11	2	2 to 4 years, undergraduate/postgraduate	£1,155		£2,400
Interdenominational / Ecumenical / Non-denominational										
Abundant Life Leadership Academy	-	-	100	-	18	20	1 or 2 years, undergraduate	£1,400		n/a
Adelaide College	20	10	-	10	20	10	3 years	n/a		n/a
All Nations Christian College	-	-	180	0	72	108	Certificate, Diploma, BA, MA, PhD	£3,813	£7,948	£3,135
Belfast Bible College	95	70	40	100	80	60	3 months to 3 years, Cert to PhD	£2,980		£3,980
Bible College of Wales	20	15	-	4	10	8	1 to 3 years, certificate / diploma		£4,400	
Birmingham Christian College	-	-	-	60	50	50	1 to 3 years, full-time BA, Bth, MA 5-10 yrs part-time. Also MPhil, Dmin, PhD.	£3,450		n/a
Capernwray Bible School	185	10	-	0	70	106	1 year college diploma		£4,385	
Centre for Youth Ministry	-	-	-	200	-	-	BA Hons Degree in youth & community work and applied theology		variable	
	-	-	-	350	-	-	National certificate in Christian youth work		variable	
Christ for the Nations UK	40	40	-	40	9	12	2 years undergraduate	£1,806		£2,142
The College of St Mark and St John	-		5000	-	-	-	10 months–4 years undergraduate/postgraduate, short courses			£2,200
Cornhill Training Course	n/a	n/a	-	100	n/a	n/a	1 or 2 years. Bible training for ministry	£2,355		n/a
The Evangelical Theological College of Wales	-	-	25	140	150	15	Foundation/diploma/Cert HE, DipHE, BA(Hons), (Campus/distance learning, MA, DMin, MPhil, PhD)	£3,000		£1,500
Faith Mission Bible College	25	25	-	0	20	20	2 year diploma, 3 year degree	£1,995		£1,995
The Grace Project	-	-	20	-	6	8	1 or 2 years, diploma	n/a		n/a
Highland Theological College	-	-	25	-	n/a	n/a	1 year Accessa, BA, MTh, MPhil, PhD, 3–6 years part time doctoral ministry, open learning	£1,125–£2,940		n/a

Theological Colleges & Bible Schools (Full-Time)

Name	Places M	Places W	Places Resident M/W	Places Non-Res	Students M	Students W	Course Details	Fees Tuition	Fees Combined	Fees Accom.
The Independent Theological Academy	-	-	-	15	n/a	n/a	For ministers, missionaries, churchworkers	n/a		n/a
Institute for Community and Development Studies	-	-	-	n/a	n/a	n/a	1 to 4 years, certificate, MA. Community development	n/a		n/a
International Christian College, Glasgow	-	-	28	150	80	70	Foundation, undergraduate/postgraduate. Full time (1 to 4 years), part time (up to 9 years)	£3,675		£2,000
Kensit Memorial Bible College	18	0	-	0	18	0	2 years, preparation for the Christian ministry	n/a		n/a
King's Bible College Training Centre	-	-	40	0	n/a	n/a	10 months, diploma	£3,495		£2,500
King's College London, Department of Theology and Religious Studies	-	-	-	200	n/a	n/a	1 to 4 years undergraduate, diploma, postgraduate	n/a		n/a
Kingdom Faith College	n/a	n/a	-	n/a	n/a	n/a	1 to 2 year courses	n/a		n/a
London School of Theology	55	58	-	250	183	175	1 to 3 years, certificates HE to PhD	£4,077		£3,513
London Theological Seminary	25	0	-	12	33	0	2 years preparation for Christian ministry	£2,610		£4,350
Midlands Bible College	-	-	-	72	n/a	n/a	2 years, Diploma, undergraduate, short courses	n/a		n/a
Moorlands College	-	-	80	70	75	75	1 to 4 years, foundation to BA in Applied Theology	£4,341		£2,178
New Tribes Mission Bible & Missionary Training College	n/a	n/a	n/a	n/a	n/a	n/a	1 year, Biblical studies for ministry, missiology	n/a		n/a
Nexus Trust: Academy of Music Ministry			75	-	n/a	n/a	1 year	£3,000		
Oxford Centre for Mission Studies				150	n/a	n/a	Guided research and masters courses	n/a		n/a
Partnership for Theological Education	n/a	n/a	n/a	n/a	n/a	n/a	Undergraduate degrees, postgraduate	n/a		n/a
Queen's, Birmingham, The Ecumenical Foundation for Theological Education	40	40	-	0	n/a	n/a	1 to 4 years certificate, diploma, BA, MA	£6,900		£2,[illegible]70
Redcliffe College	-	-	90	10	39	41	Short courses to 3 years, cert (HE), dip (HE), BA (Hons), MA	£3,960		£3,[illegible]00
St Michael's Theological College	-	-	70	-	n/a	n/a	1 year	£4,300		£2,[illegible]40
School of Christian Life and Ministry	n/a	n/a	n/a	n/a	n/a	n/a	1 year foundation course	£2,000		n/a
Tilsley College	8	8		2	7	6	1 year		£3,300	
University of Aberdeen, Department of Divinity and Religious Studies	35	35	-	100	n/a	n/a	3 or 4 years	n/a		n/a
University of Edinburgh, Centre for the Study of Christianity in the non-Western World	-	-	n/a	n/a	30	10	Various lengths of postgraduate course	n/a		n/a
University of Edinburgh, Faculty of Divinity	-	-	444	n/a	225	219	1 to 4 years, diploma, undergraduate/postgraduate	£750		n/a
University of Glasgow, Faculty of Divinity	-	-	220	n/a	110	110	3 or 4 years, undergraduate/postgraduate	n/a		n/a
University of St Andrews, School of Divinity	-	-	200	n/a	102	84	3 or 4 years undergraduate/postgraduate	£1,050		£2,500
Lutheran										
Westfield House	-	-	12	12	n/a	n/a	5 years		£4,[illegible]55	
Methodist										
Cliff College	-	-	75	100	33	32	1–3 years, undergraduate/postgraduate	£3,970		£3,3[illegible]0
Edgehill Theological College	-	-	60	60	n/a	n/a	3 years, 2 years postgraduate	n/a		n/a
Hartley Victoria College	-	-	25	30	n/a	n/a	2 or 3 years undergraduate/postgraduate. BA, MA, MPhil, PhD	n/a		n/a
Wesley College	-	-	-	70	n/a	n/a	2 or 3 years, BA (Theology), MA,	£1,200		£1,500
Wesley House, Cambridge	-	-	-	30	n/a	n/a	1 to 3 years	n/a		n/a
Pentecostal										
Bible Life Leadership Institute	15	15	-	0	10	10	1 year, undergraduate	£750		£1,200
Centre for International Christian Ministries	-	-	-	30	n/a	n/a	2 years, Modular courses		£1,200	
Global Missions and Bible Training Institute	16	19	-	0	16	17	3 years BA		£1,500	
International Bible Training Institute	-	-	-	200	34	34	1 year, diploma		£2,000	
Peniel College of Higher Education	-	-	-	145	n/a	n/a	2 years diploma, 3 years degree	£2,300		n/a
Presbyterian										
London Theological College	n/a	n/a	-	0	4	6	1 year, Certificate in Theology	£1,200		
Reformed Theological College	-	-	-	15	n/a	n/a	3 years, for men for ministry and missionaries	£1,500		
Union Theological College	19	7	-	119	64	55	3 years undergraduate	£3,148		£2,660
The United Theological College (Wales)	30	28	-	0	n/a	n/a	3 years BD, BTh	£1,300		£1,750
Salvation Army										
William Booth College	-	-	110	5	50	40	2 years undergraduate	£2,020		£3,166
Scottish Episcopal Church										
Theological Institute of the Scottish Episcopal Church	-	-	-	24	n/a	n/a	Full time 2 or 3 years, part time 3 years	n/a		n/a
Seventh-day Adventist										
Newbold College	166	117	-	90	162	117	3 to 4 years undergraduate, 1 to 2 years postgraduate	£3,360		£2,865
United Reformed										
Westminster College, Cambridge	-	-	60	n/a	n/a	n/a	4 years	n/a		n/a
United Reformed and Congregational										
Northern College	-	-	-	-	11	11	4 years undergraduate		£8,560	
Mansfield College	-	-	30	0	n/a	n/a	3 to 4 years	£6,000		n/a

T

THEOLOGICAL COLLEGES & BIBLE SCHOOLS (FULL TIME)

Main courses offered require full-time study and are at least one year in length.
For part-time and shorter courses see Theological Colleges & Bible Schools (Part-time) on Page 431.
Training Centres & Services on Page 435.

Aberystwyth Academy of Christian Discipleship St Michael's Church, Laura Place, Aberystwyth SY23 2AU
☎ 01970 617 184 🖷 01970 610 133
E: stuart@stmikes.net
Web: www.stmikes.net
Training in practical ministries, mentoring disciples.
Rector and Course Director: Rev Stuart Bell. No full-time staff. **CC** No.1019827. Began 2002; non-denominational. Operating under Tynddol Trust. Turnover £10,000 to year end Dec 03.

Abundant Life Leadership Academy, Abundant Life Centre, Wapping Road, Bradford BD3 0EQ
☎ 01274 307 233 🖷 01274 303 008
E: academy@alm.org.uk
Web: www.alm.org.uk
Training leaders to live God-centered, people-empowered, purpose-driven lives in church and society.
Principal: Mr Stephen Matthew. Lecturers 8, Other staff 2. **CC** No.701289. Began 2000; interdenominational. Turnover n/a.

***Adelaide College**, 3 Nineyard Street, Saltcoats KA21 5HS
☎ 01294 463 911 🖷 01294 463 366
E: campaign@cbtg.org
Web: www.cbtg.org
Also missionary society at work in Great Britain, conference centre.
Administrator: Mrs Marilyn Paterson. Lecturers 6, Admin staff 12, Other staff 6. **CC** No.240168. Began 1964; interdenominational. Turnover £16,000 to year end Dec 04.

***All Nations Christian College**, Easneye, Ware SG12 8LX
☎ 01920 461 243 🖷 01920 462 997
E: info@allnations.ac.uk
Web: www.allnations.ac.uk
Providing biblical and practical training for cross-cultural mission for singles, couples and families.
Executive Director: Mr Mike Wall MBA. Lecturers 13, Other staff 22. **CC** No.311028. Began 1971; interdenominational. Turnover £1,277,000 to year end Aug 02.

†Allen Hall, 28 Beaufort Street, Chelsea, London SW3 5AA
☎ 020 7351 1296
🖷 020 7349 5601
E: secretary@allenhall.co.uk
Training men for ordination to Roman Catholic priesthood.
Rector: Fr Paul McGinn. *Vice Rector:* Rev Anthony Dwyer. *Administrator:* Mr Gerald Daly BA. Lecturers 19, Other staff 9. **CC** No.233699. Began 1568; Roman Catholic. Part of Westminster Roman Catholic Diocese Trust. Turnover £850,000 to year end Dec 02.

†The Apostolic School of Ministries, Bryn Road, Penygroes, Llanelli SA14 7PH
☎ 01269 832 069
🖷 01269 842 299
E: ehwacts@aol.com
Principal: Pastor Bryn Thomas. Lecturers 10, Other staff 4. Began n/a; Apostolic. (Previously The Apostolic Church Training School). Turnover n/a.

Margaret Beaufort Institute of Theology, 12 Grange Road, Cambridge CB3 9DX
☎ 01223 741 039
🖷 01223 741 054
E: mtc33@cam.ac.uk
Web: www.margaretbeaufort.cam.ac.uk
Principal: Marie Cooke. Academic staff 3, Other staff 6. **CC** No.1041031. Began 1993; Roman Catholic. Member of the Cambridge Theological Federation. Turnover n/a.

***Belfast Bible College**, Glenburn House, Glenburn Road South, Dunmurry, Belfast BT17 9JP
☎ 028 9030 1551
🖷 028 9043 1758
E: info@belfastbiblecollege.com
Web: www.belfastbiblecollege.com
Equipping Christians for service in mission, ministry and marketplace.
Principal: Dr David Shepherd. Lecturers 8, Other staff 6. **CC** No.XN 47242A. Began 1943; interdenominational. Turnover £700,000 to year end Aug 04.

***Bible College of Wales**, Derwen Fawr Road, Sketty, Swansea SA2 8EB
☎ 01792 203 463
🖷 01792 290 488
E: office@biblecollegeofwales.org
Web: www.biblecollegeofwales.org
Offering full, part-time and modular courses accredited by University of Wales; also conference facilities.
Chair of Trustees: Rev Alan Scotland. Resident lecturers 6, Visiting lecturers 6, Other staff 9. **CC** No.1107553. Began 1924, incorporated 2004; interdenominational. Turnover n/a.

***Bible Life Leadership Institute**, PO Box 1098, 67 Melfort Road, Thornton Heath, Thornton Heath CR7 7RT
☎ 020 8689 2244 M: 07932 938 911
🖷 020 8689 5433
E: bible@lifefamilyministries.fsnet.co.uk
Web: www.biblelifefamilyministries.org
Executive Director: Pastor Hendrick Bruce LLB. Lecturers 5, Other staff 1. **CC** No.1082522. Began 2001; Pentecostal but open to all. Turnover £3,000 to year end Apr 03.

***Birmingham Christian College**, 54 Weoley Park Road, Selly Oak, Birmingham B29 6RB
☎ 0121 472 0726 🖷 0121 471 1132
E: admin@bhxc.ac.uk
Web: www.birminghamchristiancollege.ac.uk
Training for all kinds of ministry and mission in the local church and overseas; charismatic emphasis.
Principal: Rev Dr Richard D Massey, MA, BD, PhD, ALBC. Lecturers 9, Other staff 3. **CC** No.1002205. Began 1953; interdenominational. (Previously Birmingham Bible Institute). Turnover £230,000 to year end Dec 02.

†BMS International Mission Centre, Weoley Park Road, Selly Oak, Birmingham B29 6QX
☎ 0121 683 7959 🖷 0121 683 7956
E: imca@bmsworldmission.org
Web: www.bmsworldmission.org
Director: Rev Alan Pain. Lecturers 4, Other staff 8. **CC** Began 1966; Baptist. (Previously St Andrew's Hall Missionary College, International Mission Centre). Run by Baptist Missionary Society. Turnover n/a.

***William Booth College**, Champion Park, Denmark Hill, London SE5 8BQ
☎ 020 7326 2700 🖷 020 7326 2750
E: melvyn.jones@salvationarmy.org.uk
Providing training for Salvation Army officers, by recommendation only.
Principal: Major Mel Jones. Lecturers 24, Other staff 31. **CC** No.214779. Began 1929; Salvation Army. Turnover n/a.

Bristol Baptist College, The Promenade, Clifton Down, Clifton, Bristol BS8 3NJ
☎ 0117 946 7050 🖷 0117 946 7787
E: admin@bristol-baptist.ac.uk
Web: www.bristol-baptist.ac.uk
Offering training for Baptist ministry; for youth leaders under Centre for Youth Ministry.
Principal: Rev Dr Stephen Finnamore. Lecturers 8, Other staff 5. **CC** No.1102280. Began 1679; Baptist. Turnover £273,000 to year end Jul 05.

T

***Capernwray Bible School**, Capernwray Hall, Carnforth LA6 1AG
☎ 01524 733 908 🖷 01524 736 681
E: registrar@capernwray.org.uk
Web: www.capernwray.org.uk
Biblical Christ-centred teaching and practical training and outreach; various courses, students from over 20 countries.
Principal: Mr Rob Whittaker. *Managing Director:* Rev Mark Thomas. *Business Manager:* Mr Phil Burt. Lecturers 8, Other staff 28. **CC** No.1073139. Began 1949; interdenominational. Capernwray Missionary Fellowship of Torchbearers. Turnover £1,100,000 to year end Dec 02.

Centre for Youth Ministry, PO Box 442, Swindon SN5 7JH
☎ 01793 418336 M: 07732 480 356
🖷 01793 433 288
E: admin@centreforyouthministry.ac.uk
Web: www.centreforyouthministry.ac.uk
Consortium delivering full-time Youth Community degree course with professional qualification (see Engage).
National Director: Rev David Howell. Executive staff 2, Admin Staff 2. **CC** No.1081144. Began 1996; interdenominational. Turnover £800,000 to year end Aug 06.

Chester College of Higher Education, Parkgate Road, Chester CH1 4BJ
☎ 01244 511 030
E: r.ackroyd@chester.ac.uk
Web: www.chester.ac.uk
Undergraduate, postgraduate and doctoral studies, especially Christian theology and Christian youth work.
Principal: Prof Tim Wheeler. *Head of Theology & Religious Studies:* Dr Ruth Ackroyd. *Chaplain:* Rev Lorraine Dixon. Lecturers 420, Other staff 749. **CC** No.525938. Began 1839; Anglican. Turnover £24,759,611 to year end Dec 02.

T

***Christ for the Nations UK**, The Royal Norfolk, The Esplanade, Bognor Regis PO21 2LH
☎ 01243 826 222 🖷 01243 826 325
E: grow@cfnuk.org
Web: www.christforthenationsuk.org
Also conference centre.
Director: Rev Kevin J Swadling. *Director of Studies:* Dr Judith Lee. Lecturers 8, Other staff 6. **CC** No.1064962. Began 1995; interdenominational. Turnover £140,000 to year end Dec 98.

Christ's College, Aberdeen, 25 High Street, Aberdeen AB24 3EE
☎ 01224 272 138 🖷 01224 272 136
Training for ministry in the Church of Scotland.
Master: Rev J H A Dick. Lecturers 14. **CC** No.SCO 07788. Began 1843; Church of Scotland. Turnover n/a.

***Cliff College**, Calver, Hope Valley S32 3XG
☎ 01246 582 321/584 200
🖷 01246 583 739
E: study@cliffcollege.org
Web: www.cliffcollege.org
Evangelism, training, missions, research, open learning centre, conferences.
Principal: Rev Dr Martyn D Atkins BA PhD. *Bursar:* Mr John Steer. *Dean of Students:* Rev Dr Peter Phillips. Lecturers 22, Other staff 22. **CC** No.529386. Began 1883; Methodist. Turnover £1,662,582 to year end Aug 04.

†Y Coleg Gwyn (North Wales Baptist College), Penparc, 12 New Park Road, Holyhead LL65 1PH
☎ 01248 382 079 🖷 01248 353 759
E: rss013@bangor.ac.uk
Web: www.bangor.ac.uk/rs/cglc.htm
Pastoral courses and ministerial training; theological courses in conjunction with University of Wales, Bangor.
Principal: To be appointed. Lecturers 1. **CC** No.525779. Began 1862; Baptist. (Coleg Y Bedyddwyr). Turnover n/a.

College of the Resurrection, Mirfield WF14 0BW
☎ 01924 490 441 🖷 01924 492 738
E: admin@mirfield.org.uk
Web: www.mirfield.org.uk
Offering training for Church of England ordinands and BA/MA theology and pastoral studies degrees.
Principal: Rev Christopher Irvine. Lecturers 6. **CC** Began 1902; Anglican. Turnover n/a.

The College of St Mark and St John, Derriford Road, Plymouth PL6 8BH
☎ 01752 636 700 🖷 01752 636 820
E: principalsoffice@marjon.ac.uk
Web: www.marjon.ac.uk
Principal: Dr David Baker. *Chair:* Mrs Christine Hague. *Chaplain:* Rev Cate Edmonds. Lecturers 149, Other staff 270. **CC** No.312929. Began 1840; Anglican. Turnover £17,800,000 to year end Jul 05.

Cornhill Training Course, Willcox House, 140 Borough High Street, London SE1 1LB
☎ 020 7407 0562 🖷 020 7407 0569
E: ctc@proctrust.org.uk
Web: www.proctrust.org.uk
Director: Rev Christopher Ash, MA (Cantab). Lecturers 3, Other staff 1. **CC** Began 1991; interdenominational. Turnover n/a.

Covenant College, Nettle Hill, Brinklow Road, Ansty, Coventry CV7 9JL
☎ 024 7660 2700 🖷 024 7660 3276
E: info@covenantcollege.co.uk
Web: www.covenantcollege.co.uk
Taking recommended students from fellowships of Together.
Dean of Students: Mr Nicholas Howse. Lecturers n/a, Other staff n/a. Began 1980; Covenant Ministries. Turnover n/a.

Edgehill Theological College, 9 Lennoxvale, Malone Road, Belfast BT9 5BY
☎ 028 9066 5870 🖷 028 9066 7204
E: office@edgehillcollege.org
Web: www.edgehillcollege.org
Providing ministerial training, undergraduate and postgraduate theology degrees, reconciliation studies.
Principal: Rev Richard Clutterbuck BA MA. *Director of Ministry:* Rev Dr Heather Morris BSc BD. Lecturers 6, Other staff 3. **CC** No.XN 46164. Began 1926; Methodist. Associate College of Queen's University, Belfast. Turnover £250,000 to year end Dec 04.

The Elim Pentecostal School of Ministry, Regents Park, London Road, Nantwich CW5 6LW
☎ 01270 611 550
E: info@elimschoolofministry.co.uk
Web: www.elimschoolofministry.co.uk
Ministry course for those wishing to become Elim ministers.
Director: Rev David G Woodfield MTh. Lecturers 3, Admin staff 1. Began 2002; Elim Pentecostal. Turnover n/a.

For further information see list on Pages 420 - 422

The Evangelical Theological College of Wales, Bryntirion House, Bridgend CF31 4DX
☎ 01656 645 411 🖷 01656 641 987
E: secretary@etcw.ac.uk
Web: www.etcw.ac.uk
Training men to preach and pastor, men and women as missionaries, other full-time Christian workers.
Principal: Rev Dr D Eryl Davies BA BD MA PhD. Lecturers (full-time) 5, Lecturers (part-time) 18, Other Staff 9. ***CC*** No.517324. Began 1985; interdenominational. Incorporating South Wales Bible College. Turnover £500,000 to year end Dec 05.

***Faith Mission Bible College**, 2 Drum Street, Gilmerton, Edinburgh EH17 8QG
☎ 0131 664 4336 🖷 0131 672 1322
E: college@faithmission.org
Web: www.faithmission.org
Emphasising practical training in evangelism, biblical teaching and spiritual formation in an international environment.
Principal: Rev Dr Alexander Roger. Lecturers 3, Part-time lecturers 5, Other staff n/a. ***CC*** No.SCO 05119. Began 1886; interdenominational. Turnover n/a.

Franciscan International Study Centre, Giles Lane, Canterbury CT2 7NA
☎ 01227 769 349 🖷 01227 786 648
E: info@franciscans.ac.uk
Web: www.franciscans.ac.uk
Formation for ministry in Franciscan movement worldwide and within local and universal church.
Principal: Rev Philippe Yates OFM BA MA MCL JCD. *Vice-Principal:* Sr Margaret McGrath FMSJ BA MA. Lecturers 11, Other staff 7. ***CC*** No.260851. Began 1973; Roman Catholic. Turnover £200,000 to year end Dec 00.

Global Missions and Bible Training Institute, 281 Rye Lane, Peckham, London SE15 4UA
☎ 020 7639 8619 M: 07949 945 540
🖷 020 7639 8619
E: gmbti@aol.com
President/Founder: Archbishop Paul Hackman, Dip Biblical Studies ThD. Executive staff 3, Admin staff 2. ***CC*** No.1028128. Began 1994; Pentecostal. (Previously Global Missions Bible Institute). Turnover £22,000 to year end Mar 99.

†The Grace Project, Europa Studios, Studio 21, 22 Victoria Road, North Acton, London NW10 6ND
☎ 020 8961 1687
E: info@thegraceproject.com
Web: www.thegraceproject.com
Discipleship, creative arts and distance learning courses; training people to discover new covenant Christian identity.
Director: Paul Anderson-Walsh. Lecturers 4. ***CC*** No.1094304. Began 2000; non-denominational. Magazine: *Abundant Lifestyles* (500 quarterly). Turnover £40,000 to year end Mar 02.

†Hartley Victoria College, Luther King House, Brighton Grove, Rusholme, Manchester M14 5JP
☎ 0161 249 2516
Ordination and lay education validated by Manchester University.
Principal: Rev Dr John A Harrod BSc MA PhD. *Tutors:* Rev Dr Keith Davies, Rev Dr Jane Craske. Lecturers 3. ***CC*** Began 1881; Methodist but open to all. Within the Partnership for Theolcgical Education, Manchester. Turnover £150,000 to year end Dec 00.

Heythrop College (University of London), Kensington Square, London W8 5HQ
☎ 020 7795 6600
🖷 020 7795 4200
E: enquiries@heythrop.ac.uk
Web: www.heythrop.ac.uk
Specialist College of the University of London.
Principal: Rev Dr John McDade SJ BD MA PhD. Lecturers 30, Other staff 9. ***CC*** No.312923. Began 1614; Roman Catholic but open to all. Turnover n/a.

Highland Theological College, High Street, Dingwall IV15 9HA
☎ 01349 780 000
🖷 01349 780 001
E: htc@uhi.ac.uk
Web: www.htc.uhi.ac.uk
Study of Christian faith from an evangelical and Reformed perspective; full, part-time, open learning, on-line.
Principal: Rev Dr A T McGowan BD STM PhD. *Vice Principal:* Rev Hector Morrison BSc BD MTh. Full-time lecturers 4, Part-time lecturers 3, Other staff 15. ***CC*** No.SCO 29190. Began 1994; interdenominational. Turnover n/a.

The Independent Theological Academy, Westbury Chapel, Broad Street, Wolverhampton WV1 1JD
M: 07718 684 113
Principal: Name not supplied. Executive staff 1, Other staff 5. Began 1993; interdenominational. Turnover n/a. Training ministers, missionaries and church workers.

***Institute for Community and Development Studies**, Suite 319, Day Lewis House, 324 Bensham Lane, Thornton Heath CR7 7EQ
☎ 020 8664 2600
🖷 020 8664 2656
E: aepicds@ukonline.co.uk
Promoting church-involved community development practice. MA accredited course.
Director: Dr Ampaabeng Kyeremeh. Supervisors 5. ***CC*** No.1022993. Began 1991; interdenominational. Turnover n/a.

Institute of St Anselm, Edgar Road, Cliftonville, Margate CT9 2EU
☎ 01843 234 700 🖷 01843 234 701
E: office@st.anselm.org.uk
Web: www.st.anselm.org.uk
Deepening spirituality using psychology to become fully alive and to facilitate others on this path.
Director: Rev Fr L Kofler MHM. *Registrar:* Miss Claire McGuire. *Deputy Director:* Rev Fr J McCluskey. Lecturers 25, Institute staff 30, Community 120. ***CC*** No.294625. Began 1986; Roman Catholic. Turnover £876,954 to year end Jun 05.

***International Bible Institute of London (Kensington Temple)**, KT Summit House, 100 Hanger Lane, Ealing W5 1EZ
☎ 020 8799 6162 🖷 020 8998 4361
E: info@ibiol.org
Web: www.ibiol.org
Dean of Students: Praise Olatona. Lecturers 20, Other staff 4. ***CC*** No.251549. Began 1985; Elim Pentecostal but open to all. Turnover n/a.

***International Bible Training Institute**, Hook Place, Cuckfield Road, Burgess Hill RH15 8RF
☎ 01444 233 173 🖷 01444 233 173
E: office@ibti.org.uk
Web: www.ibti.org.uk
Applied theology course and training for ministry relevant to world needs.
Administrator: Ms P Bennett. Lecturers 20, Other staff n/a. ***CC*** No.255698. Began 1947; Independent Pentecostal. Turnover n/a.

***International Christian College**, 110 St James Road, Glasgow G4 0PS
☎ 0141 552 4040 🖷 0141 552 0808
E: college@icc.ac.uk
Web: www.icc.ac.uk
Training for a range of ministries, focussing on mission, youthwork, pastoral, urban and children's ministry.
Principal: Rev Dr Tony Sargent. *Vice Principal:* Dr Ted Herbert. Lecturers 16, Other staff 10. ***CC*** No.SCO 28032. Began 1892; interdenominational. Formed by merger of Glasgow Bible College and Northumbria Bible College, Sep 1998. Turnover £500,000 to year end Dec 04.

Irish Baptist College, The Baptist Centre, 19 Hillsborough Road, Moira, Craigavon BT67 0HG
☎ 028 9261 9267 🖷 028 9261 0150
E: ibc@thebaptistcentre.org
Web: www.irishbaptistcollege.org/net/co.uk
Training for pastoral and overseas missionary work.
Principal: Dr Hamilton Moore BD MTh PhD. *Secretary/Tutor:* Rev John Birnie MPhil CertEd DipTh. Lecturers 4, Other Staff 2. Began 1892; Baptist. Turnover £187,000 to year end Dec 02.

T

Kensit Memorial Bible College, 104 Hendon Lane, Finchley, London N3 3SQ
☎ 020 8349 9408
Preparing preachers especially for the Protestant Truth Society.
Principal: Rev Philip H Eveson BA MA MTh. Lecturers 1, Other staff 3. ***CC*** No.248506. Began 1905, reconstituted 1968; interdenominational. reconstituted 1968. Turnover n/a.

***King's Bible College & Training Centre**, The Kings Centre, Osney Mead, Oxford OX2 0ES
☎ 01865 297 450
🖷 01865 297 451
E: enquiries@kbctc.org
Web: www.kbctc.org
Promoting Christian faith and training people in theology and mission.
Principal: Mr Simon Shaw. *Office Manager:* Ceri Rees. Lecturers 20, Other staff 4. ***CC*** No.1056921. Began 1983; interdenominational. Turnover £250,000 to year end Jul 02.

King's College London, Department of Theology and Religious Studies, Strand, London WC2R 2LS
☎ 020 7848 2339
🖷 020 7848 2255
Web: www.kcl.ac.uk/theorelig
Head of Department: Prof Judith Lieu. Lecturers 21, Other staff n/a. Began 1829; interdenominational. Turnover n/a.

Kingdom Faith College, Roffey Place Christian Training Centre, Faygate, Horsham RH12 4RU
☎ 01293 851 543
🖷 01293 854 610
E: info@kingdomfaith.com
Web: www.kingdomfaith.com
Principal: Rev Colin Urquhart. Lecturers 5, Other staff 10. ***CC*** No.278746. Began 1984; interdenominational. (Previously Kingdom Faith Revival College). Turnover n/a.

***London School of Theology**, Green Lane, Northwood HA6 2UW
☎ 01923 456 000 🖷 01923 456 001
E: mailbox@lst.ac.uk
Web: www.lst.ac.uk
Evangelical theological college integrating academic standards with spiritual and skills development.
Principal: Rev Dr Derek Tidball BA BD PhD. *Vice-Principal:* Miss Mary Evans. Lecturers 25, Other staff 40. ***CC*** No.312778. Began 1943; interdenominational. (Previously London Bible College). Courses validated by Middlesex University. Turnover £280,000 to year end Aug 04.

†London Theological College, c/o 46 Wordsworth Road, Wallington SM6 9RH
☎ 020 8776 7551 Ⓜ 07876 232 752
🖷 020 8659 6320
E: stewardlee@daum.net
Web: www.ltcuk.org
Academic Dean: Rev Dr Joshua Lee PhD. Lecturers 8, Admin staff 5. ***CC*** No.1078377. Began 1997; interdenominational. Turnover n/a.

London Theological Seminary, 104 Hendon Lane, Finchley, London N3 3SQ
☎ 020 8346 7587 🖷 020 8371 8783
E: principal@ltslondon.org
Web: www.ltslondon.org
Preparing men for home and overseas preaching and pastoral ministry in settled and pioneer situations.
Principal: Rev Philip H Eveson BA, MA, MTh. Lecturers 6, Other staff 2. ***CC*** No.281464. Began 1977; Evangelical Protestant. Turnover n/a.

Mansfield College, Mansfield Road, Oxford OX1 3TF
☎ 01865 270 988 🖷 01865 270 970
E: walter.houston@mansfield.ox.ac.uk
Web: www.mansfield.ox.ac.uk
Education and training for recognised denominational ministries.
Director of Ministerial Training: Rev Dr Walter Houston. Lecturers 4, Other staff n/a. ***CC*** Began 1886; United Reformed and Congregational Federation. Turnover n/a.

***Mattersey Hall**, Mattersey Doncaster DN10 5HD
☎ 01777 817 663 🖷 01777 816 195
E: office@matterseyhall.co.uk
Web: www.matterseyhall.co.uk
Training in Christian leadership, biblical studies and theology, with a charismatic emphasis.
Principal: Rev Paul Alexander. *Vice-Principal (Development):* Rev Dr Andrew Davies. *Vice-Principal (Academic):* Rev Dr Glenn Balfour. Lecturers 15, Other staff 12. ***CC*** No.1032245. Began 19[illegible]9; Assemblies of God but open to all. Turnover £500,000 to year end Dec 00.

Midlands Bible College, PO Box 21[illegible]3, Stone ST15 9WQ
☎ 08700 421 704
E: admin@midbible.ac.uk
Web: www.midbible.ac.uk
Accredited theological studies by open and distance learning, specialising in Hermeneutics and Biblical Studies.
Principal: Dr Calvin Smith BEd M[illegible]. Lecturers 12, Other staff 2. ***CC*** Began 1990; interdenominational. Turnover n/a.

Missionary Institute London, Holcombe House, The Ridgeway, Mill Hill London NW7 4HY
☎ 020 8906 1893 🖷 020 8906 4937
E: mil@mdx.ac.uk
Web: www.the-mil.org.uk
President: Rev Dr Danilo Castello. Lecturers 30, Other staff 6. ***CC*** No.269713. Began 1967; Roman Catholic. Affiliated to Leuven University, Belgium, and Middlesex University. Turnover n/a.

***Moorlands College**, Sopley, Christchurch BH23 7AT
☎ 01425 672 369 🖷 01425 674 162
E: enquiries@moorlands.ac.uk
Web: www.moorlands.ac.uk
Foundation to postgraduate degree level in applied theology; biblically-based practical training for Christian ministry.
Principal: Rev Dr Steve Bracy. *Registrar:* Miss Sharon Prior. *Bursar:* Mr Mike Coulson. Lecturers 12, Other staff 20. ***CC*** No.1092000. Began 1948; interdenominational. Turnover £1,000,000 to year end Dec 02.

For further information see list on Pages 420 - 422

***Nazarene Theological College**, Dene Road, Didsbury, Manchester M20 2GU
☎ 0161 445 3063 🖷 0161 448 0275
E: enquiries@nazarene.ac.uk
Web: www.nazarene.ac.uk
Integrating academic excellence and professional ministry skills training within a context of broadly Wesleyan-Holiness spirituality.
Principal: To be appointed. Lecturers 12, Other staff 8. ***CC*** No.526675. Began 1943; Church of the Nazarene. Incorporating Emmanuel Bible College. Turnover n/a.

New Tribes Mission Bible & Missionary Training College, North Cotes, Grimsby DN36 5XU
☎ 01472 387 711 🖷 01472 387 717
E: bmtc@ntm.org.uk
Web: www.ntm.org.uk.
One-year missiology studies for reaching unreached people groups.
Director of Biblical Studies: Joseph Bailie. *Director of Cross Cultural Communication Studies:* Dr Colin Lamb. Lecturers 12, Other staff 20. ***CC*** No.278627. Began 1980; non-denominational. Turnover included in New Tribes Mission.

Newbold College, St Marks Road, Binfield, Bracknell RG42 4AN
☎ 01344 407 407 🖷 01344 407 406
E: admissions@newbold.ac.uk
Web: www.newbold.ac.uk
Pastoral education, PhD Theology (Wales), degrees/diplomas in Business, Humanities, Behavioural Sciences, English Language, Counselling.
Principal: Dr David Penner. Lecturers 33, Other staff 32. ***CC*** No.1052494. Began 1901; Seventh-day Adventist. Turnover £2,700,000 to year end Dec 00.

†Newman College of Higher Education, Genners Lane, Bartley Green, Birmingham B32 3NT
☎ 0121 476 1181 🖷 0121 476 1196
E: c.a.wormwell@newman.ac.uk
University level education.
Principal: Mrs Pamela Taylor BA MA MPhil PGCE Dip Ed. Staff 280. ***CC*** No.528916. Began 1968; Roman Catholic. Turnover n/a.

***Nexus Trust: Academy of Music Ministry**, 71 Albany Road, Coventry CV5 6JR
☎ 024 7671 3209 🖷 024 7671 7945
E: admin@nexustrust.co.uk
Web: www.nexustrust.co.uk
Training and discipling young Christian musicians in music, worship and ministry.
Director & Head of Drums: Mr Silber. *Head of Guitar & Bible College:* Mr Richard Stephenson. Executive staff 5, Other staff 5. ***CC*** No.1073232. Began 1998; non-denominational. Turnover £364,000 to year end Aug 02.

†Northern Baptist College, Luther King House, Brighton Grove, Rusholme, Manchester M14 5JP
☎ 0161 249 2522 🖷 0161 248 9201
E: richard.kidd@lkh.co.uk
Principal: Rev Dr Richard Kidd. Lecturers 4, Other staff 6. ***CC*** No.526653. Began 1964; ecumenical. Turnover £300,000 to year end Dec 02.

Northern College, Luther King House, Brighton Grove, Rusholme, Manchester M14 5JP
☎ 0161 249 2506 🖷 0161 248 9201
Web: www.ptem.org.uk
Educating people for stipendiary ministry, non-stipendiary ministry and community development work.
Principal: Rev John M Campbell BSc PhD. Lecturers 4, Other staff 2. ***CC*** No.529253. Began 1843; United Reformed and Congregational. Turnover n/a.

* **Oak Hill Theological College**, Chase Side, Southgate, London N14 4PS
☎ 020 8449 0467 🖷 020 8441 5996
E: clareo@oakhill.ac.uk
Web: www.oakhill.ac.uk
Biblical training for contemporary ministry; for pastor-teachers, cross-cultural workers, evangelists, youth workers.
Principal: Rev Professor David Peterson MA BD PhD. *Vice Principal:* Rev Chris Green BD. Lecturers 14, Other staff 20. ***CC*** No.1076618. Began 1932; Anglican. Turnover n/a.

* **Oxford Centre for Mission Studies**, St Philip and St James Church, PO Box 70, Woodstock Road, Oxford OX2 6HB
☎ 01865 556 071 M 07808 297 043
🖷 01865 510 823
E: ocms@ocms.ac.uk
Web: www.ocms.ac.uk
Research for PhD and Masters programmes.
Executive Director: Rev Canon Dr Chris Sugden MA, MPhil, PhD. *Academic Dean:* Dr Bernard Far. *Chair of the Board of Directors:* Rt Rev Dr Hwa Yung. Academic staff 10, Admin staff 8. ***CC*** No.290112. Began 1984; non-denominational. See also Regnum Books. Turnover £585,454 to year end Dec 04.

†Partnership for Theological Education, Luther King House, Brighton Grove, Rusholme, Manchester M14 5JP
☎ 0161 224 6404
E: registrar@lkh.co.uk
Web: www.ptem.org.uk
Providing full-time and part-time study in contextual theology.
Director: Name not supplied. Lecturers n/a, Other staff n/a. ***CC*** No.1082375. Began n/a; ecumenical. (Previously Manchester Christian Institute). Turnover n/a.

Peniel College of Higher Education, 49 Coxtie Green Road, Pilgrims Hatch, Brentwood CM14 5PS
☎ 01277 372 996 🖷 01277 375 332
Web: www.pche.ac.uk
Providing full-time, part-time and correspondence courses; fully-accredited degree and diploma courses, also Masters degree.
Principal: Dr Michael S B Reid, ThD DD MA. Lecturers 10, Other staff n/a. Began 1982; Free Pentecostal. Turnover n/a.

The Queen's Foundation for Ecumenical Theological Education, Somerset Road, Edgbaston, Birmingham B15 2QH
☎ 0121 454 1527 🖷 0121 454 8171
E: enquire@queens.ac.uk
Web: www.queens.ac.uk
Training for Anglican, Methodist, United Reformed ordinands, mission partners and lay people.
Principal: Rev Canon Dr David Hewlett BA PhD. Lecturers 14, Other staff 7. ***CC*** No.528989. Began 1828; ecumenical. Turnover n/a.

***Redcliffe College**, Wotton House, Horton Road, Gloucester GL1 3PT
☎ 01452 308 097 🖷 01452 503 949
E: admin@redcliffe.org
Web: www.redcliffe.org
Providing flexible mission training in biblical, theological and cross-cultural studies; practical placements.
Principal: Rev Dr Simon Steer, BA DipTh MDiv PGCE PhD. *Fund Development Manager:* Mr Tim Lewis. *Admissions Administrator:* Mrs Debs Austin-Sparks. Lecturers 8, Other staff 12. ***CC*** No.1054907. Began 1892; interdenominational. Turnover £588,000 to year end Jul 05.

Reformed Theological College, 35 Knockbracken Road, Belfast BT8 4SE
☎ 028 9081 5782
E: rtj@rpc.org
Web: www.rpc.org
Training men for Gospel ministry and for missionary service; small classes.
Principal: Rev Prof Edward Donnelly, BA MTh. Lecturers 5, Other staff n/a. ***CC*** Began 1854; Reformed Presbyterian Church of Ireland. Turnover n/a.

Regent's Park College, Pusey Street, Oxford OX1 2LB
☎ 01865 288 120 🖷 01865 288 121
E: postmaster@regents.ox.ac.uk
Web: www.rpc.ox.ac.uk
Principal: Rev Dr Paul S Fiddes MA DPhil DD. Lecturers 8, Other staff 6. ***CC*** No.309710. Began 1810; Baptist. Turnover £1,200,000 to year end Aug 04.

***Regents Theological College**, Dept UK, London Road, Nantwich CW5 6LW
☎ 01270 615 400 🖷 01270 610 013
E: info@regents-tc.ac.uk
Web: www.regents-tc.ac.uk
Affiliated to University of Wales, Bangor.
Principal: Rev Nigel C Teen. Lecturers 13, Other staff 55. ***CC*** No.251549. Began 1925; Elim Pentecostal but open to all. (Previously Elim Bible College). Turnover £1,300,000 to year end Dec 05.

***Ridley Hall**, Ridley Hall Road, Cambridge CB3 9HG
☎ 01223 741 080 🖷 01223 741 081
E: ridley-pa@lists.cam.ac.uk
Web: www.ridley.cam.ac.uk
Training for ordained ministry, youth and community work, Licensed Readers and other lay ministries. Sabbaticals.
Principal: Rev Canon Christopher Cocksworth PhD. *Bursar:* Mr Colin MacRae. Tutorial staff 12, Other staff 14. ***CC*** No.311456. Began 1880; Anglican. Turnover £100,000 to year end Dec 02.

Ripon College, Cuddesdon, Oxford OX44 9EX
☎ 01865 874 404 🖷 01865 875 431
E: admin@ripon-cuddesdon.ac.uk
Web: www.rcc.ac.uk
Principal: Rev Canon Prof Martyn Percy. Lecturers 6, Other staff 9. ***CC*** No.309714. Began 1854; Anglican. Turnover n/a.

St Chad's College, 18 North Bailey, Durham DH1 3RH
☎ 0191 334 3358 🖷 0191 334 3371
E: j.p.cassidy@durham.ac.uk
Web: www.stchads.ac.uk
University College committed to Christian values and strong personal support.
Principal: Rev Canon Dr Joseph Cassidy. *Chaplain:* Rev Robert MacSwain. *Senior Tutor:* Dr Margaret Masson. Lecturers 15, Other staff 20. Began 1904; Anglican. Turnover £1,600,000 to year end Jul 05.

St John's College, Durham with Cranmer Hall, 3 South Bailey, Durham DH1 3RJ
☎ 0191 334 3500 🖷 0191 334 3501
E: sj-cranmer-hall@durham.ac.uk
Web: www.dur.ac.uk/st-johns.college
Principal: Rt Rev Stephen Sykes. *Warden:* Rev Canon Anne Dyer. Lecturers 13, Other staff 38. ***CC*** No.113496. Began 1909; Anglican but open to all. Turnover n/a.

***St John's College, Nottingham**, Chilwell Lane, Bramcote, Nottingham NG9 3DS
☎ 0115 925 1114 🖷 0115 943 6438
E: college@stjohns-nottm.ac.uk
Web: www.stjohns-nottm.ac.uk
Principal: Canon Dr Christina Baxter BA PhD. *Dean of College:* Rev John Coyne. Lecturers 9, Other staff 15. ***CC*** No.1026706. Began 1863 as the London College of Divinity; Anglican. Turnover £1,100,000 to year end Aug 04.

St John's Roman Catholic Seminary, Wonersh, Guildford GU5 0QX
☎ 01483 892 217 🖷 01483 894 531
E: rector@wonersh.org
Web: www.wonersh.org
Training for ordained ministry with part and full-time BTh; open to lay students.
Rector: Rev Canon K Haggerty MA STL PGCE PhD. *Bursar:* Mr Tony Lee. Lecturers 27, Other staff n/a. ***CC*** No.251342. Began 1891; Roman Catholic. Turnover n/a.

†**St Mary's College, Strawberry Hill**, School of Theology, Philosophy and History, Waldegrave Road, Twickenham TW1 4SX
☎ 020 8240 4198 🖷 020 8240 2362
E: lourdasc@smuc.ac.uk
Web: www.smuc.ac.uk
Head of Department: Fr Michael A Hays. Lecturers 9, Other staff 2. Began n/a; Roman Catholic. (Previously University of Surrey, St Mary's College). Turnover n/a.

†**St Mary's Seminary**, Oscott College, Sutton Coldfield B73 5AA
☎ 0121 321 5000
Rector: Name not supplied. Lecturers 21, Other staff 4. ***CC*** Began 1794; Roman Catholic. Turnover n/a.

St Michael's College, Llandaff, Cardiff CF5 2YJ
☎ 029 2056 3379 🖷 029 2083 8008
E: info@stmichaels.ac.uk
Web: www.stmichaels.ac.uk
Initial and in-post ministerial training (with Cardiff University); training for specialist ministries.
Principal: Rev Dr Peter Sedgwick. Lecturers n/a, Other staff n/a. Began 1893; ecumenical. (Previously St Michael and All Angels' Theological College). Turnover n/a.

St Stephen's House, 15 Marston Street, Oxford OX4 1JX
☎ 01865 247 874 🖷 01865 794 338
E: enquiries@ssho.ac.uk
Web: www.ssho.ox.ac.uk
Training men and women for ordained and other ministries, theological education and formation.
Principal: Rev Canon Dr Robin Ward PhD. *Bursar:* Mrs Shirley Gray. Lecturers 5, Other staff 7. ***CC*** No.309593. Began 1876; Anglican. Hall of Oxford University. Turnover £650,000 to year end Dec 01.

Scottish Baptist College, Block K, 202 University of Paisley, Paisley PA1 2BE
☎ 0141 848 3988 🖷 0141 848 3939
E: isabella.stevenson@paisley.ac.uk
Web: www.scottishbaptistcollege.org
Formative training for Christian ministry: BD(Hons), diplomas, modules; full and part-time.
Principal: Rev Jim Gordon. Full-time Lecturers 4, Part-time Lecturers 6, Admin staff 1. ***CC*** No.SCO 16819. Began 1894; Baptist. Turnover £92,000 to year end May 03.

Scotus College, 2 Chesters Road, Bearsden, Glasgow G61 4AG
☎ 0141 942 8384 🖷 0141 943 1767
E: officeadmin@scotuscollege.org
Web: www.scotuscollege.org
National seminary in Scotland.
Rector: Rev William R McFadden PhB STL MS. Lecturers 20, Other staff 10. Began 1985; Roman Catholic. Turnover n/a.

Selly Oak Centre for Mission Studies, The Queen's Foundation, Somerset Road, Edgbaston, Birmingham B15 2QH
☎ 0121 454 1527 🖷 0121 454 8171
E: enquire-mc@queens.ac.uk
Web: www.queens.ac.uk
Mission training for the world church and the church in Britain and Ireland.
Director: Rev Val Ogden. Lecturers 4, Other staff 7. ***CC*** No.234518. Began 1923; Anglican/Methodist. (Previously United College of the Ascension). Turnover n/a.

South London Christian College, 72a Mayeswood Road, Grove Park, London SE12 9RP
☎ 020 7703 9999 🖷 020 7703 5566
E: slcclondon@aol.com
Web: www.christiancollege.org.uk
Training to doctorate level in theology, counselling, worship and ministry.
Principal: Dr Femi Olowo. *Director:* Rev Dr David Curtis. Lecturers 22, Other staff 5. ***CC*** No.1109573. Began 1991; Assemblies of God but open to all. Extension campuses in Luton and Nottingham. Turnover £420,000 to year end Oct 04.

For further information see list on Pages 420 422

†South Wales Baptist College, 54 Richmond Road, Cardiff CF24 3UR
☎ 029 2025 5066
🖷 029 2041 1566
E: admin@swbc.org.uk
Web: www.swbc.org.uk
Undergraduate and postgraduate training for Baptist ministers. Informal training courses for church congregations.
Principal: Rev John Weaver BSc MA PhD. Lecturers 3, Other staff 5. ***CC*** No.525777. Began 1807; Baptist. Turnover n/a

***Southall School of Languages and Missionary Orientation**, Western Road, Southall UB2 5DS
☎ 020 8574 4456
M: 0771 382 995
🖷 020 8606 969
Email: info@sslmo.co.uk
Web: www.sslmo.co.uk
Director: Pastor Boyd Williams. *Secretary:* Mrs Christine Streets. Executive staff 4, Other staff 14. ***CC*** No.1068126. Began 1989; Baptist. No magazine. Turnover £200,000 to year end Dec 00.
Taught distance learning: MA in missional leadership, BA in theology; leadership, justice and development courses.

***Spurgeon's College**, 189 South Norwood Hill, London SE25 6DJ
☎ 020 8653 0850
🖷 020 8771 0959
E: enquiries@spurgeons.ac.uk
Web: www.spurgeons.ac.uk
Preparing Christians for mission and ministry in the contemporary world.
Principal: Rev Dr Nigel Wright. *Deputy Principal:* Rev Dr Ian Randall. Lecturers 25, Other staff 20. ***CC*** No.1096721. Began 1856; Baptist but open to all. Turnover £1,100,000 to year end Aug 05.

Theological Institute of the Scottish Episcopal Church, Forbes House, 21 Grosvenor Crescent, Edinburgh EH12 5EE
☎ 0131 225 6357
E: info@tisec.org.uk
Web: www.tisec.org.uk
Initial ministerial education.
Ministry Development Officers: Rev Dr Michael Fuller. Dr Kenneth Fleming. Lecturers 18, Other staff 2. Began 1810; Scottish Episcopal Church. Turnover n/a.
Initial ministerial education.

***Tilsley College**, 78 Muir Street, Motherwell ML1 1BN
☎ 01698 266 776
🖷 01698 275 418
E: college@glo-europe.org
Web: www.glo-europe.org
Training for service and mission.
Principal: Dr Stephen McQuoid. Lecturers 4, Other staff 2. ***CC*** No.CR 41802. Began 1975; non-denominational. (Previously Gospel Literature Outreach Training for Service). Turnover n/a.

***Trinity College Bristol**, Stoke Hill, Stoke Bishop, Bristol BS9 1JP
☎ 0117 968 2803 🖷 0117 968 7470
E: admissions@trinity-bris.ac.uk
Web: www.trinity-bris.ac.uk
Mission and ministry training in college context; certificate, undergraduate and postgraduate levels.
Principal: Rev Canon George Kovoor. *Vice Principal:* Rev Dr John Nolland. Lecturers 10, Other staff 37. ***CC*** No.311793. Began 1972; Anglican but open to all. Turnover £1,300,000 to year end June 05.

†Trinity College Carmarthen, College Road, Carmarthen SA31 3EP
☎ 01267 676 767
🖷 01237 676 766
E: t.hughes@trinity-cm.ac.uk
Web: www.trinity-cm.ac.uk
Principal: Dr Medwin Hughes. Lecturers 85, Other staff 120. ***CC*** No.525786. Began 1848; Anglican. Turnover n/a.

Union Theological College, 108 Botanic Avenue, Belfast BT7 1JT
☎ 028 9020 5080
🖷 028 9020 5099
E: jp.taylor@union.ac.uk
Web: www.union.ac.uk
Equipping Christians for ministry and mission in today's world.
Principal: Rev Professor J P Taylor TD MA (Glasgow, Oxon, QUB) MTh. Lecturers 6, Other staff 11. Began 1853; Presbyterian but open to all. Affiliated to Queen's University. Turnover n/a.

†University of Aberdeen, Department of Divinity and Religious Studies, Aberdeen AB24 3UB
☎ 01224 272 380
🖷 01224 273 750
E: divinity@abdn.ac.uk
Web: www.abdn.ac.uk/divinity
Head of Department: Dr Seth D Kunin BA MA PhD. Lecturers 15, Other staff 3. Began 1495; interdenominational. Turnover n/a.

†University of Edinburgh, Centre for the Study of Christianity in the non-Western World, New College, Mound Place, Edinburgh EH1 2LX
☎ 0131 650 8952
🖷 0131 650 7952
E: divinity.faculty@ed.ac.uk
Web: www.div.ed.ac.uk/prosp/pstgrad/101-worldchristianity
Director: Prof David Kerr BA MA DPhil. Lecturers 3, Other staff 4. ***CC*** Began 1982; non-denominational. Turnover n/a.

†University of Edinburgh, Faculty of Divinity, New College, Mound Place, Edinburgh EH1 2LX
☎ 0131 650 8900 🖷 0131 650 7952
E: divinity.faculty@ed.ac.uk
Web: www.div.ed.ac.uk
Principal: Professor Graeme Auld. Lecturers 27, Other staff 15. Began 1584; non-denominational. College began 1846 as Church of Scotland College. Turnover n/a.

†University of Glasgow, Faculty of Divinity, Glasgow G12 8QQ
☎ 0141 330 6524 🖷 0141 330 4943
Web: www.religions.divinity.gla.ac.uk
Dean: To be appointed. Lecturers 16, Other staff 3. Began 1452; interdenominational. Turnover n/a.

†University of St Andrews, School of Divinity, St Mary's College, South Street, St Andrews KY16 9JU
☎ 01334 462 851 🖷 01334 462 852
E: divinity@st-andrews.ac.uk
Web: www.st-andrews.ac.uk/divinity/home.html
University-level programmes for undergraduates and postgraduates in arts and divinity.
Principal of College: Prof T H Heart. Lecturers 16, Other staff 3. ***CC*** No.SCO 02201. Began 1410; College 1539 interdenominational. Turnover n/a.

Ushaw College, Durham DH7 9RH
☎ 0191 373 8517 🖷 0191 373 8504
E: tracy.maratty@ushaw.ac.uk
Web: www.ushaw.ac.uk
Rector: Rev T P Drainey. Lecturers 19, Other staff 5. ***CC*** Began 1808; Roman Catholic. Turnover n/a.

Wesley College, College Park Drive, Henbury Road, Bristol BS10 7QD
☎ 0117 959 1200
🖷 0117 950 1277
E: admin@wesley-college-bristol.ac.uk
Web: www.wesley-college-bristol.ac.uk
Providing theological education and training for lay and ordained; preparation for ministry in Methodist church.
Principal: Rev Dr Jonathan H Pye. *Director of Academic Studies and Research:* Dr Mervyn Davies. Full Time Lecturers 3. ***CC*** Began 1921; Methodist but open to all. Turnover n/a.

†Wesley House, Cambridge, Jesus Lane, Cambridge CB5 8BJ
☎ 01223 741 053 🖷 01223 321 177
E: bursar@wesley.cam.ac.uk
Web: www.wesley.org.uk
Training women and men for ministry in the Methodist church.
Principal: Rev Dr Philip Luscombe. Lecturers 2. ***CC*** No.311446. Began 1921; Methodist. Turnover £400,000 to year end Aug 02.

Westcott House, Jesus Lane, Cambridge CB5 8BP
☎ 01223 741 000
🖷 01223 741 002
E: general-enquiries@westcott.cam.ac.uk or mgvr2@cam.ac.uk
Web: www.westcott.cam.ac.uk
Ordination training and formation for the Church of England in an ecumenically-diverse theological federation.
Principal: Rev Michael Roberts MA MDiv. *Vice Principal:* Rev Angela Tilby. *Director of Studies:* Rev Dr Victoria Raymer. Lecturers 5, Other staff 8. ***CC*** No.311445. Began 1881; Anglican. Turnover £700,000 to year end Dec 02.

T

Westfield House, 30 Huntingdon Road, Cambridge CB3 0HH
☎ 01223 354 331 🖷 01223 355 265
E: regquirk@aol.com
Web: homepage.ntlworld.com/westfield.house
Teaching theology within a confessional Lutheran framework, including preparation for ordination.
Preceptor: Rev Reginald C Quirk BA BD MPhil (Cantab). Lecturers 3, Other staff 1. **CC** No.220466. Began 1962; Lutheran. Turnover £100,000 to year end Dec 02.

Westminster College, Cambridge, Madingley Road, Cambridge CB3 0AA
☎ 01223 741 084 🖷 01223 300 765
E: mr258@cam.ac.uk
Web: www.westminster.cam.ac.uk
Training ministers for the United Reformed Church; history archives; conference venue.
Principal: Rev Dr Stephen Orchard MA PhD. Lecturers 5, Other staff 10. **CC** No.XR 80624. Began 1899; United Reformed. Member of Cambridge Theological Federation. Turnover n/a.

†Whitefield College of the Bible and Theological Hall of the Free Presbyterian Church of Ulster, 117 Banbridge Road, Gilford, Craigavon BT63 6DL
☎ 028 4066 2232 🖷 028 4066 2232
Principal: Dr John Douglas. Lecturers 13, Other staff 4. **CC** No.XN 59402. Began 1979; Free Presbyterian. Turnover n/a.

Wilson Carlile College of Evangelism (Church Army), Wilson Carlile Campus, Cavendish Street, Sheffield S3 7RZ
☎ 0114 278 7020 🖷 0114 279 5863
E: training@sheffieldcentre.org.uk
Web: www.churcharmy.org.uk
University-validated programme for mission-shaped training for clergy, laity and evangelists.
Principal: Rev David Jeans MA, MPhil. *Director of Studies:* Rev Gary Wilton. Lecturers 2, Other staff n/a. **CC** No.226226. Began 1882; Anglican. Turnover £650,000 to year end Dec 02.

Wycliffe Hall, 54 Banbury Road Oxford OX2 6PW
☎ 01865 274 200 🖷 01865 274 215
E: enquiries@wycliffe.ox.ac.uk
Web: www.wycliffe.ox.ac.uk
Evangelical theological college training men and women for ministry in the church and the world.
Principal: Rev Richard Turnbull BA MA PhD CA. *Director, Oxford Centre for Evangelism and Apologetics:* Rev Prof Alister McGrath DD MA DPhil. *Development Officer:* Mr Mark Tindall. Teaching Staff 16, Other staff 13. **CC** No.309703. Began 1877; Anglican. Turnover £1,677,000 to year end Dec 05.

T

For further information see list on Pages 420 - 422

THEOLOGICAL COLLEGES & BIBLE SCHOOLS (PART-TIME)

By Denomination
Tuition fees per annum unless stated otherwise
Colleges which did not supply any of this information are not listed here.

Name	Students	Course details	Fees
Anglican			
Lincoln Theological Institute for the Study of Religion and Society	n/a	Postgraduate research, MA	n/a
St Albans and Oxford Ministry Course	68	3 years. Ministerial and lay training.	£4,173 (associate student £2,650)
St John's Extension Studies	1,600	Biblical and theological studies, religious education, pastoral counselling, crosscultural mission	n/a
Anglican, Methodist, United Reformed			
Carlisle and Blackburn Diocesan Training Institute	n/a	3 years. For ordinands and lay people	£4,450
Eastern Region Ministry Course	98	Full- and part-time. For ordinands and lay people	n/a
The North East Oecumenical Course (NEOC)	42	3 years for ordinands and lay people	£2,040
North Thames Ministerial Training Course	Unlimited	For ordinands and lay people	n/a
South East Institute for Theological Education (SEITE)	Unlimited	3 years. Ministerial and lay training	£3,621
South West Ministry Training Course	Unlimited	Part-time, for ordinands	n/a
West Midlands Ministerial Training Course	60	For ordinands and lay people	£4,200
Apostolic Episcopal Free Church			
Anglian Ecclesiastical and Theological Seminary	n/a	Ministerial training; spiritual healing, counselling	n/a
Church in Wales			
South Wales Ordination Course	6	For non-stipendiary ministers	n/a
Free Church of Scotland			
Free Church College	30	3 years, diploma; part-time courses, postgraduate	£1,750
Interdenominational / Ecumenical / Non-denominational			
Central School of Religion	n/a	1 to 5 years. For ministers, graduates, church musicians, lay preachers.	Variable
Christ the Redeemer College	47	Varying length, for ministers	n/a
Covenant Bible College	9	1 year part-time or full-time. Biblical theology, diploma of biblical studies or Christian ministries	n/a
The East Midlands Ministry Training Course	n/a	Part-time MA/Diploma/Certificate Courses; theological & pastoral studies	n/a
East Midlands School of Christian Ministry	100	1 or 2 years. Theology; correspondence courses in Greek, Hebrew	£70
Emmaus Bible School UK	n/a	Studies in over 120 languages. For missionaries and missions	n/a
Greenwich School of Theology	n/a	2 or 3 years. Theology by distance learning at undergraduate and postgraduate level.	£850
Hampstead Bible College	100	NVQs in Biblical studies, City and Guilds Further Education Teacher training, Information Technology	n/a
Kingdom Faith Church, Lamplugh House	25	10 weeks	£800
Mallon De Theological College	n/a	Open, distance learning in theology	n/a
Manchester Christian College/Training Centre	50	3 years, degrees	£966
The Missionary Training Service	76	Mission & cross cultural skills, various courses	n/a
Moorlands College	150	Distance learning, year courses, placement based BA, MA	Variable
Northern Ordination Course	n/a	Ministerial training	n/a
The Open Theological College	n/a	6 years part-time distance learning Honours degree in theology	n/a
Sarum College	n/a	Short courses in theological education and training	n/a
S.E.A.N. International (UK)	n/a	Theological Education by Extension, basic level students, local churches, group study	n/a
STETS Southern Theological Education and Training Scheme	100	Ministerial and lay training	n/a
Theological Training Course	n/a	4 years, for preaching and pastoral ministry. 2 residential weeks per year	£191
West of England Ministerial Training Course	100	For ordinands and readers	n/a
West Sussex Bible Correspondence College	100	College certificate	From £45
YMCA, George Williams College	n/a	For youth and community workers	n/a
Methodist			
Edgehill Christian Education Centre	n/a	Part-time/correspondence. Theological access course	Variable
Pentecostal			
Christ the Redeemer Bible College	47	Varying length, for ministers	n/a
International Bible Institute of London (Kensington Temple)	134 full-time 1,700 part-time	1 or 2 year Diplomas	n/a
Irish Pentecostal Bible College	20	American accredited degrees	n/a
The Maria Morley Crawcrook Pentecostal College	n/a	1 year part-time/distance learning for ordination or lay vocations	n/a
New Life Bible School	40	1 or 2 years, for lay people	n/a
Religious Society of Friends			
Woodbrooke Quaker Study Centre	70	2 days to 1 year, adult education, research	£110 per course
Reformed and Congregational			
Cranmer Memorial and Reformation Theology College	n/a	1 to 3 years. Theology: diploma, general ordination, licentiate, fellowship courses	n/a

THEOLOGICAL COLLEGES & BIBLE SCHOOLS (PART TIME)

Main courses offered do not require full-time study and/or are less than one year in length
For full-time and longer courses see Theological Colleges & Bible School (Full-time) on Page 420.
For other training courses see Training Centres & Services on Page 435.

†Anglian Ecclesiastical and Theological Seminary, 50 Bells Place, Coleford GL16 8BX
☎ Number not supplied
Ordination training for the Apostolic Episcopal Free Churches Alliance.
Principal: Most Rev Dr Bruno Von Ehrenberg MD, D.Hom, DD, OSC. Lecturers 3. Began 1995; Apostolic Episcopal Free Churches. No magazine. Turnover n/a.

Carlisle and Blackburn Diocesan Training Institute, Church House, West Walls, Carlisle CA3 8UE
☎ 01228 522 573 🖷 01228 815 400
E: admin@cbdti.org.uk
Web: www.cbdti.org.uk
Training for all categories of ordained ministry, also local Reader training.
Principal: Rev Canon Tim Herbert, BA, MPhil, PhD. Lecturers 4. Began 1978; Anglican, Methodist, Salvation Army and United Reformed but open to all. (Previously Carlisle Diocesan Training Institute). Affiliated to St Martin's College, Lancaster. No magazine. Turnover n/a.

Central School of Religion, 49 Upper Tooting Park, London SW17 7SN
☎ 020 8675 0180 🖷 020 8675 0180
Training for ministers and graduates, church musicians, lay preachers.
Director of Studies: J Pinnington MA, DPhil, DD. No full-time staff. Began 1896; non-denominational. No magazine. Turnover n/a.

***Christ the Redeemer College**, CRBC House, 6 Kennington Lane, London SE11 4LS
☎ 020 7735 7100 M: 07958 651 792
🖷 020 7735 7187
E: crbcgroup@aol.com
Web: www.thecrbc.org
Theological and life skills training.
Principal: Pastor Daniel Akhazemea FCA PGD. Executive staff 1, Admin staff 2. ***CC*** No.3762755. Began 1998; non-denominational. (Previously Christ the Redeemer Bible College). Magazine: *CRBC News* (3,000 quarterly). Turnover £50,000 to year end Dec 00.

T

†*Covenant Bible College, 214 Elephant and Castle Shopping Centre, London SE1 6TE
☎ 020 7701 9959 / 7277 0272
M: 07712 079 263 🖷 020 7277 0824
E: covbibleco@aol.com
Web: www.covbibleco.org.uk
Director: Rev Paul Jinadu. *Provost:* Rev Gbenro Adewunmi. Lecturers 4, Admin staff 3. ***CC*** No.1004343. Began 1988; New Covenant Church but open to all. Magazine: *Inspired*(Circulation & frequency n/a). Turnover n/a.

Cranmer Memorial Bible College and Seminary, PO Box 20, Bexhill-on-Sea TN40 2ZH
☎ 01424 734 345 M: 07764 475 216
E: cmbc1@freenetname.co.uk
Theological training of men for the Reformed Protestant ministry; distance learning.
Principal: Rev Dr P J Gadsden. Lecturers 7, Other staff n/a. Began 1936; Reformed and Congregational. Incorporating the Institute of Evangelical Protestant Research and Development. No magazine. Turnover n/a.

The East Midlands Ministry Training Course, Room C90, School of Education, University of Nottingham, Jubilee Campus, Wollaton Road, Nottingham NG8 1BB
☎ 0115 951 4854 🖷 0115 951 4817
E: emmtc@nottingham.ac.uk
Part-time diploma course in theological and pastoral studies for students remaining in regular work.
Principal: Rev Canon Michael J Taylor MA STB PhL PhD. Lecturers 3, Other staff 2. ***CC*** No.512143. Began 1973; interdenominational. No magazine. Turnover n/a.

East Midlands School of Christian Ministry, Elim Church Centre, Ashby Road, Loughborough LE11 3AF
☎ 01509 234 306
E: richard@schoolofministry.org.uk
Web: www.schoolofministry.org.uk
Providing Christian ministry training for busy people; theology, correspondence courses, NT Greek, OT Hebrew.
Principal: Mr Richard Lee DipTh. Part-time lecturers 13, Other staff 5. ***CC*** No.251549. Began 1992; non-denominational. No magazine. Turnover £7,000 to year end Jun 00.

Eastern Region Ministry Course, 5 Pound Hill, Cambridge CB3 0AE
☎ 01223 741 026 🖷 01223 741 027
E: secretary@ermc.cam.ac.uk
Web: www.ermc.cam.ac.uk
Training for ministry across eastern England and Europe by dispersed learning and centre-based teaching.
Co-Principals: Rev Dr Malcolm Brown, Rev Canon Dr Mike Butterworth. Lecturers 6, Other staff 2. ***CC*** No.1090989. Began 1977; Anglican, Methodist, United Reformed. (Previously East Anglican Ministerial Training Couse). No magazine. Turnover n/a.

Edgehill Christian Education Centre, 9 Lennoxvale, Malone Road, Belfast BT9 5BY
☎ 028 9068 6938 🖷 028 9068 2153
E: ecec@irishmethodist.org
Web: www.irishmethodist.org/ecec
Lay training centre: theological access course (accredited), part-time classes, correspondence courses.
Coordinator: Mrs Elaine Barnett. Lecturers 2, Other staff 4. ***CC*** No.XN 46164. Began 1984; Methodist but open to all. No magazine. Turnover £60,000 to year end Dec 04.

Emmaus Bible School UK, Carlett Boulevard, Eastham, Wirral CH62 8BZ
☎ 0151 327 1172/6153/7373
🖷 0151 327 1592
E: info@emmausuk.org.uk
Web: www.emmausuk.org.uk
Offering studies in over 120 languages used by missionaries and missions worldwide. 93 English speaking studies.
UK Director: Mr David A Thompson. Executive staff 1, Other staff 8. ***CC*** No.267322. Began 1951; interdenominational. Magazine: *By the Way* (2,000 quarterly). Turnover n/a.

Free Church College, 15 North Bank Street, The Mound, Edinburgh EH1 2LS
☎ 0131 226 5286 🖷 0131 220 0597
Web: www.freescotcoll.ac.uk
Offering 3 or 4 year Bachelor of Theology course; Master of Theology degree.
Principal: Rev Prof Donald Macleod MA. Lecturers 5, Other staff 3. ***CC*** No.SCO 12925. Began 1843; Free Church of Scotland. No magazine. Turnover n/a.

Greenwich School of Theology, 29 Howbeck Lane, Clarborough, Retford DN22 9LW
☎ 01757 702 191 🖷 01777 703 526
E: woody.gst@btopenworld.com
Web: www.gschooltheol.com
Teaching theology at a distance; individually-guided study in cooperation with North-West University, South Africa.
Registrar: Mr C Woodall BA (Hons) MA. Full-time staff 4. ***CC*** No.1097904. Began 1958; interdenominational. Turnover £36,541 to year end Dec 02.

Hampstead Bible College, 224 Walworth Road, London SE17 1JE
☎ 020 7708 2185 M: 07957 113 9[illegible]5
🖷 020 7708 2206
E: admin@hampsteadbiblecollege.org
Web: www.hampsteadbiblecollege.org
Full and part-time, day courses; biblical studies, FE teacher training, basic IT, ***CC****NA, MCSE.*
Principal: Rev Jan Owbridge. Lecturers 12, Other staff 5. ***CC*** No.1050760. Began 1983; non-denominational. (Previously Hampstead Bible School). No magazine. Turnover n/a.

For further information see list on Page 431

†Institute for Orthodox Christian Studies, Wesley House, Jesus Lane, Cambridge CB5 8BJ
☎ 01223 741 037 🖷 01223 741 370
E: info@iocs.cam.ac.uk
Web: www.iocs.cam.ac.uk
Centre for higher education and research in Orthodox Christian studies.
Principal: Dr Marcus Plested. *Communications Officer:* Miss Esther Hookway. Executive staff 1, Other staff 1. **CC** No.1076510. Began 1999; Orthodox. No magazine. Turnover £150,000 to year end Dec 02.

***International Bible Institute of London (Kensington Temple)**, KT Summit House, 100 Hanger Lane, Ealing W5 1EZ
☎ 020 8799 6162 🖷 020 8998 4361
E: info@ibiol.org
Web: www.ibiol.org
Dean of Students: Praise Olatona. Lecturers 20, Other staff 4. **CC** No.251549. Began 1985; Elim Pentecostal but open to all. Turnover n/a.

Irish Pentecostal Bible College, 63 Abbey Road, Millisle, Newtownards BT22 2DG
☎ 028 9186 2232 M 07814 038 330
E: david@irish-pentecostal.com
Web: www.irish-pentecostal.com
Preparing God's people for works of service.
Principal: Pastor David Carnduff MTh. Lecturers 3. **CC** No.251549. Began 2001 Pentecostal. Affiliated to Regents Theological College; member of European Pentecostal Theological Association. Turnover n/a.

Lincoln Theological Institute for the Study of Religion and Society, Department of Religions and Theology, University of Manchester, Oxford Road, Manchester M13 9PL
☎ 0161 275 8594
E: peter.scott@manchester.ac.uk
Web: www.arts.manchester.ac.uk
Supervising research projects including public health, Europe, jubilee issues, culture, women priests, hospital chaplaincy.
Director: Dr Peter Scott. Executive staff 1, Other staff 1. **CC** No.527278. Began 1997; Anglican but open to all. No magazine. Turnover £100,000 to year end Dec 98.

***Mallon de Theological College**, 11a Methley Grove, Leeds LS7 3PA
☎ No telephone
E: mallon.detc@bigfoot.com
Web: www.theocentric.net
Providing open distance learning theological courses.
Principal: Rev Steve Hakes MTh. Executive staff 1, Other staff 1. Began 1989; ecumenical. (Previously Ekklesia). No magazine. Turnover n/a.

***Manchester Christian College & Training Centre**, Chippenham Road, Ancoats, Manchester M4 6FF
☎ 0161 203 5242 🖷 0161 202 1827
E: manchesterchristiancollege@hotmail.com
Principal: Rev Samuel Arthur. Lecturers 4, Other staff 2. **CC** No.276954. Began 1978; interdenominational. No magazine. Turnover £65,000 to year end Dec 05.

***The Missionary Training Service**, Flat 5, 40 Buckingham Gate, London SW1E 6BS
☎ 020 7932 0728 M: 07903 903 458
🖷 020 7932 0728
E: coord@missionarytraining.org
Web: www.missionarytraining.org or www.trainforchrist.org
Internet and correspondence missionary training courses; multi-lingual database of evangelical training courses world-wide.
Coordinator: Rev Ian E Benson. Executive staff 1, Other staff 1. **CC** No.1073046. Began 1993; non-denominational. No magazine. Turnover £15,935 to year end Dec 04.

***Moorlands College**, Sopley, Christchurch BH23 7AT
☎ 01425 672 369 🖷 01425 674 162
E: enquiries@moorlands.ac.uk
Web: www.moorlands.ac.uk
Christian training courses based in local church/Christian organisation and college. Certificate to postgraduate level.
Principal: Rev Dr Steve Brady. Lecturers 10, Support and admin staff 21. **CC** No.1092000. Began 1948; interdenominational. Magazine: *Moorings*(Circulation & frequency n/a). Turnover n/a.

The Maria Morley Crawcrook Pentecostal College, 50 Clayton Street West, Newcastle upon Tyne NE1 4EX
☎ 0191 242 8676 🖷 0191 232 2090
E: pentecostals@crawcrook.org
Web: www.crawcrook.org
Training leaders for Pentecostal churches or groups; part-time, correspondence courses, ministerial, lay training, distance learning.
Administrators: Rev Audrey Graham, Rev Judith Gray, Rev Linda Butler. Lecturers 4, Other staff 6. Began 1979; Pentecostal but open to all. No magazine. Turnover n/a.

†New Life Bible School, Technology House, Brentfield, Harrow Road, Stonebridge, London NW10 0RJ
☎ 020 8838 5477 🖷 020 8453 0509
E: bridgepark@lcc-uk.org
Teaching and training Christians to be more effective in their ministries.
Principal: Rev Ian Christensen. Executive staff 1, Other staff 3. **CC** Began 1991; Assemblies of God. No magazine. Turnover n/a.

The North East Oecumenical Course (NEOC), Ushaw College, Durham DH7 9RH
☎ 0191 373 7600 🖷 0191 373 7601
E: neocoffice@neoc.org.uk
Web: www.neoc.org.uk
Ministerial training course for ordination and lay candidates dispersed throughout the north-east of England.
Principal: Rev Canon Trevor Pitt BA MA STM Prof Dip Post Comp Ed. *Director of Studies:* Rev Dr Michael Chester. Lecturer 1, Other staff 3. **CC** No.1084315. Began 1976; Anglican, Methodist, United Reformed. (Previously The North East Ordination Course). Magazine: *Ministry Matters* (Circulation n/a irregularly). Turnover £205,000 to year end Sept 02.

***North Thames Ministerial Training Course**, St George Church Crypt, 16 Cannon Street Road, St-George-in-the-East, London E1 0BH
☎ 020 7481 9477 🖷 020 7481 8907
E: admin@ntmtc.org.uk
Web: www.ntmtc.org.uk
Part-time course for ordinands, and for lay ministry trainees in theological and pastoral studies.
Principal: Preb David Sceats MA. Executive staff 3, Other staff 12. **CC** Began 1994; Anglican, Methodist, United Reformed. No magazine. Turnover n/a.

Northern Ordination Course, Luther King House, Brighton Grove, Rusholme, Manchester M14 5JP
☎ 0161 249 2511 🖷 0161 248 9201
E: office@thenoc.org.uk
Web: www.noc.org
Ministerial training for Ordination.
Principal: Rev Dr Christopher Burdon. *Administrator:* Mrs E M Liddle. Lecturers 5, Other staff n/a. **CC** No.1067982. Began 1970; interdenominational. No magazine. Turnover £370,000 to year end Dec 04.

†The Open Theological College, University of Gloucestershire, Francis Close Hall, Swindon Road, Cheltenham GL50 4AZ
☎ 01242 532 837 🖷 01242 532 801
E: otc@glos.ac.uk
Web: www.glos.ac.uk/otc
Part-time distance learning for honours degree in theology.
Course Leader: Dr Trevor Cooling. Full-time staff 4. Began 1992; interdenominational. Part of the University of Gloucester. No magazine. Turnover n/a.

†St Albans and Oxford Ministry Course, Church House, North Hinksey, Oxford OX2 0NB
☎ 01865 208 260 🖷 01865 790 470
E: admin@saomc.fsnet.co.uk
Web: www.saomc.org.uk
Part-time courses in Christian education and ministry for ordinands and non-ordinands.
Principal: Rev Dr Mike Butterworth. *Vice Principal:* Rev Gerald Hegarty. Lecturers 2, Other staff 3. **CC** No.1041832. Began 1972; Anglican, Methodist, United Reformed. No magazine. Turnover £300,000 to year end Aug 00.

For further information see list on Page 431

Sarum College, 19 The Close, Salisbury SP1 2EE
☎ 01722 424 800 🖷 01722 338 508
✉: hospitality@sarum.ac.uk
Web: www.sarum.ac.uk
Providing award-bearing and short courses in theological education; training for adults of all denominations.
Principal: Rev Tim Macquiban. *Residential Services Manager:* Mrs Linda Cooper. Lecturers 9, Other staff 21. ***CC*** No.309501. Began 1864; ecumenical. (Previously Salisbury and Wells Theological College). Magazine: *Sarum College Newsletter* (2,000 half-yearly). Turnover n/a.

***S.E.A.N. International**, Missionary Mart, 1st Floor, 105 Stafford Road, Wallington SM6 9AP
☎ 020 8773 3948
✉: sean_international@compuserve.com
Web: www.seaninternational.net
Producing basic Certificate/Diploma TEE leadership-training materials; 70 languages in 120 countries.
International Coordinator: Miss Gloria Dean. Executive staff 1, Other staff 7. ***CC*** No.286965. Began 1976; interdenominational. Magazine: *Spread* (2,000 half-yearly). Turnover n/a.

South East Institute for Theological Education (SEITE), Ground Floor, Sun Pier House, Medway Street, Chatham ME4 4HF
☎ 01634 846 683 🖷 01634 819 347
✉: administrator@seite.co.uk
Web: www.seite.co.uk
Training for ministers, part-time courses for lay people: two centres in south-east England.
Principal: Rev Dr Jeremy Worthen. Lecturers n/a, Other staff n/a. ***CC*** No.288011. Began n/a; Anglican, Methodist, United Reformed. No magazine. Turnover n/a.
Also at: 48 Union Street, London SE1 1TD
☎ 020 7378 7880 🖷 020 7378 7882
And: University of Kent, Darwin College, Canterbury CT2 7NY
☎ 01227 764 000 🖷 01227 475 470

†South Wales Ordination Course, The Rectory, 19 Main Road, Portskewett, Caldicot NP26 5SG
☎ 029 2056 3379
Training course for non-stipendiary ministers for the Church in Wales.
Course Director: Rev Glyn Austin. Executive staff 1, Other staff 4. Began 1970; Church in Wales. (Previously Monmouth Ordination Course (NSM) and Llandaff Ordination Course). No magazine. Turnover n/a.

†South West Ministry Training Course, North Petherwin, Launceston PL15 8LW
☎ 01566 785 545 🖷 01566 785 749
✉: enquires@swmtc.org.uk
Part-time training for ordinands.
Principal: To be appointed. Executive staff 1, Other staff 4. ***CC*** No.1056606. Began 1981; Anglican, Methodist, United Reformed. No magazine. Turnover n/a.

STETS Southern Theological Education and Training Scheme, 19 The Close, Salisbury SP1 2EE
☎ 01722 424 820
🖷 01722 424 811
✉: swheway@stets.ac.uk
Web: www.stets.ac.uk
Preparing Anglican, Methodist, United Reformed ordinands; developing education and training for all God's people.
Principal: Rev Canon Vernon White. Training staff 9, Admin staff 3. ***CC*** No.1059977. Began 1997; ecumenical. (Previously Southern Dioceses Ministerial Training Scheme). No magazine. Turnover £522,000 to year end Aug 05.

Theological Training Course, Evangelical Movement of Wales, Bryntirion, Bridgend CF31 4DX
☎ 01656 655 886
🖷 01656 665 919
✉: office@emw.org.uk
Web: www.emw.org.uk
Preparation for preaching and pastoral ministry.
Principal: Rev Graham S Harrison BA MA BLitt. No full-time staff. ***CC*** No.222407. Began 1972; nondenominational. No magazine. Turnover n/a.

For further information see list on Page 431

Wesley Centre, Oxford, Westminster Institute of Education, Oxford Brookes University, Harcourt Hill Campus, Oxford OX2 9AT
☎ 01865 488 377 🖷 01865 488 317
E: wco@brookes.ac.uk
Web: www.brookes.ac.uk/schools/wco
Specialising in distance learning theology and religion programmes.
Head: Ms Alison Le Cornu. Teaching staff 9, Admin staff 3. Began 2003; Methodist foundation but interdenominational. (Previously Wesley And Methodist Studies Centre). Part of Oxford Brookes University. Magazine: *Wesley Centre Newsletter* (500 quarterly). Turnover n/a.

†West Midlands Ministerial Training Course, The Queen's Foundation for Ecumenical Theological Education, Somerset Road, Edgbaston, Birmingham B15 2QH
☎ 0121 454 8597 🖷 0121 454 8171
Training for Anglican, Methodist and United Reformed ordinands and lay people.
Dean: Rev Dr Anthony McLelland. Lecturers 3, Other staff 1. **CC** No.528989. Began 1973. No magazine. Turnover £100,000 to year end Aug 96.

†West of England Ministerial Training Course, University of Gloucestershire, Francis Close Hall, Swindon Road, Cheltenham GL50 4AZ
☎ 01452 300 494 🖷 01452 300 494
E: admin@wemtc.freeserve.co.uk
Web: www.wemtc.freeserve.co.uk
Training candidates for ordained and reader ministry in Gloucester, Bristol and Ludlow.
Principal: Name not supplied. *Vice Principal:* Rev Keith Crouch. Executive staff 3, Part-time lecturers 20. **CC** No.1071183. Began 1964; ecumenical. Linked to University of Gloucestershire. No magazine. Turnover £200,000 to year end Aug 02.

***West Sussex Bible Correspondence College**, 21 Rye Ash, Three Bridges, Crawley RH10 1RL
☎ 01293 520 288
E: peterinewman@onetel.com
Web: www.wsbccbiblestudy.uktutors.co.uk
Biblical, theological and historical Bible studies on Old and New Testaments for lay Christians.
Principal: Mr Peter I Newman. No paid staff. Began 1998; interdenominational. No magazine. Turnover n/a.

Woodbrooke Quaker Study Centre, 1046 Bristol Road, Selly Oak, Birmingham B29 6LJ
☎ 0121 472 5171 🖷 0121 472 5173
E: enquiries@woodbrooke.org.uk
Web: www.woodbrooke.org.uk
Adult religious education, conference and retreat centre for Quakers and others; also restaurant.
Director: Jennifer Barraclough. *Head of Education:* Helen Rowlands. Lecturers 6, Other staff 19. **CC** No.313816. Began 1903; Religious Society of Friends. No magazine. Turnover n/a.

***WYSOCS (West Yorkshire School of Christian Studies)**, Outwood House, Outwood Lane, Leeds LS18 4HR
☎ 0113 258 9300 🖷 0113 258 1309
E: admin@wysocs.org.uk
Web: www.wysocs.org.uk
Courses in understanding worldviews for mission, biblical perspectives for special subjects; also Thinking Space *gap year.*
Hon Secretary: Mrs Ruth Hanson. Part-time staff 3. **CC** No.271987. Began 1986; non-denominational. No magazine. Turnover £30,000 to year end Jul 04.

†YMCA, George Williams College, 199 Freemasons Road, Canning Town, London E16 3PY
☎ 020 7540 49001 🖷 020 7511 4900
Web: www.ymca.ac.uk
Providing professionally qualifying and access courses for youth and community workers.
Principal: Ms Mary Crosby. Academic staff 11, Admin staff 11. **CC** No.1044624. Began 1970; interdenominational. No magazine. Turnover n/a.

TRAINING CENTRES & SERVICES

The 222 Trust, 24 Old Street, Clevedon BS21 6BY
☎ 01275 797 999
🖷 01275 349 299
E: charles@living-waters.org.uk
Web: www.living-waters.org.uk
Charles and Joyce Sibthorpe's teaching and preaching ministry based on 2 Timothy 2:2.
Executive Officer: Mr Charles Sibthorpe. Executive staff 2. **CC** No.327866. Began 1987; interdenominational. Magazine: *On Eagles Wings* (1,000 every four months). Turnover £17,000 to year end Sept 04.

9:38, 2 Roger Bacon Lane, Oxford OX1 1QE
☎ 01865 204 879
E: admin@ninethirtyeight.org
Web: www.ninethirtyeight.org
Encouraging people to consider a lifetime in Christian ministry; promoting the idea of Apprenticeship Schemes.
Administrator: Mr Matthew Morgan. Admin staff 1. **CC** No.1092881. Began 1995; interdenominational. No magazine. Turnover £32,000 to year end Dec 04.

Adventist Discovery Centre UK, Stanborough Park, Garston, Watford WD25 9JU
☎ 01923 672 606
🖷 01923 894 835
E: adc@adventist.org.uk
Web: www.discoveronline.org.uk or www.totalhealth.org.uk
Free correspondence courses on the Bible, family and health for the general public.
Principal: Pastor Dalbert Elias. Executive staff 1, Other staff 4. **CC** No.1044071. Began 1947; Seventh-day Adventist. No magazine. Turnover n/a.

†All Souls' Resources, All Souls' Church, 2 All Souls' Place, London W1B 3DB
E: pam.glover@allsouls.org
Web: www.allsouls.org or www.christianityexplored.com
Evangelism course: Christianity Explored; *small group Bible studies:* Open Home Open Bible, Book by Book.
Resource & Communications Co-ordinator: Pam Glover. Admin staff 4. **CC** Began 1976; Anglican. No magazine. Turnover n/a.

Alpha Course, Holy Trinity Brompton Church, Brompton Road, London SW7 1JA
☎ 0845 644 7544
🖷 020 7052 0204
E: alphaoffice@alpha.org
Web: www.alphacourse.org
A 15-session, 10-week practical introduction to the Christian faith, primarily for non-church goers; worldwide.
Executive Director: Miss Tricia Neill. Executive staff 7, Other staff n/a. **CC** Began 1977; interdenominational. Magazine: *Alpha News* (250,000 every four months). Turnover n/a.

***Arrow Leadership Programme**, CPAS, Athena Drive, Tachbrook Park, Warwick CV34 6NG
☎ 01926 458 458
🖷 01926 458 459
E: arrow@cpas.org.uk
Web: www.cpas.org.uk
Teaching, mentoring and application focusing on leadership; deepening commitment to long-term service.
Director: Rev James Lawrence. Executive staff 1. Began 1999; Anglican. Part of Church Pastoral Aid Society. No magazine. Turnover included in CPAS.

T

For further information see list on Page 431

Bamardi Management & Training, 6 Crown Close, Leverington, Wisbech PE13 5PN
☎ 01945 475 392 M: 07971 419 919
E: bamardi@waitrose.com
Supporting churches and charities with management and training resources; church quiet days, away weekends.
Principal: Miss Diana Bailey. Executive staff 1, Admin staff 1. Began 1999; interdenominational. No magazine. Turnover n/a.

Barnabas Training Consortium Ltd, 2 Dukes Court, Bognor Road, Chichester PO19 8FX
☎ 01243 771 102 🖷 01243 776 321
E: info@btctraining.co.uk
Web: www.btctraining.co.uk
Offering professional courses in pastoral care, counselling and supervision to a degree level.
Director: Mrs Rosemary Pavey. Executive staff 3, Admin staff 1. Began 1993; non-denominational. Magazine: *E-mail bulletin.* Turnover £50,000 to year end Nov 02.

T

***BeaconLight Trust**, 150 High Street, Banstead SM7 2NZ
☎ 01737 353 313 🖷 01737 360 680
E: info@beaconlight.co.uk
Web: www.beaconlight.co.uk
Providing training courses and counselling to promote biblical Christian faith and lifestyle.
Chairman: Rev Dr Paul Adams. Executive staff 1, Other staff 2. ***CC*** No.1047046. Began 1995; non-denominational. No magazine. Turnover £13,000 to year end Jun 05.

Bradford Churches for Dialogue and Diversity, St Paul's Church, St Paul's Road, Manningham, Bradford BD8 7LS
☎ 01274 488 144
🖷 01274 488 144
E: admin@bcdd.org.uk
Web: www.bcdd.org.uk
Providing training for mission in multi-faith Britain; specialising in Muslim-Christian relations; tailored courses.
Principal: Dr Philip Lewis. Executive staff 1, Admin staff 1. ***CC*** No.1110761. Began 2005; ecumenical. No magazine. Turnover £25,000 to year end Apr 06.

Catholic Bible School, Nutbourne House, Farm Lane, Nutbourne, Chichester PO18 8SD
☎ 01243 371 766/377 331(SOS prayer line) 🖷 01243 371 459
E: info@catholic-bible-school.org
Web: www.catholic-bible-school.org
Spiritual direction, Christian counselling, guided prayer and Saturday study days.
Directors: Mr & Mrs Geoff & Gina Poulter. Executive staff 2, Other staff 4. ***CC*** No.262679. Began 1988; Roman Catholic. No magazine. Turnover n/a.

†**CCM**, Moggerhanger Park, Park Road, Moggerhanger, Bedford MK44 3RW
☎ 01767 641 005
🖷 01767 641 515
E: ccm@the-park.net
Web: www.the-park.net
Providing inservice leadership training; publishing; coordinating Moggerhanger Park Ministries, Clapham Sect / Wilberforce connections.
Joint Directors: Rev Dr & Mrs Clifford & Monica Hill. Executive staff 2, Other staff 5. ***CC*** No.1022698. Began 1992; interdenominational. (Previously Centre for Contemporary Ministry). No magazine. Turnover £62,000 to year end Dec 0[illegible].

***Centre for Islamic Studies and Muslim-Christian Relations**, London School of Theology, Green Lane, Northwood HA6 2UW
☎ 01923 456 160
🖷 01923 456 001
E: cis@lst.ac.uk
Web: www.lst.ac.uk
Providing undergraduate and postgraduate training, seminars and consultancy services to facilitate Christian-Muslim relations.
Director: Prof P Riddell. Staff included in London School of Theology 4. ***CC*** No.312778. Began 1985; interdenominational. (Previously Carey Institute for Islamic Studies). No Magazine. Turnover included in London School of Theology.

* **Centre for Contemporary Christianity in Ireland**, Howard House, 1 Brunswick Street, Belfast BT2 7GE
☎ 028 9032 5258
M: 07921 265 935
🖷 028 9043 4156
E: info@contemporarychristianity.org
Web: contemporarychristianity.org
Equipping the church through research, resources and learning / training events to serve a changing Ireland.
Director: Mr David W Porter. *Programme Director:* Mr Derek Poole. Executive staff 3, Other staff 4. ***CC*** No XR 8[illegible]80/1. Began 1988; non-denominational. (Previously Evangelical Contribution on Northern Ireland (ECONI)). Magazine: *Lion & Lamb* (2,000 half-yearly) Turnover n/a.

***Christian Discipleship International**, 250 St Helens Road, Hastings TN34 2[illegible]E
☎ 01424 433 357
E: cdi@clix.pt
Training and equipping church leaders in evangelism and discipleship to fulfil the Great Commission.
Executive Director: Rev F Piedade. Executive staff 1, Other staff n/a. ***CC*** No.1039779. Began 1994; non-denominational. (Previously Christ Alive Ministries). No magazine. Turnover n/a.

*__Christian Research__, Vision Building, 4 Footscray Road, Eltham, London SE9 2TZ
☎ 020 8294 1989
Fax 020 8294 0014
E: admin@christian-research.org.uk
Web: www.christian-research.org.uk or www.ukchristianhandbook.org.uk
Offering day briefings, staff colleges, management and research-based seminars for Christian leaders, strategic thinking; consultancy.
Executive Director: Dr Peter Brierley. *Administrator:* Mrs Gwen Gowers. Executive staff 3, Other staff 3. ***CC*** No.1017701. Began 1993; interdenominational. (Previously MARC Europe). Magazine: *Quadrant* (2,600 every two months). Turnover £260,000 to year end Dec 05.

Christian Resources International, 12 Ellesmere Road, Colwyn Bay LL29 8RP
☎ 01492 530 528
Fax 01492 534 558
E: christianresourcesint@yahoo.com
Web: www.christianresources international.com
Offering foundation Scripture teaching courses.
Secretary: Ms Esther Wintringham. Executive staff 2, Other staff 2. Began 1993; Free evangelical. Magazine: *Forerunner* (Circulation n/a quarterly). Turnover n/a.

Church of England Training Officers
Each Diocese has a range of training officers for ordained and lay people. Contact them via the appropriate Diocesan Office. See pages 155 to 162.

College of Preachers, 14a North Street, Bourne PE10 9AB
☎ 01778 422 929
Fax 01778 422 929
E: administrator@collegeofpreachers.org.uk
Web: www.collegeofpreachers.org.uk
Organising training courses to help, encourage and stimulate those engaged in the ministry of preaching.
Director: Rev Dr Stephen I Wright. *Administrator:* Mrs Karen Atkin. Executive staff 2, Other staff 1. ***CC*** No.220764. Began 1960; ecumenical. Magazine: *The Journal* (2,000 half-yearly). Turnover £151,369 to year end Dec 01.

*__Connect: Using Skills, Changing Lives Ltd__, Glenwood Church, Circle Way West, Llandeyrn, Cardiff CF23 6UW
☎ 029 2033 7880
M 07977 918 632
Fax 029 2033 7881
E: r.bishop@glenwoodchurch.org
Web: www.glenwoodchurch.org
Training future leaders, mentoring; church/community-based hands-on experience; missional accredited.
Director: Rev Rob Burns. Executive staff 1, Admin staff 2. Began 2001; interdenominational. No magazine. Turnover £15,000 to year end Dec 05.

*__Cormack Consultancies__, King's Gate, St Mary's Tower, Birnam, Dunkeld PH8 0BJ
☎ 01350 728 715 Fax 01350 728 716
E: drdavecormack@aol.com
Web: www.cormackconsultancies.co.uk
Strategic consulting, training to church, mission, business worldwide; certificated counselling training to postgraduate diploma.
Managing Director: Dr David Cormack. *Director of Counselling:* Mrs Edith Cormack. Executive staff 3, Other staff 5. Began 1985; non-denominational. No magazine. Turnover £250,000 to year end Mar 01.

*__Darash Trust__, Darash Centre, Ashwells Road, Brentwood CM15 9SE
☎ 01277 374 844 Fax 01277 374 881
E: newhcchurch@aol.com
Web: www.newharvest.org.uk
Forwarding the Christian faith through conferences, seminars, training and missions.
Chairman: Rev David Matthews. Executive staff 1. ***CC*** No.1008795. Began 1991; interdenominational. No magazine. Turnover £85,000 to year end Sep 00.

*__The DCI Trust__, 4 Home Farm Lane, Colston Bassett, Nottingham NG12 3FQ
☎ 01949 811 90 Fax 01949 811 18
E: support@dci.org.uk
Web: www.dci.org.uk
Training and equipping leaders and churches for mission, social action, micro-commerce to create local funding.
Director: Dr Les Norman. *Webmaster:* Mr Graham Crosbie. Executive staff 5, Other staff 30. ***CC*** No.1001236. Began 1987; non-denominational. (Previously DCI World Christians). Turnover £76,000 to year end Jun 05.

Decade Ministries, Farncombe View, Hungerford Hill, Lambourn, Hungerford RG17 8NP
☎ 01488 710 77 Fax 01488 710 77
E: roy@decadeministries.co.uk
Web: www.decadeministries.co.uk or www.churchsupplies.org.uk or www.allageworship.com
Providing training for clergy and leaders; also visuals for all-age worship, school assemblies and evangelism.
Director/Evangelist: Rev Roy Weaver. Executive staff 2, Other staff 3. Began 1990; Independent. No magazine. Turnover £70,000 to year end Oct 02.

Disciple Course, Disciple Office, 4 John Wesley Road, Werrington, Peterborough PE4 6ZP
☎ 01733 325 002 Fax 01733 384 180
E: disciple@mph.org.uk
Web: www.disciple.gb.com
Bible study programme taking participants through the Bible in 34 weeks.
Chief Executive: Mr Martin Stone. Executive staff 1. Began 1996; ecumenical. No magazine. Turnover n/a.

T

***DNA**, Rayleigh House, 32 High Street, Great Bookham, Leatherhead KT23 4AG
☎ 0870 2424 558 M: 07905 625 195
Fax 0870 2424 558
E: releasethelife@dna-uk.org
Web: www.dna-uk.org
Intensive year of personal discipleship, mission and leadership development in the context of local church.
National Administrator: Mr Tim Raynes. *Team Leader:* Mr Pete Gilbert. Executive staff 4. ***CC*** No.327160. Began 1982; Pioneer. (Previously Pioneer DNA). No magazine. Turnover n/a.

Engage, PO Box 442, Swindon SN5 7JH
☎ 01793 418 336 M: 07732 480 356
Fax 01793 433 288
E: admin@centreforyouthministry.ac.uk
Web: www.centreforyouthministry.ac.uk
National Certificate in Christian Youth Work: day conference / distance learning course for Christian youth workers.
National Director: Rev David Howell. Executive staff 3, Other Staff 1. ***CC*** No.1081144. Began 1996; interdenominational. No magazine. Turnover included in Centre for Youth Ministry.

***Equip**, Bawtry Hall, Bawtry, Doncaster DN10 6JH
☎ 01302 710 020 Fax 01302 710 027
E: info@equiptraining.org.uk
Web: www.equiptraining.org.uk
Providing training for Christians in intercultural ministry and local church leadership.
Director: Nigel Spencer. Staff 2. ***CC*** No.225364. Began 1989; interdenominational. No magazine. Turnover £17,500 to year end Dec 04.

Equipping the Church, 26 Lottbridge Drove, Eastbourne BN23 6NT
☎ 01323 437 755 Fax 01323 411 970
Web: www.equippingthechurch.co.uk
Providing resources for the church and individual; range of products that facilitates their growth.
Manager: Mr Paul Owen. Executive staff 2, Other staff 8. ***CC*** Began n/a; non-denominational. No magazine. Turnover n/a.

European Training Programme (UK Campus), Wycliffe Centre, Horsleys Green, High Wycombe HP14 3XL
☎ 01494 682 209 Fax 01494 682 300
E: etp_uk@sil.org
Web: www.eurotp.org/uk
Training for cross-cultural ministry: language learning, language development (including linguistic analysis), literacy, scripture translation.
Director: David Morgan. Executive staff 3, Other staff 12. Began 1953; non-denominational. No magazine. Turnover n/a.

***Faith to Faith**, Carrs Lane Church Centre, Carrs Lane, Birmingham B4 7SX
☎ 0121 633 8860
E: office@faithtofaith.org.uk
Web: www.faithtofaith.org.uk
Helping churches relate to and communicate with people of other faiths through consultancy, training, research.
Director: Dr Helen Reid. Executive staff 2. ***CC*** No.1070875. Began 1998; non-denominational. Magazine: *Faith to Faith* (2,000 every four months). Turnover £13,000 to year end Aug 00.

Farnham Castle, International Briefing & Conference Centre, Castle Street, Farnham GU9 0AG
☎ 01252 721 194 Fax 01252 711 283
E: conf@farnhamcastle.com
Web: www.farnhamcastle.com
Specialising in intercultural briefing and training, intensive language tuition; residential / day conferences, weekend retreats.
Chief Executive: Mr James Twiss. *General Manager:* Alan Ball. *Director of Marketing:* Mr Jeff Toms. Executive staff 3, Other staff 35. ***CC*** No.313648. Began 1953; non-denominational. (Previously Centre for International Briefing). Magazine: *Intercultural Focus News* (Circulation & frequency n/a). Turnover £1,571,000 to year end Sep 02.

Foundation for Church Leadership, 4 Portal Road, York YO26 6BQ
☎ 01904 787 387 M: 07814 775 368
E: director@churchleadershipfoundation.org
Web: www.churchleadershipfoundation.org
Supporting, encouraging and inspiring church leaders as they tackle new challenges in leadership.
Director: Ven Malcolm Grundy. Executive staff 1. ***CC*** No.1099165. Began 2003; ecumenical. No magazine. Turnover n/a.

***Four Twelve Ministries**, PO Box 6494, Loughborough LE12 8WA
☎ 01509 621 780
E: four.twelve@ntlworld.com
Providing apostolic support and networking for ministries and churches; UK and overseas.
Director: Mr Bryan Spence. Executive staff 2, Admin staff 1. ***CC*** No.1058105. Began 1996; interdenominational. (Previously 4:12 Ministries). No magazine. Turnover £92,000 to year end Jun 04.

***Freedom in Christ Ministries**, PO Box 2842, Reading RG2 9SZ
☎ 0845 230 2677 Fax 0845 230 2679
E: info@ficm.org.uk
Web: www.ficm.org.uk
Equipping church leaders to establish their people free in Christ.
Executive Director: Mr Steve Goss. Executive staff 2, Admin staff 2. ***CC*** No.1082555. Began 1999; non-denominational. No magazine. Turnover £130,000 to year end Dec 04.

***Fruitful Tree**, Park Business Centre, 5 La Belle Place, Glasgow G3 7LH
☎ 0845 833 0657 M: 07795 014 889
Fax 0141 331 1992
E: info@fruitfultree.co.uk
Web: www.fruitfultree.co.uk
Nurturing faith, growth and leadership through strategic development programmes, self assessment tools and biblical training.
Managing Director: Mr Iain MacLeod. Executive staff 1, No other staff. Began 2004; non-denominational. No magazine. Turnover n/a.

†Full Gospel Revival Centre, 19 Milner Road, Sherwood, Nottingham NG2 3EE
E: fullgospelrevivalcentre@hotmail.com
Counselling and Bible courses in conjunction with Nottingham University.
Overseer: Bishop S E Thomas. Executive staff 6, Admin staff 3. Began n/a; Pentecostal. No magazine. Turnover n/a.

T

Healthy Church UK, PO Box 100, Sandy SG19 1ZR
☎ 01767 692 938
🖷 0871 277 1249
E: philip@healthychurch.co.uk
Web: healthychurch.co.uk
Helping local churches to improve their health especially through Natural Church Development.
Director: Rev Dr Philip Walker. Executive staff 1. Began 2003; non-denominational. Magazine: *He@lthychurch.mag.uk* (600 quarterly). Turnover £34,373 to year end Dec 04.

***Heartcry**, 2 Shirelake Close, Oxford OX1 1SN
☎ 01865 728 410
M: 07793 582 009
E: office@heartcry.org.uk
Web: www.heartcry.co.uk or www.londonprayer.net
Training, equipping local church and conferences; working for community change, prayer, prophetic teaching, finance, healing.
Founder: Mrs Rachel Hickson. Executive staff 2, Other staff 4. ***CC*** No.1076993. Began 1993; interdenominational. No magazine. Turnover n/a.

Bryn Hughes Training, Consultancy and Mentoring, 3 Pound Bank Close, West Kingsdown, Sevenoaks TN15 6UA
☎ 01474 854 774
🖷 01474 854 774
Web: www.church-matters.com
Training, consultancy and mentoring, especially to churches, missions and charities.
Director: Mr Bryn Hughes. Executive staff 2. Began 1992; non-denominational. No magazine. Turnover n/a.

†**Human Ecology**, 11 Nantwich Road, Middlewich CW10 9HE
☎ 0870 141 7077
🖷 0870 141 7077
E: info@humanecogroup.com
Web: www.humanecogroup.com
Coaching teams and executives in organisations for performance development, working with future Christian leaders.
Managing Director: Rev Simon Walker. Executive staff 3. Began 2002; interdenominational. No magazine. Turnover n/a.

Ichthus Christian Fellowship Training Courses, 7 Greenwich Quay, Clarence Road, Greenwich, London SE8 3EY
☎ 020 8694 7171
🖷 020 8694 7172
E: training@ichthus.org.uk
Web: www.ichthus.org.uk
Courses in evangelism (including short-term summer course); church planting, leadership training with specialist streams (one year).
Training Manager: Debbie Forster. Executive staff 3, Other staff 4. ***CC*** No.1099412. Began 1975; non-denominational. No magazine. Turnover n/a.

Institute for Christian Training, Union Theological College, 108 Botanic Avenue, Belfast BT7 1JT
☎ 028 9020 5085
E: ict@union.ac.uk
Web: www.union.ac.uk/ict
Part-time and evening training courses for ministers, elders, church members; distance learning courses.
Director: Dr T D Alexander. Executive staff 1, Other staff 1. Began 1980; Presbyterian Church in Ireland but open to all. (Previously Magee Institute for Christian Training). No magazine. Turnover £75,000 to year end Dec 00.

†***The Joshua Project**, Joshua House, 27 Crestbrooke, Northallerton DL7 8YP
☎ 01609 771 027 M: 07712 323 027
E: kingsley@thejoshuaproject.co.uk
Offering 7-session course and follow-on course on location in churches.
Principal: Rev Kingsley N Armstrong. Executive staff 1. Began 1996; interdenominational. No magazine. Turnover n/a.

Journey: Explorations into Discipleship, Ashram Press, 178 Abbeyfield Road, Sheffield S4 7AY
☎ 0114 243 6688
E: ashramcommunity@hotmail.com
Web: ashram.org.uk
Guided tour in following Jesus as a radical in today's world; 6 to 9 month courses.
Coordinator: Rev Dr John Vincent. All voluntary staff. Began 2000; ecumenical. (Previously Journey: A Contemporary Exploration in Discipleship). No magazine. Turnover n/a.

Kingdom Faith Church, Lamplugh House, Thwing, Driffield YO25 3DY
☎ 01262 470 282/806
🖷 01262 470 536
E: thewayofthespirit@lamplugh.com
Holding The Way of the Spirit training courses for north-east England; day or weekend.
Pastor: Kevin Rumney. Executive staff 1, Other staff 2. ***CC*** No.278746. Began 1991; interdenominational. Turnover n/a.

***Lindisfarne Mustard Seed Project**, Lindisfarne Retreat, Marygate, Holy Island, Berwick-upon-Tweed TD15 2SD
☎ 01289 389 249 🖷 01289 389 249
E: raysimpson@bigfoot.com
Web: www.aidan.org.uk
Supporting the Community of Aidan and Hilda on Lindisfarne; retreats, consultations, soul-friending; Celtic Christian roots.
Founder: Rev Ray Simpson. Executive staff 1, No other full-time staff. ***CC*** No.1054649. Began 1996; interdenominational. Magazine: *LMSP Newsletter* (340 quarterly). Turnover £13,000 to year end Dec 00.

***London Institute for Contemporary Christianity**, St Peter's, Vere Street, London W1G 0DQ
☎ 020 7399 9555 🖷 020 7399 9556
E: mail@licc.org.uk
Web: www.licc.org.uk
Producing educational videos, DVDs and CDs; resource centre; Christian training materials from courses and events.
Executive Director: Mr Mark Greene.
Director of Operations: Mr John Baker.
Executive staff 2, Other staff 13. ***CC*** No.286102. Began 1982; non-denominational. (Previously Institute for Contemporary Christianity). Magazine: eg (5,000 every four months), *Workwise* (3,000 quarterly). Turnover £557,612 to year end Mar 04.

***Medical Service Ministries**, PO Box 13, Newton Abbot TQ13 8WZ
☎ 01647 440 113 🖷 08701 315 594
E: resources.msm@btopenworld.com
Web: www.preachandheal.org
Providing funding for personal and community health care training for Christian workers.
Secretary: Mr Lionel Holmes. Executive staff 1. ***CC*** No.234037. Began 1903; interdenominational. (Previously Missionary School of Medicine). No magazine. Turnover £12,000 to year end Sept 05.

***N.able**, 30 Haynes Road, Westbury BA13 3HD
☎ 01373 823 013
E: office@nable.info
Web: www.nable.info
Training programmes for missions, evangelists, church leadership.
Office Manager: Jonathan Brooks-Martin. Admin staff 1, Other staff n/a. **CC** No.264278. Began 2005; non-denominational. No magazine. Turnover n/a.

Nehemiah Bible Training Centre, The Oasis Christian Centre, Ysgubor Wen Road, Dwygyfylchi, Penmaenmawr LL34 6PS
☎ 01492 621 151 / 623 229
M: 07754 592 248
E: nehemiah@igoasis.fsnet.co.uk
Web: www.go.org
Ten correspondence courses on biblical topics.
Principal: Rev J M Levy. Other staff n/a. **CC** No.1048524. Began n/a; interdenominational. No magazine. Turnover n/a.

†*The New Hope Trust, Faith Acres, Peterhead AB42 3DQ
☎ 01779 838 251 🖷 01779 838 549
E: info@newhopetrust.org
Web: www.newhopetrust.org
Offering training, conference facilities; undertaking missions, humanitarian youth and children's work.
Managing Director: Ms Wendy Smith. Executive staff 1, Other staff 19. **CC** No.276520. Began 1974; interdenominational, Full Gospel. (Previously New Hope Bible College). Turnover £261,000 to year end Dec 02.

North of England Institute for Christian Education, Carter House, Pelaw Leazes Lane, Durham DH1 1TB
☎ 0191 384 1034
E: jeff.astley@durham.ac.uk
Web: www.durham.ac.uk/neice
Providing theoretical and empirical research in Christian education; theology study days, publications and educational support.
Director: Rev Prof Jeff Astley. Executive staff 2. **CC** No.513106. Began 1981; interdenominational. No magazine. Turnover n/a.

†the:park, Park Farm, Dereham Road, Bawdeswell, Dereham NR20 4AA
☎ 07004THEPARK
🖷 01362 686 208
E: thepark@dovetrust.com
Web: www.theparkonline.org
Courses and training for trustees, leaders, managers in any church or charity; meeting venue.
Director: Mr Keith Colman. Executive staff 3. Began 1982; interdenominational. No magazine. Turnover included in The Dove Trust.

†Possibilities, 77 Priory Road, Alcester B49 5EA
☎ 01789 765 634
🖷 01789 765 634
E: cliffupsd@aol.com
Providing training, consultancy and mentoring for individuals groups, churches and Christian organisations.
Director: Mr Cliff Hayward. Executive staff 1, Admin staff 1. Began 2000; interdenominational. No magazine. Turnover n/a.

†Post Green Community Trust, East Holton Farm House, Holton Heath, Poole BH16 6JN
☎ 01202 777 213
Promoting the Gospel, unity and community; helping people with mental/physical disability; annual teaching event.
Chairman: Sir Thomas Lees. Executive staff 1, No other staff. **CC** No.231175. Began 1975; interdenominational. Associated with East Holton Charity. No magazine. Turnover £20,000 to year end Dec 02.

Posters Plus, 7 Belvedere Drive, Belvedere Hill, St Saviour, Jersey JE2 7RN
☎ 01534 737 171
E: yvonne@posterplus.org.uk
Web: www.postersplus.org.uk
Training/encouraging church members to explore fresh ways of making posters to attract and inspire others.
Administrator: Mrs Yvonne Coppock. Admin staff 1. Began 1999; interdenominational. No magazine. Turnover n/a.

***Prayer for the Nations**, PO Box 15027, London SE5 9ZU
☎ 0845 130 9797 M: 07834 356 06[illegible]
🖷 020 7346 0137
E: info@pfnonline.com
Web: www.prayerforthenations.com
Leadership and Bible training; correspondence and spiritual growth courses; strategic events.
Principals: Rev Rod Anderson, Rev Julie Anderson. Lecturers 20, Full time staff 5. **CC** No.326994. Began 1983; interdenominational. (Previously Strategic Prayer School). Magazine: *Watchman's Journal*(Circulation & frequency n/a). Turnover £200,000 to year end Jul 00.

***Preachers' Help**, PO Box 34, Welwyn Garden City AL7 3BW
☎ 01707 390 410
E: geoffrey-stonier@hotmail.com
Web: preachershelp.com
Helping preachers to increase the biblical content of Gospel ministry through free distance-learning courses and literature.
Director: Rev Dr Geoffrey Stonier. Executive staff 1, Other staff 3. **CC** No.1071608. Began 1995; interdenominational. No magazine. Turnover £5,000 to year end 99.

Prepared for Service, 25 Felton Road, Lower Parkstone, Poole BH14 0QR
☎ 01202 738 416
E: pfsatcarey@aol.com
Web: www.fiec.org.uk
Two-year modular training programme working in partnership with evangelical churches also located in Reading and Chesterfield.
Administrators: David & Laraine Cook. Admin staff 2. **CC** No.263354. Began 1994; FIEC. No magazine. Turnover n/a.

The Proclamation Trust, Willcox House, 140 Borough High Street, London SE1 1LB
☎ 020 7407 0561 📠 020 7407 0569
E: pt@proctrust.org.uk
Web: www.proctrust.org.uk
Advancement of the Christian gospel; training to preach and teach the gospel of Jesus Christ.
Chairman: Mr Andrew C Green. *President:* Mr David Jackman. Executive staff 4, Other staff 5. **CC** No.1094952. Began 1986; non-denominational. Incorporating Cornhill Training Course. No magazine. Turnover £300,000 to year end Dec 04.

Purpose Ministries, Worthy Park Grove, Abbots Worthy, Winchester SO21 1AN
☎ 01962 882 082 📠 01962 882 082
Training courses in person-to-person evangelism and leading Bible discussion groups.
Director: Rev David Steele. Executive staff 1, Other staff 1. **CC** No.326081. Began 1982; interdenominational. No magazine. Turnover n/a.

Rapha Workshops, 3 Stranhope Road, Deal CT14 5AB
☎ 01304 239 621
E: Rapha@f2s.com
Teaching biblical discipleship wholeness journey from a toxic past to new life in Christ.
Director: Miss Susan Williams. Executive staff 2, Admin staff 7. Began 1993; non-denominational. No magazine. Turnover £75,000 to year end Apr 05.

***Release Foundation**, Oakwood Court, Spring Hill, Arley, Coventry CV7 8FF
☎ 01676 540 808 📠 01676 540 606
E: enquiries@releasefoundation.com
Web: www.releasefoundation.com
Serving churches through an innovative learning process; enabling Christians to recognise and release God-given potential.
Training Director: Rev Christopher Spicer. *Administrator:* Mr Ralph Coleman. Executive staff 1, Admin staff 4. **CC** No.1073329. Began 1998; interdenominational. No magazine. Turnover £119,418 to year end Dec 01.

Resource Christian Counselling, Green Pastures, East Street, Hambledon, Portsmouth PO7 4RY
☎ 0845 129 7221 📠 0845 129 7221
Web: www.resourcechristiancounselling.org
Training in pastoral care and counselling; referrals to accredited counsellors.
Administrator: Mrs Anne Porter. Executive staff 1, Admin staff 1. **CC** No.1065919. Began 1985; non-denominational. (Previously Christian Counselling International UK). ACC, NOCN accredited. No magazine. Turnover £10,000 to year end Mar 05.

†***Ridley Hall Foundation**, Ridley Hall, Cambridge CB3 9HG
☎ 01223 741 080 📠 01223 741 081
E: rah41@cam.ac.uk
Web: www.ridley.cam.ac.uk
Relating Christian faith to business; seminars at Ridley Hall and nationwide; regular publications.
Director: Dr Richard Higginson. Executive staff 1, No other full-time staff. **CC** No.311456. Began 1989; non-denominational. Magazine: *Faith in Business* (400 quarterly), produced jointly with Industrial Christian Fellowship. Turnover n/a.

Royal School of Church Music, Cleveland Lodge, Westhumble, Dorking RH5 6EW
☎ 01306 872 800 📠 01306 887 260
E: enquiries@rscm.com
Web: www.rscm.com
Teaching and helping, through courses and publications, all those concerned with music in worship.
Director: Prof John Harper. **CC** No.312828. Began 1927; ecumenical. Magazine: *Church Music Quarterly* (Circulation n/a quarterly). Turnover n/a.

***The RZIM Zacharias Trust**, 97a St Aldates, Oxford OX1 1BT
☎ 01865 203 951 📠 01865 203 950
E: office@zactrust.org
Web: www.zactrust.org
Involved in evangelism, apologetics, training; aiming to reach the sceptic with the Gospel.
European Director: Mr Michael Ramsden. Executive staff 2, Other staff 5. **CC** No.1067314. Began 1998; non-denominational. (Previously Zacharias Trust). Magazine: *Just Thinking* (65,000 every four months). Turnover £334,000 to year end Dec 04.

†**St George's College Jerusalem**, 112 Strensall Road, Earswick, York YO32 9SJ
☎ 01904 763 071 📠 01904 763 071
Operating residential centre in the Holy Land for field work, study and reflection.
UK Secretary: Rev Paul Conder. Admin staff 1. Began 1975; Anglican but open to all. Magazine: *British Friends of St George's Update* (300 annually). Turnover £2,413 to year end Dec 02.

St George's House, Windsor Castle, Windsor SL4 1NJ
☎ 01753 848 848 📠 01753 848 849
E: sgh@stgeorges-windsor.org
Web: www.stgeorgeshouse.org
Residential consultations in an atmosphere of reflection for open debate, meeting and discussions.
Warden: Mr Andrew Carter. *Director of Studies:* Dr Martin Gaskell. Executive staff 7, Other staff 10. **CC** No.1071186. Began 1966; ecumenical. Magazine: *Annual Review* (2,500 annually). Turnover £750,000 to year end Aug 05.

Sandhams, 11 The Terrace, Canterbury CT2 7AJ
☎ 07973 216 449 📠 01227 479 755
E: psandham@aol.com
Facilitating dialogue at vision and change forums, leadership conferences, strategic planning events, senior team workshops.
Managing Partner: Mr Paul Sandham. Executive staff 1, Admin staff 1. Began 1999; non-denominational. No magazine. Turnover n/a.

***Satya Bhavan (South Asian Concern)**, PO Box 43, Sutton SM2 5WL
☎ 020 8770 9717 📠 020 8770 9747
E: info@southasianconcern.org
Web: www.southasianconcern.org
Training, research and outreach among South Asians in the UK, South Asia and the diaspora.
Director: Mr Robin Thomson. Executive staff 2, Other staff 1. **CC** No.1002270. Began 1994; interdenominational. No magazine. Turnover n/a.

Seeds, 30 Grasvenor Avenue, Barnet EN5 2BZ
☎ 020 8364 9652 M: 07971 332 267
E: seeds30@aol.com
Web: www.seedscreative.org.uk
Encouraging creative, artistic skills and discussion of contemporary issues in schools and churches.
Chairperson: Mr Chris Norris. No full-time staff. **CC** No.326262. Began 1982; interdenominational. No magazine. Turnover £25,000 to year end Apr 03.

***TASK (Training and Advice for Service in the Kingdom)**, 13 School Road, Bradenham, Thetford IP25 7QU
☎ 01760 440 200
E: enquiries@taskgb.co.uk
Web: www.taskgb.co.uk
Advising and training Christians to work effectively in secular and cross-cultural positions overseas.
Director: Mr Roger G Wells. Executive staff 1, No other full-time staff. **CC** No.1068212. Began 1994; interdenominational. No magazine. Turnover £6,000 to year end Oct 05.

The Telling Place, St Wilfrid's Enterprise Centre, Royce Road, Hulme, Manchester M15 5BJ
☎ 0161 227 0377
E: info@the tellingplace.org
Web: www.thetellingplace.org
Developing a network of Christian storytellers; offering training and resources.
Executive Officer: David Ward. Executive staff 2. ***CC*** No.1107125. Began 1998; interdenominational. Working in partnership with Northumbria Community and Bible Society. Magazine: *Telling Tales* (Circulation n/a three times a year). Turnover n/a.

TnT Ministries, 29 Buxton Gardens, Acton, London W3 9LE
☎ 020 8992 0450 🖷 020 8896 1847
E: trevor@tntministries.org.uk
Web: www.tntministries.org.uk
Training people to teach the Bible to children; providing Sunday School materials and training videos.
Director: Mr Trevor Blundell. Executive staff 2. ***CC*** No.1102864. Began 1993; non-denominational. No magazine. Turnover n/a.

John Truscott, 69 Sandridge Road, St Albans AL1 4AG
☎ 01727 832 176 🖷 01727 832 176
E: john@john-truscott.co.uk
Web: www.john-truscott.co.uk
Advice and training in organisation and people-skills to churches, ministers and mission agencies.
Church Consultant & Trainer: Mr John Truscott. Executive staff 1. Began 1999; interdenominational. No magazine. Turnover n/a.

***Unlock**, Unlock House, 336a City Road, Sheffield S2 1GA
☎ 0114 276 2035 🖷 0114 276 2035
E: office@unlock-urban.org.uk
Web: www.unlock-urban.org.uk
Resourcing Christians in urban areas (non-book culture) to share Good News in their neighbourhoods.
Chief Officer: Dawn A Lonsdale. Executive staff 1, Other staff 3. ***CC*** No.313454. Began 1972; interdenominational. (Previously Evangelical Urban Training Project). No magazine. Turnover £40,000 to year end Dec 04.

***Urban Presence**, 17 Upper West Grove, Chorlton-on-Medlock, Manchester M13 0BB
☎ 0161 273 7900
E: paul@urbanpresence.org.uk
Web: www.urbanpresence.org.uk
Recognition and resourcing of inner-city churches and Christians in the mission field on their doorsteps.
Chair of Trustees: Rev Dr Dwight Swanson. Executive staff 2. ***CC*** No.1069404. Began 1992; non-denominational. No magazine. Turnover n/a.

Urban Theology Unit, 210 Abbeyfield Road, Sheffield S4 7AZ
☎ 0114 243 5342 🖷 0114 243 5356
E: office@utusheffield.fsnet.co.uk
Web: www.utusheffield.fsnet.co.uk
Training ministers and lay people for urban work, new styles of church work, theology.
Director: Rev Christine Jones. Executive staff 2, Other staff 2. ***CC*** No.505334. Began 1969; ecumenical. No magazine. Turnover £127,000 to year end Aug 04.

Warham Trust, Home Farm House, Malshanger, Basingstoke RG23 7ET
☎ 01256 781 121
E: Panddic@surfaid.org
Web: www.warham.org.uk
Developing the Network Church and facilitating its connection with traditional, local expressions of church.
Missioner: Rev Peter Irwin-Clark. Executive staff 2, Other staff n/a. ***CC*** No.1033830. Began 2003; interdenominational. No magazine. Turnover n/a.

***Web Evangelism Guide**, 44 Twyford Road, Willington, Derby DE65 6BN
☎ 01283 702 334 🖷 01283 702 334
E: guide@web-evangelism.com
Web: www.web-evangelism.com
Training resource to help Christians and churches use the web for evangelism.
Editor: Mr Tony Whittaker. Executive staff 1. ***CC*** No.237005. Began 1998; interdenominational. Part of SOON Ministries/WEC International. Magazine: *Web Evangelism Bulletin* (13,000 every two weeks, by email). Turnover n/a.

Workshop: Applied Christian Studies, 104 Townend Lane, Deepcar, Sheffield S36 2TS
☎ 0114 288 8816
M: 07881 541 432
🖷 0114 288 8817
E: office@anvil.org.uk
Web: www.workshop.org.uk
Training for busy Christians; one weekend a month, September to July; five regional centres.
Programme Coordinator: Noel Moules. Executive staff 3. ***CC*** No.1010[illegible]54. Began 1983; interdenominational. Part of Anvil Trust. No magazine. Turnover n/a.

***Youth With A Mission - England (Education and Training)**, Highfield Oval, Ambrose Lane, Harpenden AL5 4BX
☎ 01582 463 216
🖷 01582 463 213
E: enquiries@oval.com
Web: www.ywam-england.com
Training in missions and ministry, 10 locations in England and Wales.
Directors of Training: Mr John Peachey (DTS), Mr Steve Sullivan (Further Training). Lecturers 35, Other staff 100. ***CC*** No.264078. Began 1972; interdenominational. Magazine: *Life-changing Discipleship Training* (Circulation & frequency n/a). Turnover n/a.

Zion Teaching Ministries, Jacobs Well, [illegible]8 Curbar Road, Great Barr, Birmingham B4[illegible] 2AU
☎ 0121 605 0353
M 07906 689 128
E: dheysmith@aol.com or ztmglobal@aol.com
Promoting Christian education through seminars, school audio / video and Bible notes.
Directors: Rev Richard Hey-Smith. Executive staff 2, Other staff 1. Began 198[illegible]; interdenominational. Linked to Operation Rescue and World Outreach Bible Academy. No magazine. Turnover n/a.

T

EXTRA INFORMATION

The Handbook essentially lists organisations in the UK which would ascribe to the Trinitarian position described on Page 4. The groups included here (except the Late Entries on Page 455) do not satisfy the Trinitarian criterion for inclusion but are included for information purposes

X

OTHER CHURCHES & RELIGIOUS HEADQUARTERS

†The Aetherius Society, 757 Fulham Road, London SW6 5UU
☎020 7736 4187 / 7731 1094
🖷020 7731 1067
E: info@innerpotential.org
Web: www.innerpotential.org
Director: Name not supplied. Staff 5. Began 1955. Magazine: *Cosmic Voice* (Circulation n/a periodically), *Newsletter* (Circulation n/a periodically). Turnover n/a.
Also at: The Inner Potential Centre, 36 Kelvedon Road, London SW6 5BW
☎020 7736 4187

†Brahma Kumaris, Global Co-operation House, 65 Pound Lane, London NW10 2HH
☎020 8727 3350 🖷020 8727 3351
E: bk@bkwsugch.demon.co.uk
Web: www.bkpublications.com or www.btwsu.org.uk
UK and Europe Director: Sr Jayanti. *Programme Coordinator:* Sr Maureen. No paid staff. *CC* No.269971. Began 1937. Magazine: *Retreat* (3,500 half-yearly). Turnover £100,000 to Dec 96.

The Buddhist Society, 58 Eccleston Square, London SW1V 1PH
☎020 7834 5858 🖷020 7976 5238
E: info@thebuddhistsociety.org
Web: www.thebuddhistsociety.org
Registrar: Mrs Louise Marchant. Admin staff 3. *CC* No.208677. Began 1924. Magazine: *The Middle Way* (3,000 quarterly). Turnover n/a.

†Cherubim and Seraphim Church Council, 175 Earlham Grove, Forest Gate, London E7 9AP
☎020 8534 5101 🖷020 8534 0378
Church General Secretary: No name supplied. Executive staff 4. *CC* Began 1965. Magazine: *The Light* (Circulation n/a quarterly). Turnover n/a.

Christadelphians, 404 Shaftmoor Lane, Hall Green, Birmingham B28 8SZ
☎0121 777 6328 🖷0121 778 5024
E: orders@thechristadelphians.com
Web: www.thechristadelphians.com
Editor: Mr Michael Ashton. Executive staff 2, Other staff 9. *CC* No.240090. Began 1864. Magazines: *The Christadelphian Magazine* (Circulation n/a monthly), *The Dawn Ecclesial* (850 monthly)..
Christadelphian Publications, 66 Carlton Road, Nottingham NG3 2AP
☎0115 958 7208
E: editor@christiadelphians.com
Manager: Mr A Cave.

†The Church of Christ, Scientist (Christian Science Church), 9 Elysium Gate, 126 New Kings Road, London SW6 4LZ
☎020 7384 8600 🖷020 7371 9204
E: cs@compub.org
Web: www.christianscience.com
District Manager, Committees on Publications: Mr Tony Lobl. Admin staff 1, Other staff 5. *CC* Began 1879. Magazines: *Christian Science Journal* (Circulation n/a monthly), *Christian Science Sentinel* (Circulation n/a weekly), *Christian Science Monitor* (Circulation n/a daily). Turnover n/a.

†The Church of Jesus Christ of Latter-day Saints (Mormons), Church Offices, 751 Warwick Road, Solihull B91 3DQ
☎0121 712 1200 🖷0121 712 1126
E: mclavertymw@ldschurch.org
Web: www.lds.org
Area President: Mr Harold G Hillam. Executive staff 3, Admin staff 80, Serving ministers n/a. *CC* Began 1837. Magazine: *The Ensign* (7,000 monthly). Turnover n/a.

†The Church of Scientology, Office of Special Affairs, Saint Hill Manor, East Grinstead RH19 4JY
☎01342 318 229 M: 07950 968 351
🖷01342 325 474
Web: www.scientology.org
Public Affairs Director: Mr G Wilson. Serving ministers 150, Other staff 500. Began 1952. Magazines: *Freedom* (40,000 quarterly), *Auditor* (120,000 monthly), *Advance* (120,000 every two months). Turnover n/a.

Churches of God, UK, 23 Walcott Road, Billinghay, Lincoln LN4 4EG
☎01526 861 217
E: coguk@aol.com
Web: www.cgom.org or www.abcog.org
UK Co-ordinator: Mr James McBride. Executive staff 1, Admin staff 1, Serving ministers 1. *CC* No.283358. Began 1978. (Previously Church of God International). Magazine: *New Horizons* (2,500 every two months). Turnover £5,000 to year end Dec 04.

†Community of Christ, 1a Jubilee Buildings, Outram Street, Sutton-in-Ashfield NG17 1DE
☎01623 553 861
E: djwaring@cofchrist.org.uk
Web: www.cofchrist.org.uk
British Isles President: Rev David Waring. Executive staff 2, Admin staff 4, Serving ministers 2. *CC* No.255657. Began 1863. (Previously Reorganized Church of Jesus Christ of Latter Day Saints). Magazine: *Region Courier* (450 five times a year). Turnover n/a.

†Creme: Maitreya, Share International, Tara Press, PO Box 3677, London NW5 1RU
☎020 7482 1113 🖷020 7267 28[illegible]1
Web: www.shareintl.org or www.share-international.org
Author & Editor: Mr Benjamin Creme. No full-time staff. Began 1974. Non-profit organisation run by volunteers. Magazine: *Share International* (Circulation n/a periodically). Turnover n/a.

†Family Federation for World Peace, 43 Lancaster Gate, London W2 3NA
☎020 7723 0721 🖷020 77[illegible]4 2262
General Secretary: Mr D Franklin. Executive staff 1, Other staff 200, Serving ministers 53. *CC* No.256598. Began 19[illegible]8. (Previously Unification Church Holy Spirit Association for the Unification of World Christianity)). Magazine: *The Family Times* (10,000 quarterly). Turnover £100,000 to year end Dec 02.

†Federation of Jain Organisations in the UK, 11 Lindsay Drive, Harrow HA3 0TA
☎020 8204 2871 🖷020 893[illegible] 2353
E: vinod@kapashi.freeserve.co.uk
Co-ordinator: Mr Vinod Kapashi. Admin staff 1, Other staff n/a. Began n/a. No magazine. Turnover n/a.

†Friends of the Western Buddhist Order (FWBO), Madhyamaloka, 30 Chantry Road, Moseley, Birmingham B13 8DH
☎0121 449 3700 🖷0121 449 3780
Leader: Ven Sangharakshita. Members of the order 1,050. *CC* Began 1968. Magazines: *Dharma Life* (6,000 every four months), *Lotus Realm* (Circulation n/a quarterly).
Information office: London Buddhist Centre, 51 Roman Road, London E2 0HU
☎020 8981 1225
Press office: 12 Park Road, Moseley, Birmingham B13 8AB
☎0121 449 8272

General Assembly of Unitarian and Free Christian Churches, Essex Hall, 1 Essex Street, London WC2R 3HY
☎020 7240 2384 🖷020 7240 3089
E: ga@unitarian.org.uk
Web: www.unitarian.org.uk
General Secretary: Mr Jeffrey J Teagle. *Executive Officers:* Mr John Crosskey, Mrs Ingrid Tavkar. Serving ministers 77, Other staff 4. *CC* No.250788. Began 1928. Magazines: *The Inquirer* (2,300 fortnightly), *The Unitarian* (2,000 monthly). Turnover £600,000 to year end Dec 04.

X

The General Conference of the New Church, 59 Campernell Close, Colchester CO7 0TB
☎01206 303 800
E: michaelhindley@generalconference.org.uk
Web: www.spiritualwisdom.org.uk
Chief Executive: Mr Michael Hindley. *Senior Minister:* Rev Ian Russell. Executive staff 2, Admin staff 2, Serving ministers 9. *CC* No.253206. Began 1787; incorporated 1872. Magazines: *Lifeline* (400 ten times a year), *Outlook* (2,000 quarterly). Turnover £580,000 to year end Dec 04.
Also at: Swedenborg House, 20 Bloomsbury Way, London WC1A 2TH
☎020 7229 9340
And: New Church College, 25 Radcliffe New Road, Radcliffe, Manchester M26 1LE
☎0161 766 2521 Fax 0161 796 1142

The Greater World Christian Spiritualist Church, 3 Conway Street, London W1T 6BJ
☎020 7436 7555 Fax 020 7580 3485
E: greaterworld@btconnect.com
Web: www.greaterworld.com
National President: Rev Megan Long. Executive staff 2. *CC* No.212369. Began 1921. No magazine. Turnover n/a.

†Hindu Centre, 39 Grafton Terrace, London NW5 4JA
☎020 7485 8200 Fax 020 8200 0931
General Secretary: Prof Bharadwaj. Executive staff 14, Other staff 7. *CC* Began 1935. Magazine: *Sruti* (1,000 monthly). Turnover n/a.

International Churches of Christ, 9 Derby Street, Manchester M8 8QE
☎Number not supplied
E: info@icoc.org.uk
Web: www.iccmissions.org.uk
Administrator: Name not supplied. Admin staff 3, Other staff 5. Began 1982. (Previously London Church of Christ (LCC)). No magazine. Turnover n/a.

†International Society for Krishna Consciousness, Bhaktivedanta Manor, Hilfield Lane, Aldenham, Watford WD25 8EZ
☎01923 856 173 Fax 01923 850 818
E: Shachee@pamho.net
Web: www.iskon.org.uk
Governing Body Commissioner: Shiva Rama Swami. *President:* Mr Vipramuklya Swami. Executive staff 40, Other staff 450. *CC* No.259649. Began 1969. Magazine: *Back to Godhead* (150,000 every two months). Turnover n/a.

†Islamic Cultural Centre & London Central Mosque, 146 Park Road, London NW8 7RG
☎020 7724 3363 Fax 020 7724 0493
E: info@iccuk.org
Web: www.iccuk.org
Director General: Dr Ahmed el Dubiyon. Executive staff 1, Other staff n/a. Began 1944. Magazine: *Islamic Quarterly* (1,200 quarterly). Turnover n/a.

Islamic Foundation, Markfield Conference Centre, Ratby Lane, Markfield, Leicester LE67 9SY
☎01530 244 944 Fax 01530 244 946
E: i.foundation@islamic-foundation.org.uk
Web: www.islamic-foundation.org.uk
Director General: Dr M Ahsan. Admin staff 30. *CC* Began 1973. Magazines: *Muslim World Book* (Circulation n/a quarterly), *Review* (2,000 quarterly), *Encounters* (1,000 half-yearly). Turnover n/a.

†Jehovah's Witnesses, Watch Tower House, The Ridgeway, London NW7 1RN
☎020 8906 2211 Fax 020 8371 0051
E: pr@wtbts.org.uk
Web: www.watchtower.org
Contact: Name not supplied. Admin staff 30. *CC* No.1077961. Began 1900. Magazines: *The Watchtower* (Circulation 25,203,000 monthly worldwide), *Awake!* (22,755,000 twice-monthly worldwide).
Ireland: Newcastle, Greystones, Co Wicklow, Republic of Ireland

†Jewish Communities in the United Kingdom, Board of Deputies of British Jews, 6 Bloomsbury Square, London WC1A 2LP
☎020 7543 5400 Fax 020 7543 0010
E: info@bod.org.uk
Web: www.bod.org.uk
Chief Executive: Mr Neville Nagler. *President:* Mr Henry Grunald QC. Executive staff 1, Other staff n/a. Began 1760. No magazine. Turnover n/a.

†The Lord's Witnesses, PO Box 1AL, London W1 1AL
☎020 7481 8430 Fax 020 7702 4176
E: helpdesk@lordswitnesses.com
Web: www.bibledecoded.com
Contact: Mr Tony Moore. Staff n/a. Began n/a. No magazine. Turnover n/a.

†Musama Disco Christo Church, 40 Brailsford Road, Tulse Hill, London SW2 2TE
☎020 8671 5099 Fax 020 8674 9309
E: musamachurchuk@aol.com
Superintendent Minister (UK): Rev Jerisdan H Jehu-Appiah. Executive staff 3. *CC* No.328063. Began 1978. Magazine: *The Gospel Ministry* (250 quarterly). Turnover £15,000-20,000 to year end Mar 03.

The Muslim Educational Trust, 130 Stroud Green Road, London N4 3RZ
☎020 7272 8502 Fax 020 7281 3457
E: info@muslim-ed-trust.org.uk
Web: www.muslim-ed-trust.org.uk
Director: Mr Ghulam Sarwar. Executive staff 3, Other staff 2. *CC* No.313192. Began 1966. Magazine: *Reflect* (Circulation n/a every four months). Turnover n/a.

National Spiritual Assembly of the Bahá'ís of the United Kingdom, 27 Rutland Gate, London SW7 1PD
☎020 7584 2566 Fax 020 7584 9402
E: opi@bahai.org.uk
Web: www.bahai.org.uk
Chair: Dr Shirin Tahzib. *Secretary of the National Spiritual Assembly:* Dr Kishan Manocha. *Secretary for External Affairs:* The Hon Barnabas Leith. Staff 15. *CC* No.250851. Began 1923. Magazine: *Bahai Review* (Circulation & frequency n/a). Turnover £1,300,000 to year end Dec 04.

†The Pagan Federation, BM Box 7097, London WC1N 3XX
M: 07986 034 378 Fax 01223 323 299
E: secretary@paganfed.demon.co.uk
Web: www.paganfed.org.uk
President: Ms P H Jones. No paid staff. Began 1971. Magazine: *Pagan Dawn* (6,600 quarterly). Turnover n/a.

†The Spiritualist Association of Great Britain, 33 Belgrave Square, London SW1X 8QB
☎020 7235 3351 Fax 020 7245 9706
President: Mrs S Blair. Admin staff 3. *CC* Began 1872. Magazine: *Service* (3,500 every four months). Turnover n/a.

†Sukyo Mahikari, 20 Suffolk Road, South Norwood, London SE25 6EG
☎020 8771 7417 Fax 020 8771 9441
Director: Name not supplied. Staff n/a. *CC* Began 1983 in the UK. (Previously Mahikari). No magazine. Turnover n/a.

†The Theosophical Society in Great Britain, 50 Gloucester Place, London W1U 8EA
☎020 7935 9261 Fax 020 7935 9543
E: theosophical@freenetname.co.uk
Web: www.theosophical-society.org.uk
National President: Mr Colin Price. Executive staff 4. *CC* Began 1888. Magazine: *Insight* (1,200 every two months). Turnover n/a.

United Lodge of Theosophists, 62 Queen's Gardens, London W2 3AL
☎020 7723 0688/7262 8639
Fax 020 7262 8639
E: ult@ultlon.freeserve.co.uk
Web: www.ultlon.freeserve.co.uk
Leader: Name not supplied. Admin staff 2. Began 1925. Magazine: *Theosophy and the Theosophical Movement* (Circulation & frequency n/a). Turnover n/a.

The World Sikh Foundation (Sikh Cultural Society of Great Britain), 33 Wargrave Road, Harrow HA2 8LL
☎020 8864 9228
Managing Editor: Mrs H B Bharara. Executive staff 1, Other staff n/a. *CC* No.1054913. Began 1960. Magazine: *The Sikh Courier International* (3,000 quarterly). Turnover n/a.

†Zoroastrian Trust Funds of Europe, 88 Compayne Gardens, London NW6 3RU
☎020 7328 6018 Fax 020 7625 1685
E: secretary@ztfe.com
Web: www.ztfe.com
President: Mr Dorab Mistry. Staff n/a. Began n/a. No magazine. Turnover n/a.

MULTI-FAITH ORGANISATIONS

†The Association for Pastoral and Spiritual Care and Counselling, 1 Regent Place, Rugby CV21 2PJ
☎08704 435 252 🖷08704 435 160
E: bacp@bacp.co.uk
Web: www.bacp.co.uk
Working at the interface between psychotherapy and spirituality/religion; supporting counsellors/others working in faith settings.
Chair: Rev Tony Bryer. No full-time staff. *CC* Began 1973. Magazine: *Reflections* (500 every four months). Turnover n/a.

Building Bridges Pendle, 19 Market Square, Nelson BB9 7LP
☎01282 719 303 🖷01282 700 607
E: BuildABridgeNow@aol.com
Building understanding and mutual acceptance between people of faith through work, prayer and study.
Project Manager: Mr Rauf Bashir. Executive staff 7. *CC* No.1078273. Began 1998. (Previously Building Bridges). Magazine: *Building Bridges: Interfaith Matters* (1,200 quarterly). Turnover n/a.

College of Health Care Chaplains, 49 Chesterton Park, Cirencester GL7 1XS
☎01285 643 660 Mobile 07771 723 060 🖷01285 643 660
E: chcc@chrweb.co.uk
Web: www.healthcarechaplains.org
Professional association for health-care chaplaincy.
Registrar: Mr Chris Webber. Staff n/a. Began 1991. Magazine: *Journal of Health Care Chaplaincy* (1,200 quarterly). Turnover n/a.

East Northamptonshire Faith Group, East Northamptonshire Council, Cedar Drive, Thrapston, Kettering NN14 4LZ
☎01832 742 236 🖷01832 734 839
E: rsyms@east-northamptonshire.gov.uk
Encouraging and resourcing local churches and other faith groups to serve their local communities.
Voluntary Sector Development Office: Mr Richard Syms. No full-time staff. Began 2002; interdenominational but open to all faiths. (Previously East Northamptonshire Churches Group). No magazine. Turnover £4,000 to year end Mar 05.

Focolare Movement, Focolare Centre for Unity, 69 Parkway, Welwyn Garden City AL8 6JG
☎01707 323 620 🖷01707 336 413
E: info@focolare.org.uk
Web: www.focolare.org.uk
International movement for unity, through dialogue between Christians, with people of other faiths and non-believers.
Men's Delegate: Mr Tim King. *Women's Delegate:* Cathy Grue. No full-time staff. *CC* No.279072. Began 1964. Magazine: *New City* (1,000 monthly). Turnover n/a.

†Inner Cities Religious Council, Office of The Deputy Prime Minister, 4/K/10 Eland House, Bressenden Place, London SW1E 5DU
☎020 7944 3704
🖷020 7944 3729
E: icrc@odpm.gov.uk
Web: www.urban.odpm.gov.uk/community/faith/index.htm
Forum for faith communities and Government with an emphasis on regeneration.
Secretary: David Rayner. Executive staff 3. Began 1992. No magazine. Turnover n/a.

The Inter Faith Network for the United Kingdom, 8a Lower Grosvenor Place, London SW1W 0EN
☎020 7931 7766
🖷020 7931 7722
E: ifnet@interfaith.org.uk
Web: www.interfaith.org.uk
Links over 110 member organisations; promoting mutual respect and understanding between faith communities in the UK.
Director: Mr Brian Pearce OBE. Full-time staff 4. *CC* No.1068934. Began 1987. No magazine. Turnover £250,000 to year end Dec 04.

International Association for Religious Freedom - British Chapter, Upper Chapel, Norfolk Street, Sheffield S1 2JD
☎0114 276 7114
Supporting the principles and work of the International Association for Religious Freedom; seminars, meetings.
Chairman: Rev Geoffrey Usher. No full-time staff. Began 1962. (Previously IARF British Members Group). No magazine. Turnover £1,400 to year end Dec 02.

†Multifaith and Multicultural Mediation Services, Global Green University, Camlad House, Forden, Welshpool SY21 8NZ
☎01938 580 319
E: iipsgp@clara.net
Web: www.educationaid.net
Providing interfaith mediation and peacebuilding consultancy and education.
Coordinator: Dr Thomas C Daffern. Admin staff 2. Began 1996. No magazine. Turnover n/a.

Science and Religion Forum, St James' Vicarage, 280 Walshaw Road, Bury BL8 1PY
☎0161 762 5219 M: 07958 692 [illegible]54
🖷0870 912 1164
E: info@srforum.org
Web: www.srforum.org
Exploring the relationship between scientific knowledge and religious faith and practice through publications and conferences.
Contact: Rev Phil Edwards. No full-time staff. *CC* No.1034657 Began 19[illegible]1. Magazine: *Reviews* (400 half-yearly). Turnover £18,000 to year end Dec 02.

Suffolk Inter-Faith Resource (SIFRE), Suffolk College, Rope Walk, Ipswich IP4 1LT
☎01379 678 615
E: d.capey@sifre.org.uk
Web: www.sifre.org.uk
Raising inter-faith awareness; diversity training; meetings, conferences, resources.
Hon Faiths Officer: Mrs Cynthia Capey. Executive staff 1, Admin staff 1. *CC* No.1042612. Began 1994. No magazine. Turnover £20,000 to year end Mar 03.

†Three Faiths Forum, Star House, 104 Grafton Road, Kentish Town, London NW5 4BD
☎020 7485 2538 🖷020 7485 4512
E: Sidney@Sternberg-foundation.co.uk
Web: www.threefaithsforum.org.uk
Bringing the three Abrahamic faiths (Christianity, Islam, Judaism) together to understand and respect each other.
Coordinator: Mr Sidney Shipton. Executive staff 2, Admin staff 5. *CC* No.1092465. Began n/a. No magazine. Turnover £50,000-100,000 to year end Dec 02.

†World Congress of Faiths, London Inter Faith Centre, 125 Salusbury Road, London NW6 6RG
☎020 8959 3129 or 01403 257 801 🖷020 8959 3129
E: enquiries@worldfaiths.org
Web: www.worldfaiths.org or jtabick@lineone.net
Encouraging interfaith understanding and co-operation.
Chair: Rabbi Jackie Tabick. Admin staff 1. *CC* Began 1936. Magazine: *World Faiths Encounter* (800 every four months). Turnover n/a.

X

OTHER ORGANISATIONS AND AGENCIES

HELP LINES

Al Anon, 61 Great Dover Street, London SE1 4YF
☎020 7403 0888 🖷020 7378 9910

†Alcoholics Anonymous Helpline
☎0845 769 7555

†Childline
☎0800 1111 (24 hours)

Cot Death Helpline, Artillery House, 11 Artillery Row, London SW1P 1RT
🖷020 7222 8002

†Cruse Bereavement Line
☎0870 167 1677 For ages 12 to 18 0808 808 1677

†Eating Disorders Association, 103 Prince of Wales Road, Norwich NR1 1DW
☎0870 770 3256 Text 07977 493 345

FRANK
☎0800 776 600 (24-hours)

LIFE National Hotline
☎0800 849 4545 (9am-9pm) Text 07786 200 330

Marriage Care
☎020 7371 1341

National Missing Persons Helpline, Roebuck House, 284 Upper Richmond Road West, London SW14 7JE

†NSPCC Child Protection Helpline
☎0808 800 5000 (24-hours)

Salvation Army Family Tracing Service, 101 Newington Causeway, London SE1 6BN
☎0845 634 4747 or 020 7367 4747

†Samaritans
☎0845 790 9090 (24-hours)

Saneline, 1st Floor Cityside House, 40 Adler Street, London E1 1EE
🖷020 7375 2162

†Scope - The Cerebral Palsy Society, Library and Information Unit, 6 Market Road, London N7 9PW
☎0808 800 3333 (9am-9pm Mon-Fri, 2pm-5pm Sat, Sun, Bank Hols)

Healthwise, 101 Woodside Business Park, Shore Road, Birkenhead CH41 1EP
🖷0151 649 3401

Womens Aid National Domestic Violence
☎08082 000 247

ORGANISATIONS AND AGENCIES

ACAS, Advisory, Conciliation and Arbitration Service, Brandon House, 180 Borough High Street, London SE1 1LW
☎0845 747 4747
Minicom 0845 606 1600
Web: www.acas.org.uk

ACEVO (Association of Chief Executives of Voluntary Organisations), 1 New Oxford Street, London WC1A 1NU
☎0845 345 8496 🖷0845 345 8482
📧: info@acevo.org.uk
Web: www.acevo.org.uk

Action Aid, Hamlyn House, MacDonald Road, London N19 5PG
☎020 7561 7561 🖷020 7272 0899
📧: mail@actionaid.org.uk
Web: www.actionaid.org.uk

Age Concern, England, Astral House, 1268 London Road, London SW16 4ER
☎0800 009 966 (7am-7pm) or 020 8765 7200
Web: www.ageconcern.org.uk

Air Training Corps, HQ Air Cadets, RAF Cranwell, Sleaford NG34 8HB
☎01400 261 201
Web: www.aircadets.org

Al Anon, 61 Great Dover Street, London SE1 4YF
☎020 7403 0888 🖷020 7378 9910
Web: www.al-anonuk.org.uk

Alcoholics Anonymous, PO Box 1, Stonebow House, Stonebow, York YO1 7NJ
☎01904 644 026
Web: www.alcoholics-anonymous.org.uk

Amnesty International, The Human Rights Action Centre, 17 New Inn Yard, London EC2A 3EA
☎020 7033 1500 🖷020 7033 1503
Web: www.amnesty.org.uk

ARCISS, Association of Research Centres in Social Sciences, 8 Spens Crescent, Perth PH1 1PE
☎07810 201 935
📧: lucie/hayes@stir.ac.uk
Web: www.arciss.ac.uk
Administrator: Lucie Spens.

†Army Cadet Force, TA Centre, 10 Stone Buildings, Lincoln's Inn, London WC2A 3TG
☎020 7242 3480 🖷020 7242 3484
📧: ceoneacf@reserve-forces-london.org.uk
Web: www.armycadets.com

Arts Council of England, 2 Pear Tree Court, London EC1R 0DS
☎0845 300 6200 🖷020 7608 4100
Web: www.artscouncil.org.uk

ASA (Advertising Standards Authority Ltd), Mid City Place, 71 High Holborn, London WC1V 6QT
☎020 7492 2222 🖷020 7242 3696
📧: enquiries@asa.org.uk
Web: www.asa.org.uk

Automobile Association, Contact Centre, Lambert House, Stockport Road, Cheadle SK8 2DY
☎0800 197 6173 🖷0161 488 7300
📧: customer.servics@theAA.com
Web: www.theaa.com

Barnardos, Tanners Lane, Ilford IG6 1QG
☎020 8550 8822 🖷020 8551 6870
📧: dorothy.howes@barnardos.org.uk
Web: www.barnados.org.uk

Board of Inland Revenue, New Wing, Somerset House, Strand, London WC2R 1LB
☎020 7438 6622
Web: www.inlandrevenue.gov.uk

The Booksellers Association of Great Britain and Ireland, Minster House, 272 Vauxhall Bridge Road, London SW1V 1BA
☎020 7802 0802 🖷020 7802 0803
📧: mail@booksellers.org.uk
Web: www.booksellers.org.uk

The British Computer Society, 1 Sanford Street, Swindon SN1 1HJ
☎01793 417 417 🖷01793 480 270
📧: bcshq@hq.bcs.org.uk
Web: www.bcs.org.uk

The British Council, 10 Spring Gardens, London SW1A 2BN
☎0161 957 7755 🖷0161 957 7762
📧: general.enquiries@britishcouncil.org
Web: www.britishcouncil.org

British Film Institute, 21 Stephen Street, London W1T 1LN
☎020 7255 1444
Web: www.bfi.org.uk

British Institute of Management (Chartered Management Institute), Management House, Cottingham Road, Corby NN17 1TT
☎01536 204 222 🖷01536 201 651
📧: enquiries@managers.org.uk
Web: www.managers.org.uk
Also at: 3rd Floor, 2 Savoy Court, Strand, London WC2R 0EZ
☎020 7497 0580 🖷 020 7497 0463

British Library, 96 Euston Road, London NW1 2DB
☎0870 444 1500
Web: www.bl.uk
Also at: Newspaper Library, Colindale Avenue, London NW9 5HE
And: Boston Spa, Wetherby LS23 7BQ

British Museum, Great Russell Street, London WC1B 3DG
☎020 7323 8000 Minicom 020 7323 8482
📧: information@thebritishmuseum.ac.uk
Web: www.thebritishmuseum.ac.uk

X

Other Organisations and Agencies

***British National Temperance League**, Westbrook Court, 2 Sharrow Vale Road, Sheffield S11 8YZ
☎0114 267 9976 🖷0114 267 9976
E: info@bntl.org
Web: www.bntl.org

British Red Cross, UK Office, 44 Moorfields, London EC2Y 9AA
☎0870 170 7000 🖷020 7562 2000
E: information@redcross.org.uk
Web: www.redcross.org.uk

Cabinet Office, 70 Whitehall, London SW1A 2AS
☎020 7276 1234
Web: www.cabinet-office.gov.uk

Cancer Research Campaign, PO Box 123, Lincoln's Inn Fields, London WC2A 3PX
☎020 7242 0200 🖷020 7269 3100
Web: www.cancerresearchuk.org

CARE (Cooperative for American Relief to Everywhere, Inc), 10 Rushworth Street, London SE1 0RB
☎020 7934 9334 🖷020 7934 9335
Web: www.careinternational.org.uk

Carers National Association, 20 Glasshouse Yard, London EC1A 4JT
☎020 7490 8818 🖷020 7490 8824
E: info@ukcarers.org
Web: www.carersuk.org

CBI (Confederation of British Industry), Centre Point, 103 New Oxford Street, London WC1A 1DU
☎020 7379 7400
Web: www.cbi.org.uk

Central Office of Information, Hercules House, Hercules Road, London SE1 7DU
☎020 7928 2345 🖷020 7928 5037
Web: www.coi.gov.uk
See also Office for National Statistics.

Centre for Longitudinal Studies, Institute for Education, 20 Bedford Way, London WC1H 0AL
☎020 7612 6860 🖷020 7612 6880
E: cohort@cls.ioe.ac.uk
Web: www.cls.ioe.ac.uk

Charities Advisory Trust, Radius Works, Back Lane, Hampstead, London NW3 1HL
☎020 7794 9835 🖷020 7431 3739
E: people@charitiesadvisorytrust.co.uk
Web: www.charitiesadvisorytrust.co.uk

Charities Aid Foundation, 25 Kings Hill Avenue, West Malling ME19 4TA
☎01732 520 000 🖷01732 520 001
E: enquiries@caf.charitynet.org
Web: www.cafonline.org

The Charity Commission, Harmsworth House, 13 Bouverie Street, London EC4Y 8DP
☎0845 300 0218 Minicom 0845 300 0219 🖷020 7674 2300
Web: www.charity-commision.gov.uk

Child Poverty Action Group, 94 White Lion Street, London N1 9PF
☎020 7837 7979 🖷020 7837 6414
E: staff@cpag.org.uk
Web: www.cpag.org.uk

Child Support Agency, PO Box 55, Pedmore House, Brierley Hill DY5 1YL
☎0845 713 3133 Minicom 0845 713 8924
E: cas-nel@childsupportagency.gsi.gov.uk
Web: www.csa.gov.uk

Childline, 45 Folgate Street, London E1 6GL
☎020 7650 3200/0800 1111 🖷020 7650 3201
Web: www.childline.org.uk

Commission for Racial Equality, St Dunstan's House, 201 Borough High Street, London SE1 1GZ
☎020 7939 0000 🖷020 7939 0004
E: info@cre.gov.uk
Web: www.cre.gov.uk

Commonwealth War Graves Commission, 2 Marlow Road, Maidenhead SL6 7DX
☎01628 634 221 🖷01628 771 208
E: casualty.enq@cwgc.org
Web: www.cwgc.org

Community Service Volunteers (CSV), 237 Pentonville Road, London N1 9NJ
☎020 7278 6601
E: information@csv.org.uk
Web: www.csv.org.uk

Competition Commission, Victoria House, Southampton Row, London WC1B 4AD
☎020 7271 0100
E: info@competition-commission.gsi.gov.uk
Web: www.competition-commission.org.uk

Conservative Campaign Headquarters, 25 Victoria Street, London SW1H 0DL
☎020 7222 9000
Web: www.conservatives.com

Countryside Agency, John Dower House, Crescent Place, Cheltenham GL50 3RA
☎01242 521 381
Web: www.countryside.gov.uk

Cruse - Bereavement Care, Cruse House, 126 Sheen Road, Richmond TW9 1UR
☎020 8939 9530 🖷020 8940 7638
E: helpline@crusebereavementcare.org.uk
Web: www.crusebereavementcare.org.uk

Cult Information Centre, BCM Cults, London WC1N 3XX
☎0870 777 3800
Web: www.cultinformation.org.uk

Department for Constitutional Affairs, Selborne House, 54 Victoria Street, London SW1E 6QW
☎020 7210 8500
E: general.queries@dca.gsi.gov.uk
Web: www.dca.gov.uk

Department for Culture, Media & Sport, 2 Cockspur Street, London SW1Y 5DH
☎020 7211 6200
E: enquiries@culture.gov.uk
Web: www.culture.gov.uk

Department for Education and Skills, Sanctuary Buildings, Great Smith Street, London SW1P 3BT
☎0870 000 2288
E: info@dfes.gsi.gov.uk
Web: www.dfes.gov.uk

Department for Environment, Food and Rural Affairs (DEFRA), Library Enquiry Desk, Room 320, Nobel House, 17 Smith Square, London SW1P 3JR
☎0845 9335 577
E: helpline@defra.gsi.gov.uk
Web: www.defra.gov.uk

Department for International Development, 1 Palace Street London SW1E 5HE
☎0845 300 4100 🖷01355 843 63[illegible]
E: enquiry@dfid.gov.uk
Web: www.dfid.gov.uk

Department for Transport, Great Minster House, 76 Marsham Street London SW1P 4DR
☎020 7944 8300 🖷020 7944 9643
Web: www.dft.gov.uk

Department for Work and Pensions, Room 540, The Adelphi, 1 John Adam Street, London WC2N 6HT
☎020 7712 2171 🖷020 7712 2386
Web: www.dwp.gov.uk

Department of Health, Richmond House, 79 Whitehall, London SW1A 2NL
☎020 7210 4850 Minicom 020 7210 5025
E: dhmail@doh.gsi.gov.uk
Web: www.dh.gov.uk

Department of Trade & Industry, 1 Victoria Street, London SW1H 0ET
☎020 7215 5000 Minicom 020 7215 6740
Web: www.dti.gov.uk

Design Council, 34 Bow Street London WC2E 7DL
☎020 7420 5200 🖷020 7420 5300
E: info@designcouncil.org.uk
Web: www.design-council.org.uk

Direct Mail Advertising, 3 Wallis Court Fleming Way, Crawley RH10 9DA
☎0870 777 1416 🖷0870 777 1417
E: info@dmamas.co.uk
Web: www.dmams.co.uk

Direct Marketing Association (UK) Ltd, 70 Margaret Street, London W1W 8SS
☎020 7291 3300 🖷020 7323 4426
E: info@dma.org.uk
Web: www.dma.org.uk

Duke of Edinburgh's Award, Gulliver House, Madeira Walk, Windsor SL4 1EU
☎01753 727 400 🖷01753 810 666
E: info@theaward.org
Web: www.theaward.org

Eating Disorders Association, 103 Prince of Wales Road, Norwich NR1 1DW
☎0870 770 3256 Text 07977 493 345
E: helpmail@edauk.com
Web: www.edauk.com

English Heritage, Customer Services Department, PO Box 569, Swindon SN2 2YP
☎0870 333 1181 🖷01793 414 926
E: customers@english-heritage.org.uk
Web: www.english-heritage.org.uk

English Nature (Nature Conservancy Council for England), Northminster House, Peterborough PE1 1UA
☎01733 455 000 🖷01733 568 834
E: enquiries@english-nature.org.uk
Web: www.english-nature.org.uk

Environment Agency, Millbank Tower, 25th Floor, 21 Millbank, London SW1P 4XL
☎08708 506 506 or 0800 807 060 (emergency hotline) or 0845 988 1188 (fl
E: enquiries@environment-agency.gov.uk
Web: www.environment-agency.gov.uk

Equal Opportunities Commission, Arndale House, Arndale Centre, Manchester M4 3EQ
☎0845 601 5901
🖷0161 838 8312
E: info@eoc.org.uk
Web: www.eoc.org.uk

FAIR (Family Action Information and Resource), BCM Box 3535, PO Box 12, London WC1N 3XX
☎01642 898 412
🖷01642 643 707
Web: www.fair-cult-concern.co.uk

Foreign & Commonwealth Office, King Charles Street, London SW1A 2AH
☎020 7008 1500
Web: www.fco.gov.uk

Forestry Commission, 231 Corstorphine Road, Edinburgh EH12 7AT
☎0131 334 0303
🖷0131 334 3047
E: enquiries@forestry.gsi.gov.uk
Web: www.forestry.gov.uk

The Foundation for the Study of Infant Deaths, Artillery House, 11 Artillery Row, London SW1P 1RT
☎020 7222 8001
🖷020 7222 8002
E: fsid@sids.org.uk
Web: www.sids.org.uk

Friends of the Earth, 26 Underwood Street, London N1 7JQ
☎020 7490 1555
🖷020 7490 0881
E: info@foe.co.uk
Web: www.foe.co.uk

Gamblers Anonymous, PO Box 88, London SW10 0EU
☎0870 050 8880
Web: www.gamblersanonymous.org.uk

Gingerbread, 307 Borough High Street, London SE1 1JH
☎020 7403 9500 🖷020 7403 9533
E: office@gingerbread.org.uk
Web: www.gingerbread.org.uk

Girlguiding UK, 17 Buckingham Palace Road, London SW1W 0PT
☎020 7834 6242 🖷020 7828 8317
E: website@girlguiding.org.uk
Web: www.girlguiding.org.uk

Government Office for the East of England, Eastbrook, Shaftesbury Road, Cambridge CB2 2DF
☎01223 372 500 🖷01223 372 501
E: enquiries.goeast@go-regions.gsi.gov.uk
Web: www.go-east.gov.uk

Government Office for the East Midlands, The Belgrave Centre, Stanley Place, Talbot Street, Nottingham NG1 5GG
☎0115 971 2759 🖷0115 971 2404
E: enquiries.goem@goem.gsi.gov.uk
Web: www.goem.gov.uk

Government Office for London, Riverwalk House, 157 Millbank, London SW1P 4RR
☎020 7217 3328 🖷020 7217 3450
E: enquiries.gol@go-regions.gov.uk
Web: www.go-london.gov.uk

Government Office for the North East, Citygate, Gallowgate, Newcastle upon Tyne NE1 4WH
☎0191 201 3300 🖷0191 202 3998
E: general.enquiries.gone@go-regions.gsi.gov.uk
Web: www.go-ne.gov.uk

Government Office for the North West, City Tower, Picadilly Plaza, Manchester M1 4BE
☎0161 952 4000 🖷0161 952 4099
E: gonwmailbox@gonw.gsi.gov.uk
Web: www.gonw.gov.uk

Government Office for the South East, Bridge House, 1 Walnut Tree Close, Guildford GU1 4GA
☎01483 882 255 🖷01483 882 259
Web: www.go-se.gov.uk

Government Office for the South West, 2 Rivergate, Temple Quay, Bristol BS1 6ED
☎0117 900 1700 🖷0117 900 1900
E: swcontactus@gosw.gsi.gov.uk
Web: www.gosw.gov.uk

Government Office for the West Midlands, 5 St Philips Place, Colmore Row, Birmingham B3 2PW
☎0121 212 5050
E: enquiries.team@gowm.gsi.gov.uk
Web: www.go-wm.gov.uk

Government Office for Yorkshire & the Humber, PO Box 213, City House, New Station Street, Leeds LS1 4US
☎0113 280 0600 🖷0113 283 6394
E: yhenquiries@goyh.gsi.gov.uk
Web: www.goyh.gov.uk

Greenpeace Ltd, Canonbury Villas, London N1 2PN
☎020 7865 8100 🖷020 7865 8200
E: info@uk.greenpeace.org
Web: www.greenpeace.org.uk

The Guide Dogs for the Blind Association, Hillfields, Burghfield Common, Reading RG7 3YG
☎0118 983 5555
E: guidedogs@guidedogs.org.uk
Web: www.gdba.org.uk

Guinness Publishing, 338 Euston Road, Regent's Place, London NW1 3BD
☎020 7891 4567 🖷020 7891 4051
E: gworlds@itl.net

HM Revenue and Customs, Thomas Paine House, Angel Square, Torrens Street, London EC1V 1TA
☎0845 010 9000
Web: www.hmrc.gov.uk

Hammersmith & Fulham Libraries, Fulham Library, 598 Fulham Road, London SW6 5NX
☎020 8753 3877
E: www.ibhf.gov.uk

Healthwise, 101 Woodside Business Park, Shore Road, Birkenhead CH41 1EP
☎0151 649 3400 🖷0151 649 3401
E: info@healthwise.org.uk
Web: www.healthwise.org.uk

Help the Aged, 207 Pentonville Road, London N1 9UZ
☎020 7278 1114 🖷020 7278 1116
E: info@helptheaged.org.uk
Web: www.helptheaged.org.uk

The Henley Centre, 11 St John Street, London EC1M 4PJ
☎020 7955 1800
E: betterfutures@henleycentre.com
Web: www.henleycentre.com

Henley Management College, Greenlands, Henley-on-Thames RG9 3AU
☎01491 571 454 🖷01491 571 635
E: enquiries@henleymc.ac.uk
Web: www.henleymc.ac.uk

Home Office, Direct Communications Unit, 2 Marsham Street, London SW1P 4DF
☎020 7035 4848 🖷020 7035 4745
E: public.enquiries@homeoffice.gsi.gov.uk
Web: www.homeoffice.gov.uk

Hunger Project, 2 Bishopbourne, 134 Westbourne Terrace, London W2 6QB
☎07985 647 082 🖷020 7225 3573
E: ekaterina.mitiaev@thp.org
Web: www.thehungerproject.org.uk
Also at: 70 Margaret Street, London W1W 8SS
☎020 7291 3300 🖷 020 7323 4165

Other Organisations and Agencies

Independent Police Complaints Commission, 90 High Holborn, London WC1V 6BH
☎08453 002 002 🖷020 7404 0430
E: enquiries@ipcc.gsi.gov.uk
Web: www.ipcc.gov.uk

INFORM (Information Network Focus On Religious Movements), London School of Economics, London WC2A 2AE
☎020 7955 7654 🖷020 7955 7679
E: inform@lse.ac.uk
Web: www.lse.ac.uk

Information Commissioner's Office, Wycliffe House, Water Lane, Wilmslow SK9 5AF
☎01625 545 745 🖷01625 524 510
E: mail@ico.ysi.gov.uk
Web: www.informationcommissioner.gov.uk

Institute of Business Ethics, 24 Greencoat Place, London SW1P 1DX
☎020 7798 6040 🖷020 7798 6044
E: info@ibe.org.uk
Web: www.ibe.org.uk

Institute of Directors, 116 Pall Mall, London SW1Y 5ED
☎020 7839 1233 🖷020 7930 1949
E: enquiries@iod.com
Web: www.iod.com

Institute of Economic Affairs, 2 Lord North Street, Westminster, London SW1P 3LB
☎020 7799 8900 🖷020 7799 2137
E: inquiries@iea.org.uk
Web: www.iea.org.uk

Institute of Fundraising, Park Place, 12 Lawn Lane, London SW8 1UD
☎020 7840 1000 🖷020 7840 1001
E: enquiries@institue-of-fundraising.org.uk
Web: www.institute-of-fundraising.org.uk

Intellect (Computing Services and Software Association), Russell Square House, 10 Russell Square, London WC1B 5EE
☎020 7331 2000 🖷020 7331 2040
E: info@intellectuk.org
Web: www.intellectuk.org

Jewish Education Bureau, 8 Westcombe Avenue, Leeds LS8 2BS
☎0870 8008 532 M: 07725 691 184
🖷0870 8008 533
E: jeb@jewisheducationbureau.co.uk
Web: www.jewisheducationbureau.co.uk

Jubilee Plus, NEF, 3 Jonathan Street, London SE11 5NH
☎020 7820 6350
Web: www.jubilee2000uk.org

Labour Party Head Office, 16 Old Queen Street, London SW1H 9HP
☎0870 590 0200
E: info@new.labour.org.uk
Web: www.labour.org.uk

HM Land Registry, Lincoln's Inn Fields, London WC2A 3PH
☎020 7917 8888 🖷020 7955 0110
Web: www.landreg.gov.uk

Les Cedres, 17 Voie de Wissous, 91300, Massy France
☎00 33 1 69 30 00 67
🖷00 33 1 69 30 54 56
E: info@lescedres.com
Web: www.lescedres.com

Liberal Democrats, Head Office, 4 Cowley Street, London SW1P 3NB
☎020 7227 1224 🖷020 7799 2170
E: info@libdems.org.uk
Web: www.libdems.org.uk

Library Association, 7 Ridgemount Street, London WC1E 7AE
☎020 7255 0500
Textphone 020 7255 0505
🖷020 7255 0501
E: info@cilip.org.uk
Web: www.la-hq.org.uk

LIFE - Save The Unborn Child, Life House, 1a Newbold Terrace, Leamington Spa CV32 4EA
☎01926 421 587/311 667/316 737
Text 07786 200 330 🖷01926 336 497
E: care@lifeuk.org or info@lifeuk.org
Web: www.preghelp.org.uk or www.lifeuk.org

Macmillan Cancer Relief, 89 Albert Embankment, London SE1 7UQ
☎0808 808 2020 Textphone 0808 808 0121
E: cancerline@macmillan.org.uk
Web: www.macmillan.org.uk

Market Research Society, 15 Northburgh Street, London EC1 0JR
☎020 7490 4911 🖷020 7490 0608
E: info@mrs.org.uk
Web: www.mrs.org.uk

Mechanical Copyright Protection Society Ltd (MCPS), 29 Berners Street, London W1T 3AB
☎020 7580 5544
Web: www.mcps.co.uk

MENCAP, 123 Golden Lane, London EC1Y 0RT
☎020 7454 0454 🖷020 7696 5540
Web: www.mencap.org.uk

Mental Health Foundation, UK Office, 9th Floor, 20 Upper Ground, London SW1 9QB
☎020 7803 1100 🖷020 7803 1111
E: mhf@mhf.org.uk
Web: www.mentalhealth.org.uk

MIND (National Association for Mental Health), 15 Broadway, London E15 4BQ
☎020 8519 2122 🖷020 8522 1725
E: contact@mind.org.uk
Web: www.mind.org.uk

Ministry of Defence, The Ministerial Correspondence Unit, Floor 5, Zone A, Main Building, Whitehall, London SW1A 2HB
☎020 7128 9000
E: public@ministers.mod.uk
Web: www.mod.uk
No replies by Email, must include a postal address.

National Assembly for Wales, Cardiff Bay, Cardiff CF99 1NA
☎029 2082 5111
Web: www.wales.gov.uk

National Association of Citizens Advice Bureaux, Myddleton House, 115 Pentonville Road, London N1 9LZ
☎020 7833 2181 🖷020 7833 4371
E: consortancy@nacab.org.uk
Web: www.nacab.org.uk

National Centre for Social Research, 35 Northampton Square, London EC1V 0AX
☎020 7250 1866 🖷020 7250 1524
E: info@natcen.ac.uk
Web: www.natcen.ac.uk

National Children's Bureau, 8 Wakley Street, London EC1V 7QE
☎020 7843 6000 🖷020 7278 9512
Web: www.ncb.org.uk

National Council for One-Parent Families, 255 Kentish Town Road, London NW5 2LX
☎020 7428 5400/0800 018 5026 (helpline) 🖷020 7482 4851
E: info@oneparentfamilies.org.uk
Web: www.oneparentfamilies.org.uk

National Council for Voluntary Organisations (NCVO), Regent's Wharf, 8 All Saints Street, London N1 9RL
☎020 7713 6161/0800 2798 798 (helpdesk) 🖷020 7713 6300
E: ncvo@ncvo-vol.org.uk
Web: www.ncvo-vol.org.uk

National Federation of Young Farmers Club, YFC Centre, National Agriculture Centre, Stoneleigh Park, Kenilworth CV8 2LG
☎024 7685 7200 🖷024 7685 7229
E: post@nfyfc.org.uk
Web: www.nfyfc.org.uk

The National Lottery Commission, 101 Wigmore Street, London W1U 1QU
☎020 7016 3400
E: h.sear@natlotcomm.gov.uk
Web: www.natlotcomm.gov.uk

National Missing Persons Helpline, Roebuck House, 284 Upper Richmond Road West, London SW14 7JE
☎0500 700 700
E: sightings@missingpersons.org
Web: www.missingpersons.org
Visitors by appointment only.

National Trust, PO Box 39, Warrington WA5 7WD
☎0870 458 4000 🖷020 8466 6824
E: enquiries@thenationaltrust.org.uk
Web: www.nationaltrust.org.uk

X

Newspaper Publishers Association, 34 Southwark Bridge Road, London SE1 9EU
☎020 7207 2200

The Newspaper Society, Bloomsbury House, 74 Great Russell Street, London WC1B 3DA
☎020 7636 7014 🖷020 7631 5119
E: ns@newspapersoc.org.uk
Web: www.newspapersoc.org.uk

Northern Ireland Office, 11 Millbank, London SW1P 4PN
☎028 9052 0700
Textphone 028 9052 7668
Web: www.nio.gov.uk

NRG Group Ltd, 4 Rushmills, Northampton NN4 7YB
☎01604 732 700 🖷01604 624 812
Web: www.nrggroup.co.uk

NSPCC (National Society for the Prevention of Cruelty to Children), Weston House, 42 Curtain Road, London EC2A 3NH
☎0808 800 5000
Textphone 0808 800 5000
🖷020 7825 2750
E: help@nspcc.org.uk
Web: www.nspcc.org.uk

Ofcom, 2a Southwark Bridge Road, London SE1 9HA
☎020 7981 3000 🖷020 7981 3333
Web: www.ofcom.org.uk

Office for National Statistics, Customer Contact Centre, Room 1.015, Cardiff Road, Newport NP10 8XG
☎0845 601 3034 Minicom 01633 812 399 🖷01633 652 747
E: info@statistics.gov.uk
Web: www.statistics.gov.uk
See also Retail Price Index.

Office of Gas and Electricity Market (OFGEM), 9 Millbank, London SW1P 3GE
☎020 7901 7000 🖷020 7901 7066
E: library@ofgem.gov.uk
Web: www.ofgem.gov.uk

Office of Fair Trading, Fleetbank House, 2 Salisbury Square, London EC4Y 8JX
☎08457 224 499 or 020 7211 8000
🖷020 7211 8800
E: enquiries@oft.gsi.gov.uk
Web: www.oft.gov.uk

Office of Water Services (OFWAT), Centre City Tower, 7 Hill Street, Birmingham B5 4UA
☎0121 625 1300
Minicom 0121 625 1422
🖷0121 625 1400
E: enquiries@ofwat.gsi.gov.uk
Web: www.ofwat.gov.uk

Office of the Deputy Prime Minister, Eland House, Bressenden Place, London SW1E 5DU
☎020 7944 4400 🖷020 7944 9645
E: enquiryodpm@odpm.gsi.gov.uk
Web: www.odpm.gov.uk

Office of the Rail Regulator, 1 Waterhouse Square, 138 Holborn, London EC1N 2TQ
☎020 7282 2000 🖷020 7282 2040
E: rail.library@orr.gsi.gov.uk
Web: www.rail-reg.gov.uk

Ordnance Survey, Romsey Road, Southampton SO16 4GU
☎0845 605 0505 🖷023 8079 2615
E: customerservices@ordnancesurvey.co.uk
Web: www.ordinancesurvey.o.uk

OXFAM, Oxfam House, John Smith Drive, Cowley, Oxford OX4 2JY
☎0870 333 2700 🖷01865 312 600
E: oxfam@oxfam.org.uk
Web: www.oxfam.org.uk

Pensions Ombudsman, 11 Belgrave Road, London SW1V 1RB
☎020 7834 9144 🖷020 7821 0065
E: enquiries@pensions-ombudsman.org.uk
Web: www.pensions-ombudsman.org.uk

Performing Rights Society, 29 Berners Street, London W1T 3AB
☎020 7580 5544
E: enquiries@prs.co.uk
Web: www.prs.co.uk

The Periodical Publishers Association, Queen's House, 28 Kingsway, London WC2B 6JR
☎020 7404 4166 🖷020 7404 4167
E: info1@ppa.co.uk
Web: www.ppa.co.uk

The Prince's Trust, 18 Park Square East, London NW1 4LH
☎0800 842 842
Minicom 020 7543 1374
🖷020 7542 1200
Web: www.princes-trust.org.uk

Public Records Office, Kew, Richmond TW9 4DU
☎020 8876 3444
Web: www.pro.gov.uk

Publishers Association, 29b Montague Street, London WC1B 5BL
☎020 7691 9191
Web: www.publishers.org.uk

RAC, Great Park Road, Bristol BS32 4QN
☎08705 722 722
Web: www.rac.co.uk

RADAR (Royal Association for Disability and Rehabilitation), Unit 12, City Forum, 250 City Road, London EC1V 8AF
☎020 7250 3222
Minicom 020 7250 4119
🖷020 7250 0212
E: radar@radar.org.uk
Web: www.radar.org.uk

Relate Marriage Guidance, National Headquarters, Herbert Gray College, Little Church Street, Rugby CV21 3AP
☎0845 456 1310 or 01788 573 241
🖷01788 535 007
E: enquiries@relate.org.uk
Web: www.relate.org.uk

Retail Price Index, Consumer Prices General Inflation, Floor D2/16, 1 Drummond Gate, London SW1V 2QQ
☎020 7533 5874 🖷020 7533 5863
Web: www.ons.gov.org.uk

Rights of Women, 52 Featherstone Street, London EC1Y 8RT
☎020 7251 6577 🖷020 7490 5377
E: info@row.org.uk
Web: www.rightsofwomen.org.uk

Joseph Rowntree Foundation, The Homestead, 40 Water End, York YO30 6WP
☎01904 629 241 🖷01904 620 072
E: info@jrf.org.uk
Web: www.jrf.org.uk

Royal National Institute for Deaf People, Speedfix House, 19 Featherstone Street, London EC1Y 8SL
☎0808 808 0123
Minicom 0808 808 9000
🖷020 7296 8199
E: informationline@rnid.org.uk
Web: www.rnid.org.uk

Royal National Institute for the Blind, 105 Judd Street, London WC1H 9NE
☎020 7388 1266 🖷020 7388 2034
E: helpline@rnib.org.uk
Web: www.rnib.org.uk

Royal National Lifeboat Institute (RNLI), West Quay Road, Poole BH15 1HZ
☎0800 543 210
Web: www.rnli.org.uk

RSPB (Royal Society for the Protection of Birds), The Lodge, Potton Road, Sandy SG19 2DL
☎01767 680 551
Web: www.rspb.org.uk

RSPCA, Enquiries Service, Wilberforce Way, Southwater, Horsham RH13 9RS
☎0870 333 5999 🖷0870 753 0284
Web: www.rspca.org.uk

St John Ambulance Brigade, 27 St John's Lane, London EC1M 4BU
☎0870 010 4950 🖷0870 010 4065
Web: www.sja.org.uk

Salvation Army Family Tracing Service, 101 Newington Causeway, London SE1 6BN
☎0845 634 4747 or 020 7367 4747
E: family.tracing@salvationarmy.org.uk
Web: www.salvationarmy.org.uk

The Samaritans, PO Box 9090, Stirling FK8 2SA
☎08457 909 090
E: jo@samaritans.org
Web: www.samaritans.org

SANDS (Stillbirth and Neonatal Death Society), 28 Portland Place, London W1B 1LY
☎020 7436 5881 🖷020 7436 3715
E: helpline@uk-sands.org
Web: www.uk-sands.org

SANE, 1st Floor Cityside House, 40 Adler Street, London E1 1EE
☎020 7375 1002 or 0845 767 8000 (12noon-2am) ℻020 7375 2162
E: london@sane.org.uk
Web: www.sane.org.uk

The Save The Children Fund, 1 St Johns Lane, London EC1M 4AR
☎020 7012 6400 ℻020 7012 6963
Web: www.savethechildren.org.uk

Scope - The Cerebral Palsy Society, Library and Information Unit, 6 Market Road, London N7 9PW
☎0808 800 3333 (9am-9pm Mon-Fri, 2pm-6pm Sat, Sun, Bank Hols)
E: cphelpline@scope.org.uk
Web: www.scope.org.uk

Scottish Executive, St Andrew's House, Regent Road, Edinburgh EH1 3DG
☎0131 556 8400/08457 741 741 (enquiries) Minicom 0131 244 1829
℻0131 244 8240
E: ceu@scotland.gov.uk
Web: www.scotland.gov.uk

The Scout Association, Information Centre, Gilwell Park, Bury Road, Chingford, London E4 7QW
☎0845 300 1818 or 020 8433 7100
℻020 8433 7103
E: info.centre@scout.org.uk
Web: www.scoutbase.org.uk

The Sea Cadet Corps, 202 Lambeth Road, London SE1 7JF
☎020 7928 8978 ℻020 7928 8914
E: schq@sea-cadets.org
Web: www.sea-cadets.org

Shelter, 88 Old Street, London EC1V 9HU
☎0845 458 4590 ℻020 7505 2030
E: info@shelter.org.uk
Web: www.shelter.org.uk

Social Research Association, 175 Gray's Inn Road, London WC1X 8UP
☎020 7812 0634
E: admin@the-sra.org.uk
Web: www.the-sra.org.uk

Sport England, 3rd Floor, Victoria House, Bloomsbury Square, London WC1B 4SE
☎08458 508 508 ℻020 7383 5740
E: info@sportengland.org
Web: www.sportengland.org

The Strategic Planning Society, Buxton House, 7 Highbury Hill, London N5 1SU
☎0845 056 3663 ℻0870 751 8216
E: membership@sps.org.uk
Web: www.sps.org.uk

Survival International, 6 Charterhouse Buildings, London EC1M 7ET
☎020 7687 8700 ℻020 7687 8701
E: info@survival-international.org
Web: www.survival-international.org

Teetotallers Nationwide Publicity Register, 9 The Lodge, 3 Blackwater Road, Eastbourne BN21 4JF
☎01323 638 234

HM Treasury, The Correspondence & Enquiry Unit, 2/W1 HM Treasury, 1 Horse Guards Road, London SW1A 2HQ
☎020 7270 4558 ℻020 7270 4861
E: public.enquiries@hmtreasury.gov.uk
Web: www.hm-treasury.gov.uk

TUC (Trades Union Congress), Congress House, 23 Great Russell Street, London WC1B 3LS
☎020 7636 4030 ℻020 7636 0632
E: info@tuc.org.uk
Web: www.tuc.org.uk

United Nations Information Centre, 21st Floor, Millbank Tower, 21 Millbank, London SW1P 4QH
☎020 7630 1981 ℻020 7976 6478

Victim Support, Cranmer House, 39 Brixton Road, London SW9 6DZ
☎020 7735 9166 ℻020 7582 5712
E: contact@victimsupport.org.uk
Web: www.victimsupport.org.uk

VisitBritain, Thames Tower, Black's Road, London W6 9EL
☎020 8846 9000 ℻020 8563 0302
Web: www.visitbritain.org

Voluntary Service Overseas, 317 Putney Bridge Road, London SW15 2PN
☎020 8780 7200
E: infoservice@vso.org.uk
Web: www.vso.org.uk

Women's Aid Federation England (WAFE), PO Box 391, Bristol BS99 7WS
☎0117 944 4411 ℻0117 924 1703
E: info@womensaid.org.uk
Web: www.womensaid.org.uk

Women's Royal Voluntary Service (WRVS), Garden House, Milton Hill, Steventon, Abingdon OX13 6AD
☎0845 601 4670 or 01235 442 900
℻01235 861 166
E: enquiries@wrvs.org.uk
Web: www.wrvs.org.uk

World Development Movement, 25 Beehive Place, London SW9 7QF
☎020 7737 6215 ℻020 7274 8232
E: wdm@wdm.org.uk
Web: www.wdm.org.uk

World Wide Fund for Nature (WWF-UK), Panda House, Weyside Park, Godalming GU7 1XR
☎01483 426 444 ℻01483 426 409
Web: www.wwf-uk.org

RADIO & TELEVISION – BBC

BBC Corporate Headquarters & National Radio Stations: Radio 1, Radio 2, Radio 3, Radio 4, Radio 5 Live, BBC Broadcasting House, Portland Place, London W1A 1AA
☎020 7580 4468
Info 0161 200 2020
Web: www.bbc.co.uk

BBC Television Headquarters, Television Centre, Wood Lane, London W12 7RJ
☎020 8743 8000
or 0161 200 2020

BBC News Centre, Television Centre, Wood Lane, London W12 7RJ
☎020 8743 8000
E: emily.buchanan@bbc.co.uk
Web: www.bbc.co.uk
Religious Producer: Emily Buchanan.

BBC Religion & Ethics, BBC Broadcasting Centre, 2 St Peter's Square, Leeds LS9 8AH
☎0113 244 2131
E: ashley.peatfield@bbc.co.uk
Web: www.bbc.co.uk
Head of Religion & Ethics: Michael Wakelin. *Editor:* Ashley Peatfield.

BBC World Service, PO Box 76, Bush House, Strand, London WC2B 4PH
☎020 7240 3456
or 0161 244 3252
℻0161 244 3276
Web: www.bbc.co.uk

REGIONAL OFFICES

English Regions, Room 129, Henry Wood House, 3 Langham Place, London W1A 1AA
☎07739 920 216
E: naomi.wellings@bbc.co.uk
Web: www.bbc.co.uk
Religious Affairs Correspondent: Naomi Wellings.

Northern Ireland, Broadcasting House, 25 Ormeau Avenue, Belfast BT2 8HQ
☎028 9033 8000
℻028 9033 8814
E: bert.tosh@bbc.co.uk
Web: www.bbc.co.uk
Religious Producer: Bert Tosh.

Scotland, Broadcasting House, Queen Margaret Drive, Glasgow G12 8DG
☎0141 338 2000
℻0141 338 2513
E: anna.magnusson@bbc.co uk
Web: www.bbc.co.uk
Senior Religious Producer: Anna Magnusson.

Wales, Broadcasting House, Llantrisant Road, Llandaff, Cardiff CF5 2YQ
☎029 2032 2000
℻029 2032 2758
E: Lisa.Hawkins@bbc.co.uk
Web: www.bbc.co.uk
Religious Producer: Lisa Hawkins.

BBC LOCAL RADIO STATIONS

Asian Network, 9 St Nicholas Place, Leicester LE1 5LB
☎0116 251 6688 🖷0116 253 2004
E: devan.maistry@bbc.co.uk
Web: www.bbc.co.uk/asiannetwork
Religious Producer: Devan Maistry.

Coventry and Warwickshire, Priory Place, Coventry CV1 5SQ
☎024 7655 1000
E: stewart.kingscott@bbc.co.uk
Web: www.bbc.co.uk/coventry
Faith Producer: Stewart Kingscott.

Essex, 198 New London Road, Chelmsford CM2 9AB
☎01245 616 000 or 07976 796 201
E: chris.bard@bbc.co.uk
Web: www.bbc.co.uk/essex
Faith Producer: Rev Chris Bard.

Hereford & Worcester, Hylton Road, Worcester WR2 5WW
☎01905 337 230
E: andy.haynes@bbc.co.uk
Web: www.bbc.co.uk/herefordandworcester
Faith Producer: Andy Haynes.

London, PO Box 94.9, Marylebone High Street, London W1A 6FL
☎020 7208 9350
E: jumoke.fashola@bbc.co.uk
Web: www.bbc.co.uk/london
Faith Producer: Jumoké Fashola.

Radio Berkshire, PO Box 104.4, Reading RG4 8FH
☎0118 946 4200
E: harriet.lloyd@bbc.co.uk
Web: www.bbc.co.uk/radioberkshire
Faith Producer: Harriet Lloyd.

Radio Bristol / Somerset Sound, PO Box 194, Bristol BS99 7QT
☎0117 974 6701
E: liz.parker@bbc.co.uk
Web: www.bbc.co.uk/radiosomerset
Faith Producer: Liz Parker.

Radio Cambridgeshire, Broadcasting House, 104 Hills Road, Cambridge CB2 1LD
☎01223 259 696 or 07812 026 251 🖷01223 460 832
E: susan.bowden-pickstock@bbc.co.uk
Web: www.bbc.co.uk/radiocambridgeshire
Faith Producer: Susan Bowden-Pickstock.

Radio Cleveland, PO Box 95FM, Newport Road, Middlesbrough TS1 5DG
☎01642 340 660
E: mark.turnbull@bbc.co.uk
Web: www.bbc.co.uk/tees
Faith Producer: Mark Turnbull.

Radio Cornwall, Phoenix Wharf, Truro TR1 1UA
☎01872 475 263
E: naomi.rowe@bbc.co.uk
Web: www.bbc.co.uk/radiocornwall
Faith Producer: Naomi Rowe.

Radio Cumbria, Annetwell Street, Carlisle CA3 8BB
☎01228 592 444
E: ian.timms@bbc.co.uk
Web: www.bbc.co.uk/radiocumbria
Faith Producer: Ian Timms.

Radio Derby, PO Box 104.5, Derby DE1 3HL
☎01332 375 032
E: jan.rogers@bbc.co.uk
Web: www.bbc.co.uk/radioderby
Faith Producer: Jan Rogers.

Radio Devon, Broadcasting House, Seymour Road, Mannamead, Plymouth PL3 5BD
☎01752 260 323
E: pippa.quelch@bbc.co.uk
Web: www.bbc.co.uk/radiodevon
Faith Producer: Pippa Quelch.

Radio Gloucestershire, London Road, Gloucester GL1 1SW
☎01452 308 585 M: 07743 064 734
E: richard.atkins@bbc.co.uk
Web: www.bbc.co.uk/radiogloucestershire
Faith Producer: Richard Atkins.

Radio Guernsey, Television House, Dulwer Avenue, St Sampson's, Guernsey GY2 4LA
☎01481 200 600
E: colin.leray@bbc.co.uk
Web: www.bbc.co.uk/radioguernsey
Faith Producer: Colin Le Ray.

Radio Humberside, 9 Chapel Street, Hull HU1 3NU
☎01482 331 443
E: blair.jacobs@bbc.co.uk
Web: www.bbc.co.uk/radiohumberside
Faith Producer: Blair Jacobs.

Radio Jersey, 18 Parade Road, St Helier, Jersey JE2 3PL
☎01534 837 260
E: lynsey.beahan@bbc.co.uk
Web: www.bbc.co.uk/radiojersey
Faith Producer: Lynsey Beahan.

Radio Kent, Mount Pleasant Road, Tunbridge Wells TN1 1QQ
☎01892 675 605
E: lynn.wallis-eade@bbc.co.uk or radio.kent.sunday@bbc.co.uk
Web: www.bbc.co.uk/radiokent
Faith Producer: Lynn Wallis-Eade.

Radio Lancashire, 26 Darwen Street, Blackburn BB2 2EA
☎01254 841 013
E: joe.wilson.01@bbc.co.uk
Web: www.bbc.co.uk/radiolancashire
Faith Producer: Joe Wilson.

Radio Leeds, Broadcasting House, Woodhouse Lane, Leeds LS2 9PN
☎01274 841 058
E: russell.walker-brown@bbc.co.uk
Web: www.bbc.co.uk/radioleeds
Faith Producer: Russell Walker-Brown.

Radio Leicester, Epic House, Charles Street, Leicester LE1 3SH
☎0116 251 6688
E: natalie.martin@bbc.co.uk
Web: www.bbc.co.uk/radioleicester
Faith Producer: Natalie Martin.

Radio Lincolnshire, Radio Buildings, Newport, Lincoln LN1 3XY
☎01522 511 411
E: sue.edwards@bbc.co.uk
Web: www.bbc.co.uk/radiolincolnshire
Faith Producer: Sue Edwards.

Radio Manchester, PO Box 951, Oxford Road, Manchester M60 1SD
☎0161 244 3007
E: mike.shaft@bbc.co.uk
Web: www.bbc.co.uk/manchester
Faith Producer: Mike Shaft. (Previously GMR).

Radio Merseyside, 55 Paradise Street, Liverpool L1 3BP
☎0151 794 0963
E: wayne.clark@bbc.co.uk
Web: www.bbc.co.uk/radiomerseyside
Faith Producer: Wayne Clarke.

Radio Newcastle, Broadcasting Centre, Barrack Road, Newcastle upon Tyne NE99 1RN
☎0191 232 4141
E: chris.hodder@bbc.co.uk
Web: www.bbc.co.uk/radionewcastle
Faith Producer: Chris Hodder.

Radio Norfolk, Norfolk Tower, Surrey Street, Norwich NR1 3PA
☎01603 284 762
E: tony.mallion@bbc.co.uk
Web: www.bbc.co.uk/radionorfolk
Faith Producer: Tony Mallion.

Radio Northampton, Broadcasting House, Abington Street, Northampton NN1 2BH
☎01327 706 145
E: martin.heath@bbc.co.uk
Web: www.bbc.co.uk/radionorthampton
Faith Producer: Martin Heath.

Radio Nottingham, London Road, Nottingham NG2 4UU
☎0115 902 1896
E: celia.kellett@bbc.co.uk
Web: www.bbc.co.uk/radionottingham
Faith Producer: Celia Kellett.

Radio Oxford, PO Box 95.2, Oxford OX2 7YL
☎08459 311 444
E: alison.booker@bbc.co.uk
Web: www.bbc.co.uk/radiooxford
Faith Producer: Alison Booker.

Radio Sheffield, 54 Shoreham Street, Sheffield S1 4RS
☎0114 267 5466
E: dean.pepall@bbc.co.uk
Web: www.bbc.co.uk/radiosheffield
Faith Producer: Dean Pepall.

Radio Shropshire, 2 Boscobel Drive, Shrewsbury SY1 3TT
☎01743 248 484
🖂: kate.tebby@bbc.co.uk
Web: www.bbc.co.uk/radioshropshire
Faith Producer: Kate Tebby.

Radio Solent, Broadcasting House, Havelock Road, Southampton SO14 7PW
☎023 8063 1311
🖂: tim.daykin@bbc.co.uk
Web: www.bbc.co.uk/radiosolent
Faith Producer: Tim Daykin.

Radio Stoke, Cheapside, Hanley, Stoke-on-Trent ST1 1JJ
☎01782 208 080
🖂: lamont.howie@bbc.co.uk
Web: www.bbc.co.uk/radiostoke
Faith Producer: Lamont Howie.

Radio Suffolk, Broadcasting House, St Matthew's Street, Ipswich IP1 3EP
☎01473 340 734
🖂: rachel.sloane@bbc.co.uk
Web: www.bbc.co.uk/radiosuffolk
Faith Producer: Rachel Sloane.

Radio WM, Pebble Mill Road, Birmingham B5 7SD
☎0121 567 6059
🖂: michaela.howard@bbc.co.uk
Web: www.bbc.co.uk/radiowm
Faith Producer: Michaela Howard.

Radio Wiltshire / Radio Swindon, Broadcasting House, Prospect Place, Swindon SN1 3RW
☎01793 513 652
🖂: sue.davies.01@bbc.co.uk
Web: www.bbc.co.uk/radiowiltshire
Faith Producer: Sue Davies.

Radio York, 20 Bootham Row, York YO30 7BR
☎01904 540 338
🖂: adam.tomlinson@bbc.co.uk
Web: www.bbc.co.uk/radioyork
Faith Producer: Adam Tomlinson.

Southern Counties Radio, Broadcasting Centre, Guildford GU2 7AP
☎01273 320 428
🖂: alex.strangewayes-booth@bbc.co.uk
Web: www.bbc.co.uk/southerncounties
Faith Producer: Alex Strangewayes-Booth.

Three Counties Radio, PO Box 3CR, Luton LU1 5XL
☎01582 637 444
🖂: ian.pearce@bbc.co.uk
Web: www.bbc.co.uk/threecounties
Faith Producer: Ian Pearce.

RADIO & TELEVISION - INDEPENDENT

INDEPENDENT NATIONAL TELEVISION COMPANIES

Channel 3 (ITV), 200 Gray's Inn Road, London WC1X 8HF
☎020 7843 8000 🖷020 7843 8158
🖂: dominic.crosby-holland@itv.com
Web: www.itv.com
Religious Producer: Dominic Crosby-Holland.

Channel 4, 124 Horseferry Road, London SW1P 2TX
☎020 7396 4444 🖷020 7306 8794
🖂: aahmed@channel4.co.uk
Web: www.channel4.com
Religious Producer: Aaqil Ahmed.

Channel 5, 22 Long Acre, London WC2E 9LY
☎020 7550 5555 🖷020 7550 5554
Web: www.channel5.co.uk
Religious Producer: Nick Wilson.

INDEPENDENT REGIONAL TELEVISION COMPANIES (CHANNEL 3)

Anglia Television Ltd, Anglia House, Norwich NR1 3JG
☎01603 615 151 🖷01603 631 032
🖂: miketalbot@granadamedia.com
Web: www.itvregions.com/anglia
Religious Producer: Mike Talbot.

Border Television plc, The Television Centre, Durranhill, Carlisle CA1 3NT
☎01228 525 101 🖷01228 541 384
🖂: btvnews@itv.com
Web: www.itvregions.com/border

Central Region, Central Court, Gas Street, Birmingham B1 2JT
☎0870 600 6766 🖷0121 634 4740
Web: www.itvregions.com/central

Channel Television Ltd, The Television Centre, Al Pouquelaye, St Helier, Jersey JE1 3ZD
☎01534 816 816 🖷01534 816 777
🖂: broadcast@channeltv.co.uk
Web: www.channeltv.co.uk

GMTV Ltd, London Television Centre, Upper Ground, London SE1 9TT
☎020 7827 7000 🖷020 7827 7001
🖂: newmedia@gm.tv
Web: www.gm.tv

Granada Television Ltd, Quay Street, Manchester M60 9EA
☎0161 832 7211 🖷0161 827 2180
Web: www.itvregions.com/granada

London, London Television Centre, Upper Ground, London SE1 9LT
☎020 7620 1620 🖷020 7261 8163
Web: www.itvregions.com/london

Meridian, Forum 1, Solent Business Park, Whiteley, Fareham PO15 7PA
☎023 8022 2555 🖷023 8033 5050
Web: www.itvregions.com/meridian

Scottish Television Ltd, Cowcaddens, Glasgow G2 3PR
☎0141 300 3704 🖷0141 300 3030
🖂: viewer.enquiries@stv.tv
Web: www.stv.tv
Also at
(Previously Grampian Television Ltd).
Queen's Cross, Aberdeen AB15 2XJ
☎01224 846 846 🖷 01224 846 800

Tyne Tees Television Ltd, The Television Centre, City Road, Newcastle upon Tyne NE1 2AL
☎0191 404 8700 🖷0191 404 8710
Web: www.itvregions.com/tyne_tees

Ulster Television plc, Havelock House, Ormeau Road, Belfast BT7 1EB
☎028 9032 8122 🖷028 9024 6695
🖂: newsroom@utv.plc.com
Web: www.u.tv

Wales, Television Centre, Culverhouse Cross, Cardiff CF5 6XJ
☎029 2059 0590 🖷029 2059 7183
Web: www.itvregions.com/wales

West Country Region, Language Science Park, Western Wood Way, Plymouth PL7 5BG
☎01752 333 333 🖷01752 333 444
Web: www.itvregions.com/westcountry

Yorkshire Television Ltd, The Television Centre, Leeds LS3 1JS
☎0113 243 8283 🖷0113 243 3655
Web: www.itvregions.com/yorkshire

INDEPENDENT NATIONAL RADIO STATIONS

Classic FM, 30 Leicester Square, London WC2H 2LA
☎020 7343 9000 🖷020 7344 2700
🖂: enquiries@classicfm.com
Web: www.classicfm.com

Talksport, 18 Hatfields, London SE1 8DJ
☎08704 202 020
Web: www.talksport.net

Virgin Radio, 1 Golden Square, London W1F 4DJ
☎020 7434 1215 🖷020 7434 1137
🖂: enquiries@virginradio.co.uk
Web: www.virginradio.co.uk

NATIONAL PRESS RELIGIOUS CORRESPONDENTS

The Daily Express, The Northern & Shell Building, Number 10, Lower Thames Street, London EC3R 6EN
☎020 7928 8000 📠020 7620 1654
E: rachel.baird@express.co.uk
Web: www.express.co.uk
Home Affairs Correspondent: Miss Rachel Baird.

Daily Mail, Northcliffe House, 2 Derry Street, London W8 5TT
☎020 7938 6000
E: s.doughty@dailymail.co.uk
Web: www.dailymail.co.uk
Social Affairs Correspondent: Steve Doughty.

The Daily Telegraph and **The Sunday Telegraph**, 1 Canada Square, Canary Wharf, London E14 5DT
☎020 7538 7359
E: jonathan.petre@telegraph.co.uk
Web: www.telegraph.co.uk
Religion Affairs Correspondent: Jonathan Petre.

The Guardian, 119 Farringdon Road, London EC1R 3ER
☎020 7278 2332
E: stephen.bates@guardian.co.uk
Web: www.guardian.co.uk
Religious Correspondent: Stephen Bates.

The Independent, 191 Marsh Wall, London E14 9RS
☎020 7005 2000
E: a.akbar@independent.co.uk
Web: www.independent.co.uk
Religious Affairs Correspondent: Arifa Akbar.

The Observer, 119 Farringdon Road, London EC1R 3ER
☎020 7278 2332
E: dennis.campbell@observer.co.uk
Web: www.observer.co.uk
Social Affairs Correspondent: Dennis Campbell.

Press Association Ltd, 292 Vauxhall Bridge Road, London SW1V 1AE
☎08701 203 200
E: martha.linden@pa.press.net
Web: www.pa.press.net
Religious Correspondent: Martha Linden.

The Sunday Times, 1 Pennington Street, London E98 1XY
☎020 7782 5000
E: christopher.morgan@thetimes.co.uk
www.thetimes.co.uk
Religious Correspondent: Christopher Morgan.

The Times, 1 Pennington Street, London E98 1XY
☎020 7782 5000
E: ruth.gledhill@thetimes.co.uk
Web: www.thetimes.co.uk
Religious Correspondent: Ruth Gledhill.

LATE ENTRIES

Apostle Designs, Front Street, Tudhoe, Spennymoor DL16 6TG
☎0845 644 0268 M: 07900 247 187
📠0845 644 0269
E: studio@apostledesigns.co.uk|
Web: www.apostledesigns.co.uk
Providing graphic design, corporate identity and web design with an ethical approach.
Senior Designer: Mrs Claire Clark. Executive staff 1. Admin staff 1. Began 2004; Anglican. No magazine. Turnover £14,000 to year end Jun 05.

Carnforth Resthaven, 103 Norfolk Road, Margate CT9 2HX
☎01843 280 753 M: 07949 206 268
E: eileenmutanhu@btinternet.com
Web: www.carnforth-resthaven.co.uk
Providing accommodation for retreats for up to 35 people; for groups and churches.
Managing Director: Ms Eileen Mutanhu. Executive staff 1, Other staff 2. Began 2005; interdenominational. No magazine. Turnover £3,800 to year end Apr 06.

Centre for Christian Law and Freedoms, PO Box 1041, Barton, Cambridge CB3 7WY
☎01223 264 544 M: 07979 837 714
E: pauldiamond@cclf.org.uk
Web: www.cclf.org.uk
Offering funded legal advice and services for cases seeking to preserve Christian values.
Barrister: Mr Paul Diamond. Executive staff 1, Admin staff 1. Began 2006; non-denominational. No magazine. Turnover n/a.

Chalet Retreats, 30 De Mowbray Way, Morpeth NE61 3RE
☎0800 066 4995 📠0870 479 7698
E: holidays@chaletretreats.co.uk
Web: www.chaletretreats.co.uk
Christian ski and snowboard holidays in the Paradiski.
Director: Mr Ben Simpson. Executive staff 1, Other staff n/a. Began 2006; interdenominational. No magazine. Turnover n/a.

CHASTE, PO Box 983, Cambridge CB3 8WY
☎0845 456 9335
E: contact@chaste.org.uk
Web: www.chaste.org.uk
Working against sexual exploitation in trafficking in Europe, Africa, UK; training, advocacy, networking, pastoral recovery.
Chief Executive Officer: Rev Dr Carrie Pemberton. Executive staff 1, Other staff 4. **CC** No.4862586. Began 2004; ecumenical. Churches Alert to Sex Trafficking Across Europe. Magazine: Chaste (1,550 monthly by E). Turnover £20,000 to year end Dec 05.

Chipukizi wa Yesu Trust, 5 Overton Park, Dyce, Aberdeen AB21 7FT
☎01224 722 691
E: office@chipukizi.org.uk
Web: www.chipukizi.org.uk
Providing education, Christian teaching and relief of poverty in Liuli and surrounding villages in Tanzania.
Trustee: Mr John MacCormack. No full-time staff in UK. **CC** No.SCO 26743. Began 1997; non-denominational. No magazine.

Chronicle Accountants Ltd, 1d Market Street, Whaley Bridge, High Peak SK23 7AA
☎01663 734 736 📠01663 719 739
E: enquiries@chronicleaccountants.co.uk
Web: www.chronicleaccountants.co.uk
Accountants and small business advisers; Quickbook advisers; tax, payroll, bookkeeping, VAT.
Director: Mr Glenn Leathley. Executive staff 1, Admin staff 1. Began 2002; non-denominational. No magazine. Turnover £50,000 to year end Dec 05.

Community of the Resurrection, Mirfield WF14 0BN
☎01924 494 318 📠01924 490 489
E: community@mirfield.org.uk
Web: www.mirfield.org.uk
Community of priests and laymen; pastoral ministry in UK, South Africa; retreats, teaching, counselling.
Superior: Fr George Guiver. Community n/a. Began n/a; Anglican. No magazine. Turnover n/a.

The CREDO Storytelling Trust, 80 Elsham Road, London W14 8HH
☎Mob 07930 255 697
Promoting and celebrating the oral tradition of biblical storytelling through events and training workshops.
Creative Director: Ms Shan Stephens. All voluntary staff. **CC** No.1082703. Began 2000; ecumenical. No magazine. Turnover £3,000 to year end Dec 05.

Late Entries

Devotum, Folly Farm, South Holmwood, Dorking RH5 4NH
☎01306 888 251
E: gvdl@devotum.co.uk
Web: www.devotum.co.uk
Designing, manufacturing and distributing handmade religious statues sculpted by David Cope.
Sole Trader: Mrs Gillian Van Der Lande. Executive staff 1. Began 2006; interdenominational. No magazine. Turnover : first year of operation.

DLK Daniel Lelliott Krauze, 35 St Lukes Road, Maidenhead SL6 7DN
☎01628 630 123 🖷01628 674 629
E: enquiries@dlkarchitects.com
Web: dlkarchitects.com
Architects with an approach to church building design as an evangelistic tool.
Managing Director: Mr Neil Barr. Executive staff 3, Other staff 12. Began 1965; non-denominational. No magazine. Turnover £650,000 to year end Aug 05.

***Every Nation Church**, Rofel House, 1d Colet Gardens, Hammersmith, London W14 9DH
☎020 8748 7576 🖷020 8748 9587
E: mail@everynation.co.uk
Also Bible School course.
Operations Director: Mr Darren Parker. Admin staff 1, Serving ministers 12, Other staff 17. **CC** No.1102293. Began 1993. Magazine: 20Twenty (1,500 quarterly). Turnover £1,100,000 to year end Jun 05.

Five Cha Media, 65 Connington Crescent, London E4 6LB
☎020 8523 9777 M: 07918 166 761
E: info@fivechamedia.com
Web: www.fivechamedia.com
Independent Gospel music label partnering with studios, artists and composers from Africa and elsewhere.
Proprieter: Mr David Shenfield. Executive staff 1, No other staff. Began 2006; interdenominational. No magazine. Turnover : first year of operation.

Frontline Debt Advice, Parkland, Parkland Road, Cowes PO31 7LZ
☎01983 240 763 🖷01983 619 970
E: admin@frontlinedebtadvice.org.uk
Web: www.frontlinedebtadvice.org.uk
Offering free debt and welfare benefit advice by Christians to all requiring assistance; also training.
Project Manager: Mr John O Stevens. Executive staff 1, No other paid staff. Began 1989. No magazine. Turnover £10,000 to year end Mar 05.

***Hants & Dorset Christian Youth Camps**, 3 Mortimer Road, Ealing, London W13 8NG
☎No phone
Web: www.hdyc.org.uk
Organising young people's camping holidays.
Hon Treasurer: Name not supplied. **CC** No.275265. Began 1944; interdenominational. No magazine. Turnover £35,000 to year end Sep 05.

***Kensington Temple Institute of Education**, KT Summit House, 100 Hanger Lane, Ealing, London W5 1EZ
☎020 8799 6168 🖷020 8998 4361
E: info@ktioe.org
Web: www.ktioe.org
'A' Level tutorial college accredited with OCR Accredited Higher Education and Postgraduate courses.
Dean: Dominic Desouza. Executive staff 1, Other staff 2. **CC** No.251549. Began 2004; Elim Pentecostal. Magazine: Revival Times (5,000 monthly). Turnover n/a.

Chris Knott Insurance, Grove Mills, Cranbrook Road, Hawkhurst TN18 4AS
☎0800 917 2274 🖷01580 752 401
E: enquiries@chrisknott.co.uk
Web: www.chrisknott.co.uk
Offering a sustainable income generation scheme to churches and charities.
Director: Mr Chris Knott. Executive staff 7, Admin staff 28. Began 1983; non-denominational. No magazine. Turnover £1,600,000 to year end Jan 06.

The Lighthouse Group, Head Office, 353 Great Horton Road, Bradford BD7 3BZ
☎01274 570 232 🖷01274 501 724
E: info@thelighthousegroup.co.uk
Web: www.thelighthousegroup.co.uk
Educational charity working with young people in crisis.
Chief Executive: Mr Tim Morfin. National Director: Mr Michael Royal. Marketing & Funding Co-ordinator: Mr Paul Chenery. Executive staff 4, Admin staff 23. **CC** No.1074114. Began 1987; interdenominational. (Previously The Lighthouse Outreach). No magazine. Turnover £500,000 to year end Dec 05.

M&M Associates, 18 Lampeter Close, Woking GU22 7TD
☎01483 764 357 M: 07721 385 443
🖷01483 764 357
E: malcolm@fidge100.freeserve.co.uk
Providing help with encouragement, recruitment, selection, psychometric profiling, team building, individual and organisational development.
Consultant: Mr Malcolm Fidge. Executive staff 1, Other staff 1. Began 2002; non-denominational. No magazine. Turnover £3,000 to year end Mar 05.

Matt 5-9, 9 Thorne Park, Ilfracombe EX34 8NG
☎01271 879 824 M: 07970 553 723
E: matt5v9@btinternet.com
Web: www.matt5-9.co.uk
Website for those involved or interested in resolving conflict and healing harm in the church.
Organiser & Trainer: Mr Matt Wilcox. Admin staff 1. Began 2006; non-denominational. No magazine. Turnover : first year of operation.

Overcomers Outreach UK, 11 Cromwell Road, Southbourne, Bournemouth BH5 2JN
☎01202 433 937 M: 07749 058 8[illegible]5
E: e.bundred@tesco.net
Web: www.overcomersoutreach.co.uk
Christian group meetings throughout UK using 12 Steps and Scripture to aid recovery from addiction.
Public Information Officer: Mr E A Bundred. Executive staff 1, Other staff n/a. Began 1994; non-denominational. No magazine. Turnover n/a.

PEP Architects Ltd, 3rd Floor Tring House, 77 High Street, Tring HP23 4AB
☎01442 827 106 M: 07711 355 9[illegible]9
🖷01442 827 403
E: mail@peparchitects.co.uk
Web: www.peparchitects.co.uk
Architects working for churches of various denominations; repairs, alterations, new buildings.
Director: Mr Robert Thompson. Executive staff 2, Admin staff 2. Began 1996; non-denominational. No magazine. Turnover £120,000 to year end Sept 05.

John Phillips, 2 The Chimes, Benfleet SS7 1HS
☎01268 752 409 M: 07812 [illegible]84 87[illegible]
🖷01268 752 409
E: john.f.phillips@lineone.net
Advising on employment law and handling sensitive staff issues; also in-house management training.
HR Consultant: Mr John Phillips. Consultant 1. Began 1996; Methodist. No magazine. Turnover £8,000 to year end Apr 05.

John Pickering, 14 New Houses, Piccadilly Road, Chesterfield S41 0EJ
☎01246 230 406
E: pickjohn@gmail.com
Web: www.heavenspeace.com/johnpickering
Writing and performing Christian songs, using music as an evangelistic tool.
Director: Rev John Pickering. Musician 1. Began 2006; interdenominational. No magazine. Turnover n/a.

Praise Communion, 23 Cowper Road, Rainham RM13 9TT
☎01708 253 463 M: 07949 5[illegible]1 054
E: uk@praisecommunion.org
Web: www.praisecommunion.org
Prayer for peace of the UK and its youth.
Presiding Minister: Rev Michael Adekoya. No full-time staff. Began 2006; interdenominational. No magazine. Turnover : first year of operation.

X

Pump Aid, 17 Station Road, Barton Under Needwood, Burton-on-Trent DE13 8DR
☎01283 716 111
M 07831 683 549
E: karenmercer@pumpaid.org
Web: www.pumpaid.org
Relieving poverty in Africa using appropriate and sustainable technology to provide clean drinking water.
Sponsorship Co-ordinator: Mrs Karen Mercer. International Director, Africa: Mr Ian Thorpe. Executive staff 1, Admin staff 1. **CC** No.1077889. Began 1995; interdenominational. No magazine. Turnover £334,000 to year end Mar 05.

St Thomas Bookshop, 23 Soper Grove, Basingstoke RG21 5PU
☎01256 456 527
E: alison.elkin@btopenworld.com
Books ordered on request.
Manager: Mrs Alison Elkin. No full-time staff. Began n/a; interdenominational. Turnover £12,000 to year end Dec 05.

Sanctuary, PO Box 8953, Chelmsford CM2 9WN
☎0870 991 1876
M: 07900 501 246
Fax 0870 116 2131
E: info@sanctuaryuk.com
Web: carefulgrace.org.uk
Helping churches appropriately support and disciple sex offenders in their congregations through training and support.
Executive Director: Mr Richard Foot. Executive staff 1. Other staff n/a. Began 2005; non-denominational. Careful Grace Ministries. No magazine. Turnover : first year of operation.

***The Savoury World of Rice**, 2 Riverside Drive, Calver, Hope Valley S32 3XE
M: 07739 535 500
E: rice@brianandmaria.fsnet.co.uk
Web: www.brianrice.info
Entertainment-based evangelistic ministry that includes stand-up comedy, magic and live music.
Chief Executive Officer: Mr Brian Rice. Evangelist 1. Began 2000; non-denominational. No magazine. Turnover £2,500 to year end Apr 05.

Springs Christian Book Store, 84 High Street, Clacton-on-Sea CO15 6PL
☎01255 475 075
E: themarshes@tiscali.co.uk
Manager: Andy Marsh. Executive staff 1, Other staff n/a. Began n/a; interdenominational.

Street Ministries, 54 The Firs, Alston CA9 3RW
☎01434 382 308 M: 07706 679 430
E: thestreetsinger@hotmail.com
Web: myspace.com/thestreetsinger
Promoting the Gospel using street music and poetry; also with local churches by invitation.
Street Evangelist: Mr Trevor Reed. Evangelist 1. Began 1984; non-denominational. (Previously The Branch of the Vine). No magazine. Turnover n/a.

Tricks For Truth, PO Box 54923, London W3 8XS
☎020 8354 0292 Fax 020 8354 0292
E: tricksfortruth@ntlworld.com
Web: www.tricksfortruth.com
Providing visual aids and illusions; training for Christian workers.
Director: Mr Steve Macbeth. Staff 1. Began 1990; non-denominational. No magazine. Turnover n/a.

U-Turn, 297 Brockley Road, Brockley, London SE4 2SA
☎020 8694 6125 Fax 020 8694 6125
E: uturn@recovery20.fsnet.co.uk
Residential recovery programme for people with a serious desire to recover from addictive behaviour.
Project Manager: Mr Richard Mitchell. Executive staff 1, Other staff n/a. **CC** No.1013750. Began 1991; non-denominational. No magazine. Turnover n/a.

The Vine Christian Bookshop & Gifts, 37 Church Hill Road, East Barnet, Barnet EN4 8SY
☎020 8216 3778 Fax 020 8216 3778
E: info@vinechristianshop.co.uk
Proprietors: Mr & Mrs H & D Yau. Admin staff 2. Began 2005; ecumenical. Turnover n/a.

Woodleigh Christian Care Home, Norfolk Drive, Mansfield NG19 7AG
☎01623 420 459 Fax 01623 460 381
E: care@woodleighcare.co.uk
Web: www.woodleighcare.co.uk
Nursing, residential, respite and day care for people aged over 60 in a Christian environment.
Home Manager: Miss Samantha Eves. Executive staff 1, Other staff n/a. Began 1989; interdenominational. No magazine. Turnover n/a.

Words of Light, 37 Edenside Road, Bookham, Leatherhead KT23 3JB
☎01372 457 671 Fax 01372 457 671
E: sales@wordsoflight.co.uk
Web: www.wordsoflight.co.uk
Producing candles which can be personalised for gifts; bespoke service available.
Director: Mr David Harber. Executive staff 1, Other staff 2. Began 1998; non-denominational. No magazine. Turnover £45,000 to year end Mar 05.

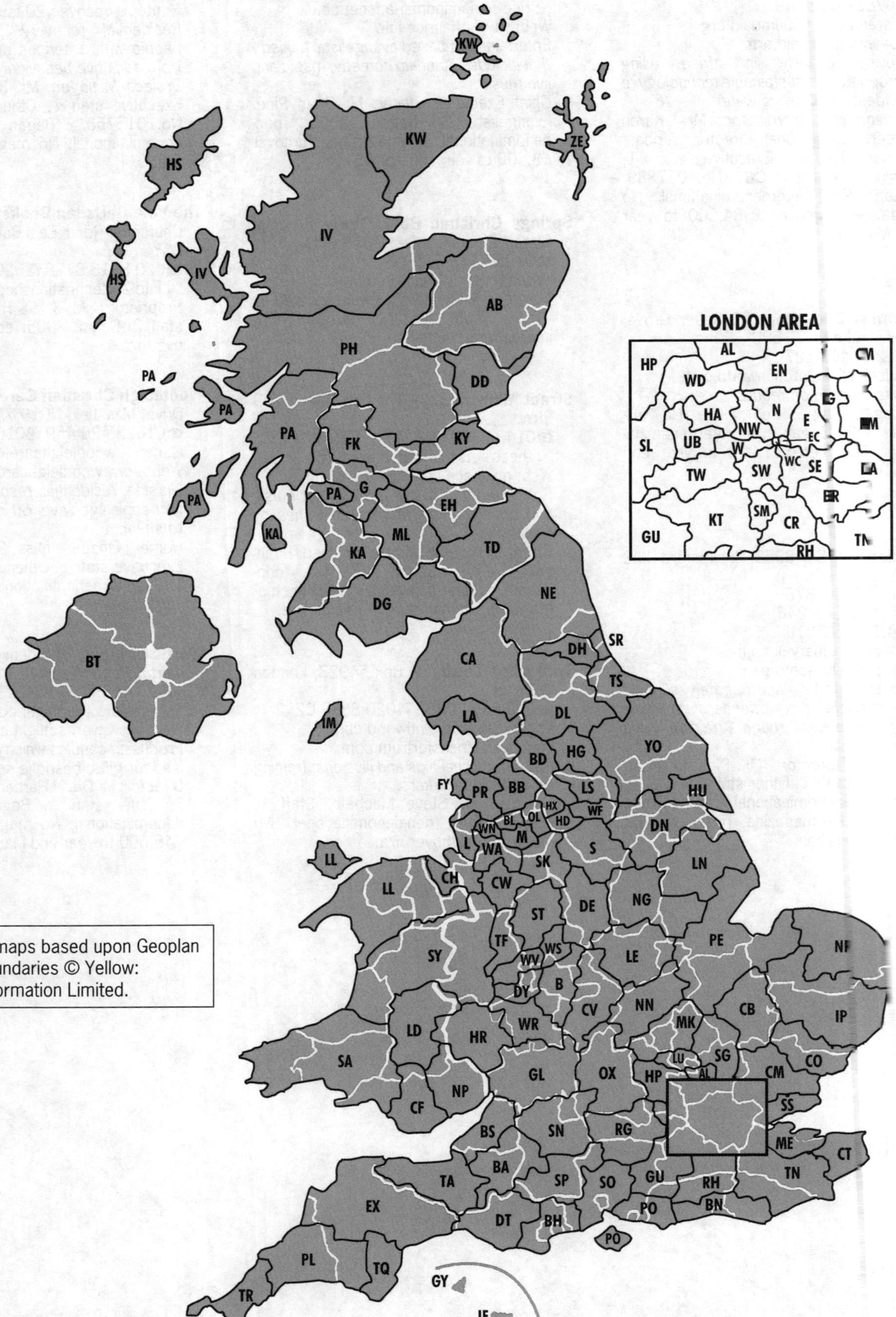

© Postcode maps based upon Geoplan Postcode Boundaries © Yellow: Marketing Information Limited.

INDEXES

HOW TO USE THE LOCATION INDEX

This Location Index groups together entries located at the same address, whether or not they are part of the same organisation. It is based on postal addresses and thus uses Postcodes and Post Towns within the countries of the UK. Up to and including the 1998/99 editions of the *Handbook* the Location Index was based on counties. These are no longer used in either the entries or the Location Index as in many cases they are no longer part of a correct postal address.

COUNTRIES

Countries are listed in the following order:
England
  London
Channel Islands
Isle of Man
Northern Ireland
Republic of Ireland
Scotland
Wales

Organisations are listed alphabetically by country for Northern Ireland, Scotland and Wales on Pages 516 to 520.

POSTCODES

Within each country, Postcodes are listed in alpha/numeric order within countries using the first part of the Postcode. London is the only exception: the London Postcodes are grouped together for ease of use, and are listed at the end of all other England entries. The map on page 458 shows the location of all Postcodes in the UK, and also the correlation between Postcodes and the 'old' counties.

POST TOWNS

The first half of the Postcode is followed by its Post Town eg AL St Albans. The list below gives in alphabetical order each Post Town which has an organisation listed in the *Handbook*, showing the 'old' county and the page number on which it may be found in the Location Index. The following list (on Page 466) gives in alphabetical order the 'old' counties showing the Postcodes found within it.

Please note
Three Postcodes straddle national borders and may therefore be found under two countries:
CH can be found in England and Wales
SY can be found in England and Wales
TD can be found in England and Scotland.

POST TOWNS BY COUNTY & POSTCODE

Post Towns by County & Postcode

Post Town	'Old' County	Postcode	Page
Dinas Powis	South Glamorgan	CF	514
Dingwall	Ross-shire	IV	511
Dolgellau	Gwynedd	LL	514
Dollar	Clackmannanshire	FK	510
Doncaster	South Yorkshire	DN	480
Dorchester	Dorset	DT	480
Dorking	Surrey	RH	493
Dornoch	Sutherland	IV	512
Douglas	Isle of Man	IM	507
Dover	Kent	CT	478
Downham Market	Norfolk	PE	491
Downpatrick	Co Down	BT	508
Driffield	North Humberside	YO	501
Droitwich	Worcestershire	WR	500
Dromore	Co Down	BT	508
Dronfield	South Yorkshire	S	493
Dudley	West Midlands	DY	480
Dulverton	Somerset	TA	497
Dumfries	Dumfriesshire	DG	509
Dunblane	Perthshire	FK	510
Dundee	Angus	DD	509
Dunfermline	Fife	KY	512
Dungannon	Co Tyrone	BT	508
Dunkeld	Perthshire	PH	513
Dunmow	Essex	CM	477
Dunoon	Argyll	PA	512
Duns	Berwickshire	TD	512
Dunstable	Bedfordshire	LU	486
Durham	Co Durham	DH	479
East Boldon	Tyne and Wear	NE	488
East Grinstead	West Sussex	RH	493
East Molesey	Surrey	KT	484
Eastbourne	East Sussex	BN	474
Eastleigh	Hampshire	SO	496
Edenbridge	Kent	TN	497
Edgware	Middlesex	HA	483
Edinburgh	Edinburgh	EH	510
Egham	Surrey	TW	499
Elgin	Morayshire	IV	512
Ellesmere Port	Cheshire	CH	477
Ellon	Aberdeenshire	AB	509
Ely	Cambridgeshire	CB	476
Enfield	Middlesex	EN	480
Enniskillen	Co Fermanagh	BT	508
Epping	Essex	CM	477
Epsom	Surrey	KT	484
Erith	Kent	DA	479
Exeter	Devon	EX	480
Exmouth	Devon	EX	480
Falkirk	Stirlingshire	FK	510
Falmouth	Cornwall	TR	498
Fareham	Hampshire	PO	492
Faringdon	Oxfordshire	OX	495
Farnborough	Hampshire	GU	482
Farnham	Surrey	GU	482
Felixstowe	Suffolk	IG	484
Feltham	Middlesex	TW	498
Ferndale	Mid Glamorgan	CF	513
Fishguard	Dyfed	SA	515
Fivemiletown	Co Tyrone	BT	508
Fleet	Hampshire	GU	482
Folkestone	Kent	CT	478
Forfar	Aberdeenshire	AB	509
Forsinard	Caithness	KW	511
Fort William	Inverness-shire	PH	512
Fraserburgh	Aberdeenshire	AB	509
Frinton-on-Sea	Essex	CO	477
Frodsham	Cheshire	WA	499
Frome	Somerset	BA	472
Gateshead	Tyne and Wear	NE	488
Gerrards Cross	Buckinghamshire	SL	495
Gillingham	Kent	ME	487
Glasgow	Glasgow	G	510
Glastonbury	Somerset	BA	472
Glenrothes	Fife	KY	512
Glossop	Derbyshire	SK	494
Gloucester	Gloucestershire	GL	481
Godalming	Surrey	GU	482
Gosport	Hampshire	PO	492
Grange-over-Sands	Cumbria	LA	485
Grangemouth	Stirlingshire	FK	510
Grantham	Lincolnshire	NG	489
Gravesend	Kent	DA	479
Great Missenden	Buckinghamshire	HP	483
Great Yarmouth	Norfolk	NR	490
Greenford	Middlesex	UB	499
Greenock	Renfrewshire	PA	512
Gretna	Dumfriesshire	DG	510
Grimsby	South Humberside	DN	480
Guernsey	Channel Islands	GY	507
Guildford	Surrey	GU	481
Guisborough	North Yorkshire	TS	499
Haddington	East Lothian	EH	510
Hailsham	East Sussex	BN	474
Halesowen	West Midlands	B	472
Halifax	West Yorkshire	HX	483
Halstead	Essex	CO	477
Haltwhistle	Northumberland	NE	488
Harlow	Essex	CM	477
Harpenden	Hertfordshire	AL	471
Harrogate	North Yorkshire	HG	482
Harrow	Middlesex	HA	482
Harwich	Essex	CO	477
Haslemere	Surrey	GU	482
Hassocks	West Sussex	BN	474
Hastings	East Sussex	TN	498
Havant	Hampshire	PO	492
Haverfordwest	Dyfed	SA	515
Hawick	Roxburghshire	TD	512
Hawkhurst	Kent	TN	498
Hayes	Middlesex	UB	499
Hayle	Cornwall	TR	498
Haywards Heath	West Sussex	RH	493
Heathfield	East Sussex	TN	497
Heckmondwike	West Yorkshire	WF	497
Helensburgh	Dunbartonshire	G	511
Helston	Cornwall	TR	498
Hemel Hempstead	Hertfordshire	HP	483
Henfield	West Sussex	BN	474
Henley-in-Arden	West Midlands	B	472
Henley-on-Thames	Oxfordshire	RG	492
Hereford	Herefordshire	HR	483
Herne Bay	Kent	CT	478
Hertford	Hertfordshire	SG	494
Hessle	North Humberside	HU	483
Hexham	Northumberland	NE	488
Heywood	Lancashire	OL	490
High Peak	Cheshire	SK	494
High Wycombe	Buckinghamshire	HP	483
Hillsborough	Co Down	BT	508
Hinckley	Leicestershire	LE	485
Hindhead	Surrey	GU	482
Hitchin	Hertfordshire	SG	494
Hoddesdon	Hertfordshire	EN	480
Holt	Norfolk	NR	489
Holyhead	Gwynedd	LL	514
Holywood	Co Down	BT	507
Honiton	Devon	EX	481
Hook	Hampshire	RG	493
Hope Valley	Derbyshire	S	494
Horley	Surrey	RH	493
Hornchurch	Essex	RM	494
Horsham	West Sussex	RH	493
Houghton le Spring	Tyne and Wear	DH	479
Hounslow	Middlesex	TW	498
Hove	East Sussex	BN	474
Huddersfield	West Yorkshire	HD	483
Hull	North Humberside	HU	483
Hungerford	Berkshire	RG	492
Huntingdon	Cambridgeshire	PE	491
Huntley	Aberdeenshire	AB	509
Hythe	Kent	CT	478
Ilford	Essex	IG	483
Ilfracombe	Devon	EX	481

Post Town	'Old' County	Postcode	Page
Ilkeston	Derbyshire	DE	479
Ilkley	West Yorkshire	LS	486
Ingatestone	Essex	CH	477
Inverkeithing	Fife	KY	512
Inverness	Inverness-shire	IV	511
Inverurie	Aberdeenshire	AB	509
Ipswich	Suffolk	IP	484
Irvine	Ayrshire	KA	511
Isle of Bute	Isle of Bute	PA	512
Isle of Cumbrae	Isle of Cumbrae	KA	511
Isle of Iona	Isle of Iona	PA	512
Isle of Harris	Isle of Harris	HS	511
Isle of Lewis	Isle of Lewis	HS	511
Isle of Mull	Isle of Mull	PA	512
Isle of Skye	Isle of Skye	IV	512
Iver	Buckinghamshire	SL	494
Ivybridge	Devon	PL	492
Jedburgh	Roxburghshire	TD	512
Jersey	Channel Islands	JE	507
Johnston	Renfrewshire	PA	512
Keighley	West Yorkshire	BD	473
Keith	Banffshire	AB	609
Kelso	Roxburghshire	TD	512
Kendal	Cumbria	LA	485
Kenilworth	Warwickshire	CV	478
Keswick	Cumbria	CA	475
Kettering	Northamptonshire	NN	489
Kidderminster	Worcestershire	DY	480
Kidlington	Oxfordshire	OX	490
Kilbirnie	Ayrshire	KA	511
Killin	Perthshire	FK	510
Kilmacolm	Renfrewshire	PA	512
Kilmarnock	Ayrshire	KA	512
Kilwinning	Ayrshire	KA	511
King's Lynn	Norfolk	PE	491
Kings Langley	Hertfordshire	WD	499
Kingsbridge	Devon	TQ	498
Kingston upon Thames	Surrey	KT	484
Kingussie	Inverness-shire	PH	513
Kinross	Kinross-shire	KY	512
Kirkby Stephen	Cumbria	CA	476
Kirkwall	Isle of Orkney	KW	512
Knighton	Powys	LD	513
Knottingley	West Yorkshire	WF	500
Knutsford	Cheshire	WA	499
Kyle	Ross-shire	IV	512
Lairg	Sutherland	IV	512
Lampeter	Dyfed	SA	515
Lanark	Lanarkshire	ML	512
Lancaster	Lancashire	LA	485
Lancing	West Sussex	BN	474
Larbert	Stirlingshire	FK	510
Largs	Ayrshire	KA	511
Larne	Co Antrim	BT	508
Launceston	Cornwall	PL	492
Leamington Spa	Warwickshire	CV	478
Leatherhead	Surrey	KT	484
Ledbury	Herefordshire	HR	483
Leeds	West Yorkshire	LS	486
Leicester	Leicestershire	LE	485
Leigh	Lancashire	WN	499
Leigh-on-Sea	Essex	SS	496
Leighton Buzzard	Bedfordshire	LU	486
Leiston	Suffolk	IP	484
Leominster	Herefordshire	HR	483
Letchworth	Hertfordshire	SG	494
Leven	Fife	KY	512
Lewes	East Sussex	BN	474
Leyburn	North Yorkshire	DL	479
Leyland	Lancashire	PR	492
Lichfield	Staffordshire	WS	500
Lincoln	Lincolnshire	LN	485
Lingfield	Surrey	RH	493
Linlithgow	West Lothian	EH	510
Liphook	Hampshire	GU	482
Lisburn	Co Antrim	BT	508

Post Town	'Old' County	Postcode	Page
Liss	Hampshire	GU	482
Littleborough	Lancashire	OL	490
Littlehampton	West Sussex	BN	474
Liverpool	Merseyside	L	484
Llanbedr	Gwynedd	LL	514
Llandrindod Wells	Powys	LD	514
Llandudno	Gwynedd	LL	514
Llandysul	Dyfed	SA	515
Llanelli	Dyfed	SA	514
Llanfairfechan	Gwynedd	LL	514
Llangollen	Clwyd	LL	514
Llanidloes	Powys	SY	515
Llanymynech	Powys	SY	515
Loanhead	Midlothian	EH	510
London	London	E, EC, N, NW, SE, SW, W, WC	501–507
Londonderry	Co Londonderry	BT	508
Loughborough	Leicestershire	LE	485
Loughton	Essex	IG	484
Lowestoft	Suffolk	NR	490
Ludlow	Shropshire	SY	497
Luton	Bedfordshire	LU	486
Lutterworth	Leicestershire	LE	486
Lydney	Gloucestershire	GL	481
Lyme Regis	Dorset	DT	480
Lymington	Hampshire	SO	496
Lyndhurst	Hampshire	SO	496
Lynton	Devon	EX	481
Lytham St Annes	Lancashire	FY	481
Macclesfield	Cheshire	SK	494
Machynlleth	Powys	SY	515
Maghera	Co Londonderry	BT	508
Maidenhead	Berkshire	SL	495
Maidstone	Kent	ME	487
Maldon	Essex	CM	476
Malmesbury	Wiltshire	SN	496
Malpas	Cheshire	SY	497
Malton	North Yorkshire	YO	500
Malvern	Worcestershire	WR	500
Manchester	Greater Manchester	M	486
Mansfield	Nottinghamshire	NG	489
March	Cambridgeshire	PE	491
Margate	Kent	CT	478
Market Harborough	Leicestershire	LE	486
Marlborough	Wiltshire	SN	495
Marlow	Buckinghamshire	SL	495
Maryport	Cumbria	CA	476
Matlock	Derbyshire	DE	479
Meifod	Powys	SY	515
Melksham	Wiltshire	SN	495
Melrose	Roxburghshire	TD	512
Melton Mowbray	Leicestershire	LE	485
Merthyr Tydfil	Mid Glamorgan	CF	514
Mexborough	South Yorkshire	S	494
Middlesbrough	Cleveland	TS	498
Middlewich	Cheshire	CW	479
Midhurst	West Sussex	GU	482
Milford Haven	Dyfed	SA	515
Milton Keynes	Buckinghamshire	MK	488
Milnthorpe	Cumbria	LA	485
Minehead	Somerset	TA	497
Mirfield	West Yorkshire	WF	500
Mitcham	Surrey	CR	477
Mitcheldean	Gloucestershire	GL	481
Mold	Clwyd	CH	514
Monmouth	Gwent	NP	515
Montgomery	Powys	SY	515
Morden	Surrey	SM	495
Morecambe	Lancashire	LA	485
Morpeth	Northumberland	NE	488
Motherwell	Lanarkshire	ML	512
Musselburgh	Midlothian	EH	510
Nairn	Inverness-shire	IV	511
Nantwich	Cheshire	CW	478
Nelson	Lancashire	BB	473

Post Towns by County & Postcode

Post Town	'Old' County	Postcode	Page
Nethy Bridge	Inverness-shire	PH	512
New Malden	Surrey	KT	484
New Milton	Hampshire	BH	473
Newark	Nottinghamshire	NG	488
Newbury	Berkshire	RG	492
Newcastle	Co Down	BT	508
Newcastle	Staffordshire	ST	497
Newcastle upon Tyne	Tyne and Wear	NE	487
Newcastleton	Roxburghshire	TD	512
Newent	Gloucestershire	GL	481
Newhaven	East Sussex	BN	474
Newmarket	Suffolk	CB	476
Newport	Gwent	NP	515
Newport	Isle of Wight	PO	492
Newport Pagnell	Buckinghamshire	MK	488
Newquay	Cornwall	TR	498
Newry	Co Down	BT	508
Newtown	Powys	SY	515
Newton Abbot	Devon	TQ	498
Newton Aycliffe	Co Durham	DL	479
Newton-le-Willows	Merseyside	WA	499
Newtownabbey	Co Antrim	BT	508
Newtownards	Co Down	BT	507
North Sheilds	Tyne & Wear	NE	488
North Walsham	Norfolk	NR	490
Northallerton	North Yorkshire	DL	479
Northampton	Northamptonshire	NN	489
Northwich	Cheshire	CW	479
Northwood	Middlesex	HA	482
Norwich	Norfolk	NR	489
Nottingham	Nottinghamshire	NG	488
Nuneaton	Warwickshire	CV	478
Oakham	Leicestershire	LE	486
Oban	Argyll	PA	512
Okehampton	Devon	EX	481
Oldbury	West Midlands	B	472
Oldham	Lancashire	OL	490
Omagh	Co Tyrone	BT	508
Ongar	Essex	CM	477
Orkney	Isle of Orkney	KW	512
Ormskirk	Lancashire	L	485
Orpington	Kent	BR	474
Ossett	West Yorkshire	WF	500
Oswestry	Shropshire	SY	497
Otley	West Yorkshire	LS	486
Oxford	Oxfordshire	OX	490
Oxted	Surrey	RH	493
Paignton	Devon	TQ	498
Paisley	Renfrewshire	PA	512
Peel	Isle of Man	IM	507
Pembroke	Dyfed	SA	515
Penarth	South Glamorgan	CF	514
Penicuik	Mid Lothian	EH	510
Penmaenmawr	Gwynedd	LL	514
Penrith	Cumbria	CA, LA	476, 485
Penzance	Cornwall	TR	498
Pershore	Worcestershire	WR	500
Perth	Perthshire	PH	513
Peterborough	Cambridgeshire	PE	491
Peterhead	Aberdeenshire	AB	509
Petersfield	Hampshire	GU	482
Petworth	West Sussex	GU	482
Pevensey	East Sussex	BN	474
Pewsey	Wiltshire	SN	495
Pinner	Middlesex	HA	482
Pitlochry	Perthshire	PH	513
Plymouth	Devon	PL	491
Polegate	East Sussex	BN	474
Pontefract	West Yorkshire	WF	500
Pontypool	Gwent	NP	514
Pontypridd	Mid Glamorgan	CF	513
Poole	Dorset	BH	473
Port Talbot	West Glamorgan	SA	514
Porthcawl	Mid Glamorgan	CF	513
Porthmadog	Gwynedd	LL	514
Portree	Isle of Skye	IV	512
Portrush	Co Antrim	BT	509

Post Town	'Old' County	Postcode	Page
Portsmouth	Hampshire	PO	49[illegible]
Portstewart	Co Londonderry	BT	50[illegible]
Potters Bar	Hertfordshire	EN	48[illegible]
Prenton	Merseyside	CH	475
Prescot	Merseyside	L	485
Prestatyn	Clwyd	LL	514
Presteigne	Powys	LD	513
Preston	Lancashire	PR	49[illegible]
Princes Risborough	Buckinghamshire	HP	483
Pulborough	West Sussex	RH	49[illegible]
Purley	Surrey	CR	477
Pwllheli	Gwynedd	LL	514
Radlett	Hertfordshire	WD	499
Rainham	Essex	RM	494
Ramsey	Isle of Man	IM	507
Ramsgate	Kent	CT	478
Rayleigh	Essex	SS	496
Reading	Berkshire	RG	492
Redcar	Cleveland	TS	499
Redditch	Worcestershire	B	472
Redhill	Surrey	RH	493
Redruth	Cornwall	TR	498
Reigate	Surrey	RH	493
Retford	Nottinghamshire	DN	480
Rhyl	Clwyd	LL	514
Richmond	North Yorkshire	DL	479
Richmond	Surrey	TW	498
Rickmansworth	Hertfordshire	WD	499
Riding Mill	Northumberland	NE	488
Ringwood	Hampshire	BH	473
Ripley	Derbyshire	DE	479
Ripon	North Yorkshire	HG	483
Robertsbridge	East Sussex	TN	497
Rochdale	Lancashire	OL	490
Rochester	Kent	ME	487
Rochford	Essex	SS	496
Romford	Essex	RM	493
Romney Marsh	Kent	TN	497
Romsey	Hampshire	SO	496
Ross-on-Wye	Herefordshire	HR	483
Rossendale	Lancashire	BB	473
Rotherham	South Yorkshire	S	494
Royston	Hertfordshire	SG	494
Rugby	Warwickshire	CV	478
Rugeley	Staffordshire	WS	500
Ruislip	Middlesex	HA	482
Rushden	Northamptonshire	NN	489
Ryde	Isle of Wight	PO	492
Rye	East Sussex	TN	497
St Albans	Hertfordshire	AL	471
St Andrews	Fife	KY	512
St Asaph	Clwyd	LL	513
St Austell	Cornwall	PL	492
St Helens	Merseyside	WA	499
St Ives	Cornwall	TR	498
St Leonards-on-Sea	East Sussex	TN	498
St Neots	Cambridgeshire	PE	491
Saffron Walden	Essex	CB	476
Sale	Cheshire	M	487
Salford	Lancashire	M	487
Salisbury	Wiltshire	SP	496
Saltash	Cornwall	PL	492
Saltburn-by-the-Sea	Cleveland	TS	499
Saltcoats	Ayrshire	KA	511
Sandbach	Cheshire	CW	479
Sandhurst	Surrey	GU	482
Sandown	Isle of Wight	PO	492
Sandwich	Kent	CT	478
Sandy	Bedfordshire	SG	494
Sawbridgeworth	Hertfordshire	CM	477
Scarborough	North Yorkshire	YO	500
Scunthorpe	South Humberside	DN	480
Seaford	East Sussex	BN	474
Seaton	Devon	EX	480
Sevenoaks	Kent	TN	498
Shaftesbury	Dorset	SP	496
Sheffield	South Yorkshire	S	494

Post Town	'Old' County	Postcode	Page
Shefford	Bedfordshire	SG	494
Shepperton	Middlesex	TW	499
Shepton Mallet	Somerset	BA	472
Sherborne	Dorset	DT	480
Sheringham	Norfolk	NR	489
Shetland	Isle of Shetland	ZE	513
Shifnal	Shropshire	TF	497
Shipston-on-Stour	Warwickshire	CV	478
Shoreham-by-Sea	West Sussex	BN	474
Shrewsbury	Shropshire	SY	496
Sidcup	Kent	DA	479
Sidmouth	Devon	EX	480
Sittingbourne	Kent	ME	487
Skipton	North Yorkshire	BD	473
Sleaford	Lincolnshire	NG	489
Slough	Berkshire	SL	494
Smethwick	West Midlands	B	221
Solihull	West Midlands	B	472
South Croydon	Surrey	CR	477
South Petherton	Somerset	TA	497
South Queensferry	West Lothian	EH	510
South Shields	Tyne and Wear	NE	488
Southall	Middlesex	UB	499
Southam	Warwickshire	CV	479
Southampton	Hampshire	SO	496
Southend-on-Sea	Essex	SS	496
Southminster	Essex	CM	477
Southport	Merseyside	PR	492
Southsea	Hampshire	PO	492
Southwell	Nottinghamshire	NG	489
Spalding	Lincolnshire	PE	491
Spennymoor	Co Durham	DL	480
Spilsby	Lincolnshire	PE	491
Stafford	Staffordshire	ST	496
Staines	Middlesex	TW	499
Stalybridge	Cheshire	SK	494
Stamford	Lincolnshire	PE	491
Stanford Le-Hope	Essex	SS	496
Stevenage	Hertfordshire	SG	494
Steyning	West Sussex	BN	474
Stirling	Stirlingshire	FK	510
Stockport	Cheshire	SK	495
Stocksfield	Northumberland	NE	488
Stockton-on-Tees	Cleveland	TS	499
Stoke-on-Trent	Staffordshire	ST	496
Stone	Staffordshire	ST	496
Stonehaven	Kincardineshire	AB	509
Stonehouse	Gloucestershire	GL	481
Stornoway	Isle of Lewis	HS	511
Stourbridge	West Midlands	DY	480
Stowmarket	Suffolk	IP	484
Strabane	Co Londonderry	BT	508
Stranraer	Wigtownshire	IV	509
Stratford-upon-Avon	Warwickshire	CV	478
Strathcarron	Ross-shire	IV	512
Strathaven	Lanarkshire	ML	512
Stroud	Gloucestershire	GL	481
Sudbury	Suffolk	CO	477
Sunbury-on-Thames	Middlesex	TW	498
Sunderland	Tyne and Wear	SR	496
Surbiton	Surrey	KT	484
Sutton	Surrey	SM	495
Sutton Coldfield	West Midlands	B	472
Sutton-in-Ashfield	Nottinghamshire	NG	489
Swaffham	Norfolk	PE	491
Swanage	Dorset	BH	473
Swanley	Kent	BR	475
Swansea	West Glamorgan	SA	515
Swindon	Wiltshire	SN	495
Tain	Ross-shire	IV	512
Tarbert	Argyll	PA	512
Tamworth	Staffordshire	B	472
Tarporley	Cheshire	CW	478
Taunton	Somerset	TA	497
Tavistock	Devon	PL	492
Teddington	Middlesex	TW	498
Teignmouth	Devon	TQ	498
Telford	Shropshire	TF	497

Post Town	'Old' County	Postcode	Page
Templecombe	Somerset	BA	472
Tenby	Dyfed	SA	515
Tetbury	Gloucestershire	GL	481
Tewkesbury	Gloucestershire	GL	481
Thame	Oxfordshire	OX	491
Thetford	Norfolk	IP	484
Thirsk	North Yorkshire	YO	500
Thornton Heath	Surrey	CR	477
Thurso	Caithness	KW	511
Tilbury	Essex	RM	494
Tiverton	Devon	EX	481
Tomatin	Inverness-shire	IV	511
Tonbridge	Kent	TN	497
Torpoint	Devon	PL	492
Torquay	Devon	TQ	498
Tranent	East Lothian	EH	510
Tring	Buckinghamshire	HP	483
Trowbridge	Wiltshire	SN	495
Truro	Cornwall	TR	498
Tunbridge Wells	Kent	TN	497
Turriff	Aberdeenshire	AB	509
Twickenham	Middlesex	TW	499
Tywyn	Gwynedd	LL	514
Uckfield	East Sussex	TN	497
Ulverston	Cumbria	LA	485
Upminster	Essex	RM	494
Uttoxeter	Staffordshire	ST	497
Uxbridge	Middlesex	UB	499
Ventnor	Isle of Wight	PO	492
Virginia Water	Surrey	GU	482
Wadebridge	Cornwall	PL	491
Wakefield	West Yorkshire	WF	500
Wallasey	Merseyside	L	476
Wallingford	Oxfordshire	OX	491
Wallington	Surrey	SM	495
Walsall	West Midlands	WS	500
Walsingham	Norfolk	NR	489
Waltham Cross	Hertfordshire	EN	480
Walton on the Naze	Essex	CO	477
Walton-on-Thames	Surrey	KT	484
Wantage	Oxfordshire	OX	491
Ware	Hertfordshire	SG	494
Warley	West Midlands	B	472
Warminster	Wiltshire	BA	472
Warrington	Cheshire	WA	499
Warwick	Warwickshire	CV	478
Washington	Tyne and Wear	NE	488
Waterlooville	Hampshire	PO	492
Watford	Hertfordshire	WD	499
Wedmore	Somerset	BS	475
Welling	Kent	DA	479
Wellingborough	Northamptonshire	NN	489
Wells	Somerset	BA	472
Welshpool	Powys	SY	515
Welwyn	Hertfordshire	AL	471
Welwyn Garden City	Hertfordshire	AL	471
Wembley	Middlesex	HA	483
Wemyss Bay	Renfrewshire	PA	512
West Bromwich	West Midlands	B	472
West Byfleet	Surrey	KT	484
West Drayton	Middlesex	UB	499
West Kilbride	Ayrshire	KA	511
West Linton	Peeblesshire	EH	510
West Malling	Kent	ME	487
West Wickham	Kent	BR	474
Westbury	Wiltshire	BA	473
Westcliff-on-Sea	Essex	SS	496
Westerham	Kent	TN	498
Westgate-on-Sea	Kent	CT	478
Weston-super-Mare	Avon	BS	475
Wetherby	West Yorkshire	LS	486
Weybridge	Surrey	KT	484
Weymouth	Dorset	DT	480
Whitburn	West Lothian	EH	510
Whitby	North Yorkshire	YO	500

Post Town	'Old' County	Postcode	Page
Whitchurch	Shropshire	SY	497
Whitehaven	Cumbria	CA	476
Whitland	Dyfed	SA	515
Whitley Bay	Tyne and Wear	NE	488
Whitstable	Kent	CT	478
Widnes	Cheshire	WA	499
Wigan	Lancashire	WN	499
Wigton	Cumbria	CA	475
Willenhall	West Midlands	WV	500
Wilmslow	Cheshire	SK	495
Wimborne	Dorset	BH	473
Winchester	Hampshire	SO	495
Windermere	Cumbria	LA	485
Windsor	Berkshire	SL	495
Winscombe	Somerset	BS	475
Wirral	Merseyside	CH	476
Wisbech	Cambridgeshire	PE	491
Witham	Essex	CM	477
Witney	Oxfordshire	OX	491
Woking	Surrey	GU	482
Wokingham	Berkshire	RG	493
Wolverhampton	West Midlands	WV	500
Woodbridge	Suffolk	IP	484
Woodford Green	Essex	IG	483
Woodhall Spa	Lincolnshire	LN	48[illegible]
Worcester	Worcestershire	WR	49[illegible]
Workington	Cumbria	CA	476
Worthing	West Sussex	BN	474
Wotton-under-Edge	Gloucestershire	GL	481
Wrexham	Clwyd	LL	513
Yarm	North Yorkshire	TS	499
Yelverton	Devon	PL	492
Yeovil	Somerset	BA	472
York	North Yorkshire	YO	501

COUNTIES BY POSTCODE AND POST TOWNS

'Old' County	Postcode	Post Towns
Aberdeenshire	AB	Aberdeen
		Ellon
		Forfar
		Fraserburgh
		Huntley
		Inverurie
		Peterhead
		Turriff
Angus	DD	Arbroath
		Dundee
Argyll	PA	Ballachulish
		Cairndow
		Campbeltown
		Dalmally
		Dunoon
		Oban
		Tarbert
Avon	BA	Bath
	BS	Bristol
		Clevedon
		Weston-super-Mare
Ayrshire	KA	Ardrossan
		Ayr
		Darvel
		Irvine
		Kilbirnie
		Kilmarnock
		Kilwinning
		Largs
		Saltcoats
Banffshire	AB	Buckie
		Keith
Bedfordshire	LU	Dunstable
		Leighton Buzzard
		Luton
	MK	Bedford
	SG	Sandy
		Shefford
Belfast	BT	Belfast
Berkshire	RG	Bracknell
		Hungerford
		Newbury
		Reading
		Wokingham
	SL	Ascot
		Maidenhead
		Slough
		Windsor
Berwickshire	TD	Duns
Buckinghamshire	MK	Buckingham
		Milton Keynes
		Newport Pagnell
	HP	Amersham
Buckinghamshire	HP	Aylesbury
		Beaconsfield
		Chesham
		Great Missenden
		High Wycombe
		Princes Risborough
		Tring
	SL	Gerrards Cross
		Iver
		Marlow
		Slough
Caithness	KW	Forsinard
		Latheron
		Thurso
Cambridgeshire	CB	Cambridge
		Ely
	PE	Chatteris
		Huntingdon
		March
		Peterborough
		St Neots
		St Ives
		Wisbech
Channel Islands	GY	Guernsey
	JE	Jersey
Cheshire	CH	Chester
		Congleton
	CW	Crewe
		Ellesmere Port
		Middlewich
		Nantwich
		Northwich
		Sandbach
		Tarporley
	M	Sale
	SK	Alderley Edge
		Cheadle
		High Peak
		Macclesfield
	SK	Stalybridge
		Stockport
		Wilmslow
	SY	Malpas
	WA	Altrincham
		Frodsham
		Knutsford
		Warrington
		Widnes
Clackmannanshire	FK	Alloa
		Dollar
Cleveland	TS	Middlesbrough
		Redcar
		Saltburn-by-the-Sea
Cleveland	TS	Stockton-on-Tees
Clwyd	CH	Deeside
		Denbigh
		Mold
		Abergele
		Colwyn Bay
		Corwen
		Llangollen
		Prestatyn
		Rhyl
		St Asaph
		Wrexham
Co Antrim	BT	Antrim
		Ballyclare
		Ballymena
		Ballymoney
		Carrickfergus
		Larne
		Lisburn
		Newtownabbey
		Portrush
Co Armagh	BT	Armagh
		Craigavon
Co Down	BT	Banbridge
		Bangor
		Castlewellan
		Downpatrick
		Dromore
		Hillsborough
		Holywood
		Newcastle
		Newry
		Newtownards
Co Durham	DH	Consett
		Durham
	DL	Barnard Castle
		Bishop Auckland
		Darlington
		Newton Aycliffe
		Spennymoor
Co Fermanagh	BT	Enniskillen
Co Londonderry	BT	Coleraine
		Londonderry
		Maghera
		Portstewart
Co Tyrone	BT	Clogher
		Cookstown
		Dungannon
		Fivemiletown
		Omagh
Cornwall	EX	Bude
	PL	Bodmin
		Camelford
		Callington

'Old' County	Postcode	Post Towns
Cornwall	PL	Launceston
		St Austell
		Saltash
		Wadebridge
	TR	Falmouth
		Hayle
		Helston
		Newquay
		Penzance
		Redruth
		St Ives
		Truro
Cumbria	CA	Alston
		Appleby-in-Westmorland
		Brampton
		Carlisle
		Keswick
		Kirkby Stephen
		Maryport
		Penrith
		Whitehaven
		Wigton
		Workington
	LA	Ambleside
		Coniston
		Grange-over-Sands
		Kendal
		Milnthorpe
		Ulverston
		Windermere
Derbyshire	DE	Alfreton
		Ashbourne
		Bakewell
		Belper
		Derby
		Ilkeston
		Matlock
		Ripley
	S	Chesterfield
		Hope Valley
	SK	Buxton
		Glossop
Devon	EX	Axminster
		Barnstaple
		Bideford
		Braunton
		Colyton
		Crediton
		Cullompton
		Exeter
		Exmouth
		Honiton
		Ilfracombe
		Lynton
		Okehampton
		Seaton
		Sidmouth
		Tiverton
	PL	Ivybridge
		Plymouth
		Tavistock
		Torpoint
		Yelverton
	TQ	Buckfastleigh
		Kingsbridge
		Newton Abbot
		Paignton
		Teignmouth
		Torquay
Dorset	SP	Shaftesbury
	BH	Bournemouth
		Christchurch
		Poole
		Swanage
		Wimborne
	DT	Blandford Forum
Dorset	DT	Bridport
		Dorchester
		Lyme Regis
		Sherborne
		Weymouth
Dumfriesshire	DG	Canonbie
		Dumfries
		Gretna
		Newton Stewart
Dunbartonshire	G	Helensburgh
Dyfed	SA	Ammanford
		Cardigan
		Carmarthen
		Fishguard
		Haverfordwest
		Lampeter
		Llandysul
		Llanelli
		Milford Haven
		Pembroke
		Tenby
		Whitland
	SY	Aberystwyth
East Lothian	EH	Haddington
		Tranent
East Sussex	BN	Brighton
		Eastbourne
		Hailsham
		Hove
		Lewes
		Newhaven
		Pevensey
		Polegate
		Seaford
	TN	Battle
		Bexhill-on-Sea
		Crowborough
		Hastings
		Heathfield
		Robertsbridge
		Rye
		St Leonards-on-Sea
		Uckfield
Edinburgh	EH	Edinburgh
Essex	CB	Saffron Walden
	CM	Billericay
		Braintree
		Brentwood
		Chelmsford
		Dunmow
		Harlow
		Ingatestone
		Maldon
		Ongar
		Southminster
		Witham
	CO	Clacton-on-Sea
		Colchester
		Frinton-on-Sea
		Halstead
		Harwich
		Walton on the Naze
	EN	Epping
	IG	Barking
		Buckhurst Hill
		Ilford
		Loughton
		Woodford Green
	RM	Dagenham
		Hornchurch
		Rainham
		Romford
		Tilbury
		Upminster
	SS	Basildon
Essex	SS	Benfleet
		Canvey Island
		Leigh-on-Sea
		Rayleigh
		Rochford
		Southend-on-Sea
		Stanford-Le-Hope
		Westcliff-on-Sea
Fife	KY	Cupar
		Dunfermline
		Glenrothes
		Inverkeithing
		Leven
		St Andrews
Glasgow	G	Glasgow
Gloucestershire	GL	Cheltenham
		Cinderford
		Cirencester
		Coleford
		Gloucester
		Lydney
		Mitcheldean
		Newent
		Stonehouse
		Stroud
		Tetbury
		Tewkesbury
		Wotton-under-Edge
Greater Manchester	M	Manchester
	OL	Ashton-under-Lyne
Gwent	NP	Abergavenny
		Abertillery
		Blackwood
		Chepstow
		Cwmbran
		Monmouth
		Newport
		Pontypool
Gwynedd	LL	Arthog
		Bala
		Bangor
		Blaenau Ffestiniog
		Conwy
		Dolgellau
		Holyhead
		Llanbedr
		Llandudno
		Llanfairfechan
		Penmaenmawr
		Porthmadog
		Pwllheli
		Tywyn
Hampshire	BH	New Milton
		Ringwood
	GU	Aldershot
		Alton
		Bordon
		Farnborough
		Fleet
		Liphook
		Liss
		Petersfield
	PO	Fareham
		Gosport
		Havant
		Portsmouth
		Southsea
		Waterlooville
	RG	Basingstoke
		Hook
	SO	Alresford
		Eastleigh
		Lymington

Counties by Postcode and Post Towns

'Old' County	Postcode	Post Towns
Hampshire	SO	Lyndhurst
		Romsey
		Southampton
		Winchester
	SP	Andover
Herefordshire	HR	Hereford
		Ledbury
		Leominster
		Ross-on-Wye
Hertfordshire	AL	Harpenden
		St Albans
		Welwyn
		Welwyn Garden City
	CM	Bishop's Stortford
		Sawbridge-worth
	EN	Barnet
		Hoddesdon
		Potters Bar
		Waltham Cross
	HP	Hemel Hempstead
	SG	Baldock
		Hertford
		Hitchin
		Letchworth
		Royston
		Stevenage
		Ware
	WD	Borehamwood
		Kings Langley
		Radlett
		Rickmansworth
		Watford
Inverness-shire	IV	Beauly
		Tomatin
	PH	Aviemore
		Croy
		Fort William
		Inverness
		Kingussie
		Nairn
		Nethy Bridge
Isle of Bute	PA	Isle of Bute
Isle of Cumbrae	KA	Isle of Cumbrae
Isle of Harris	HS	Isle of Harris
Isle of Iona	PA	Isle of Iona
Isle of Lewis	HS	Stornoway
Isle of Man	IM	Castletown
		Douglas
		Peel
		Ramsey
Isle of Mull	PA	Isle of Mull
Isle of Orkney	KW	Orkney
Isle of Shetland	ZE	Shetland
Isle of Skye	IV	Isle of Skye
		Portree
Isle of Wight	PO	Bembridge
		Cowes
		Newport
		Ryde
		Sandown
		Ventnor
Kent	BR	Beckenham
		Bromley
		Chislehurst
		Orpington
		Swanley
		West Wickham
	CT	Canterbury
		Deal
		Dover
		Folkestone
		Herne Bay
		Hythe
Kent	CT	Margate
		Ramsgate
		Sandwich
		Westgate-on-Sea
		Whitstable
	DA	Dartford
		Erith
		Gravesend
		Sidcup
		Welling
	ME	Aylesford
		Chatham
		Gillingham
		Maidstone
		Rochester
		Sittingbourne
		West Malling
	TN	Ashford
		Hawkhurst
		Romney Marsh
		Sevenoaks
		Tonbridge
		Tunbridge Wells
		Westerham
Kincardineshire	AB	Banchory
		Stonehaven
Kinross-shire	KY	Kinross
Kirkcudbright-shire	DG	Castle Douglas
Lanarkshire	ML	Airdrie
		Biggar
		Carluke
		Coatbridge
		Lanark
		Motherwell
		Strathaven
Lancashire	BB	Blackburn
		Burnley
		Clitheroe
		Nelson
		Rossendale
	BL	Bolton
		Bury
	FY	Blackpool
		Lytham St Annes
	L	Ormskirk
	LA	Broughton-in-Furness
		Carnforth
		Lancaster
		Morecambe
		Penrith
	M	Salford
	OL	Heywood
		Littleborough
		Oldham
		Rochdale
	PR	Chorley
		Leyland
		Preston
	WN	Leigh
		Wigan
Leicestershire	LE	Ashby-de-la-Zouch
		Coalville
		Hinckley
		Leicester
		Loughborough
		Lutterworth
		Market Harborough
		Melton Mowbray
		Oakham
Lincolnshire	DN	Barnetby
	LN	Lincoln
		Woodhall Spa
Lincolnshire	NG	Grantham
		Sleaford
	PE	Bourne
		Spalding
		Spilsby
		Stamford
London	E, EC, N, NW, SE, SW, W, WC	London
Merseyside	CH	Prenton
		Wallasey
		Wirral
	L	Birkenhead
		Bootle
		Liverpool
		Prescot
	PR	Southport
	WA	Newton-le-Willows
		St Helens
Mid Glamorgan	CF	Aberdare
		Bridgend
		Caerphilly
		Ferndale
		Merthyr Tydfil
		Pontypridd
		Porthcawl
Middlesex	EN	Enfield
	HA	Edgware
		Harrow
		Northwood
		Pinner
		Ruislip
		Wembley
	TW	Ashford
		Brentford
		Feltham
		Hounslow
		Isleworth
		Shepperton
		Staines
		Sunbury-on-Thames
		Teddington
		Twickenham
Middlesex	UB	Greenford
		Hayes
		Perivale
		Southall
		Uxbridge
		West Drayton
Midlothian	EH	Bonnyrigg
		Loanhead
		Musselburgh
Morayshire	IV	Elgin
Norfolk	IP	Thetford
	NR	Attleborough
		Cromer
		Dereham
		Great Yarmouth
		Holt
		North Walsham
		Norwich
		Sheringham
		Walsingham
	PE	Downham Market
		King's Lynn
		Swaffham
North Humber-side	HU	Beverley
		Cottingham
		Hessle
		Hull
	YO	Bridlington
		Driffield
North Yorkshire	BD	Skipton
	DL	Bedale
		Leyburn
		Northallerton

'Old' County	Postcode	Post Towns
North Yorkshire	DL	Richmond
	HG	Harrogate
		Ripon
	TS	Guisborough
		Yarm
	YO	Malton
		Scarborough
		Thirsk
		Whitby
		York
Northamptonshire	NN	Corby
		Daventry
		Kettering
		Northampton
		Rushden
		Wellingborough
Northumberland	NE	Alnwick
		Ashington
		Bedlington
		Cramlington
		Haltwhistle
		Hexham
		Morpeth
		Riding Mill
		Stocksfield
	TD	Berwick-upon-Tweed
Nottinghamshire	NG	Mansfield
		Newark
		Nottingham
		Southwell
		Sutton-in-Ashfield
	DN	Retford
Oxfordshire	OX	Abingdon
		Bampton
		Banbury
		Bicester
		Burford
		Chipping Norton
		Didcot
		Faringdon
		Kidlington
		Oxford
		Thame
		Wallingford
		Wantage
		Witney
	RG	Henley-on-Thames
Peeblesshire	EH	West Linton
Perthshire	FK	Dunblane
		Killin
	PH	Blairgowrie
		Crieff
		Dunkeld
		Perth
		Pitlochry
Powys	LD	Brecon
		Builth Wells
		Knighton
		Llandrindod Wells
		Presteigne
	SY	Llanidloes
		Llanymynech
		Machynlleth
		Meifod
		Montgomery
		Newtown
		Welshpool
Renfrewshire	PA	Greenock
		Johnston
		Kilmacolm
		Paisley
		Wemyss Bay
Ross-shire	IV	Dingwall
Ross-shire	IV	Kyle
		Strathcarron
		Tain
Roxburghshire	TD	Hawick
		Jedburgh
		Kelso
		Melrose
		Newcastleton
Shropshire	SY	Craven Arms
		Ludlow
		Oswestry
		Shrewsbury
		Whitchurch
	TF	Shifnal
		Telford
	WV	Bridgnorth
Somerset	BA	Bruton
		Frome
		Glastonbury
		Shepton Mallet
		Templecombe
		Wells
		Yeovil
	BS	Wedmore
		Winscombe
	TA	Bridgwater
		Chard
		Dulverton
		Minehead
		South Petherton
		Taunton
South Glamorgan	CF	Barry
		Cardiff
		Cowbridge
		Dinas Powis
		Penarth
South Humberside	DN	Barton-on-Humber
		Grimsby
		Scunthorpe
		Doncaster
South Yorkshire	S	Barnsley
		Dronfield
		Mexborough
		Rotherham
		Sheffield
Staffordshire	B	Tamworth
	DE	Burton-on-Trent
	ST	Newcastle
		Stafford
		Stoke-on-Trent
		Stone
		Uttoxeter
	WS	Lichfield
		Rugeley
Stirlingshire	FK	Falkirk
		Grangemouth
		Larbert
		Stirling
Suffolk	CB	Newmarket
	CO	Sudbury
	IG	Bury St Edmunds
		Felixstowe
	IP	Brandon
		Ipswich
		Leiston
		Stowmarket
		Woodbridge
	NR	Beccles
		Bungay
		Lowestoft
Surrey	CR	Camberley
		Caterham
		Croydon
		Mitcham
		Purley
Surrey	CR	South Croydon
		Thornton Heath
	GU	Cranleigh
		Farnham
		Godalming
		Guildford
		Haslemere
		Hindhead
		Sandhurst
		Virginia Water
		Woking
	KT	Addlestone
		Chertsey
		Chessington
		Cobham
		East Molesey
		Epsom
		Kingston upon Thames
		Leatherhead
		New Malden
		Surbiton
		Walton-on-Thames
		West Byfleet
		Weybridge
	RH	Dorking
		Horley
		Lingfield
		Oxted
		Redhill
		Reigate
	SM	Banstead
		Carshalton
		Morden
		Sutton
		Wallington
	TW	Egham
		Richmond
Sutherland	IV	Dornoch
		Lairg
Tyne and Wear	DH	Houghton le Spring
	NE	Blaydon-on-Tyne
		Boldon Colliery
		East Boldon
		Gateshead
		Newcastle upon Tyne
		North Shields
		Ryton
		South Shields
		Washington
		Whitley Bay
	SR	Sunderland
Warwickshire	CV	Alcester
		Bedworth
		Kenilworth
		Leamington Spa
		Nuneaton
		Rugby
		Shipston-on-Stour
		Southam
		Stratford-upon-Avon
		Warwick
West Glamorgan	SA	Port Talbot
		Swansea
West Lothian	EH	Bathgate
		Linlithgow
		South Queensferry
		Whitburn
West Midlands	B	Birmingham
		Cradley Heath

Counties by Postcode and Post Towns

'Old' County	Postcode	Post Towns
West Midlands	B	Halesowen
		Henley-in-Arden
		Oldbury
		Smethwick
		Solihull
		Sutton Coldfield
		Warley
		West Bromwich
	CV	Coventry
	DY	Brierley Hill
		Dudley
		Stourbridge
	WS	Walsall
	WV	Willenhall
		Wolverhampton
West Sussex	BN	Arundel
		Hassocks
		Henfield
		Lancing
		Littlehampton
		Shoreham-by-Sea
		Steyning
		Worthing
West Sussex	GU	Midhurst
		Petworth
West Sussex	PO	Bognor Regis
		Chichester
	RH	Billingshurst
		Burgess Hill
		Crawley
		East Grinstead
		Haywards Heath
		Horsham
		Pulborough
West Yorkshire	BD	Bradford
		Keighley
	HD	Brighouse
		Huddersfield
	HX	Halifax
	LS	Ilkley
		Leeds
		Otley
		Wetherby
	WF	Dewsbury
		Heckmondwike
		Knottingley
		Mirfield
West Yorkshire	WF	Ossett
		Pontefract
		Wakefield
Wigtownshire	DG	Stranraer
Wiltshire	SN	Calne
		Chippenham
		Devizes
		Malmesbury
		Marlborough
		Melksham
		Pewsey
		Swindon
		Trowbridge
	SP	Salisbury
	BA	Bradford-on-Avon
		Warminster
		Westbury
Worcestershire	B	Bromsgrove
		Redditch
	DY	Kidderminster
	WR	Broadway
		Droitwich
		Malvern
		Pershore
		Worcester

LOCATION INDEX

For map see page 458, lists by town & county pages 460-470

For map see page 458, lists by town & county pages 460-470

For map see page 458, lists by town & county pages 460-470

For map see page 458, lists by town & county pages 4[illegible]0-4[illegible]0

For map see page 458, lists by town & county pages 460-470

For map see page 458, lists by town & county pages 460–70

Location Index - England

For map see page 458, lists by town & county pages 460-470

Location Index - England

For map see page 458, lists by town & county pages 460-470

For map see page 458, lists by town & county pages 460-470

Location Index - England

For map see page 458, lists by town & county pages 460-470

Location Index - England

For map see page 458, lists by town & county pages 460–70

For map see page 458, lists by town & county pages 460-470

Location Index - England

Location Index - England

For map see page 458, lists by town & county pages 460-470

 For map see page 458, lists by town & county pages 460-470

For map see page 458, lists by town & county pages 460-470

Location Index - England

For map see page 458, lists by town & county pages 460-470

LOCATION INDEX

For map see page 458, lists by town & county pages 460-470

Location Index - England

For map see page 458, lists by town & county pages 460-470

For map see page 458, lists by town & county pages 460-470

Location Index - England

For map see page 458, lists by town & county pages 460-470

LOCATION INDEX

For map see page 458, lists by town & county pages 460-470

Location Index - England

For map see page 458, lists by town & county pages 460-470

For map see page 458, lists by town & county pages 460-470

Location Index - England

For map see page 458, lists by town & county pages 460-470

For map see page 458, lists by town & county pages 460-470

Location Index - London

For map see page 458, lists by town & county pages 460-470

SW2 London

SW3 London

SW4 London

SW5 London

SW6 London

SW7 London

SW8 London

SW9 London

SW10 London

SW11 London

SW12 London

SW14 London

SW15 London

SW16 London

Location Index - London

For map see page 458, lists by town & county pages 460-470

CHANNEL ISLANDS

ISLE OF MAN

NORTHERN IRELAND

For map see page 458, lists by town & county pages 460-470

Location Index - Northern Ireland

For map see page 458, lists by town & county pages 460-470

Location Index - Scotland

For map see page 458, lists by town & county pages 460-470

Location Index - Scotland

For map see page 458, lists by town & county pages 460-470

Location Index - Wales

For map see page 458, lists by town & county pages 460–470

For other SY Postcodes see England

COUNTRY INDEX

NORTHERN IRELAND – INDEX OF ORGANISATIONS

REPUBLIC OF IRELAND – SEE PAGE 510 OF LOCATION INDEX

SCOTLAND – INDEX OF ORGANISATIONS

Country Index

WALES – INDEX OF ORGANISATIONS

INDEX OF ADVERTISERS

All advertisers with a colour advert in pages i-xxxii also have a black and white advert on the page shown.

HOW TO USE THE MAIN INDEX

The Main Index includes the following items for all the organisations listed in the *Handbook*:

– Organization names, alternative names, known old names and commonly used abbreviations.
– Names of all people listed.
– Ecclesiastical titles by town eg; 1) Bath, Archdeacon of 2) Abernethy, Presbytery of. Where the title relates to a Diocese it is not included separately eg; Bishop of Bath and Wells cannot be found under Bath in the Main Index, but instead under Church of England Diocese of Bath and Wells.
– Magazine titles, unless the title is so similar to the organisation names that they appear in the same place in the index eg; *Adrenaline* (magazine) is not listed separately from Adrenaline.
– Imprints of publishers.
– Subject areas of work. Subjects are only listed when they appear other than in the relevant category eg; computers are not listed by subject if the organisation concerned is in the Computer and Business Service category. The word used as a subject entry will be found in the description of work of one or more organisations on the page number given.
– Names of organisations which have closed or not been traced in the past 10 years, with the year it occurred.
– To help distinguish organisations of similar name, the town is given for Bookshops, Conference Centres, Guest Houses and Hotels, and other similar organisations. Towns are otherwise listed in the Location Index and in the list on Page 569.
– Advertisements are listed for the relevant organisation. These are also listed in the Index of Advertisers on Page 560.
– Category names (in bold) eg; Elderly people is a subject entry, but **Elderly People (Residential Homes for)** is a category

The index is constructed on the word principle, that is the order of entries is determined by the alphabetical sequence of the word in each entry rather than the letters, recognising spaces between words. Thus Alpha Book Shop comes before Alpha Bookroom, since Book precedes Bookroom word for word.

Roman numeral pages are in the colour section.

MAIN INDEX

Main Index

Main Index

Main Index

Main Index

Main Index

Main Index

Main Index

Main Index

Main Index

Main Index

Main Index

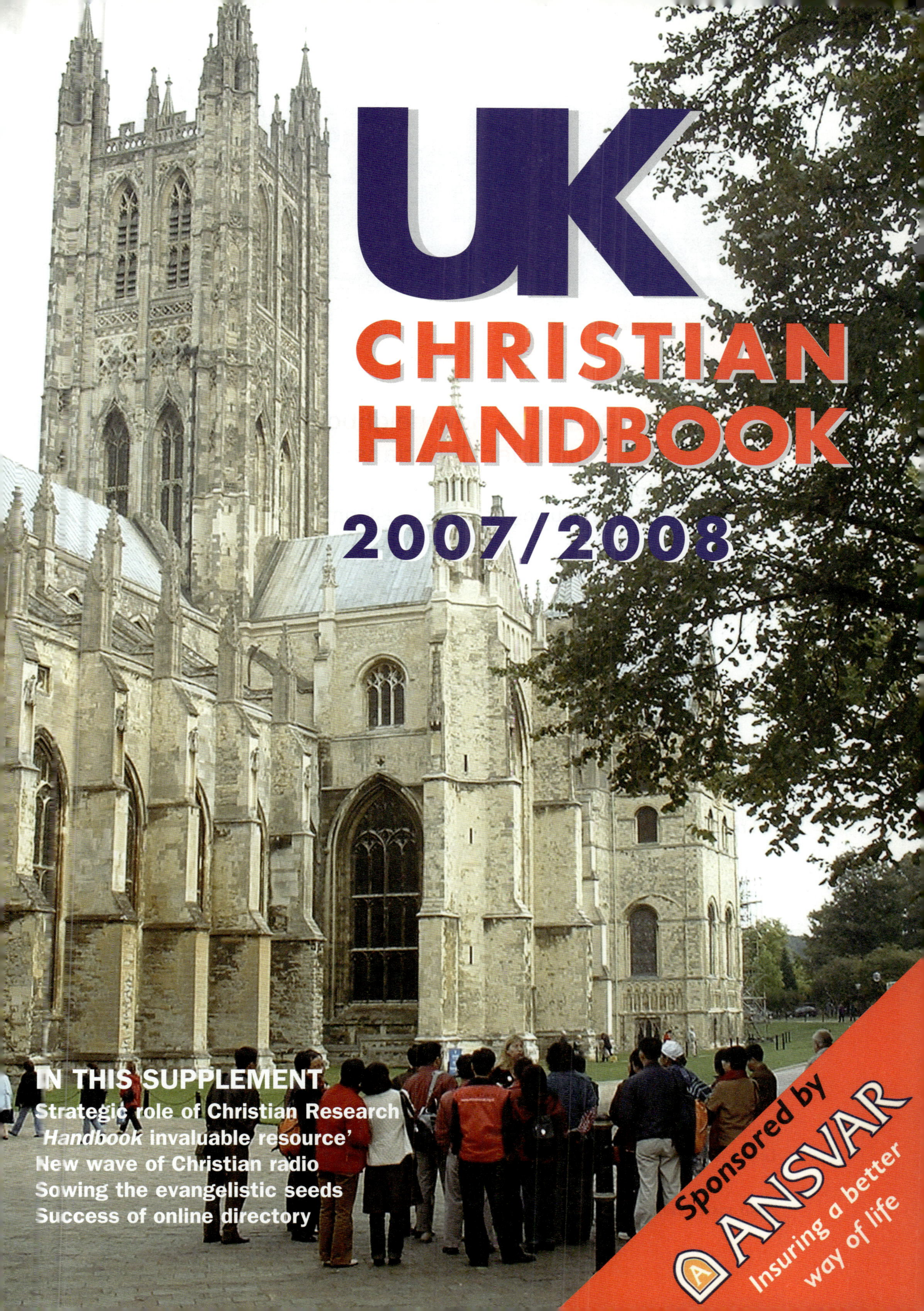
UK
CHRISTIAN
HANDBOOK
2007/2008
IN THIS SUPPLEMENT
Strategic role of Christian Research
'Handbook invaluable resource'
New wave of Christian radio
Sowing the evangelistic seeds
Success of online directory
Sponsored by
ANSVAR
Insuring a better way of life

Unique benefits of the UK Christian Handbook

The *UK Christian Handbook* has established a reputation for its reliability and accuracy, earning it the nickname of 'the yellow pages' of the Christian world.

The latest edition for 2007/08 contains information on nearly 5,000 Christian organisations and services, compared with just 2,400 entries in the first combined edition less than 25 years ago.

The *UK Christian Handbook* offers a number of unique benefits. It is:

- **Comprehensive** - it covers all Christian denominations and virtually all aspects of Christian life in the UK
- **Up to date** - every organisation listed is contacted to provide their latest information for each edition
- **Specifically Christian** - those listed are Trinitarian Christian and provide a distinctly Christian service or product
- **Accurate** - an average entry contains approximately 40 pieces of information, each of which is double-checked for accuracy
- **IT friendly** - 83% of those listed now have e-mail (77% last edition) and seven out of ten (70%) have their own websites - up from 59% last time
- **Thoroughly indexed** - there is a location index so that users can find organisations in their area and a general index which includes a subject index, previous names of organisations, names of magazines and even all the names of people listed.

Heather Wraight

Heather Wraight, Editor of the *UK Christian Handbook* said: "The *Handbook* reveals the breadth of what is going on in the Christian scene in the UK and as this special supplement reveals, it is vibrant serving both the church and society."

She said that the latest edition of the *Handbook* reflected a number of revealing trends. A total of 38 Christian care homes were no longer listed because they had either been acquired by secular organisations or had been forced to close, at least partly, because of the capital costs involved in satisfying changes required by legislation.

Legislation requiring improved accessibility had also made it impossible for a number of smaller Christian conference centres to continue, while the number of Christian guest houses and hotels had also decreased since the last edition.

"On a more positive note, Methodist Homes for the Aged have opened 21 new homes since the last edition providing follow on care for the elderly or disadvantaged who are not well enough to live at home," she added.

The problems experienced in Christian publishing are reflected in the fact that 12 publications had closed down since the last edition, although the number of organisations offering media production services had increased, reflecting the growth of the internet and associated technology.

There had also been a welcome increase in the number of relief and development agencies, particularly smaller agencies offering specialist services.

Heather added that the online version of the *UK Christian Handbook* had significantly increased awareness of the directory and welcomed the huge increase in the numbers of visitors to the website – see story on page xiv.

Organisations and individuals who purchase a copy of the new *UK Christian Handbook* will receive three months free subscription to the online directory.

Contact details: Christian Research, Vision Building, 4 Footscray Road, Eltham, London SE9 2TZ.
Tel: 020 8294 1989 Web: www.christian-research.org.uk

SPECIAL OFFER
Buy a copy of the *UK Christian Handbook* and receive three months subscription to the online directory FREE

IN THIS SUPPLEMENT

UK Christian Handbook 'an invaluable resource'

Information contained in the *UK Christian Handbook* is highly appreciated by a wide variety of users – from individuals to large multi-national organisations.

One of the largest individual users of the *Handbook* is Tearfund, the leading relief and development charity, which works in partnership with Christian agencies and churches worldwide.

TEARFUND
CHRISTIAN ACTION WITH THE WORLD'S POOR

Based at its headquarters in Teddington, Tearfund's 300 staff have access to 30 copies of the *UK Christian Handbook*.

Graham Fairbairn, Tearfund's deputy chief executive, said: "There are not many days go by without me turning to the *Handbook* for information on a particular organisation or agency.

"We work with partner organisations around the world and often need to obtain reliable information at very short notice. The *UK Christian Handbook* is the source that I turn to for that information.

"We have had copies of the *Handbook* ever since it was first published and have found it to be an invaluable resource. It has been continually improved and enhanced over the years. I ensure I always keep my own copy close by.

"It is enormously useful and helpful and I am very aware of the care that the *Handbook* staff take in making sure that the information is both accurate and also correctly referenced.

"The clarity of the information together with its ease of use and ease of referencing makes the *UK Christian Handbook* an extremely important tool for Tearfund."

For Rev George Fisher of St Thomas' Church, Blackpool, the *UK Christian Handbook* has been a valuable resource for more than 10 years.

"I always keep the latest version in my own office, but ensure that the previous issue is passed to the church office for their use," said Rev Fisher.

"I use the *Handbook* several times each month to find information and data on a wide variety of organisations," he added.

"The beauty of the *Handbook* is its ease of use and clarity of presentation. The index is very clear and comprehensive, making it easy to track down the information you need very quickly.

"In my job I need to get information or telephone numbers for different dioceses, colleges and a variety of other organisations and I know the *Handbook* will have that information for me.

"I prefer the hard copy to the online version as it is so handy and easily accessible," he added.

New brand of Christian broadcasting set to hit the airwaves

A new wave of Christian broadcasting is about to spread across Britain as part of the Government's plans to broaden radio listenership.

More than 100 community groups have been granted licences to broadcast for five years by Ofcom, the official Government regulator.

Among these are a number of Christian groups who have been successful in securing FM licences in several locations in England, as well as Scotland and Northern Ireland.

Groups representing other faiths, such as Muslim, have also been quick to see the opportunity and in some cases they have been granted licences as well.

One of the pioneers in community Christian broadcasting is the Cross Rhythms multi-media ministry, based in Stoke-on-Trent.

It was originally birthed in Plymouth through its sister organisation Cornerstone Vision, one of the collaborative partners in the production of the *UK Christian Handbook*.

In 2002 Cross Rhythms was one of a handful of groups who were invited to take part in the original trial to evaluate the benefits of community radio.

Based on the Cross Rhythms' experience and those of the other pilot stations, Ofcom in 2004 invited applications from groups across the country for community FM radio licences.

Nearly 200 applications were received and the first licences were granted in the spring of 2005. Among the first to receive its five year licence was Cross Rhythms, whose distinctive style of community radio had impressed the regulators.

As part of an ongoing collaborative strategy, two other Christian groups in Plymouth and Stockton-on-Tees have been granted licences to broadcast under the Cross Rhythms banner.

Chris Girdler, a member of the successful Christian group in Plymouth said: "We were greatly assisted in preparing our application by the Cross Rhythms team in Stoke-on-Trent and have modelled our programme content and style on the successful template they have developed.

• continued on page vii

CROSS RHYTHMS CITY RADIO 101.8FM
the new sound on the street

Cross Rhythms City Radio has been broadcasting in Stoke-on-Trent since 2002

Community radio opportunities

• continued from page vi

"With technical and programming support from Stoke-on-Trent we can set up and run the new station in Plymouth at far less cost than a stand-alone station - and it will sound very professional from day one.

"The station in Plymouth will be governed locally, but will benefit from all the experience and skills of the Cross Rhythms team in Stoke-on-Trent."

This successful brand development offers a form of 'franchise' opportunity for other Christian groups who may be considering applying for a community radio licence when applications for the next round of stations takes place in late 2006.

In addition to the three Cross Rhythms stations, licences have also been granted to Christian groups in Bournemouth (Hope FM), Dewsbury (Branch FM), Shine Banbridge County Down (Shine FM) and Cumbernauld (Revival Radio).

Another Christian broadcaster, Day One Radio based in Wolverhampton, has been awarded a local DAB (digital) licence under separate legislation.

The *UK Christian Handbook* lists organisations like these radio stations, along with many others who work in their local communities.

Community radio is a third tier of broadcasting which complements the mix of radio services already provided by the BBC and commercial radio.

The characteristics of community radio are distinct from commercial radio in that the services cover a smaller geographical area - in this case a 10km footprint across the city - and are provided on a not-for-profit basis focusing on the delivery of specific social benefits to enrich a particular geographic community or community of interest.

Contact details: Cross Rhythms City Radio, Conway House, Cheapside, Stoke-on-Trent, ST1 1HE. Tel: 08700 118008. Website: www.crossrhythms.co.uk

Sowing the seed with evangelistic resources

A West Sussex based company is making a big impact by providing a wide range of innovative resources for outreach and evangelism both in the UK and the rest of the world.

Verité Creative Marketing, one of the strategic partners involved in the *UK Christian Handbook*, is now in its fourth year.

In an age when the internet and mobile technology are growing in their scope and reach, the team at Verité have found that there is still strong demand for evangelistic tools such as booklets and newspapers especially when they are linked to websites like www.re-jesus.co.uk

Chris Powell, who founded Verité, said: "Like the Parable of the Sower we all need seeds to enable us to sow. We see our role as the producers of quality seeds which can be sown in a variety of ways and situations for the benefit of the Kingdom."

Chris and his team work in a spirit of collaboration with many different organisations in the production of high-quality evangelistic material.

• continued on page xii

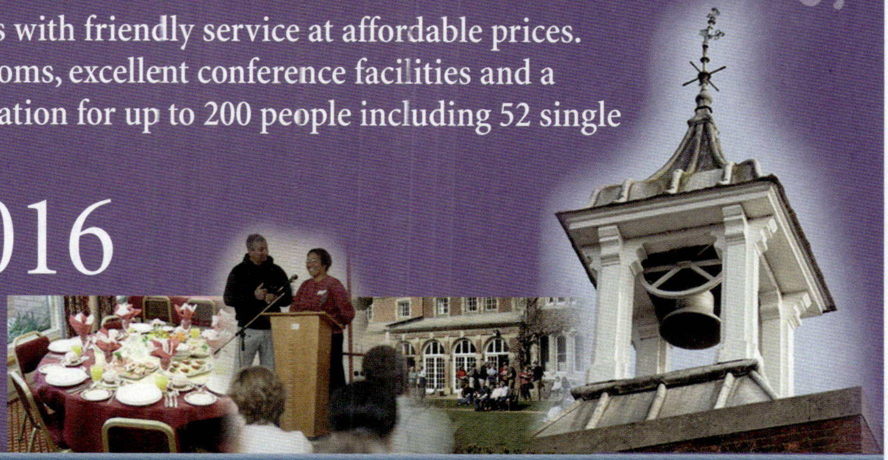

Evangelistic resources

• continued from page x

A recent example was the production of a booklet called *'KickOff 2006'* linked to the World Cup in Germany. A total of 90,000 copies were produced and sold in the UK, 500,000 distributed in Germany and up to one million more produced in more than 20 different languages around the world.

"The World Cup is a global event watched by literally billions of people and the production of 'KickOff 2006' enabled us to get the gospel message to literally all four corners of the world in an eye-catching and popular format," said Chris.

Verité worked in partnership with the Deo Gloria Trust, Christians in Sport, Major Sports Event Partnership USA, Kickoff Germany and the Christian Enquiry Agency UK in the concept and production of the booklet.

"In addition to handling the overall project management we also created graphic files which were made available to Christian organisations around the world so that they could produce their localised versions," he added. "We clear all copyright and send complete graphic files out for free to allow local translation and printing."

Verité also produced 6,500 DVDs for the World Cup featuring three different programmes and co-ordinated all the packing, design and distribution of the material for use in Arab speaking countries.

Work is already under way on evangelistic material linked to the Cricket World Cup in the West Indies and the Rugby World Cup in South Africa in 2007.

"The key to success in this field is discerning and deciding how to maximise the evangelistic opportunity provided by major sporting and other high-profile events. This inevitably requires creativity, marketing skills and the collaborative will to make it work," said Chris.

Verité has more than 50 customers and collaborative partners with whom it currently works. All Verité partners in the UK are listed in the *UK Christian Handbook*. Verité is also a part owner of Trinity Vision, the UK's leading Christian DVD provider and produces newsletters, magazines and publications for a variety of Christian organisations and ministries. Its range of services includes high quality graphic design, printing, warehousing and product fulfillment.

The UK's longest-established evangelistic newspaper is also now part of the Verité stable: *Challenge* newspaper, which celebrates its 50th anniversary in 2008. "We were delighted to take over responsibility for publishing *Challenge* in 2004," said Chris. "We distribute 50,000 copies of the testimony-based tabloid every month to churches and mission organizations throughout the UK.

"*Challenge*, combined with our other publications, results in the production and sowing of around 1.5 million 'seeds' every year," he added.

Contact details: Verité CM Ltd., 8 St John's Parade, Alinora Crescent, Goring-by-Sea, West Sussex BN12 4HJ. Tel: 01903 242975. E-mail: chrispowell@veritecm.com. See Verité's special offers on Page x.

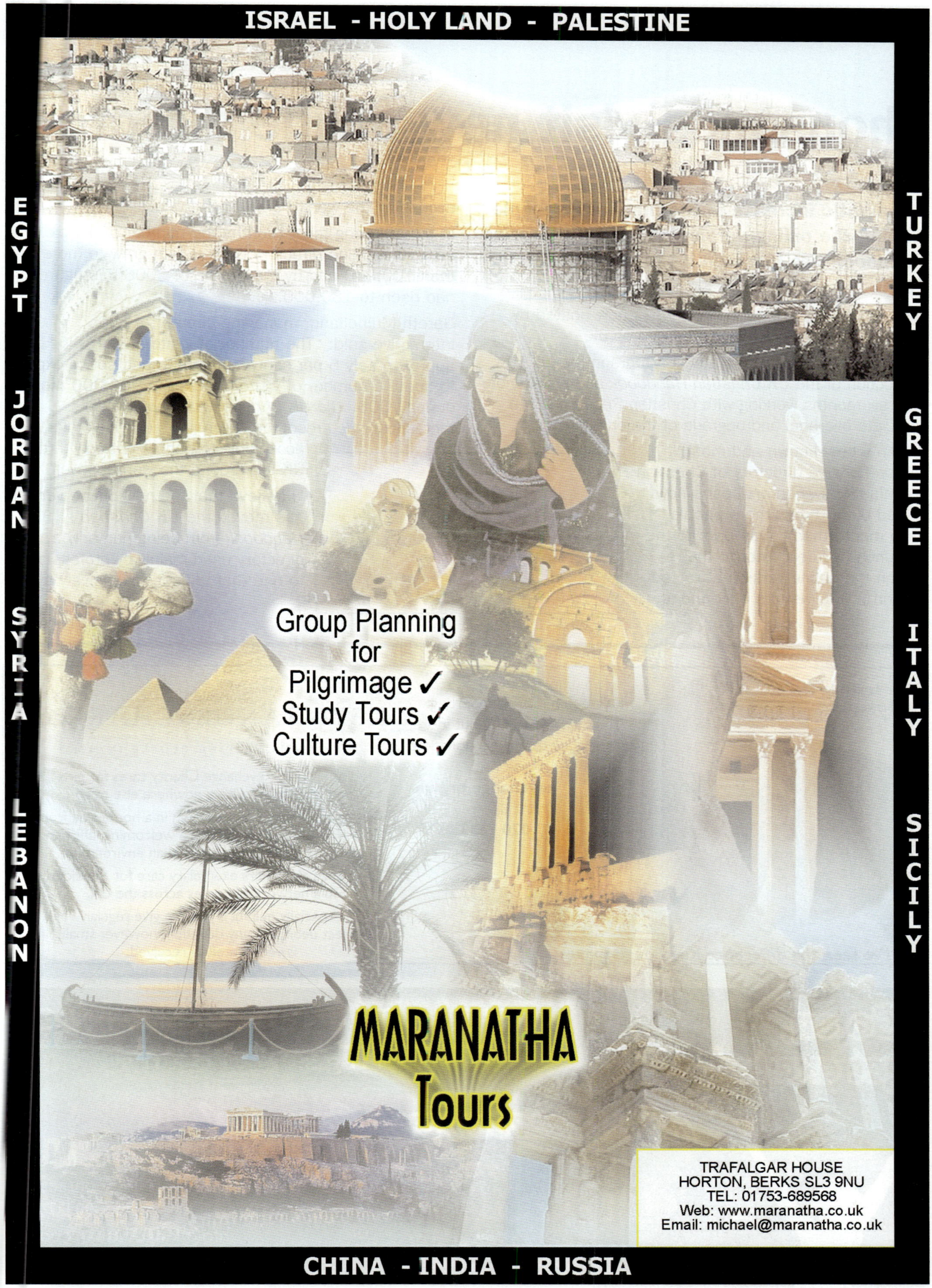
ISRAEL - HOLY LAND - PALESTINE
EGYPT
JORDAN
SYRIA
LEBANON
TURKEY
GREECE
ITALY
SICILY
Group Planning
for
Pilgrimage ✓
Study Tours ✓
Culture Tours ✓
MARANATHA
Tours
TRAFALGAR HOUSE
HORTON, BERKS SL3 9NU
TEL: 01753-689568
Web: www.maranatha.co.uk
Email: michael@maranatha.co.uk
CHINA - INDIA - RUSSIA

Thousands visit new online directory

A dramatic increase in the number of people visiting the online version of the *UK Christian Handbook* has followed its total re-launch in 2005.

The *UK Christian Handbook Online* is now hosted by Eden Interactive on its website Eden.co.uk.

Eden is one of the collaborative partners in the production of the *UK Christian Handbook* and spent more than six months working with Christian Research on a complete overhaul and upgrade of the online version.

Britain's best-known and most comprehensive directory of Christian organisations and services is now visited by 50 times more people each month than it was prior to the re-launch by Eden. Prior to the re-launch the online version attracted around 2,000 visitors each month accessing the wealth of information available.

In the following three months the number of people using the online directory each month grew to more than 100,000 and by the middle of 2006 this figure had risen to 180,000.

Gareth Mulholland, managing director of Eden Interactive said: "The number of visitors is growing by approximately 5 per cent each month and so we expect to see the number of visitors pass the 200,000 mark during 2006. *The UK Christian Handbook* is a fantastically rich resource which in its online version is accessible to people not only in the UK but around the world as well.

eden interactive ltd

"I believe that the new online version has moved the *UK Christian Handbook* from being primarily a directory used mainly by professionals to one that is used extensively by

• continued on page xvi

Success of new online directory

• continued from page xiv

individuals as well.

"We have made it much easier to use, which means that at any moment of the day there are likely to be between 10 and 15 people searching the directory for information.

"The online handbook has greatly enhanced the impact and popularity of Eden.co.uk."

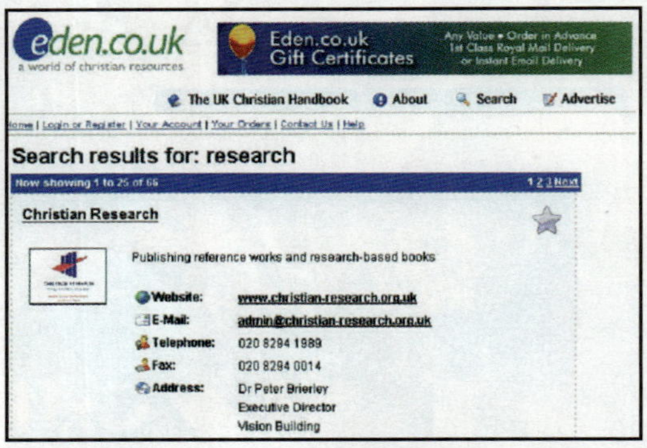

He said that the information in the directory was updated each month by Christian Research, which maintained the quality and accuracy of the data.

Further growth in the number of visitors will be achieved by syndicating the website to other Christian organisations who will link with Eden.co.uk, said Gareth.

He said that the Eden.co.uk website had been developed to provide a central platform for a wide variety of Christian information including the directory, training resources, books, DVDs, CDs, events and vacancies.

Eden Interactive, which is based in Chester, was formed in 1998 and employs a team of 16 full time and part time staff. It specialises in digital communications and marketing, including website design, animation, e-commerce, cd-roms, search engine promotion and e-mail newsletters.

Contact details: Eden Interactive, Chester Enterprise Centre, Hoole Bridge, Chester CH2 3NE. Tel: 0845 222 3336. Websites: www.eden-interactive.com and www.eden.co.uk

Strategic role of Christian Research

Christian Research often hits the headlines when they release new church attendance statistics. But who are they and what do they do?

Christian Research are probably best known in two ways: as publishers of the *UK Christian Handbook*, sometimes called the Yellow Pages of the Christian world, or for their data which gives a comprehensive picture of church membership and attendance across the UK.

Their aim is to help Christian leaders with the insight and skills needed for strategic planning for growth. In other words, they don't simply want to supply information, they want to help people use it effectively - whatever that means in their particular context.

Dr Peter Brierley started and still runs the small organisation which is based in south east London. He was formerly a statistician at the Cabinet Office, but for over 20 years he has used his expertise to serve the Christian community, mainly in the UK though occasionally wider afield.

Census results out in September

The largest projects Christian Research undertakes are national Church Censuses. The latest one, the 2005 English Church Census, will be published in *Religious Trends* No 6 in September this year – at about the same time as the *UK Christian Handbook* is published. *Religious Trends* will contain the detailed statistical results of the Census, while the interpretation and implications will be in *Pulling out of the Nosedive*.

Christian Research is a membership organisation, and one of the key benefits of membership is a significant discount on *Religious Trends* and the *Handbook*. (For more information about membership please see page xxxi).

Quadrant, a six-page bulletin of information culled from both Christian and secular sources is also mailed bi-monthly to members.

Dr Brierley and his Assistant Director, Heather Wraight (who also edits the *Handbook*), regularly offer Briefings based on their latest research, sometimes in partnership with others. Road shows with the results of the 2005 English Church Census will be held in 11 locations around England in October and November 2006.

Their seminar on *Reaching and Keeping Tweenagers* is so popular that it has been run 20 times in recent years.

Christian Research is an independent organisation which works with any denomination, and in particular seeks to serve Christian leaders.

To join the Christian Research Association, or for details of Christian Research's publications or services contact Christian Research, Vision Building, 4 Footscray Road, Eltham, London SE9 2TZ.
Tel: 020 8294 1989 Fax: 020 8294 1885
Email: admin@christian-research.org.uk www.christian-research.org.uk

The *UK Christian Handbook, Religious Trends* and *Pulling out of the Nosedive* are published in September 2006. Order them on page xxxii.

'Exceptionally committed ...'
Maxie Richards, The Maxie Richards Foundation
'Invaluable help and advice ...'
David Black, Chairman, The Haven Kilmacolm
'Professionalism and support of the highest value ...'
David Tierney, Director, The Lighthouse Foundation
'MR Associates have provided an excellent consultancy service to Teen Challenge UK for several years. We value their expert and professional approach to Housing Benefit Issues.' John E J Macey, Executive Director, Teen Challenge UK
'When I was introduced to MR Associates, I didn't anticipate the positive impact they would have on our charity. I would not hesitate to recommend their service to other housing providers - their professionalism, yet personal, straight talking approach have made them indispensible to Mercy Ministries UK.' Kerry Slater, Chief Executive, Mercy Ministries UK
Get Professional and Experienced Help in the Supported Housing Sector
M.R. Associates has an enviable track record working with Christian Supported Housing providers across the UK and understands the challenges of operating in this complex and ever-changing environment.
M.R. Associates provides a wide range of advisory and professional services including assisting providers to establish new projects, advising on policy development, Supporting People Services Reviews, and working to maximise and protect its clients' revenues. We have established a leading reputation for increasing the revenue of organisations and provide this service on a 'no win no fee' basis, only invoicing once additional revenue has been realised. We have never failed in a single case to increase revenue substantially.
In Scotland M.R. Associates also specialises in providing expert assistance and advice on the regulatory regime operated by the Care Commission.
M.R. Associates is a valued and trusted partner to the Supported Housing Sector. To find out how we can help your organisation, contact us at
M.R. Associates
T: 01475 522962 E: info@mrassociates.org.uk W: www.mrassociates.org.uk
Advisors to the Supported Housing Sector

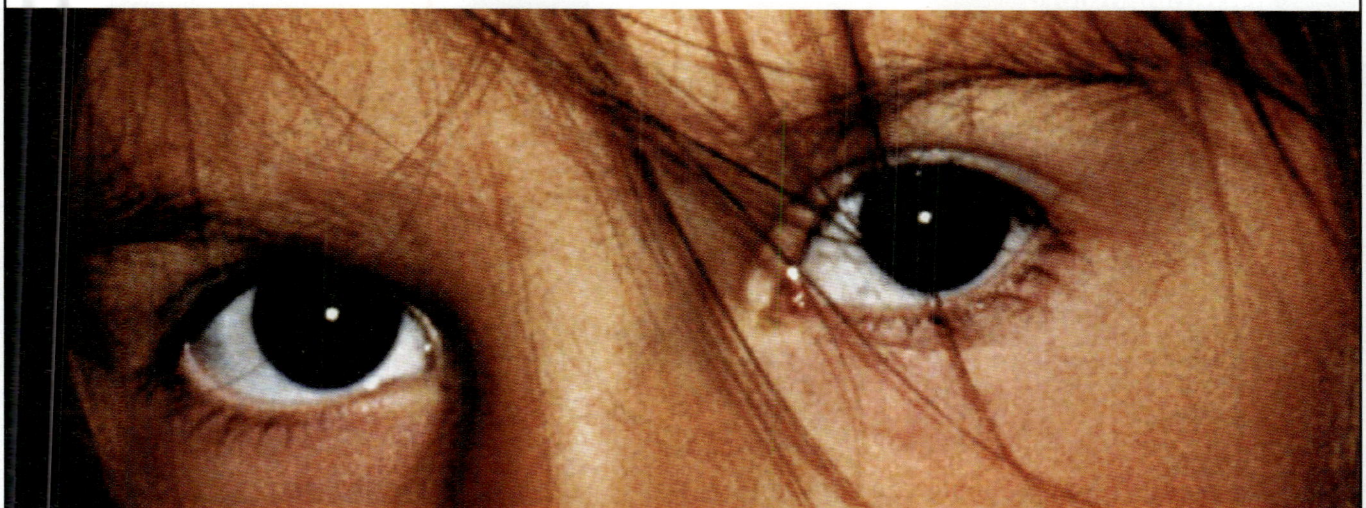

Speaking to the mountain

The Problem

No U.K. revival in Britain since the Hebrides (late 40's) People thinking "Church" is a building and not a body; I Cor.3:16,17
Concord with Belial; II Cor. 6:15-18
Widespread Toleration of Jezebel; Rev. 2:20
Removal of the Landmarks; i.e. Wesley, Wigglesworth, Jeffreys etc.; Deut. 19:14; Job 24:2,13; Prov. 22:28; 23:10,11; Hos. 5:10; I Sam. 15:23
Widespread confusion over the "new" Bible Versions portraying strange doctrines – Dan.3:25 in NIV declaring Jesus as a son of the gods!
Altars made with hands; Heb. 9:24; II Cor. 6:16; Eph. 5:30; Jer. 3:14; II Peter 1:4; Col. 1:12; Rom. 8:30; Heb. 3:14
Lack of missions commitment with the seeking of deliverance rather than the Deliverer; Matt. 6:33; Eze. 44:15; Luke 6:38; Job 36:11; Col. 1:18
The god of mammon with its Sunday afternoon shopping adherence; The asking of God to bless human plans for as in the days of Eli – the word of God seems scarce. I Sam. 1-4

God's Answer: The Prophets who rise up …

1) Possessing a concern for justice and righteousness, often being prompted to speak on behalf of God and the expectations of His Word
2) Engaging in Intercessory Prayer sensing strategic plans for spiritual warfare of which there could be no human awareness
3) Possessing an uncanny boldness and sensitivity to communicate corrective message to God's people, both corporately and personally
4) Having a zealousness on knowing that God's name is misrepresented by the "church" or other "Christians"
5) Often experiencing spiritual direction and promptings with information that could not be humanly gained

From the book: Understanding the Fivefold Ministry edited by Matthew D. Green. Charisma House 2005.

Rev David P. Griffiths is such a Prophet - Seer
Web: www.sonsofgod.co.uk *Email:* lcmi1@aol.com
Life Changing Ministries International, PO Box 106,
Colwyn Bay, Wales, LL28 4XJ
Tel: 01492 544394 *Fax:* 01492 545211

For verily I say unto you, That whosoever shall say unto this mountain, Be thou removed, and be thou cast into the sea; and shall not doubt in his heart, but shall believe that those things which he saith shall come to pass; he shall have whatsoever he saith. Mark 11:23

BEHEAD THOSE WHO INSULT ISLAM

Order Form

NOTE: join Christian Research now and get the members' discount on these book orders immediately

MEMBERSHIP (see over for information about membership). I want to join Christian Research as a:

○ Corporate Member for £58	○ Personal Member for £25
Please also send me ONE COPY	Please also send me ONE COPY
☐ *UK Christian Handbook* at £24.50 (inc p&p)	☐ *UK Christian Handbook* at £36.75 (inc p&p)
☐ *Religious Trends* No.6 at £19 (inc p&p)	☐ *Religious Trends* No. 6 at £25 (inc p&p)
☐ Both for £40 inc p&p	☐ Both for £60 inc p&p

NON-MEMBERS

UK CHRISTIAN HANDBOOK

☐ Please send me ☐ copy (ies) at £49 each (inc p&p)

RELIGIOUS TRENDS NO. 6

☐ Please send me ☐ copy (ies) at £34 each (inc p&p)

SPECIAL OFFER: BUY BOTH AND SAVE £8

☐ Please send me ☐ copy (ies) of both *UK Christian Handbook* and *Religious Trends* for £75 (inc p&p)

MEMBERS & NON-MEMBERS *PULLING OUT OF THE NOSEDIVE*

☐ Please send me ☐ copy (ies) at £10 each (inc p&p)

ALL THESE BOOKS ARE PUBLISHED SEPTEMBER 2006

PAYMENT (CHOOSE ONE)

☐ Please invoice me/my church organisation

☐ I enclose a cheque for £ ☐ made payable to Christian Research

☐ Card payment Mastercard/Visa No:

Expiry ☐ ☐ (mm/yy) Security Code ☐☐☐

Signature

YOUR DETAILS

Name

Tel no (in case of queries)

Address

Postcode

Return to: Christian Research, Vision Building, 4 Footscray Road, Eltham, London SE9 2TZ T: 020 8294 1989 F: 020 8294 0014
E: admin@christian-research.org.uk W: www.christian-research.org.uk

Please note: Your details are held on a database. Please tick the box if you do not wish us:

☐ To release your details to reputable third parties

☐ To send you information about other Christian Research products and services

Main Index

D

Main Index

Main Index

Main Index

F

Main Index

Main Index

Main Index

Main Index

I

Main Index

Main Index

L

Main Index

Main Index

M

M', Mc and Mac are all treated as Mac, and the next letter in the name determines the order of the entry, whether or not it has a capital letter. Other words and names beginning with mac follow.

Main Index

Main Index

Main Index

Main Index

O

Main Index

Main Index

Main Index

S

Main Index

Main Index

Main Index

Main Index

Main Index

V

Main Index

Main Index

Main Index

Main Index